GUIDE

THIRTEENTH EDITION

by
Karen L. Ertel
Bloomberg BNA

**Bloomberg
BNA**
Arlington, VA

Library of Congress Cataloging-in-Publication Data

Ertel, Karen.
    Grievance guide / by Karen L. Ertel. -- 13th ed.
        p. cm.
    Rev. ed. of: Grievance guide / by the BNA editorial staff. 12th ed. c2008.
    ISBN 978-1-61746-095-1
    1. Grievance procedures--United States.   I. Bureau of National Affairs
(Arlington, Va.)   II. Grievance guide.   III. Title.

    HD6972.5.G74 2012
    658.3'155--dc23

                                                                    2012040989

Published by Bloomberg BNA, 1801 S. Bell Street, Arlington, VA 22202
bna.com/bnabooks

ISBN 978-1-61746-095-1

Printed in the United States of America

PREFACE

The Bureau of National Affairs, Inc., published the first edition of *Grievance Guide* some 50 years ago to provide employers and labor unions a picture of how arbitration works in the real world. Since that time, BNA has gone through many changes, including an acquisition by Bloomberg in 2011. In this thirteenth edition of *Grievance Guide*, Bloomberg BNA continues the tradition of summarizing thousands of cases to illustrate the key factors and overarching themes that arbitrators focus on in reaching their decisions.

Although the intervention of neutral third parties to settle disputes has a long and varied history, arbitration of labor disputes had its formal beginnings in the 1940s, when unions and employers needed a way to quickly resolve labor-management disagreements and avoid hindering the country's war effort. From those experiences emerged the publication *War Labor Reports*, which was introduced by BNA in 1942. This publication changed to *Labor Arbitration Reports* at the war's end. *Grievance Guide* was introduced at the end of the following decade as a summary of the approaches documented in these publications, and has served as a practical resource for employers and unions ever since.

This thirteenth edition of *Grievance Guide* represents the collaborative efforts of BNA editors throughout the years with an overlay of updates from my own research in BBNA's *Labor Arbitration Reports*, which is a component of BBNA's *Labor Relations Reporter*. Because this book is a compilation of selected arbitration opinions over many years, I would like to thank the people who contributed to the past editions, as well as those who assisted me with this one.

The twelfth edition was prepared by Kurt D. Naasz, the assistant managing editor of BNA's human resources publishing division. Besides revising that prior edition, he assisted in my research efforts when I began this two-year project. BNA editors AnnTherese Carlozzo, Loretta Kotzin, and Paul Stelter also contributed to the twelfth edition.

I would like to give special thanks to Kenneth May, the senior editor of BBNA's *Labor Arbitration Cases*, editor-in-chief of the seventh edition of *How Arbitration Works* and reviser of the third edition of *Just Cause: The Seven Tests*, and our BBNA resident expert on arbitration. Ken provided much of the content for the revisions in this edition and helped direct my research.

In addition, Erik Brown, Elliott Dube, Cathleen Schoultz, and many other Bloomberg BNA editors contributed content of this edition. Finally I would like to thank Leslie A. Goldman, Managing Editor of the *Human Resources Library*, and Timothy J. Darby, Product Director of Bloomberg BNA's book division, for their help and support throughout this project.

Karen Ertel
Assistant Managing Editor
Daily Labor Report
November 2012

Most collective bargaining agreements contain clauses that call for arbitration as the last step of a formal grievance process. If labor and management cannot settle a particular grievance on their own, arbitration allows a neutral third party to formulate an award that resolves the issue. By agreeing to allow their disputes to be resolved in this manner, labor and management can avoid the kind of strife that might otherwise lead to work stoppages, and as well forestall criticism from their own constituency over what otherwise might be labeled an unjustified compromise. While the parties thus give up some control of the process, arbitration generally occurs only after attempts to resolve the issue themselves have failed, and has the advantage both of having the decision taken out of the hands of the parties and of being (usually) final and binding.

Just as no two collective bargaining agreements are alike in every detail, no two arbitrators are identical. However they are guided by these common concepts:

● The function of arbitrators is to interpret the meaning of the collective bargaining agreement and apply its provisions to the specific facts and circumstances of a given dispute.

● The outcome must reflect the intent of the parties that negotiated the collective bargaining agreement. Arbitrators may not alter or ignore certain contract terms with an eye toward imposing their own brand of justice.

● Arbitrators are not bound by precedent, but they typically consult the decisions of other arbitrators in developing the rationale for their awards.

● While arbitration awards must draw their essence from the collective bargaining agreement, arbitrators are not precluded from looking beyond the four corners of the contract for guidance. When interpreting ambiguous contract terms, for example, arbitrators commonly seek clarification by examining prior grievance settlements between the parties, past practice within the workplace, and relevant industry customs.

● Arbitrators sometimes seek guidance from external statutes, such as Title VII of the 1964 Civil Rights Act, the Americans with Disabilities Act, and the Family and Medical Leave Act. This is particularly true where such laws are incorporated by reference in the collective bargaining agreement.

● When fashioning their awards, arbitrators also have the leeway to take into account the impact on productivity, morale, labor-management relations, employer reputation, and other considerations.

Notwithstanding the many factors that influence their awards, arbitrators ultimately are charged with giving force to the rights and obligations agreed to by the parties through the process of collective bargaining and contract negotiations. The chapters that follow examine how those rights and obligations play out in connection with a broad range of issues and a wide variety of factual situations.

How to Use This Book

As noted above, arbitrators are not bound by precedent, but they typically consult the decisions of other arbitrators in developing the rationale for their awards.

This thirteenth edition of *Grievance Guide* presents short synopses of arbitrators' decisions in a broad range of situations and workplaces. For each arbitration case referenced, *Grievance Guide* includes a citation to the full text of the arbitrator's ruling. Bloomberg BNA publishes the full text of these arbitrators' awards in *Labor Arbitration Reports,* available in print as part of BBNA's *Labor Relations Reporter* service. Thus, a citation such as 121 LA 229 is a reference to Vol. 121 of *Labor Arbitration Reports,* page 229. The arbitrators' rulings also are available on the Web as part of Bloomberg BNA's *Labor and Employment Law Resource Center* and on Bloomberg Law.

New to this edition are a detailed table of contents to the entire book, summary tables of contents at the start of each chapter, and LA CDI (Labor Relations Cumulative Digest Index) references to the location of the topics discussed in most chapters. For example, the chapter on Absenteeism & Tardiness references LA CDI 100.552507 (public employees); 118.6361–.6367. These index numbers direct the reader to other cases on the topic in BBNA's *Labor and Employment Library* or its *Resource Center* (online). Thus, the arbitration opinions on absenteeism for public-sector employees can be found at 118.6361 in the BBNA library or resource center. *Grievance Guide* will be used most effectively in conjunction with these other BBNA services.

Another useful resource is the National Academy of Arbitrator's annual Proceedings, published by Bloomberg BNA and also available in electronic form, without charge, at *http://naarb.org/proceedings/index.asp.* Articles published in the *Proceedings* are cited to on occasion both by advocates in arguing their positions and by arbitrators in their awards.

In addition, specific types of recurring workplace problems are discussed in treatises such as *Elkouri and Elkouri: How Arbitration Works* and *Discipline and Discharge in Arbitration,* both published by BBNA.

CONTENTS

Part 2. Discharge and Discipline: Categories

Part 3. Safety and Health

Part 4. Seniority and Its Application

Part 5. Disability

Part 8. Vacations

Part 10. Health Care Benefits

Part 11. Management Rights

Part 12. Union Rights

Part 13. Strikes and Lockouts

Part 14. Union Security

Part 15. Dues Checkoff

Part 16. Wages and Hours

Part 1

Discharge and Discipline:
In General

I. Just Cause for Discipline

OVERVIEW

A basic principle that arbitrators apply in reviewing employee discipline is the "just cause" standard.

Even where collective bargaining agreements do not specifically invoke this standard, arbitrators tend to follow the tenets of just cause in judging the appropriateness of disciplinary actions taken against workers.

SUMMARY OF CASES

A. Seven Tests of Just Cause

Aside from examining the facts and circumstances of each particular case, arbitrators typically weigh a number of routine considerations in determining whether management has acted fairly in disciplining employees. Years ago, one arbitrator expressed these considerations as a series of questions, widely known as the "seven tests of just cause discipline":

● Was the employee adequately warned of the consequences of his or her conduct? The need to warn the employee may be waived for certain kinds of conduct—e.g., insubordination, drinking on the job, or stealing employer property—that are so serious that the employee is expected to know the conduct is punishable.

● Was the employer's rule or order reasonably related to efficient and safe operation of its business?

● Did management investigate before administering the discipline? The investigation normally should be conducted before the decision to discipline is made. Where immediate action is required, however, an appropriate response would be to suspend the employee pending investigation with the understanding that he or she will be restored to the job and paid for time lost if absolved.

● Was the investigation fair and objective?

● Did the investigation produce substantial evidence or proof of guilt? Although arbitrators might require conclusive proof or evidence beyond a reasonable doubt in some cases—e.g., where the alleged misconduct is of such a criminal or reprehensible nature as to stigmatize the employee and seriously impair chances for future employment—they usually apply less stringent standards. For example, a common benchmark in arbitration cases is to require proof of guilt by a preponderance of evidence.

● Were the rules, orders, and penalties applied evenhandedly and without discrimination? If enforcement has been lax in the past, management cannot suddenly reverse its course and begin to crack down without first warning employees of its intent.

● Was the penalty reasonably related to the seriousness of the offense and the worker's employment record? On the one hand, the discipline should be tailored to fit the infraction. On the other hand, the prior conduct of each employee should be evaluated, enabling management to impose lesser or greater penalties in light of the individual's employment record.

In addition to the questions outlined above, arbitrators sometimes cite the following factors in resolving grievances over disciplinary actions:

• *Rule of reason*—Even in the absence of a specific contractual provision requiring just cause for discipline, a collective bargaining agreement protects employees against unjust discipline and permits a challenge to any employer procedure that threatens to deprive employees of their rights.

• *Internal equity and consistency*— The pattern of enforcement must be consistent, with employees judged by the same standards, regardless of whether employers discipline on a case-by-case basis or use a set of rules. This does not mean, however, that the same penalty always must be given for the same offense.

Arbitrators generally agree that employers enjoy reasonable discretionary powers to prescribe rules of conduct. At the same time, arbitrators have suggested that employers have an obligation to make employees aware of these rules, either by direct publication or by consistent enforcement. Arbitrators also have contended that employers should regard industrial discipline as corrective rather than punitive, and they should avoid arbitrary or hasty action when disciplining employees.

For more information about just cause see Adolph M. Koven & Susan L. Smith, *Just Cause: The Seven Tests* (BNA Books, 3d ed. 2006, revised by Kenneth May).

B. Just Cause Determinations

If management has acted in good faith after a proper investigation and fixes a penalty that is consistent with similar cases or what would be considered fair, an arbitrator should not attempt to second guess management, an arbitrator ruled. If the causes for discipline appear to be fair, the grievant must suffer the consequences of the misconduct (*Smith & Wesson-Fiocchi Inc.*, 60 LA 366).

Along these lines, arbitrators have concluded that just cause existed for discipline of:

• a bus driver who was suspended for one day because she did not report for work on a day for which she had requested but had been denied personal leave to go on a bicycle outing. Despite her contention that the discipline should have been an oral warning, which was the first step of the disciplinary process, an arbitrator ruled that there were no mitigating factors that would justify reducing the penalty, which was not arbitrary or an abuse of discretion (*Nassau County School District*, 125 LA 610);

• a cable splicing technician worker who was discharged after he allegedly told his supervisor, "You have a family that you want to go home to every night and I have a family that I want to go home to every night," while the manager quoted the worker as saying, "but if I don't get my respect, one of us won't be going home . . .". An arbitrator ruled that the worker intentionally intimidated and threatened his supervisor and the employer had just cause to discharge him (*AT&T Services Midwest*, 129 LA 249);

• a restaurant worker who was fired after violating rules that prohibited harassing behavior and abusive or profane language directed at customers and coworkers. An arbitrator found just cause for discharge based on several factors, including the employee's record of prior discipline for rude and discourteous behavior, as well as the fact that the employer had established reasonable rules, had notified employees of the consequences for violating them, and had conducted a full and fair investigation of the employee's misconduct (*Mirage Hotel-Casino*, 128 LA 344);

• a home-delivery meal driver who was discharged for failing to deliver hot meals to some senior citizens, since he tried to falsify records and the misconduct was so egregious that it threatened the senior citizens' health (*Bay County Division on Aging*, 98 LA 188);

• an employer who conducted an investigation because an employee hung an Aryan Nation poster on a workplace bulletin board and fired the employee after discovering that he had downloaded the poster from his office computer and had also visited more than 100 white supremacist and pornographic Web sites while at work (*Tesoro Refining & Marketing Co.*, 120 LA 1299);

- a warehouse worker who was fired when he failed to count inventory by hand, as instructed, resulting in a 70 percent inaccuracy rate (*Adelphia Communications*, 120 LA 467);
- a worker who was fired for secretly growing marijuana on company property. In addition to citing the criminal nature of the offense, an arbitrator said the employee had been untruthful and refused to take responsibility for his actions, undermining the union's argument for mitigation (*Green Bay Packaging Co.*, 119 LA 1185).

By contrast, if employers take disciplinary action against employees without adhering to just cause principles, arbitrators are unlikely to uphold the penalties imposed. For example, disciplinary actions were overturned or reduced in the following cases where:

- a bus driver on duty who received an emergency cell phone call about a family member was terminated. In 2009, the employer had instituted a first offense firing discipline policy based on safety recommendations from both the National Safety Council and the Federal Transit Administration to prohibit cell phones calls on buses "except in emergency situations." But it failed to continue providing an emergency telephone number for family use provided under its 2005 policy. Because the 2009 policy was vague and lacked mandatory language to clearly set forth a policy and procedure for when cell phones could be used, if at all, while bus drivers were on duty the employer lacked just cause to fire the driver and the termination reduced to suspension without back pay (*Jax Transit Management Corp.*, 129 LA 110).
- an employee who nodded off when he had no work to do on his first day of light duty was summarily discharged pursuant to a no-sleeping rule that the employer had unilaterally imposed solely for its light duty

room. An arbitrator called the rule "questionable" and determined that the employer lacked just cause to impose such a severe penalty for a first offense (*Harrah's Las Vegas Inc.*, 129 LA 133).

- a 10-year employee, investigated by his employer for possible involvement in a workplace theft, was fired for alleged dishonesty about criminal charges from 17 years earlier. Any incomplete or inaccurate information the employee provided about the criminal charges during the investigation or when applying at the company did not amount to willful omissions or lies, which meant that the employer lacked sufficient evidence to support just cause for termination (*Xcel Energy*, 128 LA 289);
- an operator of a street sweeper was fired for failing to properly care for company equipment, but the employer lacked documentation of any prior warnings and did not produce convincing evidence that the employee failed to perform required maintenance on the street sweeper he operated (*Minuteman Sweeping*, 120 LA 1154);
- a gun was discovered in an employee's vehicle in violation of a rule against weapons on company property, and the employer fired the worker without meeting the minimum requirement of interviewing him. At arbitration, the employee credibly testified that the gun belonged to his wife, and she had forgotten to remove it after the couple had gone on a morning hunting trip, while the employee himself had removed his bow and arrows in compliance with the no-weapons rule (*Weyerhaeuser Co.*, 120 LA 1146); and
- an employee was discharged for her hostility toward a co-worker, but management had not given the employee an opportunity to correct her behavior (*Datex-Ohmeda*, 119 LA 995).

II. Disciplinary Procedures [LA CDI 100.15 (public employees); 118.25]

_____ **OVERVIEW**_____

In resolving disputes over employee discipline, arbitrators do not concern themselves merely with whether workers are guilty of misconduct. They also consider the procedures used to administer work rules and impose discipline.

As part of their disciplinary procedures, employers are generally expected to apply certain standards of due process, such as conducting an investigation and affording employees an opportunity to respond to accusations against them. Collective bargaining agreements often specify additional requirements that must be satisfied.

The following list identifies several actions that, if taken by employers, reduce the likelihood of having discipline overturned at arbitration:

• Employers should make employees aware of workplace rules and policies before holding them accountable for violations. Special efforts should be taken to inform new employees of work rules, and all employees should be notified of policy changes. Management can use various means of communicating rules and policies, such as orientation sessions, employee handbooks, bulletin board postings, and e-mail notices.

• Managers and first-line supervisors should be well-versed in workplace policies and disciplinary procedures. Rules can easily be undermined by a failure to ensure consistent enforcement.

• Employers should gather facts and evidence before imposing discipline. For example, an investigation should be conducted and witnesses should be interviewed to elicit all sides of the story. Objective evidence should be relied upon, not baseless accusations or unfounded assumptions.

• Obligations for involving the union in the disciplinary process should be carefully observed. Many collective bargaining agreements require notification about disciplinary actions and union participation in meetings with employees. In addition, *Weingarten* (see F, Union Representation below) protections may apply to investigatory interviews.

• Disciplinary action should be taken within a reasonable period, although discipline is sometimes held up while a union completes its own investigation. Where serious misconduct is alleged, the employer can remove the employee from the premises and place him or her on suspension, without inference of guilt, pending the investigation's outcome.

SUMMARY OF CASES

A. Workplace Rules and Policies

Management has the authority to establish rules of conduct as long as they are reasonable and consistent with the collective bargaining agreement (97 LA 542, 93 LA 1082, 90 LA 625, 88 LA 1164).

Once promulgated, the rules can be challenged through grievance procedures and voided if they are unreasonable, arbitrary, discriminatory, vague, or ineffective (97 LA 675, 96 LA 122).

One test of a rule's validity is whether it reasonably relates to a legitimate objective of management (55 LA 283), but even reasonable rules have been held unenforceable if they are applied discriminatorily (26 LA 934) or infringe unduly on an employee's private life (18 LA 400).

• In one case, an arbitrator found an employer's dress standards discriminatory where male employees on the day shift had to wear neckties, male employees on the second shift did not have to wear them, and female employees could dress as they pleased. The rule failed the reasonableness test, because the necktie requirement was apparently based on the personal taste of the department head, the arbitrator held (*Union Tribune Publishing Co.*, 70 LA 266).

• An employer's rule excluding all food items from a communications room, unless employees had a medical reason for eating, was overly broad, an arbitrator found. It was already a common practice for employees to keep mints, cough drops, and hard candies at their desks in case their mouths got dry, and they should have been permitted to bring in breakfast or energy bars for a quick snack during their 10-hour work-days, according to the arbitrator (*Valley Communications Center*, 119 LA 1767).

• An arbitrator ruled that an employer did not have just cause to discharge an employee for violating an employer's rule against committing "any unsafe act" when he smoked on a parked forklift. The employer's safety and health guide specifically outlawed smoking in certain areas of the plant, while refueling, or within 50 feet of the refueling station, which limited the scope of the general prohibition against unsafe acts (*Georgia-Pacific Corrugated LLC*, 126 LA 698).

• A public utility did not have just cause to issue a written reprimand to a supervisor because one of his foremen brought his crew to have breakfast at a restaurant close to the service center, an arbitrator ruled. There was no rule, regulation, policy, or procedure governing breakfast, and the concept of just cause did not support disciplining a supervisor because one of his foremen ate breakfast with his crew every morning, when eating breakfast on the job was common conduct at the time, the arbitrator said (*JEA*, 128 LA 1046).

• A transit company policy barring drivers from using cell phones had defects, an arbitrator found, even though the rule was reasonably related to its purpose in protecting the driver, passengers, and the general public from the consequences of an accident. However the arbitrator found that the policy was vague and lacked mandatory language to clearly set forth when cell phones could be used when drivers were on duty. Further, the arbitrator said, the policy did not include exceptions for emergencies, or methods for family members of employees to contact them with urgent messages (*Jax Transit Management Corp.*, 129 LA 110).

● *By contrast*, an arbitrator held that a ready mix concrete company could prohibit its drivers from possessing cell phones while working. In finding the ban reasonable, the arbitrator cited the nature of the work and the fact that the employer had no means of checking adherence to an earlier policy, which permitted drivers to carry cell phones as long as they did not use them while on duty. The arbitrator also cited concerns about issues such as safety, productivity, and the public image projected by the drivers. In addition, the reasonableness of the expanded policy was supported by the employer's willingness to make exceptions in certain situations, such as when a driver had a family member with a serious illness or a wife in the last trimester of pregnancy (*Ozinga Illinois RMC Inc.*, 123 LA 198).

● An arbitrator upheld the discharge of an employee who illegally downloaded movies at work, finding he violated work rules barring theft or misappropriation of company property, misuse of company tools, unauthorized entry into company property, interfering with others in performance of work, and engaging in unauthorized personal work (*Haynes International*, 129 LA 559).

● Another arbitrator upheld a new requirement obligating leadmen and other employees in positions of authority to take action to stop any instances of harassment that they observed. The arbitrator noted that the policy was adopted after the affected employees held two days of meetings, its import was clear, and it was directly related to a legitimate business purpose (*American Mail-Well Envelope*, 105 LA 1209).

B. Communication of Rules

When evaluating the adequacy of disciplinary procedures, arbitrators often consider whether employers have informed employees about workplace rules and the consequences for violating them.

At the same time, arbitrators do not insist that employers take any specific approach to promulgating or communicating rules prior to disciplining employees.

For example, one arbitrator observed that many workplaces operate without formal rules, relying instead on employees having a modicum of common sense (*Davey Co.*, 60 LA 917).

Other arbitrators have held that:

● plant rules need not be put in writing (*Ohio Power Co.*, 50 LA 501);

● an employer could rely on the "grapevine" to announce a disciplinary policy (*Pacific Northwest Bell Telephone Co.*, 48 LA 498); and

● there is no one way of either setting or publicizing rules; they can become effective through experience and practice (*Eastern Air Lines*, 44 LA 459).

Nevertheless, management can establish firmer footing by effectively articulating workplace rules and policies, especially if they involve requirements that employees would not necessarily expect or understand absent adequate communication.

● In one case, an arbitrator overturned the discipline imposed on a librarian who sent out an e-mail message criticizing her school's new curriculum plan. Because the employer had no rules on e-mail usage, the librarian could not reasonably be expected to know she lacked the right to use the e-mail system the way she did. "It is well established that just cause requires that employees be informed of a rule, the infraction of which may result in disciplinary action, unless the conduct is so clearly wrong that specific reference is not necessary," the arbitrator said (*Conneaut School District*, 104 LA 909).

● Another arbitrator overturned the discharge of two employees who failed to indicate on a company questionnaire that they received coverage through a spouse's health plan in addition to the company's plan. Not only did the employees lack a clear understanding of the questionnaire, but they had never been informed that double coverage was improper, the arbitrator found (*Warner Jewelry Case Co.*, 87 LA 160).

● Where a company did not meet its contractual obligation to post a policy, an arbitrator decided that it lacked just cause to impose 30-day suspensions on two drivers who received speeding tickets, even though that was the penalty prescribed in the policy (*Foster Food Products*, 98 LA 854).

● *By contrast*, an employer adequately notified employees that downloading pornography was contrary to its standards through posting, mailing, distribution, the intranet, and incorporation by reference in another document. However the discharge of a 15-year employee who downloaded pornography was reduced to a suspension, where he did not save pornography on the intranet, nor did he e-mail it within or outside of the plant (*BASF Catalysts*, 129 LA 571).

● An arbitrator upheld an employee's termination for excessive Internet usage where his employer had a clear policy against such conduct, the employee had been advised that personal use of the Internet must be limited to non-work time, and he was warned after a previous incident of computer misuse that further problems would likely result in discharge (*Department of Veterans Affairs*, 122 LA 106).

C. Consistent Rule Enforcement

Where management has winked at violations of a rule, it should announce its intention to require observance of the rule before it hands out heavy penalties. This is especially true where the rule applies to conduct that is not inherently objectionable or clearly wrong, since lax enforcement can cause employees to think that management permits the conduct in question (94 LA 297, 93 LA 302, 66 LA 953).

● An employer improperly suspended an employee under a rule that had not been enforced for five years, an arbitrator ruled. When reviving the dormant rule, the employer was required to treat it as a new rule, the arbitrator said, adding that a verbal notice to the union that a "crackdown" would begin did not satisfy the employer's contractual obligation to post new rules (*Georgia-Pacific Corp.*, 89 LA 1080).

● An employee who violated a rule against making personal toll calls from work should not have been discharged, an arbitrator ruled. Finding that supervisory employees also had engaged in the practice, the arbitrator said "it is often held that employees should not be disciplined where

they have been led by members of supervision to believe that violation of a rule will be tolerated and condoned and where employees may logically be led to believe that the rule has either been discarded or relaxed to the point that violation will not subject the employee to discipline" (*General Telephone Co.*, 86 LA 138).

● An employer's inconsistent enforcement of an absenteeism policy—where one employee received a two-week suspension for his policy infraction while two similarly-situated co-workers received three-day suspensions—violated the employer's contractual obligation to impose discipline evenhandedly, an arbitrator held (*Interpack Corp.*, 87 LA 1232).

● An employer lacked just cause to fire an employee over the distribution of an e-mail with sexual content where company guidelines prohibiting such e-mails were "completely negated" by past practice, an arbitrator ruled. He noted that supervisors commonly used the company's e-mail system to send sexually charged jokes and other inappropriate messages, which gave rank-and-file workers the right to believe that such actions were condoned by the company (*Chevron Products Co.*, 116 LA 271).

D. Due Process Rights

Arbitrators generally agree that employers should incorporate basic notions of fairness and "industrial due process" in their disciplinary procedures. For example, employers are expected to investigate alleged misconduct and give employees a chance to tell their side of the story.

● One arbitrator called due process "an integral part" of just cause, and said a primary reason arbitrators have included certain due process rights within the concept of just cause is to help the parties prevent the imposition of discipline where there is little or no evidence to support the action. By engaging in a reasonable investigation of charges against employees prior to implementing discipline, employers can prevent a rush to judgment and avoid situations where they become exposed to grievances and liability for improper disciplinary actions (*Osborn & Ulland Inc.*, 68 LA 1152).

• An arbitrator found that a last chance agreement that was imposed on an employee was invalid, since it had no ending date and gave her no access to the grievance procedure if she was discharged. The remedy was to set the last chance agreement aside (*School District of the City of Flint*, 128 LA 609).

• An employer did not have just cause to fire an employee for her role in a workplace altercation, where she did not explain her side of the story, an arbitrator decided. When faced with allegations of wrongdoing, the employee told a supervisor to "do what she has to do," and the supervisor immediately fired her. Ordering the employee's reinstatement based on the lack of a fair and thorough investigation, the arbitrator said the supervisor reacted in an emotional manner rather than fulfilling her obligation to find facts, hear both sides, and make a neutral objective judgment (*Lincoln Lutheran of Racine, Wis.*, 113 LA 72).

• A school district did not give a discharged media specialist proper notice of a meeting before the school board, where the notice said that the employee did not "relate well" to students and "was not always pleasant." The arbitrator said more specific allegations were needed, and that the general allegations were "impossible to defend against." Finding the school district acted arbitrarily, capriciously, and discriminatorily in discharging the employee, the arbitrator reinstated her with back pay. The arbitrator retained jurisdiction stating that, should the school district seek to discharge the employee in the future, it must adhere to proper procedures, which included:

• providing a statement of specific acts or omissions it alleged to justify the employee's discharge,

• supplying other relevant information that will enable her to assess and contest allegations,

• affording her the opportunity to confront the evidence against her and adduce any evidence in her defense, and

• providing a concise statement of facts as found, and reason or reasons for its decision, should it decide to discharge her (*Griggsville-Perry School District*, 127 LA 1542).

• A city waited too long to discharge an employee who was on workers' compensation leave, when it waited ten months to discharge him. The employer claimed that the employee was no longer an employee while on leave. The arbitrator said that an employee on leave is still an employee, and the delay could affect witnesses' memories (*Municipality of Anchorage*, 128 LA 1153).

E. Union Involvement

Where a contract calls for notice of disciplinary action to be given to the union, arbitrators are likely to require strict compliance with such a provision. They operate on the theory that a worker's rights are seriously abridged if the union is not given a chance to get in on the ground floor.

• Even if the disciplined employee clearly was guilty of misconduct, the penalty may be mitigated if the union was not given proper notice. Thus, one arbitrator ordered a discharged employee reinstated without back pay where the employer failed to adhere to the contractual requirement of consultation with the union over discharges (*Hayes Mfg. Corp.*, 17 LA 412; see also 94 LA 7, 86 LA 503, 65 LA 690, 64 LA 425, 64 LA 67).

• Another arbitrator ruled that an employer that had failed to comply with notice requirements had to give an employee pay for time lost between the date of his discharge and the date of the first grievance meeting, even though his discharge was for just cause (*National Lead Co.*, 13 LA 28).

F. Union Representation

Arbitrators sometimes overturn or reduce penalties imposed on employees if their employers have failed to follow contractual procedures regarding union presence at disciplinary meetings. Arbitrators also have concluded that employees are entitled to union representation when an employer is conducting a preliminary investigation, based on the theory that this is the beginning stage of a potential disciplinary process (66 LA 581, 60 LA 1066, 60 LA 832, 60 LA 9).

The U.S. Supreme Court addressed this issue in *NLRB v. J. Weingarten Inc.* (420 U.S. 251, 88 LRRM 2689 (1975)), finding that employees have a right to union representation in certain situations. Specifically, the court said such a right exists when an employer is conducting an investigatory interview that could lead to disciplinary action.

In other situations, however, *Weingarten* protections do not come into play. For example, arbitrators have held that union representation is not required during employer searches, in meetings whose purpose is to administer discipline that has already been decided upon, or during employee questioning that does not involve a risk of potential discipline (120 LA 1729, 98 LA 355, 87 LA 568, 84 LA 562, 83 LA 1248).

[See also Part 12, Union Rights.]

● A collective bargaining agreement mandated that a union steward be allowed to attend any meeting "where possible disciplinary measures may be taken" and gave the union the right to notice "prior to any discharge" and "to be present when formal charges are made." An employee was given a disciplinary notice for neglecting to perform scheduled maintenance of a forklift. A union steward was present then but not at subsequent meetings when the employee was suspended and discharged. Despite conceding that the employee's negligence warranted discharge, an arbitrator ordered reinstatement with back pay based on the employer's failure to ensure a steward's presence when it suspended and discharged the employee (*S and J Ranch*, 103 LA 350).

● A quarry did not have just cause to immediately suspend a grievant following his refusal to accept his supervisor's assignment to work out of his classification in a "pit" loading large stones, even though the penalty imposed did not violate the collective bargaining agreement's disciplinary progression, an arbitrator ruled. The quarry failed to conduct a "thorough investigation," provide union written notification of discipline, or ensure that a union steward was present for steps three through five of the progression as required by agreement (*County Line Stone Co.*, 128 LA 1807).

● An employer failed to meet its *Weingarten* obligation when it denied union representation to an employee who was ordered to write out an explanation about damaged property, an arbitrator held. Although the employee was not at risk of discipline in connection with the property damage, he was threatened with discipline for refusing to provide a signed statement. Finding that the threat of discipline triggered the employee's right to union representation, the arbitrator overturned the employer's subsequent decision to fire the employee for insubordination (*Ralphs Grocery Co.*, 101 LA 634).

● Similarly, an arbitrator held that an employee could not be punished for refusing to discuss a performance matter with her supervisor in the absence of a union representative. The employee legitimately believed that the discussion was for the purpose of conducting an investigatory interview that could lead to discipline, the arbitrator found, and the collective bargaining agreement made the presence of a union representative at disciplinary discussions mandatory if an employee so requested (*Pacific Bell*, 92 LA 127).

● On the other hand, the duty to allow union representation was not breached when an employer immediately suspended an employee for an alleged theft, an arbitrator ruled. The employee did not request union representation during that brief initial session—which was the normal procedure used by the company to get employees off the premises in potentially serious cases while gathering information and deciding further steps to take—and he received union representation at a subsequent meeting in which his possible discharge was discussed, the arbitrator noted (*Union Tank Car Co.*, 104 LA 699).

● An arbitrator ruled that an employer did not violate the due process rights of an employee, even though she did not have a union representative and witness when her supervisor alleged that she refused to go to human resources for a random drug test, where she did not request a union representative or stay long enough for a representative or other member of management to be called to scene (*Kellogg Co.*, 124 LA 1674).

● An arbitrator ruled that a discharged employee was not improperly denied union representation rights at two meetings with management, where he voluntarily went to management for the first meeting to report an incident in which he had mixed chemical waste, and, at the next meeting, called to discuss the incident, he made no request for union representation, nor did he consult with the union steward before preparing a written statement (*Chemical Solvents Inc.*, 129 LA 888).

• No violation occurred where employees waived an employer's offer to have a union representative attend a meeting at which they received suspensions that had already been decided upon by management based on its direct observation of the employees' safety infractions, an arbitrator held. Even if the employees changed their minds and asked for a union representative, they would not have been entitled to one unless they held the view that the meeting was an investigation that could form the basis of some future discipline, the arbitrator noted (*CMP Inc.*, 106 LA 437).

• In another case, the presence of a steward shielded an employer from a claim that it failed to meet due process standards when it interviewed an employee without first warning him that he could face discipline. The employer met its *Weingarten* obligation by including a union steward in the meeting, an arbitrator ruled, and the employer had no legal or contractual obligation to inform the employee that he could be subject to discipline pending the outcome of the investigatory process (*United Airlines Inc.*, 120 LA 1810).

III. Proving Misconduct [LA CDI 94.60543]

OVERVIEW

In most disciplinary cases, particularly those involving discharge, management generally has the burden of proving guilt or wrongdoing, particularly where a collective bargaining agreement requires "just cause" for discharge.

The amount or degree of proof required to prove misconduct, however, is not a cut-and-dried matter. It may vary with the severity of the alleged offense, the type of evidence at hand, and the individual arbitrator's analysis of particular facts in a given case.

Strict observance of legal rules of evidence is usually not necessary, unless expressly requested by the parties.

SUMMARY OF CASES

A. Determining Degree of Proof

In disciplinary and discharge hearings, the degree of proof required by arbitrators to substantiate allegations against employees can vary according to the type of offense involved. When employees face particularly serious accusations—e.g., those involving criminal or morally reprehensible misdeeds—arbitrators often invoke the common law standard of "proof beyond a reasonable doubt" (64 LA 1099, 66 LA 619). For other allegations, arbitrators commonly require lesser standards of proof, including "a preponderance of the evidence," "clear and convincing evidence," or "evidence sufficient to convince a reasonable mind of guilt" (77 LA 978, 77 LA 569, 77 LA 483, 77 LA 210, 75 LA 574, 74 LA 877, 74 LA 737).

● An employer applied an arbitrary and capricious standard for discharge where collective bargaining agreement did not contain a just cause provision. The arbitrator said that "it is a foundational principle of labor arbitration that, in the search for the collective agreement's intent, a general reservation of managerial rights does not necessarily reserve to management the power to exercise that right arbitrarily, capriciously, or discriminatorily (*Griggs-ville-Perry School District*, 127 LA 1542).

● The burden of proof was clear and convincing evidence of dishonesty in a case in which a 35-year employee with a good work record was discharged after she did work at home without getting prior authorization. The employer argued that the arbitrator should apply the "clear and convincing evidence" standard while the union argued for a standard of proof "beyond a reasonable doubt." The arbitrator stated, "Consistent with my policy in termination cases, it is only necessary that the Company's proof be clear and convincing and based on a preponderance of the evidence in order to sustain the discharge action. The concept of just cause implies no more than this. Of course, this assumes that the Company's actions must not be arbitrary, discriminatory, or unreasonable." Finding the grievant made mistakes in connection with events leading to her discharge, but there was not just cause for discharge, the arbitrator ordered reinstatement but without back pay or benefits (*Safeway Stores*, 128 LA 257).

● An arbitrator decided that the proper standard of proof was that of "clear and convincing evidence" in a case where an employee was discharged for allegedly pulling a knife on a co-worker during an argument. "Virtually all arbitrators agree that proof merely by a preponderance of evidence is not sufficient where an employee has been charged with a crime or discharged for violence, theft, gross insubordination, unlawful discrimination or other reasons that reflect upon his honesty, character or desirability of employment," the arbitrator said. Citing the inadequacy of the employer's investigation and the lack of sufficient evidence in the case, the arbitrator overturned the discharge (*City of Hollywood, Fla.*, 122 LA 335).

● Similarly, an arbitrator indicated that there is widespread agreement that the "preponderance of evidence" standard is not sufficient where employees have been discharged for reasons that reflect on personal character or affect future employment prospects. Accordingly, the arbitrator said the appropriate quantum of proof was that of clear and convincing evidence in reviewing allegations that an employee mistreated a helpless nursing home patient. The employee's discharge was overturned because the arbitrator did not reach the point where he was fully convinced of the employee's guilt based on evidence presented at the arbitration hearing (*Barton Center, Senior Health Management, LLP*, 121 LA 249).

● Another arbitrator addressed the standard of proof for cases of employee theft, saying, "While some arbitrators require proof by clear and convincing evidence, many others hold that proof should be made beyond a reasonable doubt." The arbitrator went on to suggest that if a case is based on circumstantial evidence, the circumstances relied upon should be consistent with a theory of guilt and inconsistent with any theory of innocence. Concluding that the employer failed to support its charge of theft "by any standard of proof that may be applied," the arbitrator ordered reinstatement with back pay for the accused employee (*General Telephone Co. of Southwest*, 79 LA 102).

● *By contrast*, a heightened burden of clear and convincing evidence was not appropriate in a case in which an employee threatened co-workers, an arbitrator ruled. The employee told her shop steward that she would kill two co-workers if she lost her job due to other charges of offensive statements that she made at work, which they had brought against her. The arbitrator said that the heightened burden was not bargained for, her conduct was not a crime, and termination was not the equivalent of a criminal conviction (*Dixie Consumer Products LLC*, 128 LA 545).

● The penalty of discharge was too severe for an employee who allegedly participated in an attempt to steal company-owned property, since the employer failed to establish the worker's guilt beyond a reasonable doubt, an arbitrator ruled. The "drastic nature of the sanction of discharge" requires a higher standard of proof, the arbitrator said, emphasizing that not only is a discharged employee out of a job, but he also faces reduced opportunities for future employment where allegations of dishonesty are concerned (*Daystrom Furniture Co. Inc.*, 65 LA 1157; see also 75 LA 588).

● On the other hand, an arbitrator decided that an employer met the burden of proof necessary to discharge an employee who was found to have deliberately falsified her time card just a few days after management warned all employees to use caution in completing their time cards. According to the arbitrator, the employer showed by a preponderance of the evidence that it had satisfied the following elements: "a valid rule existed for the safe and efficient operation of the employer's facility; Grievant was aware of the rule; Grievant violated the rule; there was a full, complete and impartial investigation; the discipline imposed was not excessive; and other employees upon similar violations were similarly treated" (*Vertex Aerospace LLC*, 120 LA 767; see also 122 LA 413).

B. Types of Evidence

In discipline and discharge cases, evidence presented during arbitration hearings can take various forms. Arbitrators tend to weigh a number of factors in making determinations about the credibility of evidence offered by management and unions. For example, arbitrators might consider:

● any conflict or contradiction in the evidence,

● any inconsistency in the testimony of accused employees and other witnesses, and

● the source of the witnesses' testimony—whether it is firsthand knowledge or merely hearsay and gossip.

Management should have enough facts in hand to establish just cause at the time of discipline or discharge. Efforts to build a strong case by extensive research after a grievance is filed could be a waste of time, since arbitrators often hold that management's case must stand or fall on the basis of facts it had when it took disciplinary action (12 LA 108, 10 LA 117, 1 LA 153).

This does not mean, however, that employers have to gather all the relevant facts and information before taking steps to address misconduct. A common approach used by management is to suspend employees pending further investigation. Even if management informs employees that the likely outcome will be minor discipline, it is generally within its rights to impose a stiffer penalty if its accumulation of further evidence shows just cause for such a penalty.

Arbitrators have found investigations were inadequate in cases in which:

● a chemical plant did not properly investigate before it discharged an employee for intentionally sleeping on the job, because it did not interview the grievant or any of the firsthand witnesses, and it wasn't clear the sleeping was intentional. The employee was reinstated without back pay (*BASF Corp.*, 128 LA 1233).

● management officials had made up their minds before they heard the grievant/police officer's evidence, even though they properly gave him an opportunity to present his evidence. "Due process during the investigation means management's mind is open, that its position on the important question of guilt or innocence is not polarized," the arbitrator said. "Any discipline imposed where a faulty and inadequate investigation is conducted must be overturned because of procedural deficiency" (*City of Sandy*, 129 LA 669).

● a correctional officer's discharge for falsifying his employment application was improper, where the correctional center delayed 28 months after completion of the application to notify the officer that he was being investigated and took another 16 months to complete investigation (*Federal Detention Center Miami*, 123 LA 1236).

● a county did not have just cause to discharge a firefighter/paramedic whose drug test showed she had morphine in her system, where the medical review officer did not do independent research to see if the medications the firefighter said she was taking could have metabolized into morphine. There was no other evidence, such as of prior drug abuse, to suspect that employee used drugs (*Orange County Florida*, 123 LA 1464).

● *By contrast*, an employer thoroughly and properly investigated a bus driver accused of falsifying a time card, where it gave the driver an opportunity to respond, interviewed all employees involved, and reviewed its own data and records to see if the driver's account of events was credible (*Oahu Transit Services Inc.*, 123 LA 814).

● An employee's confessions of workplace alcohol and drug use were admissible, even though he was interviewed for more than four hours before he made admissions, because he was repeatedly told he could leave the room if he wished. (*University of California, Berkeley*, 123 LA 1426).

● The investigation of an employee who sent sexual text messages to co-workers was fair. Even though the employer did not give the grievant the names of those who claimed that they had asked him to stop sending messages, the union and grievant had not asked for those names, the arbitrator pointed out, and the sexual harassment policy under which the grievant was disciplined protected those who were offended by the activity but felt awkward about objecting to it. The grievant's discharge was reduced to a long-term suspension by the arbitrator (*Sara Lee Foods*, 128 LA 129).

● A county-operated nursing home did not have to conduct its own investigation of two employees it discharged for smoking marijuana in a parked car on the home's premises, where the employees admitted the offenses to police and tested positive for marijuana. The arbitrator said that an independent investigation would only be a "formality" and was not needed (*Friendship Ridge*, 128 LA 116).

1. Post-Discharge Evidence

In some cases, arbitrators are willing to consider facts that emerge after disciplinary action has been taken. While arbitrators are reluctant to uphold a harsher penalty than what would have been justified by the information management had at the time it acted, arbitrators also are reluctant to ignore "after-acquired evidence" or "post-discharge evidence" that sheds new light on how a particular case should be resolved.

● An employee who was discharged because of customer complaints would have been entitled to a lesser penalty but for information that came to light after his termination, an arbitrator held. Evidence of additional problems—beyond the handful of complaints on which the discharge decision was based—revealed a pattern of conduct toward customers that was far more serious than previously known and showed that the employee was unfit to service the company's customers, the arbitrator said in denying reinstatement (*BFI Gardena Div.*, 121 LA 289).

● Another arbitrator allowed an employer to present evidence of post-discharge conduct to buttress its case against an employee. While on suspension pending termination for violating the company's policies on profanity and workplace violence, the employee telephoned a company official and made remarks that were loud, angry, threatening, and laced with profanity. This evidence was appropriate to consider because it had a direct connection and relevance to the employee's earlier conduct and the subject matter of the case, the arbitrator noted in upholding the discharge (*Kapalua Land Co.*, 121 LA 1269).

● A union that alleged disparate treatment in the discipline of an employee was allowed to present evidence showing that another worker subsequently received a lesser penalty for the same type of violation, an arbitrator ruled. Even though the evidence could not be applied to the analysis of past practices or factors used by management in making its discipline decision against the employee in question, it does serve to provide another example of the employer's inconsistent application of its discipline policy, the arbitrator observed in converting the employee's discipline to a lesser penalty (*Rhodia Inc.*, 120 LA 1392).

● An arbitrator refused to accept additional evidence from a union in another case alleging disparate treatment. In defending an employee who was fired for cursing at his boss, the union attempted to introduce evidence at the arbitration hearing on discipline issued to other employees who had confrontations with their supervisors. Evidence generally cannot be presented for the first time at the hearing, the arbitrator noted, because that would undermine one of the main purposes of multi-step contractual grievance procedures, which is to give the parties an opportunity to fully weigh relevant information and engage in discussions that can bring the grievance to a resolution (*MeadWestvaco Corp.*, 117 LA 1287).

● After-acquired evidence showing falsification of an employment application was disallowed by an arbitrator in a case where an employee was terminated for unsatisfactory conduct. The arbitrator refused to require the union to address the issue of application fraud at arbitration, noting that it was not part of the conduct for which the employee was discharged nor part of the matter grieved (*Lenox Hill Hospital*, 102 LA 1071).

C. Witnesses

One of the most important types of evidence is the testimony of witnesses, particularly when they describe the facts and circumstances upon which disciplinary action was based (77 LA 721, 75 LA 1147, 73 LA 771, 73 LA 610, 71 LA 1109, 71 LA 949).

One arbitrator devised the following criteria to be used to determine the credibility of witnesses' testimony, including:
● the relative strength of their recollections,
● the consistency in testimony given on the same subject at different times during hearings and in different settings,
● the showing of obvious bias or prejudice,
● the showing of emotional stress or other feelings that would impair ability to respond to questions carefully and accurately,
● evasiveness,
● the quality and reasonableness of testimony, and
● the existence of corroborating testimony (*Safeway Stores Inc.*, 96 LA 304).

Arbitrators sometimes bring in outside experts for impartial study of the disputed matter (6 LA 218, 18 LA 447, 21 LA 573). For example, arbitrators have accepted testimony of handwriting experts and have based their awards principally on such testimony.
● An employee's discharge for sexual harassment was upheld by an arbitrator after a handwriting expert determined that the employee was responsible for a note scrawled on a bathroom stall about a co-worker. While the note by itself could have supported the employer's disciplinary action, the arbitrator said a finding of

just cause for discharge was "inescapable" when evidence of other harassing conduct aimed at the co-worker was also taken into account (*Escalade Sports*, 118 LA 1761).
● In a case involving the discharge of an employee for allegedly writing and posting three obscene notices slandering female employees, the arbitrator ignored the employee's refusal to take a lie detector test, holding that he was within his rights in so refusing. The arbitrator did, however, rely on the testimony of a handwriting expert in upholding the discharge. He noted that the examiner's qualifications as an expert were substantial and that his identification of the employee as the author was both positive and firm (*Seaview Industries Inc.*, 39 LA 125).

1. Witness Interviews

● A health care center did not have just cause to discharge an employee it accused of refusing an order to weigh residents, because it did not interview her. If it had, she would have told them that she refused the order in jest, the arbitrator said (*Whispering Pines Health Care Center,* 125 LA 827).
● An employer did not have just cause to discharge an employee who failed a drug test, in part because it did not interview him and give him time to explain, to consider his work record and whether rehabilitation, which the arbitrator eventually ordered, was more appropriate. The arbitrator noted that failure to give the employee an opportunity to give his side of the story "constitutes an abuse of the Company's discretion," which is "inconsistent with the principles of just cause." He said that the employer acted arbitrarily in other ways, and observed that just cause does not necessarily require "a company to give some kind of hearing before administering discipline" (*Kohler Printing Inc.*, 125 LA 137).
● *By contrast,* an employer had just cause to discharge an employee for theft, even though it did not interview him. The arbitrator noted that if the discharged employee "had provided the same explanation he gave at the arbitration hearing, the likelihood that the Company would have accepted it is nil." The arbitrator also expressed

his view that "a failure to specify charges or to solicit input from the employee before a disciplinary decision does not automatically taint the action" (*Tube City LLC*, 124 LA 1212).

D. Unnamed or Biased Accusers

Some arbitrators have refused to sustain discipline based on charges by persons whom the employer refused either to identify or produce at the arbitration hearing. In one such case, an arbitrator said an employer's failure to call an employee's supervisor to testify about the events leading to the employee's discharge "seriously weakens the credibility of significant pieces of evidence the company has introduced" (*Cal-Compack Foods*, 105 LA 865; see also 105 LA 1089, 88 LA 75).

On the other hand, in a case where an employee's discharge was based on the report of a professional "spotter" employed to detect irregularities, an arbitrator held that the employer did not have to produce the spotter at the hearing, because this would have destroyed his effectiveness, which was the result, in part, of his anonymity (*Shenango Valley Transportation Co.*, 23 LA 362).

Although employees sometimes claim that they have been "set up," arbitrators generally agree that there is no reason to presume that supervisors would unjustifiably select and accuse employees of misconduct. When faced with conflicting testimony from employees and their accusers, arbitrators tend to recognize that accused employees have "a strong incentive for denying the charges," in that they stand immediately to gain or lose in the case (*Grand Union Co.*, 48 LA 812).

However, evidence of ulterior motives or ill will against employees usually prompts arbitrators to scrutinize accusers' testimony for signs of bias (60 LA 206, 63 LA 244, 64 LA 304).

For example, an arbitrator overturned the discharge of an employee who was apparently subjected to retaliation after turning in a foreman for being intoxicated on the job. Two other employees accused the employee of being a "goof-off," but one of the accusers was the foreman's broth-

er-in-law and the other was his neighbor. The arbitrator refused to put any stock in the testimony of the foreman's allies and instead credited the testimony of other employees who said they had never had any trouble working with the discharged employee (*Scientific Data Systems Inc.*, 53 LA 487).

E. Searches

Evidence obtained through searches typically is beyond question if the searches have been conducted with employees' permission. In recognition of this fact, collective bargaining agreements often address management's right to conduct searches. For example, a contract's drug and alcohol provisions might require workers to consent to searches as a condition of employment (121 LA 1729, 120 LA 1587).

Even if employees have not given their consent, they have limited expectations of privacy in the employment context, and arbitrators are likely to accept evidence obtained through searches unless the employers' conduct was egregious or in violation of the concepts of fair play.

● The search of an employee's lunch box, which he had left in an open tool locker, was justified based on a reasonable suspicion that the employee had taken company property, an arbitrator held. After the employee was seen in a parts room removing some items that had nothing to do with the work he was assigned, a supervisor searched the employee's lunch box and found the items. In upholding the employee's termination, the arbitrator said that the search was supported by reasonable cause and was not a dramatic intrusion on the employee's privacy (*American Welding & Mfg. Co.*, 89 LA 247).

● Discharge was also upheld by an arbitrator in a case where a supervisor found marijuana in the zippered compartment of a wallet that an employee had lost. The arbitrator rejected the argument that the inspection of the zippered compartment constituted an improper search, even though the supervisor could have identified the wallet's owner by looking only at the open portion of the wallet (*Rust Engineering Co.*, 85 LA 407).

• An employee's privacy rights were not violated when his employer searched the home of his ex-wife, at her invitation, and discovered company property on the premises, an arbitrator held. The ex-wife's accusation that the employee had been taking company property over a period of years gave the employer reasonable cause for the search, the arbitrator said in upholding the employee's discharge (*Exxon Co., U.S.A.*, 101 LA 777).

• Another arbitrator concluded that an employer was within its rights to use a drug detection dog to search the vehicles of employees. The arbitrator found that the search technique was justified, based on a supervisor's reasonable belief that there might be a drug problem among employees at the facility (*Georgia Power Co.*, 93 LA 846).

• On the other hand, an arbitrator ruled against an employer that had allowed security personnel at one of its plants to inspect employee vehicles for contraband such as drugs and firearms. The security personnel were looking through the windows of vehicles in the plant parking lot and, on occasion, instructing employees to allow a search of the interior or face discipline. The arbitrator ordered the employer to discontinue the practice, pointing out that the union contract allowed searches within the plant's gates but required the consent of employees for vehicle searches in the parking lot (*U.S. Steel Corp.*, 121 LA 1557).

F. Surveillance

Many arbitrators have allowed employers to conduct video surveillance of employees in order to monitor their work or prevent wrongdoing. Objections to surveillance often focus on whether it violates employees' privacy rights. As is the case with searches, however, arbitrators are likely to accept evidence obtained through video surveillance of employees.

• Videotape evidence of an employee committing safety offenses was admissible, despite contention that parties had agreed that videotaping would not be used for disciplinary actions, an arbitrator said. There was no testimony as to the history of discussions on the surveillance issue, the grievant apparently did not contest the use of the videotape, and there was no claim that the videotape was inaccurate or altered (*Rock-Tenn Co.*, 127 LA 390).

• Video evidence that a discharged employee had entered an information technology room to which he was not entitled access to perform a sex act was admissible, despite the contention that the employer had used camera for surveillance without bargaining with union, an arbitrator ruled. The camera was not used for monitoring employees but was being tested in a high-security room (*Bluffton Motor Works LLC*, 125 LA 1596).

1. Time Cards

• An employer may not make regular and systemic review of data generated by a card swipe security system for the purpose of disciplinary charges, where a collective bargaining contract provides the time sheet as the initial source by which an employee's presence on the premises is established, an arbitrator ruled. Security system data may only be used if review of the time sheet submissions and other separate evidence creates a reasonable suspicion that an employee has violated some rule or policy (*Michigan Education Association*, 124 LA 1322).

• Video tapes that purported to show that an employee did not punch in as his card indicated are not admissible, where only "enhanced reading of the tape," was available and had not been shown at the third step of the grievance procedure. (*Good Humor-Breyers Ice Cream*, 126 LA 178) (Arb. 2009).

• Rejecting a hotel employee's privacy objections, an arbitrator allowed into evidence a videotape of the employee having sex with her supervisor. After becoming concerned about theft in the hotel's banquet office, management installed a hidden surveillance camera in the office's ceiling. Although the employee claimed that she had an expectation of privacy when she engaged in sex in the locked office, the arbitrator pointed out that at least a dozen other employees had keys to the office and could have abruptly entered, which meant that the employee consented to at least a limited invasion of her privacy (*Wyndham Franklin Plaza Hotel*, 105 LA 186).

• An employer's video surveillance of its time-clock area was found permissible by an arbitrator in a case involving the discharge of employees for falsifying time cards. The employer had notified employees about the installation of the videotaping system and said it would be used for time card audits. The arbitrator upheld discharge of fifteen employees based on video evidence showing that upon their arrival, some punched more than one card, while others showed up late for work but used the already punched cards to report their time (*Casting Engineers*, 76 LA 939).

• Use of a television surveillance system was knocked down by another arbitrator, but only on the ground that installation of the cameras was a substantial enough change in working conditions to require negotiation with the union. The arbitrator did not close the door to the use of closed circuit cameras as a supervisory tool. In fact, he rejected the union's claim that this constituted an unlawful invasion of privacy or spying (*EICO Inc.*, 44 LA 563).

• Video surveillance conducted away from the workplace provided evidence to support an employee's discharge for attendance policy violations. Although the employee called in to say he would be staying home to care for his sick wife, which would have constituted excused leave, investigators hired by the employer videotaped him packing up and going on a hunting trip with his father-in-law. An arbitrator upheld the discharge, finding no "untoward invasion of privacy" in connection with the surveillance, all of which was conducted outdoors and in the open (*Interstate Brands Corp.*, 121 LA 1580).

• Another arbitrator found that an employer had reason to conduct surveillance of an employee who was suspected of engaging in other employment while taking a leave of absence. The videotape obtained by the employer showed that the employee was indeed performing outside work during leave, which justified his discharge, the arbitrator held (*Cenex Harvest States*, 120 LA 775).

G. Polygraph Tests

Arbitrators have expressed differing views on polygraph tests. In a number of cases, arbitrators have accorded at least some weight to polygraph results or to employees' refusal to submit to lie detector tests. Traditionally, however, arbitrators have been reluctant to rely on the results or infer guilt when employees decline to be tested. In deciding to discount polygraph results, some arbitrators have referred to state law restrictions or court rulings on their admissibility as evidence.

[Many states have passed laws that restrict the use of polygraph tests in employment situations. At the federal level, the Employee Polygraph Protection Act includes a broad prohibition against testing applicants and employees. However, one exemption under the law allows for testing current employees as part of private-sector employers' investigations into workplace theft or other incidents causing economic loss, so long as employers have reasonable suspicion that the employees were involved in the incidents, and examinees receive pretest written notice detailing the incidents being investigated and the basis for the employers' suspicion. EPPA does not preempt state or local laws or collective bargaining agreements that impose more restrictive provisions than the federal law.]

• One arbitrator rejected the argument that polygraph evidence should be admitted to corroborate the truthful demeanor of a discharged police officer, not for evidence of the ultimate issue of fact. The arbitrator noted that most arbitrators and courts have rejected polygraph tests as unreliable and said that truthful demeanor is an issue of fact to be decided by the arbitrator (*City of Oakland*, 128 LA 231).

• An arbitrator held that a nursing home had a right to require an employee to submit to a polygraph test as part of its investigation of an assault and robbery on its premises. The arbitrator contended that a polygraph test is a legitimate tool that an employer can use in such an investigation, and the evidence already gathered by the nursing home provided it with a reasonable suspicion that the employee had committed the crime (*Orthodox Jewish Home for the Aged*, 91 LA 810).

• A different arbitrator held that polygraph tests could be offered to employees on a voluntary basis when there was reason to suspect them of dishonesty, and the employer could consider the failure to take the tests as an additional factor in determining whether to proceed with disciplinary action (*Lag Drug Co.*, 39 LA 1121).

● Similarly, other arbitrators have held that polygraph results can provide helpful supplemental evidence, or may be considered as a factor of evidence rather than the sole basis of proof (88 LA 1019, 77 LA 1259, 64 LA 453, 43 LA 450, 39 LA 883, 39 LA 470).

● Still others have said that employees' refusal to submit to tests cannot be used against them, especially where employers are fishing for a guilty party among a group of employees and have not yet accused any particular person (73 LA 304, 39 LA 470, 32 LA 44).

● Another arbitrator completely rejected polygraph tests. Citing the fact that courts had ruled them inadmissible as evidence in criminal and civil cases, the arbitrator concluded that the same rule should apply to arbitration proceedings (*Continental Air Transport Co. Inc.*, 38 LA 778; see also 75 LA 574, 75 LA 313, 71 LA 1202, 70 LA 909, 68 LA 581).

● Similarly, an arbitrator discounted the use of polygraph results in a proceeding involving a discharge for theft, where state law forbade the reference to, or use of, polygraph tests in court proceedings (*Deer Lakes School District*, 94 LA 334).

IV. Types of Penalties [LA CDI 100.5501–.5523 (public employees); 118.01–.41]

OVERVIEW

It is universally recognized that management, in executing its operational responsibilities, has the right to establish and enforce standards of conduct and performance. Inherent in the right to enforce those standards is the power to discipline or discharge employees who fail to meet management's reasonable expectations.

A primary consideration for arbitrators in the review of discipline and discharge cases is whether the penalties imposed by management are in keeping with the seriousness of employees' offenses. Numerous arbitrators have expressed the view that some offenses justify immediate discharge, while other offenses demand lesser penalties. For offenses that do not warrant discharge, the most common penalties are warnings and reprimands, which can be oral or written, and suspensions.

Collective bargaining agreements frequently call for a sliding scale of penalties based on the seriousness of the misconduct. In addition, many provide for progressive discipline, which is a system of escalating penalties designed to give employees opportunities to learn from their mistakes and improve their conduct. A typical progressive discipline policy would impose the following penalties: oral warning, written warning, suspension, and discharge. Termination normally would occur after repeated incidents of misconduct, although summary discharge still could be triggered by offenses such as theft, violence, intoxication, or gross insubordination.

Arbitrators generally agree with the premise that discipline should be corrective rather than punitive. Even if a contract does not provide for progressive discipline, arbitrators often hold that employees should have a chance to correct problematic conduct before suffering the ultimate penalty of termination.

In addition to considering prior discipline and the seriousness of an offense in deciding whether penalties imposed on employees are appropriate, arbitrators typically look for various mitigating issues, such as the possibility of double jeopardy and the failure of management to:

- provide adequate warning about the potential consequences of the conduct in question,
- impose discipline evenhandedly based on a fair investigation and sufficient evidence of guilt, and
- give due consideration to workers' employment records in deciding on the penalty.

SUMMARY OF CASES

A. Progressive Discipline

In general, progressive discipline is based on the premise that penalties short of discharge allow employees a chance to correct problematic behavior and remain productive members of employers' workforces.

As one arbitrator explained, the policy of progressive discipline "does not mean that for any given employee each penalty must necessarily be more severe than the immediate preceding one, regardless of the offense involved." Progressive discipline means that "progressively more severe penalties may be imposed on each given employee each time any given offense is repeated." The arbitrator added that progressive discipline also means "that after a specified number of offenses, regardless of whether the offenses are identical or not, the company may have the right to discharge the given employee." Finally, the arbitrator said these interpretations of progressive discipline "avoid the inequitable meting out of discipline, and at the same time serve the dual purpose of progressive discipline—namely, the discouragement of repeated offense by employees—and the protection of the right of the company to

sever completely its relationships with any employee who by his total behavior shows himself to be irresponsible" (*Bell Aircraft Corp.*, 17 LA 230).

A contractual requirement to apply progressive discipline does not mean, however, that employers must always take incremental action or proceed through the escalating scale of penalties in lock-step fashion. For example, offenses such as stealing or drunkenness on the job are regarded as so serious that no specific warning or prior disciplinary action need precede discharge. Employees are presumed to know that such serious offenses trigger termination (66 LA 286, 27 LA 768).

- If progressive discipline were to apply to every case, one arbitrator noted, an employee who brutally assaulted his foreman or a fellow employee would get off with a warning if it were only his first offense. Thus, he held, the schedule of penalties spelled out in the contract was intended to apply to the offenses referred to and other violations of specific contract provisions and was not intended to apply to other offenses, including serious infractions of plant rules (*Alliance Machine Co.*, 48 LA 457).

● An employer need not give an employee who physically threatened his supervisor the benefit of progressive discipline, an arbitrator ruled. Since such an offense is sufficiently serious to justify immediate discharge, no employee should be required to feel physically threatened at work, and, when a threat is directed toward a member of management, the employer's legitimate authority to operate in an orderly and safe manner is undermined (*Detroit Thermal LLC*, 129 LA 1364).

Four employees who repeatedly used improper computer keying were discharged with just cause, another arbitrator held. In this case, management discovered that the employees manipulated company software while operating forklifts equipped with computer screens and keyboards used to assign and track in-house goods. The employer accused the employees of using a keying sequence that artificially inflated their productivity figures, which were used to determine both bonus payments and discipline. The arbitrator found that the employees "did not engage in run-of-the-mill, minor misconduct, for which progressive corrective discipline is normally applied," but rather, engaged in dishonest misconduct warranting summary dismissal (*Ralphs Grocery Co.*, 117 LA 833).

Contracts giving employers the right to discharge for cause or mentioning certain offenses that are grounds for discharge usually do not preclude management from imposing lesser forms of discipline. On the other hand, if contracts mandate progressive discipline, arbitrators might refuse to uphold other types of penalties that are not contemplated as part of the progressive discipline structure.

● An arbitrator rejected the penalty imposed on a teacher who told his students that the school principal was a racist. The teacher had already received an oral warning and written reprimand for earlier incidents of unprofessional conduct, and his employer wanted to issue another written reprimand—in lieu of an unpaid suspension—provided that the teacher would undergo anger management training and write letters of apology for his actions. While converting the discipline to a three-day suspension to keep the penalty in line with contractual guidelines, the arbitrator also gave the teacher the option of undergoing the training and writing the apology letters, as proposed by the employer, in order to have his discipline reduced to a written reprimand (*Palm Beach County School Board*, 114 LA 780).

● Another arbitrator held that discharge was not justified for an employee who refused to apologize to a payroll clerk. When the employee went to pick up his paycheck, the clerk kept him waiting for several minutes while she carried on a personal telephone conversation. The employee finally lost his patience and broke the connection to get the clerk's attention. The clerk complained about the employee's conduct, and he was ordered to apologize. Although the employee was unnecessarily rude to the clerk, he should not have been fired, the arbitrator said, finding that the employer was out of line in requiring the employee to say he was wrong when he felt he was not (*Magnavox Co. of Tenn.*, 28 LA 449).

B. Warnings

Except where employees are guilty of serious misconduct, arbitrators in general agree that some form of warning should precede discharge (75 LA 819, 75 LA 1254, 64 LA 778, 64 LA 563).

A clear warning about the consequences faced by employees is particularly important if they have been let off lightly for past offenses and management intends to crack down on future offenses (77 LA 940, 65 LA 894). A discharge for a "last straw" offense might be set aside unless workers were warned previously that they would be dealt with more severely (74 LA 814, 65 LA 829, 64 LA 981).

Under a system of progressive discipline, even an oral warning carries importance, as it can lay the foundation for subsequent discipline of a more severe nature. However, the line sometimes gets hazy between disciplinary warnings and counseling designed simply to help employees improve their performance.

● An employer's failure to distinguish performance counseling from warnings warranted the reduction of a penalty that was based in part on an employee's prior disciplinary record, an arbitrator held. In the employer's notice of disciplinary action against the employee, it stated that she had been "warned and warned" again, but the arbitrator found that the employer was lumping nondisciplinary counseling together with actual discipline imposed on the employee. Consequently, the arbitrator concluded that the employee had not reached the stage of the progressive discipline process that would have warranted the penalty imposed by the employer (*Housing and Community Services Agency of Lane County*, 121 LA 1121).

● Finding that a "verbal reminder" was a type of formal disciplinary action, an arbitrator ruled that the penalty had to be imposed in accordance with contractual disciplinary procedures. An employer and union disagreed as to whether a verbal reminder received by an employee after five chargeable absences constituted the first step of progressive discipline. Although the contract treated "counseling" as a corrective action that would not be subject to the procedural requirements for discipline, the attendance policy expressly defined a verbal reminder as a disciplinary action, the arbitrator found. Because the verbal reminder was not issued to the employee within the contractually mandated timeframe for disciplinary action, the arbitrator overturned the penalty (*Regional Transit District*, 116 LA 826).

● Another arbitrator overturned oral warnings issued to employees under an attendance policy that their employer unilaterally implemented before negotiating its first contract with the union. Finding that the absences triggering the warnings occurred when the employees requested and were given permission to take leave, the arbitrator concluded that the employees were not guilty of any misconduct warranting discipline (*Career Systems Development Corp.*, 113 LA 920).

C. Suspension

A suspension, which is typically the most severe penalty short of discharge, can be imposed for a serious first-time offense that is not flagrant enough to warrant summary

dismissal, or for repeated misconduct of a less serious nature. Under a system of progressive discipline, a suspension normally follows the imposition of oral or written warnings.

As is the case with other forms of corrective discipline, a suspension is commonly viewed by arbitrators to serve the purpose of rehabilitating employees. According to one arbitrator, the goal of suspension is to restore employees to an acceptable level of production or behavior (*Northern Ohio Red Cross Blood Service*, 90 LA 393).

Employers generally have some leeway in deciding on the length of suspension. Factors that come into play in determining appropriate duration include:

● the seriousness of the offense,

● employer disciplinary policies and past practice,

● workers' employment records and prior discipline, and

● the existence of mitigating circumstances (105 LA 332, 103 LA 424).

D. Discharge

Discharge is the most severe penalty available to employers and is not corrective in nature. Such penalty enables employers to rid themselves of incorrigible workers either because such workers have committed a single intolerable offense or because they have reached the final step in the progressive discipline process.

Arbitrators commonly review discharge cases with an extra degree of care, particularly when termination occurs for reasons that reflect upon employees' character or desirability for future employment elsewhere (122 LA 335, 121 LA 249, 65 LA 1157).

● Discharge was too severe a penalty for an employee who did not properly report that he had slipped on some ice and fallen while at work, an arbitrator held. The employee did not believe he was seriously injured, but he did see a doctor and have an X-ray of his arm several days later. After a plant manager learned of the incident, the employee was fired for failing to follow accident-reporting requirements. In overturning the discharge, the arbitrator noted that the employee had mentioned the fall to his boss the day after it happened. The arbitrator also pointed to witness testimony about past practice, which indicated that no other employee had ever been discharged for violating the accident-reporting rule (*Luzenac America Inc.*, 121 LA 1089).

● On the other hand, discharge was justified for a warehouse loader who forgot to properly store some 140 boxes of honey mustard packets, an arbitrator decided. His employer said the failure to refrigerate the packets could have posed a health risk to customers. Under a system of progressive discipline, the loader had already received a verbal warning, written warning, and suspension for poor work performance, so his latest infraction constituted grounds for automatic termination, the arbitrator found (*Golden State Foods*, 117 LA 632).

E. Last-Chance Agreements

In some cases, employees whose conduct has become intolerable are given an opportunity to enter into "last-chance agreements." Typically, last-chance agreements are negotiated with employers, unions, and employees, and they establish specific conditions for continued employment, making it clear to employees that failure to turn things around will result in discharge.

Last-chance agreements can have advantages for both employers and employees. In most cases, employees have already engaged in misconduct that would justify termination, and the agreements essentially enable employees to save their jobs. When employers sign last-chance agreements, they give up the right to discharge employees for misconduct that has already occurred, but they gain the power to summarily dismiss the employees if the requirements of the agreements are not met. In addition, such dismissal usually is not subject to normal contract terms—e.g., just cause and grievance procedures—that are designed to protect employees.

In some instances, arbitrators who overturn employee discharges will order conditional reinstatements and last-chance agreements for the employees. That was the award issued by one arbitrator who decided that discharge was too severe for an employee who violently pushed away the

arm of a human resources director, and also swore vehemently at the woman, when she nudged the employee awake after he fell asleep during a safety meeting (*Hendrickson Trailer Suspension Systems Inc.*, 121 LA 375).

● The appropriate penalty for a 31-year employee who committed two safety violations in a 12-month period was demotion to a position that minimized his exposure to safety hazards, coupled with a last-chance agreement. The arbitrator noted that the parties had agreed to demotion in negotiations as an option, the employee's long service had to be taken into account, and this would serve to protect him and his co-workers from harmful mistakes (*HH Sumco*, 125 LA 965).

Despite the existence of last-chance agreements, employers' efforts to terminate employees are not automatically upheld by arbitrators. In one case, an arbitrator held that an employer failed to meet the burden of proof necessary to support the discharge of a hotel employee who allegedly smoked in a guest room while she was on a last chance agreement. Another employee who was in the room did not corroborate the allegation. In addition, the union noted that it would make no sense for the accused employee to commit "professional suicide" by engaging in such conduct when company policy allowed liberal time for smoking. The arbitrator ordered the employee reinstated, finding that even with a last-chance agreement in place, she could not be discharged without sufficient evidence of wrongdoing (*Taj Mahal*, 118 LA 978)

F. Discharge or Resignation?

In some cases, employers contend that employees resigned, while employees claim to have had no intention of resigning. When presented with such cases, arbitrators must decide whether to treat the situation as a voluntary quit or as a discharge subject to the usual tests of just cause.

If the facts and circumstances support a reasonable conclusion that employees intended to resign, the matter may be treated as a voluntary quit. This generally holds true even if employees never came right out and stated a desire to resign (97 LA 297, 96

LA 585, 93 LA 1047, 92 LA 930, 92 LA 259, 90 LA 1194, 90 LA 149, 86 LA 1160, 86 LA 888).

The fact that employees leave work without permission because of dissatisfaction over something that has occurred does not necessarily mean that management is justified in treating the situation as a voluntary quit (97 LA 297, 88 LA 1265, 88 LA 597, 86 LA 144, 82 LA 569). As one arbitrator stated, "the overwhelming weight of authority holds that there is no voluntary quit by reason of an employee's refusal to perform work to which he is assigned. Unless some affirmation of an intent to quit the job is manifested by the employee, the employer's subsequent refusal to let the employee continue his status constitutes a discharge rather than a resignation" (*Oklahoma Furniture Mfg. Co.*, 24 LA 522; see also 41 LA 913, 115 LA 1495).

● Nevertheless, one arbitrator ruled that an employee voluntarily quit by storming out of work one day after learning that he did not get a job on which he bid. The arbitrator held that the employee was not justified in leaving the plant without either punching out or notifying his foreman (*Owens Manufacturing Inc.*, 63 LA 585).

● Another arbitrator reached a similar conclusion regarding an employee who left on vacation during a busy period when his employer wanted him at work. An increase in workload prompted the employer to cancel vacations that had been scheduled to begin in August. The employer contacted the employee when he failed to call in for his work assignment, and the employee said he was going ahead with his planned vacation. The employer warned him that failure to report for work as scheduled would be construed as a voluntary quit. Agreeing with the employer, the arbitrator observed that employees may select their leave dates provided the dates are agreeable to management, but the employee in this case clearly did not meet that criterion (*B.B.D. Transportation Co. Inc.*, 66 LA 64).

● On the other hand, an employee whose military training extended beyond a return-to-work date—specified in a memo granting a leave of absence—did not voluntarily quit his job, an arbitrator held.

Although the memo stated that failure to report would be considered a resignation, the arbitrator found that the employee did not demonstrate a clear and unequivocal intent to sever the employment relationship (*Rustco Products Co.*, 92 LA 981; see also 96 LA 216).

● Another arbitrator decided that an employee who offered to resign was in fact constructively discharged. The employee made the offer following the employer's indication of its dissatisfaction with his performance, and the arbitrator said it was reasonable for the employee to assume that the employer was really telling him that he might as well look for another job. The arbitrator also pointed to an admission made by the employer's plant superintendent, who said the employee would have been terminated had he not resigned (*Rodman Industries Inc.*, 59 LA 101).

G. Demotion

Many arbitrators disapprove of demotion as a disciplinary measure. It permits unequal penalties for similar offenses, they reason, and may have side effects more drastic than the intended punishment, as was the case where a demoted employee subsequently lost his job because of the change in his seniority status (*Lukens Steel Co.*, 42 LA 252).

Nevertheless, a number of arbitrators have allowed demotions for such matters as carelessness and negligence, poor work attitudes, and incompetence (74 LA 1131, 74 LA 991, 66 LA 588, 60 LA 197, 59 LA 988). In such cases, the arbitrators' approval of the employers' action frequently is grounded in the theory that demotion is not really a form of discipline but an adjustment required by employees' inability to do their jobs (*Carnegie-Illinois Steel Corp.*, 17 LA 328).

● Demotion was justified for a 14-year employee who performed unsatisfactorily as the head of a grocery store's meat department, an arbitrator held. Although the employer could not point to specific defects in the employee's handling of the department, he was demoted after several weeks of posting the lowest profit margin across the company's 39 stores. The arbitrator upheld the demotion, but he clearly did not view it as discipline. Instead, he treated the employee's 15 weeks as a department head as a trial period during which the employee failed to demonstrate his ability to handle the job (*Hart's Food Stores Inc.*, 43 LA 934).

H. Restitution

Arbitrators sometimes hold that employees can be required to make restitution as a means of remedying misconduct.

● One arbitrator held that an employee of a package delivery company was justly required to reimburse the company for his negligent loss of a parcel containing a $12,000 diamond ring. The employee had left the parcel unattended, and it was stolen. Dismissing the union's contention that the employee's actions were due to insufficient training and not negligence, the arbitrator held that the loss was solely attributable to the employee's failure to follow proper safekeeping procedures for high-value parcels (*United Parcel Service Inc.*, 105 LA 637).

● Another arbitrator required that an employee make restitution to his employer for disability benefits he had improperly received. The employer discharged the employee after a videotape showed him engaging in physical activity while he was out on disability leave. The arbitrator awarded reinstatement but refused to grant back pay and ordered the employee to make restitution for disability pay to which he was not entitled (*Solutia Inc.*, 121 LA 26).

● A hospital's requirement for nurses to make up any days they missed when scheduled for weekend work was a proper form of restitution, an arbitrator decided. Many employees regard weekend work as a burden, and those who shirk their duties would be shifting that burden to co-workers, the arbitrator said. The requirement to make up weekend work amounted to restitution and not punishment, the arbitrator found, because the hospital was trying to restore all employees to the position in which they should have been (*Armstrong County Memorial Hospital*, 116 LA 188).

● On the other hand, an arbitrator disallowed an employer's attempt to take deductions from the paychecks of sales employees when the money they received from customers came up short of the total they should have collected. The deductions, which would have made the sales employees insurers against normal business losses, were not an allowable form of discipline and would have reduced the employees' wages below the pay rates set forth in the union contract, the arbitrator held (*Pepsi-Cola General Bottlers Inc.*, 92 LA 1272).

I. Double Jeopardy and Delays

It is a well recognized principle that discipline should be reasonably prompt and that a penalty, once announced, should not be increased absent evidence that the offense was more serious than it initially appeared to be. In addition, arbitrators have held that employees are entitled to expect full discipline within a reasonable time and to assume that the penalty received is the complete one.

The principle of double jeopardy has been applied by arbitrators to prohibit the imposition of two successive penalties for the same offense, such as a written warning and a suspension (76 LA 758, 12 LA 129, 59 LA 414, 90 LA 435, 96 LA 657, 97 LA 8, 97 LA 60, 97 LA 393, 97 LA 774, 98 LA 102).

● One arbitrator said that the legal double jeopardy rule assumes that a full hearing has been held and that disclosures at that hearing are the basis for the penalty imposed. Nonetheless, "normal industrial plant disciplinary procedures" do not contemplate the kind of hearing that is the basis of the legal rule, he said, upholding the discharge of employees who already had been laid off for participating in a wildcat strike where evidence obtained after the layoff showed that they actually instigated the job action (*International Harvester Co.*, 13 LA 610; see also 74 LA 1012, 81 LA 564, 83 LA 833, 85 LA 302, 91 LA 544, 97 LA 121).

1. Court and Employer Penalties

Arbitrators generally agree that penalties imposed in court do not preclude employers from imposing their own penalties for the same conduct. Similarly, when employees have been arrested for conduct that occurred while they were on the job, arbitrators have permitted employers to take disciplinary action without waiting for a court determination of guilt.

● If an employee has paid a fine or served a jail sentence for acts committed in connection with his or her job, management still has the right to impose discipline for those acts, one arbitrator concluded. The arbitrator also noted, however, that the legal punishment can be taken into consideration in evaluating the severity of the penalty imposed by management (*Westinghouse Electric Corp.*, 26 LA 836).

● Another arbitrator ruled that a branch of the U.S. military was justified in imposing a three-day suspension on an employee after the worker pleaded guilty and was convicted of making fraudulent claims against the government. According to the arbitrator, the double jeopardy defense does not apply where the misconduct of the employee also amounts to a violation of the law (*Department of the Air Force*, 74 LA 949).

2. Delays and Staggered Discipline

Management may delay imposing a penalty for a reasonable time, but arbitrators sometimes find that excessive delay is almost the same as double jeopardy because employees then have the threat of the penalty hanging over them for months (*Ashland Oil & Refining Co.*, 28 LA 874).

On the other hand, where management penalizes a group of workers by suspending them, arbitrators typically rule that management can stagger the suspensions so that the workers are not all off at the same time.

● In one case where workers struck in violation of the contract, an arbitrator reasoned that if management suspended everyone at once, the result would be a work stoppage, the very thing the disciplinary action was intended to penalize (*United States Steel Corp.*, 40 LA 598).

● Another arbitrator came to a similar conclusion, adding that although management was not free to schedule the discipline "at its convenience" any time after the stoppage, it was entitled to reasonable latitude in deferring the suspensions (*Bethlehem Steel Co.*, 39 LA 686).

J. Back Pay

An employee who was wrongfully suspended for six months was given interest on her back pay award. The arbitrator said that interest was appropriate in "cases such as the present one." He noted that the employee took out a loan on her house on which she paid interest. She had late fees on her credit card, the arbitrator continued, and she believed that her credit rating has been harmed. The arbitrator also quoted *Atlantic Southeast Airlines*, 101 LA 515, 525 (Nolan, 1993) for the proposition that "[T]here is no logical reason why labor arbitration remedies should differ from those applied, for example, by the National Labor Relations Board" (*Wackenhut Corp.*, 124 LA 1345).

● An employee of a company that serviced aircraft was reinstated with 75 percent back pay after a near-accident he had with an airline truck. He should not have been discharged for the accident, the arbitrator ruled, but he might have defused the incident if he had been cooperative with the airline's supervisor (*Gate Gourmet Inc.*, 125 LA 80).

K. Conditional Reinstatement

● The reinstatement of an employee who was discharged without just cause for dishonesty in her accusations about a company medical director was conditioned on her being examined and being declared fit by a licensed psychologist agreed to by the parties. The arbitrator stated that the employee's behavior and attitude toward the medical director raised genuine questions about her emotional stability and "emotional instability on the part of workers in the dangerous confines of a steel plant can create serious risks" the arbitrator observed (*United States Steel Corp.*, 125 LA 449).

L. Management Also at Fault

When responsibility for the circumstances giving rise to employees' discipline or discharge can be attributed partly to management, arbitrators are likely to reduce the penalty imposed by employers.

● An arbitrator overturned the discharge of a 32-year employee who was accused of gross negligence for emptying the contents of a storage tank, which contained more than $30,000 worth of raw materials. The employee's verbal instructions from a supervisor involved more than one tank, and the supervisor conceded that he might have mentioned the wrong tank when telling the employee which one to pump out. Finding that management should have exercised more caution—both in giving the employee his work assignment and in appropriately locking and tagging the tank that was supposed to be left undisturbed—the arbitrator held that management shared some of the fault for the incident and ordered the employee reinstated without back pay (*Engelhard Corp.*, 122 LA 81).

● Another arbitrator ordered reinstatement without back pay for an employee who was fired for attendance problems. The employee had been told that he could leave work early without any penalty beyond a suspension that he had already received, but the employer had miscalculated. Even though the employee had accumulated enough occurrences under the employer's attendance system to trigger termination, the arbitrator found that discharge was not warranted because of mistakes made by the employer in tracking and communicating the employee's status under the attendance system (*Unibus Inc.*, 110 LA 597).

● On the other hand, an arbitrator refused to attribute partial responsibility to an employer that terminated an employee at the conclusion of a 26-week period of leave following an injury. The employer informed the employee of the time limit on the initial period of leave, and it was her responsibility to inquire about her options and make a timely application if she hoped to receive an extended leave, the arbitrator noted in upholding her termination (*Boise Cascade Corp.*, 110 LA 826).

Part 2

Discharge and Discipline: Categories

I. Absenteeism & Tardiness [LA CDI 100.552507 (public employees); 118.6361–.6367]

OVERVIEW

Arbitrators agree that excessive absenteeism or tardiness provides just cause for discharge. Arbitrators also concur, however, that no simple formula can be used in all instances to determine when the point of excessiveness has been reached.

In the absence of fixed standards for weighing the issues involved with absenteeism and tardiness, most arbitrators adopt a case-by-case approach. As such, their determinations on the appropriateness of disciplinary actions taken against employees usually hinge on the particular facts and circumstances of each case.

Despite all the variations that come into play, the decisions that arbitrators render in absenteeism and tardiness cases often take into consideration common factors, such as:

- the duration and frequency of employees' absenteeism and tardiness (105 LA 913, 95 LA 1169, 94 LA 409, 74 LA 623, 64 LA 12);
- the reasons for the employees' attendance problems (123 LA 1571, 98 LA 57, 74 LA 1185, 64 LA 672);
- the attendance records of other employees (114 LA 321, 112 LA 941, 107 LA 1006, 64 LA 483);
- whether employers have clear disciplinary policies relating to attendance that are known to all employees and applied fairly and consistently (77 LA 249, 65 LA 919, 63 LA 1315); and
- whether employees are adequately warned that disciplinary action could result from a failure to improve their attendance (98 LA 1203, 98 LA 105, 72 LA 347, 71 LA 744, 71 LA 129, 63 LA 148).

SUMMARY OF CASES

A. Discharge for Absenteeism and Tardiness

Arbitrators generally agree that employees with attendance problems should be put on notice and given an opportunity to improve before the discharge penalty is invoked (72 LA 347, 64 LA 1283). Other factors that arbitrators commonly consider in reviewing these types of cases include length of service, past record and the nature of prior absences, the extent to which employees' absences exceed the norm, the effect upon efficiency and morale, and future prospects for dependability.

If an employee with a good work record's performance changes, arbitrators might take the work record into account in deciding the proper penalty.

- An arbitrator determined an agency did not have just cause to discharge a bus driver who was absent without leave for 30 days, and reduced his discharge to a 30-day suspension. The driver had been employed for 10 years, had received a total of 13 commendations, and around the time he took the leave, was subject to unusual workplace and homelife stressors, causing him to act in an unusual and uncharacteristic manner (*Greater Cleveland RTA*, 128 LA 1238).

- An employer had proper cause for discipline but not to issue two 30-day suspensions to a firefighter who was absent without just cause and misrepresented the reason for his absence, an arbitrator found. The employee called in sick more than nine

hours before his scheduled graveyard shift, but then attended a basketball game that evening. The grievant had received the tickets as a present and had no intention of going to work after the game. Because the employee had 30 years of service with a good work record and no prior evidence of absenteeism or discipline, the suspensions were converted to three days each, served concurrently (*U.S. Steel Corp*, 126 LA 460).

- A city did not have just cause to discipline a firefighter who called in sick with a sore wrist and then was videotaped doing things like washing his car. These ordinary activities, the arbitrator said, "fall short of establishing that [Appellant] was able to perform his duties, tasks, and functions as a Firefighter..." (*City of Rialto*, 125 LA 550).

- An employer that operated facilities for individuals with disabilities did not have just cause to discharge an employee for leaving 15 or 30 minutes early without permission, even though the employer's strong policy reasons against allowing employees to leave early were understandable, the arbitrator said. Among other things, the employee had worked an "excessive number of hours"—nearly 30—partly because she had been "mandated" to work an additional shift, the employee had not slept during a four-hour break between shifts, and the employee had completed all of her work. The arbitrator also noted that the employer did not conduct a full and proper investigation (*Axis MN Inc*, 27 LA 698).

• An agency did not have just cause to discharge an employee who called in sick with a migraine and was seen at a mall within an hour after his shift, since, the arbitrator said, "the evidence fails to prove by any stretch anything more than a coincidence" (*Ohio Turnpike Commission*, 124 LA 1239).

• *By contrast*, an arbitrator found an employer had just cause to discharge an employee for neither reporting for work nor notifying the employer that she would not be reporting on a particular date, after the employer had instructed her to report. The collective bargaining agreement stipulated that five unexcused absences within a 12-month period would be cause for discharge, the employee had been disciplined for a large number of attendance violations during her less than year of employment, and fact that she was receiving short-term disability benefits at time of discharge did not override agreement's absenteeism policies (*Veolia Transportation Services*, 127 LA 16).

B. Documentation of Need for Leave

When employees miss work to care for sick family members, their absences often are protected under the Family and Medical Leave Act or similar state laws. If these statutory protections come into play, employers must excuse the absences and cannot consider them alongside other attendance violations in penalizing employees for absenteeism.

• Employees who want to use leave must apply for it properly or they may be discharged for absenteeism. For example:

• An arbitrator ruled that an employer had just cause to discharge single parent who had child care responsibilities, where he did not apply for personal leave to cover his absences (*Lockheed Federal Credit Union*, 123 LA 1192).

• Another arbitrator found an employer had just cause to discipline employee who took off work due to his knee injury for which he was eligible for FMLA leave because he did not provide required recertification forms (*Supervalu*, 123 LA 1721).

• *By contrast*, an employer did not have just cause to discharge employee for violating the employer's attendance policy, where

human resources manager abused her discretion in denying grievant's application for Family and Medical Leave Act leave, as she did not give him a chance to revise his medical certification, improperly found application to be defective, and failed to comply with the FMLA in determining that his medical condition was insufficiently serious (*Interstate Brands Corporation*, 128 LA 428).

C. Reasons for Absenteeism

A central task for arbitrators in reviewing absenteeism cases is to balance employees' expectations of job security against employers' rights to require acceptable levels of job attendance. The resolution of such cases often turns on whether employees have provided reasonable or justifiable excuses for being absent from work.

Some of the causes of employee absenteeism include illness or injury, illness of a family member, weather conditions, personal business, religious observances, alcoholism, and imprisonment.

1. Illness or Injury of Employee

Personal illnesses and injuries commonly cause employee absences. Although it is reasonable for employees to be excused for absences due to sickness and accidents, arbitrators have upheld termination if employees' attendance records have fallen below an acceptable range for an extended period of time. In the end, a lack of dependability usually constitutes a potent argument in favor of termination, regardless of the underlying reasons for employees' attendance problems.

As arbitrator Thomas Watkins of the Federal Mediation and Conciliation Service stated in an arbitration upholding the discharge of an employee who took excessive sick leave, "there can be no reasonable assertion that any employer need tolerate an employee who has become so unreliable as to be of no value in the workplace . . . [and] may have actually become a handicap to the organization" (*Medco Health Solutions*, 128 LA 1734).

• An employer had just cause to discharge an employee for absenteeism, where his medical problem was discovered after he was dismissed, an arbitrator ruled. Even though he had brain surgery four months after his discharge, the employer did not and could not possibly have known of the grievant's medical condition until several months after he was discharged, and his disease may have occurred within a few weeks of diagnosis (*OmniSource Corp.*, 129 LA 818).

● An employer had just cause to discharge an employee for absenteeism, despite the contention that he was under a doctor's continuous care for a variety of ailments, where he was not under continuous care for a year after he first went to a doctor for the health problem. The arbitrator found the employee had race horses and could go to a race track when he allegedly could not get to work. Finding the employee had accumulated the requisite points to be terminated, the arbitrator noted, that "[p]eople who 'game' the system often find themselves becoming so comfortable with the game they forget minor specifics, such as points accumulated within a special period of time, as cited herein. Such persons almost always are terminated—eventually (*Volvo Parts North America*, 129 LA 1473).

● An arbitrator ruled that an employer had just cause to discharge a diabetic employee, who had already been suspended for absenteeism, after he was absent for another day, even though on the following day he requested a vacation day for the absence. The collective bargaining contract gave the supervisor the discretion to grant a vacation day in case of emergency, but the supervisor had denied the request due to employee's poor record and the fact that he waited more than half a day to make the request. The grievant presented a doctor's note for the first time at the hearing and it did not state that the doctor saw the grievant on the day he took off (*FCI USA*, 126 LA 1710).

● An employer had just cause to discharge an employee for excessive absenteeism, even though the employee attributed his frequent absences to chronic migraine headaches, an arbitrator determined. On one occasion, the employee suffered a migraine at work and left to go to a hospital. When he returned to work two days later, his supervisor told him to report for duty the

following Monday. He failed to do so and was fired for excessive absenteeism. In protesting the termination, the union argued that the employer should have told the employee that his absences could have been covered under the Family and Medical Leave Act. Rejecting that assertion, the arbitrator said the employee was in fact properly terminated for violating the attendance policy in the collective bargaining agreement. Regardless of the employee's disabling migraines, the employer had a right to expect regular attendance, arbitrator declared (*GAF Building Materials Corp.*, 114 LA 1528).

● Discharge also was upheld for an employee who had been absent because of illness 14 or 15 weeks out of a six-month period. In upholding the discharge, the arbitrator said "no plant can operate profitably unless it can count upon fairly regular attendance of employees." The arbitrator added that any situation that "results in or tends toward unprofitable operations is against the best interests not only of the Company but of employees themselves" (*Celanese Corp. of America*, 9 LA 143; see also 97 LA 653, 95 LA 1169, 94 LA 41, 74 LA 205, 74 LA 362, 74 LA 681, 74 LA 623, 74 LA 531).

● *By contrast*, an employer did not have just cause to discharge a 21-year employee, where he and his wife were beset with illness problems that slowly dragged him into a "vortex" of procedural/attendance rules violation, an arbitrator ruled. First the employee's wife had a heart attack, then the employee had a pulled groin muscle and muscle spasms, and the doctor prescribed medication that made him feel like he was "there but not there." The arbitrator found the penalty for discharge for this particular employee was "wholly inappropriate" and reinstated him with back pay (*Multi Packaging Solutions*, 127 LA 1377).

● An arbitrator found the discharge was too harsh a punishment and an employer did not have just cause to discharge a machine operator who suffered from a chronic illness for reaching the dismissal threshold under a no-fault attendance policy when she was assessed three points for consecutive days missed because her employer denied her a subsequent request for Family and Medical Leave Act leave. The arbitrator found that where the use of sequential absences to discharge the employee denied her progressive discipline, the company failed to consider her physician's letter expanding upon her situation submitted at the third step. Further the employer failed to consider whether the penalty was disproportionate for a 29-year employee with a good record and a chronic illness of arthritis. However, because the grievant was "cavalier" about some of the paperwork requirements, she did not receive back pay or benefits from the date of discharge to her reinstatement (*Bemis Co.*, 129 LA 24).

● An arbitrator ruled that the discharge of an absent employee was without just cause, even though, under the terms of his last chance agreement, justification for any absence was to be determined "at the sole discretion of the Company." The agreement also stated that grievant may be required to provide "written justification of absences. . .", which he did with a doctor's note of treatment on the day he reported off (*U.S. Steel Corp.*, 128 LA 1308.)

● An arbitrator decided that discharge was premature and possibly without just cause for an employee whose off-duty back injury had caused sporadic absences. The arbitrator rejected claims by the employer that it had responsibility to protect the worker and itself from risk of further injury. Although there was no indication that the employee's absenteeism would improve, the arbitrator noted that the doctor's statements did not place any limitations on the employee's post-recovery work activities (*Delta–Macon Brick & Tile Co. Inc.*, 92 LA 837).

● Another arbitrator reinstated an employee where the employer's attendance-control policy in the collective bargaining agreement recognized the mitigating nature of the employee's illness—in this case, a chronic kidney ailment—in determining the proper discipline. The arbitrator said that valid "no-fault" attendance policies must distinguish between "malingering and honest misfortune" (*Owens-Brockway Packaging Inc.*, 96 LA 950; see also 98 LA 112).

2. Illness of Family Member

Arbitrators often take into account the rights afforded to employees under the Family and Medical Leave Act and similar state laws that provide for job-protected leave due to serious health conditions. [See also Part 6, Chapter VI, on the Family and Medical Leave Act.]

● An employer did not have just cause to discharge a 21-year industrial worker who accumulated extended work absences while ministering to serious illness problems, first after his wife's heart attack and later, his own health issues. Ultimately he was discharged pursuant to a work rule calling for automatic termination for failure to report for work or to call in for three consecutive days, this behavior being classified as job abandonment. The arbitrator ruled the discharge was inappropriate under the circumstances and reinstated him with back pay (*Multi Packaging Solutions*, 127 LA 1377).

● A hospital did not have just cause to discharge a nurse who had Crohn's disease and rheumatoid arthritis, for absenteeism, even though two physicians who made independent medical reviews of the grievant's condition from her record of absences decided that she was not entitled to Family and Medical Leave Act leave for her time off. The medical reviewers had not been informed that she had a chronic condition, the arbitrator said, and the hospital had, for six years, accepted her conditions and knew she required time off from work (*St. Elizabeth Health Center*, 129 LA 161).

● A charge of AWOL should not have been made against an employee who stayed home to care for his depressed daughter who was suicidal, since he was protected by an FMLA and a collective bargaining contract (*Dept. of Veterans Affairs Med. Ctr.*, 123 LA 1571).

● Discharge was not warranted for an employee who left work and tended to her husband during a period of hospitalization, an arbitrator ruled. The employee's absences would have been excused under the Family and Medical Leave Act, but she did not submit the doctor's certification of her husband's health condition within 15 days, as required by her employer. The arbitrator found that the husband's hospitalization lasted the entire four-day period during which the employee missed work, and although she promptly requested the required documentation, her husband's doctor delayed in completing it. Considering those circumstances, as well as the employee's excellent work record during 13 years with the employer, the arbitrator ordered reinstatement with back pay (*Lozier Corp.*, 121 LA 1187).

• Reinstatement with back pay also was ordered for an employee who took time off to care for daughter with asthma. The arbitrator noted that excused leave under the Family and Medical Leave Act is not designed exclusively for medical treatments and doctor visits. Rather, the law also allows an employee to take time away from work to provide for the "personal needs" or "psychological comfort" of a family member with a serious health condition. Emphasizing that the employer already had documentation on file from a doctor certifying that the daughter's health condition called for such care, the arbitrator held that the employee's termination for absenteeism was not justified (*Rock Tenn Co.*, 121 LA 1079).

• *By contrast, a*n arbitrator ruled that an employer had just cause to discharge an employee for excessive absenteeism, even though his final two unexcused absences were due to his brother's hospitalization and his oversleeping as a result of a medical condition. The collective bargaining agreement excused absence due to hospitalization only of spouse, child, or parent, the grievant failed to invoke the FMLA until after his discharge, and the company had consistently disallowed retroactive substitution of vacation for unexcused absence (*Red Spot Paint & Varnish Co. Inc.*, 128 LA 81).

• The Family and Medical Leave Act did not protect an employee who falsely claimed that he was staying home to care for his wife. The employee called in to say he needed to miss work because his wife was suffering from a migraine, but investigators hired by his employer videotaped him packing up and going on a hunting trip with his father-in-law. The two days of work missed by the employee were properly treated as unexcused absences, which put the employee over the limit specified in the employer's attendance policy, the arbitrator ruled. Thus, the employer was justified in discharging the employee, the arbitrator found (*Interstate Brands Corp.*, 121 LA 1580).

3. Weather Conditions

On occasion, bad weather or other calamities make it difficult for employees to report to work. But even where an "Act of God" is considered a reasonable excuse for absence, there can be difficulties in determining how long the condition provides an acceptable excuse.

• A coal mine did not violate a collective bargaining contract when it applied its no-fault attendance policy to employees during a winter storm, an arbitrator ruled, where a significant number of bargaining-unit employees were able to appear for duty, another rather large group accepted one of three paid contractual day options, and the product inventory was not sufficient to allow the employer to meet the demands of consumers while discontinuing production (*Big Ridge Inc.*, 126 LA 1057).

• An arbitrator ruled that an employer had just cause to discharge an employee who was absent for two consecutive days without the employer's consent, where the collective bargaining contract provided that employees could be discharged for conduct "other than for proven sickness," and the employee took off work due to inclement weather, but did not provide a doctor's slip (*Consolidation Coal Co.*, 128 LA 1693).

• *By contrast,* an employer acted unreasonably and unjustly when it issued absenteeism points to an employee who did not come to work during a level three snow emergency, an arbitrator ruled, where employees had not exhibited abusive or excessive absenteeism and those absent did not know, nor should have known, that they could have safely traveled during the emergency (*H. J. Heinz Co.*, 125 LA 1738).

• Under an absentee control program that assigned "points" to employees for certain types of tardiness and absences, but imposed no penalties for "Acts of God," an employer wrongly assigned points to employees who were absent from work one day after a severe winter storm, an arbitrator ruled. Management contended that strict enforcement of the absence program was necessary and that conditions did not have a "sufficient impact" on the total workforce to be considered an Act of God, since 80 percent of the employees were able to report for work the day after the storm. However, the arbitrator maintained that the company could have extended the Act-of-God allowance to the 20 percent who were still hindered by snow and ice that day, without impairing the overall effectiveness of the absence program (*Environmental Elements Corp.*, 70 LA 912; see also 95 LA 906).

4. Religious Beliefs

In some cases, the attendance problems of employees are connected with their religious beliefs. The ability of employers to penalize employees in such situations can be circumscribed by the ban on religious discrimination under Title VII of the Civil Rights Act of 1964 and by similar bans under state laws.

Federal guidelines issued by the Equal Employment Opportunity Commission call for employers to "reasonably accommodate" the religious needs of their employees when this can be done without undue hardship to the business.

● An arbitrator upheld the discharge of a Seventh-day Adventist, despite the claim that the employee's absences were due to her religious beliefs. According to the arbitrator, the employee was aware of the attendance policy at the mushroom farm where she worked, as well as the direct conflict between her religious beliefs and her mandatory work schedule. Although her employer tried to accommodate her request to be excused from Saturday work, the perishable nature of produce necessitates that it be harvested on schedule. The arbitrator concluded that excusing the employee from all Saturday work would have posed an undue hardship on the employer, and reassigning the employee to a position that did not require Saturday work would have violated the seniority rights of other employees (*Moonlight Mushrooms Inc.*, 101 LA 421).

● After an employee's religious discrimination charges in connection with his absences had already been rejected by state and federal agencies, the arbitrator refused to disturb his discharge. The employee observed a faith that treated the Sabbath, from sundown Friday to sundown Saturday, as the period of rest. Management offered a number of possible accommodations to address the conflict between the employee's religious observances and requirements for Saturday work, but the employee continued accumulating unexcused absences and was discharged. In denying the employee's grievance, the arbitrator noted that he lacked jurisdiction to consider the issue of religious discrimination, because the employee's claims had already been dismissed by the state civil rights agency and the Equal Employment Opportunity Commission (*JPI Transportation Products Inc.*, 93 LA 716).

● *By contrast,* an arbitrator reduced a suspension to a written warning for an employee who refused to work on Good Friday so she could attend church with her family. Rejecting the argument that the employee was subjected to religious discrimination, the arbitrator said the employee's faith as a Roman Catholic did not preclude her from working on Good Friday, which meant that her actions arose out of religious preference rather than religious obligation. Nevertheless, the arbitrator determined that a one-day suspension was too severe, in part because the employee had an unblemished 10-year employment record (*Bronx-Lebanon Hospital Center*, 90 LA 1216).

● Another arbitrator held that an employee's Navajo beliefs constituted a mitigating factor that warranted overturning his discharge for leaving work without permission. The employee left because of severe personal problems, and his failure to tell anyone resulted from the conviction—based in Navajo tribal and religious beliefs—that his problems were not for non-Navajo ears, the arbitrator said in ordering reinstatement without back pay (*Public Service Co. of New Mexico*, 98 LA 23).

5. Alcoholism

Alcoholism is widely recognized as an illness, and many employers have developed programs aimed at spotting and rehabilitating alcoholics, especially in the wake of the Americans with Disabilities Act. At the same time, however, employers are not obligated to retain indefinitely employees whose alcoholism keeps them from working on a regular basis. [For arbitral standards and decisions concerning employee alcoholism, see Part 2, Chapter XIV titled "Intoxication and Alcoholism."]

6. Imprisonment

● Arbitrators are by no means unanimous in their attitude toward absences caused by confinement in jail. Some have excused imprisoned employees for their absences, while others have upheld the ultimate penalty of discharge. Many arbitrators fall somewhere in the middle, taking the view that an appropriate response depends on the facts and circumstances of each particular case.

Factors mentioned by arbitrators as having an influence on their decisions in such cases include the following: the duration of the absences; the ease or difficulty of having the absent employees' duties performed by others; the nature of the employees' criminal actions; the employers' past practices with respect to absenteeism generally and to arrest-caused absences specifically; the employees' length of service, prior discipline, and record of dependability; and the effect the employees' reinstatement would have on workplace morale (96 LA 216, 94 LA 1206, 89 LA 1150, 87 LA 1273, 87 LA 691, 87 LA 500, 86 LA 1237, 74 LA 860).

● An arbitrator overturned the discharge of an employee who was arrested for allegedly selling drugs, even though the employee had entered into a "last-chance agreement" because of earlier attendance problems. The terms of the agreement called for termination if the employee incurred even a single absence in the six-month period. When the employee was arrested and missed work, he was fired. However, the criminal case against him was subsequently dropped. The arbitrator rejected the argument that the last-chance agreement justified the employee's termination. Under the employer's attendance policy, employees could not be penalized for absences beyond their control, the arbitra-

tor noted. Applying this distinction to the employee's situation, the arbitrator said the employee must be presumed innocent of the dropped charges, which were the reason he missed work. Adding that the last-chance agreement could not override the contractual requirement of "good and sufficient cause" for discharge, the arbitrator ordered the employee reinstated (*Orpack-Stone Corp.*, 102 LA 545).

● Reinstatement also was ordered for a long-term employee who was sentenced to a year and a day in prison after being arrested in a local movie house on a morals charge. Upon his release, the employee began receiving treatment from doctors and psychiatrists for "sociopathic personality disturbance, sexual deviation." The arbitrator overturned the employee's termination, despite conceding that the employee's mental illness had manifested itself in a way that was repugnant and unlawful. According to the arbitrator, the illness did not impair the employee's ability to do his job, the company failed to show that the employee's absence had affected the efficiency of his department, and there was no basis for finding that his return would result in bad feelings or tensions in the department. In combination with these factors, the arbitrator pointed to the employee's spotless 37-year employment record in finding that the company lacked just cause for discharge (*U.S. Steel Corp.*, 41 LA 460).

● Another arbitrator overturned the discharge of an employee who was jailed on drunk driving charges but reported his absence as sick leave. Ordering the employee reinstated, the arbitrator reasoned that although the employee's claim of illness was an "incomplete" explanation, the employee, because he *was* legitimately too sick to come to work, did not intend to deceive the employer (*Indianapolis Water Co.*, 102 LA 316; see also 88 LA 167).

● *By contrast,* an arbitrator upheld the discharge of an employee with a poor work record who went to prison on a felony conviction. The employee hoped to receive work release, and his union suggested granting his vacation leave or leave of absence until the work release came through. However, his employer had already terminated his employment and refused the union's request. According to the arbitrator, the employer had no reason to consider the employee's imprisonment to be in error or forced upon him for reasons beyond his control. Moreover, the arbitrator said, management "is not required to sit idly by and, in effect, carry an employee who is serving a jail sentence for acts committed against . . . society." Finding that the employer had no contractual obligation to place the worker on leave, the arbitrator concluded that the worker's confinement, in light of his prior discipline and "significant absenteeism problem," warranted discharge (*United States Steel Corp.*, 69 LA 225; see also 91 LA 1225, 79 LA 6, 73 LA 196, 72 LA 613).

D. Notice, Documentation Requirements

Most employer attendance policies require notice when employees are going to be absent, as well as a justifiable excuse for their absences. Employees generally do not meet their obligations by giving notice of absence without a good excuse. Likewise, a good excuse does not necessarily justify absence without notice.

To verify that employees have valid excuses for their absences, employers sometimes establish documentation requirements as part of their attendance policies. For example, employers might insist on a doctor's note as a way to guard against false claims of sickness or to ensure that employees are fit to resume working after an extended absence. Arbitrators tend to uphold documentation requirements unless they are deemed unreasonable.

1. Lack of Notice

It is a common practice among employers to require that employees give notice of their absences. Regardless of employees' reasons for missing work, failure to meet this requirement can justify discipline (98 LA 23, 81 LA 657, 63 LA 1262, 60 LA 680).

● An arbitrator ruled that an employer did not have just cause to discharge an employee after he accumulated a certain number of attendance points, where the discharge-causing the absenteeism incident resulted in his point total surpassing an amount linked to a three-day suspension, which was bypassed in his case. The employees were not put on notice of their point status unless a disciplinary step was reached. The arbitrator reinstated the employee on a "last chance" basis with a slightly reduced point total and without back pay (*Marsco Glass Products*, 127 LA 668).

● A county building inspector did not improperly take time away from his duties to attend to personal business during working hours when he stopped by his mother-in-law's house three times to check on a roofing job, even though he did not record time off to do so, where he asked permission of supervisor to make stops and had no reason to believe that he had to ask permission each time, and his work schedule was flexible and he had no reason to understand that he had to record 15 to 38 minutes of these three visits as time off (*County of Sacramento*, 125 LA 1500).

If employees miss work for several days without reporting in, their situation likely will be treated as a "voluntary quit." In these types of cases, arbitrators sometimes order reinstatement of employees who had good reasons for failing to inform management of their whereabouts (96 LA 216, 95 LA 881).

● An employer's discipline of an employee was reasonable after he failed to show up for work, did not call in, and had no good excuse, an arbitrator ruled. The company's attendance rules required employees to give the employer notice when missing work and provided that unreported absences would be punished by a one-day suspension. According to the arbitrator, "the obligation to report an absence, barring a legitimate excuse, is unchallengeable." Consequently, the only issue left to decide was whether the penalty was legitimate, and the arbitrator said he was obligated to defer to the employer's judgment on the matter (*Smith & Loveless Inc.*, 116 LA 235).

● An employee who had a drinking problem was properly discharged for violating the absence notification requirements of a last-chance agreement, an arbitrator decided. The employee was absent for more than one week and failed to comply with the provision in the agreement requiring him to contact one of two general supervisors about any intended absence and circumstances involved (*United States Steel Corp.*, 63 LA 274; see also 74 LA 507).

2. Defective Notice

Employees often have excuses for violating the notice requirements of their employers' attendance policies. When reviewing such cases, arbitrators commonly overturn discipline if employees can show that they made a sincere, good-faith effort to provide notice of their absences but were unable to meet their employers' requirements.

● An employer had proper cause to discharge an employee for eight unexcused absences, even though she was not suspended for her seventh absence, where each day of unexcused absence constituted a separate absence. The arbitrator said that suspension was not a right or entitlement under the employer's policy, her seventh and eighth absences took place on consecutive work days, and the human resources director previously had told her that two more days of her unexcused absence would result in discharge (*Bay Valley Foods*, 127 LA 1463).

● An employee wanted to extend his vacation and mailed a letter to his employer at the end of his originally scheduled time off to give notice of his intentions. The employer's rule specified that absence without notice "for three consecutive working days" meant termination. The employee's letter was mailed within the three-day period, but the employer did not receive it until later. The arbitrator held that the employee did not meet the notice requirement, because the employer needed to receive notice within the three-day period (*Lear Siegler Inc.*, 48 LA 276).

● *By contrast*, an arbitrator ruled that a transit company did not have just cause to discharge a bus driver for incurring a seventh unexcused absence in a rolling 12-month period, where the company failed to counsel the driver for each absence after her second as required by the collective bargaining agreement, there was substantial confusion among the parties as to which

absences were unexcused and about her total number of absences, and the company's policy regarding accepting ex post facto documentation was inconsistent (*Pace South*, 128 LA 383).

A school did not have just cause to issue a second "sick leave warning letter" to an educational assistant, even though his absences were in excess of average, an arbitrator ruled. The parties intended that there be "reasonable suspicion of sick leave abuse" before such letter could be issued, the assistant did not take more sick leave than he had earned under contract, and the principal who issued the letter testified that "abuse" was not suspected (*Milwaukee Board of School Directors*, 127 LA 1354).

3. Documentation Following Absence

In addition to demanding that employees provide notice of their absences, employers frequently insist on a doctor's note or some other form of documentation upon the employees' return to work. This type of requirement is often reserved for employees who are suspected of abusing their leave privileges, but some employers impose across-the-board documentation requirements as part of their attendance policies.

● An arbitrator held that an employer had just cause to discharge a diabetic employee, who had already been suspended for absenteeism, after he was absent for another day, even though on the following day he requested a vacation day for absence. The collective bargaining contract gave the supervisor discretion to grant the vacation day in case of emergency, but the supervisor denied the request due to the employee's poor record and the fact that he waited more than half day to make the request. Moreover, the grievant presented a doctor's note for the first time at the hearing and it did not state that the doctor saw the grievant on the day he took off, and his wife, who was supposed to call in and allegedly forgot, did not testify (*FCI USA Inc.*, 126 LA 1710).

● An employer properly discharged an employee who failed to provide the required medical documentation following an extended absence, an arbitrator held. The employee, who already had accumulated the maximum allowable points under the employer's no-fault policy and was on notice that further attendance violations would trigger discharge, missed six consecutive days of work because of an asthma flare-up. The employee did not see a doctor during this absence, and after she attempted to return to work without a doctor's note, she was discharged. Although she had paperwork on file that would have allowed her absences to be excused under the Family and Medical Leave Act, the employer's attendance policy also required employees to supply a doctor's return-to-work statement following illness-related absences exceeding four consecutive days, the arbitrator noted. The employee was unable to resume working without the statement, which triggered the unexcused absences that justified her discharge, the arbitrator found (*Whirlpool Corp.*, 121 LA 272).

● *By contrast*, an arbitrator converted a 10-year bus driver grievant's discharge to a disciplinary suspension, with loss of seniority and other contractual benefits for the period of his abandonment from employment because his conduct in abandoning his job was bizarre and out of character. The driver had phoned supervisors to say he was not feeling well, then cut off communications and reported to work a month later, presenting a return-to-work note signed by a doctor from a clinic, but could produce nothing to document the reasons for his month-long absence. Rather, he relied on advice given a year earlier from his physician, who counseled that if he should feel stressed, he "should take time off" from work and it became clear during arbitration that driver's depression affected his health and judgment (*Greater Cleveland RTA*, 128 LA 1238).

● Another arbitrator held that an employer acted unreasonably when it established a new rule requiring all employees to provide a physician's statement verifying that their absences due to illness were "excused." Although the new rule followed standard industry practices and the employer had a legitimate concern for preventing the abuse of sick leave, it covered employees with good as well as bad absenteeism records and thus went beyond the realm of reasonableness, an arbitrator decided (*Altec Corp.*, 71 LA 1064).

E. Tardiness

Tardiness typically is viewed as a less serious offense than an unexcused absence or absence without notice. Nevertheless, excessive tardiness can reach the point of rendering workers no longer suitable for employment. Employees with poor attendance records commonly are disciplined for combination of absenteeism and tardiness, suggesting that the two problems tend to be intertwined (77 LA 947, 76 LA 1066, 76 LA 324, 74 LA 290, 74 LA 205, 72 LA 347, 71 LA 129).

Recognizing the detrimental impact tardiness can have on efficiency and morale, arbitrators generally uphold the right of management to take disciplinary action to address the problem. As with absenteeism, the program of progressive discipline—e.g., counseling, warning, suspension—generally is viewed as the proper way to encourage delinquent employees to mend their ways (97 LA 708, 95 LA 983, 93 LA 441, 91 LA 339, 91 LA 231, 90 LA 131, 89 LA 1237).

1. Establishing Tardiness

In some situations, the determination of whether employees are unacceptably late for work can be difficult to make. In these types of cases, arbitrators might have to evaluate contractual provisions and employer practices to decide the circumstances under which employees should be counted as tardy.

● An employer did not have just cause to discharge an employee under a no-fault attendance policy when he was assessed one-quarter point for finishing the log-in process 11 seconds late, an arbitrator found. Where leniency or exceptions were allowed under the policy, and the employee's excuse was that he was detained by the police for barely going over the speed limit, he may have begun logging in prior to his start time, and the length of time he was tardy was extremely short, the arbitrator found (*Goebel Fixture Co.*, 128 LA 1324).

● An employer did not have just cause to discharge a grocery store checker for chronic tardiness, an arbitrator found, citing several mitigating factors. The employee, who had worked at the store for 30 years, was discharged under the employer's absenteeism policy after she was late to work 10 times in one year. The final incident of tardiness involved her being three minutes late. The union protested, contending that the last tardiness event was beyond her control and therefore exempted from consideration under company rules. The arbitrator disagreed with that contention but said the employer failed to abide by its past practice of excusing late arrivals to work of five minutes or less. This especially would apply in the employee's case, the arbitrator said, because more than half of her disciplines for tardiness had been for being less than five minutes late for work. This factor plus her nearly 30 years of seniority prompted him to order the employee reinstated with full seniority but without back pay (*Albertson's Inc.*, 115 LA 46).

● An employee who clocked in but was not at his workstation by the time his shift began should not have been counted as tardy, an arbitrator held. According to the contract, the "standard day shift" ran from 7:30 a.m. to 4:00 p.m. The employer construed this to mean that workers had to be at their workstations by 7:30, and it issued a notice stating that they would be considered late if they failed to clock in before then. One worker repeatedly clocked in at exactly 7:30 and was eventually fired. The arbitrator overturned the discharge, finding that the contract did not specify whether the workday began at the time clock or at the workstation. According to the arbitrator, without a specific contractual provision on the matter, there was no basis for the company's rule requiring employees to clock in before the start of their shifts (*Pacific Airmotive Corp.*, 28 LA 761; see also 95 LA 248, 92 LA 658, 85 LA 207).

● *By contrast,* an employer had just cause to charge an employee with one occurrence under a no-fault attendance policy for arriving six minutes late for his Saturday shift, even though the Saturday shift started one-half hour earlier than weekday shifts, an arbitrator found. It was the employee's responsibility to be informed of shift starting times, the sched-

ule was posted in an accessible location, an earlier start time on Saturday was traditional, and the employer's policy makes no exceptions as to amount of time by which employee is tardy, the arbitrator said (*Vons* 128 LA 43).

2. Tightening Rules on Tardiness

Employers sometimes attempt to tighten their rules on tardiness or stiffen penalties for rule violations. When this occurs, unions commonly raise objections and seek to remedy the situation through arbitration.

● One arbitrator took a position that new rules on tardiness must be judged on their merits as well as how they compare with past practice. The case arose when the employer issued a rule stating that employees would be discharged if they were tardy 12 times in a 12-month period. The arbitrator found a conflict with past practice, in that the rule did not require warnings to precede discharge, while every other rule promulgated by the employer in the past eight years called for prior warnings. Moreover, the penalty of discharge had never been invoked on the basis of as few as 12 instances of tardiness in a 12-month period, the arbitrator noted. Although "chronic tardiness" can reasonably be defined in terms of a fixed number of instances of tardiness, the arbitrator found that it was unreasonable to do so where the number of instances of tardiness was reduced from the number allowed in the past, where notices were not issued to employees, and where the rules made no provision for a graduated system of penalties (*The Maccabees*, 27 LA 99).

● By promulgating a rule setting new discipline for tardiness, an employer violated a collective bargaining agreement provision requiring shop rules and penalties to remain unchanged for the duration of the contract, an arbitrator held. The employer's action was an improper modification of offenses and penalties under the contract, the arbitrator found (*Wolverine Aluminum Corp.*, 74 LA 252).

F. Other Attendance-Related Issues

In addition to addressing reasons for absences, notice and documentation requirements, and problems surrounding tardiness, arbitration decisions commonly touch on other attendance-related issues. Some of these include absences on days that employees normally would not be scheduled to work, employees' failure to report to work as expected after time off, the impact of past leniency or inconsistency on the enforcement of attendance policies, and the effect of unionization on the continuation of past policies or implementation of new ones. Arbitrators' findings on these issues are discussed below.

1. Absence on Usual Day Off

Absenteeism rates often rise when management schedules work on a Saturday, holiday, or other day that is not the normal workday. Arbitrators are in agreement, however, that as a general principle, the right to schedule work belongs to management, and normal attendance rules can be applied to employees when they are legitimately expected to show up on what would normally be a day off.

Even where contracts give employees the right to decline to work on a Saturday or holiday, arbitrators usually have held that once employees accept assignments to work on such a day, their duty to their employers is the same as it would be on a regular work day (118 LA 1079, 29 LA 672, 12 LA 770, 11 LA 947).

2. Failure to Return to Work

Absenteeism problems sometimes arise when employees have had time away from work and do not return when they are expected. For example, such situations can occur because employees overstay their vacations or fail to report on a specified return-to-work date following a layoff or injury. Arbitrators tend to judge these situations as they would any other absenteeism case, with particular attention to the reason for the absence and the consistency of the employers' enforcement of failure-to-report or leave-stretching prohibitions.

● Discharge was warranted for an employee who failed to report to work following a reinstatement award, despite his contention that the position being offered was not equivalent to the one he previously

held, an arbitrator decided. Instead of resorting to self-help in violation of the "obey now, grieve later" principle, the employee's proper course of action would have been to report to work on the specified date while awaiting arbitral clarification on the position to which he was entitled, the arbitrator observed (*H.J. Heinz Co.*, 97 LA 489; see also 96 LA 740).

● An employee did not return to work until one week after the end of her scheduled two-week vacation. She claimed that she could not get transportation back from the distant place where she spent her vacation unless she waited for her husband to finish his three-week vacation. Discharge of the employee for violating the company's rules was upheld by an arbitrator who said the employee probably had deliberately chosen not to return to work on time. In any event, she had demonstrated an irresponsible attitude toward her job (*Packaging Corp. of America*, 42 LA 606).

● *By contrast*, in a case in which an employee overstayed her vacation by a week, the arbitrator found that her excuse was good enough to warrant reducing her discharge to a suspension without pay. The reason for her absence was that she was attempting to save her marriage, which the arbitrator felt outweighed the employer's need for her presence (*Vellumoid Co.*, 41 LA 1129; see also 74 LA 847).

● Just cause did not exist to discharge an employee for "unauthorized absences" following an automobile accident, even though he did not report to work on the first date specified in the medical release, an arbitrator ruled. When the employee reported for work, it was one week after the date specified in the doctor's release for light-duty work but one week prior to the earliest date that he would have been released for regular duties. In overturning the employee's discharge, the arbitrator noted that the worker was entitled to a period of readjustment following his traumatic injury, and the employer had told him on similar occasions in the past that no light-duty work was available (*Dyncorp Fort Rucker Division*, 97 LA 572; see also 98 LA 194, 96 LA 38, 95 LA 1135, 95 LA 881, 95 LA 784).

3. Ambiguous or Inconsistent Enforcement Policy

Arbitrators generally do not condone inconsistency on the part of management when it comes to the enforcement of attendance policies. If, for example, attendance requirements receive only lip service for a period of time, arbitrators are likely to find that employees have a reasonable basis for believing that their absenteeism and tardiness will go unpunished. Past leniency or lax enforcement does not necessarily bar employers from cracking down on attendance problems, so long as they give effective notice of their intentions and deal with employees in an evenhanded manner.

● An agency did not have just cause to discharge an employee who took unpaid leave for vacation, where she was under the mistaken impression that doing so would not affect her status as an employee who was at the last stage before discharge in an attendance policy, an arbitrator ruled. This impression was given mostly by assurances of union officials, but also by management officials who did not follow through on their statement that they would take care of the problem. The grievant was reinstated with a last-chance agreement (*Bi-State Development Agency*, 126 LA 986).

● In an effort to get an employee with excessive absenteeism to mend his ways, management sent him a total of five "final" warnings over a three-year period. It ultimately fired him. Overruling the discharge, the arbitrator noted that the "final" warnings all read exactly alike. Thus it was not surprising that the employee did not think anyone actually was concerned about his absences. If somewhere along the line management had let the employee know that it meant business, either by a specific warning or disciplinary suspension, then discharge for subsequent absences probably would have been upheld. Instead, management had completely nullified the effectiveness of its warnings by repeatedly threatening discharge and then taking no disciplinary action, the arbitrator concluded (*Greer Limestone Co.*, 40 LA 343).

● However, an employee's discharge for absenteeism and tardiness was justified, even though other employees had escaped punishment, an arbitrator decided. The union reviewed a huge volume of time cards and discovered high rates of tardiness for two other workers, neither of whom were discharged. In light of the employer's lax enforcement with respect to these workers, the union said, the employee's discharge amounted to disparate treatment. The arbitrator disagreed, finding that the other workers were not comparable to the employee. In all likelihood, they reported to one of the employer's units that lacked a direct supervisor, and management was "completely unaware" of their tardiness, the arbitrator said. In contrast, the employee had received numerous instances of counseling and progressive discipline for both tardiness *and* absenteeism, and a comparison within the employee's unit showed he had the worst attendance record by far. Lacking evidence that management knowingly failed to enforce its attendance standards with respect to similarly-situated employees, the arbitrator refused to overturn the employee's discharge (*Georgia-Pacific Corp.*, 118 LA 577).

G. Effect of Unionization

Unionization can affect the ability of employers to continue past attendance policies or implement new ones. Without union consent or contract language permitting the policies in question, arbitrators are likely to decide that they are unenforceable.

● An arbitrator overturned the discipline issued to employees under an attendance policy that their employer unilaterally implemented before negotiating its first contract with the union. Finding that the absences triggering the warnings occurred when the employees requested and were given permission to take leave, the arbitrator concluded that the employees were not guilty of any misconduct warranting discipline. The arbitrator also rejected the employer's argument that its attendance policy, which predated the collective bargaining agreement, should be recognized as past practice. Past practice can only exist if it has been "mutually acknowledged and practiced by both the employer and the union" over an extended period of time, the arbitrator said (*Career Systems Development Corp.*, 113 LA 920).

● Another arbitrator ruled that a company had no right, after signing its first contract, to start docking workers for tardiness. Nobody had ever been docked for tardiness before the contract was signed, and the company had agreed that no clause in the contract would be interpreted to "imply any lowering of the working conditions heretofore existing." Pointing out that the language of the contract specifically stated that workers would retain all rights, privileges, and benefits they previously enjoyed, the arbitrator refused to uphold the docking policy (*Hellenic Lines Ltd.*, 39 LA 31; see also 97 LA 988).

II. Abusive Behavior [LA CDI 100.552510 (public employees); 118.640]

[*Editor's Note:* This chapter covers abusive behavior toward employers and supervisors. For other instances of abusive behavior, see Part 2, Chapter XXIII, Workplace Violence.]

OVERVIEW

The ability of employers to control operations in an efficient manner rests partly on the assumption that employees will show respect for their supervisors. Consequently, arbitrators agree that employers do not have to tolerate abusive behavior aimed at supervisors or other members of management, particularly where it has the potential to undermine authority and cause a breakdown in workplace discipline.

The types of abusive behavior that can trigger disciplinary action range from talking back to supervisors and using profanity to making threats or committing assaults. In addition to the severity of the offense, arbitrators weigh various factors in considering the appropriateness of penalties imposed for abusive behavior. These include employees' past disciplinary records, the circumstances leading to the abusive behavior, and the possibility that supervisors instigated the incidents or shared some responsibility for what transpired.

Some types of abusive behavior are considered grounds for summary dismissal. For example, arbitrators typically uphold the penalty of discharge for acts of physical violence, and they often do the same in cases where employees have directed threats or abusive language toward management representatives (51 LA 633, 51 LA 688, 63 LA 765, 63 LA 1130,

65 LA 631, 65 LA 1119, 66 LA 206, 67 LA 426, 92 LA 3, 93 LA 1277, 95 LA 895, 97 LA 121). "Where this type of grievous on-the-job misconduct occurs," one arbitrator stressed, an employer is obligated in the protection of its employees "to mete out stern disciplinary action promptly and consistently" (51 LA 462).

SUMMARY OF CASES

A. Physical Assault

Assaults on supervisors are typically treated as grounds for dismissal unless mitigating circumstances are present. Even if an assault does not occur on company property or during working hours, it can be treated as a dischargeable offense, so long as it is work-related and has its roots in the employer-employee relationship.

One arbitrator described a worker's assault on a supervisor as "the antithesis of civilized conduct and the behavior code of employment" (51 LA 462). Another arbitrator maintained that threats by an employee to inflict bodily harm on a supervisor are "a potent form of intimidation no less serious than actual physical attack" (50 LA 232).

In cases in which employees are accused of physically abusing supervisors, arbitrators generally consider the type of assault and degree of violence involved, as well as who the aggressors were and whether workers acted in self-defense.

● Discharge of an employee was warranted, even though there was some evidence that the supervisor swore at the grievant during an argument, where the grievant pushed the supervisor, which resulted in red marks around the supervisor's neck and chin, and a "cuss" word would be considered nothing more than shop talk, an arbitrator ruled (*Packaging Corp. of America*, 129 LA 1476).

● An employer had just cause to discipline an employee, where he "crossed the line" by orally and physically challenging a supervisor's authority in front of all his coworkers an arbitrator ruled (*Courier-Journal*, 126 LA 195).

● Discharge was justified for an employee who had a fight with his supervisor, even though the supervisor might have struck the first blow, an arbitrator decided.

Remarking that the employee exceeded his right to self-defense by chasing the supervisor with a piece of iron after the fight had ended, the arbitrator ruled that the use of a dangerous weapon constituted an aggravated infraction of the plant rules (*Southern Iron & Equipment Co.*, 65 LA 694).

● An arbitrator upheld the discharge of a delivery truck driver who assaulted his supervisor during an argument that occurred when the supervisor tried to improve the driver's efficiency. While the employee's frustration and anger at repeatedly being told that his work was not up to par might have been understandable, his frustration was no excuse for the method he used to manifest his emotions, the arbitrator decided, asserting that a contrary conclusion would invite "industrial anarchy" (*United Parcel Service Inc.*, 67 LA 861).

● *By contrast*, an arbitrator decided that a worker was improperly discharged for kicking a supervisor, who had bent over to pick up something he had dropped, on the grounds that the kick was a "spontaneous kind of horseplay without malice or evil intent or any feeling of animosity or anger." Although the employer argued that the kicking incident jeopardized the "respect, consideration, and loyalty" that the supervisor needed to function on the job, the arbitrator found the contrary to be true. There was much "playing around" in the "relaxed" atmosphere of the worksite, the arbitrator pointed out, declaring that a "playful kick can be a compliment among friends" (*Tyrone Hydraulics Inc.*, 75 LA 672).

● An arbitrator ruled that an employer did not have just cause to terminate an employee for making physical contact with his supervisor as they were walking, despite the supervisor's contention that it was a deliberate shove, where both the employee and a co-worker in the vicinity testified that the supervisor abruptly stopped walking and thus caused the employee to bump into him accidentally (*FMC Technologies Measurement Solutions*, 125 LA 1576).

• A grocery store did not have just cause to discharge a checker for directing profanity at a manager during a meeting on a policy regarding restroom breaks, even though she was clearly insubordinate, where the employee had no prior discipline and her behavior was totally out of character, she thought she had permission to leave her checkstand, and she promptly offered a sincere apology; the employee was reinstated without back pay (*Safeway Inc.*, 126 LA 1249).

• Another arbitrator held that just cause did not exist to discharge an employee for fighting with his supervisor after being given a work assignment. Even though he conceded that he had struck the supervisor in the face and threatened to throw him from a catwalk, this was the only blemish on the employee's outstanding 20-year work record. Moreover, the arbitrator said, the young supervisor's management style was harassing and provocative (*Ball-Incon Glass Packaging Corp.*, 98 LA 1).

B. Off-Duty Misconduct

Off-duty assaults, as noted above, typically are viewed by arbitrators in the same light as on-premises misconduct. One arbitrator acknowledged that public authority is available to deal with those who willfully commit assault and battery. Nevertheless, an employer still retains the right to maintain discipline and protect supervisors from retaliatory action by disgruntled employees, whether it occurs on employer property or away from the premises, the arbitrator declared (*U.S. Steel Corp.*, 35 LA 227).

• An employer had sufficient evidence to discharge an employee for assaulting a supervisor at a gas station, even though the employee claimed that he had been at a dentist's office when the altercation allegedly occurred, an arbitrator held. The supervisor, who had admonished the employee shortly before the end of his shift, stated that when he stopped for gas after work, the employee approached him, shouted and cursed at him,

shoved him twice, and punched him on the arm several times. The arbitrator credited the supervisor's testimony, noting that the employee did not have any corroborating witnesses to support his story about being at a dentist's office. Even more telling, according to the arbitrator, was the fact that a co-worker testified that the employee had come to work the next day and bragged about his assault on the supervisor. Concluding that the employee had committed one of the universally recognized types of serious misconduct that warrants summary dismissal, the arbitrator upheld the discharge (*Texas Arai Inc.*, 113 LA 750).

• An employee who struck a supervisor at his home was properly terminated, an arbitrator decided. After an argument on the job, the employee and his supervisor agreed to meet at a nearby parking lot to "box it out." The employee was unable to find the supervisor at the lot and went to his residence, where he punched him. The employee's "aggressive" behavior was the "culmination of a brooding resentment" toward his supervisor, the arbitrator found. Stressing that the worker had "plenty of time to reflect and back off," the arbitrator decided that the employee's discharge was justified (*Texstar Automotive Distribution Group Inc.*, 74 LA 210).

• An employer had just cause to discharge an employee for off-duty misconduct of writing an insubordinate abusive blog aimed at a supervisor, an arbitrator ruled, since courts have generally viewed employee "speech" on public Internet blogs as another form of oral communication, which, if derogatory, could justify termination. Offensive comments were directed toward a German-national plant manager and his nationality, and the manager filed a complaint over the comments (*Baker Hughes Inc.*, 128 LA 37).

C. Threats and Intimidation

In determining the propriety of disciplinary action in situations where employees have threatened or intimidated supervisors, arbitrators tend to consider the following:

• Was the employee's language directed toward the supervisor in an insulting manner and in front of other employees?

• Did the employee intend to, or could the employee, carry out the threat of bodily harm?

• Was the employee provoked?

• Was the employee's threat ambiguous or not?

Employees typically face stiff penalties if they make threats of violence against members of management, but arbitrators sometimes overturn or reduce the penalties if employees have not made a genuine threat, have a good work record, have been provoked, or if other extenuating circumstances exist.

• An employer need not give an employee who physically threatened a supervisor the benefit of progressive discipline, since such offense is sufficiently serious to justify immediate discharge, no employee should be required to feel physically threatened at work, and, when threat is directed toward a member of management, an employer's legitimate authority to operate in an orderly and safe manner is undermined, an arbitrator ruled (*Detroit Thermal LLC*, 129 LA 1364).

• An employer had just cause to discharge an employee who intentionally intimidated and threatened his supervisor, since acts of intimidation and instilling of fear are totally unacceptable in the workplace setting, and the misconduct was even more egregious because it was aimed at a supervisor, an arbitrator ruled (*AT&T Services*, 129 LA 249).

• An employer had just cause to discharge an employee who threatened to shoot his supervisor if he was discharged and then, after discharge, was convicted of telephone harassment for posting defamatory and malicious content on a website (*United Telephone Company of Ohio*, 127 LA 339).

• An employer had just cause to discharge an employee with 33 years of service who, following the discharge of a co-worker for playing a cartoon theme over the shop radio frequency, attempted to coerce a supervisor into rescinding discharge by threatening to claim that he had been injured when the supervisor threw open the door of the break room to discover the origin of the music. The arbitrator said that if the grievant had acknowledged what he had done and that it was unacceptable behavior, "discharge might not have been justified for an employee with 33 years of service and no citable disciplinary record. But Grievant did not take that course. Instead he went forward with his charade of having been injured" and flatly denied making any effort to coerce the supervisor (*United States Steel Corp.*, 125 LA 545).

• An employer had just cause to discharge an employee who made allegedly threatening comments to a manager in the aftermath of bitter contract negotiations, even though the grievant's comments referred to an unnamed "someone" committing violence, the manager did not think that the grievant meant harm, and his specific intent was unknown, an arbitrator ruled. The manager reacted to statements by sharing the experience with a supervisor within less than an hour of the incident and, other individuals, if they knew of the statements, could reasonably have had an apprehension of harm (*Exide Technologies*, 129 LA 857).

• Discharge was warranted for an employee who verbally abused and pushed his supervisor and later said he had an assault rifle and was going to "kick someone's ass," an arbitrator held. The threatening comments were not made directly to the supervisor but rather in the presence of co-workers. Nevertheless, those comments, following the employee's battery of his supervisor, suggested an escalation of anger and a threat of violence, "which is to be taken very seriously," the arbitrator said (*Department of the Air Force*, 118 LA 1429).

• An arbitrator ruled that a supervisor's questioning of an employees' competence and reliability did not excuse the grievant for physically threatening the supervisor. Even though the supervisor's actions were somewhat tactless, they were within the scope of his authority, were job-related, and were not a personally physical threat to the grievant. Moreover, the supervisor's orders to the employee to perform tasks below his skill level did not excuse him for making physical threats to the supervisor, because even the most skilled employees are expected to take on reasonable responsibilities that are below their skill level, the arbitrator said.

• An employee who voiced a willingness to assault his supervisor was properly discharged by an employer that strictly banned threats of violence, an arbitrator decided. After a friend was fired for absenteeism, the employee commented that if he faced similar consequences from his own supervisor, he would "beat his ass." The employee, who was on probationary status for attendance problems at the time, violated the employer's zero-tolerance workplace violence policy in making the comment, the arbitrator held. Even if the employee did not actually intend to harm his supervisor, he still violated the policy, which covered actual and implied threats of bodily harm, whether or not they were made in jest, the arbitrator found (*Modine Mfg. Co.*, 121 LA 1457).

• An arbitrator ruled that an employee who had threatened to have his foreman killed by a hired assassin was properly discharged. The arbitrator emphasized that the employee's threat against the foreman's life, which was made in front of co-workers, had "a chilling effect on the entire workforce." If the employee's conduct went unpunished, the arbitrator reasoned, then other workers might be tempted to engage in similar misbehavior without fear of reprisal (*Protective Treatments Inc.*, 61 LA 1292).

• A worker was terminated for just cause after he followed his supervisor's car one morning, swerved in front, and then threatened to kill him, an arbitrator found. Dismissing the worker's denials of the incident, the arbitrator found that the supervisor's "positive testimony" carried more weight. Furthermore, the arbitrator noted, the employee had a history of run-ins with various supervisors and had recently been suspended for absenteeism (*Central Soya Co. Inc.*, 74 LA 1084).

• An employee was properly discharged after a confrontation that culminated with his foreman dying of a heart attack, an arbitrator ruled. Although the worker argued that he was not guilty of an "assault" because he had not physically attacked the foreman, the arbitrator decided that the discipline was just. The argument, coupled with the worker's shaking a rod in front of the supervisor's face as a "weapon to threaten or intimidate" the foreman, put "great stress" on the deceased. "Making verbal threats and poking the rod into a supervisor's face" were sufficient grounds for discharge, "just as pulling a knife would be enough," the arbitrator reasoned, pointing out that in the latter case there would be "no question that a supervisor would not have to be stabbed before a discharge [was] proper" (*Quality Electric Steel Castings Inc.*, 74 LA 558).

• *By contrast*, an employee's discharge was reduced to a suspension because his threat that he "was going downtown" and was "going to take care of this [supervisor] thing" referred to filing an NLRB charge, which he did. But his threat was meant to intimidate, which required some discipline, according to the arbitrator (*Bosal Industries*, 124 LA 165).

• An employer did not have just cause to terminate an employee for suggesting to coworkers that he put Visine in his supervisor's coffee to induce diarrhea and then offering a supervisor coffee, which the supervisor did not drink. The employer did not establish that the employee had notice of policies that he allegedly violated, the employee did not have an opportunity to defend himself, and there was no evidence that the threat, which was indirect, was carried out. The penalty was reduced to a written reprimand (*Lewis County*, 126 LA 1336).

• An arbitrator ruled that discharge was not warranted for an employee who got into a heated discussion with his supervisor and said, "[Y]ou think you're a little bad ass, you think you can kick my ass?" Even though the employee was an extremely large man, the arbitrator observed, his supervisor did not feel threatened, as evidenced by the fact that he felt safe enough to turn his back to the employee and walk away at the pinnacle of their argument. Lacking evidence that a genuine threat existed or that the employee had any history of violence, the arbitrator ordered reinstatement with back pay (*Harbison-Walker Inc.*, 119 LA 624).

• Discharge was too severe for an employee who made an ambiguous threat to his supervisor and apologized shortly thereafter, an arbitrator found. After spending a difficult night keeping his sister safe from her abusive husband, the employee arrived for work and mentioned to his supervisor that he was tired. The supervisor warned him not to sleep on the job, and the employee responded, "If I bring my 44-Magnum, can I go to sleep then?" While conceding that threatening a supervisor constitutes serious misconduct, the arbitrator found the employee's comment somewhat ambiguous, because he did not directly threaten the supervisor. Pointing also to the employee's tumultuous previous night, his 18 years of service without any prior discipline, and the fact that he showed unwavering remorse for his actions, the arbitrator ordered reinstatement without back pay (*Wayne State University*, 111 LA 986).

● Reinstatement also was ordered for an employee who made threatening remarks to his supervisor following mechanical malfunctions that caused tensions to rise. After the employee called a mechanic over for a second time one morning, the supervisor came to ask why production was being held up. The employee indicated the problem was the mechanic, whom he referred to as "white boy." When the supervisor admonished the employee about making racial comments, the employee put one arm around the supervisor's shoulder and drew him close. The employee complained about the supervisor pressuring him, and he said he could get someone to knock the supervisor down and tell him not to harass the employee. An arbitrator found that the threat was borne out of frustration with the particular day's events, and the employee did not have the propensity to carry it out. Adding that the employee had a 14-year record of unblemished service, the arbitrator reduced the employee's discharge to an unpaid suspension (*Pepsi-Cola Co.*, 104 LA 1141).

D. Abusive Language

In general, arbitrators do not expect employers to tolerate employees' verbal abuse of managers. Use of profane and obscene language by employees does not necessarily justify severe discipline, but if such language is used to embarrass, ridicule, or degrade supervisors, it would be considered an insubordinate act, especially if other employees were present to hear it. One arbitrator observed that profanity, when coupled with a refusal to obey a supervisor's directive, can constitute grounds for discharge (*Hastings Mfg. Co.*, 26 LA 713).

Abusive language can take other forms. For example, an arbitrator pointed out that discipline would be warranted if an employee responds to a supervisor's directive by arguing and calling the supervisor a name. The arbitrator also described other name-calling scenarios that would justify disciplinary action: the employee calls the supervisor a name in front of other employees; the employee calls the supervisor a name privately but afterward brags to other employees about telling off the boss; or the employee calls the supervisor a name privately, is warned by the supervisor, but continues to indulge in the name-calling (*Arkansas Louisiana Chemical Corp.*, 35 LA 887).

In some cases, arbitrators have overturned or reduced disciplinary penalties imposed on employees in view of mitigating factors, such as long years of service and a good work record, past acceptance by employers of "shop talk" that includes profanity and name-calling, or reciprocal use of such language by supervisors (25 LA 439, 27 LA 611, 39 LA 58, 39 LA 661, 39 LA 849, 64 LA 751, 64 LA 1065, 65 LA 25, 94 LA 1087).

1. Profanity

● An employer did not act in an arbitrary or unreasonable manner when it discharged an employee, who wrote "FU" on a board on which he was supposed to place his initials after finishing a task, despite his contention that FU meant "finished unit," where FU was an expletive, which is tantamount to challenging management's authority to direct workforce (*Trane Co.*, 129 LA 1417).

● Discharge was warranted for an employee who used obscene terms in suggesting that his foreman perform an act of indignity upon himself, an arbitrator decided. The foreman told the employee he would be given a warning for such language and started to walk away, but the employee repeated the remark with emphasis. Between 10 and 20 employees were in the vicinity at the time. The arbitrator conceded that profanity was commonly used at the plant, but he distinguished the ordinary banter and shop talk from the employee's use of a profane and vulgar expression with the intent to degrade and insult the recipient. Adding that the morale of the entire workforce could be undermined if such disrespectful insubordination were permitted, the arbitrator upheld the discharge (*Paragon Bridge & Steel Co.*, 43 LA 864).

• An arbitrator upheld the discharge of an employee who unleashed a stream of profanity at a supervisor. The arbitrator noted that other employees were known to use profanity as adjectives or adverbs, which was not the same as the employee's abusive, deprecating speech. Moreover, the employee had a history of lashing out and had been disciplined repeatedly in the past for abusive behavior, the arbitrator observed (*County of Allegany*, 121 LA 582).

• An employer had just cause to assess an employee a three-day suspension for use of profanity/abusive language to a supervisor when he called the supervisor a "fucking liar" and continued to interrupt him with comments that the supervisor was living in a "fantasy" or in a "dream world." The grievant argued that a written warning was a more appropriate penalty, but the arbitrator upheld the suspension (*Ohio Power Co.*, 129 LA 1753).

• Discharge was too severe for an employee who used obscene language and made a vulgar gesture toward a foreman after a series of mechanical breakdowns left the shop in turmoil, an arbitrator ruled. Finding that the employee's misconduct was connected with the "frustration, excitement, and confusion that prevailed," the arbitrator reduced the discharge to a three-day suspension (*Mead Packaging Co.*, 74 LA 881).

Discharge was too severe for an employee who went into a rage at a grievance meeting held to discuss her alleged use of foul language toward her supervisor. Insisting that it could not condone or tolerate this type of behavior, the employer discharged the worker for "gross insubordination." Reducing the penalty, the arbitrator pointed out that the

worker was a well-trained, long-term employee who had held several positions within the company. Under the circumstances, the arbitrator concluded, she deserved a "last chance" to correct her unacceptable behavior (*TRW Inc.*, 76 LA 782; see also 94 LA 610, 94 LA 767, 94 LA 1075).

2. "Liar"

Abusive language in the form of name-calling also can trigger discipline or discharge. For example, calling a supervisor a "liar" usually is regarded as a major offense.

• One arbitrator confirmed the seriousness of an employee calling a supervisor a liar. The arbitrator upheld the penalty of discharge, even though the employee had an "erroneous impression" that led him to think the supervisor had told an untruth (*Pacific Mills*, 3 LA 141).

• Another arbitrator noted that "most people would consider the accusation 'liar' to be more abusive and contemptuous than some casual vulgarism." In that case, the employee not only called his supervisor a liar in front of union and employer officials, but also refused to follow work assignments and even sprayed his foreman with a high-pressure hose. Finding that the worker's conduct was "no simple incivility," but rather "an egregious expression of contempt for supervisory authority," the arbitrator ruled that the employer was within its rights to terminate the employee (*ITT Continental Baking Co.*, 75 LA 764).

• In another case, an employee managed to hold onto his job after calling his foreman a "damn liar" only because he had a good work record and because there were no other employees within hearing at the time. Furthermore, there was some evidence that the foreman had initiated the use of abusive language (*Higgins Industries Inc.*, 25 LA 439).

3. Discriminatory Comments

• An employer had just cause to discharge an employee for making a racially motivated threat against a supervisor in a bar, where the threat was very serious given concern of all parties for safety in the workplace, the employee had previously been disciplined for similar actions, he had only two and one-half years with the employer, and he showed no remorse (*Integrated Metal Technology Inc.*, 125 LA 1659).

An employer has been found, in expedited arbitration, to have just cause to discharge an employee who was involved in an altercation with a co-worker, and who then called two managers "fucking fags" (*AT&T Mobility*, 129 LA 1284).

● An employee committed national origin discrimination and supervisory insubordination, where he wrote a blog on his personal computer in which he referred to upper management, which included a German-national plant manager, as "German, green card terminator. . ." and wrote "I could have sworn that Hitler committed suicide." Employer had just cause to discharge the employee for writing the insubordinate and abusive blog aimed at the supervisor, where the offense was serious, the employee showed no remorse, and he would be unable to work with the manager (*Baker Hughes Inc.*, 128 LA 37).

● An arbitrator overturned the discharge of an employee who, in a one-on-one meeting with his new boss, referred to the replacement of his old supervisor by saying that he hoped they had not lost Bin Laden only to get the Taliban. The employee admitted that he meant the new supervisor might be worse than his predecessor. Although the employee's comment was insubordinate and deserved formal discipline, the arbitrator found discharge inappropriate and reduced the penalty to a 10-day suspension (*AEP*, 117 LA 1818).

E. Disrespectful Attitude

Few things are likely to annoy supervisors more than employees who always reply with flip or sour remarks when told to do something. However, it often is difficult to draw a line between harmless, minor griping and defiance or disrespectfulness that would undermine discipline. And it is not at all rare for supervisors to put up with questionable remarks for a period of time before finally getting angry and taking action.

● Employer had just cause to suspend employee for shift in which he was insubordinate to supervisor, where he boasted as he was leaving that he'd get free night's pay from this, thereby further attempting to undermine and disrespect supervisor's managerial authority (*Courier-Journal*, 126 LA 195).

● One arbitrator ordered the reinstatement of an employee who became argumentative during a meeting with two managers and refused to lower her voice despite being told three times to do so. According to the arbitrator, the employee had a history of being loud, argumentative, and defiant, which her employer tacitly condoned by issuing nothing more than a verbal warning for such behavior in the past. In this instance, the arbitrator said, one of the managers "stoked the coals of unacceptable conduct" by calling the employee a liar and repeatedly telling her that she should quit if she did not like her working conditions. The arbitrator also noted that neither manager warned the employee that a failure to lower her voice could result in termination (*City of Gary Human Relations Commission*, 120 LA 244).

● An employee who had been with a company for 20 years talked virtually all the time, even when nobody else was around. He always insisted on having the last word and almost invariably would go off muttering disapprovingly when given an order. Twice in one day, his foreman's orders drew "I-know-my-job" retorts, which led to an exchange that culminated in discharge. An arbitrator reduced the discharge to a suspension, conceding that the employee had engaged in misconduct on the day of his discharge, but adding that his conduct on innumerable occasions in the past might similarly be characterized as objectionable. A slight variation in his 20-year theme should not precipitate anything so drastic as discharge, the arbitrator concluded (*Armour Agricultural Chemical Co.*, 40 LA 289).

F. Disparaging Remarks About Company Management

Disparaging remarks about employers, individual supervisors, or management in general are not unheard of in employee conversation. In many cases, such remarks are not considered grounds for disciplinary action.

• After a company tightened its enforcement of certain rules, two employees were discharged for making derogatory remarks about the company president and failing to observe the rules. Upon being terminated, one of the employees used profanity in directly addressing the company president. An arbitrator found little to support the company's charges of rule violations. Regarding the employees' derogatory remarks, meanwhile, the arbitrator said no one could show that such remarks were uncommon, that the statements were malicious in character, or that they affected morale and productivity. Although the use of profanity in addressing the company president was disrespectful, this conduct occurred after the employees were fired and could not properly be used as grounds to sustain their termination, the arbitrator concluded (*Top World*, 51 LA 1285).

• A worker was improperly discharged for criticizing management policies at a stockholders' meeting, an arbitrator held. The employee was the son of a woman who owned 49 percent of the company's common stock, and he attended the meeting as her representative after she became ill. During the meeting, the worker criticized management policies and challenged the competence of the company's president and other officials. The company subsequently discharged the employee, contending that his "attitude toward work had changed considerably" and that he had begun to act more like a manager than an employee. According to the arbitrator, the employee was "registering complaints and criticism not as an employee, but rather as the representative of his Mother." Consequently, the arbitrator ruled, the remarks were not proper grounds for discharge (*Hopwood Foods Inc.*, 74 LA 349).

G. Mitigating Circumstances

Sometimes when employees engage in abusive behavior, arbitrators overturn or reduce the disciplinary penalties imposed because of the existence of mitigating circumstances. In many cases, arbitrators conclude that the actions of management representatives have provoked employees' abusive behavior or helped to create situations in which personality conflicts were more likely to flare up.

• Discharge of an insubordinate employee was reduced to 20-day suspension without back pay, even though he went off and aggravated a dispute with a supervisor, struck a stretcher box, and hit a vending machine. The grievant had 18 years of seniority with almost no discipline, his brother had just been hospitalized because of an auto accident, the grievant had been ill, his post-traumatic stress disorder may have contributed to his behavior, and he eventually apologized (In re SWVA, Inc., 129 LA 1173).

• Discharge was too severe for an employee who used abusive language after being provoked by a supervisor, an arbitrator held. The employee was known for being quiet and laid-back, while the supervisor was known for being loud, profane, aggressive, and prone to calling people names. Concluding that the supervisor provoked the incident when he used profanity and called the employee "big dummy," the arbitrator reduced the employee's discharge to a suspension (*Basic*, 121 LA 642).

• An arbitrator overturned a three-day suspension and final warning issued to an employee after a confrontation with a supervisor. Past relationships often reveal mitigating factors, the arbitrator observed, and in this case, there was a history of bad blood between the employee and the supervisor who accused him of threatening behavior. While it was undisputed that the employee raised his voice during their confrontation, there was no evidence that he made any kind of threat or menacing gesture. Moreover, the arbitrator found that the supervisor was antagonistic and sarcastic to the employee. Finding additionally that the company conducted an inadequate investigation and denied the worker's right to confront his accuser, the arbitrator overturned the discipline (*Chevron-Phillips Chemical Co.*, 120 LA 1065).

• An arbitrator held that an employee's depression was a mitigating factor that warranted overturning his discharge. The employee was very ill and had sought medical help, but his physician had cancelled a scheduled appointment, the arbitrator noted. Despite the employee's ensuing violence and insubordination, the arbitrator ordered reinstatement based on the condition that the employee obtain two opinions from doctors stating his fitness to resume working (*American National Can Co.*, 106 LA 289).

● Another arbitrator decided that a supervisor precipitated an argument with an employee who had requested emergency leave to attend to a family crisis. The supervisor wanted more information before approving the leave, and when the employee refused to provide details about the family emergency, the two got into an argument. According to the arbitrator, the supervisor had engaged in a pattern of harassment, and his "excited" response to the employee's remarks contributed substantially to the heated nature of the discussion. Concluding that the supervisor's own "intemperate" conduct in dealing with a subordinate constituted unacceptable workplace behavior, the arbitrator overturned the reprimand the employee had received (*Veterans Administration*, 75 LA 733; see also 81 LA 176, 81 LA 385, 90 LA 1302, 91 LA 482, 91 LA 905, 92 LA 28, 92 LA 340, 92 LA 521, 92 LA 871).

III. Damaging Employer Property [LA CDI 100.552513 (public employees); 118.643]

OVERVIEW

When making determinations about incidents resulting in damage to employer property, arbitrators typically distinguish accidental acts from situations where employees show deliberate or malicious intent. In general, arbitrators attach greater seriousness to intentional damage caused by actions such as vandalism or sabotage than to accidental damage caused by carelessness or negligence (see also the chapter titled "Negligence").

In cases where deliberate or malicious intent is proven, the actual dollar value of the property damage takes on relatively little significance, and many arbitrators uphold the ultimate penalty of discharge even if the damage is slight (94 LA 979, 77 LA 865, 73 LA 538, 72 LA 704). Conversely, arbitrators commonly find that just cause for discharge does not exist in cases involving unintentional damage, provided that employees are not guilty of gross negligence (74 LA 257, 73 LA 98, 68 LA 1341).

SUMMARY OF CASES

A. Intent

The presence of deliberate intent or gross negligence are the primary factors weighed by arbitrators in determining the appropriate discipline for employees who damage employer property. This factor separates malicious behavior from mere carelessness or negligence, in which damage results not so much from a purposeful move to destroy as from a failure to follow procedures. If evidence establishes that employees have willingly and knowingly damaged employer property, arbitrators generally uphold the right of management to impose discipline as it sees fit.

• A shipyard had just cause to discharge a crane operator—who used a crane to move steel panel without the help of a rigger and damaged a ladder up on a landing panel—for "[g]ross negligence which results in injury to oneself or others," even though no person was injured. The crane operator knew that the panel's size would reduce his visibility and that other employees were still in the area, yet he took the panel into a dark area and did not wait for help before twice attempting to land it. As such the arbitrator found that his "repeated, aggravated gross negligence with resulting property damage" was not tolerable.

However the shipyard did not have just cause to discharge a rigger—who hooked up the steel panel to the crane and then went to the bathroom without getting a replacement rigger or advising the crane operator to do so, and in whose absence the operator damaged the ladder up on the landing panel—for "[g]ross negligence which results in injury to oneself or others." No person was injured, the rigger acknowledged his error, the parties did not intend for "others" to include the shipyard itself, and it was the operator's choice to proceed without a rigger. The rigger's penalty was reduced to a written reprimand with three days off without pay (*Jeffboat LLC*, 127 LA 1121).

• A pulp and paper mill had just cause to discharge a 33-year employee for violating its rules regarding insubordination and "thoughtless conduct which endangers employees or results in damaged property" because the employee refused to comply with a directive to extinguish fire in a kiln. The grievant was responsible for monitoring the area in which the fire broke out, and his refusal was in retaliation for his prior demotion. When asked why he stood at the window and let the fire ball burn, he said it wasn't his job to put out the fire, and the collective bargaining agreement stipulated that the first violation of either rule warranted discharge (*Abitibi Bowater Inc.*, 126 LA 1524).

• A city had just cause to discharge a custodian who caused minor damage to a bookshelf while driving a carpet extractor and failed to report the incident to his employer, where another employee had been discharged for a similar offense and the grievant had also failed to inform the city of his divorce so that his ex-wife could stay covered by his health insurance, and he twice had been caught sleeping on the job (*City of Eugene*, 124 LA 1724).

• Discharge was justified for a worker who tampered with a lock box fitted over the thermostat controlling the temperature in his work area, an arbitrator decided. Although this was "not the most destructive of acts," it constituted "willful" property damage, the arbitrator found. Management "is entitled to insist that employees respect the employer's property and to protect that property from abuse. Every worker's job is potentially threatened when employees engage in needless acts of vandalism against their employer's tangible property," the ar-

bitrator said (*National Car Rental System*, 72 LA 704).

• An arbitrator ruled that an employee was properly discharged for hitting and breaking the glass face of a malfunctioning time clock, even though the worker maintained that he had not intended to break the clock. While granting that the worker "was frustrated and irritated, perhaps justifiably so in view of the history of malfunction of the clock," the arbitrator declared that "nevertheless, there was no justification for his action." The worker "intended to strike the clock, that deliberate act damaged Company property, and his discharge was for proper cause," the arbitrator concluded (*National Services Industries Inc.*, 73 LA 538).

• A worker caught using a hammer to bang on a soft-drink machine was properly suspended for the intentional destruction of company property, an arbitrator held. The employee claimed that he had been handed the hammer "as a joke" during his unsuccessful attempts to retrieve his money from the nonfunctional machine and that he had used the hammer without contemplating "any damage which might occur to the machine." Dismissing the worker's contention that he should not be disciplined because the element of intent was lacking, the arbitrator found that regardless of whether the employee thought the whole affair was a "joke," it was "plain that he was intentionally hitting the machine with a heavy tool" (*The Flexible Co.*, 48 LA 1227).

• *By contrast*, a meat processing plant did not prove that a discharged employee intentionally misfed pork bellies through an injector machine, and the grievant was reinstated with back pay. Despite the supervisor's eye witness testimony that he saw the employee holding one belly over the other, which would violate procedures if fed into the machine that way, the supervior did not see if he fed them through machine that way, and the grievant's version of events was just as believable. Further, the meat was tested and met specifications with no waste, the grievant knew the proper method of feeding meat into the machine and had no motive to do otherwise, he did not finish work early, and he had no history of working in a careless or reckless manner (*Kraft Foods Inc.*, 129 LA 1717).

• An airline did not have just cause to discharge an employee who backed a baggage cart into the wing of an aircraft, despite the airline's zero tolerance policy involving aircraft damage, where the damage was minimal, the airline did not always discharge employees who damaged aircraft, and in three very similar cases an arbitrator had reduced discharge to suspension. The employee was suspended without pay for 14 weeks and was entitled to back pay from two days prior to the decision until his reinstatement (*Allied Aviation*, 125 LA 1468).

• An arbitrator ruled that a transit agency did not have just cause to discharge a driver who moved a camera behind his seat, because he stretched and moved the camera unintentionally, and two drivers who were discharged for similar violations did not act comparably—one placed tape over the camera lens and the other tampered with fare boxes (*Pinellas Suncoast Transit Authority*, 129 LA 1614).

• An arbitrator ruled that a county sheriff did not have just cause to suspend a deputy for eight hours for violating a departmental rule against reckless operation of a cruiser or putting the civilian population at risk of injury or property damage or for negligent operation of a cruiser when, in the high-speed pursuit of a suspect who had abducted a woman in a neighboring city, he drove off a sharp drop-off at the end of a country road, which resulted in $2,000 damage to the cruiser. The pursuit took place on a deserted country road, the officer was neither aware of the drop-off nor advised by his commanding officer, and the grievant captured the suspect (*Marion County Sheriff's Office*, 126 LA 90).

• Distinguishing "premeditated effort" from a "loss of restraint," an arbitrator overturned the discharge of a worker who broke the glass on a malfunctioning vending machine while trying to retrieve his purchase. Finding it "commonplace for human beings to bang on or kick a machine which does not deliver the promised goods," the arbitrator decided that the "provocation offered by the machine" plus the employee's otherwise clean work record militated

against termination (*Goldblatt Tool Co.*, 74 LA 257).

• A lack of malicious intent prompted another arbitrator to overturn the discharge of an employee who damaged a refrigerator. The employee was the victim of a practical joke, in which a co-worker coated his drinking straw with a foul-tasting medicated cream. When the employee took a sip and gagged, several co-workers started laughing. The employee reacted by throwing his soda and denting the refrigerator. The employer contended that he violated a rule against the malicious and intentional destruction of company property. The arbitrator disagreed, finding that the employee's brief flare-up was not malicious, and the damage to the refrigerator was unintended and relatively minor. Discharge was overly harsh under the circumstances, much like "revoking a driver's license for overstaying a parking meter, the arbitrator said in reducing the penalty to a five-day suspension (*Whirlpool Corp.*, 115 LA 622).

B. Vandalism

Vandalism, by definition, involves a malicious intent to cause damage or destruction, so when employees vandalize employer property, arbitrators generally agree that discipline is warranted. On the other hand, inconsistent enforcement can undermine employers' ability to impose the ultimate penalty of discharge. If acts of vandalism have gone unpunished in the past, arbitrators are likely to conclude that employees lacked fair and sufficient notice of the consequences for their actions.

• Discharge was too severe for an employee caught painting the words "peace, love, and brotherhood" on a door frame, an arbitrator decided. Employees had never been warned about graffiti, and management had allowed scrawls and drawings to remain on the walls for extended periods of time. This inaction may well have contributed to the worker's lack of concern about a rule prohibiting this type of activity, the arbitrator found. Although management has the prerogative to decide what will be allowed to appear on its walls and what the penalties for infractions of the rules will be, these rights cannot be exercised arbitrarily and inconsistently, the arbitrator observed, concluding that the extreme penalty of outright dismissal was far too harsh a punishment for this particular, and first-time, offense (*Russell Stanley Corp.*, 66 LA 953).

● Another arbitrator overturned an employee's discharge after he shook and kicked a vending machine but did not damage it. The arbitrator dismissed the employer's charge of "vandalism," because even "if there was malice, there was certainly no defacement or destruction." Furthermore, the employee's conduct was in accordance with "applicable mores," which hold that "vending machines are most imperfect creatures, subject to being physically abused, without penalty, when they malfunction," the arbitrator observed (*Cosden Oil and Chemical Co. Inc.*, 68 LA 1341).

● Where a prohibition was well communicated, management was justified in suspending a worker for vandalism, an arbitrator held. In that case, the employer had experienced several acts of vandalism in its restrooms, including episodes in which workers caused toilets to overflow by deliberately stopping them up with rolls of toilet paper. Security guards conducted surveillance on one of the restrooms. The guards stuffed a roll of toilet paper in one of the toilets and posted a sign on it saying "do not use." Later, an employee entered the restroom, removed the sign, and relieved himself. By the time the guards entered the restroom, the employee had flushed the toilet several times, causing it to overflow. Although the employee denied responsibility, the arbitrator upheld his suspension. Pointing out that the employee did not offer to help clean up the mess when confronted by the guards, the arbitrator concluded that the worker's denial of responsibility displayed a primary concern over culpability, fault, responsibility, and blame, rather than a primary concern over minimizing the damage (*General Electric Co.*, 74 LA 161).

● A one-day suspension was warranted for an employee who painted over the word "No" on a company "No Parking" sign, an arbitrator held. A security guard saw the employee spray-painting the sign one day after the employee had been warned not to park his truck in unauthorized spaces. The

employee received a five-day suspension for destroying company property, based on the guard's testimony. Although painting the sign was "immature and inappropriate," the arbitrator said it did not rise to the level of "destruction." Nonetheless, defacing company property warranted some punishment, the arbitrator explained, ruling that the suspension should be reduced from five days to one (*Southern Indiana Gas and Electric Co.*, 112 LA 186).

C. Sabotage

Sabotage is a particularly distasteful offense, arbitrators concur, in that it aims to deliberately subvert the employer's operations. Even if employees are not guilty of the act itself, they can face discipline for conspiring with co-workers to commit sabotage or cover it up.

● An employer properly suspended all five workers on a crew after none would admit responsibility for sabotaging a piece of equipment, an arbitrator ruled. Following a lunch break, the crew reported that the machine they had been using was broken. Upon discovering that an electrical hookup was missing from a control panel, a supervisor decided that sabotage had occurred because the wire had been manually removed. When all the employees denied any knowledge of the sabotage, management suspended the entire crew. Sabotage indeed took place, the arbitrator agreed. While acknowledging that the evidence implicating the employees was "entirely circumstantial" and the company did not consider "the nature of the involvement of individual crew members," the arbitrator pointed out that the wire tampering could not be "explained reasonably except by assigning the blame to one or more members" of the crew. Even if some crew members were not directly involved, all were "guilty of conspiring to obstruct the Company's investigation of the matter," the arbitrator decided (*Koppers Co.*, 76 LA 175).

● Discharge was appropriate for a supermarket employee who put metallic items in his employer's microwave ovens to destroy them, an arbitrator held. On one occasion, someone wrapped three foil ketchup packets in a paper towel and left them cooking in a microwave until the oven melted down. About a week later, store employees saw a suspicious-looking person in sunglasses putting something in a microwave and setting the timer all the way to 10 minutes. The item was a wad of aluminum foil wrapped in a paper towel. After management identified the culprit as an employee, he was fired. "In the pantheon of cases involving discharge for intentional sabotage, this case must rank near the top," the arbitrator said. "There literally should be no question in anyone's mind," he added, that the employee placed the damaging materials in the microwaves and set them to an inordinately long cooking time in an effort to maliciously destroy company property (*King Soopers Inc.*, 118 LA 218).

● Discharge was warranted for a computer programmer who caused the loss of a large quantity of data with an improper shutdown of his employer's computer system, an arbitrator ruled. The employer had previously received complaints from co-workers about the employee's temper and work habits and had warned the employee about bringing the system down without advance warning. The employer eventually brought in a computer specialist from another area to analyze the system, and he discovered various irregularities in the way the employee was running the system. At that point, the arbitrator said, the employee knew "he would never again have a free rein to run the system the way he had in the past." The improper system shutdown occurred shortly thereafter, causing a number of employees to lose several hours worth of work. Finding that the employee intentionally caused the loss of data, the arbitrator concluded that his continued employment would have been a deterrent to his employer's efficiency and effectiveness (*El Toro Marine Air Station*, 102 LA 685).

● Intentionally starting a fire to dramatize an allegedly unsafe working condition was sufficient cause for discharging an employee, an arbitrator decided. On the day when an air pollution inspector was observing working conditions in another part of the plant, a worker deliberately threw oil-soaked lead scraps into a vat filled with molten lead, starting a fire that shot flames four to five feet in the air. When the employee admitted starting the fire in order to get the inspector to take a look at conditions in his work area, he was discharged. The arbitrator noted there was no dispute about the employee's actions or why he took them; however, he continued, "the 'good' motive to improve unpleasant or even unhealthy conditions of work" is "wholly disproportionate to the seriousness of this conduct." Furthermore, the worker's self-righteous attitude about what he had done could be reasonably interpreted as a harbinger of further hazardous acts, the arbitrator noted, concluding that, under these conditions, the employer was justified in discharging the worker (*F.E. Olds & Son*, 64 LA 726).

● In another case, an employee threw a wad of paper into an assembly line and stuffed fries into a batter machine. Concluding that these were acts of "sabotage," an arbitrator upheld the employee's discharge (*J.R. Simplot Co.*, 103 LA 865).

● *By contrast*, an employer did not have just cause to discharge an employee it accused of purposely dumping a large number of oversized rocks in a clay feeder system, where the employer relied on an incomplete investigation in making the discharge decision, there were no eyewitnesses testifying that the grievant dumped the rocks, and the employer failed to provide a plausible motive for the grievant's alleged transgression. Further, the record showed that the clay feeder system had "been beleaguered with" rock issues before and after the incident in question (*Cemex Inc.* 128 LA 1301).

● Management erred in firing a worker for sabotage where the evidence did not conclusively establish his guilt, an arbitrator held. One night outside the employer's premises, a security guard saw a man throw what looked to be a lighted object into a trash bin. A second guard also observed someone walking along a street near the bin shortly after the first guard called for assistance. The employee was subsequently discharged based on an identification made by one of the guards. The arbitrator overruled the discharge, since the employee had an alibi for his whereabouts at the time of the incident, and because the guard's identification was highly doubtful, given that he had made his observation from about 100 yards away on a street that was poorly lit (*Greyhound Lines-West*, 61 LA 44).

● An employer acted prematurely in discharging an employee for conspiracy to commit sabotage, an arbitrator held. The employer's plant had been plagued by several incidents of sabotage, including a fire. Two workers admitted to setting the fire and implicated a third employee in the conspiracy. That employee was then indicted by civil authorities and discharged by the employer. The arbitrator ordered reinstatement, finding that the indictment only raised a presumption of guilt, and the employer acted on the basis of doubtful information. Given that the employee was with the two workers when they discussed setting the fire but did nothing to prevent it, however, the arbitrator found him negligent and withheld back pay from the reinstatement order (*Donaldson Co. Inc.*, 60 LA 1240).

IV. Discourtesy [LA CDI 100.552517 (public employees); 118.646]

OVERVIEW

Employees are expected to be courteous and respectful while performing their job duties, particularly when serving the public. As a general rule, arbitrators uphold discipline in situations where employees are guilty of rudeness or abuse, if the following conditions are met:

- the evidence convincingly supports the allegations of discourtesy (95 LA 771, 83 LA 224, 71 LA 805); and
- adverse consequences, such as "public embarrassment" or disruption of operations, have resulted from the abusive behavior (98 LA 102, 95 LA 771, 94 LA 983, 93 LA 24, 82 LA 1186).

This section examines arbitration cases involving employees' discourtesy toward customers and members of the public as well as cases involving employees' complaints of discourteous behavior on the part of management. Discourteous behavior that employees direct at supervisors, including profanity, disrespectful attitudes, and name-calling, generally constitutes insubordination, and is discussed in the chapter titled "Abusive Behavior."

SUMMARY OF CASES

A. Evidence and Due Process

Arbitrators typically agree that employee discourtesy justifies disciplinary action. When discourtesy cases hinge on second-hand information in the form of customer complaints, however, unions commonly object that such "hearsay" evidence does not provide a proper basis for discipline. They also tend to argue that employees are deprived of due-process rights if their accusers are not available for questioning at arbitration hearings.

Although arbitrators accord hearsay evidence less weight than firsthand knowledge to which witnesses can testify, they are reluctant to fault employers for sparing customers from involvement in arbitration proceedings. After all, it does not make good business sense to enable employees to confront their accusers when the attainment of that procedural goal would come at the cost of inconveniencing customers who already feel they have been subjected to discourteous or abusive behavior.

When faced with these competing interests, arbitrators often look to issues such as credibility and corroborating witness testimony, the past record of employees, and the quality of evidence showing misconduct. For example, one arbitrator said it is a "sound and good practice" for employers to have a "policy of obtaining written complaints" from customers that document an employee's guilt before taking disciplinary action (*Safeway Stores Inc.*, 64 LA 563).

● An employee with a poor record was properly fired on the basis of customer complaints, even though the employee and her union were not permitted to review the complaints or contact the complaining customers, an arbitrator decided. Before meeting with the employee and her union steward, supervisors spoke to three customers who complained about the employee. Although the union argued that this "hearsay" evidence could not be used to justify the employee's discharge, the arbitrator found that the union was given sufficient information regarding the substance of the charges. "No one will ever be able to be absolutely certain of what happened on these occasions," the arbitrator said, but the employee's long list of prior oral and written warnings and suspensions for discourtesy to customers showed that she was unable to correct her behavior in response to the progressive discipline imposed by the employer (*Fred Meyer Inc.*, 117 LA 1063).

● Reinstatement would have been in order for another employee, based on the limited number of complaints his employer knew about when it fired him, but an arbitrator upheld discharge because of further complaints that came to light after the employee's termination. The additional evidence revealed a pattern of conduct toward customers that was far more serious than

previously known and showed that the employee was unfit to service the company's customers, the arbitrator said in denying reinstatement (*BFI Gardena Division*, 121 LA 289).

● *By contrast*, an arbitrator ruled that a cell phone video clip of a bus driver, which was taken by the son of the agency owner who complained of driver's conduct, was inadmissible, even though the clip was presented at a step three grievance hearing and a collective bargaining contract required complainants to appear at step three hearings as well as arbitration. The son did not appear at the step three hearing, the clip was essentially equivalent to hearsay written statements from agency's personnel, and the clip was taken by a close relative of the complainant, and not by a disinterested third party (*Greyhound Lines Inc.*, 126 LA 1743).

● An arbitrator reduced the discharge of an employee, who was subject to customer complaints for derogatory comments and related offenses while working on the customer's worksite, to time off without pay and return to work on a last-chance agreement, where the employer went from a contemplated written warning to discharge in his punishment, he had no warnings issued with regard to his spotty work record, and he was assigned and satisfactorily worked jobs for three months after the incident that led to his discharge (*Siemens Power Generation*, 126 LA 441).

● An airport van driver was improperly discharged for complaints about his driving, an arbitrator ruled. Although hearsay evidence is acceptable in cases based on customer complaints, the evidence in this case was inconsistent and included multiple layers of hearsay, the arbitrator noted. A motorist called the company to report that the van driver had cut him off in traffic, then the complaint was put in a memorandum, and the memorandum was sent to the location where the driver worked. According to the arbitrator, this constituted "hearsay at least thrice removed." Adding that a passenger in the driver's van did not corroborate the claims outlined in the motorist's complaint, the arbitrator said the employer lacked sufficient evidence to support discharge and ordered the employee reinstated with back pay (*SuperShuttle of Los Angeles Inc.*, 118 LA 1552)

● An employer could not justify terminating two employees on the basis of hearsay in the form of a customer's e-mails, an arbitrator decided. The employer, a provider of contract services to air carriers, terminated the two employees after they were banned from working on the account of the only customer the employer had in the geographical area. Although the customer's wishes had to be respected, the employer's case against the employees rested solely on the e-mails, which the arbitrator referred to as hearsay evidence without "probative value." While acknowledging the employer's reluctance to request the customer's participation in the arbitration proceedings, the failure to call upon witnesses who could testify about the complaints against the workers deprived them of "an opportunity to cross-examine the accuser to test the truthfulness of the charges," the arbitrator said. Because reinstatement was not a practical remedy in this case, the arbitrator ordered back pay, less any earnings the two workers had from other sources following termination (*Worldwide Flight Services Inc.*, 121 LA 445).

1. Adequate Warning

Arbitrators are less likely to sustain discipline or discharge for discourteous or improper behavior if employees have received inadequate warning that their employers will not tolerate such behavior.

● One arbitrator set aside the suspension of an employee who allegedly violated an "unwritten" hospital policy by using improper language and talking in a "loud excited voice" about a movie celebrity who was on the premises. Declaring that management had not defined prohibited behaviors nor "given proper advance notice of the rules," the arbitrator said that absent clearly promulgated policies, the employer could justify the discipline only by showing that adverse "consequences" resulted from the employee's behavior (*Rochester Methodist Hospital*, 72 LA 276).

● Despite an employee's record of rude behavior toward customers, an arbitrator overturned her discharge because of

deficiencies in the way her employer handled the matter. The employer had received both oral and written customer complaints, but the employee had not been informed of the complaints as they were being received, which "lulled" her into thinking that the behavior was acceptable, the arbitrator said. Furthermore, the employer failed to give the employee "an opportunity to explain her version of the incidents which resulted in the complaints," the arbitrator said (*Apollo Merchandisers Corp.*, 70 LA 614).

B. Categories of Employment

1. Cashiers, Retail Workers

Customer complaints about discourteous or rude behavior commonly arise in the retail sector. Because customer satisfaction plays such an important role in the ability of retail employers to remain competitive, complaints about discourtesy from cashiers or other retail workers are treated with great seriousness.

● An arbitrator ruled that a sports concessions operator had just cause to discharge a vendor who used profanity and yelled at an inebriated customer who had repeatedly used racial slurs, even though the vendor had been a good employee for six years. The employer's training and policies instructed employees about how to handle difficult customers and did not include exclusions or mitigating circumstances, and the grievant willfully violated three fundamental rules of customer relations (*Illinois Sportservice Inc.*, 124 LA 21).

● An arbitrator upheld the discharge of a supermarket cashier for discourteous conduct, even though a complaining customer did not testify at arbitration. The cashier had a record of discipline for rudeness and had received a "final warning" about her behavior. She was fired after a customer called a store manager and told him she would not shop there anymore because of how the cashier had treated her. The union argued that the cashier was denied her due-process rights because the customer was not available at the hearing for cross-examination. However, the arbitrator said the case did not hinge on the details of the complaint, because its mere existence triggered termination under the final warning. "It is not the ruling of this Arbitrator that a retail employer need never produce a complaining customer to sustain the discharge of a rude cashier," but termination was clearly justified in this case based on the cashier's long history of complaints, the employer's fair and thorough investigation of the matter, and the employee's lack of credibility, among other factors, according to the arbitrator (*Schnucks Markets Inc.*, 118 LA 715).

● Discharge was proper for a department store employee who failed to follow store procedures and displayed unbecoming conduct toward fellow employees and customers, an arbitrator ruled. The employee had been warned about her undesirable actions, and evidence showed that she disregarded the employer's regulations regarding proper behavior. Because the employee had been adequately warned that her continued flouting of company rules would result in dismissal, the arbitrator concluded that discharge was reasonable (*Goldman's Department Store Co.*, 65 LA 592).

● An arbitrator ruled that an employee of a retail grocery chain was justifiably discharged for repeatedly insulting customers, because on two earlier occasions the employee had narrowly escaped termination for similar behavior. Reasoning that the employee's history was "rife" with incidents involving conduct that intimidated and embarrassed customers, the arbitrator decided that it was very "doubtful" that the employee would improve his conduct if given yet another chance (*Great Atlantic and Pacific Tea Co.*, 71 LA 805).

2. Health Care Workers

The health care industry is another area in which charges of discourtesy and abuse are frequent, but health care workers operate under slightly different circumstances, because the patients with whom they interact sometimes misinterpret actions or may be out of control themselves. As a result, arbitrators are careful to scrutinize the validity of charges filed by complainants, and they commonly consult employees' past records to determine if there were previous instances of abusive or discourteous behavior.

● An arbitrator found a nursing home did not have just cause to discharge a nurse's aide in response to a patient complaint, where the the patient was on medication, had difficulty focusing on one subject, could not independently identify the grievant, made inconsistent statements, and there was no redness or bruising on the patient's body (*Washington Square Healthcare Center*, 127 LA 1473).

● A nursing home did not have just cause to discharge a certified nursing assistant for abusing a resident who was at risk of falling when out of his wheelchair, and the arbitrator reduced the penalty to a written warning. The employee had pushed the wheelchair with the resident in it out of his room so that co-workers could see him if he attempted to walk, his subjective anguished reaction was insufficient to show abuse, considering his dementia with psychosis, her words to him at the time indicated nothing more than concern about his safety, and she erred only by briefly speaking to him too loudly (*AHF/Central States Inc.*, 126 LA 1165).

● An arbitrator overturned the discharge of a certified nursing assistant who allegedly mistreated a nursing home patient by refusing to reposition the patient's head. The only evidence against the employee was an accusation made by the patient, but three other employees testified that the patient made similar accusations against them. Lacking "clear and convincing evidence" that the employee engaged in patient abuse, the arbitrator ordered reinstatement with back pay (*Barton Center, Senior Health Management, LLP*, 121 LA 249).

● An arbitrator overturned a hospital employee's discharge for abuse following a scuffle in which the employee struck a mental patient. Management failed to establish that the employee had intentionally or maliciously abused the patient, the arbitrator found. Finding no evidence of prior sadistic behavior or improper treatment of patients by the employee, the arbitrator held that discharge was too severe and reduced the discipline to a suspension (*Faribault State Hospital*, 68 LA 713).

● A nurse's aide who allegedly directed obscene language at a patient while lifting her abruptly from her bed was improperly discharged following a superficial investigation of the matter, an arbitrator ruled. Pointing out that the employee was tired after a "long and arduous" shift, the arbitrator decided that the discipline was "overly harsh." Although the employee "may have acted without the highest degree of reasonableness and care to which the patient was entitled," the arbitrator declared, her actions were not "maliciously intended," but rather were the "result of normal human frailty" (*Viewcrest Nursing Home*, 72 LA 1240; see also 53 LA 350).

• An arbitrator set aside a written reprimand for an employee who was accused of abusing a mental patient with curses and threats, because other staff personnel testified that they never heard the employee make any threats or use any curse words. The complaints of "mental patients must be viewed with caution," the arbitrator said, adding that even those who are "well" sometimes misinterpret the actions of others (*Veterans Administration Medical Center*, 74 LA 830).

• By contrast, a nursing home nursing assistant committed patient abuse, where she admonished a resident in a berating tone to intimidate her, which fell within the definition of abuse generally and verbal abuse specificallym as contained in her employer's abuse and neglect policy. Specifically, witnesses testified that the grievant pointed her finger across the hall at a resident and yelled, "You don't ever talk to me that way when I'm taking care of you. You will not treat me that way . . . You will not talk to me and treat me like that when I'm taking care of you. You understand me?" The resident, who was known by other staff to be a pleasant patient, immediately burst into tears and said she was sorry, she didn't know what she did. The arbitrator ultimately decided that while the nursing home had just cause to suspend the grievant for a week, it did not have just cause to discharge her, because her prior write-up was for neglect and not intentional abuse, and just cause calls for suspension, but not termination (*Ridgewood Healthcare Center*, 128 LA 955).

• An arbitrator ruled that a nursing care provider had just cause to discharge

an employee for getting angry at a nursing home resident and calling her stupid after she asked for drink, where multiple witnesses testified that incident took place, the employee knew that her conduct was improper, and she previously had been suspended for being disrespectful to another resident and verbally counseled for being loud with residents (*GMG Inc.*, 125 LA 1537).

• An arbitrator credited the testimony of a mental patient in upholding an employee's discharge for failing to report patient abuse. The patient, who was a paranoid schizophrenic, reported that a housekeeping employee had sexual relations with her, and she said two other employees knew about it. The employer fired all three, citing rules against sexual contact with residents and a policy that subjected employees to dismissal for neglecting to report incidents of patient abuse. One of the employees denied any awareness of the incident, and his union argued that the testimony of a mental patient with paranoid schizophrenia must be considered "inherently unreliable." The arbitrator rejected that argument and sustained discharge, noting that the union merely speculated that the patient was mistaken and presented no evidence to show that she was imagining things, particularly at a time when she was taking her medication (*Park House LTD*, 118 LA 1560).

3. Drivers

Strict standards on courteous behavior typically apply to employees who work as drivers, especially those who operate buses or other forms of public transportation. Recognizing that drivers often work in an unsupervised capacity, arbitrators generally accept the premise that their conduct must withstand scrutiny where public interactions are concerned, even when faced with provocation.

• A bus company had just cause to issue a long-term suspension to a driver, even though it did not have just cause to discharge him because some of the charges made by a customer were not proven, an arbitrator ruled. The driver asked the rider if she lived with her family, spouse, boyfriend, or friends, and he also hugged the passenger. The arbitrator said the driver's job is not to be a friend, conversationalist, counselor, or questioner into the personal lives of passengers—it is to safely drive the bus (*Rochester City Lines Co. Inc.*, 128 LA 725).

● A transit system had just cause to issue a one-week suspension to a bus driver who ran ahead of schedule, an arbitrator ruled, where a bus that runs ahead of schedule could miss passengers who have not yet arrived at bus stops (*Ben Franklin Transit*, 129 LA 1451).

● An agency had just cause to issue a five-day suspension to a bus driver, where, in 10 blocks, he lost his composure, usurped authority of a bus aide and interfered with her ability to perform her duties, and screamed and berated a group of young children (*Erie Metropolitan Transit Authority*, 129 LA 865).

● A bus company had just cause to discharge a driver who did not follow established procedures of staying in a "safety zone" of the driver's seat in dealing with a difficult passenger, where the driver confronted, intimidated, and had physical contact with the passenger (*Valley Transit*, 127 LA 1399).

● *By contrast,* an agency did not have just cause to issue a 10-day suspension to a bus driver for an alleged confrontation with a passenger, where discipline was initiated based upon a hearsay complaint, without any investigation, an arbitrator ruled. The agency failed to provide the grievant and union at least three days of notice prior to holding a pre-disciplinary hearing, the agency failed to inform the grievant in writing of the precise charges against him at least three days prior to the hearing, and the testimony against the grievant at the hearing was based on hearsay evidence (*Erie Metropolitan Transit Authority*, 129 LA 865).

● An arbitrator ruled that a transportation operator did not have just cause to discharge a bus driver for engaging in a physical confrontation with a passenger, where the passenger, after gesturing obscenely to driver, initiated contact by at least touching the driver on the neck. The driver acted appropriately in exiting the bus and attempting to restrain the passenger until a law enforcement official could be located, the arbitrator found (*MV Transportation Inc.*, 127 LA 1333).

● A bus operator who physically ejected two passengers from his bus after an argument over transit rules was properly discharged, an arbitrator ruled, even though the employee contended that he had been provoked when one of the passengers hit him on the head. Finding that the employee's unsupervised job required him to interact with members of the public who might engage in "every conceivable mode of conduct," the arbitrator agreed that management could not depend on the employee to demonstrate reasonable and controlled behavior in his dealings with the public (*Metropolitan Atlanta Rapid Transit Authority*, 72 LA 723).

● Another arbitrator upheld a written warning for an employee who worked as an attendant on a bus that transported individuals with mental retardation and developmental disabilities. The incident prompting discipline arose when a passenger tried to hit and bite the employee. Observing that the employee was trained to handle this type of situation and was not allowed to raise her voice or intimidate passengers, the arbitrator concluded that the employer justifiably disciplined the employee for shouting at the unruly individual (*Summit County*, 121 LA 1681).

● A telephone company employee who assaulted two teenage boys after they threw snowballs at his van was improperly discharged, an arbitrator ruled. Although the employee should have "held his temper" rather than engage in conduct that was "bound to reflect unfavorably upon the company," the arbitrator found that the employee clearly had been provoked. The fact of provocation did not excuse the employee's conduct, but it went "far to mitigate against the imposition of the most severe penalty at the company's command," the arbitrator said in reducing the penalty to a 30-day suspension (*New Jersey Bell Telephone Co.*, 68 LA 931; see also 57 LA 773).

4. Law Enforcement

● *A* city had just cause to demote a police sergeant, where he used vulgarity with members of the public and tried to lecture a younger one, and he made an obscene gesture to a neighbor while he was off duty (*City of Lorain* , 127 LA 235).

- *By contrast,* the U.S. Border Patrol did not have just cause to suspend an officer for seven days for unprofessional language and conduct toward members of the public when, in response to the comment of the owner of a building that housed the station, the officer said that the station would close down following an investigation into fraud, an arbitrator ruled. The officer's disclosure of confidential information rather than her demeanor was just cause for discipline, and a three-day suspension was appropriate given that it was the officer's first incident with the public (*Department of Homeland Security,* 126 LA 1629).

- An arbitrator ruled that a township did not have just cause to issue a counseling letter to a police officer who improperly used his flashlight when he struck the bed of a truck that was not stopping at a roadblock. The officer had a reason to believe that the driver of the truck intended to run a roadblock, the officer tried other means to get the driver to change the truck's direction, the officer had never been trained on the procedure he was to follow if a vehicle tried to run a roadblock, and the officer had a six-year record with no discipline (*Hamburg Township,* 126 LA 887).

5. School Districts

- A school district acted arbitrarily, capriciously, and discriminatorily when it discharged a paraprofessional for "deficiencies" in that she did not "relate well" to students and "was not always pleasant," an arbitrator ruled. The district did not give her adequate notice of her "deficiencies," it gave her a hearing only after the school board decided to dismiss her, and it held her job hostage to the happenstance of a potentially biased or misinformed parental complaint (*Griggsville-Perry School District* , 127 LA 1542).

- A school district did not have just cause to suspend a bus driver for "discourteous treatment of the public," where, when parents of students he was keeping in his bus to determine who released an offensive odor approached, he was all business, matter-of-fact, in control at all times, his tone was even, he used deferential language to parents, released children when asked, identified himself when asked, and immediately reported potential complaints to the office by radio (*Oak Hills Local Schools,* 128 LA 475).

6. Waitstaff

- An arbitrator found that a restaurant had just cause to discharge a food server for harassment of and abusive language toward customers and co-workers, where several witnesses testified as to his misconduct, including his referring to customers using racial slurs and ignoring a customer's request for service, and he was a longtime employee who previously had been warned regarding rudeness (*Mirage Hotel-Casino,* 128 LA 344).

C. Employer Discourtesy

Complaints of discourtesy are not lodged exclusively against rank-and-file employees. Some cases call into question the conduct of management.

- An employer violated its contractual obligation to promote a harmonious relationship between the company and the union by refusing to discipline a foreman who verbally and physically abused an employee, an arbitrator decided. Although agreeing with the employer's argument that the union had no right to tell management how to discipline its supervisors, the arbitrator ruled that the foreman was guilty of abusive conduct. Management was obligated to take steps to ensure that such conduct did not occur in the future, the arbitrator concluded (*San Antonio Packing Co.,* 68 LA 893).

- A complaint about supervisory conduct lacks validity if it is based on an employee's perceptions rather than factual evidence, according to one arbitrator. The employee contended that a manager breached a workplace policy on "dignity and respect" when he left the door to his office open and leaned back in his chair with hands behind his head while talking with her. The arbitrator found that the employee failed to present any "objective facts" showing that the manager "intentionally" failed to conduct himself respectfully during the session (*Veterans Administration Medical Center*, 75 LA 793).

● Another arbitrator decided that casual remarks between supervisors about the behavior of a subordinate did not violate a contract provision requiring management and employees to show mutual respect for each other. While emphasizing that "it goes without saying that criticism of employees is best left to private discussion," the arbitrator stressed that the supervisors had meant the remarks "lightly." He noted that "to call the situation disrespectful would be tantamount to ruling that supervisors cannot supervise" (*Veterans Administration Hospital*, 71 LA 856).

V. Dishonesty & Theft [LA CDI 100.552525 (public employees); 118.648]

OVERVIEW

Cases on employee dishonesty cover a variety of improprieties, such as making phony excuses for absences, lying on job applications, falsifying time cards, and stealing employer property. Arbitrators treat most forms of dishonesty as serious misconduct that warrants severe consequences. For example, proof of theft usually justifies summary dismissal, even for a first offense. Arbitrators also tend to sustain discharge in cases where employees knowingly falsify documents or make deliberate misrepresentations to management with the goal of achieving some type of personal gain.

Because discharge for dishonesty or theft carries with it a stigma that can diminish the reputation of employees and affect their future employment prospects, arbitrators often require employers to substantiate charges of wrongdoing with "clear and convincing evidence" or "proof beyond a reasonable doubt." These are higher standards than a "preponderance of evidence," which is the norm for cases that do not involve allegations of morally reprehensible conduct. (For further discussion on issues related to proof and evidence in arbitration cases, see the chapter titled "Proving Misconduct.")

In general, arbitrators share the view that all acts of dishonesty are unacceptable, but they sometimes overturn or lessen the penalties imposed by employers when the evidence does not establish an intent to lie or steal. Other mitigating factors that arbitrators sometimes consider in cases of dishonesty or theft include the employees' length of service, their prior disciplinary record, and the amount of harm done to their employers.

SUMMARY OF CASES

A. Falsification of Job Applications

Arbitrators generally agree that the falsification of employment applications constitutes serious misconduct, particularly where the falsification is deliberately intended to deceive management representatives who are making hiring decisions. On the other hand, arbitrators have excused employees for inadvertently omitting information, leaving ambiguous questions blank, or responding inaccurately because of memory lapses.

Even if employees knowingly falsify application forms, some arbitrators refuse to sustain discharge if employees have worked for a substantial period of time before the falsification is discovered. One arbitrator noted that when the passage of time brings increasing seniority, advancing age, and the accumulation of a positive work record, "the good employee who is discharged after some time is likely to suffer a much heavier penalty than the one who is refused employment in the first instance" (*Ryan Aeronautical Co.*, 29 LA 182; see also 59 LA 255, 26 LA 575, 21 LA 560, 17 LA 230).

In contrast, other arbitrators hold that employers should not lose their right to invoke discharge if employees' fraudulent representations in application forms are not discovered for several months or even several years. Rather, arbitrators commonly apply a four-part test to determine whether discharge is appropriate in such cases:
- Was the employee's misrepresentation willful?
- Would the misrepresentation have been material to the employer's decision to hire the employee?
- At the time of discharge, did the misrepresentation remain material to the individual's continued employment?

- Did the employer act promptly and in good faith once it discovered the misrepresentation?

One of the early arbitrators to use this four-part test noted that time limitations on termination "have been applied where the misrepresentation was not serious or had ceased to be relevant" to the employment of the worker in question. "Where, however, the misrepresentation was serious and of continuing importance to the employment, no limitations period was recognized," the arbitrator explained (*Tiffany Metal Products Mfg. Co.*, 56 LA 135; see also 97 LA 286, 91 LA 1193).

1. Employment History and Qualifications

Arbitrators typically sustain discharge for the falsification of job applications if employees omit or misrepresent material information about their employment history or qualifications. In some cases, arbitrators find that discharge is not reasonable given the nature of the discrepancies.
- An employer should not have fired a worker who it unknowingly hired at two different facilities, an arbitrator ruled. In 2003, the worker was hired by Sodexo at Montclair University, N.J., as a cook, working from 7:00 a.m. to 3:00 p.m. Later in the afternoons, she also worked for Chartwells Corp. in the East Orange, N.J., School District. The employer accused the cook of "omission and material misrepresentation during the hiring process" and argued that she "falsely concealed the fact of her employment at Sodexo's unit at Montclair State," and thus it had just cause to discharge her. Finding the grievant did not try to hide her dual employment situation, the arbitrator said, "If the grievant had

intended to hide her employment at Montclair, it seems unlikely that she would have listed Montclair University on one side of the form, and Sodexo with a street address and phone number on the other side. The employer should have read the grievant's application more carefully."

"I can only assume that the employer acted negligently, since, with three different readers, not one person read the grievant's application carefully enough to notice that she was currently employed by Sodexo," the arbitrator said in upholding the grievance and ordering reinstatement and back pay (*Sodexo at East Orange School District*, 127 LA 1513).

• A waiter was properly discharged for falsifying a job application that required him to list his last three jobs, an arbitrator held. The employee failed to mention his most recent employment at a restaurant where he was discharged after two weeks. The hiring manager for the new employer testified that he would have called to check the waiter's work record at the previous job. The arbitrator found that the omission was deliberate, relevant to the hiring decision, and material to the waiter's continued employment. Adding that the employer acted promptly in firing the waiter after discovering the omission, the arbitrator concluded that discharge was appropriate in spite of the fact that the waiter had developed a stake in his job during the months that elapsed since he falsified his application (*Wine Cellar*, 81 LA 158; see also 93 LA 124, 65 LA 797, 62 LA 389, 55 LA 581, 34 LA 143, 12 LA 207).

• Another arbitrator overturned the discharge of an employee who omitted his most recent employer when filling out his job application. In this case, the application form asked for three previous employers but did not specify that they had to be the "most recent," the arbitrator noted. Lacking sufficient evidence to demonstrate that the employee deliberately falsified the application, the arbitrator ordered reinstatement with back pay (*Rite Aid Distribution Center*, 115 LA 737).

• Discharge was too severe for an employee who lied about his educational qualifications, an arbitrator ruled. On his original application and subsequent forms, the employee falsely indicated that he held multiple college degrees. Although he possessed an adequate combination of training, experience, and education to qualify for his initial job, he subsequently moved up to a job for which he was not qualified. According to the arbitrator, the employee's falsification justified discipline and removal from the higher-level job, but discharge was not warranted. Emphasizing that the employee's misrepresentations were not material to his initial employment, the arbitrator converted the penalty to a suspension and ordered reinstatement without back pay to the lower-level job (*City of Miami*, 107 LA 12).

• In contrast to cases involving applicants who have overstated their qualifications, one case dealt with an employee who concealed his post-secondary education because he knew the employer had a policy of refusing to hire people with college degrees for "blue collar" jobs. Although the employee misrepresented his education, which included a bachelor of arts degree, a master's degree, and work toward a doctorate, an arbitrator refused to uphold the employee's discharge, concluding that the falsification did not result in injury to the employer because the employee had demonstrated his competence on the job (*Hofmann Industries Inc.*, 61 LA 929).

2. Criminal Convictions

Numerous arbitration cases involve employees accused of falsifying employment applications to conceal past criminal convictions. This type of dishonesty normally constitutes an offense justifying immediate discharge, without the benefit of progressive discipline. Arbitrators sometimes overturn discharge, however, based on considerations such as whether the convictions are material to the workers' employment, whether workers must acknowledge convictions that have been expunged or sealed, and whether a period of satisfactory employment renders prior convictions irrelevant.

[A number of states have laws that prohibit employers from asking questions about applicants' arrest records, since basing hiring decisions on such questions can have a disparate impact on minorities. Questions about criminal convictions are permitted, although some courts have held that employers cannot automatically disqualify a candidate on the basis of convictions, requiring instead that employers demonstrate that workers' convictions would make them unsuitable for certain types of employment.]

• An employer had just cause to discharge an employee for failing to mention a prior conviction, even though more than five years had passed since he falsified his employment application, an arbitrator ruled. The employer discovered the prior conviction while investigating the employee for other workplace misconduct. Despite the employee's five-year employment record, the arbitrator expressed an unwillingness "to conclude that an employer who is deliberately misled by an employee loses its right to invoke reasonable disciplinary actions simply because it had not discovered the employee's fraud for a period of time, provided the falsification would have borne on the employee's initial employment." In deciding that discharge was warranted, the arbitrator first determined that the employee deliberately falsified his application. Second, the arbitrator found that the conviction would have been material to the employer's decision to hire the employee. Third, the arbitrator determined that the misrepresentation remained material to the employee's continued employment, because the passage of time did not change the seriousness of the offense or the employer's policy not to hire applicants who had committed serious crimes. Fourth, the arbitrator found that the employer acted promptly by discharging the employee on the same day that it confirmed his criminal conviction (*Huntington Alloys Inc.*, 74 LA 176; see also 116 LA 526, 115 LA 1077, 110 LA 733, 104 LA 1121, 93 LA 738, 91 LA 1193, 65 LA 797).

• An employer did not have just cause to discharge an employee for lying on two separate job applications and during the investigation of a copper theft, where the employee did not willfully omit a misdemeanor charge from applications, an arbitrator ruled. He included a more serious felony charge on each application, and his statement during the investigation that he had not been arrested in 20 years—when it actually had been 17 years—was a miscalculation. The worker's mixing up of dates and charges "can hardly be viewed as a terminable offense when the employer made no attempt to follow up, no effort to seek clarity, but instead speciously concluded that this 'lie' could justify the termination," the arbitrator stated, in ordering reinstatement (*Xcel Energy*, 128 LA 289).

• Although an employee's failure to admit to a felony conviction was deliberate and material, an arbitrator refused to sustain discharge where an employer failed to act promptly after the falsification came to light. Four months after the employee completed his job application form, a security investigation report came back showing a prior conviction for robbery. The employer did not fire the employee until nine months later. While acknowledging that "falsification of an employment application regarding the applicant's criminal record is one of the most firmly established grounds for discharge," the arbitrator said it is unacceptable for employers to learn of application falsifications, retain the employees to "see how they work out," and then fire them several months later for the original incident. Because the employee in this case was not faultless, however, the arbitrator ordered reinstatement without back pay and converted the penalty to a disciplinary suspension (*Veterans Administration Medical Center*, 91 LA 588).

• Another arbitrator overturned the discharge of an employee who failed to report his conviction for assault in college based on a mistaken belief that it had been expunged. According to the arbitrator, the employee demonstrated poor communication and language skills, and his conduct suggested he was "someone who does not understand the importance of accuracy, is negligent about how he characterizes events, who conveniently forgets unpleasant or difficult facts, and who tries to blame others for his own problems." But even though the employee's testimony raised credibility issues, the evidence did not convincingly prove that he intentionally lied in his employment application, the arbitrator held. Finding that the employee believed the conviction had been expunged from his record, thereby relieving him of an obligation to report it, the arbitrator ordered reinstatement without back pay (*City of Minneapolis*, 106 LA 564).

• Discharge also was overturned for an employee who failed to acknowledge a youth-offender conviction and a separate conviction for "driving under the influence." The employee reasonably believed that the youth-offender conviction had been expunged, an arbitrator found. In addition, the arbitrator decided that there was no nexus between the DUI conviction and the employee's job, and the evidence was conflicting as to whether the employer required applicants to list DUI convictions (*Freightliner Corp.*, 103 LA 123).

• Another arbitrator overturned the discharge of a nursing home employee who did not reveal her misdemeanor convictions. The arbitrator noted that the employee had a six-year employment record without incident, her convictions did not involve violence or patient abuse, and state law said a five-year work history without incident demonstrated rehabilitation. The arbitrator also observed that discharge was not specified as the penalty for application falsification in the employee handbook that was in place when the employee was hired (*Glenshire Woods*, 121 LA 1665).

3. Medical Information

Employers commonly request medical information as part of the hiring process in order to determine workers' suitability for the jobs they seek. The Americans with Disabilities Act of 1990 restricts the kinds of questions that can be included in job applications and interviews, but many employers require workers to fill out separate medical questionnaires after extending a conditional offer of employment. In general, arbitrators treat misrepresentations on such questionnaires the same way they treat the falsification of job applications.

• An employer had just cause to discharge an employee who falsified a medical questionnaire to hide a prior back injury, an arbitrator decided. After repeated rejections from other companies, the employee decided he would no longer disclose the injury because he suspected he was experiencing disability discrimination. When the employer offered him a job, which was conditioned upon his successful completion of a medical examination, the employee falsified a medical history form to conceal his back injury. The employee worked successfully for several months in a position requiring heavy labor, but then he had an accident that caused an unrelated neck injury. His back injury subsequently came to light, and the employer fired him for falsification. Noting that "employees with disabilities have faced unusual difficulties in the hiring process," the arbitrator said the employee had a right to be free from disability discrimination. At the same time, the arbitrator said, the employer had an "unquestioned right to expect truthful answers from its employees with respect to matters material to their employment." The information about the employee's back "was clearly material to the placement decision," the arbitrator stressed, and it remained relevant because of the possible risk of injury to the employee and others by virtue of any continuing weakness in his back. Adding that the employer followed the procedures of the ADA by making a conditional employment offer before requiring a medical history and examination, the arbitrator concluded that discharge was appropriate (*Boise Cascade Corp.*, 105 LA 223).

• An employer had just cause to discharge an employee for concealing his history of seizures, an arbitrator ruled. The employee's misrepresentations on a medical questionnaire, which he completed after receiving a conditional job offer, were discovered a few weeks later when he had a seizure at work. The arbitrator acknowledged that a fear of disability discrimination prompted the employee's dishonesty, but the employer's medical inquiries were "material and relevant to the job he was to perform; to the interests of the employer in meeting its responsibility to provide a safe work environment to all its employees, including the grievant; and to meet its legal obligations under the Americans with Disabilities Act to accommodate disabled individuals," the arbitrator found. The result of the falsification was unfortunate, the arbitrator added, because there was no evidence to suggest that honest answers would have deterred the employer, which was already accommodating another worker with a similar condition (*Colgate-Palmolive Co.*, 116 LA 397).

● An arbitrator upheld the discharge of an employee who refused to work in a confined space because he was claustrophobic. The duties of the employee's job were explained by the company, including the necessity to work in closely confined spaces, and a required medical questionnaire asked specifically about claustrophobia, the arbitrator observed. Rather than reveal that he had claustrophobia, the employee gave false and misleading information, the arbitrator determined. Noting that the questionnaire warned that falsification would provide grounds for discharge, the arbitrator concluded that the employee's material misrepresentation of his medical information warranted termination (*Archer Daniels Midland Co.*, 118 LA 153).

● In a case involving the exaggeration of a medical condition, an arbitrator upheld discharge for an employee who refused to work at acceptable levels after recovering from an occupational accident. The employee, who had undergone surgery and months of therapy, only returned to work when ordered to do so because the employer learned that he had been dropped from his rehabilitation program for lack of effort. The employer eventually fired the employee after having his medical condition and ability to perform work reviewed at various times. According to the arbitrator, medical evidence showed that the employee was deliberately exaggerating his complaints about pain and self-limiting his movements. Adding that the employee was warned he would face discharge for purposely slowing his output and refusing to perform assigned tasks at an acceptable level, the arbitrator found that the employer had just cause for discharge (*Cramer Inc.*, 110 LA 37).

[For more arbitral standards and decisions concerning medical information and impairments, see Part 5, Disability.]

B. Falsification of Work Records

Arbitrators generally agree that the falsification of records in order to claim credit for work not done is a serious offense. Discharge will not necessarily be sustained, however, in the absence of proof that employees deliberately intended to deceive their employers.

● An arbitrator upheld the discharge of an employee who manipulated the counter on a machine she was operating in order to inflate the number of parts she had tested. A co-worker reported the discrepancy to management, and an investigation revealed a large gap between the figure on the counter and the number of parts actually tested. The evidence convincingly showed that the employee manipulated the counter and then falsified her production logs to coincide with that figure, the arbitrator found, adding that the falsification appeared to have been motivated by a desire to avoid discipline for failure to meet minimum production requirements (*Robert Bosch Corp.*, 117 LA 1406; see also 96 LA 823).

● An employer had just cause to discharge an employee who falsely certified that he had performed daily safety checks on the garbage truck he drove, an arbitrator ruled. The employee's failure to perform the checks came to light after his truck caught on fire and was destroyed, causing an estimated loss of more than $200,000. The employer fired the employee for negligence and the falsification of safety inspection forms. The arbitrator concluded that discharge was warranted, even in the absence of a prior warning, based on clear and convincing evidence of the employee's false certifications that he had been performing daily safety checks mandated by federal regulations (*Waste Management Inc.*, 120 LA 175; see also 100 LA 67, 86 LA 999).

● *By contrast*, an arbitrator reduced another employee's discipline to a written warning after he made incorrect log entries. While filling out records required for compliance with his employer's quality standards, the employee made entries in the log for two future weeks. The mistakes were caught during an internal audit, and the employer charged the employee with falsification of company records. "Falsification carries with it the element of a dishonest intent," the arbitrator said, but the evidence in this case showed that the employee lacked a deliberate intent to deceive his employer. Adding that the employee was not trying to mask any shortcomings and stood to gain nothing from his incorrect entries, the arbitrator concluded that he should have been charged with failing to follow proper procedures rather than the more serious offense of falsification (*ITW CIP Stampings*, 117 LA 1777).

● An employee who filled out his production record to reflect completion of a specified period of incentive work, even though part of the time was spent training new employees, was improperly discharged for dishonesty, an arbitrator ruled. Emphasizing that the employer's system for recording and distinguishing between "incentive" and "training" was confusing, the arbitrator concluded that the employer charged the employee with committing a crime but failed to prove the worker's guilt beyond a reasonable doubt (*H. R. Terryberry Co.*, 65 LA 1091).

C. Falsification of Time Records

● Arbitrators commonly uphold discharge for the falsification of time records, especially since a failure to accurately report time worked can be viewed as an act of theft. Even if employers fail to prove a deliberate attempt to falsify time records, employees can face discharge for keeping overpayments to which they are not entitled.

● An arbitrator ruled that a city had just cause to discharge an employee who did not work a full 80 hours per pay period, engaged in non-work related matters of a personal nature during work, used his city-issued cell phone for personal use, and changed stories and made inconsistent statements (*City of Columbus*, 127 LA 466).

● An employer had just cause to discharge an employee for falsely claiming time worked in a higher job classification, an arbitrator ruled. The employee submitted her time card with a hand-written document stating that she had spent half of one shift performing the higher-paying work. However, an investigation showed that she had been using a computer station to perform her regular duties during the period in question. Finding that the employee deliberately falsified her time card with the intent to deceive her employer, the arbi-

trator upheld discharge (*Vertex Aerospace LLC*, 120 LA 767; see also 76 LA 1216).

● Discharge was called for when a maintenance technician for a cable company made two false reports about the length of his lunch breaks, an arbitrator decided. While conceding that discharge might have been deemed too harsh under a normal just cause standard, the arbitrator upheld the penalty because the parties' collective bargaining agreement mandated discharge for the falsification of any work-related report (*Time Warner Cable*, 119 LA 261).

● An arbitrator upheld the discharge of an employee who accepted pay for three days when he was off duty, even though there was no proof that he conspired with anyone else in a time-card punching scheme in order to claim credit for time not worked. According to the arbitrator, the employee's dishonesty in taking the overpayments essentially amounted to theft (*Yellow Freight System Inc.*, 106 LA 1062).

● An employer had just cause to discharge an employee who had punched out a co-worker's time card to enable her to receive overtime pay when she had not worked the necessary hours, an arbitrator ruled. The employee's misconduct constituted "immoral conduct," the arbitrator found, which was subject to immediate discharge under the parties' collective bargaining agreement (*Georgia-Pacific Corp.*, 104 LA 1213).

● *By contrast*, an arbitrator overturned the discharge of an employee for punching a co-worker's time card 30 minutes early, which was done because the employee believed the co-worker was sick. The employee's action was devoid of any intention to cheat the employer, the arbitrator reasoned, and the employer's past practice allowed employees to punch each other's cards (*Park 'N Fly of Texas Inc.*, 64 LA 1009).

● Another arbitrator ordered reinstatement without back pay for two employees who falsified time cards. On one occasion, the employees punched their time cards to reflect half-hour lunches when in fact they had taken two-hour lunches. On another occasion, one of the employees punched his co-worker's time card so he could leave early for deer hunting. In refusing to sustain discharge, the arbitrator cited the unblemished work records of the employees, the fact that the employer had previously allowed employees to leave early without punching out, and the absence of a rule specifying discharge as the penalty for falsifying time records (*Great Atlantic & Pacific Tea Co. Inc.*, 63 LA 79).

● An employer lacked just cause to discharge an employee whose time card reflected a small discrepancy in her starting time, an arbitrator ruled. The employee marked her starting time as 3:03 p.m. instead of 3:08 p.m. It was conceivable that the employee was trying to avoid a warning based on her late arrival, the arbitrator said, but the evidence showed that mistaking 3:08 for 3:03 was "not only possible, but was likely the probable explanation" of the employee's error. There was no evidence that the employee avoided any work effort or obtained any money to which she was not entitled, the arbitrator observed. Adding that there was no showing of any similar errors in the past, the arbitrator said this appeared to be a "singular initial mistake." Although the employer argued that its policy on time-card falsifications mandated discharge even for a first offense, the arbitrator said discharge for a mere mistake or inadvertent error does not comport with the just cause standard and ordered reinstatement with back pay (*Safeway Stores Inc.*, 114 LA 1551).

1. Absence Claims

Arbitrators tend to treat false claims regarding absences with the same seriousness as misrepresentations about time worked. While absence-related cases often focus on falsifications as unacceptable acts of dishonesty, arbitrators sometimes uphold discharge based on the reasoning that employees have attempted to obtain time off or paid leave benefits to which they are not entitled, making their misconduct tantamount to stealing.

● An employer had just cause to discharge an employee who provided a fraudulent doctor's note, an arbitrator held. After discovering that the employee had submitted an unsigned doctor's note to cover

absences when he was serving a short jail sentence for driving under the influence, the employer demanded that the employee provide a signed statement from his doctor to support his claim of an illness during that time period. The employee did not comply and was fired. The arbitrator upheld the employee's discharge, finding that the employer reasonably concluded that he had submitted falsified documentation (*ATC/VanCom*, 121 LA 1601).

● In a similar case, an employer discharged an employee after he attempted to fabricate an illness to avoid discipline for going bowling instead of working required overtime. An arbitrator upheld the employee's discharge, noting that "arbitral authority holds termination for such deception is appropriate" (*American Steel Foundries*, 113 LA 730; see also 110 LA 782, 74 LA 1052, 73 LA 722).

● Discharge was justified for an employee who falsely claimed leave in order to work a second job, an arbitrator held. The employee had obtained the second job while on layoff, and he decided to keep both jobs after being recalled. When a shift change brought his two job schedules into direct conflict, the employee began requesting leave for reasons such as illness, the death of a friend, and an alleged need to care for his mother. Although the employee's long and unblemished record demonstrated that he was once a valued employee, his employer was justified in firing him for stealing time and money by falsely claiming paid leave, the arbitrator concluded (*United Airlines*, 122 LA 232; see also 111 LA 673).

● *By contrast*, an arbitrator overturned the discharge of an employee who called in sick after working another job. The employer conceded that the employee was suffering from severe hemorrhoids, but it argued that the employee's claim that he was too sick to work—after working his part-time job earlier in the day—constituted a deliberate falsification aimed at improperly securing sickness and accident benefits. Distinguishing the employee's conduct from situations where workers call in sick at one job so they can work somewhere else during the same time period, the arbitrator found that the employee's ability to work his part-time job in the morning was not inconsistent with his claim that he was too sick to work later in the day. Adding that the employer did not have a policy against moonlighting and the employee met his obligations by calling in and providing a valid doctor's excuse when he was absent, the arbitrator ordered reinstatement with back pay (*Western Rubber Co.*, 83 LA 170).

• An arbitrator reduced an employee's discharge to an 18-month suspension after he called in sick on a day when he did not want to drive to work because of snowy conditions. Although the arbitrator characterized the employee's conduct as "deceitful, manipulative, and disingenuous," he also found that the employer based its termination decision in part on an erroneous charge. According to the arbitrator, the employer accused the employee of a "refusal" to perform assigned work, which wrongly suggested that he was guilty of willful disobedience when he did not show up for work (*Mail Contractors of America Inc.*, 120 LA 582).

[For more arbitral standards and decisions concerning justifiable excuses and documentation of absences, see Part 2, Chapter I, Absenteeism & Tardiness.]

D. Falsification Related to Benefits

False statements to obtain health insurance or other benefits also constitutes serious misconduct. In cases where employees falsify documents or make misrepresentations with the intent of improperly securing benefits or benefit-related payments, arbitrators generally agree that discharge is warranted (117 LA 935, 96 LA 644, 87 LA 160, 85 LA 643, 82 LA 604, 65 LA 623, 63 LA 768).

Allegations of benefits fraud, like other charges of dishonesty or theft, can reflect on employees' moral character and affect their future employment prospects. As a result, arbitrators generally require a higher standard of proof than a mere preponderance of evidence (100 LA 948, 95 LA 759, 64 LA 1099).

Some benefits-related cases involve the discharge of employees who have made false statements in order to obtain unemployment compensation to which they were not entitled. One arbitrator reasoned that false claims for unemployment benefits provide grounds for discharge if the false statements constituted fraud and theft under a particular contract; they were intentional and repeated; and they served to significantly raise employers' unemployment compensation contribution rate (*Leestown Co. Inc.*, 102 LA 979; see also 122 LA 630).

Many other cases involve employees making misrepresentations in order to obtain health insurance coverage under employer plans for individuals who do not meet the eligibility requirements. For example, arbitrators have upheld discharge in cases where:

• a city had just cause to discharge an employee who did not inform it of his divorce so that he could keep his ex-wife on his health insurance, among other offenses (*City of Eugene.*, 124 LA 1724).

• an employee did not tell her employer that she had divorced her husband, which allowed him to remain on the employer's health plan (*United Assn. of Plumbers & Steamfitters*, 116 LA 710);

• a 27-year employee falsified medical insurance forms to provide health coverage for his ex-wife (*Airfoil Forging Textron*, 106 LA 945);

• an employee designated his fiancee and her kids as his wife and stepchildren to claim health benefits for them before they became eligible through marriage, which was not scheduled to take place for another 18 months (*Bi-state Development Agency*, 96 LA 1090); and

• an employee falsely listed her live-in boyfriend as her husband on medical and dental insurance forms for three years (*Southwestern Bell Telephone Co.*, 95 LA 46).

E. Theft and Pilferage

Stealing is among the most serious forms of employee misconduct, and arbitrators unanimously believe that breaching the employer-employee bond of trust through acts of theft warrants severe consequences. In general, employers do not need specific rules to warn employees that theft is a dischargeable offense, but clear policies can prevent ambiguities from arising when stolen items are of small value or when employees claim that they thought items had been thrown away or were meant for the trash.

For example, one arbitrator upheld an employer's decision to discharge a fast-food attendant for stealing a 58-cent can of orange juice, noting that the employer had a clear policy against theft. The arbitrator, who emphasized that theft of company property can erode profitability and jeopardize the employment security of an employer's entire workforce, illustrated the strict stance that has been taken against pilferage of minor items by citing other cases in which employees were discharged for stealing an onion, a damaged tomato, and four to five pounds of grapes (*Greyhound Food Management Inc.*, 89 LA 1138; see also 122 LA 413, 93 LA 604, 79 LA 833, 79 LA 79, 77 LA 113, 63 LA 858, 62 LA 405, 43 LA 1218, 22 LA 573).

By contrast, other arbitrators have ruled that discharge is too severe for taking items of small value, especially where employees have a good employment record or an intent to steal is not clearly proven. Examples of such cases include the following:

● An arbitrator reinstated a supermarket employee who took and ate a 99-cent pie without back pay. Management had not asked the employee if he had paid for the pie, as it had been in the habit of doing. The arbitrator also observed that the work rules stated that discipline for theft was "up to and including discharge." He concluded that discharge was not warranted here and that the supermarket had "applied an atomic bomb to do the job of a fly swatter" (*Kroger Co.*, 124 LA 1633).

● Where an employee tried to steal two light-fixture covers from work, an arbitrator converted discharge to a disciplinary suspension because of the employee's 11 years of service without any record of prior misconduct and because the work rule covering theft specified a range of discipline from written reprimand to discharge (*General Electric Co.*, 75 LA 473).

● Discharge was set aside for a school custodian who stole a dollar. Citing the custodian's 20 years of service as a mitigating factor, an arbitrator decided to offer him an opportunity for rehabilitation by ordering reinstatement, provided that the custodian would sign a statement in which he admitted responsibility for the theft, promised to refrain from similar acts, and acknowledged that any future violation would be cause for immediate dismissal (*East Liverpool Board of Education*, 105 LA 161).

● An arbitrator upheld an employee's grievance entirely after she was fired for "theft and vandalism" and improperly removing company property in violation of work rules. She had taken home grommets and speaker wires to help create an exhibit for a workers' compensation case. The arbitrator ruled that the employer did not have just cause to discharge the employee for theft, where she did not have an intent to deprive the rightful owner of the items, the employer admittedly would have given her these items had she asked for them, and her attorney could have subpoenaed them (*Federal Signal Corp.*, 128 LA 1587).

● A security guard who left her post early was not guilty of theft, since she did not have an intent to steal, but patterned her behavior after another employee, an arbitrator ruled, overturning her discharge. However, she was guilty of leaving work early, and the arbitrator reduced her discharge to a nine-month suspension and last-chance agreement (*Broward Sheriff's Office*, 127 LA 1503).

1. Expense Account Reimbursement

● In addition to the outright taking of property, a broad concept of theft can encompass the falsification of reimbursement forms or expense accounts for personal gain. For example, one arbitrator held that discharge was warranted for an employee who submitted a false reimbursement request to his employer under a policy that allowed workers to receive $35 per year toward the cost of safety shoes. The employee had purchased a pair of hunting boots but claimed that they were safety boots. While acknowledging that upholding discharge could cause permanent damage to the employee's reputation and future employability, the arbitrator found that the employee had a clear intent to defraud the employer, which justified "the most severe form of discipline" (*Potlatch Corp.*, 82 LA 445; see also 81 LA 393, 74 LA 939).

• An arbitrator reinstated a 35-year employee, who had worked for 20 years as an inventory control clerk and received consistently high marks in her performance evaluations, who was discharged after she requested and received her manager's approval to purchase a replacement Rolodex, but while purchasing the Rolodex, also bought two ink cartridges for her home computer. She requested and received reimbursement from her employer for the entire expense. Questioned later as to why she charged the company for ink cartridges for her personal use, the employee said that she sometimes worked at home and needed the cartridges to do work for her employer. At a meeting with a security investigator for the company at which a representative of Local 99 of the United Food and Commercial Workers Union was also present, the employee admitted that she did not have authorization to buy the ink cartridges but again argued that former managers had allowed reimbursement for that expense and that she was acting under what she believed to be a "past practice." Nevertheless, she offered to reimburse the company for the cost of the ink cartridges.

The employee was discharged for misuse of funds, merchandise, and property, and for dishonesty. Finding she had no intent to defraud the company, the arbitrator reinstated her with back pay (*Safeway Stores, Inc.*, 128 LA 257).

2. Circumstantial Evidence of Theft

Circumstantial evidence may be sufficient to justify discharge for theft or pilferage.

• In one case, an employee was seen secreting employer products on her person by a co-worker who notified a plant guard. The guard notified a supervisor, who directed her to recover the items from the employee; however, the employee and the guard were alone when the goods were recovered. The stolen items were returned to the processing line and so disappeared as evidence. The employee later denied the guard's testimony concerning the theft. An arbitrator

sustained the discharge, ruling that the testimony of the co-worker, the guard, and the supervisor provided sufficient circumstantial evidence to prove the employee's guilt (*Max Factor & Co.*, 61 LA 886).

• Another arbitrator suggested that if a case is based on circumstantial evidence, the circumstances relied upon should be consistent with a theory of guilt and inconsistent with any theory of innocence. The arbitrator overturned the discharge of an employee—who had a piece of company-owned telephone equipment in his car that he said he was planning to deliver to a supervisor—because his employer did not offer convincing proof that he intended to steal the item (*General Telephone Co. of Southwest*, 79 LA 102).

3. Theft-Related Searches

Most arbitrators agree that the constitutional protections against illegal searches and the use of evidence obtained from such searches are not applicable to the workplace, particularly if the searching employer has probable cause to believe that a theft has occurred (66 LA 307, 51 LA 469, 50 LA 65).

• The search of an employee's lunch box, which he had left in an open tool locker, was justified based on a reasonable suspicion that the employee had taken company property, an arbitrator held. After the employee was seen in a parts room removing some items that had nothing to do with the work he was assigned, a supervisor searched the employee's lunch box and found the items. In upholding the employee's termination, the arbitrator said that the search was supported by reasonable cause and was not a dramatic intrusion on the employee's privacy (*American Welding & Mfg. Co.*, 89 LA 247).

• An employee's privacy rights were not violated when his employer searched the home of his ex-wife, at her invitation, and discovered company property on the premises, an arbitrator held. The ex-wife's accusation that the employee had been taking company property over a period of years gave the employer reasonable cause for the search, the arbitrator said in upholding the employee's discharge (*Exxon Co., U.S.A.*, 101 LA 777).

● An employer was entitled to tighten up its security rules and begin inspecting the purses of female employees as they were leaving work, an arbitrator decided. Despite the union's contention that the searches were an affront to the employees' dignity, the arbitrator concluded that management had a right to search the purses because they might contain stolen property (*AMF/Harley-Davidson Motor Co. Inc.*, 68 LA 811).

● An employee's refusal to comply with an employer's search policy, which had already been upheld at arbitration, was treated as an offense equivalent to theft by another arbitrator. Even though the employee had 24 years of service with no prior record of discipline, the arbitrator upheld his termination for refusing to allow an inspection of his lunch box to determine if he had stolen anything (*Cleveland-Cliffs Iron Co.*, 110 LA 314).

● On the other hand, one arbitrator held that an employer did not have the right to search employees' lunch bags for stolen goods. The workers' privacy rights clearly included the right to be free from such searches, the arbitrator declared (*Anchor Hocking Corp.*, 66 LA 480).

4. Arrests for Theft

Arbitrators do not necessarily agree that arrests for theft of employer property, in and of themselves, provide sufficient grounds for discharging employees. When relying solely on arrests in making their disciplinary decisions, employers face the possibility that employees will be awarded reinstatement with back pay if the charges are dropped or employees are acquitted (62 LA 901, 39 LA 1242, 39 LA 859, 35 LA 77). On the other hand, where employers make an inquiry into the facts and have substantial evidence of guilt, arbitrators are likely to uphold discharge regardless of the outcome of criminal proceedings against employees (76 LA 133, 61 LA 663, 44 LA 711, 38 LA 93, 32 LA 44, 31 LA 674).

● Emphasizing his obligation to decide a case only on the record before him, an arbitrator upheld the discharge of a 21-year employee who was discharged and also prosecuted for theft. In an effort to find out who had been stealing company and employee property, the employer treated some money with a special dye that turns purple on contact with skin. The employer put the money in an envelope, which was addressed from one worker to another, and left it on a desk. The employee was discharged and subsequently arrested after he was discovered with purple dye on his skin. While the union argued that a court had given the employee "another chance" after his criminal prosecution, the arbitrator said he was not compelled to do the same because different standards apply to the arbitration forum, and "what a court of law may have done in any particular case does not necessarily go to what is appropriate to do in an industrial setting" (*Monsanto Co.*, 105 LA 923).

● An employer had just cause to discharge a 25-year employee who admitted to stealing large amounts of company property over a period of several years, even though he was acquitted of a theft charge based on evidence that he had kleptomania, an arbitrator ruled. A court determined that the employee could not be found culpable of a crime because of his condition, but the arbitrator said kleptomania was not a recognized defense that could protect the employee from the application of a company rule mandating discharge for theft (*Kaiser Aluminum & Chemical Corp.*, 99 LA 609).

● Another arbitrator overturned the discharge of an employee who was arrested for theft after a search of his home by police and company officials recovered employer property. The case was dismissed in court because the search warrant and the search were improper. In reversing the discharge, the arbitrator cited a lack of direct evidence that the items recovered in the employee's home had been taken by him. The only evidence, the arbitrator noted, was the testimony of three persons, two of whom were admittedly hostile toward the employee (*Imperial Glass Corp.*, 61 LA 1180; see also 71 LA 1113).

F. Making False Statements

● A city had just cause to discharge a crane shovel operator for making false allegations against its demolition department by stating, at a training workshop, that the city would punch a hole in a building, then take a picture and have it declared an "emergency demolition," an arbitrator ruled. Even though no harm came from the statement, in that there was no loss of funding, the statement could have jeopardized the city's demolition program (*City of Flint*, 125 LA 955).

• An arbitrator upheld the discharge of a twenty-five year employee who whited out a clearance form to hide the fact that he had not performed certain safety-related required procedures. The arbitrator discounted the employee's work record, the fact that he was under stress, and that his grandmother had just died. The arbitrator observed that "[T]he Company needs workers who can operate in stressful circumstances and who are not even tempted to change official records to cover up their mistakes" (*Georgia Power Corp.*, 125 LA 97).

• An agency had just cause to discharge a gardener, whose job included driving agency vehicles, for not having a valid driver's license, despite a contention that progressive discipline should be applied, an arbitrator ruled, denying the grievance entirely. Not having a valid license violated agency policies and procedures, and the rules clearly required having a valid license, and there was no evidence that the agency has not consistently discharged employees who did not have a valid license. "It is clear" that employees who drive employer vehicles are required to have a valid driver's license and to report to management any license suspension or restriction and that failure to do so will result in discipline up to and including termination, the arbitrator emphasized. Although the gardener "had at least some surface plausibility for believing that he was functioning with a valid driver's license," the fact is that he should have known this was not the case (*Santa Clara County Housing Authority*, 127 LA 449).

• *By contrast*, an employer did not have a basis for discharging an employee for testifying dishonestly in an investigation of the company's medical director, the employee was interviewed the day after she fell, an arbitrator ruled, and her visibly upset demeanor was not likely to produce the most convincing evidence of her deliberate deceit (*United States Steel Corp.*, 125 LA 449).

• A 30-year county project manager for a gas fueling station did not act "with a deceitful state of mind" when he timely filed, through a professional colleague, an end-of-job report with a state agency, an arbitrator ruled, lowering his firing to a nine-month suspension, and ordering him reinstated without loss of seniority, but without back pay. The report implied that the project was complete per grant guidelines, even though the manager knew that the board of supervisors would not approve rates at which the county would sell the product and that the billing software would not be installed by the grant deadline. The state agency's manager for the grant was aware of these deficiencies, had indicated that as long as the station was operational grant objectives had been met, and testified that the grievant had not attempted to deceive the agency (*County of Orange*, 128 LA 1101).

G. Lie-Detector Limitations

Although many states have passed laws that restrict the use of polygraph tests in employment situations, federal law permits private-sector employers to use polygraph tests as part of their investigations into workplace thefts. Even if employers can justify the use of lie-detector tests by demonstrating a reasonable suspicion that employees were involved in theft, however, most arbitrators agree that lie-detector testing is not reliable enough to serve as the sole basis for establishing employees' guilt (see, for example, 88 LA 1019, 77 LA 1259, 64 LA 453, 39 LA 893, 39 LA 470).

• An employer improperly discharged employees who failed to pass a polygraph test to determine their involvement in theft of silver bars used by the employer, an arbitrator decided, where management claimed that the employees took the test voluntarily, but the employees believed that they had to take the test (*Bunker Ramo Corp.*, 76 LA 857).

• One arbitrator discounted the use of polygraph results in a proceeding involving a discharge for theft, where state law forbade the reference to, or use of, polygraph tests in court proceedings (*Deer Lakes School District*, 94 LA 334).

● Another arbitrator completely rejected polygraph tests. Citing the fact that courts had ruled them inadmissible as evidence in criminal and civil cases, the arbitrator concluded that the same rule should apply to arbitration proceedings (*Continental Air Transport Co. Inc.*, 38 LA 778; see also 75 LA 574, 75 LA 313, 71 LA 1202, 70 LA 909).

VI. Dress & Grooming [LA CDI 100.552529 (public employees); 118.639]

_____ **OVERVIEW**_____

What is desirable or necessary by way of dress and grooming standards varies from employer to employer depending on the nature of the business and the type of work being performed by different employees. Therefore, the approach to setting and enforcing standards can range from a single code handed down by top management for all employees to separate codes for each employee group.

Rules on dress and grooming often stem from employer concerns about public image or safety and health, but stringent dress codes and appearance requirements can meet with resistance if they seem to infringe unnecessarily on employees' personal rights. Arbitrators generally acknowledge that dress and grooming habits change with the times, and they prohibit unreasonable or arbitrary interference by management with employees' hair or clothing styles.

On balance, however, arbitrators recognize management's legitimate business reasons for regulating the personal appearance of employees. When deciding how much leeway employees should have in making their own choices about clothing, jewelry, hair styles, and facial hair, arbitrators often rule that job-related considerations override individual preferences.

In dealing with discipline for violations of dress and grooming standards, arbitrators make these points:

• The standards must be clear, unambiguous, and consistently enforced.

• The standards must be reasonably related to legitimate business needs, which can include the need to keep employees from being distracted by revealing or offensive attire and outlandish or bizarre personal appearances.

● The standards must be reasonably attuned to contemporary mores and attitudes toward dress and grooming. As styles change, employers might have to adjust their standards.

SUMMARY OF CASES

A. Management Right to Establish and Enforce Reasonable Rules

In general, employers have the power to establish and enforce requirements for personal appearance when there is a contractual right to adopt reasonable rules of conduct. To determine if a particular dress or grooming standard meets the test of reasonableness, arbitrators tend to consider additional factors, including the nature of the employers' business and the degree of public exposure employees encounter in their jobs (93 LA 855, 92 LA 1161, 64 LA 783, 64 LA 376, 51 LA 292).

As proof of reasonableness, arbitrators often require employers to show that their dress and grooming standards have a bearing on their public image or on health and safety (91 LA 624, 77 LA 807, 70 LA 28, 66 LA 439, 63 LA 345, 62 LA 357, 62 LA 175, 61 LA 645, 55 LA 1020). As an additional consideration, most arbitrators agree that dress codes and appearance requirements must be clear, unambiguous, and consistently enforced (64 LA 940, 63 LA 345, 62 LA 175, 52 LA 1282).

One arbitrator outlined the following questions for testing the soundness of an employer's grooming standards and the validity of discipline imposed under them:

● Did the collective bargaining agreement restrict, prohibit, or qualify the employer's right to establish grooming standards?

● Was the rule adequately communicated to all employees?

● Did the affected employees have an adequate opportunity to comply with the employer's grooming requirement?

● Was there sufficient evidence to establish that the employee's violation of the grooming code created a health or safety hazard or that it was injurious to the employer's public image?

Based on the answers to these questions, the arbitrator affirmed the suspension of an employee who refused to cut his hair in compliance with the employer's standards (*American Buslines Inc.*, 64 LA 471).

However, the employer has to provide notice and be specific about the requirements.

● A police department lacked just cause to issue three-day suspension to an officer for insubordination for failing to obey an order to trim his mustache in compliance with the department's appearance policy, an arbitrator found. The officer did not willfully disobey the order, as he trimmed his mustache in compliance with the department policy of which he had notice, but the department failed to notify officers of a subsequent modification of the policy and merely posted it on a server, and the officer later trimmed his mustache to department's specifications (*Sylvania Township*, 126 LA 1601).

● An arbitrator ruled that a school district did not have just cause to issue a warning to a teacher for wearing sunglasses and hat at a training session, where the district made the discipline decision before investigating, it announced the rule without notice, and did not fully investigate the grievant's claimed medical rationale for glasses (*Plumas Unified School District*, 130 LA 53).

● A county had just cause to discipline a correctional officer, where he allowed his hair to be trimmed by a maximum-security inmate using a contraband razor, an arbitrator found. The grievant had placed himself in a position of vulnerability, and compromised prison security (*Solano County Sheriff's Department*, 129 LA 449).

B. Justification Requirements

What evidence do arbitrators require from employers to justify their dress and grooming standards? According to one arbitrator, employers have been required in some cases to present direct evidence that employee appearances caused a loss of business or provoked complaints from the public, whereas employers have been permitted in other cases to make reasonable business justifications for their appearance standards without providing empirical proof (*City of East Detroit*, 61 LA 485).

● An arbitrator refused to sustain various clothing prohibitions that an employer wanted to add to its safety rules, finding that the employer failed to show a sufficient magnitude of safety risks to justify the new restrictions. The employer's original rules prohibited employees from having loose clothes, dangling hair, or jewelry around moving machinery. The additional restrictions included a ban on wearing so-called beach clothes—such as shorts, tank tops, short skirts, see-through blouses, and open-toed sandals—when walking from the plant gates to individual work areas. The arbitrator found that these prohibitions were "not directly related to safety," because upon entering the plant gates, employees traveled some 300 feet down a clearly marked pedestrian walkway that was supposedly safe. The arbitrator said expanding the original rule in this regard constituted "unreasonable interference with the personal freedom of the employees to come and go from and to their work places without unreasonable regimentation" (*Babcock & Wilcox*, 73 LA 443).

● Unwritten rules of dress that a company applied to a group of computer technicians also were found unreasonable. After a new manager ordered the computer workers to start wearing "suitable attire," an employee was sanctioned for showing up in baggy shorts. An arbitrator rejected the company's justification based on public image, finding that the computer workers provided technical services under a contract with a single client and had minimal contact with the client's employees. Adding that the new manager "took it upon himself to set the standards which met his own notions of propriety, and which do not reflect any requirements imposed by the customer," the arbitrator said the company failed to provide evidence that would justify requiring the computer workers "to dress for success like a herd of certified public accountants or corporate attorneys" (*Computer Science Corp.*, 87 LA 1302).

● On the other hand, an arbitrator held that an employer acted reasonably in requiring its training department employees to wear "business-casual attire." The policy came into question when one trainer requested permission to wear jeans and athletic shoes while conducting classroom sessions. The business-casual policy was reasonable, an arbitrator decided, finding that it was "founded in considered thought and reflection" and represented "a sound exercise of business discretion" (*American Airlines Inc.*, 120 LA 1796).

C. Bargaining Requirements

In some cases, appearance standards cannot be imposed unilaterally by management, and employers must bargain over policy changes that would establish new dress and grooming requirements for employees.

● An arbitrator found that a hospital did not violate a collective bargaining contract when it changed the dress code, because the statement in the contract that employees "shall abide" by a dress code did not implicitly elevate the dress code to the status of a contractual provision (*Heritage Valley Health System*, 124 LA 481).

● A police department did not violate the collective bargaining agreement, which allowed mustaches, when it unilaterally modified its appearance policy to require that mustaches be "neatly trimmed and proportioned" and "not extend past crease of mouth," an arbitrator found. Even though the proposal to allow the department to regulate the "type and size" of mustaches had been rejected in recent bargaining, the proposal clarified a pre-existing right of the department to manage the workforce through its appearance policy, and department's modifications to policy were reasonable (*Sylvania Township*, 126 LA 1601).

● An arbitrator rejected a department store's attempt to unilaterally impose a dress code on employees in one of its departments. The arbitrator found that dress requirements were a mandatory subject of bargaining under the employer's contract with the union representing its retail employees, and the parties had bargained successfully regarding such requirements for more than a dozen departments and many employee classifications. Moreover, the arbitrator said, the affected employees were courteous, neat, and well-groomed, demonstrating their professional standards and suitability for retail sales work. The case might have been closer if the workers were slovenly or the contract were silent on clothing requirements, the arbitrator said, but the facts showed that the employer's imposition of the dress code was an impermissible violation of its bargaining obligations (*Macy's*, 108 LA 489).

● Dress code guidelines published by a new prison warden could not be enforced absent formal implementation through bargaining, an arbitrator held. A month after arriving at the prison, the warden published his "expectations" in a staff newsletter. He listed various types of clothing that would be considered inappropriate for nonuniformed employees, including jeans and athletic shoes, which had been allowed under a clearly established past practice. According to the arbitrator, the employer did not cross the line by simply publishing the warden's expectations, but it would have committed a contract violation if the guidelines were enforced as a policy or rule of conduct. Adding that the past practice regarding jeans and athletic shoes could not be erased by virtue of the new warden's arrival, the arbitrator said the employer would have to bargain with the union to modify the existing dress code (*Federal Bureau of Prisons*, 113 LA 715).

● A credit union's implementation of a new policy on casual dress days triggered an obligation to bargain over clothing allowances for employees, an arbitrator held. Although the policy was reasonable and properly implemented, its specificity regarding the type and color of mandated clothing had the effect of forcing employees to purchase a new type of "uniform" to wear on casual days, the arbitrator said. Reasoning that this had an impact on employees' union-negotiated wages, which could not be

reduced unilaterally, the arbitrator ordered the employer to bargain over various cost-related issues, including who would pay for the mandated clothing, how many clothing items each employee would be allotted, and who would shoulder the responsibility for clothing damaged at work (*Aerospace Community Credit Union*, 112 LA 58).

D. Public Image

The connection between workers' appearance and their employers' public image is strongest where employees have direct contact with customers or members of the public. There is general agreement among arbitrators that employers have a legitimate interest in requiring employees to maintain certain standards of dress and grooming if their jobs include such contact (102 LA 641, 69 LA 141, 68 LA 31, 64 LA 471).

● An employer's desire to present a "clean shaven, clean cut image" to its customers was upheld by an arbitrator, who ruled that management had the right to prohibit employees from wearing beards. Absent "specific studies," the employer could only claim "somewhat empirically" that its chosen image was "at least part of its touchstone of success as seen in its rising position in the market," the arbitrator said. Nevertheless, the arbitrator decided that maintenance of this image formed a "reasonable" basis for the no-beard rule (*Randall Foods No. 2*, 74 LA 729; see also 79 LA 835, 77 LA 953, 77 LA 705).

● An arbitrator upheld a restaurant's policy requiring waitresses to have blond hair or wear blond wigs while working. The restaurant, which had won numerous awards for its fine cuisine, elegant decor, and superior service, considered the hair requirement an important ingredient in the image it wanted to portray. Noting that the appearance of the waitresses had developed into a kind of trademark for the restaurant over a period of 18 years, the arbitrator said the hair requirement furthered a legitimate management objective of providing customers a distinctive dining atmosphere (*Mister A's Restaurant*, 80 LA 1104).

As in cases from the 1960s and 1970s that involved conflicts over beards and long hair, the arbitrator said, this case pit-ted management's business arguments for grooming restrictions against the employee's right to maintain a hair style that expressed his identity and personal image. While acknowledging that general attitudes about certain grooming styles have prompted arbitrators to uphold restrictions imposed by employers even in the absence of proof regarding the negative reactions of customers, the arbitrator decided that the employee's hair style in this case was not so extreme as to warrant an inference, without further proof, that it would injure his employer's public image. Because the employer lacked objective evidence to prove just cause for discipline, the arbitrator overturned the employee's suspension and ordered reimbursement of his lost earnings (*Lucky Stores Inc.*, 91 LA 624; see also 87 LA 201, 77 LA 973, 73 LA 1209, 73 LA 850, 72 LA 588).

● Although an employer acted reasonably in banning tongue rings, it did not have just cause to fire an employee for refusing to stick out her tongue to prove she was in compliance with the rule, an arbitrator decided. The employee had her tongue pierced around the time she began working as a grocery clerk at age 16. Months later, the grocery store banned tongue rings, which are stud-like jewelry with metal balls at each end. Usually, a manager simply asked workers whether or not they were wearing tongue rings, and those found wearing the jewelry were told to remove it. On one such occasion, after the employee denied wearing a tongue ring, she was ordered to stick out her tongue as proof that she had answered truthfully. She refused to comply, and the store director fired her for insubordination.

Based on the assumption that some customers would likely be offended if they could see metal jewelry flashing in the mouths of supermarket employees, the arbitrator found that the rule against tongue rings was reasonable. The arbitrator added, however, that the employer was not justified in requiring an invasive form of investigation to determine if the employee was violating the rule. The arbitrator stressed that the employee was embarrassed and offended by "the unusual request to look into

the private space of her mouth." Without "reasonable suspicion" that the employee was lying about wearing a tongue ring, the order that she open her mouth and extend her tongue so a manager could check her "private, personal space" was unreasonably intrusive, the arbitrator said in ordering reinstatement with back pay (*Albertson's Inc.*, 115 LA 886; see also 96 LA 736).

● In contrast, an arbitrator held that an employer had just cause to fire a shuttle bus driver who refused to put on his name badge. During 15 years of driving shuttles at an international airport, the employee had worked for a series of different owners, the latest of which implemented new rules on employee dress and deportment. Soon thereafter, the employee was subjected to discipline of increasing severity because of management concerns over his uniform and obedience to supervisors. After a series of incidents, he received a "last chance" deal brokered by his union to keep his job. Shortly thereafter, he refused an order to pin his name badge on his shirt and walked away from the supervisor who had given the order. The arbitrator upheld the employee's termination, noting that the rules specifically required name badges and the last-chance agreement was unambiguous in requiring adherence to all lawful instructions (*Shuttleport Inc.*, 117 LA 492).

E. Health and Safety Concerns

It has long been established that employers can impose requirements related to employees' grooming and attire where doing so has a direct bearing on the health and safety of the workforce or the public. For example, food workers can be required to take precautions regarding their hair to avoid food contamination, police officers can be required to wear distinctive uniforms that make them easily identifiable to the public, and employees who work around moving machinery can be required to avoid loose clothes, jewelry, and dangling hair.

● A meat packing company's rule prohibiting the wearing of wigs and hair pieces in the plant for reasons of sanitation was upheld by an arbitrator on the grounds that such items fall into the same category as "street clothing," barred from the plant as a possible source of contamination (*Mar-hoefer Packing Co. Inc.*, 51 LA 983).

• A fruit-processing employer properly discharged an employee for refusing to trim his long mustache, an arbitrator ruled. The employer's grooming rule was designed to protect the employer's products against hair contamination, the arbitrator noted, rather than to regulate employee appearance (*Tree Top Inc.*, 66 LA 8).

• The disciplinary action imposed on a firefighter, whose "long and excessively bulky" hair allegedly violated the department's grooming standards, was not upheld by an arbitrator, because the evidence failed to establish that the worker's hair interfered with the proper wearing of headgear or that the employee's hair style exposed him to added personal injury (*City of Los Angeles*, 66 LA 694).

• An employer overstepped its bounds in demanding that all workers in its plant wear safety shoes, an arbitrator said, noting that contractual provisions on safety shoes only applied to one employee group. Although an Occupational Safety and Health Administration regulation mandated safety shoes for employees "working in areas where there is a danger of foot injuries due to falling or rolling objects, or objects piercing the sole," the arbitrator said the employer failed to identify areas presenting such hazards, and the OSHA rule did not mandate a plant-wide requirement (*Packaging Corp. of America*, 114 LA 809).

1. No-Beard Rules

In many cases involving restrictions on facial hair, the safety issue is whether employees must be clean shaven to ensure the proper functioning of respirators or other types of masks that fit on the face (104 LA 376, 97 LA 226, 78 LA 327, 74 LA 412, 69 LA 824, 68 LA 912).

• One arbitrator ruled that an employer was justified in requiring a pilot to shave off his beard because his facial hair could interfere with the proper functioning of the oxygen masks that members of the flight crew were supposed to use in the event of cabin depressurization (*Pacific Southwest Airlines*, 77 LA 320).

• Termination was justified for an employee who refused to shave his beard as required by a rule prohibiting facial hair in the area where a respiratory face mask was sealed, an arbitrator held. Rejecting the argument that the policy was driven by the employer's desire that employees be clean shaven, the arbitrator said the evidence established that a better seal could be achieved between the face and the mask in the absence of facial hair. Even though a good seal could be achieved if a bearded employee had enough time to properly adjust the mask, the arbitrator concluded that in an emergency situation, time is of the essence, and additional time might be disastrous to the worker and fellow employees (*Hess Oil Virgin Islands Corp.*, 75 LA 770).

• Without proper testing, an employer did not have a sound basis for determining that an employee's beard would prevent him from getting a positive seal with a fresh air mask, an arbitrator decided. Management had relied on visual observation to conclude that the employee's beard interfered with the functioning of the mask, but the arbitrator held that visual observation was insufficient in light of clear evidence that facial hair did not automatically prevent a positive seal. The proper way to determine if the employee could wear the mask safely over his beard, the arbitrator said, was to conduct a test of the device's sealing ability on the worker (*Phillips Petroleum Co.*, 74 LA 400).

• Another arbitrator concluded that an employer's respirator-related shaving rule should have been narrower. The employer established a respirator policy when it began using acids as part of its food manufacturing processes. In light of OSHA regulations requiring a good seal without interference from facial hair, the employer's policy required employees to be clean shaven if there was a "chance" they would have to use a respirator. Noting that blanket policies of this type have been found unreasonable, the arbitrator said employers are required, when possible, to draw a line between employees who need to shave and those who do not, even if it would be more convenient to require all employees to be clean shaven. Emphasizing that the employer could have designated employees on each shift to be responsible for duties involving respirators, the arbitrator overturned the employer's policy on the basis that it was overly broad (*Mission Foods*, 111 LA 501; see also 82 LA 1084, 80 LA 765).

F. Revealing or Offensive Attire

When setting standards on dress and grooming, employers sometimes include prohibitions on revealing, indecent, or offensive attire. Most arbitrators agree that employers are within their rights to ban such attire on the basis that it can be provocative and distracting and, in some circumstances, can fuel harassment complaints.

• An employer had just cause to suspend an employee for three days after she violated a Friday dress-down policy by wearing a tank top with spaghetti straps that exposed a significant portion of her breasts, an arbitrator ruled. When the employee was confronted about violating the employer's dress standards, which prohibited "revealing or tight outfits," she became loud and discourteous and subsequently refused her supervisor's order to meet with him about the situation. Concluding that the employee was negligent about complying with her employer's dress standards and was guilty of insubordination, the arbitrator upheld the suspension (*City of Lake Worth*, 121 LA 228).

• An employee who violated an employer's dress code by wearing short shorts to work was properly discharged under a last-chance agreement prompted by earlier misconduct, an arbitrator found. The employer allowed employees to wear shorts, provided they were at least mid-thigh length. On two work days in succession, the employee wore shorts that did not comply with the employer's dress code. She was fired after three separate managers spoke to her about her attire. The arbitrator found that discharge was justified under the last-chance agreement, which called for the employee's termination if she committed any violation warranting discipline (*Consolidated Container Co.*, 121 LA 557).

• An employer had a right to prohibit an employee from wearing a shirt that was considered a violation of its rule against crude and vulgar pictures and slogans on tool and lunch boxes and T-shirts, an arbitrator said. The shirt in question came from a Hooters restaurant and was emblazoned with the slogan "More Than A Mouthful," which likely referred to the breasts of Hooters waitresses, known for their meager attire. The employer acted reasonably in applying its ban on "indecent dress" to avoid the impression of a permissive atmosphere or tolerance of provocative and distracting pictures and slogans, the arbitrator held. Adding, however, that the employee had worn the same shirt on a number of previous occasions without any adverse consequences, the arbitrator determined that the employer lacked just cause to impose discipline without first warning her that the shirt would no longer be tolerated (*Clarion Sintered Metals Inc.*, 110 LA 770).

• Discipline was warranted for a Hispanic employee who refused repeated orders regarding a piece of clothing that offended a number of her African American co-workers, an arbitrator held. The offensive item was an African print scarf that the employee tied on her head. Following a previous incident involving a similar scarf, several co-workers complained and attached their signatures to a letter stating that the employee's wearing of the scarf made a mockery of Aunt Jemima and "was disrespectful to the black race." The second incident occurred less than a week later, while management was still investigating the original complaints. Despite being warned about her behavior, the employee refused management's orders to remove the scarf and was fired. The arbitrator converted the discipline to a final written warning and ordered reinstatement without back pay, provided that the employee would apologize for her actions and undergo sensitivity training (*USCP-Wesco Inc.*, 109 LA 225).

• A company acted reasonably in issuing a rule to prohibit attire that would reflect unfavorably on the company or its employees, an arbitrator held. The rule was prompted by an incident in which two employees came to work in shirts that depicted a little man urinating on the company. Although many "strange scenarios" could be imagined in which the company might apply the rule unfairly, the rule itself was reasonable, the arbitrator found. The time to assess the rule's application would be after a specific set of facts arises, at which point the union could grieve any perceived misuse of the rule, the arbitrator said (*Intertec Systems LLC*, 114 LA 1785).

G. Discrimination and Accommodation

Dress and grooming standards sometimes give rise to discrimination and accommodation issues based on factors such as gender, race, and religion. (see also chapter on Harassment).

● An arbitrator ruled that a Native American teacher who was ordered to take off his hat at a meeting was not a victim of religious discrimination, where other staff were asked to remove their hats, which did not have religious symbols, and the school district did not specifically target religious symbols for removal from the grievant's clothing, body, or lifestyle (*Plumas Unified School District*, 130 LA 53).

● An arbitrator ruled that a necktie requirement imposed by one department head in a company was inconsistent with a contractual ban on sex discrimination. The union protested that the employer's dress policy had "gradually degenerated" into letting female employees wear anything they wished, including jeans, sweaters, tank tops, and other informal apparel. Observing that not only were female employees allowed to "go with the vogue," but the company had launched a public relations campaign in which male employees were photographed wearing "all sorts of attire," the arbitrator concluded that the necktie rule was "arbitrary, capricious, and totally inconsistent" and that it was "predicated upon the personal taste of one department head" (*Union Tribune Publishing Co.*, 70 LA 266; see also 117 LA 515).

● An airline employer did not discriminate against a male ramp agent by requiring him to tuck his long hair beneath a hat, an arbitrator ruled. The arbitrator rejected the argument that the employer applied its standards discriminatorily by allowing female ramp agents to wear long hair that was not subject to the same requirement.

The law does not prohibit employers from having separate grooming standards for male and female employees in the same job, the arbitrator found (*Southwest Airlines*, 107 LA 270).

● An arbitrator held that an employer properly prohibited a receptionist of Mexican heritage from wearing nose jewelry, despite her contention that the jewelry was a reflection of her culture. The employer's action was proper under a contractual provision allowing it to "adopt reasonable rules of conduct," the arbitrator decided, adding that the employer did not violate a nonbias requirement in the contract because federal civil rights laws do not protect an employee's ability to express his or her cultural heritage in the workplace (*The Motion Picture & Television Fund*, 103 LA 988).

● Discharge was warranted for an employee who wore a turban instead of a cap that was part of her uniform, even though she claimed that her refusal was prompted by her Islamic faith. The employee asserted that she was required to cover all her hair while in public, but evidence showed that she sometimes failed to cover her hair or wore head coverings that did not satisfy the religious tenets she described. Consequently, the arbitrator said the employer was under no obligation to accommodate the employee's professed head-covering requirement, because it did not fall in the category of "sincere religious beliefs to which all else is subordinate or upon which all else is ultimately dependent" (*Alameda-Contra Costa Transit District*, 75 LA 1273).

● In another religious accommodation case, an arbitrator ordered a hospital to consider an exception to a dress rule that required operating room employees to wear pants. A female technician requested an accommodation because her religion did not allow women to wear pants. The arbitrator ordered the hospital to give the employee the chance to design an alternative uniform rather than be transferred from the operating room (*Hurley Hospital*, 70 LA 1061).

● An employer did not have just cause to discharge a Muslim employee who, after several years of dressing in the same manner, was ordered to start tucking in his shirt at work, an arbitrator ruled. When confronted by a new department head, the employee said the normal dress code did not apply to him because his religion required his shirt to remain untucked so it would cover his private parts. Nevertheless, the manager ordered immediate compliance with the employer's appearance policy. The employee became loud and argumentative and was subsequently fired. The arbitrator found it understandable that the manager's order, which conflicted with "a serious religious obligation," would be upsetting and offensive to the employee. Although the employee was informed that he could provide documentation supporting an accommodation, he was directed to violate the tenets of his religion until he could secure such documentation, which was not a reasonable order, the arbitrator said. Concluding that discharge was not justified, the arbitrator awarded the employee reinstatement with back pay (*Liberty Medical Center Inc.*, 109 LA 609).

● An employer improperly refused to test whether a proper seal of a respirator could be achieved by an employee who wore a beard because he had pseudofolliculitis, a common condition among African Americans that is aggravated by shaving, an arbitrator held. After being ordered to shave his beard to achieve a good respirator seal, the employee raised the issue of discrimina-tion and claimed that he should be allowed to test whether the breathing equipment would function adequately with a beard. Agreeing with the employee, the arbitrator ordered the employer to conduct empirical tests of the respirator's sealing ability. Allowing the employer to apply its no-beard rule uniformly without conducting such tests, the arbitrator maintained, would effectively bar many African American males from rightful employment because of a skin condition specific to their race (*Niagara Mohawk Power Corp.*, 74 LA 58; see also 100 LA 1084).

● Another arbitrator ordered an employer to accommodate employees who could not wear standard respirators because of medical restrictions. While upholding a general policy requiring employees to remain clean shaven or use their own money to buy more expensive respirators that would work with beards, the arbitrator acknowledged that standard "half-mask respirators" would not work properly for some employees because of legitimate medical reasons. "Where such reasons are documented by reliable medical evidence," the arbitrator said, the employer would be obligated to provide a different type of respirator that would accommodate the problem at no cost to employees (*Miss. Power & Light Co.*, 92 LA 1161).

VII. Drug Abuse [LA CDI 100.552545 (public employees); 118.653]

[*Editor's Note:* See also Part 2, Chapter XIV, Intoxication & Alcoholism.]

OVERVIEW

Public policy condones and encourages employer efforts aimed at keeping drugs out of the workplace and preventing safety risks posed by drug-impaired employees. In keeping with these goals, arbitrators generally support management's right to prohibit the use, possession, sale, or distribution of drugs at work and to invoke discipline or discharge against employees for drug-related offenses, including on-the-job impairment caused by prescription medications.

Despite taking a strict stance against drug-related offenses, many employers also offer programs to assist employees with drug problems. An example of the balance between rehabilitation and penalization can be seen in last-chance agreements that condition the continued employment of substance abusers on the successful completion of drug treatment programs. A similar balance shows up in the Americans with Disabilities Act of 1990, which treats drug addiction as a disability but does not protect employees who currently are engaged in illegal drug use.

The issues that arbitrators focus on in determining the proper penalty for drug-related offenses include whether:

• a drug-abuse policy has been established and clearly communicated to employees;

• employees' use or possession of drugs had, or was likely to have, a negative effect on safety;

• discipline was based on sufficient proof, such as corroborating evidence to support witness testimony;

• discipline was consistently meted out for drug involvement and was on a par with discipline for alcohol-related offenses; and

• off-duty drug involvement, arrests, or convictions had negative workplace ramifications.

SUMMARY OF CASES

A. Enforcement of Drug Policies

As with other types of offenses, arbitrators generally uphold discipline for drug-related activities that violate workplace rules, provided the rules have been communicated to employees and enforced in a consistent manner.

• An arbitrator found that the employer's zero-tolerance policy was reasonable. He noted that the policy banned the illegal use of prescription drugs but not the use of legally prescribed medication. The policy, the arbitrator said, allowed employees to avoid punishment by seeking treatment, and allowed management to forego discharge for employees whose drug use it discovers if they agree to treatment (*Quebecor World*, 123 LA 1222).

• An employer had just cause to discharge an employee who tested positive for marijuana on a random test under a provision of a collective bargaining contract that gave the employer the sole discretion to determine if an employee failing a drug test should be terminated, an arbitrator said, even though the employer had to act in good faith, where the employer had consistently applied the discharge penalty (*Temple-Inland Inc.*, 126 LA 856).

• An arbitrator ruled that an employer had just cause to discharge an employee who—during work time, on public streets, and while she was in the employer's uniform—purchased marijuana at a known drug location and reentered the employer's vehicle before being arrested for possession, where she had prior notice that her conduct violated the employer's drug-free policy and work rule, and misconduct could have caused "catastrophic" liability for the employer and undermined a reasonable observer's confidence in the employer's personnel (*Time Warner Cable of New York City*, 125 LA 664).

• Citing management's failure to ensure that employees understood its prohibitions against using or being under the influence of intoxicants on its premises, an arbitrator overturned the discharge of an employee who had brought marijuana into the plant. "To be a basis for proper disciplinary action against an employee," the arbitrator pointed out, "a rule must be reasonable in nature, clearly published, and it must be known to the employee." Although employees were given copies of the rules, the arbitrator noted, there was no follow-up to ensure that they had read them. "It is a risky assumption," the arbitrator pointed out, "for a firm to give rules to employees in a written form and expect them to read and understand them without some type of follow-up to confirm reading and clarity of understanding" (*Ethyl Corp.*, 74 LA 953).

• *By contrast*, an arbitrator ruled that an employer did not have just cause to discharge an employee for testing positive for marijuana following a minor work accident, where there was no bargaining over drug testing, which was a mandatory bargaining subject, and—assuming the employee handbook was incorporated into the collective bargaining agreement—neither "reasonable cause" nor "post-accident" circumstance for drug testing applied (*Premier Mfg. Support Services Inc.*, 127 LA 1679).

• An employer improperly discharged an aircraft engine assembler who failed two drug tests, an arbitrator ruled, because the employer lacked evidence that the employee violated the collective bargaining agreement's "peculiar" language explicitly prohibiting employee drug use or possession "in the workplace," "while performing work," and "during working hours." Although discharge would normally be upheld in such a situation, the arbitrator said the employee's positive test results could not be equated with proof that he used or possessed drugs while he was at work or that he was in an impaired physical condition while performing his safety-sensitive job. In limiting his review to the scope of the contract language, the arbitrator declared that he had no "roving commission" to implement either federal policy against drug use or any particular level of aviation safety concern, regardless of how clearly justified either might be (*Textron Lycoming*, 104 LA 1043).

● Another arbitrator held that an employer lacked just cause to fire a production worker because the employer's policy gave employees an opportunity to undergo drug rehabilitation and retain their jobs unless they were actually caught using drugs at work. The employee was supposedly seen smoking marijuana at work, but the only witness was a supervisor who subsequently lost his job for falsifying records.

Because the former supervisor did not appear at the arbitration hearing, there was no way to test his credibility based on cross-examination and observation of his testimony, the arbitrator pointed out. Despite other evidence of the employee's drug use, the employer did not prove that he committed the dischargeable offense of smoking marijuana at work, the arbitrator said. Thus, the arbitrator ordered the employer to adhere to its own policy and allow the employee to save his job by entering an approved program of rehabilitation (*Keystone Steel & Wire Co.*, 119 LA 440).

B. Last-Chance Agreements

A common step that employers and employees take in lieu of discharge for drug-related offenses is to enter into last chance agreements. Arbitrators typically sustain summary dismissal if employees do not remain drug-free or abide by other terms specified in the agreements. In general, ar-

bitrators share the view that the only question to decide is whether employees have violated the agreements, because overturning discharge in such cases could discourage employers from offering substance abusers a last chance to salvage their jobs.

● An arbitrator ruled that an employer had proper cause to discharge an employee who relapsed and used cocaine during a layoff after remaining drug-free while under the terms of a last-chance agreement prior to his temporary layoff. Despite the employee's contention that he should be entitled to another opportunity for rehabilitation, the arbitrator pointed out that the collective bargaining agreement provided that a drug-using employee "will be offered an opportunity for rehabilitation in lieu of discipline pursuant to a Last Chance Agreement," which did not mean he should be given multiple opportunities (*United States Steel Corp.*, 127 LA 969).

● Although an employer had not consistently fired other workers for their drug-related offenses, an arbitrator upheld the discharge of an employee who was subject to a last-chance agreement. The employee would have been terminated for his numerous attendance violations, but the employer offered him a last-chance agreement because he admitted to having a drug problem. Within two weeks, the employee violated the agreement in several ways, such as missing work, skipping a drug treatment session, and engaging in illegal drug use.

The union tried to save the employee's job by claiming disparate treatment, but the arbitrator said the employee's situation could not be compared directly with those of other workers who were retained by the employer. Discharge was justified for the employee's various violations of the last-chance agreement, which unambiguously spelled out the conditions the employee had to meet to keep his job, the arbitrator found (*General Electric Co.*, 91 LA 400).

C. Safety Considerations

Generally, arbitrators are stricter in upholding discipline levied against employees if their drug use or impairment endangers co-workers or the public.

• An employer had just cause to discharge a maintenance mechanic who failed a drug test prior to returning from sick leave, an arbitrator ruled. The employer had "reasonable suspicion" to test him due to his admitted use of prescription pain killer during sick leave, his job as maintenance mechanic was a safety sensitive position, he knew he was required to take a medical examination prior to his return, and he admittedly smoked marijuana the day before taking the test (*BWay Manufacturing*, 127 LA 1665).

• A city bus driver who had been involved in an accident while on her route was justly dismissed after a blood test and urinalysis revealed the presence of habit-forming drugs in her system, an arbitrator concluded. Although lacking "absolute proof" of the employee's drug use, "to allow an employee who has taken drugs to continue to drive a bus would pose a danger to the public," the arbitrator said, and "it is unthinkable" that such an employee should be allowed to continue in the job (*Washington Metropolitan Area Transit Authority*, 82 LA 150).

• A police dispatcher who admitted to using cocaine off the job was properly dismissed, said an arbitrator who declared that "it is incompatible with the functions of a police communications dispatcher to have a person employed in the role admittedly taking cocaine or other controlled substances." Moreover, because a person in that job "receives telephone calls from the public regarding possible life-threatening situations which must be rapidly analyzed," the arbitrator said, the job requires "full concentration of the dispatcher's faculties while in the performance of their duties and the use of controlled substances such as cocaine impairs that function" (*San Francisco Police Department*, 87 LA 791).

• *By contrast*, an arbitrator ruled that an employer did not have just cause to discharge an employee who caused an on-site accident resulting in injury to herself and then tested positive for marijuana and Valium use, where the employer did not prove that other employees—who merely had been suspended after testing positive for drugs following their involvement in on-site accidents—were less negligent than she or had engaged in less serious drug use, and the employer did not notify the workforce of any change in its disciplinary pattern (*Trane Co.*, 125 LA 725).

• A chemical plant employee whose job was not "in a sensitive area" was unjustifiably discharged for smoking marijuana on the premises, an arbitrator held. Arguing that its business required alert employees, management insisted that an employee under the influence of drugs could "cause an erroneous mixture of chemicals" that might result in "explosions or fires." The arbitrator, however, pointed out that the employee worked "in the boiler house, unloading and shoveling coal," rather than in a sensitive area where there would be the "possibility of dangerous mistakes" (*Hooker Chemical Co.*, 74 LA 1032).

D. Nature of Abused Drug

If employees' behavior or performance at work becomes affected by prescription medications, rather than illicit substances, arbitrators still tend to sustain discipline where workplace rules prohibit on-the-job impairment.

• A county did not have just cause to discharge an employee in whose desk it found marijuana, since she had a card allowing her to use it for medical purposes (*Monterey County*, 123 LA 677).

• Three longshoremen were found in a drug test to have used artificial marijuana. However, the collective bargaining agreement specified drug testing only for seven specific drugs, so the discharges of two of the longshoremen were overturned. The third had already gone to drug rehabilitation and had been reinstated. The arbitrator said that he could not "ignore evidence of drug use that is of record in this case," so he ordered the two other longshoremen to go to drug rehabilitation as a condition of reinstatement (*P&O Ports Louisiana*, 129 LA 1023).

• An arbitrator reduced the discharge of an employee who tested positive for off-duty marijuana use 11 years after he enrolled in an employee assistance program for methamphetamine to a disciplinary suspension, where the employee had 26 years of service and was clean for 11 years, had no discipline problems and freely admitted his marijuana use after failing the test, and a suspension 11 years before was not part of her personnel record (*Augusta Newsprint Co.*, 125 LA 531).

• An arbitrator ruled that a school board did not have just cause to discharge a cancer-stricken employee for failure to perform duties satisfactorily and insubordination after her medications rendered her sporadically incapable of performing normally. She was a 10-year employee with no history of performance problems, she was not a recreational drug abuser, she checked herself into a rehabilitation program after being discharged, and she was only indirectly guilty of insubordination by coming to work when she was not fully able to work. The arbitrator reduced her discharge to a time-served suspension without back pay and allowed the school board to require a medical exam including a medical screen to verify her fitness, said she must participate in an aftercare program for at least one year and provide the board with a list of her medications and timely update it, and allowed the board to randomly drug test her up to four times in the year after reinstatement (*Scottsboro Board of Education*, 126 LA 1732).

• An employee was not excused from discharge for cashing both his regular and replacement pay checks because he used Oxycontin. The arbitrator found no evidence that "Oxycontin does in fact inhibit one's freedom of choice to such an extent as to relieve a person of responsibility for his actions" (*United States Steel Corp.*, 124 LA 326).

• An employee was properly given a three-day disciplinary layoff when management determined that he reported to work under the influence of drugs, an arbitrator decided. The employee objected to the discipline, claiming that the drug was Valium and that it had been prescribed for him by his physician. Whether the employee's behavior was adversely influenced by his "taking medicine as prescribed or using drugs without benefit of prescription is not relevant to the fact that the employee was under the influence and therefore a risk in

the workplace," the arbitrator said (*FMC Corp.*, 80 LA 1173).

E. Evidence of Drug Involvement

1. Witnesses

When employers discipline employees based on the testimony of witnesses to the employees' drug use or possession, arbitrators often look for corroborative evidence of drug involvement before enforcing disciplinary measures. The types of witnesses most commonly relied upon in such cases are undercover agents, supervisors, and co-workers.

• An arbitrator ruled that a county did not have just cause to discharge a school bus driver who tested positive for marijuana, despite testimony from her former mother-in-law that she had personally seen the driver smoke marijuana, where the mother-in-law testified that the driver had "done wrong" by leaving her son and was not credible. The county was required to prove that the driver knowingly ingested marijuana, and since it did not, the county was required to reinstate her with back pay to date of award. However the arbitrator also ruled that the driver must complete a rehabilitation program prior to reinstatement to her safety-sensitive position, because she knowingly drove the bus with marijuana in her system on the day after she unknowingly consumed brownies laced with marijuana (*Washington County Bd. of Educ.*, 124 LA 1317).

2. Undercover Agents

When employers have hired undercover agents as part of anti-drug campaigns to detect drug use and possession in the workplace, arbitrators usually weigh the testimony of undercover agents in light of their expertise and the other evidence presented, including contrasting testimony from accused employees.

• An arbitrator overturned the discharge of an employee that was based on the unsupported testimony of an undercover agent. Noting that "the accused must always be given the benefit of substantial doubts," the arbitrator asserted that "dismissal for alleged criminal conduct may not be upheld when the sole evidence supporting the charge is the uncorroborated testimony of an undercover informant." Corroboration could include samples of the drugs allegedly used by the employees, laboratory analyses, photographs, or tape recordings, the arbitrator pointed out (*Pacific Bell*, 87 LA 313; see also 97 LA 271, 95 LA 813, 83 LA 580).

● Two employees were unjustly discharged for alleged drug use based solely on reports from an undercover agent that "were filtered down to the employer management by and through the agent's supervisor," an arbitrator held. Without "some type of corroboration" of the agent's reports, which might have been either "direct or circumstantial," the testimony of employees must be "superior," the arbitrator reasoned. To allow a job to be "damaged or tarnished or taken away by uncorroborated and unsubstantiated evidence," the arbitrator maintained, "would be to allow an employer to act arbitrarily and capriciously and unreasonably in many instances" (*Pettibone Ohio Corp.*, 72 LA 1144).

● Another arbitrator ruled that an employer, relying on evidence of an undercover detective, properly discharged four employees for possession and use of marijuana on employer premises. The testimony of the detective was "firsthand information where the incidents testified to were backed up by reports written daily," declared the arbitrator. Moreover, the undercover detective's "demeanor, the impression that his testimony was truthful, his memory, his perception," and his prior experience as a police officer showed that his testimony was "accurate and credible," the arbitrator concluded, ruling that the discharges were for just cause (*Consumer Plastics Corp.*, 88 LA 208).

● An arbitrator upheld the terminations of several employees who had been discharged for on-the-job drug and alcohol use based on the uncorroborated testimony of an undercover agent who "passed" a polygraph test. The arbitrator accorded "significant weight" to the fact that the agent's testimony was supported by the polygraph results, while all the accused employees refused to submit to the test (*Georgia Pacific*, 85 LA 542).

3. Supervisors or Co-workers

Management personnel or co-workers also may testify regarding employees' drug use or possession. In such cases, arbitrators consider the strength of the testimony based on what the witnesses claim to have observed.

● An employer had just cause to discharge an employee for insubordination and having marijuana on the employer's property, where the employer had found marijuana on its premises, a K-9 dog led the manager and union steward to the employee's vehicle, the dog's handler—who initially asked him to open the door to his vehicle—was clearly identified as a private company representative and not a law enforcement officer to whom the warrant requirement would have applied, and the grievant's refusal of the manager's subsequent order to open the door amounted to "self-help" (*Southern Standard Cartons Inc.*, 125 LA 1811).

● An arbitrator upheld the discharge of four employees who were witnessed by four supervisors smoking a marijuana cigarette among them. The "chain of circumstances pointing to the guilt of the grievants goes far beyond conjecture and suspicion," the arbitrator declared. The four supervisors testified that they smelled the "pervasive and unmistakable odor of marijuana" and observed the employees deeply inhaling the smoke as they passed the marijuana cigarette back and forth while looking "suspiciously from side to side before lighting or inhaling from the cigarette," the arbitrator noted (*Cascade Steel Rolling Mills Inc.*, 78 LA 753).

● An employer had just cause to dismiss an employee after two supervisors discovered her smoking what they thought was a marijuana cigarette in the women's locker room, an arbitrator said. The supervisors testified that they found part of a marijuana cigarette on the floor of the locker room, which smelled of marijuana smoke (*Dobbs Houses Inc.*, 78 LA 749; see also 88 LA 633, 75 LA 642).

● *By contrast*, an arbitrator overturned the discharge of an employee discovered by a supervisor in a company exercise room, which smelled of marijuana. Management must show "good and sufficient evidence to support the charges [of drug use]," the arbitrator said, but in this case, the supervisor was not able to say irrefutably that the odor he smelled came from the employee's smoking in the exercise room. If the company's argument in favor of discharge were upheld—even though "significant doubt" remained as to the employee's guilt—it would be tantamount to shifting the burden of proof to the employee, making him guilty until proven innocent, the arbitrator said (*Owens-Corning Fiberglas Corp.*, 86 LA 1026).

● An employer improperly suspended an employee after a co-worker reported finding marijuana on the employee's chair, an arbitrator decided, because that evidence and a subsequent investigation did not conclusively establish that the employee had marijuana in his possession (*Air Force Logistics Command*, 75 LA 597).

F. Equal Treatment for Abusers

Arbitrators sometimes compare the discipline given to drug abusers with the discipline employers have levied against alcohol-abusing employees, often overturning or softening discipline given drug abusers if they have been treated more harshly.

● One arbitrator ruled that an employer did not have just cause to discharge an employee who caused an on-site accident, resulting in injury to herself, and then tested positive for marijuana and Valium use, where the employer did not prove that other employees—who merely had been suspended after testing positive for drugs following their involvement in on-site accidents—were less negligent than she or had engaged in less serious drug use, and the employer did not notify the workforce of any change in its disciplinary pattern (*Trane Co.*, 125 LA 725).

● In the case of three employees discharged on their first offense of smoking marijuana on their employer's premises, an arbitrator found that the employees were indeed guilty of violating the employer's drug and alcohol policy. The arbitrator, however, noted that the employer regularly applied progressive discipline—not automatic dismissals—for employees' first offenses in using alcohol on employer property. The arbitrator held that "alcoholism in industry, and as a social problem, is far more debilitating, costly, and destructive than marijuana. There is no rational or reasonable basis for treating them as distinct. Therefore to treat alcohol abuse with progressive discipline and treat drug abuse with immediate discharge is improper" (*Mallinckrodt Inc.*, 80 LA 1261).

● Two employees who smoked marijuana on the roof of their office during work hours were properly discharged rather than offered counseling through an employee assistance program, as an alcoholic co-worker had been offered, an arbitrator ruled. Even though the EAP had been designed to treat both alcohol and drug-abuse problems, the arbitrator declared that the employer had not treated the two cases disparately because the co-worker was an admitted alcoholic, while the dismissed drug users "denied they had a drug problem and maintained that they were recreational users" (*Central Ohio Transit Authority*, 88 LA 628).

G. Off-Duty Drug Use

When considering drug-related activities that employees engage in while away from work, arbitrators commonly decide on the appropriateness of discipline or discharge after taking into account the workplace ramifications of employees' off-duty conduct. One arbitrator said discharge is inappropriate "unless the behavior renders the employee unable to perform his duties or appear at work; or the behavior leads to the refusal of other employees to work with the employee" (*General Telephone Co. of Calif.*, 87 LA 441).

● A county did not have just cause to discharge a deputy probation officer, even though she used marijuana off duty and apparently lied to management personnel about it, where there was no nexus between her drug use and her job performance, there was little evidence that she engaged in threatening behavior with co-workers, she was a long-term employee with a reasonably good work record, and she went into drug rehabilitation until she lost her health insurance. The arbitrator reinstated her without back pay after successful completion of drug treatment and an official declaration of complete abstinence from drug use (*County of Solano*, 128 LA 1703).

● An arbitrator ruled that a teacher should not have been disciplined for possession of marijuana, where drug police seized the marijuana at the teacher's mother's home, not the teacher's. However the school board had good and just cause to discharge a teacher who got into a mid-week late hour bar brawl with a student, even though the teacher would have avoided discipline if the fight had not been with a student. The arbitrator found that teachers arrested for possession of marijuana, shoplifting, and driving under the influence remained employed, but fighting with a student in a bar at 2 a.m. is a more serious offense (*Monroe County Board of Education*, 129 LA 948).

● An employer did not have just cause to discharge an employee for testing positive for cocaine after claiming back pain, where he was absent from work when employees were educated about the substance abuse testing program and thus he was unaware that drug test was required any time an injury was reported or that he could avoid discipline by coming forth with his cocaine problem prior to detection. Even though he should have known that he should not use illegal drugs, he was unaware of the consequences of his drug use and the availability of rehabilitation, which were spelled out in the policy (*Dynamet Inc.*, 126 LA 903).

● An arbitrator reduced the discharge of a city employee who had marijuana in his car to a one-day suspension. The arbitrator noted that the employee did not bring the drug into the workplace, which did not include the parking lot, and that possession of 3.7 grams of marijuana under Oregon law is "a violation, not a crime, akin to littering . . ." (*City of Portland*, 123 LA 1444).

● An arbitrator ruled that a county-operated nursing home had just cause to discharge two employees for smoking marijuana in a parked car on the home's premises, even though the home did not conduct an investigation, where employees admit-

ted to doing so to a police officer, they tested positive for marijuana, the home clearly communicated that such offense warranted discharge, and investigation would have been a formality (*Friendship Ridge*, 128 LA 116).

● An arbitrator upheld the discharge of an employee whose use of illegal narcotics outside of work interfered with his job performance. The arbitrator ruled that the employee's "drug-induced" condition "rendered him unfit to perform his work," and therefore, the employee violated "the contractual prohibition against the use of illegal narcotics." Even though there was no evidence to show that the employee used the drugs while on duty, the arbitrator concluded that the employer had the right to discharge the employee "without opportunity to rectify or change his offending behavior" (*Lick Fish and Poultry*, 87 LA 1062).

● An employee was justly discharged when he reported to work under the influence of drugs he took while off-duty, an arbitrator decided. When the employee arrived at work, management noticed that he was "walking like he was somewhat in pain" and he appeared "droopy-looking." After a urinalysis revealed the presence of drugs in his system, the employee admitted to using marijuana over the previous weekend and was subsequently discharged. The arbitrator reasoned that because the employer's policy prohibited employees from reporting to work while "under the influence of illegal drugs," the employee was justly disciplined, although his use of marijuana had occurred while he was off duty (*Houston Lighting & Power Co.*, 87 LA 478).

H. Arrest on Drug Charges

If employees are arrested on drug charges, arbitrators are reluctant to uphold termination in the absence of other evidence of wrongdoing or a clear indication that the arrest itself—without a conviction—has an adverse workplace impact.

● An employer unjustly suspended an employee without pay after his arrest in connection with local drug trafficking, said an arbitrator. "We have not regressed to the point where the presumption of innocence until proven guilty is abandoned," insisted the arbitrator. The employer was "precipitous" in suspending the employee, said the arbitrator, stressing that no charges had been levied against the employee and a "real investigation" had not been conducted by the employer (*Times Mirror Cable Television*, 87 LA 543).

• Discharge was not justified for an employee who missed work because of his arrest for allegedly selling drugs, an arbitrator held. The employee had entered into a last-chance agreement as a result of earlier attendance violations, and his employer contended that the absence caused by his arrest triggered automatic termination under the agreement. Rejecting this argument, the arbitrator said the employee had to be presumed innocent of the drug charges, which were later dropped, and he could not be penalized for an absence beyond his control. Adding that the last-chance agreement could not override the contractual requirement of "good and sufficient cause" for discharge, the arbitrator ordered the employee reinstated (*Orpack-Stone Corp.*, 102 LA 545).

• Another arbitrator ruled that an employee's dismissal was proper, even though the drug charges against him were dismissed. The employee was arrested for possession of cocaine while employed as the manager of a community center, a position described by the arbitrator as requiring "great contact with the community, where success is based on trust and leadership." Despite acknowledging that police arrest "is not a basis for determining guilt," the arbitrator upheld the employee's dismissal, finding that the community center "would suffer and that its programs would be undermined if a facility manager who had had drug involvement were reinstated" (*Wayne State University*, 87 LA 953, see also 76 LA 387).

• Discharge was reduced to a suspension for an employee who was arrested in connection with the manufacture of drugs in his home. In overturning discharge, an arbitrator noted that the employer was not identified in news accounts of the incident, no co-workers expressed a reluctance to work with the employee, the employee's prior disciplinary record was nearly spot-

less, and the employee technically did not violate a rule requiring discharge for felony convictions because his cooperation with police resulted in all charges against him being dropped (*Mobil Oil Corp.*, 95 LA 162).

I. Conviction on Drug Charges

Arbitrators typically uphold discharge for drug-related convictions that violate employer rules or have negative workplace ramifications. When a court tempers the sentence by, for example, suspending part of it or permitting a work release, however, arbitrators sometimes require that management show similar leniency.

• An employer did not have just cause to discharge an employee for his convictions for possession of marijuana with intent to sell, despite his employer's concern that the employee may have distributed marijuana to coworkers, an arbitrator ruled. There was no proof that the employee sold or used drugs, he passed several drug tests, his convictions did not publicly affect the company, and he had been a long-term employee with no prior discipline. The arbitrator reinstated the employee with a suspension (*Morton Salt Co.*, 125 LA 346).

• An employee who received a suspended sentence for a drug-related conviction was entitled to conditional reinstatement by his employer, absent "specific and compelling evidence" that his conviction was "harmful to the interests of the company or other employees," an arbitrator ruled. Although management argued that the employee "could be a destructive influence on other employees," that his "continued employment would be damaging to the employer's reputation," and that reinstatement might "cause other problems such as absenteeism and tardiness," the arbitrator dismissed these objections as "either hypothetical or speculative" (*Intalco Aluminum Corp.*, 68 LA 66).

• An employer was justified in firing a worker who was convicted of three drug-dealing felonies and, in extensive publicity about the case, was identified as an employee of the employer, an arbitrator decided. The arbitrator said common sense alone should be enough to tell the employee that a drug conviction could result in her discharge, even though the employer had no formal rule prohibiting illicit off-premises drug activity. If the employer were required to reinstate the employee, her continued employment would have a negative impact on the employer beyond the severe, adverse effects caused by the publicity of her case, the arbitrator said in upholding discharge (*Haskell of Pittsburgh Inc.*, 96 LA 1208).

● Harm to a soft-drink distributor's business interests justified the discharge of an employee after his arrest and guilty plea for conspiracy to sell the drug known as ecstasy, an arbitrator ruled. Noting that customers of the company had read newspaper articles and recognized the employee as one of the company's delivery drivers, the arbitrator said the decision to discharge the employee was made in order to preserve the company's market share in a highly competitive business (*Delta Beverage Group Inc.*, 96 LA 454).

● An arbitrator upheld the dismissal of an employee who was convicted of selling cocaine. Rejecting the employee's argument that he was unjustly discharged, given that the sale took place neither on employer premises nor on employer time, the arbitrator ruled that just cause existed for the discharge "because of the impact [of the arrest] on the employer's product, its reputation, employee safety, plant security, and production and discipline" (*Martin-Marietta Aerospace*, 81 LA 695; see also 88 LA 425, 68 LA 697).

VIII. Drug Testing [LA CDI 100.552545 (public employees); 118.653]

OVERVIEW

With so many employers relying on drug testing as a means of detecting drug use and discouraging employees from reporting to work in an impaired state, the volume and variety of arbitration cases in this area continue to expand.

Among the most common drug-testing issues addressed by arbitrators are whether:

• employers have the authority to implement drug-testing requirements unilaterally;

• zero-tolerance policies trump standards of just cause, allowing summary dismissal without consideration of anything besides a failed drug test;

• employers have a right to impose testing requirements in the absence of special safety considerations or conditions that provide probable cause for testing;

• testing positive for drugs proves that employees' job performance is impaired;

• privacy rights are unjustifiably intruded upon when employees are subjected to certain testing procedures;

- test refusals or adulteration of samples can be treated the same as failed tests; and
- protocols for the handling and testing of samples are properly followed, producing reliable results.

SUMMARY OF CASES

A. Negotiation of Testing Policies

Employers that unilaterally implement drug-testing policies often encounter objections from the unions representing their workers. A common argument in such cases is that employers lack the authority to impose testing requirements without union-management negotiations. Arbitrators, however, are divided over whether bargaining is a necessary precursor to the implementation of testing policies.

In one case, an arbitrator said the mutual refusal by an employer and union to negotiate in good faith over changes in drug testing protocols must end. The collective bargaining agreement contained a drug and alcohol provision requiring testing of employees who worked in the warehouse or drove trucks and stipulated that "urine samples are preferred and will be used whenever possible. Breathalyzer is the desired means of alcohol detection." The agreement further stated that "at any time during the life of this agreement should the company decide to change or alter" the drug and alcohol policy, "the parties will negotiate in good faith with respect to said desired change prior to the company making any such desired change."

The employer came to believe that under some circumstances urine and breathalyzer tests were either inaccurate, unreliable, or impossible to administer, and proposed the use of hair analysis, in which a subject's chest hair is collected and tested. The union protested that this was overly invasive and a violation of the CBA.

The employer's position was that the use of the terms "preferred" and "desired" to describe urinalysis and breathalyzer testing, respectively, left the company with the option of choosing other forms of testing with or without the union's approval. The union insisted that only urinalysis and

breathalyzer testing be used until the issue was negotiated.

The union accused the employer of failing to negotiate, while the employer charged that the union's only response to its request to negotiate was "follow the contract." The union filed a grievance and an unfair labor practice charge with the National Labor Relations Board over the employer's unilateral implementation of a change in drug and alcohol testing.

"The position of the union ... was not any better than that of the company," the arbitrator said. "The evidence was that on at least one and maybe more occasions the response to the company's request for a change in testing was 'follow the contract.' The problem with this position is there was a dispute as to what the contract meant for the parties to follow. Therefore telling the company to follow the contract could do no more than be irritating."

The arbitrator ordered the parties to engage in good faith negotiations regarding changes in the drug and alcohol testing program that relied on anything other than observation urinalysis or breathalyzer (*Gateway Distribution Co. Inc.*, 128 LA 436).

- An arbitrator overturned the discharge of an employee who tested positive for marijuana following a minor work accident, because there had been no bargaining over drug testing, which was a mandatory bargaining subject, and—assuming the employee handbook was incorporated into the collective bargaining agreement—neither the "reasonable cause" nor "post-accident" circumstance for drug testing applied under the facts of the case (*Premier Mfg. Support Services Inc.*, 127 LA 1679).

- Another arbitrator overturned the discharge of an employee who failed a drug test for the first time, because the policy does not mandate termination, the policy was not a product of collective bargaining, the decision to decline to refer the employee to rehabilitation was not a product of informed judgment, the union's approach in discussions of the policy was that employees should be provided a second chance, and in some cases employees had not been discharged for failure of a first test (*Kohler Printing Inc.*, 125 LA 137).

● One arbitrator held that an employer committed a contract violation when it imposed testing requirements without union input. The union objected that the employer's new substance abuse policy constituted new work rules and, as set out in the contract, could not be implemented without union-management negotiations. Calling the employer's policy "improper," the arbitrator said although "there is no doubt that there is more drug abuse in our present day society," the employer cannot "overlook a contractual clause" requiring negotiations in connection with the establishment of new work rules (*Hobart Corp.*, 88 LA 905).

● An employer's unilaterally implemented drug-testing policy violated a contract provision requiring the employer to treat employees "fairly and equitably," an arbitrator held. The testing policy was objectionable, said the arbitrator, because it mandated testing for employees whose work had no bearing on safety and who did not work with the public, provided that uncooperative employees could be charged with insubordination, dictated the testing method to be used despite the availability of many methods, did not allow employees to test a portion of their sample by a lab of their choosing, and did not mandate that the employer verify positive test results with a confirmatory test (*Bay Area Rapid Transit District*, 88 LA 1).

● Another arbitrator decided that an employer exercised traditional management rights when it unilaterally implemented a policy on drug and alcohol testing. The propriety of the policy came into question after the employer fired an employee for repeatedly refusing to sign a form acknowledging his receipt and awareness of the testing policy. The union argued that the employee was right not to sign the acknowledgement form because the employer

should have bargained over the testing requirements. Upholding the discharge, the arbitrator ruled that "there is no question but that the employer had the right to implement this drug and alcohol test policy. It is clearly an exercise of management's right and was an integral part of the employer's responsibility to maintain safety, efficiency, and discipline in the workplace" (*Concrete Pipe Products Co. Inc.*, 87 LA 601).

● Rule changes imposing stringent drug testing requirements were properly implemented by an employer at an ammunition plant, an arbitrator found, emphasizing the special safety considerations involved in the case. The employer launched its testing program after anonymous testing revealed that employee drug use was widespread. The rule changes, which mandated immediate discharge following positive drug tests, were justified on the basis of the serious threat posed by "highly explosive materials being produced at the plant," the arbitrator observed. In his ruling, the arbitrator specifically stressed the appropriateness of random drug testing, noting that the time for believing that employee drug use could be detected by outward signs of impairment "has long since run." The arbitrator did order two modifications, however, requiring the employer to confirm positive test results before removing employees from their jobs and striking down random testing of those returning from leaves of absence, which was deemed an improper attempt to control employees' off-duty conduct (*Day & Zimmermann Inc.*, 94 LA 399).

B. Zero-Tolerance Policies

Some employers implement "zero-tolerance policies" that call for summary discharge whenever employees fail drug tests, but arbitrators do not always uphold termination in such cases.

● One arbitrator overturned an employee's discharge under a zero-tolerance policy because his employer failed to give him an opportunity to explain his failed drug test. The employee took a pain medication called Darvocet, which was prescribed for his wife. He had a history of intermittent pain following serious leg surgery two years earlier, and although his doctor had prescribed a similar drug, the employee took the medicine so infrequently that he had allowed his prescription to lapse six months earlier. The evidence indicated that the employee had taken a small amount of Darvocet and had performed his job duties the day of the test without any signs of impairment. The employee's discharge over the drug test was the only disciplinary action taken against him in 20 years of service with the employer.

The arbitrator refused to sustain the employee's discharge based largely on the conclusion that the zero-tolerance policy did not trump contractual language requiring just cause for discipline. Unlike the just cause provision in the contract, the zero-tolerance policy was adopted by the employer as an exercise of management rights and did not result from "a formal bilateral process of negotiation" between the parties, the arbitrator noted. Finding that the employee was entitled to the due process rights implicit in the just cause standard, the arbitrator faulted the employer for not conducting a fair investigation and failing to give the employee a chance to explain his conduct before subjecting him to discipline. Adding that the employee's conduct was not so outrageous or dangerous as to warrant summary discharge, the arbitrator reduced the discipline to a three-week suspension (*Newspaper Agency Corp.*, 119 LA 926).

● An employer's zero-tolerance policy could not automatically trigger discharge for a failed drug test without regard to extenuating circumstances, an arbitrator held. The case arose when an employee with an exemplary 16-year record tested positive for marijuana. His wife had been a regular user of the drug for 30 years, and he smoked from her marijuana cigarette during a New Year's Eve party. Prior to that incident, he had always passed the random drug tests required by his employer.

The arbitrator said summary discharge under the employer's zero-tolerance policy conflicted with the express contractual language requiring just cause for discipline. Asserting that progressive discipline is a central principle under the just cause

standard, the arbitrator concluded that the employee's isolated instance of misconduct presented a classic case for corrective discipline as opposed to summary termination. "The Grievant was, and can be again, a valuable and economically productive member of the work force; he recognizes his instance of wrongdoing and will not repeat it," the arbitrator said. Adding that "discharge was a disproportionate penalty summarily imposed without regard to any extenuating, mitigating circumstances and without regard for the Grievant's impeccable record and long service," the arbitrator reduced the employee's discipline to a two-week suspension (*Interstate Brands Companies*, 120 LA 356).

● *By contrast*, another arbitrator held that a single positive drug test provided just cause for discharge under a policy that was unilaterally implemented by an employer. The employer's previous policy, which had been negotiated with the union, allowed employees to retain their jobs after a first offense if they entered into an employee assistance program. The employer had approached the union with a proposal for a zero-tolerance policy, but the union refused to negotiate, so the employer unilaterally made the change. When an employee subsequently failed a random drug test, the union contended that the employer was still bound by the prior policy and could not fire him for a first-time offense.

Although the parties had negotiated the previous policy, it was not incorporated in the collective bargaining agreement, the arbitrator found. Nor was the employer obligated to continue the prior policy as a binding past practice, the arbitrator held, citing a zipper clause that said the written contract constituted "the entire agreement between the parties." For matters not covered in the contract, the parties did have the right to enter into negotiations and reach separate binding agreements, which is what the employer attempted to do when it proposed the zero-tolerance policy, the arbitrator noted. The union's refusal to negotiate constituted a bargaining impasse, the arbitrator said, which gave the employer the right to make the change unilaterally. Thus, the arbitrator held that the employee's discharge under the policy was justified (*ConocoPhillips Co.*, 121 LA 1025).

C. For-Cause Testing

Arbitrators readily agree that probable cause exists to subject employees to drug testing if they exhibit behaviors that suggest impairment, such as loss of motor control, slurred speech, glazed eyes, and an unsteady gate. Cause for testing also exists where employees are reasonably suspected of being in possession of illicit substances on employer premises or engaging in drug use while on duty.

In addition to testing individual employees based on actual observations of suspicious workplace conduct, employers often establish other requirements, such as post-accident testing or broader policies tied to safety considerations. Though arbitrators are not unanimous on the subject, they are more likely to uphold such policies—and the discipline imposed under them— where employers provide sound reasons to support the testing and also ensure that their requirements are clearly articulated and consistently enforced.

Without proper testing, an employer may not terminate a worker for violating drug and alcohol prohibitions. In one case, a 12-year employee who won performance awards and regular merit raises in recognition of her good work began to show evidence of impairment at work. After going through the proper channels, the employee was taken for drug testing; however, on the way to the test, the employee told the manager that she could not pass the test because she had taken Xanax that day—a prescription drug often used for panic disorders that produces side-effects of sleepiness, impaired speech, and abnormal coordination. Instead of proceeding with the drug test, the manager referred the worker to the employer's employee assistance program, where the worker was placed on administrative leave while undergoing the EAP course. Days later, while on administrative leave, the worker was arrested by the police for "public intoxication." A year after the employee successfully completed the EAP course, her supervisor again received complaints that the employee was impaired at work. The manager took the employee to an independent testing facility for a drug test to verify her impairment. The employee could not give the required amount of urine needed for a proper test, although she stayed there for over three hours trying to give enough urine. She was then placed on administrative suspension, followed by a disciplinary hearing, and terminated for violating employer drug and alcohol policies.

While the record had ample evidence that the employee had problems, in light of the lack of just cause, the arbitrator ordered reinstatement provided the employee undergo treatment at the employer's expense with an EAP counselor, as well as submit to certain testing while on administrative suspension without pay during EAP treatment. When the EAP counselor recommended that the grievant be reinstated, the arbitrator ordered, she was placed in a position at the rate of pay and seniority she had at discharge (*City of Norman, Okla.*, 127 LA 1649).

1. Post-Accident Testing

Post-accident testing is a feature of many employer policies, but arbitrators do not agree that all accidents provide sufficient cause to require employees to undergo testing.

● One arbitrator ordered an employer to cease enforcement of a blanket policy on post-accident testing, reasoning that an accident does not necessarily give an employer reasonable suspicion of drug use. According to the arbitrator, an automatic requirement to undergo testing in the wake of an accident, without a reasonable suspicion that drugs were involved, would negate employees' rights to privacy and due process. Concluding that the testing requirement constituted a contract violation, the arbitrator instructed the employer to limit post-accident testing to situations where supervisors had a reasonable basis for believing that employees were under the influence of intoxicants (*Stone Container Corp.*, 95 LA 729; see also 91 LA 1186).

● Another arbitrator held that an employer had just cause to discharge an employee who failed a drug test after he lacerated his hand and was taken to an urgent care facility. The employer's drug testing policy, which required the testing of employees involved in accidents requiring off-site medical care, was reasonable where the employees worked in the vicinity of potentially hazardous industrial equipment and the policy's distinction between minor and serious accidents provided a reasonable basis to test, the arbitrator ruled (*Jefferson Smurfit Corp.*, 106 LA 306).

● Just cause existed to discharge an employee who tested positive for marijuana following an accident, an arbitrator ruled, even though the accident was not his fault and he showed no signs of impairment. The employee was working as the motorman on a commuter train when a woman committed suicide by jumping in the path of his train. His employer sent him for drug testing after the incident, in accordance with its procedures for post-accident testing. The arbitrator upheld the employee's termination based on a positive reading for marijuana, finding that the accident properly triggered the testing requirement. Responsibility for the accident was not at issue, the arbitrator added, "since the fact of a serious accident, in itself, is deemed sufficient" to warrant drug testing in the safety-sensitive transportation industry (*Chicago Transit Authority*, 96 LA 1165; see also 91 LA 213, 82 LA 150).

● *By contrast*, an arbitrator ruled that a 24-year employee at an aluminum manufacturing plant was improperly discharged based on a positive drug test following a minor accident that occurred while he was operating a front-end loader. Although language on post-accident testing had previously been incorporated in collective bargaining agreements between the parties, there was no longer any written rule stating that accidents involving mobile equipment provided cause for drug testing, the arbitrator found. In addition, the employer did not provide sufficient evidence to support its contention that it had a consistent past practice of requiring drug tests following incidents similar to the employee's

accident, the arbitrator said. The arbitrator awarded the employee reinstatement with back pay, but he also cautioned that the decision should not be viewed as a deterrent to the establishment and enforcement of rules requiring post-accident testing (*Ormet Corp.*, 117 LA 334).

2. Safety Considerations

Many employers impose testing requirements on the basis of legitimate safety concerns. Some testing programs apply specifically to employees in safety-sensitive jobs, while other programs have broad application in work environments that pose unusual threats to employee and public safety.

● Discharge was warranted for an employee at an oil refinery who failed a drug test, an arbitrator decided. The test, which was ordered after the employee reported for work showing obvious signs of impairment, revealed the presence of multiple prescription medications in sufficient amounts to indicate drug abuse. In addition to the incident in question, witnesses testified that the employee had a history of on-the-job impairment, and his behavior had prompted complaints from co-workers who were concerned that he posed a safety threat. Acknowledging that "the nature of the work in a refinery is potentially explosive," the arbitrator determined that the employee committed a dischargeable offense by reporting to work under the influence of drugs "in such a potentially dangerous environment" (*Citgo Petroleum Corp.*, 88 LA 521).

● An employer was justified in firing an employee who failed a drug screening that was carried out under a policy that required random testing of employees in safety-sensitive jobs, an arbitrator held. The employee, who worked as a bus mechanic, tested positive for opiates and morphine after using a drug for which he had no prescription on file. The positive test properly triggered the employee's termination in accordance with the employer's testing policy, the arbitrator held. Although the policy included an exception for workers with information on file indicating their use of prescription drugs and their ability to perform their jobs without impairment while taking such drugs, the employee lacked the necessary medical documentation and was therefore in violation of the policy, the arbitrator found (*Greater Cleveland Regional Transit Authority*, 119 LA 1759).

D. Kinds of Testing

Many arbitrators refuse to uphold policies that call for random testing, finding that they conflict with the just cause standard or improperly infringe on the privacy rights of employees. Nevertheless, such requirements often receive approval based on the existence of special safety issues, a history of drug problems, or other relevant factors.

1. Random Testing

● An arbitrator struck down an employer's policy on random drug testing, finding that it violated the principles of just cause by requiring employees to give evidence against themselves without a preliminary showing of reasonable suspicion. The arbitrator rejected the employer's arguments that random testing was warranted as a means of addressing workplace drug problems, promoting safety, and reducing workers' compensation costs. Deciding that employee privacy interests outweighed the potential for workers' compensation savings, the arbitrator stressed that without giving the workers something in return, the company could not "expect its hourly employees to contribute to its cost saving efforts by subjecting their bodies to drug testing without cause." Moreover, the employer only presented generalized evidence about existing drug problems, and the work at the employer's plant did not involve "materials that are inherently dangerous or pose a threat to the community at large," the arbitrator said (*MII Inc.*, 115 LA 1461; see also 113 LA 886, 113 LA 862, 96 LA 596, 90 LA 1161).

● A contractual prohibition against employee discipline without "proper cause" precluded an employer from imposing random drug and alcohol testing, an arbitrator decided. The employer's right to establish plant rules was limited in that such rules could not conflict with the provisions of the parties' collective bargaining agreement, the arbitrator pointed out. Focusing on the contract's "proper cause" language, the arbitrator said employees were entitled to a presumption of innocence unless the employer could produce evidence to prove they were guilty of wrongdoing. Random testing would turn that rule on its head by shifting to employees "the burden of proving their innocence of drug or alcohol use without the necessity of a preliminary showing of probable cause or reasonable suspicion," the arbitrator said in striking down the random testing requirement (*Ohio Star Forge Co.*, 110 LA 705).

● An employer could not bypass bargaining and unilaterally implement a policy that would give management the right to test any employee at any time for drug or alcohol use, an arbitrator ruled. The employer had a history of implementing rules addressing issues that were mandatory subjects of bargaining, and the union had never before demanded negotiations over the changes initiated by management. Nevertheless, the arbitrator found that the employer's rulemaking power still had its limits. Noting that the testing requirements involved in this case went "far beyond" earlier rule changes invoked by the employer, the arbitrator rejected the unilateral implementation of random testing and instructed the employer to give the union an opportunity to address the matter of drug testing in good-faith negotiations (*Phelps Dodge Copper Products Co.*, 94 LA 393)

● Another arbitrator upheld a program requiring periodic and random testing of all personnel who were granted unescorted access inside the security fence of a nuclear power plant. The arbitrator said the testing requirements were an appropriate response to the "unacceptable risk" that drug use might affect employees' fitness for duty and lead to a possible nuclear accident. Adding that expert testimony established the effectiveness of random testing as a deterrent to employee drug use, the arbitrator said the "overwhelming public benefit derived from insuring a drug-free environment at a nuclear facility is more than sufficient to outweigh the small inherent risk that innocent employees may be unjustly accused of using drugs" (*Arkansas Power & Light Co.*, 88 LA 1065).

● An employer properly implemented random testing, an arbitrator held, where safety considerations in an extremely hazardous work environment outweighed intrusions into employee privacy. Prior to adding new requirements for random testing at its chemical plant, the employer had a program that allowed individual employees to be tested on the basis of probable cause. After new evidence revealed that drug use in the workplace had continued and was more pervasive than management previously realized, the employer concluded that its "for cause" testing program was ineffective. The arbitrator agreed with that conclusion and held that the decision to implement random testing was reasonable based on the employer's need for a more effective testing tool (*Dow Chemical Co.*, 91 LA 1385).

● In a similar case, an arbitrator held that a refinery did not violate a collective bargaining agreement when it implemented a random drug and alcohol testing program after a policy of reasonable-cause testing proved unsuccessful. The employer had bargained in good faith before implementing random testing and had established a need for the policy based on employees' documented substance abuse problems, the arbitrator observed (*Atlas Processing Co.*, 106 LA 172; see also 89 LA 716).

● A hospital had just cause to request a nurse's consent to random drug testing in light of her history of drug problems and a proven lack of persistence in seeking rehabilitation, an arbitrator ruled. Pointing out that there is "no certain 'cure' for addiction to mood-altering chemicals," the arbitrator upheld the testing order, noting that the risks and probabilities of the nurse's resuming drug use "must be evaluated in the context of the job responsibilities," which could involve life-threatening situations for her patients (*Deaconess Medical Center*, 88 LA 44; see also 116 LA 497, 106 LA 97, 91 LA 363).

E. Off-Duty Testing

When employers take disciplinary action against employees on the basis of off-duty testing, they tend to be on shakier ground than they would be if the testing were conducted on an actual work day.

● One arbitrator reduced the discharge of an employee who tested positive for off-duty marijuana use 11 years after he enrolled in an employee assistance program for methamphetamine use to a disciplinary suspension, where the employee had 26 years of service and was clean for 11 years, had no discipline problems and freely admitted his marijuana use after failing the test, and a suspension he had received 11 years before was not part of his personnel record (*Augusta Newsprint Co.*, 125 LA 531).

● Another arbitrator overturned the discharge of an employee who failed a drug test on a Sunday, a few days before his scheduled return from a leave of absence for medical reasons. The arbitrator compared return-to-work testing with random testing and cited "considerable doubt" about the propriety of discipline imposed under such circumstances. According to the arbitrator, "an employee's extended absence, in most cases due to no fault of his own, provides no reason to believe that the returning employee is more likely to be a drug user than any other employee." Even if a worker on leave has used drugs, "what an employee does on his own time is his own business, unless that conduct implicates the employment relationship," the arbitrator said. Although the employer had a rule prohibiting workers from reporting to work under the influence of drugs, the employee could not be fired under that rule when he was not permitted to report to work, the arbitrator held. Nonetheless, reinstatement with back pay was not warranted, the arbitrator found, deciding that the employer could defer the employee's actual return until he tested negative for drugs (*Wheatland Tube Co.*, 119 LA 897).

● Even though an employee was subject to the terms of a reinstatement agreement upon completing a drug treatment program, his employer was not justified in placing him on permanent suspension after he failed a random drug test on a day he was off work, an arbitrator ruled. The parties' collective bargaining agreement did not prohibit off-duty drug use, according to the arbitrator. Finding that the terms of the employee's agreement did not supersede the provisions of the contract, the arbitrator ordered reinstatement with back pay, provided that a physician could certify the employee as fully capable and drug free (*New Orleans Steamship Assoc.*, 105 LA 79).

● *By contrast,* another arbitrator held that an employer had just cause to discharge an employee who tested positive for amphetamines during an off-work, random drug test. In this case, the employee had previously been suspended for taking drugs and had been given a second chance, under which he was put on indefinite probation and was required to undergo random drug testing and rehabilitation. Despite conceding that it would have been more appropriate for the employer to administer the test while the employee was at work, the arbitrator upheld the employer's decision to discharge the employee for failing the off-duty test (*BHP Coated Steel Corp.*, 106 LA 387).

● Reimbursement of lost wages from outside employment was not required in a case where off-duty testing interfered with employees' second jobs, an arbitrator held. The employer had already required employees to undergo testing on two earlier occasions but had informed the employees ahead of time when the tests were scheduled. For a third test, the employer provided notification in the morning and required workers to provide samples the same day. Two employees requested reimbursement of income allegedly lost from outside employment due to the lack of advance notice. Rejecting the workers' complaint, the arbitrator said nothing in the bargaining agreement required advance notice of testing or reimbursement of wages allegedly lost from outside employment (*Wooster City Board of Education*, 102 LA 535).

F. Proof of Impairment

A common argument put forth by unions in the wake of employees' positive drug tests is that the test results, on their own, do not prove on-the-job impairment and should not constitute sufficient cause for discipline or discharge. Arbitrators sometimes heed such arguments, but they also consider other factors, such as whether employer policies require proof of impairment before discipline can be meted out.

● One arbitrator ruled that an employer had just cause to discharge an employee who tested positive for marijuana on a random urine test, despite contentions that he passed later tests, where: hair test contradicted the results of the urine test, there was no evidence of handling of samples at laboratories, and the grievant's use of Advil and Tylenol the night before the test could have produced a false positive, because other tests were taken a week later and the drug could have disappeared from the grievant's system, the hair test is not as accurate, sample handling was adequate as long as it was handled properly until it was placed in the hands of a qualified independent testing laboratory, and the gas chromatography test, which was used by the laboratory, is virtually 100 percent accurate in detecting marijuana (*Temple-Inland Inc.*, 126 LA 856).

● An arbitrator rejected the passive inhalation theory for explaining why an employee tested positive for marijuana and cited a number of scientific studies, found from the Internet, to buttress his view (*Comprehensive Logistics Inc.*, 123 LA 1409).

● One arbitrator overturned the discharge of an employee who tested positive for cocaine after he exhibited erratic behavior at work. Even though the test showed the employee was using drugs, without "proof of either the inadequacy of work performance, intoxication, or the creation of a risk of harm, the proof that an employee used cocaine is insufficient to constitute just cause" for discharge, the arbitrator said (*Kroger Co.*, 88 LA 463; see also 88 LA 91).

● Another arbitrator rejected an employee's argument that his discharge following a positive drug test was not justified because his job performance was unimpaired. The arbitrator ruled that the employer acted in a "fair, reasonable, and contractually permissible manner" by discharging the employee. The employer's policy permitted it to dismiss employees who were found using drugs, and the arbitrator concluded that the employee's positive test result provided sufficient proof of drug use (*Indianapolis Power and Light Co.*, 87 LA 826).

● In a case involving post-accident drug testing, an arbitrator upheld discharge despite the absence of independent proof showing on-the-job impairment. An employee cut his arm while working with a power tool and was taken to a hospital for stitches. While there, he submitted to a drug test in accordance with a policy mandating post-accident testing for any on-the-job incident resulting in outside medical treatment or damage to company property. The arbitrator said the employer's policy, which unambiguously stated that termination would result from a failed drug test, justified the employee's discharge even without other proof of impairment. Noting that the employee had a significant amount of marijuana metabolites in his system, the arbitrator said the test result alone suggested "the distinct possibility of on-duty impairment or at least a close 'nexus' between off-duty drug use and being on-duty, both of which are widely understood to threaten fundamental employer interests" (*Frito-Lay Inc.*, 109 LA 850).

G. Refusing to Test

A refusal to submit to a drug test is often considered just cause for discharge, either because the refusal constitutes insubordination or because it is viewed as the equivalent of a failed test.

For example, a supervisor told a four-year yard lift truck that he had been selected as one of 10 workers for a random drug test by urine sample to detect marijuana, PCP, cocaine, opiates, or methamphetamine. When told he had been selected for the test, the driver replied, "Oh, I'm not worried about that." The tester motioned the driver to follow him, but as the tester stopped to speak to another employee, the driver continued walking. The tester assumed that the driver had walked to the plant medical room for testing, but instead the driver clocked out and drove away. The driver later claimed he was confused about when and where he was to be tested.

At the arbitration hearing, the driver provided the results of a drug test indicating a negative finding for the five drugs. He said he choose a hair sample drug test because he understood that the results went back further than a urine test and he wanted to emphasize his clean record. The argument that the driver "did not know that he needed to go for testing" when asked "does not make sense," the arbitrator said. Why would a supervisor tell the grievant he had been chosen for random drug testing, "if it was not at that time?" the arbitrator asked. "If it was for the next day (when work was not scheduled) or the next week, it would defeat the purpose of being random." Finding that the employee's actions in walking away, clocking out, and leaving the plant without taking the drug test "were tantamount to a refusal to be drug tested," the arbitrator denied the grievance (*Koppers Inc.*, 127 LA 1389).

● An employer had just cause to discharge an employee for violating a last-chance agreement by refusing to take a random drug test, an arbitrator ruled, because the employee's claims bordered on the preposterous! The employee claimed he could only urinate once per day at 8:30 a.m., but neither the family physician's note nor urologist's report supported this claim, and the nurse on duty reported that the employee showed signs of impairment on the day he refused to take the test (*Lorillard Tobacco Co.*, 125 LA 1390).

● Where reasonable cause existed to suspect drug use, an employer acted appropriately in terminating an employee for not submitting to testing, an arbitrator ruled. After the employee was reported for driving erratically on his return trip from making deliveries for a soft-drink company, three supervisors observed signs of impairment in his appearance and behavior. The employee refused to submit to drug testing and was subsequently fired. Although other explanations were offered for most of the factors upon which the employer based its suspicions of drug use, "that does not make the Company's suspicions any less reasonable," the arbitrator declared. Adding that the "purpose of the drug screen is to resolve the element of doubt that may inhere in the

Company's information and observations," the arbitrator ruled that the employee's refusal to submit to testing provided just cause for discharge (*Coca-Cola Bottling Group*, 97 LA 343).

• *By contrast*, an arbitrator overturned the discharge of an employee who refused to take a drug test after a manager observed him smoking what appeared to be a marijuana cigarette. Although the employer had reasonable grounds to order the drug test and to discipline the employee for his refusal to take the test, the terms of the collective bargaining agreement required progressive discipline, the arbitrator pointed out. Accordingly, the arbitrator reduced the employee's discipline to a written warning (*Warehouse Distribution Centers Inc.*, 90 LA 979).

• One employee who refused to undergo testing was awarded reinstatement with back pay. The employee had driven two co-workers to a neighboring town after work, and while they were gone, the employer checked the co-workers' unattended vehicles and noticed some marijuana. When they returned, the employee agreed to a search of his car, and the employer found a partially smoked marijuana cigarette in the backseat ashtray. In subsequent questioning, the employee acknowledged that the two co-workers commonly used marijuana, but he denied any personal involvement. The employer ordered the employee to submit to a drug test or be fired for insubordination. Unable to obtain any assurance from the employer that a negative result would keep him from being fired, the employee offered to resign. He tried to rescind his resignation later that day, but the employer refused.

The employer's rules prohibiting the use or possession of drugs on company property did not provide a legitimate basis for an ultimatum requiring the employee to undergo testing or be discharged, an arbitrator held. When the employee returned to drop off his co-workers, his presence was "totally unrelated to his employment," the arbitrator found. "It follows, therefore, that the [employer] had no authority to address instructions to him which he was required to follow at the risk of being insubordinate," the arbitrator said. If not for those instruc-

tions, the arbitrator continued, the employee would have had no reason to resign in the first place. Consequently, the arbitrator ruled that the employee could not be held to a resignation that resulted from an improper application of the employer's rules (*Texas Utilities Generating Co.*, 82 LA 6).

H. Volunteering to Test

Discharge was not warranted for an employee who volunteered to take a drug test in an effort to substantiate his account of how he came into possession of some cocaine, an arbitrator held.

A nearly empty vial of cocaine was found in a bag of the employee, who worked as a flight attendant, when he went through an airport security check. The employee said he found the vial with some trash on a previous flight and intended to hand it over to a company agent. The police were summoned, and the employee requested immediate drug testing to prove he was telling the truth about having found the vial. Additionally, another flight attendant testified that the employee had told her about finding the vial prior to the security check, and she said she had assured the employee that he could simply turn it in before his next flight.

The employee's immediate offer to undergo testing supported his story, the arbitrator said, noting that the employee wanted to prove he was not a drug user and "had nothing to hide." The arbitrator also noted that the employee's explanation of how he came into possession of the vial was reasonable and supported by the testimony of the other flight attendant. Moreover, the authorities decided not to prosecute the employee for drug possession, deciding there was insufficient evidence of illegal conduct. Concluding that these factors mitigated against discharge, the arbitrator ordered the employee's reinstatement (*Southwest Airlines*, 118 LA 1697).

I. Privacy During Test Procedures

Depending on the particular circumstances involved, arbitrators sometimes decide that certain drug-testing procedures unreasonably intrude upon the privacy of employees.

● An employee who refused to submit to urinalysis in the presence of a nurse was unjustly discharged, an arbitrator held. Because the employee would have had to undress fully to provide the specimen and was refused a request for a robe, she refused to submit to the test and was fired. Because the employee would have had to undress completely, the arbitrator maintained that the presence of the witness was "more than usually embarrassing," and the refusal to allow her to wear a robe "made the conditions of the test unreasonably onerous" (*Union Plaza Hotel*, 88 LA 528).

● A drug-testing program that permitted an official to observe an employee urinating and required employees to report all prescription medicines they were taking was unreasonable, an arbitrator decided. The policy was implemented over objections of the union, which called the procedures an invasion of privacy. With regard to the specimen collection procedure, the arbitrator said if it is possible for an employee to alter a specimen, then the "circumstances or location should be changed rather than requiring observation of urination." The arbitrator ordered the parties to negotiate the testing procedures into a "reasonable form" (*Sharples Coal Corp.*, 91 LA 1065).

J. Sample Problems, Testing Protocols

Arbitration cases sometimes focus on the technical side of drug testing. For example, the integrity of samples provided by employees and the reliability of the procedures used to handle and analyze samples can be key factors in determining the validity of disciplinary actions imposed on employees.

1. Problems with Test Samples

Absent mitigating circumstances, arbitrators generally agree that severe consequences are appropriate if employees have tampered with their test samples in an effort to avoid the detection of drug use.

● An arbitrator upheld the discharge of an employee for adulterating drug samples, even though he was a long-term employee with a good record, where the tester conducted four readings in two different tests and could not obtain an acceptable sample.

Misconduct that breaches substantial employer interests will not be excused based on years of service, the arbitrator said (*Howard Industries Inc.*, 129 LA 1297).

● An arbitrator upheld the discharge of an airline mechanic who adulterated his test sample. The employee became subject to "no-notice testing" after entering into an employee assistance program because of drinking and drug problems. About seven months later, he was fired for supplying a urine sample containing a chromium compound. The employee later admitted that he had kept an adulterating agent in his toolbox and added it to his sample in an effort to mask the presence of a painkiller. Although the adulteration of test samples was not listed as a dischargeable offense, the arbitrator said it was reasonable to consider the employee's action the same as a refusal to test, which was specifically prohibited. At a minimum, the employee's conduct constituted "a failure to cooperate," the arbitrator said, because providing the adulterated sample was "a subterfuge to the Company's moral and legal obligation to ensure air travel is as safe as possible" (*Continental Airlines*, 120 LA 980; see also 113 LA 712).

● Termination also was upheld in the case of an employee who, after a prior positive drug test and an opportunity for rehabilitation, adulterated a test sample by adding nitrites. "An employee's action to adulterate a urine specimen is equivalent to cheating the system, an untenable and unacceptable act," according to the arbitrator who decided the case. "Such deliberate dishonesty to avoid detection of the use of illegal substances is a serious offense, and one for which severe action may be warranted," the arbitrator declared. Adding that the employee's conduct was "particularly egregious" in light of his employer's past offer of rehabilitation, the arbitrator said termination was justified (*North Star Steel*, 114 LA 234).

● An employee was properly terminated for providing a laboratory with a "substituted specimen" that did not "exhibit the clinical signs or characteristics associated with normal human urine," an arbitrator ruled. When the employee was told to report to the laboratory for a random drug test, he drove himself and, on the way there, stopped and went into a bathroom with another employee. At the laboratory, the employee was allowed to keep his clothes on and enter a bathroom alone to produce his urine specimen. Finding no evidence of unreliable procedures on the part of the laboratory, the arbitrator held that the test results showing a substituted specimen provided proper grounds for termination (*County of Wayne*, 118 LA 417).

• *By contrast*, another arbitrator overturned the discharge of a firefighter who adulterated his urine sample. The employee testified that he had become anxious about an upcoming drug test after inhaling secondhand marijuana smoke during a fishing trip. A neighbor in whom he confided gave the employee nitrite powder, which he added to his urine specimen when he was tested. The employer allowed the employee to explain himself after it learned of the adulteration but still fired him under its zero-tolerance drug policy. According to the arbitrator, the employee's conduct was tantamount to a refusal to test, which called for "disciplinary action up to and including dismissal" rather than summary discharge under the employer's policy. Given the employee's eight-year record of discipline-free employment, the fact that his attempt at deceiving the employer "was in no way characteristic of him," and testimony from other witnesses supported his account of passive inhalation of marijuana, the arbitrator held that discharge was too severe a penalty and awarded the employee reinstatement without back pay (*Pasadena Paper Co.*, 117 LA 549; see also 115 LA 418).

2. Soundness of Test Procedures

Challenges to drug testing are sometimes based on employees' claims that unsound or careless testing procedures are responsible for producing questionable or false results. Such claims commonly focus on issues such as chain of custody and the reliability of the testing methods used by employers.

• One arbitrator pointed out that a crucial evidentiary test for workplace substance abuse is the soundness of testing protocols. In upholding the discharge of an employee, the arbitrator commended the "very careful and thorough" testing procedure implemented by the employer. The procedure required the employee to undergo both blood and urine tests, the arbitrator noted, and the samples were submitted to two separate labs, each of which corroborated the positive findings of the other (*Citgo Petroleum Corp.*, 88 LA 521).

• An arbitrator rejected an employee's claim that his suspension based on a positive drug test was unjust because the employer could not prove that it maintained a careful "chain of possession" regarding the specimen. The employer exercised "due care" in securing the sample and properly identifying it as the employee's, the arbitrator noted, adding that greater requirements for proper identification of the sample "might well result" in a program that would be impossible to carry out (*Union Oil Co. of Calif.*, 87 LA 297).

• Despite the existence of a chain-of-custody error, an arbitrator sustained an employee's termination for a failed drug test. The employee, who had become subject to random testing after admitting he was addicted to cocaine, provided a urine specimen at his employer's medical facility. A nurse prepared two sample kits, which were kept briefly in a refrigerator near the nurse's station before being shipped to two separate labs. Both samples came up positive. However, the union noted that one of the kits had been improperly sealed, and it argued that the sample could have been switched while it was in the unlocked refrigerator. Rejecting those arguments, the arbitrator found that the way the nurse sealed the one kit was merely a "technical" chain-of-custody violation, and the probability of someone switching the sample in the refrigerator—which was in full view of the constantly attended nurse's station—"would seem to border on the impossible." Adding that backup tests on the other sample clearly confirmed the positive results, the arbitrator found just cause for discharge (*Shell Oil Co.*, 93 LA 273; see also 114 LA 1811).

• *By contrast*, another arbitrator gave an employee a chance to retest after his original urine sample was not handled according to the proper protocol for chain of custody. After the collection of the employee's urine specimen, there was a break in the chain of possession. Notwithstanding the fact that the employee also provided blood samples, which tested positive for marijuana, the arbitrator said the fairness of the testing procedure was compromised by the mishandling of the urine specimen. The arbitrator ordered a new test and said the employee would be entitled to reinstatement without back pay if the results showed that he was free of controlled substances (*Roadway Express Inc.*, 87 LA 1010).

● A truck driver who tested positive for marijuana was entitled to reinstatement with back pay based on a failure to follow procedures laid out under Department of Transportation regulations, an arbitrator ruled. A lab verified the positive test but skipped the DOT requirement of obtaining a medical review officer's certification before informing the employer of the results. Under the DOT regulations, which were incorporated by reference in the parties' contract, the MRO must review positive test results, ensure the chain of custody was proper, explore alternative possibilities that might account for the positive results, give the tested employee a chance to explain the results, and certify the positive test before the results are transmitted to the employer. According to the arbitrator, "the Medical Review Officer is regarded as the 'lynch pin' of the drug testing process," and leaving the MRO out of the process compelled a finding that discharge was improper (*Schwebel Bakery Co.*, 118 LA 1028).

● Reinstatement also was ordered for a bus driver who was unable to have a backup sample tested because it spilled in transit to a lab. Emphasizing that the opportunity for a backup test was guaranteed under the collective bargaining agreement, the employer's drug and alcohol policy, and federal regulations on the testing of transportation workers in safety-sensitive jobs, an arbitrator said the employee's discharge could not be upheld based solely on the original test results, which were positive for cocaine. Because of public safety considerations, however, the arbitrator ordered the employee's reinstatement to a non-driving job on an interim basis and gave the employer the option of demanding the completion of a rehabilitation program and imposing random testing for up to two years (*Metropolitan Transit Authority*, 116 LA 19).

3. Types of Testing Procedures

● A 16-year operating technician at U.S. Steel Corp. returned to work after a year of hospital care. He submitted to alcohol and drug testing, and while his urine sample tested negative, his hair sample tested positive for marijuana. The technician admitted to smoking marijuana years earlier and to still socializing occasionally with others who smoked marijuana but denied recent use and suggested that blood transfusions he received while hospitalized during his layoff may have come from donors who used marijuana.

The technician was discharged for drug use but offered rehabilitation and a return to work under a last-chance agreement. The worker chose not to accept the offer, and the union, arguing in part a lack of just cause in light of what it called the questionable circumstances of the testing.

The arbitrator said "the record evidence established that [the employee's] hair test utilized scientifically accepted methods for evaluating his drug use." The employee, "having decided not to accept rehabilitation in lieu of discipline pursuant to a Last Chance Agreement, must now bear the consequence of his decision," the arbitrator said in denying the grievance entirely (*U.S. Steel Corp.*, 128 LA 581).

● An arbitrator upheld the use of hair testing for drugs, observing that "[H]air testing and saliva testing are universally accepted and relied upon for workplace testing . . . (*Bowater Inc.*, 123 LA 673).

Arbitrators ruled employers had just cause to discipline employees under the following circumstances:

● an employer had proper cause to discharge an employee who tested positive for marijuana on a hair test, where the test used scientifically accepted methods for evaluating drug use and chain of custody was unbroken, and the employee declined an offer of rehabilitation and last-chance agreement (*U.S. Steel Corp.*, 128 LA 581).

• an employer had just cause to discharge an employee who tested positive for marijuana on a random urine test, despite contentions that he passed later tests, a hair test contradicted results of the urine test, there was no evidence of handling of samples at laboratories, and the grievant's use of Advil and Tylenol the night before the test could have produced a false positive, where other tests were taken a week later and the drug could have disappeared from the grievant's system, a hair test is not as accurate, sample handling was adequate as long as it was handled properly until it was placed in the hands of a qualified independent testing laboratory, and a gas chromatography test, which was used by the laboratory, is virtually 100 percent accurate in detecting marijuana (*Temple-Inland Inc.*, 126 LA 856).

• *By contrast*, an employer did not have just cause to suspend an employee for a positive "rapid screening" drug test, where the employer would not have accepted advance doctor's certification that employee's prescribed drug dosage would not impair his ability to perform his work safely, the employer would not accept a medical review officer's determination that the employee had a legal prescription for the drug for which he tested positive without a nonimpairment statement from the employee's doctor, and it failed to inform the employee in advance that he would need such doctor's statement to return to work (*Falls Stamping & Welding Co.*, 125 LA 267).

IX. Electronic Communications and Technology

OVERVIEW

Workplace rules and policies commonly target the personal use of computers and electronic communications, including social media, e-mail, and cell phones. In addition, many policies on electronic communications strictly prohibit activities involving sexually explicit, discriminatory, or otherwise offensive content.

Employers have established these policies to address problems such as wasted work time and reduced productivity. Other concerns include risks to the integrity of workplace computer networks, exposure to lawsuits as a result of sexually explicit or discriminatory content, and safety hazards associated with the use of cell phones while driving.

Most arbitrators agree that employers are justified in disciplining employees for violating electronic communications policies or misusing company-provided computer resources. In the absence of repeated or egregious misconduct, however, such infractions are not necessarily viewed as grounds for dismissal. For arbitrators to sustain discharge, employers usually must show that work rules or policies prohibit the activities in question, and they must show that the rules have been clearly communicated and consistently enforced. Otherwise, arbitrators tend to overturn or soften the penalty.

SUMMARY OF CASES

A. Policy and Enforcement Issues

Employees may face discipline up to discharge for improper use of computer resources and other electronic communications infractions. To uphold discipline in such cases, arbitrators generally require that employers:

• establish clear rules or policies specifying prohibited conduct,

• adequately communicate the rules and warn workers of the consequences for violations,

• consistently enforce the rules, and

• avoid giving workers the impression—through lax enforcement or participation in prohibited conduct by management employees—that violations will be tolerated.

Where employers do not follow these basic tenets in the establishment and enforcement of policies on the use of computers and electronic communications, arbitrators are likely to overturn or reduce discipline, as several of the cases below illustrate.

• Discipline was not warranted for a librarian who sent out an e-mail message criticizing her school's new curriculum plan, an arbitrator held, because the employer had no rules for the use of its e-mail system. The librarian sent the message to 37 other librarians. Although the school principal had encouraged his staff to pursue outside resources for guidance regarding the curriculum changes, he objected to the librarian's negative tone in describing the plan and issued a written reprimand for her use of the school's e-mail system to air her personal opinions.

"It is well established that just cause requires that employees be informed of a rule, the infraction of which may result in disciplinary action, unless the conduct is so clearly wrong that specific reference is not necessary," the arbitrator said. In this case, the employer admitted that it had no rules on e-mail usage, and the librarian's conduct could not be characterized as a clear-cut or blatant misuse of the e-mail system, the arbitrator found. (*Conneaut School District*, 104 LA 909).

• In the case of an employee who had not been properly notified of his employer's Internet policy, termination was too severe a penalty for a sexually graphic e-mail, an arbitrator decided. Several workers in the employer's security department shared a computer. A female co-worker saw the graphic e-mail on a computer monitor that had been left on, and she was offended by it. After an investigation of the incident, the employee was terminated for violating the employer's Internet and sexual harassment policies. However, the union contended that the employee was charged with violating a policy he had never seen.

The employee's conduct did not justify termination, the arbitrator held, especially since there was no evidence that the employee had been given a copy of the Internet policy before the incident. Although his actions did violate the company's sexual harassment policy, of which he was aware, other workers who engaged in activities involving sexually graphic e-mail had only received suspensions, the arbitrator noted, ordering the employee reinstated without back pay (*PPG Industries Inc.*, 113 LA 833).

• An employer's lax enforcement of its e-mail policy prompted an arbitrator to overturn an employee's termination. As part of an investigation into sexual harassment allegations against another worker, the employer selectively reviewed the e-mail activities of certain personnel, including a manager who had sent numerous inappropriate messages to dozens of people. Many of them went to the employee, who in turn forwarded some of the messages to his home e-mail account. Following the investigation, the employee was the only member of the bargaining unit fired for sending and receiving inappropriate e-mails.

Emphasizing that e-mail violations were condoned and also committed on a regular basis by three managers with whom the employee dealt, the arbitrator reasoned that their conduct signaled tolerance of such actions and provided sufficient evidence of lax enforcement to preclude the employee's termination under the employer's e-mail policy. Moreover, the employer failed to consider the fact that the employee had limited his activity by sending inappropriate messages only to his home e-mail account, which meant that no co-workers could have been affected by those communications, the arbitrator said. Finding that the employer's treatment of the employee was fundamentally unfair, the arbitrator ordered reinstatement with back pay (*Snohomish County*, 115 LA 1).

• An employer that did not strictly or consistently enforce its e-mail policies lacked just cause to fire an employee over the distribution of an e-mail with sexual content, an arbitrator ruled. The e-mail originated with a supervisor, but the employee in turn shared the e-mail with three other workers. One or more of those workers also forwarded the e-mail, until eventually someone complained. When the company traced the message back to the employee, he was fired.

Although company guidelines prohibited such e-mails, the arbitrator found that past practice "completely negated" the company's posted policies. The arbitrator noted that supervisors commonly used the company's e-mail system to send sexually charged jokes and other inappropriate messages, which gave rank-and-file workers the right to believe that such actions were condoned by the company. In the case at hand, the employee sent an inappropriate e-mail to a limited number of co-workers, not anticipating that it would be forwarded on to others who might be offended. Deciding that the employee's offensive conduct was "entirely accidental," the arbitrator reduced his discipline to a three-day suspension (*Chevron Products Co.*, 116 LA 271).

• In another case, an arbitrator overturned the discharge of an employee who had committed earlier e-mail infractions but was not adequately warned that further violations would result in termination. Following an incident in which the employee e-mailed a racially offensive newsletter to company offices in China, he was counseled about various incidents in which he demonstrated insensitivity toward ethnic, gender, and diversity issues. The employee also was caught sending horse racing results through the employer's e-mail system and ordered to stop. The employee was subsequently fired after the employer discovered that in two weeks' worth of e-mails, only 10 percent of his messages were work-related, and the other e-mails included more racing results and references to the inappropriate newsletter he had previously sent.

According to the arbitrator, the employer failed to define "serious misconduct" sufficiently at the time of the first infractions to give the employee adequate warning that he could be fired immediately for any subsequent offenses. Consequently, the arbitrator overturned the discharge and ordered the employee reinstated under a last-chance agreement (*AlliedSignal Engines*, 106 LA 614).

• *By contrast*, an arbitrator held that an employee's termination for excessive Internet usage was justified where his employer had a clear policy against such conduct. After the employee's Internet usage became noticeable to his boss, she requested a 10-day review of his activities, which revealed that he was accessing the Internet for personal reasons at various times throughout the day. The employee had been advised that his employer's policy allowed limited personal use of the Internet during non-work time. In addition, he had previously received a suspension for misuse of computer resources and was warned that further problems would likely result in discharge. When confronted about his activities, the employee claimed he was technically in compliance with his employer's policy. Because he was entitled to a 30-minute lunch period and two 15-minute rest breaks, he argued, that gave him 60 minutes of non-work time that he could divide up for his personal Internet usage throughout the day.

The arbitrator rejected the employee's argument, pointing out that he did not track his time on the Internet, and the review of his online activities showed personal Internet usage in excess of 60 minutes on one of the days in question. Moreover, the arbitrator found that the collective bargaining agreement did not give employees unbridled freedom to take lunch and rest breaks whenever they wanted or to divide up the allotted time in any way they saw fit. Emphasizing the employee's awareness of the Internet policy and his prior discipline for computer misuse, the arbitrator held that discharge was warranted (*Department of Veterans Affairs*, 122 LA 106).

B. Social Media/Internet

Because the world of social media is evolving, employers often are confused about how to write policies protecting themselves and employees are unsure what they can post on Facebook, Twitter, or other forms of electronic communication on the Internet. Typically the conduct on social media or other websites is off-duty misconduct, a subject covered in Part 2, Chapter XVI. First Amendment and privacy issues may be raised as well.

● The Michigan Court of Appeals upheld the Michigan State Tenure Commission's reinstatement of a middle school teacher who was discharged because pictures of her simulated sex act with a mannequin—which were taken at a private party—were posted on the Internet and misinterpreted. The court deferred to the commission's expertise in holding that the adverse effects of the publicity from her off-duty conduct, which did not involve students, did not provide just cause for discipline (*Land v. L'Anse Creuse Public School Board of Education*, 30 IER Cases 1511 (Mich. Ct. App.) (unpublished)).

Two years earlier, in the same case, an arbitrator upheld the school board's right to suspend the teacher with pay pending the commission's hearing, but said that the school board did not have just cause to discipline the teacher (*L'Anse Creuse Public Schools*, 125 LA 527).

One arbitrator ruled that a Head Start program had just cause to discharge a teacher who created a Facebook page to complain about her workplace. Even though the employer did not have a specific social media policy at time, the employee's posts tended to undermine the working relationship with the center administrator, classroom partners, and parents of children in the classroom. Further, the arbitrator said, common sense should have told the grievant that she was engaging in conduct that would not have been approved of by co-workers or management (*Vista Nuevas Head Start*, 129 LA 1519).

● Another arbitrator ruled that an off-duty blog on MySpace aimed at an employee's German-born plant manager provided just cause for termination. The manager received an envelope addressed to the company containing a printout of the employee's blog, which stated, "Ask any [employee] what they think of the upper management. You might (hear) the words ... German, green card terminator or some other four letter words that I won't etch down on the scrolls. That's enough said on that subject. I could have sworn that Hitler committed

suicide. Is there such a thing as reincarnation?"

The employee was terminated for off-duty conduct creating a hostile work environment and harassment. The union noted that the blog did not name the manager, who in fact did not testify at arbitration, and maintained that there is no work rule prohibiting alleged inappropriate use of a personal computer at home and that harassment prohibitions only apply on company premises. Noting that the mechanic's supervisor was the only German-born manager at the facility, the arbitrator said that "harassing conduct directed at a supervisor certainly amounts to insubordination" and denied the grievance entirely (*Baker Hughes Inc.*, 128 LA 37).

● A grievant's Facebook message to his mother-in-law stating that he would "see [father-in-law] at the plant" and to "watch for me" did not constitute a material breach of his last-chance agreement, which defined a violation as engaging in "any conduct related to any disciplinary offenses on his record," an arbitrator ruled. He had no such similar offense, and the statement that this was his "final opportunity" to become a satisfactory employee did not create an independent violation, the arbitrator found, but said the grievant's conduct merited a 30-day suspension (*U.S. Steel Corp.* 130 LA 461).

C. Sexual or Obscene Content

When employees misuse computer resources by engaging in activities that involve sexual or obscene content, their conduct can have a number of adverse effects on their employers. In addition to reducing their own productivity, employees who spend time at work viewing, downloading, sending, or receiving sexually explicit content can disrupt the efficiency of co-workers, expose workplace computers to viruses, and overload employer networks. If e-mail or Internet abuses result in co-workers receiving or viewing sexually explicit content against their will, employees' inappropriate activities also can create a hostile work environment and give rise to sexual harassment claims.

Arbitrators do not necessarily put such conduct on a par with other workplace behaviors—such as violence, theft, and gross insubordination—that are so discredited as to warrant summary dismissal. Nevertheless, discharge is commonly upheld for employees who egregiously or repeatedly misuse company-provided computers, Internet access, or e-mail systems for activities involving sexual content.

• An employer had just cause to discharge an employee who downloaded pornography from the Internet and introduced sexually explicit material into the company's e-mail system, some of which was sent to friends outside the company, an arbitrator ruled. In firing the employee, the employer cited policies that barred workers from using the company computer, e-mail, and Internet resources to seek, send, or receive pornographic material. Claiming that such conduct had gone unchecked for a long time, the union argued that the employer provided inadequate notice that the employee's activities could result in discharge.

The arbitrator rejected the union's argument. "Employees received repeated instructions regarding limitations with the computer system and they had to be aware that the Company took pornography in the workplace very seriously," the arbitrator said. Even though other workers received lesser discipline for their part in sending and receiving inappropriate material, the employee's abuse was flagrant and repeated. The arbitrator added that the company had a right to keep its computer system clean and efficient, and "its abhorrence of the misuse of its computers on its time is perfectly acceptable" (*A. E. Staley Manufacturing Co.*, 119 LA 1371).

• An employer properly discharged an employee for his regular access during work of pornographic websites with violent content, an arbitrator ruled. Following an investigation of office Internet use, the employer disciplined 25 workers for accessing, viewing, and distributing adult content during the workday via the Web and e-mail. The employee in question claimed that he was singled out for termination because he was the only one who accessed violent pornography.

The arbitrator said the employer used a "rational, systematic plan" to evaluate the Internet policy violations and to mete out discipline. For example, the employer considered it more serious to send than to receive pornographic e-mails, and even more serious to actively search the Web for pornographic material. The employer could reasonably conclude that "more offensive misuse warranted a more severe penalty," the arbitrator found. Determining that the employer "reasonably applied a carefully considered and rational set of factors" to the employee's conduct, the arbitrator upheld discharge (*State of Minnesota Department of Administration*, 117 LA 1569).

• An employee was properly discharged after she called over her co-workers to look at an obscene e-mail, an arbitrator held. The content of the e-mail prompted complaints to management by a number of the employee's co-workers. The employer subsequently fired the employee based on the e-mail incident, her record of using vulgar language and making sexual comments in the presence of co-workers, and her extensive prior discipline and repeated warnings for inappropriate language and other misconduct.

The e-mail incident violated the employer's policies on unlawful harassment and computer misuse, the arbitrator found. Considering that incident along with the employee's other misbehavior—which had a disruptive effect, created an environment "charged with tension and stress," and seriously impaired the morale of co-workers—the arbitrator determined that discharge was justified (*Nord Center*, 121 LA 1158).

• An employer had just cause to discharge an employee who used the Internet at work to access pornography involving minors, an arbitrator decided. The employer audited the employee's Internet activities after someone complained that he was viewing child pornography. The audit revealed that in the span of one day the employee spent several hours on the Internet visiting a number of sexually explicit websites, some of which depicted girls that appeared to be under the age of 18. In contesting the employee's subsequent termination, the union pointed out that another worker had been allowed to retain his employment with a one-year probationary period after viewing sexual content on the Internet.

The case at hand differed from that of the worker who retained his job, the arbitrator said, because the employee was fired not only for accessing inappropriate sites, but for visiting sites that showed minors in pornographic displays. Adding that the employee assumed the risk that he would be viewing illegal content when he accessed sites with names like "Uncensored Teens" and "Wet Girls," the arbitrator held that termination was justified (*Xcel Energy*, 119 LA 26).

● An arbitrator upheld the suspension of an employee who amassed more than 1,300 hits on sexually explicit websites while investigating his employer's Internet access policy. Although workers' access to sexually explicit sites was previously blocked, the employer unilaterally changed its policy by allowing open access but relying on Internet monitoring to detect workers' visits to such sites. The employee, who served as the local union president, went to the office on two Sundays to use the Internet and check if the employer had changed its policy without the union's involvement. The employee subsequently informed the employer that he planned to file a grievance over the Internet access policy. Three weeks after that, he was confronted about the websites he had visited. The employer eventually gave him a five-day suspension.

Without delving into the propriety of the employer's policy change, which was the subject of a separate grievance, the arbitrator rejected the employee's argument that his Internet activities were acceptable because they related to union business. The employee said he conducted his investigation during off hours to avoid exposing co-workers to sexually explicit content. However, his numerous hits on more than 30 websites "went far beyond" what was necessary to determine that the employer had changed its policy, the arbitrator said in upholding the suspension (*U.S. Department of Agriculture*, 118 LA 1212).

By contrast, some arbitrators have been reluctant to discharge employees who download pornography because the proof was ambiguous, in that it is possible the pornography was in the form of pop-ups.

● One arbitrator ruled that an employer did not have just cause to discharge an employee after they discovered child pornography on his computer. Police personnel and the union's expert concluded that the few pornographic images found on the computer were not placed there by the grievant, but could have been pop-up advertisements. The employee's job involved data analysis, programming, and Internet usage (*AK Steel*, 125 LA 903).

● One arbitrator reduced the discharge of a 15-year employee who downloaded pornography to a suspension. The arbitrator was unwilling to discipline with discharge for a first offense, and the employee did not save the pornography on the internal intranet, nor did he e-mail it within or outside of the plant (*BASF Catalysts LLC*, 129 LA 571).

● An arbitrator reduced the discharge of an employee for sending "thousands" of sexually related texts to co-workers to a long-term suspension, because the employee admitted that what he did was wrong, said he would not repeat it, and was a long-time employee who was first the person "caught" under a new company policy (*Sara Lee Foods*, 128 LA 129).

D. Offensive or Discriminatory Content

As is the case with computer-related activities involving sexually explicit content, conduct that involves offensive or discriminatory content also can give rise to grave discipline. Arbitrators generally uphold severe consequences for such conduct, recognizing its potential to disrupt the workplace and create liability risks for employers.

● A city had just cause to discipline an employee who used the city's computer while on duty to access and print offensive and discriminatory racial and ethnic "jokes," an arbitrator ruled. The employee had previously shown disregard for city policies, but his suspension of 20 work days was reduced to a five-day suspension, because the employee did not intend to make that material available to other employees and had inadvertently left four pages jammed in the copier (*City of Fort Lauderdale*, 125 LA 1249).

● Discharge was warranted for an employee who went on the Internet at work and printed out a poster from a white supremacist hate group, an arbitrator decided. After the employee hung the poster on a workplace bulletin board, his employer investigated his computer activities. The employee was subsequently fired for violating various policies, including a ban on accessing content of a "discriminatory or offensive nature."

The employee "egregiously and repeatedly" violated his employer's rules against the misuse of company computer equipment by intentionally accessing numerous hate sites and other inappropriate content on the Internet, the arbitrator found. Adding that hanging a poster from a hate group contributed to a hostile work environment, the arbitrator upheld the employee's termination (*Tesoro Refining & Marketing Co.*, 120 LA 1299).

● An employer was justified in firing a worker for posting racist messages on an external website, an arbitrator held. The employee, who admitted to engaging in personal use of the Internet at work for up to an hour a day, was found to have sent racially derogatory messages to a "chat room." Citing other harassment charges against the worker in the previous year, the employer said she both violated its anti-harassment policies and ignored its explicit warnings against harassing others. In her defense, the employee claimed that she did not know that her messages could be traced back to the company. In addition, the union argued that the employee had a bipolar condition that contributed to her behavior.

In upholding the termination, the arbitrator said that the employee's defense was not valid because her repeated sending of offensive e-mails flouted previous warnings and was not the sort of spontaneous, impulsive behavior that could be explained by her bipolar condition (*M T Detroit Inc.*, 118 LA 1777).

● A five-day suspension was appropriate for an employee who used company e-mail to distribute copies of a calendar containing denigrating photos of obese and disabled people, an arbitrator held. The union argued that although the calendar was offensive, suspension was excessive given the employee's 35 years of service and the company's tolerance of widespread use of its e-mail system for purposes unrelated to work. The arbitrator upheld the suspension, accepting the employer's argument that the calendar violated company anti-discrimination policies and citing a lack of evidence that offensive materials had been e-mailed in the past without disciplinary consequences. The arbitrator also found that mitigation of the employee's discipline on the basis of seniority would "establish an unacceptable standard" (*Southern California Edison*, 117 LA 1066).

E. Computer Control Issues

The extent of management's control over workplace computers and systems sometimes comes into question as a result of conflicts involving computer security or counterproductive behavior on the part of individual employees. Recognizing the right of management to assert control over company computers, arbitrators commonly uphold discipline where employees abuse their technological know-how by violating access rights or engaging in activities that undermine co-workers or management.

● An employer had just cause to discharge an employee who used the company Internet to illegally download copyrighted full-length movies onto his own personal laptop, monopolizing 88.42 percent of the available company's bandwidth during the third shift. Upholding the discharge, the arbitrator determined that the grievant violated several company rules: misappropriating the company's Internet system to download movies, in violation of rules regarding theft or misappropriation of company property; misuse of company property, by personally employing the company's Internet system to engage in illegal conduct; and "unauthorized entry into company property (*Hayes International*, 129 LA 559).

● An employee was properly discharged for accessing management computer files, an arbitrator ruled. Not only did the employee access the confidential and privileged files of management officials, but he printed out some of the files, shared the information with co-workers, and also taught other employees how to access the files. According to the arbitrator, the dissemination of this information caused mischief and undermined the morale of management and rank-and-file employees. Although improper access to the files might have been understandable if it happened once or twice, said the arbitrator, the evidence showed that the employee spent six to eight hours per week accessing the files over a period of several months, which takes on a "far more serious dimension." Concluding that the employee's conduct "caused an irreparable breach" in the employer-employee relationship, the arbitrator upheld termination (*Hoosier Energy Rural Electric Cooperative Inc.*, 116 LA 1043; see also 93 LA 969).

● Just cause existed to discharge a computer programmer who undermined the work of fellow employees in the way he ran his employer's computer system, an arbitrator ruled. The employer had received complaints about the programmer's work habits and had told him he could no longer shut the system down without prior approval and advance warning to other employees. The employer eventually brought in a computer specialist to analyze the system, and he discovered various irregularities in the programmer's work. At that point, the arbitrator said, the programmer knew "he would never again have a free rein to run the system the way he had in the past." The programmer's termination was prompted shortly thereafter by an improper system shutdown that caused the loss of several hours worth of work. Finding that the employee intentionally caused the loss of data, the arbitrator decided that his continued employment would have been a deterrent to his employer's effectiveness and efficiency (*El Toro Marine Air Station*, 102 LA 685).

● Another arbitrator overturned the discharge of an employee who accessed files that had been stored on his employer's network by a worker in the information systems department. While exploring the internal network, the employee accessed the files and found a program called "Splitter." He downloaded a copy of the program because he thought it would help him manage his own computer data. He also found a file containing pornographic pictures. He accessed the files again later to report his findings to a shop steward. The employee's supervisor, with whom the employee had a strained relationship, fired him for violating computer security rules, contending that he "hacked" into the other worker's files and downloaded unauthorized software when he copied the "Splitter" program.

After eight and one-half years with an exemplary record, the employee became subject to a pattern of harassment at the hands of his new supervisor, the arbitrator found. The employee's exploration of the company's internal network, which led to the access of the inappropriate files, was done with assurances from his supervisor that such activities were permitted, the arbitrator noted, adding that there was nothing clandestine or malicious in the employee's actions. According to the arbitrator, the employee should have been commended for reporting what he had discovered, but instead his supervisor "recklessly used the information as a sword by which to nail the grievant." Concluding that the employee was wrongfully discharged, the arbitrator ordered reinstatement with back pay and benefits, plus interest (*Boeing-Irving Co.*, 113 LA 699).

● An employer lacked just cause to fire an employee for dragging his feet in complying with a new policy that prohibited personal passwords on company computers, an arbitrator decided. Following an incident in which some supervisors were impeded by an unknown password when they wanted to perform a computer operation, the company decided that personal passwords would no longer be allowed. Management asked a union committeeman to inform the employee and other workers of the policy. A manager subsequently discovered that the employee still had a password on his computer, and the union president said he would speak with the employee. The next day, the employee discussed the matter with a supervisor. According to the supervisor, the employee said he still had the password in place and would not remove it until he got an explanation of the reason behind the request.

However, the employee did remove the password later that same day.

The employer characterized the employee's actions as "grossly insubordinate," but the arbitrator disagreed. While acknowledging that the employee did not comply with the new policy upon receiving notice of it, the arbitrator said "it is axiomatic that a Union Committeeman cannot give a direct order to a bargaining unit employee that he is duty bound to obey upon pain of being discharged." When the employee did discuss the matter with a supervisor, he made a "somewhat defiant statement" about not removing the password, but even that conversation was "bereft of any element of a direct order," the arbitrator found. Deciding that the employee could not be charged with insubordination, the arbitrator ordered reinstatement with back pay (*Saint Gobain Norpro*, 116 LA 960).

F. Cell Phone Usage

To address concerns about productivity and safety issues, many employers impose restrictions on cell phone usage at work.

● A county had just cause to issue a one-day suspension to an assistant prosecuting attorney who spent part of the time she was in juvenile court using her cell phone to send text messages. The arbitrator considered this to be "unprofessional conduct." (*Wayne County*, 127 LA 874).

1. Workplace Security Issues

Some industries, such as airports and prisons, strictly prohibit the use of cell phones for security reasons, and the penalty for violation is often discharge.

● One arbitrator upheld the discharge of an airport custodian who used a company-provided cell phone 46 times to call Haiti following the devastating earthquake in Haiti in January 2010. His primary motive was to check on his mother, whose leg was broken in the earthquake. The employee handbook stated that personal calls be authorized only for use in case of an emergency, such as fire or a life-threatening situation, unless prohibited by the airport. The employee handbook further stated that unauthorized calls that resulted in a monetary charge were the responsibility of the em-

ployee who made the call and that any violations could result in disciplinary action, up to and including termination. The custodian believed his use of the employer's phone imposed no financial cost to the employer because he used prepaid phone cards that he purchased for approximately $2 each. The cards, however, proved insufficient to cover all charges for the calls, resulting in a $442 discrepancy in the usual phone bill of the employer.

The employee was aware that there was a telephone policy in the employer's work rules and that he was also violating airport security, but he had no intent to steal from the employer. Although the arbitrator found the employee was not in violation of the employer's theft policy, the arbitrator denied the grievance and let the termination stand because the grievant "engaged in a pattern of wrongfully utilizing the employer's cell phone." (*N & K Enterprises*, 128 LA 688).

● Discipline of a correctional officer who brought a cell phone to the facility was with just cause, despite his contention that cell phones in the facility were commonplace, where he knew that they were prohibited by rule and it was a criminal misdemeanor to possess a cell phone in jail without authorization. Rather than conform to the rules, the grievant clearly decided to flaunt the rules. He openly showed his cell phone to another employee to demonstrate a new game he had on the phone, and he actively used his cell phone to send and receive text messages throughout the day while on duty. The arbitrator found the grievant's conduct conveyed a disregard for the employer's rules and had the potential effect of underming the employer's authority (*Solano County Sheriff's Department*, 129 LA 449).

By contrast, another arbitrator ruled that a 10-year airline ramp agent who violated work rules by using a cell phone for emergency medical reasons should be disciplined with a simple oral warning rather than a final written warning. The agent, who had spoken with the physician treating his fiancee, who was undergoing chemotherapy for cancer, called his finacee to tell her what the doctor said. The worker was accused in part of violating the employer's cell phone work rules, and in light of two related warnings over cell phone use in the past, given a final written warning.

In reducing discipline to an oral warning, the arbitrator reasoned that "the grievant was in the rear of an aircraft when he used his cell phone" and could not be seen by the company's customers, was not in any immediate danger and could not cause harm to others by using his cell phone, and the call occurred when he could not unload the aircraft, because he had to wait for a co-worker to arrive (*Southwest Airlines*, 128 LA 1628).

2. Drivers

● An employer had just cause to discharge a driver of a bus for developmentally disabled passengers who took a personal cell phone call while driving in violation of an employer rule, even though she had a very good work record and the call she received was about her mother's illness, an arbitrator ruled. The grievant had been warned not to use her cell phone when operating her vehicle, her inattention resulted in a citizen complaint to the agency that works with developmentally disabled passengers, its superintendent testified he would no longer permit the grievant to drive its clients, and the phone call was not an emergency (*First Transit Inc.*, 128 LA 586).

● An employer properly fired an employee who used a cell phone while driving a bus, a board of arbitrators ruled. The employee had received counseling and discipline for a prior cell phone violation and other misconduct, yet she repeated the same infractions a few weeks later. In upholding the employee's termination, the board of arbitrators said the decision was based on an "overall performance record that reflects a pattern of unwillingness to conform to critical work rules that serve to ensure the safe operation of her bus" (*Kansas City Area Transportation Authority*, 127 LA 1196).

● *By contrast*, an arbitrator held that another employer did not have just cause to fire a driver after a supervisor saw him using a cell phone while operating a bus. The employer had a policy restricting the unauthorized personal use of cell phones while on duty, and it claimed that the driver's actions posed obvious safety risks. However, the employee said he only used the cell phone because the radio on his bus was not working and he was trying to reach the dispatcher. Based on the evidence presented, the arbitrator said it was more likely than not that the employee had given an accurate account of what happened, and therefore the charge against him was not supported (*Winston-Salem Transit*, 123 LA 1185).

● An employee with a prior record of safety infractions was improperly fired after being accused of improper use of a cell phone, an arbitrator decided. In ordering reinstatement with back pay, the arbitrator noted that the employer permitted other workers to make limited use of cell phones on the job, and the purpose of the employee's call, which was to discuss his child's school problems, had to be considered a legitimate reason for using the phone (*Tremco Inc.*, 124 LA 229).

X. Gambling [LA CDI 100.552527 (public employees); 118.650]

OVERVIEW

Gambling of some type occurs in most organizations, typically consisting of relatively innocuous activities, such as sports pools, but occasionally involving serious criminal conduct, as in the case of organized "numbers" rackets. In deciding on discipline for alleged on-premises gambling, arbitrators typically consider a couple of key factors.

• Was the evidence connecting employees to the gambling substantial and convincing? Arbitrators look to see if the evidence supports charges that workers have engaged in prohibited activities on company property or time (95 LA 148, 51 LA 707, 45 LA 247, 41 LA 823, 39 LA 859, 18 LA 938, 12 LA 699).

• Did the nature of the offense justify the penalty? Although some gambling activities warrant severe discipline, arbitrators are not likely to uphold termination for a first offense in the absence of egregious misconduct (95 LA 937, 52 LA 945, 49 LA 1262, 28 LA 97, 22 LA 210, 16 LA 727, 12 LA 21). Similarly, even though employers might tolerate sports pools or holiday turkey raffles, that does not prevent them from cracking down on employees involved in illegal bookmaking or numbers operations (33 LA 175, 22 LA 210, 17 LA 150, 13 LA 235).

SUMMARY OF CASES

A. Rationale for Discipline

Management is within its right to promulgate and enforce rules against on-premises gambling, most arbitrators concur, because, as one employer put it, "organization and morale would be seriously affected" if such activity were permitted. As phrased by the employer in that case, "the evils which run concurrently with gambling, namely ill feeling, cheating, fighting, and the lure of 'easy money,' could disintegrate a highly productive workforce and reduce its efficiency beyond measure." If the "company and its employees are to reap the benefits of successful operation," that employer emphasized, "any factors which curtail industrial efficiency and production must be completely eliminated" (*Brown Shoe Co.*, 16 LA 461).

Based on similar reasoning, arbitrators have upheld discipline where employers are able to show that workers engaged in gambling on company premises, even though they may have been on their own time.

• A worker who engages in illegal activity on company property—even during his free time—is not carrying out his responsibilities as an employee, according to one arbitrator. Although management was unable to prove that the worker in this case was writing numbers on company time, the arbitrator upheld the discharge because the "numbers slips" found on the employee demonstrated that he was conducting his activities at the plant.

Dismissing the worker's arguments that the discharge was unwarranted because the activity took place "off-the-clock," the arbitrator declared that "during all times that an employee is on company property, he must be deemed to be an employee" and must "conduct himself properly in discharging his responsibilities as such employee." In short, the arbitrator concluded, the worker, while at the plant, "may not engage in illegal activities whether he does so on his 'free time' or not and whether he uses company property (i.e., a company telephone) or not in order to further his illegal activities" (*Jones & Laughlin Steel Corp.*, 29 LA 778).

• Another arbitrator sustained the discharge of an employee for running an illegal numbers racket on company property, despite evidence that he conducted the gambling on his own time. Because the gambling took place inside the plant, it was "inextricably bound up with his employment status," the arbitrator ruled (*Bethlehem Steel Co.*, 45 LA 646).

• In contrast, an arbitration board overruled the dismissal of another employee who was arrested on company property with numbers slips in his possession and who subsequently pleaded guilty to a gambling charge. Dismissing management's allegations that the existence of the slips showed that the worker had engaged in the illegal activity on its premises, the board concluded that such possession did not constitute clear proof that "there had been gambling or accepting of wagers" by the worker on company property (*Jenkins Bros.*, 45 LA 247).

• Even though an employer had clear proof of gambling at work, inadequate warning about the possible consequences of such conduct prompted an arbitrator to overturn an employee's discharge. Based on an anonymous tip, a management representative went to the company's plant one night and obtained photographic evidence of the employee and some supervisors gambling at cards on company time. All of them lost their jobs. However, the arbitrator noted that the company handbook contained no proscriptions about gambling. In fact, many employees at the plant bet on Super Bowls, lotteries, etc., and the winners of these bets were posted at the time clock. Although gambling is a serious offense, "the fact that the supervisors were participants lent an aura of permissiveness to the gambling," the arbitrator added, ordering the employee reinstated without back pay (*Yokohama Tire Corp.*, 117 LA 5).

B. Nature of the Offense

1. Organized Gambling

Generally, organized gambling is viewed as a serious offense by arbitrators. Given that charges of criminal conduct may be involved, however, arbitrators require that management meet stringent standards of proof to sustain a discharge decision. Thus, where an employee was apprehended with hundreds of dollars in small bills and change and a sheet of lottery numbers, an arbitrator upheld his discharge (*Bethlehem Steel Co.*, 45 LA 646).

• Another arbitrator decided that an employee's guilty plea to charges of illegal gambling on company property was just cause for discharge, because the employee's otherwise good work record did not outweigh the fact of his misconduct (*Jenkins Bros.*, 45 LA 350).

• The discharge of an employee for allegedly engaging in a numbers racket on company time and property was set aside by an arbitrator because management failed to meet its burden of proof. While agreeing with the employer regarding the "harmful effects of playing numbers," the arbitrator declared that he did not "believe an employee, especially one with long seniority, should lose his job for engaging in the numbers racket, unless there is substantial and convincing proof that the employee did so act" (*Chrysler Corp.*, 12 LA 699).

2. Unorganized Gambling

On the other hand, unorganized gambling meets with greater leniency from arbitrators.

● Employees involved in a "check pool" on company time and property were improperly discharged, an arbitrator decided, despite a work rule prohibiting on-premises gambling. Although the employer argued that termination was justified under a rule intended to guarantee that standards of "good conduct" were followed, the arbitrator said the rule was not properly applied in the case at hand, given that the pool was not shown to be detrimental to these standards. In addition, management properly should have followed its own policy of issuing warnings for violations of conduct rules instead of terminating the workers for a first offense, the arbitrator said (*Black Diamond Enterprises Inc.*, 52 LA 945).

● A board of arbitration upheld the discharge of three employees caught playing poker. Dismissing the workers' protests, the board pointed out that management twice before had warned them about gambling on company time and property (*Brown Shoe Co.*, 16 LA 461).

XI. Garnishment [LA CDI 118.641]

OVERVIEW

When garnishment plunges employers into the midst of employees' personal financial difficulties, it can create various clerical and administrative headaches for employers.

Contemplating the burdens associated with garnishment, one arbitrator said it is natural that employers would want "to avoid the time, inconvenience, and expense of extra bookkeeping, extra accounting procedures, the necessity to file written returns with the attaching officer, as well as the additional trust liability for the funds that [they are] required to hold and [their] statutory liability for any failure to hold and to pay according to the instructions of the attaching officer" (*American Brass Co.*, 35 LA 139).

Nevertheless, arbitrators have expressed differing views on how much is too much when it comes to garnishment. For example, a rule permitting discipline for repeated garnishments was found unreasonable by one arbitrator to the extent that it conflicted with statutory protections for employees (*PMC Specialties Group*, 97 LA 444), whereas other arbitrators have accepted rules providing that more than one garnishment would constitute grounds for discharge.

The federal Consumer Credit Protection Act makes it unlawful to discharge employees for garnishment from a single indebtedness, first-time tax levies, Chapter 13 bankruptcy orders, and family or child support orders. Many state laws are more expansive, in that they do not mirror the CCPA's "single indebtedness" limit with regard to protecting employees against discharge for garnishments.

To be upheld at arbitration, a rule on garnishment not only needs to conform with statutory requirements, it also must be:

• reasonably predicated on saving employers from inconvenience, cost, liability, or the imposition of other serious burdens;

• reasonable in terms of the penalty assessed for infractions;

• applied without bias; and

• clear, unambiguous, and known by employees (*General Telephone Co. of Wisconsin*, 48 LA 1331).

Even when these conditions are met, arbitrators sometimes find that extenuating or mitigating circumstances warrant overturning or reducing the discipline imposed by employers. Such circumstances might include situations where employees lacked knowledge of the debts in question, had compiled otherwise unmarred work records, made arrangements to discharge their debts or resolve wage attachments, or fell into debt because of income losses caused by chronic layoffs.

SUMMARY OF CASES

A. Rules and Warnings

Rules and warnings are two items that arbitrators typically look for in reviewing garnishment-related cases. Arbitrators are unlikely to overturn discipline carried out in accordance with garnishment rules that have been properly implemented and consistently enforced. Even if employers lack specific rules on the subject, discipline probably will be upheld for employees who have been warned but have failed to take remedial action to address their garnishment problems.

• A union employer had just and sufficient cause to discharge a receptionist for blocking her employer's receipt of three notices garnishing her wages, an arbitrator ruled, even thought there was no direct evidence of wrongdoing. The arbitrator found that it was highly unlikely that the three notices were not delivered due to random happenstance, as the employer's incoming mail went through the receptionist, she was experiencing severe financial problems, and she knew that the debtor was going to be garnishing her wages. However because the employer failed to provide her with a 30-day written notice of its intent to discharge her per the collective bargaining agreement, the arbitrator ruled the employer must provide back pay for the number of days its notice was deficient. This was despite the argument that an exception was called for due to the receptionist's egregious conduct, because the agreement provided no exceptions to the 30-day notice requirement (*United Teachers-Los Angeles*, 128 LA 491).

• An employer's failure to enter into negotiations over a garnishment rule prompted an arbitrator to strike down the rule. The employer had unilaterally implemented a rule change calling for the discipline of employees who incurred more than one wage garnishment within 36 months, but the union did not learn of the rule or the discipline imposed by the employer for excessive garnishments until a member of the bargaining unit complained about it. According to the arbitrator, the collective bargaining agreement between the parties not only mentioned union negotiations in connection with new or modified rules, it also required the employer to engage in negotiations before making any changes in working conditions. Finding that the employer skipped this step in violation of the contract, the arbitrator rescinded the rule and overturned disciplinary actions the employer had imposed under it (*City of Cincinnati*, 122 LA 622).

• An employer properly discharged an employee who violated a plant rule by causing three garnishments to be served on the employer within 12 months. The rule was reasonable, according to the arbitrator, because the employer was not obligated to undertake the administrative burden of dealing with employees' financial problems outside of work (*Federal Paper Board Co. Inc.*, 60 LA 924).

• One arbitrator upheld an employee's discharge in the absence of a rule concerning garnishments. After the employee had received counseling and verbal warnings over his repeated garnishments, his employer issued a written warning that said a "recurrence of two garnishments in one week will result in immediate termination." The employee subsequently was discharged for violating this provision. Stressing that the employer had attempted to assist the employee in his financial difficulties through counseling, the arbitrator said discharge was justified when the employee continued to show irresponsibility and created administrative expense for his employer (*Lear Siegler Inc.*, 63 LA 1157).

• An employer acted within its rights in discharging an employee whose wages were garnished three times in less than four years, an arbitrator ruled. The employee argued that the dismissal was unlawful, interpreting a labor secretary opinion letter to hold that if an interval between garnishments exceeds one year, discharge based on the second levy would constitute termination for one garnishment. Noting that the Consumer Credit Protection Act protects "those with only one indebtedness on which garnishments have been issued," the arbitrator said it was "impossible to read into it any protection for the employee who has had multiple garnishments for multiple indebtednesses." The employee had been counseled after the first garnishment, warned after the second that an additional levy would result in dismissal, and given a week in which to prove his claim that the third wage order was in error, the arbitrator noted, adding that "there was certainly nothing precipitous about management's action in this case" (*BBC Manufactured Buildings Inc.*, 77 LA 1132).

• An arbitrator upheld a three-day suspension imposed on an employee for incurring eight garnishment orders in as many months. The employee was a "chronic offender in the area of garnishments," the arbitrator noted, pointing out that one year previously, he had been given a one-day suspension for incurring five wage attachments. Furthermore, prior to the latest suspension, the employee had been warned by management that additional orders would result "in discipline up to and including discharge." Observing that the employee "made no effort to seek outside help in the form of personal bankruptcy or a trusteeship to take care of his financial problems" until the employer was faced with yet another garnishment order, the arbitrator concluded that the suspension was reasonable (*Diem and Wing Paper Co.*, 72 LA 850).

• An employer had cause to fire an employee whose indebtedness resulted in multiple court orders and garnishments, an arbitrator held. Management counseled the employee about his financial problems and finally warned him that one more garnishment order would result in discharge. When another order was issued and the employee was terminated, he protested that it was unfair to fire someone for being in "a financial bind." The arbitrator upheld the discharge, noting that the employee "entangled" the employer "in the mesh" of his problems "throughout virtually the entire period" of his employment. Just as "employees resist employer control and discipline for off-premises, nonwork related incidents," the arbitrator concluded, so "employers should have a corollary right to be free from measurable expense and involvement" in employees' personal problems (*Shawnee Plastics Inc.*, 71 LA 832).

• An arbitrator ruled that an employer had just cause to discharge an employee who refused to make peace with the Internal Revenue Service, which had issued a levy against his wages. Based on his belief that the withholding of income taxes was unconstitutional, the employee submitted a tax form claiming 14 dependents, none of whom he had. In addition, he threatened to sue the employer if it withheld any money from his paycheck. The employee argued that the Consumer Credit Protection Act precluded his firing over the garnishment, and he claimed that he had made a tax protest that was protected by the First Amendment to the U.S. Constitution. The arbitrator rejected those arguments and upheld discharge. Noting that the employer had a legal obligation to comply with the dictates of the IRS, the arbitrator said the employee had "no right to impose the consequences" of his philosophy about income taxes upon the employer (*Las Vegas Building Materials Inc.*, 83 LA 998).

• A company was justified in discharging an employee who had only one garnishment but also had caused numerous delinquent credit complaints to be sent to the company, despite management's repeated counseling, an arbitrator ruled. The employee protested that the termination violated the Consumer Credit Protection Act's prohibition against discharge for garnishment for one indebtedness, but the arbitrator found that the single garnishment was not the sole reason for the termination. Emphasizing that "the cause of termination was a protracted record of financial irresponsibility" that had caused unreasonable demands to be placed on the company, the arbitrator said federal law could not be construed so as to make the employee "invulnerable to consequences of unacceptable patterns of behavior" (*Continental Air Lines Inc.*, 57 LA 31; see also 77 LA 1132, 72 LA 850, 71 LA 832).

B. Disciplinary Actions Overturned

Arbitrators sometimes find that employers have improperly invoked the penalty of discharge against employees in garnishment-related cases.

● One arbitrator ruled that management had no right to fire an employee whose pay was garnished for three weeks in a row under a single court order. Workers whose wages were attached were punished by warnings for the first two offenses and discharge for the third. In this case, the arbitrator held that three withholdings under one court order could not be considered three separate offenses (*Bagwell Steel Co. Inc.*, 41 LA 303; see also 71 LA 538).

● Discharge was not warranted for an employee who was the subject of two garnishment orders in less than two weeks, an arbitrator decided. The employer had a rule calling for a warning after one garnishment and immediate discharge after a second. However, the employee's situation was governed by a state law that allowed no more than one garnishment to be carried out against a worker within a 30-day period, which meant that the second garnishment "became a nullity" when it was received by the employer so shortly after the first, the arbitrator determined. Concluding that the employer could not legally fire the employee on the basis of only one valid garnishment, the arbitrator ordered reinstatement with back pay (*Columbus Nursing Home Inc.*, 82 LA 1004).

● Discharge also was overturned by another arbitrator, despite 21 garnishments against an employee. In this case, the employer admitted that its rule on the matter was not usually applied in such instances and would not have been invoked except for other complaints against the employee, including poor attendance and criminal misconduct (*Rexall Drug Co.*, 65 LA 1101).

● Another arbitrator decided that termination was improper where an employer's warning to an employee about his garnishments was clouded by a conversation concerning an unrelated suspension. In overturning discharge, the arbitrator also noted that management had delayed a month before communicating with the union about the employee's possible discharge (*Virginia American Waterworks*, 63 LA 912).

1. Extenuating Circumstances

Extenuating or mitigating circumstances sometimes lead arbitrators to overturn terminations for garnishment. In one case, for example, an arbitrator nullified an employee's termination for three wage attachments because of circumstances that included family illness (*American Airlines Inc.*, 47 LA 108).

● An employer improperly discharged an employee for incurring two garnishments, an arbitrator ruled, despite a work rule providing that more than one garnishment would constitute just cause for discharge without warning. The termination "fell short of what was 'just,'" the arbitrator found, because of four extenuating factors: the employee had a good record; the garnishments resulted from debts that the employee had merely co-signed; management failed to inform the employee of possible programs for making voluntary wage deductions or to help him in any other way, as it had done with another employee in similar circumstances; and the employee had since "demonstrated his responsibility by diligently paying off debts on a basis accountable to the creditors" (*Delta Concrete Products Co.*, 71 LA 538).

XII. Horseplay [LA CDI 100.552510 (public employees); 118.645]

OVERVIEW

When addressing incidents of employee horseplay or practical jokes, arbitrators often make a distinction between lighthearted frivolity that involves only a remote possibility of injury and conduct that involves malicious intent or a high risk of harm. Even if the latter type of conduct does not have injurious consequences, it typically warrants a harsher penalty than more benign horseplay.

SUMMARY OF CASES

A. Severity of Conduct

The following arbitration rulings illustrate the distinction between relatively harmless horseplay or practical jokes and conduct that is more serious in nature.

• A non-union employer substantially followed its policies and procedures when it discharged an employee who drove a company golf cart into a high pile of sand, an arbitrator ruled, despite the contention that the employee's conduct was mere horseplay that should merit a final warning. The arbitrator reasoned that golf carts are known to be unstable and potentially dangerous vehicles, piles of sand are inherently unstable, the grievant risked the possibility of serious injury to himself or his passenger, and he risked serious damage to the machine parts of the cart (*Target Corp.*, 128 LA 1665).

• A hotel had just cause to discharge an employee for affixing two fake security cameras to the ceiling of a work room, even though the employee admitted the act and said she intended no harm but wanted to play a "practical joke" on co-workers,

where the act was premeditated, the only plausible motivation was to scare, aggravate, or otherwise disrupt employees on the following shift, the conduct contributed to a "tense" environment among workers, and discharge served the hotel's legitimate business interest in deterring similar conduct (*Greenbriar Hotel Corp.* 129 LA 371).

• Discharge was appropriate for an employee who flung a 63-year-old co-worker over his shoulder and carried him the length of the plant where they worked, causing serious injury to the older man's back, an arbitrator ruled. In addition to acknowledging the employer's duty to protect the safety of its workers, the arbitrator noted that the employer had a rule providing for disciplinary action up to termination for horseplay or unsafe behavior. Although other workers had received lesser forms of discipline for incidents of horseplay, the arbitrator found that those incidents did not involve injury. Moreover, the employee admitted engaging in physical behavior with his smaller co-workers on previous occasions, suggesting a pattern of dangerous horseplay that warranted discharge, the arbitrator held (*Muskin Inc.*, 89 LA 297).

● An employee who paraded a live snake through the workplace was justifiably discharged, an arbitrator held. The employee captured the snake in the road when he was returning from a work assignment, and a foreman told him to find a container in which to keep it until the end of the shift. The employee held the snake out in front of him as he marched through various work areas until he finally located a can. One co-worker, who had a heart condition and a profound fear of snakes, fled at the sight of the animal, pushing other workers out of his way. "That some people are frightened by snakes, even though the fear may be irrational, must be acknowledged and known to reasonable persons," the arbitrator declared. Emphasizing that the employee's behavior created "real potential for injury or harm," the arbitrator concluded that the discharge "was for just cause and equitable in the circumstances" (*J.R. Simplot Co.*, 67 LA 645).

● An arbitrator upheld the discharge of an employee who sneaked up on a co-worker and put him in a choke hold. Although the aggressor attempted to save his job by characterizing the incident as a playful wrestling match, the arbitrator said the horseplay initiated by the employee was more akin to "physical violence," which justified his termination (*Tone Brothers Inc.*, 118 LA 957).

● *By contrast*, an arbitrator overturned the discharge of an employee who pulled back a supervisor's chair, causing her to fall. The employee's conduct showed a lack of judgment, the arbitrator found, but it was not shown to have been a malicious act. The arbitrator reduced the discipline, concluding that a 10-week suspension would be sufficient to impress upon the culprit that employees have an obligation to "conduct themselves as mature individuals, rather than as light-hearted juveniles" (*Fisher Electronics Inc.*, 44 LA 343; see also 75 LA 672, 54 LA 281, 48 LA 1278).

● An arbitrator ruled that an employer did not prove it had just cause to suspend a grievant for driving a forklift into a truck close to another employee, scaring her, and

laughing about it. There were no other witnesses besides the accuser, the safety manager stated that she did not believe that the grievant did it, and the grievant had had no discipline in 37 years, was the union president, and had long served on the safety committee (*Kraft Global Foods Inc.*, 128 LA 1530).

● An arbitrator reinstated a firefighter who took his lieutenant's credit card, went to a convenience store, and used an ATM to request a cash withdrawal. Although the employer contended that the employee's conduct amounted to theft, the arbitrator accepted the employee's explanation that he was pulling a prank on the lieutenant, who was known for being miserly. Several pieces of evidence supported the firefighter's explanation, including his healthy financial status and the fact that he did not have the personal identification number that would have been needed for an actual withdrawal using the credit card, the arbitrator observed. Concluding that the incident was "a bad practical joke that got out of hand," the arbitrator reduced the firefighter's discharge to a disciplinary suspension (*City of Philadelphia*, 122 LA 277).

● Discharge was not warranted for an employee who threw a pie in the face of a management consultant, an arbitrator decided, finding that the employee was mistakenly under the impression that the consultant was willing to participate in practical jokes. There was an excellent working relationship at the plant among employees, managers, and union officials, due in part to the presence of room in the plant for a "little fun," the arbitrator noted. Considering all the circumstances, the arbitrator held that the employee deserved another chance to demonstrate his worth (*Clay Equipment*, 73 LA 817).

● Despite the safety hazards created by horseplay involving a "water cannon," an employer was not justified in issuing three-day suspensions to all 43 employees in one department when none of them would divulge who was responsible for blasting a worker in the face, an arbitrator decided. Noting that the employer's investigation did not yield any evidence indicating which employees were directly involved or had knowledge of the incident, the arbitrator said, "Suspicion is no substitute for proof in the just cause context." All of the employees were "entitled to a presumption of innocence despite the fact that it is almost a matter of absolute certitude that some of them, if not a majority of them, could be held accountable if more information was available," the arbitrator said in overturning the discipline (*Hoechst Celanese Celco Plant*, 111 LA 760).

1. Fire Hazards

Even when characterized as pranks or practical jokes, incidents involving fire tend to pose a serious risk of physical harm and property damage. In general, arbitrators agree that such incidents constitute grave misconduct.

● A chemical plant had just cause to discharge an employee who brought a taser to work and used it in horseplay in the break room, an arbitrator ruled. The employee did not have a "hot work" permit allowing him to bring in an instrument that could ignite materials in the plant, and the employee had a poor work record (*Zeon Chemicals*, 125 LA 1281).

● Discharge was justified for an employee involved in burning toilet paper in a women's bathroom to set off a plant fire alarm, an arbitrator ruled. The employee and one of her co-workers made a torch out of toilet paper, ignited it, and applied the flame to a fire detection unit, triggering the alarm system and transmitting a signal to the local fire department, which dispatched firefighters to the plant. In addition to creating a fire hazard and rendering the alarm system inoperative for a period of days, the incident disrupted production at the plant and interfered with the ability of the fire department to respond in the event of an actual fire at some other location, the arbitrator noted in upholding termination (*Abbott & Co.*, 76 LA 339).

● A grocery retailer had just cause to discharge a meat cutter for lighting a co-worker's apron on fire, an arbitrator decided. The employee claimed that horseplay was common in the workplace, and he attempted to equate his conduct with actions such as throwing eggs and tomatoes. Given the severity of the employee's conduct and the danger it posed to his co-worker, however, the arbitrator found that summary dismissal was warranted (*Kroger Co.*, 75 LA 290).

● An arbitrator upheld the discharge of an employee who dropped lighted cigarettes into the pockets of two co-workers. Other horseplay occurred at the plant, such as blowing workers' hats off with an air hose or throwing pieces of rubber. After the employee was hit on the head one day with a piece of rubber, he retaliated by surreptitiously dropping a cigarette in his co-worker's back pocket. Another worker noticed smoke coming from the victim's pocket and stopped him as he was about to enter a spray booth where highly combustible paints, lacquers, and solvents were used. The employee pulled the same prank on another co-worker, who was working on a cutting machine at the time. The arbitrator distinguished these incidents from the other types of horseplay at the plant, finding that the employee created a dangerous fire hazard and showed a serious disregard for the personal safety of others (*Decar Plastics Corp.*, 44 LA 921; see also 75 LA 305).

B. Penalty Reductions

In addition to considering the potential for injury or property damage caused by incidents of horseplay, arbitrators take into account various other factors when deciding whether or not to uphold disciplinary actions imposed by employers. When arbitrators reduce penalties levied for horseplay, they typically do so because of the following types of reasons:

● mitigating circumstances, such as employees' long years of service and past record of good conduct;

● disparate treatment, where employers impose uneven penalties for similar offenses committed by different employees; and

● shortcomings in rule enforcement evidenced by factors such as prior laxness, management participation in horseplay, insufficient warning of potential consequences for misconduct, or a lack of progressive discipline.

For example, one arbitrator overturned the discharge of an employee whose horseplay actually resulted in injury to a co-worker and could have caused damage to equipment. Citing the employee's unblemished record, the arbitrator held that a disciplinary suspension without pay was adequate punishment (*Butler County Mushroom Farms Inc.*, 41 LA 568).

● Another arbitrator overturned the discharge of an employee who hid a co-worker's car, largely because an earlier prank of a similar nature had gone unpunished. The employee hid the car by moving it some 75 yards with a forklift. He characterized the incident as a practical joke, but the company took a sterner view, calling it a malicious misuse of company property that constituted a blatant disregard for safety. In a previous incident involving a forklift, three employees had raised a manager's car and set it on some blocks so that the wheels simply spun in place when the manager attempted to drive off. Noting that the perpetrators of that prank "received no discipline whatever," the arbitrator concluded that the employee in the instant case was disproportionately penalized. Adding that no harm was done to the co-worker, her car, or the forklift, the arbitrator converted the discharge to a two-week suspension (*Webcraft Games*, 107 LA 560).

● Discharge was too severe for a welder with an unblemished record who tossed a hammer, injuring a co-worker's arm, an arbitrator held. The employee testified that a group of co-workers had been playing practical jokes on him and throwing things at his back while he was trying to work. He said he tossed the hammer at a parts tub and was not even aware that it ricocheted into one of the workers. The arbitrator credited the employee's testimony and reduced the penalty to a suspension. Noting that the incident was provoked by the co-workers' harassment, the arbitrator concluded that the employee suffered a momentary lapse in judgment and was not likely to engage in such conduct again. Adding that progressive discipline is preferred for workers with otherwise clean records, the arbitrator said termination was not appropriate for the employee's first disciplin-

ary offense (*Trailmobile Inc.*, 113 LA 182; see also 96 LA 828, 91 LA 1402).

● A deputy sheriff's horseplay with his handgun did not justify discharge, an arbitrator ruled. The deputy was guilty of repeatedly violating a policy that prohibited the removal of a handgun from its holster except "in the performance of duty, or in the course of routine maintenance, or during training," the arbitrator observed. Nevertheless, termination was not justified, because the deputy had never received any formal warnings or other discipline for his conduct, the arbitrator found. In reducing the discipline to a 30-day suspension, the arbitrator observed that "horseplay without an intent to cause harm is not usually thought to be so severe as to obviate the possibility of a change of behavior and warrant immediate discharge" (*County of Washington*, 122 LA 725).

● Emphasizing the corrective purpose of discipline, an arbitrator ordered an employer to rescind the transfer of an employee who had been "teasing" his female co-workers. The employer had transferred the employee from the third shift to the first shift, with attendant loss of his shift differential. For the action to have a rehabilitative value, the employee deserved a chance to return to the third shift and prove that he profited from the experience, the arbitrator observed (*Sobel Metal Products Inc.*, 54 LA 835).

● An arbitrator overturned the discharge of a worker who smeared red ink on a machine handle. The arbitrator agreed with the employer's contention that it was justified in imposing severe punishment on violators of a three-times posted rule against horseplay. The arbitrator added, however, that the employee had five years' service with a good record and readily confessed to the transgression when asked about it. Although the offense was serious, it was not "sufficiently heinous to support a summary discharge," the arbitrator concluded (*Southeast Container Corp.*, 69 LA 884).

C. Racial or Sexual Conduct

In some cases, the line between horseplay and racial harassment or sexual harassment becomes difficult to discern, and arbitrators must closely examine the events that occurred and the contentions of the parties to determine the nature of the misconduct, as well as its seriousness.

● An arbitrator ruled that an employer did not have just cause to discharge a male employee who put his fingers in the hole of the crotch area of the coveralls of a male 70-year-old co-worker, even though there perhaps was bodily touching. The arbitrator found sex had little or nothing to do with the actions, which were not in violation of company sexual harassment policy, although it was bullying behavior that violated company policy and was something more than mere joking (*Equistar Chemicals LLP,* 126 LA 1480 (Arb. 2009)).

● An arbitrator ruled that an employer did not violate a collective bargaining agreement when it discharged a black employee who referred to a fellow black employee as an Uncle Tom Boy, called another female staffer "a white she devil," told a black employee who had a white wife that she was not one of his "white bitches," and had previously been counseled regarding "racially charged language." "Those comments were racially charged, created a work environment wherein her co-workers found it difficult to work around her, and potentially subjected the employer to liability had it not taken steps to rectify the situation," the arbitrator said. The employee had been previously counseled regarding "racially charged language," and was aware such comments would not be tolerated, the arbitrator stated in denying the grievance entirely (*Franklin County Residential Services Inc.,* 128 LA 590).

● Despite an employee's contention that he merely engaged in lighthearted horseplay, an arbitrator found that his conduct toward an African-American co-worker was properly treated as racial harassment. The employee approached the co-worker with a cloth bag on his head and asked, "How do you like my do-rag? What it be?" According to the arbitrator, the employee's conduct revealed his intent to ridicule speech and apparel stereotypically associated with African-Americans. Adding that the employee was well aware that

the co-worker previously had complained about racist comments in the workplace, the arbitrator decided that the employee's misconduct warranted the issuance of a last-chance agreement (*Customized Transportation, Inc.,* 102 LA 1179).

● *By contrast,* an employee who hit a female co-worker on the shoulder was not guilty of sexual harassment, an arbitrator decided. According to the arbitrator, the employer felt compelled to take decisive action against the employee in light of its policy against sexual harassment and its obligation to provide a safe workplace. However, the arbitrator found that the employee was engaged in horseplay when he hit his co-worker's shoulder, and he was not acting in anger and meant no harm. Adding that the co-worker had often participated in horseplay herself, the arbitrator awarded the employee reinstatement without back pay (*Eagle-Picher Industries Inc.,* 101 LA 473).

● Discharge was excessive for an employee who used her employer's photographic equipment to take pictures of her bare breasts, an arbitrator ruled. She intended the pictures for her boyfriend, and no one in the company other than management officials directly involved with the case ever saw them. Although the employer contended that the employee's conduct could be considered obscene and in violation of laws prohibiting indecent exposure and sexual harassment, the arbitrator held that her behavior was "analogous to intentional horseplay, but without malice or intent to injure anyone." Finding that the employer "precipitously dismissed the viability of progressive discipline," the arbitrator reduced the discharge to a two-month suspension (*Eaton Corp.,* 112 LA 705).

● Another arbitrator overturned the discharge of two employees accused of sexually harassing a young male who was working with them for the summer. They allegedly called the summer employee into a room, turned off the lights, and threatened him with sodomy. The summer employee complained a few days later, and the two regular employees were fired. While acknowledging that horseplay of a sexual nature might have occurred on other occasions, the employer argued that the incident at hand differed in that the victim lodged a complaint, and the actions he described amounted to unlawful harassment. However, the arbitrator reduced the penalties to suspensions, finding that there was no clear evidence of any intent to consummate a sexual act, the employer had permitted horseplay even of a "simulated sexual nature," and its supervisory employees had taken part in such behavior (*Coca-Cola Bottling Co.*, 106 LA 776).

XIII. Incompetence [LA CDI 100.552535 (public employees); 118.651]

OVERVIEW

Incompetence, unlike carelessness or negligence, generally is not treated as a disciplinary problem because the usual remedies of warnings and suspensions are ineffective when the employee is, in truth, incapable of doing the work.

Although this type of situation does not involve culpability for wrongdoing, one arbitrator explained, discharge still can be supported if an inability to perform the work causes the employment relationship to become "so impaired that it is not reasonable to require an employer to continue that relationship." Allowing such a situation to persist would impair an employer's ability to make a profit, grant wage increases, and continue to provide jobs, the arbitrator said.

Before terminating employees for "nonculpable reasons," however, employers must warn them of possible consequences and work with them "to try to correct or remove the thing that is destructive to the employment relationship," the arbitrator said. Nondisciplinary discharge would be warranted if "the cause that impairs the employment relationship is chronic" and "there is no reasonable prognosis that the cause can be removed within a reasonable period of time." Applying this reasoning, the arbitrator upheld the discharge of a worker whose output was consistently substandard even after her employer had counseled and warned her about her productivity for more than a year (*Florsheim Shoe Co.*, 74 LA 705; see also 91 LA 293).

Other arbitrators similarly have upheld termination where employers repeatedly have counseled employees about problems with poor performance or incompetence (96 LA 556, 91 LA 1347, 91 LA 1014, 91 LA 593). This emphasis on counseling also underlies arbitral decisions to sustain discipline short of discharge, such as a reprimand or suspension, where the discipline is designed to function as a warning to the employee (74 LA 274, 73 LA 385).

Discipline is likely to be overturned, however, where employers cannot substantiate allegations of incompetence, have neglected to give employees the proper training or supervision necessary for doing their jobs correctly, have failed to give employees adequate warning and an opportunity to improve poor performance, or have established unreasonable performance standards or output requirements (120 LA 690, 118 LA 861, 97 LA 1196, 97 LA 1145, 97 LA 1045, 97 LA 931, 97 LA 549, 97 LA 12, 96 LA 957, 92 LA 850).

Even where workers clearly are incapable of meeting job requirements, employers sometimes can serve their own best interests in terms of hiring expenses and workforce morale by moving employees to other jobs they can handle. Employers do not necessarily have a free hand in reassigning employees, however, especially if such action would constitute a demotion. For example, one arbitrator overturned the demotion of an employee for incompetence, finding that his employer lacked the contractual authority to impose a demotion (*Colonial Brick Corp.*, 120 LA 1073; see also 121 LA 1203).

SUMMARY OF CASES

A. Evidence and Due Process

Generally, as well as requiring an employer have just cause for discharging or disciplining employees, employers have an obligation to give employees adequate training and advance warning before disciplining them for incompetence.

● An arbitrator ruled that an airline did not have just cause to discharge a call center representative who shirked her job duties on one shift, where she had a 14-year record as a fine employee, and another employee who had committed the same offense had been warned rather than summarily fired. The arbitrator emphasized that the employer erred when it did not give the employee the opportunity to explain her conduct and reinstated the employee without back pay (*Air Canada*, 126 LA 965).

● A power company did not have just cause to discharge a second-class technician for incorrectly operating a bypass switch by himself without authorization or qualification to do so and then failing to communicate the problem properly to the dispatcher, an arbitrator ruled. The employee eventually fixed the problem with the dispatcher's help and with no injuries or equipment damage, he had no prior discipline, the incident

did not show that progressive discipline would be ineffective, and the company did not discharge other employees for mistakes that paralleled his (*Central Maine Power Co.*, 127 LA 85).

● An arbitrator overturned the discharge of a food services company employee for four violations in the area of food preparation in three weeks. The grievant was a long-term employee who previously had not been disciplined, violations—of which evidence was meager—were minor, as none of them resulted in injury to customer or damage to the company's reputation, and the company could have merely pointed out violations to the employee and asked him to be more aware of its expectations (*Aramark Corporation*, 128 LA 449).

● An arbitrator overturned the discharge of a bilingual Russian emigre for poor work performance because her employer had neglected to give her special training that would emphasize her need to understand cultural differences and tasks associated with her job as a state economic assistance worker (*County of Hennepin*, 105 LA 391).

● *By contrast*, an arbitrator upheld the discharge of a credit union teller for failing to lock the cash drawer before leaving work. The union did not contest the teller's commission of the offense, the teller had received a three-day suspension for the same offense 10 months earlier, and the teller had been warned that discharge was the next step (*Madison Cnty. Fed. Credit Union*, 128 LA 244).

● A power plant had just cause to discharge its chief operator for unsatisfactory performance when, on consecutive days, she made mistakes that first led to a small power outage and then to an island-wide outage, an arbitrator ruled. Even though she violated no specific rule and was under stress due to her husband's health, she failed to exhibit focus, temperament, and judgment and a chief operator must respond effectively to unforeseen events that could have serious consequences. In upholding the discharge, the arbitrator also noted that the operator already had been disciplined three times for similar incidents (*Maui Electric Co. Ltd.*, 127 LA 1173).

● A community college had just cause to suspend a senior librarian for violating instructions, an arbitrator ruled, even though she had not been specifically told that she was subject to discipline for failure to follow instructions. A 20-year employee, as she was, "surely knew that she was not free to decide for herself what work she would or would not do," the arbitrator observed (*Community College of Allegheny County.*, 124 LA 1398).

● An arbitrator ruled that a company that operates and maintains mechanical systems in government buildings had just cause to discharge an employee who had released a large quantity of refrigerant into the air, where he did not initially have the skills and experience necessary for the position and was hired in error, and it was unreasonable for the employer to incur the time and expense to bring the employee to journeyman standards (*Northern Management Services Inc.*, 128 LA 744).

● An employer had just cause to discharge a furnace stocker who did not properly account for data on a production sheet, an arbitrator ruled. The requirement of doing so was a reasonable rule, the company quality operating procedures set forth data

requirements, and this was the grievant's fourth offense in a rolling 12-month period (*NLMK Indiana*, 128 LA 1142).

● An arbitrator upheld the discharge of an employee who loaded a customer's truck without washing a bucket from the previous load, which contaminated the load and angered the customer. On top of this mistake, the grievant had a long history of poor performance and customer complaints, two suspensions, and had been transferred to another shift "in lieu of discharge" (*National Lime and Stone Co.*, 128 LA 1714).

● An employer had just cause to discharge an employee for incompetence without giving him the benefit of full progressive discipline, an arbitrator ruled. Unlike misconduct, poor workmanship that results from genuine incompetence is not a subject for progressive discipline, because progressive discipline cannot reasonably be expected to have a corrective effect, the arbitrator declared. The employee had been counseled seven times in under nine months, the arbitrator noted, providing ample notice of management's concerns about his work. The arbitrator added that the employee could not blame his performance problems on the employer's training, which was adequate for dozens of other workers who had received less training than the employee (*Sterling Steel Co., LLC*, 120 LA 152).

● An arbitrator ruled that an employee's continuing inventory errors provided just cause for termination. The employer took great pains to train the employee initially, the arbitrator found. In addition, "no less than four supervisors offered him assistance to correct his mistakes and at least two actually assisted him with the inventory," the arbitrator observed. Despite these efforts and the imposition of progressive discipline, the employee continued to make large errors. According to the arbitrator, the employer was under no obligation to retain the employee after giving him several opportunities to perform up to acceptable standards (*Armstrong World Industries Inc.*, 121 LA 996).

B. Performance Standards

Cases of incompetence or substandard output often hinge on performance measures established by employers. This is particularly true of cases involving employees who hold production jobs. One arbitrator observed that employers have "regularly been held to be entitled to set production standards and discharge an employee for failure to meet them provided the standards are fair and reasonable" (*Allied Employers Inc.*, 65 LA 270; see also 95 LA 182, 92 LA 862).

Arbitrators also agree in theory that employers have the right to tighten work standards and require better performance, even if this is a break from past laxness. To bring about such a reversal of past practice, however, employers may have to do more than merely exhort employees to do better. Discipline of workers who continue to produce at the old standards may not be upheld if the new standards have not been clearly defined and communicated to the employees (12 LA 527, 8 LA 282).

In addition, arbitrators have emphasized that employers should not enforce their standards mechanically but instead should apply them on an individualized basis, taking into consideration the facts and circumstances surrounding each employee's case. For example, an arbitrator held that just cause did not exist to discipline several employees, despite their failure to meet reasonable production quotas. Noting that discipline was automatically imposed without any inquiry into why the employees' output fell short, the arbitrator faulted management for going "strictly by the numbers" and failing to examine "either justness or cause" (*Orrville Products Inc.*, 88 LA 204).

● An arbitrator upheld the discharge of a college facilities operations technician for unsatisfactory performance in terms of both productivity and attendance. The employee was on a 90-day performance improvement plan (PIP), and the union argued the employer did not comply with the plan in terms of past practice, because there was no progress meeting 45 days into the plan, and the employer allowed the employee to work 12 or 13 days after the plan's completion. The arbitrator found the employee had a regular meeting during the PIP period, the halfway point was a holiday weekend, the grievant fully satisfied only 10 of 21 PIP

elements, and she was not taken advantage of by being given extra time caused by the vacation and illness of the college vice president. Rather, that time gave the grievant extra time to demonstrate her performance abilities, the arbitrator said (*Washtenaw Community College*, 128 LA 51).

● An arbitrator found that an agency did not violate a collective bargaining agreement when it reassigned a lead psychologist to a position as clinical psychologist, without loss of pay, even though reassignments were not to be made as punishment, and the reassignment occurred soon after the grievant was suspended. Management had concerns that the grievant did not have the critical thinking skills or insight into his own behavior that was needed for a lead position, and he had problems interacting with others, for which he had been disciplined (*Department of Veterans Affairs*, 129 LA 1335).

● Written reprimands were justified for a group of workers who failed to achieve adequate output, in spite of their contention that they had done "the best they could" with "faulty equipment," an arbitrator ruled. Even granting that there had been equipment problems, the arbitrator said, the employees never advised their supervisor of the faulty machinery and thereby wasted the opportunity to get it repaired without "significant loss of production" (*Wallace-Murray Corp.*, 73 LA 385).

● An arbitrator upheld a three-day suspension imposed on an employee who had been warned several times about his low production but continued to work at a pace that was vastly inferior to that of even temporary employees. Stressing that "maintenance of high efficiency is important to the profitability of the Company and the continued jobs of the employees," the arbitrator declared that "continued low production" on the part of any one worker "cannot be condoned." In this case, the arbitrator found that the employer's decision to suspend the employee in question was "neither arbitrary nor capricious" but rather "could be viewed as lenient." Cautioning the employee that the employer was using "progressive discipline" in an effort to drive home the lesson, the arbitrator emphasized that unless he "immediately" improved, he could "expect to be discharged without any hope of reinstatement" (*Lash Distributors Inc.*, 74 LA 274).

1. Sales Employees

● As is the case with production workers, sales employees often have output levels to meet and can become subject to discipline or discharge for failing to reach quotas established by their employers. Because sales performance can be influenced by a number of variables beyond employees' control, however, arbitrators are likely to scrutinize discharges based on poor sales records to determine whether employees are actually responsible for the shortfalls in their output. For example, one arbitrator overturned the discharge of an employee for a decline in his ice cream sales, because the employer failed to show that the decline was the employee's fault (*Russell Creamery Co.*, 21 LA 293).

● Discharge was overturned for a saleswoman who, despite leading her region in sales for several months, failed to meet quotas for two quarters in a one-year period. A combination of circumstances made the achievement of the quotas unrealistic, an arbitrator found, noting that almost everyone in the same classification as the employee failed to reach their quotas during the period in question. "One sign of a reasonable standard is that employees are given feedback on their performance that actually helps them reach it," the arbitrator added, but that did not happen in this case. Concluding that the employer had enforced an unreasonable standard, the arbitrator ordered the employee's reinstatement (*Watts Health Care Foundation*, 112 LA 780).

● By contrast, an arbitrator ruled that a potato chip company had proper cause for terminating a route sales representative based upon the handbook and established policy, where the salesman failed, from the first hire, to keep his truck inventory organized and to control sales on his route, and continued this pattern despite repeated warnings (*Frito Lay Co.*, 127 LA 385).

● An arbitrator found that an employer had just cause to discharge a route

salesman for failing to remove expiring or expired product from convenience store shelves (*Interstate Brands Corp.*, 128 LA 280).

● Another arbitrator ruled that an employer was justified in discharging an employee because of his flagging sales. Although the employee argued that economic conditions slowed his sales, the arbitrator decided that the true cause of the decline was the employee's "lack of application or lack of sales ability," as evidenced by the fact that his sales record "averaged only about two-thirds that of his assistant" and "ranged as low as approximately one-third." Absent evidence that the assistant was a "super salesman," the arbitrator said the discrepancy could only be explained by the employee's unsuitability to the job (*Allied Employers Inc.*, 65 LA 270).

2. Health Care Workers

● An arbitrator overturned the discharge of a nurse, who had failed to observe procedures regarding the security of controlled substances, finding it was an excessive penalty. The arbitrator found that no actual harm to patients had ensued. Moreover the agency failed to explain how the nurse's offenses constituted such an intolerable error as to justify the penalty of removal for the first offense, rather than the lesser discipline of suspension, especially in light of the facility's contractually established preference for progressive discipline (*Department of Veterans Affairs*, 128 LA 1281).

● An arbitrator ruled that a nursing home did not have just cause to discharge a licensed practical nurse for her first offense of losing a controlled substance, where two other nurses were not discharged for committing that offense for first time. The grievant, who had three minor unrelated offenses on record, was reinstated with suspension (*Consulate Healthcare of Cheswick*, 129 LA 828).

● A week-long suspension, not discharge, was the proper penalty for a nursing home nursing assistant who verbally abused a patient, an arbitrator ruled. The nursing assistant had been discharged for "pointing, yelling, and . . . berating" a patient, leaving the patient in tears. This conduct was verbal abuse, the arbitrator found, but it was not physical abuse. The nursing home's policy was that the penalty for verbal abuse was a warning for the first offense. However, because the nursing assistant had a disciplinary record that included one write-up for neglect, her discipline, the arbitrator concluded, should be a suspension, for the two offenses combined (*Ridgewood Health-care Center*, 128 LA 955).

● An arbitrator overturned the discharge of a registered nurse despite rejecting the argument that her performance problems were attributable to inadequate training. The employee had worked for many years as a lower-level nurse before passing her RN test and getting promoted. In the higher-level job, however, she was counseled a number of times, suspended for two weeks, and finally discharged. The union argued that mitigating circumstances, such as inadequate training and poor supervision, could explain the employee's poor performance. While disagreeing with that argument, the arbitrator held that termination was too harsh a penalty. Deciding that the employee was simply overwhelmed by her new position as an RN, the arbitrator ordered the employee returned to her lower-level nursing job (*County of Santa Clara*, 113 LA 1148).

XIV. Intoxication & Alcoholism [LA CDI 100.552545 (public employees); 118.653]

OVERVIEW

Most employers have policies that treat on-the-job intoxication as a serious offense that calls for termination or severe discipline. Discipline or discharge also can be triggered by the possession or consumption of alcohol at work.

In general, arbitrators agree that employers have a right to take disciplinary action against employees who violate reasonable policies on alcohol possession, consumption, or intoxication. When reviewing such cases, however, arbitrators also tend to consider the possibility that employees' behaviors stem from underlying problems with alcohol dependency. In recognition of the fact that alcoholism is an illness, some arbitrators prefer remedies that focus on the rehabilitation of employees through a combination of corrective discipline and treatment programs.

Even if arbitrators are sensitive to the disabling effects of alcoholism, that does not mean they will demand that employers turn a blind eye to alcohol-related infractions, particularly if such infractions have an actual or potential adverse impact on any of the following:

- employee reliability, behavior, and performance;
- the safety of co-workers or the public;
- workplace morale; and
- employer operations or relationships with customers and other third parties.

SUMMARY OF CASES

A. Anti-Alcohol Policies

Not all employees who commit alcohol-related infractions are alcoholics, and those who are alcoholics do not necessarily deserve special treatment. In fact, the Americans with Disabilities Act specifies that employers are within their rights to enforce alcohol policies and hold alcoholics to the same standards of conduct and performance as other workers.

Several arbitrators have pointed out that rules against intoxication, alcohol possession, and drinking on the job make good sense. As with other types of offenses, arbitrators generally uphold discipline for violations of alcohol-related rules, provided the rules have been communicated to employees and enforced in a consistent manner.

Generally, arbitrators uphold discharge for intoxication where employees' behavior endangers other workers, poses a hazard to public safety, or creates a risk of damage to property or equipment. The degree of danger or the attitude of erring employees toward rehabilitation are sometimes factors in determining if discharge should be sustained.

● An employee was properly discharged under an electric company's policy that provided "zero tolerance" for alcohol possession or consumption at work, an arbitrator held. In firing the employee for leaving a six-pack of beer in a company refrigerator, the employer emphasized that it strictly forbade such conduct in the interest of safety. Moreover, the employee in question was a union official who not only knew of the company's zero-tolerance policy, but also participated in contract negotiations and signed off on the policy language. Under the circumstances, the arbitrator said, there was no choice but to uphold the employee's discharge (*Alpena Power Co.*, 112 LA 1008).

● A transit agency had the right to discipline a "body man painter" who failed a random alcohol test. The job of painting buses required use of dangerous tools and was considered a safety-sensitive position (*Greater Peoria Mass Transit District*, 129 LA 801).

● A utility service had just cause to discharge a 32-year lineman who had beer at dinner on work time, despite contention that he was not adequately warned of consequences of drinking alcohol on the job, where employees inherently know, or should know, that they are not permitted to drink beer while on duty, and policies include that use of alcohol on the clock is not permitted, and impairment is not the sole relevant factor (*United Electric Cooperative Inc.*, 128 LA 759).

● An employer properly discharged an alcoholic employee who worked in an underground mine where even brief lapses in basic mine safety practices could lead to serious injury or death, an arbitrator decided. The arbitrator rejected the argument that the employee could undergo rehabilitation and be reinstated, finding that the risks involved in the employee's occupation made his return to work inappropriate (*Asarco Inc.*, 76 LA 163).

● A heavy equipment operator was properly discharged for intoxication when he drove a road grader into a creek, injuring himself and damaging the grader. Although the employee claimed that he was an alcoholic and was willing to undergo rehabilitation, the arbitrator pointed out that whether or not the employee's intoxicated condition was the result of alcoholism, he "should have recognized his condition and the danger it presented." Instead, the employee went ahead to operate dangerous equipment, thereby "deliberately jeopardizing" his safety, as well as the safety of his fellow employees and the equipment itself, the arbitrator noted. "Under these extreme circumstances, the company has an unchallengeable right to punish such conduct severely as a deterrent to ensure that it will never happen again," the arbitrator concluded (*Freeman United Coal Co.*, 82 LA 861).

● An arbitrator ruled that an employee who was drunk while on duty and fell over the edge of the barge on which he was working was improperly discharged despite management's claims that the accident "severely jeopardized" the employee's life and the safety of others. Noting that the employee admitted he had an alcohol problem, became an active member of Alcoholics Anonymous, stopped drinking, and had no prior disciplinary or poor performance record, the arbitrator reduced the discharge to a 60-day suspension (*Ohio River Co.*, 83 LA 211).

• *By contrast,* discharge of a driver whose random alcohol test revealed .029 ng/ml was reduced to suspension without pay for over four months the driver had been off work, despite language prohibiting the arbitrator from modifying the agreement, since the arbitrator had authority to reduce a penalty that was excessive so as to violate just cause, and the employee had 13 years of commendable service with no prior positive alcohol or drug test results (*Middendorf Meat Co.*, 128 LA 897).

• An arbitrator ordered reinstatement without back pay for an employee who drank beer in his employer's parking lot during a break and returned to work under the influence of alcohol. In overturning the termination, the arbitrator emphasized that a company policy in effect at the time did not specify that such conduct would result in discharge. The arbitrator also noted that the employee had 24 years of service, he was not a problem employee and did not have a drinking problem, and this was his first alcohol-related offense (*U.S. Smokeless Tobacco Mfg.*, 120 LA 1587; see also 96 LA 1185).

Another arbitrator held that discharge was too severe for an employee who had a bottle of liquor in his knapsack at work. The employee said he had forgotten about the liquor, which he had obtained from a friend for a party. The arbitrator ordered reinstatement under a last-chance agreement after a review of other rulings on the subject. The review revealed that "arbitrators are reluctant to sustain the discharge penalty" for a relatively senior worker who commits a first offense involving alcohol, the arbitrator said, unless the worker has a poor employment record or management has pointedly warned employees that rules calling for discharge based on alcohol possession or consumption will be rigidly enforced (*Quaker Oats Co.*, 96 LA 419).

B. Evidence of Intoxication

When employees are accused of intoxication, disputes often arise as to whether the evidence regarding their state of sobriety is sufficient to support disciplinary action. In some cases, arbitrators have refused to rely on mere opinion evidence, requiring instead that employers produce evidence that specifically describes various details of appearance and conduct showing that workers were in fact under the influence of alcohol (85 LA 1127, 85 LA 251, 83 LA 1323).

1. Alcohol Testing

• The results of blood-alcohol tests or Breathalyzers can serve as proof of intoxication, but discharge is not a foregone conclusion in cases that involve alcohol testing. As illustrated by the examples below, arbitrators sometimes overturn termination because employers lack valid test results showing that employees were under the influence of alcohol.

• An arbitrator ruled that a city did not prove by a preponderance of evidence that it had just cause to discharge an employee for repeatedly being under the influence of drugs or alcohol, where city did not test her for alcohol, she was unable to give a urine specimen as part of the drug test, and neither the personnel manual nor the collective bargaining agreement covered such an inability (*City Of Norman*, 127 LA 1649).

• An arbitrator ruled that an employer violated a collective bargaining agreement when it sent an employee, who tested below .04%, which was a level above which discipline is given, but above .02% on an alcohol test, home for the entire day. The arbititrator found that test takers might not need an entire 24-hour period to get below the .02% level, at which it would have been safe to perform safety sensitive functions, and employees who test below .04% should be given one opportunity at their option to be retested sometime during the remaining portion of their shift.

The employer also violated the bargaining agreement when it retested the employee it had sent home the previous day because he tested between .02% and .04% on the alcohol test, the arbitrator said, since automatic testing was not based on reasonable suspicion and there was no logical inference that every employee who tested below .04% and was not subject to discipline would continue to test above .02% a day later when they returned to work (*Temple-Inland, Inc.*, 129 LA 1529).

• An arbitrator ruled that a transit agency did not have just cause to discharge an employee who tested above the 0.08% level on a random alcohol test, even though the agency had adopted a policy combining the rule stated in its handbook, which was a zero tolerance for alcohol use, and a substance abuse policy that offered rehabilitation for first-time offenders. The agency procedure violated the negotiated substance abuse policy and was not discussed in advance with the union (*Greater Peoria*, 129 LA 801).

• An arbitrator ruled that the results of a horizontal gaze nystagmus (HGN) test given to an off-duty police officer at the scene of an accident should not have been relied upon, where the police department did not offer any evidence of whether the officer who gave the test had undergone training in the administration and grading of an HGN test nor did it offer evidence of whether any training offered on the test met National Highway Traffic Safety Administration standards.

The arbitrator also said that the results of a "one leg stand" and "walk and turn" tests given to the officer at the scene should not have been relied upon, reasoning it is not uncommon for people involved in accidents to be shaky and lose coordination, and the officer complained of back and neck pain from the accident.

However, the arbitrator allowed evidence of a breath test from a preliminary alcohol screening device in a hearing about the police officer's discharge, despite contentions that test results are used only in court to demonstrate probable cause to arrest, and that the device was not regularly inspected. The arbitrator reasoned that arbitrations and administrative hearings have different standards of evidence than courts, and the device was found to be working within the prescribed tolerances when tested eight months before the officer's automobile accident and five months after.

In the end the arbitrator ruled that the police department did not have cause to dis-charge the officer, even though the breath test from the preliminary alcohol screening device showed that he had a blood alcohol level of more than twice the legal limit after the automobile accident, because the operator did not follow the test requirements that he observe the subject for 15 minutes before testing, and the officer testified that he was suffering the effects of the airbag being deployed, and was still coughing up dust and powder particles (*Honolulu Police Department*, 127 LA 148).

• A township did not have just cause to discharge a police officer who obtained answers to a recertification examination for operation of a breathalyzer but did not necessarily use them, even though his actions were wrongful and the local press reported alleged widespread cheating at the test. Testing for a renewal permit was not taken seriously by the testers, the test-taking scandal did not result in invalidation of any convictions based on the result of testing, giving the test was a small part of the grievant's job, and the highway patrol officers who committed similar or more egregious offenses were almost all returned to their jobs (*Jackson Township*, 126 LA 1226).

• An arbitrator overturned the discharge of an employee who was not given a blood test even though management judged him to be intoxicated after observing his unusual "walking and talking patterns." A blood test "quite clearly" was in order in this case, the arbitrator said, adding that no one knew for certain if the employee had been under the influence because he was never tested. "To discharge a person for suspected but unconfirmed intoxication is to discharge unjustly," the arbitrator asserted (*Durion Co.*, 85 LA 1127).

• Termination was not warranted for an employee who repeatedly came to work smelling of alcohol, because testing did not show alcohol in his bloodstream, an arbitrator held. After being sent home on a previous occasion, the employee received a written warning and was sent to a clinic for blood-alcohol testing the next time he reported to work smelling of alcohol. The test came back negative. Nevertheless, the employee was fired two weeks later when he once again showed up smelling of alcohol. The arbitrator said the employer acted prudently in keeping the employee from working and requiring testing, but it lacked just cause to fire the employee merely for smelling of alcohol because he showed no signs of impairment and tested negative for alcohol. The arbitrator awarded the employee reinstatement with back pay but also ordered him to get a professional alcohol abuse assessment within 30 days (*DynCorp*, 114 LA 458).

2. Refusal to Submit to Testing

• An arbitrator ruled that an employer did not have just cause to discharge an employee for refusing to take an alcohol/substance abuse test after he stated that he was too ill to continue an assignment. The collective bargaining agreement required a sufficiently identifiable likelihood that an employee have a serious problem caused by substance abuse in order for the employer to have "reasonable cause" to challenge his fit-for-duty status with a test. Although two supervisors indicated there was such a likelihood their observations were attributable to other normal situational responses, the supervisors' observations and independent nature of those observations were questionable, the arbitrator said (*United Parcel Service*, 126 LA 1088).

• A delivery driver was unjustly discharged for refusing to submit to a blood test, an arbitrator ruled. A supervisor smelled alcohol on the driver's breath, and when the driver admitted to drinking a beer at lunch—after having two traffic accidents that day—the supervisor asked the employee to submit to a blood test. The driver refused to take the test and was discharged for insubordination. Overturning the termination, the arbitrator pointed out that the employer could not fire the employee for insubordination because he was not warned that his refusal to undergo the test would be an admission of intoxication or that it would result in his dismissal (*Signal Delivery Service Inc.*, 86 LA 75).

• In a similar case, an arbitrator awarded reinstatement to an employee who refused to submit to testing. A supervisor smelled alcohol on the breath of the employee, who admitted to drinking some beer before reporting to work. Because the em-

ployee refused to submit to testing, however, the employer lacked sufficient evidence to prove he was intoxicated. The arbitrator ordered reinstatement but denied the employee back pay, deciding that in not taking the blood test, the employee was "forestalling an independent evaluation of his condition, which was reasonably suspect" (*Foote & Davies Inc.*, 88 LA 125).

• *By contrast*, an employer had just cause to discharge a drunk employee who refused to take a drug test, despite his contention that the employer's substance abuse policy required that he be offered rehabilitation, an arbitrator ruled. The policy also stated that the employer had the right to require testing of an employee who was "under influence of alcohol," and those who, like the grievant, refused to take the test "may be disciplined up to and including discharge" (*U.S. Tsubaki Inc.*, 125 LA 353).

• An arbitrator upheld the discharge of an employee who was fired for drinking but refused to submit to testing. The arbitrator noted that refusals to undergo testing have been held by many arbitrators to constitute implied admissions of guilt. In this case, however, the arbitrator upheld the employee's discharge on the basis of witness testimony that clearly showed he was intoxicated on the day of his dismissal (*Cal Custom/Hawk*, 65 LA 723; see also 77 LA 1180, 76 LA 144).

C. Evidence of Alcohol Possession

When workplace policies or rules clearly forbid alcohol possession on employer property, management may use the discovery of alcoholic beverages as the basis for disciplinary action. As indicated by some of the rulings below, however, arbitrators do not always sustain the discipline imposed by employers in such situations.

• An arbitrator ruled that a grocery retailer did not have just cause to discharge an employee for drinking two ounces of wine at a sampling table while on duty, where her misconduct was not sufficiently serious, and suspension would have corrected the problem in light of her 31-year employment history during which she had only two verbal reprimands and one written reprimand (*Schnuck Markets Inc.*, 125 LA 1079).

● An arbitrator ruled that a casino did not have just cause to discharge a cocktail server who failed an alcohol test. The employer did not have the requisite "reasonable cause to believe that [the employee was] under the influence of alcohol," even though her manager's suspicions were aroused when he saw her drinking out of cup that he says he retrieved out of a tub filled with other drinking glasses, and tequila shots were missing from the top of the bar. The employee had been working her shift for three hours without incident, the arbitrator said, and had not contributed to an accident, which was a factor for determining "reasonable cause" (*Caesar's Palace*, 130 LA 373).

● *By contrast*, an arbitrator ruled that an employer had just cause to discharge a production employee for being under the influence at work, where the supervisor observed that his eyes were red and smelled alcohol on his breath, his Breath Alcohol Test was .119g/dL, he worked in a safety-sensitive job operating, monitoring, and troubleshooting equipment in a dangerous environment, and he continued to question his impairment (*Corning Inc.*, 129 LA 1813).

D. Rehabilitation v. Discharge

In the absence of strictly enforced policies requiring termination for alcohol-related offenses, arbitrators usually favor progressive discipline as a means of correcting misconduct and warning employees with drinking problems that they need to seek treatment. Even in the wake of termination, some arbitrators are inclined to reinstate alcoholic employees if there is a possibility of rehabilitation.

In such cases, arbitrators generally require employees to show that they have taken meaningful action to address their alcoholism. In addition, continued employment is often conditioned on the successful completion of a treatment program and participation in counseling or Alcoholics Anonymous meetings.

● An arbitrator awarded conditional reinstatement to an employee who became intoxicated and urinated on a co-worker. The incident occurred after an off-duty evening of beer drinking when the employee and co-worker were sharing a motel room while on assignment cleaning toxic waste tanks. The union said the employee, despite admitted periodic blackouts, had been employed for 20 years without complaint, and the company knew of his drinking but took no corrective action. The arbitrator acknowledged that the employee's actions were "disgusting and repulsive," and his blackouts were exceedingly worrisome, especially in such a hazardous occupation. Citing his long, discipline-free record of employment, however, the arbitrator ordered reinstatement for the employee, provided that he complete an alcohol abuse rehabilitation program at his own expense and apologize to the co-worker (*K & D Industrial Services Inc.*, 112 LA 820).

● Another arbitrator reinstated an alcoholic employee even though his employer had "sufficient just cause" to fire him for attendance problems prompted by his alcoholism. According to the arbitrator, the employer knew that the employee's poor attendance record was the result of his alcohol-abuse problems, and other alcohol-dependent employees had been given second chances to improve their records. In overturning termination, the arbitrator noted that the employee recognized his alcoholism and had taken self-help measures to control it (*Youngstown Hospital Assoc.*, 82 LA 31).

By contrast, an arbitrator ruled that a company was not required to reinstate an excessively absent employee when he successfully completed an alcohol rehabilitation program because he had not disclosed his alcoholism until after he was discharged. Finding that because there was nothing in the labor agreement "exculpating an employee from his actions due to the fact that it is subsequently learned that they were due to chronic alcoholism," the arbitrator ruled that although the employee was "on the way to fully resolving his alcohol abuse problems," he has "no right to require this company to reinstate or rehire him" (*Bemis Co. Inc.*, 81 LA 733; see also 90 LA 399, 86 LA 430).

● An alcoholic employee's refusal to continue participating in a treatment program justified his termination, an arbitrator decided. Rejecting the employee's argument that he had agreed merely to enroll in the program, not to complete it, the arbitrator said that it would be "absurd" to expect any beneficial results from treatment that was started but not finished. The arbitrator also noted that while in the program, the employee refused to cooperate to the point that he had been asked to leave the institution. Deciding that management had taken all "reasonable" measures to help the employee deal with his "acute and chronic" alcoholism, the arbitrator ruled that termination was warranted (*National Gypsum Co.*, 73 LA 228).

● Another arbitrator emphasized that even though alcoholism is an illness, it is an illness that only the patient can "cure." The arbitrator upheld the discharge of an alcoholic employee who had been given repeated opportunities to bring his drinking problem under control and had failed too often for the arbitrator to conclude that all would be well if only he were given another chance (*Caterpillar Tractor Co.*, 44 LA 87).

1. Employee Assistance Programs

The availability of employee assistance programs can be useful for dealing with drinking problems. Employees can go to EAPs on their own to get help with their alcoholism on a confidential basis, or management can make EAP referrals, thereby letting employees know that they must address underlying problems with alcohol abuse that interfere with their ability to meet acceptable standards of conduct and performance.

In some cases, EAP referrals can be required as a precursor to termination.

● For example, one arbitrator found that an employer had a past practice of referring employees to an EAP when they were suspected of abusing alcohol. Consequently, the arbitrator overturned the termination of an employee, even though his intoxication was substantiated by a blood-alcohol test and the parties' collective bargaining agreement gave the employer the right to either discharge or discipline employees in such situations (*Georgia-Pacific Corp.*, 108 LA 43).

● In a similar case with the opposite outcome, an arbitrator rejected the contention that a hospital was required to offer EAP services to an employee. Testing of the employee was ordered after two co-workers reported that he was impaired. A breathalyzer test showed a blood-alcohol level of 0.158, but the employee refused to submit to a urinalysis to test for drugs. In upholding the employee's termination, the arbitrator relied on language in the collective bargaining agreement, which said employees who test positive for alcohol "may" be offered EAP enrollment, while employees who refuse to undergo testing "shall" be discharged (*Battle Creek Health System*, 121 LA 1640).

2. Last-Chance Agreements

In some instances, employees who commit alcohol-related offenses can save their jobs by entering into last-chance agreements. Although employers commonly initiate such agreements, they also can be ordered by arbitrators as part of a conditional reinstatement award.

● One arbitrator ordered reinstatement under a last-chance agreement for an employee who tested positive for alcohol after scraping the bumper of a co-worker's car in his employer's parking lot. The employee had a 0.02 blood alcohol concentration, which was the testing laboratory's minimum threshold for impairment. In giving the employee another chance, the arbitrator noted that he had a clean record during his five years with the employer, the damage to both vehicles was very minor, the parties' collective bargaining agreement failed to set a minimum blood-alcohol level for being under the influence, and the employee showed no signs of intoxication at the time of the accident (*City of Las Vegas Housing Authority*, 112 LA 259).

● An employer did not have just cause to discharge an employee, who was accused of alcohol use that was prohibited by his last-chance agreement, even though a police report indicated that several people said that he was intoxicated at a second bar to which he went in the evening, an arbitrator found. The employee brought a mug of soda with him to the first bar, and the accuracy of hearsay statements in the police report did not prove he had been drinking. However, the remedy for the employee was reinstatement without back pay, because even if he drank soda at the bars to which he went, his conduct was at the very least reckless (*U.S. Steel Corp.*, 128 LA 1308).

When reviewing cases in which employees have failed to abide by the terms of a last-chance agreement, arbitrators generally uphold summary dismissal provided that the agreement is valid and employers have observed standards of due process in substantiating that a violation of the agreement has in fact occurred.

● An employer gave an employee a last-chance agreement after repeatedly counseling and disciplining him because of absenteeism stemming from a drinking problem. When the employee began drinking again and had another string of absences, he was discharged. An arbitrator emphasized the weight of the employee's last-chance agreement in refusing to set aside the discharge. When such an agreement has been reached, the arbitrator said, any decision about whether to give the employee an additional chance must rest entirely within the discretion of the employer. To rule otherwise could make employers reluctant to offer last-chance agreements in the future, thus jeopardizing the ability of other employees to salvage their own jobs by entering into such agreements, the arbitrator observed (*Mohawk Rubber Co.*, 47 LA 1029).

● An arbitrator ruled that an employer had just cause to discharge an employee for violating a last-chance agreement by either reporting to work under the the influence of alcohol or consuming alcohol while on the job, even though his blood alcohol concentration of .06 percent was below the .08 percent identified in the substance abuse policy as "under the influence." The random screening occurred seven hours after the employee arrived at work, and a reasonable application of scientific extrapolation showed that he either had to have reported to work with a BAC of at least .17% or consumed alcohol while at work (*Square D Company*, 126 LA 1293).

● A failure to wear safety glasses triggered the termination of another employee whose problems with alcohol led him to enter into a last-chance agreement. The employee had completed a rehabilitation program, but the last-chance agreement also called for a one-year probation during which any rule violations would constitute grounds for dismissal. An arbitrator refused to disturb the termination after confirming the validity of the agreement based on the following factors: a union representative was present when the employee signed the agreement, which he did of his own free will; the agreement's requirements, including the duration of the probationary period, were reasonable; and the employee understood the provisions of the agreement (*Gaylord Container Corp.*, 97 LA 382; see also 87 LA 973, 65 LA 803, 56 LA 319).

● An employee was properly discharged after he failed to attend counseling sessions required under a last-chance agreement, an arbitrator ruled. The employee had entered into the agreement after he reached the point of losing his job due to chronic tardiness, which he blamed on a drinking problem. Rejecting the argument that the employee did not understand his responsibility to continue with counseling, the arbitrator noted that letters were sent to the employee about his failure to comply with the requirements, yet he failed to take any action for more than two months. Even if there was some miscommunication early on, the employee "could not simply sit and wait . . . without some follow-up or contact to see what he was to do next," the arbitrator declared (*Fort James Corp.*, 113 LA 742).

E. Off-Duty Drinking

Under normal conditions, the consumption of alcohol outside of working hours does not have a direct impact upon the employer-employee relationship and therefore is not subject to discipline. However, stricter standards sometimes apply to employees in certain jobs or under certain circumstances.

● An arbitrator ruled that a township had just cause to discharge an off-duty police officer who was arrested for driving under the influence, claimed that he had not been drinking when he had failed a field sobriety test, refused to take another test, and pleaded "not guilty" to the charges, even though he had seven years of unblemished service, where he would have to be considered suspended from employment for the six months his driver's license was suspended, and the township would have to make "Brady" disclosures to all defendants in cases in which he would be involved that he had lied in the past (*Perrysburg Township*, 129 LA 472).

● An arbitrator ruled that a corrections facility had just cause to discharge a corrections officer for his off-duty misconduct while intoxicated, even though other intoxicated officers received lesser punishments, where the grievant used a dangerous weapon in his crimes, went beyond threats, descending into violent action, placing his victims in fear for their lives (*Minnesota Department of Corrections*, 130 LA 235).

● An airline had just cause to discharge a flight attendant flying on a pass privilege who, under the influence of alcohol and prescription drugs, engaged in significant misbehavior including falling onto other passengers, taking liquor from beverage cart, and smoking in the lavatory, an arbitrator ruled. Despite her claim that the discipline should be reduced because one drug she was taking could cause people to engage in abnormal behavior without being aware of what they are doing, the flight attendant's condition was nonetheless a result of very poor judgment, she violated work rules, and her smoking violated the law and posed a significant risk to others (*Airtran Airways*, 128 LA 295).

● An employee who consumed alcohol while she was off duty for four hours was justifiably suspended, an arbitrator ruled. The employee drank beer during the off-duty interval of her split shift in violation of a company policy prohibiting the consumption of alcohol at any time during a tour of duty. The arbitrator rejected the argument that the policy was inherently unreasonable, in light of the employer's emphasis on its employees' relations with the public. Adding that the company had adequately communicated the policy to employees and evenhandedly enforced it, the arbitrator decided that a 10-day suspension was appropriate for the employee's violation of

the policy (*General Telephone Co. of California*, 77 LA 1052).

● An employee who had been with a company for 25 years and had an obvious drinking problem was justly discharged for off-duty drinking, an arbitrator decided. After issuing the worker several written warnings, the company finally discharged him for being drunk on company property. Subsequently, the company agreed to take him back if he promised to discontinue his drinking, attend AA meetings regularly, and follow doctor's orders. Nearly a year later, the worker was again terminated after company officials saw him drinking beer in a tavern while off duty. The arbitrator upheld the discharge based on the worker's employment history and attitude, which indicated that he did not intend to improve his conduct in regard to the use of alcohol (*Emge Packing Co. Inc.*, 52 LA 195).

F. Holiday Drinking

Arbitrators sometimes make allowances for employees who are caught drinking alcoholic beverages on the job during the holiday season.

● One arbitrator held that an employer was not justified in discharging an employee who was caught drinking whiskey at work on the last day before a Christmas shutdown. A supervisor had observed the employee, amidst co-workers, drinking from a pint-size bottle filled with a whiskey-colored liquid. Although condemning the conduct of the employee, the arbitrator maintained that "justice tempered with mercy" should be the standard for reviewing discipline in such cases. Stressing that the employee had a long, "unblemished" work record and that drinking on the last day before the Christmas holidays was "customary" on the job, the arbitrator reduced the discharge to a suspension (*Wagner Electric Corp.*, 57 LA 10).

● Another arbitrator decided that an employer properly suspended a truck driver for drinking alcoholic beverages during a warehouse party on the last working day before Christmas, and for breaking a lock on a plant gate while attempting to retrieve his vehicle. The arbitrator held, however, that management was not justified in completely barring the employee from ever driving a company truck again. The "core" question, the arbitrator stressed, was whether the employer's disciplinary action fit the entire picture. Although conceding that the employee "slipped and slipped rather badly" by acting irresponsibly at the Christmas party, the arbitrator noted that, in a "candid moment," most people would admit that they had engaged in similar conduct. "If we were all angels at all times," the arbitrator concluded, "we would sprout wings and fly up to Heaven" (*Ashland Oil Inc.*, 59 LA 292).

XV. Negligence [LA CDI 100.552535 (public employees); 118.651]

[*Editor's Note:* See also Part 2, Chapter XIII, Incompetence.]

OVERVIEW

Negligence, carelessness, and inattention to duty commonly give rise to employee discipline. While arbitrators do not require employers to wait for employees to cause major damage, injuries, or losses before taking decisive action, they generally agree that corrective discipline is in order for such offenses. In some cases, however, a single incident can trigger discharge, depending on the nature and seriousness of the misconduct.

The offenses of negligence and carelessness are generally characterized as acts or omissions that run counter to what reasonably prudent and diligent employees would do under similar circumstances. If employees exhibit a wanton disregard for the destructive or injurious consequences of their actions, they can be charged with gross negligence.

When reviewing cases of negligence and carelessness, arbitrators commonly consider mitigating factors such as employees' years of service and past conduct in deciding whether to uphold the discipline imposed by employers. Arbitrators also tend to consider the following points:

- the likelihood of employees repeating their negligent or careless behavior;
- the attitude of erring employees, in particular the desire and ability to learn from their mistakes;
- the actual or potential harm resulting from the misconduct;
- the impact on other employees; and
- whether outside factors contributed to the situation, such as defective machinery or work processes, inadequate training, or the actions of other personnel.

_____ **SUMMARY OF CASES** _____

A. Gross Negligence

To sustain termination for negligence or carelessness in the absence of repeated warnings and prior discipline, management usually must be prepared to prove that employees are guilty of gross negligence—that is, an almost willful disregard or complete inattentiveness to work activities despite the opportunity to foresee the likely consequences of their actions (97 LA 542, 94 LA 21, 91 LA 1284, 91 LA 1162).

● An arbitrator ruled than an employer had just cause to discharge a lead painter who claimed to have knowledge of corrosion, corrosion removal, and aircraft stripping and painting, for gross negligence, because he left rudder parts in a vat of stripper for almost 48 hours instead of 15–20 minutes as stated in the specification. The employee admitted he did not read the specification and this negligence caused over $13,000 worth of damage. Not only did the company incur the monetary loss, but it also affected the company's reputation with customers (*Sabreliner Corp.*, 129 LA 1533).

● An employer properly discharged a worker for gross negligence after she failed to follow proper procedures in an emergency situation, an arbitrator held. Instead of closing a valve that fed gas to a heater where the flame had gone out, the employee panicked and ran for help, which allowed the gas to build up and caused an explosion. The employee argued that discharge was too severe because she had only one week of experience in her new assignment, but the arbitrator noted that she had received eight weeks of training in emergency procedures. Following this "thorough training," the arbitrator said, the employer had a right to expect the employee's adherence to its procedures, especially where the correct response to the emergency entailed "simply shutting off a valve." The arbitrator concluded that termination was justified in light of the damage and the potential for injury that the employee's actions had caused (*Hess Oil Virgin Islands Corp.*, 72 LA 81; see also 102 LA 321).

● Discharge was justified for an employee whose negligence allowed a company van to get stolen, causing a loss to his employer of nearly $20,000, an arbitrator decided. The van was stolen from outside the employee's home, where he had left it unlocked with the keys inside. According to the arbitrator, the employer had well-established rules on the responsibilities of employees who were entrusted with company equipment. Adding that company policies provided ample notice that discharge could result from the type of offense committed by the employee, the arbitrator upheld the employee's termination (*Charter Communications*, 118 LA 1206).

● A defense contractor properly discharged an employee after his negligence led to the scrapping of a highly classified device that was intended for installation in a high-performance U.S. Navy aircraft, an arbitrator ruled. The employee had paperwork and other indicators telling him precisely what to do at the next step in the device's production, yet he subjected the device to a process that effectively destroyed it. Noting that the employee's failure to use due care cost his employer more than $200,000 and caused a setback in its delivery schedule, the arbitrator found that discharge, without the benefit of progressive discipline, was warranted (*Marion Composites*, 115 LA 1203).

● *By contrast*, an arbitrator overturned the discharge of a machinist with an unblemished record who made a costly error. Although management argued that the employee was guilty of gross negligence, the arbitrator ruled otherwise because the error did not involve willfulness or recklessness or a wanton disregard for life, health, or property. Rather, the arbitrator said, it amounted to an oversight on a simple step in a complicated process, something that could have happened to anyone. Discharge was not warranted for this first offense, the arbitrator decided, especially considering the employee's honesty in reporting the mistake, his tenure, and his sense of responsibility. Instead, the arbitrator concluded, a two-week suspension was appropriate (*Ingalls Shipbuilding Corp.*, 37 LA 953; see also 97 LA 386, 96 LA 585).

● A hospital did not have just cause to discharge an employee who mistakenly released the wrong body to a funeral home, an arbitrator ruled. The employee was fired for gross negligence after he failed to follow the hospital's policy for identifying a body before releasing it. The union objected, claiming that only one other worker under the current collective bargaining agreement had been discharged over a similar incident, and that worker had a disciplinary history. The employee in this case had a clean record, and although he did not follow the proper procedures, there was some dispute as to whether he was entirely responsible for the mix-up or whether another worker also was involved. Concluding that the employee's conduct was not grossly negligent or willful, the arbitrator reduced the discharge to a five-day suspension (*UPMC Presbyterian*, 114 LA 986).

● Termination was too severe for a custodian who created a fire hazard, an arbitrator held. The employee used a building storeroom as a "shack," where he connected more than one appliance to an extension cord and caused a fire by leaving a space heater running for several hours. Despite finding that the employee was guilty of gross negligence, the arbitrator overturned his termination. The employer was aware that other custodians maintained similar shacks in other buildings, the arbitrator pointed out, and yet it did not discipline them for negligence or address their unsafe use of electrical appliances, even in the aftermath of the fire. Adding that the employee had a long and relatively clean work history, the arbitrator ordered reinstatement without back pay (*San Francisco Housing Authority*, 118 LA 283).

● Lax enforcement by management also prompted the reinstatement of another employee, who was discharged for negligence over the theft of a company car that he had momentarily left unattended with the motor running. Although the employer had a rule against leaving a running vehicle unattended, an arbitrator found that management did not address the issue "on a regular basis." Declaring that the employer was "as much at fault" as the employee when his failure to adhere to the rule led to the car's theft, the arbitrator reduced the employee's discipline to a lengthy suspension (*Servair Inc.*, 76 LA 1134).

B. Repeated Negligence or Carelessness

Cases of discharge for negligence commonly involve repeated offenses rather than a single transgression. In general, arbitrators uphold management's right to discharge employees if they are guilty of persistent negligence or carelessness and have previously received warnings or discipline for inattention to their job duties (116 LA 531, 114 LA 65, 101 LA 749, 96 LA 609, 94 LA 1080, 74 LA 1008).

● An arbitrator ruled that a hospital had just cause to suspend a nurse for four days for failing to properly document a patient's liver biopsy specimen, exceeding the limits on the amount of overtime hours she could work under the hospital's policy after being instructed not to do so, and twice being tardy to work and misstating her arrival time. The nurse admitted to her failure to document the specimen, there was no evidence that she would have left patients unattended if she had not exceeded overtime limits, she had past attendance problems as well as a three-day suspension, and thus it was reasonable for the hospital to move to the next step of the progressive discipline system (*Jackson Memorial Hospital/PHT*, 126 LA 723).

● An employer had just cause to discharge a furnace stocker for a company that produced hot rolled steel coils who did not properly account for data on a production sheet, an arbitrator ruled. The grievant failed to sign the production schedule long sheet moving a slab on the company's computer inventory system out of available inventory and into another area called the "slab charging window." As a result of this error, the production line had to be stopped. The arbitrator found that the tracking requirement was a reasonable rule, the company quality operating procedures set forth data requirements, and it was the grievant's fourth offense in a rolling 12-month period (*NLMK Indiana*, 128 LA 1142).

• In light of an employee's past record, discharge was warranted for an incident of carelessness that caused only $17 worth of damage, an arbitrator ruled. In upholding the employee's termination, the arbitrator noted that the employee had reached the discharge step in the progressive discipline process due to repeated incidents of carelessness and poor performance in the past (*Union Foundry Co.*, 120 LA 161).

• An employer was justified in discharging a mill worker who negligently caused the dumping of thousands of pounds of industrial paint, an arbitrator held. Noting that the employee's record included "repeated and admitted violations of safety rules either by deliberate action or by gross negligence," the arbitrator decided that termination was appropriate after lesser discipline failed to change the worker's conduct (*W. C. Richards Co.*, 64 LA 382).

• An employer properly discharged a clerical employee for persistent neglect of her responsibilities, an arbitrator decided. The employee consistently carried on personal conversations rather than taking business calls, was frequently absent from her work area, and took inordinate lengths of time—up to nine months in one case—to process invoices, thereby causing the employer to lose substantial discounts for timely payments. Finding that the employee made no attempt to improve her performance despite verbal and written warnings from her supervisor, the arbitrator ruled that management was under no obligation to keep on a worker who "did not diligently apply herself" to her job (*General Electric Co.*, 74 LA 1278).

C. Neglect of Duty or Responsibility

When dealing with isolated incidents of ordinary negligence—that is, carelessness or neglect of duty that lacks the severity to constitute gross negligence—arbitrators are likely to approve discipline short of discharge, provided the discipline is imposed in accordance with established policies and there is sufficient evidence to support the charge (119 LA 1293, 119 LA 637, 112 LA 587, 97 LA 66, 97 LA 60, 95 LA 873, 93 LA 302).

• An employer did not have just cause to suspend a 12-year employee with no disciplinary history for admitting an unauthorized vehicle onto the employer's premises without complying with the employer's entry procedure, an arbitrator ruled, where his conduct was not grossly negligent. The employee had been promoted to a position responsible for granting entry to vehicles only six weeks before the incident, and the incident would not have occurred if his assistant had read pertinent paperwork. The arbitrator reduced the suspension to a letter of reprimand (*Missouri American Water Co.*, 126 LA 1821).

• An arbitrator overturned the discharge of an employee who was fired for not properly closing a water valve, which contributed to a costly workplace shutdown. Even though the employee was negligent in not checking the valve indicator to ensure that the valve was closed, his failure was not repeated, willful, or intentional, and was only one of several causes of the shutdown, the employee had 31 years of employment and a non-problematic recent work history, and a similarly situated employee was not discharged for failing to open another valve. The arbitrator reduced the penalty to 24 hours off without pay (*US Magnesium LLC*, 126 LA 1572).

• A hospital health care associate was negligent, where her job included changing batteries in telemetry packs in patients' rooms, she did not observe the signal stating that a patient's pack needed a new battery, and the patient later died. However, the hospital did not have just cause to suspend the health care associate, the arbitrator said, where other employees who were more culpable in failing to see that the battery was changed only received written warnings. The arbitrator reduced her penalty to a written warning (*St. Joseph Health Center*, 129 LA 408).

• A reprimand was warranted for an employee who failed to monitor several government contracts, resulting in more than $65,000 in overpayments to contractors, an arbitrator decided. Failing to find one "scintilla" of evidence supporting the employee's claim of extenuating circum-

NEGLIGENCE

stances, the arbitrator ruled that the employee's neglect of duty justified an official reprimand, which was the most severe form of discipline specified for a first offense of this type (*General Services Administration*, 75 LA 1158).

● Management improperly disciplined two workers in a case of "group responsibility," an arbitrator decided. Because an operation that normally was performed by one of two workers was not carried out, the employer incurred several thousands of dollars in damages. It then disciplined both of the workers. Overturning the penalties, the arbitrator came out strongly against holding an entire crew responsible for performing a task that management had not specifically assigned to any one individual. Such a practice would carry discipline to the extreme by permitting punishment of a group whenever individual responsibility could not be pinpointed, the arbitrator declared, pointing out that responsibility for assigning duties rests with management (*International Nickel Co. Inc.*, 44 LA 376).

D. Accidents and Recklessness

While arbitrators generally agree that accidents resulting from negligence or carelessness serve as a legitimate basis for disciplining employees, they also agree that harsher discipline is warranted for accidents caused by reckless behavior. However, employers sometimes have difficulty establishing recklessness, which can be defined as deliberate or intentional behavior without a reasonable regard for obvious risks.

Even in the absence of recklessness, a series of accidents can provide grounds for termination. In fact, employers occasionally argue that they should be allowed to discontinue the employment of workers because they are "accident prone."

1. Accident Proneness

Arbitrators have expressed differing views regarding whether employees' involvement in repeated accidents can support the conclusion that they pose a liability risk justifying termination.

One arbitrator said management has the right to fire an "accident-prone" employee if it can show that the worker meets the definition of one who has "a greater number of accidents than would be expected of the average individual under the same conditions" or who has "personality traits that predispose to accident[s]." Before resorting to termination, the arbitrator added, management also must explore whether the employee's accident proneness can be corrected.

In the case at hand, an employee was discharged after filing an inordinate number of insurance claims for on-the-job injuries. Rather than establishing accident proneness, however, the evidence suggested that the employee "had only a propensity to file claims in instances where most employees would have been satisfied with receiving merely first-aid treatment," the arbitrator said. To address the situation, the arbitrator suggested returning the employee to work with a warning that "while she should report all accidents, she should not exaggerate them." Such an approach "would shed light on whether her propensities might be remedied," the arbitrator said, whereas "without such experience, it is not clear that she was sufficiently 'accident prone' to warrant discharge as too burdensome an employee" (*Georgia-Pacific Corp.*, 52 LA 325).

Another arbitrator argued that industrial discipline, particularly the supreme penalty of discharge, should not be based on the notion that an employee merely is "accident prone." Workers may unluckily be involved in a series of accidents for which they are completely blameless, the arbitrator observed, while others, who act recklessly, somehow escape accidents. According to the arbitrator, it is not the former group that deserves discipline, but the latter. Using this reasoning, the test for discipline is not whether employees have been involved in accidents, but whether they are so careless and inefficient as to justify the conclusion that they are not safe and competent workers (*Interstate Bakeries Corp.*, 38 LA 1109).

2. Recklessness

Recklessness is considered a more serious offense than ordinary negligence, especially when it leads to accidents resulting in injuries or property damage. To sustain charges of recklessness, arbitrators typically require a showing that employees have knowingly engaged in risky behavior while demonstrating indifference about the potential harmfulness of their actions or callousness toward the safety of co-workers.

• One arbitrator upheld the suspensions of two employees who attempted to cut a sliver of metal off a sheet of steel while holding one end, which led to an accident that broke one employee's finger. The employees were taking a shortcut in order to save time even though they were not being rushed by management and knew what they were doing was dangerous, the arbitrator said. Noting that the resulting accident could have resulted in dismemberment, the arbitrator held that the employees were justly suspended for their "self-evidently reckless and negligent" conduct (*Rock-Tenn Co.*, 110 LA 1109).

• Despite concluding that an employee acted recklessly when he knowingly entered a blasting area, an arbitrator overturned his termination and ordered reinstatement without back pay. According to the arbitrator, the employee committed an intentional violation of a known safety rule. However, other workers had received lesser penalties for similar misconduct, which prompted the arbitrator to decide that the employee had "not quite gone over the line" that would trigger forfeiture of his job (*Pacific Power & Light Co.*, 119 LA 1404).

• An employer improperly charged an employee with the "major infraction" of recklessness after he was injured at work, an arbitrator ruled. The employee was using a remote-controlled hoist to lower a rack of 50-pound posts into a "rinse tank" when one of the posts came loose, bounced off the tank, and struck him. Lacking any evidence to indicate that the employee's conduct leading up to the accident was deliberate, the arbitrator held that he should not have been disciplined for recklessness. At worst, the employee's actions amounted to inadvertence or inattention, the arbitrator said in reducing the discipline to an oral

warning for carelessness (*Trinity Industries*, 120 LA 265).

3. Driving Accidents

Driving accidents are special cases. The dangers implicit in the careless or negligent operation of a vehicle typically weigh heavily in arbitrators' decisions on the propriety of discipline imposed on employees who are involved in such accidents.

"Arbitrators are ordinarily reluctant to disturb disciplinary discharges . . . if it means the return to the highway of an employee who may be dangerous to himself, to others, and where the legal and financial interests of the Company are potentially at stake," one arbitrator observed. Termination has been upheld, the arbitrator said, if employees are guilty of gross negligence or willful and wanton conduct, have a record of numerous accidents, or are involved in transporting dangerous materials. On the other hand, the arbitrator continued, termination has been overturned where the alleged negligence was not conclusively proven; the incident presented no danger to the public; the negligence was ordinary, rather than gross, in nature; or special conditions, such as bad weather, were a contributing cause in the accident.

Applying this reasoning, the arbitrator overturned the termination of a worker who had a driving accident on the job, even though he had been suspended previously because of an accident. The arbitrator took into account the terrain and weather conditions that were present in the employee's second accident and found that his actions were "not so clearly negligent ... as to warrant discharge." Furthermore, the worker's record of "one prior minor accident in no way is comparable to the pattern of cases where discharge has been sustained because of a great number of accidents" caused by negligence, the arbitrator concluded (*Kaiser Sand and Gravel Co.*, 50 LA 571).

• An arbitrator reduced the discharge of a truck driver who hit a telephone pole when a cloud of dust blew in the window and the driver failed to keep both hands on the wheel and bring the truck to a complete stop. Even though the driver's reckless reaction constituted gross negligence and he had had another accident four months prior to the accident, the accident did not violate the "extreme cases" provision of the bargaining agreement that would justify the bypass of progressive discipline. The arbitrator reduced his penalty to a one-month suspension without back pay, last-chance agreement, and back pay from the end of the suspension to his return (*Triangle Construction & Maintenance Inc.*, 128 LA 1126).

• An arbitrator overturned the discharge of an employee who allowed the fuel truck he was driving to collide with a passenger airplane. The employee had stopped several feet short of the plane when he approached it for refueling, but he failed to engage the emergency brake, and the fuel truck rolled into the plane. The collision resulted in a flight delay and personal injury payments to the plane's pilots, who claimed they suffered "whiplash" type injuries. The arbitrator found that the penalty of termination was excessive, in part because the accident did not result in damage to the truck or the plane. Adding that the employee was a good worker with five years of service and the incident was not the result of aggressive or reckless behavior, the arbitrator reduced the discharge to a suspension (*Allied Aviation Fueling Co.*, 122 LA 274).

• An arbitrator reduced the discipline imposed on an employee who backed a forklift truck into another worker. The arbitra-

tor determined that the employee's offense was more serious than a "disregard of the safety rules," which would have been considered a minor infraction, but could not be characterized as intentional misconduct or recklessness, inasmuch as his conduct did not amount to "a callous and conscious disregard of the safety of his fellow employees." Concluding that the employee's accident involved an inattention to his surroundings and a failure to exercise due care, the arbitrator held that the appropriate discipline was a seven-day suspension (*Grand River Rubber & Plastics Co.*, 116 LA 1434; see also 118 LA 1411).

• *By contrast*, a forklift operator was properly discharged for causing an accident that injured a co-worker, an arbitrator ruled. The employee was driving a forklift truck when he collided with another forklift truck driven by a co-worker. In the accident, the co-worker suffered a deep gash to his forehead that required several stitches. After conducting an investigation, the employer concluded that the employee had been speeding and had failed to yield the right of way to the co-worker. Finding that the evidence supported the charges against the employee, who previously had been warned about his driving, the arbitrator upheld the employee's discharge for negligence and disregard for safety (*Economics Laboratory Inc.*, 77 LA 73; see also 122 LA 259, 121 LA 1133).

XVI. Off-Duty Misconduct [LA CDI 100.552505 (public employees); 118.634]

[*Editor's Note:* See also Part 2, Chapters VII. Drug Abuse; IX. Electronic Communications and Technology; XVII. Outside Employment & Moonlighting.]

OVERVIEW

As a general rule, arbitrators frown on attempts by employers to exert dominion over employees' activities or conduct while away from work. One arbitrator declared that employers should not discipline employees for off-duty activities because "to do so would constitute an invasion of the employee's personal life by the employer and would place the employer in the position of sitting in judgment on neighborhood morals, a matter which should be left to civil officials" (*Menzie Dairy Co.*, 45 LA 283).

Despite agreeing in principle that the private lives of employees should remain beyond employers' control, arbitrators also acknowledge that off-duty misconduct can serve as the basis for discipline or discharge when it affects the employment relationship in a negative way. For the most part, arbitrators concede that employers have just cause to take disciplinary action in situations where off-duty misconduct:

- causes a loss of business or damages the reputation of employers;
- impairs the offending employees' ability to perform their jobs; or
- leads to the refusal or reluctance of other employees to work with the offending employees.
- When off-duty misconduct impinges on legitimate business interests by causing these types of harmful effects, employees' right to privacy usu-

ally takes a back seat to the right of employers to protect their interests by invoking discipline or discharge. If, however, a nexus between employees' outside activities and the workplace is not evident, arbitrators typically refuse to uphold discipline.

SUMMARY OF CASES

A. Reach of Employer Policies

When employers take the position that employees must be held accountable for off-duty actions that conflict with workplace rules or policies, arbitrators often have to decide if the rules or policies validly apply to the conduct in question.

● Employers cannot hold employees accountable for off-duty conduct unless the conduct produces untold work related consequences, and proof must exist that the behavior harms the employer's reputation, behavior renders the employee unable to perform the duty, and the behavior leads to refusal, reluctance, or inability of other employees to work with him (*Monroe County Board of Education*, 129 LA 948).

● One arbitrator held that an employer improperly fired an employee who failed a drug test that he took while he was off duty because of an injury. The employer attempted to justify the discharge on the basis that the employee could have returned to work while under the influence of drugs, which would have been a rule violation. However, the arbitrator did not accept that argument. "Even if an employee on an extended absence does ingest illegal drugs, what an employee does on his own time is his own business, unless that conduct implicates the employment relationship," the arbitrator said. "While the use of illegal drugs is a violation of criminal law, an employer has no greater role as an enforcer of criminal law than it does in regulating whether an off-duty employee curses, goes to church, or cheats at cards," the arbitrator declared (*Wheatland Tube Co.*, 119 LA 897).

● A retirement home improperly invoked a no-gifts rule in firing a certified nursing assistant who received $10,000 from a resident while providing private off-duty services, an arbitrator held. The retirement home had discontinued its practice of scheduling and supervising

the performance of off-duty services, and a separate company had taken over those functions. This had the effect of making the CNA an independent contractor while performing off-duty services, which meant she was not subject to the employer's no-gifts rule when she received the $10,000, the arbitrator found. Adding that the CNA's off-duty conduct did not harm the employer's reputation or product, render her unable to perform her job duties, or cause other employees to refuse to work with her, the arbitrator overturned the termination (*Admiral at the Lake*, 121 LA 19).

1. Threats, Fighting, and Assaults

Heightened awareness and apprehension about workplace violence have prompted many employers to adopt policies that take a strict stance against threats, fighting, and assaults. Arbitrators generally agree that discipline is warranted for employees who direct threatening or violent behavior toward co-workers, even if such conduct occurs while off duty.

● An employer had just cause to discharge an employee who phoned a co-worker at home and threatened to beat him with a baseball bat, an arbitrator held. The employer fired the employee under its workplace violence policy, which stated that threats or violence against fellow employees would not be tolerated. Although the union argued that the policy was not meant to apply to off-duty conduct, the arbitrator said termination was appropriate because of the incident's "critical nexus" with the workplace. The arbitrator stressed that the employee's presence in the workplace would not only make the threatened co-worker fearful, it would also be likely to cause a ripple effect among other employees, "thereby destroying the workplace harmony" (*Procter & Gamble Co.*, 114 LA 1185; see also 114 LA 1024, 74 LA 1084, 57 LA 725).

• An employer properly suspended two employees who got into a fight on the sidewalk adjacent to their employer's plant after the end of their shift, an arbitrator ruled. The employer's work rules did not mention off-duty, off-premises conduct. However, the arbitrator pointed out that the employer prohibited fighting among employees without limiting the applicability of the prohibition to actions occurring at work (*O. B. Williams Co.*, 87 LA 534; see also 114 LA 475, 88 LA 157, 83 LA 760, 82 LA 172).

2. Challenge to Policies

In addition to contesting the ability of employers to apply workplace rules or policies to particular off-duty incidents, unions sometimes challenge the validity of the policies themselves.

• One company instituted a rule barring employees from engaging in off-duty conduct that would reflect badly on the company, but the union objected that the new rule "could be so overreaching as to apply if an employee got intoxicated at a golf outing." An arbitrator held that the rule was reasonable on its face, regardless of the hypothetical scenarios that could be "conjured up." Adding that all policies have the potential to be misapplied, the arbitrator said any unjust application of the rule would have to be "grist for the mill" of future arbitrations (*Intertec Systems LLC*, 114 LA 1785).

• An arbitrator upheld an employer's policy that addressed off-duty activities involving drugs. The policy stated that suspension or discharge could result from the off-duty, off-premises use, possession, distribution, or sale of controlled substances if the retention of an offending employee would have an adverse effect on the employer's business or employee relationships. The arbitrator said the policy did not improperly extend the employer's jurisdiction beyond the workplace, since an actual showing of a negative impact on the employer was required before discipline could be imposed (*Schnuck Markets, Inc.*, 102 LA 1016).

• Another arbitrator found that a hotel's policy barring fraternization between off-duty employees and hotel guests was reasonable. The arbitrator pointed out that a prior policy allowing employees to patronize the hotel's nightclub had led to problems with off-duty workers becoming involved in altercations, drug offenses, and other misconduct. Rather than completely barring employees from enjoying the hotel's facilities, the policy allowed off-duty employees to register as guests themselves, the arbitrator observed. This distinction between being an employee and a paying guest was important, the arbitrator said, because it served to protect the hotel from legal liability for the activities of off-duty employees (*KSL Grand Wailea Resort Inc.*, 120 LA 833).

• On the other hand, an arbitrator struck down a policy calling for the discipline of an employer's drivers whenever they incurred off-duty moving violations. The policy was unreasonable because it could jeopardize employees' jobs even if their off-duty driving did not affect their ability to perform their duties, the arbitrator found. Instead of automatically invoking discipline based on a rigid policy, the employer should determine the connection between employees' off-duty driving and their jobs on a case-by-case basis, the arbitrator said (*Coca-Cola Bottling Co. of Mid-America Inc.*, 101 LA 576).

B. Adverse Impact

As noted above, arbitrators look for a nexus between employees' outside activities and the workplace when reviewing cases involving off-duty misconduct, and they typically decline to sustain discipline or discharge if employers cannot clearly demonstrate an adverse impact on the employment relationship.

• The lack of an adverse workplace impact prompted an arbitrator to overturn the discharge of an employee who pled guilty to a drug charge. The arbitrator noted that there was no damage to the employer's reputation due to news media coverage, the company suffered no economic harm in the market place, other workers did not object to the employee's reinstatement, and the employee's misconduct did not implicate his ability to perform his job duties. The arbitrator also noted that the employee had 16 years of service and the evidence indicated that he had "minimal" involvement with drugs (*Champion International*, 96 LA 325; see also 78 LA 1311).

● An employer did not have just cause to discharge an employee based on two off-duty misdemeanor arrests for alleged drunk and disorderly conduct, where there was no proven factual connection between the arrests and the workplace, an arbitrator held. The employer failed to conduct a proper investigation and discharged the employee before his case went to trial, the arbitrator pointed out. Adding that the ultimate disposition of the charges did not support the employer's contention that safety would have been compromised by the employee's presence in the workplace, the arbitrator ordered reinstatement with back pay (*Space Gateway Support*, 118 LA 1633)

● Reinstatement with back pay also was awarded to an employee who was convicted of two felony counts of insurance fraud involving his personal property. The employee's job did not involve handling money, an arbitrator noted, and off-duty dishonesty was not a dischargeable offense under the collective bargaining agreement. In addition, the arbitrator observed that the employee's off-duty misconduct did not have a negative effect on production, workforce morale, the employer's community image, or other legitimate business interests (*S.B. Thomas Inc.*, 106 LA 449)

● *By contrast*, an arbitrator upheld the discipline imposed on a school bus driver for a careless driving citation she received while off duty. The arbitrator said the driver's motor vehicle records were relevant to her job of transporting children (*School Board of Orange County, Fla.*, 108 LA 216).

● The connection between off-duty misconduct and job performance was emphasized by an arbitrator in upholding the discharge of a hotel bellman who pled guilty to involvement in the sale of a stolen handgun. The employee's duties included the possession of a master key that afforded access to valuable items, and his continued employment by the hotel once it knew of his misconduct would have increased the hotel's risks of liability, the arbitrator noted. In addition, evidence showed that the bellman's supervisor and fellow employees no longer had confidence in him (*Hilton Hawaiian Village and Hotel*, 76 LA 347).

● Another arbitrator ruled that the discharge of an employee for his off-duty behavior was warranted because the misconduct stamped him as an individual who was capable of resorting to violence and, therefore, potentially dangerous to co-workers (*Central Packing Co. Inc.*, 24 LA 603).

● Similarly, an arbitrator held that a hospital was justified in discharging a food service worker following his conviction for the off-duty stabbing of his ex-wife's boyfriend, where the worker had a history of angry confrontations on the job, other employees were concerned about his return, and a kitchen would not be a suitable work environment for someone who tended to use sharp objects to attack others when angry (*North Oakland Medical Centers*, 106 LA 488)

● An employer was justified in discharging three employees who were found guilty in court of possessing supplies that were part of another employer's shipment of goods, an arbitrator decided. In upholding the terminations, the arbitrator noted that the employer's operations were closely linked to the theft area, the employees previously were suspected of stealing employer property, and the employer's business interests were substantially harmed in view of the small size and close-knit character of the community (*Inspiration Consolidated Copper Co.*, 60 LA 173).

● An arbitrator held that an employer had just cause to suspend a bargaining unit employee for striking a salaried employee during an off-duty incident in a bar, where the unit employee had called the salaried employee a "scab" for having worked in a unit job during a lockout some 15 months earlier. The arbitrator reasoned that the employer's labor relations had been affected by such name-calling and that a failure to discipline the employee could cause the employer's salaried workers to be concerned if a future strike or lockout occurred. Allowing the employee to escape discipline also could give other unit employees the impression that attacks on salaried workers would not be taken seriously (*Central Illinois Public Service Co.*, 105 LA 372).

C. Public Employees

1. Public Perception/Morality Issues

• A firefighter, who had been a rapper since high school, continued his sideline with the fire department's permission, and even did some raps that encouraged fire prevention. However, in one of his raps, he mentioned "turning pigs into bacon bits," by luring the police into burning buildings, which got the attention of the local news media and the local police. He was discharged for refusing to end his relationship with his recording company. The arbitrator held that the firefighter engaged in constitutionally protected speech. The arbitrator also noted that the demonstrations and disruptions feared by the fire department never materialized. The firefighter also did his primary job of fighting fires satisfactorily, the arbitrator noted. However, the arbitrator limited back pay up until the date the employee posted a newspaper story about himself and this incident on his recording company's website as an act of defiance. In addition, the arbitrator ruled the firefighter was not to appear under his own name or stage name in any performance in which firefighters or police officers were mentioned. Overall, the arbitrator said that city rules governing the work in which an employee may engage off-duty must be reasonable and reasonably enforced, and the essential characteristic of the rules is that they must be designed to assure the employee's physical, mental, and ethical capacity to effectively perform the primary city job. (*City of Philadelphia*, 127 LA 1384).

• A city had just cause to suspend a police officer who appeared on television to complain about a disciplinary action taken against a fellow officer. The department rules forbade officers appearing on television without departmental approval. The arbitrator said that the officer's statements did not "address a matter of public concern . . ." (*City of Weslaco*, 123 LA 1397).

• An employer did not have just cause to discharge an employee for allegedly violating a work rule prohibiting conduct that violates the common decency or morality of the community. The employer argued that there was a risk that the grievant, who allegedly took a shot at someone in a bar, would do the same in the workplace. However, the police report did not definitively establish that the grievant took a shot at another person in a bar, and the employer cited no evidence that the employee had committed a violent act in his 12 years in the workplace (*U.S. Steel Corp.*, 128 LA 1308).

• The negative impact on public perception is not sufficient by itself to provide just cause for a public employee's discharge (*Minnesota Department of Corrections*, 130 LA 235).

2. Police Officers

Arbitrators ruled that police officers were unfairly disciplined in the following cases:

• A city did not have just cause to suspend a police officer—who took his upset wife's cell phone away from her and met with resistance in trying to hug her, which prompted her to call deputy sheriffs to their house—for failing to use sound judgment and disobeying the law, where he was not aggressive toward her, he asserted that his hugging her had calmed her in the past, and he was not required to tell the police chief about the investigation of the situation inasmuch as he was not aware that his wife initially made a domestic violence complaint, which she later withdrew (*City of Houston*, 126 LA 250).

• A city did not have just cause to discharge an off-duty police officer for discrediting the department by frequenting a bar that is a known hangout for gangs, where many police officers also visited the bar and no other officer had been disciplined for doing so (*City of El Paso*, 124 LA 1583).

• An arbitrator ruled that a city did not have just cause for a three-day suspension of a police officer for trespass or bringing discredit upon her department, where the officer admitted confronting her ex-boyfriend in his home. The boyfriend testified that the officer had "free roam" of his home and did not indicate that she was unwelcome or should leave on the day in question, the matter did not become public as the ex-boyfriend declined to press charges, involvement in a domestic quarrel is not enough to conclude that the officer violated any law or departmental rule, and the officer's exercise of poor judgment did not amount to wilful dishonoring of the department (*City of Rockford*, 124 LA 1416).

• *By contrast*, an arbitrator ruled that a city had just cause to suspend a police officer for 15 days for behavior that tended to bring discredit or embarrassment to the department for an incident in another city in which he appeared intoxicated and for which he paid a fine and agreed to pretrial diversion for resisting arrest, even though the public intoxication charge was dropped, where the city is not required to present evidence that is beyond a reasonable doubt and the incident brought embarrassment to the department (*City of Houston*, 123 LA 1821).

• An arbitrator held a city had just cause to demote a police sergeant, where he used vulgarity with members of the public and tried to lecture younger ones and he made an obscene gesture to a neighbor while he was off duty (*City of Lorain*, 127 LA 235).

• A county sheriff's department had just cause to terminate a corrections deputy for striking up a relationship with a convicted felon during the period between her prior termination and reinstatement, sending him money while he was in jail, continuing the relationship after her reinstatement, and being untruthful when discussing it with members of the department, an arbitrator ruled. The employee was put on notice based on her first termination that the convicted felon was an individual of "questionable character" by department's standards, and the employer's policy did not constitute an unwarranted invasion of her privacy (*Berrien County*, 126 LA 938).

D. Just Cause for Discipline

Arbitrators ruled than employers did not have just cause to discipline employees in the following cases:

• An employer did not have just cause to discharge a female employee for violating its nepotism policy by marrying the son of another employee, where two highly-skilled male employees were exempted from the policy after she was discharged, less-skilled employees in her office—most of whom were presumably women, the arbitrator said—were less likely to be exempted, and the employer had engaged in unintentional discrimination (*Black River Electric Cooperative*, 127 LA 878).

• The discharge of a city police officer who lived with her boyfriend outside of city limits did not involve the issue of how the employee spent her off-duty time, where the issue was not that she had a boyfriend, but about how little time she spent in her home in the city (*City of Taylorville*, 129 LA 616).

• An agency did not have just and sufficient cause to discipline an employee for off-duty misconduct, even though he admitted pushing his former girlfriend down to the ground during a domestic dispute, where she first came at him with a knife (*Federal Bureau of Prisons*, 127 LA 686).

• A school district did not have just cause to discipline a teacher, who was involved in salacious activity off duty that was filmed without her knowledge and distributed on the Internet, where the activity did not directly involve either the school or her capacity to teach (*L'Anse Creuse Public Schools*, 125 LA 527).

• *By contrast*, an arbitrator ruled a school board did not violate the Alabama Teacher Tenure Act, which allows cancellation of contracts on grounds of immorality or "other good and just cause," when it cancelled an elementary school teacher's contract for off-duty misconduct after the board learned that she appeared nude and semi-nude on easily accessible websites, some of which referred to explicit sexual acts. Teachers are generally held to a higher standard in their personal lives due to their role as educators and caretakers of children, the decision was not arbitrary or irrelevant to maintaining an efficient school system, and such conduct made her unfit to resume her job, the arbitrator said (*Phenix City Board of Education*, 125 LA 1473).

• Citizenship and Immigration Service did not have just cause to discharge an employee whose husband was an illegal alien, an arbitrator ruled, but found some discipline was appropriate for her failure to notify management in clear and unequivocal terms that she was cohabiting with an illegal alien. The employee had made good-faith efforts to get his status changed once she found out about it, and she had an outstanding 20-year record; her discharge was reduced to suspension for time off work (*Dep't of Homeland Security*, 126 LA 1761).

● An arbitrator upheld the discharge of a high school teacher because he failed to take reasonable steps to maintain the custody and control of obscene, nude photographs of him taken by his wife. His wife posted the pictures on websites that were accessible to students and the teacher's credibility and status as a role model was irreparably damaged (*Warren City Bd. of Educ.*, 124 LA 532 (Arb. 2007).

E. Effect of Arrest

As some of the preceding examples demonstrate, arbitrators generally will not uphold termination for off-duty misconduct based solely on an arrest. On the other hand, most agree that employers are justified in suspending employees pending the resolution of criminal charges. In such situations, the suspension can be viewed as an act of self-defense on management's part aimed at preventing the impairment of legitimate business interests (48 LA 379, 45 LA 498).

● One arbitrator found that an employer was within its rights to establish a rule automatically subjecting employees to immediate suspension without pay if they were indicted or arrested for a felony. Rejecting the union's argument that the rule was unfair and unjust in that it convicted an employee before he had a chance to show his innocence, the arbitrator agreed with the employer that some of an employee's off-duty behavior could relate directly to the conduct of a business and therefore be subject to employer rules (*Virginia Chemicals Inc.*, 65 LA 760).

● Suspension was clearly warranted in the case of a driver-salesman who was arrested on a variety of obscenity charges, an arbitrator held, because of the possible damage to the employer's image and good will if it continued to employ the man. Noting that the employee's job necessitated a close personal relationship with customers, the arbitrator reasoned that the seriousness of the charges increased the risk of employer harm if the employee were allowed to continue working while awaiting his trial (*Menzie Dairy Co.*, 45 LA 283).

● Another arbitrator stopped short of upholding an employee's suspension, even though police had found nearly $250,000 worth of marijuana at his residence. The employee's company had a drug-free workplace program and a policy that called for termination upon conviction, but it also had a 30-year practice of allowing employees to remain on the job while awaiting the outcome of charges that were pending against them, the arbitrator noted (*Babcock & Wilcox Co.*, 102 LA 104).

● Two employees were indicted for committing criminal acts of violence against nonstrikers during a strike. When they returned to work after the strike, the employer suspended them. The employees emphatically denied their guilt, and several months passed without a trial date being set. An arbitrator conceded that an initial suspension was justified, because the employer reasonably could conclude that the employees' return at the time would disrupt plant operations. On the other hand, suspension should not have continued beyond 60 days without the employer making its own investigation and taking appropriate disciplinary action, the arbitrator held (*Plough Inc.*, 54 LA 541).

● An employer's indefinite suspension of an employee who killed someone in a fight was not appropriate in the absence of a proper investigation, an arbitrator ruled. In reviewing the incident, the employer did not request information from the arresting officers, did not attend the employee's indictment or bail hearing, and never questioned the employee or investigated his claim of self-defense, the arbitrator observed. The off-duty incident did not harm the employer's business or reputation, the arbitrator added, and all of the employee's co-workers signed a petition seeking his return to work, which showed they did not feel he posed a danger to them (*U.S. Food-service*, 114 LA 1675).

• In a case where an employee was arrested for allegedly assaulting his wife, an arbitrator found that his suspension until the charges were dismissed more than four months later was not justified. The employee had only been jailed for one night, which meant that he remained available to work, but his employer refused to allow his return until after the county prosecutor dismissed the charges against him. According to the arbitrator, the employer relied on inaccurate information from the prosecutor's office in handling the situation and failed to conduct an adequate investigation into the employee's alleged misconduct. Emphasizing that a "good faith but mistaken belief that misconduct has occurred will not suffice to sustain disciplinary action," the arbitrator ordered the employer to rescind the suspension and reimburse the employee for his lost wages (*Fluor Hanford Inc.*, 122 LA 65).

• A university had just cause to fire a custodian who was arrested for possession of cocaine just one block from the school's campus, an arbitrator ruled. The union argued that the custodian's off-duty arrest did not warrant termination. However, the arbitrator said the fact that the custodian was arrested off-campus was irrelevant, because there was a "tangible" relationship between his off-duty misstep and the university's obligation to maintain both a drug-free environment and an untarnished public image. In fact, the arbitrator asserted, the university was obligated to discharge the custodian because, based on his irrational behavior at the time of his arrest, the university could reasonably have assumed that he was a chronic drug user who would put students at risk (*Western Michigan Univ.*, 115 LA 628).

F. Conviction Considerations

Arbitrators often uphold discharge for off-duty misconduct that results in a criminal conviction, especially where work rules or contract provisions call for termination in such situations. In the absence of an established policy dictating the response to a conviction, arbitrators tend to observe the same principles that apply to other types of off-duty conduct, requiring a workplace nexus and harm to employer interests in order to sustain discipline or discharge.

• The usual prerequisites for imposing discipline on the basis of off-duty misconduct—such as showing an adverse impact on the workplace—were not necessary in the case of an employer that had a negotiated rule mandating discipline for "conviction of a felony involving drugs," an arbitrator held, because the employer and union had made the rule part of their collective bargaining agreement. Nevertheless, the arbitrator decided not to sustain the termination of an employee who was convicted of possessing illegal drugs. In reducing the penalty to a suspension for the first-time offender, the arbitrator noted that off-duty possession and use of drugs was not as serious an offense as such misconduct on employer premises (*Nugent Sand Co.*, 71 LA 585).

• Another arbitrator ordered the reinstatement of an employee who had been fired by his employer after accepting several thousand dollars in return for allowing a drug manufacturing operation to be set up in his home. The employer had a policy stating that conviction of a drug-related felony would result in discharge, the arbitrator noted, but the criminal charges against the employee were dropped when he cooperated with the police. Even though the employee admitted his misconduct when testifying about the drug operation and his name was widely published by the media, these factors did not support termination independent of the policy, according to the arbitrator. The employer was not identified in news accounts of the incident, the arbitrator added, and no co-workers expressed any reluctance about working with the employee (*Mobil Oil Corp.*, 95 LA 162).

• *By contrast*, an arbitrator decided that an indefinite suspension was appropriate for a route salesman whose conviction for drunk driving rendered him uninsurable. It would not be reasonable to require the employer to keep the employee on the payroll when driving was a necessary requirement of his job, the arbitrator held (*De De Beverage Co. Inc.*, 85 LA 891; see also 107 LA 219, 97 LA 801).

• Discharge was appropriate for an employee of a chemical plant who was convicted of arson, an arbitrator ruled, citing the "danger of repetition of an incendiary act in the working environment where flammable and explosive chemicals are always present" (*Occidental Chemical Corp.*, 97 LA 585).

• Another arbitrator decided that an employee's burglary conviction provided just cause for discharge, where the off-duty misconduct raised serious doubt about the employee's trustworthiness to work in his employer's retail store (*Safeway Stores Inc.*, 74 LA 1293)

• A gas company employee convicted of embezzlement at his part-time job was properly discharged, an arbitrator ruled. The arbitrator said the employer was "understandably concerned" about the risk of bad public relations, especially because its employees held a strong position of trust with respect to customers' homes. The fact that this particular employee did not have access to customers' residences was not known to the general public, the arbitrator pointed out (*New Haven Gas Co.*, 43 LA 900).

G. Effect of Acquittal

An acquittal does not necessarily preclude employers from taking their own action against employees for off-duty misconduct. Regardless of an acquittal in a criminal trial, one arbitrator explained, the findings of a disciplinary proceeding may establish that an employee did, in fact, commit the act in question. In such cases, the arbitrator said, "it matters not that the rigorous protection in the criminal law has saved the individual from criminal penalties because such fact does not constitute a bar to the employer's right to protect itself or its other employees" (*New York City Health & Hospitals Corp.*, 76 LA 387).

• An arbitrator upheld the discharge of an employee for damaging employer property, even though a jury had acquitted the employee of the criminal charge of malicious destruction of property. The arbitrator held that the jury's action did not foreclose him from making his own judgment on the evidence presented to him,

observing that he did not know what evidence or arguments were presented in the criminal action, which rules of law were applied, and which elements of evidence persuaded the jury to reach the verdict it did. According to the arbitrator, "in the absence of a contrary stipulation by the parties, determinations by other tribunals of issues arising on the same facts are not binding on arbitrators" (*Chrysler Corp.*, 53 LA 1279; see also 54 LA 541).

• On the other hand, an arbitrator held that an employer may not ignore an acquittal to which it objects if it has agreed to base its disciplinary decision on the outcome of a trial. "It is essential to good labor-management relations," the arbitrator stressed, "that grievance settlements not be disturbed in the absence of a conclusive showing of changed conditions" (*Standard Oil Co.*, 13 LA 799).

• Another arbitrator ruled that an employer could not renege on its agreement to return a police officer to the payroll if he were acquitted of morals charges. The employer asserted that the agreement did not constitute a binding contract and, in any event, the settlement had been made by the former chief of police, who had retired prior to the officer's acquittal. Rejecting these arguments, the arbitrator found that at the time the agreement was made, the since-retired police chief had full authority to settle grievances and impose discipline, and the employer was bound by that settlement. Furthermore, the arbitrator pointed out, "even though given ample opportunity," the employer was unable to show "any conclusive change in the circumstances which would permit them to rescind the agreement" (*City of Pontiac, Mich.*, 77 LA 765).

H. Off-Duty Sexual Activities

In cases involving off-duty sexual activities, employers often contend that they are justified in taking decisive action, because the continued employment of workers who have engaged in behaviors regarded as immoral or repugnant by society can jeopardize employee and customer relations. However, arbitrators commonly refuse to enforce discipline in such situations—even in the context of criminal activities of a sexual nature—unless employers can show how the off-duty conduct harms their business interests.

● One arbitrator said it is a fundamental principle of workplace justice that an employee's private life is none of the employer's concern except when there is demonstrable deleterious impact in the workplace. Thus a city did not have just cause to discharge a firefighter who admitted to meeting a paramour/co-worker in the archive room and also kissing her on the cheek during work hours on several occasions, where nothing more sinister could be drawn from those facts. Thus the discharge of a firefighter who appeared in uniform while off duty at a hotel where he was to meet his lover was without just cause, where he did not bring discredit to the department, and there was no rule regulating when and where uniforms were to be worn (*City of Quincy*, 126 LA 767).

● One arbitrator awarded reinstatement to a female employee who was fired for having an affair with a co-worker. Upon learning that the employees, both married, had become intimately involved, management gave them the option of resigning or being fired. While the man chose to resign, the woman refused to accept the ultimatum and was subsequently discharged. The arbitrator dismissed the employer's contention that the discharge was necessary in order to protect the organization's good name. Instead, the arbitrator agreed with the employee that her private life had no adverse effect on the organization or on her job performance (*Operating Engineers*, 68 LA 254).

● Similarly, an arbitrator held that an employer erred in discharging two married employees for "unbecoming conduct" after catching them in an embrace. The conduct did not occur on the employer's time, did not affront any customer, and was not the subject of complaint by any fellow employee, the arbitrator noted in overturning the employees' terminations (*Williams Bros. Markets*, 64 LA 528).

● Another arbitrator ordered the reinstatement of a gay employee who gave a party in his home that included a "lesbian show." Several co-workers were among the party guests, and someone subsequently reported to a company executive that there had been drugs and "homosexual activities" at the party. However, the arbitrator found that there was no relevance to the workplace in the conduct at the party or the employee's homosexual status. The arbitrator found that the employer failed to establish "good cause" for discharge, which was the standard required under the collective bargaining agreement. "Management's disapproval alone does not satisfy" the contractual standard, the arbitrator said (*Ralphs Grocery Co.*, 77 LA 867).

● An arbitrator overturned the discharge of a male police officer, whose affair with a civilian under investigation was characterized as obstruction of official business. The arbitrator said there was no indication that the affair "obstructed official business," and the employer had no right to intrude in the officer's private life, given its commitment in the bargaining agreement to take disciplinary action only in cases of "serious" off-duty misconduct. To provide a legitimate basis for terminating the officer, the arbitrator said, the employer would have to have developed a formal, written notice that consorting with the woman during the investigation was a dischargeable offense (*City of Toronto*, 102 LA 645).

● In another case, a hospital security guard was sentenced to three months in jail for kissing and fondling a stranger when he was off duty. The employer argued that termination was warranted because 60 percent of the hospital's staff were women and the employee posed "a threat to their security and respectful treatment." An arbitrator rejected that argument, noting that the employer could not identify a single staff member who viewed the employee as a threat. Moreover, a petition urging the employee's reinstatement was signed by more than 100 employees, a majority of whom were women. Adding that published accounts about the off-duty incident did not reveal that the employee worked for the hospital, the arbitrator found that the employer failed to prove any adverse impact on its operations, employees, or reputation (*Virgin Islands Dept. of Health*, 97 LA 500).

• An arbitrator ordered the reinstatement of an employee who sought to return to his job after serving a nine-month jail sentence for a morals charge at a motion picture theater. The arbitrator noted that the employee had a 37-year, unblemished work record; the nature of the offense did not impair the employee's ability to perform his job; the underlying psychiatric problem that led to the offense did not, in itself, render the employee unfit for further employment; and aside from supposition, it was not shown that operations would be impaired by any resentments or tensions on the part of supervisors or fellow employees (*United States Steel Corp.*, 41 LA 460).

• An arbitrator awarded conditional reinstatement to an employee who pled guilty to a charge of taking indecent liberties with a nine-year-old girl and who spent about eight months in a state mental hospital. The employee's record of 16 years' employment without prior incident was cited as some indication that he could continue as a satisfactory employee, while the fact that he had been a factory employee was seen as minimizing any adverse affect on the morale or efficiency of other employees, as well as the public at large. The arbitrator also emphasized the employee's lack of public contact, acknowledging that the outcome of the case might have been different if the employee had been a retail clerk in a toy store (*Armco Steel Corp.*, 43 LA 977).

• A police officer who was fired following an incident involving a 14-year-old babysitter was entitled to reinstatement with back pay, an arbitrator decided. The officer was convicted of fourth-degree sexual misconduct and indecent exposure, but the arbitrator noted that there were no complaints of misconduct issued while the officer was on duty; he was remorseful and committed to resolving his pedophilia, as evidenced by his enrollment in a treatment program; and the director of the program testified that the officer did not pose a threat to society and had an encouraging prognosis (*City of St. Paul, Minn.*, 101 LA 265).

• On the other hand, discharge was appropriate for an employee who was convicted of incest, because there was evidence that fellow employees would no longer work with him, an arbitrator found. In upholding the employee's termination, the arbitrator also cited the fact that the company had received adverse publicity in connection with the employee's conduct (*Lone Star Gas Co.*, 56 LA 1221).

• In another case, where an airline purser was arrested once in an altercation arising from his taking pictures of nude males in a hotel room, an arbitrator converted a discharge to a 90-day suspension. When the employee subsequently pleaded guilty to criminal charges involving the photographing of a nude minor, termination was upheld. The cumulative effect of these incidents exposed the airline to potential damage, the arbitrator said, noting that "some people may be given pause" in riding planes "under the control of persons who are so inept at managing their own affairs" (*Northwest Airlines Inc.*, 53 LA 203).

XVII. Outside Employment & Moonlighting [LA CDI 100.552560 (public employees); 118.6482]

OVERVIEW

When employees take second jobs or pursue personal business ventures, their activities can result in discipline or discharge under contract provisions that ban outside employment. Even in the absence of such a ban, moonlighting can trigger disciplinary action if it leads to violations of workplace rules or otherwise proves harmful to the primary employer's interests.

Arbitration rulings have found that outside employment can provide justification for disciplinary action if:

• the issue of dishonesty is raised, such as when employees fraudulently claim sick leave in order to perform outside work (104 LA 673, 91 LA 1261, 91 LA 647, 90 LA 16, 83 LA 48, 67 LA 606, 66 LA 177);

• moonlighting adversely affects workers' primary employment by causing such problems as poor performance, absenteeism, tardiness, neglect of routine job duties, or failure to work overtime (89 LA 1062, 66 LA 1071, 66 LA 177, 62 LA 779); and

• a conflict of interest or direct competition exists between the outside employment and the primary job, especially where trade secrets or special skills are involved (104 LA 312, 94 LA 841, 87 LA 1140, 86 LA 1073, 85 LA 286, 82 LA 1259).

SUMMARY OF CASES

A. Moonlighting Policy Implementation

If employers want to clamp down on moonlighting, they may have to engage in collective bargaining before they can implement new restrictions. Arbitrators are more likely to sustain unilateral policy changes, however, that focus specifically on preventing employees from taking a second job with a competitor or engaging in outside activities that compete with their primary employers' business interests.

● An employer committed a contract violation when it unilaterally banned employees from engaging in outside employment while on leave, an arbitrator ruled. The employer argued that the rule was necessary to prevent employees from abusing leave under the Family and Medical Leave Act. The arbitrator noted that collective bargaining agreements frequently contain prohibitions on moonlighting, but the contract in question did not address moonlighting in connection with leave. Furthermore, there was an "established past practice" of allowing moonlighting at the company, the arbitrator ruled, ordering the employer to bargain over the matter (*Dexter Co.*, 121 LA 628).

● Another arbitrator held that an employer had the right to establish a rule against working for a competitor. In applying such a rule, a company is not required to establish beyond doubt that an employee's moonlighting has damaged its business or led to a financial loss, the arbitrator said, maintaining that management can take action against an offending employee where it "reasonably" infers that the outside employment might lead to disclosure of information or the use of special skills (*Ravens-Metal Products Inc.*, 39 LA 404).

● A supplier of heating and air conditioning equipment was justified in banning employees from engaging in outside work that involved installing or servicing such equipment, an arbitrator ruled. The policy was intended to keep employees from competing with the heating and air conditioning contractors who made up the employer's customer base. Although "the law abhors restrictions on the rights of individuals to pursue business opportunities and gainful employment," employees nonetheless have a duty to their employers and risk losing their jobs by engaging in activities that run counter to their employers' interests, the arbitrator observed. Finding that the policy in this case barred employees from engaging in a particular type of outside employment so they would not jeopardize relations with customers, on whom the employer relied for repeat business, the arbi-

trator said the policy's narrow restrictions on moonlighting were reasonably geared toward protecting the employer's business (*Brauer Supply Co.*, 97 LA 526).

1. Conflict-of-Interest Policies

Some employee activities do not involve any form of competitive threat but instead create conflicts of interest that can adversely affect employers. Many employers have conflict-of-interest policies.

● An employer did not have just cause to discharge a truck driver who worked one day for another company, where the employer's conflict-of-interest policy did not prohibit all employment with outside firms, as the driver employee would not seem to be in a position to "influence" the employer's business decisions for personal gain, and the driver was not scheduled to work that day. The arbitrator reduced his penalty to a disciplinary suspension for his time off after discharge, because the driver knew that moonlighting was wrong and tried to hide from the employer's official, who happened to see him driving for the other company, and the driver's explanation of events that day was unconvincing (*R.W. Sidley Inc.*, 126 LA 897).

● A city did not have just cause to discharge a firefighter, whose outside career as a rapper it had approved, for his rap that included a five-second phrase that suggested that police officers should be lured into burning buildings, an arbitrator ruled. The officer's performance was constitutionally protected speech, demonstrations and disruptions did not occur, the grievant was a satisfactory firefighter, and his performance use by a fire prevention program was a mitigating factor (*City of Philadelphia*, 127 LA 1384).

● A city had just cause to discharge a loan representative who approved three loans through the city's home buyer assistance program on which she also acted as the seller broker, an arbitrator ruled. Her actions violated the city's prohibition of conflicts of interest, federal regulations regarding such loans, and the city's secondary employment program. In a three-party transaction such as that found in a real estate transaction, the arbitrator explained, a single individual serving two of the three parties has a conflict of interest. Each party must either represent him or herself or have a separate representative. As a representative of the seller, the arbitrator went on, the grievant had a duty to obtain terms most favorable for the seller. "As the representative of the City, the [grievant] had the responsibility of insuring that the amount loaned to the Buyer was appropriate," the arbitrator noted, concluding that the grievant "could not and should not have attempted to serve two principals at the same time" (*City of Fort Worth*, 124 LA 989).

2. Conflicts of Interest in Journalism

● A news agency properly discharged a journalist under a policy prohibiting activities that created a "clear conflict of interest," an arbitrator determined. While reporting on his employer's financial difficulties and bankruptcy, the employee received permission to use the information he gathered in writing a book. However, the arbitrator found that the employer had cause to fire the employee for violating its conflict standards because the book commented in a critical and derogatory manner about the employer and its efforts to save the business (*United Press International Inc.*, 94 LA 841).

● A newspaper publisher had the right to fire its drama critic for accepting outside work as a press agent for a summer theater and allowing her name, which was also the name of her column in the newspaper, to be used in promoting the summer theater, an arbitrator decided (*Tribune Publishing Co.*, 42 LA 504).

● Another arbitrator held that a newspaper publisher had the right to give a reporter a choice between his job with the paper and an outside job as editor of a union weekly that espoused political views contrary to the newspaper's editorial policy (*Niagara Falls Gazette*, 41 LA 899).

● On the other hand, a publisher did not have the right to order an advertising salesman to quit a night job in a local department store, an arbitrator ruled. The publisher contended that advertising business from other retailers could be affected if they viewed the salesman's connection

with the department store as a conflict of interest. The arbitrator rejected that argument and directed the publisher to make the employee whole for wages he lost when he relinquished his part-time employment (*Lowell Sun Publishing Co.*, 43 LA 273).

● Another arbitrator held that a publisher improperly discharged two circulation managers for operating a local beer tavern. The arbitrator rejected the company's contention that a bias against beer existed in a large segment of the community, noting that the sole test of community morals is that which has been crystallized by statute or ordinance into positive mandate. Without any question about the legality of beer production or sales, the arbitrator concluded that the employees were not engaged in activities of a detrimental nature to the newspaper (*Memphis Publishing Co.*, 48 LA 931).

B. Leave Abuse and Dishonesty

Arbitrators typically find that employers have just cause to discharge employees who lie about being sick or make fraudulent use of leave so they can engage in outside employment. Such transgressions usually are treated as unacceptable acts of dishonesty rather than simple attendance violations.

● The limitation on self employment while an employee is on leave of absence applies to work done at any time of day, one arbitrator said, despite the contention that it applies only to work done when an employee would normally be working for the employer, where the collective bargaining agreement states that the limitation is against "engaging in other employment, including self employment, during a leave of absence . . . ," and the purpose of the provision was to limit abuse of leave.

Thus an employer had just cause to discharge an employee, who was on leave for depression, for violating the limitation on self employment while on leave of absence, where during the course of the day on leave he shopped for, delivered, and unloaded roofing materials for his roofing business (*Ace Hardware Corp.*, 126 LA 1354).

● Discharge was justified for an employee who falsely claimed leave in order to work a second job, an arbitrator held. The employee had obtained the second job while on layoff, and he decided to keep both jobs after being recalled. When a shift change brought his two job schedules into direct conflict, the employee began requesting leave for reasons such as illness, the death of a friend, and an alleged need to care for his mother. Although the employee's long and unblemished record demonstrated that he was once a valued employee, the arbitrator said, his employer was justified in firing him for stealing time and money by falsely claiming paid leave (*United Airlines*, 122 LA 232; see also 111 LA 673).

● An employer properly discharged an employee who admittedly lied when he denied working at another company during a period when he was on sick leave because of injuries sustained in an automobile accident, an arbitrator ruled. According to the arbitrator, the employee showed "a clear intent to deceive [the employer] for the purpose of obtaining a personal benefit" (*I. B. Goodman Mfg. Co.*, 62 LA 732).

● An employer had just cause to discharge an employee who took three days off to harvest his corn crop despite a specific order to report to work, an arbitrator decided. The potential economic loss that would result from failing to proceed with the harvest did not excuse the worker's failure to fulfill his obligation to the employer, the arbitrator found (*Dryden Manufacturing Co. Inc.*, 66 LA 1071).

● In a similar case, an arbitrator found that a worker was properly discharged for doing farm work while on sick leave. The employee's activities during his period of sick leave constituted a business venture for profit that was prohibited by the bargaining agreement, the arbitrator held, noting that the employer had a clearly stated rule that did not permit leaves of absence for the "purpose of any other employment or business venture" (*Farmland Foods Inc.*, 67 LA 606).

● *By contrast*, a city violated a collective bargaining agreement and the Family and Medical Leave Act when it prohibited a police officer from working secondary employment while on FMLA leave, an arbitrator said. Although the FMLA regulations allow employers to maintain policies barring secondary employment, the city began enforcing the policy with the grievant, the arbitrator found. Despite the city's contention that it had the right to invoke a new policy in response to a new situation and immediately apply that policy, the arbitrator disagreed. "A reading of 29 C.F.R. §825.312(h) makes it clear the Employer may continue a uniformly applied policy governing secondary employment, not institute a policy for the first time upon an employee working secondary employment while on FMLA leave," the arbitrator said, and ordered the city to pay make-whole monetary damages to the employee (*City of Warrensville Heights*, 126 LA 1313).

● An arbitrator overturned the discharge of an employee who called in sick after working at a part-time job earlier the same day. The employer conceded that the employee was suffering from severe hemorrhoids, but it argued that the employee's claim of sickness after working elsewhere constituted a deliberate falsification. Distinguishing the employee's conduct from situations where workers call in sick at one job so they can work somewhere else during the same time period, the arbitrator found that the employee's ability to work his part-time job in the morning was not inconsistent with his claim that he was too sick to work later in the day. Adding that the employer did not have a policy against moonlighting, the arbitrator ordered reinstatement with back pay (*Western Rubber Co.*, 83 LA 170).

● An arbitrator ruled that a police officer's indefinite suspension for working without permission while he was on job-related medical leave was dismissed on the grounds that a city failed to comply with a state-law requirement that a written, signed complaint be given to the officer. A Garrity warning, which requires employees to answer questions under penalty of discharge but prohibits using answers for criminal investigation, did not constitute a complaint because it contained no affirmative statements that the officer violated any of the listed department rules (*City of Lubbock*, Texas, 125 LA 554)

● A city had cause to discipline a fire captain for violation of the city's policy on outside employment and state law on conflict of interest when, without informing the city, he accepted employment as a sales representative for a manufacturer of fire engines while he simultaneously served as the city's agent for purchase of a fire engine. However the arbitrator reduced his discharge to a demotion to firefighter and a six-month suspension without pay, where the modified penalty appropriately balanced the employer's compelling interest in its conflict-of-interest policy and seriousness of offense against the employee's 20-year history without discipline and excellent work record (*City of Sumner*, 123 LA 1249).

• An employee who missed work on several occasions because of arm and neck pains was awarded reinstatement by an arbitrator on the condition that he stop working in any outside business for one year. The employee was fired when management discovered that he was working at a garage on the days he had called in sick. Although finding that the worker's outside venture had interfered with his regular job, the arbitrator concluded that the worker's prior satisfactory job performance and length of service warranted his receiving a second chance (*Microdot Inc.*, 66 LA 177).

C. Working for Competitors

Arbitrators generally concede that employers have the right to bar employees from working for competitors during their off hours. Such employment unfairly gives competitors the benefit of training and experience provided by the primary employer and also creates a risk that employees will reveal trade secrets or other proprietary information, such as business plans, sales figures, or new designs.

Despite the detrimental effects that can result from employment by a competitor, arbitrators often require employers to give employees a chance to give up their outside employment before resorting to termination.

• A truck driver who worked one day for another company was given a disciplinary suspension for his time off after discharge, even though his employer did not have just cause to discharge him, where the driver realized that moonlighting was

wrong and tried to hide from the employer's official who happened to see him driving for other company, and the driver's explanation of events that day was unconvincing (*R.W. Sidley Inc.*, 126 LA 897).

• An employer that required all employees to disclose any moonlighting activities improperly discharged a worker for failing to reveal his part-time job with a competitor, an arbitrator ruled, because the employer had terminated the worker without giving him a chance to resign from the second job. Other employees in similar situations had been allowed an opportunity to relinquish their outside interest before any disciplinary action was invoked, the arbitrator noted (*William Feather Co.*, 68 LA 13).

• After learning that two of its workers had accepted part-time employment with a competitor, an employer gave them a formal warning that any further activity of that sort would be cause for discharge. An arbitrator ruled that the employer was justified in barring the outside work but decided that the warnings were not justified. The employer had the right to forbid the outside employment, the arbitrator said, but it could not impose discipline concurrent with giving notice of its policy (*Mechanical Handling Systems Inc.*, 26 LA 401; see also 47 LA 372).

D. Personal Business Ventures

Personal business ventures that put employees in competition with their employers or create conflicts of interest do not have to be tolerated, arbitrators agree. If employees engage in activities aimed directly at taking business away from their employers, arbitrators typically uphold termination (57 LA 1258, 55 LA 1044, 53 LA 1176).

• An arbitrator ruled that a discharged business enterprise specialist was guilty of the charge of improper use of his work computer for his private business and teaching position, despite his contentions that he used materials that related to training for both his regular job and teaching assignment, and that he did not profit financially from teaching. The school examination found on the computer had very little relationship to the subjects in job training, and he acknowledged that he received compensation for teaching (*State of Ohio*, 125 LA 1509).

● An employer had just cause to discharge workers who were soliciting business for private gain on company time and working in competition with their employer, an arbitrator held. "[N]o employee needs to be told that if he is soliciting company customers on company time and property for a competing business, that he runs a great risk of losing his job," the arbitrator declared. "It is an established rule of employment law," the arbitrator added, "that an employee may not use for his own benefit, and contrary to the interest of his employer, information obtained in the course of the employment" (*Alaska Sales and Service Co.*, 73 LA 164; see also 74 LA 1066).

● *By contrast*, another arbitrator converted a discharge to a disciplinary layoff where an employee had been siphoning business from his employer. In this case, the employer had a specific rule forbidding employees to solicit during working hours with the intent of obtaining work ordinarily performed by the company. Nevertheless, noting such mitigating factors as the employee's good record and the absence of any evidence that the employer had actually lost money, the arbitrator held that giving the worker a second chance would benefit both the company and society (*Heinrich Motors Inc.*, 68 LA 1224; see also 75 LA 1092).

● Discharge was improper where an employee was not given a reasonable opportunity to disengage himself from a business that his primary employer considered a conflict of interest, an arbitrator ruled. Although the employer contended that the worker's part ownership in a local bar competed with its retail business, the arbitrator decided that the employer had failed to prove that the bar was a competitor. If the worker's interest in the operation competed with his primary job, the arbitrator noted, then the employer should have allowed the worker a chance to give up his ownership interest in the bar (*Albertson's Inc.*, 65 LA 1042; see also 96 LA 1).

● Another arbitrator held that an employee had to make a choice between his job and his outside business activity. The employee worked as a salesman for a wholesale distributor of cigarettes but also had an interest in a private vending machine business that served the employer's retail customers. Because the employee's outside activity created a conflict of interest, the arbitrator held that the employer could discharge the employee if he refused to terminate "those outside but closely related business activities, which cause economic harm to the employer" (*Phillips Brothers Inc.*, 63 LA 328).

E. Other Adverse Effects

Moonlighting that does not involve working for a competitor or otherwise conflict with the primary job usually is not regarded as just cause for discharge, in the absence of contractual prohibitions on outside employment.

● In the course of preparing reprimands for an employee's spoiled work, management stumbled onto the fact that he was moonlighting. The reprimands were changed to a discharge when the employee refused to give up his second job. An arbitrator set aside the discharge because management had insufficient backing for its conclusion that it was injured by the worker's other job. Although his two jobs allowed him only about five hours of sleep a day, his foreman saw no signs that the employee was suffering from lack of sleep and instead had given him rapid promotions. There also was no showing that he was less efficient or produced more spoiled work than other employees (*United Engineering & Foundry Co.*, 37 LA 1095).

● An arbitrator held that an employer improperly discharged a flight attendant whose "Bohemian" lifestyle and work as a professional artist were described in a magazine feature article that identified him as working for the employer. Even though the employee failed to get the required prepublication review, approval, and permission from the employer, the arbitrator pointed out, neither the employee's artistic endeavors nor the article constituted work "detrimental to, or in conflict with, the company's interest" (*Trans World Airlines Inc.*, 93 LA 167).

● In contrast, an arbitrator held that an employer properly issued a written reprimand to an auxiliary engineer who published an article in a newspaper that suggested the employer had an atrocious safety record, despite the claim that the employee's action was entirely without malice (*San Diego Gas & Electric Co.*, 82 LA 1039).

XVIII. Refusal to Obey Directives [LA CDI 100.552540 (public employees); 118.6521, 118.658]

OVERVIEW

Most cases of insubordination involve a refusal to follow the directives of duly designated members of management or a failure to comply with established procedures. When reviewing the propriety of discipline in such cases, arbitrators generally consider not only the magnitude of the offense and earlier occurrences of such behavior, but also whether:

- the orders or procedures in question were clearly expressed,
- employees were made aware of the possible consequences of their actions, and
- discipline was applied in a nondiscriminatory and progressive manner.

Even in the presence of clear directives coupled with warnings about failing to comply, employees sometimes feel they have unassailable reasons for objecting to the rules, orders, or procedures laid down by management. Rather than resorting to "self help" in such situations, however, employees generally are required to carry out management's directives and seek redress after the fact through the grievance process.

This approach—commonly known as "obey now, grieve later"—applies in most, but not all, cases. One notable exception is when compliance by employees would entail unusual health or safety risks. Arbitration and court rulings alike have confirmed that employees have a right to refuse work that they reasonably believe to be highly dangerous. Arbitrators also have recognized exceptions when observance of the "obey now, grieve later" standard would result in substantial harm that could not be remedied satisfactorily after the fact and when employees reasonably believe that management directives are illegal, unethical, or immoral.

SUMMARY OF CASES

A. General Rules

Violations of clearly expressed orders typically constitute insubordination and provide grounds for discipline, but not necessarily discharge. One arbitrator noted that insubordination in its broadest form is not an offense that is so self-defining and of such gravity as to warrant immediate termination, since insubordination takes on many forms and degrees of seriousness (*Huttig Building Products Inc.*, 128 LA 1251).

• An arbitrator observed that a supervisor must be the judge of when, and of what, tasks are to be performed. The case at hand involved a service employee who claimed that he was too busy to comply with his supervisors' instructions. Although the pressure of dealing with the public may increase the potential for friction, the arbitrator emphasized, it does not warrant abandoning the standard of "obey now, grieve later." It would be destructive of proper labor-management relations, the arbitrator concluded, to allow employees to be the final judge of what instructions they would follow or honor (*National Lawyers Club Inc.*, 52 LA 547).

• Another arbitrator noted that arbitrators have the authority to modify the penalty of discharge of insubordinate employees, even though shop rules state that the penalty for such conduct is discharge, where arbitrators' decisions often balance what is fair and what is necessary in fashioning remedies, the collective bargaining agreement specifically authorizes the arbitrator to modify the discharge penalty, and the parties implicitly provided such authorization (*Clayton & Lambert Mfg. Co.*, 129 LA 353).

• Another arbitrator stated that the general rule that a supervisor's instructions must be carried out promptly and must continue to be followed is excepted when: (1) compliance with an instruction poses a reasonable danger to the employee's health, (2) obeying the instruction denies the employee a right to file a claim with the employer for pay, (3) compliance with the instruction could not be remedied through grievance procedure, and (4) the employee was denied a right to the presence of a union steward or otherwise deprived of a right to file or process a grievance (*United Parcel Service*, 127 LA 1412).

1. Refusal to Obey Directives

• An arbitrator ruled that an employer had just cause to discharge an employee for violating its rules regarding insubordination and "thoughtless conduct which endangers employees or results in damaged property" by refusing to comply with a directive to extinguish a fire in a kiln. The employer was responsible for monitoring the area in which the fire broke out, and the arbitrator found that his refusal was in retaliation for a prior demotion, and a collective bargaining agreement stipulated that a first violation warranted discharge (*Abitibi Bowater Inc.*, 126 LA 1524).

• An arbitrator ruled that a hospital had just cause to discipline a nurse for insubordination, where he threatened to leave his shift if he were assigned an extra patient, refused to go see a superior after being informed that she wanted to speak with him, and then told her in person that he was too busy to report to her office (*Desert Springs Hospital Medical Center*, 127 LA 727).

• An arbitrator upheld the discharge of an 18-year employee for insubordination, where she had failed to follow instructions and displayed a disrespectful and unprofessional manner, had previously been disciplined for similar behavior, and professional conduct towards co-workers was the enforced norm with the employer (*United Parcel Service*, 127 LA 1412).

● An arbitrator found an employer had just cause to discharge an employee who refused to follow her supervisor's instructions, which he repeated three times, to work in a certain area with another employee, where, absent safety considerations, the employee must do as instructed and grieve later, and the employee testified that she was aware of a work rule which provides that an employee who refuses to follow a supervisor's order is subject to immediate discharge (*Trane Inc.*, 127 LA 1659).

● A rental car shuttle company had just cause to discharge an operator who refused to stop transmitting on a two-way radio system when told to do so by a dispatcher and who sent e-mail to the employer's client complaining about the employer, an arbitrator ruled. The arbitrator found that the grievant had engaged in a continuing effort to undermine the employer's relationship with the client even after the client suggested he bring his complaints to the employer and union instead of the client, and he had committed similar offenses earlier (*First Transit Inc.*, 128 LA 138).

● An employee was properly suspended for insubordination after improperly parking her car. The employee was asked to move her car after parking in an area reserved for motorcycles, but she refused to do so. The employee then refused to accept a ticket from a safety manager for parking illegally, and she remained defiant when she was directed by her supervisor to report to a senior manager's office where she would be given a memo directing her to move her car. The employer argued that the employee was "flagrantly" insubordinate, but the union insisted that the worker should not have been required to report to the manager's office unless a union representative was allowed to accompany her.

It has long been established that an employee first must follow an order and then turn to the grievance procedure for further relief, the arbitrator declared, upholding the disciplinary action. Pointing out that an "air of insubordination" surrounded the employee's conduct, the arbitrator con-

cluded that the worker's "open defiance" of management's directives constituted just cause for discipline (*Federal Correctional Institution*, 75 LA 295; see also 96 LA 633, 96 LA 212, 93 LA 203).

By contrast, an arbitrator found that an employer did not have just cause to discipline an employee for insubordination for allegedly refusing an order to empty his pockets, where the employer had the burden of proving that insubordination occurred, and the employee explained that he did not empty his pockets because they were sewn into his pants, but that he took everything out of them (*United Telephone Company of Ohio*, 127 LA 339).

● A health care center did not have just cause to discharge an employee it accused of refusing an order to weigh residents, because it did not interview her. If it had, she would have told them that she refused the order in jest, the arbitrator said (*Whispering Pines Health Care Center*, 125 LA 827).

● An employee was improperly discharged for a string of insubordinate acts over a 20-minute period, an arbitrator ruled, because he was not warned about the consequences of persisting in his insubordination. The employee first refused his supervisor's directive to adjust the brakes on a piece of machinery. His supervisor told him to report to a manager, which he also refused to do. He was then told to clock out and leave, but he stayed put until police came and removed him. The employer treated the incident as five individual acts of insubordination based on the employee's refusals to fix the machine, report to the manager, stop working, clock out, and leave the premises.

The arbitrator rejected the argument that the employee's insubordination constituted a single violation because it took place in a span of 20 minutes. Rather, the arbitrator found that the employee committed several violations when he failed to comply with his supervisor's instructions regarding "several distinctly different tasks or acts." At the same time, however, the arbitrator found that the supervisor committed a "procedural error" when he "failed to forewarn" the employee "of the grave consequences of his disobedient behavior." Stressing that such a warning "might have shocked" the employee "back to his senses," the arbitrator said the supervisor's lapse warranted setting aside the termination (*St. Regis Paper Co.*, 75 LA 819; see also 98 LA 131, 97 LA 592, 95 LA 302, 93 LA 773).

• An employee was improperly suspended over a disputed order involving his time card, an arbitrator held. The employee, a union steward, attended a grievance meeting that started a half hour before the end of his shift. At the end of the two-hour meeting, the employee clocked out. His supervisor subsequently changed the employee's time card to reflect the time he had stopped working rather than the time he had left work. The employee refused to sign the time card, claiming that the card had been "tampered with." Following the employee's repeated refusals to initial the card, management suspended him for insubordination.

The supervisor's insistence that the employee sign the card "in the face of his fear of signing away his claim" for pay "served no legitimate business purpose and did not constitute a valid work order," the arbitrator declared, especially in light of the fact that the employer could calculate the employee's pay in any way it thought proper. Because the employee had not refused a valid work order, the arbitrator continued, he could not be guilty of insubordination. Stressing that an "essentially trivial" incident "ought not result in serious consequences," the arbitrator decided that the employer did not have "proper cause" to suspend the worker (*Kilsby Tubesupply Co.*, 76 LA 921).

• An employer did not have just cause to fire an employee for receiving help with a task after being directed to avoid such help, an arbitrator ruled. The employee worked at a public housing facility, and his job performance came under scrutiny when a new supervisor arrived. After a party at the building, residents voluntarily helped the employee stack folding chairs. The supervisor later castigated him for allowing their help, citing liability concerns. A few days later, she found him fixing a burned out light, and a resident was holding the bulb. She terminated him for insubordina-

tion based on her earlier directive about residents helping out. According to the employee, the resident showed up and held the bulb without permission or prompting. Finding that the evidence did not support the allegations and that the supervisor failed to apply progressive discipline, the arbitrator awarded the employee reinstatement with back pay (*Seattle Housing Authority*, 117 LA 1611).

2. Refusal to Carry Out Assignments

• An arbitrator ruled that an employer had just cause to discharge an ambulance driver for insubordination, where she argued with her supervisor, clocked out, and left the premises after being instructed to hold over to take another run (*American Medical Response*, 129 LA 1005).

• Another arbitrator ruled that an employer had proper cause to discipline but not to discharge a firefighter technician for failure both to respond to an emergency fire call and to comply with a written supervisory directive, when he failed to answer a call two minutes before the end of a shift and left work, where firefighters who have not clocked out are required to respond and the fire chief had issued a written directive that they stay until they are released by a supervisor, but he had 30 years of service with virtually no disciplinary record. The firefighter was reinstated with a concurrent 30-day suspension (*U.S. Steel Corp.*, 126 LA 460).

• An employer had just cause to discharge a commercial truck driver for failing to follow a police officer's orders by driving a truck that had been deemed out of service (OOS), failing to follow federal regulations by not conducting thorough pre-trip inspections, and failing to put safety first by driving the truck on public highways with 10 safety violations, an arbitrator ruled. The OOS violations could clearly be noted during pre-trip inspections, officers had sufficiently advised him about OOS status, and his conduct amounted to "refusal to do a work assignment" that rendered written notice unnecessary (*Arkhola Sand & Gravel Co.*, 128 LA 65).

• Discharge was warranted for an employee who refused to carry out an assignment because he objected to the pay rate for the work in question, an arbitrator held. The employee, who also served as a shop steward, received incentive pay when performing his normal duties. One day, when he was told to perform other work, he asked if he would receive his average incentive rate. His supervisor said he would be paid the base rate, which was much lower. A confrontation ensued, in which the employee pointed out that the same pay issue had come up previously and remained unresolved. When the employee said he did not intend to do the work, his supervisor responded by telling him to carry out the assignment and file a grievance afterwards. Rather than follow his supervisor's instructions, the employee left the plant.

The employee clearly stood in violation of the "work now, grieve later" standard when he refused to carry out his supervisor's directive, the arbitrator found. The employee's conduct, which amounted to a labor-management confrontation on the shop floor that resulted in an unnecessary workplace disruption, "is exactly what this standard is designed to prevent," the arbitrator said in upholding termination (*Leggett and Platt Inc.*, 120 LA 122).

• An arbitrator ruled that an employer had cause to discipline but not to discharge an employee who refused to work on a rail switch, where he resorted to self-help because he was arguably asked to perform work belonging to another craft or classification. There was no evidence of a safety concern, the employee did not identify himself as a shop steward when he approached managers about their working at the switch, and he had a special obligation to uphold the collective bargaining agreement due to his role as a steward. However the employer did not have cause to discharge him because he was not told that his refusal could lead to discipline, and a prior award stated that an employee must be "adequately notified" of "grave disciplinary consequences flowing from [his or her] refusal"; The employee was reinstated with suspension and no back pay for time off work (*Bemis Co. Inc.*, 127 LA 499).

A gas company did not have just cause to discharge a customer service represen-

tative who refused an assignment, where the dispatcher never put the servicewoman to the test of whether she was refusing to complete the assignment, never used words like "order" or "direct," never asked the grievant whether she was refusing, and did not "insist" that she finish calls. The arbitrator reinstated the employee without back pay (*Equitable Gas Co.*, 127 LA 865).

3. Refusal to Follow Rules and Procedures

A failure to comply with established rules or proper procedures typically leaves employees open to discipline.

• An employee who refused to report to his supervisor at the beginning and end of his shifts was properly discharged. The worker was warned of the consequences of noncompliance but repeatedly refused to follow the check-in procedures on the grounds that the rule was unreasonable and discriminatory because it applied only to a two-employee unit. "The mere fact that an order is directed at two people does not *per se* render it discriminatory," the arbitrator said. Noting that management often had difficulty locating the workers in the unit because of their inability to answer pages when performing certain tasks, the arbitrator decided that the check-in rule was reasonable. Despite his supervisor's warnings, the employee "continued to flout the rule," the arbitrator stressed, upholding the worker's discharge (*Washington Hospital Center*, 75 LA 32).

• A teacher who required his students to complete an examination during a bomb threat was properly issued a one-day suspension for failing to comply with established procedures. The teacher protested the discipline, arguing that false alarms were common at the school and that it was within his "judgment to allow the students to complete" the important exam. The arbitrator said the teacher's actions were "most serious" and his judgment in the situation "clearly faulty" when he endangered the pupils by requiring them to stay in the building. Adding that the teacher "deliberately and willfully" disobeyed "clear and reasonable policy and legal guidelines," the arbitrator found that the one-day suspension was appropriate (*Whitehall-Coplay School District*, 76 LA 325).

● An employee who refused to sign a form was properly discharged for insubordination, an arbitrator decided. When the work of employees involved special tools, their employer required them to sign a voucher that said a sum equivalent to the value of the company-issued tools would be deducted from their pay in the event that the equipment was not returned. The employee refused to sign such a voucher, even though his supervisor told him to do so, and he was fired. Stressing that he had "never" signed for a tool before and "was not starting now," the employee said he refused to comply because he believed the voucher amounted to a "blank check" for the company to make unauthorized deductions from his wages.

According to the arbitrator, the employee's attitude "amounted to a deliberate defiance of the legitimate exercise of managerial authority in terms of the requirement that employees sign for the tools and materials they are issued." Rejecting the worker's argument that signing the voucher was equivalent to signing a "blank check," the arbitrator stressed that there was "no evidence that the employer had ever made improper or unauthorized deductions from employee paychecks in the past as a result of their having signed the voucher" (*Budd Co.*, 75 LA 281; see also 43 LA 46, 40 LA 562).

● *By contrast*, an arbitrator overturned the discipline that was imposed on a Spanish-speaking employee for insubordination, finding that a language barrier kept the employee from understanding a documentation procedure required by his employer. The employee had been told to sign a document, the purpose of which was to confirm that supervisors had given the employee safety instructions. According to the arbitrator, the employer did not have just cause to suspend the employee for refusing to sign the document, because the employee in good faith did not understand why he had to sign it (*Bud Antle Inc.*, 106 LA 101).

● An employee who failed to follow policy changes and new procedures at a detached clinic where she was the sole laboratory technician was improperly discharged for insubordination, an arbitrator ruled. Because the employee was located five miles from her supervisor, she had to exercise more independent judgment than might otherwise have been required, the arbitrator noted, adding that the physical separation undoubtedly made effective communications difficult and contributed to a number of misunderstandings. Furthermore, the arbitrator pointed out, the employee, upon challenging the policy changes, had been assured by her supervisor that she could continue to use her discretion regarding the facility's operating procedures. Under the circumstances, discharge was not warranted, the arbitrator concluded (*Permanente Medical Group*, 52 LA 217).

B. Work Schedules and Overtime

Cases involving discipline for insubordination often deal with employee refusals to work when they are needed. Absent specific contract provisions to the contrary, arbitrators generally agree that it is within management's province to establish employees' regular schedules and decide when they will perform call-in duties and overtime work.

[See also Part 16, Wages and Hours, C. Overtime Work & Pay]

● A college had just cause to discharge a professor who refused to teach a course because of a conflict with her personal schedule, an arbitrator ruled. The college required its instructors to have a class load of 15 hours, which translated to five classes, but the professor objected that an afternoon class would interfere with her ability to pick up her daughter from day care. The arbitrator decided that the evidence of insubordination supported termination, because the professor defied a directive in refusing to accept a fifth class that she would have had to teach in the afternoon. Emphasizing the difficulty the professor faced in balancing her work and family responsibilities, however, the arbitrator went on to recommend that the college rehire the professor if she could adjust her personal life in a way that would accommodate her job requirements (*Bevill State Community College*, 121 LA 609).

● A seven-day suspension was warranted for a flight attendant who refused an extension of duty that would have added another flight to the ones she was originally scheduled to work, an arbitration board held. The flight attendant refused the extension because of a dental appointment and a problem with baby-sitting arrangements for her children. Nevertheless, the arbitration board found that she was obliged to accept the additional flight. In upholding the suspension, the arbitration board noted that flight attendants "are required to have flexible personal schedules in order to accommodate their employers' requirements" with regard to staffing flights and avoiding the delays that occur when a plane lacks the personnel needed to make up a flight crew (*Piedmont Airlines Inc.*, 103 LA 751).

• Discharge was warranted for a police officer who refused to follow a lieutenant's order to finish his shift rather than leaving early, an arbitrator found. In addition to disobeying a direct order, the officer used profanity and was disrespectful toward the lieutenant. The arbitrator pointed out that the officer had been disciplined previously for insubordination and said the latest offense "was so glaring that no express notice need be given that discharge could be a consequence" (*City of Alton*, 121 LA 1288).

• A conflict that arose when a supervisor called an employee to report for unscheduled work did not rise to the level of insubordination that would justify termination, an arbitrator ruled. The employee, whose job made him subject to call-in duties, was contacted while receiving a hair treatment and directed to report to work immediately. The employer claimed the employee refused and hung up on his supervisor, but the employee did report within an hour. When management subsequently confronted him to impose discipline, an argument ensued and the employee allegedly shouted profanities. Finding that the testimony did not support the severity attributed to the incidents by the employer, the arbitrator determined that the appropriate penalty for the employee's insubordination was a written warning (*Bunge Corp.*, 111 LA 1201).

• An arbitrator reversed the discharge of a union trial-board member for insubordination after he left work without permission to attend a union convention. The employer was required to grant a leave of absence to any employee "designated by the union" to attend a convention "or other official union business," the arbitrator found. The timing of the situation did not allow the employee to follow the "obey now, grieve later" rule, because internecine union politics made a swift resolution of the member's predicament unlikely before the convention, the arbitrator observed (*Dole Refrigerating Co.*, 96 LA 787).

1. Overtime Requirements

While agreeing that employers generally have the right to require employees to work overtime, arbitrators also have placed certain limitations on that right. For example, one arbitrator asserted that compulsory overtime must be of reasonable duration; commensurate with employee health, safety, and endurance; and ordered under reasonable circumstances (*Texas Co.*, 14 LA 146).

Another arbitrator said "reasonable excuses for not working overtime must be accepted" (*American Body & Equipment Co.*, 49 LA 1172). Still another arbitrator required a number of conditions to be met before disciplining employees for refusing overtime, including the following:

• advance notice of overtime requirements must be given except in emergencies;

• overtime must be assigned first to qualified employees who are willing to work extra hours; and

• only if there are not enough willing workers may unwilling employees be required to work overtime (*Sunbeam Electric (P.R.) Co.*, 41 LA 834).

2. Health and Endurance

Claims of physical inability may provide grounds for overturning disciplinary action taken against employees for refusing to work overtime. As one arbitrator stated, "that genuine illness is a proper excuse for nonperformance of a work assignment—overtime or regular—goes beyond reasonable question" (*United States Steel Corp.*, 63 LA 608).

• An employee who had a recent history of disability and severe back pain was justified in refusing to obey a supervisor's order to work overtime because of the "serious hazard" posed by such work, an arbitrator decided (*Pet Dealers Supply Co.*, 60 LA 814).

● In recognition of a "fatigue factor," an arbitrator ruled that an employer improperly suspended an employee who had already worked 12 hours and refused an order to work two additional hours. The employee contended that he had become fatigued and was concerned about his safety. Noting that the employee worked around a constantly moving line and machinery, the arbitrator said he could "well appreciate the danger, because of fatigue, to anyone required to work there continuously for more than twelve hours." Adding that the evidence showed that no other workers in the employee's department had ever been required to work more than 12 hours in one day, the arbitrator said the employee "was excused from any obligation to comply with the order" to work the additional hours (*Quaker Oats Co.*, 84 LA 1085).

● In another case, an arbitrator found that management properly disciplined an employee who claimed that he could not work overtime because he was "sick" from the heat. The worker's "excuse of sickness," the arbitrator decided, was "for the sole purpose of avoiding overtime work and did not represent a true account of his physical condition at the time such excuse was made" (*Becton, Dickinson & Co.*, 60 LA 913).

3. Religious Conflicts

Employees' religious beliefs and practices may lead to scheduling difficulties. Although employers are required to make reasonable accommodations for sincerely held beliefs, religious conflicts do not automatically constitute a valid reason for refusing to work overtime.

● One arbitrator held that employees' refusal to work on Christmas Eve and New Year's Eve was not punishable as insubordination in view of the "peculiar and sacred" place those holidays occupy in the culture and in view of the irretrievable loss that would result if the employees followed the "obey now, grieve later" rule (*Kaiser Steel Corp.*, 31 LA 567).

● In upholding the discharge of an employee who refused overtime because

he had "certain duties to perform as a minister," another arbitrator ruled that "this very high calling does not entitle an employee to exceptional consideration" (*Food Haven Inc.*, 62 LA 1246).

● In another case involving religious conflicts, an arbitrator insisted that "chaos" would follow if an employee were permitted to "determine for himself, for reasons sufficient to him, whether he will regularly not work on a workday" that "management has the right to schedule" (*Combustion Engineering Inc.*, 49 LA 204).

4. Personal Hardship

Personal inconvenience or hardship resulting from extra work requirements also is cited as an excuse for refusing overtime. Depending on the severity of the hardship, arbitrators may accept the excuse as a valid reason for the refusal.

● In one case, an arbitrator held that an employee's personal needs warranted deference. The arbitrator acknowledged that emergencies and other circumstances can give rise to overtime requirements that outweigh "all but the very most vital needs of a good faith employee." At the same time, however, the arbitrator observed that in most cases there must be some give and take between employer and employee to reach a "common sense" adjustment of overtime problems. With that reasoning, the arbitrator found that the employer was unjustified in demanding that the employee report for work on the day her house was being moved to a new location (*Southwestern Bell*, 61 LA 202).

● *By contrast*, another arbitrator ruled that an employer had the right to reject an employee's attempt to be excused from overtime on a permanent basis because of a conflict with his car pool arrangements. An exemption from overtime duty was not warranted, the arbitrator found, even though the employer had encouraged employees to form car pools and was required by contract to excuse employees from overtime if the overtime would cause hardship or serious inconvenience (*American Can Co.*, 65 LA 12).

● A two-day suspension was warranted for an employee who refused to report for an emergency weekend overtime because of a purported conflict with "personal business," an arbitrator decided. After warning the employee that failure to respond to the company's emergency would be grounds for discipline, the employer issued a two-day suspension and a final warning notice when the employee did not report for the weekend overtime. The arbitrator upheld the employee's suspension for refusing to work without providing a plausible explanation. However, the arbitrator set aside the final warning, finding that it was not called for under the employer's progressive discipline program (*Phillips Petroleum Co.*, 116 LA 1251).

C. Safety and Working Conditions

The leading exception to the "obey now, grieve later" doctrine arises when employees have reasonable cause to believe that the work they have been told to perform is unusually hazardous.

[See also Part 3, Safety and Health, A. Safety.]

While some arbitrators have taken the position that workers must prove the existence of unsafe conditions to justify their refusal to obey orders, most agree that employees are protected if they have a good-faith belief that the situation is abnormally dangerous, even if in actuality conditions are safe. As one arbitrator put it, discipline should not be imposed on an employee who is "sincere in his belief of danger and so long as he makes a 'reasonable' appraisal of the potential hazards" (*A.M. Castle & Co.*, 41 LA 666; see also 67 LA 486, 30 LA 648).

● Applying this reasoning, an arbitrator awarded reinstatement to an outside electrician who refused to throw two high voltage switches unless another outside electrician were present. In support of its decision to fire the employee for insubordination, his employer insisted that the refusal to obey an order based on safety factors could not be justified absent evidence of actual danger. The arbitrator rejected that argument, concluding that a refusal to obey an order may be justified by a good-faith fear for personal safety, whether or not a hazard really exists. Stressing that the employee's fear was "real" enough,

the arbitrator overturned his termination (*Hercules Inc.*, 48 LA 788).

● A worker was improperly suspended for insubordination after refusing to operate a vehicle he believed was in an unsafe condition, an arbitrator ruled. After experiencing problems over a prolonged period of time with the brake system on the vehicle, the worker told his supervisor that he had no desire to continue operating it. When the employee was once again assigned to the vehicle, he said he would "rather not" operate it. He was then suspended for disobedience. Finding, however, that the worker's desire not to operate the vehicle was based on a legitimate concern for his personal safety, the arbitrator decided that the suspension was unjust (*Georgia-Pacific Corp.*, 75 LA 808; see also 98 LA 72).

● Another arbitrator refused to uphold the discipline of an employee who refused an assignment for safety reasons, even though the employee did not claim that he was avoiding a danger to himself. The arbitrator held that the employee was unjustifiably disciplined for insubordination when he refused to work with another worker who performed his job in such a way as to endanger the safety of others (*Midland Structural Steel Corp.*, 30 LA 38).

● *By contrast,* an arbitrator upheld the suspensions imposed on a group of employees who refused to work in the presence of an acid mist. Their employer had offered to provide respirators to protect the employees from the mist, but they contended that use of the respirators would not reduce the danger of the acid. According to the arbitrator, the employees showed only that there were "abnormal conditions" in the work area, not that such conditions were "abnormally dangerous." The employees could not assume that the respirators would have been ineffective, the arbitrator added in upholding their suspensions (*Bunker Hill Co.*, 65 LA 182).

1. Hazardous Versus Uncomfortable

If working conditions are merely uncomfortable instead of hazardous, arbitrators are not likely to excuse a refusal to carry out a work order or assignment. At some point, however, conditions can become so bad as to make it unreasonable for management to require employees to continue working.

● The latter type of situation was found by an arbitrator in a steel fabricating plant where the heat was turned off for renovation during the winter and the thermometer dipped to 20 degrees. Disciplinary suspensions of workers who walked out were set aside by the arbitrator (*Berger Steel Co. Inc.*, 46 LA 1131).

● In another case, seven employees who were working on overtime told their foreman they were going home on a day when the temperature in the plant approached 100 degrees. Their foreman told them they were making a mistake, but they left nevertheless. They were subsequently terminated.

An arbitrator agreed with the company that the employees had violated the well recognized standard that prohibits employees from leaving without permission, whether they are performing regular or overtime work. Mitigating circumstances were found here, however. For example, the arbitrator said the foreman's vague response to the employees was at best only a half warning. He probably could have forestalled the walkout if he had told the employees that they had a duty to remain and that they would be disciplined if they left without permission, the arbitrator observed, reducing the discharges to two-week disciplinary layoffs (*Phelps Dodge Aluminum Products Corp.*, 52 LA 375).

● An arbitrator found that an employer's use of portable toilets at a shipyard was not a serious threat to the safety and health of employees because there was no evidence that the toilets were unsanitary. The employees had objected to the toilets, claiming that it was unpleasant to use such facilities without the benefit of hot and cold running water. The arbitrator concluded that the employees failed to prove that any disease or ailment had been contracted by the use of the facilities and that, therefore, there was no basis for their complaint (*National Steel and Shipbuilding Co.*, 64 LA 466).

2. *Medical Restrictions*

In some cases, restrictions or limitations owing to a medical problem, injury, or dis-

ability can excuse employees from carrying out assigned work.

● An arbitrator held that an employee who had tendonitis was not insubordinate when she refused a work assignment with the reasonable belief that she physically could not perform the work because of her documented medical condition (*Stockham Valve and Fittings Inc.*, 102 LA 73).

● Discipline was not warranted for an employee at a manufacturing facility who objected to operating two punch presses simultaneously, an arbitrator held. The employee had been injured previously and, after she began operating the two machines, she complained that the work hurt her shoulders. The arbitrator noted that the employee, who also served as a union official, met with management about the assignment. Although she thought the operation of two presses at the same time was unreasonable and possibly unsafe for her, she did in fact return to the assignment after meeting with management, and she continued to work until quitting time. Under the circumstances, the employer was not justified in disciplining the employee for insubordination, the arbitrator found (*Time-O-Matic Inc.*, 118 LA 1459).

● Another arbitrator ruled that an employer had just cause to terminate an employee who claimed that medical restrictions prevented him from performing janitorial work. The employer had assigned the employee to clean bathrooms and locker rooms, contending that the assignment did not exceed the employee's lifting, bending, and twisting limitations owing to a back problem. After the employee repeatedly refused to perform the work, he was terminated for insubordination. The arbitrator said the employee's restrictions might have made it unsafe for him to perform some types of work, but the evidence indicated that the janitorial assignment fell within his restrictions. Thus, the employee had no legitimate excuse for refusing the work and was justifiably discharged, the arbitrator held (*U.S. Steel Corp.*, 120 LA 1801).

● Despite an employee's claim that medical problems prevented him from working extended shifts, his employer had just cause to fire him for insubordination, an arbitrator ruled. The employer extended its shifts to nine hours to fill a large order on time, but the employee said he could only work eight-hour shifts because of a health problem. Subsequently, on four workdays, the employee worked his regular shift and went home. Management warned that he must provide documentation of his health problem to be excused, but the employee never complied. The arbitrator concluded that the employer had just cause for discharge by "a wide margin" based on the employee's insubordination on at least nine occasions, including "four when he refused to work overtime, four times when he refused to provide a medical slip, and once when he refused to grant a release of medical information." (*Key Rock Energy*, 115 LA 462).

● An employee who claimed extreme nervousness moved her work area farther away from the noisy area of the plant despite her foreman's order to remain until she substantiated her complaint with a doctor's slip. An arbitrator upheld the employee's discharge, finding that she repeatedly disobeyed orders to stay at her regular workstation, ignored a warning of discharge, and "acted with full knowledge of the consequences" (*Scripto Inc.*, 48 LA 980).

D. Conflicting Laws or Regulations

Arbitrators are reluctant to sustain disciplinary actions when employees fail to obey management directives because of a good-faith and reasonable belief that their compliance would conflict with a valid right, law, or regulation.

● A pilot should not have been fired for insubordination after he decided to refuse a flight, because he based his decision on a regulation limiting the number of hours pilots could remain on duty, an arbitration board ruled. Employees do not have to follow management directives that are illegal, the arbitration board noted. Concluding that the pilot acted reasonably in determining that he was barred from beginning a flight that would have caused him to ex-

ceed 16 hours of duty in a 24-hour period, the arbitration board found that the pilot "met the qualifications for the illegality exception to the 'obey now, grieve later' rule" and therefore was entitled to reinstatement with back pay (*Pan American Airways Corp.*, 116 LA 757).

● Discharge was not warranted where an employee of an armored car service refused to cut the seal on a bag of currency, an arbitrator held. The employer implemented a new procedure requiring employees to open damaged bags and count the currency inside, because it suspected that some currency was being extracted when bags got holes in them. A few days later, when the employee encountered a damaged bag and was told to follow the new procedure, he refused to do so, insisting that "tampering" with the seal would be illegal. The arbitrator noted that the employee had been taught by directive and custom of 11 years' duration that he should never break the "sacrosanct" seal of any bag. While acknowledging that management did not order the employee to perform an illegal act, the arbitrator said discharge was not appropriate where the employee had a good-faith belief that legal complications could arise if he obeyed the order (*Brinks Inc.*, 76 LA 1120).

● Another arbitrator overturned the discharge of an employee who was ordered to participate in an instructional session but refused to attend without a union representative. After getting into a loud argument with a co-worker, the employee was ordered to undergo training and counseling to improve her future conduct. The employee demanded union representation, but she was mistaken in her belief that Weingarten rights applied to the instructional session. Deciding that the employee should not have been fired for insubordination, the arbitrator said refusing to ignore a supposed legal right is not equivalent to failing to comply with management directives regarding the performance of work duties (*Health Care and Retirement Corp.*, 105 LA 449).

XIX. Sexual Harassment [LA CDI 100.552510 (public employees); 118.640]

OVERVIEW

Employers have a legal obligation to prohibit sexual harassment in the workplace, and they face the prospect of costly litigation whenever their workers fall victim to this type of behavior at the hands of fellow employees. In recognition of the grave implications such behavior can have, employers and arbitrators alike tend to treat sexual harassment as serious misconduct that warrants termination or other severe discipline.

Under Title VII of the Civil Right Act of 1964, sexual harassment is considered a form of unlawful gender-based discrimination. There are two categories of sexual harassment:

• *Hostile environment harassment* occurs when an employee is subjected to a pattern of unwelcome conduct in the workplace that creates a hostile, intimidating, or offensive work environment. It should be noted that the conduct need not be of a specifically sexual nature, it need only be gender-based.

• *Quid pro quo harassment,* from the Latin phrase meaning "this for that," typically involves an individual with managerial authority demanding sexual favors from an employee in exchange for bestowing job-related benefits, which might include special treatment or something as basic as staying employed.

When sexual harassment cases go to arbitration, they typically involve grievances challenging discipline imposed on the alleged harassers. In comparison, grievances seeking remedies on behalf of the victims of sexual harassment are quite rare. Additionally, the vast majority of arbitration cases involve hostile environment harassment, because workers covered by union contracts seldom hold positions in which they can be accused of quid pro quo harassment.

Discipline for sexual harassment can stem from a wide range of conduct, such as sexual remarks or propositions, gender baiting or hazing, obscene gestures, physical touching, and computer activities or electronic communications that are sexual in nature. To constitute hostile environment harassment in violation of Title VII, such behaviors generally have to be unwelcome and sufficiently severe or pervasive as to interfere with or alter the conditions of the victims' employment.

While arbitrators commonly refer to these legal standards when ruling on sexual harassment cases, their decisions do not necessarily hinge on the requirements or definitions established under Title VII. On the contrary, arbitrators draw their authority from collective bargaining agreements, and they are more concerned with the enforcement of contractual work rules than the application of external law. If workplace rules or policies on sexual harassment are more stringent than Title VII—for example, barring any and all conduct that can create a hostile work environment—employees who violate those rules can be subject to disciplinary action even if their behavior does not rise to the level of unlawful sexual harassment.

SUMMARY OF CASES

A. Discharge or Discipline Upheld

Employers commonly subject employees to severe consequences for engaging in conduct that either creates a hostile environment or simply violates work rules and policies on sexual harassment. Arbitrators are likely to uphold discharge or discipline decisions based on a wide range of behaviors, including the following:

● sexual, crude, or suggestive language directed at co-workers (107 LA 331, 106 LA 371, 88 LA 791);

● unwanted sexual advances or persistent requests for dates (114 LA 725, 113 LA 129, 82 LA 921);

● obscene gestures (122 LA 892, 103 LA 248, 90 LA 1230, 78 LA 985, 78 LA 690);

● suggestive physical contact or inappropriate touching (105 LA 718, 97 LA 957, 85 LA 246);

● grabbing, fondling, or kissing co-workers (112 LA 120, 104 LA 125, 102 LA 737, 101 LA 982, 99 LA 969, 82 LA 640);

● exposing oneself to co-workers (101 LA 1151, 86 LA 1253);

● giving sexually graphic written materials to co-workers (121 LA 1411, 102 LA 161);

● making sexual jokes (121 LA 54, 112 LA 1050, 104 LA 779, 86 LA 249); and

● engaging in computer activities that involve pornography (119 LA 1371, 119 LA 26, 118 LA 1212, 117 LA 1569).

1. Cases Involving Discharge

Arbitrators have sustained terminations in numerous cases stemming from accusations of sexual harassment. Some common factors that arbitrators tend to cite in upholding discharge include the existence of rules or policies prohibiting sexual harassment, advance warning for employees of the potential consequences of violations, and employers' observance of proper procedures in establishing proof of misconduct and meting out discipline.

● A female police officer was discharged for a number of offenses. Contributing to her problems was the fact that she had been placed on administrative leave for calling a fellow female officer "flat chested," which the arbitrator said "no doubt" was sexual harassment. The officer had trouble adjusting to the workplace after she returned from the leave (*City of San Carlos*, 127 LA 1609).

• An arbitrator ruled a school had just cause to discharge a girl's softball coach/hall monitor, where he had highly improper conversations with a female student about sexual positions and anal sex, and he had improperly touched a female student 18 years earlier, which bolstered the current complaint (*Canton City School District*, 129 LA 86).

• A township had just cause to discharge an assistant fire chief who sexually harassed a subordinate and two wives of subordinates, where he made inappropriate comments about their sex lives, and grabbed them. The arbitrator found that even though he had close to five years of service without any discipline, he irreparably damaged his employment relationship with the department (*Brookfield Township*, 129 LA 1794).

• An employer acted properly in firing an employee who created a hostile environment for one co-worker and also sexually harassed other female employees, an arbitrator ruled. The employee had been making sexual advances toward the co-worker for months, but she did not complain to management until the employee's unwanted behavior increased in intensity. The employer promptly looked into the matter, and its investigation revealed the veracity of the co-worker's allegations as well as several other incidents of sexual harassment, all of which were corroborated by other witnesses. In addition to citing this pattern of harassment, the employer cited the employee's relatively brief and checkered service record with the company as justification for its decision to fire him.

In upholding the employee's termination, the arbitrator noted that the employer had a policy prohibiting sexual harassment, and the employee's receipt of the policy, as well as its communication to him in training sessions, served as proper notice that his conduct could result in termination. Additionally, the arbitrator found that the employer evenhandedly applied its policy by meting out consistent punishment for

violations. Given the employee's service record, the seriousness of his misconduct, and his apparent lack of remorse, the arbitrator determined that he was "not a candidate for rehabilitation" and termination was "not excessive" (*Carolina Telephone & Telegraph Co.*, 118 LA 1712).

• An employee who directed a sexually loaded remark at a female co-worker over his employer's intercom was properly discharged, an arbitrator held. In the wake of an argument, the employee used the intercom to call out to the co-worker, "Blow me." The arbitrator agreed with the employer's conclusion that the employee violated its sexual harassment policy, which said "all our employees should be able to enjoy a work environment free of discrimination and harassment" and made violations punishable by discipline "up to and including immediate discharge." The union argued that the employer acted out of fear of litigation, but the arbitrator refused to hold that against the employer. The employer hoped to be a law-abiding citizen in enforcing its policy, the arbitrator noted, and one benefit of following the law is freedom from litigation. Adding that the employee had been advised of the policy and the penalties for noncompliance, the arbitrator upheld his termination (*AMG Industries Inc.*, 106 LA 322).

• An employer had just cause to fire an employee, where he touched, stared at, and made unwanted solicitations to several female co-workers, an arbitrator decided. The employee had received training on sexual harassment and clearly was advised that his employer prohibited the type of conduct in which he engaged, the arbitrator emphasized. Discharge was warranted even though some of the employee's conduct took place while he was off duty, the arbitrator added, noting that employers have an interest in protecting their workers from sexual harassment at the hands of fellow employees regardless of where the harassment occurs (*Thyssenkrupp Budd Co.*, 121 LA 164).

• An arbitrator found that a sales representative's conduct during a meeting at a hotel constituted sexual harassment. One female co-worker alleged that the employee poked and eventually kissed her in trying to find out the room number of another woman. A second female co-worker said the employee had grabbed her buttocks and responded with obscenities when she asked him to leave her alone. The employee eventually went to the room of a third female co-worker, where he allegedly grabbed the woman's roommate, pulled her on top of him, and passed out on the bed. The arbitrator upheld the discharge, holding that the meeting was held to further the employer's business interests, and therefore, the employee was properly held accountable for his misconduct (*Superior Coffee and Foods*, 103 LA 609).

● An incident involving relatively mild conduct provided an adequate basis for terminating an employee who was subject to a last-chance agreement, an arbitrator ruled. The employee previously had been disciplined for improperly touching three female co-workers and was warned that any future violations of his employer's sexual harassment policy would result in immediate discharge. The employee's termination occurred after a male colleague falsely claimed to be going for drinks with a female co-worker. Upon hearing this, the employee gently put his hands on the female co-worker's shoulders for perhaps two seconds and asked, "Why are you going out with [him] when you are not going out with me?" The female co-worker was frightened and began crying.

Based in part on the emotional reaction of the female co-worker, the arbitrator concluded that the employee engaged in misconduct that violated his "last and final warning status." While noting that the employee was friends with the co-worker and it was extremely unlikely that he meant her any harm, the arbitrator said the employee made a mistake in the way he abruptly touched her, and he "knew or should have known that he could not afford to make another mistake in touching female employees" (*Interstate Brands Corp.*, 120 LA 865).

● In another case, an arbitrator held that an employer had just cause to fire an employee for unwanted physical contact with a supervisor. The employee reportedly approached the supervisor at a company Christmas party, began rubbing her back, and ignored her two times before finally complying when she told him a third time to stop. When confronted about the incident, the employee denied engaging in the complained of conduct. However, the employer interviewed several witnesses who corroborated the supervisor's version of what happened. The arbitrator found that discharge was warranted under a company policy that called for immediate dismissal based on any improper conduct that "adversely affects the employee's relationship with fellow employees," including supervisors (*Pepsi-Americas Inc.*, 120 LA 1793).

● An employee's demeaning sexual comment to a gay co-worker provided just cause for discharge, despite the employee's contention that the remark was meant as a joke, an arbitrator held. The employee's comment was an offensive reference to the co-worker's homosexuality, the arbitrator found, and it violated an employer policy that incorporated the language of a city ordinance prohibiting harassment based on "sexual or affectional preference." Adding that management's attempts to eliminate harassment must be given due deference, the arbitrator upheld the employee's termination (*Fry's Food Stores of Arizona Inc.*, 99 LA 1161).

● Just cause existed to discharge a female employee under a rule against sexual harassment for writing anonymous letters that accused a female co-worker of sexual infidelity with her supervisor, an arbitrator concluded. The letters were examined by a handwriting expert, who definitively established that the employee wrote them. The employee was "incontestably guilty" of harassment that was calculated to "bring disrepute" to the co-worker and created "a psychologically repressive work environment," the arbitrator found. Although not "unmindful" of the employee's exemplary record during 32 years of service, the arbitrator said it was not a mitigating factor in this case because the misconduct was not only "heinous," but also "in most respects more serious than other forms of sexual harassment" prohibited by the employer (*Schlage Lock Co.*, 88 LA 75).

• An employer had just cause to discharge a gay employee based on his explicit recounting of his sexual encounters and his threats and propositions to three male co-workers, an arbitrator held. The co-workers had repeatedly informed the employee that his stories and conduct were unwelcome, the arbitrator found, and they testified that his conduct was repugnant, embarrassing, and intimidating for everyone in their immediate work area. In upholding the employee's termination, the arbitrator also pointed out that the employer had a policy prohibiting such conduct, and the policy had been explained to the employee as recently as one month prior to his termination (*Hughes Aircraft Co.*, 102 LA 353).

• Discharge was appropriate for an employee who admittedly asked sexually explicit questions and made sexual requests of three female co-workers. An arbitrator upheld termination even though a sexually permissive atmosphere pervaded the workplace and the employee had never been informed of his employer's sexual harassment policy. The employee admitted that his behavior was wrong and unacceptable in the workplace, the arbitrator noted, yet he persisted in his unwelcome and intimidating conduct after the female co-workers rejected his advances. In addition, the victims were frightened by his repeated harassment, and there was no evidence that the employee's behavior would change if he were reinstated, the arbitrator found (*Steuben Rural Electric Corp. Inc.*, 98 LA 337);

2. Cases Involving Lesser Discipline

Arbitration cases in which employers have responded to sexually harassing behavior with discipline short of termination are somewhat less common than discharge cases, but arbitrators are no less likely to uphold the discipline imposed.

• An arbitrator unheld a city's demotion of a male police corporal, who had a female subordinate remove her duty belt and unbutton her shirt, then removed her shirt from her shoulder and placed his hand inside her ballistic vest. Despite contentions there was a safety need for the officer to adjust her vest, his actions violated rules describing conduct unbecoming for police officers, and there was no real safety need to adjust the female officer's vest (*City of Mission*, 126 LA 1372).

• An arbitrator ruled that a university had just cause to suspend a professor for one quarter for violating its policy against sexual harassment by showering unwanted attention on a female student through physical and verbal behavior that unreasonably affected her performance. There had been no similar incidents in the professor's 19 years with the university and he had been designated three years prior as professor of the year. The suspension was upheld because the arbitrator found that the professor continued to insist that he had done nothing wrong and the university appropriately decided that any lesser penalty would fail to impart a message that such conduct was considered serious (*California State University*, 128 LA 404).

• An arbitrator ruled an employer had just cause to discipline an employee for sending sexual text messages to co-workers, despite his contention that he sent messages only to co-workers who had sent him similar messages, where two co-workers denied that they had sent the grievant such messages, the grievant sent "thousands" of sexual messages, and it was doubtful that he could be sure they were all sent only to employees who had sent him messages. However, the arbitrator reduced the discharge to a long-term suspension, because the employee acknowledged that what he had done was wrong and said that if reinstated he would not repeat the conduct, and termination is too harsh for the first employee "caught" (*Sara Lee Foods*, 128 LA 129).

• An arbitrator upheld an employer's discipline of an employee who transmitted an email of a tattooed male nude figure, even though most recipients were not offended, where one was. The arbitrator reasoned that it could not be ruled out that a co-worker by chance walking by the computer terminal at the time the attachment was opened could have observed the email and been offended (*American Red Cross*, 125 LA 1696).

• A male officer was suspended for three days with just cause for violating the agency sexual harassment policy through remarks that created an intimidating, hostile, or offensive environment. After seeing a female officer off-work at a pool, he telephoned her at work to "compliment" her on her tan and bikini and to ask about unseen tattoos. He also made comments about her physical characteristics to another female officer. The grievant had already been disciplined three times, including once for personal boundary/touching issues (*Minnesota Department of Corrections*, 127 LA 273).

• A university had just cause to suspend for one term a teacher, who had been a professor of the year for three years, for violating its sexual harassment policy. He showered unwanted attention on a female employee by holding, touching, and kissing her, obstructed her movements to escape, and made comments to the effect that her beauty was distracting. The penalty was warranted, the arbitrator held, because the professor continued to insist that he had done nothing wrong, and any lesser penalty would send the message that the misconduct was not considered serious (*California State University*, 128 LA 404).

• A 20-day suspension was appropriate for an employee who "bluntly solicited" a female co-worker, an arbitrator ruled. The employee on several occasions, both on and off the job, told the co-worker that he wanted to have oral sex with her. The co-worker did not respond to the employee's advances, would "hide" from the employee when he came to her work area, reported the incidents to her supervisor, and submitted a written statement to the employer detailing the misconduct. Management suspended the employee for "disruptive harassment" for his "unceasing efforts" to win the co-worker's submission.

The arbitrator concluded that the misconduct "interfered" with the co-worker's job performance, adding that the facts "established to a degree of certainty one rarely encounters" a hostile, abusive, and intimidating work environment. The employer had a legal obligation to take "immediate and appropriate corrective action," the arbitrator pointed out in upholding the suspension (*Veterans Administration Medical Center*, 87 LA 405).

• In a case of same-sex harassment, an arbitrator found that an employer properly suspended an employee for his repeated questioning of a co-worker about whether he wanted oral sex. The employee had received proper notice that such conduct was prohibited, the arbitrator found, pointing out that he previously had been reprimanded for violating a policy barring disrespectful conduct and obscene language directed at co-workers, and he also had been trained on avoiding sexual harassment. Although the employee contended that the training only dealt with harassment of persons of the opposite sex, the arbitrator stressed that some forms of misconduct are considered so egregious that they justify disciplinary action even if an employer has not issued specific work rules prohibiting the misconduct (*Department of Veterans Affairs*, 113 LA 961).

• An employer properly issued a two-day suspension to an employee accused of "spreading vicious rumors" about a female co-worker who spurned his romantic attentions, an arbitrator held. The co-worker had refused the employee's repeated requests for dates and eventually stopped speaking to him. Even though no physical contact between the two had transpired, the employee later told some female workers that the co-worker had become angry because he had fondled her. Upon learning of the remarks, the co-worker lodged a harassment complaint against the employee for "spreading vicious rumors." While acknowledging that the employee had an impressive record free of any prior discipline, the arbitrator said the suspension imposed on the employee was an appropriate response to his remarks. Not only are such statements "generally recognized as demeaning and a vicious degradation of character," it is clear that the employee's remarks would have had an adverse effect on the female co-worker's standing in the workplace, the arbitrator observed (*Social Security Administration*, 81 LA 459).

B. Penalties Overturned or Reduced

In other cases, arbitrators have overturned or reduced the discipline imposed on employees for allegedly engaging in sexual harassment. While arbitrators sometimes find that the evidence against employees does not support the charges, they often determine that the penalties assessed by employers are excessive because of one or more mitigating factors, such as:

- long service or a good work record without prior disciplinary problems (85 LA 11, 83 LA 570, 80 LA 19, 71 LA 54);
- procedural shortcomings in management's efforts to substantiate allegations of sexual harassment (122 LA 33, 88 LA 1292, 82 LA 25);
- inconsistent enforcement or an environment of tolerance caused by management's participation in or failure to address conduct of a similar nature (119 LA 737, 112 LA 877, 106 LA 776, 106 LA 360, 101 LA 107, 94 LA 297, 92 LA 1090);
- ambiguousness of the misconduct or a lack of evidence that the behavior was unwelcome or offensive (122 LA 1298, 112 LA 257, 111 LA 554, 86 LA 254); and
- a likelihood that the conduct in question amounted to an isolated incident that would not recur or that lesser discipline would result in rehabilitation of the offending employees (114 LA 819, 109 LA 768, 108 LA 787, 79 LA 940).

1. Punishment Found Inappropriate

The following are examples of cases in which arbitrators overturned or reduced the punishment meted out by employers.

- An arbitrator found that an employer did not have just cause to discharge an employee who called a male co-worker a "faggot" and said that he heard of the co-worker's "evening gown weekend." The grievant was a friend of the co-worker, who had recently revealed his homosexuality, and the grievant was concerned that his friend's flamboyant behavior would get him in trouble. The arbitrator observed that the statements were not hate-related. Nevertheless, the grievant was suspended for his time off and given a last-chance agreement (American Airlines Inc., 125 LA 1025).
- A college did not have just cause to discipline a professor for his classroom behavior, even though he made assorted sexual innuendoes and ethnic slurs that were found to be offensive by some students, and

had been warned in writing about such conduct two years earlier, an arbitrator ruled. He was also an award-winning tenured teacher with a gift for making students learn; he was reinstated without back pay. (City Colleges of Chicago, 126 LA 1801).

- An employee was accused of repeatedly propositioning a female co-worker and making many sexually suggestive remarks. The harassment was so persistent and upsetting, the co-worker said, that she felt ill and had to leave work early. She complained to management, and the employee was fired. An arbitrator found that the employee sexually harassed the co-worker, unreasonably interfered with her work, and created a hostile work environment. However, the arbitrator said, there were mitigating factors in the case, including the employer's lack of a written policy on preventing sexual harassment, the lack of sensitivity training on the subject for the employees, and the absence of any warnings of the consequences of engaging in such behavior. Because of these mitigating factors, the arbitrator ordered the male employee's discharge reduced to an unpaid disciplinary layoff (Commercial Printing Co., 115 LA 393).
- A company's lack of a specific policy against sexual harassment also contributed to another arbitrator's decision to overturn an employee's termination. During a power outage at work, the employee had hovered around and briefly touched a female co-worker. The company's employee handbook did not directly address sexual harassment, but it did state that discharge could result from "threatening or gross intimidation of other employees" or "immoral conduct or indecency." According to the arbitrator, the employee's offense did not fall into either category. Noting that the employee had 25 years of service with no prior discipline for similar misconduct, the arbitrator ordered reinstatement without back pay, concluding that discipline short of discharge would be adequate to demonstrate to all employees the company's firm resolve with respect to sexual harassment (Sugardale Foods Inc., 86 LA 1017).
- An employer's failure to follow appropriate progressive discipline steps prompted an arbitrator to overturn an

employee's termination, despite proof that he had sexually harassed three female co-workers. Although the employee had twice been warned about his behavior—which was limited to banter and kidding remarks with sexual innuendo—the second warning was much the same as the first and therefore did not constitute a clear and forceful "final warning," the arbitrator found. Based on this error and on the fact that the employee's misconduct was not egregious, the arbitrator ordered reinstatement with partial back pay (*Dow Chemical Corp.*, 95 LA 510).

• Another arbitrator awarded reinstatement with back pay to an employee who was fired for making obnoxious sexual comments to a female co-worker. The employee contended that the co-worker did not object to his remarks, but rather was a willing participant in and sometimes the initiator of such behavior. Emphasizing that the co-worker did not appear as a witness at the arbitration hearing and no one else gave testimony refuting the employee's contentions, the arbitrator held that the employer failed to establish that the employee engaged in unwelcome conduct that would rise to the level of sexual harassment (*TNT Logistics North America Inc.*, 121 LA 1434).

• Discharge was too severe a penalty for a male police officer with 17 years of service who sexually harassed a female co-worker, an arbitrator found. The officer was accused of unfastening the bra straps of the female co-worker while the two were parked in a city van. Management believed the female officer's allegations and decided to fire the officer. The employer had just cause to discipline the male officer, but not to discharge him, the arbitrator said, given the officer's 17-year, discipline-free employment record and the fact that the employer's policy on sexual harassment did not require such a drastic punishment, especially for a first offense. The arbitrator reduced the discipline to a one-year suspension (*City of Boston*, 116 LA 906).

• Discharge was reduced to a seven-month suspension for an employee who allegedly pinched a female co-worker's breast while making a "kissing" sound.

The arbitrator who decided the case cited the following mitigating circumstances: the employee's 28 years of employment; the absence of past disciplinary problems in the employee's record; and the female employee's failure to report the incident when it occurred. The arbitrator warned, however, that the reduction in the penalty "should not be construed to lessen the seriousness of the conduct," nor be understood in any way to relieve the employer of its duty to protect employees from sexual harassment (*Dayton Power and Light Co.*, 80 LA 19).

• Discharge was not warranted for an employee who continued to send letters, flowers, and gifts to a female co-worker despite her protestations, an arbitrator held. Asserting that public policy does not mandate discharge for sexual harassment, but merely requires that the hostile work environment be eliminated, the arbitrator determined that the appropriate discipline under the circumstances was a written notice of violation of the employer's policy against sexual harassment (*KIAM*, 97 LA 617).

• Similarly, another arbitrator concluded that an employee's sexual banter and innuendoes warranted a one-week suspension instead of termination. Despite the duty of employers to keep their workplaces free from sexual harassment, not all offenses warrant termination, the arbitrator declared (*Mead Corp.*, 113 LA 1169).

• In a case involving the harassment of a gay co-worker, an arbitrator overturned termination in part because the harasser apologized after realizing that the co-worker had been offended. A female employee asked the worker about his family status, and when he told her he was gay, she said she suspected as much because he "sounded feminine." The female employee also used pejorative terms in referring to the co-worker, but when she asked if he was bothered, he avoided answering directly. During a subsequent discussion in which the employee and the gay co-worker expressed conflicting opinions, she said his view was different because he was gay. He asked what being gay had to do with it, and she said he was "a minority" because "a majority of men are not gay." He took offense, left work early, and subsequently brought the issue to the attention of a manager.

The employee asserted that she did not intend to denigrate the co-worker or create an offensive working environment, and she apologized once she recognized that her comments were upsetting to him. These factors mitigated against her discharge, the arbitrator held. While acknowledging that the employee's actions were "indisputably inappropriate," the arbitrator concluded that they did not rise to such an egregious level as to justify termination. Consequently, the arbitrator ordered reinstatement, but without back pay (*The Kroger Co.*, 117 LA 1601; see also 116 LA 1687).

• An arbitrator found that a three-day suspension was too severe for a leadman who violated his employer's sexual harassment policy, which required him to stop situations involving sexual content and report them to a supervisor. The employee looked at a "girlie" magazine that had been brought to work by a co-worker. He neither attempted to stop other employees from looking at the magazine, which was explicitly sexual in content, nor alerted a supervisor to its presence. Noting that the employer issued verbal warnings to other workers involved in the incident, including the one who brought the magazine into the workplace, the arbitrator determined that a verbal warning also was the appropriate penalty for the leadman's role in the incident (*American Mail-Well Envelope*, 105 LA 1209; see also 107 LA 910).

C. Harassment of Third Parties

Many arbitration cases address incidents in which employees are accused of sexually harassing third parties, such as customers, clients, independent contractors, and other nonemployees. As the following cases illustrate, arbitrators often find that such incidents provide sufficient reason to terminate or otherwise discipline employees.

• Termination was appropriate for a bus driver who was reported by a 13-year-old passenger for making sexual advances toward her (*Oahu Transit Services Inc.*, 122 LA 161).

• A university had just cause to fire a custodian based in part on his sexual ha-

rassment of two female students, which included trapping one of them in a bathroom and refusing to let her out (*Central Michigan University*, 99 LA 134).

• An employment guidance counselor was properly fired for making sexual comments to the clients of a county Human Services Department with the intention of possibly developing sexual relationships with them (*County of Ramsey, Minn.*, 86 LA 249).

• A district representative for a newspaper company was properly suspended based on his unwelcome advances, offensive questions, and comments of a sexual nature aimed at several female independent contractors who worked as paper carriers (*Dayton Newspapers Inc.*, 100 LA 48).

• A food manufacturing company had just cause to discharge an employee for making sexual propositions while visiting retail stores in order to deliver the company's products (*Nabisco Foods Co.*, 82 LA 1186).

• Similarly, a delivery driver's sexual remarks and other offensive comments while making a delivery at a bar constituted grounds for termination (*Lohr Distributing Co.*, 101 LA 1217).

• A power company properly discharged an employee for repeatedly visiting a female customer, asking increasingly personal and prying questions, and making sexual advances toward her (*American Electric Power*, 114 LA 501).

• A telephone repair technician was properly discharged for making obscene and harassing telephone calls to a customer (*Southern Bell Telephone & Telegraph Co.*, 75 LA 409).

• *By contrast*, termination was reduced to a six-month suspension for a city maintenance worker who offended several female passersby by calling out to them and emitting whistles and other sounds (*City of Rochester, N.Y.*, 82 LA 217).

• A three-day suspension was reduced to a written reprimand for an employee who attended a training session conducted by a female independent contractor and made offensive allusions to the instructor's torso when he filled out a course-evaluation form (*Michigan Dept. of Transportation*, 104 LA 1196).

D. Other Issues in Harassment Cases

A number of other issues tend to surface in connection with sexual harassment cases, including divergent views about the standard of proof employers should be required to meet, the necessity of weighing conflicting testimony from alleged victims and accused harassers, and whether victims should be granted leeway in meeting deadlines for filing complaints.

1. Employer's Burden of Proof

Although the standard normally applied in arbitration cases is proof by a preponderance of the evidence, some arbitrators have required employers to meet more stringent requirements in proving sexual harassment, reasoning that such charges are particularly serious because of their potential to affect the reputation and future job prospects of accused employees. For example, a number of arbitrators have required employers to provide "clear and convincing evidence" to substantiate charges of sexual harassment (116 LA 1331, 115 LA 1225, 110 LA 737, 104 LA 818, 100 LA 316).

While it is quite rare to apply the even loftier standard of "proof beyond a reasonable doubt," one arbitrator asserted that this was the appropriate burden for an employer to meet in a sexual harassment case. According to the arbitrator, a charge of sexual harassment clearly involves an accusation of moral turpitude that carries an enormous social stigma, and it is not overly dramatic to say that in some cases an employee's life is on the line, because substantiation of the misconduct can damage the person's standing in the community and destroy important personal and professional relationships (*King Soopers Inc.*, 86 LA 254; see also 85 LA 11).

2. Conflicting Testimony

One of the unique aspects of sexual harassment cases is that many of them hinge on weighing the testimony of alleged victims against the conflicting testimony of accused harassers. In such situations, arbitrators rely heavily on credibility determinations in deciding which version of events to believe. In some instances, the accusers themselves

become subject to discipline based on evidence showing that they have intentionally lodged false complaints.

An arbitrator ruled an employer did not have just cause to discharge an employee for sexual harassment, because the complainants who alleged the most serious offenses against him were not present at the hearing, those complainants' interview statements were not in the form of sworn affidavits, and the "quality" evidence showed only that the employee regularly maked off-color comments. The penalty was reduced to a one-week suspension (*University Hospital Inc.*, 126 LA 1719).

● Termination was warranted for an employee who was accused of embracing and kissing a co-worker, an arbitrator concluded, even though there were no witnesses and the two individuals told completely different stories. The arbitrator found the accused employee "to be a thoroughly unbelievable witness," and thus accepted the victim's version of the incident. "Employees have the right to be safe from abusive actions and it is the duty and responsibility of the company to give them this protection and further, to discipline and even discharge those employees whose misconduct justifies such a penalty," the arbitrator concluded (*Care Inns Inc.*, 81 LA 687).

● An arbitrator upheld the suspension of a male employee accused of improperly touching a female employee, despite inconsistencies between the female victim's oral and written accounts of the incident. Noting that the woman might have been so traumatized by the experience that her recollection of it was clouded, the arbitrator ruled that the inconsistencies in her accounts of what happened did not undermine the basic truthfulness of her charges (*Fisher Foods Inc.*, 80 LA 133).

● On the other hand, an arbitrator ruled that an employee was not insulated from punishment and could not make a valid case for retaliatory discharge after she lodged a false complaint of sexual harassment against her supervisor. The employee, who had a poor record and had received numerous warnings about her lax attention to her job, had been overheard telling a co-worker that she was going to "get" her supervisor. She accused him of sexual harassment, but when the matter was investigated, there was unanimous praise for the man, who had never had any complaints brought against him. By contrast, the employee had a history of fighting, making racial slurs, and sleeping on the job. The company fired her for dishonesty.

Even if the employer's action had the potential to have a chilling effect on legitimate claims of sexual harassment, it was taken for good reason, and the employee's termination was in no way retaliatory, the arbitrator determined. Such dishonesty "is commonly regarded as a first-offense dischargeable violation," the arbitrator pointed out. Furthermore, although the employer cited only the false statements as a reason for the discharge, the totality of the employee's work record, as well as her demeanor at the arbitration hearing, disqualified her "from continuing to work with others," the arbitrator concluded (*Mrs Baird's Bakeries Inc.*, 114 LA 59).

● Another arbitrator ruled that an employee was improperly suspended for allegedly making false claims of sexual harassment. The arbitrator said that although the alleged victim (who previously had been raped) may have exaggerated one claim and incorrectly stated a second, she had not done so intentionally intending to deceive or defraud (*Defense Mapping Agency*, 92 LA 653).

3. Delays in Filing Complaints

Arbitrators have ruled that delays in filing sexual harassment complaints may not be a bar to arbitration.

● In one case, an allegedly harassed employee failed to complain the first time the harassment occurred. She later left the employer, and the only remedy sought was that the "sexual remarks and verbal abuse stop." An arbitrator found that grounds for a grievance existed as long as the employee found the workplace hostile because of the actual sexual harassment or the threat of embarrassment. Moreover, the arbitrator said, public policy not only favors arbitrability as opposed to the forfeiture of rights, but also favors the resolution of sexual harassment complaints (*Burnett & Sons*, 102 LA 743).

● In another case, an arbitrator ruled that an employee's delay in filing a sexual harassment complaint should be attributed to "harmless error," because sexual harassment victims may not complain immediately as a result of the embarrassment, humiliation, and stigma attached to filing such a complaint—the underlying thinking that the harassed individual provoked or encouraged the improper conduct. The arbitrator reasoned that the employee should not lose standing to make the complaint that resulted in the arbitration (*George Koch Sons Inc.*, 102 LA 737).

XX. Sleeping & Loafing [LA CDI 100.552555 (public employees); 118.654]

OVERVIEW

Generally, arbitrators uphold termination for employees caught sleeping on the job only if the sleeping is recurrent or there is some exacerbating factor (111 LA 577, 91 LA 443, 86 LA 907). If, however, employers have work rules that make sleeping on the job a firing offense or there is an established practice that makes it so, then arbitrators usually sustain termination based on only one incident (98 LA 183, 81 LA 1263, 77 LA 1143, 74 LA 115).

In addition, discharging employees for a first offense is usually regarded as justified if the act of sleeping on the job poses a danger to fellow workers, to persons in the offending employees' care, or to company equipment (81 LA 955, 76 LA 232, 73 LA 705).

Ultimately, however, employers have the burden of proving that accused employees were in fact sleeping, rather than just resting their eyes. Employers also must show that they have consistently imposed discipline against employees caught sleeping, because discrepancies in applying rules against sleeping on the job give arbitrators reason to overturn termination (95 LA 452, 91 LA 30, 90 LA 1053, 88 LA 991, 64 LA 77, 61 LA 686, 27 LA 137, 19 LA 380, 14 LA 907).

In cases that involve loafing, meanwhile, arbitrators typically hold that discharge is too severe for a first offense. Instead, employers are expected to make use of corrective discipline and warn employees that their jobs are in jeopardy if the loafing persists (119 LA 372, 118 LA 632, 96 LA 149).

SUMMARY OF CASES

A. Penalty for Sleeping

Generally, arbitrators agree in principle that discharge is warranted for employees who are caught sleeping on the job in cases where employers have strictly enforced rules against such conduct. In the absence of a specific no-sleeping rule, arbitrators tend to weigh factors such as the type and degree of responsibility involved in the jobs of offending employees and the circumstances under which they fell asleep.

A supervisor acted reasonably and within his authority when he ordered an employee to go home because the supervisor believed that the employee was sleeping during a training session, where the supervisor observed the grievant sleeping, and the grievant had attended a meeting 13 days previously in which he was told that sleeping would not be permitted "during work hours." (*Detroit Thermal LLC*, 129 LA 1364).

1. Intentional Sleeping

A worker who makes deliberate preparations and hides out in order to take a nap—sometimes referred to as "nesting"—would deserve more severe treatment than someone who is ill or tired for a good reason and involuntarily drops off while trying to work.

● An arbitrator ruled an employer did not have just cause to discharge an employee for the offense of "intentional sleeping," even though he admittedly fell asleep in a chair, where he did not make a substitute bed and was not discovered in a hidden or inaccessible area while he was supposed to be working; he was reinstated without back pay (*BASF Corp.*, 128 LA 1233).

● An employer did not have just cause to discharge a 14-year employee who slept on the job, but did not nest, where he was a few feet from the break room and was found by a supervisor on routine inspection, an arbitrator ruled. He had not changed clothes, taken off his shoes, or darkened the room, and he was not there for an extended period of time. The arbitrator reinstated him without back pay (*American Airlines Inc.*, 128 LA 1151).

2. First Offense

● An agency had just cause to discharge two employees for sleeping on the job, even though it was their first offense, an arbitrator ruled, where the agency had a rule that indicated that discipline for sleeping on the job could include discharge. The employees were found in prone or semi-prone positions across their vehicle seats, their vehicle was parked in a darkened area, they appeared startled when the doors were opened, and they were dishonest about the incident (*U.S. Army Fleet Support*, 126 LA 580).

● An arbitrator ruled that an employer had just cause to discharge an employee for sleeping on the job, even though the employee had a long record of good service, where the employer had issued a reasonable plant rule providing that a first-time offense of sleeping on the job constituted grounds for termination. The arbitrator reasoned that any employer has the right to expect that their employees stay awake while at work in order to perform the jobs for which they are paid (*Manley Brothers of Indiana Inc.*, 106 LA 442).

● Another arbitrator found that sleeping while hazardous work was in progress was grounds for firing an employee, even though it was the first time the employee had been disciplined for sleeping on the job (*PPG Industries Inc.*, 110 LA 372).

● A health care worker at a residential treatment center for depressed and schizophrenic patients was properly fired for a first offense of sleeping on the job, an arbitrator held. After the employee was found sleeping in a lounge chair in the center's secluded, darkened living room, he was fired for violating a no-sleeping rule. The arbitrator noted that all cases of sleeping on the job are not equal. In this instance, the employee's misconduct should be elevated to a "much higher level" because his work was in a mental health facility where many patients were at high risk of harming themselves or others, the arbitrator observed. Given this heightened standard, progressive discipline was not in order (*Horizons of Michigan*, 115 LA 1672).

• A company had just cause to suspend an employee for approximately six months without pay and place him on a 12-month last-chance agreement for violating a sleeping-on-duty rule when he inadvertently fell asleep, where the employee, though not deliberately hiding, was in an area he had been told to vacate when his duties were finished (*Johnson Controls*, 129 LA 348).

• A nursing home had just cause to discharge a housekeeper for sleeping on the job, despite her contention that she sat down in a chair due to chest pains, because a supervisor caught her in the chair with her eyes closed, and the grievant did not claim that she had chest pains or deny that she was sleeping on the job the arbitrator found (*Bortz Health Care*, 126 LA 1239).

• *By contrast*, an employer did not have just cause to summarily discharge an employee for sleeping on the job in the "light duty" room, where progressive discipline should have been applied, an arbitrator ruled. The arbitrator reasoned that the no-sleeping rule was unilaterally imposed solely for the light duty room under a questionable rationale, and this was the first such offense for the employee on his first day of light duty, and reduced the discharge to a final written warning (*Harrah's Las Vegas Inc.*, 129 LA 133).

• An arbitrator ruled that a company did not have just cause to discharge an employee for sleeping on the job, even though a plant rule provided that violation "will normally be handled . . . [by] discharge," where the word "normally" implied that the company would examine mitigating circumstances, and recent meetings on enforcing rules did not provide adequate notice to employees that sleeping would result in summary discharge. Over a 28-year period penalties for sleeping on duty had ranged from no discipline to a six-month suspension with a last-chance agreement, and the employee inadvertently fell asleep and did not seek out a hiding place (*Johnson Controls*, 129 LA 348).

• An employer did not have a reasonable and sufficient cause to discharge a 31-year employee who fell asleep on the job due to a panic attack, an arbitrator ruled, where he had a nearly spotless disciplinary record, and the employer should have resorted to progressive discipline. The arbitrator decided the employer could request that the grievant submit to a medical evaluation to see if he is on proper medication prior to his reinstatement (*Georgia Power Co.*, 129 LA 481).

B. Sleeping During Break

Can employees be disciplined for sleeping during lunch breaks or rest periods? The answer to this question may depend on whether the employees took steps to make sure they would wake up before the break was over, thus indicating their intention of not overstepping the rules and only sleeping during the time when they were not required to work. If the circumstances show that employees might have slept past the end of their allotted break or rest period, arbitrators are more likely to uphold disciplinary action.

• An arbitrator ruled that an employer had just cause to issue a one-day suspension to an employee who fell asleep in her work truck in a public area, even though she was on an unpaid lunch break when discovered. She violated an employee work rule on "expectations" as to employee conduct during "work breaks and lunches," and an employee sleeping in a public area does not project a positive image of the company (*AT&T Services Inc.*, 125 LA 1601).

• A three-day suspension was too harsh a penalty for a worker who fell asleep in a break room, an arbitrator ruled. The employee had been assigned to light duty because he had rheumatoid arthritis. He generally worked independently while on these light-duty assignments, and one day, he worked through his scheduled break time and took his break later. After being discovered sleeping in the break room, he was suspended for three days because he did not have his supervisor's permission to go on break at that time. The arbitrator noted that there were several mitigating factors that rendered the punishment too harsh: the employee, by choosing to sleep in the break room, was clearly not trying to hide; the employee had been with the company for several years and had a good work history; and his sleeping posed no threat to other workers. The employee also was authorized to determine the order in which he performed his daily tasks, the arbitrator said, reducing the suspension to just one day (*AAA Plumbing Pottery Corp.*, 115 LA 351).

C. Proof of Sleeping on Job

Most arbitrators agree that discipline for sleeping on the job must be supported by convincing evidence that employees were in fact asleep (83 LA 468, 81 LA 1009).

However, one arbitrator said that actual "clinical proof" of sleeping is not required to constitute a sleeping violation, since clinical proof would require the presence of a physician or use of sophisticated sleep equipment (*Zeon Chemicals*, 129 LA 1687).

● An employee was working in the cab of a crane when several people saw his head nodding and his eyes shut. Although the employee's foreman arrived within a matter of minutes and found the employee awake, he received a two-week suspension for sleeping on the job. The employee admitted he had been drowsy, but he said his eyes were shut only because they were smarting from the oil and brake fluid in the crane cab. The union contended that from the 25- or 30-foot distance from which the employee was observed, no one could tell whether he was really asleep. An arbitrator found the discipline unjustified. The witnesses only assumed the employee was asleep, the arbitrator said, because they were not close enough to be sure (*John Deere Ottumwa Works*, 27 LA 572).

● An employee failed to respond after being paged twice on a plant's public address system, and a supervisor subsequently discovered him lying on a pile of plastic-covered bags on the roof of the plant. Although the employee explained that he was merely resting to relieve a toothache, he was nevertheless fired for sleeping on the job. An arbitrator held that the employer had not met the burden of proof needed to support the charges against the employee. The supervisor testified that the employee's eyes were open and he was lucid when he was found, the arbitrator noted, and there was no evidence that the employee had actually prepared the "bed" on which he was rest-

ing, leaving in doubt the "premeditated" nature of his action (*Coastal Resin Co.*, 61 LA 686; see also 71 LA 1041).

D. Mitigating Factors

In determining whether the discipline imposed for sleeping on the job is warranted, arbitrators may consider a number of mitigating factors, such as the employment record of offending employees, whether they inadvertently fell asleep, and whether discomfort or medical issues played a part in the situation (95 LA 1006, 91 LA 443, 86 LA 1096, 81 LA 1200, 77 LA 1200, 76 LA 643).

● An employee was discharged for sleeping on the job and for verbally abusing a supervisor who tried to awaken him. The employee had mistaken the supervisor for a lower-level employee and apologized for his behavior after learning the identity of the supervisor. Finding that the employee's conduct caused no harm and that he did not realize that he was insulting a supervisor, the arbitrator ruled that the employee's work record and lack of prior disciplinary action were sufficient reasons to warrant reinstatement (*Union Carbide Corp.*, 66 LA 702).

● An employee who had taken codeine for a toothache was hit in the groin by a valve arm he was polishing. He claimed that he had lain down to relieve the pain. After the employee was discovered lying across some packing boxes in a corner of the shop where the lights were off, his employer fired him. An arbitrator overturned the discharge, rejecting the employer's argument that the lights had been turned off in order for the employee to escape detection. The sleepless night the employee had endured because of his toothache was considered a mitigating factor. In addition, the arbitrator faulted the employer for failing to conduct an investigation into the employee's reasons for falling asleep (*Crown Cork & Seal Co. Inc.*, 64 LA 734).

● An employer properly discharged an employee for on-the-job sleeping even though it was caused by various medical problems, including obesity, an arbitrator decided. The employer had the right to expect the employee to present himself "fit for work," according to the arbitrator, who pointed out that the presence of an employee who is asleep at work is not conducive to an employer's public image. Adding that the employer attempted rehabilitative measures and progressive discipline to correct the employee's behavior, the arbitrator concluded that under the circumstances discharge was warranted (*City of Iowa City*, 72 LA 1006).

1. Sleep Apnea

Employees sometimes have difficulty staying awake on the job because of sleep apnea, which is a breathing problem that interferes with the ability to sleep soundly at night, typically resulting in sleepiness throughout the day. As illustrated by the examples below, arbitrators are not inclined to view the disorder as a valid excuse for sleeping on the job.

● After an employee of a power company had several incidents of falling asleep at work, including one in which his error caused a power blackout, he was counseled and agreed to be examined by a neurologist chosen by the company. No special medical problems were detected but he was told to contact the neurologist if his sleep problems persisted. Based on the neurologist's report, the company notified the employee that further incidents could lead to termination. The employee was observed falling asleep at work on three more occasions and was fired.

When the employee was subsequently diagnosed with sleep apnea, the union contested his termination, arguing that his misconduct was caused by his medical condition and was involuntary. However, an arbitrator upheld the termination in spite of the employee's post-discharge diagnosis. The worker did not seek medical help until after he was terminated, the arbitrator noted, and there was no evidence to suggest that it was the employer's responsibility to determine the cause of his problems. The arbitrator also cited the nature of the employee's job and his failure to contact the neurologist about the recurrence of his sleeping problems as factors supporting termination (*Texas Utilities Electric Co. Production Div.*, 103 LA 152).

● Another arbitrator awarded reinstatement without back pay to an employee who had twice been discovered sleeping during breaks. The employee had been diagnosed with sleep apnea, which caused his excessive sleepiness, but he had failed to follow the recommended treatment to control the sleep disorder. Because the employee slept while on break, discharge was not warranted, the arbitrator ruled. Adding, however, that the employee's productive value was diminished because of his failure to address his medical condition, the arbitrator decided not to award the employee back pay as part of his reinstatement order (*EG & G Mound Applied Technologies*, 102 LA 60).

E. Loafing

1. Notice

In general, arbitrators treat loafing as a performance problem, and they usually expect employers to warn workers and give them an opportunity to correct their behavior before resorting to discharge.

● An arbitrator ordered the employee's reinstatement with back wages, less two weeks' pay for a disciplinary layoff. The employer's charges against the employee were that he loafed on the job, causing him to neglect his duties, which in turn resulted in economic losses for the company. The employer argued that discharge was appropriate because the employee's deficiencies had been noted previously and had been addressed by reinstructing the employee on the performance of his duties.

In ordering the reinstatement, the arbitrator found that the employer had reinstructed the employee in his duties but had not specifically warned him that his job was at risk at the time of that reinstruction, as was customary. The arbitrator also found that the irregularities complained of were no greater than those of other employees who had been reprimanded or laid off but not discharged (*International Minerals & Chemical Corp.*, 4 LA 127).

● *By contrast*, another arbitrator upheld the termination of an employee who had been warned repeatedly about loafing and other misconduct. The employee had a history of abusing phone privileges, engaging in long conversations unrelated to work, and taking too much time for breaks. As a result of co-worker complaints about the employee's loafing, as well as her tendency to use offensive language and talk explicitly about sex, her manager issued a memorandum emphasizing the need to restrict personal phone calls, limit breaks, and avoid vulgar language and discussions about "personal relationships." Instead of mending her ways, however, the employee persisted in her misconduct. Her termination was finally precipitated by an incident involving an obscene email that she showed several co-workers.

The employee had been warned on numerous occasions about loafing, inappropriate language, and other policy violations, the arbitrator found, and "had been advised that future instances of such misconduct could lead to termination." Based on the fact that she demonstrated "an unwillingness or inability to correct her behavior," the arbitrator concluded that termination was warranted (*Nord Center*, 121 LA 1158).

2. Discipline for Loafing

Arbitrators upheld discipline for loafing in the following cases, finding:

- an employer had just cause to suspend an employee for five days for insubordination and loafing, where the employee was observed working on a puzzle during work time, she failed to request additional work as instructed, and the next higher step in progressive discipline was warranted given her disciplinary record (*State of Iowa*, 124 LA 1174).
- an ambulance company had just cause to discharge two employees for loafing for nearly one hour between calls involving transporting hospital patients across the street for treatment, despite their contention that employees had to wait for the doors to be opened at the emergency room and intensive care unit and for the first patient's bed to be remade after his treatment, where a nurse told a manager that the first patient had returned without undue delay and that the employees had left 30 to 60 minutes earlier, and the employees waited one-half hour before informing a dispatcher of the alleged bed-making delay (*American Medical Response*, 127 LA 705).
- a gas company acted properly when it moved to discipline a meter reader for loafing, where, among other things, he habitually took longer than is reasonable to go from stop to stop, other employees had been discharged for similar offenses, and he was offered an opportunity to defend himself at a pre-disciplinary hearing with union representation afforded. However, the meter reader's suspension for loafing was reduced from 10 days to five days, where he had almost 40 years of service, and the employer improperly considered old discipline, which was only a blemish on his record (*Equitable Gas Co.*, 125 LA 673.
- *By contrast*, an arbitrator overturned the discharge but gave the employee a 30-day suspension—a banquet bartender—even though she sat on an ice caddy for a short period of time, where this was a minor infraction, and the manager who complained that she was not properly standing behind the bar did not realize that service had been pushed back from the announced starting time. The banquet bartender, who was discharged without just cause, was reinstated with a 30-day suspension, even though her one offense that was proven was a minor lapse, where she was subject to a last-chance agreement (*Grand Sierra Resort & Casino*, 126 LA 1466).

XXI. Strike-Related Activities [LA CDI 100.80 (public employees); 118.6604]

OVERVIEW

Work stoppages may present a wide range of disciplinary situations, including the following:

• **Unlawful job actions, such as wildcat strikes, as well as contractually prohibited work stoppages and slowdowns**—In such circumstances, discipline is warranted by the sole fact of the walkout or slowdown and may be applied either to all participants or only to those who initiated or prolonged the job action (97 LA 1006, 96 LA 294, 93 LA 1097, 90 LA 24, 89 LA 880).

• **Offenses committed during an authorized strike**—Although employees may not be punished for taking part in a lawful work stoppage, any misconduct that occurs during the walkout is grounds for disciplinary action, provided that there is concrete evidence to support the charges (94 LA 929, 90 LA 969, 90 LA 502, 89 LA 126, 87 LA 394, 87 LA 188).

• **Misconduct aimed at strikebreakers following a settlement**—When strikers return to work and come into contact with individuals who crossed the picket line, hostile feelings toward strikebreakers can give rise to harassing or intimidating behavior, which in turn can give rise to disciplinary action (114 LA 1495, 113 LA 952, 77 LA 1259).

The following discussion examines in greater detail how arbitrators view these types of situations and the factors they consider in weighing discipline imposed for strike-related activities.

SUMMARY OF CASES

A. Unlawful Work Stoppages & Slowdowns

Arbitrators may allow employers to take disciplinary action against employees even in the absence of concrete evidence to prove that they acted jointly to engage in improper work stoppages or slowdowns. Once employers show a likelihood that employees took concerted action, arbitrators can require individual workers to come up with evidence to explain why they should not be disciplined for deliberately slowing their work pace or engaging in unlawful work stoppages.

● According to one arbitrator, "the employer is required only to establish a prima facie case based on circumstantial evidence which would lead the reasonable person to conclude that the employees' actions were more probably concerted." At that point, "the burden of coming forward with evidence to rebut such prima facie presumption shifts to each employee because each employee would be best able to produce substantiating or corroborating evidence to support any contrary contention." In the case at hand, the arbitrator decided that management adequately supported its allegations that 21 employees were involved in an unlawful work stoppage when none of the workers could provide any alternative explanation for failing to report for work on the day in question. Accordingly, he concluded, the employer was justified in issuing disciplinary layoffs (*Longview Fibre Co.*, 69 LA 1182).

● Three-day suspensions were appropriately levied against employees who engaged in a group "sick-out," another arbitrator held, precisely because the workers could not support their claims of illness with medical certificates. Although the employees argued that the employer could only require doctors' statements in case of an extended illness, the arbitrator ruled that management was within its rights to demand the documentation and impose discipline for lack thereof because it legitimately suspected the workers of "abusing the sick leave privilege" (*Barbers Point Federal Credit Union*, 76 LA 624).

● Discharge was appropriate for two employees who asked co-workers to engage in a slowdown, an arbitrator decided. The employees worked for a drug store chain as stockers, and the contract stated that the company did not have to give employees a full day's pay if there was insufficient work for an eight-hour shift. After the two employees repeatedly solicited co-workers to slow their pace and make the work last a full eight hours, they were fired for violating a contract clause barring strikes and slowdowns. The arbitrator upheld the terminations even though the co-workers refused to participate in a slowdown. The contract's prohibition against strikes and slowdowns specified that violating the provision "in any way" would provide "immediate cause for discharge," the arbitrator noted (*Walgreen Co.*, 100 LA 468).

● A worker was properly discharged for limiting her production, an arbitrator decided, finding that her work record and working conditions indicated that the decline in production was caused by a "deliberate slowdown." Stressing that management had imposed the ultimate penalty of discharge only as a last step in a series of progressive disciplinary measures, the arbitrator rejected the worker's claim that her 33 years of service militated against discharge. Although agreeing that "long service with a good record weighs heavily in favor of an embattled employee," the arbitrator concluded that, nonetheless, "no union, company, or arbitrator can always and forever shield an employee from a contractual result of an act of pure folly in a context where the ultimate result was known or should have been known to the individual employee" (*Martinsburg Mills Inc.*, 48 LA 1224).

● *By contrast*, a manufacturer did not have just cause to discharge a 32-year employee with two prior instances of discipline, an arbitrator ruled, because it failed to prove that she instructed co-workers to slow their production down. However the arbitrator found there was proof that her abusive conduct toward her co-workers created an intimidating work atmosphere and she slowed down production by her own conduct, and gave her a one-year suspension (*Yaskawa America*, 129 LA 321).

• Another arbitrator ruled that a school district was precluded from asking for doctors' notes for teachers who may have been involved in sick out to protest district actions, where the district heard rumors of a sick out but did not warn teachers that they would need doctors' notes if they called in on day of alleged sick out (*School District of City of Detroit*, 124 LA 33).

• Long service has led arbitrators to overturn discharge for prohibited slowdowns or work stoppages. For example, one arbitrator converted a worker's dismissal for a deliberate slowdown to a four-week layoff, citing the worker's extensive record of satisfactory performance (*Reed Roller Bit Co.*, 29 LA 604; see also 8 LA 1).

• In another case, an arbitrator held that a union did not engage in an unlawful work stoppage when 23 employees refused to work in response to confusion over an employer's newly published policy change. The arbitrator ruled that there was no evidence of employee concerted activity and it was not clear that employees had acted with one mind. Also, the arbitrator pointed out that there was neither a classic sit-down strike nor an absolute refusal to work by all employees (*The Virgin Island Telephone Corp.*, 101 LA 273).

1. Honoring Picket Line

Refusing to cross a picket line also may be grounds for discipline where such action leads to a violation of contract provisions banning interference with work performance or operations.

• Based on the no-strike clause of its collective bargaining agreement, an employer was justified in suspending workers who refused to cross another union's peaceful picket line to perform their duties, an arbitrator decided. Although the employees argued that the no-strike agreement did not apply, the arbitrator ruled that their refusal to perform their duties was, in fact, a work stoppage in violation of the contract provision that specifically stated there would be "no strike, work stoppage, slowdown, or any other interference with or imped-

ing of work." By agreeing to this provision, the employees had waived their statutory rights to refuse to cross a picket line, the arbitrator found, concluding that their actions warranted two-day suspensions (*Monongahela Power Co.*, 64 LA 1210).

• Another arbitrator held that management properly disciplined its inspectors for reporting late to their assignments because they had honored an informational picket line. The parties' bargaining agreement specified that employees were "responsible for not taking sides or personally becoming involved in an industrial dispute between the management and the employees of the official establishment or plant to which they are assigned." Rather, in such cases they were to report to work "as scheduled" unless "otherwise directed by their supervisor."

There was "no question" that the employees were aware of both the contract provision and their assignments yet "voluntarily" chose to honor the picket line and thus report late, the arbitrator declared, finding the employees "guilty as charged." As for the propriety of the discipline, the penalty imposed was a one-day suspension for "failure to follow instruction to report as scheduled," the arbitrator noted, stressing that "had the agency so desired, the charge could have been that of engaging in an unlawful activity—a strike—with the statutory penalty of discharge." When "weighed against the offense committed," the arbitrator concluded, the penalty was not too severe (*U.S. Dept. of Agriculture*, 75 LA 36).

• Despite the existence of a no-strike/no-slowdown agreement, an arbitrator reinstated a worker discharged for honoring a picket line set up by another union at the worksite. The controlling factor in this case was a second contract provision that barred disciplinary action against an employee who "refuses to go through or work behind any primary picket line, including primary picket lines at the company's place of business." Finding that the picket line was an extension of one set up at the company's wholly owned subsidiary and thus was properly classified as a "primary" line, the arbitrator ruled that the employee's actions were protected from reprisal (*Coca Cola Bottling Co.*, 72 LA 73; see also 89 LA 1227, 84 LA 5, 72 LA 706, 69 LA 1024).

2. Wildcat Strikes

Wildcat strikes are grounds for severe discipline, arbitrators overwhelmingly agree, absent any indication that the workers were prevented from reporting to the job through "duress, coercion, intimidation, or the like." Declaring that "willing participation in a work stoppage is among the most heinous of industrial offenses," one arbitrator stressed that dismissal in such circumstances would not be "too severe" a penalty or one that would "shock the conscience" of an arbitrator.

Accordingly, that arbitrator ruled that management was justified in dismissing 132 workers who refused to end a wildcat strike in the face of union officials' instruction to return to the job. Finding no evidence that any of the employees were prevented from showing up for work, the arbitrator concluded that each thus was an "employee responsible" for the unauthorized strike as defined under the contract and appropriately subject to the agreement's provision authorizing discharge for unlawful work stoppages (*American Air Filter Co. Inc.*, 47 LA 129).

● For practical purposes, however, most employers do not go to the extreme of discharging all wildcat strikers. As one arbitrator explained, "a company that is the victim of an unlawful strike cannot be expected to 'cut off its nose to spite its face' by firing all participants" (*Charles Mundt & Sons*, 46 LA 982).

● One employer properly disciplined wildcat strikers by charging them all with five absences under its absence control program, regardless of how much work they actually missed. Both the "literal application" of the employer's absenteeism policy and a strict assessment of discipline for violating the no-strike clause "would have resulted in the termination of the majority" of the employees, management pointed out, with the result that the organization would have suffered the "same detrimental effect on production as the unauthorized work stoppage itself."

Finding it a "fundamental prerogative of management to select the form and extent of disciplinary action as long as it is not specifically restricted from doing so by the agreement, as long as cause is demonstrated, and as long as equal treatment is accorded," the arbitrator agreed with the employer that it had "discretion to apply the absentee policy as it chooses in the context of a wildcat strike, whether the application be literal, something less stringent than literal application, or no application at all" (*Kennecott Copper Corp.*, 77 LA 505).

● Most cases dealing with wildcat strikes involve selective discipline, and arbitrators are asked to decide if employers acted properly in disciplining only certain strikers or whether in doing so they acted in an arbitrary, capricious, or discriminatory manner. Especially where the employer has selectively applied the discharge penalty, some arbitrators may require clear proof that the workers thus disciplined deserved being singled out because they were either instigators of unlawful activity or at least more active in it than other employees. Absent such evidence, the dismissals may be overturned (67 LA 1250, 61 LA 148).

● Other arbitrators do not set such strict "rules" and will uphold the propriety of selective discipline under a wider range of circumstances (93 LA 1097, 77 LA 505, 66 LA 626, 63 LA 677, 61 LA 896, 55 LA 1159, 53 LA 75, 53 LA 45).

● "No agreement provision and no obligation to justice compels the company to discipline in every case of employee misconduct," one arbitrator declared. "Inequality of treatment in disciplinary matters does not amount to unjust discrimination if there are rational grounds for distinguishing between those to be disciplined and those not to be disciplined," the arbitrator maintained, stressing that "it is only where the grounds for distinction are irrational, arbitrary, or whimsical that disciplining of some employees and not others may be looked upon as unjust and discriminatory" (*Ford Motor Co.*, 41 LA 609).

● In another case, however, an arbitrator held that management erred in discharging four of 26 wildcat strikers. Although acknowledging the employer's right of discretionary punishment in such cases, the arbitrator pointed out that the discipline should have been applied to a "representative group" rather than levied in a completely arbitrary manner. If the company had conducted a thorough investigation, the arbitrator noted, it would have found that other employees had greater responsibility for the walkout and were more deserving of discipline (*Homer Laughlin China Co.*, 67 LA 1250).

B. Use of Selective Discipline

The instigation of a work stoppage or slowdown by employees, as noted above, generally is regarded as proper justification for the application of selective discipline.

• Holding that the initiators of a walkout bear a heavier responsibility for the misconduct than other strikers, an arbitrator sustained management's move to suspend only the first employees to leave work. The arbitrator found that the selective discipline was further justified in that the company could not have given all 800 workers disciplinary layoffs without shutting down its plant (*Goodyear Atomic Corp.*, 27 LA 321).

• Three employees were properly discharged for attempting to prevent co-workers from reporting to the job and inciting a wildcat strike to protest what they considered to be prior unjust discipline, an arbitrator ruled. Rejecting the employees' contention that the stoppage was justified because management had failed to respond to their legitimate grievances, the arbitrator upheld the employer's argument that the workers had flagrantly violated the contract. Stressing that one of the most serious and disruptive acts an employee can perform is to lead a wildcat strike, the arbitrator concluded that in inciting the unlawful activity, the workers knew they had embarked on a dangerous course of action (*National Mine Service Co.*, 69 LA 966; see also 65 LA 709).

• Another arbitrator ruled that a worker was properly dismissed for causing an unauthorized work stoppage following a dispute with his supervisor. Any disagreement "with company policy or the actions of his supervisors" should have been pursued "through the grievance procedure," the arbitrator ruled, declaring that an employee who "disregards the contractual dispute settlement mechanisms and engages in self-help subverts the fundamental nature of the collective bargaining relationship." Because the worker "knowingly caused a work stoppage" in violation of the contract, the arbitrator concluded, the discharge was warranted (*Traverse City Iron Works*, 76 LA 21).

• *By contrast*, another arbitrator reinstated five workers who were discharged for organizing an unlawful strike because the contract's no-strike clause failed to specify, and management had not warned them, that they could be dismissed for their actions. Besides failing to make clear the range of discipline possible, management officials "stood or sat idly by while employees around them argued about walking out" and some supervisors even "actively encouraged the walkout" (*Superior Switchboard & Devices Divisions*, 75 LA 1107; see also 96 LA 294).

• Where the evidence did not support management's allegations that an employee had attempted to incite a walkout, an arbitrator ordered the worker's reinstatement. Not only was the crewman who made the accusations an unreliable witness, the arbitrator pointed out, but also there were no signs of job desertion to corroborate the story (*Payne & Keller of Louisiana Inc.*, 70 LA 114).

1. Union Leadership

Union leadership may be a basis for selective discipline in cases where shop stewards or union officials have not carried out their responsibility of promoting adherence to contract clauses that prohibit strikes and slowdowns. In such cases, arbitrators consistently have held union leaders to a higher standard of responsibility than ordinary bargaining unit members.

• "A shop steward's duty in the face of an unauthorized work stoppage is well settled," one arbitrator declared, explaining that "not only should he make a determined effort to prevent the stoppage before it begins, but upon its development must actively and unequivocally attempt to bring an end of the stoppage at the earliest possible moment." The arbitrator added that "only in this way can the steward comply with his responsibility to uphold the integrity of the contract and its orderly processes for dispute settlements" (*United Parcel Service Inc.*, 47 LA 1100).

● Another arbitrator similarly stressed that union officials have "an especial obligation to refrain from committing overt acts designed to encourage others to walk out or stay out." Pointing out that such officials have been "chosen to be custodians of the agreement, guardians of its rights, and monitors of its obligations within the prescribed procedures," the arbitrator concluded that "hence, if they engage in overt acts which flout the agreement's most solemn obligations, they engage in a specific class of acts which set them apart from the rank and file" (*Mack Trucks Inc.*, 41 LA 1240).

● Declaring that union officials must give more than "lip service" to their obligation to prevent unlawful work stoppages, an arbitrator ruled that an employer properly imposed more severe discipline on union delegates than on rank-and-file workers for participating in a stoppage. The contract specified that "in the event of an unauthorized slowdown, boycott of overtime, or any other form of strike," union officials were to "immediately notify participating employees that the conduct is in violation of the agreement" and "instruct participating members to resume normal operations at once."

Nevertheless, the arbitrator found, the union delegates not only failed to honor this pledge but even went so far as to encourage the members in their recalcitrance by actively taking part in the work stoppage. Rejecting the delegates' contention that complying with the contract provision would have meant acting "as double agents," the arbitrator pointed out that one "can't have his cake and eat it too." Having accepted the honor of the titled delegate position and the accompanying leadership, the arbitrator concluded, the officials "must accept the responsibilities of the position" (*New Jersey Bell Telephone Co.*, 77 LA 1038; see also 68 LA 618, 49 LA 27, 43 LA 608, 41 LA 732).

● An arbitrator held that termination was warranted for a union steward after he and nearly 20 other workers refused to perform assigned work until required certificates from the Occupational Safety and Health Administration were posted. Rejecting the steward's claim of being singled out for punishment, the arbitrator said the steward assumed a leadership role in the work stoppage by speaking to union members on the day of the event, and his entire course of conduct indicated an intent to obstruct normal operations rather than to raise legitimate safety concerns (*National Maintenance & Repair Inc.*, 101 LA 1115).

● On the other hand, where union officials have attempted to prevent or halt a work stoppage without success or where they are not contractually bound to take such affirmative action, arbitrators have overturned discipline selectively levied against them (64 LA 1210, 64 LA 425, 55 LA 1159).

● An employer improperly suspended a union steward for demonstrating "negative leadership" by standing outside the plant gate rather than reporting for work during an unlawful job action, an arbitrator decided. Although the steward came to the plant on all three days of the unlawful strike, he went home after being unable to get through the blocked entrance, the arbitrator found. Observing that the steward had not carried a picket sign and had never before been disciplined during his eight years of employment, much less involved in an unlawful strike, the arbitrator concluded that the charges against him were "arbitrary" and "unjust" (*Powermatic/Houdaille Inc.*, 65 LA 1245).

● A union official who eventually tried to halt a wildcat strike was improperly discharged, an arbitrator ruled. In light of the official's initial participation in the unlawful action, the arbitrator concluded that a one-year probation was in order (*Cyclops Corp.*, 45 LA 560; see also 73 LA 9).

C. Misconduct During Lawful Strikes

Where work stoppages are lawful, employees still face the prospect of being disciplined by their employers for any misconduct that occurs as part of the strike. Although the term "misconduct" covers a multitude of offenses, from taunting strike-breakers to assaulting supervisors, one arbitrator outlined the following criteria for judging the propriety of discipline in cases that involve strike-related violence:

- "What is the extent of participation? In any mob situation the degree of involvement of the individual in any action taken is important."
- "What was the nature of the violence? This has both quantitative and qualitative aspects. Participation in several incidents is more serious than in only one. Some actions are more reprehensible than others. Shouting insults and shoving are of a different order from striking a person."
- "Was the violence provoked? To the extent that the violence is retaliatory and defensive, it is less culpable than if undertaken as an act of aggression."
- "Was the violence premeditated or undertaken on the spur of the moment? Premeditated violence is the more inexcusable."
- "What will be the impact of the punishment? Discharge is more of a penalty for an old man than a young one; for a long service employee than a short service employee."
- "Was the disciplinary action discriminatory? A company is under some obligation to treat persons similarly situated in a comparable, although not necessarily identical, manner (*Cudahy Packing Co.*, 11 LA 1138).

Expanding on these guidelines, another arbitrator stated that reviews of strike-related misconduct should be influenced by the following considerations:

- "How serious was the offense in terms of injury to persons or damage to property?"
- "Were remedies-at-law available and were they involved?"
- "Was the conduct destructive of good employee-employer relations?"
- "Was the conduct destructive of good community relations?"
- "Will the discipline restore good relations, or is it the result of a spirit of vindictiveness?"

- "Was the conduct such that the employee could be reabsorbed into the work force?" (*J.R. Simplot Co.*, 64 LA 1061)
- A striking employee who verbally and physically abused a supervisor at a local social club was justifiably discharged, an arbitrator ruled. The employee's behavior was particularly blameworthy in that the incident occurred away from the picket line and thus was not the result of "inflamed group passions," the arbitrator found. Reinstating the worker in the face of the damage to the employer-employee relationship, the arbitrator concluded, would be a "visible and highly public vindication" of the abusive behavior (*General Telephone Co. of Kentucky*, 69 LA 351; see also 92 LA 578).
- An employer was justified in discharging a picketing striker for "streaking," "mooning," and using racial slurs against replacements, under a strike settlement agreement authorizing dismissal only for picket-line misconduct "that would be considered serious under normal working conditions." The arbitrator rejected the worker's arguments that even if he were guilty of the allegations, such behavior was not so serious as to warrant discharge. Rather, finding that "any one of these three actions would constitute misconduct if engaged in within a plant operating normally," the arbitrator specified that "any would create a major disturbance, interrupt production, upset plant discipline, and bring opprobrium to the company." Furthermore, while the use of racial epithets alone "might or might not be considered serious enough to warrant immediate discharge within a plant," the arbitrator stressed, "occurring on a picket line such language can only be calculated to injure the company, its standing in the community, and to reflect discredit upon the public relations image of the company and union alike" (*H & L Tooth Co.*, 66 LA 1020).
- An employer had just cause to fire a striker who threw screws at company vehicles, even though his discharge letter did not specifically mention that act, said one arbitrator. The employee was seen by a hired guard dropping screws onto an exit driveway in front of an 18-wheel truck leaving the plant. Days later, a manager took

photos of the strikers, which were shown to the guard, who identified the employee as the striker he saw depositing screws. Subsequently, the company fired the employee, but the union pointed out that the termination letter made "no mention" of screws. Emphasizing that the case hinged on the credibility of those involved, the arbitrator decided that termination was warranted (*Merchants Metals Inc.*, 117 LA 1).

● An arbitrator upheld an employer's discharge of a strike shift leader who on four occasions taunted and threatened drivers who were crossing a picket line and then repeatedly lied about his misconduct, even though the incidents constituted only 15 minutes of a three-year strike (*Bayou Steel Corp.*, 108 LA 513).

● A striking employee was, however, improperly discharged for tire-slashing because management failed to "continue and complete a comprehensive investigation of the matter sufficient to establish the employee's culpability." Although the employer offered "circumstantial" evidence suggesting that the worker may have been responsible for the damage, it did not meet the "burden of proof" necessary to sustain the dismissal, the arbitrator concluded (*Collins Foods International Inc.*, 77 LA 483; see also 74 LA 726).

1. Mitigating Factors

Mitigating factors also may lead an arbitrator to reinstate a worker discharged for picket line misconduct.

● Citing a "satisfactory" work history, one arbitrator reduced to a six-month suspension the termination penalty levied against a worker for throwing ball bearings through the window of a guard house during a strike. Although the company argued that the employee was a "rabble rouser" whose return to the workforce could "create the possibility of discord and hostility rather than enhance a peaceful, working relationship," the arbitrator found no evidence "of prior acts of hostility toward the company nor damage to company property that would tend to justify the apprehension of the company were he to be reabsorbed into the workforce." Management's "stated objective for the disciplinary action"—de-

terrence of future such incidents—could be better accomplished "by a lengthy suspension without pay and accompanied by a stern reprimand," the arbitrator concluded (*Charter International Oil Co.*, 75 LA 929).

● An arbitrator reduced to lengthy suspensions the discharges imposed on two employees for strike offenses, finding that the misconduct was not so "grave" as to prevent the employees' being "reabsorbed into the workforce." The first employee, who threatened a contractor performing work at a picket site, deserved a four-month disciplinary layoff, the arbitrator decided, while the second, who kicked in the side panel of a company pick-up truck, deserved a five-month suspension (*General Telephone Co. of Kentucky*, 69 LA 351).

● An employer that chooses to continue to operate its plant during a strike, regardless of the fact that such action historically invites violence, may not be justified in discharging employees for picket line misconduct, according to some arbitrators. In two similar cases, arbitrators reduced dismissals to disciplinary layoffs, based on the theory that a company that elects to "continue operations and engage replacements" during a strike "cannot escape a share of responsibility for the militancy and aggressiveness of the strikers." Violence usually occurs only when management decides to utilize strategies of replacing striking workers and deploying armed guards, one arbitrator noted, deciding that by taking on the historical "inevitability" of violence in pursuing such options, an employer is guilty of "contributory negligence" that militates against outright dismissal (*Washington Scientific Industries Inc.*, 67 LA 1044 and *J.R. Simplot Co.*, 64 LA 1061).

D. Post-Strike

A residue of antagonism and bitterness commonly lingers beyond the end of a strike, even if the parties have pledged to restore good relations and refrain from acts of retribution as part of a strike settlement agreement. These emotions sometimes give rise to acts of misconduct in the form of hostile behavior directed at strikebreakers.

Most arbitrators agree that such misconduct justifies disciplinary action, particularly where returning strikers have been warned against harassing or intimidating strikebreakers. Unless the offense is of an extremely serious nature, however, arbitrators generally will not sustain a discharge for post-strike misconduct. The reasoning underlying many arbitration decisions in these cases is similar to that applied to cases involving misconduct that occurs while strikes are in progress.

● Although "some form of discipline" was warranted, discharge was too severe for a returning striker who directed abusive language toward new hires taken on as strike replacements, an arbitrator ruled. Upon returning from a six-month strike, several workers repeatedly referred to the new hires as "scabs" and made threatening remarks to them. One employee, who had been "counseled" for his abusive language, was fired after he arrived at work wearing a T-shirt with a caption that made obscene reference to the strikebreakers. Although the employer argued that discharge was an appropriate response to the employee's continuing course of intimidating conduct, the arbitrator said counseling "does not suffice for disciplinary action intended to correct the misconduct and apprise the employee of the seriousness of his actions." Absent explicit warning that discharge would result if the employee continued to intimidate the new hires, the arbitrator concluded, suspension was a more appropriate discipline (*Chromalloy American Corp.*, 72 LA 838).

● An arbitrator overturned the discharge of a hospital employee accused of harassing co-workers who had continued working during a strike. The arbitrator concluded that the employer had not treated the employee fairly as compared with non-strikers who also engaged in antagonistic behavior following the strike. Some of the individuals who complained about the employee had instigated confrontations, yet the employer did not impose discipline on any of them, the arbitrator observed. In addition to this inequity, the arbitrator found that the employee had not received "full and fair warning" that his behavior could result in discipline, nor was he "afforded his right to know of the specific charges brought against him and to confront his accusers." Noting further that the employee had a long record of service without disciplinary problems, the arbitrator awarded him reinstatement with back pay (*Akron City Hospital*, 113 LA 146).

● Another arbitrator overturned the discharge of a flight attendant for her behavior toward employees who had worked during a strike. The employee in question was working as the lead attendant on her first flight following the conclusion of the strike when she engaged in behavior that showed "some degree of hostility," the arbitrator observed. She lacked the "professional demeanor" required under company standards, the arbitrator found, but the evidence did not clearly indicate that she engaged in intentional wrongdoing that would warrant termination. As a factor calling for mitigation of the discipline, the arbitrator pointed to the fact that the airline had continued to operate during the "bitter and acrimonious strike," and the terms of the settlement were "extremely disadvantageous to the union." Through its actions, the company contributed to the "hostility and bitterness" of returning employees and "cannot complain" if some of the anger of returning strikers spilled over in the days following their defeat, the arbitrator declared. "In the absence of prior discipline, and given the nature of the circumstances," the arbitrator concluded, the appropriate discipline was a letter of warning (*Continental Airlines*, 77 LA 368).

● On the other hand, an arbitrator upheld a 10-day suspension for an employee whose post-strike misconduct included staring at a strike replacement worker and joining a co-worker in fabricating a story about being threatened by the replacement worker. The employee's actions constituted harassment and intimidation in violation of the parties' return-to-work resolution, the arbitrator pointed out, adding that employees had been warned that violations could lead to discharge (*AS Mid-America Inc.*, 101 LA 1177).

● Similarly, an arbitrator upheld the suspensions of five employees who engaged in post-strike "staring" tactics against replacement workers. The arbitrator decided that the discipline was justified because the employees had been sufficiently warned about and directed to stop the harassment (*La Crosse Telephone Corp.*, 65 LA 1077).

● Another arbitrator held that an employer was justified in disciplining an employee for his remarks to a replacement worker immediately following a strike. During the month-long work stoppage, the employer's trucks were operated by drivers from another company. On the day following settlement of the strike, a driver was having difficulty starting a truck when the employee laughed and said he hoped the truck blew up. As it turned out, the truck would not start because the gas tank had been filled with water. Although there was no evidence connecting the worker to the sabotage, management issued him a five-day suspension for his misconduct.

The arbitrator held that the employee's comments were "inflammatory and threatening" and found that such remarks in the wake of the strike naturally stirred up the driver's concern and apprehension. Although the employee's comments were "further magnified by the fact that an act of sabotage had taken place," his discipline should have reflected his "actual involvement" in the post-strike misconduct, the arbitrator added, reducing the length of the employee's suspension from five days to two (*Emery Industries Inc.*, 72 LA 110).

XXII. Union Activity [LA CDI 118.664]

OVERVIEW

In cases involving alleged insubordination or rule violations by employees who also serve as union stewards or officers, arbitrators generally look to see whether the offenses were committed when the employees were acting in their official union capacity or merely as rank-and-file workers. If employees are not properly performing representational duties when they become insubordinate, they can be subjected to the same disciplinary actions as other workers because the behavior does not constitute concerted protected activity under the National Labor Relations Act (122 LA 1273, 92 LA 3, 63 LA 765, 62 LA 432).

If, however, employees are discharging the duties and responsibilities required of them as union representatives, arbitrators often excuse them from abiding by normal standards of employee conduct, including the "obey now, grieve later" doctrine. Arbitrators commonly hold that union representatives should be shielded from discipline if they oppose management or refuse to follow directives that conflict with union rights.

Exceptions to discipline have even been extended to union representatives for insolence, outbursts, and abusiveness, particularly when confronting management on behalf of other members of the bargaining unit. Arbitrators grant a degree of latitude to union stewards and officers for the behavior they engage in during such confrontations, drawing a distinction between union advocacy and insubordination.

SUMMARY OF CASES

A. Grievance Investigation, Processing, and Bargaining

If union representatives, pursuant to the contract, seek to leave their posts to investigate grievances, management cannot withhold permission unreasonably. In general, the prerogatives of management do not include deciding whether disputed matters constitute legitimate grievances that are subject to investigation. On the other hand, union stewards can be subject to discipline if they engage in union-related activities without management consent or authorization under the contract.

● A union steward asked his foreman for a pass to investigate the discharge of a probationary employee. His foreman refused and referred him to the general foreman. The general foreman argued that the discharge of a probationary employee was not a grievable issue and told the steward to go back to his job or risk discharge. The steward refused and was fired.

An arbitrator set the discharge aside, saying there "is a clear distinction between the case of a supervisor telling an employee to go back to his job, and a supervisor telling the union to stop investigating a grievance." When the duly authorized representative of the employer told the duly authorized representative of the union to stop investigating a grievance, the employer was issuing orders to the union, and it was the steward's duty, as a representative of the union, to insist on the union's rights. If the steward had been rough, rowdy, or belligerent in his attitude, some disciplinary action might have been warranted, but that was not the case here (*International Harvester Co.*, 16 LA 307).

● In another case, a union steward asked for and was denied by his foreman permission to attend a meeting between a company executive and two employees. At break time, the steward went to the meeting anyway. Although he returned to his post by the end of the break period, the company fired him for insubordination. An arbitrator reversed the discharge, noting that the steward had not been given reprimands for such conduct. The foreman who refused the employee permission to attend the meeting also admitted that he did not think the steward was guilty of insubordination (*General Fireproofing Co.*, 61 LA 389).

● An employer lacked just cause to discipline a union steward who joined two employees in initiating grievance meetings with their supervisor. Both employees came to the steward with concerns about schedule changes, and she advised them that the first step of the grievance process was to have an informal discussion with their supervisor. Within a week of each other, the employees asked the supervisor if she could meet with them for a few minutes, and she agreed on both occasions. The supervisor, who was new to her job, was thrown off

guard when the steward joined each meeting and informed her that they were first-level grievance discussions. The supervisor complained to upper management, and the steward was placed on unpaid leave while the matter was investigated. The employer disciplined the steward with "documented counseling," asserting that the meetings were not properly scheduled and amounted to "ambushes."

In both instances, the employees approached the supervisor, who agreed to the meetings, and the steward attended at the employees' request in order to help them present their grievances, the arbitrator noted, emphasizing that this right was guaranteed by the collective bargaining agreement. Although the employer argued that the meetings should have been scheduled in advance, the agreement did not specify how the oral discussions at the first step of the grievance process were supposed to be initiated, the arbitrator observed. Consequently, the arbitrator held that the employer had no basis for disciplining the steward or placing her on suspension without pay during its investigation (*Alta California Regional Center*, 116 LA 44).

● An arbitrator ruled an employer violated a collective bargaining agreement and section 8(a)(3) of National Labor Relations Act when it disciplined a union business manager/employee for using company equipment to copy information to be used in bargaining, where the employer knew what the grievant was doing and wanted to frustrate his efforts (*Intermountain Power Services Corp.*, 127 LA 942).

● *By contrast*, an arbitrator upheld the suspension of a steward who refused a repeated order to return to his work station after being denied admittance to an injury-review meeting between management and a member of the bargaining unit. The steward had no right to attend the meeting because no formal grievance had been filed, the arbitrator concluded (*Ethyl Corp.*, 96 LA 255; see also 95 LA 909, 90 LA 856, 88 LA 145).

● Another arbitrator upheld the termination of a union steward who disobeyed an order to stop working on union business during company time. The employer stated that the steward consistently refused to comply with supervisory directives and insisted on displaying a combative and defiant attitude in the presence of co-workers. The employer's statements were echoed by several employees and even a union representative, all of whom testified that the steward was uncooperative and insubordinate.

Considering the weight of the evidence against the steward, the arbitrator found that discharge was justified after she refused to perform her assigned tasks and continued to work on union business when she was not authorized to do so. The arbitrator faulted the steward for believing that her insubordinate behavior was justified because it was her "job" to help other workers. "Her job was to produce product for her employer, when, where, and how she was told!" the arbitrator declared (*Mountaintop Baking Co.*, 115 LA 861).

B. Leave for Union Business

Contract provisions concerning union leave vary greatly, and the outcome of arbitration decisions on whether employees are entitled to time away from work for union business depends not only on the particular contract clause, but also on the facts and context of each case, often with reference to the good faith of both parties (*C & D Batteries Inc.*, 32 LA 589; see also 122 LA 532, 117 LA 905, 111 LA 52, 101 LA 610, 96 LA 787, 80 LA 201, 80 LA 1055, 78 LA 969, 76 LA 648, 75 LA 66, 71 LA 349, 71 LA 696, 64 LA 709, 58 LA 253, 54 LA 1130).

• Employers are entitled to enough information regarding the nature of the union business involved and the probable duration of the absence to permit them to make an intelligent choice as to granting or denying leave. Internal union affairs and "secrets" need not be divulged (118 LA 491, 78 LA 8, 69 LA 831, 64 LA 1274, 50 LA 1140, 42 LA 632, 35 LA 873, 32 LA 589, 11 LA 569).

• Leave for union business may encompass organizational activity outside the bargaining unit at a plant affiliated with the employer (80 LA 403, 74 LA 916, 74 LA 501, 74 LA 396, 64 LA 975, 58 LA 253, 50 LA 1140, 35 LA 873). On the other hand, such leave rarely covers political activities engaged in by union representatives (104 LA 30, 76 LA 648, 64 LA 1089, 37 LA 249, 8 LA 350, 5 LA 428).

• An employer may approve leave for union business on a conditional basis in certain circumstances (41 LA 739, 37 LA 475, 37 LA 249, 36 LA 400).

• Past practice has influenced arbitrators' decisions in granting or denying leave for union business (110 LA 916, 76 LA 1273, 75 LA 66, 70 LA 887, 43 LA 670, 15 LA 611, 14 LA 574, 11 LA 1074, 11 LA 569).

C. Confrontations With Supervisors

Although union representatives have a duty to advocate on behalf of members and contest management actions that violate the contract or deny workers' rights, they may be subject to discipline if they become excessively insubordinate and abusive toward supervisory personnel. No clear consensus exists among arbitrators regarding how much leeway union representatives should be granted when engaging in confrontational behavior. In general, however, standards for behaving respectfully toward supervisors are stricter when union representatives confront management personnel in the presence of other employees.

• An arbitrator ruled that a hospital had just cause to issue reprimands to union stewards who "became overly emotional and loud in a sensitive patient area" in an effort to force a meeting with a supervisor over the alleged harassment of an employee, which had not been fully resolved in an earlier meeting with the supervisor (*Stanford Hospital*, 124 LA 1025).

• An employer did not have just cause to issue a verbal warning to a union steward who verbally attacked a "substitute supervisor" who intruded on discipline meeting, where the steward was acting as a union representative and was not attacking the supervisor solely for her own purposes, the grievant did not resort to harsh language until near the end of the confrontation when provoked, and this was the seventh time she had to ask the supervisor to stay out of disciplinary meetings, but the first time she used abusive language (*Arandell Corp.*, 129 LA 681 (Arb. 2011)).

• An employer had just cause to suspend a shop steward for insubordination after he yelled at a supervisor and then left work, an arbitrator found. The steward approached the supervisor at the start of his shift and asked to address a gathering of workers about an upcoming shutdown. When the supervisor refused permission, the steward argued with him all the way to the assembly room where the meeting was going to take place, and several co-workers witnessed the steward yelling at the supervisor. In response to the steward's belligerent behavior, the supervisor took him to a separate area and told him to wait there until the meeting's conclusion. Within a few minutes, the steward left, walking through the assembly room where the supervisor was speaking, and clocked out.

Although the incident might have been avoided if the steward had been allowed to speak, it was within management's authority to deny him permission to address the gathered employees, the arbitrator observed. Concluding that the steward was clearly insubordinate in his rude and hostile behavior toward the supervisor, as well as his refusal to wait for the supervisor until he finished his talk, the arbitrator upheld the suspension (*Siemens Auto. Corp.*, 117 LA 398).

● Another arbitrator upheld the suspension of a union steward for his abusive and threatening language. When the steward requested permission to speak with a co-worker, a supervisor asked what they were going to discuss. According to the supervisor, the steward became angry and uttered profanities. When a manager later asked the steward to explain his behavior, the steward denied using profane language and said the supervisor was a liar. The manager then noted that other supervisors had made similar complaints about the steward and stressed that such language was "uncivilized." In response, the steward said to the manager, "You can kiss my ass." The steward was suspended for three days.

Acknowledging that "the right of the union steward to do his job properly must be protected," the arbitrator said that "mere militancy or zealousness on his part will not justify punishment, nor can a steward be limited to the language of polite society in fulfilling his role." On the other hand, "management cannot function properly if employees who are also union stewards can with impunity verbally insult and abuse members of management," the arbitrator said in upholding the suspension (*Hobart Corp.*, 75 LA 907; see also 91 LA 482, 90 LA 462, 88 LA 512, 81 LA 1115, 81 LA 888, 81 LA 821).

● In an argument over a grievance, a foreman and steward exchanged angry words. The foreman then warned the steward that if he continued his display of bad temper, "he had better punch his time card and leave." The employer subsequently issued the steward a letter of warning for his conduct.

An arbitrator upheld the discipline. While noting that a "steward cannot be disciplined for actively pursuing grievances or presenting his arguments in a positive manner," the arbitrator declared that "a distinction must be drawn between presenting arguments in a positive manner and being argumentative." The arbitrator also differentiated between attacking the logic of a decision and attacking the person responsible for the decision. "Moreover, we cannot ignore tone of voice or attitudes. These may be just as important as the words used," the arbitrator said (*Westinghouse Electric Corp.*, 38 LA 1226).

● *By contrast*, another arbitrator overturned the discipline imposed on a union committeeman who used loud and vulgar language during a grievance meeting with a manager. Objectionable language and abusive behavior can justify discipline for insubordination under normal circumstances, but many arbitrators have recognized that some immunity applies to stewards who engage in such actions in the context of carrying out their representational duties, the arbitrator noted. While stopping short of condoning the employee's outburst, the arbitrator concluded that he had not crossed "a line between vigorous advocacy and gross conduct" (*The PQ Corp.*, 106 LA 381; see also 114 LA 1161).

● In deciding the case of a local president who was trying to protect the rights of a co-worker, an arbitrator said union representatives often have been excused from discipline for conduct that occurs in the heat of the grievance representation process, but they do not enjoy absolute immunity when they engage in abusive or insubordinate behavior.

Believing that an employee had wrongly been denied overtime, the local president contradicted a supervisor's directive and told the employee to report to work anyway. The two wound up in the supervisor's office, where the president's behavior included cutting the supervisor off, becoming argumentative, and refusing an initial request to report to the company's HR manager.

The arbitrator said termination was not warranted for the local president's conduct. Although management is not expected to tolerate insubordination, the standard for what is considered insubordinate language or conduct "may differ depending whether it occurred in or out of the grievance representation process," the arbitrator noted. To avoid thwarting that process, "arbitrators are reluctant to uphold discipline of union stewards for normally considered abusive language and conduct when it occurs in heated exchanges with supervisors concerning grievances," the arbitrator said in reducing the penalty to a two-month suspension (*Ciba Specialty Chemicals Corp.*, 119 LA 1452).

• An employer did not have just cause to discharge a union officer for his insulting comments and verbal attacks on management during a meeting where he was representing a co-worker who faced possible discipline for attendance problems, an arbitrator ruled. The comments of the union officer included calling the company's HR director a puppet, making disparaging remarks about the company CEO, and referring to the vice president of operations as an idiot. Additionally, in arguing that some absences are unavoidable and should not be grounds for discipline, the union officer referenced personal information about the co-worker's supervisor, who had suffered a miscarriage.

Although the union officer's remarks were disconcerting to the management representatives in attendance at the meeting, they were not overheard by members of the bargaining unit and did not disrupt the employer's operations, the arbitrator noted. Notwithstanding the union officer's questionable approach, he appeared to act out of "militancy or zealousness" in trying to resolve the co-worker's attendance problems, the arbitrator added. Consequently, the officer's behavior did not cost him the protection to which he was entitled as a union representative, the arbitrator concluded, awarding him reinstatement with back pay (*Adams-Columbia Electric Cooperative*, 117 LA 1765).

• Where a steward was discharged for using profane language during a joint labor-management meeting and threatening the employer's "managerial control," an arbitrator disagreed with management's view of the incident and ordered reinstatement. The employer conceded that the profane language alone would not have justified discharge in the context of the meeting but added that it drew the line at the steward's comment that he would tell management how to run its plant.

The arbitrator reasoned that although such outbursts are undesirable, they are also sometimes unavoidable. In the context of the meeting, the arbitrator concluded that there was no real threat to management's control because, despite the verbal threat, management was free to do as it pleased, subject to the grievance machinery (*Kaiser Engineers Inc.*, 63 LA 1051; see also 96 LA 56, 89 LA 361, 85 LA 716).

• An arbitrator held that an employer did not have just cause to discharge a local union president who grabbed a security officer's shoulder and directed obscene language at a management representative in a dispute over how an outside union agent should have been escorted from the employer's premises. The arbitrator pointed out that the union president was a long-term employee, she was upset and acted impulsively, she did not assault or threaten the security guard after he asked her to remove her hand from his shoulder, she did not have a propensity for violence, and there was no evidence that other employees would be reluctant to work with her if she were reinstated to her former job (*Army and Air Force Exchange Service*, 105 LA 332).

D. Disrupting Management Authority

Aside from engaging in direct confrontations with members of management, union representatives sometimes take other actions that have the effect of disrupting or undermining management authority. In many cases, arbitrators agree that discharge is warranted for such actions.

● An arbitrator held that a steward's discharge for insubordination was appropriate after he took several actions that usurped and disrupted management authority. The steward's transgressions included intervening in the work scheduling of a co-worker because he felt she was not qualified for the work, instructing a worker to leave her post and take refuge in a bathroom so she could avoid an interview with a company official, and informing several employees that they did not have to continue working beyond 12 hours, which resulted in four employees leaving work. According to the arbitrator, the steward was properly terminated for his unacceptable activities, which "clearly violated recognized and acceptable norms of behavior imposed upon any employee irrespective of their Union status" (*Pechiney Plastic Packaging Inc.*, 115 LA 1042).

● The acting president of a local union was justly fired after he told a co-worker to refuse to perform a driving job, an arbitrator ruled. The driving job had become vacant, and another employee had successfully bid on the position. When the company failed to move the employee into the position, he complained to the acting union president. To help the employee, the acting president told other workers that they should stop filling in on the job, which presumably would prompt the company to place the successful bidder in the position.

After one worker agreed to perform the driving job two days in a row, he was told by the acting president that he could face union charges and lose his union card if he did not refuse the assignment. The company

fired the acting president, arguing that his actions were prohibited under the collective bargaining agreement. The arbitrator agreed, finding that the acting president had violated the contract by intimidating the worker and attempting to disrupt production. Even though his goal of helping the successful bidder was totally unselfish "and even praiseworthy," the proper mechanism for resolving the dispute was the grievance process, the arbitrator said (*Linderme Tube Co.*, 116 LA 837).

● In a case involving a union steward's misstatements concerning an employer's actions toward its Vietnamese employees, which purportedly compromised the employer's relationship and credibility with the employees, an arbitrator ruled that the steward's statements were such that they lost their protected status. Upholding the steward's discharge, the arbitrator cited the negative impact of the misstatements on the employer's reputation, as well as their potentially disruptive effect on plant operations, discipline, and labor-management relations (*Mid-West Chandelier Co.*, 102 LA 833).

● Discharge also was warranted for a chief steward who repeatedly interrupted a company president during an information meeting about a bonus plan, an arbitrator decided. Noting that the steward refused to comply with the president's order to hold his questions until the end, the arbitrator concluded that the steward's tenacious badgering was an attempt to undermine the president's authority in the presence of a roomful of employees. When the steward was ejected, he motioned to other employees to follow him out of the meeting, which was also an act of defiance that supported his discharge for insubordination, the arbitrator found (*Converters Paperboard Co.*, 108 LA 149).

XXIII. Workplace Violence [LA CDI 100.552510 (public employees); 118.640]

[*Editor's Note:* For violence or threats against supervisors, see II. Abusive Behavior, in this section.]

OVERVIEW

Fighting and assaults have long been condemned as serious forms of misconduct, not only because of the safety implications but also because of the negative impact on employer operations and employee morale. Increasing awareness and apprehension about workplace violence also have prompted many employers to adopt strict policies against threatening or abusive behavior, as well as bans on weapons in the workplace.

Arbitrators generally agree that severe discipline is warranted for employees who commit acts of workplace violence, make threats against fellow employees, or possess weapons on employer property. Even where employers have adopted "zero-tolerance policies" to address these types of misconduct, however, arbitrators sometimes recognize mitigating factors or other special circumstances as a basis for overturning or reducing the discipline imposed on employees.

SUMMARY OF CASES

A. Fighting and Assaults

In cases that involve fighting and assaults, arbitrators commonly hold that, absent mitigating circumstances, management has the right to invoke the discharge penalty (121 LA 782, 119 LA 1576, 118 LA 437, 117 LA 1327, 116 LA 161, 97 LA 356).

● An arbitrator ruled that a production employee at a company that manufactured packaging containers was properly discharged for fighting with another em-

ployee, even though the other employee was only suspended. The grievant struck the co-worker when the co-worker told the grievant, "don't ask me for anything anymore." The arbitrator found that the grievant had no right to act out as he did, no matter how provocative the statement might have been (*Crown Cork & Seal USA, Inc.*, 129 LA 495).

● An employer properly terminated an employee, who was under a last-chance agreement for stealing time, for pushing a co-worker, despite the contention that the employer needed to prove it had just cause to discharge the employee for any acts other than another offense of stealing time. The agreement stated that "Any. . . failure to meet all the duties and responsibilities associated with your job" would result in discharge, and the employee had failed to meet his responsibilities when he committed acts of violent behavior (*Cleveland Electric Illuminating Company*, 130 LA 101).

• An agency had just and sufficient cause to discharge an employee, even if he did not start an altercation with his co-worker and despite the grievant's contention that he acted in self-defense, an arbitrator found, reasoning that the grievant was bigger than the co-worker, the grievant had followed the co-worker out to a dock and had pulled a knife out and snapped it open. Had the knife remained in the grievant's pocket, the arbitrator said, he would not have been subject to the removal action (*Department of Defense*, 128 LA 1183).

• A company had just cause to fire an employee who jumped a co-worker and wrestled him to the ground, an arbitrator decided. The company's initial decision was to terminate both men over the altercation, but it later decided to reinstate the worker who had not been the aggressor in the incident. The union argued that the other employee should have been reinstated as well, claiming that he had merely engaged in a friendly wrestling match. The arbitrator disagreed, citing the company's zero-tolerance policy that included a "no-touch" clause in physical confrontations, as well as evidence that this was not a case of friendly horseplay. Given the company's careful assessment of what happened, its decision was neither arbitrary nor unfair, the arbitrator determined (*Tone Brothers Inc.*, 118 LA 957).

• Another arbitrator upheld the termination of an employee who threw a steel gage in response to a co-worker's provocation, because the employee's action could have resulted in serious bodily harm. The arbitrator acknowledged that the incident was precipitated by the tormenting behavior of the co-worker. Moreover, management contributed to the problem by failing

to maintain adequate discipline and decorum in the work environment. However, the arbitrator concluded that the employee's action in response to the situation "was beyond any measure of reason." When he hurled the heavy gage at the co-worker, "he engaged in a malicious, violent, act surpassing the characterization of justifiable anger," the arbitrator determined (*AGCO Corp.*, 119 LA 1505).

Even while condemning workplace violence, however, many arbitrators have reduced discharges to less drastic penalties when it is shown that employees were provoked into fighting or there is insufficient evidence of fault. In such cases, one arbitrator said, an employer reasonably could discharge the instigator without discharging the employee who finally resorted to violence to protect himself (*Goodyear Decatur Mills*, 12 LA 682).

• An arbitrator ruled that a county with a zero-tolerance policy toward violence did not have good cause to discharge an employee for fighting with a co-worker, when the co-worker had only been suspended over the fight. The evidence about who instigated the fight was inconclusive as the only two witnesses were the participants (*County of Sacramento*, 125 LA 712).

• A warehouse employee at a water and electric company who was involved in an altercation with a co-worker was not guilty of assault, even though the grievant pushed the co-worker on the chest, causing her to fall back, an arbitrator ruled. There was nothing in the co-worker's statement claiming or even suggesting that she was experiencing any "apprehension of bodily harm," which was a necessary element of proof in the assault charge. The employer did not have just cause to discharge the employee involved in the altercation, where its only proof that she committed battery was a photo showing that the other employee had a bruise on her arm (*Kansas City Board of Public Utilities*, 129 LA 1089).

• An employer did not have just cause to discharge a grievant for fighting, an arbitrator ruled, where the complaining employee's testimony alone was insufficient to establish that the grievant placed his hands around the employee's neck. The employee was less than credible in other parts of his testimony, but because the record established that the grievant poked his finger in the complaining employee's chest, pushed him, and "got in his face," his conduct merited 30-day suspension with back pay limited to a 50 percent of his pay for 14 remaining months (*Ecolab Inc.*, 128 LA 922).

• An arbitrator ruled that a group home for the mentally ill did not have just cause to discharge a residential aide who had a scuffle with a co-worker, where the grievant had been provoked by the co-worker and did not hit her, no client was in danger of being harmed by the grievant's conduct, and the home was not exposed to liability (*Nord Center*, 129 LA 1760).

• An arbitrator overturned the discharge of an employee who struck a co-worker with a pipe. The co-worker had called the employee names and threatened him with a piece of timber. In trying to avoid the encounter, the employee had twice walked away before starting to fight. "It should be obvious that an employee suffering an unprovoked attack should not be expected to calmly keep his hands by his side while being clobbered," the arbitrator asserted, maintaining that when fighting is a "reasonable self-defense" mechanism, it does not constitute just cause for discharge. Finding that the employee's conduct was provoked, but that his self-defense measures were excessive under the circumstances, the arbitrator reduced the discharge to a two-month suspension (*Central Foundry Co.*, 63 LA 731).

• An employer did not have just cause to discharge an employee who pulled a knife during an argument with a co-worker who taunted the employee and used racial slurs, an arbitrator ruled. The knife was a small one that the employee used for tasks required in his job, and he drew it out because he was frightened, not because he was being aggressive, the arbitrator found. Even though the co-worker provoked the employee and did nothing to avoid the encounter, he was not disciplined, which meant that the employee's termination amounted to disparate treatment, the arbitrator ruled. Adding that the employee had a good work record during his nine years

with the employer and had never before been involved in a similar incident, the arbitrator awarded him reinstatement with back pay (*Welch Foods Inc.*, 73 LA 908; see also 119 LA 341).

1. Mitigating Factors

• Arbitrators often consider the amount and type of physical contact involved when deciding whether or not to sustain discipline or discharge for workplace violence. For example, one thoughtless blow or an open-handed shove might warrant less severe treatment than misconduct of a more violent, deliberate, or prolonged nature (122 LA 1477, 119 LA 1633, 118 LA 675, 102 LA 377).

• Some types of verbal abuse, such as racial slurs or cursing, can be counted as mitigating factors when they precipitate an altercation (119 LA 405, 117 LA 660).

• Mitigation may be found in a failure by management to head off an impending conflict, such as where it knows of bad blood between employees and fails to take steps to address the problem (76 LA 244, 65 LA 487).

• The length of service and overall work record of employees also can weigh in their favor (105 LA 648, 98 LA 1, 76 LA 1249, 60 LA 1305).

• Arbitrators sometimes consider whether a violent incident indicates that employees have vicious tendencies or dangerous propensities toward such conduct. An employee's medical or psychological condition may or may not be viewed as a mitigating factor calling for a reduction in discipline (89 LA 432, 83 LA 966, 75 LA 12, 53 LA 283).

B. Threats of Violence

When arbitrators review cases that involve threats of violence or abusive language, much depends on the manner and spirit of the remarks in question. A test used by many arbitrators is whether the conduct created a safety threat or caused apprehension in other employees.

• One arbitrator said a critical element to consider when employees have been charged with using threatening language is how the remarks were perceived.

In the case at hand, a hospital employee commented that she would "take it outside the hospital" in dealing with a supervisor and that supervisor "did not know who he was messing with." Emphasizing that the employee's words reasonably were perceived as a threat of possible assault, the arbitrator upheld the employee's discharge (*Mercy Hospital and Medical Center*, 120 LA 1514).

• An employer properly discharged an employee who made comments to one of her co-workers about "going postal," an arbitrator decided. The employee made the same or similar comments more than once, and when the co-worker tried to discourage such thoughts, the employee affirmed her threat by saying, "I'm not suicidal, I'm homicidal." In addition to making these comments, the employee had a history of mental illness and discipline for behavior that left co-workers feeling "threatened and fearful," the arbitrator noted in upholding her termination (*Lansing Community College*, 122 LA 1392).

• A pharmacy benefit management company had just cause to terminate an employee, where he initially did not report his two separate arrests for off-premises illegal drug possession, and, during a phone call with his manager, angrily said that he wanted to "take care" of the then-unknown employee who had notified company of the arrests (*Express Scripts Inc.*, 126 LA 1299).

• An employer properly invoked its zero-tolerance policy in discharging an employee for threatening and violent behavior, an arbitrator held. The employee threatened a co-worker who refused to move from a seat in the break room at a table where the employee had left his drink. He took off toward his work area, slamming his fist into a nearby tool locker. Other workers told management they felt unsafe because of the employee's violent outburst. The company fired the employee, claiming he had violated its zero-tolerance policy on violence. In protesting the discharge, the union noted that the employee was under psychiatric care and taking prescribed, anti-psychotic medication to resolve anger management problems. Even though the employer's policy did not *require* termination in each case involving threats of violence, the arbitrator found that the totality of the circumstances gave the employer just cause to discharge the employee (*Whirlpool Corp.*, 115 LA 33).

• An employer had just cause to fire a bakery employee for threatening a co-worker, an arbitrator ruled. The co-worker had hidden the employee's tools as payback, he said, for similar behavior by the employee. When the employee found out what happened, he began chasing the co-worker and threatened to hurt him. Several bystanders said they believed the employee would have harmed the co-worker if he could have caught him. The employer fired the employee, citing a policy that called for the immediate termination of any employee who threatens a co-worker. Stressing that the employer had a duty to prevent the type of behavior in which the employee engaged, the arbitrator determined that the termination was justified. Discharge has been upheld, the arbitrator added, in many cases involving threatening and intimidating conduct less serious than that of the employee (*Interstate Brands Corp.*, 116 LA 1414).

• An employer had just cause to discharge an employee who said she would kill a co-worker, an arbitrator found. The employee began seeing a psychiatrist following a mental breakdown, and she told the psychiatrist she had suicidal thoughts and felt the urge to harm her supervisor and a number of co-workers. Several weeks later, after returning to work part-time, the employee told a colleague she would kill a male co-worker if he did not stop disturbing her. The employee's psychiatrist had warned the employer to take the employee's threats seriously; thus, it fired the employee and provided 24-hour security for the co-worker and the employee's supervisor. Although the union argued that the abrupt discharge violated the employee's due process rights, the arbitrator decided that the employer was only following the psychiatrist's advice in the way it responded to the employee's threat (*Alabama Power Co.*, 116 LA 157).

• Termination was warranted for an employee who said he would shoot people at work, an arbitrator ruled. The employee, who worked as a customer service representative in a call center, reportedly proclaimed, "I'm going to bring myself a gun tomorrow and start shooting me some folk." The arbitrator found that the employee's statement violated an employer policy that expressly prohibited threats of violence in the workplace. Termination was warranted given the seriousness of the employee's violation and the employer's "responsibility for the safety of all employees," the arbitrator concluded (*SBC Midwest*, 122 LA 1; see also 121 LA 1821, 118 LA 1735, 117 LA 1382).

• *By contrast*, another arbitrator overturned the discharge of an employee who made a comment about bringing a gun to work. The employee performed finishing work on metal tubing, and he often complained about the way the materials came to him from two co-workers whose job it was to cut the tubing. All three of them had been warned about bickering, but the employee's supervisor felt that the two co-workers were more the instigators. The employee's termination was prompted by his comment one day to a colleague that he "better duck if I bring in my .44." Although the employee admitted to owning a .44 caliber handgun, he said the comment was a joke between friends.

The arbitrator acknowledged "that any remark about bringing a gun to work raises a red flag of alarm or concern, particularly in today's age of increasing reports of violence and shootings at the workplace." However, he said a number of factors militated against discharge, including the following: the gun remark was made in jest privately to a friend and was not a threat to the two co-workers; those workers baited the employee, causing his agitation; despite its awareness of the two co-workers' role as the main instigators, management failed to take positive action to address the cause of the situation. Adding that the employee "was entitled to greater consideration by the company for his record of 21 years, with no prior disciplines," the arbitrator reduced the discipline to a three-day suspension (*Garelick Manufacturing Co.*, 122 LA 1576).

• In another case, an employer's failure to show that a threatening remark posed a genuine danger prompted an arbitrator to overturn an employee's discharge.

Upon returning from a three-day suspension, the employee remarked in the presence of the company safety director that he would kill his supervisor. The company had a zero-tolerance policy with regard to violence and fired the employee the next working day after company officials were told of the incident. The union argued that the employer's delay in responding showed that the threat was not taken seriously and therefore was not covered by the zero-tolerance policy. According to the arbitrator, the safety director's failure to notify company officials of the incident for an entire work day, as well as her failure to call the police or take any action whatsoever, undermined the employer's claim that the threat was genuine. The arbitrator ordered reinstatement but refused to award the employee back pay (*Ryder/ATE*, 111 LA 1038; see also 95 LA 895).

C. Off-Duty Violence or Threats

Ordinarily, employees are not subject to discipline for their actions while away from work. However, arbitrators generally agree that employers have a right to take disciplinary action in situations where off-duty misconduct involving violence or threats affects the employment relationship in a negative way.

Some arbitrators have noted that employers have an obligation to maintain order and safety on their premises, which includes more than just the plant. Therefore, discharges have been sustained for assaults that take place in employer parking lots and when employees are leaving company property (50 LA 407, 30 LA 948, 29 LA 820).

• A corrections facility had just cause to discharge a corrections officer who was convicted of criminal misdemeanors for off-duty conduct, where he disabled another man's automobile brakes, forced entry into a home at night, had a drunken rampage, threatened violence, and unlawfully imprisoned his former girlfriend and her current boyfriend (*Minnesota Dept. of Corrections*, 130 LA 235).

• An employer had just cause to discharge an employee who phoned a co-worker at home and threatened to beat him with a baseball bat, an arbitrator held. The employer fired the employee under its workplace violence policy, which stated that threats or violence against fellow employees would not be tolerated. Although the union argued that the policy was not meant to apply to off-duty conduct, the arbitrator said termination was appropriate because of the incident's "critical nexus" with the workplace. The arbitrator stressed that the employee's presence in the workplace would not only make the threatened co-worker fearful, it would also be likely to cause a ripple effect among other employees, "thereby destroying the workplace harmony" (*Proctor & Gamble Co.*, 114 LA 1185; see also 114 LA 1024, 74 LA 1084, 57 LA 725).

• *By contrast,* an arbitrator overturned the suspension of a county sheriff who did not have just cause to suspend a deputy for violating the sheriff's off-duty policy when the deputy pursued in his patrol car a customer at a small grocery store who drove off without paying, subsequently rammed the patrol car, and tried to run down the deputy. The officer violated a policy against making arrests while off duty for offenses such as misdemeanor theft, and there was a contention that the officer was personally involved in the underlying incident and should have merely reported it to on-duty personnel. However, the arbitrator found there was clearly something wrong with the drive-off customer and the deputy's pursuit showed a legitimate concern for public safety rather than a personal concern over a $42 theft, and reduced the suspension to a written warning (*Lawrence County Sheriff*, 125 LA 304).

• An off-duty fight between two employees during a poker game was not just cause for discipline absent any harm to the employer. "No evidence takes this case outside the general rule that off-duty indiscretions do not permit discipline," the arbitrator ruled, emphasizing that there was no proof whatsoever that the employees were unable to work together after their off-duty altercation or that any other employee refused to work with either of them (*Honeywell Inc.*, 68 LA 346).

D. Weapons in the Workplace

Arbitrators generally agree that management has the right to forbid employees from bringing firearms and other weapons to work. On the other hand, arbitrators may be unwilling to uphold disciplinary actions against employees who bring weapons onto their employers' premises in cases where rules prohibiting such conduct have not been promulgated or posted (69 LA 613, 64 LA 291) or consistently enforced in the past (77 LA 845, 46 LA 1161).

• Discharge was warranted for a bus driver who violated his employer's no-weapons rule, an arbitrator decided. The driver was reported by a passenger for brandishing a knife in a threatening manner, and a police search of the driver's bus turned up a kitchen knife with a five-inch blade. The driver was fired in spite of his claim that he did not know how the knife had gotten on the bus. The arbitrator found that the employer had strictly enforced its no-weapons rule by uniformly terminating workers who violated it. Adding that the rule was "essential in securing the overall safety of employees, passengers, and the general public," the arbitrator upheld the driver's termination (*Metropolitan Transit Authority*, 122 LA 945; see also 79 LA 508).

• Another arbitrator upheld the termination of an airport maintenance worker following the discovery of a loaded gun in his vehicle when it was parked in the employee parking lot. The employee violated a clear policy against possessing a firearm on employer property, the arbitrator found, adding that the policy was appropriate in light of the heightened security concerns applicable to a busy airport (*Airport Authority of Washoe County*, 119 LA 920).

• An employer properly fired an employee who carried a concealed weapon at work and threatened a management official, an arbitrator ruled. The employee had uttered threats, profanities, and racial slurs about his supervisor in front of co-workers. When reporting to company offices for a subsequent disciplinary meeting, the employee stopped at a guard station, pulled out a knife, and said he was going to cut the company's director of human relations. Refusing to accept the employee's claims that he was "joking" and "showing off," the arbitrator upheld the employee's termination

(*Smurfit-Stone Container Corp.*, 121 LA 1154; see also 109 LA 796).

● An employer had just cause to discharge an employee after finding a loaded handgun and open liquor bottles in a search of his car while it was parked in a company parking lot, an arbitrator ruled. The employee had left the gun and liquor in his car following a family gathering. The arbitrator acknowledged that there was no threat of danger from the employee, who did not intend to use the gun or liquor while at work. However, the employer had imposed and strictly enforced a total ban on weapons and alcohol in the workplace, the arbitrator noted, and making an exception for the employee based on his lack of intent would have rendered the rules useless (*Marathon Petroleum Co.*, 93 LA 1082; see also 76 LA 26).

● *By contrast*, other arbitrators have held that discharge is not warranted where employees inadvertently have brought weapons onto employer property. For example, one arbitrator awarded reinstatement to a teacher who had stowed a handgun in a backpack for a Saturday visit to a gun club, but then forgot to remove it before going to work on Monday. "The seriousness of bringing a gun to school is not disputed," the arbitrator said. Adding, however, that a "measured response" to the infraction was required by the just cause standard, the arbitrator reduced the discipline to a lengthy suspension (*Shaler Area School District*, 119 LA 570; see also 120 LA 1146, 117 LA 1403).

● Another arbitrator overturned the discharge of an employee who brought a gun to work, noting that the collective bargaining agreement said the offense of possessing a firearm on employer property "may," but not "shall," result in discharge. The arbitrator ordered the employee reinstated, but without back pay, because although the gun was unloaded and the employee was merely showing it to people, the employee's offense was a serious one (*Interstate Brands Corp.*, 104 LA 993).

Part 3

Safety and Health

I. Safety [LA CDI 100.552575 (public employees); 118.659]

[*Editor's Note:* See also Part 2, Chapter VI, Dress & Grooming; Part 2, Chapter XV, Negligence; and Part 2, Chapter XIV, Intoxication & Alcoholism. For a discussion of cases involving charges of insubordination when employees refuse to perform unsafe work, see Part 2, Chapter XVIII, Refusal to Obey Directives.]

OVERVIEW

Arbitrators generally acknowledge that management has the right to issue and enforce rules that are reasonably related to the purpose of ensuring a safe and healthful workplace (122 LA 1038, 95 LA 705, 84 LA 972).

Discharge may be justified where employees have persistently violated safety rules in spite of progressive discipline. Arbitrators also have upheld immediate discharge for serious safety infractions, particularly those that endanger other workers.

Safety rules must be consistently enforced. Where there has been lax or irregular enforcement of safety rules, arbitrators have refused to uphold discipline on the grounds that employees have been subjected to inequitable or arbitrary treatment.

In some cases, employers' responsibility to provide safe working conditions is used as the basis to challenge management decisions on issues such as work assignments and staff reductions. Without evidence of actual safety risks, however, arbitrators are unlikely to interfere with the right of management to make such decisions.

SUMMARY OF CASES

A. Reasonableness of Safety Rules

Safety rules must be reasonable in scope and application, arbitrators have held. Accordingly, arbitrators have rejected rules that are overly broad or that impose unnecessary requirements or restrictions on employees.

● An arbitrator refused to sustain various clothing prohibitions that an employer wanted to add to its safety rules, finding that the employer failed to show a sufficient magnitude of safety risks to justify the new restrictions. The employer's original rules prohibited employees from having loose clothes, dangling hair, or jewelry around moving machinery. The additional restrictions included a ban on wearing so-called beach clothes—such as shorts, tank tops, short skirts, see-through blouses, and open-toed sandals—when walking from the plant gates to individual work areas. The arbitrator found that these prohibitions were "not directly related to safety," because upon entering the plant gates, employees traveled some 300 feet down a clearly marked pedestrian walkway that was supposedly safe. The arbitrator said expanding the original rule in this regard constituted "unreasonable interference with the personal freedom of the employees to come and go from and to their work places without unreasonable regimentation" (*Babcock & Wilcox*, 73 LA 443).

● An employer overstepped its bounds in demanding that all workers in its plant wear safety shoes, an arbitrator said, noting that contractual provisions on safety shoes only applied to one employee group. Although an Occupational Safety and Health Administration regulation mandated safety shoes for employees "working in areas where there is a danger of foot injuries due to falling or rolling objects, or objects piercing the sole," the arbitrator said the employer failed to identify areas presenting such hazards, and the OSHA rule did not mandate a plant-wide requirement (*Packaging Corp. of America*, 114 LA 809).

● In a similar case, an arbitrator concluded that an employer's respirator-related shaving rule should have been

narrower. The employer established a respirator policy when it began using acids as part of its food manufacturing processes. In light of OSHA regulations requiring a good seal without interference from facial hair, the employer's policy required employees to be clean shaven if there was a "chance" they would have to use a respirator. Noting that blanket policies of this type have been found unreasonable, the arbitrator said employers are required, when possible, to draw a line between employees who need to shave and those who do not, even if it would be more convenient to require all employees to be clean shaven. Emphasizing that the employer could have designated employees on each shift to be responsible for duties involving respirators, the arbitrator overturned the employer's policy on the basis that it was overly broad (*Mission Foods*, 111 LA 501; see also 82 LA 1084, 80 LA 765, 74 LA 412).

B. Discharge for Safety Infractions

Because plant safety violations may have dire consequences, arbitrators often take a strict view and uphold discharge for a single safety infraction, reasoning that the seriousness of employees' offenses warrant termination without the benefit of progressive discipline.

● A salt mine had just cause to discharge an employee who was subject to a last-chance agreement and who violated a safety rule requiring immediate reporting of a chemical release, an arbitrator ruled, even though he had almost 28 years of seniority, since there is a limit to an employer's toleration of a grievant's violation of safety rules (*Morton Salt*, 128 LA 557).

● An employer had just cause to discharge a 37-year foreman, because the foreman did not properly instruct a journeyman on how to handle a job site and stay out of a danger zone and the journeyman entered the danger zone and was seriously injured, an arbitrator found. The grievant may be held to a higher—almost supervisory—standard as a foreman, he has a history of safety infractions, as senior employee he should have known better and been more careful, and he was not even willing to concede that he may have done something incorrectly (*Public Service Co. of Colorado*, 129 LA 361).

• A refinery had good and sufficient cause to discharge an employee whose premature action in untightening bolts led to ignition of fire that resulted in damage to company property and loss of production exceeding $65 million, an arbitrator found. The arbitrator reasoned that even though the employee had 20 years of satisfactory service, 20 years was not a surety bond for continued employment when failure to follow proper procedure has major consequences in terms of equipment repairs causing lost production and associated loss of revenue (*LyondellBasell*, 129 LA 1291).

• An arbitrator found that an employer had just cause to discharge an employee, where he committed four safety violations in three or four minutes by not following the company's requisite de-energizing and lock-out procedures, and there were no mitigating factors, such as a spotless work record, offered into evidence (*Rock-Tenn Co.*, 127 LA 390).

• An employer had just cause to discharge an employee for deliberately violating safety rule, an arbitrator ruled, where the employee removed and exchanged an electronic temperature control module from one soup kettle to another in violation of a work rule providing that only maintenance personnel were authorized to perform electrical maintenance. The employee also failed to completely power down equipment and was a short-term employee with a less than satisfactory record (*Sandridge Gourmet Salads*, 128 LA 1211).

• An employer had just cause to discharge an employee for his first offense of safety rules aimed at the prevention of fires and explosions at a paint and resin manufacturing plant, an arbitrator held. Stressing the employer's emphasis on the importance of following the rules, the arbitrator said he was "struck by the many and various different ways by which the company's management repeatedly conveys this message to the employees." These included publication of the rules in a safety handbook, signs and schematics posted on the walls to remind employees of the proper procedures, and

even a memorandum from the plant manager informing workers that there would be "zero tolerance" for violating the rules. Concluding that the employee "was very conversant" with the rules and that his actions could have resulted in serious injury to himself and others, the arbitrator decided that termination was warranted (*PPG Industries Inc.*, 122 LA 1250).

• An employer did not act arbitrarily in firing an employee for a lockout violation, an arbitrator found. After the press he was operating malfunctioned, the employee climbed into the machine in an effort to fix it, but he did not follow appropriate lockout procedures to ensure that the machine would not accidentally activate while he was inside it. The employer had placed lockout violations at the top of a "Taboo List" of rules that could be punished with immediate discharge, the arbitrator observed, and the employee had signed an acknowledgement form regarding the list of dischargeable offenses less than five months before the incident occurred. While conceding that strict enforcement of the lockout rule "ends with harsh results," the arbitrator held that the employer acted reasonably when it invoked the discharge penalty in response to the employee's violation (*Benteler Automotive Corp.*, 121 LA 733; see also 122 LA 171).

• *By contrast*, an employer did not have cause to discharge an employee who was cleaning a robot head while it was moving in violation of a lock-out procedure, even though training on safety procedures had been extensive and professional, where at least some line supervisors knew that employees cleaned robot heads without locking them and did not punish those employees. The arbitrator reinstated the employee without back pay and with a 30-day suspension (*International Automotive Components*, 128 LA 1723).

• A manufacturer did not have just cause to discharge an employee for a second violation of a lock-out tag-out rule requiring that machinery be locked and at "zero energy state" before working on or around the machine, even though this was a rule "considered so serious" that "most serious disciplinary action is warranted" and the employee had received a warning that another violation would "result in termination." The arbitrator found that the collective bargaining agreement provided that warnings were not effective for more than 12 months, the employee's second offense occurred outside the 12-month period, and there was past practice of requiring two violations of lock-out tag-out rule for discharge (*Georgia-Pacific Corp. LLC*, 129 LA 433).

● An arbitrator ruled that an employer did not have just cause to discharge a truck driver who negligently failed to reinsert one support pole on a trailer and for use of abusive language, where the grievant received no notice that his negligence created a "major safety hazard," there was not a reasonable basis for imposing "indefinite suspension" during investigation, the employer did nothing to dispel the grievant's belief that indefinite suspension was unwarranted, management had not made an apparent effort to interview the grievant or steward to determine any aggravating or mitigating circumstances surrounding the grievant's abusive language, and the employer failed to provide the grievant with "corrective action notice" form stating the basis of his termination. The arbitrator reinstated the grievant without back pay, subject to a 12-month probationary period (*Huttig Building Products Inc.*, 128 LA 1251).

C. Progressive Discipline

Although certain safety violations can provide just cause for immediate discharge, arbitrators commonly expect employers to enforce their safety rules through the imposition of progressive discipline.

● One arbitrator decided that a company's revocation of a grievant's forklift operating license for hitting a beam with the tip of his fork constituted discipline subject to the just cause standard, despite the company's claim that it could take unilateral action on safety matters. The company-wide safety rules and plant code of conduct both indicated that safety violations were typically dealt with through the disciplinary process and the company's third-step answer cited unsafe operation of forklift as "justification for this discipline" (*Anchor Hocking LLC*, 128 LA 1206).

● Discharge was not warranted for an employee's third safety infraction involving forklifts, an arbitrator held. The employee had received a verbal warning for his first offense and a written warning for his second offense. His employer skipped the third step under its progressive discipline policy, which would have been a suspension, and fired the employee after his third offense. The arbitrator acknowledged the appropriateness of skipping steps of the progressive discipline process under some circumstances, but he found that the behavior of the employee in this case "was not so heinous as to justify the Company's rush to apply the discharge penalty." Accordingly, the arbitrator reduced the penalty to a suspension (*Cargill Animal Nutrition*, 120 LA 1665; see also 94 LA 152).

● An employee's failure to follow proper procedures for transferring hazardous waste did not warrant the issuance of step-four discipline under an employer's system of progressive discipline, an arbitrator ruled. The employee had previously been disciplined with a "Casual Reminder" and "Routine Reminder" under the employer's five-step policy. For the employee's latest infraction, the employer skipped the third step, which would have been a "Formal Reminder," and issued the employee a "Decision Making Leave," which was the last step before termination. The union argued that the employee was treated more severely than other workers who committed similar infractions, and the company had never before bypassed any of the steps in the progressive discipline policy. Finding that the employer did not apply its step-by-step scheme fairly and consistently, the arbitrator reduced the discipline to a "Formal Reminder" (*Rhodia Inc.*, 120 LA 1392).

● *By contrast*, an arbitrator upheld the discharge of an employee who had sustained a number of injuries as the result of failing to wear proper safety equipment and failing to observe appropriate safety precautions. The arbitrator observed that the employer's system of rules provided "for progressive disciplinary actions for successive violations of the rules and regulations, which include safety regulations." The arbitrator concluded that "the safety rules requiring the use of protective equipment are reasonable," and added that because they are reasonable, and because the collective bargaining agreement "specifically permits the establishment of rules and regulations, it is the duty of all employees" to abide by these rules (*Vulcan-Hart Corp.*, 78 LA 59; see also 98 LA 357, 94 LA 777).

D. Consistency of Enforcement

When overturning or reducing discipline for safety violations, arbitrators often fault employers for failing to ensure consistent enforcement or uniform application of their rules.

● An arbitrator reduced a written warning and a 90-day prohibition against driving an employer's trucks to a written warning for an employee who drove a tractor-trailer erratically and unsafely, in violation of a reasonable safety rule that authorized both warnings and disqualifications as penalties, because two previous rule violators were not disqualified from the same task (*Seaway Food Town*, 94 LA 389).

● Another arbitrator overturned the termination of an employee who ran a forklift into a pole, causing substantial structural damage to the warehouse where he worked. The employee failed to exercise ordinary prudence to ensure that the blind spots created by the vehicle's masts did not conceal hazards in his path, but he did not recklessly disregard basic safety standards as his employer alleged, the arbitrator found. Noting that other workers were treated far less severely for safety infractions of similar seriousness, the arbitrator reduced the employee's discipline to a one-day suspension (*Straits Steel and Wire Co.*, 96 LA 798).

● An employer improperly disciplined an employee who failed to use a safety belt as prescribed by a rule that management had allowed to lie dormant for at least 20 years, an arbitrator held. "In fairness, and desire to promote favorable employee relations," maintained the arbitrator, "the employer should have given notice of its intent to enforce seat belt usage and the nature of discipline to be administered for noncompliance." In the absence of such a warning, the employer's action lacked equitability, the arbitrator said in overturning the dis-

cipline (*U.S. Army Corps of Engineers*, 86 LA 939).

● An employer committed a contract violation by not requiring its supervisory employees to wear the same protective equipment that workers were required to wear during periods when they were exposed to the same risks, an arbitrator determined. The arbitrator noted that the bargaining agreement specifically stated that "all levels of supervision of the company, the employees, and the union will cooperate fully to promote safe practices, health conditions, and the enforcement of safety rules and procedures." When supervisors "are exposed to the same risks but do not observe the same safety rules that line employees are required to observe," the arbitrator said, the supervisors "are clearly violating" the agreement. "Such a violation by a foreman may not only endanger the foreman himself," observed the arbitrator, but "it may also endanger employees with whom he is working" (*Noranda Aluminum Inc.*, 78 LA 1331).

E. Worker Knowledge of Safety Rules

In reviewing discipline imposed by employers for safety violations, arbitrators occasionally find that employees were not adequately informed of the rules they were accused of violating.

● One arbitrator found that a company did not have just cause to issue a five-day disciplinary suspension to a customer systems technician for a "preventable accident" in which an automatic garage door that periodically closed lowered onto the boom of his truck when he was entering a garage and ripped the door from brackets. Although the supervisor reported that the technician should have gotten out of the vehicle and hit the reset button located inside the garage to reset the timer, this was an unwritten rule, and the company had no clear policy for the employee to follow as to entering the garage when the door was already open (*AT&T Services Inc. Midwest*, 129 LA 435).

● An employer's improper posting of a safety rule prompted an arbitrator to overturn the discharge of another employee. The employer had fired the employee under a contract provision stating that a refusal to comply with posted rules provided cause for termination. However, the arbitrator pointed out that the rule was posted in the lunchroom and not in the employee's department, and the posting was in Spanish, but the employee only knew English (*Smurfit Recycling Co.*, 103 LA 243).

• An arbitrator found an employer did not have just cause to discharge a haul truck driver for abandoning a burning truck without staying a few more seconds to hit the emergency off switch or activate the manual fire suppression system, which was what he was trained to do. Discussing fire procedures in a training session is not the same experience as employing them in the midst of a flaming haul truck cab, the arbitrator said, and the seemingly life or death choice he made in the flame-laden truck cab did not justify the decision to discharge him (*Asarco LLC*, 127 LA 753).

• *By contrast, a* nuclear power plant had just cause to issue three-day suspension to an employee who violated safety rules by not getting approval before doing maintenance work on guarded equipment. The arbitrator said that even if the grievant did not knowingly violate the rules, that kind of conduct is not acceptable in a nuclear plant where warnings must be noticed and obeyed without delay (*Indiana Michigan Power*, 126 LA 1780).

• An arbitrator found that an employer had just cause to discharge a 31-year employee who did not follow lockout procedures for a high pressure water line, even though his supervisor and manager were present during the procedure, where neither told the grievant not to lockout the machine, he had prior discipline for a lockout violation and four written warnings for other matters, there were training programs on safety concerns, and the employer had a zero tolerance rule for lockout procedure violations (*IAC Sheboygan LLC*, 126 LA 1665).

F. Ensuring Safe Working Conditions

Some arbitration cases focus on whether employers have taken actions that violate their obligation to ensure safe working conditions. If the evidence does not adequately establish the existence of safety risks, however, arbitrators usually leave such actions undisturbed in deference to management rights and employers' authority to control business operations.

• An arbitrator found that a school board did not violate a collective bargaining agreement that ensured every effort would be made to provide safe working conditions when it assigned an unaccompanied, female teacher to supervise a study hall in an isolated auditorium. The arbitrator noted that teachers who previously supervised the study hall by themselves had not complained to the employer, and the actions of students who were assigned to the study hall did not support the contention that conditions were unsafe. While acknowledging the importance of safety, the arbitrator said the evidence was not sufficient to override management's rights and require a response "to the anxieties of an individual teacher" (*Washington Local Schools Board of Education*, 104 LA 1185).

• Pulling maintenance employees off some shifts at a steel plant was not a violation of an employer's safety and health obligations, an arbitrator ruled. Although maintenance employees had been available during all production shifts in the past and on some occasions had provided critical assistance in connection with workplace accidents, the plant's equipment and operations had become safer over the years, the arbitrator noted. Weighing the added safety benefits against the costs of keeping the staffing requirement in place, the arbitrator concluded that having maintenance employees work during every shift was a "luxury" the employer could not afford and which had become unnecessary in light of the plant's existing safety record (*Southwestern Ohio Steel Inc.*, 116 LA 1128; see also 116 LA 1718).

• *By contrast*, an arbitrator held that an electric company could not reduce the number of employees assigned to perform street light maintenance using bucket trucks. Traditionally, crews of two employees performed such work, but the company attempted to change that practice by assigning only one worker to a bucket truck. Finding that the company's safety regulations required at least two employees to be assigned to each bucket truck, the arbitrator ruled that the company committed a contract violation in failing to assign two-person crews to perform the work in question. Consequently, the arbitrator ordered the company to discontinue using single-member bucket truck crews for street light maintenance (*New York State Electric & Gas Corp.*, 111 LA 339).

• Another utility committed a contract violation in requiring two employees to perform electrical work in hazardous conditions, an arbitrator decided. The employees were directed to convert a customer's residence from aerial to underground electrical service on a day when it was misty and snowing. Under the contract, however, the employer was prohibited from requiring the employees to perform the work in inclement weather. Concluding that the weather created hazardous conditions for working on energized circuits, the arbitrator ordered the employer to abide by the contract in the future and cease to assign work on energized circuits during similar periods of inclement weather (*South Central Power Co.*, 119 LA 1680).

G. Failure to Use Safety Equipment

• An employer did not have just cause to discipline an employee for not wearing his hard hat at work, where the employer did not give him an opportunity to discuss the allegation at or near the time a snapshot of him without a hard hat on was taken and explain his conduct. The arbitrator reduced the employee's discharge to a 60-day suspension (*Zeon Chemicals LP*, 129 LA 1687).

• An arbitrator held that an employer did not have just cause to discharge an employee for not wearing a protective face shield while pumping chemicals because the employer failed to prove it expressly alerted the employee to a "supposed" general rule requiring face shields when handling any chemicals. No documents distributed to employees contained such a rule, a training video communicated the opposite message by showing employees handling chemicals wearing only goggles, and no supervisor notified the employee of the rule, the arbitrator found (*Cone Mills Corp.*, 104 LA 833).

• A penalty of a final written warning plus a five-day suspension was too severe for a mine employee who completed a work task by crossing an icy catwalk and coal pile without a harness, an arbitrator ruled, even though the collective bargaining agreement allowed for discipline for rule violations that could result in serious personal injury. The employer's prolonged failure to clean up a coal pile undermined its assertion that safety was paramount and the use of a harness was not specifically mandated by the employer or the state government. However, the arbitrator upheld the employer's oral warning to the grievant because of his failure to at least attempt to notify his supervisor about dangerous conditions (*Mississippi Lime Co.*, 126 LA 4).

• A bus company had proper cause to discharge a driver who drove without wearing a seat belt, an arbitrator ruled, where the rule was reasonable and consistent with state law, the driver had previously failed to wear a seat belt on more than one occasion, he had worked for the company for six years and had an unclean record, and safety violations are a serious offense (*Veolia Transportation Services*, 128 LA 906).

H. Vehicle Violations

• An arbitrator ruled that a bus company did not have just cause to discharge a driver solely because he stopped a bus well past the stop line and blocked the crosswalk at a red light. The arbitrator found that the employer presented no written rule, policy, explanation, or definition of what constituted running a red light, which was a dischargeable offense. However, the arbitrator also found that the bus company had just cause to discharge the driver, because he had been suspended for a preventable accident within the preceding 30 days and was working under a last-chance agreement, and the handbook provided that two safety-related violations in 12 months will result in discharge (*First Transit Inc.*, 128 LA 935).

• An employer had just cause to discharge a bus driver for releasing a brake and allowing the bus to move forward when at least one pedestrian was in a crosswalk in front of it, even though the driver then applied the brake and thus avoided hitting anyone. The arbitrator found that the grievant previously had entered into a settlement agreement stipulating that discharge would result from her committing a serious disciplinary infraction (*Veolia Transportation*, 125 LA 1334).

• An arbitrator found that an employer had just cause to terminate a bus driver for parking a bus in a manner that violated a safety rule, despite the union's contention that the termination decision was untimely because the employer made it more than five days after learning about the incident. The driver previously had been suspended multiple times due to safety rule violations and misconduct toward customers, the arbitrator found. Further, the union waited until the day of the arbitration hearing to raise the timeliness issue, which the arbitrator found was inappropriate, and the collective bargaining agreement's language was unclear as to when the employer would become aware of any incident giving rise to discipline (*ShuttlePort California LLC*, 125 LA 1297).

• An employer had just cause to discharge a commercial truck driver for failing to follow police officers' orders by driving a truck that they had deemed out of service (OOS), failing to follow federal regulations by not conducting thorough pre-trip inspections, and failing to put safety first by driving the truck on public highways with 10 safety violations. The arbitrator's findings indicated OOS violations could clearly be noted during pre-trip inspections, officers sufficiently advised the grievant about OOS status, and his conduct amounted to "refusal to do a work assignment" that rendered written notice unnecessary (*Arkhola Sand & Gravel Co.*, 128 LA 65).

I. Smoking

• An employer did not have just cause to discharge an employee for smoking on a parked forklift near a propane tank and storage room full of combustible paper, one arbitrator found, despite the employer's contention that "common sense" should have told the employee that this behavior was unacceptable and could result in discharge. The arbitrator reasoned that smoking is not misconduct involving moral turpitude, the employer's safety policy only warned against smoking when refueling or when batteries were nearby, operators were never told that this rule was meant to ban all smoking on forklifts, and training manuals were silent on the subject (*Georgia-Pacific Corrugated LLC*, 126 LA 698).

• A medical center had just cause to issue a verbal warning to an employee who smoked in an unauthorized area when he visited the center while he was on leave of absence, where he had been given informal counseling for smoking in an unauthorized area previously. The arbitrator found the counseling was for a first violation and that this was the grievant's second such violation by and under the employer's progressive discipline and therefore a verbal warning was appropriate (*California Pacific Medical Center*, 125 LA 1255).

II. Smoking Restrictions [LA CDI 124.70]

OVERVIEW

Generalizations about arbitration rulings on smoking restrictions are difficult to draw, in part because employer rules and societal views on smoking have changed significantly over the years. Many employers once granted workers unfettered smoking privileges, but limitations and bans have become increasingly common, paralleling, to some extent, increasing awareness about the hazards of tobacco usage and the health risks associated with secondhand smoke.

Despite mounting evidence about tobacco's harmful effects, arbitrators do not automatically uphold smoking restrictions. If collective bargaining agreements confer certain smoking rights on employees, for example, arbitrators are reluctant to sustain employer policies that conflict with those rights.

In a number of smoking-related cases, meanwhile, arbitrators have reached opposite conclusions while considering seemingly identical situations. For instance, arbitrators are divided on the question of whether employers are required to bargain with unions before introducing new smoking restrictions. Some hold to the view that the ability to smoke at work constitutes a term or condition of employment, which would make smoking restrictions a mandatory subject of bargaining. Other arbitrators treat smoking as a privilege that employers have unilateral authority to grant or deny.

For the most part, however, arbitrators tend to base their decisions on the reasonableness of the restrictions in question, and they typically uphold restrictions that are supported by substantial business-related justifications. Similarly, arbitrators are likely to uphold reasonable discipline imposed on employees for violating valid workplace smoking policies.

SUMMARY OF CASES

A. Smoking Restrictions Upheld

The weight of arbitration decisions in favor of smoking restrictions has increased over the years as employers have taken a more aggressive stance on tobacco usage and arbitrators have become more favorably inclined toward no-smoking policies.

In sustaining the restrictions imposed by employers, many arbitrators have voiced the opinion that smoking is not a term or condition of employment, but rather a privilege that management can revoke for legitimate business reasons. This is particularly true where collective bargaining agreements do not specifically address smoking but do include management rights provisions that give employers unilateral authority over the establishment of workplace rules.

● For example, one arbitrator ruled that an employer's new policy that totally prohibited tobacco in the workplace was not discriminatory, stating that tobacco use is more generally recognized as a privilege, not a right. Moreover, even though in past decisions addressing smoking bans, there had been an inclination to uphold partial bans to protect non-smokers while supporting designated smoking areas for smokers, this middle ground is quickly disappearing, the arbitrator said, as more states have implemented total bans of smoking in buildings. The arbitrator went on to say the prohibition is supported by a desire to promote better health for all employees (*Dexter Foundry Inc.*, 126 LA 1607).

● An employer did not violate a collective bargaining agreement by unilaterally implementing policies that prohibited smoking initially and the use of any form of tobacco subsequently, an arbitrator held. The employer had reserved the right to amend previously published smoking regulations to achieve the ultimate goal of a smoke-free workplace and the policies were reasonable and consistent with the evolving evidence of health hazards. Further, the union waived any right to bargain when it pursued a grievance instead of demanding that the employer bargain over the workplace smoking ban (*Rotek Incorporated*, 127 LA 924).

● An employer did not violate a collective bargaining contract when it unilaterally changed smoking policies to eliminate allowing smoking during short, non-scheduled breaks, despite a contention of past practice requiring supervisors to give such breaks, an arbitrator held. The union's acquiescence in rules giving supervisors the discretion to give such breaks did not require them to do so and the rule was reasonable, because breaks would be hard to police as to length. Further, the arbitrator said, there was the issue of encouraging unhealthful habits and the possibility of exponential untidiness in the smoking area (*Kautex Textron*, 124 LA 785).

In one case where an employer prohibited smoking anywhere on its property, the business justifications for the ban encompassed many of the reasons commonly referenced in other cases on smoking restrictions. They included preserving employee health and safety, improving productivity, eliminating fire risks, reducing absenteeism, and cutting health insurance costs.

Based on those justifications, an arbitrator upheld the employer's smoking ban. The arbitrator also found that the ban was reasonable because the employer had historically retained discretionary authority over smoking on company property, had met with and adopted suggestions from the union about the new policy, and had sponsored smoking cessation classes on company time prior to implementing the ban (*Rolls-Royce Energy Systems Inc.*, 120 LA 223).

● A dental insurance company was justified in implementing a total ban on smoking, an arbitrator ruled. The employer had begun issuing smoking restrictions nearly 20 years earlier and had ratcheted up the restrictions on several occasions. Originally, employees were allowed "to smoke whenever and wherever they wished," the arbitrator noted, but through a progression of rule changes, the employer eventually prohibited indoor smoking, then restricted where employees could smoke outside its buildings, and finally banned the use of tobacco on its premises, in company-owned vehicles, and in personal vehicles parked on company property.

As part of his opinion, the arbitrator allowed that a smoking ban can constitute a mandatory subject of bargaining by virtue of its impact on workers' terms and conditions of employment. However, the arbitrator sidestepped the question of whether the employer committed an unfair labor practice by unilaterally implementing the ban, noting that his authority was limited to the interpretation and application of the parties' collective bargaining agreement. Under the agreement, the employer had "the unilateral right to establish rules, and thereafter to modify or amend them," the arbitrator said. In contrast, the arbitrator found that employees did not have a right to smoke on the employer's premises. Stressing that the mission of the company involved improving oral health and that smoking presented a health hazard the company did not want "to promote or condone," the arbitrator concluded that the ban on tobacco usage "was a reasonable exercise of managerial authority" (*Delta Dental Plan of Michigan Inc.*, 122 LA 203).

● An employer that prohibited indoor smoking was justified in expanding its policy to ban the use of tobacco products anywhere on its premises, an arbitrator held. In challenging the rule change, the union contended that workers should be allowed to continue smoking outdoors during breaks. However, the arbitrator said the employer could broaden its smoking ban to help accomplish the objectives of improving the overall health of its workforce and reducing substantial costs associated with employees' use of tobacco. The broader ban also was appropriate, the arbitrator said, because the narrower policy had proved to be unenforceable. In addition, employees were given adequate notice of the ban, they were offered smoking cessation classes and products, and the policy did not discriminate against any unit employees, the arbitrator pointed out (*Plasti-Line Inc.*, 114 LA 1240).

● In upholding an employer's total ban on smoking, another arbitrator not only cited the detrimental health effects of tobacco smoke, but also emphasized the property rights of employers. While the arbitrator acknowledged that other rulings have considered the extension of smoking bans to outside areas "unfair and capricious," he disagreed with that conclusion. "It is universally acknowledged," he said, that secondary smoke is detrimental to those around it, and even if outside smoke dissipates, the smokers themselves face negative health effects. According to the arbitrator, an employer need not assume these increased health risks or exacerbate the problem by allowing smoking on company premises. Also stressing that property law gave the company authority over the activities on its premises, the arbitrator asserted that the employer had "the absolute right to prohibit smoking on its property and in those areas it controls either through ownership or through lease" (*Norris Plumbing Fixtures*, 104 LA 174).

● Declaring that workers did not have a contractual right to smoke anywhere and anytime, an arbitrator upheld an employer's decision to prohibit smoking in employee work areas. In light of the "growing body of information about the health risks associated with tobacco use," the arbitrator said, it is not surprising that numerous arbitrators have upheld smoking restrictions based solely on concerns for employees' health. The arbitrator noted that the employer in this case gathered specific evidence on its health expenses attributable to smoking, which exceeded $1 million per year. Other factors supporting the reasonableness of the policy, included the following: the employer voiced its intention to make its facilities smoke-free during contract negotiations the previous year; employees received notice of the policy three months before it took effect; the employer provided free on-site smoking cessation programs; and the policy applied equally to all employees, visitors, and vendors (*Timkin Co.*, 108 LA 422).

● Citing contract language that reserved the right of management to issue reasonable work rules, an arbitrator decided that an employer was not obligated to adopt the proposals for a smoking policy that were offered by a joint labor-management committee. Instead of following the committee's recommendations, the employer instituted a more restrictive policy that limited smoking to lunch and break periods in two designated areas. The restrictions were not overly burdensome, the arbitrator said, noting that the policy struck a balance between the interests of smokers and nonsmokers, and the designated smoking areas were sufficient to accommodate the number of people who wanted to use them during specified times (*Tomkins Industries Inc.*, 112 LA 281).

● Another arbitrator upheld a similar policy that was unilaterally instituted by an employer after a discarded cigarette caused a fire. Emphasizing the safety concerns that gave rise to the policy, the arbitrator found that the employer was justified in prohibiting employees from smoking at their workstations. Also, restricting smoking to break times was not unreasonable, the arbitrator said, given management's concern about the "impact on production" if employees were permitted to leave their workstations whenever they wanted to smoke (*Morelite Equipment Co.*, 88 LA 777).

B. Smoking Restrictions Overturned

Despite increasing awareness about the hazards of smoking and the health risks posed by secondhand smoke, arbitrators do not consistently uphold the policies implemented by employers. On the contrary, arbitrators often overturn workplace smoking restrictions because:

● they conflict with the terms of a collective bargaining agreement;

● employers have implemented smoking policies unilaterally rather than bargaining with a union; or

● the policies are deemed unreasonable, overly burdensome, arbitrary, or capricious.

Among the policies most commonly struck down by arbitrators are those that extend smoking restrictions to outdoor areas. In a case involving an employer's premises-wide smoking ban, for example, an arbitrator commented that eliminating smoking inside the employer's plant reasonably fostered the objective of maintaining a safe and healthful work environment, whereas prohibiting smoking outside the plant was not reasonable since tobacco smoke "readily dissipates" outdoors, and "an employee smoking in his or her own car has no discernible effect on the health or safety of others" (*VME Americas Inc.*, 97 LA 137; see also 96 LA 506, 96 LA 122, 94 LA 894).

● An arbitrator held that a fire department violated a collective bargaining agreement by unilaterally implementing a total ban on smoking within any enclosed facility of the department. Even though the action was taken after the county enacted an ordinance banning most public indoor smoking, the agreement excepted "fire apparatus floors" from the general smoking ban on county property and provided that conflicting ordinances would be preempted by agreement. The arbitrator ruled that the public policy reflected in the ordinance did not justify overriding the government's commitment to defer the impact of the new legislation for the term of the agreement (*Kansas City Fire Department*, 126 LA 609).

● Rejecting an employer's unilateral expansion of a smoking ban to all company property, an arbitrator ordered the employer to restore a policy that allowed smoking in an outdoor "lean-to" shelter. The arbitrator pointed out that the company had agreed as part of the settlement of an earlier grievance to provide the smoking shelter, and that the settlement agreement had become an implied term of the parties' collective bargaining agreement once it survived a subsequent round of contract negotiations. Agreeing with the union's argument that smoke dissipates outside and does not affect the health or safety of others, the arbitrator concluded that the company lacked a legitimate business-related justification for depriving employees of the contractual "benefit" of the smoking shelter (*Campbell Group*, 102 LA 1031).

● An employer's no-smoking policy that ended a 20-year practice of using outside smoking areas was overturned by another arbitrator. The arbitrator concluded that the unilateral rule change constituted a violation of the parties' collective bargaining agreement, which lacked a management rights clause and stipulated that any "privilege" not addressed in the contract and enjoyed by employees would continue (*Cross Oil & Refining of Arkansas*, 104 LA 757).

● An arbitrator held that a no-smoking policy at a manufacturing facility violated a collective bargaining agreement and past practice, where the history of smoking at the particular facility established a term or condition of employment over which the employer was obligated to bargain, and the union involved had successfully challenged the employer's earlier attempt to ban smoking in a break room (*Basler Electric Co.*, 94 LA 888).

• In another case, an arbitrator ordered an employer to submit a disputed no-smoking policy to a union-management safety committee. The arbitrator noted that the policy was driven by safety concerns, and the purpose of the contractually established committee was to make recommendations for improving workplace safety. Although the committee did not have the authority to "veto" rule changes initiated by the employer, the arbitrator said, the employer violated the contract by implementing the new policy without first referring the proposal to the committee for its review and suggestions (*H-N Advertising & Display Co. Inc.*, 88 LA 329; see also 102 LA 872).

C. Discipline for Smoking Violations

When deciding whether or not to uphold the discipline imposed on employees for smoking violations, arbitrators tend to consider the restrictions that were violated, the circumstances of the incidents in question, and the presence or absence of any mitigating factors.

• Back-to-back smoking incidents constituted sufficient grounds for the termination of an employee who worked around airplanes, an arbitrator concluded. The employee was seen with a cigarette in a no-smoking area. She was ordered to extinguish that cigarette but lit another one a short time later. She was subsequently discharged. While observing that smoking in prohibited areas was not "expressly provided as a cause for discharge," the arbitrator pointed out that there are certain "critical areas," such as the aircraft fueling site, where smoking is perilous and "constitutes legal malice" (*Gladieux Food Services Inc.*, 70 LA 544).

• An employer had just cause to fire an employee who inadvertently carried a lighted cigarette into a manufacturing plant, an arbitrator held. The employer had banned smoking in the plant in an effort to eliminate fire hazards, and its policy subjected violators to immediate discharge. One day on her lunch break, the employee lit a cigarette after exiting the plant, but then real-

ized that she had left her lunch behind. She forgot to put out the cigarette when she went back inside the plant to retrieve her lunch, and the employer fired her. Although the employee's violation was unintentional, the arbitrator concluded that her conduct created just as much of a fire hazard as a conscious violation of the no-smoking rule. Adding that the employer was "entitled to view violations of the rule as a most serious matter," the arbitrator upheld the employee's termination (*Century Products Co.*, 101 LA 1).

• *By contrast*, another arbitrator overturned the discharge of an employee who inadvertently lit a cigarette in a clearly marked no-smoking area. The employee quickly extinguished the cigarette upon realizing his mistake, but a supervisor witnessed the incident and fired the employee on the spot. Even though management convincingly demonstrated the hazardousness of the employee's conduct, the arbitrator said "consideration must be given to mitigating circumstances." The employee had an exemplary record and was "horrified" by his unconscious act of lighting the cigarette, the arbitrator pointed out. Finding that the employee did not have the "guilty mind" required to commit the dischargeable offense of intentionally smoking in the restricted area, the arbitrator ordered reinstatement without back pay (*Converters Ink*, 68 LA 593).

• Discharge was too severe for a 30-year employee who was observed with a lit cigarette in his hand while working around hydrochloric acid, an arbitrator ruled. The employer's safety rules prohibited smoking around hazardous materials, but the acid was classified as nonflammable, and the plant's heating system contained two overhead heaters that had gas pilot lights with exposed flames. Concluding that the employee's termination was arbitrary and capricious, the arbitrator reduced the discipline to a suspension. Smoking in the facility may have been hazardous, the arbitrator said, but the employer could hardly justify immediate termination for smoking in the same area where exposed pilot lights burned (*Van Waters & Rogers Inc.*, 102 LA 609).

● Discharge was not warranted for an employee who took an unauthorized cigarette break outside the plant where he worked, an arbitrator determined. A prior arbitration award upheld a policy that banned smoking inside the plant to protect the health of nonsmokers and reduce fire hazards. However, those objectives were not affected by the employee's infraction, which amounted to leaving work without permission, the arbitrator observed. Adding that the employee had 14 years of service with just two prior instances of minor discipline, the arbitrator decided that the appropriate penalty was a six-month suspension (*Barnstead-Thermolyne Corp.*, 107 LA 645).

● A 15-day suspension was inappropriate for a school custodian who smoked at work, an arbitrator ruled. Because of complaints that custodians were loafing, the school district installed a surveillance camera in a maintenance shed at the school. The custodian was caught on videotape smoking during a break for a total of seven minutes. Meanwhile, a number of his fellow employees were videotaped smoking and watching television in the shed instead of performing their job duties. The arbitrator found that the custodian's suspension was too severe under the school district's progressive discipline policy. Moreover, the arbitrator noted that a fellow employee was caught on videotape shirking his duties and committing numerous smoking violations, but he received the same discipline as the custodian. Adding that the employer had been lax in enforcing its rules against smoking on school grounds, the arbitrator reduced the custodian's discipline to a written reprimand (*Bloom Township High School District No. 206*, 119 LA 321).

Part 4

Seniority and Its Application

I. Seniority [LA CDI 100.56 (public employees); 117.201]

OVERVIEW

Although specific contract terms vary, the seniority provisions under collective bargaining agreements typically give greater protections and privileges to those employees who have worked in an organization or a particular "seniority unit" the longest. In many cases, seniority dictates the handling of layoffs, promotions, transfers, shift choices, overtime assignments, and vacation preferences.

Generally, seniority is based on an employee's length of service. In some situations, however, seniority determinations and individual rankings on seniority lists can become problematic, such as when two or more employees have the same start date, when employees undergo job or classification changes, when employees experience interruptions in employment, when companies change ownership, or when different groups of employees are combined.

Because seniority plays a key role in securing the rights of employees—including their competitive rights in relation to one another—it is not surprising that disputes occasionally arise over seniority determinations. This chapter examines how arbitrators address a range of seniority-related issues, including the problematic situations noted above.

SUMMARY OF CASES

A. Seniority Units

Seniority rights apply to specific groups or units as defined under collective bargaining agreements, either specifically or by interpretation. In some cases, the seniority rights of employees apply on a companywide basis, but seniority rights also can be limited to a particular division, plant, department, or occupational classification.

• The units in which employees accumulate and exercise seniority rights do not have to be the same. For example, employees might accrue seniority on a companywide basis, but its exercise might be limited to a particular department, shift, or job classification. Employees also can have different seniority accruals for different purposes. For instance, companywide seniority is typically used to determine employees' benefit rights, but seniority within a smaller unit often governs such issues as layoffs, vacation preferences, and overtime assignments (107 LA 448, 103 LA 363, 100 LA 1051, 96 LA 1211, 91 LA 763).

• The accrual of seniority may vary for different classifications of employees. For example, one arbitrator ruled that a two-track seniority system for regular and temporary employees was acceptable (*Hazelwood Farm Bakeries Inc.*, 92 LA 1026), while another arbitrator upheld a separate seniority system for employees on restricted duty (*Lear Corp.*, 108 LA 592).

• Employees who transfer or change jobs can receive new seniority starting dates and lose the seniority accumulated in a former unit. For instance, when an employee with five years of service transferred to a new plant, her date of entry into the bargaining unit at the new plant was properly used for purposes of determining her seniority rights under the plant's collective bargaining agreement, an arbitrator found. At the same time, however, the arbitrator held that the employee's original hire date applied for purposes of benefits, because the agreement could not take away entitlements accrued outside the bargaining unit (*Arco Chemical*, 102 LA 1051).

• In one case where the seniority unit was not clearly specified under a collec-

tive bargaining agreement, an arbitrator allowed an employer to make seniority determinations on a companywide basis in the interest of operational efficiency. The arbitrator rejected the union's argument that the employer should go by the seniority of employees within a given classification when conducting layoffs. Citing the seasonal nature of the work and the varied skills of the employees, the arbitrator found that classification seniority would have limited the employer's flexibility in a way that was not mandated by the contract (*Great Lakes Homes Inc.*, 44 LA 737).

B. Seniority Starting Date

Although most collective bargaining agreements contain seniority clauses, they do not always include specific language on the commencement and accrual of seniority rights. In the absence of a contractual definition of seniority, the term is "commonly understood to mean the length of service with the employer or in some division of the enterprise" (*Curtiss-Wright Corp.*, 11 LA 139).

Arbitrators generally hold that seniority begins to accumulate on the first day of work or the date of hire. If employees share the same seniority date, however, disputes can emerge over their seniority standing relative to one another.

• One arbitrator gave equal seniority to employees with the same length of service. The union had urged that employees' relative seniority standing should follow the order in which they received their physical examinations, but the arbitrator ruled that seniority should not be measured in units of less than one day (*Standard Oil Co. of Ind.*, 3 LA 758).

• Where a contract simply stated that length of service was to be calculated from the date employees began to work, an arbitrator refused to put one worker higher on a seniority list than a co-worker who started on a later shift the same day (*Bethlehem Steel Co.*, 26 LA 567).

• Under a collective bargaining agreement that was more specific on the order of seniority, meanwhile, an arbitrator awarded a higher seniority standing to a worker who clocked in before a co-worker who was hired on the same date (*Robertshaw-Fulton Controls Co.*, 22 LA 273).

- In a case where employees were hired and began to work on the same day and on the same shift, another arbitrator held that an employer appropriately ranked the employees on a seniority list according to the order in which they were called and told to report to work (*Armstrong Rubber Co.*, 74 LA 301).

- Where two employees with the same seniority date competed for a vacant position, an employer was justified in giving the job to the employee who was deemed to be better qualified, an arbitrator held. The candidates were evaluated by a committee consisting of two management members and a bargaining unit member, who unanimously agreed that one of the candidates was more qualified than the other. Because the collective bargaining agreement did not specify how to decide between two workers with equal seniority, the arbitrator concluded that consideration of the candidates' qualifications was a legitimate way to break the "tie" (*St. Louis Park School District*, 90 LA 542).

- Where a layoff decision had to be made between two workers with equal seniority, an arbitrator held that the toss of a coin should serve as the final tie breaker if a joint committee could not agree on which employee to retain (*McCall Corp.*, 49 LA 183).

C. Employment Status Changes

Seniority-related questions often arise in connection with employment status and classification changes, such as when employees switch from part-time or temporary status to regular full-time employment or if they move into the bargaining unit from nonunit jobs.

- An arbitrator ruled that an employer did not violate a collective bargaining contract when it failed to credit an operations department employee with seniority for the time he worked in the maintenance department, where the contract had three separate seniority lists for the employer's three separate departments, and the employer had created disincentives to keep employees from transferring from the maintenance department (*Murphy Oil USA*, 124 LA 1203).

- A part-time employee promoted to full-time status was entitled to seniority from the date of hire, not the date of promotion, an arbitrator ruled. Although the contract excluded part-time employees from some benefits, it was amended to establish a part-time seniority list and specifically defined seniority as beginning on the hiring date. Thus, the arbitrator concluded, the employer's past practice of counting seniority only from the date of full-time employment was overridden by the agreement (*Columbus Retail Merchants Delivery*, 65 LA 825).

- An employer acted arbitrarily in how it established the seniority dates of two employees who formerly worked part-time, where it used the date that one employee achieved full-time status as his seniority date but used the original hiring date of the other employee, an arbitrator ruled. Instead of going by either of those dates, the arbitrator devised a different method for determining the employees' seniority. He converted the part-time schedule of each employee to a percentage of the full-time workweek, then calculated proportionate seniority credits. For example, one employee had worked 15-hour weeks for 16 years; after translating the 15-hour schedule to roughly 37 percent of a 40-hour week, the arbitrator gave that employee a seniority credit of approximately six years for the period of his part-time employment (*Pepsi-Cola Bottling Co.*, 97 LA 1011).

- An employer was justified in ignoring length of service when it decided between two part-time employees for promotion to a full-time job, an arbitrator held. Because the collective bargaining agreement in this case provided that part-time employees did not accrue seniority, the arbitrator concluded that the employer acted appropriately in selecting the employee who had better qualifications instead of the one who had longer service as a part-time worker (*Pace Fox Valley Division*, 101 LA 912).

- The seniority of an employee who was initially supplied to a company by a temporary agency should have been based on his original starting date rather than the date he became a permanent employee, an arbitrator ruled. Finding that the company was a joint employer at the outset because it exercised complete control and direction over the employee's work, the arbitrator determined that it was appropriate to include the period of temporary employment for seniority purposes (*Metz Baking Co.*, 100 LA 671).

● An employee who was hired on permanently at a company after two separate stints as a temporary worker was entitled to seniority as of his first hiring date, an arbitrator decided. The employer waived probation for the employee because he had completed it "the first time around," and the collective bargaining agreement provided for continuous service credit to be granted back to the date of hire upon completion of probation, the arbitrator noted (*Inland Container Corp.*, 93 LA 1297).

● *By contrast*, another arbitrator refused to count the period of temporary employment toward the seniority of employees at another company, because the collective bargaining agreement specifically denied contractual rights to temporary workers (*Alltel Pennsylvania Inc.*, 108 LA 872).

● An employer acted improperly when it laid off several employees with greater unit seniority while retaining long-service workers who had come into the unit from nonunit jobs, an arbitrator ruled. The employer contended that flexibility in its operations demanded use of the date of employment as the basis for everyone's seniority, rather than the date of employees' entry into the unit. Reversing the employer's action, the arbitrator ruled that seniority rights under the contract were based on date of entry into the unit (*Elmar Electronics Inc.*, 64 LA 912).

D. Seniority of Demoted Supervisors

Movement between supervisory positions and bargaining unit jobs also can create uncertainty about seniority. In the absence of contractual language stipulating how to handle such situations, arbitrators are divided on whether to give employees seniority credit for time spent in supervisory positions.

● Some arbitrators have held that supervisors continue to accumulate seniority after promotion unless the contract specifically states otherwise (70 LA 1246, 62 LA 1013, 43 LA 228, 34 LA 285, 31 LA 137, 25 LA 595).

● Other arbitrators have ruled that seniority ceases to accumulate during the period when employees hold positions that are not covered by collective bargaining agreements, because seniority is strictly a contractual right (99 LA 620, 79 LA 48, 32 LA 892, 31 LA 859, 31 LA 200).

● Still others have held that employees forfeit all their seniority when promoted because, in effect, they have voluntarily resigned from the unit (100 LA 534, 40 LA 388, 27 LA 30, 26 LA 898).

● There is more apparent agreement among arbitrators that supervisors who have never been members of the bargaining unit are entitled to no seniority credit when they move into bargaining unit jobs (41 LA 583, 33 LA 150, 32 LA 274, 29 LA 828).

● In a case that involved conflicting contract provisions, an arbitrator held that an employer properly counted an employee's prior seniority in deciding the order of layoffs, even though he had spent four years in a supervisory job before returning to the bargaining unit. The current collective bargaining agreement provided that seniority would be forfeited after 12 months in a supervisory job, but the provision did not apply in this instance because it was adopted after the employee had left the bargaining unit, the arbitrator said. Under the terms of the agreement that existed when the employee originally took a supervisory job, his accumulated seniority was not subject to divestment, the arbitrator found (*Great Lakes Diesel Co.*, 75 LA 1077; see also 70 LA 1217, 65 LA 544).

E. Employment Interruptions

Employees usually retain their seniority rights during layoffs and periods of approved leave. This is particularly true in the case of military leave, because federal and state laws protect the employment and seniority rights of individuals who take leaves of absence for military service (75 LA 696, 63 LA 750).

In some cases, however, collective bargaining agreements set limits on how long employees can be away from work without losing seniority. For example, arbitrators have upheld employees' loss of seniority under contract provisions providing for the forfeiture of accumulated seniority after a period of extended layoff, such as one year (84 LA 376, 84 LA 27). Arbitrators have issued similar rulings with regard to employees who experience employment interruptions due to injury or illness (103 LA 877, 83 LA 1165, 81 LA 366).

• In an unusual case, an arbitrator ruled that taking seniority rights from a returning a veteran would violate a collective bargaining contract, which provided that veterans were entitled to the rights and privileges provided by the Uniformed Services Employment and Reemployment Rights Act, even though the veteran quit before he joined the military. The veteran abruptly resigned from his job as a mover on June 15, 2006, and formally enlisted in the Navy on Aug. 14, 2006. After serving in the military and getting an honorable discharge, the veteran sought to return to the company with full seniority benefits, but the company offered him employment as a new hire.

The union filed a grievance on behalf of the veteran alleging the employer violated the seniority provisions of the bargaining agreement and sought relief of reinstatement with seniority benefits. The evidence indicated the veteran had told several employees that he was planning to enlist before he quit, the employer interviewed its own employees and consulted extensively with experts on USERRA, including the U.S. Department of Labor, on the question of what constituted sufficient notice under USERRA, and voluntarily reinstated the veteran.

After the employee won his right to reinstatement, the union filed another grievance alleging the employer violated the identical seniority provisions of the contract, seeking relief on behalf of those who lost employment opportunities due to the employer's decision to reinstate the veteran. This grievance was denied. The arbitrator reasoned that once the union filed the grievance supporting reemployment, it abandoned its right to argue the opposite point of view in a later grievance, and the resolution of the first grievance became a procedural bar to preclude further hearing on the "sufficiency of notice" argument (*3 MD Relocation Services LLC*, 129 LA 836).

• One arbitrator decided that an employer properly denied an employee seniority for the eight months of his layoff, where the relevant contract language stated that "seniority is continuous service with the employer, compiled by time actually spent on the payroll, plus properly approved absences." Concluding that the layoff was a period spent off the payroll and not an approved absence, the arbitrator upheld the denial of seniority (*Firestone Tire and Rubber Co.*, 61 LA 136; see also 72 LA 609, 72 LA 240).

• An employee who refused an offer of recall from layoff was improperly deprived of seniority, an arbitrator ruled. When the employee refused reinstatement on the night shift because of a conflict with his religious obligations, the employer took away his seniority, arguing that the contract clearly provided for seniority denial in such cases. An arbitrator overturned the action, finding that the employer had violated Equal Employment Opportunity Commission guidelines requiring employers to accommodate the religious needs of employees unless doing so would pose an undue hardship on the business (*American Forest Products Corp.*, 65 LA 650).

• When considering the question of whether outside employment during a leave of absence triggers a loss of seniority, an arbitrator held that seniority should remain intact unless a contract clause forbids the taking of outside work (*Goodyear Tire & Rubber Co.*, 5 LA 234; see also 72 LA 663, 63 LA 941).

• Another arbitrator ruled, however, that an employee may not accumulate seniority simultaneously with two employers and that an employee forfeited his employee status during a layoff by working for another employer (*Fairchild Engine & Airplane Corp.*, 3 LA 873).

1. Unauthorized Absences

Most collective bargaining agreements forbid unauthorized absences, and arbitrators have upheld the termination of workers' seniority—and employment—for relatively short absences without a valid excuse (94 LA 325, 79 LA 1012). Lacking contractual provisions calling for termination, however, arbitrators are inclined to protect employees' accumulated seniority if they have been absent without authorization for a good reason.

● An employee was absent for one week without permission at Christmas time. On his return, the employer claimed it was rehiring the employee so that his seniority would begin at the day he was rehired. The arbitrator agreed with the employer that granting or denying leave was a management prerogative that could not be questioned unless employer action was unreasonable or discriminatory. In this case, however, the arbitrator ruled that because the absence was for good cause, there should be no break in the employee's seniority (*Pittsburgh Metallurgical Co. Inc.*, 12 LA 95).

F. Ownership Changes and Mergers

Ownership changes and plant mergers can present unique challenges with regard to seniority determinations. Although employees usually retain their original seniority dates in cases where new owners simply take over existing operations, things become more complicated when groups of employees are combined. Reluctant to strip affected employees of their seniority rights, a number of arbitrators have devised methods for integrating the seniority of formerly separate employee groups.

● Even though a sales contract called for a buyer to assume a seller's labor obligations, an arbitrator held that the buyer's original workforce would have suffered an unfair disadvantage if the employees at the newly acquired organization were allowed to retain all of their accrued seniority when the two groups were merged into a single seniority list. The arbitrator decided that the seller's workers should retain full seniority as it applied to employee benefits, but their competitive-status seniority was reduced to protect the interests of the buyer's original workforce. For the merged seniority list,

those employees from the acquired company who had accumulated at least two years of seniority were allowed to retain one-half their seniority, and those with less seniority went to the bottom of the list (*Country Belle Cooperative Farmers*, 48 LA 600; see also 66 LA 1029).

● Following the merger of two plants that had separate seniority lists, an arbitrator devised a method for creating a combined list that took into account employees' length of service as well as their individual positions on the separate lists. The arbitrator reasoned that ranking employees by length of service alone would be unfair to workers in the plant where length of service was relatively low, while slotting employees solely on the basis of their numerical positions on the original lists would be unfair to those in the plant where length of service was relatively high. To strike a balance, the arbitrator numbered everyone in order of length of service and also ranked them according to their positions on the plant-specific seniority lists, then he took the average of the two numerical rankings to determine each employee's position on the combined seniority list (*Moore Business Forms Inc.*, 24 LA 793).

● Another arbitrator decided that the most equitable method for determining seniority was to make a pool of the combined jobs resulting from a merger, with each group getting a proportionate share of it. After determining that the work performed by the transferred employees amounted to 70 percent of what they had contributed before the merger, the arbitrator credited the transferred workers with seven-tenths of their seniority at the midpoint date of the transfers (*Sonotone Corp.*, 42 LA 359).

● Where two merged plants were covered by a multi-employer agreement that confined seniority rights to each separate plant, an arbitrator gave seniority preference to workers in relation to the types of operations they performed prior to the merger. Those whose work was similar at both plants should be assigned from both seniority lists in the proportion that such workers at each plant bore to the total number of workers at both plants, the arbitrator directed (*Superior Products Co.*, 42 LA 517; see also 72 LA 458, 71 LA 476).

G. Seniority and Probation

The attainment of seniority status and the accompanying contractual protections typically occurs upon completion of an initial probationary period. As illustrated by the following case examples, small variations in contract language can make a big difference in determining whether or not employees have completed probation.

● Under one contract, new employees had to serve a 30-day probationary period, and they could be fired during that period without the protection of the contract's just cause provision. One employee clocked out on his 30th day of work and received notice later that evening that he was fired. An arbitrator concluded that the employee had become subject to the just cause provision when he clocked out that day because the probationary period had come to a close and seniority had begun to accrue, which meant that full status as an employee also was achieved at that time (*Lyon Inc.*, 24 LA 353).

● Interpreting a contract that defined the probationary period as 45 "working days of actual service with the employer," an arbitrator decided that an employer could not exclude overtime or weekend work from the calculation of seniority. The arbitrator reached this conclusion despite the fact that the employer and union had reached an informal, verbal agreement providing that only straight time would be counted toward the completion of probation (*Hoover Ball & Bearing Co.*, 64 LA 63).

● Another arbitrator held that an employee had completed her probationary period during two separate terms of employment under a contract stipulating that probation would last "for the first month" of employment. The employee had worked less than a month, was discharged, was rehired shortly thereafter, and worked another three weeks. Given that the periods of employment were separated by only 17 days, the arbitrator decided that the employer had an ample opportunity to judge the employee's suitability for the job (*Kreisler Industrial*, 27 LA 133).

● *By contrast*, an arbitrator decided that an employer was justified in restarting the clock for a probationary employee who was rehired, because the contract in that case defined the probationary period in terms of "continuous employment" (*Armstrong Cork Co.*, 23 LA 366).

● An agreement indicating that employees would be on probation until they "performed work" on 30 days within any three-month period led an arbitrator to hold that days on which an employee had been sent home because of bad weather could be discounted in figuring his probationary period. It might have been different, the arbitrator noted, if the agreement had stated the probationary period in terms of time employed (*Bethlehem Steel Co.*, 27 LA 300).

H. Union Officials' Seniority

Superseniority for shop stewards and other union officials is a kind of special seniority that is not based on length of service. It supersedes normal seniority in certain situations, such as layoffs and transfers, in the interest of protecting employees who are capable of providing effective union representation.

● One arbitrator held that an employer committed a contract violation in laying off a shop steward while other employees in his department retained their jobs. A superseniority clause in the contract required the steward to be shielded from layoff as long as at least two other employees remained in the department. Finding that the steward's improper layoff continued for a period of more than six months before other department members also lost their jobs, the arbitrator ordered a make-whole remedy, which included back pay and interest minus the steward's earnings from other sources during the period of the improper layoff (*Contempo Design Inc.*, 120 LA 1317).

● Another arbitrator found that an employer disregarded its contractual obligations in unilaterally transferring union stewards to different company locations and leaving some locations without designated union representatives. The parties' contract provided for one employee at each location to serve as a union representative who could negotiate with the employer in order to settle grievances, and the contract also granted employees superseniority while serving in that capacity. Finding that the employer violated the contract when it transferred the stewards without regard to their seniority standing, the arbitrator ordered the employer to return them to their original locations (*Mikocem LLC*, 121 LA 1377).

● On the other hand, an arbitrator held that an employer did not commit a contract violation in refusing to grant superseniority to an employee who was elected to a grievance committee position after he was already laid off. Under the contract in question, grievance committee members were entitled to superseniority in layoff situations but not recalls, the arbitrator pointed out, and thus the employer acted appropriately in recalling a worker who had 13 more years of seniority than the committeeman when a position opened up as the result of another employee's retirement (*AmeriMark Building Products Inc.*, 104 LA 1066).

1. Loss of Superseniority

Arbitrators generally agree that superseniority only lasts as long as employees continue to serve in an official capacity as union representatives. For example, an arbitrator ruled that a local union president, who had kept his job during a layoff because of superseniority, should have been bumped upon leaving office. Concluding that the employee was no longer entitled to retain a position "out of seniority order" once he ceased to occupy a protected union office, the arbitrator ordered the former union president's removal from the job so it could be awarded to the most senior qualified worker on layoff status (*Lockheed Aeronautical Systems Co.*, 94 LA 137; see also 75 LA 263, 25 LA 174).

I. Challenging Seniority Standings

Arbitrators generally agree that employees are allowed to dispute the seniority standings of fellow workers in addition to challenging their own seniority dates. For instance, in one case where employees had the right to file grievances over the inter-

pretation and application of a contract, and the contract prescribed the method of computing seniority, an arbitrator determined that the incorrect listing of a seniority date was a contract violation that any employee could protest (*Republic Steel Corp.*, 18 LA 907).

When employees lodge complaints related to seniority standings, an issue that often surfaces is whether the usual time limits on grievances apply. Arbitrators have reached different conclusions as to how long employees retain the right to challenge seniority errors.

● Absent a specific contractual restriction, one arbitrator said employees have a right to complain about errors in seniority lists at any time. The employer in the case had given an employee credit for too much seniority in his department, and the error went unchallenged for nine years. When another worker filed a grievance over the error so that he could move up a notch on the seniority list, the employer cited a contract provision stating that grievances must be filed within 30 days of the occurrence of the events involved. The time limit did not apply in this situation, the arbitrator held, because if it was a contract violation to give an employee extra seniority credit in the past, it also was a violation to continue giving him the extra credit. However, preferences that had been given to the employee in the matters of promotion, demotion, and layoffs were beyond challenge, the arbitrator ruled (*Bethlehem Steel Co.*, 23 LA 538).

● Another arbitrator held that an employer could be required to provide partial back pay to an employee who was laid off before a junior co-worker, even though the mistake went undetected for more than three years. Under the contract, a 30-day time limit normally applied to grievances seeking back pay, but there was no way for the employee or the union to be aware of the error until 40 months after the employee's layoff, which was when the employer posted a seniority list that included an incorrect seniority date for the employee (*Kelsey-Hayes Co.*, 85 LA 774).

● *By contrast*, another arbitrator held that after a posted seniority list had gone unquestioned for a long period of time, errors on the list could not be corrected even though there was no "statute of limitations" in the contract (*Creamery Package Mfg. Co.*, 31 LA 917).

1. Responsibility for Seniority Error

Responsibility for an error on a seniority list rests with the party that prepared it.

- An employer prepared a seniority list, considered final and binding when a copy was given to the union. The list was incorrect, and an arbitrator held that the union was not jointly responsible for the mistake. The rule that the list was final and binding applied only to a correct list, and because the employer had the sole responsibility for preparing the list, it also had the sole responsibility for any errors, the arbitrator concluded (*Bethlehem Fabricators Inc.*, 41 LA 6).

II. Order of Layoff [LA CDI 100.68 (public employees); 117.1133]

OVERVIEW

Most collective bargaining agreements stipulate that seniority plays a role in determining the order of layoffs. Some contracts make seniority the primary consideration, while others give seniority less weight than ability and other factors. When disputes arise over the order of layoffs, arbitrators must look to the particular contractual language negotiated by the parties to see how seniority applies to the case at hand.

Broadly speaking, there are three basic types of seniority clauses:

• "strict seniority," in which the order of layoffs is determined on a strict seniority basis;

• "sufficient ability," in which seniority dictates the order of layoffs except in situations where senior employees lack the ability to do the available work; and

• "relative ability," in which the relative ability of employees governs the order of layoffs, but seniority becomes the deciding factor if employees are substantially equal. (See Elkouri & Elkouri, *How Arbitration Works*, 873 (Sixth Edition 2003)).

Whereas the application of strict seniority to layoffs is relatively straightforward, layoff procedures governed by a combination of seniority and ability are more problematic and, consequently, account for most of the arbitration cases in this area.

In general, the same considerations apply to the bumping rights of senior employees. While this chapter focuses on disputes over the order of layoffs, arbitration cases addressing the right to displace junior employees are discussed in a separate chapter, titled "Bumping Rights."

SUMMARY OF CASES

A. Seniority Versus Ability

Strict seniority clauses protect the employment of workers with the greatest length of service by making seniority the controlling factor in determining the order of layoffs (121 LA 1569, 98 LA 651, 83 LA 346, 75 LA 625). Seniority within a particular job classification—as opposed to seniority across an entire bargaining unit—may be used in making such determinations (119 LA 826, 118 LA 1615).

In addition to seniority, the ability of employees often plays a part in layoff decisions. At the very least, collective bargaining agreements might make exceptions to strict seniority for certain positions that require specialized training, skills, or experience (127 LA 1751, 127 LA 744, 123 LA 254, 121 LA 1471, 102 LA 940, 87 LA 572, 78 LA 951).

1. Sufficient Ability

To ensure that retained employees can keep operations running, collective bargaining agreements commonly state that layoffs will be executed by inverse order of seniority so long as the remaining employees are able to perform the available work.

In resolving cases that involve these "sufficient ability" clauses, arbitrators generally require the qualifications of employees to be measured against job requirements. In other words, the outcome hinges on whether senior employees are qualified for a particular job, not whether they are more or less qualified than junior employees.

● An arbitrator ruled than an employer violated a collective bargaining agreement by laying off an engineer after bypassing four less senior employees. The relevant clause in the bargaining agreement was a *"sufficient ability"* seniority clause and not a *"relative ability"* clause, the agreement applied seniority rights to layoffs "where the qualifications are equal," and the engineer met all qualifications (*St. Catherine University*, 127 LA 528).

● One arbitrator overturned an employer's layoff of a mechanic who had greater seniority but lesser qualifications than another mechanic who was retained. The collective bargaining agreement said the least senior employee in a given classification would be the first one laid off, provided that remaining employees could perform the available work. The contract did not provide for the more qualified employee to be retained, the arbitrator stressed. Acknowledging, however, that the junior mechanic had usually handled the electrical tasks that needed to be done, the arbitrator said the employer could require a trial period during which the senior mechanic would have to demonstrate his ability to perform the available work (*Cable Manufacturing & Assembly Co. Inc.*, 118 LA 1234).

● An employer erred in laying off production workers without first determining if they could handle maintenance work that was being performed by junior employees, an arbitrator ruled. To evaluate the production employees, the employer was required to judge their ability "against some minimal requirements of the particular job" rather than comparing them "against any particular job incumbent," the arbitrator instructed. For employees who met the minimum standard, the employer then had to provide "a reasonable familiarization period" in which they would have the opportunity to demonstrate their ability to do the maintenance work, the arbitrator said (*Lackawanna Leather*, 113 LA 603).

● *By contrast*, an arbitrator upheld an employer's retention of four junior employees under a contract provision that said seniority governed the order of layoffs except when senior employees lacked needed qualifications that junior employees already possessed. The arbitrator cited evidence showing that each of the four employees had skills or qualifications that senior employees lacked. At the same time, however, the arbitrator overturned other layoff decisions that the employer made without properly following the requirements of the contract (*Temple Inland*, 123 LA 206).

● An arbitrator ruled that a cement company did not violate a collective bargaining contract when it assigned two employees who were immediately qualified to perform work at a packhouse during a shut-down instead of two more senior employ-ees. The contract provided that in tempo-rary shutdowns, layoffs for unskilled work were to be by seniority, for skilled work by "ability and experience," and that senior displaced employees had the option to "ac-cept work available" at the plant "for which they are qualified." The company estab-lished that skilled employees were needed to properly load out weight on trucks and to ensure correct specifications for multiple customers, and the senior employees had little recent experience at the packhouse (*Ash Grove Cement Co.*, 129 LA 723).

● An arbitrator ruled that an employ-er did not violate a collective bargaining agreement stating that seniority governed in layoff "where skill and ability to perform the remaining work is relatively equal . . . ," when it laid off a senior welder but retained a junior welder because she also was a lead-er who taught, trained, and tested welders, had excellent written and verbal communi-cation skills, and spoke Spanish, which was an advantage in that job (*Jeffboat LLC*, 128 LA 1359).

● Senior warehouse workers were properly laid off instead of a junior employ-ee who held the position of "working fore-man," an arbitrator held. Although regular warehouse employees occasionally filled in for the working foreman, the arbitrator said the ability to serve in that role on a stopgap basis did not mean those employ-ees possessed the qualities that manage-ment considered essential to the long-term performance of the job. Noting that per-sonal motivation and leadership potential were the key characteristics identified by management, the arbitrator said the junior employee possessed both qualities while the senior employees were found wanting in those areas (*Bechtel Power Corp.*, 73 LA 128).

● Another arbitrator upheld an em-ployer's layoff of a senior employee who had failed to become proficient in the use of new technology. Emphasizing the em-ployer's contractual right to have sufficient qualified employees to perform necessary work on all shifts at all times, the arbitrator decided that the employee's lack of compe-tency on the new technology justified his layoff because work involving the old tech-nology was becoming less and less available (*Type House + Duragraph*, 102 LA 225).

2. Relative Ability

Many contracts allow layoff decisions to be made by comparing employees with one another. Under so-called "relative ability" clauses, employers are permitted to retain junior employees who possess superior abil-ity. If employee qualifications are substan-tially equal, then the individual with more seniority must be retained.

When assessing the relative ability of employees, management can take into ac-count differences in a number of areas, such as skills, experience, attendance and disci-plinary records, efficiency, physical fitness, special training, aptitude, and efficiency. At the same time, however, minor differences in ability usually do not justify giving pref-erence to junior employees.

● An arbitrator ruled that a school dis-trict did not violate a collective bargaining agreement, which had a "relative ability" clause, when it laid off a senior teacher in-stead of junior teachers. The senior teacher was licensed to teach mathematics but had a computer background and taught courses in that area; the junior teachers both had four years of experience teaching mathematics courses. The arbitrator ruled that the dis-trict could consider the "competency" of the teachers in determining which of them to lay off, despite the contention of a past practice of not doing so, because there was no mutuality in the district's decision not to consider "competency" in previous teacher reductions in force. The standard of review in determining whether the junior teachers were more competent to be retained in the layoff was whether there was substantial evidence that the competency of each of the two junior teachers was clearly superior to the grievant's competency to teach the as-signed classes (*Centennial School District*, 129 LA 970).

● Citing contract language that said layoffs would be carried out on the basis of seniority, skill, and ability, an arbitrator held that superior productivity was an ap-propriate deciding factor in the retention of a junior employee (*Leach Manufacturing Co. Inc.*, 79 LA 1251).

● Another arbitrator ruled that a junior worker could be retained in preference to a senior worker, who required a much greater amount of supervision in performing the job in question (*Copco Steel & Engineering Co.*, 12 LA 6).

● Distinguishing between two employees who were classified as master mechanics, an arbitrator held that the retention of the junior employee was warranted because of his unique ability, developed over the course of many years, to maintain and repair special equipment that was extremely important to his employer's manufacturing operations (*Sandusky International Inc.*, 118 LA 916).

● Another arbitrator ruled that an employer was justified in retaining a junior employee under a contract that said skill, ability, and attendance would be considered in layoffs. The union argued that two senior workers who were laid off had better attendance records than the retained employee. Although the junior employee had been minimally tardy, the employer contended that his superior skills and abilities outweighed his minor attendance problem. According to the arbitrator, the employer had the exclusive right to make layoff determinations so long as it did not act in an arbitrary manner, and the decision to lay off the two senior workers was not arrived at arbitrarily (*H & K Dallas Inc.*, 108 LA 600).

● Under a contract that allowed an employer to make layoff decisions on the basis of ability, physical fitness, absenteeism, and job knowledge, an arbitrator upheld the layoff of a senior employee who had the highest absenteeism rate in his department, even though his absences resulted from an on-the-job injury and were excused. The arbitrator pointed out that the contract simply referred to absenteeism and did not make a distinction between different types of absences for layoff purposes (*Virgin Islands Industrial Maintenance Corp.*, 117 LA 1397).

● An employer was justified in laying off an employee with 15 years of service based on his substandard dependability

and questionable ability to deliver a quality product in a timely fashion, an arbitrator found. Noting that the employer considered the employee's conduct, attendance, trustworthiness, and consistency in evaluating his relative ability and dependability, the arbitrator concluded that these factors provided a proper basis for determining that the employee was inferior to the junior employees who were retained by the employer (*American Lithographers*, 121 LA 993).

● *By contrast*, an arbitrator decided that the layoff of a senior employee instead of a junior co-worker was not appropriate in a case where an employer based its decision on only one of many functions the workers performed. There was nothing in the contract to allow the employer to judge an employee on the basis of that one function, and the performance of that function had never been a condition of continued employment, the arbitrator pointed out (*National Broadcasting Co.*, 61 LA 872).

● Under a contract that said seniority would prevail in layoffs if ability and competency were equal, an employer acted arbitrarily by laying off a senior employee and retaining junior employees who were not substantially superior in ability, an arbitrator ruled. When layoff decisions are made by comparing employees, "approximate or near equality" is sufficient to bring seniority into play, the arbitrator said. In the case at hand, the employer made its layoff decision without the input of the supervisor who was in the best position to evaluate the employee. Based on that supervisor's testimony and other evidence that established the employee's competency in comparison with the junior employees, the arbitrator found the employee's layoff improper and ordered his reinstatement (*Rainier Port Cold Storage Inc.*, 79 LA 441).

● An employer committed a contract violation by laying off a senior warehouse employee based on the type of work he performed, an arbitrator ruled. The employer tried to make a distinction between two types of warehouse jobs, but under the collective bargaining agreement, "a warehouseman is a warehouseman," the arbitrator observed. Without any evidence to show that the senior employee was inferior to the junior warehouse workers who were retained, the arbitrator said the employer had no justification for laying him off. The arbitrator awarded the senior employee reinstatement with back pay, including lost overtime (*Triangle Construction & Maintenance Inc.*, 120 LA 559).

• Another arbitrator ruled that an employer committed a contract violation by retaining a junior mechanic and laying off a senior one who was deemed inferior because he had never worked on certain machines that the junior mechanic had. The arbitrator stated that, as a general rule, employees within the same classification should be deemed to have relatively equal ability and skill for layoff purposes, especially when their duties are the same (*Poloron Products of Pa.*, 23 LA 789).

3. Employee Assessments

When the order of layoffs is based at least in part on ability, disputes sometimes arise over the methods employers use to assess or evaluate employees. Systems for rating employees generally meet with the approval of arbitrators so long as they are valid and properly related to job performance.

• One arbitrator ruled that an employer's use of a point system for making layoff decisions was reasonable, even though length of service only accounted for a maximum of 10 out of 100 available points. The contract stated that the factors management would consider, in descending order of importance, were efficiency, economy of work, satisfactory performance, physical fitness, and length of service. Before conducting layoffs, the arbitrator noted, management spoke with a union business agent, who was the one who suggested a point system. Moreover, the points allocated to each factor followed the order of importance stated in the contract, and each of the factors on which employees were evaluated bore "a fundamental relationship to the needs of production," the arbitrator commented in upholding the system (*Wilson Trophy Co.*, 104 LA 529).

• An arbitrator upheld an assessment method that categorized employees as marginal, average, or above average, so that those in the lowest tier would be laid off first. Using a "special performance profile," first-line supervisors evaluated employees who worked for them, and successively higher levels of management reviewed the evaluations to make sure they reflected ability, skill, and qualifications but not other factors. Management then conducted layoffs by seniority, starting with employees in the marginal group. The arbitrator upheld the three-tier system, finding no evidence that it violated the contract (*Houston Lighting & Power Co.*, 103 LA 179).

• An arbitrator ruled that an employer was not obligated "to follow a rigid objective review in connection with layoff decisions" under a contract that permitted the consideration of ability, skill, efficiency, qualifications, experience, attendance, accident record, developmental potential, knowledge, physical performance, and job performance "as determined by the employer." The union contended that the employer's layoff selections should have been reversed because management had not reviewed the personnel files of employees as part of the assessment process. However, the arbitrator found that the employer was not arbitrary or capricious in relying on the judgment of supervisory personnel who were "well familiar" with the work skills and employment history of all the affected employees (*Farm Fresh Catfish Co.*, 91 LA 721).

• Where the retention of a pair of junior employees under a relative ability clause was based on the opinions of supervisors who were "responsible for the efficient performance of the unit," a company's layoff of employees with more seniority could not be overturned, an arbitrator ruled. Even though the company may have erred in its assessment of one employee's qualifications, the arbitrator said, there was "no indication that it was not acting in good faith, or that its judgment was arbitrary, capricious or unreasonable, the only instances which would justify arbitral interference" (*Standard Havens Inc.*, 92 LA 926).

• Another arbitrator upheld an employer's basing ability measurements on a unilateral merit-rating plan. The arbitrator decided that the plan could be used because it included factors properly related to measurement of ability and skill and there was no evidence that the factors were rated incorrectly (*Merrill-Stevens Dry Dock & Repair Co.*, 17 LA 516).

● On the other hand, a merit-rating plan that used such factors as cooperation, safety habits, personal habits, and attitude toward superiors was not a fair way to evaluate employees for layoff purposes, an arbitrator ruled, because those factors were not the same as ability to perform a job (*Western Automatic Machine Screw Co.*, 9 LA 606).

● In a case involving the first-time use of tests to show the relative efficiency of employees, an arbitrator held that an employer could not lay off a senior employee based on his low efficiency rating. Efficiency comparisons could be used in the future, however, provided that the ratings were valid and management informed employees ahead of time about its intentions, the arbitrator ruled (*McEvoy Co.*, 42 LA 41).

B. Superseniority in Layoffs

Collective bargaining agreements commonly make exceptions to normal layoff procedures by conferring superseniority on shop stewards and other union officials to ensure that remaining workers continue to receive effective union representation following layoffs.

One arbitrator commented that the superseniority granted to union representatives is not related to their functions as productive workers but stems from their special status in administering the collective bargaining agreement. Consequently, ability and productivity considerations do not allow employers to ignore the superseniority of employees whose retention is mandated because of the representational duties they perform (*Freed Radio Corp.*, 9 LA 55; see also 97 LA 792, 2 LA 622).

In addition, arbitrators have barred employers from imposing transfers during layoff situations that would result in union stewards being moved from the particular department or shift where they have been serving as representatives (73 LA 13, 64 LA 1080). On the other hand, arbitrators have held that superseniority does not give stewards the right to stay in their existing jobs, as long as they remain in the same area where they have been performing their representational duties (18 LA 780, 17 LA 291, 13 LA 628).

While recognizing the importance of union representation for remaining employees, arbitrators also recognize that the specific terms of each collective bargaining agreement determine the extent to which superseniority applies. Where a given contract article grants superseniority to shop stewards and then limits the application of seniority by the ability factor, for example, arbitrators have upheld layoffs of shop stewards who cannot perform the required work (23 LA 379, 8 LA 1030).

1. Designations by Management

Some contracts also give management the right to designate some employees as having superseniority so they will be excluded from layoffs.

Under a contract that permitted an employer to grant superseniority to a certain number of employees of its own choosing, an arbitrator upheld an employer's retention of an employee who lacked regular seniority standing. The contract stated that seniority status would be attained after 30 days on the job, but one of the employees designated by the employer had not yet worked that long. The union argued that superseniority could not be given to a worker who had no seniority at all. The arbitrator sided with the employer, noting that the contract allowed the employer to retain on its "working force" a certain number of employees "without regard to their seniority." Despite the short tenure of the employee in question, he was a member of the working force, the arbitrator found, and the phrase "without regard to their seniority" meant that seniority was not a factor at all (*Bethlehem Steel Co.*, 28 LA 808).

C. Layoff of Probationary Employees

Under most contracts, probationary employees must be laid off before employees who have attained seniority rights (119 LA 500, 77 LA 1075). Where collective bargaining agreements do not include such requirements, arbitrators may uphold the retention of probationary employees in lieu of regular employees, particularly if seniority is not a governing factor in layoffs or if probationers possess needed skills (113 LA 880, 107 LA 763, 91 LA 1275, 85 LA 24).

• One arbitrator ruled that an employer properly retained probationary employees who were qualified to perform the duties of their electrical tester jobs, instead of permitting their displacement by more senior employees, given that the senior employees lacked the qualifications to do the work (*Eaton Corp.*, 65 LA 671).

• An employer had the right to retain a probationary employee who had experience in operating certain machines, instead of recalling laid-off senior employees who did not have the ability to run the machines, an arbitrator held, because under the contract the employer was entitled to keep qualified employees on the job (*Bellows International*, 65 LA 1280; see also 68 LA 1032).

• Under a special apprenticeship agreement, an arbitrator determined that an apprentice was immune to ordinary reductions in force, despite the fact that he was still on probation, because making him subject to layoff by seniority would have frustrated the purpose of the apprenticeship (*California Metal Trades Assn.*, 27 LA 105).

• When employers select workers for layoff from among a group of probationary employees, the order of layoffs does not matter, arbitrators have held, because length of service is not a deciding factor if the employees have not yet acquired any seniority rights (14 LA 963, 6 LA 760)

D. Temporary or Emergency Layoffs

Employers often are allowed more leeway with temporary or emergency layoffs than they would have in executing indefinite layoffs, since many arbitrators are inclined to exempt brief layoffs from the application of potentially cumbersome seniority rules (61 LA 506, 43 LA 1092, 41 LA 970, 12 LA 763, 4 LA 533).

Examples of situations in which arbitrators have allowed employers to disregard seniority rules include:

• a three-day layoff caused by an acute gas shortage (*Atlantic Foundry Co.*, 8 LA 807);

• a temporary shutdown caused by a breakdown in equipment (*United Engineering and Foundry Co.*, 31 LA 93); and

• an eight-day layoff precipitated by a heavy snowfall (*Riverton Lime & Stone Co.*, 8 LA 506).

In the absence of contract clauses making layoff rules inapplicable to temporary or emergency situations, however, some arbitrators have held that ordinary layoff procedures must be followed even where the lack of work only lasts a few hours or one or two days (95 LA 1024, 64 LA 256, 59 LA 984, 21 LA 400, 30 LA 441).

• Where it was not shown that application of seniority rules would have caused a hardship, an arbitrator ruled that an employer should have gone by seniority in executing an emergency layoff. The arbitrator found nothing in the contract to authorize the employer's unilaterally established rule that layoffs did not include periods of less than three days (*Yale and Towne Mfg., Co.*, 40 LA 1115; see also 74 LA 844).

• In a case involving a two-day plant shutdown in order to take inventory, an arbitrator held that the seniority requirements associated with layoffs had to be observed. The arbitrator decided that the shutdown "constituted a slack work period 'resulting in layoffs of employees' within the meaning of the agreement." Therefore, seniority had to be considered, and the employer erred in laying off workers who had more seniority than some of the employees put to work to take inventory, the arbitrator ruled (*Warren City Mfg. Co.*, 7 LA 202; see also 65 LA 471).

• *By contrast*, another arbitrator held that a shutdown for inventory purposes was a temporary cessation of operations and not really a layoff. Therefore, management did not have to go by seniority when selecting the employees it wanted to help take inventory (*Caterpillar Tractor Co.*, 7 LA 554; see also 74 LA 89).

III. Layoff Notice & Pay [LA CDI 100.70 (public employees); 117.109]

OVERVIEW

In delineating procedures for layoffs, many collective bargaining agreements specify that employers must provide advance notice to affected employees. The required amount of notice commonly ranges from 24 hours to a few days or even weeks.

If employees are laid off without proper warning, they usually become entitled to pay in lieu of notice. Some contracts express this requirement as an "either-or proposition," meaning that employers must provide the required amount of notice or pay employees for an equivalent number of days. Other contracts stipulate that employees are entitled to compensation only for the shortfall in the notice period. For example, if a contract requires three days' notice and employees are informed of layoffs two days ahead of time, they would be entitled to one day of pay to make up the difference.

When disputes arise in connection with layoff notices, they often center around the adequacy of notices and the applicability of notice requirements to short-term or temporary layoffs. Perhaps even more common are disputes concerning sudden layoffs prompted by unforeseen problems. In many such cases, arbitrators excuse a failure to meet the normal notice requirements, especially where contracts make exceptions for emergency situations.

SUMMARY OF CASES

A. Notice or Pay Required?

Exceptions to requirements for providing advance notice of layoffs or pay in lieu of notice are commonly included in collective bargaining agreements. Such exceptions typically come into play when layoffs are caused by emergencies or events beyond management's control, such as machine breakdowns, power outages, fires, and floods. Other circumstances in which arbitrators have excused the failure to provide advance notice of layoffs include strikes affecting operations, unforeseen materials shortages, snowstorms, unexpected business or financial crises, and gas shortages requiring plant shutdowns (67 LA 699, 62

LA 962, 50 LA 290, 51 LA 1151, 49 LA 1140, 12 LA 726, 5 LA 295).

If contracts do not explicitly provide for exceptions, do employers remain obligated to provide layoff notices or pay in lieu thereof? Some arbitrators have ruled that contractual commitments hold sway in the absence of explicit exceptions for emergency layoffs (29 LA 706, 18 LA 227). Expressing the opposite view, one arbitrator held that notice requirements only apply in situations where management reasonably can give notice, and an employer is not liable for pay in lieu of notice in emergency situations (*International Harvester Co.*, 14 LA 134).

• Despite the lack of a contractual exception for emergencies, an arbitrator excused a union employer from providing two weeks' advance notice or two weeks' pay in lieu of notice when its offices were forced to shut down temporarily because of last-minute problems with a planned relocation. Through no fault of the employer, its new offices were not available for use by the time its old offices had to be vacated. The union representing the affected employees said the employer committed a contract violation by laying employees off without notice, but the arbitrator said the provision on layoff notices was not intended to apply to the situation at hand, which involved emergency conditions beyond the control of management that only lasted a limited time. Consequently, the employer had no obligation to provide pay in lieu of notice, the arbitrator ruled (*International Association of Machinists*, 73 LA 1127).

• Under a contract that required advance notice of a layoff except in emergencies, an arbitrator held that there was an emergency within the meaning of the contract when an employer had to lay off several workers on short notice because of a work slowdown in one department. The arbitrator said the employer did not have to give the workers layoff pay because the layoff was neither planned nor desired by the employer (*Lone Star Steel Co.*, 28 LA 465).

• An employer was not required to provide layoff notices when a lack of work prompted supervisors to send employees home and keep them off duty for more than a day, an arbitrator ruled. In settling a prior grievance, the union had agreed that the normal requirements for 24 hours' notice of layoffs or a day of pay in lieu of notice did not apply to lack-of-work situations, where supervisors would be allowed to keep employees off the job for up to five days on a departmental basis due to equipment failure, acts of nature, or other conditions beyond the employer's control. Finding that the company had a right to invoke the lack-of-work procedures in the situation at hand, the arbitrator said the affected employees were not entitled to layoff notices or pay in lieu of notice (*Ameriwood Industries*, 122 LA 1018).

• *By contrast*, an arbitrator held that a layoff without notice due to a lack of work constituted a violation of a contract that required three days' advance notice of layoffs "except where such notice is impossible." Because the contract did not explain the word "impossible," the arbitrator applied its ordinary definition and concluded that only an emergency of major proportions would excuse a failure to provide the required notice. Decline or even cessation of orders did not qualify as such an emergency, the arbitrator decided (*Mobil Chemical Co.*, 50 LA 80).

• Similarly, an arbitrator found that an employer was liable for two days' pay after notifying a union and employees of layoffs on the morning the layoffs were implemented. The arbitrator ruled that the contract clearly required two days' advance notice of layoff to the union or an immediate written explanation for the lack of notice. Because the employer did not furnish a written explanation until the union requested it three weeks later, the arbitrator said, there was no emergency (*York International Corp.*, 93 LA 1107).

• One employer that failed to provide proper notice of layoffs was obligated to give the affected workers 40 hours' pay, an arbitrator ruled. Citing contract language that mentioned "extenuating circumstances," the employer argued that payment should not have been required due to the financial difficulties the company was having. The arbitrator refused to accept that defense, noting that the employer's financial condition had been poor for some time.

The reasons behind layoffs invariably relate to financial considerations, the arbitrator added, and allowing such concerns to override a requirement to provide pay in lieu of notice would effectively "void all payments where a layoff is involved" (*International Playing Card and Label Co.*, 116 LA 717).

B. Adequacy of Layoff Notices

When disputes arise over the adequacy of layoff notices, a common question is whether employees have received sufficient information about impending layoffs in order to plan for the time when they will have no income from their primary employment. In such cases, arbitrators often hold that employers must direct notices to the individual attention of affected employees, giving them specific warning that their jobs are in jeopardy.

• An arbitrator ruled that a notice requirement was not met by an employer that repeatedly told a union at their regular joint meetings that there was a possibility of a layoff. Notices "have to be clear and specific," the arbitrator said, and employees must be made aware that layoffs are in store for them as of a certain date. In this case, however, the employer did not notify individual employees of the prospect of losing their jobs.

In deciding on an appropriate remedy, the arbitrator rejected the notion that all employees were entitled to an award of two weeks' pay for the employer's failure to meet its obligation of providing two weeks' advance notice, because some employees were not laid off that long. Instead of receiving pay for the notice violation plus additional pay for any time worked during the period in question, employees were entitled to a total of two weeks' pay covering both time worked and layoff time, the arbitrator held (*Phillip's Waste Oil Pick-Up & Road Oiling Service Inc.*, 24 LA 136).

• An arbitrator ruled that an employer did not satisfy a notice requirement by providing a general notice to a union about an impending layoff without identifying those to be laid off. Reasoning that the purpose of the advance notice requirement was to give employees an opportunity to look for other work, the arbitrator said the employer was required to list those employees to be affected (*Donaldson Co. Inc.*, 21 LA 254).

• Even where a layoff was to last a matter of days, an arbitrator held that an employer did not meet its notification obligation by providing a general notice to the affected department that some employees would be laid off. The arbitrator emphasized that the affected individuals were supposed to be specifically told in advance that they were to be laid off (*Anaconda Aluminum Co.*, 65 LA 498).

• Another arbitrator, however, decided that an employer satisfied its contractual obligations by posting notices stating that there "may be" layoffs. In rejecting the argument that the notices were inadequate because they were "tentative and speculative," the arbitrator said the lack of certainty in the wording did not defeat the purpose of alerting workers to the possibility of layoffs so they could plan for other employment (*Yaffe Printing Co.*, 101 LA 1019).

1. Timing of Notices

When contracts require advance notice a certain length of time prior to layoffs, can nonworking days be counted as days of notice? At least one arbitrator has ruled that they cannot. Noting that the notice period is intended to give affected workers time to secure other employment, the arbitrator said this purpose would be defeated if nonworking days could be counted in the notice period (*Hoke Inc.*, 3 LA 748).

• Another arbitrator ruled that an employer had to pay eight hours' wages to employees who were laid off without receiving notice at least one working day in advance, despite the employer's contention that it could not give the required notice because employees were not in the plant due to a vacation shutdown. The arbitrator likened the vacation shutdown to a weekend. If employees were to be laid off, the arbitrator said, then they should have been notified at or before the start of their shifts on the last day they actually worked (*Magnavox Co.*, 64 LA 686).

• *By contrast*, an arbitrator held that an employer satisfied its obligation to provide at least 24 hours' notice of layoffs, even though workers were informed at 3:30 p.m.

on a Friday that they would be laid off effective 6:00 p.m. Saturday. Because Saturday was not a scheduled working day, the union maintained that the employer had not given workers sufficient advance notice of the layoff. Rejecting the union's position, the arbitrator found that the notice requirement merely meant that layoffs could become effective no sooner than 24 hours after the posting of a notice, and there was no clear past practice governing Friday layoff notices (*White Metal Rolling and Stamping Corp.*, 65 LA 771).

C. Temporary or Short-Term Layoffs

Some employers seek to excuse shortcomings in layoff notifications by arguing that the usual requirements do not apply to temporary or short-term layoffs. As evidenced by the examples below, arbitrators are likely to reject such arguments when they are not supported by explicit contract language.

● One employer contended that a contract clause on layoff notices applied to permanent layoffs, so its obligation to provide two weeks' advance notice should have been waived for a temporary layoff. Disagreeing with the employer, an arbitrator said a layoff is a layoff whether it is permanent or temporary. If a distinction were to be made between the two, it should have been expressly stated in the collective bargaining agreement, the arbitrator maintained (*International Paper Co.*, 60 LA 447).

● In another case, workers were laid off without warning for only two days but were awarded a week's pay for the violation. The outcome seemed harsh in light of the brief duration of the layoff, an arbitra-

tion board conceded, but it would not have seemed so if the layoff had lasted longer. According to the arbitration board, the employer's obligation under the contract was clear and unqualified, requiring that workers either receive one week's notice or a week's pay in lieu of notice (*General Baking Co.*, 28 LA 621).

● In a case involving a three-day plant shutdown, an arbitrator rejected an employer's argument that it had merely shortened the workweek as opposed to laying off employees. Concluding that a layoff is a layoff "whether it be for a short period of time or for an indefinite period," the arbitrator held that the shutdown triggered the employer's obligation to provide three days of advance notice. Finding that the employer had in fact provided notice of the shutdown two days ahead of time, the arbitrator awarded each of the affected employees one day of pay to make up the difference (*Exide Corp.*, 98 LA 626).

● On the other hand, an arbitrator ruled that an employer did not violate its contractual notice obligations when unforeseen parts shortages forced three separate one-day shutdowns. According to the arbitrator, the contract clause on layoff notices "seems to be aimed at a much more permanent situation such as a 'reduction in force' rather than a parts shortage which occurs without warning." Finding that the contract did not address situations in which the employer had no knowledge of pending layoffs until just before they happened, the arbitrator said the shutdowns caused by the parts shortages did not trigger the normal requirement of providing two days' advance notice of layoffs (*Tower Automotive Inc.*, 120 LA 1121).

IV. Bumping Rights [LA CDI 117.113 et seq.]

_____ **OVERVIEW** _____

Layoffs and bumping often go hand in hand as employees exercise their seniority rights to displace junior co-workers. Although the idea of protecting senior employees from layoffs sounds straightforward, the application of bumping rights can give rise to many questions. For example, how much of a choice do employees have when bumping? Are they limited to particular classifications and departments, or can they move anywhere they want? Are employees required to displace their least senior co-worker, or can they bump anyone with less seniority than themselves?

In the absence of detailed contract provisions addressing the intricacies of seniority and bumping rights, arbitrators frequently are called upon to resolve disputes involving these types of questions.

Disagreements over employees' suitability for particular jobs also are prevalent, because employers commonly block requested bumps based on ability and similar factors. In such cases, senior employees do not necessarily need superior qualifications to displace junior co-workers, especially if layoff and bumping provisions merely require them to have sufficient ability to meet basic job requirements. Where ability plays a central role in bumping decisions, arbitrators often find that senior employees are entitled to a trial period in which to demonstrate the adequacy of their skills.

Conflicts surrounding bumping rights can also focus on a range of other issues, including whether:

- employees can bump into higher-rated jobs;
- efficiency concerns preclude bumping when layoffs are brief;
- employers or employees bear the responsibility for initiating bumping; and
- employees have a right to refuse a bump if it would mean moving into a less desirable position or a lower pay grade.

SUMMARY OF CASES

A. Existence of Bumping Rights

Although many collective bargaining agreements contain detailed clauses on layoffs and bumping, others do not specifically address the existence of bumping rights. When interpreting agreements of the latter type, arbitrators often find that the job protections conferred by contractual seniority provisions give laid-off employees an implicit right to displace their junior co-workers.

- Bumping rights were implied under a contract that established a plant-wide seniority system and gave preference in layoff situations to senior employees who were qualified to perform the available work, an arbitrator held. The parties' collective bargaining agreement did not expressly set forth any bumping rights. "However, most arbitrators have held that bumping rights are implicit in a contract providing for the application of seniority when the work force is reduced," the arbitrator said. "At a minimum," the arbitrator added, an employee targeted for layoff "is entitled to be evaluated for any bargaining unit positions within the employee's occupational classification for which the employee is qualified by virtue of experience, skill and efficiency" (*Matanuska Electric Association Inc.*, 107 LA 402; see also 14 LA 938, 13 LA 843, 8 LA 816).

- An employer should have permitted an employee to bump into a different job when his position was abolished, an arbitrator held, even though there were no bumping procedures specifically detailed in the parties' collective bargaining agreement. The employer contended that bumping had never been allowed. Nevertheless, the arbi-

trator concluded that the employee should have been given the opportunity to displace a junior co-worker based on the contract's seniority clause, which stated that "the last employee hired shall be the first to be laid off" (*Cerro Gordo Care Facility*, 80 LA 11).

- On the other hand, where a collective bargaining agreement's provisions on bumping had been eliminated during contract negotiations, an arbitrator found that laid-off employees lacked the right to displace other workers. The deletion of the bumping provisions was one of the few contract changes made, the arbitrator noted. "To imply something as critical as bumping into the [collective bargaining agreement] in this context would be contrary to the parties' intent," he said (*Kaiser Fluid Technologies Inc.*, 114 LA 262; see also 3 LA 535).

B. Scope and Application of Rights

Much more common than disputes over the existence of bumping rights are conflicts over the scope and application of bumping rights. Where collective bargaining agreements provide for both plant-wide and departmental seniority, for example, departmental rights usually take precedence, with arbitrators allowing employees to invoke their plant-wide rights only after bumping opportunities within their own departments have been exhausted (38 LA 939, 30 LA 472, 3 LA 205).

- Where a collective bargaining agreement provided only for departmental seniority, an employer was justified in refusing to let employees exercise bumping rights on a plant-wide basis, an arbitrator ruled. The union maintained that past practice contradicted the contract's departmental restrictions, noting that plant-wide bumping rights had previously been granted under a special agreement. But the arbitrator said if there had been a past practice of allowing plant-wide bumping, there would have been no need for a "special agreement." Such agreements "are limited and confined to the matter dealt with" and do not modify a labor contract's terms or create a binding past practice unless the parties clearly express such an intent, the arbitrator stated (*Norwalk Furniture Corp.*, 100 LA 1051).

● Similarly, another arbitrator found that employees' bumping rights were limited to positions within the department where they maintained posted job rights. In this case, seniority was established on a plant-wide basis as well as a departmental basis, but specific procedures for layoffs and bumping had not been written into the parties' collective bargaining agreement. Thus, the arbitrator relied on past practice in concluding that bumping rights were properly limited by department (*United States Steel Corp.*, 65 LA 283).

● A state university system was justified in limiting the scope of employees' bumping rights to the "seniority pools" that were specified under the parties' collective bargaining agreement, an arbitrator held. The bargaining unit covered custodial, maintenance, and crafts and trades employees at three different campuses, and the employees were separated into a number of different shops at each location. Because of the contract's emphasis on "seniority pools," which were confined to individual shops, the arbitrator determined that laid-off employees lacked the right to bump across shops or locations (*University of Alaska*, 120 LA 237).

● Under a contract that allowed laid-off employees to bump junior co-workers in their "job series," an employee could not move into a job that was substantially dissimilar from her own, an arbitrator ruled. The term "job series," as used in the contract, referred to jobs requiring similar skills, knowledge, and ability, beginning with an entry-level position and providing for a progression of pay at each higher level, the arbitrator noted. The employee, who held a so-called "coordinator" position,

had nowhere to bump because her job was "singularly classified, and not part of any series," the arbitrator found (*Tillamook County*, 119 LA 279).

● Although laid-off maintenance employees could use their plant seniority to move over to production jobs, they were only allowed to bump into "base rate" or entry-level positions, an arbitrator held. This bumping limitation protected production workers who had bid into higher level jobs, the arbitrator said, and it also served as a trade-off for the fact that employees from other classifications could not bump into maintenance positions (*Ralston Purina Co.*, 74 LA 584; see also 84 LA 952).

● A hospital properly denied the bumping requests of laid-off nurses under a contract that granted employees bumping rights "in their classification," an arbitrator decided. If the parties had intended to give the nurses bumping rights throughout the bargaining unit, the contract would have omitted the words "in their classification," the arbitrator reasoned. Rather than being included "to take up space," those words served to delimit the bumping rights of laid-off employees, the arbitrator declared (*St. Vincent Mercy Medical Center*, 117 LA 785).

● *By contrast*, an arbitrator held that an employer wrongfully denied an employee's request to bump into a different job classification. In denying the move, the employer cited contract language that said seniority within a given job classification would be used as the basis for conducting layoffs. However, the arbitrator determined that the language in question referred to the order of layoffs and did not restrict bumping rights. Nothing in the contract prohibited employees from bumping into a different classification where they were qualified to perform the work, the arbitrator said, adding that a contrary ruling would have vitiated employees' seniority rights, which applied across the entire bargaining unit (*Brentwood Medical Associates*, 118 LA 1313).

● An employer committed a contract violation when it only allowed an employee to bump within her own department, an arbitrator ruled. In this case, contractual seniority provisions were ambiguous, but the arbitrator favored a broad interpretation that granted bumping rights based on the employee's bargaining-unit seniority. In so ruling, the arbitrator noted that seniority rights, carrying with them the promise of continued employment, "have long been recognized as among the most valuable rights that an employee can earn under a collective bargaining agreement" (*DynCorp Technical Services Group*, 93 LA 1192).

1. Terms of Contract

● An arbitrator ruled that an employer was within its rights when it retained six junior employees in the department after layoff, even though an agreement had a clause limiting layoffs out of seniority order to eight days, where that provision did not limit another provision that allowed deviations from seniority when a junior employee's qualifications were essential for the job, and retained employees were the only ones who had completed training for departmental jobs (*Trane Inc.*, 127 LA 1751).

● An arbitrator ruled an employer did not violate a collective bargaining contract when it laid off a senior warehouse employee, despite contentions that he was qualified for the job and knew it better than the retained junior employee, because the contract gave the employer the right to "give primary consideration" to employees' qualifications, and it did so through an evaluation by the employee's supervisor that was not slanted or biased against the grievant (*Leica Biosystems*, 126 LA 1697).

● An arbitrator ruled an employer violated a collective bargaining agreement by laying off an engineer after bypassing four less senior employees, where the agreement applied seniority rights to layoffs "where the qualifications are equal," and the engineer met all the qualifications (*St. Catherine University*, 127 LA 528).

2. Notice of Bumping Rights

● An arbitrator ruled that a county violated a collective bargaining agreement when, upon approving elimination of the grievant's technician position at a recreation center to which he had been transferred one month earlier, it failed to inform

him that he qualified to bump into a foreman II position occupied by a junior employee, and the grievant should have been awarded that position on the date he met with the labor relations manager regarding bumping procedures (*St. Lucie County*, 127 LA 471).

C. Control Over Bumping Options

Where collective bargaining agreements do not dictate specific bumping scenarios, questions can arise about employees' ability to exercise choice regarding the jobs into which they move. Do employers control the particulars, or do employees have a say in the matter? Arbitrators have ruled both ways on this issue, as illustrated by the examples below.

● Under a contract that permitted bumping in any department, one arbitrator ruled that an employee's choice was limited to picking a classification. Management had the right to decide which job within the classification the senior employee would fill, the arbitrator said (*Fulton-Sylphon Co.*, 2 LA 116).

● Another arbitrator found that employees lacked the right to bump into any classification they chose under a contract specifying that laid-off workers would replace the least senior employees in "Labor Grades A, B, C, & D in the department" (*Franklin Electric Co.*, 122 LA 1421).

● An employer was justified in requiring a first-shift employee to move to the second shift when exercising his bumping rights under a contract that provided for the displacement of the co-worker with the lowest seniority in the pertinent classification or department, an arbitrator held. Employees had previously been allowed to exercise their bumping rights on a shift-wide basis. As a rise in layoffs made it increasingly burdensome and disruptive to allow bumping within a single shift, however, the employer insisted on strict adherence to the use of plant-wide seniority in bumping. According to the arbitrator, the language of the contract clearly contemplated plant-wide seniority and did not "give employees the option of bumping according to present or preferred shift, or to create the 'domino' effect entailed in shiftwide bumping" (*Western Paper Products Inc.*, 81 LA 953).

- An employer did not commit a contract violation when it assigned laid-off employees to locations and work areas that were different than those of the workers they displaced, an arbitrator decided. The parties' labor contract did not require bumping employees to receive the same assignments as the displaced workers, the arbitrator noted, and nothing in the contract granted employees the right to request or obtain specific job assignments (*Linn County*, 119 LA 47; see also 102 LA 1102).

- *By contrast*, an arbitrator found that a school district violated a collective bargaining agreement by moving employees to new locations without letting them bump into positions of their own choosing. The employer argued that a contract provision on involuntary transfers applied to the employees, who were displaced as the result of a school closing. However, the arbitrator held that the contract's bumping provisions had to prevail in such a situation, or else the employer would be able to avoid giving employees their preferences in all bumping situations simply by invoking the transfer provision and involuntarily moving the affected workers (*Warren County School District*, 121 LA 506).

- Where a contract permitted qualified employees to displace anyone with less seniority to avoid layoff, an arbitrator held that an employer could not deny an employee his choice of jobs on a work crew. The employee requested a particular job on the crew but was given another that carried the same classification and wage rate. The arbitrator found that there was a difference between the two jobs because of nonwage factors, which made one seem more desirable to the employee. Noting that past practice had been to post individual jobs on the crew for bidding, the arbitrator concluded that the employee was entitled to choose the particular job he wanted (*Dayton Steel Foundry Co.*, 29 LA 191).

1. 'Less Senior' Versus 'Least Senior'

Another question that sometimes arises in connection with bumping is whether employees can displace anyone junior to them or only their "least senior" co-worker. In disputes of this type, arbitrators tend to base their decisions on the specific wording of the applicable contract provisions.

- Under a contract that mandated the displacement of the co-worker with the least seniority, a laid-off secretary had no choice but to bump into a part-time job, an arbitrator ruled. The language of the contract clearly stated "that it is 'the least senior employee' in the classification who may be bumped," the arbitrator pointed out. The employee could not bump a less senior secretary from a full-time job when the secretary with the least seniority held a part-time position, the arbitrator found (*Kenton City Board of Education*, 121 LA 688).

- An employer was justified in limiting an employee's bumping rights to the job in her occupational group that was held by the worker with the least seniority, an arbitrator held. The contract did not permit the employee to bump into just any job held by someone with less seniority, the arbitrator emphasized. Thus, when the employee was unable to do the job that was held by the only co-worker she was entitled to bump, the employer had the right to lay her off while continuing to employ others with less seniority, the arbitrator found (*Ford Motor Co.*, 1 LA 462).

- Despite an employer's past practice of requiring employees to bump into positions held by co-workers with the least seniority, an arbitrator determined that the language of the parties' collective bargaining agreement did not support such a requirement. The contract used the phrase "less senior employee," which could not be construed to mean "least senior" and could not be overridden by a conflicting past practice, the arbitrator held. "To rule otherwise would be to change the clear and unambiguous language of the contract," the arbitrator said (*Pittsburg and Midway Coal Mining Co.*, 87 LA 1107; see also 76 LA 1017).

- Under a contract that simply made seniority the governing factor in layoffs, an arbitrator decided that an employee could bump any junior co-worker in an equal or lower classification. The employee was not limited to bumping only the most junior employee, the arbitrator held. If that were the intent of the parties, they should have said so in the contract, he reasoned (*Warren Petroleum Corp.*, 26 LA 532).

D. Ability, Skills, Qualifications, and Prior Experience

Collective bargaining agreements commonly give at least some weight to employees' ability, experience, skills, and qualifications as part of the bumping process. At one end of the spectrum are contracts that prevent job incumbents from being displaced by laid-off employees with inferior ability and skills, and at the other end are contracts that grant automatic bumping rights on the basis of seniority so long as the laid-off employees can meet the basic requirements of the position in question.

● Under a contract that made seniority the deciding factor if employees were relatively equal in ability, an arbitrator decided that an employer should have allowed laid-off employees to bump into unskilled jobs. The work involved was relatively simple, and the senior employees would have been capable of stepping in and handling the required tasks even if they had never held the positions previously, the arbitrator found (*Olin Corp.*, 80 LA 1279).

● An arbitrator ruled that a county violated a collective bargaining agreement when it did not allow a senior clerical assistant to bump into the junior assistant's position, despite the employer's contention that the grievant lacked the necessary computer skills of database maintenance and troubleshooting to fill the junior assistant's job. The county had attempted to impose job duties that were outside the scope of a clerical assistant's duties (*Mason County*, 126 LA 1182).

● An arbitrator rule that an employer violated a collective bargaining contract that required bumping an employee who had the "present ability" to do the job, when it refused to allow a laid-off employee to bump into a position in a finishing classification, even though the employee had never held the position in the classification on a full-time basis. The employee had worked in that department on temporary assignments, the revised job descriptions did not refer to any specific high-level requirements that were in the new job description

that were not in the old description, and the grievant offered unrebutted testimony that he could do all the work of the position (*Penn-Union Corp.*, 128 LA 875).

● An arbitrator ruled that an employer should not have laid off senior employees in favor of junior employees who were trained and qualified to keep certain units in operation. The bargaining agreement provided that senior employees selected for layoff may bump into another job in the department for which they could qualify within a reasonable period of time, and the employer's untimely offer of retraining prevented senior employees from exercising this right (*Cytec Industries*, 127 LA 1722).

● An employer committed a contract violation when it denied two employees the right to displace junior employees in jobs for which they were eligible and qualified, an arbitrator ruled. One employee had been kept from bumping into a job that he was "unquestionably capable of performing," the arbitrator said. Management considered him unable to do the work because he had complained of a sore back several weeks before the layoff, the arbitrator noted, but the evidence did not show that he was physically unfit for the job. The other employee had the "basic ability" to handle a junior employee's responsibilities and should not have been excluded because of safety considerations, where the job in question did not involve inherent dangers, the arbitrator found (*Hanna Mining Co.*, 80 LA 905).

● An employer improperly blocked an employee from bumping into a job based on his failure to meet a set of "ideal" requirements that were known only to the manager overseeing the position, an arbitrator ruled. Although the contract gave the employer broad authority in determining qualifications and ability, it could not exercise that authority arbitrarily and capriciously, the arbitrator declared. In this case, the employee met all the listed requirements for the position and was wrongfully denied the bump based on "secret" qualifications, the arbitrator concluded. Seniority and bumping rights are critical rights, but if an employer were "permitted to have unfettered discretion in adding newly created prerequisites before a bump can be authorized," the arbitrator said, it would undermine "the entire notion of seniority" (*Wayne County Community College District*, 121 LA 493; see also 108 LA 801).

• *By contrast*, an arbitrator upheld an employer's right to lay off certain group leaders for one program without regard to seniority, where the agreement allowed selection of group leaders on the basis of qualifications and layoffs were simply another form of selection. The union was unable to obtain strict application of seniority for layoffs in bargaining, and the arbitration award involving similar language in the agreement between the union and employer in a different location held that the employer had the right to remove group leaders at any time without regard to seniority (*Lockheed Martin*, 123 LA 1405.

• An arbitrator ruled an employer did not violate a bargaining contract when it laid off senior members of "Fabricator A" instead of junior members of "Senior Fabricator" classification, because the retained employees possessed the skills needed to do more complex work (*Art Iron Inc.*, 127 LA 746).

• Similarly, an employer did not violate a collective bargaining contract, which provided that junior employees would be retained in layoffs if they had "talents necessary to maintain efficient operation of the department," an arbitrator ruled, when it laid off senior employees, because junior employees best had the ability to perform certain job duties (*Hennegan Company*, 127 LA 597).

• An arbitrator upheld an employer's right to lay off a senior six-year margarine line employee in favor of a junior sanitation employee for a week, even though the senior employee had worked in the sanitation department for the first six months of his career, and another senior employee had been assigned there for "light duty," because the grievant had no recent experience or training in sanitation work, the tasks and training process in sanitation had changed considerably after the grievant left, and the employee doing "light duty" did not replace the junior employee (*Ventura Foods, LLC*, 124 LA 1332).

• An arbitrator ruled that a school board did not violate the Alabama Fair Dismissal Act when it laid off a repairman

with seven years of service who installed and maintained security alarms, despite the contention that the board's policy for reductions in support personnel provided that employees would be discharged in reverse order of seniority gave the repairman the right to bump junior employees in other divisions of the maintenance department. The board had been compelled to cut the budget, all employees in the security subdivision were let go, and the policy cited protected senior employees within a certain job classification, but did not confer the right to bump junior employees in other classifications or departments (*Mobile County School Board*, 128 LA 1275).

• An employer did not have to grant an employee's request to bump into a job in its foundry that required skills he did not possess, an arbitrator held. After determining that the employee was not qualified for the chosen position, the employer offered a lower-level job, which the employee refused. He then went on layoff before being allowed to bump into a different foundry job. In concluding that the employee had no right to the original foundry job, the arbitrator pointed out that the position included requirements that the employee could not satisfy by virtue of his prior experience. The employer had the authority to determine the skills needed for the position, and there was no evidence that it arbitrarily created unnecessary job requirements in order to keep the employee from bumping into the job, the arbitrator said (*Chromalloy-Sturm Machine Co. Inc.*, 84 LA 1001).

• Under a contract that allowed bumping only if "in the company's opinion" employees were qualified "at that time" to perform the available work, an employer properly refused to allow two employees to bump into positions they held temporarily in the past, an arbitrator found. Based on the quality of the employees' work during their temporary assignment to the jobs, along with the fact that the positions had recently been restructured and the duties expanded to encompass the use of new technology, the arbitrator found that the employer was justified in concluding that the employees were not qualified to perform the requisite tasks (*Worldsource Coil Coating Co. Inc.*, 102 LA 17).

● A television station was justified in refusing to let a floor director bump into a design specialist job, an arbitrator held. The employee lost her job when a show was discontinued, and the employer determined that she lacked the skills required to work as a design specialist. The arbitrator agreed with the employer, finding that the employee did not have the training and experience needed for the design specialist position, which was significantly different from the floor director job in terms of education, function, and creativity (*Twin Cities Public Television*, 117 LA 97).

● Under a contract that permitted employees to bump into different departments only if "their job descriptions are similar, or the qualifications are less," a storekeeper did not have the right to move to an account clerk position, an arbitrator ruled. The two positions involved distinctly different duties, and the required qualifications for an account clerk, which included "college level course work in computers, bookkeeping and office administration or equivalent experience," were not less than those required for a storekeeper, the arbitrator determined (*City of Escanaba*, 122 LA 1217).

1. Experience Requirements

Under some contracts, the bumping options available to employees are limited according to their prior experience. In other words, they cannot move into a position unless they have held that particular job or performed the same duties in the past. The following are examples of cases in which arbitrators have ruled on employers' enforcement of these types of experience requirements.

● When negotiating a new contract, one employer had bargained for the inclusion of a provision stipulating that laid-off employees could bump into a position if company records showed that they had at least 30 workdays of experience in that job. When the company proposed the experience requirement, however, it knew that it lacked detailed records on employees' prior work experience. In light of this fact, an arbitrator decided that it was "unreasonable, arbitrary, and capricious" to make the

execution of employees' bumping rights contingent on having the requisite experience "as shown on Company records" (*W.E. Plechaty Co.*, 84 LA 571).

● Another employer's labor contract allowed employees to bump into positions provided that they had performed the work within the last three years. An arbitrator determined that a laid-off employee was permitted to bump into a higher-rated lead person job even though he had never formally held that position in the past. Although the evidence suggested that the junior employee who was being displaced from the job had superior qualifications, the arbitrator said the outcome of the case turned on the question of whether the senior employee had the prior experience required under the contract. Finding that the senior employee had indeed done the job, albeit for only eight days, the arbitrator decided that he met the experience requirement and had demonstrated the skills needed for the position (*The Dial Corp.*, 120 LA 856).

● An arbitrator upheld an employer's decision to deny a laid-off forklift mechanic the opportunity to bump into a maintenance department classification involving hydraulic repair work. Both positions were highly skilled and technical, the arbitrator noted, but they required different knowledge and experience, as evidenced by the establishment of separate apprenticeship standards and training programs for each. The arbitrator determined that it was a reasonable exercise of management's discretion to permit employees to bump into such craft positions only if they had previously held the classification or completed an apprenticeship program for the classification. Because the employee in question did not meet either prerequisite, his bumping request did not have to be granted, the arbitrator found (*Allied Tube & Conduit Corp.*, 122 LA 1735).

2. Testing Issues

Employers occasionally raise the issue of testing in conjunction with the bumping process as a means of assessing employees' skills and ability, but few arbitrators have held that such testing is appropriate.

• One arbitrator ruled that an employer could not base any bumping decisions on a skills inventory test for clerical employees. The employer had the right to use the test in connection with hiring and promotions, the arbitrator found, but not in the context of layoffs or reductions in force. According to the arbitrator, applying the test to the bumping process could conceivably cause qualified clerical workers to be blocked from bumping into positions they previously had performed successfully, which represented a conflict with the employees' contractual seniority rights (*Central Michigan University*, 102 LA 787).

• Another arbitrator held that an employer did not violate a collective bargaining agreement, which allowed employees affected by layoffs to bump into positions for which they had the necessary skills, qualifications, and abilities, when it blocked trainees from obtaining jobs as mechanics after they declined to take a test of practical skills that could have demonstrated that they met the job requirements (*IMC-Agrico Co.*, 116 LA 1645).

• An arbitrator held that an employer could require testing to determine a senior employee's qualifications for a position to which he wished to bump. In this case, employees had the right to bump "any employee" with less seniority, "providing that the employee doing the bumping is qualified in that job classification," the arbitrator noted, and the parties' contract did not restrict the means the employer could use in determining qualifications (*International Salt Co.*, 91 LA 710).

• An arbitrator ruled that an employer could not require that a senior non-probationary employee pass an endurance component of a physical abilities' test to exercise his bumping rights into an order selector's position, where failure on the test would have established that the employee would be excessively fatigued in the job but would not show that he is unable to perform the "essential duties" of the job, the employer had not amended the job description of order selector to reflect the fact that a selector must possess a specific level of aerobic capacity, and the bumping involved a reduction in force of limited duration from which the employee would be recalled to an old job in a short period of time (*Supervalu Inc.*, 124 LA 1368).

E. Trial and Training Periods

Where collective bargaining agreements make bumping rights contingent on ability and similar factors, disputes sometimes focus on employees' entitlement to a period in which they can learn their new duties and demonstrate the adequacy of their skills. Contract clauses on bumping often provide for these so-called trial periods, alternatively referred to as orientation, familiarization, and break-in periods.

In many cases, arbitrators find that employers are required to offer such periods (113 LA 603, 96 LA 1069, 82 LA 721, 82 LA 655, 82 LA 213, 75 LA 1001). Some arbitrators have even found that employees are entitled to a period of training so they can gain the proficiency needed in their new jobs (120 LA 1522, 113 LA 1060, 98 LA 209, 93 LA 400, 86 LA 741, 81 LA 1248). However, other arbitrators have held that senior employees, in order to exercise their bumping rights, must possess the ability to perform the job in question without the benefit of any training or trial period (121 LA 95, 114 LA 980, 94 LA 1190, 67 LA 282, 65 LA 901, 44 LA 694, 44 LA 24).

• In one case, an employee slated for layoff exercised her bumping rights by choosing a job she had never before performed. After a week's trial, she was informed that she lacked the ability to do the job satisfactorily and was laid off. The union protested, saying that she had not been given enough time to become familiar with the new job and that, even if her disqualification was proper, she should have been offered an opportunity to bump into another job. However, an arbitrator found that the layoff was proper, because the employee had been given a reasonable opportunity to demonstrate her ability and the contract did not provide for repeated bumping. The employee was largely responsible for her poor selection of a job to bump into, the arbitrator added, noting that she had purposely passed up a job she knew she was capable of doing (*U.S. Slicing Machine Co.*, 22 LA 53).

● An employer was justified in preventing one laid-off employee from bumping into a furnace operator job while another worker was undergoing a break-in period for the same job, an arbitrator held. When both of the laid-off employees sought to move to the position of furnace operator, only the one with greater seniority was allowed to proceed with the bumping process, which called for a 10-15 day period of "adequate supervision and adequate instruction" in which the employee could demonstrate that he had "the skill and ability to perform the job." Because the employer had to have a minimum contingent of qualified workers to keep its furnace running, it was not required to let the employee with lesser seniority bump an incumbent from the furnace operator job while the qualifying period for the other laid-off worker was under way, the arbitrator decided (*Magellan Aerospace Corp.*, 120 LA 945).

● Under a contract that granted laid-off employees the right to bump into positions that could be performed with a minimal break-in period, an employer did not have to let a senior employee displace a skilled worker who held an inspector position, an arbitrator decided. The phrase "minimal break-in period" meant a brief period of three or four days in which workers could familiarize themselves with a job, but the senior employee would have needed a few months of training in order to perform the inspector job, the arbitrator determined (*Dentsply International Inc.*, 85 LA 24; see also 86 LA 54).

● On the other hand, an arbitrator found that an employer was in violation of a collective bargaining agreement when it insisted that employees were limited to a break-in period lasting no more than four days. The contract mandated bumping of the least senior employee in a classification, and the individual who was supposed to be displaced in this instance held a highly skilled job as an electronic instrument technician. The arbitrator found that the job could not be designated as immune from the contract's bumping requirements, and the employer could not require

a maximum break-in period of four days under the circumstances (*Mead Corp.*, 79 LA 493).

F. Upward Bumping [LA CDI 117.1135]

A question that sporadically emerges during layoffs is whether the bumping rights enjoyed by senior employees permit them to displace junior co-workers who hold higher-rated jobs. Although arbitrators have refused to allow senior employees to bump into higher-rated classifications in many cases, upward bumping has been approved in certain situations.

Arbitrators have cited the following reasons in upholding upward bumping:

● collective bargaining agreements contained layoff provisions that were broad (30 LA 886, 20 LA 394, 14 LA 502);

● there was no practice of prohibiting upward bumping, or past practice supported upward bumping (103 LA 306, 21 LA 214); and

● upward bumping did not conflict with contractual promotion provisions (29 LA 439, 12 LA 738).

In denying upward bumping, meanwhile, arbitrators often emphasize that a layoff may not be used as a means of achieving a promotion. The rationale here seems to be that a promotion can be sought only when a vacancy exists, and the process of obtaining a higher-rated job must be governed by the promotion clause of a collective bargaining agreement; therefore, bumping into a higher-rated job would amount to a violation of contractual promotion provisions (76 LA 899, 72 LA 719, 71 LA 295, 25 LA 417, 23 LA 789, 15 LA 891).

Arbitrators also tend to shy away from approving bumps into higher-rated jobs where such moves are not sanctioned by past practice, even if a collective bargaining agreement would allow upward bumping (38 LA 128, 30 LA 815, 30 LA 1, 23 LA 220).

● One arbitrator denied an upward bump under a contract providing that all promotions to higher classifications should be given to the most senior qualified employee who bids for "the vacancy." An employee who received a layoff notice tried unsuccessfully to bump into a higher-rated classification held by a co-worker with less seniority. In upholding the employer's refusal to grant the upward bump, the arbitrator maintained that there was not a single reported arbitral decision extending permission, approval, or even toleration of upward bumping as a means of achieving a promotion in violation and defeat of the specifically agreed promotion requirements of a collective bargaining agreement (*K.L.M. Royal Dutch Airlines*, 60 LA 1053).

• An arbitrator upheld the denial of an upward bump to an employee who was not qualified to perform the higher-rated work. The employee could perform only about 20 percent of the job he sought, and the contract did not provide for the training he would have needed to successfully carry out the duties of the position, the arbitrator found (*United Telephone Co. of Ohio*, 60 LA 805; see also 111 LA 665).

• Another arbitrator upheld an employer's refusal to bump an employee into the top job on a mill crew. Historically, the employer contended, employees had never been permitted to bump into top jobs that they actually had not performed. According to the arbitrator, established past practice and failure of the contract to provide a training period for bumping supported the company's right to turn down employees it deemed to be unqualified (*Empire-Reeves Steel Corp.*, 44 LA 653; see also 103 LA 433).

• Where a contract stated that both ability and seniority were determining factors in bumping, an arbitrator decided that a senior employee with the required ability could replace a junior employee in a higher-rated job, because junior employees had to be laid off first during a reduction in force. The arbitrator said contractual promotion provisions were irrelevant in determining employees' job rights in a layoff except to the extent that they could assist with the interpretation of contractual layoff clauses (*Greater Louisville Industries Inc.*, 44 LA 694).

• An employee who had unsuccessfully attempted to obtain a higher-rated position through the job bidding process was subsequently entitled to bump into the position during a layoff, an arbitrator ruled. The employee had been deemed qualified for the position when he bid on it, but a ju-

nior employee with superior qualifications was selected for the job. According to the arbitrator, the criteria originally used to select the junior worker no longer applied when the senior employee was attempting to bump into the job. Citing the "essential and basic significance of seniority as a job preserving right," along with the fact that the parties' collective bargaining agreement did not expressly prohibit upward bumping, the arbitrator found that upward bumping was implicitly permitted as an exercise of the employee's seniority rights (*Metalloy Corp.*, 91 LA 221).

• An arbitrator found that a mechanic who lost her job due to a lack of work was eligible to bump into a higher-rated position. Her employer had compiled a list of 20 lower-rated jobs for bumping purposes, and she had to select one of them or face termination as a "voluntary quit." The employee was not offered another mechanic position, even though she was senior to other mechanics and therefore had bumping rights within her classification. Beyond those rights, however, the arbitrator noted that the contract permitted plant-wide bumping of a junior employee in "any other job," if the employee doing the bumping was qualified. Emphasizing the word "any," the arbitrator said upward bumping was "clearly countenanced" by the contract. As a remedy, the arbitrator awarded the employee temporary reinstatement, with back pay, to a position equivalent to the one she previously held, and he also ordered the employer to give the employee "a fair opportunity" to prove herself in the higher-rated job in which she had initially expressed an interest (*Diamond International Corp.*, 81 LA 797).

G. Bumping During Brief Layoffs

Recognizing the upheaval that bumping can cause, arbitrators commonly excuse employers if they do not allow employees to exercise their normal bumping rights during brief layoffs. In the interests of efficiency, some collective bargaining agreements carve out specific exclusions for layoffs that are brief in duration (66 LA 609, 43 LA 1092, 15 LA 172). In the absence of such exclusions, arbitrators are more likely to find that seniority and bumping rights remain in force during short-term layoffs (96 LA 117, 40 LA 1115, 35 LA 299, 21 LA 400, 9 LA 399).

● An arbitrator found that a cement company did not violate a collective bargaining contract when it assigned two employees who were immediately qualified to perform work at a packhouse during a shutdown instead of two more senior employees. The contract provided that in temporary shutdowns layoffs for unskilled work were to be by seniority, for skilled work by "ability and experience," and that senior displaced employees had the option to "accept work available" at the plant "for which they are qualified. The company established that skilled employees were needed to properly load out weight on trucks and to ensure correct specifications for multiple customers, and senior employees had little recent experience at the packhouse (*Ash Grove Cement Co.*, 129 LA 723).

● One arbitrator upheld an employer's refusal to honor the bumping requests of employees who were laid off for three and one-half days. The employees claimed that a contract provision calling for plant-wide seniority gave them the right to displace junior co-workers in different job classifications. However, the arbitrator found that other language in the contract precluded bumping in layoffs lasting less than four days. Citing the impracticality of moving employees in and out of jobs in connection with brief layoffs, the arbitrator said "[s]uch a futile and inefficient realignment of the work force was undoubtedly intended never to be" (*Bristol Steel and Iron Works Inc.*, 73 LA 573).

● Another arbitrator rejected an employee's grievance concerning a two-day layoff, stating that "in the absence of relatively clear contract language to the contrary, the parties should not be held to have intended to authorize a general disruption of operations, and the complications and difficulties of a sequence of bumps, merely because an employee is laid off for a fixed period of only a few days" (*United Screw & Bolt Corp.*, 42 LA 669).

● An employer did not have to allow bumping when electrical problems prevented some employees from working for part of one day, an arbitrator held, finding that the layoff provisions of the parties' collective bargaining agreement were not intended to cover such a situation (*Rotorex Co.*, 99 LA 190).

● *By contrast*, an arbitrator found that an employer committed a contract violation by laying off an employee during a one-day shutdown of one of its production lines while allowing junior employees in the same classification to continue working elsewhere in its plant. The employer contended that the displacement of junior employees should not be required for a brief shutdown, but the arbitrator said the employer had an obligation to ensure that "whatever work is available goes to the senior employees first." Seniority rights had to be respected notwithstanding the issues of "convenience, practicality and feasibility," which were matters to be addressed at the bargaining table, the arbitrator concluded, borrowing a phrase from an arbitration decision rendered many years earlier (*Pepsi-Cola Portsmouth Bottling Co.*, 95 LA 1024).

● An employer should have permitted bumping in connection with a four-day layoff, an arbitrator ruled. The parties' collective bargaining agreement provided an exception to the application of bumping rights in layoffs lasting less than four days, and the employer contended that it had originally expected the affected employees to be idled for three days. Nevertheless, the arbitrator held that the employees were wrongfully denied their bumping rights. In addition to citing the layoff's actual duration, the arbitrator noted that the employer had consistently permitted employees to bump during short-term layoffs in the past and had not informed the union of its intention to enforce the contractual exception that applied to layoffs of less than four days (*Central Aluminum Co.*, 103 LA 190).

H. Responsibility to Initiate Bumping

Questions sometimes emerge with regard to the responsibility for initiating the bumping process. Do employers have to start the bumping machinery in a layoff, or are the affected employees required to put in claims for jobs to which they are entitled? Arbitrators' rulings in such cases depend largely on the specific circumstances involved.

● One employee had been laid off for five months before he was recalled to a different job. A week later, he bid for and was awarded a job as a rivet heater being held by a junior employee. He also put in a claim for back pay to cover the period of his layoff, arguing that he should have replaced the junior rivet heater at that time. An arbitrator denied the claim for back pay, finding that the employee had some obligation to be diligent in asserting his bumping rights, either by himself or through his steward. If he did not do so, the arbitrator said, he should not be permitted to collect back pay from his employer, because that would mean the employer was paying twice for the work—once to the employee who had been on layoff, and once to the employee who kept the job (*General American Transportation Corp.*, 15 LA 672).

● Another arbitrator reached an opposite conclusion where an employee was bumped from his job by a senior employee and did not realize that he had a right to another job that he had previously bid for but declined to accept. When the employee learned of his right to the other job three weeks later, the employer refused to move him into it and argued that the employee had waited too long to file a grievance asserting his claim to the job. Remarking that the employee could not have known of his right despite reasonable diligence, and so could not have asserted his claim earlier, the arbitrator decided that the grievance was timely filed and proper, because it was filed one day after the employer refused to bump the employee into the desired job (*Dayton-Walther Corp.*, 64 LA 645).

I. Right to Refuse Downgrading

Layoff situations occasionally give rise to disputes over the rights of employees to refuse a bump if it would mean moving into a less desirable position or a lower pay grade. Some arbitrators have found that employees can elect to be laid off rather than downgraded.

● An arbitrator ruled that union committeemen, who should not have been laid off due to their super-seniority rights, were not required to mitigate their damages by bumping, where positions into which they would have bumped paid less (*Stroh Die Casting Co.*, 127 LA 713).

● Two employees' jobs were eliminated during a reduction in force, and they were offered lower-rated jobs on the basis of their seniority. They refused to take the jobs and were discharged. The company said the discharges were for just cause because the men had refused the only work available to them. However, an arbitrator decided that the right of senior employees to bump into lower jobs was not the same as a requirement that they take such jobs. In the absence of clear contract language requiring them to take available work or be discharged, the arbitrator concluded that they were free to request layoffs and subsequently rehire in line with their seniority. He ordered the company to change the separation status of the employees from discharge to layoff (*Caterpillar Tractor Co.*, 23 LA 313).

● Another arbitrator held that employees could continue to elect layoff rather than demotion, despite the introduction of a supplemental unemployment benefit plan, where this right of election had existed in the past (*United Engineering & Foundry Co.*, 47 LA 164).

● *By contrast*, an arbitrator found that a laid-off employee lost her job rights when she refused to bump into positions that provided less pay or were considered too physically demanding. The arbitrator noted that language had been removed from the parties' collective bargaining agreement that would have allowed the employee to choose a layoff period of 120 days and receive unemployment compensation benefits during that period. Under the revised contract, the employee no longer had the right to elect a temporary layoff in lieu of exercising her bumping rights, the arbitrator determined (*Sperry & Rice Manufacturing Co. LLC*, 122 LA 1665).

V. Worksharing [LA CDI 117.32]

OVERVIEW

During business slowdowns, employers commonly lay off employees to keep the size of the workforce in balance with the reduced supply of full-time work. As an alternative, employers sometimes distribute the available work in equal shares by cutting back employees' hours or shortening the workweek.

Where collective bargaining agreements neither condone nor forbid worksharing, arbitrators commonly uphold the practice, especially if employers have sound business reasons for choosing hours reductions over layoffs. In many cases, however, arbitrators reject worksharing arrangements implemented unilaterally by employers, reasoning that across-the-board cutbacks in hours conflict with the seniority rights conferred by collective bargaining agreements.

SUMMARY OF CASES

A. Worksharing Arrangements Upheld

When unions object to worksharing arrangements, they commonly argue that employers have an obligation to impose layoffs so that senior employees can continue working full-time schedules. In the absence of contractual workweek guarantees, however, arbitrators often find that management's authority over hours and schedules allows a certain degree of flexibility in this area, particularly where financial and operational considerations make worksharing preferable to layoffs.

One arbitrator conducted a thorough analysis of prior cases involving worksharing and identified the following standards for determining whether employers are justified in reducing the workweek in lieu of instituting layoffs:

• Unilateral reductions in hours are not permitted if employers and unions have included provisions in their collective bargaining agreements that expressly guarantee employees eight hours per day or 40 hours per week. The ability of employers to implement worksharing also can be constrained by contract language delineating specific reasons for which hours can be reduced or requiring union consent in such matters.

• When contracts define the normal workweek, they do not necessarily create an obligation to provide employees a certain amount of work. Employers can deviate from the normal workweek in the presence of abnormal conditions so long as the changes are temporary in nature and based on sound business reasons, such as plant efficiency, product quality, and economic considerations.

● Collective bargaining agreements with seniority provisions for layoff purposes do not automatically mean that employers must resort to layoffs during slack periods. Rather than precluding worksharing, such seniority clauses provide employees with a relative claim to available work when employers implement layoffs.

In the case at hand, the arbitrator upheld a unilateral workweek reduction that an employer imposed on its clerical employees while trying to weather a decline in business caused by unfavorable economic conditions. Although the contract defined the regular workweek as five consecutive eight-hour days, it did not expressly guarantee a minimum amount of work, nor did it contain any language requiring union consent or delineating specific conditions that had to be present before work hours could be changed, the arbitrator found. The arbitrator also noted that the employer imposed the schedule change as a temporary measure and did not use the reduction in hours to circumvent the seniority provisions of the contract (*Ampco-Pittsburgh Corp.*, 80 LA 472).

Below are additional examples of cases in which arbitrators have upheld worksharing arrangements imposed by employers.

● An arbitrator ruled that a manufacturer did not violate a collective bargaining agreement when, in response to a downturn in business, it reduced work hours of employees in select groups each week from 40 to 32 hours, resulting in less senior employees working more hours than senior employees. There was no reduction in the number of employees working in any unit and no indicia of "layoff," and a reduction in work hours was permitted by agreement (*PPG Industries Inc.*, 126 LA 1529).

● Finding that senior employees had no entitlement to schedules that would assure them of eight-hour workdays, an arbitrator held that an employer was justified in reducing hours so it could maintain its two-shift system during an economic downturn. Contractual language stated that the employer "shall have no responsibility or obligation to furnish any minimum number of hours of work per week or per day to its employees," the arbitrator noted in upholding the reduction in hours (*Dixie Container Co.*, 65 LA 1089).

● In a similar case, an arbitrator rejected a union's argument that junior employees should have been laid off so that senior employees could work a full 40-hour week. The arbitrator ruled that the contract clearly gave the employer the right to divide work equally in the event of insufficient demand (*Industrial Garment Manufacturing Co.*, 65 LA 875).

● An employer was justified in reducing the workweek to 35 hours under a contract that gave management the unlimited right to schedule production, an arbitrator ruled. The reduction was reasonable during a temporary business slowdown, the arbitrator concluded, rejecting the union's argument that a reduction to a 32-hour workweek was the only exception to the "regular 40-hour week" (*Rex Chainbelt Inc.*, 52 LA 852).

● A paper mill did not violate a collective bargaining agreement when it reduced maintenance mechanics' hours from 80 every two weeks to 72, even while continuing to use outside contractors to perform some maintenance work, an arbitrator decided. In this case, the collective bargaining agreement stated that there was no guarantee of 40 hours of work per week and that schedules were subject to change based on product demand and operating efficiencies. The arbitrator said the employer met the conditions stated in the agreement for outsourcing work and there was an insufficient connection between the mill's outsourcing and the reduced hours, given the mill's financial situation (*Georgia-Pacific Corp.*, 120 LA 1035).

● An arbitrator found that a worksharing plan that alternated three- and four-day workweeks was not barred by a collective bargaining agreement defining "week" as a seven-day period beginning on Monday, because the provision referring to "week" was only for bookkeeping purposes and did not define the workweek. The arbitrator further held that the employer met its obligation to discuss its worksharing plan with the union. The plan was the subject of three meetings and one telephone conversation, details of the plan were fully communicated, and the employer fully explored alternatives offered by the union, the arbitrator observed (*Cone Mills Corp.*, 86 LA 992).

● Even though a collective bargaining agreement included a guarantee of a 40-hour workweek, an arbitrator held that an employer did not violate the contract by temporarily reducing some employees' schedules rather than instituting layoffs during a business downturn. The contract allowed for an exception to the 40-hour schedule in the event of plant shutdowns. The employer's action could be considered a "partial shutdown," the arbitrator said, noting that the agreement did not distinguish between partial and complete shutdowns (*Interstate Brands Corp.*, 121 LA 143).

● An employer in the motion picture industry was justified in changing the status of employees so they would no longer be guaranteed a 40-hour workweek, an arbitrator held. After suffering a business reduction due to a strike, the employer converted some employees from weekly employees, who were guaranteed at least 40 hours of work per week, to daily employees, who only were guaranteed four hours per day. Based on the collective bargaining agreement's "plain language," the arbitrator found that the employer had the "managerial discretion" to make the status changes and cut hours rather than laying off employees according to seniority (*Burbank Studios*, 92 LA 1094).

● An employer was justified in reducing the workweek of proofreaders from five days to four days under a contract provision stating that the employer's right to shorten or lengthen hours would not be restricted, an arbitrator held. The arbitrator disagreed with the union's claim that past practice should govern the decision, finding that a single instance in which the least senior person had been laid off under similar circumstances was not sufficient to constitute past practice (*Rochester Monotype Composition Co. Inc.*, 77 LA 474).

1. Group Affected by Worksharing

An issue that sometimes arises in disputes over worksharing is whether hours can be cut for one group of employees while other groups are still operating on a full schedule.

● An employer had the right to schedule a four-day workweek for employees in its manufacturing department during a time period in which a regular workweek was scheduled for employees in its parts depot and export departments, an arbitrator decided, where the contract gave the employer the right to schedule four-day workweeks upon compliance with certain requirements. Pointing out that the manufacturing employees on the four-day workweek were not on layoff but on a contractually permissible shortened workweek, the arbitrator concluded that the fact that the depot and export employees were not placed on a four-day workweek did not convert the scheduling change into a reduction in force that required application of layoff procedures (*Hyster Co.*, 66 LA 522).

● An employer properly scheduled its most junior first-shift employees for a four-day workweek in an attempt to avoid a "full-scale" layoff, even though there were employees with less seniority on the second shift. At issue was whether the employer's action constituted a layoff or a reduction in hours of work. The arbitrator agreed with the employer's contention that only a reduction in work hours had occurred. Consequently, the arbitrator held that the employer was not obligated to allow senior employees on the first shift to bump junior employees on the second shift because the seniority rights governing layoffs and bumping did not apply to the situation at hand (*Eagle Crest Foods Inc.*, 95 LA 482).

B. Worksharing Arrangements Rejected

In some cases, arbitrators refuse to uphold worksharing arrangements on the basis that they conflict with contract terms governing the hours of work. In other cases, arbitrators conclude that cutbacks in hours are tantamount to layoffs. Thus, where contractual provisions make seniority a controlling factor in layoff situations, they reject across-the-board schedule reductions that affect senior and junior employees alike.

● An employer violated a collective bargaining agreement when it reduced the workweek from five eight-hour days to four eight-hour days during a period of economic problems, an arbitrator ruled. While acknowledging the employer's "desire to stay flexible," the arbitrator found that the contract explicitly stated that senior employees were to be protected from reductions in employment through the layoff of more junior workers in situations where there was not enough full-time work to go around (*Northwest Automatic Products Inc.*, 117 LA 465).

• Where a letter of understanding specified that senior employees would have the first opportunity to work a full schedule and junior employees would be laid off to protect the employment of senior employees, an arbitrator held that an employer was prohibited from implementing a reduction in hours. Even though the contract did not guarantee a certain amount of work, it defined the regular schedule as 40 hours per week, the arbitrator noted. Based on the obligations outlined in the letter of understanding, the arbitrator ordered the employer to refrain from reducing the hours of senior employees "except in cases of emergency or where it is clearly unavoidable" (*Fisher Nut Co.*, 89 LA 1313).

• An arbitrator held that a public utility lacked the authority to reduce the workweek during a period when it was experiencing financial problems. By implementing an across-the-board reduction of the workweek, the employer circumvented its contractual obligations, which called for layoffs in order of seniority in response to such a situation, the arbitrator found. To remedy the contract violation, the arbitrator ordered the employer to make up for the losses in pay experienced by employees whose seniority would have kept them from being laid off during the period in question (*Arkansas-Missouri Power Co.*, 74 LA 1254).

• An employer suffering a significant reduction in business committed a contract violation when it reduced the workweek for all employees by closing its plant on Fridays and scheduling employees for less than a full week's work, an arbitrator ruled. Noting that the contract defined a "regular workweek" as consisting of five days and 40 hours, the arbitrator found that the employer's action constituted a layoff, and the employer was required to follow seniority in making layoffs (*Yaffe Printing Co.*, 101 LA 1019).

• An arbitrator ruled that an employer violated a seniority layoff clause when it instituted one- and two-day plant shutdowns. The arbitrator rejected the employer's contention that a separate clause concerning "changes in customer requirements" was applicable. According to the arbitrator, that clause concerned only "unforeseen, unpredictable, unplanned and unanticipated conditions," which the present situation—a slow business period—was not (*Tecumseh Products Co.*, 65 LA 471).

• Another arbitrator awarded back pay to senior employees to reflect the amount of work their employer improperly assigned to junior employees during a business lull. The employer claimed that the seniority protections applicable to layoff situations did not constrain its ability to schedule employees for "short-time" work when production demands became irregular and unpredictable. Rejecting that argument, the arbitrator found that the reduced work schedules were tantamount to layoffs, and the employer committed a contract violation by failing to give due consideration to seniority in scheduling employees to perform the available work (*Lufkin Industries*, 90 LA 301).

• A municipal employer reduced the workweek by cutting one eight-hour day each week for all bargaining unit members rather than laying off some employees, saying that it was a management right to schedule employees as it deemed necessary to serve the needs of the community. An arbitrator held that the employer committed a contract violation in cutting the workweek. Under the contract, the employer could not change work schedules without the consent of the union except in emergency situations. Because the events necessitating a reduced work schedule were foreseeable, no true emergency existed, the arbitrator found (*Ambridge Borough*, 73 LA 810).

1. Contract Terms Allow Reduced Hours

Even in cases where the terms of collective bargaining agreements permit reduced work schedules, arbitrators sometimes find that employers have failed to comply with contractual requirements for implementing worksharing.

• An employer could not institute layoffs while operating on a reduced schedule, an arbitrator held. A contractual provision allowed the employer to reduce the work schedule to 32 hours per week for a period of up to six weeks per year if business conditions necessitated cutbacks. Although the same contract provision allowed the employer to resort to layoffs if further cutbacks were needed, it stated that employees who remained on the job would be entitled to a 40-hour workweek. The union objected to the proposed layoff of six employees during a period when the employer had instituted the 32-hour schedule, contending that the employer had to choose between a reduction in hours and a reduction in force. Agreeing with the union, the arbitrator found that the contract required the employer to discontinue the reduced schedule if any regular employees were to be laid off (*Rotex Inc.*, 79 LA 726; see also 64 LA 1085).

● A steel mill improperly reduced employees' hours during a period of sluggish demand for its products, an arbitrator found. The employer had no special requirements to meet as long as employees worked an average of at least 32 hours per week. When decreases below that level were imminent, the employer was supposed to meet with the grievance committee and decide between a reduction in force and an equal distribution of work among employees. In the event the parties could not agree, the contract required layoffs. Without obtaining the agreement of the grievance committee, the employer kept a group of more than 100 employees working less than 32 hours per week for a period of eight weeks. Finding that the employer failed to follow the required steps, the arbitrator ordered the employer to make the affected employees whole for the wages they lost as a result of the improper reduction in their hours (*USS, Division of USX Corp.*, 100 LA 827).

● Where a union and employer had negotiated a contract clause stating that "either the hours per day or the days per week could be reduced by mutual agreement," an arbitrator held that the employer could not institute a four-day workweek in the face of union objections. The employer argued that

the contract gave it the right to implement worksharing, and the union's role was limited to approving either a reduction in hours per day or days per week. The arbitrator disagreed, finding that the employer had to have the union's consent before proceeding with any form of worksharing. Given that there was no consent by the union, the employer's proper course of action was to implement layoffs by seniority, the arbitrator concluded (*Aro Corp.*, 55 LA 859).

● One collective bargaining agreement stated that when it became necessary to make layoffs involving employees with two or more years of service, operations would be reduced to a single shift or to a 32-hour week before further layoffs were made. An arbitrator held that this clearly required the employer to lay off all employees with less than two years' service before reducing the workweek to 32 hours (*Aetna Ball & Roller Bearing Co.*, 22 LA 453).

● Another agreement required an employer to reduce the workweek to 32 hours before any layoffs could occur. The employer claimed it could make layoffs to eliminate the night shift instead of reducing hours as long as the volume of work did not drop enough to justify instituting a 32-hour week. An arbitrator ruled that the employer could not lay off employees as long as there was enough work to keep everybody working for 32 hours or more per week (*Babcock Printing Press Corp.*, 10 LA 396).

● Similarly, a contract stated that when work slowed down in any department, an employer would be required to reduce hours to 32 per week for 30 days before making any layoffs. The employer reduced the workweek for one class of employees within a department, but not for others. An arbitrator said this action was a violation of the contract because the employer could not implement a reduction of hours for one class of employees while maintaining regular schedules for other classes of employees in the same department. The arbitrator awarded pay for the time lost by those employees whose hours were cut (*Mueller Brass Co.*, 3 LA 271).

VI. Recall From Layoff [LA CDI 117.121]

OVERVIEW

The interplay between seniority and ability is a major theme in recall situations, just as it is in determining the order of layoff and the bumping rights of employees. In many disputes over recalls, unions object that employers have violated laid-off employees' seniority rights by denying them available work, while employers counter that junior employees have been properly recalled on the basis of their skills, qualifications, efficiency, experience, or similar factors.

The outcome of such disputes usually depends on the balance struck between seniority and ability in the applicable contract language. At one end of the spectrum are collective bargaining agreements requiring recall by seniority, though many such agreements allow exceptions in the event that senior employees lack necessary skills or the ability to handle the available work. At the opposite end of the spectrum are contracts that emphasize ability and mention seniority merely as a means of deciding between employees who are substantially equal in terms of their skills and ability.

In addition to disagreeing about the amount of emphasis seniority should receive, unions and employers often lock horns over the type of seniority used in conducting recalls. For example, one party might claim that plant-wide seniority should be used in determining who returns to work first, while the other party might argue that recalls should be conducted according to employees' seniority within a particular department or job classification.

Other questions that frequently surface in recall situations include the following:

• Do shop stewards or other union officials have superseniority that gives them special recall rights?

• What procedures must employers use in providing notification of recalls, and how much time do employees have to respond to recall notices?

• Are employees required to accept any job offered to them, or can they reject an undesirable position and still retain their recall rights?

• Can employers impose fitness standards in connection with recalls or require employees to undergo examinations before returning to work?

This chapter provides numerous examples of arbitration cases addressing the issues mentioned above and, in so doing, illustrates the factors arbitrators typically consider in resolving recall-related disputes.

SUMMARY OF CASES

A. Seniority Versus Ability

Seniority almost always plays a role in determining the order of employees' recall from layoff, but it is seldom the only consideration. Some collective bargaining agreements allow employers to consider ability in certain situations, such as where senior employees lack the necessary skills or experience to perform the available work, while other contracts go even further, making ability the predominant factor governing the order of recall. When the resolution of recall-related disputes hinges on the balance between seniority and ability, arbitrators must examine the applicable contract language to determine if the appropriate weight has been given to each factor.

• Although a contract referenced skills and qualifications as criteria affecting the order of layoff, an employer did not have the right to apply the same criteria to its recall procedures, an arbitrator ruled. Noting that the contract contained a separate clause that mentioned seniority alone as a consideration in recall decisions, the arbitrator said employees had to be recalled strictly according to their seniority. Thus, the employer committed a contract violation by recalling junior employees with special training, the arbitrator found (*Hughes Aircraft Co.*, 101 LA 415).

• An arbitrator upheld an employer that did not recall four senior employees, but retained junior employees who had skills and abilities to perform and complete the job requirements in a workmanlike manner (*Bruns Belmont Construction Inc.*, 125 LA 505).

• Where a contract contained a general seniority clause but was silent on the issue of how seniority would factor into recalls, an arbitrator determined that an employer had an obligation to recall a senior employee who had sufficient ability to perform the available work. Despite the absence of a contract clause specifying a recall procedure, the arbitrator decided that the employer could not bypass the senior employee just because a junior employee was somewhat more proficient (*Laher Battery Production Corp.*, 11 LA 41).

• A past record of poor attendance did not justify an employer's refusal to rehire a laid-off employee under a contract that made seniority the controlling consideration in recalls, an arbitrator found. The employer should not have factored the employee's attendance record into its recall decision, the arbitrator decided, because this was something that should have been disposed of at the time the absences occurred. Such a past offense could not be used as the basis for indefinitely denying future job opportunities, the arbitrator held (*The Cleveland-Cliffs Iron Co.*, 24 LA 599).

• An arbitrator determined that an employer should have recalled laid-off senior employees who required some training on new, complex machinery rather than bring back junior employees who had been taught to use the machines before the layoff. In a case where recalls were to be conducted according to seniority and ability, but qualifications were not explicitly mentioned in the recall clause, the arbitrator decided that basic ability to learn to do the work as well as a training period were implied in the contract (*Thiokol Corp.*, 65 LA 1265; see also 76 LA 932, 76 LA 575, 76 LA 540).

• An arbitrator held that an employer committed a contract violation when it recalled a number of employees without giving due consideration to seniority. The parties' collective bargaining agreement provided that laid-off employees would be recalled to work on the basis of their "length of service and the ability to step into and perform the work of the job at the time the job is awarded." Finding that a number of laid-off employees who met the rehire criteria had been passed over in favor of workers with less seniority, the arbitrator ordered the employer to provide back pay to the employees who should have been recalled (*Sunnyside Coal Co.*, 104 LA 886).

● An employer failed to follow proper recall procedures when it shut down production in order to go back and correct defective work, an arbitrator ruled. To correct the defects, the employer recalled junior employees from its rework department, which was being phased out. However, the parties' collective bargaining agreement provided that senior employees would have priority as long as they were qualified to perform the work. Recalling the junior employees without the union's consent constituted a contract violation, the arbitrator said, noting that the employer failed to show that the senior employees were not qualified to handle the work (*Flxible Corp.*, 94 LA 158).

● On the other hand, where a contract said the ability of employees would have to be equal before seniority could come into play, an employer had no obligation to recall a senior worker ahead of junior employees who were capable of performing certain tasks that the senior worker could not do, an arbitrator ruled. The employee could only prevail if the evidence showed that he was able to handle all of the work performed by the junior employees, but the employee and the union failed to meet that burden, the arbitrator found (*Latrobe Construction Co.*, 114 LA 311).

● Under a contract that based the order of recall on seniority, provided that senior employees were qualified for the available positions, an employer was justified in recalling a junior employee for a job as a pump specialist based on his relevant experience, an arbitrator decided. The union argued that a senior employee should have

received a trial period to determine whether she was capable of performing the work, but the arbitrator noted that the contract only called for trial periods in job bidding situations. Recall from layoff is very different, the arbitrator declared, because the need to maintain efficiency is heightened in periods when the workforce has undergone a contraction. Adding that "employees who exercise recall rights must be able to do the job without undue delay," the arbitrator said the employer was not required to give the job to the senior employee, who would have needed training to become qualified for the position (*Aurora Pump*, 120 LA 1522).

● In another case, an arbitrator ruled that an employer had the right to recall a junior employee instead of a senior worker to do shop tasks and repair work on a railroad crane. The junior employee had done most of the original work on the crane when it was custom-built for a customer, and the customer had specifically asked that the junior employee do the repair work, the arbitrator observed (*T. Bruce Sales*, 81 LA 481).

● An arbitrator upheld an employer's refusal to recall a senior typesetter from layoff because he lacked the proper computer skills to operate a newly installed computer publishing system. The parties' labor contract gave the employer the right to have "sufficient qualified employees" to perform necessary work on all shifts at all times, the arbitrator said, adding that the senior employee also failed to practice on a computer on his own time or take outside computer courses as was contractually required and as other employees had done (*Type House + Duragraph*, 102 LA 225).

● Under a contract that gave precedence in recalls to employees with superior ability, an employer was justified in passing over a senior employee who had been rated by supervisors as having the lowest capability and skills among the workers on its recall list, an arbitrator held. The employer and the union apparently recognized the potential detriments of making seniority the predominant factor in retention and recall decisions, as evidenced by the fact that their contract gave primary emphasis to the skills and capability of employees, relegating seniority to a secondary consideration that would only come into play if ability was equal, the arbitrator observed. Because the employer's assessment of the senior employee ranked him as the least qualified employee subject to recall, "his seniority was not applicable to the decision process," the arbitrator concluded (*A-1 Door and Building Solutions*, 123 LA 1286).

• Under a similar contract, which made seniority the deciding factor only if ability, skill, and efficiency were equal, an arbitrator found that an employer was justified in recalling two junior employees to their jobs while bypassing five senior employees. The union argued that the senior employees were qualified for the positions. However, the arbitrator found that they would have needed a break-in period before they could do the work proficiently, whereas the junior employees were the most efficient on the jobs in question at the time of recall. In light of the fact that the contract made seniority controlling only where efficiency already was equal, the arbitrator denied the grievance (*Curtis Companies Inc.*, 29 LA 50).

• An employer did not commit a contract violation by having employees perform overtime while a senior worker, who was experienced in the tasks, remained on layoff, an arbitrator held. According to the arbitrator, the employee's recall rights would have been triggered only if a recall or hiring added to the number of employees in his former classification. Determining the size of the workforce is a basic right of management, and ordering the employer to rehire the employee would have interfered with that right, the arbitrator concluded (*Avco Corp.*, 63 LA 288).

• Another arbitrator found that an employer was justified in not recalling a senior employee under a contract that based recall on seniority so long as an employee could "do the job in a reasonably efficient manner." A dispute arose when a junior employee, who was the only qualified operator of a new machine, went to work on a less advanced machine while the new one was being repaired. A laid-off senior employee claimed he should have been recalled to work on the older machine, but the arbitrator disagreed. Although the junior employ-

ee was prevented from operating the new machine while it was being repaired, working on that piece of equipment was a major part of his duties, the arbitrator noted (*Eagle-Picher Industries Inc.*, 65 LA 1108).

• An arbitrator determined that an employer that shut down operations to do equipment repairs and laid off all employees for five days did not violate its labor contract by recalling certain junior employees before recalling more senior workers whose crew was on a regularly scheduled day off. The standard reverse-order recall did not apply in this case because all employees were laid off at the same time, and recall by seniority would have conflicted with other contract language, the arbitrator said. In addition, work time and time off would be balanced among the various crews very quickly because the junior employees soon would be on their regularly scheduled day off while the affected senior crew worked, the arbitrator observed (*Asarco Inc.*, 102 LA 795).

B. Type of Seniority Used in Recalls

Unions and employers sometimes disagree over the type of seniority that should be used to determine the order of recalls. Although plant-wide seniority is likely to allow the earliest possible return to work for those employees with the greatest overall length of service, collective bargaining agreements commonly stipulate that recalls are to be based on seniority within a particular department or job classification, which effectively narrows the pool of positions available to senior employees.

• An arbitrator held that an employer properly relied on an employee's seniority within her department as the basis for recalling her ahead of an employee from another department who had an earlier date of hire. The parties' collective bargaining agreement clearly and unambiguously stated that "seniority shall be by departments," and the employer fully complied with the agreement in conducting the recall, the arbitrator said (*Interior Inc.*, 117 LA 1425).

• An employer was justified in recalling the most junior of a group of workers while employees from other classifications with more seniority remained on layoff, an arbitrator ruled. The parties' collective bargaining agreement provided for the use of seniority within job classifications in conducting layoffs, stating that reductions in force would be made "on a classification basis plant-wide." The phrase "plant-wide" referred to the scope within which the "classification basis" would operate, the arbitrator said, meaning "that throughout the plant, reductions in force shall be made by seniority within those classifications to be reduced." In reference to recalls, the contract required the order of layoffs to be reversed, and the use of classification seniority remained in effect, the arbitrator found. Thus, the recalled employee, though junior to other laid-off employees from other classifications, was brought back to work in conformance with the parties' labor agreement, the arbitrator held (*Miba Bearings U.S. LLC*, 119 LA 826).

• An employer did not commit a contract violation by overlooking plant-wide seniority when recalling an employee to its shipping department, an arbitrator ruled. When another employee argued that she was entitled to the job based on her plant-wide seniority, the employer defended its action by pointing out that the recalled employee had worked in the shipping department and had the experience necessary to handle the job without extensive training. Although the contract specified the use of plant-wide seniority in most recall situations, it also stated that employees had to "meet the qualifications" of the position into which they wanted to move, the arbitrator noted. Shipping was not specifically mentioned as a department that would be exempt from the application of plant-wide seniority, but the recall of the junior employee was warranted because of the unique training and experience required in the job, the arbitrator decided (*Kellogg's Snacks*, 119 LA 1365).

• In another case, an employer applied plant-wide seniority in recalling a maintenance mechanic to perform general production work, but an arbitrator determined that the decision constituted a violation of a production employee's seniority rights. The parties' collective bargaining agreement required the employer to keep the senior-

ity of production workers and mechanics separate. Regardless of the maintenance mechanic's plant-wide seniority, he should not have been recalled to perform production work while anyone from that department remained on layoff, the arbitrator held (*Crane/Cor Tec Co.*, 91 LA 763).

• An employer violated its labor contract when it kept an employee on layoff and brought in someone from another job classification to perform work in the employee's classification, an arbitrator ruled. The employer pointed out that the worker who was brought in possessed critical skills in a related classification, and, even though there was not enough work in that area to keep him occupied on a full-time basis, his retention was important to the employer's operations. According to the arbitrator, however, the contract expressly required layoffs and recalls to be conducted according to seniority within individual job classifications. The arbitrator acknowledged that the employer had valid reasons for wanting to retain the other worker while trimming its payroll, but the evidence showed that there was enough work in the laid-off employee's classification to justify his recall. Thus, the arbitrator ordered the employer to reinstate the employee and make him whole (*Associated Universities Inc.*, 105 LA 1041).

• When an employer combined two groups of workers for seniority purposes, a laid-off employee moved up the dovetailed seniority list far enough to trigger his recall, an arbitrator found. During contract negotiations, the parties agreed to combine the pipefitter and welding classifications, which resulted in the dovetailing of two formerly separate seniority lists. Because the contract also provided for the execution of layoffs, bumping, and recalls in order of seniority, the laid-off employee's movement up the combined list gave him the right to return to work and displace another worker who was now lower on the dovetailed seniority list, the arbitrator decided (*Pennwalt Corp.*, 90 LA 756).

C. Superseniority for Union Officials

Many collective bargaining agreements provide "superseniority" for shop stewards and other union officials as a way of maintaining continuity in representational activities such as grievance processing and contract administration. Although disputes over superseniority usually focus on keeping union representatives from being swept up in layoffs in the first place, conflicts over the application of superseniority to recalls can also arise under certain circumstances. For example, arbitrators might be asked to determine whether employees gain special recall rights if they are elected to union office while on layoff.

• One arbitrator held that an employer was justified in failing to recall an employee who acquired superseniority when he was elected to union office while on layoff. The employer did not have to recall the employee until there was a job opening for which he was qualified, the arbitrator said, noting that the purpose of superseniority was to ensure continuity in the administration of the contract, not to make jobs for union representatives (*Queen City Industries*, 33 LA 794; see also 75 LA 261).

• Stewards who represented assemblers could not claim that their superseniority gave them precedence in recall when the assemblers were recalled to work in a different type of job, an arbitrator ruled. The jurisdiction of the stewards did not extend to other categories of jobs, and thus their superseniority did not come into play when the assemblers were recalled to work in another capacity, the arbitrator reasoned (*Textron Inc.*, 83 LA 931).

• An arbitrator held that an employee who was elected to a grievance committeeman position while on layoff was not entitled to be recalled ahead of a more senior employee. According to the arbitrator, contract language granting superseniority applied only to the order of layoff and was silent on the issue of recall from layoff. Any "provision granting superseniority protection must be narrowly construed within the specific contractual grant of such protection," the arbitrator said, pointing out that in this instance contract provisions on superseniority were clearly limited, and recall from layoff was to be awarded based solely on normal seniority (*Amerimark Building Products Inc.*, 104 LA 1066).

• *By contrast*, another arbitrator held that employees gained immediate recall rights by virtue of being elected as stewards while on layoff. The parties' collective bargaining agreement gave stewards superseniority over other employees on their shift, as well as the right to remain in the group they represented. The employees' assumption of the role of steward automatically entitled them to preferential seniority, the arbitrator found, adding that the employer's refusal to recall the newly elected stewards frustrated the rights of bargaining unit members to be represented by individuals of their own choosing (*Lydall Eastern Inc.*, 85 LA 329).

• A steward should have been recalled on a construction project once an employer brought two carpenters back to work, an arbitrator decided. The union had assigned a third carpenter as job steward when two other carpenters were originally assigned to the construction project. After the carpenters' work was suspended to allow other trades to do their jobs, the steward was denied recall even though one of the original carpenters and another were rehired. The employer argued that it was a specialty contractor that only had to have a "shop steward" to serve as steward for all jobs requiring fewer than three workers. The arbitrator disagreed, finding there was no contract language requiring a shop steward to perform all the functions of a steward (*Master Builders' Association of Western Pennsylvania Inc.*, 63 LA 664; see also 74 LA 987).

• Under a contract that did not provide for an assessment of employees' relative ability but instead gave recall precedence to union representatives with a basic capability to handle the work in question, an employer improperly passed over a grievance committeeman for a temporary assignment and instead brought in another employee who had longer service and was considered better able to perform the work, an arbitrator found. The evidence did not support the employer's contention that the grievance committeeman could not handle the assignment, which involved reviewing and sorting records from part of the employer's operations that had been shut down. Even if the other employee had superior ability, the contract still required the recall of the grievance committeeman, the arbitrator held, ordering the employer to make the committeeman whole for all monies lost (*United States Steel Corp.*, 85 LA 1113).

D. Recall Scheduling, Notification, and Response

Collective bargaining agreements commonly specify a particular method for employers to use in providing notification of recalls, as well as deadlines for responding to the notices. Disputes involving such provisions tend to arise when employees fail to respond within the required time frame, leaving arbitrators to decide whether deficient recall notices caused the problem or the employees themselves were at fault.

• An arbitrator ruled that employees laid off in 2007 are entitled to be recalled more than three years later in fall of 2010, even though a collective bargaining contract ratified in the spring of 2010 said that recall rights were for a "period equal to the length of this Agreement," where the term for the agreement in effect in 2007 was for five years. The arbitrator found that the parties never discussed their "intentions" concerning how a change in a contract term would impact recall rights, which affected 71 laid-off employees. Forfeiture of recall rights should not occur absent language permitting no other reasonable conclusion and showing the "unmistakable intention" to work such a forfeiture, the arbitrator said, finding the recall rights were those established in the prior five-year contract (*CertainTeed Corp.*, 128 LA 1092).

• An employer should not have unilaterally changed its layoff scheduling practices, from automatically reassigning temporarily laid-off employees to lower classifications while paying them at their higher regular classification pay rate to permitting laid-off employees to bid on work in a lower classification at that classification's pay rate, an arbitrator ruled. The agreement stipulated that employees working out of the classification "shall" be paid at a higher classification pay rate unless they volunteered to work out of classification, the laid-off employees were not truly "vol-

unteering" for lower-classification work, and the past practice was to use the higher regular-classification pay rate (*American Spirit Graphics Corp.*, 126 LA 802).

• An employer that failed to provide proper recall notification could not penalize an employee who missed a deadline for returning to work, an arbitrator ruled. Although the parties' collective bargaining agreement specified that recalled employees would be notified by registered letter, the employer merely sent a union steward a request to inform employees to come to the plant for recall. The steward failed, however, to tell one employee, and she was permanently laid off when she did not report to the plant within a contractually established five-day period. The arbitrator decided that the employee had not been notified as prescribed by the contract, or for that matter, in any way at all, and ordered that she be reinstated with full seniority and back pay (*Ohmer Corp.*, 13 LA 364).

• An arbitrator overturned an airline's termination of two pilots who did not respond to recall notices until about three weeks after they were sent. The parties' collective bargaining agreement expressly stated that employees were required to respond with seven days of receiving notification of a recall. Because of the delay in the employees' response, the airline treated them as having voluntarily resigned. However, the employees had been out of town when the notices were sent. According to the arbitrator, the airline had no right to terminate the pilots' employment, because the contract allowed them seven days to respond after "receipt" of notification, and they met that deadline after they returned home and actually got the recall notices (*Pan American Airways Corp.*, 119 LA 1814).

• In a case where a recall notice was not properly delivered to an employee, an employer could not hold the employee responsible for failing to respond on time, an arbitrator determined. The employer complied with contractual requirements by mailing a notice to the apartment house where the employee lived, but through postal service error, the notice went to the wrong unit. When the employee failed to report on time, the employer stripped him of his seniority, which meant he no longer had a right to return to work. While noting that the employer technically met its obligation in providing the recall notice, the arbitrator said the employee's failure to receive the notice was not his fault. Consequently, the arbitrator ordered the employer to restore the employee's seniority and give him back pay (*Levinson Steel Co.*, 23 LA 135).

● In another case, an arbitrator overturned an employer's termination of an employee who failed to respond to a recall notice within 72 hours. The employer had sent one telegram notifying the employee he was up for rehire, and when there was no response, dispatched a second telegram telling the employee to report back to work the next day. Because the employee was out of town, however, he did not find the telegrams until later, and when he reported for work he learned that he had been fired for failing to respond within 72 hours of the first notice. The arbitrator overturned the discharge, finding that it was reasonable for the employee to have expected the second telegram to grant him a second 72 hours, which expired on the afternoon of the day he reported for work (*Ameron Inc.*, 64 LA 517).

● *By contrast*, an arbitrator ruled that an employer was justified in refusing to rehire a laid-off employee. The employer had sent the required notice of recall to the employee, but the employee failed to provide the contractually required response in which he would state his desire to return to work. Responsibility for adhering to contractual requirements runs both ways, the arbitrator observed, concluding that absent any discriminatory intention or result, the employer legitimately refused to rehire the employee (*Challenge-Cook Bros. Inc.*, 65 LA 533).

● Similarly, an arbitrator upheld the termination of an employee who apparently either intentionally avoided receiving a recall notice or at least ignored it and its requirements (*Blackmer Pump Co.*, 20 LA 238).

● Where a contract gave workers 24 hours to respond to recall notices, an employer was justified in treating an employee's failure to respond within that time frame as a voluntary quit, an arbitrator ruled. Noting that the employee had been through the layoff and recall process many times, the arbitrator dismissed the union's contention that the employee was unfamiliar with the contract's recall notice and voluntary-quit provisions. It was the employee's responsibility to know the terms and conditions of the contract and what he should do when recalled, the arbitrator said (*The Stroh Brewery Co.*, 92 LA 930).

● An airline did not commit a contract violation by terminating a pilot who refused a second recall, an arbitrator held. In this case, the employee had the option of refusing a job but remaining a viable candidate for recall as long as there were enough junior pilots to fill the employer's roster. In a telephone conversation with the company's chief pilot, when the employee asked if he would have a secure future with the employer if he returned, he was told no such assurances could be made. The various options and alternatives were clearly laid out for him in that exchange, the arbitrator said, and when he rejected the second recall offer, he knew or should have known that he was triggering contract provisions that mandated his termination (*Air Transport International LLC*, 119 LA 429).

1. Pay Issues Related to Delays

Employees sometimes claim that they are entitled to compensation when they experience delays in returning to work because of recall notification problems. As illustrated by the following examples, arbitrators' rulings in such cases depend largely on the applicable contract language and the circumstances causing the delays.

● An employer was not obligated to compensate two employees for work time they lost when initial recall letters sent by their employer did not reach them, an arbitrator ruled. The employer used a two-step notification procedure consisting of an initial contact by telephone or first-class mail, followed, if necessary, by a certified letter sent a week later. When the return of two employees was delayed because they did not receive their initial recall letters, the union contended that the employer should have sent the initial notices using certified mail. While acknowledging that the employees lost pay through no fault of their own, the arbitrator rejected the union's contention that the employer should be required to make them whole. The parties' collective bargaining agreement merely obligated the employer to use reasonable means of notifying employees of a recall, and that requirement was satisfied by the employer's two-step procedure, which had worked effectively in recalling numerous other workers over a period of years, the arbitrator said (*Warren Molded Plastics Inc.*, 76 LA 739).

• Where a telephone call from an employer did not constitute proper recall notification, an arbitrator found that an employee's layoff lasted long enough to make him eligible for severance pay. Under the parties' collective bargaining agreement, the severance pay entitlement kicked in after six weeks of layoff. The employer called the employee after five weeks, but the employee did not get the message and only found out about the recall when he received written notification a week later. After returning to work, the employee claimed he was due severance pay because he had been out of work for six weeks. The arbitrator agreed in spite of the fact that the employer had attempted to reach the employee at the five-week point. Because the contract required written notification, the telephone call to the employee did not trigger recall, the arbitrator said, ordering the employer to give the employee severance pay (*Manville Forest Products Corp.*, 92 LA 681).

E. Refusal to Accept Proffered Job

Disputes occasionally arise in recall situations because employees are faced with moving into lower-paying or undesirable jobs. If collective bargaining agreements do not give employees a choice in the matter, the refusal to accept a proffered job can trigger the loss of their recall and seniority rights. In many cases, however, arbitrators find that employees are entitled to hold out for better positions or at least keep their former pay rates.

• An employer committed a contract violation by stripping a laid-off employee of

his seniority after he rejected a recall for two days of work per week, an arbitrator ruled. The parties' collective bargaining agreement contained a guarantee of 40 hours' work per week for full-time employees, and the employer's past practice was to interpret "guarantee" to mean that employees were entitled to 40 hours in any week in which they worked, the arbitrator found. In overturning the employer's action, the arbitrator awarded the employee back pay as well as a contract-signing bonus that he would have received if he had been properly recalled (*S & S Meat Co.*, 97 LA 873).

• An employer could not bypass a senior employee for recall after he insisted on waiting for a position in his own department rather than accepting another job his employer offered him, an arbitrator held. When the employee's department began conducting recalls, the employer brought in workers with less seniority, asserting that the employee had waived his right to recall by refusing the other job. Under the parties' collective bargaining agreement, however, employees were permitted to take a layoff instead of a transfer to another department, the arbitrator noted. Thus, he concluded that the employee could refuse the job offer in a different department without losing his right to be recalled to his own department in line with his seniority (*International Harvester Co.*, 22 LA 773; see also 88 LA 639).

• Although an employee had accepted an assignment to a lower-rated position in a layoff situation, he was subsequently entitled to exercise his recall rights and return to his former labor grade, an arbitrator decided. The employee had lost his position as a welder and gone from labor grade nine to labor grade one. Although there were no openings for welders, he claimed the right to return to labor grade nine when a job as a press operator became available. The employer argued that the employee only had a right to return to the welder job, but the arbitrator disagreed. He said recalls had to be conducted in reverse of layoffs, which meant that the employee was entitled to move back up through the grades until he returned to his former grade, even if that meant switching to a different job than the

318 GRIEVANCE GUIDE

one he previously held (*Johnson Controls Inc.*, 84 LA 629).

● After returning from layoff to a lower-paying job, an employee was entitled to receive his former wage rate for 15 days, an arbitrator found. The parties' collective bargaining agreement allowed employees to retain their former pay rates for 15 consecutive working days after transferring to lower-rated jobs, and the union contended that the employee's situation should have been treated as a transfer because he was required to accept the job offered by the employer or lose his seniority. The employer, which had paid the employee at his former rate for only five days, claimed that the pay requirement for transfers did not apply in recall situations. The arbitrator rejected the employer's argument and sided with the union, noting that the word "transfer" meant shifting or changing from one job to another, which fit the employee's situation even though he was on layoff when his job change was put into effect (*National Can Corp.*, 25 LA 177).

● An employer did not violate a collective bargaining contract when it reassigned an employee who worked at the Branson facility to perform some deliveries at the Springfield facility, even though there was an employee on layoff there, where assignment was temporary and was consistent with business needs, an arbitrator ruled. And, in bargaining, the employer had rejected a union proposal that the employee on layoff had to be offered work before any transfer would be permitted (*Nattinger Materials Co.*, 126 LA 1655).

● Similarly, another arbitrator ruled an employer was within its rights when it did not return the former union president to a position as salesman but gave him an open position as a merchandiser, where there was nothing in the contract to indicate that he was on leave during his nine years as president or that he could bump back into that job. The employer had discontinued placing the president's name and seniority date on the seniority lists it regularly posted and furnished to the union, which the union did not protest (*R.L. Lipton Distributing*, 126 LA 1502).

● After eliminating a production line, an employer was justified in recalling the affected employees to lower-rated positions and reducing their pay, an arbitrator ruled. The union contended that the employees' wages should have been protected, citing contract language providing that "[w]hen an employee is assigned to work on a job that is in a level lower than his regularly classified level, he shall be paid at the rate of his regularly classified level." However, the arbitrator found that the language in question referred to temporary assignments. It did not apply to the recalled employees, because they were permanently reassigned following the elimination of their former jobs, the arbitrator said (*Masonite International Door Fabrication Services*, 121 LA 1464).

F. Fitness Standards and Examinations

Arbitrators generally agree that, absent specific contract bans on the practice, employers can require employees to submit to physical examinations or other types of tests in conjunction with recalls, particularly if layoffs have lasted for an extended period of time. When employers apply examination requirements or fitness standards to returning employees, however, arbitrators generally agree that they cannot be more stringent than those applied to workers who are still on the job (22 LA 632, 11 LA 364, 8 LA 1015).

● An employer committed a contract violation by refusing to recall an employee based on his high blood pressure, an arbitrator ruled. When the employer had the employee undergo medical tests, it found that his blood pressure was higher than what was allowed for new employees but within the range allowed for current employees. According to the arbitrator, the contract contained no provision for denying recall rights to a laid-off employee whose physical condition would have been acceptable if he were still working for the employer (*Allegheny Ludlum Steel Corp.*, 25 LA 214).

● An employer did not follow proper procedures when it refused to rehire a senior employee because of his past medical problems, an arbitrator ruled. Rather than relying on the employee's old medical information, the employer should have required a new medical examination at the time of the recall, because its practice with other workers was to base fitness determinations on their current medical information, the arbitrator said in ordering the employee's reinstatement (*National Lead Co.*, 42 LA 176).

• An arbitrator found that a dump-truck driver who lost his left hand and forearm in an accident while on layoff should have received the same recall opportunities as anyone else. The arbitrator noted that the employee had been fitted with a prosthetic device that enabled him to pass driving tests and drive a tractor. More rigorous standards could not be applied to the employee, but if doubts about his fitness for the job were to materialize later, his continued employment could be affected just as any other employee's would be, the arbitrator concluded (*Murphy Construction Co.*, 61 LA 503).

• Where an employer normally gave recalled employees "more tolerant treatment" in medical examinations than new hires, it could not subject a laid-off employee to the same examination as that given new hires and then deny him reinstatement on the basis of the examination's results, an arbitrator ruled. Adding that the employer's refusal to recall the employee was also based on the possibility of a recurrence of past back trouble, not on his present condition, the arbitrator decided that the employee was entitled to be rehired (*Weatherhead Co.*, 42 LA 513).

• In another case, even though an employee's physical condition was the same at the time of recall as it was when he was laid off, an arbitrator held that the employer could refuse to put him back to work for health reasons. The 300-pound employee had a heart murmur, and the employer's medic said it would endanger his health to resume working. According to the arbitrator, the fact that the man worked until he was laid off was no sign he was not endangering his health but merely indicated that the employer had not realized his condition was so serious. When the employer found out, it was justified in refusing to recall the employee, the arbitrator concluded (*Bethlehem Steel Co.*, 26 LA 514).

Part 5

Disability

I. Disability [LA CDI 100.552565 (public employees); 118.665]

OVERVIEW

When reviewing cases that involve workers with disabilities, arbitrators typically take their cues from the Americans with Disabilities Act of 1990 (42 U.S.C. § 12101 et seq.) and the ADA Amendments Act (ADAAA), effective Jan. 1, 2009. The ADA's prohibitions against disability-based discrimination in employment serves as a useful guide for arbitrators, even when they must apply the provisions of a specific collective bargaining agreement in resolving such cases.

For employees to be protected by the ADA as "qualified individuals with disabilities," they must have a covered disability and meet the qualification standards for the job in question. If employees lack a covered disability or cannot perform a job's essential functions, with or without reasonable accommodation, they are not entitled to the ADA's protections.

The issue of reasonable accommodation arises time and time again in disability-related arbitration cases. Under the ADA, employers must accommodate the known physical or mental limitations of otherwise qualified workers with disabilities unless the accommodations would pose an undue hardship. Before making accommodations, employers are entitled to request medical information substantiating employees' disability status.

Besides looking to the ADA for guidance in disability-related cases, arbitrators sometimes refer to the Rehabilitation Act of 1973 and state laws. The ADA's employment discrimination provisions mainly apply to private-sector employers and labor organizations, while the Rehabilitation Act's provisions cover government employers, colleges and universities, employers with more than $10,000 in federal contracts or subcontracts, and recipients of federal funds.

The ADA and the Rehabilitation Act use the same regulations for prohibiting disability-based discrimination in employment, but the Rehabilitation Act also includes affirmative action requirements for the hiring and advancement of workers with disabilities. State laws against disability bias sometimes extend broader protections, such as covering workers who are excluded under the ADA and the Rehabilitation Act.

SUMMARY OF CASES

A. Lack of Protected Status

Employees must meet two separate requirements in order to be considered "qualified individuals with disabilities" under federal law. First, employees must have a covered disability, which can be defined generally as a physical or mental impairment that substantially limits a major life activity, such as walking, seeing, hearing, speaking, or working. Second, they must meet the qualification standards for the job in question. If employees do not meet these requirements, they fail to qualify for protected status under the employment discrimination provisions of the ADA and the Rehab Act.

Some employees lack protected status because their impairments pose a direct threat to health or safety that cannot be removed through reasonable accommodation. Also excluded are workers with disorders caused by the current use of illegal drugs. Alcoholism is a covered disability, but employers can hold alcoholics to the same standards as other employees. For that matter, employers never have to reduce the performance standards for a job's essential functions in order to accommodate workers with disabilities.

● An arbitrator ruled that a city was not obligated to provide an electrician who had a 50-pound lifting restriction with a reasonable accommodation under the requirements of the pre-amendment Americans with Disabilities Act. The arbitrator found that courts had not deemed restrictions of 25 pounds or more to a be significant limitation to a recognized major life activity of lifting, and the fact that the employer perceived the employee as unable to perform

his job did not mean that it regarded him as having an impairment that substantially limited a major life activity (*City of Minneapolis*, 125 LA 558).

● An arbitrator rejected a claim that an employee's reassignment violated the ADA, finding that the worker did not qualify as disabled. The employee had a medical restriction that limited him to nine and one-half hours per day, and the employer transferred him to an untrained job so he could more easily be replaced by surplus workers when his shift ran long. The arbitrator rejected the argument that the employee was entitled to an accommodation in his former position. The employee was not protected by the ADA as a "qualified individual with a disability," the arbitrator said, because he did not have a physical or mental impairment that substantially limited any major life activities. The arbitrator found that when the employer reassigned the employee, it properly exercised its right to efficiently manage operations without violating any ADA or contract provisions (*Del Monte Foods*, 121 LA 1100).

● Despite physical impairments that hindered an employee's ability to climb or stand for prolonged periods, he did not have an ADA-covered disability, since his restrictions did not substantially limit any major life activities, an arbitrator decided. Notwithstanding the employee's lack of protected status, the arbitrator found that the employer's efforts to reassign the employee met the ADA's requirements. The employer could not be faulted for offering positions that required an interview or test, because the ADA does not require employers to abandon their nondiscriminatory standards defining qualifications, prerequisites, and entitlements to transfers, the arbitrator observed. When the employee turned down those offers and instead suggested the creation of a special job tailored to his limitations, the employer was justified in discharging him, the arbitrator said, noting that the ADA does not require the creation of a new position (*GTE North Inc.*, 113 LA 665).

• An inability to perform a job's customary duties disqualified another employee from ADA protection, an arbitrator found. The employee suffered an on-the-job injury that rendered him unable to perform his core job functions, even with reasonable accommodations. The employer discharged the employee based on its determination that he was not a "qualified individual with a disability" as defined under the ADA. The arbitrator agreed with that determination but found that the employer faced a broader obligation under a contract provision requiring it to return employees to their regular jobs following work-related injuries or "place such employees on other work if possible." In light of that provision, the arbitrator held that the employee was entitled to retraining for a different job that fit his work restrictions (*Techneglass Inc.*, 120 LA 722).

• An employer did not run afoul of the law by discharging an alcoholic employee for absenteeism, an arbitrator ruled. As a threshold requirement, employees with disabilities must be able to perform the essential functions of their jobs, but they cannot do so when they are absent, the arbitrator noted. In this case, the employee was not discharged because of his disability but because of his prior discipline and unexcused absences, the arbitrator said, and the employer was not required to excuse the employee's alcohol-related absences as an accommodation for his disability (*Andex Industries Inc.*, 111 LA 615).

• Termination of employment was appropriate for a receptionist who could not perform the essential functions of her job, an arbitrator ruled. The employee had a history of mental problems, and her employer had explored various accommodation options. Because of the employee's disability, however, she could not remember what she did, said, or was told to do, and she made numerous mistakes in areas such as filing, scheduling, handling mail, and answering telephone calls, the arbitrator said. Such conduct would not be tolerated from someone without a disability, the arbitrator said. Noting that the purpose of disability discrimination laws "is to treat disabled employees just like everyone else," the arbitrator said there was no reason to hold the employee to a "lesser standard" than her co-workers (*Wayne County*, 110 LA 1156).

• After an employee had two seizures at work, his employer acted reasonably in discharging him out of fear of possible injury to himself and others, an arbitrator ruled. Medical testimony from a doctor failed to show that the seizures could be fully controlled in the future, and there was no other job at the plant to which the employee could be transferred, the arbitrator concluded (*Weber Manufacturing Co. Inc.*, 63 LA 56).

• Another arbitrator held that an employer was justified in placing an employee on temporary layoff because his disability posed a safety threat. The employee had diabetes and worked as a driver. After the employee went off his diet, the employer removed him from his job because of the risk that he could go into a diabetic coma while driving. Citing the employer's right to remove employees with conditions that could endanger themselves or their co-workers, the arbitrator upheld the temporary layoff (*Boeing Co.*, 106 LA 650).

B. Medical Evidence

In an effort to protect disabled workers from discrimination, the Americans with Disabilities Act limits the situations in which employers can request medical information or examinations. In general, disability-related inquiries and medical exams are allowed when employers have a "reasonable belief, based on objective evidence," that employees pose a direct health or safety threat or their ability to perform essential job functions has become impaired by a medical condition. Employers also can request medical information from employees who seek to return to work following a leave of absence.

In addition, when employers receive accommodation requests, they can require reasonable medical documentation to determine the existence of a covered disability, ascertain employees' functional limitations, and substantiate the need for accommodations. Employers cannot ask employees for all of their medical records or request extra information after receiving sufficient documentation from employees' doctors. If employers lack sufficient medical information, however, employees must cooperate in making the necessary documentation available, or their employers will not be obligated to provide reasonable accommodations.

● A hospital acted properly in demanding an independent medical examination to substantiate a condition that allegedly prevented an employee from working overtime, an arbitrator held. The employee had seen a general practitioner, who provided doctor's slips restricting the employee to eight hours of work per day because of anxiety. Faced with a need to have employees put in more overtime hours, the hospital referred the employee for a psychologist's evaluation to substantiate his medical restrictions. When the employee failed to get the second opinion, the hospital suspended him. According to the arbitrator, the request for an examination by a psychologist was reasonable, because a condition such as anxiety should be diagnosed by a medical specialist who is trained in behavioral science and capable of conducting an evaluation based on specific criteria established by the American Psychiatric Association. The employee's suspension, which was lifted once he went through with the exam, was justified under the circumstances, the arbitrator found (*Fairmont General Hospital Inc.*, 119 LA 134).

● After repeatedly making mistakes in counting inventory, an employee could not avoid termination by giving his employer an unsupported diagnosis of attention deficit hyperactivity disorder, an arbitrator ruled. At earlier steps of the progressive discipline process, the employer had offered the employee additional training and suggested that he take advantage of the

company's employee assistance program, but the employee did not avail himself of either option. The employee did seek medical advice after his final inventory mistake, and he then contended that his performance problems were attributable to a diagnosis of ADHD. Observing that the employee failed to present supporting documentation to substantiate the diagnosis, however, the arbitrator held that the evidence submitted by the employee was not sufficient to show that his poor performance was caused by a medical condition (*Armstrong World Industries Inc.*, 121 LA 996).

● An employee could not escape discipline by claiming her tardiness was caused by sleep apnea, an arbitrator held. The arbitrator found that the employee could not establish a claim of discrimination against her employer when she had not produced medical information about her alleged disability before she was suspended. "In this case, there is no evidence to demonstrate that the illness of sleep apnea ... prevented her from setting an alarm clock and waking up at a designated hour," the arbitrator added (*Federal Bureau of Prisons*, 120 LA 1755).

● An arbitrator ruled that an employer properly transferred a partially disabled employee to light-duty status because the employer had adequate medical evidence that the employee should be transferred to such an assignment. In addition, the arbitrator said, the employer had the legal obligation to transfer the employee to light duty in order to protect the employee's own safety and health, as well as the safety and health of co-workers (*ITT Automotive*, 105 LA 11).

● *By contrast*, an employer did not have just cause to discharge an employee with a heart condition after a company doctor and the employee's own physician gave conflicting opinions about the employee's ability to continue working, an arbitrator decided. Both medical opinions were plausible, but the company doctor acknowledged that there were shortcomings in the information he used to evaluate the employee's limitations. Given the employee's 26-year tenure, he was entitled to another evaluation by an independent heart specialist who could resolve the situation with an un-biased medical opinion, the arbitrator held (*Noranda Aluminum Inc.*, 119 LA 217).

● An arbitrator ruled an employer did not have just cause to discharge a driver because his job restrictions barred him from using and lifting blocks weighing up to 60 pounds and using a boom jack, because the employer waited 40 days from the date of the report of the functional capacity exam that limited him to 50 pounds of lifting before discharging him, he continued to work during that 40-day period, and drivers commonly help each other with booming (*Coreslab Structures Inc.*, 129 LA 329).

1. Return to Work

If employees have received a doctor's note clearing them to return to work following injuries or illnesses, that documentation generally entitles them to reinstatement, even if their employers doubt that they are fully ready to resume working. On the other hand, employees sometimes jeopardize their reinstatement rights by making inconsistent statements about their ability to work. For example, if employees have made a claim of total disability in order to receive Social Security benefits, that can be used as evidence that they are no longer qualified to perform the essential functions of their jobs.

● An employer violated the reinstatement rights of an employee who was unconditionally cleared to return from disability leave, an arbitrator ruled. The employee had experienced on-the-job injuries requiring several months of recovery and rehabilitation. Following a series of return-to-work releases with restrictions the employer could not accommodate, the employee eventually provided a doctor's note clearing him for normal duty. The employer ordered its own fitness-for-duty examination, and the employee was unconditionally released to return to work. However, the employer said the employee's old job was no longer available and, after another six months of unpaid disability leave, offered him a position outside the bargaining unit. According to the arbitrator, the employee was entitled to reinstatement once an employer had medical evidence of the employee's ability

to perform the essential functions of his job. Even if the employer argued that the employee was injury prone, the evidence did not show that his reinstatement would pose a direct threat to himself or others, the arbitrator noted. Adding that the employee had the seniority to bump back into his old job, the arbitrator concluded that the employer had no contractual basis for refusing reinstatement at the time of the unconditional release, or for later placing the employee in a new job outside the bargaining unit. Consequently, the arbitrator ordered back pay and gave the employee the choice of returning to his old bargaining-unit position or keeping the new job (*Huron County*, 116 LA 1808).

● After failing to seek a second opinion, an employer had no basis for rejecting a return-to-work release provided by an employee's doctor, an arbitrator ruled. Between on-the-job back injuries, the employee had worked intermittently with some restrictions. Following his latest injury, the employer refused to permit his return on the date his physician cleared him for work. Without sending the employee for an examination by a company doctor to determine if his return would pose a health hazard, the employer lacked a proper basis for deciding that the employee was unable to perform the functions of his position, the arbitrator held. To remedy the unjustified delay in the employee's return, the arbitrator ordered back pay for the period from the doctor's release until the employee actually resumed working (*Akzo Nobel Coatings Inc.*, 119 LA 732).

● An employer acted improperly in preventing an employee from returning to work because of a lifting restriction, an arbitrator decided. The employee's doctor imposed a 40-pound lifting limitation after he injured his shoulder at work. The employer contended that it was not required to offer a light-duty position and told the employee he would not be able to work until all medical restrictions were lifted. Emphasizing the distinction between creating a light-duty job and modifying an existing position to accommodate a disability, the arbitrator said the employee's lifting limitation did not preclude him from performing his job's essential functions. "An employee may not be denied an employment opportunity because his disability prevents performance of incidental or marginal duties," the arbitrator stated, ordering reinstatement with back pay (*Canton Township*, 121 LA 259).

● *By contrast*, an arbitrator ruled an employer did not violate a collective bargaining contract when it terminated an employee who had back and groin injuries and could only return to work in a four-hour work role, because the employer's policy required employees return to eight-hour shifts. The limitation to eight-hour shifts for returning injured employees had been established three years prior to the grievant's submission of his medical releases, and was set after an assessment of the employer's operation revealed a hardship created by using four-hour work rules as a basis for scheduling employees (*Anchor Hocking LLC*, 129 LA 1619 (Arb. 2011)).

● An employer had just cause to discharge an employee who claimed total disability in order to receive Social Security benefits, an arbitrator held. The employee took a leave of absence from work and applied for Social Security disability benefits after experiencing acute kidney problems. His doctor indicated that he could make a recovery if he received a kidney transplant, but she could not provide a return-to-work date. According to the arbitrator, discharge was justified in the absence of a medical release or any other evidence to indicate that the employee would be able to resume working. The attestations the employee made in order to qualify for Social Security disability benefits provided "conclusive evidence" that he was permanently disabled and unable to work in any capacity, the arbitrator said (*Borough of Trafford*, 122 LA 230).

C. Reasonable Accommodation

Reasonable accommodation can be thought of as the removal of barriers that prevent disabled workers from performing essential job functions. Examples of reasonable accommodations include making facilities accessible, modifying equipment, restructuring jobs, modifying work schedules, and reassigning disabled workers to vacant positions.

In general, employees are responsible for informing their employers of the need for accommodations, and the parties are expected to engage in an interactive process to arrive at a feasible solution. As part of the process, employers are entitled to request medical information about employees' disabilities and functional limitations.

Accommodations are not reasonable if they pose an undue hardship. In other words, employers are not required to provide accommodations that would be overly expensive or difficult to implement. Furthermore, employers are not required to grant specific accommodations requested by employees if other solutions can meet their needs.

● According to one arbitrator, the interactive process that is used to arrive at an appropriate accommodation involves a shared responsibility between the employer and employee. "The need for open and ongoing communications is a major part of the accommodation process," the arbitrator observed (*Department of Housing and Urban Development*, 116 LA 1364).

● In providing a reasonable accommodation, an employer is not required to assign another worker to perform any essential functions of a disabled employee's job, nor is it required to bump another worker or create a new job, another arbitrator decided. Moreover, an employee does not have the right to pick what the accommodation will be. "So long as a reasonable accommodation is provided, an employee may not dictate the terms of what work she will or will not accept," the arbitrator said (*Consentino's Brywood Price Chopper*, 104 LA 187).

● Although its accommodation efforts failed, an employer made sufficient attempts to enable an employee with back problems to return to work, an arbitrator found. The employee could not perform the requisite tasks of his old maintenance mechanic job because of permanent lifting and bending restrictions. The employer made two attempts to find the employee another suitable job. After neither one worked out, the employer "was faced with the fact that there were no other vacant positions to offer," the arbitrator observed. Although the employee suggested restructuring his old job to fit his restrictions, the arbitrator said the employer was not required to offer a position specially designed to meet the employee's needs. Thus, the arbitrator concluded, the employer committed no violations in terminating the employee's employment (*Maintenance & Industrial Services Inc.*, 116 LA 293).

• A technician who was discharged for failing to return to work following a six-month medical leave of absence that her employer—a hospital—voluntarily extended to 10 months for stress-related symptoms stemming from a conflict with her supervisor was not denied a reasonable accommodation, because she was not "disabled" as matter of law. She claimed inability to work with her former supervisor but was otherwise able to work, the hospital changed her duties to lighten her workload, extended her leave, and assisted in trying to find an alternate position for her (*John Muir Health Systems*, 126 LA 257).

• An employer was within its rights to discontinue past arrangements that had allowed a disabled employee to retain the same position for more than four years without performing all of its essential functions, an arbitrator ruled. Because the past accommodations went beyond what was reasonable, the employer did not violate the ADA when it ended the special arrangements and removed the employee from the position, the arbitrator decided. As an alternative accommodation, the employer offered another assignment, but the employee rejected it. At that point, the arbitrator said, the employer was not required to continue offering other reassignments (*King Soopers Inc.*, 115 LA 207).

• Lacking a feasible accommodation for an employee who was unable to meet the physical requirements of his job, an employer had just cause for discharge, an arbitrator ruled. The employee had a degenerative knee condition, and his doctor said he should limit standing, kneeling, and climbing to blocks of 15 to 30 minutes. To follow his doctor's recommendations, the employee would have needed two breaks every hour or so, the arbitrator observed. Concluding that such an accommodation would not be reasonable, the arbitrator upheld the employee's discharge (*Case Corp.*, 113 LA 1).

• Another arbitrator held that an employer met its obligation to provide a reasonable accommodation when it offered an employee with a bad knee a position in its painting department. The employee had rejected the employer's offer, claiming he was unable to climb stairs because of his disability and was allergic to certain chemicals used in the painting department. The arbitrator noted that the employee had climbed stairs at home without further damaging his knee and had failed to provide medical evidence of his alleged paint allergies (*Riester and Thesmacher Co.*, 107 LA 572).

• A school district had just cause to charge more than 30 days against a teacher's sick leave balance during a period when the parties were unable to arrive at a reasonable accommodation, an arbitrator ruled. The teacher suffered from diabetes and hypertension, and the employer questioned his fitness to resume working following a lengthy absence. During an initial return-to-work meeting, the employer mentioned a possible assignment as a study hall and lunch monitor. The teacher subsequently provided a doctor's certification based on the assumption that he would work as a monitor, but such an assignment was never officially offered. Although the teacher later resumed classroom duties, he objected to the loss of sick leave when he could have returned earlier as a monitor. "In order for a *possible* accommodation to be a *reasonable* accommodation," the arbitrator said, "it must at least enable the employee to perform the essential functions of the job. The essential function of a teacher is to teach. A schedule that would assign a teacher no teaching duties whatsoever is not a reasonable accommodation that the District would be required to adopt" (*Berlin Brothers Valley School Dist.*, 121 LA 866).

• "Removing an obviously disabled man from a place of unusually hazardous exposure for him" is "the 'right' thing" to do, an arbitrator asserted, but the outright firing of a disabled employee is doing the "right thing in the wrong way." Rather, management should reassign the worker to a more accommodating position. In the case at hand, the arbitrator determined that no such position was currently available, so he ordered the disabled employee placed on layoff status (*Vulcan Mold & Iron Co.*, 40 LA 1266; see also 92 LA 1228).

1. Demotion

When presented with clear evidence that disabilities are interfering with employees' job performance or pose safety hazards, arbitrators will sustain a demotion to another position, especially if such an action permits employees to maintain employment.

● Management was within its rights to demote an employee whose heart condition prevented him from competently performing his job duties, an arbitrator ruled. When the employee returned to work after heart surgery, he was allowed two trial periods to build back up to normal output levels. However, evaluations showed that he was not performing satisfactorily, and he was demoted to a lower position. The worker charged that he had not been given a fair opportunity to show what he could do. The arbitrator disagreed, stressing that the employee had been given ample time to demonstrate his abilities, yet other employees were outperforming him by as much as two to one (*Haven-Busch Co.*, 74 LA 1205).

● An employee at a weapons plant was properly demoted from his position as a quality assurance technician after a medical assessment revealed that he was no longer capable of meeting the functional requirements essential to the job, an arbitrator held. The employee, who had 33 years of service with the company, was referred for the assessment after a supervisor raised concerns about his physical condition. The arbitrator found that the employee's fitness-for-duty demotion was warranted based on the results of the medical assessment, which showed that he was significantly impaired. "Management has the right and responsibility to take corrective action when an employee has a medical disability that endangers the employee's own safety or that of others," the arbitrator observed (*BWXT Pantex LLC*, 120 LA 385).

D. Seniority Versus Accommodation

The accommodation rights of employees with disabilities sometimes come into conflict with the seniority rights of their co-workers. This often occurs when employers offer reassignment as a reasonable accommodation. If the reassignment of disabled employees results in the bumping of senior co-workers, arbitrators typically overturn the accommodation to avoid undermining contractual seniority systems.

● An arbitrator refused to uphold a disabled employee's reassignment to the day shift when that accommodation entailed bumping a more senior co-worker to the swing shift. "The law is very clear," the arbitrator stated, "that an employer is not required to disturb a bona fide seniority system in order to reasonably accommodate a disabled employee." The arbitrator added that "if an accommodation conflicts with seniority rights governed by a Collective Bargaining Agreement, the accommodation must be held unreasonable" (*Mason & Hanger Corp.*, 111 LA 60; see also 110 LA 673).

● An employer went too far in trying to comply with the ADA when it bumped an employee from a job to which she had just been promoted, even though she was still on probationary status, an arbitrator decided. The employee had successfully bid on the job and was performing satisfactorily when the employer put a junior bidder in the job as an accommodation for her lifting restrictions. Once the employer posted the position and the senior employee was awarded the job, her contractual seniority rights took effect, the arbitrator said, and the employer could not bump her from the job without violating the collective bargaining agreement. The arbitrator ordered reinstatement and back pay for the wages the senior employee lost when she was bumped from the position (*Alcoa Building Products*, 104 LA 364).

● Another arbitrator ruled that an employer's light-duty accommodation policy violated a collective bargaining agreement's seniority provisions. To justify its bumping of senior employees to accommodate workers who needed light-duty work, the employer pointed to language negotiated with the union that said "all things being equal," seniority would be the factor that decided who would fill a job. The employer argued that the phrase "all things being equal" gave it authority to consider physical ability in assigning jobs. Rejecting that argument, the arbitrator held that permitting the displacement of workers from jobs won through hard-earned seniority rights would cripple the seniority system negotiated by the parties. A vacancy does not occur whenever the employer finds it "convenient or economical" to bump an employee out of a bid position and place an injured worker in the slot, the arbitrator stressed. If the employer wished to acquire the power to unilaterally bump workers out of their positions, it had to negotiate that right with the union, the arbitrator stated (*Thomson Consumer Electronics Inc.*, 103 LA 977).

● During a reduction in force, an employer improperly retained a disabled employee as a clerk in its tool room, an arbitrator ruled. The employer reassigned a senior employee from the clerk position to a lower paying job while allowing the disabled employee to stay in the position because of her medical restrictions. The arbitrator noted that the employer showed "compassion and good intentions" in attempting to provide a reasonable accommodation, but keeping the less senior employee in the clerk position violated the collective bargaining agreement. To remedy the situation, the arbitrator ordered the senior employee reassigned to the clerk position with back pay. While admitting that the decision might adversely affect the less senior employee, the arbitrator said he hoped the parties would find another way to accommodate her, even though he was precluded from doing so (*Olin Corp.*, 103 LA 481).

E. Mental Illness

Mental illnesses, like physical impairments, constitute covered disabilities under federal law if they cause substantial limitations in major life activities. Employees with disabling mental illnesses qualify for protected status under the law provided that they can perform the essential functions of their jobs, with or without reasonable accommodation, and do not pose a direct threat to health or safety.

Arbitrators commonly uphold the discharge of employees with mental illnesses based on legitimate performance or safety issues. However, employers are not entitled to discharge employees based on unfounded fears that their mental illnesses create undue risks in the workplace (61 LA 121, 28 LA 333, 26 LA 295).

● An arbitrator ruled that an agency violated the labor contract when it failed to accommodate an employee who had bipolar and attention deficit disorders, even though the agency and its "reasonable accommodation committee" claimed they did not receive enough medical information to make a judgment. The arbitrator found there was no provision in the agreement for the creation of such a committee, and at the hearing the agency's EEO manager was unable to state what additional medical information was needed. Stating that "reasonable job accommodation should be an interactive process, not a stalling process," the arbitrator sustained the grievance, ordering that the grievant be made whole by restoring her to her former grade with all back pay and benefits. Retaining jurisdiction, the arbitrator also remanded the case to the parties to determine if a reasonable accommodation could be found for the grievant and to determine what, if any, damages should be imposed upon the medical center for discriminating against the grievant in its handling of her request for a reasonable job accommodation (*Department of Veterans Affairs*, 123 LA 1571).

● Discharge was not appropriate for an employee with obsessive compulsive disorder, an arbitrator held, because her employer failed to provide her with reasonable accommodations. The psychiatrist who was treating the employee informed the employer of her OCD and suggested that she "work in an environment that does not require intensive coordination with other employees or the requirement of meeting the public." Although the employer transferred the employee a number of times, it failed to inform her supervisors about her OCD or put her in a work environment with the accommodations her psychiatrist recommended. Under the circumstances, the arbitrator found that the employer lacked just cause to terminate the employee for shortcomings in her job performance. The arbitrator ordered reinstatement with back pay and directed the employer "to provide reasonable and effective accommodation upon this employee's reinstatement" (*Department of the Air Force*, 109 LA 989).

● Reinstatement also was ordered for an employee who experienced excessive absenteeism because of depression. After the worker's termination, he received medical treatment that brought his disability under control. Noting that the worker went on to perform well elsewhere and also had been a good worker in his old job, except for the absenteeism caused by his bout with acute depression, the arbitrator determined that he should be allowed to return to his former position. However, the arbitrator refused to award back pay and required quarterly reports from the employee's doctor to show the employer that the employee's depression was being treated (*Interstate Power & Light Co.*, 121 LA 307).

● *By contrast*, another arbitrator refused reinstatement for an employee who was terminated because of attendance violations, even though he had been diagnosed with "major depressive disorder." In this case, the evidence suggested that the employee had stopped taking his medications and was no longer under the care of a physician. Additionally, the arbitrator noted that the employee had long been a problem for the company, and his lack of reliability also had a negative impact on the co-workers he was supposed to relieve at the changeover in shifts (*Armstrong World Industries Inc.*, 114 LA 540).

● An arbitrator ruled that an employer had just cause to discharge an employee who had bipolar disorder and had been medically determined to be unable to perform her job, even though her original physician stated that she could return to work, where a later independent medical examiner came to a different conclusion, and the union did not ask that the employee be reexamined (*Dairy Fresh of Alabama Inc.*, 130 LA 137).

● An arbitrator ruled that an employer had just cause to discharge a drunk employee who suffered from bipolar disorder, where his misbehavior was the result of alcohol abuse and not his medical disorder (*U.S. Tsubaki Inc.*, 125 LA 353).

● An arbitrator upheld the discharge of a schizophrenic employee who was fired for threatening co-workers, despite a doctor's testimony that the employee had resumed taking his medication and was able to function normally, where the damage had been done, and the employer could not afford to jeopardize the safety and well-being of employees in the plant (*Anchor Hocking*, 125 LA 312).

● Discharge was an appropriate response to the insubordinate behavior of an employee who, as a result of a car accident, was prone to outbursts, had various cognitive deficits, and lacked normal workplace inhibitions, an arbitrator ruled. Considering the nature of the employee's disability and the fact that he was on medication that could not control his behavior, the arbitrator sustained the employee's discharge, concluding that his employer was not required to retain someone who was "so disabled as to demonstrate incapacity to consistently carry out his required job." The arbitrator said he would have considered placing the worker on sick leave until his disability had been treated had it been claimed that the employee's condition was subject to cure or control (*National Linen Supply*, 107 LA 4).

● A schizophrenic employee was properly discharged for his violent behavior at work, an arbitrator ruled. After the employee was hospitalized and diagnosed as a paranoid schizophrenic, management tried to place him only in low-stress situations. Over time, however, the employee began exhibiting hostile and aggressive behavior on the job and claimed he was being picked on by co-workers. At one point, he was suspended for shoving and choking a general foreman. The employee was allowed to return to work, but he subsequently grabbed a co-worker, pushed him against a wall, and shouted at him. Management then decided to fire the employee, although it understood that his behavior was induced by the illness. In upholding the discharge, the arbitrator cited medical evidence indicating that the employee's illness caused him to "manifest paranoid thought processes focused primarily on the work situation" and that returning him to work would likely trigger repeat behavior (*Babcock & Wilcox Co.*, 75 LA 12; see also 92 LA 1291).

• Another arbitrator held that a manic-depressive employee was discharged with just cause. The employee's bipolar disorder caused explosive behavior that could not be controlled even though it might be regulated through medication under close medical supervision, the arbitrator observed (*Rohm and Haas*, 104 LA 974).

F. Vision Impairments

Many employers take vision impairments into consideration when determining whether workers are suitable for particular jobs. Arbitrators typically hold that vision impairments can be used as a basis for disqualifying employees from a position if the impairments interfere with the safe performance of the job's essential functions.

• Demotion was justified for a mill-wright at a sawmill after his slow work revealed that he was visually impaired, an arbitrator decided. The employee had performed his millwright duties safely for nine years, but he told his supervisor that he had only one good eye and worked slowly out of concern that he would get hurt if he worked any faster. According to the arbitrator, reassignment of the employee was warranted after two ophthalmologists examined him and recommended that he not work around moving belts, saws, gears, chippers, and cranes (*Potlatch Corp.*, 97 LA 1001).

• Similarly, an arbitrator held that an employer properly reassigned a crane operator to another job when, following an accident, it discovered that the employee had "zero depth perception." Dismissing the employee's argument that the accident was caused by the poor condition of the crane, the arbitrator stressed that regardless of whether this allegation were true, "the requirement of good depth perception for anyone operating the crane is a reasonable requirement," but "particularly if the crane is in poor condition" (*Foster Wheeler Corp.*, 54 LA 871).

• On the other hand, an employer did not have just cause to discharge a maintenance mechanic who had glaucoma, an arbitrator held. The employer removed the employee because of safety concerns. However, the employee had received treatments that allowed the interoccular pressure in his eyes to remain stable within normal ranges for the past seven years. Although he had lost some peripheral vision, he was cleared by his ophthalmologist to operate slow-moving vehicles in the employer's warehouse, and he had a good record with no on-the-job accidents. While acknowledging that the employer made a good-faith effort to resolve what it believed to be a potentially hazardous situation, the arbitrator said the employer had no legitimate basis for removing the employee from his job. Consequently, the arbitrator ordered reinstatement with back pay (*SuperValu Inc.*, 119 LA 1377).

• In a similar case, an arbitrator overturned the discharge of an employee who was "industrially blind," largely because it appeared that the employee had made an amazing adjustment to his disability and had worked for years without mishap (*United Gas Improvement Co.*, 40 LA 799).

• One employer, suspecting that poor eyesight on the part of some employees was causing them to produce a lot of defective work, set up a new vision-testing program. For some jobs, the vision requirements were raised. Several workers could not pass the new tests for their jobs and were discharged. An arbitrator decided that the discharges were not for good cause under the contract and ruled that the workers could keep their jobs as long as they continued to meet the standards in effect at the time they were hired (*Connecticut Telephone & Electric Corp.*, 22 LA 632).

G. Chemical Sensitivity, Allergies

In cases involving chemical sensitivity or allergies, arbitrators commonly find that the measures required to protect employees from exposure exceed what is reasonable. Arbitrators generally agree that discharge is an appropriate last resort if employers are unable to devise feasible solutions for accommodating affected employees.

• A hospital was not required to change the general disinfectant cleaner used throughout its facility because one employee was allergic to it, an arbitrator held. The employee's allergy caused several flare-ups and rashes, and she eventually stopped working. After she had been off work for a year, the hospital terminated her employment. According to the arbitrator, the hospital had provided the employee with some accommodations, but her allergic reactions intensified. In addition, it looked into other disinfectants but concluded that the product it was using was the best option, based on effectiveness, availability, and cost. In the absence of persuasive evidence that any reasonable solution existed that would accommodate the employee's allergic condition and meet the hospital's legitimate business needs for an effective and environmentally safe general disinfectant, the arbitrator concluded that the hospital did not violate disability accommodation requirements or just cause principles in terminating the employee (*South Peninsula Hospital*, 120 LA 673).

● To accommodate a high school teacher who was hypersensitive to fragrances, a school district did not need to institute a fragrance-free campus policy or remove more than 100 lockers outside her classroom in order to prevent students from using fragrances in her vicinity, an arbitrator held. The arbitrator also rejected the suggestion that a security guard be posted near the teacher's classroom between periods to protect her from being "assaulted" by students spraying fragrances on her door. Instead, the arbitrator ordered the installation of oscillating surveillance cameras as a more effective deterrent and suggested that the teacher consider moving to a portable classroom, which would lessen her exposure (*Culver City Unified School District*, 110 LA 519).

● An employer was justified in discharging an employee who was unable to do her job because of an allergic reaction to the nitroparaffin chemicals she worked with, an arbitrator held. Despite receiving special protective gear, the employee continued to experience "contact dermatitis" on her hands. The employer gave the employee every manner of protective gear required under the agreement, the arbitrator said, but it was under no obligation to transfer her to a job outside the bargaining unit as a way to eliminate her chemical exposure. The employee was not protected by the ADA, the arbitrator added, because she did not have an impairment that substantially limited a major life activity (*Angus Chemical Co.*, 102 LA 388).

H. Obesity and Hypertension

Arbitrators agree that employers have just cause for termination if obesity and high blood pressure, either on their own or in combination, prevent employees from doing their jobs. In a number of cases, however, arbitrators have found that employers overstepped their bounds in terminating obese or hypertensive employees. For example, one arbitrator ordered the reinstatement of an employee, despite her obesity and high blood pressure, where her condition had not affected her job performance in any way (*Magnavox Co.*, 46 LA 719).

● Despite five major job-related injuries, an obese employee should not have been demoted from his machinist job to a janitorial position, an arbitrator held. The employee, who weighed 300 pounds when he was hired and 428 pounds at the time of his last occupational injury, had never been warned about his job performance, his history of injuries, or his weight. On the contrary, the arbitrator found, his employer had tolerated his obesity by reassigning certain duties that were difficult for him to perform. In rejecting the employer's contention that the employee's obesity posed a hazard, the arbitrator cited a lack of evidence showing a connection between the employee's weight and his injuries and also noted that the employee was returned to work without any medical restrictions. Thus, the arbitrator overturned the demotion and ordered the employee made whole for any loss in wages he incurred (*Man Roland Inc.*, 97 LA 175).

● Another arbitrator ordered the reinstatement of an employee with hypertension who was fired for refusing assigned work and leaving without permission. The employee had become upset after receiving a work assignment that he believed to be excessive and unreasonable, and he claimed that he felt sick because of his hypertension, which flared up with stress. The employee found another worker to cover for him and went home early. The arbitrator emphasized the seriousness of the employee's misconduct but found that his hypertension had to be taken into consideration as well. Concluding that discharge was not warranted, the arbitrator ordered reinstatement. However, he withheld back pay and required the employee to provide the employer with a physician's statement indicating the employee's ability "to perform all the functions of his job in a reasonable manner" (*SMG*, 118 LA 1239).

● An employer was not required to "make work" for an obese employee when medical restrictions prevented him from performing his normal duties, an arbitrator held. The employee's obesity placed great strains on his back muscles, making it difficult for him to bend, stoop, or lift objects that weighed more than 10 pounds. Although management attempted to assign work to him that fell within these narrow limitations, the arbitrator said, the employee "was frequently not cooperative," and supervisors "were beginning to run out of things" for the employee to do. According to the arbitrator, an employer is not obligated to retain a worker who is unable "to perform enough useful productive work to warrant his continued employment." The arbitrator gave the employee a last chance to reduce his weight so he could resume his job duties without restrictions, adding that management would be justified in discharging the employee if he failed to take advantage of the opportunity (*Reynolds Metals Co.*, 71 LA 1099).

● An employer had just cause to discharge an obese employee who was deemed "unfit for work," an arbitrator decided. The employee had been hospitalized after repeatedly falling asleep on the job. When he returned to work, management warned him about the need to improve his condition, but he again started falling asleep at work after returning to his old habits of staying up late and consuming large quantities of junk food. Management tried counseling the employee and imposing corrective discipline, but the problem continued. The arbitrator concluded that discharge was appropriate after management's "consistent program of progressive discipline" and the worker's

repeated failures to take advantage of the opportunities given him. According to the arbitrator, the employer had "a right to expect" the employee to present himself "fit for work" (*City of Iowa City*, 72 LA 1006).

I. Epilepsy

In some cases involving the employment of epileptics, arbitrators have ruled against discharge based on the mere existence of the disability when employers lacked evidence of a safety hazard. For jobs that involve driving, meanwhile, regulatory compliance obligations sometimes force employers to exclude epileptic employees even if medication can keep their seizures in check.

● An employer acted improperly when it fired an epileptic employee in response to a comment made by a government safety worker, an arbitrator decided. In seven years with the company, the employee never had any epileptic-related accidents. He refused to operate forklifts or climb ladders and regularly took medicine that helped control his seizures. Nevertheless, the employer fired him after an Occupational Safety and Health Administration staffer commented that epilepsy "constituted a dangerous condition." The arbitrator ordered reinstatement, citing medical testimony that the employee could work safely in the plant. While sympathizing with the employer's safety concerns, the arbitrator said the time to decide whether or not the worker's continued employment constituted a hazard would be when an injury resulted from his condition (*Samuel Bingham Co.*, 67 LA 706).

● Discharge was upheld, however, in the case of a crane operator who passed out and fell during his seizures. Hazards to himself and others existed in his continued employment, the arbitrator noted, pointing out that impartial medical experts had advised the employer against retaining the worker. Not only were there no other jobs at the plant for the worker to perform safely, but he also lacked a long and satisfactory record, the arbitrator observed (*Acme Galvanizing Inc.*, 61 LA 1115).

● Another arbitrator held that an employer was justified in discharging an employee for failing to indicate he had epilepsy when he filled out his employment application. The employer discharged the employee because of his falsification of the application, not because of his disability, the arbitrator emphasized. The employer had made reasonable accommodations for another worker who experienced seizures, but the employer never had the opportunity to offer any accommodations in the employee's case because he deliberately withheld information about his condition (*Colgate-Palmolive Co.*, 116 LA 397).

● An employee with a history of epileptic seizures was properly discharged from her job as a city bus driver, an arbitrator ruled. The employee was prescribed anti-seizure medication following her last seizure, and after an 11-month leave of absence, she presented a release from her doctor that cleared her to return to work. The employee then underwent a Department of Transportation physical examination, however, and the medical examiner determined that she was not fit to work as a commercial driver because of guidelines disqualifying individuals who take anti-seizure medicine. In light of the medical examiner's determination and the heightened safety concerns that apply to providers of public transportation, the arbitrator agreed that the employee was no longer qualified to work as a commercial driver (*Greater Cleveland Transit Authority*, 121 LA 327).

● On the other hand, an arbitrator overturned the disqualification of another epileptic driver who had received a state waiver allowing him to drive commercial trucks within the state. The employee worked as a delivery driver for a soft drink company but was barred from that job when he was diagnosed with epilepsy. After a year without any seizures, the employee attempted to return to his former position, and he received a waiver from a state agency to requalify for his commercial driver's license. The company still barred him from the job, however, relying on federal regulations that preclude people with epilepsy from working as commercial drivers. According to the arbitrator, the employee was entitled to the delivery job based on the state's determination that he could resume his driving duties without causing a safety concern. The arbitrator ordered the employee made whole for any earnings he lost while he was improperly denied reinstatement to his former position (*Coca-Cola Bottling Co. of Michigan*, 116 LA 737).

Part 6

Leave

I. Arranging Leave

OVERVIEW

In most unionized workplaces, employees are eligible for various types of paid leave, such as vacations, sick leave, bereavement leave, and leave for jury duty or court appearances. Unpaid leaves of absence also can be made available in certain circumstances, allowing employees to miss work for extended periods of time without losing their jobs.

When employees need or want to be away from work, they typically must follow certain procedures to obtain approved leave. If employees do not satisfy proper requirements for arranging leave, they can incur unexcused absences and put themselves at risk of being disciplined or discharged for attendance infractions.

The arbitration cases discussed in this chapter deal primarily with the process of requesting and receiving authorization for leave. This chapter also addresses disputes that arise in connection with employees' return to work and cancellations of approved leave.

For a discussion of arbitration rulings on discipline for attendance infractions, see Part 2, Chapter I, Absenteeism & Tardiness. For a discussion of cases dealing with arrangements for time off under the Family and Medical Leave Act, see Chapter XI, Family and Medical Leave.

SUMMARY OF CASES

A. Leave Arrangement Procedures

When employees want to arrange leave from work, they usually have to follow specific rules and procedures. In some cases, these rules and procedures are negotiated by unions and employers as part of the collective bargaining process. In others, they are established unilaterally by management and are not spelled out in labor agreements.

While questions sometimes arise about the right of management to issue rules that dictate how employees go about obtaining leave, the most common source of disputes is the application of requirements that already exist. For example, arbitrators often are asked to decide if leave has been properly requested or if employees are in fact eligible for a particular type of leave. Because of the many variations in leave policies and how they apply to the situations of individual employees, arbitration decisions in this area tend to hinge on the facts and circumstances of each case.

• One arbitrator decided that an employer had a right to stop allowing the substitution of vacation days for what would otherwise be unexcused absences. The substitutions enabled employees to use vacation days without having filled out vacation request forms in advance. The employer discontinued the practice in the face of increased competition, maintaining that it had to tighten its leave policies to remain fully staffed. According to the arbitrator, the contract clearly allowed the employer to limit employees' ability to make the vacation substitutions. The change was not "arbitrary or capricious," the arbitrator added, but "motivated by business needs" (*Donaldson Co. Inc.*, 119 LA 561).

• Another arbitrator held that a school board was justified in denying a half day's vacation to a custodian who took the leave without proper approval. The custodian called the school board's business manager one morning but was only able to speak with a secretary about leaving work early that day. He made arrangements for a co-worker to cover for him and dropped a leave form in the mail, which the business manager received and denied the following day. In upholding the denial, the arbitrator said allowing employees to take time off without obtaining proper consent would negate the employer's right to approve or deny vacation requests. Although the employer had a pattern of accommodating last-minute vacation requests from employees with good attendance records while showing less tolerance for employees with excessive sick leave usage, the arbitrator said that pattern did not amount to unfair discrimination. The arbitrator overturned the employer's decision to dock the custodian's pay for the half day he missed, however, finding that the use of paid personal leave was appropriate for the absence in question (*Cuyahoga Falls City School District Board of Education*, 114 LA 1565).

• An employee's incarceration following a conviction for drunk driving did not constitute an "emergency" that would qualify for special leave arrangements, an arbitrator ruled. In recognition of the employee's value, his employer persuaded a judge to offer enrollment in an employee assistance program as an alternative to jail time. The employee did not avail himself of that opportunity, however, and was terminated due to the absences he incurred during his incarceration. The arbitrator found "no question" that termination was warranted, despite the fact that the employee requested a leave of absence or change in vacation to cover his time in jail. The actions that led to the employee's incarceration "were voluntary and in no way qualify as an 'emergency' situation" that would enable the employee to receive a leave of absence or to reschedule his approved vacation dates, the arbitrator said (*Sasol North America Inc.*, 119 LA 591; see also 79 LA 973, 35 LA 581).

• An employee could not escape termination for absenteeism by claiming that he should have been granted leaves of absence to cover several of the days he missed work without calling in or properly notifying a supervisor, an arbitrator held. The clear language of the contract allowed leaves of absence for sickness or accident provided employees furnished proof of their condition and made written application for the leave, the arbitrator observed. However, the employee did not submit the required form, nor did he make an oral request in lieu of a written application. In upholding discharge, the arbitrator not only emphasized the employee's failure to take the actions needed to receive a medical leave of absence, but also his failure to act in a manner that would lessen the impact of his frequent absences on his employer's operations (*DynCorp Technical Services*, 116 LA 1345).

• *By contrast*, an arbitrator held that a school district erred in denying a sabbatical to a teacher based on his refusal to provide requested documentation. The teacher gave his employer a brief doctor's note recommending that he be granted a year off for "health restoration." The employer asked for more details and still considered the teacher's documentation insufficient after he supplied a second doctor's note. The teacher cited his right to privacy in refusing to supply further information. The arbitrator found that the school district's demands conflicted with its own policies, which provided that an employee requesting a sabbatical for health restoration only had to supply "an official supporting medical statement and recommendation from his/her physician" (*West Branch Area School District*, 114 LA 1543).

• An employer was arbitrary and capricious in refusing to approve time off for an employee who received a court order to attend a pretrial hearing conference on her divorce, an arbitrator ruled. Although the employer had a policy that allowed time off if employees received a court-issued summons, the employer told the employee that her court order did not qualify. The arbitrator disagreed, noting that the order compelled the employee to appear in court for the pretrial conference. After the employee's absence, the employer argued that she was not entitled to time off because her court appearance was scheduled in the afternoon, which did not conflict with her schedule on the midnight shift. The arbitrator rejected that argument based on when it was raised. The outcome might have been different if the employer had questioned the necessity of the absence ahead of time, but its failure to do so deprived the employee of the chance to make different arrangements, the arbitrator pointed out (*OleTex Inc.*, 116 LA 1001).

• In a dispute over how to classify a day off, an arbitrator said an employee's situation could be treated as a "leave of absence" even though it was at odds with a provision in the collective bargaining agreement. The contract provision set out procedures for requesting leaves of absence lasting more than six days, stating that employees had to seek permission in writing. Although the employee's request was made orally, the employer erred in treating the day he missed in the same way it would treat absenteeism, the arbitrator found. Emphasizing the difference between absenteeism and being off duty with permission, the arbitrator held that the contract provision in question implied that a shorter leave period did not require a written request (*Emge Packing Co.*, 15 LA 603).

• In another case involving an informal leave request, an employee was absent for an extended period of time after obtaining oral permission from management. The employee, on returning to work, was notified by the employer that he had lost his seniority rights because the leave authorization had not been put in writing. Although a contract provision stated that the employer "agrees that leave shall be in writing and a copy thereof sent to the union," an arbitrator held that the leave was authorized and that the employee did not lose his seniority rights (*Gem Electric Mfg. Co. Inc.*, 11 LA 684).

• A teacher was entitled to "assault leave" after being struck by a student while trying to break up a fight in her classroom, an arbitrator ruled. The teacher, who was injured in the fight and later diagnosed with post-traumatic stress disorder, began an extended period of leave after the incident. Although she filled out an assault report for her employer, reported the incident to the police, and discussed the matter with employer representatives, her time away from work was treated as workers' compensation leave and sick leave. The employer said the teacher did not properly request assault leave and was not eligible for such leave because the student unintentionally struck her while trying to hit someone else. The fact that the student intended to injure someone else did not mean the teacher was not a victim of assault, the arbitrator declared. Regarding the process of applying for assault leave, the arbitrator found no evidence that the employer had disseminated a policy on the matter, whereas the teacher credibly testified that she requested the leave. Consequently, the arbitrator decided that the teacher was entitled to the leave benefits, which included full salary, full payment of her medical expenses, and no deductions from sick leave during the period of her incapacity resulting from the assault (*Chicago Board of Education*, 118 LA 349).

B. Adequacy of Notice

In cases involving notice about leave, employers commonly argue that a lack of adequate notice cancels employees' right to leave and exposes them to discipline or discharge. As evidenced by the examples below, however, arbitrators do not always agree with the way employers enforce notice requirements.

• In one case, an arbitrator held that an employer unjustly terminated an employee who had notified her supervisor that she was in the hospital after having a reaction to some medication. A contract provision required a written leave request for absences from illness lasting more than five working days, and the employee was terminated on the sixth day for failing to meet this requirement. During the first five days, however, the employee, her mother, and her husband had called five times to advise her supervisor of the employee's plight. When the employee's husband spoke with her supervisor on the fifth day, "it must have been apparent to all concerned that a leave of absence would be necessary," the arbitrator observed. Noting that the employer had initiated leaves of absence on prior occasions without requiring written requests, the arbitrator held that the employee technically met the requirements of the contract by making it known that she could not return to work within the five-day period (*Amana Refrigeration Inc.*, 73 LA 133; see also 112 LA 125).

• Another arbitrator overturned the termination of an employee who missed work for three days after his mother-in-law died suddenly one weekend. Funeral services were held on a Monday, and the employee asked his adult son to contact his employer to explain his absence. A co-worker who attended the funeral showed the employer a copy of the funeral program on Tuesday, but the employee's son failed to call in as requested. Because the employee was absent for three days without notice, the employer treated his situation as a voluntary quit. At the same time, the employer gave the employee funeral leave pay for the days he was gone. "Notwithstanding the son's failure," the arbitrator held, the employer had "constructive notice" that the employee was absent because of the death of a family member. The "determinative factor" in the case was the granting of paid funeral leave, the arbitrator said, noting that the employer could not grant such leave while also taking the position that the employee

was absent without notice (*Fawn Engineering Corp.*, 118 LA 1).

• In a case involving leave for union business, a contract required "reasonable notice" to the proper employer official before employees could leave their work areas. The employer unilaterally established a policy stating that "reasonable notice is deemed to be 48 hours," but the union objected after an employee was suspended for violating the new rule. An arbitrator found that the employer could not change the notification requirement without the union's input. When the "reasonable notice" clause was inserted in the contract, it became a proper subject for bargaining, the arbitrator said, and management could not unilaterally fix its meaning (*Ampco Metal Inc.*, 3 LA 374).

• On the other hand, an employer with a rule against combining personal and vacation days was justified in disciplining an employee for failing to provide proper notice about a two-week absence that included both types of leave, an arbitrator ruled. The employee planned her two-week absence three months ahead of time and submitted a form for the use of three personal days. When a management official questioned her about the purpose of the leave, she said it was for "personal business." At some point in time, the employee also left an undated note for her supervisor listing all the days she would miss work. The employee's insufficient note might not have warranted discipline on its own, the arbitrator observed, but when asked about her request for personal leave, the employee "was required to be more forthcoming." She knew she would be using the leave in conjunction with vacation, and telling management it was for personal business "was, to be charitable, imprecise," the arbitrator said in finding that a verbal warning was justified for the employee's infraction (*North Central Board of Education*, 104 LA 399).

C. Return to Work After Leave

At the conclusion of leave, conflicts sometimes emerge over employees' responsibility to notify their employers about returning to work. Disputes also can arise if employees are ready to return from leave but are not allowed to resume working right away.

• In one case, an employer instituted a new call-in requirement for workers returning from leave. The employer already required employees to call in before returning from a leave for illness or injury, but the policy was expanded to include leave for other reasons, such as vacation and jury duty. The union objected that the employer had imposed a new employment term without negotiation, but the arbitrator refused to overturn the policy. Management had the right to control operations and direct the workforce except where that authority was specifically limited by the contract, the arbitrator noted, and there was nothing in the contract that prohibited the call-in requirement (*Hawaiian Electric Co.*, 117 LA 1433).

• Just cause did not exist to discharge an employee for "unauthorized absences" following an automobile accident, even though he did not report to work on the first date specified in a medical release, an arbitrator ruled. When the employee reported for work, it was one week after the date specified in a doctor's release for light-duty work but one week prior to the earliest date that he would have been released for regular duties. In overturning the employee's discharge, the arbitrator noted that the employee was entitled to a period of readjustment following his traumatic injury. Moreover, the employee had asked the doctor who was treating him if he could go back to work earlier, but he was advised that it might do him harm, the arbitrator observed (*DynCorp Fort Rucker Division*, 97 LA 572).

• In a case that involved leave stretching, an employee mailed a letter to his employer to give notice that he wanted to extend his vacation. The employer's attendance rules specified that absence without notice "for three consecutive working days" meant termination. The employer did not receive the letter until more than three days after the end of the employee's scheduled vacation, and he was fired for absence without notice. The employee did not meet the notice requirement by mailing the letter, an arbitrator found, because the employer needed to receive notice within the three-day period (*Lear Sieglar Inc.*, 48 LA 276).

• Another arbitrator ruled that an employer was not justified in preventing an employee from working for one week after he overstayed an overseas vacation by a day. The delay was caused by a missed connection on the employee's return flight. Although the employee failed to notify his employer of the delay, which constituted an unapproved extension of leave, this was insufficient cause to place him on an alternate work schedule that began one week later, the arbitrator decided. According to the arbitrator, the employer's action amounted to an unwarranted suspension (*Potlatch Corp.*, 63 LA 816).

• An employer was entitled to "reasonable" lead time in reinstating an employee after a lengthy absence, but making the employee wait two weeks was excessive, an arbitrator ruled. The employer claimed that the nature of its operations made it impossible to act more quickly in reinstating the employee when he announced after six months that he was ready to return to work. Noting the length of the absence, the arbitrator allowed that it was not feasible to reinstate the employee immediately. However, one week should have been enough time to figure out where best to place the employee, the arbitrator decided, ordering the employer to pay the employee for one week's lost wages (*Crawford Clothes Inc.*, 12 LA 1104).

D. Leave Cancellations

Cancellations or changes in approved leave are fairly uncommon and usually occur only when employers have pressing reasons, be they emergency situations or discovering that employees have misused or lied about their need for leave. Less common are cases addressing the right of employees to cancel their own approved leaves.

• An employer properly cancelled a pharmacist's approved annual leave because of the pharmacy's inability to cope with an extensive backlog of unfilled prescriptions, an arbitrator held. The employee had followed proper procedures to secure annual leave, but ongoing staff shortages created an emergency situation that prompted the employer to cancel his leave rather than have other pharmacists work overtime. The arbitrator upheld the leave cancellation, noting that the unusual and unexpected situation required prompt attention, and the employer did not have adequate reserves to resolve the problem because of recent budgetary cuts (*Department of Veterans Affairs Medical Center*, 101 LA 377).

● Discharge was inappropriate for an employee who failed to return to work when his employer cancelled his medical leave, according to an arbitrator. After a back injury at work, the employee had been granted several separate medical leaves of absence. When the employer saw the employee's picture in a local newspaper announcing that he had won a fishing contest, it cancelled his leave and ordered him to resume his duties. When the employee failed to report for work, he was fired. Finding that the employer acted hastily, without any proof that the employee was malingering, the arbitrator ordered the employee reinstated with back pay (*Snyder General Corp.*, 88 LA 1153).

● An arbitrator held that an employer was not obligated to accede to an employee's request to cancel administrative leave. The employee, a tenured first-violinist in a symphony, had an opportunity to join a touring performer for a number of concert dates, and she requested an administrative leave. The normal duration for an administrative leave was one year, but the employee returned before the end of that time and asked to resume working with the symphony. She claimed that she had previously spoken with the symphony's executive director about the ability to rescind her leave or work as a substitute. The executive director denied ever agreeing to either option. The arbitrator found that the contract did not give the employee the right to cancel her leave, and there was no conclusive evidence of an oral agreement to the contrary. Citing other evidence showing that administrative leaves were intended to last a full year without exceptions, the arbitrator decided that the employee was not entitled to resume working before her leave concluded (*Pacific Symphony Association*, 108 LA 85).

II. Paid Sick Leave [LA CDI 100.5201 (public employees); 116.25]

[*Editor's Note*: See also Part 1, Discharge and Discipline: In General; Part 5, Disability; and Part 10, Health Care Benefits.]

OVERVIEW

The vast majority of unionized employers provide benefits that allow employees to continue receiving pay when they are unable to work because of illness, injury, or medical appointments. These benefits are susceptible to abuse, however, which is why contract language and policies on paid sick leave commonly spell out eligibility criteria and make the granting of such leave subject to reasonable verification requirements.

This chapter discusses the issues that arbitrators consider when resolving disputes over employees' eligibility for paid sick leave, including the validity of employer requests for proof of illness and the adequacy of doctors' notes provided by employees. Other subjects addressed in this chapter include:

- the falsification of sick leave claims;
- the availability of sick pay during strikes, layoffs, and leaves of absence unrelated to illness;
- the interplay between paid sick leave and compensation from other sources;
- physical or mental evaluations of employees returning from sick leave; and
- involuntary sick leave.

SUMMARY OF CASES

A. Eligibility for Sick Leave

Arbitrators generally allow employers to require information from employees in order to determine their eligibility for paid sick leave, and leave denials are likely to be upheld if they are reasonable and consistent with applicable contract terms. On the other hand, arbitrators are likely to side with employees if employers contravene contract provisions on paid sick leave or act arbitrarily in refusing to grant such leave.

● An arbitrator upheld an employer's refusal to give sickness and accident benefits to an employee who was off work due to a rib fracture, where her physician wrote on the return-to-work form that the employee needed light duty, and prior awards had held that a physician must certify that an employee has "total disability" to receive S&A benefits (*U.S. Steel Corp.*, 127 LA 366).

● One arbitrator upheld an employer's denial of sick pay to three employees who sought leave extensions but refused to authorize access to their private medical records. Although it is up to employees to decide whether they are too sick to report for work, it is the employer's prerogative to determine if they can receive paid sick leave, the arbitrator said. To be eligible, the employees had to provide some sort of proof, especially when the need to extend leave was seen as "suspicious," the arbitrator said. Absent "unusually harsh or capricious" actions by the employer, the employees had to follow proper procedures and provide proof that their leave should be extended, the arbitrator found (*Lloyd Noland Foundation Inc.*, 74 LA 1236).

● An arbitrator upheld the discontinuation of sick leave for an employee who refused to provide information about a second job. The employee was using sick leave because he was experiencing excessive stress, and his employer suggested that the second job could be the source of his stress. The arbitrator rejected the employee's assertion that such information was both private and irrelevant. The employee's second job could be regarded as much more stressful than his primary employment, the arbitrator noted, and the employee had a "duty to cooperate with legitimate employer investigations" (*South Central Power Co.*, 119 LA 1417).

● A union employer was justified in refusing to grant sick leave to an employee on the dates he wanted to schedule elective surgery, an arbitrator decided. Citing the nature of the procedure, which could easily have been rescheduled, the arbitrator held that the employer could refuse to grant sick leave because the employee was needed at the time to help conduct a membership drive (*Indiana State Teachers Association*, 104 LA 737).

● Two employees who missed their Saturday shifts were properly denied sick leave by their employer, despite the fact that they provided doctors' notes, an arbitrator ruled. Absent any contract language specifically allowing or disallowing the employer's actions, the arbitrator said he was forced to rely on a "consistent, extensive, interpretation of the contract . . . that Saturday absentees are not eligible for sick leave" (*H.D. Lee Company Inc.*, 76 LA 1261).

● *By contrast,* an arbitrator ruled that an employer violated a collective bargaining agreement in terminating an employee for absenteeism after denying him sick leave for a nine-day absence following a motorcycle accident. The contract explicitly stated that any employee who could offer medical evidence of illness or injury was entitled to 30 days of sick leave, the arbitrator said, ordering the employer to reinstate the employee with full back pay and benefits (*Hurd Lock & Mfg. Co.*, 108 LA 1212).

● An employer's new attendance policy that penalized employees for taking a day off did not violate a collective bargaining agreement, which under the designation "Leaves of Absence" provided for "sick leave for employees 'who are off work because of non-occupational illness or injury, . . . ,' where the normal meaning of the term 'leave of absence' involved an extended period of time, and that is the way the agreement was interpreted" (*Saint-Gobain*, 129 LA 97).

1. Doctors' Statements

Employers often insist on a doctor's note or similar documentation when employees claim sick leave. Some employers reserve this type of requirement for employees who are suspected of abusing their leave privileges, while others impose across-the-board requirements as part of their sick leave policies. If employees fail to follow reasonable documentation requirements, arbitrators are likely to uphold the denial of sick pay and possibly even termination.

• An arbitrator held that an employee's pattern of excessive sick leave justified his employer's insistence on proof of illness. The employee was notified that if he could not give a reason for previous absences, he would have to bring in written verification from a physician every time he used sick leave in the future. Finding that the contract's sick leave provisions did not limit the employer's right to insist on a physician's certificate when there was reasonable suspicion of sick leave abuse, the arbitrator upheld the requirement imposed on the employee (*City of Ann Arbor*, 102 LA 801; see also 118 LA 1806).

• In another case, an arbitrator decided that an employee's refusal to show that he had been examined by a doctor, even though his illness was genuine, relieved the employer of its obligation to pay him for his leave (*Phillips Petroleum Co.*, 45 LA 857).

• Where a contract required proof of illness to authenticate the need for sick leave, an arbitrator found that an employer could refuse to grant sick leave until the date an employee was actually seen by a doctor. On two occasions, an employee with a neurological condition missed several days of work because of her illness but did not see a physician until after the first day of each absence. The arbitrator held that the contractual requirement for proof of illness justified the employer's decision to treat the initial days of each absence as personal leave, because coverage under the sick leave provisions did not commence until the employee was "under the direct care of a physician effective as of the date seen by the physician" (*Federal Credit Union-East Division*, 116 LA 522).

• An employer properly discharged an employee who failed to provide required documentation following extended sick leave, an arbitrator held. The employee, who

already was on notice that any attendance violations would trigger discharge, missed six consecutive days of work because of an asthma flare-up. The employee did not see a doctor during the absence, and after she attempted to return to work without a doctor's note, she was fired. The employer's attendance policy required a doctor's statement following illness-related absences exceeding four consecutive days, the arbitrator noted. The employee was unable to resume working without the statement, which triggered the unexcused absences that justified her discharge, the arbitrator found (*Whirlpool Corp.*, 121 LA 272).

• *By contrast*, an arbitrator overturned the discharge of an employee who was absent for four days and did not bring in his doctor's note until he was healthy enough to return to work. While away from work, the employee had phoned management each day to report his illness and had visited his physician for a written note explaining the cause. When he returned to work, the plant manager told him he had no job there because, based on past practice, he had quit by being absent for three days without submitting a written note during that time. The contract, however, clearly did not require a note from a physician within the first three days of an absence, the arbitrator said, ordering the employee reinstated with full seniority and all earnings and benefits lost as a result of the termination (*Can-Clay Corp.*, 117 LA 1019).

• An employer improperly denied sick leave to an employee who brought in a doctor's note that read simply, "treated for bronchitis," and included a date on which the employee could resume working, an arbitrator ruled. The employer contended that the notice did not provide the information required to excuse the absence— i.e., that the employee was "incapable" of working. According to the arbitrator, however, when the doctor included the return-to-work date, he implied that the employee was incapable of working before that date. Thus, the arbitrator held that the employer's documentation requirements were satisfied and the employee was entitled to sick leave (*United States Steel Corp.*, 64 LA 540).

2. *Illness of a Family Member*

Although the Family and Medical Leave Act provides a right to time off when employees are needed to care for family members with serious illnesses, the law only guarantees unpaid leave. However, that does not preclude employees from receiving paid sick leave when they miss work to care for ill family members. In general, employees' eligibility for paid sick leave in such situations hinges on the contractual provisions or leave policies in force at their workplace.

● In one case, an arbitrator ruled that an employer committed a contract violation by denying an employee's request to use sick leave instead of vacation time to cover a period of four days when she missed work to care for her husband. The contract's "clear and unambiguous" language granted the employee the right to use her sick leave to care for her ill spouse, the arbitrator found. In ordering the employer to restore four vacation days to the employee and charge her accrued sick leave for the absence, the arbitrator pointed out that nothing in the Family and Medical Leave Act is intended to "diminish more generous medical leave rights granted to employees via a collective bargaining agreement" (*UAW-Legal Services Plans*, 119 LA 1217).

● An employee should not have been forced to use vacation leave rather than emergency sick leave to take his sick child to the doctor, an arbitrator held. The employee told his foreman he needed to take emergency leave to get his son medical care, and the foreman said he would "take care of it," suggesting he approved the leave, the arbitrator said. The employee later discovered that he had been charged one day of vacation leave, and the only explanation was that the foreman said he had a "gut feeling" that the there was no real emergency. If the employee determined there was an emergency involving a sick family member, he was entitled to sick leave under the terms of the contract, the arbitrator found. The question of "whether an 'emergency' exists or not is not a question of how it is viewed in the mind of the employer's deciding official or by 'gut feelings,'" the arbitrator said,

ordering the employer to restore the day of vacation to the employee and approve the sick leave (*Farmland Industries Inc.*, 102 LA 830).

● Another arbitrator held that an employer should have granted sick leave to an air traffic controller who missed work because he was exhausted after caring for his two sick children all night. The employer granted the time off but charged it to the employee's annual leave account. The arbitrator overturned the employer's decision and awarded sick leave instead. Noting that the contract provided for the use of sick leave if employees were "incapacitated," the arbitrator concluded that the employee was indeed too incapacitated by stress and sleep deprivation to work as an air traffic controller (*Federal Aviation Administration, Fort Worth Air Route Traffic Control Center*, 64 LA 45).

B. Falsified Sick Leave Claims

Arbitrators commonly hold that the falsification of sick leave claims warrants severe disciplinary action. Such conduct can provide just cause for termination where collective bargaining agreements or work rules treat dishonesty as a firing offense.

● An airline was justified in firing a flight attendant who claimed sick leave while taking a cruise, an arbitrator ruled. The employer discovered by chance that the employee was vacationing, and its investigation revealed that the employee had gone so far as to offer to pay someone to fill in for him at work. The arbitrator upheld the employee's discharge, noting that "abuse of sick leave and 'dishonesty' are potential termination offenses" under the contract and the employer's rules (*Southwest Airlines Co.*, 117 LA 160; see also 74 LA 1052, 73 LA 722).

● An arbitrator upheld the discharge of an employee who claimed to be sick when she was in fact walking a picket line. The employee, chief steward and a union local, had taken off work to picket in sympathy with another union affiliated with her local. Even though progressive discipline could have been applied, the arbitrator noted that "dishonesty, abuse of time, and receiving pay under false or misrepresented circumstances" constituted grounds for termination (*Merck-Medco RX Services of Texas LLC*, 110 LA 782).

• An employee was justly suspended for two and one-half weeks after he was discovered operating a tractor on his farm while taking sick leave, an arbitrator decided. Although the employee had been ill and was not fully recovered when he was caught doing the farm work, he was obviously not too sick to report to his job because operating a tractor was considerably more strenuous than his duties as a television engineer, the arbitrator found (*Station KMTV*, 39 LA 324).

• In another case, however, an arbitrator overturned the termination of an employee who admitted that he had performed outside "remunerative work" while drawing benefits under a sickness and accident plan. Although the employee violated the employer's rules by working in his own drive-in restaurant, it was merely the kind of "self-help contemplated" by the contract, according to the arbitrator. The penalty for engaging in such work, where not detrimental to the employee's speedy recovery, was forfeiture of benefits, not discharge, the arbitrator noted (*Corn Products Co.*, 44 LA 127; see also 44 LA 133).

• An employer lacked just cause to discharge an employee who obtained a note from her doctor for a five-day period that included a weekend when she went to Las Vegas with co-workers, an arbitrator ruled. The employee had a chronic condition called spastic colitis that commonly flared up for two to five days at a time. During the period of her absence, she had called in to her doctor and then picked up the note and some medication, but she was not seen by him. The doctor told the employer that this was not an unusual practice, but the employer concluded that the excuse about being ill was false, and it fired the employee for dishonesty.

The arbitrator found that the trip to Las Vegas did not make the employee's purported illness a lie, because the two were not mutually exclusive. Although it was possible that the employee manipulated her doctor into signing a note so she could avoid being penalized for absenteeism, it

was equally possible that the employee's spastic colitis affected her throughout the five-day period, the arbitrator pointed out. Stressing that "suspicion is no substitute for proof," the arbitrator ordered the employer to offer the employee reinstatement and make her whole for lost pay and benefits (*Sonoco Flexible Packaging*, 109 LA 824; see also 103 LA 238, 102 LA 709).

C. Sick Leave During Other Absences

Employees sometimes claim paid sick leave when other events, such as strikes, layoffs, or unrelated leaves of absence, would also prevent them from working. In such situations, arbitrators commonly look for contractual language that spells out whether or not employees are entitled to sick leave benefits.

Without specific contract terms to guide their decisions, arbitrators tend to rule one of two ways. They either hold that the lack of available work precludes a claim for sick pay, or they conclude that sick pay must be awarded if employees satisfy the underlying requirement of being unable to work because of illness or injury.

• In a case where an employer refused to grant paid sick leave to an employee during a work stoppage, an arbitrator upheld the denial because most employees were off duty as a result of the strike. The arbitrator reasoned that the purpose of a sick pay provision is to pay an employee not because he or she is sick but because illness prevents the employee from working. If no work is available, the employee is not entitled to sick pay, the arbitrator concluded (*Trans World Airlines Inc.*, 41 LA 312).

• An arbitrator upheld an employer's denial of sick leave for two employees who participated in an illegal strike while overturning the denial of sick leave for a third employee. The arbitrator reasoned that paid sick leave should be granted when workers risk losing earnings by becoming ill. For two of the employees, the arbitrator found that they would not have worked on the day in question, and therefore had no earnings to lose, because they said they would have refused to cross picket lines. For the third employee, however, the arbitrator determined that there was a legitimate and verified physical complaint and but for the employee's not being able to get the proper doctor's certification, leave normally would have been granted (*Commonwealth of Pennsylvania*, 73 LA 981).

• An arbitrator granted sick leave in the case of employees who were excused prior to a strike and whose excuses had been extended into the strike period. Other employees were denied sick leave during the strike, regardless of whether they actually were ill (*County of Santa Clara*, 65 LA 992).

• An employer improperly denied sick leave to 11 employees of one of its bargaining units for the first day another unit went on strike, an arbitrator held. Although the employer claimed that the employees were part of a wildcat strike, the arbitrator rejected the notion that sick leave requests by 11 out of 38,000 employees constituted a wildcat strike. Stressing that "there was no massive withholding of services of the sort associated with a wildcat strike," the arbitrator ordered the employer to credit each of the employees for the sick leave they were denied (*State of Ohio*, 112 LA 11).

• An employer that closed down because of a hurricane could not legitimately refuse to grant sick or injury pay to those employees who had been out on sick leave at that time, according to an arbitrator. The employer's assertion that the employees had no right to benefits on a day when they would not have been able to work even if they were well was not persuasive, the arbitrator said, holding that they were entitled to the pay because the primary cause of their unemployment continued to be their illness or injury (*Eastern Air Lines Inc.*, 41 LA 801).

• An arbitrator overturned an employer's refusal to pay an employee on temporary layoff for six days of unused sick leave. The employer argued that it could deny the sick leave because the employee did not work during the entire contract year in question, but the arbitrator said the contract clearly stated that an employee on layoff subject to recall was still entitled to accrued sick leave. Thus, the arbitrator ordered the employer to pay the employee for the six days (*The Hertz Corp.*, 101 LA 267; see also 103 LA 785).

• An arbitrator ruled that an employee on a leave of absence was entitled to sick pay. The employee continued to accrue seniority and earn holiday pay while on leave, and the arbitrator decided he was still on the "active payroll" despite the employer's contention that sick pay was only provided for employees who actually worked on a day-to-day basis. Because the contract specified that being on the active payroll was the critical issue in granting sick leave benefits, the arbitrator ordered the employer to give the employee paid sick leave (*Freightliner Corp.*, 63 LA 834).

• An employee was not entitled to use her accumulated sick leave during a sabbatical, an arbitrator ruled. The collective bargaining agreement stated that employees would receive one-half of their regular salary plus "all fringe benefits" while on sabbatical, but the arbitrator determined that sick leave was not a fringe benefit under the contract (*Allegheny Intermediate Unit*, 82 LA 187).

• Another arbitrator denied sick leave to an employee who sustained an on-the-job injury during a temporary recall from layoff. The arbitrator based his decision on contract language stating that sick pay would be granted when employees were unable to perform their scheduled work because of illness or injury. In this case, the employee returned to layoff status and had no scheduled work that would fall into the category of work he was unable to perform, the arbitrator found. Furthermore, there was no contract provision requiring sick pay during layoff, and no evidence of a clear past practice requiring sick pay under such circumstances (*American Bakeries Co.*, 64 LA 450).

D. Sick Pay and Other Compensation

Questions occasionally arise about the interplay between paid sick leave and compensation from separate sources, such as Social Security and workers' compensation. As illustrated by the cases below, eligibility for other benefits does not necessarily negate employees' entitlement to sick pay.

• One arbitrator held that an employer had no right to deduct disability payments from an employee's sick leave pay when past practice had been to grant the full amount of both benefits. Notwithstanding the fact that the combined benefits exceeded the employee's regular wages, the arbitrator found that sick pay was a negotiated benefit to which the employee had a right (*Mohawk Airlines Inc.*, 39 LA 45).

• An arbitrator ruled that an employer had no right to deprive an employee of sick pay benefits by terminating him, despite three doctors' findings that the employee had a severe disability and could receive Social Security disability benefits. The contract provided for sick leave payments for up to 52 weeks, and the arbitrator said none of the doctors refuted the possibility that the employee could return to work within that period, ordering the employer to pay him full sick leave benefits (*Witco Chemical Co. Argus Chemical Division, Halby Chemical Co.*, 61 LA 1188).

• Another arbitrator rejected an employee's claim to sick pay in addition to workers' compensation on the ground that nothing in the contract indicated the parties intended to have any sort of supplemental arrangement. To order the employer to make such payments would have the effect of amending the contract, the arbitrator concluded (*Babcock & Wilcox Co.*, 22 LA 456; see also 71 LA 1118).

E. Return-to-Work Examinations

Before allowing employees to resume their duties following extended periods of sick leave, many employers require a physical examination or psychological evaluation. Although such practices are generally regarded as a prerogative of management, most arbitrators insist that employers apply such requirements consistently without overstepping any contractual provisions that govern return-to-work exams.

• An employer could not require an employee who was out sick for six weeks to submit to a physical exam, even though the employer suspected the employee's illness could create a hazard for himself or his co-workers, an arbitrator held. The labor contract specifically stated that examinations could be required only if an employee was absent for at least 90 days, the arbitrator noted (*Buckeye Forging Co.*, 42 LA 1151).

• Another arbitrator balked at requiring an employee to consent to an employer examination when she had complied with the contractual requirement that she obtain certification for work from her own doctor and where the contract did not provide for an evaluation by the employer's doctor (*MGM Grand Hotel*, 65 LA 261).

• An employer lacked just cause to impose a 14-day suspension on an employee for refusing to submit to a psychiatric fitness-for-duty exam or produce requested medical data in a timely fashion when he sought to return to work from a lengthy sick leave, an arbitrator held. In overturning the suspension, the arbitrator noted that the employer had informed the employee in writing that the psychiatric exam would not be required if his own doctor verified that he was fit for duty, supervisors gave vague and contradictory testimony about what the employee was told he was required to do, and the deadline they claimed he was given for producing documents was unreasonable (*Federal Bureau of Prisons, Metropolitan Correctional Center*, 102 LA 238).

• When an employee sought to return from a six-month absence caused by a heart condition, his employer barred him from working based on an examination by a plant physician. The employee's personal doctor reported that he had fully recovered, but the strain involved in his former position remained a concern. Eventually, the employee was examined by a hospital's work-evaluation unit, which found that he could resume all his duties. Still, the employer said he could not have his old job back. An arbitrator found that reinstatement was called for, based especially on the findings of the work-evaluation unit. Because the arbitrator believed that the employer was motivated by concern for the employee's welfare, however, he denied back pay for the period prior to when the employee was examined by the work-evaluation unit (*U.S. Steel Corp.*, 38 LA 395).

• Another arbitrator awarded partial back pay to an employee whose ability to resume working had been disputed by an employer and a union. Each side had a doctor examine the employee, but they disagreed on whether the employee was capable of returning to work. According to the contract, the employer and union were supposed to select a third doctor to decide the issue, but neither side took any steps to do so. The arbitrator found that the employee became "re-employable" sometime during the course of the disagreement, but because the exact date was uncertain and both parties were at fault, the arbitrator cut the award of back pay in half (*Air Carrier Engine Service Inc.*, 65 LA 666).

F. Involuntary Sick Leave

Doubts about the physical or mental fitness of employees can prompt employers to impose involuntary sick leave. When this occurs, disputes can arise about management's authority to remove employees from their jobs. Even where the reasonableness of involuntary leave is not at issue, the question of entitlement to pay can become a source of disagreement.

Arbitrators are likely to uphold the right of employers to remove employees from duty based on evidence of physical or mental health problems. For example, one arbitrator described the imposition of forced leave pending full medical confirmation of an employee's fitness to work as "a reasonable temporary solution." The test of whether an employer has acted reasonably in imposing forced leave hinges largely on the safety risks involved, the arbitrator observed.

In the case at hand, the arbitrator found that an employer did not abuse its discretion in imposing leave on an employee who required psychological treatment. The arbitrator upheld the involuntary leave despite the fact that the employee was forced to use up his sick days and vacation time and then go without pay during his absence (*City of Chicago*, 97 LA 20; see also 108 LA 726, 108 LA 537, 86 LA 799).

Another arbitrator found that an employee's forced medical leave was reasonable but he was entitled to restoration of his sick leave once he was cleared to resume working. After the employee mentioned some sleep difficulties during a physical examination, he was diagnosed with a mild and correctable form of sleep apnea. He said his ability to drive was not impaired, but his employer pulled him from his duties as a heavy equipment operator on the advice of a doctor who never actually examined or interviewed the employee. While acknowledging that caution is warranted where genuine safety concerns are involved, the arbitrator said "fairness requires that the employee should be made whole for his economic loss once his claim of fitness has been vindicated." Thus, the arbitrator ordered the employer to restore 13 days of sick leave that the employee used during his "temporary medical suspension" and reimburse the employee for lost overtime earnings (*St. Clair County Road Commission*, 120 LA 496).

III. Personal, Jury Duty & Funeral Leave

OVERVIEW

Of the various types of paid time off granted under collective bargaining agreements, funeral leave, jury duty leave, and personal leave are some of the most common.

As implied by its name, personal leave is intended to cover personal situations, including those of an emergent nature, for which vacation or other forms of paid leave might not be appropriate. Although employees usually receive a certain degree of latitude in taking personal leave, many employers restrict its use in one way or another, and disputes often focus on whether or not employees have acceptable reasons for requesting time off.

In arbitration cases involving jury duty leave, a common source of contention is the amount of pay to which employees are entitled, particularly in situations where the hours of jury service do not prevent employees from reporting to work for at least part of their shifts. Some collective bargaining agreements also grant paid time off for court appearances unrelated to jury service. A question that often surfaces in connection with court leave is whether employees can use the leave for court activities in which they are serving their personal interests as opposed to fulfilling a civic duty.

In disputes over funeral leave or bereavement leave, meanwhile, arbitrators are sometimes asked to consider whether a particular individual's death qualifies for paid time off. Other issues confronting arbitrators in this area include whether weekend days can be subtracted from the amount of time employees are entitled to receive and whether employees who have a death in the family or attend a funeral while they are away from work for other reasons, such as vacations or strikes, can be denied funeral or bereavement leave.

In most instances, arbitrators' decisions in cases involving personal, jury duty, and funeral leave hinge on a close reading of the applicable contract clauses. Past practice is likely to be a determining factor where contractual language is ambiguous, however, or where the parties have developed an unwritten understanding of the terms and conditions applicable to the granting of leave.

SUMMARY OF CASES

A. Personal Leave

When disputes arise over personal leave, they usually involve claims that employers have improperly denied employees' leave requests. In making their decisions in such cases, arbitrators commonly look to contractual language, past practice, and employer policies to identify the standards applicable to personal leave and to determine if employees have satisfied the necessary conditions for receiving leave.

● An arbitrator found an employer did not violate a collective bargaining agreement in refusing to grant an employee a day of paid leave due to inclement weather, even though agreement provided for such use of paid leave. The employee tended to avoid driving in any amount of snow, she far exceeded the number of inclement weather claims of any other employee, she had initially claimed illness on the day it snowed, and her subsequent claim that her driveway was blocked by 10 inches of snow was unsupported by weather data (*AFSCME Michigan Council 25*, 126 LA 589).

● An arbitrator ruled that an employer did not violate a collective bargaining agreement when it failed to treat personal days as time worked for purposes of overtime computation, even though practice under a predecessor agreement would have done so. The new agreement repealed the past practice when it explicitly provided that union business days, vacations, and holidays count as time worked for computing overtime, but failed to mention personal days, and the union made a unilateral mistake when it failed to tell employer that its bargaining proposal did not mention personal days because they were not a problem and assumed that the past practice would continue under the new agreement (*Linett Co./Tri-Arc Manufacturing*, 124 LA 1336).

● One arbitrator held that an employer properly restricted the use of personal leave during a time of year when increased absenteeism traditionally created staffing problems. The case arose when the employer denied requests for personal leave from three employees under a new policy that required advance approval from management and specified that personal leave would only be granted for certain purposes, such as court appearances, real estate closings, weddings, and emergencies involving personal property loss. The arbitrator found that the contract gave the employer clear decision-making authority over personal leave for the time period when staffing problems usually occurred, and management had appropriately applied its new policy in denying the employees' leave requests (*Crystal Lake Elementary School District No. 47*, 113 LA 775).

● An employer properly denied an employee's request for personal leave to take time off on two Jewish holidays, an arbitrator found. Contractual language prohibited the use of personal leave for religious purposes except in unusual circumstances and allowed leave for one-time occurrences as opposed to recurring events. Noting that the observance of the holidays in question did not fit these criteria, the arbitrator upheld the employer's denial of the employee's requested leave (*School District of Beloit*, 73 LA 1146; see also 71 LA 937).

● An employer was justified in refusing to pay an employee who did not receive proper approval for personal leave before taking time off to go fishing with his father and brother, an arbitrator decided. He told a supervisor he wanted time off on a work day when personal leave normally would not have been allowed. The employee said he thought he had received the supervisor's verbal assent, but he later found out his request was denied. According to the arbitrator, personal days were intended for use in situations where employees had no choice in the matter, and advance authorization was required except in emergencies. By failing to secure proper authorization for personal leave on a work day where the employer's policy was to deny such leave absent extenuating circumstances, the employee had fallen far short of the requirements for securing the paid leave, the arbitrator held (*Carrollton Village School District*, 121 LA 530).

• *By contrast*, another arbitrator determined that an employer violated a labor contract by refusing to grant leave to an employee to attend a convention related to product distributors (the employee was himself a distributor). Looking at past instances of granting personal/business leave, the arbitrator said the employer had approved leave for reasons such as family or farm business, relocation trips, banking and investment matters, legal consultations, and handling rental property issues. The employee's request for leave, which would not have affected his job performance, should have been granted, the arbitrator concluded, ordering the employee made whole for his losses (*Saydel Consolidated School District*, 75 LA 953; see also 76 LA 673).

An employer violated a collective bargaining agreement by prorating accrual of personal leave for full-time employees instead of giving them full weeks of such leave based on years of service, an arbitrator ruled, because the employer had established past practice of not prorating full-time employees' personal leave (*Secure Solutions LLC*, 126 LA 789).

• An employer violated a collective-bargaining agreement when it required employees responding to subpoenas to take unpaid leave instead of allowing them to choose to take vacation leave, an arbitrator ruled. Even though an agreement with another local union specifically addressed that issue and banned the use of vacation leave, the arbitrator said, every bargaining agreement is unique (*Missouri Gas Energy*, 129 LA 336).

• An employer improperly denied an employee's request for personal leave to attend a papal mass in a city 150 miles away, an arbitrator held. Because the employer had granted leave at least three times for other employees to attend similar events, its denial of the employee's request was unreasonable, the arbitrator found, ordering the employer to reimburse the employee for one day's pay plus interest (*Board of Education, Geneseo Community Unit School District No. 228*, 75 LA 131).

• A unilateral policy change that would have allowed an employer to deny the use of personal leave in order to maintain adequate staffing levels was overturned by another arbitrator. Although the contract was silent on the issue, past practice had been to allow employees to decide what constituted "emergencies" justifying the use of personal leave. The unilateral policy change was improper because the employer had acquiesced in the practice of deferring to employees' judgment and because enforcing the staffing requirement would have had a "chilling effect" on the exercise of employees' rights under the contract, the arbitrator concluded (*City of River Rouge*, 65 LA 1105).

1. Falsified Leave Requests

Where there is evidence that employees have lied about the reasons for requesting personal leave, arbitrators usually uphold employers' right to impose discipline, including termination.

• An arbitrator upheld the termination of an employee who requested personal leave on short notice to attend a funeral but instead used the time to drive a tour bus. The employee had a history of prevarication and had been warned on several occasions about his behavior. Despite the employee's claim that his reasons for taking personal leave were his business alone, the arbitrator decided that termination was appropriate given the employee's history and the fact that he lied about the leave (*Meijer Inc.*, 108 LA 631).

• An employer was justified in firing an employee for being deceitful about the reasons for personal leave, an arbitrator ruled. After the employee gave his foreman a telegram stating that his mother was seriously ill, the employee asked for and was granted permission for personal leave but worked the rest of his shift. He also gave the foreman a definite return-to-work date. The employee's nonchalance spurred suspicion, and the employer hired an investigator who found out that the employee's mother was not ill, and the employee actually had gone to a convention near her home. The arbitrator agreed that the employee had lied and upheld the discharge (*International Harvester Co.*, 14 LA 980).

● A five-day suspension was appropriate for an employee who claimed sick leave after her employer denied a request for personal leave at Thanksgiving, according to an arbitrator. The employee failed to report to work for any of the three days preceding the holiday, but when she returned to work on Monday, she submitted a request for sick leave for the three days missed along with a note from a podiatrist saying she had been under his care all that time. The employee's actions warranted discipline, the arbitrator decided, noting that "her request for sick leave was being used to get the [personal] time off that was previously denied" (*North Royalton City School District Board of Education*, 116 LA 1275).

B. Jury Duty Leave

A central issue to be decided in many arbitration cases involving jury duty leave is the amount of pay to which employees are entitled. Although arbitrators recognize the importance of paid leave in removing obstacles to jury duty—including the monetary losses employees might incur as the result of missing work and the physical hardship they would face if forced to work in conjunction with performing jury service—rulings in this area are divided. When arbitrators uphold employers' pay denials, they typically do so because contractual language supports such action or because employees would have missed work anyway during the period of their jury service.

● One arbitrator upheld an employer's denial of pay to an employee on jury duty since no work was available for him because the plant was closed as the result of a heavy snowstorm. The contract specified that pay for jury duty only was required when an

employee lost work time because of jury service, the arbitrator pointed out (*FMC Corp.*, 65 LA 264).

● Another arbitrator found that an employer was not obligated to provide paid jury duty leave to an employee who was called for jury service on two days when she already was scheduled to be off work. Contract provisions stated that employees were entitled to payment for jury duty because of time lost when they otherwise would have been working. In this case, the employee was not scheduled to work, and she had no right to be reimbursed for work time she did not lose as a result of jury duty, the arbitrator concluded (*Union Eye Care Center Inc.*, 76 LA 170; see also 51 LA 1288).

● An employee was not entitled to paid leave for the hours between 7 a.m. and 9:15 a.m. on two days when he did not report for his 7 a.m. shift before going to court for jury duty, an arbitrator ruled. Although the contract specified that employees should receive the difference between their regular pay rate and whatever fee they received for serving on a jury, the arbitrator based his decision on a grievance settlement from 15 years earlier, which established that employees had to report to work before leaving for jury duty. According to the arbitrator, the reporting requirement had been consistently applied by the employer (*A.Y. McDonald Manufacturing Co.*, 100 LA 323).

● An arbitrator upheld an employer's denial of overtime pay to an employee who served on a jury for two days in one week and then filled in for a co-worker on the weekend. Under the contract, an employee had to work more than 40 hours in one week to receive overtime pay, the arbitrator said, and time spent on jury duty was not to be considered work time for the purposes of computing overtime (*Cabot Corp.*, 52 LA 575).

● *By contrast*, another arbitrator held that an employee was entitled to overtime for the hours he served on a grand jury while also continuing to work a full-time schedule. When the employee was selected for the grand jury, which was scheduled to convene on Tuesdays over a period of several weeks, his employer arranged his schedule so he would have Tuesdays off but continue to work 40 hours per week. Stressing that the contract in question required days of jury service to be counted as days worked for purposes of computing overtime pay, the arbitrator ordered the employer to pay the employee at his overtime rate for all uncompensated hours of jury service (*City of Urichsville*, 119 LA 1723).

• Interpreting a contract provision that protected employees from loss of pay due to jury service, an arbitrator held that an employer's obligation was not limited to paying only for those hours of jury duty that directly overlapped or were contiguous with an employee's scheduled work hours. In the case at hand, a second shift employee was serving on a jury in a federal case, and she had to drive some 130 miles in traveling to and from the courthouse. Considering the need to rest and prepare for jury duty as well as the requisite travel, the arbitrator decided that the employee was entitled to take a half day off with pay on two separate evenings that preceded her jury duty dates, in addition to her full shift on the actual dates of her jury service (*Iodent Co.*, 81 LA 1012).

• In a similar case, an arbitrator ruled that an employer was obligated to provide paid leave to a night-shift employee even though his shift ended an hour before his jury duty began. The labor contract called for paying employees the difference between regular earnings and jury pay when they were on jury duty. According to the arbitrator, it was necessary for the employee to be away from work if he were to report to court on time and in proper condition to fulfill his obligation as a juror (*Ozark Smelting & Mining Co.*, 27 LA 189).

1. Court Leave

Many employers give employees paid time off for court appearances unrelated to jury service, reasoning that the fulfillment of one's civic duty can also include activities such as testifying as a witness at a hearing or a trial. When employers deny requests for court leave, they often contend that employees' activities are personal in nature or do not fit the eligibility requirements for

court leave. In general, the decisions of arbitrators in such cases hinge on the specific contractual provisions governing the use of court leave.

• An arbitrator overturned an employer's denial of a half day of court leave to an employee who had been subpoenaed to testify regarding her husband's visitation rights with respect to his children by a previous marriage. In support of its decision to refuse the employee's request for court leave, the employer contended that the employee was not testifying as a disinterested witness. However, the arbitrator found that argument irrelevant to the outcome of the dispute. The critical issue, according to the arbitrator, was the fact that the contract clearly stated that an employee had only to provide a "lawfully issued subpoena for a court appearance" to qualify for court leave (*Newton Falls Exempted Village School District*, 121 LA 708).

• An employee was entitled to paid leave when he testified against his employer in proceedings before the National Labor Relations Board, an arbitrator held. The employee, who also served as local union president, was subpoenaed as a witness after the union filed unfair labor practice charges against the employer. In denying the employee's leave claim, the employer cited contract language that excluded court activities in which employees had a personal interest. In overturning the leave denial, the arbitrator noted that the employee had a duty as the president of the local union to attend the trial and represent the union's cause. Because that duty could be distinguished from any personal interest the employee might have had, the arbitrator ordered the employer to pay the employee for the leave he took minus mileage and whatever stipend he received for appearing before the NLRB (*Baker Marine Corp.*, 78 LA 794).

• *By contrast*, an arbitrator upheld an employer's refusal to pay partial wages to a number of employees who were subpoenaed by their own attorneys in a lawsuit against their employer. In spite of contractual language promising paid leave for subpoenaed employees, the arbitrator noted that the concept of a subpoena implies force of some kind. "Common sense indicates that an employee need not be 'compelled' to attend a hearing in his/her own case," the arbitrator said. Thus, the arbitrator concluded that the subpoenas in this case were merely a ploy, and he held that the employer was not obligated to "underwrite the cost of the employee-plaintiffs' litigation against it" (*Tysons Bearing Co. Inc.*, 120 LA 4).

• Another arbitrator upheld the denial of court leave for employees who appeared as witnesses in cases where they also were litigants. Although contractual language provided for paid leave when employees were subpoenaed to appear in any court, the parties' bargaining history and long understood interpretation of the contract led the arbitrator to conclude that court leave did not cover situations where employees were parties to a dispute, in which case they would only be allowed to use personal or vacation leave, compensatory time, or unpaid leave (*State of Ohio Departments of Commerce, Highway Safety, Taxation, Transportation, and Bureau of Workers' Compensation*, 100 LA 125).

• Employees who were subpoenaed to testify at the divorce trial of a co-worker were not entitled to paid court leave, an arbitrator decided. The employer contended that the contractual language on jury duty and court leave did not apply to employees who were subpoenaed by an attorney to serve as character witnesses. In upholding the denial of court leave, the arbitrator noted that the contract only covered situations where employees performed jury duty or were "subpoenaed as a witness by a U.S. Government agency" (*V.T. Griffin Services*, 120 LA 477).

• Two employees who had been subpoenaed to testify in an arbitration hearing were not entitled to use "legal leave," as opposed to personal leave, to attend the proceedings, an arbitrator ruled. Even though an arbitration hearing is one of only three forums where an employee might testify, the labor agreement pointedly left it off a detailed list of approved venues that would qualify for the use of legal leave, the arbitrator observed (*Somerset Area School District*, 119 LA 581).

• An employer had the right to deny paid leave to an employee who received a summons to appear as a defendant on criminal charges, an arbitrator held. Noting that the charges were ultimately dismissed, the arbitrator expressed sympathy for the employee but found that the denial of paid leave was appropriate because the contract did not cover situations in which employees appeared in court because of a summons. It would have been a disservice to the employer-union relationship to make a determination that distorted clear contract language, the arbitrator commented in upholding the leave denial (*National Super Markets*, 74 LA 10; see also 69 LA 1102).

C. Funeral or Bereavement Leave

Where collective bargaining agreements provide for funeral leave or bereavement leave, they usually specify that such leave will be granted in the event of the death of employees' family members. In some cases, arbitrators have to address the threshold question of how "family member" is defined in order to determine whether a particular relative's death provides a proper basis for employees to receive paid leave.

• An arbitrator ruled than an employer did not violate a collective bargaining agreement when it failed to provide bereavement leave pay in addition to holiday pay to an employee who took bereavement leave on Memorial Day when he was scheduled to work, because the agreement expressly stated that bereavement pay was not a method to provide "additional pay" and the union's evidence was too general and unspecific to establish a past practice of paying both types of pay (*Viscofan USA*, 126 LA 359).

• An arbitrator ruled that an employer did not violate a collective bargaining agreement by considering an employee to have quit voluntarily after he was absent for four consecutive work days without express written authorization. The employee had telephoned his supervisor to say that his uncle had died and that he would be absent from work, but his "uncle" was not included in list of familial relationships to which bereavement leave applied, any application for personal leave was required to be in writing and to be approved by a supervisor in writing, and the employer consistently had acted to discharge employees under the voluntary-quit standard (*Image Point*, 125 LA 1212).

• A school district violated a collective bargaining agreement when it denied bereavement leave to three teachers after the death of their close friend and told the teachers to take personal necessity leave instead, an arbitrator ruled. The agreement unambiguously entitled employees to bereavement leave after the death of any immediate family member "as defined" in the provision for personal necessity leave, which allowed for leave after the death of a close friend. The arbitrator ordered the school district and union to meet and confer over how to correct the unintended consequences of deleting the definition of "immediate family" in the bargaining agreement (*San Ysidro School District*, 127 LA 478.

• One arbitrator overturned an employer's denial of funeral leave to an employee whose half-brother had died. The employer argued that the employee's half-brother was not represented to the community as part of the employee's family unit, and therefore his death did not make the employee eligible for funeral leave. In rejecting the employer's argument, the arbitrator pointed out that several dictionaries and the state legislature defined the term brother to include half-brothers. A test based on the "family unit" should not be applied when there is a blood relationship or where a contract lists relatives covered for purposes of funeral leave, the arbitrator reasoned (*Hartman Electrical Manufacturing*, 92 LA 253; see also 95 LA 455).

• Another arbitrator held that an employer properly denied an employee bereavement leave to make funeral arrangements for his wife's stepfather. A contract clause allowed bereavement leave for deaths in the "immediate" family, defined as including a "father, mother, spouse, sister, brother, father-in-law, mother-in-law, or child." Because the deceased was not the employee's father-in-law, the leave denial was appropriate, the arbitrator ruled. While acknowledging that the employer had provided bereavement leave under

similar circumstances once before, the arbitrator noted that the grant of leave in that instance was based on misinformation and the employer's failure to check past records (*Northville Public Schools*, 104 LA 801; see also 96 LA 115, 89 LA 1285, 87 LA 1042, 86 LA 1132, 83 LA 1153).

• Where a collective bargaining agreement explicitly stated that employees could receive paid leave to attend the funeral of "immediate" family members, an arbitrator held that an employee's desire to attend the funeral of a grandparent-in-law need not be honored. Nonetheless, when the employer inadvertently approved and paid for the leave, through no deception on the employee's part, it was beyond the bounds of fairness to allow the payment to be deducted from the employee's salary seven months later, the arbitrator found, ordering the employer to reimburse the employee for the amount deducted (*National Uniform Service*, 104 LA 981; see also 76 LA 1107, 71 LA 874, 71 LA 473).

1. Timing of Leave

Aside from addressing the question of whether a particular relative's death qualifies for the use of funeral leave, arbitrators often are asked to consider the timing of leave and decide how many paid days off employees are entitled to receive. As evidenced by the examples below, disputes commonly arise when the leave period straddles a weekend or is not immediately adjacent to the date of the relative's death.

• One arbitrator held that an employee was entitled to three days of funeral leave on Monday, Tuesday, and Wednesday to attend the Wednesday funeral of his father who had died the previous Friday. The employee's paid leave had been limited to Monday, because his employer claimed that contractual language granting "up to three days funeral leave" meant up to three days following the actual death, not preceding the funeral. The arbitrator disagreed with the employer, emphasizing the fact that the contract provided for "funeral leave" rather than "death leave." Based on the language of the contract, the three days of leave had to center on the date of the funeral rather than the date the person expired, the arbitrator said (*W.G. Bush & Co.*, 65 LA 608; see also 80 LA 1305).

• An arbitrator overturned an employer's denial of death leave when an employee needed a day off to take care of estate matters a month after a relative's death. The employee, who had been off work when his relative died, was given two days of death leave before returning to work, but the employer required the employee to use personal leave when he later took the additional day off to meet with an attorney about his relative's estate. According to the arbitrator, the employer had never refused a request for such leave in 30 years, and it could not unilaterally change the longstanding interpretation that had been given to the contractual language on death leave. Thus, the arbitrator ordered the employer to restore the employee's personal leave and treat the day off as death leave (*Birch Run Area Schools*, 122 LA 1212).

• An employer improperly limited an employee to three days of funeral leave when his sister and brother-in-law died, an arbitrator ruled. The contract provided for three days off for the death of the former and one day off for the death of the latter, but the employer argued that "pyramiding of leave" was not allowed for multiple funerals. The arbitrator, however, concluded that the employee was entitled to four days of funeral leave. The contract was silent on the issue of multiple deaths, the arbitrator noted, and the employee spent the four days driving to and from the funerals, which were a substantial distance away (*Federal Glass Co.*, 65 LA 787; see also 72 LA 337).

• An arbitrator overturned an employer's decision to grant a single day of paid leave to an employee who missed work on Friday, attended his sister's funeral on Saturday, and took additional time off after the weekend. A contract clause on funeral leave provided for payment in full for time lost, not to exceed three days. According to the arbitrator, past practice did not support the employer's decision to count the employee's unscheduled weekend days as part of the three-day period. Rather, the arbitrator held that the entitlement to pay for lost work time applied to "three sequential work days including work days before the funeral and/or after the funeral." Additionally, the arbitrator ruled that the employer could not limit payments to eight hours of wages per day in cases where scheduled shifts exceeded that amount of time (*Swanson Plating Co.*, 110 LA 1207).

• Another arbitrator found that a more restrictive approach was called for where a contract allowed up to three "consecutive days" of funeral leave and only provided pay "for time absent from regularly scheduled working hours on Monday through Friday." The arbitrator limited pay to Friday for an employee who missed work prior to a Sunday funeral, and limited another employee to two days of paid leave preceding a Saturday funeral. The contract's unambiguous language on consecutive days, excluding Saturdays and Sundays, outweighed the union's argument that past practice dictated more liberal pay awards in connection with funeral leave, the arbitrator reasoned (*FMC Corp.*, 64 LA 1300).

• Similarly, an employee who requested Thursday, Friday, and Monday as bereavement leave was not entitled to be paid for Monday under a contract that granted three "consecutive days" for dealing with a family member's death, an arbitrator ruled. The normal meaning of "consecutive" is one day that immediately follows another, meaning calendar days as opposed to scheduled work days, the arbitrator held (*Gulf Printing Co.*, 92 LA 893; see also 89 LA 385, 89 LA 179).

• An employer was justified in refusing to grant paid leave when an employee needed time off after a funeral to assist relatives with their travel arrangements, an arbitrator found. The contract permitted up to three days of leave in connection with the death of an immediate family member so that employees could make funeral arrangements and attend the funeral. The employee was not entitled to use paid leave on the day after the funeral because that day did not qualify as time spent either in attending or arranging for the funeral, the arbitrator decided (*Trane Co.*, 53 LA 1108; see also 73 LA 96).

2. *Funeral Leave and Other Absences*

Disputes also are likely to arise regarding the denial of paid funeral leave in situations where employees are away from work for other reasons, such as vacations or strikes, at the time of a relative's passing.

- In one case, an arbitrator said an employer properly refused to grant an employee paid funeral leave when a relative died during a period when he was already scheduled to take a vacation. The employee's mother died shortly after his wedding, so he canceled his honeymoon and instead attended to the details of the funeral and mourning services that followed. The employer allowed a two-day extension of the employee's time off but denied pay for funeral leave. The contract language on funeral leave tied benefits to the loss of working time, and because the employee suffered no such loss, he was not entitled to receive paid funeral leave, the arbitrator held (*Maui Pineapple Co.*, 46 LA 849; see also 79 LA 82).

- *By contrast*, an employer was ordered to pay workers who attended the funeral of the child of one of them during a strike. Noting that work remained available, an arbitrator said the employees could have done their jobs if they had reported for work. Because funeral pay is compensation for time not worked because an employee is attending a funeral, and given that the employees did in fact attend the funeral, the arbitrator concluded that the presence of the strike was inconsequential (*U.S. Pipe & Foundry Co.*, 65 LA 111).

- Another arbitrator ordered an employer to grant paid funeral leave to a pair of brothers who attended their father's funeral during a plant shutdown caused by severe weather. The two employees had already received approval for funeral leave before the shutdown occurred. Even though the award had the effect of giving the employees more money than they otherwise would have received during the period in question, the arbitrator said the severe weather could not have an impact on funeral leave that was already granted (*Hillerich & Bradsby Co.*, 70 LA 950; see also 75 LA 1076).

IV. Leave for Union Business

OVERVIEW

Provisions in collective bargaining agreements that allow leave for union business vary greatly. Some give union representatives the right to take paid time during work for activities such as grievance handling and contract negotiations, while others enable employees to take leaves of absence for activities such as union meetings, training sessions, and national conventions.

Whether employees are entitled to receive leave for union business depends on the facts and circumstances of each case. Generally speaking, however, arbitrators are likely to hold that employers are justified in limiting the amount of time spent on union business and denying requests for leave to engage in union activities that are not authorized by contractual language or a past practice of the parties.

SUMMARY OF CASES

A. Disputes Over Leave Restrictions

Employers and unions often resort to arbitration to resolve disagreements about the types of activities that qualify for union leave and the amount of time employees are entitled to receive. If collective bargaining agreements lack specific guidelines and instead contain broad language on time off for union matters, arbitrators are not likely to uphold leave refusals just because a particular activity is not to employers' liking. As evidenced by some of the examples below, however, arbitrators do not always overrule the leave restrictions imposed by employers.

• An arbitrator ruled that an agency did not violate federal law or the collective bargaining agreement when it denied a newly appointed union treasurer official time to attend the union's financial officers training, even though some of the training involved preparing reports required by federal agencies which the Federal Labor Relations Authority had found was not internal union business. The agreement said that official time "may" be authorized for unit representatives to attend "training approved by the [e]mployer" on matters within the scope of the Federal Labor-Management Relations Statute, which indicates that authorizing official time for union representatives to attend training is permissive (*Dep't of the Navy*, 129 LA 1576).

• An arbitrator ruled that a city did not violate a collective bargaining agreement when it denied the request by an employee who served as the union's district representative and chief steward to attend a meeting of the civil service commission during middle of his shift without taking some form of personal leave, where the agreement granted official time to union representatives only to attend "meetings between labor and management." (*City of Hamilton*, 128 LA 68).

● One arbitrator held that an employer was justified in denying leave for an employee to serve on a political action committee. Political activity did not constitute "union business" as defined by the contract, which permitted leave for transacting union business or representing the national union, the arbitrator determined (*Anchor Duck Mills*, 5 LA 428; see also 37 LA 249).

● A school board was not required to grant teachers leave to picket another school, an arbitrator decided. Their contract permitted them to take time off for "official sessions" of their union, and they claimed that while picketing they also were engaged in such activities. However, the arbitrator found that granting them paid leave to picket another employer was so "extreme and novel" that such actions would likely have been spelled out in their contract. Finding no such language, the arbitrator concluded that the contract was designed to permit the employees to participate in internal union affairs only (*Jackson Public Schools*, 64 LA 1089).

● An employer did not commit a contract violation in refusing to grant union leave to employees so they could represent fellow employees in state workers' compensation proceedings, an arbitrator ruled. After some employees had attended seminars on workers' compensation, a union committee decided that the employees should attend workers' compensation proceedings on behalf of other union members in order to reduce the costs that would be incurred if employees received formal legal representation. Upholding the employer's refusal to release the employees for such activities, the arbitrator said representation at workers' compensation proceedings was a peripheral benefit that the union had chosen to provide its members, not official union business (*Hill-*

shire Farms Co., a Division of Consolidated Foods Corp., 88 LA 1148).

● An employer was not required to invoke call-in procedures or shut down a critical machine to enable the financial secretary of a local union to miss work so he could attend one of his union's monthly meetings, an arbitrator held. When no one volunteered to fill in for the employee, the union argued that the employer had an obligation to use its call list to obtain a replacement who could operate the machine while the employee attended the meeting. The arbitrator found that the employer was required "to make all reasonable efforts" to accommodate the leave requests of union officers so they could handle union business, but such efforts did not include utilizing the call list to find a qualified employee to cover for an officer or shutting down a machine that was critical to the employer's operations (*Wausau-Mosinee Paper Co.*, 118 LA 1473).

● An arbitrator ruled that a fire department violated the collective bargaining agreement when it asked a firefighter/union president what he was doing when he took union leave, where the agreement stated that the president "shall be granted" leave "for the purposes of discharging his official duties as Local President," and nothing in the provision authorized the department to request any particulars of leave request (*Union Township Board of Trustees*, 125 LA 1638).

● An arbitrator ruled that an agency violated a collectivebargaining agreement when it denied requests for official time without giving a specific reason instead just using the general phrase "compelling need" of a "mission requirement." However the agency did not violate the agreement when it gave specific reasons for denying requests. The arbitrator found it was absurd to use such a general phase for denying requests. The remedy for the agency's violations of the bargaining agreement by denying requests for official time without giving specific explanations was to require that specific explanations be given in the future, where other remedies, such as ordering training for agency's managers and supervisors was not appropriate (*Department of the Army*, 123 LA 1084).

• Although brief periods of time off to prepare for monthly union meetings did not qualify as leaves of absence for union business, an employer could not unilaterally discontinue its practice of granting the time off, an arbitrator ruled. Members of a local union's executive board had traditionally been allowed about two hours of unpaid time for monthly planning sessions that were held on the Wednesdays before regularly scheduled Saturday meetings. After excusing the board members for this purpose over a period of years, the employer eventually decided that the practice had become too burdensome and informed the union that employees would no longer be released from work for the planning sessions.

According to the arbitrator, the importance of releasing union officials for the performance of union business had been recognized by the parties under their contractual provisions on unpaid leaves of absence, but those provisions were not geared toward the brief periods of time off that the executive board members requested each month. Nevertheless, undisputed evidence established a past practice of excusing employees for the monthly planning sessions, and that practice was entitled to protection, the arbitrator found. Despite emphasizing the importance of the planning sessions, the arbitrator said the board members' leave entitlement was not fixed and absolute, and he ordered the parties to engage in collective bargaining to work out specific arrangements regarding the amount and timing of leave to be granted (*Weston Paper and Manufacturing Co.*, 76 LA 1273; see also 70 LA 887).

• An employer violated its labor contract by refusing to pay a bargaining committee member for travel time the day before a bargaining session in another part of the state, an arbitrator ruled. According to the arbitrator, the contract was "clear and unambiguous" in requiring the employer to offer a reasonable amount of paid leave for "direct travel to and from the location where the bargaining team member works" without restricting paid travel time only to the day bargaining was scheduled. The arbitrator ordered the employer to cease denying paid travel time to employees who needed to take travel time before the actual day of bargaining (*University of California*, 122 LA 532).

• Another arbitrator overturned a new fire chief's unilateral decision that prohibited firefighters from attending monthly union meetings while on duty, which had been allowed for some 20 years. Finding that management could not unilaterally change a known practice that had been "unequivocal and of long-standing duration," the arbitrator ordered the employer to let the employees resume attending the monthly meetings. The only condition was that the firefighters had to "be properly uniformed and ready for immediate response to emergencies" during their attendance at the meetings, the arbitrator said (*Reno-Tahoe Airport Authority*, 121 LA 1238).

• Reinstatement was not warranted for an employee who had been away from his job for 15 years, an arbitrator decided. The employee, who had been on an approved union leave, claimed that he should have been reinstated because of an agreement he had with his employer. However, the arbitrator noted that the pact had been predicated on his working for the union, and the employee had not bothered to contact the employer for nearly nine months after his position with the union ended. He also was actively pursuing a different line of work, which the arbitrator said amounted to a "constructive quit" and freed the employer from any obligation to reinstate him (*White, Williams & Co.*, 120 LA 513).

1. 'Official time' for Federal Employees

When employees of federal agencies request paid time off for union matters, the leave is typically referred to as "official time." The following cases reflect some of the disputes that can arise with respect to the use of official time.

• An arbitrator held that a federal agency committed a contract violation by denying official time to an employee who worked as an air traffic control specialist. The employee had been designated by his union as the representative for workers in another bargaining unit, but his requests for the use of official time to perform his duties were denied because he was not a member of their unit. According to the arbitrator, under both the contract and a memorandum of understanding, the union had sole authority to designate representatives, and the employer was required to grant the employee official time to fulfill the responsibilities of that role (*Federal Aviation Administration*, 120 LA 1202).

● A federal agency acted improperly in denying official time to stewards to travel to union training sessions held in conjunction with their national convention, an arbitrator decided. In justifying the move, an agency official cited pressure from Congress for the agency to cut back on the use of official time. Although "political reality must be part of the agency's lifeblood," the arbitrator acknowledged, it did not trump the terms of the collective bargaining agreement, which provided for the use of official time to attend training. "It was the parties' mutual intention as evidenced in their agreement to provide official time to travel to approved training," the arbitrator concluded, ordering the employer to make the stewards whole for their losses and post a notice for 60 days stating that it would cease the violations (*Internal Revenue Service*, 122 LA 1673).

● Another arbitrator upheld an agency's denial of paid time off and travel expenses for a union official to attend a three-day meeting on alternative dispute resolution. Although ground rules established between the parties stated that the employer would pay for a union negotiator's official time, travel, and per diem expenses to various union meetings and proceedings, the rules also specifically limited to 10 the number of sessions for which the agency was responsible. In this instance, the union had requested payment for an 11th session, which the employer properly denied, the arbitrator determined (*Defense Contract Audit Agency*, 119 LA 289).

B. Grievance and Arbitration Activities

Due to the importance of grievance processing and similar representational activities, most unions attempt to secure contractual provisions guaranteeing paid time for stewards and other union officials to spend on the performance of day-to-day union business at the workplace. In general, arbitrators rely on contract clauses and past practice to determine whether or not employers have an obligation to provide union leave for such activities.

● An arbitrator ruled that a city's motion to quash the subpoena of a police officer to be paid to attend his own disciplinary appeal hearing was denied. The criteria for mandatory payment under the state's local government code was satisfied, in that such hearings were "administrative hearing," and the officer was charged with conduct relating to his official duties and thus his appearance was "in the capacity of a . . . police officer" (*City of Paris*, 127 LA 1818).

● An employer could not unilaterally set a limit on the number of hours that employees could spend handling grievances, an arbitrator held. The arbitrator rebuffed the employer's attempt at justifying the unilateral action by claiming that its new rule was a reasonable response to excessive and increasing amounts of time being spent on grievances. The contract did not provide for a specific time limit, the arbitrator observed, but instead obligated the employer to pay for all time that was "reasonable and necessary" for handling disputes under the agreement (*Goss Co.*, 44 LA 824).

● An employer was obligated to allow a chief steward to walk through its plant as part of his paid work day so that employees could make known their grievances, an arbitrator decided. After five years of allowing the practice, the employer began objecting to the daily walk and refused to pay the employee for time spent on the activity unless he specifically requested and received permission in advance. According to the arbitrator, the employer's inaction over the years constituted tacit approval of the steward's activity that could not be changed without negotiating with the union (*American Saint Gobain Corp.*, 46 LA 920).

● An employer should not have docked a steward's pay for a half hour that he spent discussing his own grievance with a union attorney, especially in light of the fact that the employee had asked for and received his supervisor's approval for the time off, an arbitrator ruled. The collective bargaining agreement between the parties allowed stewards to spend a reasonable amount of time processing formal grievances without suffering any loss of pay or benefits. Reasoning that the contract did not exclude a steward's own grievance from the term "formal grievances," the arbitrator ordered the employer to restore a half hour of compensatory time to the employee (*County Sanitation District of Los Angeles County*, 64 LA 521).

• An employer could not deny paid time off to employees who were being deposed in a case against the employer that arose under Title VII of the Civil Rights Act of 1964, an arbitrator decided. The employees were in essence using the court system to process their grievances with the employer, and the contract specified that they were entitled to be paid for time spent in processing grievances, the arbitrator said. It also was the employer's choice that they give their depositions during working hours and, as such, the employer could not then use that decision against them, the arbitrator concluded, ordering back pay for all employees who gave depositions (*Wallace Silversmiths Inc.*, 64 LA 1119).

• On the other hand, an arbitrator refused to award stewards any pay for attending grievance sessions and labor-management meetings during times when they were not scheduled to work. Although their union pointed to a past practice of paying stewards for nonwork time spent on grievance handling, the practice had been applied inconsistently and was not binding because the agreement was clear and unambiguous about what was permitted, the arbitrator said. Stewards' pay could not be docked for time spent on grievance handling during working hours, but the contract said nothing about paying stewards for attending to grievances if they did so on their own time and was completely silent on the matter of whether they should be paid for time spent at other union meetings (*Supervalu Inc.*, 118 LA 791).

• Union stewards were not entitled to remain on the clock when providing union representation to employees during disciplinary investigations, an arbitrator held. Stewards were required to clock out to

attend grievance meetings, but the union said they should have remained on the clock when employees exercised their *Weingarten* rights by requesting a steward's presence during investigatory meetings. According to the arbitrator, however, a contract clause stating that union activities could not be conducted "during compensated work hours" meant that the stewards had no choice but to punch out while representing employees in *Weingarten* meetings (*Arizona Portland Cement Co.*, 115 LA 1279).

1. Arbitration Hearings

While arbitrators often find that paid time off for grievance handling is contractually required, they are less likely to determine that employers must provide paid union leave for employees to prepare for or attend arbitration hearings.

• One arbitrator decided that a contract clause on grievance activity applied to arbitration hearings. The contract normally required stewards to handle union business during lunch or at other times when they were not working, but it included an exception allowing stewards to receive paid time off to attend grievance meetings that the employer scheduled during work hours. Concluding that arbitration hearings were a type of grievance meeting, the arbitrator ordered the employer to grant stewards paid time off if they participated in arbitration hearings during their regular working hours. The arbitrator acknowledged that this interpretation was of little help to stewards from the night shift, who commonly used vacation time the night before an arbitration hearing or simply attended the proceedings in a tired condition, but he said he could find nothing in the parties' contract that would provide relief for that situation (*Ecolab Inc.*, 120 LA 641).

• Another arbitrator found that an employer had no contractual obligation to pay stewards for the time they spent testifying at arbitration hearings. Under the parties' collective bargaining agreement, the employer had to pay "for all time spent during working hours investigating and adjusting grievances and complaints." Although stewards were necessary participants in handling grievances, the arbitrator decided, their presence was not needed at arbitration hearings, and their involvement in such hearings did not qualify as time spent investigating or adjusting grievances (*Consolidated Industries Inc.*, 43 LA 331).

• An employer could not require the use of paid vacation time instead of unpaid leave when employees needed time off to prepare for arbitration hearings, an arbitrator ruled. The arbitrator noted that vacation was an earned benefit for personal use, and even though employees often had taken vacation days voluntarily when they needed time off in connection with arbitration hearings, workers had never been forced to use their vacation benefits. Consequently, the arbitrator ordered the employer to return to its past practice of allowing unpaid leave in such situations. In doing so, however, the arbitrator also held that such absences would be "subject to 'last minute' revocation if a significant work-related emergency arises" (*Texas Utilities Mining Co.*, 87 LA 815).

• An employer did not commit a contract violation by refusing two employees' leave requests and instead arranging their schedules so their days off would coincide with an arbitration hearing, an arbitrator found. The employees had requested unpaid leave with the understanding that their union would pay the wages they lost while missing work, but their altered schedules meant that they still worked a full week. Rejecting the employees' argument that they were entitled to leave, the arbitrator found that the employer had a longstanding practice of adjusting employees' schedules so they could participate in arbitration hearings on their days off. Once their schedules were adjusted, the arbitrator added, the employees did not have to miss work to attend the arbitration hearing and therefore lacked cause for a leave of absence (*Youngstown Vindicator Printing Co.*, 88 LA 17).

• In a dispute over the appropriate discipline for employees who missed work to testify in arbitration proceedings, an arbitrator ruled that two-day suspensions were too severe. Their employer had not received appropriate notice of their need to attend the proceedings, the arbitrator noted. Finding that the employees appeared to be innocent pawns in a labor-management tug-of-war, however, the arbitrator cut the length of their suspensions in half (*United Engineering Co.*, 64 LA 1274).

C. Leave for Local Union Officers

Employees who hold elected office in their local unions tend to face unusual demands on their time, and their leave requests often differ from those made by shop stewards or other union representatives. While recognizing that union officers can be called upon to perform a wide range of duties, arbitrators generally hold that employers are within their rights in limiting the amount of time spent on union business and denying requests for time away from work to engage in activities that are not covered under contract clauses on union leave.

• An employee who also served as local union president was justifiably issued a warning letter by his employer that said he could not continue to devote virtually all his work time to union business, an arbitrator held. Although the parties' contract granted the employee paid time for fulfilling his union responsibilities, he should not have regarded that as "carte blanche permission" to spend as much employer time as he pleased on union business, the arbitrator said. He was still an employee whether or not he also was the local union president, the arbitrator observed, adding that if the employer paid the employee his full salary while he also worked full-time for the union, that would smack of unlawful employer domination of the union (*Pratt &Letchworth*, 48 LA 1345).

• An arbitrator upheld an employer's denial of paid leave to a local union president so she could attend arbitration hearings and participate in contract talks involving bargaining units aside from the one where she was a member. Although the employee had on occasion been paid for grievance processing in other units that were part of the employer's wide-ranging business, there was "not a hint in the agreement itself" that could be "intended to signal a broader, extra-unit reach" to her rights to paid leave for fulfilling her duties as president of the local, the arbitrator concluded (*Aramark Corp.*, 121 LA 665).

● An employer did not have to approve a three-day leave of absence for a local union official who wanted the time off to organize workers at another facility operated by the employer, an arbitrator ruled. The collective bargaining agreement stipulated that union leave would be permitted "for attending union conventions, educational conferences or seminars, etc." The union argued that the term "etc." was sufficient to cover organizing activity, but the arbitrator rejected that argument. While acknowledging that broadly worded contract clauses on leave for "union business" have been held to encompass organizing and other activities involving separate locations, the arbitrator found that the contract in this case did not allow for such an interpretation because the purpose of the requested leave was not comparable to the specified activities of attending conventions, conferences, and seminars (*Amcast Automotive*, 118 LA 16).

● Similarly, an employer did not have to grant leave to a union president who wanted time off to negotiate a contract between the union and another employer, an arbitrator held. The employee had requested the time under a contract clause stating that "the business representative of the union or his agent designated in writing . . . may sit in on any and all meetings." According to the arbitrator, the clause did not give the employee the right to take time off at will while maintaining his job and was silent on any perceived right to take leave to negotiate a pact with another employer (*Leonetti Furniture Manufacturing Co.*, 64 LA 975).

● Union officers were not entitled to receive special leave for "partnership" activities when they were performing normal representational duties, an arbitrator ruled. On two occasions, the president and vice-president of a local union requested "partnership time" when they worked with other local officials on union activities during work hours, but their employer denied the requests. The arbitrator upheld the denials based on contract language that distinguished between "partnership" activities

and other union business, observing that "nothing is plainer than the fact that the former must concurrently involve representatives of both labor and management," not just labor (*Department of Veterans Affairs*, 115 LA 1432).

● An employer acted appropriately in reducing a local union president's wages to match a reduction in the workweek of his "home unit," an arbitrator decided. To avoid constant work disruptions caused by the employee's need to handle union matters, the employer had agreed to pay him full wages while allowing him to spend all his time conducting union business. The employee had been receiving six days of wages per week, but his pay was reduced when the employer cut the workweek of his home unit from six days to five. In upholding the pay reduction, the arbitrator found that the employer's promise to pay the employee for time spent on union business was specifically tied to the schedule of the unit where he worked prior to becoming the local union president (*RMI Titanium Co.*, 118 LA 947).

● An arbitrator held that a public-sector employer violated a collective bargaining agreement by forcing a local union president to take annual leave rather than unpaid leave to meet with Congressional representatives during his union's "lobby week." According to the arbitrator, "it is well established law" that lobbying Congress is an integral part of labor relations in the public sector, and the employee had a significant role to play in the week's events. By making the union officer take annual leave, the employer maintained the right to recall him to work during what the employer said was an emergency situation. The arbitrator concluded that the employee had met the appropriate criteria and should have been allowed to use unpaid leave as requested (*U.S. Army Corps of Engineers*, 104 LA 30; see also 91 LA 525).

● Tensions over a local union president's entitlement to paid time for union business prompted another arbitrator to order negotiations between management and the union on how they should handle the leave approval process. The local president was one of only seven employees in a small shop, and his requests for time away from the job were increasingly questioned by his supervisor and denied in the interest of meeting work demands. Finding that the parties had experienced a degradation of the mutual trust that was required for the proper functioning of contractual provisions on union leave, the arbitrator instructed the parties to meet and ascertain a means of achieving an "appropriate balance" between the employee's "representational demands" and management's right to make reasonable leave decisions in light of the fact that the employee constituted 14 percent of the manpower in the shop where he worked (*Department of Homeland Security, U.S. Border Patrol,* 122 LA 1547).

V. Maternity, Paternity & Adoption Leave

OVERVIEW

Collective bargaining agreements grant varying leave rights with regard to pregnancy, recuperation from childbirth, and caring for or bonding with newborns and newly adopted children. When disputes arise over employees' ability to miss work or receive paid time off in such situations, arbitrators first look to contract clauses that specifically address maternity, paternity, and adoption leave, but their decisions often hinge at least in part on other contract provisions, such as those pertaining to disability and sick leave.

In addition, arbitrators commonly take into account family leave and anti-discrimination laws. Under the federal Family and Medical Leave Act, for example, covered workers are entitled to up to 12 weeks of unpaid leave following childbirth, adoption, or the placement of a foster child, as well as leave in connection with serious health conditions, which can include pregnancy and postnatal recovery. Under federal and state anti-discrimination laws, meanwhile, employers must treat pregnancy as they would any other disability. For instance, if employers offer paid leave for other illnesses or conditions, they also must do so for pregnancy-related ailments.

While statutory protections play a role in the resolution of many leave-related grievances, they often serve as a baseline, establishing the minimum requirements that employers must meet in granting employees maternity, paternity, and adoption leave. As illustrated by the cases discussed in this chapter, arbitrators sometimes find that employees' contractual rights exceed the entitlements afforded by federal and state laws. (For a discussion of cases dealing with the full range of issues that arise under the FMLA, see Part 2, Chapter I, Absenteeism & Tardiness, and Chapter VI, Family and Medical Leave in this section.)

SUMMARY OF CASES

A. Maternity Leave

Collective bargaining agreements vary widely in their provisions concerning maternity leave. Recognizing that women can face limitations in their ability to work during pregnancy or while recuperating from delivery, some labor contracts treat the period before and after childbirth in the same way as a period of illness or disability. Other contracts are less restrictive and allow employees to take leave even in the absence of physical difficulties.

Frequently, arbitrators must interpret an array of contract provisions when resolving grievances related to maternity leave, because employees could be entitled to various types of paid and unpaid leave, as well as disability benefits. In addition, arbitrators tend to consider the impact of federal and state laws, such as the Pregnancy Discrimination Act of 1978, which amended Title VII of the Civil Rights Act to make it unlawful for employers to discriminate on the basis of pregnancy.

A school board did not violate collective-bargaining contract when it prorated sick and personal leave of a teacher for the year in which she missed work due to maternity leave, even though the contract gave all employees 10 days of sick leave, an arbitrator ruled. The provision allowing for prorating of sick leave was a more specific provision, and the arbitrator found the contract should be read to "breathe life" in to all its provisions (*Purchase Line School District*, 124 LA 440).

● One arbitrator held that an employer misinterpreted contract language on the amount of leave employees were allowed to take for maternity purposes. The employer had argued that employees were entitled to a maximum of four months' leave for prenatal, infant care, maternity leave, and sick leave. It argued that a contract clause stating that the "sum of such leaves will not exceed four months" applied to all available types of leave. The arbitrator disagreed, finding that the contract meant that pregnant employees were entitled to a prenatal and/or infant care leave of four months plus a period of sick leave if needed and attested to by a physician's statement that sick leave was necessary (*West Side Credit Union*, 77 LA 622).

● An employer committed a contract violation when it unilaterally implemented reductions in maternity leave, an arbitrator found. The employer cut maternity disability pay from six to four weeks for uncomplicated births and from eight to six weeks for Caesarian deliveries. According to the arbitrator, the reductions amounted to changes in employment conditions that should have been negotiated with the union. The arbitrator ordered the employer to make whole any employees who had been affected by the unilateral changes (*Jewel Food Stores*, 104 LA 59).

● Under a collective bargaining agreement that provided for up to one year of unpaid parental leave after the birth of a child, an employer could not unilaterally limit a pregnant employee's postnatal leave to half a year, an arbitrator found. The employer had agreed to the clause in several different contracts and had denied only one other such request. According to the arbitrator, the denial in this instance was based on the employer's "general dissatisfaction" with long leaves, which did not justify refusing the employee's request (*Ankeny Community School District*, 77 LA 860).

● An employer discriminated against a pregnant employee by placing her on leave rather than allowing her to perform light-duty work, an arbitrator decided. When she became unable to perform the various physical tasks required by her job, the employee asked for a transfer to another department and then asked to be assigned to a light-duty position. The employee went out on leave after her requests were refused, and she was without income during her pregnancy once she exhausted her sick leave and vacation benefits. Noting that a male employee had been assigned to light duty following an operation, the arbitrator asserted that the pregnant employee was not accorded fair and equal treatment and ordered the employer to pay her straight time for the period when she was denied work (*Cities Service Co.*, 87 LA 1209).

• An employer should not have classified a pregnant employee's unscheduled time off as an absence that was subject to discipline, an arbitrator found. When the employee suffered severe pain and bleeding, she sought emergency medical help and did not call her employer until two days later, when she was told she had no more sick leave available and would have to request FMLA leave. The employer treated the employee's situation as an absence without leave. The arbitrator faulted the employer for demanding proof of the need for leave in advance of what was an unforeseeable medical emergency and ordered the employee's absence converted to unpaid FMLA leave (*Department of Homeland Security*, 119 LA 833).

• A pregnant employee who failed to call in regularly during her maternity leave was wrongfully fired by her employer because it should have granted her FMLA leave, which would have obviated the need for calling in, an arbitrator ruled. The employer contended that the employee did not qualify for FMLA leave because her length of service fell short of the 12-month threshold established under the law. However, the arbitrator found there was no such mandate under the collective bargaining agreement, which would have permitted the leave. Asserting that the employee had to be treated as if she had been granted FMLA leave, thereby relieving her from the obligation to check in with the employer every three days, the arbitrator overturned the employee's termination and ordered her reinstated and made whole (*Enesco Corp.*, 107 LA 513).

• An employer should not have fired an employee for occasionally going to her husband's business while she was on FMLA leave for severe postpartum depression, an arbitrator found. The employee was seen arriving at her husband's store by a private investigator, who observed her for a few days and said the employee appeared to be working there. The arbitrator, however, determined that the employee merely was going to the store to be with other people and use the store's computer for personal household matters. Despite occasionally helping out with stocking and other tasks, she was

not actually employed, was not engaging in fraud, and should not have been fired, the arbitrator said, ordering the employer to restore her job and provide back pay (*Chippewa Valley Schools*, 121 LA 890).

• The protections of the FMLA did not apply to an employee who missed work due to pregnancy complications and other reasons, an arbitrator found. The FMLA only applies to employees who have worked at least 1,250 hours during the preceding 12 months, but the employee fell "far short" of that threshold, the arbitrator noted. Nevertheless, finding that the employer had not notified the employee that she was close to being terminated, which amounted to a failure to follow its own procedures, the arbitrator overturned the employee's discharge. He ordered reinstatement without back pay and assigned the employee four points under the employer's no-fault attendance system, which called for termination at eight points (*Electrolux Home Products*, 117 LA 46).

• An arbitrator upheld an employer's refusal to grant paid leave for a full semester to a teacher so she would be able to bond with her newborn. Given ambiguous contract language on paid leave for "maternity purposes" but clear employer rules on how and when paid maternity leave was allowed, the arbitrator determined that such leave was supposed to be granted only when a mother is "physically incapacitated as a result of pregnancy or a postpartum medically related reason." He concluded that the employer was under no obligation to provide paid leave for a new mother who is in "good enough physical health to resume work but wishes to stay at home to bond" with her newborn (*Department of Defense Dependents School*, 89 LA 105).

1. Use of Paid Sick Leave

Arbitrators often find that employees have a right to use paid sick leave during absences associated with pregnancy and childbirth.

• An employee was entitled to paid sick leave for time she was away from work because of serious medical problems associated with her pregnancy, an arbitrator ruled. The employer's past practice of only providing leave without pay to pregnant employees was not controlling, the arbitrator said, because there was "little evidence to suggest that there was mutual acquiescence" by the parties. Adding that the parties' contract forbade gender-based discrimination in the granting of benefits, the arbitrator concluded that the employer was obligated to give the employee paid sick leave for the period of time she was disabled (*Kaiser-Permanente Medical Care Program*, 64 LA 245).

● When an employer agreed to a new contract that moved a provision for a "pregnancy leave of absence" into a clause covering "sick leave of absence," it committed itself to providing paid sick leave rather than unpaid leave, an arbitrator ruled. Despite the employer's claim that it never intended for maternity leave to be provided as paid leave, the arbitrator said its intentions during contract negotiations were irrelevant in light of the clear contract language and ordered the employer to provide paid sick leave rather than unpaid leave to pregnant employees (*Scottscraft Inc.*, 64 LA 279).

● An employer improperly refused to allow an employee to use her accumulated paid sick leave to cover 13 days she took off after her doctor certified that she was unable to work because of pregnancy-related complications, an arbitrator ruled. Finding that the contract between the parties was covered by a state anti-discrimination law that forbade bias against pregnant women, the arbitrator ordered the employer to pay her for the 13 days (*Apollo-Ridge School District*, 68 LA 1235; see also 64 LA 239).

● In a similar decision, an arbitrator found that an employer had illegally discriminated against a pregnant employee by refusing to let her use accumulated paid sick leave to cover time off caused by pregnancy-related medical complications. He ordered the employer to grant the employee 21 days of pay, charged to her sick leave account, and to stop denying these benefits to all its pregnant employees (*West Allis-West Milwaukee Joint City School District No. 1*, 68 LA 644).

● Under a contract that provided unpaid maternity leave and paid sick leave for "personal illness," an employer should not have denied sick leave pay to an employee because of a pregnancy-related disability, an arbitrator ruled, despite the employer's past practice of never granting sick leave to employees taking maternity leave. A contractual clause prohibiting discrimination "with respect to any term or condition of employment" and a state law prohibiting sex discrimination were deciding factors, the arbitrator noted (*Muskego-Norway School District*, 71 LA 509).

● On the other hand, an arbitrator ruled that an employee was not entitled to use a sick leave bank to cover the time she spent caring for her newborn. The contract allowed workers to use the sick leave bank only if they were incapacitated by a severe illness or injury. The employee claimed that breast-feeding her child constituted such an illness, but the arbitrator said breast-feeding is not a sickness, and even if it were, it clearly was not among those "extraordinary physical problems" mentioned in the contract as providing a basis for using the sick leave bank (*Cheektowaga Central School Board of Education*, 80 LA 225).

2. Benefits Considerations

Some disputes focus less on employees' leave rights than on their ability to receive certain benefits while they are away from work during pregnancy or postnatal recovery. As evidenced by the following examples, eligibility for disability benefits is a common source of contention.

● Although a labor contract did not specifically mention maternity benefits, an employer violated public policy as delineated in the Pregnancy Discrimination Act when it denied disability benefits to a pregnant employee, an arbitrator said. Despite the employer's assertion that the employee did not qualify for such benefits because she was "not the victim of either an accident or an illness," the arbitrator noted that the contract provided a basis for his decision by stating that discrimination based on gender should not be tolerated. Noting that the agreement also referred to federal anti-discrimination laws, the arbitrator determined that the employee should be reimbursed for all disability benefits she was denied (*Kalamazoo Label Co.*, 95 LA 1042).

• An employer violated federal civil rights law, a state anti-discrimination statute, and its labor contract when it denied (through its insurer) disability benefits to a pregnant employee who was on temporary layoff, an arbitrator found. The employee, who had been forbidden to lift anything weighing more than 20 pounds, was put on "rotating layoff" status. Her benefit claims were denied by the company's insurer, which mistakenly assumed that she was no longer an employee. Noting that the employee, who was expecting twins, was denied benefits while they were granted to a male employee whose disability kept him off work for similarly long periods, the arbitrator concluded that the employer was bound by contract and by law to provide the employee with back benefits (*Skilcraft-Sheetmetal Inc.*, 116 LA 890).

• An employee on an unpaid maternity leave was entitled to have her insurance premiums paid by her employer, an arbitrator ruled. Although in 10 years the employer had never denied any request to continue payment of insurance premiums, it was not clear that such payments were mandatory. When the employer instituted a new policy cutting off fringe benefits once paid leave concluded, the union asserted that the employer was changing an employment condition or term that should have prompted collective bargaining. The arbitrator found that the current contract language was unclear and agreed that the matter should have been negotiated. Declaring that past practice had to be followed in such instances, he ordered the employer to reimburse the employee for any hospital expenses that should have been covered (*Greensburg Salem School District*, 76 LA 241).

3. Return-to-Work Issues

Strong job protections apply to leave that is covered by the FMLA. Nevertheless, reinstatement following maternity leave can sometimes be a contentious issue, particularly in cases that do not deal specifically with employees who are returning to work from FMLA leave.

• An employer improperly terminated an employee for failing to return to work at the expiration of maternity disability leave,

an arbitrator decided. The worker initially had requested and been granted a leave of absence without specifying an exact return date, but later, at management's request, she submitted a new leave form on which she specified both the beginning and end dates of her pregnancy disability leave. Declaring that it would be "most unfair" to hold an employee to "exactness about [a] date when there is no exactness possible in predicting either the birth date or the date of recovery," the arbitrator said the employer's claim that it was misled about the employee's return date was the result of its own "insistence on the completion of an ambiguous form under confusing circumstances." He ordered the employee reinstated and made whole (*Cooperative Optical Services*, 86 LA 447).

• Another arbitrator found that an employer's refusal to reinstate an employee following maternity leave amounted to constructive discharge. Not only did the employer deny her reinstatement, but it also laid off the employee and filled her position with a less senior employee. By refusing to reinstate the employee when she expressed her desire to return from maternity leave, the employer "constructively discharged" the worker "without any semblance of just cause," the arbitrator held, ordering the employer to reinstate the employee with back pay (*Pipe Fitters Union Local 636*, 75 LA 449).

• An arbitrator found that a school district did not violate a collective bargaining agreement, which provided that employees on maternity leave "shall return to the position previously held," when it assigned a returning speech pathologist to a different school on her return. The speech pathologist position is itinerant and the district must retain authority to assign pathologists to where they are most needed, the arbitrator said. Moreover, the agreement used the term "assignment" in other provisions to indicate that employees were to be returned to a position at same facility (*San Francisco School District*, 124 LA 347).

• An employer committed a contract violation by denying an employee who was returning from maternity leave assignment to one of seven vacancies for which she applied and was qualified, an arbitrator decided. Although the contract required the employer to give job assignment priority to employees returning to work after giving birth and taking maternity leave, the employee was not interviewed for any of the seven positions, and five of the seven vacancies were filled by employees who were lower on the priority list. Noting that the employer "undeniably failed" to give the returning employee the priority to which she was entitled, the arbitrator ordered the employer to assign her to one of the seven jobs (*Decatur School District*, 86 LA 841).

B. Paternity Leave

Arbitrators must consider contract language and statutory requirements when they decide cases involving leave for new fathers. Although paid paternity leave is relatively uncommon, unpaid leave is required under the FMLA and similar state laws. As always, arbitrators are not limited by federal or state law requirements if collective bargaining agreements are more liberal in the leave entitlements they convey.

● An arbitrator ruled that a county violated a collective bargaining agreement when it denied a corrections officer the use of more than eight days of sick leave after the birth of his child, even though the personnel office was unaware of the jail administration's understanding of the proper use of paid sick leave in paternity situations. The jail administration had repeatedly and consistently allowed corrections officers to apply more than eight days of paid sick leave to absences during the pregnancy of an officer's spouse or mate (*County of Erie*, 126 LA 1757).

● An employer's refusal to allow an employee to use accrued sick leave to take time off to care for his wife after the birth of their child violated a collective bargaining agreement, an arbitrator decided. A city employee wanted to use 90 hours of accrued sick leave to care for his wife after childbirth but was forced to use vacation time instead. Although under federal and state law only unpaid leave was required, the arbitrator noted that the city's administrative code specifically provided that employees could use accrued sick leave to care

for a spouse who was not well. Thus, the arbitrator ordered the employer to credit the employee for his lost vacation leave (*Moses Lake*, 114 LA 744).

● Another arbitrator held that an employer's failure to properly promulgate a new policy restricting the use of paid time off for paternity leave doomed its decision to deny such leave to four employees whose wives were new mothers. According to the arbitrator, the employer lacked a consistent past practice and instead had a disorganized and scattershot approach to dealing with leave requests. Had the employer properly notified the union and all employees of its new, more restrictive policy, the arbitrator said he would have found it reasonable and upheld the employer's position. Absent proper notification, however, the arbitrator refused to uphold the new policy and ordered the employer to make whole the employees for the leave they were denied or for the type of leave they were required to take in lieu of sick leave (*City of Farmington Hills*, 121 LA 569).

● *By contrast*, an arbitrator upheld a school district's denial of paid sick leave to a male teacher who had applied for FMLA leave to care for his wife and newborn daughter. Although a number of male employees had been allowed to substitute paid sick leave for unpaid family leave in the five years preceding the employee's grievance, the arbitrator asserted that where there is a conflict between past practice and unambiguous contract language, an arbitrator must abide by the agreement. In this case, the arbitrator found that the language of the contract overrode the past practice of granting paid paternity leave (*Millcreek Township School District*, 122 LA 1085).

C. Adoption Leave

When disputes arise over the leave available in connection with adoptions, they often focus on whether employees should receive the same leave entitlements as they would if they had been pregnant and given birth. Where collective bargaining agreements provide for leave based on the physical difficulties associated with pregnancy and childbirth, arbitrators are likely to find that equivalent leave entitlements do not apply to adoptions. The opposite holds true in cases where the concept of "illness" does not figure prominently in contractual leave provisions.

• An employer did not commit a contract violation by refusing to allow an employee to use paid sick leave to bond with her newly adopted baby, an arbitrator found. The employee was granted seven weeks of unpaid leave when her request for paid time off was denied. The employer argued that paid leave for maternity purposes was tied to the presence of a "sickness," which meant that the use of such leave was reserved for pregnancy, delivery, and recuperation following childbirth. The arbitrator agreed, noting that because neither the employee nor her newly adopted infant was sick, contract provisions providing for the use of sick leave by new mothers did not apply (*City of Columbus*, 102 LA 477).

• Similarly, an arbitrator held that an employer properly denied an employee's request to use paid sick leave to care for her recently adopted child. The employee had come to an arrangement by which she worked a half-day schedule for several months, but she was not permitted to use paid time off. Upholding the employer's decision to restrict the employee to the use of unpaid parental leave, the arbitrator pointed out that her adoption-related absence was not among the five authorized reasons for paid sick leave expressly allowed under the collective bargaining agreement (*Columbia Local School District*, 100 LA 227).

• Another arbitrator decided that an employee who adopted a child was eligible for unpaid maternity leave under a contract that granted up to one year off for such purposes. Although the employer insisted that the employee take personal leave and argued that she was not eligible for maternity leave because she had not given birth, the arbitrator said the contract clearly supported the employee. Had the agreement provided time off for "childbearing," the employer might have been permitted to restrict the leave to pregnant employees and women who had just given birth, but it stated that leave for maternity purposes should be granted to any employee who needed to perform the "duties" of "motherhood," the arbitrator observed (*Ambridge Borough*, 81 LA 915).

• An employer improperly forced an employee to use her accumulated vacation leave rather than unpaid family leave to care for her newly adopted daughter for three months, an arbitrator held. Although the employer insisted that to qualify for maternity or parental leave, an employee would have to undergo pregnancy and its concomitant "physical incapacity," the arbitrator determined that contract provisions that allowed absences for maternity reasons should not be seen as precluding situations "where the family unit is increased by adoption rather than natural birth" (*American Federation of Government Employees*, 71 LA 93).

VI. Family & Medical Leave

[*Editor's Note:* See also Part 2, Chapter I, Absenteeism & Tardiness.]

OVERVIEW

Since the 1993 enactment of the Family and Medical Leave Act, increasing numbers of arbitration cases have addressed the rights and obligations of employees and employers under the federal law.

The FMLA allows covered employees to take leave in connection with their own serious illnesses, the qualifying illnesses of immediate family members, the birth of a child, or the placement of a child for adoption or foster care. As amended in 2008, the FMLA also applies to certain situations involving the commencement of active military duty and the care of family members who incur serious injuries or illnesses while serving in the Armed Forces. Many states have statutes that are similar to the federal FMLA.

This chapter discusses various types of labor-management disputes that arise in connection with family and medical leave, starting with the threshold question of whether arbitrators have the authority to consider FMLA complaints. Other major topics include the following:

• the reconciliation of statutory and contractual rights, particularly where collective bargaining agreements contain provisions that are more beneficial to employees than the "minimum standards" established by law;

• requirements employees must meet to be eligible for FMLA leave;

- protections afforded employees who qualify for FMLA leave, including insulation from discipline or other adverse action based on covered absences;
- questions surrounding the use of paid leave for FMLA absences;
- the rights of employers in confronting leave falsification and abuse; and
- return-to-work issues that arise at the conclusion of FMLA leave.

SUMMARY OF CASES

A. Law and Contract Interplay

Arbitrators commonly state that they are "bound by the four corners" of labor contracts, meaning their authority is derived from collective bargaining agreements, and their purpose in resolving labor-management disputes is to interpret the contractual terms negotiated by the parties. While this would seem to limit arbitrators' ability to base their decisions on the mandates of the federal Family and Medical Leave Act or similar state laws, the reality is that arbitrators rarely shy away from considering FMLA complaints.

- Where a collective bargaining agreement incorporated FMLA leave protections by reference, an arbitrator found that it was proper to consider FMLA-related issues in overturning the termination of an employee who had chronic health problems and poor attendance. As a threshold argument, the employer contended that the arbitrator was "foreclosed from examining the FMLA violations" alleged in the employee's grievance, because "ruling on FMLA questions would be an extra contractual exercise of arbitral authority." However, the arbitrator found that the employer's argument was defeated by the labor agreement's express terms, which barred termination in violation of the agreement, incorporated federal and state laws by reference, and specifically recognized FMLA leaves as part of its medical leave provisions (*Manchester Plastics*, 110 LA 169; see also 119 LA 1007).

- Despite a contract's silence regarding the FMLA, an arbitrator decided that he had jurisdiction to address an employee's claim that he was discharged in violation of the federal leave law. After experiencing numerous absences to care for his seriously ill mother, the employee attempted to invoke his FMLA leave rights to avoid termination. His employer argued that the arbitrator had no jurisdiction to even consider the FMLA since the law was not mentioned anywhere in the parties' collective bargaining agreement. The contract did call for the arbitration of discharge cases, however, and the arbitrator said this meant he could consider "anything which bears upon or goes to prove the fairness or unfairness of a discharge." The FMLA had a direct bearing on the case, the arbitrator said, noting that it was his principal reason for setting aside the employee's termination (*Aerospace Center Support, Arnold Air Force Base*, 112 LA 108).

- Another arbitrator decided that he had the authority to consider and apply external law absent an express contractual prohibition against doing so. In this case, a bus driver requested partial days of FMLA leave, and his employer contended that he forfeited his eligibility for a full-time bus route under a policy requiring drivers to be available for their entire routes. The arbitrator rejected the employer's assertion that FMLA issues were not arbitrable as part of the employee's grievance. By including a "savings clause" in their contract—which invalidated any provisions that conflicted with applicable laws or regulations—the parties indicated their "intent that the contract should be interpreted harmoniously with external law," the arbitrator said. Finding that it was therefore appropriate to consider the conflict between the route forfeiture policy and FMLA leave protections, the arbitrator concluded that the employer could not penalize the driver for exercising his FMLA rights (*Laidlaw Transit Inc.*, 109 LA 647).

• *By contrast*, where a contract specifically restricted arbitral jurisdiction, an arbitrator determined that he lacked the authority to decide if an employer's denial of leave violated the FMLA. The collective bargaining agreement stated that contractual arbitration procedures would not apply to any claim for which there was some other method of enforcement, such as the enforcement mechanism under the FMLA, the arbitrator observed. Although the contract referenced the FMLA in one section, the arbitrator said the provision was included only for informational purposes and did not create an exception to the contract's general restriction on arbitral authority (*Board of Education of the Margaretta Local School District*, 114 LA 1057).

• Another arbitrator refused to consider whether an employer had the right to treat an employee's time off for an injury as FMLA leave. The union claimed that the employer had never before required employees to concurrently use FMLA time while taking leave for an on-duty-injury. The arbitrator decided not to address the issue, however, finding that neither party argued that there was an FMLA violation, and the dispute between the parties centered on the benefits associated with the employee's on-duty injury leave. Distinguishing between statutory and contractual rights, the arbitrator said FMLA rights were exercised "outside the four corners" of the parties' collective bargaining agreement and therefore were beyond his jurisdiction (*City of Parma Heights*, 120 LA 452).

1. Minimum Standards

The FMLA and state leave laws set out minimum standards, but the provisions in collective bargaining agreements often exceed those standards. Thus, employers cannot simply meet the statutory requirements if they have made contractual promises that are more beneficial to employees.

• An employer could not rely on FMLA standards in denying leave to a pregnant worker who had been employed for less than 12 months, an arbitrator held. The FMLA establishes a threshold of at least one year

on the payroll and 1,250 hours worked in the preceding 12 months before employees can take advantage of the leave law's provisions. However, the employer's labor contract permitted leaves of absence merely "for good cause shown." According to the arbitrator, the employer erred in rejecting the employee's leave request based on the FMLA's service requirements, because the law was not intended to displace more generous contract provisions or employer policies. The FMLA "established a floor, not a ceiling, on leave-related benefits," the arbitrator said (*Enesco Corp.*, 107 LA 513).

• Although an employee had insufficient hours in the preceding 12 months to satisfy the FMLA's service requirements, her employer lacked just cause under its own policies to fire her for absenteeism, an arbitrator decided. The employee's absence rate amounted to 19 percent of available workdays, and she had also missed 73 workdays due to a medical leave of absence and a voluntary layoff. Despite having inadequate hours to qualify for FMLA coverage, she was inappropriately penalized for some of her absences, the arbitrator found, noting that the employer's policies called for exceptions when employees missed work because of personal or family illnesses. Consequently, the arbitrator ordered the employer to reinstate the employee without back pay and give her a 90-day trial period in which to demonstrate improved attendance (*Darling Store Fixtures*, 108 LA 183; see also 117 LA 46).

• Although employers must have at least 50 employees to be subject to the FMLA, an employer that dropped below the 50-employee threshold remained obligated to meet the law's requirements, an arbitrator ruled. While conceding that the FMLA would not apply under its own terms, the arbitrator found that a provision of the parties' collective bargaining agreement incorporated the FMLA, and that provision reflected an intent to provide job-protected leave without regard to the number of workers employed at any given time (*Kodiak Electric Association*, 122 LA 1409).

• An employer committed a contract violation in using the FMLA as the basis for limiting the duration of an employee's leave, an arbitrator found. Although 12 weeks of FMLA leave is the maximum amount employees can take in a 12-month period, the parties' collective bargaining agreement contained no such limitation. Noting that the agreement was negotiated after the law was enacted, and the parties had not adopted any language tying leaves of absence to the FMLA, the arbitrator concluded that the FMLA's existence could not be used for the purpose of limiting collectively bargained language concerning leaves of absence (*City of Englewood, Ohio*, 113 LA 624).

● An arbitrator blocked an employer from deleting a contract clause that made both paid and unpaid leave available to employees in the event of injury, illness, pregnancy, or childbirth. In submitting the proposed change to interest arbitration, the employer argued that the leave clause was unnecessary in light of the rights and protections conferred on employees by the FMLA and similar state laws. Unconvinced that employees would retain the same level of leave benefits if the clause were deleted, the arbitrator said the proposed change was "a matter better left to the parties' future deliberations" (*Sibley County Sheriff's Department*, 111 LA 795).

● Another arbitrator overturned an employer's absenteeism policy in part because it did not allow employees to take FMLA leave without a risk of discipline. The employer implemented the policy unilaterally without advance notice to the union, which amounted to a contract violation, the arbitrator found. Moreover, the new policy assessed points for all absences, including "excused absences," and made no exceptions for FMLA leave. Noting that work rules implemented by management had to be "reasonable," the arbitrator said it would be a stretch to consider a policy reasonable when it failed to recognize and accommodate the FMLA (*Cargill Inc.*, 111 LA 571).

B. Eligibility for Leave

Federal and state laws outline various eligibility criteria that employees must satisfy to qualify for family and medical leave.

For example, specific situations in which employees can qualify for FMLA leave include the birth or adoption of a child or the placement of a foster child, a "serious health condition" that prevents employees from performing their jobs, and medical problems requiring employees to care for family members. The following cases illustrate how arbitrators have applied FMLA eligibility criteria to specific situations.

● An arbitrator ruled that an agency did not violate a collective bargaining agreement, which provided that it may not schedule employees to avoid paying overtime, when it changed an employee's schedule so that he worked from Tuesday through Saturday instead of his preferred schedule with Monday and Tuesday off, even though he had planned to take an FMLA day on Sunday to care for his mother, where the FMLA leave did not count toward overtime calculation, and he was offered an opportunity to work Monday overtime (*Greater Dayton RTA*, 125 LA 357).

● An employee was not eligible to take FMLA leave or paid sick leave to care for his pregnant girlfriend, an arbitrator ruled. Under the FMLA, eligible employees can take leave to care for an immediate family member, defined as a parent, spouse, or child. The employee's girlfriend did not meet the statutory definition of a relative for whom the employee could provide care, nor did she qualify as a relative under the employer's labor contract or past practice, the arbitrator found. Thus, the employee's leave options were properly restricted, with FMLA leave becoming available to him only after the birth of his child, the arbitrator ruled (*City of McAlestar, Okla.*, 114 LA 1180).

● An arbitrator ruled that an employer violated the collective bargaining contract when it required an employee to take paid vacation leave while on FMLA leave to take his child to hospital in late January, even though FMLA allowed the employer to substitute paid leave for unpaid FMLA leave, where the FMLA also required compliance with the contract, which provided that vacations had to be taken in July and from Christmas to New Year's. The arbitrator ordered the employee be given a prospective remedy, where the union had held the case for two years before advancing it to arbitration, and the employer had already paid the employee (*Big Ridge Inc.*, 128 LA 107).

• An arbitrator held that an employee could not be excused under the FMLA for missing work when his live-in companion was hospitalized. In addition to pointing out that a live-in companion is not the equivalent of a spouse under the law, the arbitrator observed that an employee who wants to take FMLA leave in connection with a family member's illness must be needed "to care for" the individual. There was no evidence that the employee was needed in such a capacity, and the FMLA does not grant leave "simply because an employee wishes to be with an ill family member," the arbitrator said (*Morgan Foods Inc.*, 106 LA 833).

• On the other hand, an arbitrator ordered reinstatement with back pay for an employee who took time off to care for a daughter with asthma. In this case, the arbitrator noted that excused leave under the FMLA is not designed exclusively for medical treatments and doctor visits. Rather, the law also allows an employee to take time away from work to provide for the "personal needs" or "psychological comfort" of a family member with a serious health condition. Emphasizing that the employer already had documentation on file from a doctor certifying that the daughter's health condition called for such care, the arbitrator said the employee's termination for absenteeism was not justified (*Rock Tenn Co.*, 121 LA 1079).

1. "Serious Health Condition"

Eligibility for FMLA leave commonly depends on the existence of a "serious health condition," which the law defines as a condition involving inpatient care or continuing treatment by a health care provider. In general, "inpatient care" means an overnight stay at a hospital or medical facility, and all subsequent treatment for the same condition also qualifies for FMLA leave. The "continuing treatment" standard, meanwhile, can apply to pregnancy and chronic conditions, as well as illnesses

resulting in a period of incapacity of more than three days and requiring at least two visits to a health care provider or only one office visit along with a continuing treatment regimen supervised by a health care provider.

• An arbitrator ruled that an employer did not have just cause to suspend an employee for the two days of absence he took to care for his wife after foot surgery, despite the employer's contention that surgery did not incapacitate his wife for three days, which would mean that she did not have a "serious health condition" covered under the FMLA. The wife was given prescription medications, was instructed to apply ice bags to the operated area 30 minutes out of every hour for the first 24 hours, was to remain on crutches for 21 days, had follow-up appointments with a doctor, and was unable to work. The employee's suspension was reduced to two days without pay, because he did not comply with the FMLA's written request rules (*Central Aluminum Co.*, 125 LA 1778).

• An employee who had back-to-back unexcused absences after reaching the termination stage of his employer's attendance program did not establish the existence of a serious health condition that would have entitled him to FMLA leave, an arbitrator ruled. The employee received a doctor's excuse four days after his absences, but the employer had a longstanding policy that prohibited backdated doctor's notes. The employee then requested an application for FMLA leave, and his doctor indicated "diarrhea, lactose-intolerance" as the employee's "serious health condition." The arbitrator, however, determined that the employee did not have a health condition that would qualify for FMLA leave. Several factors undermined the employee's FMLA claim, said the arbitrator, including the fact that he only saw his doctor once and was not prescribed a regimen of continuing treatment (*Bridgestone/Firestone Inc.*, 110 LA 929).

• An arbitrator held that an employee could not avoid termination for absenteeism in a case where the question of FMLA eligibility was not raised until late in the arbitration process and the employee's medical problems did not qualify as a "serious health condition." Although the employee had hypertension, there was no evidence that his high blood pressure required him to obtain inpatient care or continuing treatment by a health care provider, the arbitrator observed. The employee also had an episode of laryngitis and the flu, but the FMLA was not intended to cover common, short-term illnesses of that type, the arbitrator said (*G.E. Railcar Repair Services Corp.*, 112 LA 632).

• An employee who was hospitalized because of depression and who continued to receive medical treatment thereafter had a "serious health condition" within the meaning of the FMLA, an arbitrator held. Based on evidence showing that the onset of the employee's illness preceded a series of events that culminated in his discharge, the arbitrator determined that the employee should have been retroactively credited with FMLA leave and thus spared from termination (*Ohio Department of Transportation*, 115 LA 563).

• Another arbitrator decided that an employee was eligible for FMLA leave based on his daughter's serious health condition. The employee had been penalized for two absences that occurred when he was caring for his daughter, who had a chronic anxiety disorder coupled with panic attacks. Those absences should not have figured into the termination decision, the arbitrator found. Nonetheless, the arbitrator determined that the employee bore some responsibility for his predicament because he had not properly informed the employer about his need for FMLA leave. Consequently, the arbitrator ordered reinstatement but refused to award the employee back pay (*Georgia-Pacific Corp.*, 118 LA 1079).

2. Leave Request and Documentation Requirements

In some cases, employers assert that employees are ineligible for FMLA protection because they have not provided proper notice of their need for family and medical leave. Along similar lines, employers frequently contend that employees have failed to satisfy requirements for providing medical documentation to support their eligibility for FMLA leave. When faced with these

types of cases, arbitrators tend to focus primarily on the timeliness and adequacy of leave requests and medical documentation, as well as mitigating circumstances that might excuse employees' failure to follow proper procedures.

• An arbitrator ruled that an employer did not have just cause to discharge an employee for 10 incidents of absenteeism during a rolling 12-month period, where several incidents—though not the tenth one—involved gout attacks triggering eligibility for leave under the FMLA, and the union had a legitimate understanding that the attendance policy permitted challenge to any underlying incident with respect to particular grievance proceeding (*Metal-Matic Inc.*, 125 LA 1071).

• It was not reasonable for an employee to take part of a workday off as "intermittent leave" under the FMLA to care for a sick mother, since "intermittent" as a term refers to taking a day off here and there, not a few hours in the middle of a day, an arbitrator ruled (*Moorhead Public Service Commission*, 127 LA 426).

• An employee who missed work to care for her mentally and physically disabled son was protected by the Wisconsin Family and Medical Leave Act and should not have been fired for absenteeism, an arbitrator ruled. According to the employee, the need for leave arose suddenly because her son's regular caregiver was not available. However, her employer contended that the purpose of the Wisconsin FMLA was to allow workers to "schedule leave" for medical needs. The employer also contended that under the federal FMLA, employees should give 30 days' advance notice, if possible, when the need for leave is foreseeable, and otherwise they are expected to provide notice at least two days in advance "except in extraordinary circumstances." Declaring that advance notice is not required for unforeseeable or emergency situations, the arbitrator held that the employee was entitled to take a day of leave without penalty when the need to care for her son arose unexpectedly (*Tenneco Packaging*, 112 LA 761).

• In a case involving a retroactive leave request, an arbitrator found that a pregnant employee was entitled to FMLA leave when she experienced a medical emergency. The employee was absent from work for six days due to abnormal abdominal pain, bleeding, and a doctor's order for bed rest. She called in to request leave on the third day of her absence and submitted a doctor's statement substantiating her condition on the first day she returned to work. Overturning the employer's FMLA denial, the arbitrator pointed out that the employee's need for leave was not foreseeable. The employee provided notice within a reasonable period of time given the situation, the arbitrator held (*Department of Homeland Security*, 119 LA 833).

● A missed deadline for submitting a doctor's note did not provide grounds for firing an employee who had two chronic conditions that were certified for intermittent FMLA leave, an arbitrator held. The employee was off work because of one of her chronic conditions when she injured her back, causing her to miss an extra day. After failing to supply a doctor's note for that absence in a timely manner, she claimed that the oversight was caused by mental fuzziness induced by the interaction of newly prescribed medications. The arbitrator decided that the extra day of leave was protected under the FMLA. Turning to the failure to supply a doctor's note within the allotted time, the arbitrator regarded as credible the explanation provided by the employee's doctor—that the drug interaction was significant enough to have caused a degree of incapacitation for several days. In light of the circumstances, the arbitrator reduced the discharge to a disciplinary layoff without pay (*Whirlpool Corp.*, 118 LA 775).

● Another arbitrator overturned discharge in a case where an employee's doctor took responsibility for FMLA documentation problems. The employee had been absent over a 15-day period, and the employer determined that the doctor's statements provided by the employee were insufficient to support his stated reasons for not reporting to work. Not until after the employee's termination did his doctor supply adequate documentation in the form of a letter, which provided acceptable reasons for the ab-

sences and also explained that the confusion surrounding the earlier statements was his own fault. The arbitrator overturned the employee's termination, finding that the doctor's letter meant that the employee finally had complied with the employer's documentation requirements (*South Texas Nuclear Operating Co.*, 121 LA 329).

● Discharge was not warranted for an employee who left work and tended to her husband during a period of hospitalization, an arbitrator ruled. The employee's absences would have been excused under the FMLA, but she did not submit a doctor's certification of her husband's health condition within 15 days, as required by her employer. The arbitrator found that the husband's hospitalization lasted the entire four-day period during which the employee missed work, and although she promptly requested the required documentation, her husband's doctor delayed in completing it. Considering those circumstances, as well as the employee's excellent work record during 13 years with the employer, the arbitrator ordered reinstatement with back pay (*Lozier Corp.*, 121 LA 1187). See also *U.S. Postal Service*, 118 LA 666.

● *By contrast*, an arbitrator held that an employer was justified in discharging an employee who failed to meet a deadline for submitting FMLA documents concerning his wife's serious health condition. The employee had been repeatedly warned that his absences put him at risk of termination. Although the employer had given the employee an extension on the original deadline for submitting his FMLA paperwork, he did not take the forms to his wife's doctor until the day before they were due, and the person responsible for handling such paperwork was gone that day. Despite acknowledging the legitimacy of the employees' FMLA claim based on his wife's health problems, the arbitrator said the employee knew he was "cutting it close" by waiting until the last minute to take care of the required certification. Furthermore, the employer had given the employee ample warning of "dire consequences" if he failed to provide the forms, the arbitrator noted in upholding the discharge (*Degusa/Goldschmidt Chemical Corp.*, 118 LA 638).

● An arbitrator held that an employer properly refused to excuse an employee's absence under the FMLA when he failed to meet requirements for requesting leave in advance. The employee, who was at the last step in the disciplinary process for repeated absenteeism, submitted a request for FMLA leave to take his mother to a doctor's appointment but did so after the fact. Noting that nothing in the parties' collective bargaining agreement or the FMLA excused the employee from providing advance notice when the need for leave was readily foreseeable, the arbitrator said the employer was justified in firing the employee (*Integram-St. Louis Seating*, 113 LA 693).

C. Protection of Covered Absences

As evidenced by several of the cases discussed elsewhere in this chapter, employees' exposure to discipline or discharge under workplace attendance policies often hinges on whether or not their absences are covered by the FMLA. The protection of covered absences can affect other determinations as well, such as employees' eligibility for attendance bonuses or their consideration for job transfers and promotions. On the other hand, employees who take FMLA leave cannot dodge the uniform application of work rules and standards that do not unfairly penalize them for covered absences.

● In a case where an employer disciplined an employee on the basis of absences that should have been excused under the FMLA, an arbitrator declared that "it is unlawful to disadvantage an employee because she asserts her FMLA rights." The employer had a problem with the documentation the employee had provided in certifying her need for FMLA leave, but instead of pursuing an investigation of her FMLA status, the employer restricted her leave and proposed discipline. The employer's action against the employee was "fatally flawed" by the fact that it considered FMLA absences together with absences that were not covered by the FMLA, the arbitrator pointed out. While acknowledging the importance of reliable attendance, the arbitrator said "the FMLA cannot be ignored simply because the employer wants

its employees not to be ill" (*Internal Revenue Service*, 116 LA 993).

● Another arbitrator found that an employer improperly rescinded a day of FMLA leave and denied an attendance bonus to an employee who had taken time off to care for his son. The employer's refusal to excuse the absence was based on the fact that the employee had left his home for over an hour to jump start a relative's car. During that time, the employee's mother-in-law, a registered nurse, cared for his son. In essence, the arbitrator said, the employer's position was that the only valid reason the employee could leave his son in someone else's care while taking FMLA leave was to pick up prescription medication or attend to an emergency. Calling that restriction "unrealistic and unreasonable," the arbitrator said the employer had unjustly imposed what amounted to "de facto discipline" in denying the employee's attendance bonus. He ordered the employer to credit the employee for the day in question and pay him the bonus (*IKO Production Inc.*, 118 LA 887; see also 118 LA 106).

● An employer improperly factored attendance into its decision to reject the job bid of an employee who suffered migraine headaches, an arbitrator decided. The employer maintained that the employee's attendance was a legitimate consideration for the position, because excessive absenteeism could impede efficiency and affect revenues. After an outside applicant was hired for the opening, however, the union contended that the employer unfairly rejected the employee based on her absenteeism. Agreeing with the union, the arbitrator noted that attendance was not mentioned in the posted job requirements, and that factor would have lost much of its relevance if the employer had applied the FMLA and excluded the employee's migraine-related absences from consideration. The arbitrator ordered the employer to award the employee the job and make up for any difference in wages by giving her back pay from the date the transfer would have occurred (*Oxboro Clinic*, 108 LA 11).

● The protections of the FMLA could not shield a sales representative from termination for substandard performance, an arbitrator ruled. According to the arbitrator, the employee had been failing to meet monthly sales requirements long before taking FMLA leave. Her sales performance also fell short of the employer's standards her first full month back at work, even though she had recovered from her health problems and had received refresher training, the arbitrator noted. Thus, the evidence did not establish a "cause and effect" relationship between the employee's FMLA leave and her failure to meet the sales requirements, the arbitrator said in upholding the termination (*Sprint/Central Telephone Co. of Texas Inc.*, 117 LA 1321).

D. Paid or Unpaid Leave?

Numerous disputes that arise in connection with FMLA leave focus on whether sick leave, vacation, or other types of paid leave can be applied to FMLA absences. In many cases, the question that arbitrators must answer is whether employers can require the substitution of paid leave when employees would prefer to take unpaid leave. Also frequently contested is the issue of whether employees have a right to use paid sick leave while taking time off under the FMLA.

1. Forced Substitution of Paid Leave

Although the FMLA allows employers to require leave substitutions, arbitrators sometimes find that contractual provisions give employees the choice of taking unpaid leave rather than being forced to use accrued vacation or some other form of paid leave.

● One arbitrator upheld an employer's newly instituted policy requiring employees to exhaust their paid vacation, sick, and personal leave during FMLA absences before taking any unpaid leave. In addition to relying on the language of the FMLA, which permits employers to require that employees use their accrued paid leave during periods of FMLA leave, the arbitrator noted that the parties' collective bargaining agreement explicitly granted the employer the authority to modify rules related to leave (*Vie de France Yamazaki Inc.*, 116 LA 1518).

● An employer did not violate its labor contract when it required an employee to use a day of vacation instead of granting him unpaid FMLA leave, an arbitrator ruled. The employer had a well-publicized policy calling for the substitution of accrued paid leave for FMLA leave, the arbitrator noted, and nothing in the contract conflicted with the policy (*Smith and Loveless Inc.*, 119 LA 1444; see also 118 LA 275).

● Another arbitrator upheld an employer's decision to charge an employee for a week of vacation in accordance with its consistent practice of requiring vacation substitutions for periods of FMLA leave lasting five days or more. Although the substitution requirement was typically invoked for periods of continuous FMLA leave, the employee in question had reached the five-day threshold over a period of two weeks. The union contended that the substitution of paid leave in the employee's situation was at odds with a contract clause requiring vacation leave to be taken in "full weeks." The arbitrator brushed aside that argument, citing contract language that required the scheduling of vacation to be consistent with business requirements. The employer's FMLA-based leave substitution policy served a business purpose because it was "calculated to reduce the unavailability of employees," the arbitrator said (*Interstate Brands Corp.*, 117 LA 714).

● *By contrast*, an arbitrator ruled that an employer improperly subtracted 60 hours of paid leave from an employee who was covered by a collective bargaining agreement that granted workers the exclusive right to elect when they used their paid time off. The arbitrator noted that the FMLA allows for the substitution of paid leave, but the law is not intended to override more generous contract provisions. In this case, the contract precluded the employer from unilaterally forcing its employees to use accrued paid leave during any period of FMLA leave, the arbitrator found (*Union Hospital*, 108 LA 966; see also 119 LA 1797, 119 LA 1700, 107 LA 131).

● An arbitrator held that the leave provisions of a memorandum of understanding between a city fire department and a union prevailed over a city policy requiring employees who took FMLA leave to concurrently use accrued sick leave, then vacation time, then floating holidays until each type of paid leave was exhausted. The MOU gave employees the right to select the dates of vacations and floating holidays and specifically stated that it superseded any contradictory city rules or regulations, the arbitrator noted. The elimination of personal choice in the use of these types of leave impermissibly conflicted with the rights granted by the MOU, the arbitrator decided (*City and County of San Francisco*, 119 LA 596).

2. Employees' Rights Regarding Usage of Paid Sick Leave

Employees commonly claim that they should be permitted to use paid sick leave to cover their FMLA absences. Since the FMLA does not create any entitlements regarding sick leave usage, the outcome of such cases typically hinges on the leave rights granted to employees under collective bargaining agreements.

● Stressing that nothing under the FMLA prevents employers from granting more generous leave benefits than those required by law, an arbitrator held that an employee was contractually entitled to use more than two and one-half months of paid sick leave following the birth of her child. Her employer had relied on standards spelled out under the FMLA in restricting her use of paid sick leave, but the arbitrator found that the parties' collective bargaining agreement imposed less stringent requirements to qualify for leave. For example, the contract did not require employees to be under the care of a physician to obtain paid sick leave, the arbitrator noted. Adding that the employer could not apply heightened standards in situations where paid sick leave was to be substituted for unpaid FMLA leave, the arbitrator ordered the employer to reverse its improper leave denial and give the employee back pay for the period in question (*Southeast Local School District*, 112 LA 833).

● Under a collective bargaining agreement providing that employees could "use sick leave to provide care," an arbitrator found that an employer committed a con-

tract violation in restricting an employee to the use of accrued vacation time when she took FMLA leave to care for her husband. The employer argued that it was permitted by law to compel the use of accrued vacation time during FMLA absences, but the arbitrator said the contract unambiguously granted employees the right to use sick leave when caring for a spouse (*UAW-Legal Services Plans*, 119 LA 1217).

● Despite the absence of contract language granting employees the right to use paid sick leave during FMLA leave, an employer's external personnel policies and past practice dictated a finding in favor of an employee who took time off in connection with his wife's pregnancy, an arbitrator held. To remedy the violation, the arbitrator ordered the employer to reimburse the employee for any hours when he was placed on leave without pay while caring for his wife and to restore any vacation leave that had been applied toward his time off (*City of Moses Lake*, 114 LA 744).

● In a case where an employer implemented a rule providing for 50 percent sick pay during the first two days of each illness, an arbitration board held that sick pay reductions could not be imposed repeatedly on employees using intermittent FMLA leave. The rule was intended to discourage sick leave abuse, but the arbitration board distinguished casual sick leaves lasting one or two days from intermittent usage of FMLA leave based on a single underlying health condition. Asserting that it would be unreasonable to require reductions over and over again for recurring FMLA absences, the arbitration board held that the employer could not subject employees to repeated application of the 50 percent pay provision for separate periods of intermittent FMLA leave in the same calendar year (*American Airlines Inc.*, 121 LA 527).

● On the other hand, an arbitrator found that an employer was within its rights to deny an employee's request to use paid sick leave while taking FMLA leave after the birth of his child. Although several male employees had been allowed to use paid sick leave under similar circumstances in the past, the employer's labor contract specified that illness or disability was a prerequisite to obtaining paid sick leave in connection with pregnancy and childbirth. The arbitrator determined that the contract's unambiguous provisions did not grant the employee the right to use paid sick leave (*Millcreek Township School District*, 122 LA 1085).

• Another arbitrator upheld an employer's denial of an employee's request to use paid sick leave during a period of FMLA leave when she was caring for her mother. The parties' collective bargaining agreement restricted the usage of paid sick leave to situations involving illnesses of employees or their children, and it did not allow sick leave to be used in conjunction with the illnesses of other family members. Pointing out that the FMLA itself does not create such an entitlement, the arbitrator said the employer was not obligated to let the employee use paid sick leave while taking time off to care for her mother (*Puget Sound Hospital*, 109 LA 659; see also 104 LA 1127).

E. Leave Falsification or Abuse

Although covered employers are required by law to honor legitimate claims for the use of family and medical leave, they do not have to tolerate leave falsification or abuse. For instance, arbitrators are likely to uphold the discharge of employees who engage in outside employment after attesting that they need to take leave because they are unable to work. Before disciplining employees, however, employers must have proof of their dishonest or abusive actions.

• An arbitrator upheld the discharge of an employee for dishonesty regarding his use of Family and Medical Leave Act leave, where the employee stated that he had been home for two absences but a private investigator's videotape showed him visiting a friend's home during one absence and visiting a bar and watching a football game during another. The employer had issued a memorandum warning that any employee providing false information regarding FMLA leave would be discharged, and the employee had an attendance problem (*HBC Service Co.*, 127 LA 319).

• An arbitrator ruled that an employer had just cause to discharge an employee

who was late with questionable FMLA certification for days taken off, because the employee was negligent and had many days in which to meet his obligation and failed to do so (*Johnson Controls Inc.*, 124 LA 759).

• An employer had just cause to discharge an employee for taking a day off as Family Medical Leave Act leave, where his son went to school after having an asthma attack and the parent was not entitled to stay at home in case his son had another episode, an arbitrator ruled. Moreover, the grievant was not entitled to take the day off merely because his daughter was "sick" (*Volvo Parts Distribution Center*, 124 LA 416).

An arbitrator ruled an employer was justified in its decision to discharge an employee who appeared to be healthy while on FMLA leave, where the employee falsely represented that he was physically and medically unable to perform the essential functions of his job, life-threatening injuries he received three years earlier did not justify his abuse of the employer's absentee policy, he was a relatively short-term employee with a poor attendance record, he was willing to falsify records, and he had welding skills, which provided him an opportunity to get other jobs (*Union Metal Corp.*, 126 LA 1185).

• An employer unjustly fired an employee based on a presumption that he was lying when he claimed FMLA leave for a partial day absence, an arbitrator ruled. The employee, who was previously approved for FMLA leave on the basis of having chronic depression and panic attacks, did not return from lunch one day until 15 minutes before the end of his shift. When confronted, the employee first told his supervisor that he had to take an injured child to the emergency room, and he later asserted that a problem with his paycheck had caused him to become depressed. He asked his supervisor to treat his absence as FMLA leave. The employer refused to accept the employee's proffered excuses and concluded that he was abusing FMLA leave. According to the arbitrator, however, the employer could not take action against the employee based on a presumption of dishonesty that was not supported by proof. Because the employer did not conduct a proper investigation or obtain adequate evidence to challenge the employee's claim for FMLA leave, his discharge was not justified, the arbitrator held (*Nordson Corp*, 120 LA 709).

• An employer should not have fired an employee for occasionally going to a family business while she was on FMLA leave for postpartum depression, an arbitrator decided. Although the employee's FMLA documentation stated that her condition precluded her from working, the employer hired private investigators because of earlier comments she had made about helping with a new shop that her husband and his uncle were opening. The employee was seen going to the shop on two of the three days she was under observation. The employer contended that she was engaged in outside employment while on FMLA leave, but she and her husband asserted that her main purpose in going to the shop was to be with relatives while attempting to recover from her depression. Finding that the employee's explanation was entirely credible and more persuasive than the employer's evidence, the arbitrator awarded her reinstatement with back pay (*Chippewa Valley Schools*, 121 LA 890).

• *By contrast*, an arbitrator upheld the discharge of an employee who was accused of submitting false and misleading FMLA documents and inappropriately claiming total disability in order to receive medical leave and insurance benefits while working at a second job. The arbitrator found that the employee was clearly warned of the consequences of falsifying medical documents, yet he began working as a real estate agent after signing an FMLA form stating that he was "unable to perform work of any kind." Adding that the employer conducted a fair and impartial investigation before proceeding with disciplinary action, the arbitrator decided that termination was justified (*Koppers Industries Inc.*, 115 LA 152).

• Another arbitrator upheld the firing of a worker who falsely claimed he was taking FMLA leave to stay home and care for his wife. The employee called in to say he needed to miss work because his wife was suffering from a migraine, but investigators hired by his employer videotaped him packing up and going on a hunting trip with his father-in-law. The two days of work missed by the employee were treated as unexcused absences, which properly prompted his discharge under the employer's attendance policy, the arbitrator found (*Interstate Brands Corp.*, 121 LA 1580).

F. Return-to-Work Issues

Disputes related to family and medical leave sometimes focus on return-to-work issues. Reinstatement rights are a cornerstone of the statutory protections conferred on employees who take FMLA leave, but employers also have rights that they can exercise. For example, employers can require employees to obtain a fitness-for-duty certification from a doctor as a prerequisite to reinstatement, and they can insist that employees return to work in a timely manner at the conclusion of leave.

• An employer had just cause to discharge an employee for overstaying his FMLA leave, an arbitrator decided. The employee had undergone shoulder surgery and was initially expected to be out for two months. His doctor subsequently provided a revised release date that was two weeks earlier, and the employer told the employee he would be expected to return at that time. When the employee did not resume working as scheduled, the employer called and warned him that he was overstaying his leave, but the employee said he wanted to ask his doctor to approve additional time off. Although the employee eventually obtained a note from a different doctor, the employer had already decided to fire him under a policy that called for termination after failing to report to work for three days without permission. The arbitrator upheld the termination. The employee was required either to report for work by his release date or to obtain timely medical documentation calling for an extension of his leave, the arbitrator said, but he did neither (*American Standard Inc.*, 122 LA 787; see also 118 LA 806).

• An arbitrator upheld an employer's termination of an employee on FMLA leave who did not come back to work when he was supposed to and failed to provide timely replies to queries about his medical status. The employer had the right to ascertain if the employee still suffered from the medical condition that had prompted the need for leave in the first place, according to the arbitrator. The employee's repeated failures to comply with the requests for information and the insufficient response he ultimately gave the employer provided grounds for termination, the arbitrator concluded (*Big River Zinc Corp.*, 108 LA 692).

● An employer had just cause to fire an employee whose delay in providing a return-to-work certificate at the conclusion of FMLA leave caused her to incur unexcused absences, an arbitrator ruled. The employee's FMLA leave was protected, the arbitrator held, but the employer's attendance policy also required employees to supply a doctor's statement of their fitness for duty following illness-related absences exceeding four consecutive days. The employee knew of the requirement, and her doctor had informed her that he would not provide any medical certifications without first seeing her, yet she "did not even attempt to schedule an appointment until after she had been refused permission to resume her duties," the arbitrator said. In finding that the period of delay was not protected under the FMLA, the arbitrator said to rule otherwise would mean that employees could extend their leave periods "through the simple expedient of failing to produce a fitness certificate" (*Whirlpool Corp.*, 121 LA 272).

● An employer was justified in terminating an employee who had exhausted his FMLA leave and had not received a return-to-work date from his doctor, an arbitrator found. The employer notified the employee that if his doctor could certify that his medical problems were resolved and he was able to return to work, the doctor should submit documentation within a month. The doctor provided a letter that testified to the employee's return to health, but it did not specify a return-to-work date. Meanwhile, the employee applied for Social Security disability benefits, and in doing so he asserted that he was no longer able to work. Given these facts and the employee's deteriorating health, the arbitrator concluded that the employee would never be able to return to his job and agreed that termina-

tion was appropriate (*Borough of Trafford*, 122 LA 230).

● Rather than granting an additional leave of absence, an employer was justified in terminating an employee who remained unable to work after using up her FMLA leave, an arbitrator ruled. Although the employer's labor contract allowed for leaves of absence lasting up to one year, the employer was under no obligation to grant the employee additional time off, the arbitrator found. The employer's denial was reasonably based on the fact that the employee had been absent half of the time during her two and one-half years of employment, the arbitrator said (*System Sensor*, 111 LA 1186; see also 109 LA 440).

● An arbitrator upheld the termination of an employee who had been injured on the job but did not recover enough to resume working by the time his FMLA leave ran out. The employee had exhausted all other forms of leave and had been employed on a no-pay status for six months before his employer decided to terminate him. The union's contention that the employer failed to provide notice of the impending termination was without merit, the arbitrator held, because no amount of notice would have changed the fact that the employee was still unable to resume his duties after his FMLA leave ran out. An employer cannot be expected to indefinitely retain an employee who cannot perform his job, the arbitrator said in denying the grievance (*City of Harper Woods*, 121 LA 718).

● On the other hand, an arbitrator overturned the discharge of an employee who was unable to return to work after 12 weeks, because her employer had failed to meet contractual notice requirements applicable to FMLA leave. Based on the employer's failure to send the employee an "official notification" that she was deemed to be using FMLA leave, the arbitrator decided that the clock never started running on the 12 weeks to which she was entitled under the law. The arbitrator ordered the employer to grant the employee 12 weeks of properly designated FMLA leave. If a fitness-for-duty examination showed that the employee was unable to resume her duties at the end of the 12 weeks, she could be terminated at that time, the arbitrator said (*Apcoa Inc.*, 107 LA 705).

● Where an employee was blocked from returning to work after recovering from a heart attack, his employer improperly counted the additional time off as FMLA leave, an arbitrator ruled. The employer asserted that it could require a fitness-for-duty certificate before allowing the employee to resume working, but the arbitrator said such a requirement had to be explained to the employee at the onset of FMLA leave. Because the employer had not properly informed the employee of the certification requirement, it could not continue subtracting FMLA leave beyond the date that the employee asked to return to duty, the arbitrator held. To remedy the situation, the arbitrator ordered the employer to restore all of the employee's improperly charged leave and make adjustments, as appropriate, in any penalties assessed against the employee for subsequent absences (*Allegheny County*, 121 LA 1784).

Part 7

Promotion and Transfer

I. Posting of Vacancies & Bidding [LA CDI 100.70 (public employees); 119.01 et seq.]

OVERVIEW

Disputes over job posting and bidding can present arbitrators with a variety of questions. Some deal with fundamental issues, such as whether vacancies exist or particular employees have bidding rights, while others address the technicalities of posting and bidding requirements established under individual collective bargaining agreements.

In resolving disputes over the existence of vacancies, arbitrators generally allow employers the leeway to assess their staffing needs and decide when or if positions will be filled. On the other hand, arbitrators tend to look closely at certain situations—including, for example, where the duties of a position are permanently reassigned to other employees—to see if employers are circumventing their contractual obligations to post jobs for internal bidding.

Other questions addressed in this chapter include the following:
- Do posting requirements apply to temporary vacancies?
- How much detail must job postings provide?
- Under what circumstances should employees be excluded from bidding?
- Are lateral and downward bids allowed?
- Are bidders entitled to training and trial periods in their new jobs?

SUMMARY OF CASES

A. Job Posting Requirements

To decide whether posting requirements apply in a given situation, arbitrators look first and foremost to contract clauses that govern the posting and bidding process. In the absence of specific contract provisions addressing the circumstances at hand, arbitrators sometimes fall back on other sources of guidance, including the past practice of the parties and contract clauses on seniority and management rights.

• An employer violated a collective bargaining agreement, which required it post jobs when a "vacancy occurs in an operational classification," when it hired an outside applicant for the position of maintenance mechanic without posting the job internally, an arbitrator ruled. Even though the term "operational classification" had to do with production work and not maintenance work, the word "operational" was not defined in the agreement and was not used in any way that excluded the maintenance mechanic classification (*CII Carbon LLC*, 123 LA 1062).

• An arbitrator ruled that a grocery distribution center violated its collective bargaining contract when it posted a job opportunity for a full-time warehouse clerk in the frozen food warehouse as a non-union job, where union CRT clerks had done that work, in conjunction with supervisors, for about 18 years, and there were available part-time CRT clerks qualified to move up to full-time positions (*Safeway Stores Inc.*, 127 LA 1077).

• A state agency committed a contract violation when it selected an employee for a newly vacated position rather than posting the job, according to an arbitrator. Contract language was unambiguous and provided that the employer had to post any vacancy when it planned to replace an existing employee who was leaving the position, the arbitrator said (*State of Iowa, Division of Vocational Rehabilitation Services*, 120 LA 645).

• An arbitrator ruled that an employer was required to post 12 positions after changing the hours for the positions from 10 a.m. through 6 p.m. to 7 a.m. through 3 p.m. The employer had on three occasions posted jobs subject to less substantial shift-time changes, the arbitrator pointed out, and posting the jobs would give senior employees an opportunity for assignment to a more desirable shift (*U.S. Steel Mining Co.*, 97 LA 196; see also 116 LA 809).

• Allowing two employees to exchange shifts without posting their jobs was a contract violation, an arbitrator found. A day-shift employee moved to the night shift on a voluntary basis when another worker went on medical leave. When that worker returned, he asked for and was transferred to the day-shift position that was vacated by the employee who had changed shifts to fill in for him. According to the arbitrator, the contract required that "permanent transfers shall be posted for bidding." As soon as one worker permanently moved out of a shift, that created a vacancy, the arbitrator pointed out, ordering the employer to fill vacancies in the future through plant-wide bidding consistent with the contract (*Dakota Gasification Co.*, 117 LA 777).

• *By contrast*, a bakery company did not violate a bargaining contract when it did not post the position of first shift oven operator/utility for bid when the position became vacant due to retirement and gave the duties of setting oven gauges to a supervisor instead, even though the settlement agreement had placed an employee who later retired in that job. The arbitrator found there was no need for a full-time position inasmuch as the ovens had become fully automated, setting the gauges took about 10 minutes per eight-hour shift, and the position was not meant to be permanent (*Klosterman Bakery Co.*, 124 LA 1249).

• An arbitrator found an employer did not violate a collective bargaining agreement when it failed to post maintenance mechanic bid jobs by primary areas, even though it had done so at times in the past, because the past postings were a "mixed bag," and did not establish past practice (*White Wave Foods*, 129 LA 1604).

• An arbitrator ruled an employer was not required to post and fill a vacated forklift operator position, even though the bargaining agreement stipulated that bid jobs were not to be eliminated, where there was insufficient work to support the position, and the agreement did not require the posting of positions for which there was no work or specify how many forklift operators there should be at any given time (*Virbac Animal Health*, 126 LA 801).

• An employer did not violate its labor contract by moving an employee into a boiler operator job without posting the position, an arbitrator ruled. The boiler operator job had been difficult to fill because of its undesirable hours, and changes had been made to get more employees to train for the position. When a permanent vacancy occurred, the employer gave the position to an employee who had bid on an entry-level training slot for the boiler operator function more than a year earlier. Finding that the posting requirements contained in the parties' collective bargaining agreement did not apply to the situation at hand, the arbitrator concluded that the employer properly awarded the position to the worker who had undergone the training, because he was the "senior qualified employee" (*Bowater-Albertville Sawmill*, 122 LA 1330).

● An employer did not have to post three jobs transferred to a newly created department, an arbitrator determined. Despite the union's claim that past practice dictated that the employer had to keep the jobs in the bargaining unit, the arbitrator said a memorandum of agreement between the parties, which dealt with issues specific to the new department's creation, trumped any past practice (*City of Chicago*, 121 LA 1449).

1. Job Elimination or Reassignment of Duties

Although employers generally have the right to refrain from posting vacancies when reduced staffing needs or operational changes make positions superfluous, arbitrators commonly scrutinize situations where employers eliminate positions or reassign job duties to other employees. In some cases, arbitrators find that employers are circumventing their posting obligations when they take such actions.

● An employer did not violate its labor contract when it failed to post a laborer's job after the incumbent moved to another position, an arbitrator ruled. Because of changes at the employer's facilities, there was not enough work to warrant hiring a replacement in the vacated job, the arbitrator found. In addition, the parties' agreement granted the employer "the unambiguous right to regulate the amount and type of work to be performed as well as the number of employees necessary to complete that work," the arbitrator said (*Alltrista*

Consumer Products Co., 118 LA 1050; see also 118 LA 993, 113 LA 444, 49 LA 74, 46 LA 1027).

● An employer had the right to abolish a position after an employee's retirement, an arbitrator decided. In general, employers have the authority to "eliminate unneeded jobs and assign remaining tasks to other classifications" except where such action is specifically forbidden by collective bargaining agreements, the arbitrator noted. Regarding the job from which the employee retired, the arbitrator found that there was no longer enough work to warrant a full-time position, and the division of the remaining duties among other employees did not violate the posting requirements or seniority provisions of the parties' labor agreement (*Quaker Oats Co.*, 84 LA 390; see also 86 LA 1102).

● In another case, an arbitrator allowed an employer to redistribute a retired employee's duties on a temporary basis. The employer had the right to transfer the duties to two other employees in lower classifications while it retooled its computer systems, the arbitrator determined, but to ensure this was only a temporary measure, he ordered the employer to return the lost position to the bargaining unit within 90 days and follow the posting and bidding procedures required under the contract (*Ohio Brass Co.*, 62 LA 913).

● *By contrast*, an arbitrator found that an employer committed a contract violation by assigning a supervisor to perform duties that had been handled by a worker who retired. When the employee's retirement created a permanent vacancy within the bargaining unit, the contract's job posting requirements were triggered, the arbitrator determined. As a remedy for the violation, the arbitrator ordered the employer to pay the eventual successor to the job the wage rate of that position, retroactive to the date the position should have been posted (*Stanray Corp.*, 63 LA 332).

● Even though a union had agreed to let an employer use overtime and transfers to cover the duties of a position for more than two years, that did not mean there was no longer a vacancy that had to be posted, an arbitrator held. The employer argued that it had discretion in the matter because its labor contract only mandated posting "when there is a vacancy for which the Company has determined it will require a replacement." The employer could not argue that no additional help was needed, however, when it had continued to cover the position by using overtime and transfers, the arbitrator declared. Thus, the employer committed a contract violation by failing to post the vacancy, the arbitrator held (*Mohawk Rubber Co.*, 86 LA 679).

● While acknowledging the right of management to abolish positions due to lack of work, an arbitrator found that an employer was required to post a position that no longer required full-time hours. The volume of work had decreased, but the same duties were still being performed by employees in other positions on an as-needed basis, the arbitrator noted. Distinguishing between a reduction in hours and the complete elimination of a job, the arbitrator found that the employer had to fulfill its posting obligations with regard to the position, even if that meant posting it as a part-time job (*Interstate Container Corp.*, 96 LA 553).

● A health care facility could not excuse its failure to post two vacancies for certified nursing assistants by citing cost considerations and low patient occupancy levels, an arbitrator ruled. In rejecting the employer's argument that low occupancy meant there was no need to fill the positions, the arbitrator noted that the employer had begun using "relief CNAs" on a call-in basis, which indicated that the need was still there. Regarding the issue of costs, the arbitrator acknowledged that the employer had "very real financial problems," but he found that numerous factors were contributing to those problems, and the evidence did not justify the employer's refusal to post and fill the CNA vacancies based on cost considerations (*Anaconda Community Hospital and Nursing Home of Anaconda*, 114 LA 132).

2. Posting of Temporary Jobs

Unless specifically restricted by collective bargaining agreements, arbitrators

typically regard it as another of employers' rights to decide whether or not they will post and fill jobs left open as a result of employees' illnesses or other temporary absences (96 LA 1007, 90 LA 577, 85 LA 1190, 55 LA 19, 43 LA 395, 41 LA 492).

● An arbitrator upheld an employer's filling a teacher's job temporarily without posting the position. Although the union claimed that the contract required the employer to post any opening, the arbitrator concluded that "job openings" referred only to permanent jobs, not to a temporary replacement for an employee who took maternity leave (*Marion Independent School District*, 70 LA 1275).

● Posting was not required when a mining company temporarily replaced a bathhouse attendant who took leave for heart bypass surgery, an arbitrator ruled. Under the parties' collective bargaining agreement, all permanent vacancies had to be posted for five calendar days. However, instead of posting the bathhouse attendant's job, the employer chose to replace him with two other workers who shared the duties. Noting that "the company has full authority to exercise its management rights in filling" a temporary vacancy, the arbitrator said he could not "order management to post a permanent vacancy for bidding as a result of the temporary absence" of the bathhouse attendant (*Eastern Associated Coal Corp.*, 119 LA 1595).

● Relying on past practice, an arbitrator decided that an employer had the right to hire college students during summer months for unskilled work. Although the union claimed that the jobs should have been treated as temporary vacancies available to all employees, the arbitrator said there was no past practice of having such work performed only by full-time helpers, apprentices, and journeymen. He also pointed out that because of their lack of training, the students did not do any work that they were prohibited from performing (*Central Illinois Public Service Co.*, 72 LA 874).

● An arbitrator found that an oil refinery was within its rights to fill a temporary vacancy on one shift with three workers from another shift on a rotating basis so they could brush up on their skills in the more demanding job. While rejecting the employer's claim that it had "unlimited discretion" to make assignment changes, the arbitrator upheld the temporary assignments in this case. If the training issue had not been part of the equation, the union would have prevailed, the arbitrator said (*CITGO Petroleum Corp.*, 122 LA 1495).

• Another arbitrator held that an employer did not commit a contract violation by failing to post a temporary vacancy and subsequently appointing the acting replacement to the job on a permanent basis. The employee was originally selected to replace a worker who was on short-term sick leave, and because the contract specifically exempted vacancies that lasted 60 days or less from the posting requirement, the employer did not violate the agreement, the arbitrator found. Later, when it became apparent that the vacancy would become permanent, the employer posted the job but could not find a qualified candidate, the arbitrator noted. Given that the employee who was temporarily in the position had demonstrated his competence, his appointment as a permanent replacement was proper, the arbitrator concluded (*Wm. Powell Co.*, 63 LA 341).

• *By contrast*, an arbitrator rejected an employer's claim that its management rights clause permitted it to fill temporary vacancies without posting the jobs. The employer had filled a team leader position by appointing an acting team leader for an indefinite period of time, prompting another employee to file a grievance. The employer claimed that it was constrained by limits on its staffing levels, but the arbitrator said that issue was irrelevant in light of clear contract language stating that all vacancies had to be posted (*Office of Economic Opportunity*, 63 LA 692; see also 85 LA 290).

• An employer committed a contract violation by assigning an employee to perform dispatcher duties on a relief basis, because the assignments were not temporary and thus amounted to the creation of a new position, an arbitrator ruled. Even though the employee did not perform the duties every day, the arbitrator found that the employer had implicitly created a new relief dispatcher job. The arbitrator said the

employer could not make the assignments indefinitely without posting the position as a permanent vacancy and paying the applicable rate for the dispatcher duties (*Homestake Mining Co.*, 88 LA 614).

3. Information and Notification Requirements

Disputes over job postings often focus on procedural and technical issues concerning information and notification requirements. In many cases, unions contend that employers have not supplied required details about a position or have failed to use proper channels for posting or communicating about vacancies.

• An arbitrator ruled than an employer responsible for administering a child development program violated a collective bargaining agreement when, after resignation of a bus driver who had transported children to and from the employer's center and had performed custodial duties, it posted a vacancy that included custodial duties but omitted driving duties. The contract provided that where a "regular vacancy" occurs "when a replacement is needed" jobs must be posted where the unit members work, and the need for the replacement of a driver was evidenced by children's parents or guardians taking on the task of driving them to and from the center (*Community Action Commission*, 127 LA 1328).

• One arbitrator held that an employer's job postings had to identify by number the specific machine to which an employee would be assigned, rather than merely stating the category of a machine. Substantial differences existed among machines within some categories, the arbitrator noted. Moreover, the posting provisions of the parties' collective bargaining agreement required an indication of "specific equipment involved," and the employer's job postings had included machine numbers for 26 years, the arbitrator pointed out (*Riblet Products Corp.*, 93 LA 1049).

• An arbitrator decided that an employer could not unilaterally decide to list only the classifications of vacancies rather than naming specific jobs in its postings. The employer had to resume naming specific jobs in its postings, the arbitrator decided, but it did not have to re-post all vacancies that had been affected by its change in policy (*Lion Oil Co.*, 25 LA 549).

● A school district's failure to adequately describe the requirements and qualifications for an athletic director's job constituted a technical violation of its labor contract's posting provisions, an arbitrator determined. Although the employer was wrong in failing to include relevant descriptive information in the posting, the arbitrator did not require the employer to re-post the job, given that the bidders apparently knew what the position entailed (*Girard School District*, 119 LA 1476).

● An employee could not fault her employer for improper posting methods when she was unable to receive information about an opening via e-mail, an arbitrator decided. The employee had no e-mail at the time, and she claimed that she could not apply for the job because she was never informed that an opening existed. However, the arbitrator found that in addition to announcing the opening by e-mail, the employer had "posted" it on a 24-hour job recording telephone line, on the Internet, and on a job information bulletin board, which gave the employee ample opportunity to find out about and apply for the position (*Department of the Army*, 117 LA 992; see also 114 LA 1316).

● A federal agency should not have posted vacancy announcements on the Internet to recruit outside candidates without first notifying its union, an arbitrator ruled. Contract language was unambiguous and required the employer to give the union copies of vacancy announcements before advertising those vacancies in any venue, the arbitrator concluded (*U.S. Department of Veterans Affairs*, 121 LA 134).

● Another arbitrator ruled that an employer properly discharged its notification duty when it let the chairman of a local union know about its decision to reject internal applicants as unqualified prior to its hiring of an outside applicant. Although the union objected to the fact that the employer hired an external candidate before it met with the union committee, the arbitrator decided that such a meeting was not required by a strict reading of the contract

(*Semling-Menke Co.*, 62 LA 1184; see also 73 LA 516).

B. Eligibility for Bidding

After vacancies have been posted, a question that frequently arises is whether particular employees are eligible to bid on the positions. For example, many collective bargaining agreements restrict the bidding rights of new employees or require workers to wait a certain period of time between bids.

● One arbitrator held that an employer violated a contract by awarding a position to a senior bidder instead of another qualified employee. The senior bidder had been awarded another new job only 83 days earlier, the arbitrator pointed out, and the contract expressly required employees to wait at least 90 days after successfully bidding on and moving into one position before they could bid on another new job (*PSW Industries Inc.*, 97 LA 155).

● Another arbitrator held that an employer committed a contract violation by transferring a new hire into a different job when he lacked bidding eligibility. After the employer posted the job and got no bidders, it transferred the employee to the job even though he was 53 days short of working six months at his current position, as required by the contract. Rejecting the employer's claim that it was free to move the employee into the job because nobody had bid on it, the arbitrator ordered the driver to complete the remaining 53 days in his original position before bidding on new jobs. The arbitrator also reaffirmed the contract's security clause by requiring that in the future both the union and company had to agree in writing to hire a covered employee if contract bidding rules were to be bypassed (*Arkhola Sand & Gravel Co.*, 115 LA 837).

● On the other hand, an arbitrator found that a contract provision requiring employees to wait at least six months between job bids did not apply to a new employee. The arbitrator determined that the contractual waiting period did not affect the employee's eligibility to bid—even though he had not yet accumulated six months of service—because the restriction only applied to employees if they had bid on a job in the previous six months, which the employee had not done (*Mid-Central/Sysco Food Services Inc.*, 103 LA 872).

● An arbitrator upheld an employer's refusal to consider a job bid by a trainee but said the employer should have accepted the bids of two other trainees who sought positions outside job categories for which they were being trained. According to the arbitrator, a contract clause on job bidding did not limit employees' bidding rights if they had the "potential capabilities for the job." In the case of the two employees, the arbitrator decided that they were in fact qualified for the jobs. The third trainee had been in his post for less than two months, however, so the arbitrator said he would not overrule the employer's action in his case because of the brief period of employment (*Black Clawson Co.*, 64 LA 175).

1. Lateral and Downward Bids

When deciding whether employees are eligible to bid on positions at the same level or in a lower classification than their current jobs, some arbitrators have concluded that such moves conflict with the goal of using bidding procedures as a means of awarding promotions (30 LA 550, 24 LA 723, 23 LA 159, 21 LA 707). Other arbitrators, however, have emphasized seniority rights in allowing employees to make lateral and downward bids (69 LA 822, 41 LA 329, 40 LA 1305).

● In one case, an arbitrator upheld an employer's refusal to permit a downward bid. Reasoning that the employer's right to "arrange" its employees had not been expressly restricted by the contract with respect to downward bids, the arbitrator said management could reject an employee's bid for a lower-level job when such a move would adversely affect the employer's operations (*Longview Fibre Co.*, 63 LA 529; see also 83 LA 685).

● Another arbitrator found that a contract contained no language permitting downward bidding. According to the arbitrator, the agreement specified that a permanent opening had to be filled from among employees working in job classifications below that in which the opening existed. Given clear instruction from the contract,

the arbitrator held that an employee could not assert his seniority rights to "bid down" to a lower-level job (*Pittsburgh Plate Glass Co.*, 44 LA 7).

● When a senior employee asked to fill a temporary vacancy in a job rated below his own, his employer had the right to refuse him, an arbitrator ruled. The employee could not assert seniority rights to move into a lower-level job unless a local practice to that effect existed, which was not the case here, the arbitrator determined (*Bethlehem Steel Co.*, 44 LA 457).

● Although a contract clause on bidding rights referred only to "employees," an arbitrator decided that the clause applied exclusively to members of the bargaining unit and not to a supervisor who wanted to bid on a nonmanagement job. In addition to finding that the supervisor was not an employee within the meaning of the bidding clause, the arbitrator noted that he was not eligible for union membership and could not accumulate seniority under the contract (*Boardman Co.*, 41 LA 215).

● In a case where an employee retained his seniority rights after becoming a supervisor, an arbitrator found that he was eligible to bid on a bargaining unit job. The parties' collective bargaining agreement permitted the continued accumulation of seniority for one year after leaving the bargaining unit, the arbitrator noted, which meant that the promoted employee still enjoyed the same seniority rights as other workers. Thus, the arbitrator held that the supervisor could bid on the bargaining unit job (*Owens-Corning Fiberglas Corp.*, 28 LA 578).

C. Trial and Training Periods

[See also Trial and Training Periods under III. Measurement of Ability, in this section.]

When weighing seniority against ability in disputes over bidding and selection procedures, arbitrators sometimes conclude that employers cannot deny jobs to senior bidders without giving them trial or training periods in which to become familiar with their new duties and demonstrate the adequacy of their skills.

● An employer should have given a senior bidder a trial period on a job, an arbitrator ruled. Under the labor pact between the parties, senior bidders had to be given an opportunity to demonstrate with "normal supervisory instructions" that they could perform the work. Although the employee may not have been entitled to a training period under the contract, the arbitrator concluded that "normal supervisory instructions" could not be interpreted to require that the senior applicant be able, ready, and willing to take over without training or indoctrination and fulfill all the duties of the position (*John Deere Chemical Co.*, 42 LA 443; see also 73 LA 1218, 72 LA 1238, 71 LA 1171).

● Finding that a junior bidder had been improperly selected for a position, an arbitrator ordered an employer to give a senior bidder a trial period in which to demonstrate her qualifications. Although the employee who was hired outshone the senior bidder in terms of computer training, the senior employee did have a working knowledge of the company's systems and had never been found wanting as a hard worker, the arbitrator noted. Without sufficient evidence to support the conclusion that the junior employee's computer skills made her clearly superior to the senior employee, the arbitrator ordered the employer to hire the senior applicant on a trial basis with the understanding that she would have three weeks to show that "with reasonable guidance and instruction" she could perform the job satisfactorily (*Perry Judd's Inc.*, 119 LA 1662).

● An arbitrator found that an employer acted appropriately in refusing to offer a senior employee a job as an electrician, electing instead to award the position to an outside applicant. Although the senior bidder normally would have been given the job, in this instance, the employee admitted he was inadequately prepared to work on solid-state circuitry, which was key to the position for which he applied. According to the arbitrator, the employer was not required to give a job to an employee unless the person was regarded as being "trainable" for the position within a 45-day period specified in the contract (*Rotek Inc.*, 73 LA 937; see also 73 LA 935, 73 LA 20, 71 LA 479).

II. Bases for Promotion [100.70 (public employees); 119.01 et seq.]

OVERVIEW

In delineating the criteria that employers must use in awarding promotions, collective bargaining agreements typically give at least some weight to the seniority of the candidates. However, different contracts place varying degrees of emphasis on seniority as compared with employees' ability and merit. Broadly speaking, most contract clauses on promotions can be divided into three categories based on the balance they strike between seniority and ability:

• Under "sufficient-ability clauses," promotions are awarded to employees with the most seniority provided they possess enough ability to handle the job.

• Under "hybrid clauses," seniority is one of several factors that employers take into account, but it does not necessarily receive more emphasis than merit-based considerations, such as prior experience, education and special training, work and attendance records, job-related skills, and overall fitness and ability.

• Under "relative-ability clauses," promotions are awarded on the basis of superior skills and qualifications, with seniority becoming a factor only if the top candidates have substantially equal ability.

The interplay between seniority and ability is the most common issue that arbitrators address in judging the propriety of employers' promotion decisions. However, arbitrators also confront a variety of other issues in promotion-related cases. For example, promotion decisions are sometimes challenged because employers have passed over employees who serve as union representatives. Disputes also can arise if employers hire from the outside instead of promoting internal candidates. When dealing with promotions to supervisory positions, meanwhile, arbitrators might be asked to decide if employers can select any candidate they want, without taking seniority into account, or if duties that employees performed before their promotions can remain part of their jobs once they leave the bargaining unit.

For a separate discussion of arbitration cases on acceptable methods for assessing the skills and qualifications of employees, see the chapter titled "Measurement of Ability."

SUMMARY OF CASES

A. Seniority and Sufficient Ability

If collective bargaining agreements contain "sufficient-ability clauses" that emphasize seniority in establishing promotion rights, arbitrators generally agree that employers must give preference to senior employees who are capable of doing the work, even where junior employees have superior qualifications. This means employers cannot promote the most qualified candidate if another bidder with more seniority meets the minimum requirements for the job (99 LA 506, 94 LA 376, 79 LA 1147, 74 LA 106).

• An employer was not allowed to promote a junior employee to an electrician position that an employee with greater seniority was able to handle, an arbitrator held. Although the employer contended that the senior employee took an unreasonably long time to perform certain tasks, the arbitrator determined that even if he was not the most qualified bidder, the senior employee was reasonably capable of performing the higher-rated work (*American Monorail Co.*, 21 LA 589).

• A hospital violated its labor contract by failing to promote the most senior employee to the post of private-duty nurse in one of its doctors' offices, an arbitrator ruled. Despite contract language that required the promotion to go to the most qualified senior applicant, the employer claimed that it could give the post to another candidate because the physician for whom the nurse would work did not want to hire the senior employee. Contrary to the hospital's claims, however, the doctor had expressly approved all four applicants, the arbitrator said, ordering the employer to award the position to the senior employee (*Clinch Valley Clinic Hospital*, 64 LA 542; see also 96 LA 670, 75 LA 1024, 74 LA 266).

• An employer improperly denied a senior employee a position based on the fact that a junior employee was readily able to step into the job because of his familiarity with the equipment involved, an arbitrator decided. The employer should have given the more senior employee the job and let him have a short period of time to familiarize himself with the equipment rather than refuse outright to give him the position, according to the arbitrator, who ordered the employer to put the more senior employee in the job and make him whole for any wage increases he was denied (*Board of Public Utilities, Kansas City, Kansas*, 91 LA 605; see also 115 LA 1175).

• *By contrast*, an employer did not violate a collective bargaining agreement by failing to promote a candidate with the most unit-wide seniority to a full-time bartender position, an arbitrator ruled. The agreement both stipulated that "employees in the same job classification" would be considered for such a permanent vacancy and made clear the classification of seniority was determinate, only the successful candidate had a prior position in the "bartender" classification, and the unsuccessful candidate's position was in "bar back" classification (*Aquarius Hotel & Casino*, 127 LA 45).

• Another arbitrator held that an employer's promotion of a junior bidder to a "lead person" position did not violate a collective bargaining agreement that specified jobs should be awarded to the most senior bidder who had the required qualifications. Even though the junior and senior bidders for the job were virtually equal in certain critical skills, the arbitrator found that the senior bidder had particular deficits that precluded her selection, including trouble working with her supervisors, a lax attitude about quality, and more than one verbal reprimand (*Spontex Inc.*, 105 LA 254).

• An employer was justified in rejecting a senior employee for a vacancy where he could not satisfy the job's minimum qualifications, an arbitrator found. The rejected applicant lacked the requisite license for the job, the arbitrator noted, and training to get the license would have taken several years. The successful candidate had far less seniority, but he was ready to take the licensing examination at the time he was selected and passed the exam shortly after being hired, the arbitrator pointed out (*Perkins Local School District*, 121 LA 1350).

• Under a contract that recognized seniority as a determining factor in promotions if "consistent with the ability to perform the required work," an arbitrator upheld an employer's termination of trial periods for two senior employees who had been promoted to electricians' jobs. The employer cited various examples of their failings, including the fact that they negligently caused a basement to flood, took nine days to complete a four-day electrical wiring job, and connected a ground wire to a live circuit. The arbitrator agreed with management that the trial period clearly demonstrated the employees' incompetence (*ICI United States Inc.*, 65 LA 869).

• An employer properly promoted a junior bidder over a senior candidate for the position of foreman of a crew working on electrical power transmission lines, an arbitrator determined. Although the parties' collective bargaining agreement entitled the most senior employee to a promotion "even if the less senior individual is much more qualified," the more senior of the two applicants could not meet the position's minimum requirements, the arbitrator said, adding that nothing in the requirements the employer had established for the job smacked of unreasonableness (*Xcel Energy*, 121 LA 1226).

B. Promotion Under Hybrid Clauses

Rather than making seniority the controlling factor in promotion decisions, many collective bargaining agreements include it along with other considerations, such as experience, education, attendance, disciplinary history, job-related skills, and overall fitness and ability. Contract provisions of this type are known as "hybrid clauses" because they require employers, and by extension, arbitrators, to consider both seniority and ability in making determinations about promotions (98 LA 26, 97 LA 86, 97 LA 41, 96 LA 338, 96 LA 100, 95 LA 206, 94 LA 905, 94 LA 435, 93 LA 660, 93 LA 589, 75 LA 494, 75 LA 2, 74 LA 1023, 74 LA 811, 73 LA 632).

• Under a contract making seniority and aptitude more or less equal factors in promotion, an arbitrator held that an employer could not refuse a senior employee a promotion based on claims that he could not perform the job. Asserting that aptitude means the potential to learn a job, the arbitrator decided that the senior bidder should have been given a 10-day trial period to determine whether he was capable of learning the tasks associated with the position (*Vulcan Mold & Iron Co.*, 29 LA 743).

• A sheriff's office abused its discretion when it chose a junior employee for a detective position, rejecting a senior applicant, who was the most qualified for the position, an arbitrator ruled. Even though the senior employee had failed to complete assignments in a satisfactory manner because he completed them too quickly, he exceeded standards in many categories of his performance evaluations, had greater experience than the selected candidate, and had an associate's degree (*Clark County*, 128 LA 1025).

• An employer violated its collective bargaining agreement when it selected a junior employee for promotion over an equally qualified senior employee, an arbitrator held. In this case, the parties' collective bargaining agreement called for the evaluation of job bidders based on a variety of criteria, and the employer claimed that the senior candidate's interpersonal skills and technical acumen were not up to par. According to the arbitrator, however, the employer's comparison of the two employees' qualifications did "not persuasively demonstrate a significant difference between the two candidates" that would have affected "either one in his ability to communicate, lead, or work one-on-one or with teams." He ordered the employer to award the position to the senior bidder and make him whole for the period during which he had been denied the promotion (*CAE USA Inc.*, 121 LA 762).

● An employer violated its labor contract by hiring a junior employee rather than a senior worker after both had undergone special training that was supposed to lead to promotion, an arbitrator ruled. When the employer decided to give special training in inspection procedures, it initially denied training to the more senior of two equally qualified candidates. After protests by the union, the employer relented and offered the training to the senior employee, but when she completed the course, she was denied a promotion even though the more junior worker had been promoted, a difference the employer ascribed to changed job requirements. The employer's failure to consult the union at the outset as it was developing the job requirements doomed its decision, the arbitrator concluded, ordering it to pay the senior employee the earnings she lost when she was initially denied the special training (*Purolator Products Inc.*, 25 LA 60).

● Even where seniority was only a secondary factor, an arbitrator ruled that an employer could not promote a probationary employee who had better qualifications than a senior bidder. The contract stated that the employer had to select employees for promotion based on seniority, ability, and physical fitness, and if the last two factors were relatively equal, seniority would govern. Even though the probationary employee was the best qualified for the job, he had no seniority whatsoever, and the arbitrator said the agreement required that a candidate have all three criteria to some degree to be considered for promotion. As long as employees with seniority had bid for the job, the arbitrator concluded, the probationary worker was ineligible for advancement at that time (*Borden Chemical Co.*, 32 LA 697).

● An employer did not violate its labor contract when it failed to promote a senior employee with 30 years of service, according to an arbitrator. Although the employee met some of the criteria required for promotion, he was lacking in certain technical skills, had shortcomings when it came to communicating with colleagues, and had a hard time controlling his emotions. These deficits justified his employer's refusal to promote him, the arbitrator found (*Nuclear Management Co. LLC*, 121 LA 1174).

● An employer did not have to select a senior applicant for the position of laboratory assistant under a contract that treated seniority as just one of the criteria to be considered in making promotion decisions, an arbitrator held. The candidate who was passed over for the promotion claimed she had the ability to learn the tasks required in the job, but she offered no proof of greater training, education, experience, or aptitude than the less senior applicant, who was certified in the required tasks, had relevant experience, and could show he possessed the necessary abilities to perform satisfactorily, the arbitrator observed (*Empire District Electric Co.*, 118 LA 919).

● An arbitrator held that an employer's promotion of a 13-year employee over a 17-year employee for a leadership position did not violate a collective bargaining agreement. In its evaluations of the two employees, the employer had rated the junior employee higher in initiative, communication abilities, and interpersonal skills, the arbitrator noted, adding that the more senior employee's relatively longer experience was not a significant factor in his favor (*Nordson Corp.*, 104 LA 1206).

1. Education and Certification Requirements

Some arbitration cases focus on whether employees can satisfy the minimum requirements for a position rather than how their qualifications stack up against those of fellow job candidates. When this issue surfaces in connection with education and certification requirements, arbitrators commonly agree that employers are entitled to deny promotions to employees who fail to meet the standards established for particular jobs.

● One arbitrator upheld an employer's refusal to promote an employee who lacked the degree necessary to meet a position's education requirements. Denying the employee's claim that he should have been allowed to qualify for the position through on-the-job training, the arbitrator found that the employer had clearly established the need for a two-year associate's degree, and other employees who held the position were not qualified to provide on-the-job training (*Ohio Power Co.*, 94 LA 463; see also 96 LA 201, 82 LA 851).

• A mining company was justified in relying on a certification requirement to deny an employee a mechanic's job, an arbitrator ruled. The company required all its mechanics to possess an electrical certification from the Mine Safety and Health Administration, because the law mandated such certification for any employee performing electrical work. Rather than presenting an actual certification card, the employee provided the company with a letter from an instructor that said he had completed the requisite training. Finding that the letter did not "rise to the level of the electrical certification card issued by MSHA," the arbitrator said the employer properly concluded that the employee was not eligible for the mechanic's job (*Saganaw Mining Co.*, 86 LA 943).

• In another case, an arbitrator upheld an employer's requirement that applicants for promotion to certain jobs have at least a high school education or its equivalent. The educational requirement was sustained because it related to the need for mathematical skills used in the job. However, the arbitrator found that the employer acted improperly in setting a maximum age of 30 as the cutoff point for promotion eligibility regarding the jobs in question (*Ball Brothers Co. Inc.*, 46 LA 1153).

C. Ability as Primary Consideration

Where collective bargaining agreements stress ability as the primary consideration in promotion decisions, seniority only comes into play if employees are substantially equal in terms of their merit. When dealing with these "relative-ability clauses," arbitrators frequently must weigh the various criteria used in selecting employees for advancement to determine whether employers' promotion decisions are fair and reasonable (96 LA 338, 94 LA 562, 94 LA

266, 93 LA 233, 89 LA 1288, 89 LA 1035, 88 LA 420, 86 LA 111, 85 LA 393, 84 LA 23, 83 LA 960).

• In laying out ground rules for deciding if an employer was justified in promoting a junior employee over a senior bidder, one arbitrator said the employer had to show that the standards for comparison of the employees' qualifications were established in good faith and were adequate to evaluate the candidates, the criteria were applied fairly and impartially, and the decision to promote the junior employee was clearly reasonable (*Atlas Powder Co.*, 30 LA 674).

• An arbitrator found no violation of a collective bargaining agreement where an employer selected a junior candidate for promotion over a more senior applicant. The language of the contract was "clearly unambiguous" in stating that seniority was a factor only when applicants displayed more or less equal qualifications, the arbitrator said, noting that the employer was free to choose the best-qualified candidate based on "demonstrated competence." Absent any evidence of capriciousness or discrimination in deciding what constituted competence, the arbitrator found that the employer did not have to consider seniority because the candidate it chose was clearly superior to the senior applicant (*Sandia National Laboratories*, 123 LA 120; see also 91 LA 657, 91 LA 68, 89 LA 1307).

• Under a contract that made seniority the deciding factor if candidates had relatively equal qualifications, an arbitrator held that an employer gave proper emphasis to proven ability and experience in deciding whom to promote. Even though two sets of bidders seemed to have similar potential, according to the arbitrator, the contract allowed the employer to promote two junior employees who had relevant job experience and demonstrated ability while bypassing two senior workers who had neither the experience nor particular skills needed for the position (*Pittsburgh Limestone Corp.*, 6 LA 648; see also 50 LA 445).

• An arbitrator held that an employer's promotion of a junior employee over a senior bidder was justified under a contract that said seniority would be the deciding factor when applicants' skills, work records, and abilities were equal. The arbitrator noted that the junior employee had performed the jobs' duties for eight months to one year before it was posted and had an advanced degree. *By contrast*, the senior bidder had merely worked at similar jobs and taken some courses. Absent evidence that the employer had acted in a capricious, arbitrary, or discriminatory manner, the arbitrator refused to second guess the promotion decision (*South Central Rural Telephone Cooperative Corp. Inc.*, 81 LA 594).

● An arbitrator upheld an employer's decision to give a promotion to a junior bidder who had extensive experience with the duties required in the job. Under the parties' collective bargaining agreement, the employer was required to award a promotion to the most senior bidder who had the "present ability" to do the job. Only when two or more applicants were equally qualified would the employer be required to promote the one with more seniority. Unlike the successful candidate, a senior applicant had no experience regarding the performance of nearly all the position's functions, the arbitrator found (*Richmond Power and Light*, 119 LA 1257).

● An employer did not violate its collective bargaining agreement when it denied a senior employee a promotion, an arbitrator ruled. Noting that the contract made seniority the deciding factor only when applicants' abilities and experience were relatively equal, the arbitrator said the employer properly gave the promotion to a more qualified junior employee. The senior employee was not entitled to the promotion or even a trial period in the job when the junior candidate was clearly more fit for the position, the arbitrator concluded (*Pittsburgh Steel Co.*, 21 LA 565).

● An arbitrator upheld an employer's decision to promote a junior employee under a contract that said senior applicants would take precedence over junior applicants when their qualifications were generally of the same caliber. The employee who was hired was qualified to do all the tasks involved in the position and had already shown that his skills met the standards needed to take on the job, the arbitrator found, whereas the senior employee had only a glancing familiarity with the job duties and machinery involved in the work (*Ingersoll-Rand, Steelcraft Manufacturing Co.*, 117 LA 903).

● *By contrast*, an arbitrator found that an employer violated its labor contract by selecting a junior bidder for a promotion based on how he tested for the job. The employer chose the employee for a senior clerk position after he scored highest on a test with a complicated grading system, but the arbitrator held that the selection process could not end there. The employer still had to "assess whether those at the top of the applicant pool" had qualifications that were substantially equal, in which case seniority then should have determined which applicant to promote. The employer's claim that the senior applicant would have taken at least four months to get up to speed was unsupported, the arbitrator said, ordering the employer to hire and make whole the senior applicant (*Kansas City Power & Light Co.*, 104 LA 857; see also 90 LA 1020).

● An arbitrator ruled that a public utility violated the labor contract's "relative ability" provision regarding promotions when it used a structured behavioral interview as the sole criterion for selecting three successful bidders for crew leader positions who had less seniority than the grievant and failed to consider past work experience. The provision specifically required that the utility consider "knowledge" and "ability" in assessing candidates for promotion, work experience was a tangible objective factor in this process, and a human resources manager testified that it is the best indicator of future performance (*Omaha Public Power District*, 129 LA 16 (Arb. 2011)).

● Another arbitrator overturned an employer's promotion of an employee with less seniority than another qualified candidate. The contract required that a vacancy would be filled according to seniority if different bidders' skills and abilities were equal. According to the arbitrator, even though the junior employee had a broader range of experience in various departments, the senior bidder had much more education and should have been promoted (*Lockheed-Georgia Co.*, 49 LA 603; see also 72 LA 1167).

D. Bias Against Union Representatives

In some cases, employees claim that employers have unfairly passed them over for promotions because they also serve as union representatives. In general, arbitrators find that it is improper for employers to lock union representatives out of promotions unless there are bona fide work-related reasons for denying them advancement.

• In a case where an employee worked for his employer two days a week and his union three days a week, an arbitrator held that he was properly denied a promotion to a team-leader position. The arbitrator reasoned that the employee was not the best candidate for the position, which required regular attendance, because of the absences resulting from his dual status. In addition, the arbitrator noted that the employee had not even been offered to make himself available for full-time work with the employer. If he were to do so, however, the employer could not use his past attendance as a factor in denying him the position, the arbitrator concluded (*USS, A Division of USX Corp.*, 101 LA 124).

• An arbitrator upheld an employer's rejection of a union steward for promotion under a contract that gave management a free hand in judging the ability and qualifications of employees. According to the arbitrator, as long as the employer honestly believed another candidate could do the job better and there was no evidence of animus toward the union, its judgment could not be overturned (*Norwich Pharmaceutical Co.*, 30 LA 740).

• *By contrast*, another arbitrator found that an employer violated its collective bargaining agreement when it denied a promotion to an employee because he was a union steward. Not only did the employee have all the qualifications and ability to do the job, the arbitrator said, he also had been performing the tasks associated with the position for more than a year. Under the contract, the employer could not deny the employee the same rights accorded

other qualified workers, the arbitrator said, ordering the employer to promote the employee and make him whole for any lost wages (*Boeing Satellite Systems*, 121 LA 340).

• An employer violated its labor contract when it promoted two employees to jobs as "lead workers" ahead of a union steward who had more seniority and more than enough ability to do the work, an arbitrator decided. The employer justified its action in bypassing the steward by saying that although he was qualified for the job, he spent too much time on union business to be able to do the work satisfactorily. However, the arbitrator stated that only an established past practice limiting promotion of union representatives could justify bypassing the union steward. Finding no such practice, the arbitrator ordered the employer to promote the steward (*Douglas Aircraft Co. Inc.*, 23 LA 786).

• When an employee who had shown her ability to perform a job was denied the position because she could not devote full time to it due to her union duties, an arbitrator said the employer had unfairly discriminated against her. The arbitrator ordered the employer to offer the job to the employee, declaring that if employees "find that their union positions are handicaps in obtaining preferred job assignments, it will become practically impossible for the union to attract the leadership it needs to carry on its work" (*American Lava Corp.*, 42 LA 117; see also 72 LA 1151).

E. Hiring From the Outside

Collective bargaining agreements often specify that employers must first review all internal candidates for promotion before seeking to hire external applicants. If contracts do not include such restrictions, employers are free to hire outsiders even without considering internal candidates.

• An arbitrator ruled that an electric company did not violate a collective bargaining agreement when it passed over a senior lineworker B for promotion to a lineworker A position and hired an outside journeyman lineman with 10 years of experience based on his demonstration of skills required for the A position and his familiarity with the company's equipment. Even though the agreement provided that the company policy was to promote employees from within and that seniority would be given preference provided the employee had the necessary qualifications, the agreement reserved the right to hire from the outside if no employee qualified for promotion, and the grievant had not completed the 22 required skills demos and passed the progression test (*Cleveland Elec. Illuminating Co.*, 128 LA 945)

● An employer did not violate its labor contract when it hired an outsider to fill a designing job, an arbitrator decided. Although a draftsman already working for the employer claimed to be qualified for the position, the contract placed no restriction on the employer's right to hire outside applicants over internal bidders. The contractual restriction on the employer was that it had to follow certain procedures if it filled a job through promotion, the arbitrator noted (*Chrysler Corp.*, 32 LA 988; see also 85 LA 190, 85 LA 73, 84 LA 956, 84 LA 952).

● An employer was justified in filling a maintenance job with an outside applicant rather than one of a dozen internal bidders, an arbitrator ruled. Although 12 employees bid on the position, 11 agreed that they lacked the necessary qualifications, and the remaining employee failed to press his claim to the job. After the employer hired a new employee from outside, the union argued that one of the bidders should have been given a trial period on the job. Finding, however, that none of the internal bidders would have been able to handle the job, the arbitrator held that the employer was justified in filling the position with a new hire (*Atlantic Foundry Co.*, 8 LA 807; see also 96 LA 1105, 82 LA 1273, 40 LA 403, 31 LA 267).

● An employer's awarding a job to an outside applicant over a current employee did not violate a collective bargaining agreement, an arbitrator ruled. The job in question had been posted more than once, and each time the internal applicant was the lowest ranking candidate of both inside and outside job seekers, the arbitrator said. Nothing in the agreement required the employer to hire the internal candidate if he also happened to be the lowest ranking applicant, the arbitrator said (*Weaver Elementary School District*, 121 LA 1499).

● An employer acted appropriately in hiring an outside applicant for a job without even granting interviews to existing employees who expressed interest in the position, an arbitrator decided. When the employer posted a job opening, it determined that there were no in-house candidates who had any of the relevant training or experience needed for the job. Although the employer never interviewed any of the internal candidates, the arbitrator said its actions did not violate the parties' collective bargaining agreement, which only specified that qualified in-house candidates had to be considered (*Walker Manufacturing Co.*, 62 LA 1283).

● An arbitrator decided that an employer's hiring of an outside applicant instead of promoting a probationary employee was appropriate under contract language requiring internal promotions to be based on seniority. Although the employer acknowledged that the employee had the ability and qualifications for the job, the arbitrator noted that under the contract, seniority was the most important aspect of any promotion decision. As a probationary employee, the internal bidder simply had no seniority, and whatever the employee's skills and qualifications, the employer could not offer the individual the promotion, the arbitrator concluded (*Westar Energy Inc.*, 120 LA 1338).

● An arbitrator upheld an employer's hiring of an outside applicant for a millwright's position in a case where in-house bidders failed to provide any evidence of their qualifications. Although the union argued that senior employees had to receive preference for job openings if they could learn to do a job within a reasonable time period, the arbitrator said the employer had proved its immediate need for an experienced millwright, and none of the in-house bidders would have been proficient at the job for months (*Kerns Desoto Inc.*, 64 LA 1125).

● *By contrast*, an arbitrator ruled that an employer could not hire an outside applicant to fill a position for which several internal bidders were qualified. When the employer posted the vacancy, it tentatively chose one of several unit employees, but an outside candidate applied and the employer described him as "just too good to turn away." Under the contract, however, the employer could not go outside the bargaining unit unless it had exhausted the list of qualified internal candidates, the arbitrator said, ordering the employer to hire the most qualified internal bidder (*The Burdick Corp.*, 49 LA 69).

• A city committed a contract violation when it hired external applicants instead of promoting from within to fill new streetsweeper machine-operator positions, an arbitrator ruled. The arbitrator reasoned that when the city hired the new employees, they became part of the bargaining unit, and hence subject to past practice. In this case, the past practice that had developed in the department's promotional training program dictated that new sweeper operator jobs should go to certified operators with the greatest seniority. Thus, although the actual hirings may have been proper, the placement of new hires in the operator jobs was not, the arbitrator concluded (*City of Milwaukee*, 65 LA 833; see also 75 LA 511, 73 LA 1218).

• Under a contract requiring that promotions be based on length of service, training, and efficiency, an arbitrator ruled that previous training could not be a requirement for promotion into an apprenticeship program. The employer could not hire an outside applicant rather than a senior employee merely because the senior employee had not graduated from a vocational school. To deny an employee the opportunity to enter the apprenticeship program, the arbitrator said, would nullify the purpose of the program. The employer could not have both an apprenticeship program and a requirement that applicants have prior training, the arbitrator concluded (*Hershey Estates*, 23 LA 101).

F. Promotion to Supervisory Positions

Many collective bargaining agreements allow employers a free hand in selecting employees for promotion to supervisory jobs, and arbitrators tend to give less scrutiny to such selections than they give promotions involving bargaining unit jobs (40 LA 321, 6 LA 16).

Nevertheless, disputes sometimes arise over the promotion of bargaining unit members to supervisory positions, often focusing on how much weight seniority should receive in employers' decisions. Another question that commonly emerges in relation to supervisory promotions is whether employees should be allowed to retain any of the duties they performed in their bargaining unit jobs.

• One arbitrator upheld an employer's decision to promote an employee to a warehouse foreman's job over a candidate with greater seniority. The employer could show that the junior applicant had worked as a foreman for another employer, was more qualified, and had greater relevant experience than the senior employee, the arbitrator observed. The junior candidate could "hit the ground running" in just a few weeks, the employer asserted, and because the contract did not make seniority the most important factor in promotion decisions, the arbitrator concurred in the employer's choice (*SCM Corp.*, 58 LA 688).

• An employer's selection of the most junior of 45 applicants for a supervisory job violated its labor contract, according to an arbitrator, who rejected management's argument that the junior employee's "ambition" was so great a qualification that it compensated for his extremely short length of service. At least two other candidates had significant supervisory experience, the employer blew out of proportion the significance of the junior employee's "drive," it failed to prove that other applicants lacked such drive, and the contract clearly stated that seniority and bona fide qualifications should be the deciding factors in promotion decisions, the arbitrator said, ordering the employer to promote the most senior qualified candidate (*British Overseas Airways Corp.*, 52 LA 165).

• In a dispute over the work performed by a newly promoted supervisor, an arbitrator approved an employer's transfer of some of the employee's old duties that he had performed while he was a member of the bargaining unit. The arbitrator found that the duties the employee carried with him to the new position were supervisory in nature, and those functions that were not supervisory had been assumed by other employees who remained in the bargaining unit (*Crown Zellerbach Corp.*, 52 LA 1183).

• Similarly, an arbitrator ruled that an employer could assign a new supervisor the same duties he performed while in the bargaining unit where those duties were largely supervisory in nature. Because the employee already was performing as a de facto supervisor, the arbitrator dismissed the union's argument that by promoting the employee, the employer was taking work out of the bargaining unit. The arbitrator said the union should have objected earlier when the employee originally was assigned supervisory duties while he was still in the bargaining unit, not when he was made a supervisor (*Chrysler Corp.*, 23 LA 247).

• A newspaper did not violate its labor contract when it promoted two "assistant metro editors" out of the bargaining unit into supervisory positions, an arbitrator ruled. The employer had a history of shifting work and jobs from one bureau to another as different localities' needs changed to stay on top of burgeoning news sources. When two employees were promoted out of the bargaining unit, they continued to do essentially the same editing tasks plus more managerial work, and their bargaining unit jobs were abolished. The employer asserted that originally their jobs were classified as bargaining unit positions to keep the employer within a contractually required 34-person limit on managerial posts. The arbitrator agreed, noting that the abolition of the employees' former jobs "was the result of the newspaper no longer having a need for those two positions" and "was not done as an attack on the bargaining unit, but was done for valid, good faith, business needs" (*Beacon Journal Publishing Co.*, 115 LA 1263).

III. Measurement of Ability

OVERVIEW

Under most collective bargaining agreements, the two leading considerations in promotion decisions are the ability and seniority of the candidates. Unlike seniority, however, ability typically cannot be measured through the application of standard formulas or simple calculations.

Absent contract clauses that dictate specific ways of measuring ability, arbitrators usually grant employers wide latitude in how they determine employees' worthiness for promotion. For example, arbitrators have upheld the use of tests, trial periods, merit-rating systems, and interviews. They also have found it acceptable to take into account employees' experience, education, work history and performance, physical fitness, and other factors.

Despite their reluctance to second guess employers' determinations regarding employees' suitability for promotion, arbitrators do not blindly accept methods of measuring ability that produce skewed or biased results. In general, arbitrators demand fairness and objectivity on the part of employers and insist that they assess job candidates on the basis of qualities and capabilities that relate directly to the positions being sought.

SUMMARY OF CASES

A. Tests as Measure of Ability

Arbitrators commonly approve of the use of tests to see how employees stack up against position requirements and fellow job candidates (97 LA 244, 97 LA 86, 96 LA 17, 25 LA 480), but they might not allow employers to rely on test results to the exclusion of other considerations (120 LA 344, 29 LA 262).

For tests to be considered a valid means of measuring employees' ability, arbitrators generally agree that they must meet four criteria:

- they must be specifically related to the job,

- they must be fair and reasonable,

- they must be administered in good faith and without bias, and

● they must be properly evaluated (79 LA 868, 72 LA 1307).

● One arbitrator said an employer could use written tests if they were fairly evaluated and if management did not rely on minor differences in scores to block the promotions of senior employees (*Stauffer Chemical Co. Inc.*, 8 LA 278; see also 49 LA 589, 41 LA 902).

● In a case where an employer and a union had agreed that ability was a necessary ingredient in obtaining new jobs, an arbitrator decided that tests could be used to assess internal bidders. The employer had not specifically bargained away the right to use tests in the selection process, the arbitrator noted, and the tests were reasonable, administered evenhandedly, and had a meaningful and substantial relationship to the job (*Rockwell International Corp.*, 82 LA 232).

● An arbitrator upheld an employer's use of a written test to determine the qualified bidders for a vacant rebuild mechanic position. The agreement provided that such vacancies were to be awarded to the most senior "qualified" employee, the test was carefully designed by an outside consultant with considerable experience in the relevant machinery to determine whether the applicants had the basic skills requirements of the job, and there was no evidence that any of the Hispanic applicants would not understand questions that were administered in English. The arbitrator found that the employer did not violate the labor contract when it selected a junior applicant for promotion to the rebuild mechanic position, since the agreement provided that such vacancies would be awarded to the most senior "qualified" employee at the time vacancy occurs, and the junior employee was the only applicant who passed the written test for the position (*Excel Corp.*, 125 LA 641).

● Another arbitrator upheld an employer's use of tests under a collective bargaining agreement that permitted the consideration of ability, fitness, and knowledge, along with seniority, when selecting employees for promotions. The arbitrator determined that the tests used by the employer were relevant, valid, and administered in a fair and unbiased manner (*James River Corp.*, 93 LA 874).

● A city did not violate state law, which provided that the promotional applicant with the highest test score shall be promoted unless "valid reason exists for not doing so," when it bypassed the highest scorer on a test for a deputy fire chief position, an arbitrator ruled. There was testimony that the selected applicant had more experience and more certifications in the work tasks of the division (*City of McAllen*, 128 LA 148).

● An arbitrator ruled an employer did not violate a labor contract when it failed an employee on a hands-on fabrication test used for promotion to the position of first class mechanic. The union's contention was that the work area used for testing was cluttered and the grievant lacked the necessary tools and material, during the test. But the arbitrator found he had a clean working area of about 50 square feet, he did not show that any items near the work table delayed his progress significantly, he failed to prove that drill bits or any other equipment were faulty or unavailable, he drilled holes that were the wrong size, and he did not use tapping fluid (*Lorillard Tobacco Co.*, 124 LA 1611).

● Under a collective bargaining agreement that said both ability and seniority would factor into selection decisions, an employer was justified in choosing a junior bidder whose score on a test was more than twice that of a senior bidder, an arbitrator ruled. Although the employer had routinely selected senior applicants in the past, the arbitrator found no evidence of any "mutual agreement" that would establish a binding past practice to override contractual language that made ability a consideration along with seniority. Adding that testing was a rational way of assessing the candidates' ability to perform the required work, the arbitrator decided that the employer acted appropriately in selecting the junior candidate based on the results of the test (*Tecumseh Corrugated Box Co.*, 118 LA 309; see also 82 LA 1011).

● An arbitrator upheld an employer's promotion of nine junior bidders over senior candidates because the junior bidders were more qualified and did better on tests. On two previous occasions, the most senior bidder had been promoted and given a 30-day training period. However, the arbitrator noted that the parties' collective bargaining agreement mentioned employee qualifications in addition to seniority as the bases for promotion. According to the arbitrator, two instances of promoting senior bidders did not constitute a past practice sufficient to overturn the agreement. He further stated that the employer's action was permitted because the contract gave it the "sole right to determine qualifications for job bidders" (*Cleo Inc.*, 121 LA 1707).

● *By contrast*, an arbitrator held that an employer improperly disqualified a senior employee from consideration for a promotion after he failed a written test. The employer contended that the questions on the test were aimed at assessing the employee's knowledge of the work to be done. However, the arbitrator said the kind of "text book knowledge" that was needed to pass the test did not necessarily serve as an adequate indicator of the employee's ability to perform the duties required in the position. To give the employee a fair opportunity to demonstrate his ability to handle the job, the arbitrator ordered the employer to offer him a five-day trial period (*Consolidated Coal Co.*, 77 LA 785).

● An arbitrator determined that an employer improperly selected a junior bidder for a job over a senior employee who failed a written test. The parties' collective bargaining agreement required the employer to select the most senior bidder with the present ability to perform the duties of the position being sought, but the arbitrator said the written test required by the employer did not properly assess the "job performance skill" of the employees who took it. To remedy the situation, the arbitrator ordered the employer to grant the senior employee a trial period in the position and award him the job permanently if his performance proved satisfactory (*FECO Engineered Systems Inc.*, 90 LA 1282; see also 14 LA 241).

● Under a contract that required vacancies to be filled by senior bidders if they had sufficient ability to handle the work, an arbitrator ruled that an employer could not bypass a senior employee and promote one who had less seniority but a higher score on a written test. A superior score could not be used as justification to promote the junior bidder where the contract was unambiguous about seniority taking precedence, the arbitrator said (*Marquette Cement Manufacturing Co.*, 25 LA 479; see also 41 LA 856).

● A city fire department unfairly evaluated several employees' skills when they took a driving exam for a position, an arbitrator decided. The employer had a right to give "reasonable and appropriate" tests and did not intentionally skew the testing environment, but the arbitrator found that a series of equipment problems and other circumstances rendered the process unfair. He ordered the employer to allow the affected bidders to retake the exam (*City of Fort Myers, Florida*, 117 LA 1441).

1. Use of Aptitude Tests

While arbitrators usually sign off on tests that are designed to predict employees' ability to handle particular positions, they tend to question whether aptitude tests should be used in making promotion decisions, especially if the tests are general in nature and do not measure employees' present ability to perform specific duties.

● In a ruling against the use of an aptitude test, one arbitrator found that employees had been improperly denied promotions because they could not pass a general, written test that had little or no relationship to the jobs they sought. The arbitrator declared that tests "must not contain problems more difficult than must be solved on the job," nor can they contain topics or problems that are completely unrelated to the tasks involved in the position (*Latrobe Steel Co.*, 34 LA 37; see also 52 LA 633, 34 LA 46, 31 LA 1002).

● An employer committed a contract violation when it used general aptitude tests to screen out employees who applied for certain jobs, according to an arbitrator. Although the contract permitted the use of testing to determine if job bidders had "sufficient" qualifications, the arbitrator found that the failure to achieve a passing score on the aptitude tests did not mean that employees' qualifications were inadequate. The tests did not relate to the specific jobs in question but rather were designed to aid in the evaluation of aptitude and knowledge relevant to a cluster of jobs, the arbitrator pointed out. He found that the use of the tests obstructed the exercise of seniority rights under the contract's job bidding procedures, which called for promotions to be awarded to employees with the most seniority as long as they were qualified for the positions they sought (*GTE Telephone Operations*, 103 LA 1205).

• On the other hand, an arbitrator ruled that an employer did not commit a contract violation by administering an aptitude test to applicants for a training program. In addition to finding that the test was fair, reasonable, and administered without discrimination, the arbitrator emphasized that it would screen out those applicants who had little likelihood of learning the complex skills taught in the training program (*Celanese Piping Systems Inc.*, 64 LA 462).

• An employer's new policy calling for the use of aptitude tests was acceptable, an arbitrator ruled, even though the parties' collective bargaining agreement did not expressly permit the tests. The employer promised that the tests would not be used to eliminate an applicant but only as additional criteria in judging an employee's qualifications. As long as the tests were used in "precisely the manner, and given no greater weight than management's witnesses attested," the employer could proceed with its new testing policy, the arbitrator concluded (*United Carbon Co.*, 49 LA 465; see also 47 LA 552).

2. Employer's Failure to Test

In some disputes over the candidate assessment and selection process, arbitrators are faced with situations where employees have not taken tests as a result of their own or their employers' actions. If the failure to test was caused by the employees themselves, arbitrators are likely to reject their claims that they have been wrongfully denied the positions they seek. On the other hand, if employers are responsible for the failure, they will have a hard time convinc-

ing arbitrators that senior job candidates were justifiably passed over for promotion.

• An arbitrator ruled an employer did not violate a collective bargaining contract, which provided that testing be done "at time of hire and not thereafter except in connection with promotions to department head positions," when it promoted a candidate to the position of head cashier without testing applicants. The testing clause gave the employer the option to test for lead positions, but did not require testing (*Penn Traffic Inc.*, 125 LA 321).

• An employer committed a contract violation by refusing to administer a test to a job bidder for a newly created position, an arbitrator found, even though the employee had failed the same test when he applied for other positions. Reasoning that the purpose of testing was to determine the aptitude of applicants and not just their knowledge of various subjects, the arbitrator concluded that all employees who bid on jobs requiring passing test scores should have been given the opportunity to take the tests after they signed bids and before the jobs were awarded (*Dayton-Walther Corp.*, 65 LA 529).

• An employer committed a contract violation by refusing to let an employee test for a higher job classification that would include a wage increase, an arbitrator ruled. In attempting to justify its refusal to let the employee test, the employer claimed that it had the right to determine how many employees it needed in the higher classification. However, the language of the contract clearly stated that the employer had to reclassify workers and increase their pay if they could pass the test, the arbitrator observed. While concluding that the opportunity to test had to be offered, the arbitrator said the employer was not required to provide employees training that would help them pass the test (*United States Steel Corp.*, 122 LA 489).

3. Employee's Refusal to Take Test

• An arbitrator upheld an employer's refusal to promote a senior employee who proffered his experience as a substitute for a written test. Under a "contractually established" program, the test was a prerequisite to enrolling in maintenance mechanic classes that would enable an employee to learn tasks of a higher-grade job. Although the arbitrator sympathized with the employee's claims that he should be able to forego the test because of his education and experience, nothing in the collective bargaining agreement or the training program's provisions allowed employees to circumvent the testing requirement. Simply refusing to take the test was not a way to resolve any possible inconsistencies between the contract and the program provisions, the arbitrator concluded, denying the grievance (*Aristech Acrylics LLC*, 117 LA 1590).

• A refinery worker who refused to take a test was not entitled to the job she sought, an arbitrator held. The employee was out on an extended leave of absence when her employer underwent a reorganization and eliminated her former position. Upon her return, she attempted to secure a similar position but refused to take a qualifying test for the job. Although the employee had performed some of the position's duties in the past, she had done so only as a helper or assistant, not on her own, the arbitrator noted. Upholding the employer's refusal to grant the employee the job in the absence of the qualifying test, the arbitrator said the test requirement was neither unreasonable nor punitive in nature and was within management's contractual rights to run its operations and manage its workforce (*Lyondell-Citgo Refinery Co.*, 117 LA 815).

• An employee's failure to take a qualifying test before seeking a promotion did not give a company a valid basis for rejecting his job bid, an arbitrator ruled. The company's employment office administered tests, while its labor relations office oversaw the bidding process. The employee wrote on his job bid that he wanted to test, but the company said the request was not submitted through the proper channels. The company also said workers normally tested for new jobs ahead of time rather than requesting a test when bidding on a particular opening. Regardless of how the company normally handled testing, the arbitrator found no evidence suggesting that the employee should have known it would not suffice to request a test on the bid form

he submitted to labor relations. Moreover, the posting for the job did not specify that employees had to have passed the required test before they would be permitted to bid on the position, the arbitrator pointed out. Under these circumstances, the company could not treat the employee as unqualified for the job when it had not given him an opportunity to be tested, the arbitrator said (*United States Steel LLC*, 116 LA 1636).

Denying employees the opportunity to test for a position was not a contract violation where an employer screened the resumes of applicants and eliminated those individuals who lacked the minimum qualifications for the job, an arbitrator decided. Even though the contract required promotion to be based on scores in a competitive examination along with "strong consideration" given to qualified workers who met other criteria, the resume review was no different from any other screening process in which job bidders must first meet minimum job requirements before being allowed to test for a position, the arbitrator concluded (*City of St. Petersburg*, 104 LA 136).

B. Assessing Ability in Trial Periods

Arbitrators commonly view trial periods as an effective means of assessing whether employees have the ability to perform the jobs they seek. The use of trial periods is particularly prevalent under collective bargaining agreements that include so-called "sufficient-ability clauses," which require promotions to go to the bidder with the most seniority if that individual can meet the basic requirements of the position being sought. As evidenced by some of the cases summarized below, one of the questions that comes up with regard to trial periods is how long they are required to last.

• Under a collective bargaining agreement that provided for a 30-day trial period upon promotion to a new job, an arbitrator said the period had to last 30 working days, not 30 calendar days, because employees could not be "tested" when not at work (*Monmouth Consolidated Water Co.*, 23 LA 427).

• Another arbitrator ruled that three months was a reasonable period in which to determine whether an admittedly qualified employee had the proper temperament for a higher-rated job (*Seeger Refrigerator Co.*, 16 LA 525; see also 75 LA 1101, 73 LA 935).

● Five weeks was not long enough to evaluate an employee's ability in a case where there was some disagreement among managers as to whether the employee was succeeding in the job, an arbitrator held. Giving the employee an additional two weeks was a reasonable accommodation to make sure one way or another, according to the arbitrator (*Lukens Steel Co.*, 18 LA 41; see also 71 LA 1171).

● An arbitrator determined that an employer violated its contract when it denied a senior applicant a trial period on a job but instead promoted an experienced junior employee to the position. Because the contract made seniority the controlling factor in promotions if the senior employee had "the competency for the job," the employer had to promote the most senior applicant who was competent, not the most competent applicant, the arbitrator said, ordering the employer to grant the senior employee a trial period (*Beaunit Mills Inc.*, 15 LA 667).

● In a case where there was some doubt about a senior employee's fitness for a job, his employer should have granted him a trial period, an arbitrator ruled. A supervisor did not select the employee for the position because he thought the employee was too old to handle the tasks the job entailed. According to the arbitrator, however, the employee was strong and rugged, and the supervisor's assumptions did not justify rejecting him for the job. The arbitrator said trial periods are not always necessary, but he concluded that this particular employee was entitled to an opportunity to prove himself (*Ford Motor Co.*, 2 LA 374).

● Failure to make the grade during a previous trial period is enough evidence that an employee is not capable of handling a job, an arbitrator decided. In such an event, an employee is not entitled to a second trial period in the same position, the arbitrator said (*Republic Steel Corp.*, 3 LA 760).

1. Training Versus Trial Period

Unlike a period of training, which is geared toward the attainment of new knowl-edge and skills, a trial period assumes that employees already have the ability to meet job requirements and provides employers the opportunity to test that assumption. Based on this distinction, arbitrators have allowed employers to deny trial periods to those candidates for promotion who fail to meet minimum qualification requirements for the positions they seek (67 LA 678, 66 LA 1299, 66 LA 1276, 36 LA 343, 30 LA 598).

● One arbitrator emphasized the difference between a trial period and a training period in upholding an employer's promotion of a junior employee. The parties' collective bargaining agreement called for a 12-day trial period when employees were promoted, and it specified that seniority would be the determining factor in promotion decisions, "all circumstances being reasonably equal." When the employer bypassed the senior bidder for a job that required special preparation and experience, the union admitted that the employee was not qualified but argued that he should have been given a chance to show he could handle the work. The employer contended that the contractually required trial period should become available only after an employee had been selected for promotion. Siding with the employer, the arbitrator said the contract did not entitle the senior bidder to a period of on-the-job training (*Colonial Baking Co.*, 34 LA 356; see also 73 LA 937, 39 LA 336).

● An arbitrator held that a pipefitter with 15 years of experience was properly denied a trial period in a job as a model maker under a contract that called for promotion decisions to be based on seniority and ability to perform the work. The position of model maker was a highly skilled job requiring mathematical knowledge of geometry and trigonometry, the ability to set up and operate various machines, and the capacity to work from engineering blueprints in conceptualizing and fabricating prototype products. Finding "no discernible kinship of skills, knowledge, and training" between the employee's existing job as a pipefitter and the desired position of model maker, the arbitrator said the employer was justified in removing the employee from consideration and had no obligation to assign him to the job on a trial basis (*Roper Corp.*, 74 LA 962).

C. Other Measures of Ability

Evaluations of ability and fitness for promotion can take into account a wide range of factors, such as education, experience and past performance, merit and efficiency ratings, and responses during interviews. In general, arbitrators look for objectivity and relevance in the methods and criteria used to assess employees' ability and give little or no weight to unfounded opinions and subjective measures.

● An arbitrator ruled an opera company did not violate the "American Preference" clause of a labor contract, which stated that the opera must have "extraordinary artistic reasons" that would make it "necessary" to engage a foreign artist in a *non-leading* principal role, when it cast a German baritone in a "leading" role in one opera and a "non-leading" role in another. Both roles were part of one four-part work—Wagner's the Ring Cycle—and his casting in the leading role was not at issue, but the union argued there were not extraordinary reasons to cast him in the non-leading role. The arbitrator upheld the employer, ruling that the German artist had the voice quality, ability, and experience to sing both roles, and was willing to take a minor role and commit to 11 weeks for three performances, and that the opera had made a good-faith effort to employ an American first (*San Francisco Opera Association*, 129 LA 42).

● An arbitrator ruled that a school district improperly promoted a junior employee on the basis of a subjective oral interview and biased evaluation. Although the parties' collective bargaining agreement contained a "relative-ability clause" under which seniority was the deciding factor only when bidders had nearly equal qualifications, the arbitrator determined that an interview team's positive evaluation of the junior candidate was highly subjective. The team did not fairly evaluate the applicants' files, and the school's principal was biased against the senior candidate, the arbitrator added, ordering the employer to promote the senior candidate and grant him a con-

tractually required trial period (*Madison Metropolitan School District*, 103 LA 652).

● In a similar case, an arbitrator overturned an employer's promotion of a junior employee under a contract that made seniority the deciding factor if applicants' knowledge, training, and ability were substantially equal. The hiring supervisor preferred the junior bidder. However, the senior employee had a history of satisfactory performance, which the arbitrator considered a more objective measure of ability than the supervisor's opinion. Because the two employees' work experience showed that they were relatively equal in skill, knowledge, and ability, the arbitrator decided that the senior bidder had to be awarded the promotion (*Plymouth Cordage Co.*, 27 LA 816).

● An employer was justified in denying an employee a promotion after taking into account various factors and concluding that he lacked the necessary qualifications for the job, an arbitrator decided. The employer made its determination only after reviewing the employee's application, interviewing him, checking on his past employment, and considering his education. This evaluation process revealed that the employee lacked sufficient ability and experience in two key areas. According to the arbitrator, the employer's judgment regarding the employee's qualifications was not arbitrary or capricious and therefore had to be upheld (*West Virginia Wesleyan College*, 90 LA 1103).

● An employer gave due consideration to prior job experience when deciding which employees it would promote to a new position requiring a unique set of skills and abilities, an arbitrator decided. As a departure from the emphasis on seniority that normally governed the promotion process, the union agreed that the employer could base its decisions on the relative ability of the candidates while giving "appropriate weight" to their experience. The employer hired a psychologist to help with the assessment of the candidates and attributed particular importance to certain skills that were not required in the employees' existing jobs, the arbitrator noted. When the employer passed over some senior candidates with a history of satisfactory performance in their old jobs, the union objected that prior experience had been given too little weight, but the arbitrator rejected that argument. "The problem is that satisfactory performance of an old job does not make an employee the most qualified person for a new position," the arbitrator said. The employer was within its rights to judge the candidates "on the entire range of needed skills, including academic ability and personal characteristics as well as on-the-job experience," the arbitrator held (*Bowater Inc.*, 103 LA 1000).

1. Discrimination Issues

Arbitrators generally acknowledge that female employees have the right to bid on jobs traditionally held by male employees. Yet, in determining whether employees have been adversely affected because of sex discrimination, many arbitrators have refused to encroach on employers' recognized rights to judge employment qualifications and determine job tasks (67 LA 833, 67 LA 23, 66 LA 1276, 66 LA 180, 62 LA 1294).

● An arbitrator upheld an employer's denial of a promotion to a black female employee after she failed the physical exam for the position. Noting that a contract clause on promotions mentioned ability and physical fitness as key considerations, the arbitrator determined that the test was a valid assessment tool and provided a proper basis for judging the employee's suitability for promotion. Absent any indication of discrimination, the arbitrator found that the employee's inability to meet the physical requirements of the position justified the employer's decision to reject her (*United States Steel Corp.*, 65 LA 626; see also 96 LA 1033, 76 LA 432, 75 LA 148).

● An employer did not discriminate against a senior female clerk-stenographer when it passed her over for promotion to an accounting job and instead selected a male

candidate, an arbitrator ruled. Under the parties' collective bargaining agreement, candidates for promotion had to have reasonably equal qualifications before seniority would come into play. According to the arbitrator, the employer properly determined that the two applicants' qualifications were not reasonably equal, because the employee who was selected for the position already worked in the accounting department and had five years of relevant experience. Thus, the arbitrator concluded that no discrimination occurred (*Missouri Utilities Co.*, 68 LA 379).

● An arbitrator upheld an employer's promotion of a male employee to the position of "lead power clerk" over a female employee under a contract that gave primary emphasis to ability in promotion decisions. Despite the fact that the female employee had seniority and better clerical skills, the male employee had warehouse experience, which was a critical requirement in the position. Based on their various skills and training, the arbitrator concluded that the two candidates were not relatively equal and that the female employee's lack of experience in performing warehouse duties gave the employer a legitimate basis for denying her the promotion (*TU Electric*, 97 LA 1177).

● Another arbitrator held that an employer violated a contractual anti-discrimination clause when it disqualified a female job candidate because she could not perform the duties required in the position. The arbitrator found that the employer had engaged in a pattern of sex discrimination that made it impossible for the employee to receive a fair training period or objective evaluation of her abilities. The dispute displayed "classic socio-psychological motives" in terms of male resentment of the "real competition" represented by the female employee, the arbitrator said (*Braniff Airways Inc.*, 66 LA 421).

IV. Transfer [LA CDI 100.08 (public employees); 120.04 et seq.]

OVERVIEW

Many arbitrators regard the authority to transfer employees as a natural extension of management's right to direct the workforce. Arbitrators usually require that any contract provisions limiting employers' ability to transfer employees be both explicit and clear. If contracts are silent on the subject or contain ambiguous provisions, arbitrators are likely to uphold the reasonable implementation of permanent or temporary transfers, including job or classification changes, transfers to different departments or locations, and other moves.

While respecting management's control over staffing and operational matters, arbitrators often rule against employers in transfer-related cases if they overstep their authority or fail to honor employees' contractual rights. For example, arbitrators commonly find that the seniority rights of employees enable them to refuse involuntary transfers or assert claims to voluntary transfers.

Another issue addressed in this chapter is whether employees should receive higher wages or maintain the same pay rate when they move to different jobs. Transfers prompted by health and safety concerns are also discussed, as are transfers involving union officials.

SUMMARY OF CASES

A. Right to Implement Transfers

Various justifications have been accepted by arbitrators in upholding transfers implemented by management, including:

- business needs—e.g., reductions in work or technological changes (94 LA 632, 76 LA 516, 67 LA 702, 62 LA 1200);
- employees' presence creating undue hazards for themselves or others (92 LA 833, 64 LA 24);
- breakdowns in machinery making it necessary to transfer employees to other jobs or machinery (65 LA 1108, 37 LA 591, 23 LA 105);
- incompetence (62 LA 798, 45 LA 229); and
- personality clashes (69 LA 1138, 67 LA 509, 67 LA 271).

Some collective bargaining agreements make employers' authority to implement transfers subject to special conditions in order to protect employees' seniority or other contractual rights. However, arbitrators generally agree that any constraints on management's ability to move employees where they are needed must be clearly stated in contracts.

• One arbitrator ruled that an employee had to accept a transfer unless the parties' collective bargaining agreement expressly gave him the right to refuse it. Except where specifically constrained by the agreement, the employer had the right to assign work and direct its employees as it saw fit, the arbitrator held (*Phillips Oil Co.*, 18 LA 798; see also 73 LA 497).

• An employer had the right to transfer an employee to a different department whether or not she consented to the transfer, an arbitrator determined. The union contended that the transfer took place as a disciplinary action because the employee had trouble getting along with her supervisor, but the arbitrator found that nothing disciplinary could be inferred from the action. The employee suffered no loss of seniority, no cut in pay, and no change in hours or benefits, the arbitrator noted. In addition, the parties' collective bargaining agreement clearly stated that the employer had the right to change employees' assignments without regard to their needs or desires, the arbitrator observed (*Safeway Inc.*, 117 LA 1705; see also 99 LA 717, 93 LA 548, 91 LA 118).

• An arbitrator ruled that an employer did not violate its collective bargaining agreement by temporarily transferring an employee to perform work outside the bargaining unit on a voluntary basis. According to the arbitrator, the employer retained the right to move its workforce, transfer employees, and otherwise run its operations as it saw fit except to the extent that those rights were "specifically relinquished or modified" by the contract (*Delfield Co.*, 96 LA 448; see also 85 LA 511).

• An employer had the right to transfer a bus driver to a different route in response to passenger complaints about him, an arbitrator held. After earlier warnings about his behavior, the driver was switched

to a different route when another complaint was lodged by a passenger, who said the driver made her uncomfortable by discussing topics such as extraterrestrials and alien visits, handing her a personal business card, and asking her to visit his website. Given the strong emphasis that was placed on the ability of drivers to interact with passengers in a positive manner, the pattern of complaints about the employee justified his transfer, the arbitrator found (*Interurban Transit Partnership*, 120 LA 1235).

• A bakery company that transferred a driver's route from one sales branch to another did not commit a contract violation, an arbitrator held. In objecting to the transfer, the union said the contract barred unreasonable actions taken against the best interests of employees. However, the arbitrator found that the transfer could not be deemed unreasonable because management's rationale for the change was logically based on a number of cost-saving considerations. The arbitrator also noted that the contract gave management exclusive control over the company's operations, including the authority to make changes in sales routes for sound business reasons (*Perfection Bakeries*, 120 LA 888).

• Under a contract that gave an employer the right to transfer certain employees, a worker's refusal to accept a transfer constituted insubordination justifying termination, an arbitrator decided. The employee was an unskilled "utility" worker at a poultry processing plant who could be called upon to fill jobs in any part of the plant. When a supervisor directed him to move to a job involving strenuous and difficult work, however, the employee insisted on speaking with a union steward first. He was warned that he needed to work as directed and pursue a grievance later, but he still balked at accepting the transfer and was fired. According to the arbitrator, the contract clearly provided that anyone in the employee's classification could be "required to work, involuntarily, on any job other than their regularly assigned or bid job." This meant that the employee did not have the right to question or contest the transfer, the arbitrator said. Because plant rules treated a failure to abide by management's instructions as insubordination warranting summary discharge, the arbitrator determined that the employee was properly fired for failing to start working in the new job after repeatedly being directed to do so (*Tastybird Foods*, 88 LA 875).

• *By contrast*, a grocery store chain violated a collective bargaining contract when it did not honor an employee's refusal to accept a transfer to a store that was more than 20 miles from his home, even though the store in which he worked was also more than 20 miles from his home. The contract provided that employees could refuse transfers to stores more than 20 miles from their homes, and the store to which the employee was transferred was an additional eight miles from his home. The arbitrator ordered the employee to be transferred to his preferred store and reimbursed for the difference in mileage between the two stores (*Safeway Inc.*, 126 LA 961).

• A vocational school district should not have transferred an employee to a posted vacancy without her having applied, an arbitrator ruled, where the agreement article and posting required that applicants apply in writing, and the superintendent stated in a memo to her that he understood "that you prefer to stay in your current position," but that he was "formally transferring" her to new position. The arbitrator ordered that the vacancy be re-posted, and all teachers in the district be given an opportunity to bid on it (*Buckeye Joint Vocational Sch. Dist.*, 127 LA 1518).

• A school district should not have transferred teachers involuntarily after closing the school where they worked, an arbitrator ruled. The employer sent the teachers to other schools without taking into account their preferences or bumping rights. The employer claimed that bumping rights only applied if an employee was off the payroll, but the arbitrator agreed with the union that the employees in question were in fact "displaced" by the school closing, and that such a displacement triggered their bumping rights. According to the arbitrator, the teachers' involuntary transfers had to be cancelled in the next school year and their bumping rights had to be honored (*Warren County School District*, 121 LA 506).

1. Seniority Considerations

As illustrated by the cases summarized below, arbitrators often take the seniority rights of employees into consideration when dealing with disputes over transfers.

• An arbitrator decided that an employer committed a contract violation when it transferred a senior employee from his job on the first shift to a position on a newly created second shift. Although the employer contended that its management rights clause gave it the authority to assign employees to shifts, the arbitrator ruled that transfers were governed by the contract's seniority provisions. Because there were other qualified employees who had less seniority than the transferred employee, the arbitrator concluded that the employer was obligated to transfer the junior employees first (*National Lead Co.*, 59 LA 574).

• An employer should not have refused a senior employee's transfer request and placed a junior employee in a position, an arbitrator ruled. The employer maintained that its management rights clause granted it the right to assign its workforce as it saw fit, and although the arbitrator noted that the contract was silent on seniority in transfers, it was the employer's "well established, consistently followed past practice" to transfer senior employees when they made such requests. According to the arbitrator, "seniority rights are sacred to unions and their members," and past practice forms a kind of "shadow language" in contracts that must be honored. He ordered the employer to transfer the employee and pay him the amount of money he would have earned had he been transferred when the request was made (*City of Urbana*, 119 LA 1078).

• An arbitrator found that an employer violated its labor contract when it moved a senior employee from his millwright's job on one crew to a job as shift leader on a different crew and transferred a junior employee into the millwright's position. Even though the employer had the right to reassign employees from one plant to another and from one crew to another, in this case the employee was transferred from one type of job to a very different type of position. The contract required that out-of-occupation transfers be made by reassigning the most junior employee, not a senior worker, the arbitrator said, ordering the employer to make the senior employee whole (*Timken Co.*, 97 LA 146; see also 91 LA 1377).

● An employer did not violate its labor contract when it transferred a senior employee to a job in another building and assigned a junior employee to work on the senior employee's machine. The contract was silent on the issue of seniority preference as it might apply to performing given tasks or working on particular machines within a job classification, the arbitrator said. Absent specific contractual limitations, the employer had the right to assign its workforce as it pleased, the arbitrator concluded (*Crescent Metal Products Inc.*, 104 LA 724).

● In another case, an arbitrator upheld an employer's decision to transfer a junior employee into a vacant job when no eligible employees bid on the position. The parties' labor contract contained a complicated and very detailed outline of when and how seniority came into play when the employer had job openings to fill. Seniority could be exercised only within "lines of progression," which meant that workers in the "technical" line of progression could not claim seniority preference if they were interested in jobs in another line of progression. Under the contract, the employer had the right to transfer a junior employee into a vacancy that could not be filled by a qualified candidate, which was exactly what the employer had done, the arbitrator concluded (*Reed Tool Co.*, 115 LA 1057).

2. Transfers for Safety or Health Reasons

When employees have physical limitations or health problems that pose undue hazards or prevent them from performing their jobs, arbitrators usually find that employers are within their rights to address the situation by transferring the employees to different positions.

● An arbitrator upheld an employer's transfer of an employee who was involved in an accident while operating a ground-controlled crane. After the accident, the employer tested the employee and discovered that his depth perception was nil. According to the arbitrator, depth perception was a bona fide and reasonable qualification for a crane operator, and the parties' labor contract did not bar the employer from testing employees for relevant physical skills and attributes or removing them from jobs where they could pose a danger to themselves or others (*Foster Wheeler Corp.*, 54 LA 871).

● An employer did not commit a contract violation by transferring an employee to a lighter-duty and lower-paying job after he had undergone two operations, an arbitrator determined. Although the employee asked to return to full duty and supplied a note from his doctor saying he was fit for work, the employer's own physician said the employee could not safely handle his regular job. According to the arbitrator, the parties' collective bargaining agreement gave the employer the right to implement transfers "to avoid exposing employees to undue hazards to their health or safety." The arbitrator added that the employer's actions were not tainted by obvious discriminatory intent or bad faith, and the plant physician likely was more familiar with the work involved than the employee's personal doctor (*International Shoe Co.*, 14 LA 253).

● An arbitrator upheld an employer's transfer of an employee who had a medical condition that prevented him from working long hours. The employee was limited to working nine and one-half hours per day, which posed a problem when his shift ran long and the employer had to figure out how to cover his job. When the employer addressed the situation by transferring the employee to an unskilled position that was easier to cover, the union argued that the employee should have been accommodated in his old job in accordance with the Americans with Disabilities Act. The arbitrator disagreed, finding that the employee's medical condition did not rise to the level of a disability under the ADA. The employee's assignment to another position was a valid exercise of the employer's right to efficiently manage its operations, the arbitrator found (*Del Monte Foods*, 121 LA 1100).

B. Transfers Desired by Employees

In addition to handling cases involving objections to involuntary transfers, arbitrators frequently deal with disputes over transfers that are desired by employees. While arbitrators often find that employees are entitled to the desired transfers, they sometimes conclude that employers have no obligation to grant the requested moves.

● One arbitrator declared that lateral transfers could not be denied to employees simply because the positions being sought offered no better pay than the employees' existing jobs. If a new job would provide a better chance for advancement, employees should be allowed to pursue the position under normal contractual procedures for promotion and lateral transfers, the arbitrator said (*Picker X-Ray Corp.*, 42 LA 179).

● An arbitrator ruled that an employer violated a collective bargaining agreement when it did not offer lateral transfers to an unfinished new facility to employees of a closed facility. The contract language provided for transfer rights "if employer opens new facilities . . ." and the old facility closes. The employer argued that the language meant that a new facility had to be open when the first one closed to give its employees transfer rights. The arbitrator ruled this was too narrow and technical a construction of the contract language, finding: the new facility had been discussed in the bargaining transfer provision, the employer acted in bad faith and withheld transfer notification from the union, and the employer had hired some staff for the new facility and could have given employees from the closed plant temporary jobs until the new facility opened (*Sunbelt Rentals Inc.*, 125 LA 1160).

● Similarly, an arbitrator held that an employer should not have denied a senior employee's request for a lateral transfer into a job that offered him more opportunities for promotion. The employer claimed that the employee was its most efficient turret-lathe operator and could not be spared from his current duties. However, the arbitrator said as long as the employee could perform the requested job of tracer-lathe operator, the employer could not deny him the position in favor of an outside hire. An able employee should not be penalized for his ability by denying his seniority rights, the arbitrator concluded, ordering the employer to grant the transfer (*Steel Products Engineering Co.*, 47 LA 952).

● The transfer rights in a collective bargaining agreement were not triggered when a parent company permanently closed one of its subsidiaries, an arbitrator ruled. Because the contract applied solely to the parent corporation and did not treat the subsidiary's employees as part of the "company," they were not covered by the contract and therefore had no right to be transferred when they were displaced by the shutdown, the arbitrator found (*Marsh Wall Products*, 45 LA 551).

● In a case involving shift transfers, an arbitrator determined that employees could not obtain more desirable shifts by displacing workers with less seniority. Although the union argued that the seniority rights applicable in other situations should also apply to shift transfers, the arbitrator decided that nothing in the contract gave senior employees the right to wrest preferable shift assignments away from junior workers (*Kuhlman Electric Co.*, 19 LA 199).

● An auto manufacturer was not bound to transfer employees from plants where certain models were discontinued to plants that still assembled those models, an arbitrator ruled. Because the same type of work continued to be performed where the employees were located, the arbitrator determined that there was no actual transfer of operations and thus the employer was not contractually obligated to transfer the employees (*Chrysler Corp.*, 43 LA 349).

C. Pay Issues Related to Transfers

One of the questions that commonly arises in disputes over transfers is how much employees should be paid when they move into different jobs. If arbitrators cannot obtain clear answers by looking at the provisions of collective bargaining agreements, their tendency is to come down on the side of the transferred employees, especially in cases involving temporary assignments to higher-rated jobs.

• An arbitrator found that a television station violated its collective bargaining agreement when it refused to pay news writers a higher salary after temporarily transferring them to jobs as producers. The arbitrator dismissed the employer's contention that no such raises were mandated because the writers' job descriptions included a statement that they could be required to fill in for producers. According to the arbitrator, the contract specified that any employee who worked in a job that was outside the worker's "regularly assigned" position had to be paid according to the wage scale of the temporary assignment (*CBS Broadcasting Inc., KPIX-TV*, 115 LA 1300; see also 117 LA 942).

• An employer was obligated to increase the pay of an employee who was temporarily assigned to a higher grade job, according to an arbitrator. Even though the contract was silent on the matter, the employer had to pay the higher amount because its own classification system described the core duties of the higher level job, and the employee was performing those duties and should have been paid accordingly, the arbitrator concluded (*Tide Water Associated Oil Co.*, 17 LA 829; see also 63 LA 487).

• An employee who sought and was granted a lateral transfer should have received a pay increase for her new position, an arbitrator ruled. The employer claimed that no increase was required because the employee's job title, classification, and business unit were unchanged. The arbitrator, however, pointed out that the employee had to apply for the job, compete with other candidates, invoke her seniority in getting the job, and undergo two weeks of training—changes that indicated this was not "simply a reassignment," as the employer asserted. The parties' collective bargaining agreement mandated that employees who made lateral transfers and were not at their appropriate step would be granted the step increase at the new job, the arbitrator added, ordering the employer to grant the employee the wage hike (*McLaren Regional Medical Center*, 121 LA 434).

• An employee was entitled to retain his former wage rate after his employer transferred him to a lower grade job, an arbitrator held. Even though there was nothing in the parties' collective bargaining agreement about the pay rates of employees who were downgraded as a result of involuntary transfers, the arbitrator found that the issue had been addressed during contract negotiations, and management and union representatives had agreed that transferred employees would be protected from pay reductions. This "side agreement" had not been reduced to writing but was nonetheless enforceable because it had received the approval of a management official who had the authority to negotiate on behalf of the employer, the arbitrator found (*Charley Brothers*, 76 LA 854).

D. Transfers Involving Union Officials

Because most arbitrators attribute great importance to the representational duties that stewards and other union officials perform on behalf of their fellow workers, they tend to disapprove of transfers that prevent employees from fulfilling those duties. In some cases, arbitrators rely on contract provisions granting superseniority to union officials in overturning the transfers implemented by employers.

• One arbitrator held that the superseniority conferred under a collective bargaining agreement meant that union officials could not be transferred from the units they represented. According to the arbitrator, transferring a union representative who has superseniority defeats the very purpose of having such status, which is to provide continuity of representation for the units in which the officials are elected, allow them to police the contract in their departments, and make them readily available to talk to unit members and supervisors (*New York Shipbuilding Corp.*, 43 LA 741).

• Another arbitrator found that an employer disregarded its contractual obligations in unilaterally transferring union stewards to different company locations and leaving some locations without designated union representatives. The parties' contract provided for one employee at each location to serve as a union representative who could negotiate with the employer in order to settle grievances, and the contract also granted employees superseniority while serving in that capacity. Finding that the employer violated the contract when it transferred the stewards, the arbitrator ordered the employer to return them to their original locations (*Mikocem LLC*, 121 LA 1377).

• Despite finding that an employer had the authority to move a union steward to a different department, an arbitrator decided that the employee could continue to serve as shop steward in his "home" department. The employer had the right to transfer the employee and could not be forced to return him to his home department for representational purposes, the arbitrator concluded. Adding, however, that employees have the right to select their own steward, the arbitrator determined that the employer's transfer authority could not be used to eliminate the employee as the steward for the department where he used to work (*New York Shipbuilding Corp.*, 44 LA 924).

• An employer violated its collective bargaining agreement when it transferred its unit's chief shop steward involuntarily, first to the second shift and later to the third, an arbitrator ruled. Despite the employer's claim that the contract only forbade transfers outside the bargaining unit, the arbitrator found that moving the steward even within the unit but from one shift to another constituted a "transfer" as described by the contract and triggered the clause that prohibited such action (*Midland Rubber Corp.*, 18 LA 590).

• On the other hand, an arbitrator ruled that an employer did not have to transfer an employee from the second shift to the first shift just because he had been elected chief steward. Although the contract implied that the chief steward should be on the first shift, it did not say that he must work on the first shift or that the employer must transfer him from one shift to another, the arbitrator said. The employer allowed the chief steward to have unlimited access to the plant, which was all that was required by the agreement, the arbitrator observed (*Chrysler Corp.*, 42 LA 1018).

• An arbitrator upheld an employer's transfer of a union officer from her job as a dispatch clerk to another clerk's position when her union responsibilities began interfering with her job. The employer moved the employee out of her dispatch job because her frequent absences from her post affected her ability to carry out her responsibility of setting schedules for other workers. The union claimed that the transfer violated a contract clause prohibiting bias against union members, but the arbitrator disagreed, noting that the employee suffered no loss of status or pay, and her working conditions were the same as in her previous position (*Oliver Corp.*, 15 LA 65).

Part 8

Vacations

I. Vacation Eligibility [LA CDI 100.5203; 116.1551]

OVERVIEW

In determining the vacation rights of employees, arbitrators must consider the benefits promised under collective bargaining agreements alongside the eligibility criteria pertaining to those benefits. For example, employees' entitlement to vacation benefits usually depends on length of service or actual time worked.

At the heart of most eligibility disputes are questions about how much vacation employees should receive or whether they qualify for any vacation at all. These questions can be difficult to answer if employees have experienced service breaks or extended absences due to layoffs, strikes, medical problems, or other reasons. Aside from situations involving time away from work, events that commonly trigger disputes over vacation rights include employment termination and retirement, as well as shutdowns and changes in ownership.

SUMMARY OF CASES

A. Service Requirements

Employees' eligibility for vacation benefits commonly hinges on certain service requirements, such as total length of service or a minimum number of hours, days, or months worked in a given period. In most disputes over vacation eligibility, determinations with regard to service requirements play at least some part in arbitrators' decisions about the amount of vacation, if any, to which employees are entitled.

• An employee who was off work to fulfill his National Guard training was not eligible for vacation under the parties' labor contract and federal law, an arbitrator ruled. The contract required employees to have been in the employer's continuous service for at least 150 days before qualifying for a vacation, but the employee was one day short of that requirement. According to the arbitrator, although the employee's job was secure under federal law, he was not entitled to vacation time because the contract required that he actually be at work to earn vacation time. According to the arbitrator, "neither the language of the collective bargaining agreement, the past practice of this employer, nor the statutory law" made the employee eligible for vacation benefits (*Concordia Foods Inc.*, 102 LA 990).

● An employer was justified in denying vacation benefits to an employee with an irregular part-time schedule, an arbitrator decided. Contractual language required the employer to provide vacation benefits for those working a "normal schedule of 20 hours per week or more," but the employee had worked fewer than 20 hours in 17 weeks out of the year and his schedule fluctuated from week to week, the arbitrator noted. Although the employee had two periods of seven consecutive weeks when he worked more than 20 hours per week, this was not enough to meet the vacation eligibility threshold set out under the contract, the arbitrator decided (*Park Plaza Hotel*, 102 LA 400).

● An arbitrator ruled an employer was justified in denying vacation benefits to all but five employees in 2010, where the bargaining agreement provided that employees "must have received earnings in at least seventy percent of the pay periods" to be eligible for vacation in the following year. The union argued that "the pay period for purposes of the vacation should consist of allowable vacation for all workers who worked seventy percent of the time worked by the employee who worked the most." But as there was no definition of the one-year pay period, the arbitrator said the reasonable conclusion was that one year constituted the pay period (*Tube City*, 128 LA 1352).

● An arbitrator ruled an employer did not violate a collective bargaining contract when it denied vacation eligibility to employees who did not work 1,040 hours in the previous year, despite the union's contention of past practice allowing vacation under those circumstances. The arbitrator found the contract was not ambiguous, and the union presented evidence of only two employees who were allegedly told they were entitled to vacation without mention of a work requirement to support the alleged two-decades-old practice (*International Paper Co.*, 127 LA 564).

● A casino did not commit a contract violation when it reduced the vacation benefits of dealers who worked less than 1,800 hours in a year, an arbitrator found. The employer frequently allowed employees to clock out and leave early if there were more dealers than necessary to provide adequate staffing for a given shift. Based on the contract's clear language requiring 1,800 hours of work to qualify for full vacation benefits, the arbitrator found that vacation reductions were warranted for those employees who failed to accumulate the necessary hours because of the so-called "early outs" they had taken. Notwithstanding her denial of the employees' grievance, the arbitrator urged the employer to warn dealers in the future that taking advantage of early outs could cause them to fall short of the 1,800-hour threshold (*Greektown Casino*, 120 LA 25).

● An arbitrator upheld a school district's refusal to grant vacation benefits to a secretary who worked nine full months and three weeks in each of two other months. The parties' labor contract provided that all full-time employees who worked either an 11-month or 12-month schedule were entitled to paid vacations. The employee in question, however, did not work such a schedule and should have realized that she did not qualify under both contractual language and past practice, the arbitrator concluded (*Cambridge City Schools*, 123 LA 339).

● Under a similar contract, an employer was justified in refusing to grant an employee four weeks of vacation despite his 20 years of service, an arbitrator determined. The contract provided for vacation benefits if employees worked 11-month or 12-month schedules, but the employee had spent at least nine years of his tenure in nine-month positions, the arbitrator noted. The arbitrator concluded that the employer did not have to count those years toward the 20 years of service required for receiving four weeks of vacation per year (*Upper Scioto Board of Education*, 118 LA 409).

● On the other hand, an arbitrator held that a city employer could not stop granting firefighters a bonus week of vacation after 10 years of service. The bonus week had been granted for a number of years in accordance with a city ordinance, but a new collective bargaining agreement between the parties did not expressly provide for the extra vacation and stated that the terms of the agreement would supersede personnel policies dictated by ordinance. The new contract also contained a zipper clause. Nevertheless, the arbitrator found that firefighters with 10 years of service remained entitled to the bonus week. According to the arbitrator, the union had not negotiated away the bonus week of vacation, and the new contract stated that the rules, regulations, and working conditions effective upon the agreement's inception would remain in force. In addition, the zipper clause could not override past practice, the arbitrator declared (*City of Frederick*, 106 LA 298).

• Another arbitrator held that an employer could no longer require employees to have eight years of service before becoming eligible for vacation benefits. The parties had reached an oral agreement during bargaining to adopt the same contract terms in place at another company, which called for vacation benefits after one year of service. Although the collective bargaining agreement implemented by the parties mirrored the other company's contract in all other respects, it omitted the language about the one-year service requirement for vacations. Deciding that the omission did not reflect the intention of the parties during negotiations, the arbitrator ordered the inclusion of the language, which entitled employees to 40 hours of paid vacation if they worked at least 1,040 hours in the first year of employment (*Hibbing Ready Mix*, 97 LA 248).

• An employer erred in basing an employee's vacation entitlement on his overall years with the company instead of his time at a particular plant, an arbitrator decided. The employee had worked at the company for more than five years before he transferred from another location and became a member of the bargaining unit at the plant in question. When the employer credited his prior service for vacation purposes,

the union objected because of the morale and scheduling difficulties that were created. Finding that the collective bargaining agreement defined length of service as time worked at the particular plant, the arbitrator held that the employee's years with the company prior to joining the bargaining unit could not be counted for vacation purposes. Consequently, he held that the employee was not entitled to the additional week of vacation that his prior service would have earned him (*Glidden Co.*, 97 LA 470; see also 97 LA 1035).

B. Effect of Time Away From Work on Vacation Eligibility

Many disputes over vacation eligibility focus on how to treat periods of time when employees are away from work for various reasons, such as layoffs, strikes, union leave, and absences due to injury or other medical problems. Employers commonly contend that vacations have to be earned, and the underlying service requirements can only be satisfied through the accumulation of actual work time. Unions, meanwhile, tend to take the position that service is synonymous with "seniority," which is not necessarily broken while employees are away from work.

1. Effect of Layoffs

Although employees generally are entitled to all vacation benefits earned prior to being laid off, it does not necessarily follow that the time they spend on layoff can be credited toward meeting service or work requirements for future vacations (67 LA 997, 64 LA 641, 34 LA 170).

• In one case, an arbitrator decided that the key to deciding whether laid-off employees were eligible for vacation benefits was whether they were "on the payroll." In the parties' labor contract, those specific terms were used, and the arbitrator concluded that laid-off workers could not be described as being on the employer's payroll and therefore were not eligible for vacation benefits (*Globe Corp.*, 23 LA 298).

• Although employees on layoff continued to accumulate seniority, they were not entitled to vacation benefits under a contract provision granting them vacations as rewards for "satisfactory service," an arbitrator ruled. Emphasizing that the vacation provisions laid down an actual work requirement before employees became eligible for vacation benefits, the arbitrator concluded that the language pertaining to "earned vacation" negated any automatic accrual of employment benefits during a layoff (*Frye Copysystems Inc.*, 65 LA 1249).

• An employee who had experienced a 10-month layoff was not entitled to include that time as part of her "length of service" for vacation purposes, an arbitrator held. In this case, the parties had a consistent and long-term practice of not including time spent on layoff in the calculations of employees' length of service, the arbitrator found (*National Cash Register Co.*, 64 LA 103).

• *By contrast*, another arbitrator faulted an employer for deducting time spent on layoff from workers' "employment" as it related to vacation eligibility. According to the arbitrator, if the parties' contract stated that laid-off employees had the right to recall on the basis of seniority, and seniority is based on "employment," then being laid off temporarily should not affect employees' vacation rights. Employees continued to accumulate seniority while on layoff, the arbitrator said, adding that the employer could not deny vacation benefits to laid-off employees who fulfilled all other conditions to qualify for recall. They were entitled to have their layoff periods counted as employment in determining vacation credits, he concluded (*Hanchett Manufacturing. Co.*, 28 LA 235).

• An employer committed a contract violation in reducing employees' vacation benefits when they returned to work from layoffs, an arbitrator held. The employer attempted to invoke a contract provision that called for prorated vacation benefits in the event of employment termination. It argued that upon returning to work, the employees should only receive a portion of their annual vacation allotment, based on how much time they worked since their last employment anniversary. According to the arbitrator, however, the provision on prorated vacations did not apply to the laid-off employees, because the contract stated

that a break in service had to last at least a year to be treated as a termination. In the absence of any clear contract language that would limit the employees' vacation benefits, the arbitrator decided that the employer had to continue its past practice of paying full vacation benefits to those returning from layoffs (*Fabick Machinery Co.*, 104 LA 555).

• Employees who were laid off because of plant closings late in the year should have been accorded the status normally granted to employees on indefinite layoff, making them eligible for vacation time accrued during the year of the layoff, an arbitrator ruled. Despite a related contract clause stating that workers must have been actively employed at some time during the calendar year to be eligible for vacation benefits during that calendar year, the arbitrator ruled that the applicable provision was in fact another contract clause, which entitled employees to vacations if they were laid off for an indefinite time (*Continental Can Co.*, 76 LA 1212).

2. Effect of Strikes

Questions about employees' vacation eligibility sometimes arise in connection with strikes and lockouts. Given that arbitrators usually treat vacation benefits as a form of deferred compensation that employees earn continuously as they perform their jobs, those who quit during strikes or lockouts are normally deemed to be entitled to vacation pay if they have otherwise satisfied the criteria for vacation eligibility and provided proper notification of their intent to resign.

By the same token, arbitrators are likely to hold that employees do not accrue vacation credits during strikes because they are not performing the work required to earn vacation benefits. Likewise, when calculating employees' overall length of service for purposes of determining vacation entitlements, arbitrators commonly exclude the time that employees have been off the job because of work stoppages (79 LA 1294, 74 LA 1061, 70 LA 636, 66 LA 745, 49 LA 113, 49 LA 55, 48 LA 213, 47 LA 1164, 47 LA 319, 45 LA 512, 42 LA 929, 33 LA 837, 27 LA 251).

- An arbitrator ruled that an employer had the right to deduct the time that employees spent on strike in determining the employees' vacation eligibility dates under a side letter to the parties' labor contract. Despite the union's claim that the contract based vacation entitlement on "years of employment or in the trade" and strikers never ceased being employed, the arbitrator said there was evidence that during contract talks on the side letter it was decided that strike time would be treated as layoff time. The union already had agreed that layoffs generally would affect vacation eligibility dates, the arbitrator concluded, denying the grievance (*George Banta Co. Inc.*, 74 LA 388).

- In another case, an arbitrator ruled that an employer properly reduced its employees' vacation benefits to reflect the work time that was lost as the result of a strike. The contract entitled employees to receive vacation benefits based on their continuous service, and the arbitrator reasoned that vacations, like wages, had to be earned (*Ohio Power Co.*, 63 LA 1235).

- Employees who returned to work from a 13-month lockout were not entitled to vacation benefits from the previous year, an arbitrator held. When the employees returned, they were covered by a newly negotiated contract that said absences for more than six months in one year would trigger the loss of vacation eligibility for that year, the arbitrator observed, adding that the issue of vacation benefits was discussed and denied at the bargaining table (*RMI Titanium Co.*, 121 LA 990).

- An arbitrator upheld an employer's refusal to allow employees to count time spent on strike as excused absences as defined by the parties' collective bargaining agreement and as applied to the accrual of vacation time. Although the strike was legal, the arbitrator doubted that it was "excused" by the employer, adding that the employer would be subsidizing the strike if it hewed to that interpretation of the contract (*Motor Car Dealers Association of Kansas City*, 49 LA 55).

- Another arbitrator ruled that taking part in a strike, even though the job action violated the contract, was not in itself cause to deprive employees of vacation credits. In the arbitrator's view, the strikers would have forfeited vacation credits if management had fired them before the vacation credits accrued or had notified them that their return to work would be conditioned on a waiver of vacation credits (*Marathon Rubber Products Co.*, 6 LA 238).

3. Effect of Time Missed for Medical Reasons

In cases involving employees who miss work because of medical reasons, such as injuries or long-term illnesses, arbitrators usually focus on the governing contract language and employers' past practices in deciding whether vacation benefits should be granted.

- In a case where an employer and a union differed in their interpretations of ambiguous contract language, an arbitrator relied on past practice in ruling that an employee had accrued vacation while on injury leave. The contract stated that vacations were "earned," but it was unclear whether they were earned "by the sweat of one's brow" through active employment or simply by remaining on the employer's rolls and accumulating continuous service, the arbitrator said. In deciding the matter based on past practice, the arbitrator found that time away from work as a result of industrial injuries or sickness and accident claims had been treated the same as active employment for purposes of time "earned" over the course of several years (*Van Air Systems Inc.*, 110 LA 1049).

- An injured employee was entitled to vacation benefits even though he had a doctor's excuse for only the first three months of a five-month absence and his ailments were exacerbated by excessive drinking, an arbitrator held. Given the proof that the employee had suffered a real injury, and since he could not work as a result of that injury and not just because of his drinking habits, the arbitrator concluded that he was in fact due his vacation (*Chicago & Harrisburg Coal Co.*, 2 LA 56).

- An employee who was awarded total disability under workers' compensation was entitled to vacation benefits for 400 weeks during which he was to receive the workers' compensation benefits, an arbitrator ruled. Pointing out that the employee, who continued to receive benefits from the employer, was regarded as being on the employer's "payroll," notwithstanding the fact that he was not on the "active payroll," the arbitrator concluded that there was nothing in the contract to support the employer's claim that its vacation obligation was restricted to the year the employee sustained the injury (*Thomas Industries Inc.*, 61 LA 627).

● *By contrast*, an arbitrator upheld an employer's denial of vacation benefits to employees who missed work for more than a year as a result of personal disability caused by accident or sickness. The parties' collective bargaining agreement generally restricted the use of vacation time to the year in which it was earned, and the employer argued that the employees had no vacation entitlement in a calendar year when they performed no work. The union countered that other employees had received vacation benefits under similar circumstances, thus creating a binding past practice. Despite acknowledging the union's argument, the arbitrator found that there were also prior instances in which employees had not received vacation pay while away from work for an entire year due to illness or injury. Declaring that a "checkered practice is not really a practice at all," the arbitrator decided that the evidence did not establish the consistency needed to prove the existence of a binding past practice (*Elliott Turbomachinery Co.*, 119 LA 727).

● Where a contract provided that "time lost for illness" would not affect vacation benefits, an arbitrator ruled that an "injury," even though occurring on the job, was not an "illness" for purposes of computing these benefits. The parties' contract clearly distinguished between illness and injury and allowed only for time lost for the former, the arbitrator said, denying the grievance (*Modecraft Co. Inc.*, 44 LA 1045; see also 85 LA 967, 74 LA 1061).

4. Effect of Union Leave

Unless collective bargaining agreements specify otherwise, arbitrators are not likely to waive the normal service requirements for union officials or count the time spent on union business as time worked for purposes of vacation eligibility.

● An arbitrator upheld an employer's denial of vacation benefits to an employee who also served as local union president and spent many hours on union business. Under the parties' contract, eligibility for vacation benefits hinged on an employee's working at least 1,400 hours in a vacation year. The local president was 64 hours shy of the requirement, but the union claimed that all those hours were excused time off for union activity that could be included in his vacation eligibility calculations. The arbitrator, however, concluded that the contract distinguished "excused union activity" from "authorized leaves of absence," and only the latter could be included in vacation benefit calculations (*American Air Filter Co. Inc.*, 39 LA 942).

● Another arbitrator held that an employer was justified in refusing to grant vacation to an employee who had been away on union business for six months. Under the parties' labor contract, employees had to be "continuously in the service of the employer" as of the vacation eligibility date to be granted time off. The arbitrator reasoned that "continuously in the service" meant "continuously available to the employer," which the union official was not because he was working on union activities for those six months (*Chamberlain Co. of America*, 8 LA 755).

C. Termination and Retirement

Arbitrators generally agree that employees are entitled to payment for unused vacation benefits at the time of termination provided they have met contractual requirements for vacation eligibility. In settling disputes that involve departing workers, arbitrators tend to apply the same principles regardless of whether employees resign, retire, or lose their jobs involuntarily.

● One arbitrator ruled that an employer violated a collective bargaining contract when it instituted rules on "vacation allotments" without bargaining, since these rule changes were "material, substantial and significant" (*Ports America Louisiana*, 124 LA 1153).

• Another arbitrator ruled an employer was not justified when it denied an extra week of vacation to employees whose 15th anniversary took place after June 1, where the contract provided that employees with 15 or more years of service got an extra week of vacation, and past practice had been to provide that extra week computed at the time of seniority eligibility (*Johnson Controls Inc.*, 124 LA 257).

• An arbitrator ruled that an employer did not violate a collective bargaining agreement by rescinding its practice of paying vacation pay for the entire calendar year in advance for employees leaving its employ, where the agreement unambiguously stipulated that they are entitled only to "unpaid vacation monies due" them on the basis of the "number of weeks worked," and no specific term required the employer to accept requests for advances of not-yet-earned vacation pay (*Continental Structural Plastics*, 126 LA 1765).

• An arbitrator upheld an employer's denial of vacation benefits to a retiring employee who met two out of three contractual eligibility criteria. Under the contract, an employee had to be on the payroll on Jan. 1, have at least one year of continuous service as of Jan. 1, and have worked for the employer in 26 of the 52 weeks immediately preceding Jan. 1. Although the employee met the second and third requirements, he was not on the payroll as of Jan. 1 because he had retired before that date. The employee did not qualify for the vacation benefits, the arbitrator held, finding that the employer was entitled to enforce all three requirements even though it might not be entitled to do so in cases of involuntary terminations (*Rex Chainbelt Inc.*, 49 LA 646).

• Another arbitrator held that an employer was not required to grant an employee prorated vacation benefits for the year in which he resigned. The contract in this case did not include any language suggesting that "the right to a vacation is one which accrues on a daily, weekly, monthly or some other pro-rata basis," the arbitrator said. Unless specifically stated otherwise, the arbitrator asserted, "a vacation is a benefit that is considered to be earned and granted only after the completion of each year of continuous service" (*Tube City Inc.*, 117 LA 719).

• *By contrast*, an employee who was fired for chronic absenteeism was still entitled to his vacation benefits, an arbitrator ruled. The collective bargaining agreement provided vacation benefits for workers who had at least one year of service and earnings in at least 30 pay periods of the vacation year. Despite having been terminated for cause, the employee met all the criteria stated in the contract and was entitled to his vacation benefits, the arbitrator concluded (*Weaver Manufacturing. Co.*, 19 LA 325).

• An arbitrator reached a similar conclusion with regard to an employee who was discharged for cause. Although the employer had unilaterally changed its vacation policies in such a way that would have disqualified the employee from receiving benefits and had put some of those changes in a side letter, the employer and union had not agreed to include the side letter in the contract. The arbitrator found that the employee qualified for vacation benefits because the existing contract did not specifically bar such benefits in the employee's situation (*General Foods Corp.*, 18 LA 910; see also 12 LA 641).

• An employer violated its collective bargaining agreement when it failed to provide earned, prorated vacation benefits to employees who had quit, an arbitrator held. Although the employer was going through hard times, the arbitrator noted that changes in the "economy, markets, customers, and corporate fortunes" do not give an employer license to be freed from "its solemnly negotiated promises." The contract clearly did not call for employees who resigned to forfeit accrued vacation benefits, and any employees who had fulfilled the contractually required service and then quit were entitled to their earned vacation, the arbitrator concluded (*Wolverine Die Cast Corp.*, 117 LA 1002).

• An employer committed a contract violation when it refused to provide vacation benefits to an employee who retired before his anniversary date, an arbitrator ruled. Despite the employer's contention to the contrary, the arbitrator said the contract did not define a specific qualifying or vesting date, nor did contract language differentiate between accrued vacation leave on a monthly basis and earned leave based on anniversary dates. Contractual language was "much more susceptible to the union's interpretation" that vacation leave benefits were earned or vested as they were accrued on a monthly basis, the arbitrator concluded, ordering the employer to provide the vacation benefits to the retired employee (*LB&B Associates*, 114 LA 865).

D. Shutdowns and Ownership Changes

In addition to the various situations discussed above, other events that can raise questions about vacation eligibility include shutdowns and changes in ownership.

1. Shutdowns

When employees are idled or experience a permanent loss of employment as a result of business closures or partial shutdowns, arbitrators generally agree that they remain entitled to their accrued vacation benefits (76 LA 1212, 13 LA 804, 12 LA 860).

● An arbitrator determined that several employees were entitled to vacation benefits even though their company had shut down the part of its facilities where they worked. The parties' labor contract stated that employees were eligible for vacations if they had a specified period of service and were "in the employ" of their company on April 15. It also stated that workers were still considered employed for two years after a layoff. Therefore, when the plant shutdown caused the employees to be laid off just before April 15, they were nonetheless due their vacation benefits because they were still regarded as employed for another two years and because they met all the other requirements, the arbitrator found (*Botany Mills Inc.*, 27 LA 1).

● Another arbitrator held that employees were entitled to prorated vacation benefits following a plant shutdown because they were terminated through no fault of their own. It was immaterial that the contract had expired before the employees' vacation eligibility date, the arbitrator said, adding that the right to vacation benefits is earned in much the same way as wages (*Brookford Mills*, 28 LA 838).

● An employer committed a contract violation when it denied vacation benefits to a number of employees following a shutdown, an arbitrator held. Employees normally were entitled to a week of vacation at Christmas and a week of vacation in the summer, but the employer contended that the affected workers were not entitled to their summer vacation benefits because they were off the payroll at the time. The arbitrator disagreed, concluding that the employees were still on the employer's payroll as of the date when the summer vacations were to begin (*Phillip Morris USA*, 116 LA 1650).

2. Ownership Changes

If successor employers take on the collective bargaining agreements of their predecessors, they usually are obligated to count the entire length of employees' service when determining how much vacation time the employees must be granted.

An arbitrator ruled that employees of a bankrupt company that closed its plant at the end of 2009 were entitled to vacation pay earned in 2009, where the collective bargaining agreement stated that vacation pay was limited to a specific date in case of discharge, retirement, quit, layoff, and death, but not bankruptcy. Employees could not be denied an earned benefit by a situation that was totally out of their control (*Lynchburg Foundry Co.*, 128 LA 1804).

● A successor employer had to credit workers for service given its predecessor when computing vacation eligibility, an arbitrator held. The arbitrator found that the successor employer was liable for a number of reasons, including the fact that it hired all of the predecessor's bargaining-unit employees, operated in the same manner and same location, and had a labor contract that had substantially the same provisions as the predecessor's agreement (*A.B.A. Diesel Parts & Service Co.*, 62 LA 660).

● An arbitrator ruled that a successor employer obligated itself to provide paid vacations for its predecessor's employees when it wrote a letter saying they could take from one to two weeks of vacation accrued in the preceding two years, depending on their seniority. Although the employer contended that the letter said nothing about paid vacations, the arbitrator said the common and ordinary meaning of the terms used was "intrinsically associated" with paid vacations. Adding that the successor employer made assurances about vacation benefits at employee meetings, the arbitrator ruled that the employer had to provide paid vacations in keeping with previous seniority provisions (*Zenetron Inc.*, 74 LA 861).

• *By contrast*, another arbitrator upheld a successor employer's refusal to carry over vacation time employees accrued between their anniversary dates and the date that the change in ownership took effect. When the union and the successor employer met to sign a new contract, the parties agreed that employees' seniority would be carried over to the successor but that there would be no carry-over of vacation or sick days. Under the interim agreement they signed, employees were to start a new accrual period when the successor assumed control of the operations. The pact made it clear that any vacation previously accrued was the predecessor employer's responsibility, not the successor's, the arbitrator said, denying the grievance (*American Food & Vending Corp.*, 120 LA 507).

II. Vacation Scheduling [LA.CDI 100.5203 (public employees); 116.152]

OVERVIEW

For the most part, employers' authority over vacation scheduling falls under the same umbrella as other management rights associated with running a business and maintaining efficient operations. Although contract language and past practice can limit management control over vacation scheduling, arbitrators generally agree that the needs of employers with regard to meeting business demands take precedence over the preferences of employees with regard to the timing of their vacations.

When disputes arise over vacation scheduling, they commonly involve situations where employers deny the dates requested by employees or reschedule vacations that have been previously approved. In some conflicts over vacation scheduling, seniority can emerge as a deciding factor. Disputes also can arise if employers attempt to force employees to use vacation leave during shutdowns or if employee illnesses cause vacation leave and sick leave to overlap.

SUMMARY OF CASES

A. 'Subject to Business Requirements'

Where collective bargaining agreements allow employees to choose their vacation dates, the contract language typically includes a proviso stating that the timing of employees' vacations remains "subject to business requirements." When employers and employees clash over vacation dates, arbitrators are likely to uphold employers' scheduling decisions as long as they are supported by valid business reasons (94 LA 309, 67 LA 709, 61 LA 958, 59 LA 268).

● An employer did not commit a contract violation by limiting employees' ability to use their vacation leave one day at a time,

an arbitrator held. Although employees had been allowed to schedule single-day leave quite freely for many years, increasing problems caused by the practice prompted the employer to restrict employees to five single-day vacations per year. Because the contract's management-rights clause granted the employer broad powers unless "specifically limited by some express language," the arbitrator concluded that the employer's unilateral change, which was based on valid business reasons, had to be allowed (*Sealy Mattress Co.*, 121 LA 883).

● An employer was justified in refusing to let a maintenance worker take his vacation during a time when its plant was shut down for maintenance and repair, an arbitrator decided. Although the contract was silent on the matter of a worker's right to take vacations when desired, the arbitrator noted that absent specific contract language, the employer should take into account an employee's preferences but added that contractual silence also meant that the employer had more discretion in deciding when to allow the employee to take time off. Because there were no specific restrictions on the employer and because the employer did not act in a discriminatory or capricious manner, the arbitrator determined that the denial was acceptable (*Hubinger Co.*, 29 LA 459).

• An arbitrator upheld a university's unilateral change in vacation scheduling guidelines that restricted employees' flexibility in taking time off and gave supervisors final say as to whether "emergency" vacations would be granted. Despite the employer's past practice of trying to accommodate employees' vacation preferences, the labor agreement unambiguously granted the employer the right to make such decisions. According to the arbitrator, the employer could make unilateral changes in vacation policy because it retained whatever rights "it has not given away in negotiations." The contract did not "give away" the employer's right to determine the number of employees, if any, who could be spared from work at any time, the arbitrator concluded (*Ball State University*, 121 LA 774).

• An arbitrator ruled that an employer was justified in ordering 33 employees to take a one-week forced vacation during a particular week, because the management rights clause allowed the employer to manage the business in the manner it "determine[s] to be in its best interest," and the action was designed to limit layoffs and cut down on overtime in the latter half of the year. "The fact that the persons selected would have been laid off that week due to seniority, that only persons with two or more weeks of vacation remaining were picked, and that those placed on vacation retain the right to pick which of the remaining weeks would constitute the rest of their vacation, aids the finding of a reasoned use of management rights," the arbitrator reasoned (*AK Steel Corp.*, 128 LA 48).

• A meat provider did not violate a collective bargaining contract when it blacked out the week before Mother's Day from the schedule so that employees could not take vacation that week, where it had done so for at least nine or 10 years, and was acting in good faith and to meet operational needs, an arbitrator ruled (*PFG/Middendorf Meat Co.*, 126 LA 1626).

• An arbitrator ruled an employer was justified in blocking employees from taking vacations during four weeks that contained holidays, where the bargaining agreement stated that the "vacation period shall be selected by mutual consent," the union failed to eliminate the phrase during bargaining, there was a need for full shifts during those weeks, and there was a practice of limiting employees' vacations on those weeks (*Pepsi-Cola*, 128 LA 426).

• An arbitrator ruled that the number of firefighters who are allowed to take vacation on any given shift to maintain the required minimum staffing was three firefighters, despite the union's contention that it should be four firefighters. The shift size had increased from five to seven members, and two firefighters were allowed to be off when the shift had five members, where having three firefighters off was a ratio of 42 percent off, which was similar to 40 percent off, when two of the five were allowed to take vacation days (*City of Markham*, 129 LA 1544).

• An arbitrator held that an employer could continue a practice of two years' standing where it required employees to begin their vacations on Mondays. Under the collective bargaining agreement, the employer had the right to schedule vacations to maintain efficient operations. Despite the union's demand that each employee be allowed to choose which day to begin vacations, the arbitrator pointed out that the contract was unambiguous in allowing the employer to make such determinations, and the union's acquiescence in the practice for two years signaled its tacit approval (*Sinclair Refining Co.*, 12 LA 183).

• Under a contract that gave management sole authority over the timing of vacations, an employer was justified in re-scheduling the vacation of one member of a three-man crew, an arbitrator ruled. Had the employer allowed the employee to take his vacation while a second member of the crew was out of town, the arbitrator noted, the third member would have been left alone to perform work normally done by all three employees (*United Telephone Co. of Northwest*, 64 LA 906; see also 73 LA 813, 73 LA 687).

● An employer did not violate its la-bor contract when it provided vacation pay to employees but forced the vacation-ing workers to return to their duties, an arbitrator ruled. The contract specified that under unusual circumstances, the employer could "request" that some or all employees work during their vacations. Disagreeing with the union's contention that the employer could not compel em-ployees to resume working while on vaca-tion, the arbitrator said the obvious intent of the contract was to give the employer the right to require employees to return to work under unusual circumstances. In ad-dition, the arbitrator concluded that it was up to the employer to define what consti-tuted "unusual circumstances" (*Maxwell Brothers Inc.*, 5 LA 449).

● An employer was within its rights when it enforced a contract clause on vaca-tion scheduling that required employees to submit written requests rather than simply calling in to schedule vacation, an arbitrator ruled. During the life of a previous collec-tive bargaining agreement, a past practice of allowing employees to call in their vaca-tion requests had been "memorialized" un-der a memorandum of understanding. The arbitrator noted, however, that the MOU contained "sunset language" stating that the practice would remain in "full force and effect for the term of the collective bargain-ing agreement." Once that agreement was replaced by a new contract, the past prac-tice expired and the employer was entitled to enforce the requirement for written va-cation requests, the arbitrator found (*May-flower Vehicle Systems*, 121 LA 634).

● *By contrast*, an arbitrator ruled an employer violated a collective bargaining contract when it required an employee to

take paid vacation leave while on Family Medical Leave Act (FMLA) leave to take his child to the hospital in late January, even though FMLA allows an employer to substitute paid leave for unpaid FMLA leave, because FMLA also requires compli-ance with the contract, which provided that vacations had to be taken in July and from Christmas to New Year's (*Big Ridge Inc.*, 128 LA 107).

● Adoption of a new vacation policy did not give an employer the right to abandon a past practice of allowing employees and supervisors to work out vacation schedules, an arbitrator decided. Although the parties' labor contract allowed the employer to set the total number of employees who could be on vacation at one time, it did not give the employer the right to determine when particular employees were to take their va-cations, the arbitrator concluded (*Reynolds Metals Co.*, 43 LA 1150).

● An employer violated its labor con-tract when it turned down an employee's request for a specific vacation period be-cause it overlapped with that requested by a co-worker, an arbitrator held. Although the agreement provided that the employ-er's business needs had to be considered in scheduling vacations, the arbitrator found that the employer had in the past allowed overlapping vacations and added that both employees' being off work at the same time would not necessarily have impeded operations. To reject an employee's vaca-tion request, the arbitrator concluded, the employer would have to show that granting the request would adversely affect produc-tion, safety, or general employee relations (*Tin Processing Corp.*, 15 LA 568; see also 110 LA 476, 46 LA 715).

● Another arbitrator ruled that man-agement could not make a blanket denial of all vacation requests for Christmas week. Under the parties' agreement, vacations had to be taken between April 15 and Dec. 31, subject to the employer's operational needs. The employer could not unilater-ally decide to change its policy and refuse leave requests for Christmas week but had to make every effort to accommodate employees' desires for the timing of their vacations unless doing so would adversely affect production, the arbitrator held. Absent such proof, the employer should have agreed to the employees' requests, the arbitrator concluded (*Bethlehem Steel Co.*, 30 LA 899).

B. Seniority as a Factor

As in other situations where the potential exists for more than one employee to want the same thing, seniority can become a deciding factor in determining who gets preference in the scheduling of vacations. The following are examples of cases in which arbitrators addressed the issue of seniority in connection with vacation scheduling.

● An employer was justified when it scheduled employee vacations using separate seniority lists for warehouse employees and for employees working with a new mechanized distribution system, an arbitrator ruled, even though the collective bargaining agreement appeared to call for only one list. An addendum governing staffing issues arising from the installation of a new system distinguished the operations of the new system from the other warehouse operations, and the use of two lists maintained the integrity of both the addendum and the collective bargaining agreement (*Albertson's Inc.*, 127 LA 572).

● The selection of vacation dates by seniority order became a key feature of a scheduling plan that an arbitrator required an employer to implement after it refused to grant an employee his preferred vacation period. The arbitrator determined that the parties' labor contract, which granted up to 13 weeks of vacation, required further guidelines to balance employees' vacation rights against the employer's operational needs. The plan called for plant and unit quotas and allowed employees to select vacation periods within those quotas in order of seniority. The plan also permitted the employer to schedule vacations by calendar quarter because this method enabled the most employees to have time off during preferred times, such as the summer. At the same time, the arbitrator ordered the employer to make exceptions in special cases of hardship, where the granting of employees' vacation requests would not interfere with production (*Armco Steel Corp.*, 45 LA 120).

● As long as no operational problems existed, an employer should have granted senior employees' preferences for the timing of their vacations when those times conflicted with dates foremen wanted, an arbitrator ruled. Because nothing indicated that the employer assigned the vacation weeks to foremen on the basis of anticipated production needs, the arbitrator concluded that foremen had to take second choice (*Air Reduction Chemical & Carbide Co.*, 42 LA 1192).

● Another arbitrator ruled that an employer's contractual right to designate vacation schedules did not permit it to grant vacation times according to shift seniority, where the contract provided only for seniority in job classification and overall tenure (*Baltimore Sun Co.*, 103 LA 363).

● An employer's imposition of limits on the vacation schedules of transferred employees violated a collective bargaining agreement, an arbitrator found. Even though the contract specified the number of workers who could be on vacation in each department at any one time and granted times by seniority, the transferred employees had seniority in their former departments and already selected their vacation times before they volunteered to move to a different department. When the employer first refused and ultimately allowed them to keep their original vacation times, it also told the union that in the future employees who took voluntary transfers would only be allowed to pick the unselected vacation weeks available in their new departments. According to the arbitrator, the employer had to honor its past practice of allowing employees to keep their already selected vacation time (based on seniority) because changing the policy would be tantamount to making a unilateral change in the contract, which could not be allowed (*Schmidt Baking Co. Inc.*, 104 LA 574; see also 94 LA 51).

● An arbitrator upheld an employer's denial of an assistant town clerk's request for a vacation during the election season—her office's busiest time. According to the arbitrator, despite the fact that the employee had seniority, which she felt entitled her to take her vacation when she so desired, the employee's absence during that time would have meant she would miss a conference that was considered essential for her job. Although the parties' labor contract stated that vacation length was allotted based on seniority, it was silent on scheduling. Past practice had been to forbid time off when the election season was in full swing, the arbitrator said, adding that the employee had been told about the importance of the conference and had been informed about its dates well in advance (*Town of Trumbull*, 99 LA 173; see also 110 LA 476).

C. Vacations During Shutdowns

At some workplaces, vacations routinely coincide with annual shutdowns, and the requirement to use leave at the specified times is accepted without question. If employers do not make this type of vacation scheduling a standard and recurring practice, however, arbitrators might bar them from forcing employees to take vacation leave during shutdowns or periods of layoff (96 LA 445, 81 LA 254, 48 LA 1018, 32 LA 776, 31 LA 462).

• One arbitrator overruled an employer's requirement that all employees take their vacations during a two-month shutdown prompted by a lack of orders. Although the parties' labor contract required employees to schedule vacations in advance at a time acceptable to the employer, it did not grant the employer a blanket right to unilaterally reschedule those vacations, shutdown or not, the arbitrator said. Employees could not be deprived of their opportunity to specify the vacation times they wanted, the arbitrator concluded (*Koppers Co. Inc.*, 42 LA 1321).

• An arbitrator found that an employer was not free to demand that employees take one week of their vacations during a plant shutdown. Under a contract that required the employer to endeavor to comply with employees' vacation requests insofar as business needs permitted, the arbitrator noted that forcing workers to schedule vacations during the shutdown in essence resulted in the employer's "endeavoring *not* to comply with requests" for vacations other than during the shutdown, and that violated the parties' collective bargaining agreement (*Welch Grape Juice Co.*, 48 LA 1018).

• An employer could not require employees to take their vacations during a period of indefinite layoff, an arbitrator held, because to do so would miss the whole point of a vacation. According to the arbitrator, "a vacation is a period of rest between periods of work" whereas "a layoff is a period of anxiety and hardship between periods of work" (*Ford Motor Co.*, 3 LA 829).

• On the other hand, an employer had the right to schedule a vacation shutdown during the summer based on an oral agreement, past practice, and the lack of restrictive contract language, an arbitrator ruled. In opposing the move, the union pointed out that the employer had failed to secure contract language recognizing management's right to schedule vacation shutdowns. However, the arbitrator said it was not necessary to obtain such language in light of the oral agreement, the employer's longstanding past practice of scheduling vacation shutdowns for legitimate business reasons, and the lack of any limiting language in the previous agreement (*Lynchburg Foundry Co.*, 76 LA 554; see also 96 LA 445).

• Absent contract language or a binding past practice dictating otherwise, an employer had the inherent right to fix employees' vacation time, an arbitrator ruled. The employer in this case decided it no longer could afford the disruptions that accompanied parceling out employees' vacations as they wished, and it unilaterally designated the week of July 4th for a plant-wide vacation shutdown. The arbitrator overruled union objections based on past practice because that past practice had only involved negotiations between the employer and individual employees without any union involvement (*Vogt Manufacturing Corp.*, 44 LA 488; see also 30 LA 225).

• An arbitrator ruled that an employer did not violate its labor contract when it required workers to take their vacations during its facility's annual shutdown. According to the arbitrator, no testimony led him to believe that there was any understanding of contract language other than that it clearly and unambiguously stated the employer had the right to shut down the plant once a year for up to two weeks. It further stated that employees had to take their vacations during that time unless their services were needed by the employer, the arbitrator observed (*Union Tank Car Co. Inc.*, 117 LA 255).

D. Vacation Leave and Sick Leave

Vacation leave and sick leave sometimes intersect, such as when scheduled time off is disrupted by illness. The issues addressed by arbitrators in such cases can include determining which type of leave applies and deciding whether employees must be given new vacation dates in lieu of those that were scheduled.

● An employer committed a contract violation by failing to reschedule the vacation leave of an employee who fell ill and remained in the hospital throughout the period he was supposed to be off, an arbitrator ruled. Noting that sick leave and vacation leave are entirely different privileges, the arbitrator said the contract required the employer to reschedule the employee's vacation. Moreover, the arbitrator declared that the employee's name should have been automatically removed from the vacation roster once his supervisor knew he was in the hospital (*Derby Gas & Electric Co.*, 21 LA 745; see also 25 LA 94).

● In another case, an employee who was on sick leave at the time of his scheduled vacation could not have his vacation rescheduled because all available times had been allotted for the remainder of the year. The employee was entitled to vacation pay in addition to the sick pay he received during the period in question, an arbitrator held, because the contract specifically provided for such an occurrence (*Tenneco Oil Co.*, 54 LA 862).

● An employer was not obligated to continue offering employees the option of substituting vacation days for sick leave, an arbitrator ruled. In finding that the employer could dispense with the practice even though employees had long been allowed to make such substitutions, the arbitrator observed that past practices are relevant "for the interpretation of ambiguous contract language or if the contract is silent regarding some issue," but they "are not availing when clear contract language exists." Finding that the employer's rights in this case were clearly detailed in the contract, the arbitrator said those rights remained enforceable even though the employer had not been utilizing them (*Donaldson Co. Inc.*, 119 LA 561; see also 120 LA 432).

III. Vacation Pay [LA CDI 100.5203; 116.1711 et seq.]

OVERVIEW

Although vacation clauses in collective bargaining agreements tend to be specific about how much time off employees will be granted per year, they do not always include detailed provisions addressing the issues that can surface in connection with vacation pay. As a result, arbitrators are frequently called upon to provide answers to the following types of questions:

- How much vacation pay should workers receive upon separation from employment?

- Do employees have a right to vacation pay in the event of a layoff or shutdown?

- Can employees receive vacation pay while collecting workers' compensation?

- What are the appropriate wage rates to use in calculating vacation pay, and should incentives, overtime, and premium pay be counted as part of employees' wages?

- Does pay for time not worked have to be included in vacation pay calculations?

- What effect do varying pay rates or workweek changes have on vacation pay?

SUMMARY OF CASES

A. Payment for Unused Vacation

Arbitrators generally agree that employees must receive payment for all accrued but unused vacation upon separation from employment. If, however, employees have not satisfied the requirements necessary to qualify for vacation benefits, such as remaining actively employed as of a certain date, arbitrators usually have no choice but to deny their claims for vacation pay.

• An employee who quit after 13 months of employment was entitled to 15 days of vacation pay, an arbitrator ruled. The parties' contract called for 10 days of paid vacation after six months of service, which were to be used in the following six months, and another 15 days of vacation after a year of service, which were to be used in the following 12 months. Because the employee worked only one month into her second year, the employer claimed that she should receive prorated vacation pay instead of getting credit for the full 15 days that were allotted for the 12-month period. The arbitrator, however, found that the employee was entitled to payment for all of the vacation days that were credited on her first anniversary, because the history of the contract's language and the bookkeeping methods used by the employer for the previous 20 years revealed that was the norm (*Columbia Typographical Union No. 101*, 63 LA 507).

• Under a contract that said employees became eligible for vacation benefits once they had worked a certain number of days before Aug. 1 of the vacation year, employment on that date was not a prerequisite that departing employees had to satisfy in order to receive vacation pay, an arbitrator ruled. Having satisfied the requirements for length of service and number of days worked, employees who left the company prior to Aug. 1 were entitled to be paid for their unused vacation benefits, the arbitrator declared (*Telescope Folding Furniture Co. Inc.*, 49 LA 837; see also 71 LA 781).

• An employer erred in the formula it used to calculate the amount of vacation pay to which employees were entitled for the year of their retirement, an arbitrator held. To determine the amount of prorated vacation benefits the employees had accrued, the employer counted completed months of service and rounded down, essentially excluding any portion of the final month the employees worked. Finding this system unfair, the arbitrator ordered the employer to use the same approach that its accounting department had adopted for other calculations, which counted all the days up to the date of retirement and divided that total by the number of days in the calendar year (*Interstate Brands Corp.*, 121 LA 1720; see also 116 LA 1192).

• An employer could rescind its practice of paying vacation pay for an entire calendar year in advance for employees leaving its employ, an arbitrator ruled, because the agreement unambiguously stipulated that employees were entitled only to "unpaid vacation monies due" them on the basis of the "number of weeks worked," and no specific term required the employer to accept requests for advances of not-yet-earned vacation pay (*Continental Structural Plastics*, 126 LA 1765).

• Another arbitrator held that an employer did not violate its labor contract when it paid an employee who retired only the vacation pay he had accrued for working part of the year. When the employee retired effective Oct. 31, working past his anniversary date by slightly more than two weeks, the union claimed that the employer owed the retiree his full four weeks of annual vacation pay. Citing past practice, the arbitrator agreed with the employer that the calculation should reflect the portion of the year the employee worked, which meant that he was owed approximately 5 percent of the four weeks' vacation pay (*Cotter Merchandise Storage Co.*, 121 LA 1209).

• An employer was justified in refusing to provide any vacation pay for the calendar year in which a retiring employee left its payroll, an arbitrator decided. The contract granted vacation pay to employees who were on the payroll as of the beginning of the vacation year and who had worked during the vacation year, which was defined as Jan. 1 to Dec. 31. Although the employee remained on the payroll until Jan. 4, the last day he actually worked was Dec. 30. Consequently, the arbitrator found that the employee failed to work during the vacation year and therefore did not qualify for any vacation pay in that year (*Westvaco*, 67 LA 128).

• Employees who elected to retire before an annual vacation period were not entitled to vacation pay, an arbitrator decided. Even though the employees had worked the requisite number of weeks to qualify for the annual period of paid vacation, the contract stated that employees who quit before the cutoff date were not eligible for vacation benefits. According to the arbitrator, a number of factors helped determine her decision, including the fact that voluntary retirement could be construed as quitting, and eligibility rules in the contract stated that workers earned their vacation rights by being employed at the start of the annual vacation period (*York Wall Paper Co.*, 69 LA 431; see also 84 LA 863).

1. Unused Vacation of Deceased Workers

In deciding the disposition of vacation benefits upon the death of employees, arbitrators commonly find that payment for unused vacation must be made to the survivors of deceased workers.

● An employer could not legitimately refuse to provide accrued vacation pay to survivors of employees who died, an arbitrator ruled. Employees who died in December had nonetheless fulfilled the conditions for eligibility for vacation benefits, the arbitrator said, rejecting the employer's contention that the parties' labor contract disqualified such payments because it contained language that disqualified employees who quit or retired. In awarding accrued vacation benefits to the survivors, the arbitrator stated that to hold death as a disqualification would be to alter the contract unilaterally (*Pittsburgh Steel Co.*, 43 LA 860).

● An arbitrator ruled that a deceased employee's widow was entitled to his vacation pay. The contract was clear in requiring an employee to work at least 1,000 hours in one year in order to be eligible for a vacation the next year. It also provided that if a worker who had earned a vacation died before the vacation had been taken, the employer had to provide vacation pay to the surviving spouse. According to the arbitrator, even though the employee died in December of the year before he was to take the vacation, there was nothing in the contract that required him to have been on the payroll as of Jan. 1, as the employer contended. The employee had fulfilled the hours requirement, the arbitrator said, making him, and by extension his widow,

eligible for the vacation pay (*Clinton Corn Processing Co.*, 41 LA 513).

● Where a contract provided for vacation rights to be forfeited if employment was terminated prior to Jan. 1 of the vacation year, an arbitrator upheld an employer's denial of vacation pay to survivors of employees who died before Jan. 1. The union contended that termination referred only to quitting or discharge, but the arbitrator said the union's argument was without merit because death must obviously "terminate" the employment relationship (*Bethlehem Steel Corp.*, 47 LA 258).

B. Effect of Layoffs and Shutdowns

If employees have earned their vacations through the requisite amount of service to their employers and have met all other eligibility requirements, arbitrators usually regard them as having a right to their vacation pay when they are laid off or lose their jobs as a result of shutdowns.

● Employees who were terminated as a result of an employer's voluntary shutdown were entitled to prorated vacation pay for the time worked prior to the closing, an arbitrator ruled. Even though the contract required a minimum number of hours worked before employees were eligible for vacation pay, the arbitrator treated vacations as additional wages and reasoned that vacation benefits already earned under the unexpired contract could not be completely annulled by the employer's choice to close its facilities. The arbitrator said his rationale was supported by a related contract provision that granted vacation pay to employees whose time off for sick leave prevented them from working the full 1,000 hours that was normally required for vacation eligibility (*National Plumbing Fixture Corp.*, 49 LA 421; see also 85 LA 979, 51 LA 400).

● In a case where an employer and a union disputed employees' entitlement to vacation pay for the year following a shutdown, an arbitrator held that no vacation pay had to be granted to employees who had not reached their employment anniversary dates prior to the shutdown. The parties' collective bargaining agreement provided for prorated vacation pay based on how much time employees worked between their last employment anniversary and the date of termination, the arbitrator noted. With regard to those employees whose anniversary dates had passed before the shutdown occurred, the arbitrator decided that the formula used to calculate their prorated vacation pay should include not only their regular hours, but their overtime hours as well (*Brechteen Co.*, 114 LA 966).

● Another arbitrator determined that employees were entitled to prorated vacation pay even though they had not reached their individual anniversary dates when their employer unexpectedly closed its plant. The arbitrator said the vacation benefits were "deemed payable unless the [collective bargaining] agreement or past practice clearly bars payment." Rather than preventing the payment of vacation benefits, the contract stated that employees were entitled to their earned but unused vacations upon separation from employment, the arbitrator found, ordering the employer to grant paid benefits to employees who lost their jobs because of the shutdown (*A.I.M. Corp.*, 111 LA 463).

● An employer committed a contract violation when it failed to pay employees on a prorated basis for the vacation they had earned prior to being laid off, an arbitrator ruled. Finding that the contract called for prorated vacation pay whenever employees with at least one year of service were laid off, the arbitrator ordered the employer to give the affected employees vacation pay based upon the hours they worked between their employment anniversary and layoff dates (*La Grou Cold Storage Inc.*, 119 LA 1464).

● An arbitrator ruled that an employer did not violate a bargaining contract when it did not give vacation pay to employees who declined to return to work after a layoff, even though they had been about to receive vacation pay when the layoff occurred, because nothing in the contract obligated the employer to pay them, and they voluntarily chose not to return to work and receive the benefits of that employment (*Howard Industries Inc.*, 128 LA 432).

● An arbitrator held that an employee on layoff was not entitled to request deferment of lump-sum payment for vacation or sick-leave benefits until his three-year recall rights expired or upon request for payment of benefits. The parties' labor contract provided for deferral of benefits to a month selected in the next calendar year, but it did not allow deferral for the length of time requested by the employee in this case, the arbitrator found (*Sacramento, Calif.*, 82 LA 996; see also 82 LA 686).

C. Effect of Strikes

Unless contracts specifically spell out that strikes have no effect on vacation pay, arbitrators tend to rule that employees cease to accumulate vacation benefits during periods when they are off the job because of work stoppages. Their rationale is that employees earn vacation pay by providing services to employers, something they cannot do while on strike.

● An employer had the right to deduct strike time from vacation pay calculations, an arbitrator held. Under a contract that based vacation pay on "time worked," the arbitrator said the denial of vacation pay was appropriate for the time on strike when employees were not working (*Modecraft Co.*, 38 LA 1236).

● In a similar ruling, an arbitrator decided that an employer had the right to reduce the vacation pay of employees to reflect their absence from work because of a strike. The contract granted employees paid vacations based on their completing specified periods of service, the arbitrator said, noting that the parties intended "service" to mean "service rendered" or "worked," not merely being on the payroll (*Reichhold Chemicals Inc.*, 66 LA 745; see also 63 LA 1235).

● Finding that vacation pay is a form of compensation that is not earned while on strike, an arbitrator ruled that an employer was justified in excluding the period of a strike when calculating employees' vacation accruals. While distinguishing strikes from other extended absences, the arbitrator noted that the employer had also prorated vacation accruals for employees who had been away from work on leaves of absence (*Murphy Oil USA Inc.*, 92 LA 1148).

● Teachers who continued a two-week-old strike through the first three days of their scheduled one-week vacation were not entitled to vacation pay for the three-day period, an arbitrator decided. The striking teachers failed to meet the school's regulation requiring that they be on paid status for at least one of the five working days immediately preceding a vacation in order to be eligible for paid time off, the arbitrator found, adding that the regulation was consistent with the parties' collective bargaining agreement (*Hawaii Dept. of Education*, 62 LA 415).

● An employer did not have to alter its formula for calculating weekly vacation pay to account for the impact of an extended strike, an arbitrator ruled. To determine how much employees would be paid for a week's vacation, the employer normally divided employees' total earnings in the past year by 52 weeks. During the year of the strike, employees' time away from work drove down their total earnings, which in turn had the effect of significantly reducing the pay they would receive for a week's vacation. The employees' losses in vacation pay as a result of the formula could not be helped, the arbitrator said, noting that the contract dictated the use of the prior year's earnings in calculating weekly vacation pay (*Blaw-Knox Co.*, 47 LA 1164).

● *By contrast*, another arbitrator determined that an employer could not deduct strike time from vacation pay calculations. Because the parties' labor contract was silent on the matter, the arbitrator was persuaded by a past practice in which strike time counted as "active service" that figured in employees' accrual of full vacation pay (*Mobil Oil Co.*, 42 LA 102).

● An employer should not have deducted time lost because of employees' layoffs, strikes, or leaves of absence from their total years of service used to calculate vacation pay, according to an arbitrator. The parties' labor contract stated that a worker's most recent date of hire was the employee's anniversary date and that eligibility for vacation pay was computed from that date. The effect of this action was to set back anniversary dates for a number of long-time employees, the arbitrator said, adding that that would subvert the contract's intent (*Blue Box Co.*, 61 LA 754).

● An arbitrator ruled that an employer violated its labor contract when it gave returning strikers prorated vacation pay rather than letting them take time off from work. When several striking employees were reinstated in September, they asked for their vacation rights for the period of time they had worked at the beginning of the year. The employer agreed to provide vacation pay but refused to grant the workers any time off. Under "principles of equity," the arbitrator said, the employees should have been granted the time off that was their due. Adding that the employer could not have expected them to make vacation arrangements when they were out of work, the arbitrator ordered the employer to allow the employees to take off time without pay rather than being forced to take vacation pay in lieu of vacation (*Reliance Medical Products Inc.*, 99 LA 95; see also 82 LA 1156, 85 LA 997).

D. Effect of Workers' Compensation

Arbitrators' views vary on whether employees are entitled to vacation pay when they are also receiving workers' compensation or other benefits associated with injuries or illness. The outcome of such cases usually hinges on specific contract language or the existence of a binding past practice.

● An employee who in one year received 15 weeks' pay for work and 30 weeks' pay from workers' compensation was not entitled to vacation pay for that year, an arbitrator found. The contract provided that employees had a right to vacation pay if they had worked for the employer for one year and received 40 paychecks in that time. Considering the union's unsuccessful attempt during contract negotiations to include a reference to workers' compensation checks, the arbitrator maintained that "paycheck" clearly referred to payment for services provided (*Ohse Meat Products Inc.*, 48 LA 978).

● Employees who failed because of an industrial accident to accumulate contractually specified straight-time hours of work were entitled to prorated vacation pay based on actual hours worked, an arbitrator ruled. Because the labor contract clearly stated that employees were to receive vacation pay based on actual hours worked, the arbitrator concluded that the employer had to pay them for vacation credits they accrued whether or not the employees were receiving workers' compensation payments during the time they were eligible for vacation pay (*Solar Chemical Corp.*, 56 LA 99).

● An employer violated its labor contract when it did not allow two employees to accrue vacation time when they were on workers' compensation leave, an arbitrator ruled. Although the parties' labor agreement did not clearly address the issue, the arbitrator determined that the employer had a past practice of allowing employees on extended workers' compensation leave to continue to accrue vacation benefits (*Allamakee County Secondary Roads Department*, 119 LA 274).

● In a case involving an employee who was injured outside the workplace, an arbitrator ruled that his receipt of sickness and accident benefits did not prevent him from receiving vacation pay. Even though the simultaneous payment could be seen as "double compensation," the arbitrator said the parties' collective bargaining agreement neither expressly nor implicitly denied the right of an eligible employee to receive vacation benefits and sickness and accident benefits at the same time (*Airco Inc.*, 62 LA 1056; see also 91 LA 1083, 71 LA 460).

E. Vacation Pay Calculations

In determining the amount of vacation pay to which employees are entitled, arbitrators commonly grapple with questions concerning the appropriate wage rates or forms of compensation to use in the calculations. For example, questions sometimes arise about whether or not to include compensation over and above employees' base rates, such as incentives, overtime, and premium pay, or compensation for time not worked, such as holiday pay. In most cases, arbitrators derive their answers from contract terms that define the basis for calculating vacation pay or from past practices surrounding vacation pay calculations.

● An arbitrator ruled an employer should have added an "earnings protection adjustment" to its calculation of weekly vacation pay of employees who were em-

ployed at a time of 2003 restructuring and whose vacation pay was less in 2004 and 2005 due to lower incentive earnings. The collective bargaining agreement provided that employees who were employed when the restructuring took place would receive the higher of either the pay period average actual earnings per hour or the 2003 hourly vacation rate for "all hours paid in pay period." Vacation hours were "paid" hours, and applying the adjustment to vacation pay served the purpose of avoiding pay losses caused by the workplace restructuring, the arbitrator said (*United States Steel Corp.*, 123 LA 1345).

● An arbitrator concluded that under a contract basing employees' vacation pay on "gross earnings" of the preceding year, a lump sum the employer paid to "buy out" an old incentive plan had to be included in computing employees' vacation pay. The arbitrator ruled that there was no evidence to support the employer's claim that an oral agreement excluded the lump sum from calculations, and even if such a pact existed, the unambiguous, written contract superseded any oral pact. In addition, the arbitrator said, the ordinary meaning of the term "gross earnings" encompassed the lump-sum payment (*Johnson & Johnson and Ethicon Inc.*, 49 LA 841).

● An arbitrator ordered an employer to include the shift differentials received by employees in the calculation of their vacation pay. According to the arbitrator, when employees regularly—as opposed to only occasionally—worked a variety of shifts, the wage differences had to be figured into their vacation pay (*Hans Rees' Sons Inc.*, 10 LA 705).

● On the other hand, an arbitrator found that where shift premiums had not been included in vacation pay calculations for a number of years, they could not suddenly be included. The union's failure to object in the past could be seen as tacit approval of this method of figuring employees' vacation pay, the arbitrator said, denying the grievance (*Bell Aircraft Corp.*, 9 LA 65).

● Similarly, an arbitrator held that employees were not entitled to include day rates, incentive rates, and shift premiums in the calculation of vacation pay. The parties' collective bargaining agreement stated that vacation pay had to be based on average hourly earnings, but it expressly excluded overtime and other hours or pay outside employees' normal workweek, the arbitrator found (*Kensington Steel Co.*, 17 LA 662).

● Another arbitrator held that an employer was not obligated to base vacation pay on any earnings greater than 40 hours per week. Contract language clearly excluded overtime hours from vacation pay calculations, the arbitrator said, adding that the employer's basis for figuring how much vacation pay employees were due had been consistent for a number of years (*Webster Tobacco Co. Inc.*, 5 LA 164).

1. Pay for Time Not Worked

When conflicts arise over the types of earnings that should be used in calculating vacation pay, they sometimes focus on pay for time not worked. Under collective bargaining agreements that use prior compensation as the basis for determining the amounts to be paid out for upcoming vacations, employers sometimes argue that they should be able to exclude the money employees have received while on paid leave.

● One arbitrator held that an employer had to include vacation, holiday, bereavement, and jury duty pay in average straight-time earnings for the previous year for purposes of computing vacation pay. After an extensive review of previous decisions, the arbitrator found that there was a consistent trend among arbitrators that "all monetary benefits paid to an employee" should be included in employee earnings for purposes of calculating vacation pay. "Any exceptions from the generally accepted meaning of the phrase 'straight-time earnings' should be expressly set forth by specific contract language," the arbitrator declared (*Ridge Machine Co.*, 53 LA 394; see also 39 LA 148, 32 LA 270, 26 LA 105, 21 LA 769, 20 LA 579).

● Under a contract that said vacation pay was to be based on gross annual earnings, an employer could not exclude previously paid vacation benefits from its calculations, an arbitrator held. Despite the employer's contention that gross annual earnings should not include the vacation benefits, the arbitrator determined that the applicable contract language clearly established the parties' intent to consider the total amount of money earned by the employee. If they had wanted to exclude vacation and holiday pay, they would have simply referred to annual earnings not gross annual earnings, the arbitrator concluded (*Canada-Ferro Company Ltd.*, 66 LA 572).

● Another arbitrator ordered an employer to discontinue its longstanding practice of excluding the previous year's vacation pay from calculations for the current year's vacation benefits. The parties' collective bargaining agreement specified that employees' gross earnings for the 52 weeks prior to Jan. 1 of the vacation year were to be the basis for computing vacation pay for the current year. Even though the employer had been computing vacation pay in the same way for a decade, the arbitrator said the method was incorrect as was evidenced by clear contract language, which could not be overridden, especially because the union was not necessarily aware of the practice and had not formally agreed to it (*Huffman Manufacturing. Co.*, 49 LA 357).

● An employer should have included wages paid to employees for holidays in its calculations of vacation pay, an arbitrator found. Despite the employer's claim that employees could not have "earnings" while away from work because of a holiday, the arbitrator suggested that under a contract that counted vacation pay itself as part of the calculations that went into employees' next vacation package, holiday pay also had to be counted (*Master Weavers Institute*, 11 LA 745).

● *By contrast*, an arbitrator decided that adding hours paid under a previous vacation into calculations for employees' next vacation was not necessary unless the parties' labor contract clearly required the employer to use that method. In this case, the collective bargaining agreement used the words "hours worked," which could refer only to the time employees actually were at work performing their duties, the arbitrator held (*John Deere Spreader Works of Deere & Co.*, 20 LA 670).

2. Varying Pay Rates

If employees experience variations in pay as a result of moving from position to position in a given year, arbitrators can be faced with the task of determining which wage rate to use in calculating vacation pay.

● In one instance, an arbitrator upheld an employer's paying an employee vacation benefits based on the lower-paying of two jobs he held in the course of a year. The arbitrator reasoned that because the contract based vacation pay on the rate of an employee's regular job, and the employee had been permanently transferred to a lower-paying position, he was properly paid vacation benefits at that lower rate. The fact that the vacation had been scheduled before it was known that the employee would be transferred was irrelevant, the arbitrator said. The lower-rated job was the employee's regular job because he had been permanently assigned to it a week before his vacation, the arbitrator concluded (*Olin-Mathieson Chemical Corp.*, 24 LA 116).

● An arbitrator decided that employees should receive vacation pay based on the wage rates they received during the majority of the preceding year. In a case involving employees who worked at certain jobs temporarily or were assigned to different shifts or jobs on a rotating basis, the arbitrator held that the employees should be paid vacation benefits based on the rate they received the majority of the work year (*Hiram Walker & Sons Inc.*, 5 LA 186).

3. Contract Changes

Transitions from old to new collective bargaining agreements can create complications with regard to the calculation of vacation pay, particularly when wage changes are involved and the contracts are not specific about the dates or rates to be used for the calculations.

● An employer should have based its employees' vacation pay on higher wage rates established in a new collective bargaining agreement, an arbitrator ruled. When the parties drew up their new contract, it provided for substantial increases that went into effect about two weeks before the employer distributed vacation pay, which it based on the old, lower wages. Despite the employer's position that pay rates in effect when the vacations were earned should have formed the basis for its calculations, the arbitrator concluded that if the parties had meant to use a different rate for vacation purposes, they would have said so (*Lynch Corp.*, 9 LA 115; see also 116 LA 1767).

● An employer committed a contract violation by deducting nine cents per hour from its employees' base rates when calculating their vacation pay, an arbitrator ruled. After experiencing a severe business downturn, the employer negotiated wage reductions as part of a new collective bargaining agreement. Although the employer intended a similar reduction in vacation pay, the contract did not reflect that intention. Rather, it said that employees' vacation pay would be calculated on the basis of average wages in the prior year and would include any increases that took effect before employees' vacation dates. According to the arbitrator, the plain language of the contract did not allow the employer to lower employees' vacation pay when they experienced pay cuts instead of increases (*The Fenton Art Glass Co.*, 120 LA 1549).

● Under a new contract that granted retroactive wage increases, an employer should have made the higher rates applicable to employees' paid vacation, an arbitrator held. As a general rule, the arbitrator said, when a wage increase is made retroactive, it should apply to all hours for which employees have been paid. According to the arbitrator, "that rule is applicable whether such hours are those of holidays, vacations, or hours of work" (*Pioneer Alloy Products Co. Inc.*, 5 LA 458; see also 17 LA 512).

● An employer and union had to "share equally" in the benefits and penalties prompted by their failure to nail down clear contract language governing vacation pay, an arbitrator ruled. A new contract provided for a wage increase and a new vacation plan that would cut back on many employees' time off, so the parties agreed that the amount of vacation that employees would receive in the current year would be based on the terms of the old contract. They failed to discuss vacation pay, however, leaving open the question of whether the old or new wage rates would apply. The arbitrator held that both sides should have brought up the matter, and because neither side did so, the arbitrator fixed the rates at a point half way between those originally sought by the union and those desired by the employer (*Crosley Motors Inc.*, 8 LA 1024).

● Where a contract based vacation pay on hourly wage rates that were in effect on May 1, an employer did not have to include a cost-of-living increase that took effect two weeks later, an arbitrator decided. The union claimed that the wage increase would have gone into effect by May 1 had it not been for the employer's clerical problems. Despite the fact that the delay had the effect of lowering vacation pay, the arbitrator said the contract clearly pointed to using the wage rate in effect on May 1 as the basis for vacation pay (*Milwaukee Press & Machine Co.*, 65 LA 549).

● An employer did not deprive employees of any vacation pay to which they were entitled when it implemented a new collective bargaining agreement that based vacation accruals on the calendar year instead of employees' anniversary dates, an arbitrator held. In deciding the issue, the arbitrator found no need to consider past practice, prior contract language, or any other factors outside the "four corners" of the collective bargaining agreement, because the new contract clearly stated that vacation accruals would be based on the calendar year, from Jan. 1 to Dec. 31 (*U.S. Foodservice Inc.*, 122 LA 1465).

4. Workweek Changes

When variations occur in the standard workweek or in the actual hours that employees work, these irregularities can give rise to disputes over the calculation of vacation pay.

● One arbitrator determined that an employer could not reduce vacation benefits to 40 hours' pay after it cut its regular workweek to 40 hours. The parties' collective bargaining agreement specified that 48 hours was the basis for figuring vacation pay. Notwithstanding the reduction in hours and the employer's financial problems, the arbitrator said the contract was unambiguous and could not be ignored (*Kempsmith Machine Co.*, 5 LA 520).

● In a case where the normal workweek was defined as 40 hours but employees routinely worked more than that, an arbitrator held that the number of hours employees actually worked was the proper foundation on which to calculate vacation pay. The contract based vacation pay on the scheduled workweek in the previous calendar year and also defined the normal workweek as 40 hours. Reasoning that "scheduled" referred to a time established in advance and consistently adhered to, the arbitrator decided that vacation pay had to be based on the six-day week actually worked because employees usually were expected to work on Saturdays unless otherwise notified (*Cemenstone Co.*, 9 LA 41).

● An employer was justified in calculating vacation pay on the basis of the most common schedule worked by its employees rather than adding in the longer hours worked by some employees and basing vacation pay on the overall average of actual hours worked, an arbitrator ruled. Under a contract stating that vacation pay was to be based on the "weekly hours worked by the company in a majority of the workweeks of the vacation year," the union contended that the weekly average of actual hours worked by all employees should be used in computing vacation pay. The arbitrator, however, reasoned that the word "company" in the clause referred to a whole and not isolated parts of the operation. For 90 percent of workers in the employer's plant, the average weekly shifts did not exceed 40 hours, he noted, adding that the union's position would cause confusion and destroy the meaning of established work schedules (*G. C. Hussey & Co.*, 5 LA 446; see also 9 LA 35).

Part 9

Holidays

I. Eligibility for Holiday Pay [LA CDI 100.48 (public employees); 115.71]

OVERVIEW

Most collective bargaining agreements contain clauses designating several holidays that will be observed each year. Although it is usually a given that employees will receive time off on the designated days, their ability to receive holiday pay sometimes hinges on meeting certain eligibility requirements. For instance, many collective bargaining agreements make employees' eligibility for holiday pay contingent on whether they report for work as scheduled on the days surrounding holidays. The goal behind these before-and-after-holiday work requirements is to reduce absenteeism by imposing a penalty, in the form of lost pay, on any employee who engages in unauthorized holiday "stretching."

Determinations about employees' eligibility for holiday pay can become complicated under a variety of scenarios. A question that commonly faces arbitrators, for example, is whether contractual work requirements can be used to deny employees holiday pay when they are absent on the surrounding days for reasons beyond their control, such as illness or inclement weather. Similarly, arbitrators might be asked to decide whether employees remain eligible for holiday pay despite being away from work due to vacations, layoffs, shutdowns, or strikes.

In deciding these cases, some arbitrators place great emphasis on the goal of preventing holiday stretching. Reasoning that the loss of holiday pay should be reserved for employees who purposely shirk their duties, they conclude that employees are not violating surrounding-days work requirements if they experience absences through no fault of their own. Other arbitrators, however, are less concerned with the underlying purpose than with the actual language of the governing contract clauses, finding it appropriate to deny holiday pay whenever employees fail to satisfy the eligibility requirements spelled out in the clauses.

SUMMARY OF CASES

A. Work Requirements

Recognizing that employers have a right to enforce work requirements aimed at preventing massive absenteeism on the days surrounding holidays, arbitrators generally agree that holiday pay does not have to be granted to those employees who take off before or after holidays, engaging in "holiday stretching" (91 LA 345, 69 LA 604, 69 LA 189, 53 LA 1206, 51 LA 723, 49 LA 468, 48 LA 1101, 46 LA 102, 40 LA 673). [*Editor's Note*: Cases involving holiday stretching also are reported in Part II. Pay for Holiday Work of this section].

• An arbitrator upheld an employer's denial of holiday pay to an employee who failed to work as scheduled after a designated holiday. Under a contract that required an employee to work a full shift on both the working day before and the working day after a holiday, the arbitrator accepted the employer's view that when Christmas fell on a Thursday, the employee had to work the preceding Wednesday and her next scheduled day, which was the following Monday. Even though the employee was told not to work on the intervening Friday, the arbitrator reasoned that the term "working day" referred to a day on which an employee is expected to work, and for this employee that day was the Monday after the holiday (*American Thread Co.*, 10 LA 250).

• Under a contract that did not limit the hours employees could be required to work, an arbitrator found that employees who failed to report for work on a Saturday were not eligible to be paid for a holiday on the following Monday. Because they were scheduled to work that Saturday and did not, they had not met the contract's work

requirement to make them eligible for holiday pay, the arbitrator decided (*Great Lakes Spring Corp.*, 12 LA 779; see also 73 LA 777, 54 LA 923).

1. Partial Absences

• An employee who was 36 minutes late to work on the day before a holiday nonetheless was eligible for holiday pay, an arbitrator ruled. According to the contract, employees had to report for duty on the scheduled work day before a holiday to qualify for holiday pay. The agreement did not specify that employees could be disqualified for not working the entire day, the arbitrator noted (*Lake City Malleable Inc.*, 25 LA 753).

• Similarly, an arbitrator overturned an employer's denial of holiday pay to an employee based on his late arrivals preceding a holiday. Even though the parties' collective bargaining agreement was unambiguous in requiring employees to work three full shifts before a holiday, the arbitrator overlooked the employee's tardiness. The arbitrator said that because the average time missed was so minimal, the employee could not be accused of stretching his holiday, and holiday stretching was the basic concern in the relevant contract provisions (*Ogden Aviation Fueling Services*, 117 LA 1584; see also 107 LA 505, 104 LA 901, 102 LA 506).

• An employer wrongfully denied holiday pay to an employee who left work an hour early the day after Labor Day to take care of his children, an arbitrator ruled. Citing a prior decision requiring the employer to show leniency toward partial day absences before or after holidays unless employees abused the privilege, the arbitrator found that the employer's denial of holiday pay was unreasonable in the current situation, which constituted a "true emergency" (*Quebecor World*, 120 LA 365).

• An employee who received permission from her foreman to visit her doctor during a shift prior to a holiday was entitled to holiday pay, an arbitrator decided. The employee and her foreman had a good-faith understanding that if she returned from her doctor's appointment to complete her shift, she would qualify for holiday pay. Although it was unclear whether this type of partial absence violated the work requirements under the contract, the arbitrator said the employer should stand by the foreman's decision and provide holiday pay to the employee (*ITT-Phillips Drill Division*, 69 LA 437).

An arbitrator held that under a day-before-and-day-after-holiday work requirement, employees' partial absences disqualified them for holiday pay. Even though the employees were given permission to leave early on the day before Christmas, based on the parties' negotiating history and the specific contract language that had resulted, the employees were precluded from receiving holiday pay, the arbitrator concluded (*American Bemberg Corp. & North American Rayon Corp.*, 10 LA 384).

• An arbitrator ruled that an employer did not violate a collective bargaining agreement in refusing to pay holiday pay to employees who were absent for two hours or less on either the last scheduled day before or first scheduled day after a holiday without "justifiable reason," even though the employer had past practice of giving holiday pay to employees who had not demonstrated justifiable reasons for absences, because the employer ahd abolished that practice by notifying the union during bargaining of its intention to apply the language as written, and the employer was not obligated to notify individual employees of the reduction in benefits (*Commercial Vehicle Group Inc.*, 126 LA 364).

2. Failure to Work on a Holiday

Where collective bargaining agreements make eligibility for holiday pay contingent

on working as scheduled, disputes sometimes arise over how to treat employees who fail to report for a shift that actually falls on a holiday. In deciding such cases, arbitrators often look at the way employees were told about the need to report for work.

• One arbitrator ruled that an employer did not violate its collective bargaining agreement when it posted notices a week beforehand that employees were expected to work the following Monday holiday. The parties' labor contract was silent on the issue of notification, but because many vacationing employees called in to find out if work was scheduled for that holiday, the arbitrator decided that others on vacation had no valid claim to holiday pay on the ground that they had not received sufficient notice (*Bethlehem Steel Co.*, 22 LA 781).

• Another arbitrator upheld an employer's decision to declare ineligible for holiday pay employees who failed to show up for work scheduled on Christmas day. The fact that a foreman had asked the employees if they "planned" to work on the holiday was irrelevant and did not mean that they really had a choice about showing up for work, the arbitrator decided (*Bethlehem Steel Co.*, 25 LA 680).

• An employer was justified in refusing to grant holiday pay to employees who balked at reporting for holiday work after an emergency call-in, an arbitrator held. Under a contract provision that denied holiday pay to employees who were asked or scheduled to work and failed to show up, the arbitrator held that this did not require advance requests or scheduling for holiday work because the contract was unambiguous about the requirement and made no mention of advanced notice (*Firestone Tire & Rubber Co.*, 29 LA 469).

• Although an arbitrator recognized an employer's right to make changes in work schedules, he ruled that one day's notice that an employee was supposed to report for work on a holiday was not enough. Thus, in spite of a contract provision denying holiday pay for those who failed to report for work as scheduled on a holiday, the arbitrator concluded that the absent employee was eligible for holiday pay (*Bethlehem Steel Co.*, 23 LA 271).

3. Union Business

● An arbitrator determined that an employer was wrong to deny employees holiday pay when they did not meet attendance requirements as a result of being absent for union business. Although the contract made eligibility for holiday pay contingent on working the surrounding days, the contract also stated that time lost in conducting union business was to be counted as time worked for attendance and other purposes. Consequently, the arbitrator decided that the employees could not be denied holiday pay because of missing work to attend to their legitimate union duties (*International Harvester Co.*, 11 LA 1166).

● Similarly, an arbitrator ruled that employees off on union business were entitled to be treated as if they had worked for purposes of a "before or after holiday" work requirement, where the absentee control policy provided that "union business" was listed among "types of excused absences." Thus the employer violated the collective bargaining agreement when it denied employees on union business on the day before July 4 and the day after Labor Day holiday pay, even though it could do so on one-shift days when hours off would seriously interfere with operations, because the requests in question were for two-shift days when the employer could have filled vacancies, the arbitrator found (*Ball Aerosol and Specialty Container*, 129 LA 464).

● By contrast, an employer was justified in denying holiday pay for President's Day to an employee who was excused for union business on the day before the holiday, an arbitrator decided. Despite the fact that the absence had been approved, the arbitrator pointed to clear contract language stating that an employee had to work a full schedule on the day before a holiday to be eligible to be paid for it. The arbitrator added that payments were not made to other employees who took time off for union business the day before the holiday (*Hewitt Soap Co. Inc.*, 112 LA 640).

B. Effect of Absences on Eligibility

Conflicts tend to arise over eligibility for holiday pay when employees fail to satisfy surrounding-days work requirements because of reasons beyond their control. For instance, employees' entitlement to holiday pay often comes into question when they experience absences due to medical problems or inclement weather.

1. Absences for Medical Reasons

To determine whether employees remain eligible for holiday pay despite absences due to illness or injury, arbitrators typically consider the specifics of the contract clauses governing holiday pay. Some collective bargaining agreements require that employees provide a doctor's note or some other proof that they were in fact ill or injured to establish eligibility, while others allow employees merely to claim illness without providing documentation to garner their holiday pay (93 LA 537, 92 LA 571, 92 LA 228, 91 LA 1174, 81 LA 943, 81 LA 330, 73 LA 777, 73 LA 414, 72 LA 607, 71 LA 1067).

● An arbitrator upheld an employer's refusal to provide holiday pay to an employee who was absent the day before Thanksgiving and the Monday after the holiday. Normally, a worker who could provide a reasonable excuse could bypass the contract's day-before-and-day-after-holiday work requirement, but the employee did not provide the needed medical certification, and the employer had "clear and convincing evidence" that the claim of illness was bogus, the arbitrator noted (*Steris Corp.*, 123 LA 739).

● An employer was justified in refusing to give an employee holiday pay for Labor Day when he did not work the day after the holiday because he was out on unpaid industrial injury leave, an arbitrator ruled. Although the employee had earlier received holiday pay for Memorial Day despite being out on industrial injury leave, the employer's "benevolent mistake" in granting holiday pay in that instance did not constitute a past practice that would be binding in the face of contract language to the contrary, the arbitrator said (*Santa Clara Valley Transportation Authority*, 122 LA 285).

• An arbitrator upheld an employer's denial of holiday pay for an employee who had been injured in a car accident and consequently could not fulfill a contractual requirement to work the day before and the day after a holiday. The contract waived the work requirement for employees who were suffering from an illness or had been injured in a workplace accident, but the employee in question did not fall into either of those categories, the arbitrator observed (*Alside Inc.*, 42 LA 75).

• An employee who broke one of his fingers but who was certified as capable of returning to work did not qualify for holiday pay, an arbitrator held. The parties' collective bargaining agreement limited holiday pay to employees who worked the last full scheduled workday prior to and the first full scheduled workday after a holiday, and despite the employee's injury, he could have worked and qualified for holiday pay but did not, the arbitrator said, denying the grievance (*Belknap Inc.*, 69 LA 599).

• An arbitrator upheld an employer's refusal to grant holiday pay to an employee who was absent the day before Veterans' Day but refused to provide a doctor's note. Although eligibility for holiday pay was subject to working on the surrounding days, that requirement could be waived for employees if they provided a doctor's certification that they were unable to work due to illness. Although the union argued that the employer had a past practice of foregoing the requirement, the arbitrator held that the employee was properly denied holiday pay based on his failure to provide proof of illness (*Brookhaven Medical Care Facility*, 119 LA 1253).

• An employee who failed to obtain a doctor's note certifying his illness on the day after Christmas was not entitled to holiday pay, an arbitrator decided. Although the employee contended that he was too ill to see his doctor, contract language was very clear in requiring employees to provide a physician's note if they were too sick to come to work on the days surrounding a holiday. Without such documentation, the

arbitrator said, the employee was not eligible for holiday pay (*Weil-McLain Co. Inc.*, 64 LA 625).

• *By contrast*, another arbitrator held that an employee's failure to provide proof of illness did not render him ineligible for holiday pay. Noting that the contract did not provide for substantiation of an excuse to qualify an employee for holiday pay, the arbitrator concluded that the employee's post-holiday sickness constituted a legitimate excuse, absent any challenge to the truthfulness of his claim of illness (*Hubbell Metals Inc.*, 67 LA 638).

• An employer violated a collective bargaining agreement, which allowed employees to receive holiday pay if a "bona fide illness or injury prevents the employee from working the day preceding the holiday," when it did not give holiday pay to an employee who missed work on New Year's Eve due to his young son's ear infection, an arbitrator held. Despite the employer's contention that there was a past practice of not paying employees whose ill children were the cause of absence, the arbitrator found that two instances did not make a past practice, and the child's treatment at the hospital showed that the employee was "prevented" from working (*C.H. Guenther & Sons*, 129 LA 309).

• Even though an employee failed to obtain a doctor's note for a day he missed before a holiday, as required by his employer, an arbitrator awarded him holiday pay. According to the arbitrator, the employee was unaware that the day he missed was his last scheduled workday before the holiday because the work schedule had not been posted (*United States Steel Corp.*, 67 LA 97).

• An employer committed a contract violation in denying holiday pay to employees who did not satisfy a day-before-and-after-holiday work requirement because they were out sick, an arbitrator determined. Because the contract clearly waived the work requirement if employees were out sick, the arbitrator held that employees were entitled to holiday pay no matter when their illnesses began (*Bakers Negotiating Committee*, 24 LA 694; see also 98 LA 258).

• An arbitrator ruled that employees were entitled to holiday pay for holidays that occurred while they were off work because of on-the-job injuries that enabled them to collect workers' compensation. The employer argued that the employees were on "leave of absence," which disqualified them from receiving holiday pay, but the arbitrator pointed out that the contract's leave-of-absence provision only referred to unpaid leaves. The employees were on paid leave under their workers' compensation payments, the arbitrator said, and the holidays also were paid days, suggesting that the holiday pay was part of the employees' regular wages (*Walworth County*, 71 LA 1118).

• An employee who went on disability retirement immediately after the expiration of a disability leave of absence was entitled to be paid for eight holidays that occurred during the leave of absence, an arbitrator decided. Despite the employer's contention that the employee had lost all of his holiday benefits because he did not return to work for one day after the extended absence, the arbitrator determined that the employer's view of the contract missed the point of such rules, which was to prevent holiday stretching. The alleged past practice of the employer of not granting holiday pay in similar situations was not binding, the arbitrator concluded, because the employer had taken such action without the union's knowledge (*Ideal Basic Industries Inc.*, 68 LA 928).

2. Inclement Weather

Arbitrators usually look at the reality of situations involving extreme weather conditions that affect employees' ability to satisfy work requirements associated with holiday pay. A lot depends on the particular circumstances as well as the extent of employees' efforts to report for work as scheduled.

• An employer properly refused to grant an excused absence or holiday pay to an employee who was absent on the first workday after Thanksgiving because of bad weather, an arbitrator held. The employee was one of only a few workers who did not make it into work the day after the holiday, and according to the arbitrator, because the absence was unexcused, the employee's failure to meet the day-after-holiday work requirement doomed his chances of qualifying for holiday pay (*Tennessee Dickel Distilling Co.*, 69 LA 189).

• An employee who did not report for work on the first scheduled workday after the New Year's holiday was not eligible for holiday pay, an arbitrator ruled. Although weather conditions had been very bad, the employee's absence was not excused, a road blockade that would have obstructed his route to work had been lifted, and he had no valid reason for missing work. Without a valid excuse, the arbitrator held, the employee could not meet the attendance requirement to qualify for holiday pay (*Electrical Repair Service Co.*, 69 LA 604).

• On the other hand, an employee whose arrival at work was delayed by three minutes because of an ice storm on his first day back after the New Year's holiday was entitled to holiday pay, an arbitrator ruled. Although the labor agreement required employees to work their full scheduled hours on the days surrounding a holiday to be eligible for holiday pay, the arbitrator noted that the ice storm was especially severe and the employee made an "extra effort" to get to work on time. Given these facts, the arbitrator said that it was "within the true spirit of close enforcement of the contractual requirements to award holiday pay" to the employee (*Vertex Systems Inc.*, 68 LA 1099).

• A manufacturer violated its labor contract when it cited employees for being absent and denied them holiday pay when they could not get to work because of a snowstorm, an arbitrator found. The employer had granted dispensations to employees who lived in rural areas near its plant but not to workers who were city residents. According to the arbitrator, the distinction between the two groups was "arbitrary and capricious" because it was based on "geographical assumptions, not individual needs and problems." He ordered the employer to withdraw any adverse action against the employees in question and grant them the holiday benefits they had been denied (*Knauf Fiberglass GmbH*, 114 LA 304).

C. Effect of Vacations on Eligibility

When vacations and holidays overlap, arbitrators usually determine that employees are entitled to holiday pay if contract clauses focus on the issue of employers having adequate staffing. Under those clauses, employers usually are required to provide holiday pay to vacationing employees because there is no question of the employees' availability for work while on vacation.

● An arbitrator held that employees should be paid for holidays that fell during their vacations even if they chose the time of their vacations themselves. He said this was not shifting any loss to the employer, but only requiring it to pay the employees as much if they chose a vacation in which there was a holiday as they would have received if they chose one without a holiday (*Tioga Mills Inc.*, 10 LA 371; see also 93 LA 598).

● An employer should have provided holiday pay to an employee whose vacation coincided with a holiday and who returned from his vacation a day late, according to an arbitrator. The parties' labor contract provided for an extra day's pay when a holiday fell during an employee's vacation period and also stated that employees had to work the day before and the day after a holiday to be eligible for holiday pay. The employer argued that the employee did not meet the work test for holiday pay eligibility because he did not show up the day after his vacation. The employee did qualify, the arbitrator decided, because the holiday-during-vacation clause was entirely separate from the work-test clause (*Streitmann Supreme Bakery of Cincinnati*, 41 LA 621; see also 99 LA 382, 45 LA 249, 27 LA 801).

● *By contrast*, an arbitrator ruled that an employer did have to give holiday pay to an employee who had been on vacation most of the calendar week of a holiday and out sick the first work day after the holiday, and was on vacation the calendar week before the holiday, even though the contract treated vacation as time worked for certain specified purposes, such as hours of service for pension credit. The contract did not provide for holiday pay if the employee did not work the week of the holiday unless he had worked the week before, and there were no contractual provisions that treated vacation the week before a holiday as a qualifying event (*Graphic Packaging International*, 126 LA 1).

● An arbitrator ruled that an employer did not violate a collective bargaining agreement when it blocked employees from taking vacations during four weeks that contained holidays, where the agreement included a phrase that the "vacation period shall be selected by mutual consent," the union failed to eliminate the phrase in bargaining, there was a need for full shifts during those weeks, and there was a practice of limiting employees' vacations on those weeks (*Pepsi-Cola*, 128 LA 426).

● Another arbitrator decided that an employer did not have to grant holiday pay to two employees who took approved vacation leave for the day after a holiday and then were sick on the next day. The parties' contract stated that employees were eligible for holiday pay if a holiday occurred during their "vacation period" and if they worked on the day before and day after a holiday. Because the employees had taken an isolated vacation day and were not in a "vacation period," the vacation-holiday clause did not apply, the arbitrator said, and the relevant provision was the one requiring work on the days surrounding a holiday. The employees' own scheduled workdays were the issue, not the company's scheduled workdays; therefore, because they did not work on their next scheduled days, even if their absences were excused, the arbitrator said neither employee fulfilled the contractual surrounding-days work requirements to qualify for holiday pay (*CWC Kalamazoo Inc.*, 105 AL 555; see also 95 LA 381, 83 LA 612).

● An employee was not entitled to pay for a holiday that fell during a scheduled vacation, an arbitrator decided, where the employee also failed to satisfy a surrounding-days work requirement because of a strike. The employee, the arbitrator held, was not excused from working on the last regularly scheduled workday before and the first workday after his vacation, both of which were required for him to be eligible for holiday pay (*Union Carbide Corp.*, 65 LA 189).

D. Effect of Strikes on Eligibility

Arbitrators commonly reason that employees lose their entitlement to holiday pay during strikes. This principle has been applied to lawful strikes as well as those that are unauthorized or illegal (93 LA 473, 85 LA 51, 74 LA 1058, 37 LA 3, 36 LA 1276, 33 LA 681, 30 LA 671, 24 LA 560).

In some situations, however, arbitrators decide that employees should not be held responsible for their failure to satisfy before-and-after-holiday work requirements as a result of work stoppages (20 LA 349, 16 LA 317).

• One arbitrator allowed holiday pay for New Year's Eve day where a legal strike beginning on the day after a contract expired made it impossible to work the "next scheduled workday" (*A. O. Smith Corp.*, 51 LA 1309).

• Another arbitrator found that a contract did not make eligibility for holiday pay contingent on working the surrounding days, and thus employees were entitled to receive holiday pay for Christmas even though they were out because of an economic strike (*Royle & Pilkington Co. Inc.*, 18 LA 451).

• On the other hand, an arbitrator upheld the denial of holiday pay for an employee who participated in an unauthorized work stoppage. According to the arbitrator, when the employee chose "to detach himself temporarily from the contract effects" by a work stoppage running through a holiday, he forfeited the holiday benefit "just as surely as he surrenders pay on any other day of such a stoppage" (*Hellenic Lines Ltd.*, 38 LA 339).

• Employees who were on strike over Labor Day were not entitled to holiday pay, an arbitrator ruled. Even though the parties entered into a strike settlement pact that retroactively reinstated the holiday pay provision, nothing during the strike prevented the employees from complying with the employer's existing and continuing holiday work requirements, the arbitrator concluded (*Packaging Corp. of America*, 62 LA 1214).

1. Refusal to Cross Picket Lines

Generally, arbitrators agree that employees forfeit holiday pay by refusing to cross picket lines on the same basis as if they failed to meet holiday-related work requirements due to direct participation in a strike.

• An arbitrator determined that it was one thing for an employer to agree that its employees had the right to respect picket lines, but that did not mean that their refusal to cross picket lines was without consequences. Although the employees were free to honor their cohorts' pickets and miss work before and after a holiday, the arbitrator said the employer was not required to approve their absences by making them eligible for holiday pay (*Schlage Lock Co.*, 30 LA 105; see also 54 LA 754, 25 LA 687).

• Missing work because employees were honoring other workers' picket lines did not free them from a day-before-and-day-after-holiday work requirement, an arbitrator decided. A grocery store chain's labor contract mandated that to be eligible for holiday pay employees had to work the days surrounding holidays unless their absences were excused because of illness, injury, or other acceptable reasons. Honoring picket lines, although permitted and not an action that would prompt discipline, nonetheless did not qualify as an "excusable absence," the arbitrator said (*Ralphs Grocery Co.*, 121 LA 432).

• An arbitrator ruled that an employer was not obligated to pay employees for the Fourth of July holiday, which fell during a period when they were honoring picket lines of another union. Noting that the parties' collective bargaining agreement did not include any specific language requiring such payments, the arbitrator concluded that the union had to bear the economic losses during the period in question (*Pearl Brewing Co.*, 68 LA 221).

E. Effect of Shutdowns and Layoffs

Arbitrators have ruled both ways on whether employees remain entitled to holiday pay in spite of shutdowns and layoffs. If collective bargaining agreements grant holiday pay without restriction, chances are that laid-off employees qualify for it. Even in the presence of contractual work requirements, however, arbitrators do not automatically find employees ineligible to be paid for holidays that occur during shutdowns and layoffs. Factors that can decide the outcome of such cases include the specific wording of the applicable contract clauses, the timing and duration of shutdowns and layoffs, and employers' reasons for instituting them.

• In one case, an arbitrator ruled that a three-day shutdown did not free an employer from its obligation to pay employees for a holiday that occurred during the short layoff. The contract required that employees report for duty on the scheduled workdays before and after holidays rather than on the adjacent calendar days. In light of the fact that employees had worked Dec. 30 and had been told not to report again until Jan. 5, the arbitrator held that they had reported for work as required on the scheduled workdays before and after New Year's Day, and they were therefore entitled to holiday pay for that day (*Aerolite Electronic Hardware Corp.*, 10 LA 214; see also 96 LA 1218).

• Employees who were recalled from layoff about three weeks after Memorial Day were entitled to pay for the holiday, an arbitrator ruled. Under the parties' collective bargaining agreement, employees were eligible for holiday pay if their absences were the result of a short-term layoff and if they had worked within 30 calendar days of the holiday, the arbitrator pointed out (*Consolidated Aluminum Corp.*, 66 LA 938; see also 72 LA 840).

• Another arbitrator ruled that laid-off employees were entitled to holiday pay even though they did not work on the day before and the day after a holiday. His reasoning was that there would have been no reason to write a contract clause requiring employees to have earned some wages within the 30 days before the holiday if the parties had meant to exclude laid-off employees from holiday pay eligibility (*Thomas L. Leedom Co.*, 21 LA 740; see also 75 LA 729).

• Deciding that contract language trumped an employer's past practice of 14 years, an arbitrator awarded holiday pay to employees who were recalled from an extended layoff the day after Labor Day. The contract's only requirement for holiday pay eligibility was that employees had to work during the payroll week in which the holiday fell. When seven employees returned to work during the week of Labor Day after more than nine months on layoff, they qualified for holiday pay under the terms of the contract, the arbitrator concluded (*Anaconda Aluminum Co.*, 48 LA 219).

• An arbitrator held that an employer was wrong to deny holiday pay to an employee who was on disciplinary layoff immediately before and after a holiday. The arbitrator said the purpose of requiring employees to work on the days surrounding a holiday is to discourage holiday stretching. Because the employee had been ordered not to report for work, the arbitrator reasoned that he could not be held responsible for missing the days that the contract required for holiday pay eligibility (*Inland Steel Co.*, 20 LA 323).

• The equities of a layoff situation precipitated by a machine breakdown required an award of holiday pay to the affected employees, an arbitrator ruled, because the breakdown was not their fault. Given that there was no contract language requiring that employees work on the days surrounding holidays, the arbitrator determined that the employer owed them their holiday pay (*Thompson Mahogany Co.*, 5 LA 397).

• In a somewhat seasonal industry where layoffs were fairly regular, an arbitrator found that employees would suffer serious inequities if they lost holiday pay because of a brief layoff. Noting that the employees had worked throughout most of the contract year, the arbitrator concluded that the employer had to give them holiday pay despite the fact that they were on layoff (*Otto Guggenheim & Co. Inc.*, 11 LA 1130; see also 10 LA 887).

• Employees were entitled to holiday pay for Christmas, which fell on a Thursday, when they worked the day before the holiday but did not work on Friday because of a temporary shutdown, an arbitrator decided. Even though the employees failed to work the following Monday, as would normally be required to be eligible for holiday pay, the arbitrator awarded holiday pay because they worked the day before Christmas and were excused from working on the day immediately following the holiday because of the shutdown (*Reilly Tar and Chemical Corp.*, 66 LA 835; see also 75 LA 651).

• Employees who were laid off indefinitely on the afternoon of their last scheduled workday before Thanksgiving were entitled to holiday pay, an arbitrator held. Except for Thanksgiving, however, employees were not entitled to payment for the holidays that fell during their extended layoffs, the arbitrator ruled (*Premiere Corp.*, 67 LA 376).

• *By contrast*, an employer did not have to pay employees laid off on December 24 holiday pay for New Year's Eve and New Year's Day, where the contract provided that laid-off employees do not receive pay for holidays that are not within seven days of layoff, and the bargaining history confirmed that those days were "calendar days" (*Premier Mfg. Support Services*, 128 LA 267).

• An arbitrator ruled that an employer did not violate a collective bargaining contract when it gave holiday pay for only two holidays to employees laid off in December, even though there were five holidays within 30 days of their layoff and on one occasion the employer gave laid-off employees pay for all those holidays. One occasion did not make a past practice, and in the new contract the parties expanded the period laid-off employees could receive holiday pay from seven days to 30 in exchange for limiting pay to two holidays (*Silgan Closures*, 124 LA 808).

• Where an employer shut a plant down on New Year's Eve, an arbitrator held that employees were not eligible for pay for New Year's Day because they had not worked the following day as required by the contract (*California Metal Trades Association*, 11 LA 788).

• An extended shutdown relieved an employer of its obligation to provide holiday pay based on a contractual before-and-after-holiday work requirement, another arbitrator ruled. A month-long shutdown is qualitatively different from a layoff of just a few days, the arbitrator observed (*Vulcan Detinning Co.*, 4 LA 483; see also 82 LA 1170).

• Employees who did not work the last shift on the workday before the start of a two-week vacation shutdown were not entitled to holiday pay for the Fourth of July,

which fell during the shutdown, an arbitrator ruled. Despite contract language that excused justifiable absences, the arbitrator determined that the employer's past practice required employees, when holidays occurred during shutdowns, to work as scheduled before and after the holidays to be eligible for holiday pay (*Regal Ware Inc.*, 65 LA 795).

• Employees who had been laid off for an entire year were not exempt from the normal work requirements that were a prerequisite for receiving holiday pay, an arbitrator held. According to the arbitrator, a contrary ruling would have allowed the workers to claim pay for all of the holidays provided by the contract, which would have conflicted with the fundamental purpose of the work requirements (*Chrome-Rite Co.*, 12 LA 691; see also 82 LA 1170, 72 LA 528, 71 LA 609).

F. Holidays on Nonwork Days

Are employees entitled to be paid for holidays that do not fall on scheduled workdays? If collective bargaining agreements expressly state that the purpose of holiday pay is to protect employees from loss of income when they are prevented from working because of a holiday, then arbitrators usually have no choice but to deny payment for holidays on nonwork days. If contracts are not clear on this point, however, arbitrators are more likely to treat holiday pay as a negotiated benefit that employees are entitled to receive regardless of whether a holiday falls on a weekend or a regularly scheduled workday.

• In a case where a contract's holiday clause was ambiguous, an arbitrator reasoned that if he denied employees pay for holidays falling on a Saturday, he would be adding a clause to the contract that the parties did not intend to include. Emphasizing that his role was to interpret the agreement, not rewrite it, the arbitrator ordered the employer to grant holiday pay to the affected employees (*Carson Electric Co.*, 24 LA 667).

• An arbitrator found that a school district erred in refusing to grant holiday pay to custodial employees who had to work on New Years' Day when it fell on a Saturday.

Despite noting that the employer made a "good faith" effort to interpret the contract, the arbitrator noted that in the past, the employees would have been entitled to an alternative day off with pay in place of the holiday. The arbitrator decided that the employer should offer an alternative holiday in such situations, or else it would have to grant the employees holiday pay (*Capital School District*, 115 LA 147).

• *By contrast*, an arbitrator held that an employer was not required to grant holiday pay where a holiday fell on a Saturday and employees did not normally work on Saturdays. The arbitrator found that the purpose of the applicable contract language was to protect employees from loss of income when holidays fell during their regular workweek. If employees were not normally scheduled to work on a day when a holiday occurred, they were not entitled to be paid for that day, the arbitrator reasoned (*Standard Grocery Co.*, 7 LA 745).

• Another arbitrator upheld an employer's refusal to consider employees eligible for holiday pay under a contract granting pay for holidays that fell on employees' scheduled workdays. The employer's plant had been operating continuously, but a decline in orders late in the year caused the employer to revert to a five-day week. Based on the earlier pattern of Saturday work, the union claimed that holiday pay was warranted for New Year's Day when it fell on a Saturday. Disagreeing, the arbitrator stressed the contractual requirement that holidays had to fall on employees' scheduled workdays, and New Year's Day was not a scheduled workday for any of the employees (*Minnesota Mining & Manufacturing Co.*, 12 LA 165).

G. Ad Hoc Holidays

Because ad hoc holidays are relatively unusual—often based on presidential or gubernatorial orders or declarations—arbitrators' decisions on whether they should be treated as paid days off for employees tend to hinge on the fine points of holiday clauses contained in collective bargaining agreements.

• Employees of a local government should have been granted a paid holiday on the day after Christmas when the U.S. president issued an executive order closing all federal offices, an arbitrator ruled. In an earlier decision, another arbitrator had awarded a paid holiday under virtually equivalent circumstances. Even though subsequent determinations by the state's attorney general and the courts indicated that such executive orders were not applicable to state and local agencies, the arbitrator pointed out that employees' holiday rights were rooted in the parties' labor contract, and it specified that employees were entitled to holidays declared by the president (*City of Reno*, 111 LA 1043).

• Another arbitrator decided that a county government violated its labor contract when it denied employees holiday pay for Cesar Chavez Day. According to the arbitrator, although the state legislature allowed counties to forego observance of the holiday, the parties had signed a memorandum of understanding that bound the employer to a different standard. The MOU's clear and unambiguous meaning and intent was that any holiday appointed by a federal or state government had to be observed, the arbitrator concluded, ordering the employer to recognize the holiday in the future (*Butte County*, 116 LA 600).

• *By contrast*, an arbitrator ruled that an employer did not violate a collective bargaining agreement when it did not give security employees holiday pay for President Ford's funeral, even though they were provided holiday pay for President Reagan's funeral and the employer gave holiday pay to facilities and logistics employees. The employer did not authorize or designate the day of the funeral as a holiday, payment for Reagan's funeral did not establish a past practice, and the facilities and logistics employees were covered by a different agreement (*Caelum Research Corp.*, 125 LA 541).

• Similarly, an employer was not required to grant a paid holiday on a national day of mourning for a recently deceased president, an arbitrator determined. Although the definition of "holiday" in the parties' collective bargaining agreement included any day appointed or recommended by the president, the arbitrator noted that the current president had not specifically designated the day of mourning as a holiday per se. Based on the contract's list of holidays, the arbitrator added, one could infer that a paid holiday would have to recur each year, be recognized as a national holiday celebrated throughout the country, and be validated by closure of all public offices. Because "the day of remembrance is something of a different nature," the arbitrator said the employer was not required to treat it as a paid holiday (*Youngstown State University*, 122 LA 1377).

● A state police department did not have to give employees holiday pay when the president closed federal government offices to commemorate the death of former President Richard Nixon, an arbitrator ruled. The parties' labor contract defined a holiday as any day the state's governor or the current president designated as such. In this case, the president's executive order specifically allowed states to determine whether the day was to be considered a holiday for state and local government employees, the parties' contract did not set a different standard, and the state governor declined to regard the day as a holiday, the arbitrator noted (*Illinois State Police*, 106 LA 44; see also 104 LA 166).

II. Pay for Holiday Work [LA CDI 100.48
(public employees); 115.71]

OVERVIEW

Nearly all collective bargaining agreements that address the subject of holidays specify some sort of premium pay for employees who work on holidays. One issue that commonly arises in connection with holiday work is whether to allow "pyramiding," whereby employees would receive more than one type of pay for the same hours. For example, arbitrators might be asked to decide if employees should receive payment for their holiday work, plus the traditional holiday pay that is intended for those who have the day off.

Other questions that emerge in connection with pay for holiday work include whether payment for overtime hours should be calculated using holiday rates and whether employees can receive multiple forms of premium pay. Multiple premiums might apply, for example, if holiday work occurs on a weekend. (For a discussion of arbitration cases dealing with special pay rates exclusive of holiday premiums, see the chapter titled "Premium Pay.")

SUMMARY OF CASES

A. Holiday Premiums

Collective bargaining agreements typically mandate that employers give employees premium pay for work performed on holidays. In general, the extra pay serves as an economic disincentive to discourage employers from requiring holiday work, and it also recognizes the value placed on being off work on such days.

● One arbitrator ordered an employer to pay triple-time wages to two employees who worked on Labor Day. Clear contract language provided that employees who worked on certain specified holidays had to be paid at a rate of two times their regular hourly rates plus straight-time pay for the holiday itself, the arbitrator determined (*Theodore Mayer & Brothers*, 62 LA 540).

● Another arbitrator awarded triple-time pay to employees at a county landfill for holiday work. One provision of the contract called for employees to receive eight hours of straight-time pay on designated holidays, and a separate provision called for employees to receive double-time pay if they worked on a holiday. The arbitrator determined that the provisions had to be read as cumulative in the absence of specific language forbidding such an interpretation; thus, employees were entitled to the straight-time pay regardless of whether or not they worked, plus the double-time rate for all hours they put in on designated holidays (*Mason County*, 97 LA 45).

● Employees were entitled to premium pay for scheduled work on Thanksgiving even though they did not satisfy separate work requirements that were a prerequisite for receiving straight-time holiday pay, an arbitrator ruled. One contract clause granted employees double-time pay for mandated work on specified holidays, while a separate provision required employees to report as scheduled on the days surrounding holidays to qualify for regular holiday pay. According to the arbitrator, the two provisions were inconsistent and could not be interpreted in a way that would cause a forfeiture of premium pay for holiday work. Although employees could be disqualified from receiving straight holiday pay if they failed to report for duty as scheduled on the days surrounding a holiday they had off, employees were entitled to premium pay for holidays they actually worked regardless of their attendance on the surrounding days, the arbitrator said (*Rangaire Inc.*, 66 LA 755).

● In a similar case, an arbitrator held that an employer erred in denying premium pay for holiday work on the basis that employees had failed to comply with surrounding-days work requirements aimed at preventing holiday "stretching." The contract provision requiring employees to work on the day before and the day after a holiday referred only to eligibility for holiday pay for employees who did not work on a holiday, the arbitrator pointed out. A separate provision required double-time pay for all hours worked on a holiday. Finding that the two provisions were independent of each other, the arbitrator determined that employees were entitled to double-time pay for holiday work regardless of whether they worked the surrounding days (*Alpha Cellulose Corp.*, 27 LA 798).

● Night-shift employees were entitled to both holiday premiums and holiday pay when they reported several hours early for their first shift following a holiday in order to perform start-up work, an arbitrator held. Although there was no dispute that the employees were to receive regular wages for their first shift back after the New Year's holiday, the employer argued that start-up work performed between 7 p.m. and 11 p.m. on Jan. 3—a day that the collective bargaining agreement designated as a holiday—should have been compensated at a double-time rate. The arbitrator, however, decided that the employer had to grant straight-time holiday pay as well as double-time premiums for the start-up work (*ICG Castings Inc.*, 122 LA 961).

● *By contrast*, an employer was justified in denying workers triple-time wages for working on a holiday, an arbitrator decided. Given contractual silence on the question of whether employees who worked on a holiday were entitled to holiday pay in addition to premium pay, the arbitrator ruled that the contract would have to explicitly call for such payment. Otherwise, he concluded, awarding triple-time wages would result in two contract clauses being applied to the same set of hours worked (*Southern Standard Bag Corp.*, 47 LA 26; see also 39 LA 1262, 25 LA 432, 22 LA 564).

● A school district did not violate a collective bargaining agreement when it paid security and custodial staff who worked a high school football game on the day after Thanksgiving at the contractual call-in rate of time-and-one-half their regular rate of pay, despite provisions in the agreement stating that the day was a holiday payable at two-and-one-half times the regular rate, an arbitrator ruled. An addendum to the contract addressing budget problems converted that day and three other former holidays to non-paid days, to which the call-in provision applied (*Val Verde Unified School District*, 129 LA 229).

● An employer did not violate a collective bargaining agreement, which provided that employees must work their scheduled shift before, during, and after a holiday to receive holiday pay, when it did not give holiday pay to employees who took sick days on a scheduled shift before or after the holiday, even if they took Family and Medical

Leave Act leave. The arbitrator said that statutory deferral to the employer's policies excluded holiday payment (*Cuyahoga County Sheriff Office*, 129 LA 169).

● An arbitrator upheld an employer's decision to pay straight-time wages to employees who worked on unpaid holidays. Although the parties' collective bargaining agreement specified a time-and-one-half rate for employees who worked on paid holidays or on their regularly scheduled days off, the arbitrator determined that employees were not entitled to the same premium rate for working on days that the contract specifically designated as unpaid holidays (*Reynolds Wheels International*, 119 LA 1523).

● An employer did not violate its labor contract when it refused to pay a holiday premium to security officers who worked on Columbus Day, an arbitrator held. Columbus Day was one of four floating holidays that the contract distinguished from other designated holidays. Based on the contract and testimony by a member of the union bargaining team suggesting that it was clear that floating holidays were removed from the category of holidays requiring premium pay, the arbitrator concluded that those employees who worked on Columbus Day were not entitled to pay at the higher rate (*Metrohealth Systems*, 122 LA 272).

B. Premium Pay Combinations

Disputes over premium pay combinations commonly arise when holidays coincide with weekend days or the sixth or seventh day that employees work in the same workweek. In some cases, arbitrators decide that multiple forms of premium pay can apply to the same hours, but in others, arbitrators refuse to allow the pyramiding of premium pay.

● An arbitrator found that an amusement park did not violate the collective bargaining agreement when it did not give custodians holiday pay for the time of at most one hour they worked on New Year's Eve, which was a holiday. This time was prior to their regular shift, which started at midnight on New Year's Day, which was not a holiday. The employer had a system in which work days started at 4:00 p.m. of

the preceding calendar day (*Walt Disney Parks and Resorts*, 129 LA 1817).

● An employer did not violate a collective bargaining agreement by paying grievants only time-and-one-half compensation for working on a holiday but not a holiday allowance in addition, an arbitrator ruled, because the agreement stipulated that in order to qualify an employee must work the scheduled shifts preceding and following the holiday. The grievants did not and were not eligible for the allowance (*Hussey Copper Ltd.*, 126 LA 1461).

● An arbitrator ruled that an employer did not violate the collective bargaining contract when it paid employees, who worked a 48-hour week, straight time for last the 12-hour day of that week after paying them double-time holiday pay for working Thanksgiving, because the contract prohibited pyramiding of pay, employees are paid for overtime of over 40 hours for the week, and were paid at a higher scale (*Folgers Coffee Co.*, 124 LA 1623).

● Double-time wages for holiday work were not subject to the time-and-a-half multiplier that would normally apply to work performed on a Saturday, an arbitrator held. In this case, Saturday was the sixth day of the workweek and it fell on the Fourth of July. Employees who worked that day received double-time premium pay plus straight-time holiday pay. The arbitrator was asked to decide if a separate contract provision, requiring time-and-a-half premium pay for employees who worked on the sixth day of the same workweek, should apply to the holiday work, allowing employees to receive triple-time wages on top of their straight-time holiday pay. Lacking any express language in the contract that would definitively resolve the question, the arbitrator looked to the bargaining history of the parties and their intention in crafting the current contract language, which suggested that pyramiding was not allowed. Thus, the double-time rate for holiday work was not subject to the sixth-day multiplier, the arbitrator concluded (*Evanite Battery Separator Inc.*, 90 LA 225).

● A school district did not violate a collective bargaining agreement when it paid security and custodial staff who worked a high school football game on the day after Thanksgiving at the contractual call-in rate of time-and-one-half their regular rate of pay, despite provisions in the agreement stating that the day was a holiday payable at two-and-one-half times the regular rate, an arbitrator ruled. A recent addendum addressing budget problems converted this day and three other former holidays to non-paid days, to which the call-in provision applied (*Val Verde Unified School District*, 129 LA 229).

● An employer did not violate a collective bargaining agreement, which provided that employees must work their scheduled shift before, during, and after the holiday to receive holiday pay, when it did not give holiday pay to employees who took sick days on a scheduled shift before or after the holiday, even if they took Family and Medical Leave Act leave, since statutory deferral to an employer's policies excludes holiday payment (*Cuyahoga County Sheriff Office*, 129 LA 169 (Arb. 2011)).

● An employer was not required to pay triple-time wages to employees for working on Saturday holidays, an arbitrator ruled. Under the parties' labor contract, employees received time-and-a-half for Saturday work and double-time for holiday work. The union sought triple-time pay for employees who worked on Saturday holidays, but the arbitrator determined that the parties had agreed on double-time wages as the appropriate premium for holiday work. If holidays and Saturdays coincided, that did not mean employees were entitled to double the Saturday rate, the arbitrator said (*Heating, Piping & Air Conditioning Contractors New York City Association*, 11 LA 816; see also 74 LA 345).

● *By contrast*, an arbitrator ordered a city to pay an employee who was denied holiday pay for Christmas. The city violated the collective bargaining agreement when it denied the holiday even though the employee called in sick on Dec. 22 and the agreement required employees to work the day before the holiday, because the contract also provided that employees be given holiday pay if they had a normal day off on the day before the holiday, as the grievant was, and the city had consistently given holiday

pay to other employees in similar circumstances (*City of Niles*, 124 LA 1096).

● Another arbitrator decided that employees were entitled to triple-time pay for work that they performed on a Friday holiday after they rejected an offer to trade days. The issue of swapping days or treating the Friday holiday as Saturday work, which was normally paid at a time-and-a-half rate, arose in an effort to accommodate increased production needs, but the parties' collective bargaining agreement provided that Saturday holidays had to be celebrated on the preceding Fridays and triple-time wages applied to holiday work. Consequently, the arbitrator held that when New Year's Eve fell on a Saturday, the proper day to observe the holiday was the preceding Friday, and employees were entitled to triple-time pay if they worked that day. Only those employees who specifically agreed to trade days and waive triple-time holiday pay could be denied the full premium, the arbitrator concluded (*General Tire & Rubber Co.*, 71 LA 813).

● An employer violated its labor contract by denying triple-time wages to employees who worked on a Saturday holiday, an arbitrator ruled. The employees were paid time-and-a-half wages for the Saturday holiday they worked, but they contended that they were also entitled to time-and-a-half wages for having worked more than 40 hours a week. The arbitrator ruled that a contract provision prohibiting pyramiding of overtime was applicable only to daily and weekly overtime work, not holiday work, and added that the clause stating that employees were entitled to time-and-a-half "additional" wages for working certain holidays meant "additional to such other pay as would be received on the day involved." Therefore, the arbitrator concluded that the employees were entitled to triple-time pay (*Los Angeles Jewish Community Council*, 11 LA 869).

1. Past Practice

● An arbitrator ruled that police investigators were not entitled to both paid time off and holiday pay for holidays, on which they were not allowed to work, despite the contention that there was past practice of giving them such pay. The contract clearly and unambiguously stated that employees who did not work on holidays would receive only holiday pay, and the practice of paying investigators paid time off was a short-lived phenomenon (*Village of Shorewood*, 129 LA 1273).

• A county did not violate a collective bargaining agreement when it gave employees who worked on two holidays one-and-one-half times their regular rate plus the normal eight hours of holiday pay, even though employees who worked on two Christmas holidays received triple pay. The arbitrator said that mistakes of payment in two of 120 holidays in an eight-year period did not make a past practice, and the past practice could not contradict express terms of the agreement (*Franklin County Board*, 127 LA 1537).

• An arbitrator ruled that an employer did not violate a collective bargaining agreement when it did not give security employees holiday pay for President Ford's funeral, even though they were provided holiday pay for President Reagan's funeral and the employer gave holiday pay to facilities and logistics employees. The employer did not authorize or designate the day of the funeral as a holiday, payment for Reagan's funeral did not establish a past practice, and the facilities and logistics employees were covered by different agreements (*Caelum Research Corp.*, 125 LA 541).

• An arbitrator ruled that employees were entitled to be paid at two-and-a-half times their regular wage rate for working on their sixth consecutive scheduled day, which fell on Memorial Day. Despite ambiguous contract language, the arbitrator said the employer's past practice of at least five years had been to pay employees at two-and-a-half times the regular rate for working on a holiday when it was their sixth workday of a payroll week (*Epicurean Inc.*, 85 LA 1109).

C. Overtime Rates on Holidays

Another issue facing arbitrators is how overtime compensation should be handled when employees work extra hours on a holiday. Absent clear contractual prohibitions against basing overtime calculations on the increased hourly wages paid out for holiday work, arbitrators tend to rule in favor of employees' garnering overtime pay at the higher rate.

• An arbitrator decided that the 40 hours beyond which overtime was payable to employees should include the hours that employees worked on a holiday and daily hours worked in excess of the normal eight-hour day. Although he could see no bad faith on the part of the employer and despite the fact that the employer paid overtime rates for hours worked in excess of eight in any one day (rather than just for hours in excess of 40 per week) and already had paid a premium rate for work performed on the holiday, the arbitrator determined that the employer had underpaid several employees who worked on Memorial Day (*Northwest Protective Service Inc.*, 65 LA 930).

• An employer's refusal to pay employees overtime for working on Fridays in weeks with Monday holidays violated its collective bargaining agreement, according to an arbitrator. Although the employer had the option of scheduling workers in four 10-hour shifts rather than the standard five eight-hour days, that option was an exception to normal hours granted as a favor to the employer with one-week notice to the union. The option could not be used, the arbitrator said, as an incentive for the employer to avoid paying overtime by shifting to a four-day schedule on weeks with holidays (*Terreri Construction Co.*, 114 LA 1089).

• An arbitrator ruled that an employer did not violate s collective bargaining agreement, which provided overtime for Saturday work if the employee worked 40 hours in a week prior to Saturday or had excused absences for reasons including a holiday. The employer did not pay employees for working the Saturday after President's Day, even though the plant was closed on President's Day, because the agreement exempted President's Day from the list of holidays that year, and the plant was closed due to lack of business (*Tharco Containers Inc.*, 128 LA 1521).

An employer did not commit a contract violation by denying holiday premiums and paying employees only their regular overtime rates on the eve of a holiday, an arbitrator held. Even though a side agreement provided for extra pay when employees worked on the eve of a holiday, the parties had changed the definition of holidays in their collective bargaining agreement to exclude holiday eves and include only those shifts that fell on the holidays themselves. Finding that the retention of contrary language in the side agreement was a mutual mistake, the arbitrator held that employees could no longer receive additional premiums for overtime work performed on holiday eves (*St. Louis Post-Dispatch*, 92 LA 23).

D. Pay for Birthday Holidays

Some collective bargaining agreements grant birthday holidays, meaning that an employee's birthday is to be regarded as a holiday for that particular worker. Pay issues that can arise in connection with birthday holidays are sometimes as unique as the holidays themselves.

● An employer was obligated to give double-time pay to an employee for scheduled work on his birthday, an arbitrator ruled. Contending that scheduling the employee on his birthday was an error, the employer said the usual requirement to pay employees for holiday work at a double-time rate should not apply. The arbitrator disagreed. Because the contract clearly gave the employer the right to direct its workforce, and having made the choice to schedule the employee on his birthday, the employer was bound by that choice and its consequences, the arbitrator concluded (*Thomas Truck & Caster Co.*, 74 LA 1276).

● An employer did not have the right to discontinue a past practice of allowing employees to work on their birthday holidays, an arbitrator ruled. The management-rights provision of the contract did not give the employer the right to eliminate the practice unilaterally, the arbitrator said. In light of the fact that the employer did not make any effort during contract negotiations to urge the union to agree on discontinuing the practice, the employer was bound by its longstanding practice of allowing employees to work on their birthday holidays and reap the financial benefits (*United Salt Corp.*, 72 LA 534).

● Where a contract granted employees a paid day off on their birthdays, an employer could not refuse to give an employee an extra day of pay when his birthday fell on a Sunday, an arbitrator ruled. The parties' labor contract stated that if an employee's birthday fell on a regularly scheduled day off, the employee had to receive holiday pay for the day. However, the employer argued that a separate contract provision, stating that any holiday falling on a Sunday had to be celebrated the following Monday, applied to the situation. Rejecting that argument, the arbitrator reasoned that the provision relating to birthday holidays was specific to the situation and therefore controlling (*American Smelting & Refining Co.*, 65 LA 1217).

● *By contrast*, an employer was not required to pay overtime to employees who worked on their birthdays but had selected a different day on which to celebrate it, an arbitrator ruled. The contract designated the employees' birthdays as holidays, allowed employees to select a date on which to celebrate their birthdays, and provided for time and one-half for hours worked on one's birthday, and the employee who selected a different day on which to celebrate his birthday selected a new date for his recognized birthday holiday (*Domtar Industries Incorporated*, 123 LA 1009).

Part 10

Health Care Benefits

I. Health Care Benefits [LA CDI 100.5901 et seq. (public employees); 116.60]

OVERVIEW

Health care benefits have long been a source of tension in labor-management relations, particularly as the expense of providing employees with health insurance has spiraled upward. To contain their health insurance outlays, employers commonly consider strategies such as reducing benefits, shifting costs to employees, instituting managed care arrangements, and switching plan administrators. Unions, on the other hand, typically strive to maintain comprehensive health care coverage at minimal expense to bargaining unit members.

During contract negotiations, these competing interests routinely come out in the form of cost-containment proposals from management and maintenance-of-benefits proposals from unions. When disputes arise during the life of collective bargaining agreements, however, that is when arbitrators are called upon to interpret and enforce existing provisions on health insurance.

This chapter analyzes the types of questions that arbitrators have to sort out in connection with health care benefits, including the following:

● Do employers have the authority to make health plan changes without first bargaining or obtaining union consent?

● Are contractual terms outlining the payment obligations of employees and employers being applied correctly?

● Who is eligible for health care benefits and are employers allowed to deny plan coverage under certain circumstances?

SUMMARY OF CASES

A. Unilateral Health Plan Changes

Although unions often agree to health plan changes in the course of negotiating new labor contracts, it is not uncommon for employers to make unilateral plan modifications during the life of existing contracts. Arbitrators tend to overturn unilateral plan changes where collective bargaining agreements contain maintenance-of-benefits provisions, but they are likely to uphold such changes if they are contractually authorized or do not result in impermissible benefit reductions.

1. Plan Changes Overturned

To protect health insurance coverage from erosion, many collective bargaining agreements include provisions that require employers to maintain "identical," "equivalent," or "comparable" benefits to those that were in place at the time of contract ratification. In general, arbitrators overturn plan changes that conflict with such provisions. Additionally, arbitrators sometimes conclude that plan modifications amount to changes in the terms and conditions of employment, and they hold that employers cannot implement such changes without first bargaining or obtaining union consent.

● An employer unlawfully implemented a new health plan that unilaterally changed the cap on insurance premiums of bargaining unit employees who worked at least 30 but fewer than 35 hours per week from 20 percent to 50 percent, because the parties reached an oral agreement during contract negotiations that the contribution of "30 or more" part-time employees would be capped at 20 percent of the premium, and the union never waived its right to bargain over terms and conditions of employment (*American Red Cross*, 127 LA 12).

● An arbitrator ruled that an employer violated the bargaining contract when it increased employees' health care premiums, even though the employer claimed that its failure to provide the union with the required listing of the number of employees on the plan every month was not significant because the information would have been of no value to the union (*Cooper Standard Automotive*, 125 LA 1377).

● An employer did not have the right to collect retroactively from employees health insurance premium contributions that it inadvertently made in excess of what was required under a collective bargaining agreement, where the employer was responsible for the error, an arbitrator ruled (*Vanguard Car Rental USA*, 125 LA 846).

Considering the collective bargaining agreement's stipulation that there would be a 50/50 split of "cost above premiums" between the employer and employees if health premiums exceeded a total monthly cost of $629, an arbitrator ruled that an employer owed affected employees a refund of one month reflecting 50 percent of a decrease in premiums from approximately $847 to $798, because the stipulation's language provided not only for an increase in premiums but also for any decrease that would keep the total cost above the $629 cap (*Hanson Spancrete*, 125 LA 645).

● An arbitrator ruled an employer violated a collective bargaining agreement, which provided that "there will be no major . . . changes in the current level of benefits. . .," when it unilaterally changed the health plan. The document announcing the changes was titled "Summary of Major plan changes," and the director of benefits admitted during the hearing that some of the changes were major (*Schnuck Markets Inc.*, 130 LA 20).

● An arbitrator ruled an employer violated the collective bargaining contract, which provided that "benefit and coverage levels will be maintained . . ." after a change in health insurance carriers, when it changed carriers resulting in cuts in two benefits and improvements in some others, because the contract required that no benefits be cut. The arbitrator ordered the employer to either reinstate the previous carrier or adopt another plan that contains all of the existing benefit and coverage levels (*Rousselot Inc.*, 128 LA 1345)

● An employer could not raise employees' share of premiums in response to a large cost increase for major medical insurance, an arbitrator ruled. Employees had been required to pay a fixed amount for major medical for several years, and the contract stated that the employer would continue providing coverage "on the same contributory basis." According to the arbitrator, the employer's action had the effect of reducing employees' take-home pay, and changes in wages, benefits, and working conditions could not be made unilaterally during the life of the agreement. Adding that employees had the right to expect that the benefits they enjoyed when the agreement was signed would remain in effect unless they were changed by mutual consent of the parties, the arbitrator concluded that the employer violated the terms of the contract and past practice when it increased employees' payments (*TRW Inc.*, 81 LA 616).

● An arbitrator found that an employer violated its collective bargaining agreement when it changed employees' share of health insurance premiums from $10 per week to 10 percent of the total cost. The arbitrator said that the change from a dollar-denominated payment to a percentage of premium was a "qualitative difference" in the terms and conditions of employment because the amounts deducted from employee's paychecks would increase whenever insurance rates were raised by the carrier. Finding that this was more risk than was bargained for in the agreement, the arbitrator ordered the employer to refund the difference in costs to employees (*American Sand & Gravel Co.*, 118 LA 535).

● Another employer switched from purchasing coverage through an insurance carrier to providing health insurance on a self-funded basis, but it assured employees that benefits would remain identical. Two years later, when the employer attempted to require employees to begin contributing to the cost of their coverage, the union grieved. An arbitrator found that the employer had a well established policy of paying the full amount of employees' insurance premiums. Concluding that the employer could not begin requiring monthly payments from employees without first bargaining, the arbitrator ordered the employer to resume its practice of paying the entire cost of the plan (*Cahokia Flour Co.*, 95 LA 1285).

● Similarly, an arbitrator found that an employer violated its collective bargaining agreement when it increased co-payments and related items under its group health plan. The contract permitted the employer to change carriers "at its option" as long as benefits were not decreased, but it did not give the employer the power to make unilateral changes concerning costs, the arbitrator said (*Arkansas General Industries Inc.*, 116 LA 1373; see also 115 LA 1239, 110 LA 293).

● An employer did not have the authority to make benefit reductions when faced with budget shortfalls as a result of rising health insurance expenses, an arbitrator decided. After the employer began providing health care coverage on a self-insured basis, an increase in claims activity threatened its budget. However, the employer failed to reach a consensus with the union on how to address the problem. The employer then made unilateral changes, including increased co-payments, a new deductible, the elimination of some benefits, and a waiting period for coverage for new employees. Emphasizing that the contract required the level of health insurance to be maintained, the arbitrator ordered the employer to rescind the benefit reductions and compensate employees for any benefits they were denied as a result of the changes (*City of Norman*, 115 LA 827).

● An employer committed a contract violation when it changed insurance carriers and the new carrier raised employee co-payments for prescription drugs, an arbitrator held. The contract stated that the employer had the right to change carriers as long as benefits remained equivalent to those in effect as of the date of the change. The arbitrator reasoned that the drug co-pay amounts were a form of benefit and therefore had to be maintained, even though the contract did not directly specify a particular level of benefits. As a remedy, the arbitrator ordered the employer to reimburse all employees affected by the higher co-pays (*Town of Oconomowoc*, 115 LA 169).

● A change in health insurance that removed employees' ability to choose their own physicians constituted an impermissible benefit reduction, an arbitrator ruled. An employer and union had negotiated a provision allowing for a change of insurance carriers as long as employees would continue to receive comparable benefits. The employer subsequently changed carriers and began requiring all employees to obtain care through a referral system, which meant they would no longer be able to select their own physicians. The arbitrator said the employer was justified in attempting to contain costs, but the new medical plan did not provide comparable benefits. Declaring that the choice of a physician was a medical benefit that could not be eliminated unilaterally, the arbitrator ordered the employer to find and maintain new coverage that would restore employees' ability to choose their own physicians (*Joy Mining Machinery Inc.*, 114 LA 1097; see also 114 LA 975).

• Where a collective bargaining agreement expressly stated that employees would be responsible for 20 percent of hospital costs up to a specified limit, an employer could not institute a preferred provider network that required employees to pay higher amounts if they used hospitals outside the network, an arbitrator decided. The new network did not include a hospital in a town where a number of employees lived, which meant that they would have to travel some 50 miles to reach an in-network facility or incur higher out-of-pocket costs to use their hometown hospital. Concluding that the employer's unilateral implementation of the new arrangement had the effect of reducing some employees' benefits, the arbitrator ordered the employer to stop requiring higher payments for the use of out-of-network hospitals and reimburse any employees who had incurred extra costs by going outside the network (*Excel Corp.*, 106 LA 1069).

• An employer violated a collective bargaining agreement by making unilateral changes in health insurance coverage, even though the changes were beneficial to many employees, an arbitrator found. When confronted with a 23 percent premium increase, the employer eliminated one of the five plan options available to employees and instituted new, higher co-payments for brand-name prescription drugs. By offsetting some of the premium hike, these changes benefited the employer as well as those employees who had elected coverage options that required them to pay a percentage of premiums.

• The arbitrator said the employer had two legitimate courses of action when confronted with the premium increase: either accepting the hike while maintaining the benefits called for under the contract or fully apprising the union of the situation

and negotiating modifications. It was the responsibility of the union, not the employer, to make determinations about the terms that would best serve the needs of the bargaining unit as a whole, the arbitrator declared. He ordered the employer to make affected employees whole for out-of-pocket losses—both retroactively and on a continuing basis—until the parties could meet and negotiate acceptable modifications to the health insurance provisions of the contract (*Hackley Hospital*, 122 LA 138).

• Where a contract permitted changes in health insurance "to either improve the coverage provided and/or to reduce the premiums," an employer did not have the right to decrease benefits unilaterally, an arbitrator held. The language in question had been introduced some 16 years earlier and was included in each new contract as part of a larger section outlining the insurance benefits that were negotiated by the parties. According to the arbitrator, the language had never been interpreted as giving management the authority to reduce benefits unilaterally during the life of an agreement. Adding that such an interpretation would produce "a nonsensical result" and conflict with past practice, the arbitrator revoked the benefit reductions imposed by the employer (*City of Zanesville*, 101 LA 757).

2. Plan Changes Upheld

Where collective bargaining agreements do not include guarantees that lock in existing health care benefits, arbitrators are more likely to uphold employers' unilateral plan changes. In some cases, arbitrators find that contractual language specifically grants employers a certain degree of latitude in making plan modifications. Even in the absence of such language, arbitrators sometimes determine that the changes instituted by employers do not rise to the level of contract violations or mandatory subjects of bargaining.

An employer did not violate a collective bargaining agreement, which provided that the employer contribute 80 percent of premiums of "active employees," when it reduced dependent coverage to 50 percent, an arbitrator ruled, accepting the employer's definition of "active employee" as one who was "actually working and gainfully employed" at the plant (*Western Refining Co.*, 129 LA 438).

• A joint labor-management insurance committee made a change in insurance carriers that resulted in the loss of a co-pay benefit for diabetic supplies. The arbitrator upheld the change in coverage despite contentions that the employer was obligated to provide benefits at least equal to the old plan and that union members of the joint committee did not have authority to bargain on the union's behalf. A maintenance of standards clause excepted negotiated changes, the arbitrator ruled, and employee members of the committee had the authority to bargain on the union's behalf over changes in the health care program (*Dawson Metal Company Inc.*, 126 LA 545).

• An arbitrator ruled that an employer did not violate a labor contract, which provided that it pay a percentage of the premium cost of the least-expensive of health plans offered to employees as its contribution for premium costs of all employees, in whatever plan they enrolled, when it used a high-deductible plan as the least-expensive plan. Even though it had used another, more expensive plan as its benchmark plan in the prior two years, where it did so by mistake, two occasions did not make a past practice, the employer officials were ignorant of the fact that a mistake was made, and the union's expectation that the employer would use the more expensive plan as its benchmark was not based on any assurance, promise, or represenation of the employer (*Bridgeway Inc.*, 126 LA 681).

• An arbitrator upheld an employer's right to increase employees' contributions to exceed the cap on employees' health insurance premium contributions, where the collective bargaining agreement also included a cap on the employer's contribution and stipulated that premium increases would be "shared equally" by the employer and employees (*Vanguard Car Rental USA*, 125 LA 846).

• An arbitrator held that a contract's "me too" provision, which guaranteed bargaining unit members the same medical insurance as management employees, permitted an employer to implement changes requiring monthly contributions for indemnity coverage under a fee-for-service plan. The employer added two new plan options that included preferred provider networks and, at the same time, discontinued its practice of offering fully funded indemnity coverage. Employees objected to the changes because of the monthly charges for traditional indemnity coverage, but the arbitrator found that the contract did not contain a maintenance of benefits provision or any guarantee concerning contributions from employees. The employer had the latitude to make the changes in question so long as it provided bargaining unit members and management employees with the same medical benefits, the arbitrator concluded (*Browning-Ferris of Illinois Inc.*, 114 LA 1424).

• An employer did not commit a contract violation when it replaced a zero deductible health insurance plan with a high deductible plan and health savings accounts, an arbitrator ruled. The employer had promised the small unit of janitorial employees covered by the contract that they would not have to pay any premium costs and would get the same health insurance as some 1,800 company employees who were not represented by a union. The only other contractual limitation on the employer's ability to make health plan changes was a provision requiring the employer to bargain with the union before instituting "unilateral changes in wages, hours, or other terms and conditions of employment." When the new plan was unveiled, the union offered a proposal for different health insurance coverage, but the same proposal had already been rejected twice before by the employer because it would carry unacceptable costs.

The arbitrator upheld the new scheme even while expressing the belief that the janitorial employees, with their modest incomes, were not well served by the change. The new plan imposed deductibles of $2,000 for single coverage, $4,000 for a couple, and $6,000 for family coverage, and employees were supposed to use money from their health savings accounts to offset those out-of-pocket costs. Although the employer made HSA contributions of $550 for single coverage, $1,100 for a couple, and $1,650 for family coverage, that left a gap of as much as $4,350 for employees to cover. According to the arbitrator, the plan could be a "very, very bad deal" for lower wage workers with high medical expenses. Nevertheless, the employer had the contractual authority to implement the change, the arbitrator found, and by failing to offer any proposals aside from the one that the employer had previously rejected, the union effectively waived its right to bargain over the effects of the change (*Food Services of America*, 122 LA 363).

● Under a collective bargaining agreement that incorporated the terms of an external health plan document, an employer had the authority to increase employee copayments, an arbitrator ruled. The contract itself did not address employee payments or other specifics related to health benefits. Instead, it made reference to a summary plan document, or SPD, which stated that the employer could evaluate the costs of the plan and determine the amount to be contributed by each employee. According to the arbitrator, the contract and the SPD were inextricably intertwined, and the SPD gave the employer the right to amend the methods of funding health insurance. Although the union did not participate in drafting the terms of the SPD, the language that incorporated the SPD into the contract had been subject to negotiation, and that language was contained in three successive labor agreements without objection from the union, the arbitrator pointed out (*Sandusky Ltd.*, 122 LA 1195).

● An employer did not commit a contract violation when it changed third-party administrators but continued providing the same health benefits, an arbitrator held. Citing problems with the new plan administrator because of its failure to ensure the proper payment of employees' claims, the union contended that the employer did not fulfill its promise of maintaining "identical coverage." According to the arbitrator, however, the administrative problems could not be equated with a reduction in benefits, and the contract did not preclude the employer from changing plan administrators as long as covered benefits were not changed (*Stark County Sheriff*, 108 LA 394).

● Another arbitrator upheld an employer's decision to switch plan administrators despite the impact of the change on certain coverage costs. Under new cost-sharing provisions negotiated by the parties, employees could enroll in a standard plan, which was a preferred provider organization, and the employer would pay 85 percent of the cost. The employer also offered to pay an equivalent dollar amount for HMO coverage. Initially, 85 percent of the PPO cost exceeded the amounts employees had to pay for HMO coverage, but an increase in rates charged by HMOs, coupled with reduced PPO costs resulting from the change in plan administrators, meant that employees who enrolled in HMOs had to begin making substantial contributions. The union argued that the employer should switch back to the original plan administrator and allow employees to receive HMO coverage at little or no cost.

Rejecting the union's argument, the arbitrator said the employer acted in good faith in minimizing the costs associated with the standard PPO plan. In comparison to the rate hikes imposed by HMOs—which the employer could not control—the PPO savings achieved by changing plan administrators had relatively little impact on employees' payments for HMO coverage, the arbitrator found. Adding that employees' provider choices remained intact under the new plan administrator's PPO network, the arbitrator said no violation occurred in connection with the change in administrators or the rise in HMO costs (*Columbia Gas of Maryland and Columbia Gas of Pennsylvania*, 122 LA 113; see also 114 LA 944).

● Notwithstanding a contractual obligation to "maintain its existing group insurance program," an arbitrator held that past practice and a lack of timely union action permitted an employer to implement unilateral health benefit changes. According to the arbitrator, the employer had a history of implementing health plan revisions without union objections, and its latest plan changes were not grieved until several months after they were announced. Citing the union's laxity in challenging the employer's unilateral plan changes, the arbitrator allowed the revisions to remain in effect (*Associated Milk Producers Inc.*, 89 LA 1186).

● Under a contract that granted an employer the discretion to make health plan changes, an arbitrator upheld the implementation of co-payments for mail-order prescriptions. The employer's health insurance program included a standard plan and a "high option," which offered the same benefits but differed in methods of employee payment. Citing a contract provision that allowed the employer to make changes in the "standard" health plan, the union argued that the new co-payments could not be required of employees who selected the high option. Disagreeing with the union, the arbitrator found that the high option was simply another version of the employer's standard plan. Both versions were identified as a single plan by the health insurance carrier, and plan documents gave the employer "sole authority and responsibility to review and make final decisions on all benefits," the arbitrator noted. Nothing in the contract diminished the employer's right to change the particulars of the plan, the arbitrator added in upholding the new co-payments (*Friedrich Air Conditioning Co.*, 112 LA 907).

B. Interpreting Payment Provisions

Aside from resolving disputes over unilateral health plan changes, arbitrators sometimes have to determine if agreed-upon plan provisions are being applied correctly. As evidenced by the following examples, employers and unions commonly disagree over the interpretation of provisions related to payments.

● Under a health insurance plan that included a formula for an employer and its employees to share coverage costs, a decline in expenses did not mean the employer had to reduce employees' payments, an arbitrator held. The employer and union had agreed to a new arrangement whereby the employer would pay 90 percent of the costs of indemnity coverage and employees would pay the remaining 10 percent. Future increases were to be shared equally. During the first year of the cost-sharing arrangement, claims declined, but the employer did not reset employees' contribution amounts

at a lower rate. The arbitrator found that employees were not entitled to a payment reduction, because the contract only provided for the sharing of cost increases. Without a parallel clause dealing with declining costs, there was no basis for concluding that the parties had bargained insurance premium reductions into their contract, the arbitrator found (*E-Systems Inc.*, 103 LA 295).

● In another case, an employer attempted to control escalating premium costs by switching health plans. The employer wanted to move a pool of about 1,000 employees over to the new plan, but a group of 88 union-represented employees voted against the change. Based on the small size of this remaining group, the original insurance carrier hiked its rates, which had an impact on the employees because they were required to pay 12 percent of the premium costs. Their union grieved, but an arbitrator found that they were not entitled to any monetary relief. The arbitrator said the employees had a contractual right to retain the original health plan, and the employer was obligated to honor their decision. However, it was not required to offset their higher costs, the arbitrator held, noting that the employer was already paying an extra $140,000 per year in premiums over what it would have paid if the employees had agreed to change plans (*Joy Mining Machinery*, 116 LA 723).

● An employer did not commit a contract violation by requiring employees to make the same co-payment for brand-name prescription drugs that lacked generic equivalents as for brand-name drugs that had generic substitutes available, an arbitrator ruled. Evidence from the most recent contract negotiations showed that the employer intended to discontinue its previous co-pay practices and initiate a new prescription drug plan. The evidence also showed that the union accepted the revised plan without conditions. By accepting this plan, the arbitrator said, the union agreed to the company's position and "essentially negotiated away any past practices accrued from the previous contracts" (*Snap-On Tools Inc.*, 117 LA 341).

● An employer's policy of paying stipends to employees if they forfeited coverage and instead obtained health insurance through their spouses did not apply to situations where co-workers were married and both spouses received their insurance coverage through the employer, an arbitrator decided. Interpreting the contract provision on the stipends to mean that coverage obtained through a spouse would be provided by another employer, the arbitrator said giving stipends to married co-workers would be tantamount to rewriting the agreement (*Celite Corp.*, 120 LA 97).

● An arbitrator found that an employer bargained in bad faith when it convinced a union to leave language in a collective bargaining agreement that allowed for premium contributions by retirees. The employer had also verbally promised that retirees would not be required to pay insurance premiums, but it later reneged on that promise. The arbitrator said that oral agreements are as binding as written agreements and ordered refunds issued to those retirees who had incurred financial costs (*Eljer Plumbingware Inc.*, 115 LA 1720).

1. Obligations of Successor Employers

Changes in ownership can present unique challenges with regard to health insurance payment obligations when successor employers seek to scale back health insurance contributions and benefits from levels that their predecessors had agreed to provide. In such cases, arbitrators tend to look closely at successor employers' express commitments concerning insurance payments.

● A successor employer did not violate a collective bargaining agreement by failing to provide dental and vision insurance coverage to certain employees after their retiree dental and vision benefits from the predecessor employer were eliminated, an arbitrator ruled. Even though the collective bargaining agreement stated that all fringe benefits were to be provided on an aggregate equivalency basis, the fringe-benefit provision did not mention treatment of the predecessor's retirees, and the health insurance provision expressly excluded those retirees from coverage (*Magna Steyr*, 127 LA 833).

● One arbitrator held that a successor employer was liable for health insurance contributions where the employer had signed a memorandum promising "to adopt all the terms" of its predecessor's collective bargaining agreement (*Green Team of San Jose, Calif.*, 103 LA 705).

● Another arbitrator held that the labor agreement negotiated between a successor employer and a union did not require the employer to continue making health care and life insurance premium payments for employees on layoff or disability. The agreement provided that medical and life insurance coverage would apply to "active" employees. Although the predecessor employer had agreed to continue making the premium payments despite employees' lack of "active" status, the evidence did not show that the successor employer had agreed to do the same, the arbitrator said. On the contrary, the employer credibly testified that it had advised the union of its plan to discontinue such benefits during periods of layoff and disability, the arbitrator noted (*Republic Special Metals*, 120 LA 1447).

C. Eligibility for Coverage

Health insurance eligibility can also be a source of controversy. When making determinations about the availability of benefits or the application of certain plan elements to specific employees, arbitrators often have to consider the scope of contractual promises regarding health care coverage and nuances of employment status.

● One arbitrator held that an employee did not become eligible for full-time health insurance benefits as a result of working two part-time jobs with combined hours that exceeded 20 per week. Although the collective bargaining agreement defined "full time" as a position in which the employee worked 20 or more hours each week, eligibility for full-time benefits was contingent on the position held, not the actual number of hours worked, the arbitrator concluded (*Garaway Local School District Board of Education*, 101 LA 181).

● An employer did not commit a contract violation when it terminated health coverage for an employee who had been injured and was unable to return to work, an arbitrator held. The employer kept the employee on its employment rolls and continued his health care benefits for several months, even after the employee's doctor determined that he could not resume working. The employer ended his coverage a year after his injury, but the union said the move violated a provision stating that employees would continue to accumulate service during workers' compensation leave for purposes of health insurance eligibility.

According to the arbitrator, that provision referred to the fact that periods of workers' compensation leave would be counted as time worked when new employees were trying to accumulate the six months of service required for initial health plan eligibility. Ongoing eligibility was reserved for those who retained their status as employees, however, which meant that the worker in question was no longer entitled to health care coverage once it became clear that he would never be able to return to work, the arbitrator found (*Cole Brothers Contractors*, 109 LA 345).

● An arbitrator held that a striker was not entitled to sickness and accident benefits for an illness that occurred during a strike. The arbitrator based his decision on the fact that under the insurance policy, coverage ended "upon termination of employment." According to the arbitrator, the grievant was no longer employed when he joined the strike, and there was no agreement at the end of the strike to make benefits retroactive (*Rack Engineering Co.*, 76 LA 1013).

● An employer that had terminated group health coverage during a strike was not obligated to cover an employee's claim arising from an illness that occurred before he returned to work, an arbitrator ruled. Workers had been given the opportunity to convert to individual policies during the strike, but the employee had declined to do so. He became ill and was hospitalized the day before his scheduled return and was unable to report to work for another month. The arbitrator found that the employee's claim for medical benefits was without merit because the insurance carrier's booklet clearly stated that coverage would not resume "until you return to full time work

for one full day," and the parties had incorporated the booklet's language into their labor agreement (*Allied Plant Maintenance Co. of Tennessee*, 90 LA 553).

● *By contrast*, an arbitrator held that an employee who had been employed for 14 years at the time of a strike should have resumed his benefits coverage without restrictions upon ratification of a new labor agreement. The employee could not be treated as a new employee with a pre-existing condition, the arbitrator held, because the parties intended to treat all employees as they had been treated before the strike, and the only variation applied to employees who had not continued their premium payments and had experienced the onset of new problems during the period of the strike (*Domore Office Furniture*, 78 LA 1225).

● An employer could not rely on a contract provision concerning "personal" leaves of absence in attempting to shed its benefit obligations with regard to an employee on a medical leave of absence, an arbitrator ruled. The contract did not require benefits for employees on personal leaves of absence, but the arbitrator held that the word "personal" was akin to "reasons other than illness." Citing separate language that referred to leave for non-industrial illness or injury, the arbitrator said the employer remained obligated to make health and welfare benefit contributions for the employee during his medical leave (*T-M Manufacturing*, 110 LA 978).

● An employer's contractual pledge to absorb any premium increases resulting from escalating health care costs applied to an employee who was receiving continuation coverage under the Consolidated Omnibus Budget Reconciliation Act, an arbitrator decided. Federal rules allow employers to charge individuals receiving COBRA coverage 100 percent of actual premium costs plus an extra 2 percent for administrative expenses. However, the arbitrator found that the contractual protection against premium increases applied to the employee in spite of his COBRA status. The employee had been off work on short-term disability and had resigned so he could get money out of his retirement for his wife's medical bills, but the arbitrator said he remained covered by the agreement because of a provision stating that "the ability to work because of proven sickness or injury shall not result in the loss of seniority rights" (*USF Bestway Inc.*, 120 LA 1569).

1. Coverage for Nonemployees

Disputes also arise from time to time with regard to health coverage for individuals who are not employees. For example, arbitrators are commonly called upon to consider the contractual benefit rights or insurance eligibility status of dependents, spouses, domestic partners, and retirees.

• In a case where domestic partnership benefits were extended to homosexual couples living together, an arbitrator denied such benefits to opposite-sex cohabitants. Opposite-sex couples could legally marry and qualify for benefits that way, while same-sex couples were not able to legally marry, the arbitrator pointed out (*City of Kalamazoo*, 116 LA 815).

• An employer did not violate its collective bargaining agreement's anti-discrimination provision by refusing to extend an employee's health insurance coverage to his same-sex partner, an arbitrator ruled. The contractual language on insurance coverage was reasonably clear and did not equate "spouse" with "unmarried domestic partner," the arbitrator found. Moreover, the employer's practice of limiting spousal coverage to heterosexual marriages had been clear and consistent, the arbitrator noted (*Kent State University*, 103 LA 338; see also 115 LA 852).

• The grandson of a retiree's surviving spouse was not entitled to health insurance coverage under the terms of a collective bargaining agreement that covered grandchildren who were legally adopted, lived with the employee in a parent-child relationship, and met IRS dependency support requirements, an arbitrator ruled. Even though the child's grandmother claimed her grandchild as a dependent on her income tax, she had not legally adopted the child, and the child's mother lived in the house. Observing that it was not established who provided support for the child, the arbitrator ruled in favor of the employer (*TRW Inc.*, 107 LA 693).

• In a case involving an early retiree who died, an arbitrator concluded that an employer did not commit a contract violation by denying the retiree's dependents continued coverage until the time the retiree would have reached age 65. The arbitrator based his decision on a summary plan description stating that coverage for dependents ceased at the time of the subscriber's death (*Boise Cascade Corp.*, 119 LA 35).

• An employer did not commit a contract violation when the spouse of an employee was found uninsurable based on her past medical record, an arbitrator ruled. The decision to deny the application for dependent coverage was made by the employer's insurance carrier. The employer provided benefits through the carrier's plan, and if the carrier erred in its determination, the employee's dispute was with the carrier and not the employer, the arbitrator concluded (*TSC Industries Inc.*, 71 LA 787).

Part 11

Management Rights

I. Management Rights [LA DCI 100.03 (public employees); 2.08]

OVERVIEW

The issue of management rights can become rather convoluted when viewed against the backdrop of the many court rulings and National Labor Relations Board decisions that weigh employers' bargaining obligations against their authority to take unilateral actions. Under federal labor law, employers can be charged with unfair labor practices if they make changes affecting conditions of employment without first obtaining union consent or bargaining to impasse, yet they are free to act of their own accord when making some business decisions or when unions have waived their bargaining rights concerning certain matters.

Arbitration awards, though they are colored by the intricacies of federal labor law and the decisions of the courts and the NLRB, tend to take a less complicated approach to management rights. For instance, arbitrators commonly adhere to the "residual rights" doctrine, which essentially holds that unionized employers retain the same management authority as their nonunion counterparts except in those areas where their powers are constrained by statute or specific contract language.

Because the concept of residual rights carries less weight with the courts and the board than it does with arbitrators, employers have become more likely through the years to include management-rights clauses in their collective bargaining agreements. These clauses might contain details on the powers reserved to management—with the added proviso that the enumerated rights are not intended as an all-inclusive list—or simply state that employers retain all customary functions and prerogatives of management except as restricted by express contract provisions.

Even if collective bargaining agreements give employers broad discretion in certain areas, however, arbitrators are reluctant to uphold arbitrary, unreasonable, or bad-faith managerial actions that adversely affect employees. In addition, arbitrators sometimes conclude that employers are subject to implied obligations or limitations under general contract provisions, such as recognition, seniority, and wage clauses.

While the issue of management rights can arise in connection with almost any type of dispute, this chapter focuses mainly on managerial authority as it pertains to the following:

• control of operating methods, the introduction of new technology and equipment, and the relocation or discontinuation of operations;

• the right to establish standards for the quantity and quality of employees' output;

• control of job classifications, staffing, and crew sizes;

• control of work assignments and the performance of bargaining unit work by supervisors; and

• the right to establish workplace rules and policies.

_____ SUMMARY OF CASES _____

A. Extent of Management Authority and Control of Operations

Arbitrators generally express the view that employers have an inherent right to manage their businesses. For example, arbitrators have recognized the broad authority of employers to control operating methods and take unilateral action regarding the introduction of new technology and equipment. When considering the extent of management's authority over such matters, arbitrators often base their decisions on whether employers have bargained away any management rights that would exist in the absence of union representation.

• According to one arbitrator, the "underlying premise" of any collective bargaining agreement is that the employer holds onto all the rights that are not limited by contract or statute. Therefore, absent violations of the law, if the contract is silent on a particular issue or condition, the employer is free to act as it sees fit. Rejecting the argument that the employer "must have contract authority to take a particular action," the arbitrator determined that the "converse is true." For the union to prevail,

it must show that the contract either imposes obligations on the employer or constrains the employer's actions (*St. Louis Symphony Society*, 70 LA 475).

• Another arbitrator found that despite the lack of an explicit contract clause delineating the powers retained by management, an employer's right to run its operations was "inherent and ... reserved and maintained." Absent any "arbitrariness or capriciousness" in its actions, the employer was free to direct its workforce, and that right could not be "denied, rejected, or curtailed" unless the employer's actions clearly violated specific contract language, the arbitrator said (*Fairway Foods Inc.*, 44 LA 161).

• An employer did not commit a contract violation when it changed operating methods at one of its plants, an arbitrator decided. The main office of the company had warned that the plant had to reduce expenses or else production would be shifted to other locations that were more cost effective. Management held discussions with members of the bargaining unit and factored in their feedback, but the union had additional objections and argued that the employer could not unilaterally implement the changes. According to the arbitrator, the employer recognized that its competitiveness could be hindered by a requirement to obtain the union's consent before making operational changes, and thus it had never agreed to grant the union "any such veto power." Despite the impact of the operational changes, which included pay reductions and even job losses for some employees, the union failed to show a violation of the contract, and there was no evidence of bad faith or capriciousness in the employer's actions, the arbitrator said (*Pillsbury Co.*, 75 LA 523).

• A labor contract granted an employer the sole right to determine the processes used in its manufacturing operation, an arbitrator held. Because the agreement specifically allowed the employer to install new machines, the arbitrator ordered the employees to run them to their full capacity in good faith, even though it meant that their compensation per unit of output would have to be lowered under a piece rate plan. The arbitrator stated that there was sound economic justification for upholding management's right to introduce technical improvements, adding that to rule in favor of the union would negate the purpose of the management-rights clause and lead to economic stagnation (*Associated Shoe Industries of Southeastern Mass. Inc.*, 10 LA 535).

• A city government did not need to continue direct deposit of employees' paychecks by purchasing equipment and installing computer programs needed to tie into a bank's new systems, an arbitrator held. Despite the fact that the city had deposited paychecks directly into employees' bank accounts for a decade before the bank upgraded its systems, the arbitrator said the collective bargaining agreement gave management the right to decide "matters of inherent managerial policy," including how technology was used (*City of North Olmsted, Ohio*, 106 LA 865).

• In another case, an arbitrator upheld an employer's installation of equipment that resulted in job losses for certain employees. Although the employees claimed

that their seniority rights were violated, the arbitrator noted that the employer had the right to mechanize its operations by using new equipment. Because the duties the employer took away from the employees were not performed by anyone else within or outside the bargaining unit, but by a machine, the arbitrator determined that there was no connection between the operational changes and the affected workers' seniority rights (*Bethlehem Steel Co.*, 35 LA 72).

1. Moving or Discontinuing Operation

In disputes over operational decisions, management rights usually prevail unless express contract language restricts employers' actions. Nevertheless, arbitrators have ruled both ways on the question of whether employers have unilateral authority to relocate work and discontinue some or all of a facility's operations.

• Nothing in the contract terms negotiated by an employer and a union or in the parties' bargaining history precluded the employer from moving a department's operations from one of its plants to a different facility, an arbitrator ruled. The union claimed that the elimination of the department and the job classifications of the employees who worked there would constitute a violation of the recognition clause in the parties' collective bargaining agreement. Adding that it had agreed to forego part of a scheduled wage increase when bargaining over the department's creation, the union argued that the wage concession "bought" the department and should have guaranteed its continued existence at least for the duration of the agreement.

Rejecting the union's position, the arbitrator found that the employer had a history of moving operations between plants, and the union had failed during past contract talks to obtain restrictions on the employer's right to transfer work to other locations. In light of these facts, the arbitrator refused to treat the recognition clause as though it required the employer to maintain the status quo during the life of the agreement. The arbitrator also rejected the union's assertion that it "bought" the department with its wage concession, observing that the negotiations over the new department involved give and take from both parties. "In any bilateral exchange culminating in a contract," the arbitrator stated, "it can be aptly said that each party pays a price to secure the commitments of the other" (*Harvard Industries Inc.*, 91 LA 849).

• An employer could legally relocate its packaging process operation to a new nonunion location without first bargaining with a union, an arbitrator ruled. The union had little recourse, the arbitrator found, because the parties' collective bargaining agreement contained a management-rights clause that gave the employer exclusive authority to decide where to locate its plants, and the contract recognized the union as the bargaining representative of employees at the particular plant in question "and no other." In addition, the arbitrator noted that the primary reason for the move was the employer's legitimate need for more space, and nothing the union might propose in negotiations could increase the space available at the old location (*Zebco Corp.*, 104 LA 613).

• An employer had the right to transfer its bar soap operation from a plant at which employees were represented by a union to an out-of-state plant where workers were represented by a different union, an arbitrator decided. The language of the contract applied only to the plants the employer operated locally, and not to the out-of-state plant. The union argued that the transfer was tantamount to subcontracting, which was not allowed in the absence of consultations with the union, but the arbitrator rejected that argument (*Lever Bros. Co.*, 65 LA 1299; see also 71 LA 873, 71 LA 120).

• Where an employer's decision to relocate a plant was based on legitimate business reasons, an arbitrator determined that only an explicit contract provision could have prevented the move, because management's freedom to relocate was not limited by the mere existence of a contract. Nevertheless, the arbitrator found that management should have discussed the move in advance with the union and should have offered any available jobs to employees from the old site. Those who did not make the move were entitled to severance pay plus

a share of the pension fund, the arbitrator decided (*John B. Stetson Co.*, 28 LA 514).

• Another arbitrator held that an employer should not have closed its catalog merchandise distribution center and transferred functions to other cities while a labor contract was still in force. The employer relied on a letter of understanding that it claimed gave it the right to change its distribution methods in ways that might affect its distribution facilities, but the arbitrator noted that the parties had also agreed to a memorandum of understanding that prohibited relocation or closing of the plants covered by the contract. The parties' bargaining history indicated that the MOU was supposed to apply to all distribution center bargaining unit work, and its clear language could not be subverted by the letter's reference to distribution methods, the arbitrator concluded (*Sears Logistics Services*, 95 LA 229, clarified at 97 LA 421).

• A garment manufacturer committed a contract violation in transferring operations to a plant in another state by moving its equipment at night, over weekends, and without the union's knowledge, an arbitrator found. Pointing out that the contract imposed an obligation to bargain over any permanent relocations, the arbitrator directed the employer to discontinue operations in the new plant, re-establish the factory in the state from which it had moved, and pay the union for 300 employees' lost wages, vacations, and welfare-fund contributions (*Jack Meilman*, 34 LA 771; see also 36 LA 1364).

• An employer was obligated to compensate employees for their loss of pay caused by the relocation of a distribution facility to a plant in another location, an arbitrator decided. Despite the employer's claim that the management-rights clause in the parties' collective bargaining agreement gave it "absolute" discretion in operating its business, a reasonable interpretation of the contract was that "the parties intended that there will be an existing business during the term of the agreement," the arbitrator concluded (*Sealtest Dairy*, 65 LA 858).

• An employer violated its collective bargaining agreement when it closed a nonunion warehouse and transferred work to its union warehouse but continued to use nonunion drivers, an arbitrator ruled. The employer claimed that its labor contract applied only to workers at the union warehouse, a contention that the arbitrator did not accept. Delivery of all products to customers served out of the union warehouse had to be considered bargaining unit work, the arbitrator concluded, adding that to decide in favor of management rights in this case would have nullified the union's recognition clause (*Kraft Foods Global Inc.*, 122 LA 58; see also 119 LA 1193).

2. Limits on Unilateral Action

If arbitrators block or overturn unilateral management actions, they often do so because bargaining obligations apply to a particular subject. In some cases, however, arbitrators find that employers have surrendered their exclusive control over a subject as a result of prior negotiations.

● An arbitrator ruled an employer could not unilaterally reduce staffing on each of its presses from three to two-and-one-half employees, even though the agreement ambiguously referred to "scheduling procedure" and not specifically to "staffing" or "manning" requirements, because the employer had always used three employees per press, and during negotiations for the agreement the employer presented the union with a document in which the employer spelled out "3 people per press" in two locations. The arbitrator ordered the employer to make financial restitution equal to the additional wages that would have been paid if each press had been manned by three employees (*Graphic Packaging International Inc.*, 126 LA 719).

● An arbitrator ruled that a productivity improvement program could not be unilaterally implemented by an employer with a disciplinary component that altered employees' conditions of employment. The employer contended that it was exercising its exclusive right to manage the plant, but the arbitrator held that bargaining had to precede a change in working conditions. If the program had not included the disciplinary features, the employer would have been under no obligation to negotiate with the union over its implementation, the ar-

bitrator added (*Union Carbide Corp.*, 70 LA 201).

● An employer could not raise the subject of compulsory overtime during contract talks and, after failing to reach an agreement on the matter, later claim that the imposition of mandatory overtime was a management prerogative, an arbitrator held. The union had refused to agree to such an arrangement when the issue was addressed during contract negotiations, and the employer had signed the contract even though it did not contain the desired language on overtime. Were it not for these earlier events, the arbitrator said, the employer would have been able to invoke its management-rights clause and make overtime mandatory. After submitting the issue to bargaining, however, the employer could not claim that the contract's silence on the matter meant that management retained the authority to take unilateral action, the arbitrator concluded (*Sylvania Electric Products Inc.*, 24 LA 199).

● Another arbitrator ruled that an employer association could not reduce the number of electricians at a worksite from eight to five after having agreed with the union that eight would be employed. Even though there was no specific contract clause calling for a particular number of electricians, the arbitrator said that the employer could not take a subject that was within its managerial rights and submit that subject to collective bargaining, reach an agreement on it, and then repudiate the agreement (*Pacific American Shipowners Assn.*, 10 LA 736).

B. Control of Output and Quality

Most arbitrators hold that employers can take unilateral action in setting production standards or quotas as long as they are fair and reasonable (115 LA 844, 92 LA 86, 290 LA 570, 82 LA 714, 65 LA 405, 65 LA 380, 65 LA 270, 64 LA 885).

● One arbitrator determined that an employer could establish production quotas even though employees previously had been allowed to set their own standards. Nothing in the contract indicated that the parties intended the past practice to be continued indefinitely, the arbitrator noted, and the union had been notified that the change was being contemplated. There was no evidence that the new standards were unreasonable, he added, and the employer's failure to exercise a right it had under the agreement did not mean it had waived that right (*Mead Corp.*, 41 LA 1038).

● An employer had the right to use the objective yardstick of production quotas in evaluating an employee's performance, according to an arbitrator. After the employee received a warning stating that he was producing only 42 percent of the average of other employees doing comparable work, the union complained, pointing out that the contract made no reference to production or efficiency standards. The employer, however, claimed that its action was based on prerogatives granted by the contract's management-rights clause, under which it retained the right to manage the plant, direct the workforce, and suspend and discharge employees for just cause. The arbitrator upheld the employer's position, noting that the only rationale for not supporting it would be if the employer did not apply the standards in an evenhanded manner (*Menasco Mfg. Co.*, 30 LA 264).

● A bottling company's production quotas were reasonable, as was the discipline imposed on employees who failed to meet the quotas, an arbitrator ruled. The company revised its quotas for loading pallets with soft-drink cans based on a genuine business need to increase production, the arbitrator observed. Considerations the arbitrator cited in upholding the quotas included the fact that the work could be done more quickly than at the company's other facilities because of the type of product involved, as well as the fact that the workers used motorized loading equipment, which made the job easier. The arbitrator also noted that the company gave the employees four months to get up to speed before disciplining anyone for falling short of the quotas (*Coca-Cola Bottling Midwest Inc.*, 100 LA 911).

● An arbitrator held that an employer did not violate its collective bargaining agreement when it issued a suspension and final warning to a maintenance employee who fell below a mandated 35 percent call-in response rate. Although the standard had been established unilaterally, it was acceptable, the arbitrator ruled, citing the employer's implied rights and the fact that the standard was reasonable and relatively easily achieved by all other maintenance employees (*PQ Corp.*, 118 LA 568).

● Another arbitrator determined that an employer legitimately required a press operator in a metal works plant to meet a production quota within 60 calendar days or face discipline. The arbitrator described the case as unusual because the employer merely stated its expectations and voiced its concern that the employee was not working up to his abilities rather than disciplining him for not meeting the standard. The employer did nothing to harm the employee, the arbitrator concluded, adding that merely telling someone "what is expected of him is not the equivalent of any sort of punishment" that could be dealt with under grievance procedures (*Cerro Metal Products Co.*, 109 LA 993).

1. Quality Standards

Most arbitrators also treat the establishment of quality standards as an inherent function of management, recognizing that employers' continued existence depends largely on their ability to maintain adequate levels of quality.

● In one case, an arbitrator upheld an employer's institution of changes aimed at improving the quality of its products, observing that the employer's concern for quality was a genuine, necessary, and reasonable aspect of its right to control operations (*Howes Leather Co. Inc.*, 71 LA 606; see also 55 LA 84, 29 LA 161).

● A clothing manufacturer had a right to hold employees to certain quality standards, an arbitrator ruled, where decisions about whether employees met the standards were "mutually shared" by several managers, supervisors, and upper-level staff who checked garments on a random basis. Nevertheless, the arbitrator ordered the employer to reinstate an employee under a last-chance agreement after she was terminated on the basis of two separate problems, because only one of them was adequately supported by physical evidence (*Hugo Boss Cleveland Inc.*, 119 LA 1487).

• Despite the reasonableness of standards established by an employer under a new quality control system, an arbitrator refused to uphold the termination of workers who could not meet the standards. Noting that the system contained a plan for giving employees a chance to learn the new standards, the arbitrator said the employer should have given them time to improve if their performance was found wanting (*Patent Button Co.*, 43 LA 1208; see also 1 LA 20).

• *By contrast*, another arbitrator upheld a pharmaceutical company's termination of a worker for having a higher than allowed error rate. Under the management-rights provisions of the parties' collective bargaining agreement, the employer had great leeway in setting standards, the arbitrator found. The employer was not even required to provide a rationale for what constituted an acceptable error rate as long as the standard was applied even-handedly, the arbitrator added, noting that the employer's inability to "articulate the genesis of the efficiency regulation does not render the standard per se unreasonable" (*Cardinal Health Inc.*, 108 LA 1039).

C. Control of Job Classifications, Staffing, and Crew Sizes

Arbitrators generally agree that employers retain control of decisions about job classifications, staffing, and crew sizes unless specific contract provisions restrict their actions.

• An arbitrator ruled that an employer had the right to assign an employee to work as a forge truck/hook-up, even though there had been a practice of assigning both the hook-up person and the inside truck driver on a shift when more than two crews were working in the forge shop. The contract gave the employer the right to change or eliminate practices when the basis for the practice had been changed or eliminated, and operational changes gave rise to the basis for change or elimination of this practice (*Canton Drop Forge Inc.*, 123 LA 1113).

• An arbitrator ruled an employer had the right to unilaterally discontinue three job classifications and establish one with the net result that three bargaining-unit jobs

were lost, because there were no contractual provisions prohibiting those actions, the management rights clause authorized them, the actions were taken in good faith for legitimate business reasons, and five employees affected by the changes remained employed (*Roquette America Inc.*, 128 LA 103).

• Under the management-rights clause of a contract, an employer had the right to forego filling three computer jobs that it had previously posted, an arbitrator decided. The employer was under no obligation to maintain a particular number of positions at its plant, according to the arbitrator (*Computing & Software Inc.*, 61 LA 261).

• An employer did not violate its labor contract when it eliminated a job after the incumbent moved to another position, an arbitrator ruled. Because of changes at the employer's facilities, there was not enough work to warrant hiring a replacement in the vacated job, the arbitrator found. In addition, the parties' agreement granted the employer "the unambiguous right to regulate the amount and type of work to be performed as well as the number of employees necessary to complete that work," the arbitrator said (*Alltrista Consumer Products Co.*, 118 LA 1050).

• An employer had the right to abolish a position after an employee's retirement, an arbitrator decided. In general, employers have the authority to "eliminate unneeded jobs and assign remaining tasks to other classifications" except where such action is specifically forbidden by collective bargaining agreements, the arbitrator declared. Regarding the abolished job, the arbitrator said there was no longer enough work to warrant a full-time position, and the division of the remaining duties did not violate any specific provisions of the parties' labor agreement (*Quaker Oats Co.*, 84 LA 390; see also 86 LA 1102).

• An employer was within its rights to eliminate three bargaining unit positions after it modernized its operations, resulting in greater automation and consolidation of some processes, an arbitrator determined. A reading of the parties' collective bargaining agreement as a whole made it clear that the employer had the right to eliminate job classifications, according to the arbitrator.

Moreover, the employer needed to modernize in order to remain competitive, the arbitrator said (*Container Corp. of America*, 91 LA 329; see also 96 LA 844).

● Another arbitrator upheld an employer's reduction in the size of a work crew after mechanization allowed the work to be done by fewer employees. The parties' collective bargaining agreement obligated the employer to maintain a certain crew size "under present conditions," which meant that management was free to reduce the size when the "present conditions" no longer existed, the arbitrator said (*Theo. Hamm Brewing Co.*, 35 LA 243).

● An arbitrator found nothing wrong with the actions of an employer that combined the duties of three jobs into one classification and offered to negotiate with the union over a wage rate for the new job. The arbitrator said that a job-protection clause in the parties' collective bargaining agreement was primarily aimed at maintaining the pay scale, not at preventing all changes in classifications, and absent specific prohibitions, the employer's actions were allowed under the contract's management-rights clause (*Sewanee Silica Co.*, 47 LA 282).

● An employer did not commit a contract violation when it eliminated a job classification and transferred the associated duties to other, more skilled workers, an arbitrator found. No specific contract provisions forbade such a move, the arbitrator noted. The job protections granted under the contract's seniority provisions did not come into play, the arbitrator added, because employees could only exercise their seniority rights to make claims on work in the same or lower-rated classifications (*Axelson Mfg. Co.*, 30 LA 444; see also 89 LA 113, 71 LA 396).

● Following its purchase of a folding carton plant, an employer was justified in requiring pressmen to operate the cutting press machine without help, an arbitrator ruled. Because the employer made modifications to the equipment that rendered a reduction in crew size feasible and given that the existing contract did not protect or freeze the number of crew members, the arbitrator reasoned that the employer was within its rights to make the change (*Con-

tainer Corp. of America*, 65 LA 517; see also 76 LA 1099, 71 LA 185).

● A union recognition clause did not guarantee that bargaining unit work would not be changed by an employer, according to an arbitrator. An employee lost his job when the employer upgraded some computer equipment and transferred work from one department to another. Noting that the union's recognition clause extended to departments, not to types of work, the arbitrator said the employer's actions were acceptable under the contract's management-rights clause. The computer upgrade was undertaken in good faith and for sound business reasons, the arbitrator observed, adding that the union could not claim jurisdiction over a new system introduced in another department (*McCall Corp.*, 44 LA 201).

● A memorandum of understanding that created certain production coordinators' jobs also specifically granted an employer the right to "recapture" the positions for nonunit workers, up to and including eliminating the jobs altogether, an arbitrator ruled. Despite the union's contention that the elimination of a job category would have to be negotiated, the arbitrator said this job in particular was created outside the normal collective bargaining process as "a gratuitous proposal advanced by management" that could benefit both the employer and the workforce. Nothing was said in the MOU about maintaining the position, the arbitrator concluded, denying the grievance (*Pregis Innovative Packaging Inc.*, 123 LA 1761).

● *By contrast*, an arbitrator ruled that an employer violated its labor contract when it split the duties of welder-inspectors and abolished the entire classification without negotiating with the union. Despite its claims of management prerogative, the employer had to get the union's approval because its collective bargaining agreement specifically stated that job descriptions and classifications had to remain unchanged unless both parties agreed to alter them (*Lone Star Steel Co.*, 26 LA 160).

● An employer could not eliminate an employee's job in the absence of any changes in the work he did, an arbitrator held. The parties' collective bargaining agreement included a management-rights clause that gave the employer the right to make assignments to its workforce, but the contract also prohibited the employer from altering job classifications except in situations where a new job was created or substantive changes were made in the production process. In light of this prohibition, the arbitrator found that the employee's job, which had not changed in content, could not be wiped out by the employer (*Bethlehem Steel Co.*, 17 LA 295).

● Relying on contract provisions that established the rates of pay for various job classifications, another arbitrator ruled that an employer could not unilaterally eliminate a particular classification. Despite the fact that the resulting reallocation of duties would have caused little disruption and posed no undue burden on the workforce, the arbitrator concluded that the employer was required to negotiate with the union before combining or eliminating job classifications (*Kansas Grain Co.*, 29 LA 242).

● Where a contract banned a reduction in existing crew size but permitted negotiations on the number of workers in certain situations, an arbitrator held that management could not negotiate for a smaller crew. Although the contract did not expressly confine negotiations to increasing, rather than decreasing crew sizes, the arbitrator determined that it was the parties' intent to maintain the stated minimum staff levels, at least for the contract term (*Sinclair Oil Corp.*, 41 LA 878; see also 46 LA 503).

● An employer violated its contract when it decided to cut the number of employees on a work crew, an arbitrator ruled, because the contract specified a minimum crew size. In light of that express requirement, the employer had to maintain the minimum number of employees for the duration of the agreement, regardless of whether there was enough work for all the crew members, the arbitrator determined (*Weston Biscuit Co. Inc.*, 21 LA 653).

D. Control of Work Assignments

Management is typically allowed wide discretion in assigning various tasks and duties to individual workers. Arbitrators also give management wide latitude in reassigning work from one classification to another, provided the transferred duties are compatible with those already performed by the recipients of the work. Employers arguably have greater freedom if their collective bargaining agreements do not enumerate the tasks associated with specific classifications, but the existence of detailed job descriptions does not necessarily preclude employers from shifting duties around. The situations that are likely to draw the closest scrutiny from arbitrators are those in which tasks are reassigned outside the bargaining unit.

● An employer's freedom to assign work is not restricted by job descriptions unless the contract expressly says so, an arbitrator held. The purpose of job descriptions, the arbitrator said, is to describe duties for classification purposes rather than to detail each and every job requirement. Unless the collective bargaining agreement states otherwise, he added, management should be free to change duties and assignments, and the employees must perform their assigned tasks, saving their protests for the regular grievance channels (*Pittsburgh Steel Co.*, 34 LA 598; see also 61 LA 808, 53 LA 1130).

● Nothing in a collective bargaining agreement prevented an employer from assigning certain tasks to an employee in a lower classification after determining that higher skill requirements were not necessary to perform the work, an arbitrator ruled. Although the contract called for specified tasks to be performed by craft workers, the arbitrator agreed with the employer that the work in question did not require specialized skills (*General Dynamics Corp.*, 74 LA 1225; see also 21 LA 424).

● Under a contract containing an explicit management-rights clause, an employer had the authority to stop letting workers have a choice, according to seniority, of the machine they would use during their shifts, an arbitrator ruled. Because these selections were not true job vacancies but merely open production-line slots, they were not subject to the contract provisions allowing employees to exercise seniority rights, the arbitrator explained. The right to choose machines arose under a side agreement to a previous contract, and the employer had refused to renew that side agreement because senior staff regularly left the most difficult tasks for inexperienced workers, resulting in more defective products and prompting many customer complaints. The employer had the right to operate its plant so that it produced a quality product, the arbitrator concluded, denying the grievance (*Owens-Illinois Inc.*, 102 LA 1196).

• Another arbitrator ruled that an employer could give employees additional tasks when a new contract dropped the status quo provisions that had prevented unilateral changes in work assignments. Past practice had meant that the employer could not require certain employees to take on extra tasks while their machines were cycling through a process that left them with some free time. Ruling that past practice under a previous contract was not binding unless the language giving rise to that practice was written into the current contract, the arbitrator said the employer was no longer required to assign only one job at a time to the employees (*Overmyer Mould Co. Inc.*, 43 LA 1006).

• An employer had the right to take work away from a group of employees and reassign it upon introducing new equipment, an arbitrator ruled. Although the group had done the work in the recent past, the evidence did not clearly establish that the tasks in question were within the traditional scope of the group's work, the arbitrator noted, deciding that the assignment change constituted a reasonable management decision (*Detroit News*, 62 LA 313).

• An employer had the authority to assign technicians, instead of bargaining unit personnel, to develop a procedure for producing fuel rod simulators under a test program, an arbitrator decided. The union argued that because unit personnel used the same tools, instruments, and procedures as the technicians, it followed that the work performed by the technicians was bargaining unit work. According to the arbitrator, however, the parties' collective bargaining agreement specifically granted the employer the right to assign such work, and having it performed outside the bar-

gaining unit did not violate the contract's recognition clause. Adding that the union was overlooking the needs and purpose of the employer's experimental and research work, the arbitrator said a contrary ruling would have prevented the employer from engaging in essential developmental efforts (*Union Carbide Corp.*, 72 LA 1318; see also 72 LA 927).

• An employer did not commit a contract violation by having a time clerk and a die setter spend part of their day working in other job classifications when various technological changes reduced the amount of work available in their regular jobs, an arbitrator ruled. The union said the employer's actions circumvented procedures for job posting and bidding, but the arbitrator allowed the out-of-classification assignments, noting that the employees still worked in their own classifications more than half the time. If they ever reached the point where they spent a majority of their time on the other jobs, the employer would have to discontinue the existing arrangement and treat the out-of-classification positions like vacancies that were subject to normal bidding procedures, the arbitrator held (*The Fletcher-Enamel Co.*, 27 LA 466).

• An employer had the right to assign to nonunion staff the duties that its receptionists had performed prior to their jobs being eliminated as an economic measure, an arbitrator ruled. According to the arbitrator, there was no contract language expressly prohibiting the employer from shifting work to nonunit employees if the assignments were made in good faith and for good reasons. Because the work had not been performed exclusively by members of the bargaining unit, the effect on the unit was negligible, the arbitrator added (*Lake City Elks Lodge*, 72 LA 643; see also 29 LA 324, 23 LA 561).

• *By contrast*, an arbitrator determined that an employer committed a contract violation when it reassigned clerical duties to a new department outside the bargaining unit. The employer contended that clerical jobs should not have been regarded as part of the unit, but the arbitrator found no evidence that the parties had intended to limit the bargaining unit to production work.

Unless the job modifications were prompted by major technological change or the elimination of a need for the tasks themselves, the employer could not reassign the work and abolish bargaining unit jobs under the guise of management rights, the arbitrator said (*Gisholt Machine Co.*, 44 LA 840).

● An employer violated its labor contract when it assigned plant guards to perform bargaining unit work, an arbitrator held. Even though the contract's only prohibition against the assignment of work to nonunit employees was a ban on supervisors doing unit work, the arbitrator said the employer's actions were nonetheless prohibited because members of the bargaining unit had a vested right in the work. According to the arbitrator, the employer could not deprive the unit members of the work by using individuals from outside the unit to displace them (*Reynolds Metals Co.*, 26 LA 756).

● Another arbitrator held that an employer could not transfer certain tasks from one bargaining unit to another. The employees in a brewer's bottling department had manually tested the strength of drink cans for a number of years. After the employer acquired a machine that could more efficiently prepare the cans for testing, it moved the work to the plant's machinists, who were in a different bargaining unit. The arbitrator found that the nature of the work was not substantially changed by the new equipment and decided that the employer's action violated the contract's recognition clause, which gave the union jurisdiction over the customary work of the bargaining unit. He also determined that the job security clause reserved jobs in the bottling department for employees on the seniority list in that department. Despite the employer's claims that it had the right to operate its plant and make technological improvements as it saw fit, the arbitrator concluded that the resulting alterations in job duties were not permissible (*Hamm Brewing Co.*, 28 LA 46).

1. Work Performed by Supervisors

Disputes over work assignments often involve claims that supervisors have taken on duties or assignments that rightfully belong within the bargaining unit. In many such cases, arbitrators find that employers have committed contract violations by permitting supervisors to perform bargaining unit work. Under unusual circumstances, however, arbitrators are more apt to condone the performance of unit work by supervisors.

● An arbitrator ruled that a university should not have allowed two librarians promoted to supervisor to perform bargaining unit work and fail to fill their vacated unit positions, even though the agreement lacked an express provision prohibiting supervisors from doing unit work. The spirit and purpose of the agreement included protection of the unit from job erosion, and numerous arbitral decisions holding that even in the absence of such a specific proscription, recognition, seniority, and wage clauses warrant finding such a prohibition (*Yeshiva University*, 125 LA 885).

● A fire department violated a collective bargaining contract when it had firefighters and captains, instead of lieutenants—as required by the contract—respond to fires, an arbitrator ruled. Even though there was a past practice of sometimes substituting captains for lieutenants for short periods of absence, the arbitrator noted that lieutenants often were absent for entire days for various reasons, and the department had failed to present evidence that it was without notice of the absences such that it could have made substitutions in personnel (*Union Township*, 124 LA 403).

● An arbitrator ruled an employer did not have the right to direct management and salaried employees to sweep and clean its plant for a half-hour period between shifts, where the work was covered by a contract provision barring salaried employees from doing work normally performed by bargaining unit members. Cleaning did not fall under an exception for work that was "incidental and not to the exclusion of a bargaining unit employee," and the union did not intend for the prohibition to embody the philosophy of management's personal involvement with plant functions (*Ohio Module Manufacturing Co. LLC*, 126 LA 307).

● Even though an employer had the right to assign certain tasks to supervisors on occasion, a contract violation would occur if supervisors were used in a way that would deprive employees in the bargaining unit of available assignments or if supervisors performed significant amounts of unit work, an arbitrator ruled (*Fafnir Bearing Co.*, 39 LA 530).

● When the work associated with a job diminished, an employer could not lay off the bargaining unit member who held the position and use supervisors to do the remaining work, an arbitrator ruled. In its defense, the employer explained that the position was no longer a full-time job, that supervisors had done the work on the employee's days off, and that it needed to cut costs. However, the arbitrator said the supervisors simply were not permitted to do unit work on a regular basis under the parties' collective bargaining agreement. Whatever the employer's financial straits, and despite the employee's ultimately being reassigned elsewhere, the employer could not cut costs by violating the agreement, the arbitrator concluded (*The Levy Co.*, 123 LA 1735).

● An employer that owned a group of cemeteries violated its labor contract when it had a supervisor doing clerical work after a bargaining unit employee quit, an arbitrator ruled. The contract specified that only one supervisor could work at each cemetery, but the employer kept two supervisors at one of its locations and had one of the supervisors do bargaining unit tasks. The employer could have hired a temporary employee, who would not have been subject to the collective bargaining agreement, but instead it violated the contract by slotting a supervisor into the bargaining unit job, the arbitrator observed (*Mikocem LLC*, 121 LA 1377).

● An employer could not have a supervisor take over the assignments of a bargaining unit worker who was on layoff, an arbitrator held. Although the parties' collective bargaining agreement did not ban supervisors from doing production work, it did state that no employee would be temporarily transferred to a job in another department where the employee regularly handling the job was on layoff. In light of this clause, the arbitrator said the most the supervisor could do was assist a member of the bargaining unit in carrying out the laid-off worker's assignments (*Sayles Biltmore Bleacheries Inc.*, 26 LA 585).

● An employer could not assign a shipping checker's duties to a foreman without union consent, an arbitrator held. As part of their contract negotiations, the employer and union had addressed the content of the shipping checker's job and set down its description as part of the collective bargaining agreement. In light of this fact, the arbitrator said the employer would be in violation of the agreement if it acted unilaterally in assigning the associated tasks to the foreman (*Kraft Foods Corp.*, 10 LA 254).

● Another arbitrator, noting that a contract's definition of bargaining unit work was ambiguous, examined the way the definition had been applied in the past and determined that an employer could not allow supervisors to perform work normally assigned to the bargaining unit. Over a period of three years, management had progressively withdrawn supervisors from performing tasks whenever the union claimed that the work in question belonged to the bargaining unit. Because management itself had given this consistent interpretation to the contract, the arbitrator found it binding (*Los Angeles Drug Co.*, 29 LA 38; see also 75 LA 540, 27 LA 748).

● Under a contract containing a general ban on the performance of production work by supervisors, an arbitrator ruled that an employer violated the contract by assigning supervisors to such work, outside regular hours, as a way of proving that its production standards were fair. Noting that the contract did allow supervisors to perform production work for the purpose of instructing employees, the arbitrator added that the employer's actions would have been acceptable if the employees who regularly performed the work had been called in to observe the demonstration (*National Lead Co.*, 34 LA 235).

● *By contrast*, an arbitrator ruled that a publisher had the right to use its presses to train management personnel, notwithstanding the union's contention that the parties' labor contract established the union's jurisdiction over operation of the presses. The arbitrator pointed out that if the union wanted to prevent the publisher from using the presses for management training, it should have negotiated for the inclusion of specific language to that effect in the collective bargaining agreement (*Sacramento Newspaper Publishers Assn.*, 62 LA 1112).

● An arbitrator ruled that a union did not meet its burden of proving that the employer violated a provision of the collective bargaining contract providing that a supervisor may do unit work so long as the work "is not intended to displace any Parts Department employee." A manager did unit work while the employee was on layoff, and it was difficult to fathom management's "intent" and even more difficult to hold that the employee already on layoff had been "displaced" by intermittent work by a manager on a few given days (*Reco Equipment Inc.*, 126 LA 1131).

● When technological improvements resulted in a worker's duties being taken over by a machine, an employer was justified in assigning the job of monitoring the equipment to a supervisor rather than the displaced worker. Despite specific contract clauses prohibiting supervisors from doing unit work, the arbitrator said the monitoring task was closer to the normal duties of supervisors than to the work done by bargaining unit employees. At the same time, however, the arbitrator held that if supervisors were to operate the machines manually or do physical work in cleaning, repairing, or adjusting them, that would be a violation of the contract (*Goodyear Tire & Rubber Co.*, 35 LA 917).

● An employer did not violate its labor contract when it transferred supervisors to bargaining unit jobs during slack seasons, an arbitrator found. The contract clearly stated that the employer could hire or retain as many as 30 employees, in any category, if the employer determined that their special training, experience, or ability was needed. In light of the fact that the contract made the employer the "sole judge" of who needed to be retained, it had the right to make 30 transfers of nonunit employees to bargaining unit jobs as long as it did not act in bad faith, the arbitrator said (*Jefferson City Cabinet Co.*, 35 LA 117).

● A contractual ban on assigning supervisors to bargaining unit work did not apply during a strike, an arbitrator ruled. Such a ban was designed to protect the job rights of union members on duty or available for work, but it could not apply when the members in question had refused to work, the arbitrator reasoned, noting that in such a case they could not be said to be displaced by supervisors (*Texas Gas Corp.*, 36 LA 1141; see also 75 LA 1302).

● Another contract barred an employer from using supervisors in a way that would deprive bargaining unit members of work, but it allowed supervisors to perform bargaining unit tasks if all active employees were working a regularly scheduled 40-hour week. An arbitrator denied a grievance over the work performed by supervisors in the wake of a strike, finding that the employer met the contract's requirements. According to the arbitrator, the employer had made sincere efforts to induce employees to return to work after the strike but had met with limited success, and supervisors merely filled in where needed as opposed to permanently replacing any bargaining unit employees (*American Sugar Refining Co.*, 123 LA 277).

● An arbitrator held that an employer could continue to have a working foreman perform production work after he became assistant superintendent. Although the contract mentioned a limit of three supervisors, the arbitrator determined that the cap must have been meant to apply only to the number of working supervisors. The arbitrator concluded that the assistant superintendent could continue doing production work as one of the three working supervisors, and the employer was not restricted by the contract when making staffing decisions with regard to supervisors who did not perform production work (*Mt. Carmel Public Utility Co.*, 16 LA 59).

● An employer was justified in having a supervisor fill in on a shift and perform bargaining unit work, an arbitrator held, in spite of the fact that contractual provisions prohibited supervisors from regularly handling the tasks intended for unit members. In this case, the arbitrator noted that the only unit employee who was interested in working the shift already had worked two consecutive shifts, and the contract barred him from working another full shift (*Avecia Inc.*, 120 LA 368).

• An employer had the right to assign supervisors to replace a sprinkler valve that had blown off and caused water to spill into an oil room, an arbitrator decided. Despite the fact that the work customarily was done by pipefitters, the arbitrator upheld management's action, citing the fact that there was a bona fide emergency (*Diamond National Corp.*, 61 LA 567).

• Similarly, a brewery did not violate a contract ban on the performance of bargaining unit work by supervisory personnel when, during the course of repair of a malfunctioning machine by a machinist who was not wearing a safety shield, a supervisor pushed away bottles on a conveyor that were moving toward the machine, an arbitrator held. The danger of an explosion arising from the flow of the bottles constituted an emergency that permitted the supervisor to act, the arbitrator reasoned, denying the grievance (*Anheuser Busch Inc.*, 62 LA 1130; see also 71 LA 454).

• An employer did not violate its labor contract, which prohibited foremen and supervisors from doing bargaining unit work "except in an emergency, to protect life or property," when it allowed them to do unit work for a few minutes at a time for justified reasons, an arbitrator held. The contract was not clear about whether other situations to protect property and production also were covered exceptions, the arbitrator said, so the parties' past practice had to provide the basis for the ruling. Without complaint or grievance by the union, supervisors had been allowed for some time to help out on the production line in such situations as when employees took bathroom breaks, the arbitrator noted. Although the union now contested these actions, the arbitrator concluded that the grievance was without merit given the union's long silence on the matter (*Standard Furniture Mfg. Co.*, 122 LA 986).

2. Application of 'De Minimus' Principle

Arbitrators may decide to overlook a technical violation of a ban on supervisors performing bargaining unit work when violations are so minor as to warrant application of the "de minimus" principle, which calls for ignoring inconsequential violations. For instance, no substantive violation was found when one supervisor flicked a switch or when another supervisor dusted and swept an office where there was no indication that an employee was adversely affected (53 LA 706, 52 LA 49).

• A mine operator did not violate a contract when a foreman loaded roof bolting supplies found in a transport vehicle usually used to get to various sections of the mine, an arbitrator held. Even assuming that the operation of the vehicle to move the bolting supplies was work that normally would have been performed by bargaining unit employees, the supervisor's handling of the task, which took no more than 25 minutes, was allowed under the de minimus principle, the arbitrator concluded (*Consolidation Coal Co.*, 65 LA 892; see also 75 LA 569).

• Another arbitrator rejected an employer's contention that the use of supervisors to do two hours of bargaining unit work was allowed under the de minimus principle. The contract prohibited supervisors from taking on assignments normally given to unit workers except in emergencies. Although the employer claimed that a backlog of work constituted an emergency, the arbitrator said the backlog was foreseeable, and bargaining unit employees could have performed the work on an overtime basis. Accordingly, the arbitrator ordered the employer to provide two hours of overtime pay to the three most senior members on the volunteer overtime roster (*Americold Logistics LLC*, 118 LA 1720).

• Similarly, an arbitrator ruled that a coal company violated a collective bargaining contract, which generally barred supervisors from doing unit work, when it had supervisors unload between 10,000 and 12,000 tons of coal on two days union members were off work for contractual memorial days, despite the union's contention that the work was de minimus, because that argument defied common sense, the arbitrator said (*Dynamic Energy Inc.*, 129 LA 745).

• An arbitrator ruled that a hotel-casino violated a collective bargaining agreement when it laid off its restaurant's cashiers and transferred their duties to food servers, because the transferred duties were not de minimus, the agreement did not give the hotel-casino the right to combine classifications unilaterally, except as to "branded, fine dining venues," which the restaurant was not, and the single prior instance in which the employer transferred cashier duties to fountain servers at the food court did not constitute a past practice (*Caesars Palace*, 128 LA 299).

3. Work in the Media

● An arbitrator ruled that a television station violated a collective bargaining contract when it assigned an executive producer, who had previously been a reporter, to a broadcast sweeps story on a particular crime, even though the producer had contacts that enabled her to do the original story better than the unit reporter might, where the sweeps story was just an update and was not as fresh as the original (*Youngstown Television LLC*, 124 LA 589).

● By contrast, an arbitrator upheld a newspaper's right to allowing a music editor, who was a supervisor, to edit the work of freelancers, where being the music editor and supervisor were not mutually exclusive, and editors in and outside of the bargaining unit were permitted to edit freelancers' work (*Village Voice*, 123 LA 1279).

E. Control of Rules and Policies

Arbitrators consistently acknowledge that management has the right to establish workplace rules and policies, provided they are reasonable and consistent with the collective bargaining agreement (93 LA 1082, 92 LA 68, 91 LA 1251, 90 LA 729, 90 LA 625, 88 LA 1164, 77 LA 705). However, rules and policies adopted by employers have been held unreasonable and unenforceable if they are vague, ineffective, arbitrary, or discriminatory; if they are overly broad; or if they unduly infringe on the private lives of employees (97 LA 675, 96 LA 122, 95 LA 729, 93 LA 1070, 77 LA 807, 72 LA 588, 26 LA 934, 18 LA 400).

● An employer's unilateral implementation of a smoking ban was in keeping with the rights of management to promulgate workplace rules and protect employees' safety and health, an arbitrator decided. Asserting that the ban affected "conditions of employment," the union argued that the employer could not impose the new policy during the term of the parties' collective bargaining agreement unless it first negotiated with the union. The arbitrator disagreed, finding no limitation in the agreement "on the reserved right of management to establish health policy or any other work rule." The arbitrator also found that the policy was reasonable "in that it clearly relates to legitimate Company objectives, applies equally to everyone, and makes no attempt to dictate employee behavior off Company premises" (*Witco Corp.*, 96 LA 499; see also 92 LA 390, 92 LA 181, 91 LA 375, 72 LA 258).

● An arbitrator upheld a new attendance policy initiated by an employer under a contract that said "maintenance of order and efficiency are solely the responsibility of management." Although the union argued that the employer was required to bargain over the new policy, the arbitrator found that the employer's only obligation under the contract was to submit new rules to the union before they became effective, and that obligation had been satisfied (*Simpson Industries*, 104 LA 568).

● A work rule prohibiting firearms on company property was reasonable, an arbitrator found, citing management's obligation to take precautions for protecting employee health and safety (*Gardner-Denver Cooper Industries*, 76 LA 26).

● A public utility properly instituted a residency policy that restricted how far away from work employees could live, an arbitrator ruled. The policy was aimed at limiting the amount of time it would take employees to report when they were called out during emergencies. According to the arbitrator, the residency requirement was reasonably related to the employer's obligation to restore power as quickly as possible in situations involving the disruption of service. In addition, the arbitrator noted that the employer had the express right under the parties' collective bargaining agreement to adopt or revise reasonable rules in the interest of efficient operations, continuity of service, and safety (*Potomac Edison Co.*, 96 LA 1012).

● An employer had the authority to restrict employees' use of single-day vacations to five per year, an arbitrator decided. The union argued that the employer could not unilaterally alter its past practice of allowing employees to use vacation leave in one-day increments without limitation. However, the arbitrator pointed out that the parties' collective bargaining agreement contained a strong management-rights clause that gave the employer "all functions of management" unless they were explicitly limited by the agreement. Thus, the employer had reserved the right "to create and modify" rules and policies on the use of vacation leave, the arbitrator found (*Sealy Mattress Co.*, 121 LA 883).

● In upholding an employer's unilateral implementation of new safety rules, an arbitrator based his decision on the fact that the union had agreed to "unequivocal" contract language approving management's right to set safety standards (*Armstrong World Industries Inc.*, 122 LA 1038).

● *By contrast*, another arbitrator held that an employer could not bar employees from wearing beach clothes when walking to and from plant gates, in amplification of a safety rule that prohibited loose clothing or jewelry when employees were moving around machinery. The rule went substantially beyond the scope of the general rule and constituted unreasonable interference with the personal freedom of employees to come and go from their work areas, the ar-

bitrator concluded (*Babcock & Wilcox*, 73 LA 443).

● An employer's rule excluding all food items from a communications room, unless employees had a medical reason for eating, was overly broad, an arbitrator found. It was a common practice for office workers to keep mints, cough drops, and hard candies at their desks in case their mouths got dry, the arbitrator observed. In addition, the employees should have been permitted to bring in breakfast or energy bars for a quick snack, especially since they worked 10-hour days, the arbitrator said (*Valley Communications Center*, 119 LA 1767).

● An employer was prohibited from implementing a rule that would subject employees to disciplinary layoffs whenever they were more than 15 minutes late in returning from meal or rest breaks, an arbitrator held. The parties' collective bargaining agreement stated that existing rules and penalties could not be changed for the duration of the agreement. Although the employer claimed that it was issuing a new rule as opposed to modifying an existing one, the arbitrator found that the employer's practice had been to treat late returns from meal and rest breaks the same as tardiness infractions. Imposing disciplinary layoffs for such infractions would conflict with the employer's existing rules, which did not specify any penalties for employees' first two tardiness offenses and only called for a written warning after a third offense (*Wolverine Aluminum Corp.*, 74 LA 252).

II. Subcontracting & Outsourcing [LA CDI 117.389]

_____ **OVERVIEW** _____

Arbitration cases involving subcontracting and outsourcing typically pit legitimate management and labor interests against each other. On one side, employers are striving for efficient and economical operations. On the other, unions are trying to keep as much work as possible within the bargaining unit.

When considering the propriety of subcontracting, arbitrators look first and foremost at whether contract language allows or forbids the practice. In the absence of subcontracting restrictions, arbitrators generally agree that employers can contract out for the performance of work by nonemployees if the decision is made in good faith for legitimate business reasons and does not significantly harm the bargaining unit or employee interests.

To determine if subcontracting is excessively harmful, arbitrators consider various factors, such as whether it results in layoffs or job losses, substitutes for the recall of laid-off employees, or causes workers to lose hours and income. Arbitrators also look askance at subcontracting if it is used to discriminate against unions or workers.

Taken to the extreme, subcontracting has the potential to subvert collective bargaining agreements and threaten entire bargaining units. According to one arbitrator, a unit's retention of existing jobs and duties is a central assumption underlying the bargaining process. "A company and union do not bargain for wages, hours, overtime, etc., in a vacuum. They bargain for the performance of certain *work*, and set the terms of such performance. If, having set those terms, the Company can avoid compliance by the simple device of contracting, the entire contract could become a nullity," the arbitrator said (*Pet Milk Co.*, 33 LA 278).

As a separate consideration in weighing the propriety of subcontracting, arbitrators consider whether employers have given unions prior notice of the intent to outsource work. Even in the absence of contract language requiring notification or consultation with unions, arbitrators sometimes hold that employers should provide notice so the parties will have a chance to engage in meaningful discussions before subcontracting is put into effect.

SUMMARY OF CASES

A. Authority to Subcontract Work

Some collective bargaining agreements specifically address subcontracting, while others are silent on the matter. If contract language does not expressly prohibit the practice, arbitrators often find that management rights clauses give employers the authority to engage in subcontracting. However, arbitrators sometimes find that restrictions on outsourcing are implied by other contract provisions, such as recognition clauses and clauses that bar employers from transferring work out of the bargaining unit.

● An employer violated a collective bargaining agreement when it outsourced work after laying off employees who had performed it, because neither the parties' negotiations nor other language modified the agreement's stipulation that an employer "'will not contract out work' normally performed in the plant . . . whenever there are qualified Employees . . . on lay off with recall rights" (*GBC Metals LLC*, 128 LA 554).

● Under a collective bargaining agreement that prohibited an employer from assigning the work of bargaining unit employees to individuals outside the unit, an arbitrator found that shifting certain duties to an out-of-state contractor constituted a contract violation. The clause prohibiting the assignment of work outside the unit implied an agreement not to subcontract, according to the arbitrator (*National Distillers & Chemical Corp.*, 76 LA 286).

● Under a similar contract, an employer lacked the right to have a contractor clean its lot and outside bathrooms, an arbitrator determined. While conceding that the employer generally had broad discretion in subcontracting decisions, the arbitrator noted that cleaning of the lot and outside bathrooms had historically been performed by members of the bargaining unit, and the contract barred the shifting of service work to anyone outside the unit. Even though the move did not displace any current employees, the union faced a loss of bargaining unit positions when the employer decided to forego the job posting and bidding process, the arbitrator found. To remedy the situation, the arbitrator ordered the employer to restore the work to the bargaining unit and reimburse employees who lost opportunities to perform the services that were shifted to the contractor (*ATC/Phoenix Co.*, 122 LA 481; see also 120 LA 522).

● Another arbitrator relied on the recognition clause of a collective bargaining agreement in finding that an employer could not outsource for the performance of a job that had traditionally been part of the bargaining unit. The recognition clause did not list the positions for which the union would serve as employees' exclusive bargaining agent, but other contract provisions made specific reference to the job in question. Despite the absence of any express restrictions on subcontracting, the arbitrator said that if she allowed "the unilateral transfer of bargaining unit work to an independent contractor, she would be undermining all of the bargaining unit positions that have been recognized as being part of this unit. No job would be free from outsourcing" (*Port of Seattle*, 110 LA 753; see also 79 LA 1273, 42 LA 1121, 21 LA 713).

● An employer could not contract out for the performance of work that laid-off employees were capable of performing, an arbitrator decided. Although the employer had a practice of engaging in subcontracting for the short-term performance of specialty work, it had not previously done so for jobs of a permanent nature, as was the case here. Moreover, the arbitrator found, subcontracting of the work in question was inherently precluded by the parties' collective bargaining agreement, which stated that all work that fell within the experience and qualifications of employees in the bargaining unit was to be performed by the unit. The arbitrator did not order the immediate termination of the subcontracting arrangement but did require the employer to reimburse the affected employees for the hours they would have worked if subcontracting had not occurred (*American Crystal Sugar Co.*, 116 LA 916).

● An arbitrator held that a hospital's subcontracting of a backlog of medical transcription work normally performed by bargaining unit employees violated a collective bargaining agreement that obligated the employer to make a good-faith effort to preserve bargaining unit work. Pointing out that the transcription backlog had accumulated over an extended period of time, the arbitrator said the obligation of good faith was hardly satisfied when the situation that the hospital cited as justification for subcontracting was one that the hospital itself had negligently allowed to develop (*Fairmont General Hospital*, 105 LA 247).

● *By contrast*, an arbitrator upheld a manufacturer of pulp and paper products' right to subcontract 16 days of electrical work, even though three electricians had earlier been laid off, because they had elected their contractual right to refuse recalls of less than 30 days. The contract allowed laid off employees to refuse recall to jobs lasting thirty days or less. Each laid off craftsman had exercised this right and none had advised management of a desire to change his mind before the decision to hire Albany Electric was made. "The employer had every right to respect their wishes, therefore, and was under no duty to recall them before letting out the basement wall lighting," the arbitrator said (*Georgia-Pacific*, 126 LA 253).

● An arbitrator ruled that an employer did not breach a contract's union-security clause by contracting out for the performance of marginal work that was previously assigned to the bargaining unit. An underlying consideration in granting union security was to increase efficiency, and the arbitrator determined that transferring the duties in question to an outside contractor did not violate the clause because the move would foster higher levels of efficiency. Under a management rights clause, meanwhile, the contract exclusively reserved to the employer the authority to run its operations as long as its actions did not violate any other contract provisions. No provisions were violated by subcontracting the marginal work, according to the arbitrator, who also noted that the employer had repeatedly rejected various union contract proposals that would have imposed restrictions on subcontracting (*Olin Corp.*, 109 LA 919).

● An arbitrator ruled that an employer did not violate a collective bargaining agreement when it contracted out a tool room position, even though a supplemental memorandum of agreement in the contract stated that this position "will be backfilled from" the maintenance division, because the memorandum did not state that the position shall not be subcontracted, and no employee was so affected by the company's action (*Chevron Oronite Co. Inc.*, 129 LA 528).

● The recognition clause of a contract did not bar a glassware manufacturer from using a contractor to repackage its products for a pair of national retail chains, an arbitrator ruled. The recognition clause defined the bargaining unit and protected against the transfer of covered positions outside the unit, but the parties never intended it to prohibit subcontracting, the arbitrator decided. Under a separate clause that allowed for department-specific agreements, the parties had stipulated that such pacts could not conflict with the overall contract, yet they had provided for subcontracting in one departmental agreement, the arbitrator pointed out. Moreover, the arbitrator found, the employer had subcontracted repackaging work for many years, its actions did not harm the bargaining unit or show any indications of bad faith, and the cost considerations involved in the subcontracting decision were not aimed at maximizing profits but rather at retaining major customers and preserving existing jobs (*Libbey Glass Inc.*, 116 LA 182; see also 111 LA 879).

• An employer did not commit a contract violation when it eliminated a bargaining unit position and contracted out for the performance of janitorial work, an arbitrator found. In this case, the management rights clause in the parties' collective bargaining agreement specified that the employer had the authority to reconfigure and abolish jobs, and there was no conflicting provision that limited this authority, the arbitrator observed. The fact that the janitorial position was listed in the contract at the time it was written did not guarantee the position's continued existence for the full term of the contract or waive management's right to abolish the job and make other arrangements for the performance of the work, the arbitrator said (*James River Corp.*, 104 LA 475).

B. Reasonableness, Good Faith, and Other Considerations

Broad contract clauses on management rights and union recognition play a part in many subcontracting cases, but arbitrators seldom base their decisions solely on such clauses. On the contrary, the outcome typically hinges on a range of considerations, including the following:

• *Context and surrounding factors*— for each case, there are background issues such as past practice and the bargaining history of the parties that can provide arbitrators with a context in which to review subcontracting. Arbitrators also tend to weigh a variety of other factors, including whether the subcontracted work is temporary rather than permanent or involves ancillary rather than integral functions.

• *The reasons for subcontracting*— certain business justifications can persuade arbitrators to look favorably on subcontracting. For example, arbitrators are more likely to uphold subcontracting if employers lack available employees who can handle the work, if employers do not have the necessary equipment, or if the subcontracting is prompted by an unusual situation or some urgent need. Employers often cite cost savings as a reason for subcontracting, but arbitrators are not always swayed by this justification. While it is true that costs can overshadow other considerations in cases where a company's survival is at stake, arbitrators commonly reject subcontracting based solely on economic reasons, especially if employers achieve savings by laying off employees and eliminating bargaining unit jobs.

• *The impact of subcontracting*—when considering the impact of subcontracting, arbitrators focus primarily on whether it harms the bargaining unit and its members. The greater the harm, the more likely it is that subcontracting will be condemned.

In addition, various arbitrators have laid out guidelines and principles that provide a framework for evaluating the propriety of subcontracting. For instance, one arbitrator indicated that employers must act "in good faith and without deliberate intent to injure" their workers (*National Sugar Refining Co.*, 13 LA 991).

Another arbitrator insisted on applying the so-called "rule of reasonableness." Rejecting the notion that an employer could contract out bargaining unit work without limitation because its labor contract was silent on the matter, the arbitrator took the position that management "is under an implied limitation to act reasonably and in a manner that will not erode or defeat the basic purposes of the bargaining agreement and the rights it was intended to protect" (*Kenworth Truck Co.*, 73 LA 947).

For disputes in which collective bargaining agreements lack subcontracting restrictions, perhaps the most well-known guidelines came from an arbitrator who said "the general arbitration rule is that management has the right to contract out work as long as the action is performed in good faith, it represents a reasonable business decision, it does not result in a subversion of the labor agreement, and it does not have the effect of seriously weakening the bargaining unit or important parts of it" (*Shenango Valley Water Co.*, 53 LA 741).

More extensive guidelines have been developed by other arbitrators. As an example, the following list summarizes one arbitrator's ground rules for evaluating the propriety of subcontracting:

● employers cannot violate specific contract clauses or the spirit of the collective bargaining agreement;

● they have to act reasonably, in good faith, and in accordance with past practice; and

● subcontracting must be dictated by business requirements and deprive no more than a few workers of employment.

The same arbitrator also cited other factors in upholding an employer's decision to use a contractor instead of its own maintenance employees to perform electrical work over a three-month period. For instance, the arbitrator noted that the maintenance employees were not capable of handling the work, they remained fully employed and were putting in overtime during the period in question, and subcontracting was not done to eliminate any jobs or to have the work performed at a cheaper rate (*General American Door Co.*, 115 LA 1697; see also 37 LA 334).

1. Balancing of Factors

In the final analysis, the outcome of many disputes depends not only on the facts and circumstances surrounding subcontracting, but also on how much weight arbitrators give the different criteria that form the basis of their rulings. While these elements can vary greatly from case to case, one theme that repeatedly emerges is the need to balance the interests of employers against the interests of unions and the workers they represent.

● An arbitrator overturned an employer's subcontracting of janitorial work and awarded reinstatement with back pay to three employees affected by the move. After examining a host of rulings and commentaries on subcontracting, the arbitrator warned that "there is no certainty in this area, no absolute truth." Nevertheless, he declared that "all of the cases in this area attempt to strike a fair balance" by evaluating three factors: the type of work subcontracted, the reasons for subcontracting, and the impact on the bargaining unit and its members.

The arbitrator said the first factor weighed in the employer's favor, because janitorial work was not an essential part of the business, and such work "can often be done better and cheaper by outside specialists." Regarding the reasons for subcontracting, the arbitrator found that the employer's primary goal was to save money by avoiding the costly wages and benefits required under its labor contract. This factor weighed in the union's favor, the arbitrator said, because the "implied covenant of good faith and fair dealing" underlying the parties' contract imposed an obligation not to engage in subcontracting just to obtain cheaper labor. The arbitrator said the deciding factor was the impact of the subcontracting. It deprived three employees of their jobs and harmed the entire bargaining unit, in part because the union had made it a priority in contract negotiations to bargain for wage settlements that would benefit these lower-paid workers. According to the arbitrator, when the employer engaged in subcontracting and abolished the janitorial jobs, it gained back part of what it had given up during contract negotiations, while the bargaining unit "lost a crucial element of its bargain" (*Uniroyal Inc.*, 76 LA 1049).

● Another arbitrator barred an employer from subcontracting all of its truck maintenance and repair work. The arbitrator cited the "covenant of fair dealing between contracting parties," saying one party "cannot subvert the agreement by conduct seeking to deprive the other party of the bargain that was struck." This implied covenant has prompted arbitrators to reject subcontracting arrangements that deprive unions of what they have gained through collective bargaining "unless an employer can demonstrate a special business need that outweighs the loss caused the members of the bargaining unit," the arbitrator said. For instance, subcontracting would be justified in emergency situations requiring efforts beyond the capacity of available employees, the arbitrator observed, or to obtain the use of equipment that is not readily available to the employer, or even for economic reasons if the savings are considerable and subcontracting has minimal impact on employees.

In the case at hand, the arbitrator held that the circumstances surrounding subcontracting required a finding against the employer. "The work by the subcontractors was performed by the same personnel, under the same circumstances, at the same location, using the same equipment, without any explanation for the change," the arbitrator noted. This alone was sufficient to find a violation, according to the arbitrator, but he also determined that the company's elimination of its repair and maintenance unit diminished the bargaining unit and attacked the integrity of the labor agreement (*Campbell Truck Co.*, 73 LA 1036; see also 86 LA 945).

• A publisher violated the labor agreement covering its skilled mailers when it announced that it would eliminate the bargaining unit and subcontract all mailing work, an arbitrator found. The employer's action did not constitute a "reasonable business decision," since its intent was to "reduce labor costs at the expense of undermining the integrity and strength, and eventual existence, of the bargaining unit," the arbitrator said. There was no imminent threat to the company's economic survival, no need for new equipment or facilities, no time pressure for completing the work, and no emergency that might have made subcontracting necessary, the arbitrator noted. Because the subcontracting was permanent rather than temporary, the arbitrator added, even a reasonable justification would have been outweighed by the harm to the union and unit employees (*The Advertiser Co.*, 89 LA 71; see also 95 LA 344).

• In a case involving janitorial work, an arbitrator based his decision in favor of a union on a balancing of various considerations, including the fact that contracting out would be on a permanent basis and would displace five long-time employees (*Sealtest Foods*, 48 LA 797).

• An employer committed a contract violation by contracting out for extra security services during a strike, an arbitrator decided. The employer cited the emergency nature of the situation and claimed that subcontracting was more economical than hiring additional guards. Using an "inexact" balancing test to weigh the parties'

interests, the arbitrator determined that the damage to the union's representational rights exceeded the employer's operational burdens in this case. The arbitrator's decision hinged in part on the fact that the strike dragged on for several months. The employer would have been justified in avoiding the costs and difficulties of hiring more guards if it reasonably believed the strike would be brief, but management had acknowledged early on that the strike would be a lengthy one, the arbitrator noted. At that moment, the balance shifted in favor of the union, and its right to represent individuals performing bargaining unit work outweighed the employer's burdens of hiring and training more guards, the arbitrator said (*Pemco Aeroplex Inc.*, 109 LA 385).

• An employer did not have the right to unilaterally contract out bargaining unit work during a time when maintenance mechanics were on layoff, an arbitrator ruled. Even though the magnitude of the job, in addition to the rush nature of the work, justified contracting out a portion of the task, the subcontracting deprived unit employees of work they would have customarily performed, the arbitrator found. The employer contended that contracting out the work was not an effort to undermine the union, but the arbitrator emphasized that the injuries done to the workers and the potential damage to the union were of paramount importance. According to the arbitrator, the adverse effect that the subcontracting caused the unit was the same as if the employer had intended to undermine the union (*Consolidated Aluminum Co.*, 66 LA 1170; see also 119 LA 241).

• Despite the fact that an employer would have saved $350,000 a year by subcontracting pickup and delivery work, an arbitrator found that the savings involved did not justify the elimination of its transportation department and the resulting diminution of the bargaining unit. The economic justification would have carried more weight if the company's survival were at stake, but that was not the situation here, the arbitrator observed. In addition to citing costs as a reason for the subcontracting, the employer emphasized that the affected drivers were "non-core employees." However, the arbitrator found this justification troubling. If the drivers' categorization as non-core employees were accepted as a reasonable basis for subcontracting, then everyone who was not directly engaged in manufacturing the company's product could be replaced by subcontractors, the arbitrator said, and this would amount to "a serious subversion of the labor agreement and an undermining of the bargaining unit" (*Hughes Electron Dynamics*, 115 LA 473).

• On the other hand, an arbitrator upheld an employer's decision to contract out an ancillary portion of its business that was inefficient, costly, and involved the use of antiquated equipment. The employer operated a paper mill that used wood chips as raw material, some of which came from its own wood yard. However, the expenses involved in operating the wood yard were excessive when compared with industry norms. Equipment problems alone increased the employer's costs by hundreds of thousands of dollars per year. Rather than spending the $25 million that was required to bring the wood yard up to par, the employer outsourced that part of its business and absorbed the affected employees into its remaining workforce without any layoffs or pay cuts.

Even though the outsourcing decision led to the eventual elimination of more than 30 union jobs, the arbitrator found that the impact on the bargaining unit was outweighed by business necessity and surrounding factors, such as the incidental nature of the wood yard operation, an extensive past practice of contracting out work, and a bargaining history in which the employer repeatedly rejected union efforts to impose subcontracting restrictions. According to the arbitrator, contracting out the wood yard was the employer's best option for ensuring the viability of the mill and preserving the rest of the jobs in the bargaining unit. This decision constituted a "reasonable, good faith business judgment" based on factors other than labor costs, the arbitrator said, pointing in particular to the need to replace the wood yard's outdated equipment, which the contractor was willing to do at its own expense (*Packaging*

Corp. of America, 122 LA 1158; see also 112 LA 1082, 86 LA 81).

• An employer that subcontracted some out-of-state product deliveries for economic reasons did not violate its labor contract, an arbitrator ruled. The employer had drivers on layoff at the time, but they were recalled soon thereafter. Thus, the arbitrator said it was "difficult to believe that the subcontracting was done to circumvent the contract or to destroy or weaken the collective bargaining relationship." Since a union's goal in obtaining a labor contract is to provide job security and the opportunity to perform available work, any subcontracting of tasks that might otherwise be performed by the bargaining unit could be viewed as an attempt to defeat the contract's intent, the arbitrator pointed out. "On the other hand, it is equally well established that management has the right to efficiently conduct its business," which includes the right to subcontract work if it does so in good faith without trying to harm its employees, the arbitrator said.

In this case, the arbitrator found that the employer made a good faith subcontracting decision based on the savings involved. The arbitrator also noted that the employer had a past practice of subcontracting out-of-state deliveries, and there was no language in the parties' collective bargaining agreement that would bar the practice. Adding that the union had bargained for a prohibition on subcontracting but had failed, the arbitrator declared that the union could not accomplish through arbitration what it was unable to achieve through contract negotiations (*Burger Iron Co.*, 78 LA 57).

• In another case, an arbitrator upheld an employer's subcontracting of repair work but warned that the absence of contractual restrictions on subcontracting did not mean the employer had carte blanche to contract out bargaining unit work. Rather, the arbitrator subscribed to the approach delineated in *Shenango Valley Water Co.* (see above), which permits employers to engage in subcontracting if they do so reasonably and in good faith without subverting the collective bargaining agreement or weakening the bargaining unit. The employer testified that the repair work needed to occur over a weekend and that its employees had refused weekend work, thus establishing the good faith and reasonableness of its subcontracting decision, the arbitrator observed. In weighing the impact of the subcontracting, the arbitrator said neither the collective bargaining agreement nor the bargaining unit was damaged; this was an isolated incident that did not impinge on employees' regular work (*Blue Diamond Coal Co.*, 78 LA 702).

● An employer's subcontracting of cleaning services was justified in conjunction with the relocation of its main offices, an arbitrator decided. At the old location, the offices were cleaned by production technicians as a small part of their duties, and they typically did the work only when conditions became unbearable. At its new, larger location, the employer insisted on a higher quality of cleaning services due to the presence of visitors. The arbitrator agreed that increased janitorial demands warranted the use of an outside contractor. Rather than paying hourly technician rates for lackluster cleaning work, it was reasonable to pay a contractor a monthly rate for janitorial services and obtain the use of equipment and specialized abilities that the employer lacked, the arbitrator said. After weighing these and other factors, the arbitrator decided that the employer's business justifications for subcontracting outweighed the union's interests in opposing it (*Illinois-American Water Co.*, 117 LA 647; see also 101 LA 258).

● Another arbitrator upheld an employer's hiring of an outside contractor to perform night janitorial duties. The employer saved money without harming existing employees, who retained their jobs and received less onerous schedules when the night duties were contracted out, the arbitrator noted. Due to fluctuating time and manpower requirements, the arbitrator added, the overnight cleaning did not lend itself to the scheduling of regular employees. Also, the contractor was capable of performing work that was more sophisticated than what bargaining unit employees could do and that required equipment the employer did not have, the arbitrator said

(*Transit Authority of River City*, 74 LA 616; see also 104 LA 1107).

● An employer did not commit a contract violation by hiring a contractor to paint its buildings, an arbitrator decided. Several maintenance employees were on layoff when the project was carried out, and the union argued that they were entitled to the work. The arbitrator disagreed, citing a past practice of subcontracting and a bargaining history that showed no indication of a mutual intent to prohibit the practice. The arbitrator also looked favorably on the fact that the work was temporary in nature and part of a special project, because if it was continuous or involved routine maintenance, that "would tend to undermine the bargaining unit and the employment of bargaining unit employees." Furthermore, the arbitrator noted that the employer did not have all the necessary equipment, and economic considerations weighed in favor of subcontracting the work. Taken together, the evidence showed that the employer's actions were dictated by legitimate business reasons and were not intended to subvert the collective bargaining agreement, the arbitrator said (*Federal Mogul Corp.*, 82 LA 441).

2. Satisfying Contractual Conditions

Many collective bargaining agreements contain provisions that permit or restrict subcontracting under certain circumstances. For example, it is common to prohibit subcontracting if it results in layoffs. In the presence of provisions giving employers conditional authority to engage in subcontracting, arbitrators shift their attention from weighing the justifications and harmfulness of subcontracting and focus instead on determining whether the contractual conditions have been satisfied.

● An employer committed a contract violation when it entered into a vehicle leasing arrangement, an arbitrator held. The responsibility for vehicle maintenance was outsourced as part of the leasing arrangement, depriving the company's mechanics of work they had performed when the company owned the vehicles in its fleet. The arbitrator's decision hinged on the resulting personnel cutbacks, because the parties' collective bargaining agreement expressly barred the employer from outsourcing any work covered by the contract if doing so would result in layoffs of bargaining unit employees (*Sprint Communications*, 120 LA 940; see also 104 LA 246).

● In another case, a contract provision prohibited an employer from subcontracting if it had the necessary equipment and personnel and if subcontracting triggered layoffs. The employer eliminated the job of an employee who handled deliveries, and it subcontracted much of the work to parts vendors. After the employee was processed for layoff, the employer still had a vehicle for making the deliveries. An arbitrator decided that the employer's actions constituted a contract violation, in spite of the fact that the employee was reassigned to a different job (*The Levy Co.*, 123 LA 1735).

● Under a collective bargaining agreement that allowed subcontracting for economic reasons, an employer committed a contract violation when it failed to make a meaningful comparison between a contractor's bid on a job and what it would have cost for bargaining unit employees to do the same work, an arbitrator ruled. The employer did not satisfactorily explore the facts necessary to make a meaningful cost comparison, and thus it appeared that the employer acted too precipitously in deciding to subcontract the work, the arbitrator concluded (*Iowa Industrial Hydraulics Inc.*, 100 LA 1208).

● An employer committed a contract violation when it subcontracted shipping of its product to a customer's warehouse during a week when product demand was not excessive, an arbitrator found. The parties' collective bargaining agreement permitted subcontracting in an "overflow situation," but that condition was not met here, according to the arbitrator, who said the employer failed to show that it could not meet the demand with bargaining unit employees (*Midwest Coca-Cola Bottling Co.*, 116 LA 1153).

● The subcontracting of concrete-block work required for the erection of new structures violated contractual language that barred an employer from contracting out any work "normally performed by

its maintenance employees," an arbitrator held. The employer contended that the subcontracting restriction only applied to normal repair and maintenance work and not new construction, but the arbitrator rejected that argument. Historically, the maintenance workers had performed a wide variety of duties, and they had done block work as needed for 20 years with no distinction as to maintenance, construction, repair, or renovation, the arbitrator pointed out (*Champion International Corp.*, 91 LA 245; see also 97 LA 1216, 97 LA 650).

● In a case involving the removal of a 110-foot section of a coal conveyor belt, an arbitrator reached the opposite conclusion and allowed subcontracting. The union argued that maintenance mechanics from the bargaining unit were experienced with the required tasks and should have been given the project in accordance with a contract provision that barred the subcontracting of customary maintenance and repair work. However, the arbitrator decided that the employer was free to subcontract the project because it did not involve work over which the bargaining unit had jurisdiction. The union could claim repair and maintenance work but not construction or demolition work, the arbitrator asserted. Working on something that remains in use and putting it in better shape would qualify as repair and maintenance, whereas removing something entirely would not, the arbitrator reasoned, denying the union's grievance (*U.S. Steel Mining Co. Inc.*, 100 LA 856; see also 123 LA 1095, 103 LA 1099, 102 LA 631, 97 LA 214, 82 LA 725, 78 LA 262).

● Another arbitrator upheld an employer's subcontracting of over-the-road trucking work. The parties' collective bargaining agreement granted the employer the right to subcontract work after examining three conditions—whether the work could be performed as economically by plant employees, whether qualified employees were available, and whether suitable equipment was at hand—and determining that at least one of them did not exist. Having met this contractual requirement, the employer was free to lay off four truck drivers and subcontract with common carriers to perform work that was formerly done by the bargaining unit, the arbitrator determined (*Thunder Bay Manufacturing Corp.*, 121 LA 1236).

● A contract clause that prohibited subcontracting if it resulted in the displacement of bargaining unit employees was not violated when an employer contracted out maintenance work on mobile equipment, an arbitrator ruled. "Displacement" is a broader term than "layoff," the arbitrator said, because it also includes situations in which employees are reassigned but not let go. Nevertheless, the mechanic who was affected by the employer's subcontracting decision was not displaced, the arbitrator determined. Even though the mechanic no longer worked on the mobile equipment, he retained the same job classification and wage rate, the arbitrator pointed out (*A.P. Green Industries*, 117 LA 1473).

● Another arbitrator held that a tortilla manufacturer had the right to subcontract shuttle drivers' work. The parties' collective bargaining agreement allowed subcontracting "as the requirements of the business demand," provided that subcontracting did not cause layoffs and was limited to work that employees were unwilling or unqualified to perform. The arbitrator found that business requirements supported subcontracting because the employer experienced high turnover and attendance problems among drivers; difficulty in recruiting new drivers; and significant costs related to leasing, fueling, and repairing shuttle vehicles. The fact that the employer could not keep the positions filled, the arbitrator added, amounted to a situation where bargaining unit employees were unwilling to do the work. Finally, in considering whether subcontracting resulted in layoffs, the arbitrator noted that only one shuttle driver could have been protected by this provision, and he resigned prior to the implementation of subcontracting, so he was not laid off as a result of the move (*Gruma Corp.*, 120 LA 749).

● Under a contract that prohibited subcontracting if it resulted in layoffs or reductions in pay rates for bargaining unit employees, an employer was justified in contracting out weekend repair work on a boiler, an arbitrator decided. At first, the employer thought its own employees could handle the repairs on an overtime basis. After discovering the magnitude of the job, however, the employer opted to subcontract the work so the boiler could be up and running by Monday. Both manpower and time constraints supported the employer's decision, the arbitrator noted, but he said the main reason for upholding the subcontracting was that it did not violate the layoff and pay restrictions. Even if employees lost overtime pay, there was no subcontracting violation, according to the arbitrator, because the contract specifically referred to reductions in employees' rate of pay (*Midwest Generation EME LLC*, 121 LA 86; see also 97 LA 64).

C. Common Business Justifications

As noted in the previous section, arbitrators tend to approve of subcontracting if it is motivated by compelling business reasons. Justifications commonly cited by employers include costs, work demands that exceed the capacity or skills of available employees, a lack of necessary equipment, and unusual urgency or special needs.

1. Economic Reasons

Arbitrators often uphold subcontracting on the basis of economic justifications when employers' financial health is so poor that a failure to reduce costs could threaten their survival. Under less dire circumstances, however, arbitrators find it difficult to overlook the negative effects of subcontracting.

● An arbitrator upheld a public utility's right to subcontract, because the labor contract allowed the company to subcontract as long as it did not "result in reduction of staffing . . . or where it would undermine the Union's representation," when the company subcontracted the work of three locator/leak surveyors, where they bumped into other jobs, and the employer made the decision for economic reasons and not to undermine the union (*MidAmerican Energy Co.*, 129 LA 737).

● An arbitrator upheld an employer's outsourcing program that produced significant savings but also contributed to widespread job losses. Over a four-year period, shrinking demand for the company's products and extensive outsourcing caused the bargaining unit to dwindle from 160 employees to just 15. Although the parties' collective bargaining agreement permitted outsourcing when necessary for business reasons such as cost reductions and time constraints, it stated that outsourcing would be done in good faith and with the purpose of making the employer's plant a more successful and secure place to work. The union claimed that the employer failed to abide by these conditions, but the arbitrator rejected that argument.

Despite the devastating effect outsourcing had on the bargaining unit, the arbitrator determined that the appropriate test, given the stark economic realities faced by the employer, was whether outsourcing facilitated cost cutting that would enable the plant to remain open. At one point, the arbitrator noted, the employer was losing $160,000 per month, but the savings in material and labor costs from outsourcing helped the employer achieve a slim profit margin. "Unfortunately for the Union and its members, the reality appears to be that without outsourcing the Company cannot make a profit, and that without showing a profit, the Company is not likely to be a secure place to work for any bargaining unit employee," the arbitrator said (*Barko Hydraulics LLC*, 117 LA 1715).

● A company that lost $345 million in three years was legitimately driven to engage in subcontracting as part of its efforts to stop a financial free fall, an arbitrator held. The employer decided to centralize warehousing and distribution functions. It closed a number of warehouses, displacing unionized workers, and contracted with third parties that provided enhanced services and capabilities. By consolidating operations into three regional distribution centers, the employer estimated that it saved $22 million. The union objected to the employer's subcontracting and asked for the reinstatement of laid-off material handlers or the discontinuation of any subcontracting that involved material handling work. Rejecting the union's position, the arbitrator found that the employer had a legitimate need to engage in subcontracting and instituting layoffs. The employer was "overwhelmed in a collapsing sector," the

arbitrator said, and failing to implement changes "would have guaranteed business disaster" (*Nexitra LLC*, 116 LA 1780).

● A warehousing distributor and service provider for retail stores had the right to subcontract tractor/trailer delivery work and eliminate the positions of seven truck drivers when cost reductions became critical to the company's survival, an arbitrator held. In a previous ruling, the employer had been blocked from contracting out the same work, but the arbitrator in this case emphasized that the company's financial circumstances had changed. The employer had long been aware of the inefficiencies in its trucking operations, as evidenced by its previous attempt to terminate them, the arbitrator noted. "It has since suffered severe setbacks resulting in lost customers, a huge cutback in employment of management and nonunion employees, and continuing financial losses," such that the ability to achieve substantial savings by subcontracting tractor/trailer deliveries "is likely to be critical to its ability to stay in business," the arbitrator said (*Federal Wholesale Co.*, 92 LA 271).

● An employer was justified in contracting out a production segment that continued losing money in spite of a substantial investment in new machinery, an arbitrator held. The contractor had the same machinery but achieved greater output with smaller crew sizes, and its lower costs were owing to these productivity differences rather than lower pay rates, the arbitrator noted. The employer had made a sizable investment in upgrading its own equipment with the goal of keeping the work in the bargaining unit, the arbitrator pointed out, but the desired productivity improvements never materialized, and the segment in question experienced an annual loss in excess of $1.5 million. Concluding that the continued operation of this unprofitable segment could have had severe consequences for the entire bargaining unit, the arbitrator determined that the employer's subcontracting decision was made in good faith for compelling economic reasons unrelated to wage rates (*Miller and Co.*, 102 LA 197).

● *By contrast*, an arbitrator overturned an employer's decision to subcontract janitorial work for the sole purpose of saving money. The arbitrator acknowledged that employers, in shouldering responsibility for operating a viable business, must be allowed a great deal of freedom to respond to economic pressures and other forces that come to bear on their operations. However, employers assume limitations on their freedom when they recognize a union and commit to contractual terms that define the jobs, wages, and working conditions of the bargaining unit, the arbitrator observed. Balancing the parties' legitimate interests, the arbitrator determined that in order to subcontract, the employer needed reasons other than the ability to get the work "done cheaper with contract workers." The employer failed to show any "economic exigencies" that would have justified subcontracting, and there were no changes in the janitorial work or the level of skill involved that would have made subcontracting a necessity, the arbitrator held (*Armstrong World Industries Inc.*, 115 LA 410; see also 75 LA 665).

• A savings of 25 cents per unit did not justify an appliance manufacturer's decision to subcontract the production of refrigerator condensers, an arbitrator decided. As part of the arrangement, the employer moved its own capital equipment to the contractor's location, where it was used with cheaper labor to produce the condensers at a reduced cost. The resulting impact—the elimination of 29 production jobs—constituted a "substantial detriment to the bargaining unit" that outweighed the employer's economic interests, the arbitrator said. In finding that the employer's authority to engage in subcontracting was limited, the arbitrator noted that the parties' labor agreement set forth standards of wages and working conditions applicable to the jobs covered by the agreement's recognition clause, and the agreement contemplated that the work normally performed by employees in the covered jobs "would continue to be so performed as long as the work was available." To allow the company to subcontract the condenser production work and eliminate the associated jobs "would subvert and destroy the entire bargaining relationship," the arbitrator declared (*Whirlpool Corp.*, 115 LA 668).

• An employer committed a contract violation by subcontracting a portion of its product delivery work and shrinking its bargaining unit of drivers by one-third, an arbitrator ruled. The employer's decision was prompted by a widening wage gap between its unionized drivers and contract workers in the area, the arbitrator found. Weighing the job security of union-represented workers and the overall stability of the bargaining unit against the employer's interests in reducing costs, the arbitrator decided that "the relatively drastic reduction in the number of drivers (from 15 to 10) tips the balancing process in favor of the Local. Indeed, if carried to its extreme, there would appear to be little to prevent Management from completely decimating the bargaining unit" (*BP America Inc.*, 122 LA 940; see also 100 LA 1129, 92 LA 841, 86 LA 705).

2. Availability of Staff

Arbitrators typically allow employers to engage in subcontracting if they do not have enough employees to handle the amount of work that must be done or if members of the bargaining unit lack the ability to perform the required work (123 LA 267, 114 LA 250, 104 LA 547, 95 LA 1078).

• Despite emphasizing that subcontracting rights must not be exercised "with unfettered abandon," an arbitrator decided that an employer could outsource work when it was unable to meet customer demands with its own employees. According to the arbitrator, if the central purpose of outsourcing is to transfer work out of the bargaining unit, such actions "must be presumed to be an attack on the bargaining unit. To permit such an attack would render the collective bargaining process an exercise in futility, with hard won labor agreements being circumvented by outsourcing." In the case at hand, however, the arbitrator found that employees were already working significant overtime, no one was on layoff, and the size of the bargaining unit was expanding as the result of additional hiring. Moreover, the arbitrator noted, the employer had a longstanding practice of relying on outsourcing in situations where it lacked the capacity to timely perform work to meet customer demands (*Eaton Corp.*, 114 LA 1691).

• Similarly, an arbitrator held that an employer was justified in subcontracting for temporary production labor during a period when the hiring of additional employees could not happen fast enough to keep pace with production demands (*Boise Cascade Corp.*, 105 LA 1094).

• An arbitrator upheld a telephone service provider's long-term use of contract workers to supplement its permanent workforce. The area served by the company was experiencing rapid growth, and aggressive recruiting efforts could not yield enough new employees. Without the use of contractors, the arbitrator said, the company likely would have been forced to shut down significant portions of its business. There was a lack of evidence to suggest that the bargaining unit was adversely affected, according to the arbitrator, who noted that contractors worked the least desirable shifts, received no more overtime hours than regular employees, and were bumped when qualified employees expressed an interest in their positions. The arbitrator also pointed out that the company had a past practice of subcontracting for more than 20 years and had rebuffed a union attempt to secure a prohibition against subcontracting in the most recent round of contract negotiations (*Sprint/Central Telephone Co.*, 114 LA 633).

• A company that supplied fresh vegetable products to retail grocery stores was justified in subcontracting some cold storage work after receiving numerous customer complaints, an arbitrator ruled. The main problem was one of insufficient capacity. The company could not handle all the produce coming into its cooler, and the employees who loaded outgoing trucks could not keep up with the workload. The resulting delays affected the company's ability to get fresh produce to customers without losing shelf-life dates. The arbitrator found that the company's insufficient capacity gave it a compelling reason to engage in subcontracting. The company testified that customer service was its main concern, the arbitrator noted, and labor costs were not a factor in its subcontracting decision. In ad-

dition, employees continued to receive their guaranteed hours, and no one was laid off as a result of the subcontracting, the arbitrator observed (*Mann Packing Co. Inc.*, 118 LA 1221).

• An arbitrator upheld an employer's use of contract workers to fill in for regular employees when its plant experienced a dramatic increase in unscheduled absences. Due to the high levels of absenteeism, largely from employees calling in sick, output at the plant was reduced on some occasions by nearly 30 percent. The company fell behind on production deadlines, which began affecting its ability to fulfill orders and retain customers. Under the circumstances, the arbitrator said, the use of contract workers was in the best interest of both the company and the bargaining unit. The arbitrator also cited a number of other considerations in ruling for the employer, including the fact that no employees were on layoff or suffered hours reductions, the employer could not mandate enough overtime hours to make up for the high absenteeism levels, there were ample employees to compensate for normal absenteeism, and it would not have been feasible to hire more permanent employees to address a temporary spike in absenteeism (*U.S. Pipe & Foundry Co.*, 114 LA 426).

• Another arbitrator determined that an employer was justified in contracting out capping work at a landfill. According to the arbitrator, there were not enough bargaining unit employees to perform the work, employees could not be spared from their regular duties, and many employees already were working a substantial amount of overtime (*Browning-Ferris Industries of Ohio Inc.*, 118 LA 602).

• An employer properly used a construction contractor for the installation of 1,200 feet of stainless steel pipe instead of allowing the job to be performed on an overtime basis by bargaining unit employees, an arbitrator ruled. The employer was having a new plant built, and its own pipefitters performed some of the associated work when it involved black iron pipe. However, the installation of the stainless steel pipe required a type of welding that was foreign to the employer's pipefitters. Welders used by the contractor, on the other hand, were certified in the required method, and their installation of the pipe carried a one year warranty. Emphasizing the bargaining unit employees' lack of experience with the required welding method, the arbitrator concluded that the employer had a justifiable basis for subcontracting the work (*Formica Corp.*, 87 LA 117).

• In a similar case, an arbitrator decided that a mining company acted appropriately in subcontracting the fabrication and installation of two 15-foot slurry lines. Bargaining unit workers had done basic repair and maintenance tasks related to such lines, but the fabrication and installation of new lines involved tasks that they were not experienced with and had not been trained to do, the arbitrator pointed out (*Pinn-Oak Resources Preparation Plant*, 121 LA 678).

• An employer had the right to contract out tasks involved in replacing a boiler and demolishing the building that held the old boiler, an arbitrator ruled. The labor agreement provided that normal and traditional work belonged to bargaining unit employees, but the arbitrator found that a number of factors supported the decision to hire an outside contractor. Considerations cited by the arbitrator included the fact that the employer's maintenance workers had neither the time nor the skills to do all the work, no bargaining unit employees lost any assignments or pay during the project, and they were used for the project when they were available (*Rock-Tenn Co.*, 120 LA 1552).

• A successor employer did not violate its collective bargaining agreement when it contracted out mason helper work, an arbitrator ruled. The agreement was silent on whether the successor employer had to carry over job classifications from the predecessor's contract, the arbitrator noted. Thus, in the absence of a qualified bargaining unit member who could do the required tasks, the employer was not obligated to keep the mason helper work within the bargaining unit, the arbitrator decided (*Republic Special Metals*, 119 LA 1557).

• *By contrast*, an employer committed a contract violation when it failed to use employees from its maintenance depart-

ment for a project involving the installation of insulation, an arbitrator held, finding "no serious doubt" regarding the availability of personnel with skills required for the work. Several months earlier, the union had worked with the employer to effectuate cutbacks, including the layoff of 90 maintenance employees, but had made it clear that it would object to the use of contractors to do work that the laid-off employees could do. At that time, the union received an assurance from management that the maintenance employees would be used instead of contractors whenever possible. This assurance, coupled with language in the parties' contract, obligated the employer to use its maintenance employees on the insulation project, the arbitrator said. He rejected a separate argument raised by the employer, namely that it lacked sufficient supervisory personnel to oversee the workers. Asserting that collective bargaining agreements normally deal only with represented workers, the arbitrator found that contract language on the availability of personnel, equipment, and "related services" did not refer to supervisors (*Manville Forest Products Corp.*, 85 LA 85; see also 119 LA 143).

• An employer could not cite a lack of available workers as a justification for subcontracting lawn maintenance work when it had one employee on layoff and had failed to replace another employee who retired, an arbitrator held. Ruling otherwise would mean that employers could allow the size of the bargaining unit to decrease and then contract out work on the basis of insufficient personnel, the arbitrator reasoned (*Owens-Brockway Glass Container Inc.*, 106 LA 868; see also 117 LA 624).

3. Availability of Equipment

Another factor arbitrators consider is whether employers have appropriate equipment to perform the tasks that would otherwise be subcontracted (120 LA 910, 86 LA 81, 79 LA 535, 64 LA 1244, 63 LA 82, 62 LA 505).

• An employer did not violate a collective bargaining contract when it subcontracted tank washing, an arbitrator ruled, where it needed the tank room for a new bottle coating product, there were no laid-off employees, and employees who did that work retained their jobs (*Red Spot Paint & Varnish Co. Inc.*, 128 LA 973).

• An arbitrator upheld an employer's decision to subcontract lawn maintenance work after it moved to a new location with vastly larger grounds. The parties' collective bargaining agreement permitted the subcontracting of work that involved special skills, tools, or equipment the employer did not possess. A janitor used a push mower to cut the grass at the former location, but the new site, with 10 acres of land surrounding the employer's plant, required the use of a commercial mower. According to the arbitrator, this was a piece of specialized equipment that had not been needed at the former location, which clearly gave management the right to subcontract the work. The arbitrator said the employer's subcontracting decision was also bolstered by the fact that the janitor and other members of the bargaining unit were already fully utilized at the new location without caring for the grounds (*LAU Industries*, 114 LA 462).

• Another arbitrator upheld the subcontracting of work that could not be performed safely using an employer's own equipment. The arbitrator emphasized the touchiness of the subcontracting issue and acknowledged that the union "has no choice but to protest" the contracting out of work performed on the employer's premises. However, the arbitrator noted that a provision in the parties' collective bargaining agreement stated that "health and safety of the employees is the highest priority of the parties." Adding that the employer's judgment regarding the riskiness of performing the work with its own equipment had to be respected, the arbitrator denied the union's grievance (*Basin Cooperative Services*, 105 LA 1070).

• An employer was justified in contracting out various testing and analysis tasks to improve the reliability and productivity of its production equipment, an arbitrator ruled. In this case, the contracted work involved the use of computers and software, as well as a large and varied database of proprietary technological information that enabled the subcontractor to diagnose causes of equipment failure and predict maintenance needs. This database was available only as part of a comprehensive program, which included technical services performed by the subcontractor's personnel, the arbitrator noted. Although members of the bargaining unit had done the same type of work, the greater scope and sophistication of the subcontractor's database and its overall program allowed the employer to obtain a higher level of predictive maintenance service by contracting out the work, the arbitrator determined (*U.S. Steel Corp.*, 122 LA 1552).

• *By contrast*, an arbitrator ordered an employer to pay lost overtime to employees after it subcontracted unit work, despite the fact that the employer did not have the equipment the subcontractor used and the employees were not trained to operate the equipment. The parties' collective bargaining agreement prohibited the employer from subcontracting even if it had to rent part of the equipment and train the affected employees in the operation of such equipment, the arbitrator found (*Ashland Chemical Co.*, 64 LA 1244).

• A contract provision allowing subcontracting based on a lack of equipment was not satisfied when an employer's equipment fell into disrepair, an arbitrator found. With limited exceptions, the employer was prohibited from subcontracting any work that was customarily performed by members of the bargaining unit on the employer's premises. One exception permitted subcontracting if the necessary tools or equipment were not available at the employer's plant. The employer cited this exception as part of its justification for subcontracting over-the-road trucking work, because the one truck it owned was in poor condition and was being retired. The arbitrator rejected this justification, distinguishing between the absence of equipment and the replacement of existing equipment. Allowing the exception to apply to the replacement of equipment would mean that the employer could contract out any work at its plant once its existing equipment became inoperable or unusable, the arbitrator pointed out. Nevertheless, he still upheld the employer's right to contract out over-the-road trucking work. Such work was not performed on the company's premises, the arbitrator reasoned, and thus it fell outside the scope of the contractual prohibition against subcontracting (*Collis Corp.*, 95 LA 89).

4. Unusual or Urgent Situations

While arbitrators tend to look askance at the subcontracting of routine and recurring tasks, they are more inclined to allow employers to engage the services of contractors under unusual circumstances that involve special or urgent needs (105 LA 117, 93 LA 465, 80 LA 363, 74 LA 269).

● An employer had the right to contract out the fabrication and installation of a temporary water pumping system when its existing system broke down, stopping the flow of water into its corn processing plant, an arbitrator ruled. Noting that the breakdown halted work in various departments, the arbitrator found "no question that the situation presented an emergency which had to be remedied immediately." In light of the circumstances, the arbitrator approved of the employer's decision to hire a contractor with the specialized skills, equipment, and material required for the job. Rejecting the contention that pipefitters within the bargaining unit should have been assigned the work, the arbitrator noted that such a situation had never arisen before, and when the emergency occurred, there was no way to determine how long the work would take or whether the pipefitters were capable of performing the necessary tasks (*Hubinger Co.*, 75 LA 742).

● An arbitrator upheld the outsourcing of new member recruitment by a credit union that was in urgent need of additional customers. The employer had a reasonable basis for outsourcing marketing activities aimed at attracting new members, the arbitrator said, because it faced critical financial and time constraints that necessitated the expansion of membership in order to restore viability to the credit union. The employer had tried to incorporate the marketing function into the existing organizational structure, but time and expertise were in short supply and normal operations suffered as credit union staff were spread thin, the arbitrator said. After marketing activities were outsourced, the arbitrator

observed, membership began expanding much faster. The outsourcing decision was made for compelling business reasons, the arbitrator concluded, adding that the arrangement offered the credit union "a path to survival" (*Ohio Valley Federal Credit Union*, 82 LA 805).

● An employer was justified in subcontracting hazardous work on a leaking glue tank, which had to be repaired quickly using specialized equipment, an arbitrator found. The tank sprung a leak on a Saturday, and management called in a subcontractor to work on the tank so it could be back on line by the start of business on Monday. In addition to citing the urgency of the situation, the arbitrator pointed out that bargaining unit employees were not properly qualified to perform the work, which was subject to the Occupational Safety and Health Administration's "confined spacy entry" requirements. The employer's decision to contract out the repair work under the unique circumstances of this case "appears reasonable and in good faith," the arbitrator said. "It is very difficult for any neutral observer to fault responsible management that puts its employees' safety first, preserving their talents for tasks which fit more appropriately into their specific areas of expertise," he added (*Gaylord Container Corp.*, 106 LA 461).

● After several customers lost telephone service, a phone company properly called in an independent contractor on a Saturday to help correct the problem, an arbitrator held. The independent contractor had worked alongside a cable splicer from the bargaining unit on a troublesome job involving the transfer of numerous telephone lines. The loss of service involved some of the same lines, and a technician from the unit was unable to correct the problem. At that point, management decided that someone with first-hand knowledge of the lines would be helpful, and it called in the contractor after trying unsuccessfully to reach the cable splicer from the bargaining unit who had been involved in the earlier work. Another cable splicer with no prior involvement disputed the company's action, claiming a lost opportunity for Saturday overtime. The arbitrator rejected his claim, finding that the employer did not have a general need for a cable splicer, because there were only "two people who knew enough about what had been done and what troubles turned up to be of help" in effectuating the necessary repairs. Thus, the company's decision to call in the contractor was justified under the particular circumstances, the arbitrator determined (*GTE North Inc.*, 98 LA 617).

• *By contrast*, in a case in which the bargaining contract provided that the employer "agrees to notify Union of all subcontracting that might affect the bargaining unit," an employer violated the agreement when it did not notify the union of production testing subcontracting, an arbitrator ruled. The arbitrator rejected the union's contention that notice was not required if there was an "emergency condition that prevented notification" and that emergency existed in that some of the most skilled testers were unavailable, because the emergency exception referred to circumstances in which the employer was permitted to send out work because of the need for speed, which was not the situation in this case (*Haynes International Inc.*, 129 LA 1092).

• An employer violated a collective bargaining agreement when it failed to notify the union about the subcontracting of a belt repair, even if there was an emergency, an arbitrator ruled. The employer never provided formal notice, which should have been provided "as soon as practicable" in an emergency situation, and the subsequent first quarter report the employer gave the union contained little of the information specified in the agreement, and came long after a lapse of any reasonable period in which notice would have been practicable (*United States Steel Corp.*, 123 LA 1144).

• On the other hand, an arbitrator found that an employer could not justify its use of a subcontractor to repair an elevator when there was no genuine emergency. Over the years, the chains carrying the elevator had broken on numerous occasions, and employees from the bargaining unit had always performed the necessary repairs. Whenever the elevator was out of service, the employer would instead use a crane to lower materials, which posed an

inconvenience but did not slow the production process. In deciding to subcontract the work, however, the employer said the elevator breakdown was an emergency requiring immediate, round-the-clock attention, and it claimed that using its maintenance employees to make the repairs would have delayed other necessary work. The arbitrator disagreed, finding that the elevator breakdown did not constitute a bona fide emergency, because there was never an actual or threatened curtailment of production. In fact, qualified employees were available to perform the repairs without any impact on other necessary work, and a crew of maintenance workers "would have effected the repairs much faster than the time it took the contractor," the arbitrator determined (*Willamette Industries Inc.*, 106 LA 230).

D. Advance Notice of Subcontracting

• Many collective bargaining agreements include provisions requiring employers to provide advance notice about plans for subcontracting, and some go further by requiring discussions or bargaining with unions concerning such plans. Arbitrators tend to strictly enforce these requirements, because a lack of notification deprives unions of the opportunity to suggest alternative possibilities before subcontracting arrangements are put into effect (123 LA 1144, 119 LA 1569, 119 LA 1422, 117 LA 1413, 112 LA 550, 110 LA 1, 109 LA 809, 106 LA 1095, 106 LA 980, 106 LA 902, 105 LA 1214, 105 LA 869, 103 LA 619, 99 LA 366, 98 LA 13, 94 LA 695, 93 LA 666, 89 LA 349, 78 LA 710, 54 LA 1207, 53 LA 993, 46 LA 724).

• In a case in which the bargaining contract provided that the employer "agrees to notify Union of all subcontracting that might affect the bargaining unit," an employer violated the agreement when it did not notify the union of production testing subcontracting, an arbitrator ruled. The arbitrator rejected the union's contention that notice was not required if there was no actual erosion of the bargaining unit by subcontracting, because the purpose of the notice requirement and meet-and-discuss obligation was that it may lead to a change in the decision based on the facts showing possible alternative arrangements., the arbitrator said (*Haynes International Inc.*, 129 LA 1092).

• An employer violated its labor contract by failing to notify a union that it was contracting out delivery work and eliminating a truck driver position, an arbitrator ruled. The employer had been using a truck under a lease arrangement, and it had known for five years that it would subcontract the work when the lease expired. Despite the absence of a specific notification provision in the parties' labor agreement, the arbitrator found that the employer had an inherent obligation, in recognizing the union as exclusive representative of bargaining unit employees, "to keep its union apprised of changes that have an impact on unit personnel, even only one employee." Finding that the lack of reasonable notice deprived the union of its right to bargain with the employer over the effects of the subcontracting decision, the arbitrator ordered the employer to engage in bargaining and make up for the driver's reduced earnings after he was downgraded to a lower-paying job (*Witco Chemical Corp.*, 89 LA 349).

• An employer did not have the right to contract out repair work on the grounds that turnaround time was too long, where inadequate notice deprived the union of a "full opportunity to explore options to improve," an arbitrator said. In this case, the employer had mentioned its concerns and the possibility of subcontracting, going so far as to tell the union it was seeking a quote from a contractor. However, the union lacked concrete details that would have enabled it to make a counterproposal, the arbitrator found. When the employer subsequently announced that the subcontracting decision had been made, it was "a done deal" as opposed to "an open-minded invitation to review the whole of the circumstances," the arbitrator said. Concluding that the employer's actions prevented meaningful discussion about possible ways of keeping the work in-house, the arbitrator ordered the employer to return the work to the bargaining unit until a full discussion could take place on alternatives to contracting out (*American Airlines Inc.*, 120 LA 1644).

• An employer committed a notification violation when it contracted out forklift repair and maintenance work and only informed the employee who had been performing the work, an arbitrator ruled. A union committee met monthly to discuss any work that the employer wanted to have done by outside contractors, and the employer also used an "Outside Contractor Approval Form" to describe the reasons for contracting out specific jobs. Pointing out that the committee meetings gave the union "an opportunity to have its say in the matter," the arbitrator held that the employer's notification of the affected employee was not sufficient to meet its obligations under the labor agreement. "However unlikely that the Union would have been able to propose alternatives satisfactory to the company regarding the cost of forklift repairs, it was deprived of the opportunity to do so," the arbitrator said (*Allied Tube & Conduit Corp.*, 122 LA 1735).

• In another case, a hospital committed a violation by failing to provide the 30-day advance notice required under its labor agreement before subcontracting work involving the transcription of medical reports, an arbitrator ruled. In effect, the notice requirement restricted the employer's right to subcontract the work, the arbitrator reasoned (*Kaiser Foundation Hospitals*, 61 LA 1008).

• An arbitrator ruled that an employer's one-day notice to a union that it planned to subcontract bargaining unit work violated a contract because it failed to give the union time to invoke the agreement's expedited procedure before a joint, labor-management contracting out committee and also because there was no emergency situation that made subcontracting a business necessity (*Armco Steel Co.*, 102 LA 396).

• Similarly, an employer committed a contract violation when it provided notice only six days prior to subcontracting "emergency repairs" on a malfunctioning kiln, an arbitrator held, finding that a true emergency did not exist and bargaining unit employees with the requisite ability could have performed the work on an overtime basis (*U.S. Steel Corp.*, 121 LA 1317).

• *By contrast*, an arbitrator did not fault an employer for failing to provide a union with advance notice of subcontracting when problems with conveyor belts were sudden and frequent and the need for repairs was critical and immediate. The employer resorted to subcontracting because employees who could have performed the repairs were already occupied with essential work or were unwilling to accept overtime, the arbitrator observed. Under the circumstances, there was no violation when the employer failed to supply the usual "contracting-out notices" prior to having the work performed by contractors, the arbitrator decided (*USS, A Division of USX Corp.*, 115 LA 1729).

• An employer properly contracted out construction and installation of manufacturing equipment after a maintenance manager met with union officers and gave them forms with details such as a description of the project and the contractor to whom the job would be awarded. The parties' labor contract did not prohibit subcontracting but only provided that the union, when notified, had to be given an opportunity to plead its cause, which was the case here, the arbitrator said (*J.T. Baker Chemical Co.*, 76 LA 1146).

• An employer satisfied its contractual obligation to engage in consultations with a union prior to using a contractor's services for reconstructing a portion of its pump-room floor, according to an arbitrator. The union had proposed an alternative means of accomplishing the work, but the employer rejected its suggestions and went forward with its subcontracting plans. The employer was not required to obtain the union's agreement before engaging in subcontracting, the arbitrator said. Rather, the employer was merely obligated to listen to the union's arguments, weigh them, and then make its decision, the arbitrator concluded (*FMC Corp.*, 75 LA 485).

• An employer's notice to a union about subcontracting plans was sufficient, even though it did not divulge the identity of the contractors who would be performing the work, an arbitrator held. The parties' collective bargaining agreement required the employer to provide written notice describing the location, type, duration, and timetable of the work to be performed, thus enabling the union to ascertain the reasons for subcontracting. However, the arbitrator found, the employer was not required to name the contractors in its notice. Even if the union objected to other aspects of the notice, the arbitrator added, the notification complaint had to be dismissed based on the union's failure to make those objections known prior to the actual arbitration proceedings (*Reserve Mining Co.*, 74 LA 1128).

• In a similar ruling, an arbitrator determined that he was precluded from considering a union's claim regarding a notice violation when the issue was not raised within 30 days of the commencement of the subcontracted work, as required under the parties' collective bargaining agreement (*Gulf States Steel Inc.*, 111 LA 757).

Part 12

Union Rights

I. Union Rights [LA CDI 93.27]

OVERVIEW

Although most collective bargaining agreements delineate various rights and privileges that are granted to unions, arbitrators frequently have to resolve disputes over the extent of those rights and the ability of employers to place limitations on them. The cases decided by arbitrators commonly focus on union rights related to obtaining information from employers, the representation of employees during disciplinary investigations, the posting of union materials on workplace bulletin boards, access to employer premises, and the wearing of union buttons and insignia.

Arbitrators usually interpret contract provisions on such issues broadly, holding that any intended restrictions should be expressly stated. According to one arbitrator, "the law of labor relations is relatively clear that an employer has no right to interfere with an employee's performance of his valid union activities and his obligations to his union, the same as the union and employee have no right to interfere with the employer's right to manage and operate the plant" (*Greif Bros. Corp.*, 67 LA 1001).

SUMMARY OF CASES

A. Information Rights

Most arbitrators agree that unions should have any information necessary for the processing of grievances and for making sure that employers are not committing contract violations. As one arbitrator pointed out, "the object and purpose of arbitration is to arrive at a fair and just decision, and to this end parties should be assisted in obtaining competent and material evidence where such may reasonably be had" (*Chesapeake & Potomac Telephone Co. of West Va.*, 21 LA 367).

• An employer was obligated to furnish a union with copies of security reports concerning the suspension of grocery store employees for selling alcoholic beverages to minors, an arbitrator ruled. In this case, the contract specifically required the employer to divulge "all available material facts" on request. Merely allowing the union representatives to hear about the reports or read them at an adjustment board meeting was not sufficient to "facilitate openness and settlement of grievances," the arbitrator said (*Safeway Stores Inc.*, 89 LA 627).

• An arbitrator required an employer to disclose information requested by a union on an alleged past practice, despite the fact that the collective bargaining agreement did not contain a full disclosure clause. The arbitrator declared that the grievance process includes revelation of all of the facts of the case and "presumes full disclosure" (*Regional Transportation District*, 87 LA 630).

• After an employer discharged an employee for exceeding his allotted amount of sick leave, an arbitrator decided that the employer was obligated to give the union the names, addresses, initial employment dates, and seniority dates of employees who had been allowed to return to work after being absent in excess of their authorized sick leave (*Mobil Oil Corp*, 63 LA 263).

• An employer improperly assessed a service fee for supplying information that a union needed to process grievances pertaining to allegedly unsafe conditions, an arbitrator held. The employer claimed that the fee was justified because it was required to use management personnel to select the requested information from records that contained some otherwise confidential or proprietary information. The arbitrator, however, found no hard evidence that confidential or proprietary information was actually included in the records, and he decided that the time consumed in compiling the information was not of such magnitude that the union should have been obligated to shoulder some of the cost (*U.S. Steel Corp.*, 79 LA 249).

• An arbitrator upheld a grievance over a promotion decision after an employer failed to provide information during the grievance procedure or hearing that would have permitted a comparison of all the candidates' qualifications. The arbitrator noted that the collective bargaining agreement required promotion by seniority "when skill and ability are approximately equal," but the employer failed to prove that a senior employee had inferior skills and abilities and failed to rebut the employee's testimony regarding his qualifications (*Union Carbide Corp.*, 97 LA 771; see also 119 LA 616).

1. Specific Information Rights

Aside from resolving disputes over information associated with general contract enforcement and grievance adjustment, arbitrators are sometimes asked to decide if unions are entitled to certain notifications, benefits data, or other specific types of information.

• An employer did not fulfill its notice obligations with regard to the opening of a new facility when a management official mentioned the opening during a grievance hearing on an unrelated matter, an arbitrator decided, finding that the contract required the employer to provide the union with "formal" notice (*Bowman Transportation Inc.*, 88 LA 711).

• A grievance settlement entitling a union to a new project form prior to "any contractors coming onto the property" was violated when an employer unilaterally discontinued giving the form to the union, an arbitrator held. Because the agreement had been arrived at in an open and arms-length discussion and the employer had continued the practice for more than eight years, the arbitrator saw no reason for changing the practice (*Cannelton Industries Inc.*, 91 LA 744).

• Given that a union was entitled to bargain over an employer's proposed retirement plan amendments, the employer had to give the union the text of all proposed and existing amendments and all actuarial data concerning all participants, an arbitrator ruled. The actuarial information was considered absolutely necessary to evaluate the presence or absence of benefits resulting from employees' contributions, the arbitrator concluded (*Anti-Defamation League of B'nai B'rith*, 53 LA 1332).

● Under a supplementary unemployment compensation benefit trust plan providing that an employer would "comply with reasonable requests by the union for other statistical information on the operation of the plan," an arbitrator held that the union was entitled to monthly lists of names of recipients and amounts paid. The employer's contention that the lists were not "statistical information" placed an unduly narrow restriction on the term, the arbitrator said (*Mack Trucks Inc.*, 36 LA 1114).

2. Employer Actions Upheld

When arbitrators uphold the actions of employers in denying information requests, they often do so because unions lack specific contractual rights to the information or because fulfillment of the requests would be unduly burdensome. If employees overstep their bounds in obtaining information for union purposes, meanwhile, arbitrators are likely to uphold employers' disciplinary actions against them.

● Under a contract that said nothing about seniority lists, one arbitrator held that a union had a right to seniority information only when the union specifically asked for it (*Bethlehem Steel Co.*, 24 LA 699).

● Contract provisions making payroll data available on request did not require an employer to furnish such records for uncovering claims during a dispute over seniority in layoffs, an arbitrator held. The records were to be used only for testing the validity of specific claims, the arbitrator pointed out (*Employers' Council of Santa Clara County & Central Calif. Meat Processors' Assn.*, 36 LA 42; see also 77 LA 1008, 74 LA 96, 72 LA 57).

● An arbitrator held that a supermarket chain was not obligated to comply with a union's general request for layoff information. The arbitrator found that there were specific notification provisions in the collective bargaining agreement on various subjects, including termination, but none of them specified notification of layoffs (*Albertson's Inc.*, 104 LA 890).

● An arbitrator denied a union's grievance over computer tapes containing dues withholding information, because providing the material as requested would have involved computer reprogramming requiring at least two staff months of time. Noting that the information was "readily available" under the existing computer system, the arbitrator said the employer could begin furnishing computer tapes containing the requested information after completing the installation of a new computer for processing payroll and personnel data (*General Services Administration*, 80 LA 669).

● An arbitrator denied a grievance based on a university's failure to inform a union before posting a library job as a temporary position even though a contract provision said the university would provide the union with notice of its intention to introduce changes or substantially change or create new jobs. Noting that the purpose of the provision was to "ameliorate effects of technological change of the kind not involved in this case," the arbitrator said changing the duration of a job was not the same as changing a job or creating a new job (*Brown University*, 113 LA 485).

● A veterans hospital properly imposed a 14-day suspension on a pharmacist because of the information he gave a union steward as evidence in a grievance, an arbitrator ruled. The pharmacist had copied a patient's medical records without deleting the patient's name or other confidential information, which constituted a violation of the federal Privacy Act, the arbitrator found. Rejecting the contention that the pharmacist's conduct was permitted under exceptions granting the union access to medical documents in pursuit of official business, the arbitrator said that records are collected for medical treatment purposes, and the exceptions restrict the use of records to the purpose for which they were compiled (*Veterans Affairs Medical Center, San Antonio, Texas*, 97 LA 1038).

● Another arbitrator upheld an employer's discharge of a shop steward based in part on his refusal to stop looking at other employees' time cards. The arbitrator said that even though the employer had to allow the shop steward reasonable access to relevant documents in investigating grievances, the steward had to go through management when reviewing time cards, just as other stewards did, and could not just "troll" through the cards while they were on the rack (*Stone Container Corp.*, 106 LA 475).

B. Weingarten/Representation Rights

When employers conduct investigatory interviews that could lead to disciplinary action, the employees suspected of wrongdoing have a right to union representation in accordance with the U.S. Supreme Court's ruling in *NLRB v. J. Weingarten Inc.*, 420 U.S. 251, 88 LRRM 2689 (1975). Although this ruling only requires union representation to be provided upon request, many employers make it a policy to inform employees of their *Weingarten* rights and ask if they would like a union representative to be present.

In weighing the protections afforded by the *Weingarten* ruling, arbitrators have found that employees are not entitled to union representation in certain situations. For instance, arbitrators have held that *Weingarten* rights do not come into play when the focus of an investigation is to search vehicles in company parking lots without questioning the employees who own the vehicles (98 LA 355, 84 LA 562). Other examples of situations where arbitrators did not find any *Weingarten* violations include the following:

- a truck driver's purpose at a meeting was to fill out an "accident report" where the non-management employee serving as a scribe for the report rejected the grievant's assertion that he requested union representation and the branch manager did nothing to suggest interrogation of the grievant at that meeting (*Huttig Building Products Inc.*, 128 LA 1251);
- there was no investigatory interview being conducted at the time an employee was being escorted from the workplace for insubordination (*Boise Cascade Corp.*, 121 LA 1313);
- the purpose of a meeting was to administer discipline that had already been decided upon (*AFG Industries Inc.*, 87 LA 568);
- employees waived an offer of representation at a meeting where they received suspensions based on safety infractions observed by management, since the discipline

had already been decided upon and even if the employees changed their minds and asked for a union representative, they would not have been entitled to one unless they held the view that the meeting was an investigation that could form the basis of some future discipline (*CMP Inc.*, 106 LA 437);
- an employee did not ask for representation at a meeting in which management investigated her false claim that she was absent from work because of jury duty (*Cuna Mutual Insurance Society*, 117 LA 1357; see also 86 LA 350);
- there was no investigatory component in a meeting called by management to inform an employee that she had to undergo drug testing (*Birmingham-Jefferson County Transit Authority*, 84 LA 1272);
- employees were witnesses to an altercation but were not targets of the investigation (*U.S. Steel Corp.*, 120 LA 1729);
- a bus driver declined an employer's offer of having a shop steward present after he was given a statement to read and sign admitting he had not performed required daily safety checks (*Waste Management Inc.*, 120 LA 175);
- an employer immediately suspended an employee for an alleged theft, and the employee did not request union representation during that brief initial session, which was the normal procedure used by the employer to get employees off the premises in potentially serious cases while gathering information and deciding further steps to take (*Union Tank Car Co.*, 104 LA 699);
- in notifying an employee about a meeting to discuss discipline for insubordination, an employer spelled out the employee's right to union representation, but the employee did not arrange for a union steward to attend the meeting (*Library of Congress*, 73 LA 1092);
- an employee requested a meeting with management about her absenteeism, and there was no evidence that the meeting was investigatory in nature (*Bell Helicopter Textron Inc.*, 98 LA 201);
- an employee did not request representation and neither the *Weingarten* rule nor the collective bargaining agreement required the employer to ask the employee

if he wanted a steward present during the interview (*Color-Art Inc.*, 116 LA 535);

• an employer denied an employee's request for union representation during a performance evaluation, since there was no grievance or grievable event (*Anoka County, Minn.*, 84 LA 516);

• an employer interviewed an employee without first warning him that he might face discipline, since a union steward was in fact present and the employer was not obligated to inform the employee that he could be subject to discipline pending the outcome of the investigatory process (*United Airlines Inc.*, 120 LA 1810);

• an employer did not offer union representation to an employee who resigned when he was assigned to rotating shifts, since the right to union representation exists for investigatory interviews, not for a confrontational meeting following an action that the employer had the contractual right to implement (*Unnico Services Co.*, 113 LA 432);

• an employer did not honor an employee's request for union representation when he was placed on suspension "pending investigation," since the employer was not required to allow representation when no interview took place (*Boise Cascade Corp.*, 114 LA 1379);

• an employer did not ask employees who left work without their supervisor's approval if they wanted union representation when they were leaving the building, since they had already been told that they did not have permission to leave and had received union representation in earlier meetings discussing the issue (*Lear Corp.*, 110 LA 885); and

• an employer allowed an employee to have a steward present but did not allow the steward to speak and did not listen to the employee's attempt to tell her side of the story, since the employer had already decided on its course of action and was not conducting an investigation that would have triggered traditional *Weingarten* rights (*Pilgrim's Pride Corp.*, 116 LA 1441).

1. Contractual Representation Rights

Collective bargaining agreements commonly grant broader representation rights

than those called for under the *Weingarten* ruling. For example, many contracts require employers to offer union representation during all disciplinary meetings, rather than just investigatory interviews, and some make the presence of union representatives mandatory, essentially nullifying employees' ability to waive representation. Even where collective bargaining agreements are silent on the issue of union representation, arbitrators sometimes hold that *Weingarten* rights are an inherent element of due process and the just cause standard.

• In one case, a collective bargaining agreement mandated that a union steward be allowed to attend any meeting "where possible disciplinary measures may be taken" and gave the union the right to be notified prior to any discharge and to be present when formal charges were made. An employee was given a disciplinary notice for neglecting to perform scheduled maintenance of a forklift. A union steward was present then but not at subsequent meetings when the employee was suspended and later discharged. Despite conceding that the employee's negligence warranted discharge, an arbitrator ordered reinstatement with back pay based on the employer's failure to ensure a steward's presence when it suspended and discharged the employee (*S and J Ranch*, 103 LA 350).

• An arbitrator ruled a university violated a discharged employee's *Weingarten* rights, despite the lack of clarity as to what was said at the meeting, where the employee either asked for a steward and was not given one, or was misled into thinking that she was not under investigation directly when she in fact was (*University of St. Thomas*, 124 LA 1468).

• Even though an employee voluntarily waived his right to union representation, an arbitrator concluded that his employer violated a contract provision that said employees who were disciplined or discharged "shall" have the benefit of a steward's presence at the meeting. The inclusion of the word "shall" in the collective bargaining agreement placed the duty on the employer to comply with the requirement, the arbitrator determined (*Packaging Corp. of America*, 119 LA 106).

• An arbitrator ruled that an employee could not be punished for refusing to discuss a performance matter with her supervisor in the absence of a union representative. The employee legitimately believed that the discussion was for the purpose of conducting an investigatory interview that could lead to discipline, the arbitrator found, and the collective bargaining agreement made the presence of a union representative at disciplinary discussions mandatory if an employee so requested (*Pacific Bell*, 92 LA 127).

• Another arbitrator found a violation of an employee's rights even though he had not requested the presence of a union representative at an investigatory meeting about an incident for which he was later disciplined. Noting that the employer failed to inform the employee of the meeting's purpose or that it could lead to discipline, the arbitrator said the employee clearly could not have known or reasonably suspected the purpose of the meeting or the potential for discipline so that he could have asked a union representative to attend (*County of Cook*, 105 LA 974; see also 98 LA 713).

• An employer failed to meet its *Weingarten* obligation when it denied union representation to an employee who was ordered to write out an explanation about damaged property, an arbitrator held. Although the employee was not at risk of discipline in connection with the property damage, he was threatened with discipline for refusing to provide a signed statement. Finding that the threat of discipline triggered the employee's right to union representation, the arbitrator overturned the employer's subsequent decision to fire the employee for insubordination (*Ralphs Grocery Co.*, 101 LA 634).

• A shop steward had a right to union representation in a disciplinary situation, an arbitrator held, since the right applied to any disciplinary matter unrelated to his performance of union duties, and the collective bargaining agreement specifically stated that any employee subject to disciplinary action would be given the opportunity to have a shop steward present (*TAC Services Inc.*, 114 LA 1640).

• Just cause did not exist to suspend an employee for refusing to attend an injury-review meeting without union representation, an arbitrator found. Despite her employer's assurances that no discipline would result, the employee reasonably believed that she would be given a warning for failing to wear safety gloves, the arbitrator noted, based in part on the fact that the injury prompting the meeting was the result of the employee's fifth on-the-job accident (*Ethyl Corp.*, 96 LA 255).

• A municipal employer violated a collective bargaining agreement when it denied a firefighter the right to union representation at a discussion concerning his refusal to accept a job assignment, an arbitrator held. Although the fire chief testified that he simply wanted to learn the reasons for the employee's refusal, the arbitrator concluded that the discussion constituted an investigatory interview under the circumstances, and the employee reasonably could view it as a prelude to disciplinary action (*City of Edina*, 90 LA 209).

C. Bulletin Board Postings

Employers commonly provide unions with access to workplace bulletin boards for posting materials of interest to their members, including news of elections, meetings, and other union business, as well as announcements of social and recreational activities.

One arbitrator listed four criteria that could be used in weighing the appropriateness of union postings. The criteria, which the arbitrator derived from the book *How Arbitration Works* by Elkouri and Elkouri (a publication of BBNA's book division), included the following:

The subject matter of the posted document should not stray from the reasonable concept of what constitutes union business.

Documents should not have a detrimental effect on employee morale or inflame employees against each other or the employer.

Documents should not contain statements that defame the employer or are patently disloyal or detrimental to the employer.

The employer should not reject notices that clearly concern union business, even though they approach being inflammatory or adverse to the employer's interests.

In the case at hand, the arbitrator upheld the right of a fire department employee, who also served as union president, to post letters endorsing city council candidates. In reaching his decision, the arbitrator cited a state law allowing city employees to participate in political activities during off-duty hours and while not in uniform (*Midwest City Fire Department*, 100 LA 137).

Other types of postings against which employers have protested, but arbitrators have found acceptable, include the following:

● a notice urging members' support for striking members of another union (*Wisconsin Tissue Mills Inc.*, 73 LA 271);

● a notice stating that the purpose of a forthcoming union meeting was to consider strike action against the employer (*Fairchild Engine & Airplane Corp.*, 16 LA 678);

● a letter from a union international representative that attempted to avoid an imminent wildcat strike and assure members that the union would fight their grievances through legal means (*Fruehauf Corp.*, 54 LA 1096);

● a seniority list drawn up by the union after the parties had failed to agree on such a list (*Lennox Furnace Co.*, 20 LA 788); and

● a notice urging union members to register for voting (*Warren City Manufacturing Co.*, 7 LA 202).

● However, an arbitrator held that a union did not have the right to post a notice titled "Long Term Disability Facts," which contained information concerning a union-administered and sponsored long-term disability plan. The collective bargaining agreement specified that the bulletin board was for official announcements and information on social, educational, and recreational affairs. The arbitrator said the notice in question, which contained express data about the disability plan, did not fit the criteria for permissible postings (*Arcata Graphics/Kingsport*, 102 LA 429).

1. Derogatory Content

Many collective bargaining agreements allow employers to bar the posting of materials that are derogatory or objectionable in nature. When employers raise such objections, arbitrators commonly hold that unions can be prohibited from posting anything that is clearly inappropriate, slanderous, or defamatory.

● A union violated an agreement to refrain from posting material containing "any derogatory remarks" or "personal attacks on individuals" when it responded to an article extolling the safety record at an employer facility by posting criticism that referred to a safety officer by name in a disparaging, disdainful manner and called him management's "lackey" (*U.S. Army Soldier Support Center, et. al.*, 91 LA 1201).

● In one case, an arbitrator upheld the discharge of an employee for posting unauthorized inflammatory notices pertaining to his employer, where the employee had been given repeated warnings concerning other notices he had posted and had been ordered not to post the notice that led to his discharge (*Beaver Precision Products Inc.*, 51 LA 853).

● Another arbitrator upheld a chief steward's suspension for insubordination when he refused to obey an order to remove a bulletin board posting that stated that insurance coverage of an employee receiving treatment for a malignancy had been terminated, that the union had pleaded his case to "deaf ears," and that this was "just one more example of the 'people-oriented' reorganized employer." The arbitrator concluded that the posting was defamatory within the meaning of the contract (*Dalfort Corp.*, 85 LA 70).

● *By contrast*, an arbitrator found that a union representing workers at a veterans hospital did not commit a contract violation by posting a newsletter that said the hospital director had received multiple demands to bargain over the consolidation of hospital units. Although the union's contract with the Department of Veterans Affairs barred the posting of defamatory materials directed at department officials, the arbitrator said the statement about the hospital director did not constitute defamation because it was true (*Harry S. Truman Memorial Veterans Hospital*, 115 LA 482).

● A city did not have just cause to issue a one-day suspension to a police officer, who highlighted names of two fellow officers on a printout of overtime hours that was on the bulletin board and wrote the phrase, "Are you part of the 300+ club?", where orders did not specify that this kind of comment was inappropriate for bulletin boards (*City of Parma Heights*, 124 LA 1196).

2. Content Related to Organizing

Controversies often arise over the permissibility of union postings that include information related to organizing.

● One arbitrator held that contract clauses permitting the posting of union "announcements" could not be stretched to include organizing materials (*General Electric Co.*, 31 LA 924).

● Another arbitrator held that a union's posting of notices stating "Effects of Being Nonunion" and "Why Join the Union" violated a contract clause prohibiting the posting of "notices containing solicitation," because the contract's ban included soliciting for union membership. The arbitrator also held that the union's posting of a letter to its membership on the status of grievances violated the contract's no-solicitation clause, where the tone of the letter set forth reasons to join the union and thus constituted solicitation for membership (*Leggett & Platt Inc.*, 104 LA 1048).

● An employer was justified in deleting material from a union's electronic bulletin board that urged nonunion employees to join, an arbitrator ruled. The arbitrator said the posting was clearly "internal union business," which the collective bargaining agreement specifically barred the union from posting (*Naval Inventory Control Point*, 118 LA 695).

● When a union posted a listing of nonmembers under the title "Scabs," it was acting improperly, according to an arbitrator. The posting smacked of coercion and created an atmosphere of intimidation, the arbitrator pointed out. The underlying purpose was to blacklist employees, which, the arbitrator concluded, was an unlawful recruitment tactic and misuse of information (*Union Carbide Corp.*, 44 LA 554).

3. Review and Permission Requirement

Some disputes focus on whether employers can require unions to submit notices for review and approval before they are posted.

● One arbitrator decided that an employer did not violate a collective bargaining agreement or local working conditions when it began requiring limited review and approval before a union could post notices on a bulletin board it had purchased. The arbitrator ruled in favor of the employer because the union was unable to provide sufficient information regarding an alleged agreement with the company concerning the use of the bulletin board. According to the arbitrator, the employer had the right to be assured that any material posted on its premises involved legitimate union communications (*U.S. Steel Corp.*, 121 LA 1793).

D. Access to Employer Premises

Many collective bargaining agreements provide for nonemployee union representatives to come onto employer premises to investigate grievances and ensure that employers are not committing contract violations. In some cases, arbitrators have indicated that rights to visit the workplace are inherent in agreements whether explicitly guaranteed or not (36 LA 815, 32 LA 1004, 30 LA 358).

At the same time, however, arbitrators generally find that unions are not entitled to unlimited access. For example, one arbitrator outlined the following considerations with respect to workplace visits by union representatives:

● Visitation rights must be exercised at reasonable times and in a reasonable manner.

● The employer cannot legitimately interfere with the representative's business so long as the visitation rights are exercised reasonably.

● In judging the reasonableness of a visitation's timing, not only the particular hours of visitation but also the number of visitations must be considered.

● The employer can establish reasonable rules governing access to the premises as long as they do not unreasonably interfere with the legitimate purpose of the visit (*Roy Demanes & Assoc. Inc.*, 60 LA 1039).

As suggested by the factors outlined above, general standards of reasonableness can play a large part in deciding the outcome of disputes over union access to employer premises. In addition, arbitrators tend to consider the type of conduct that union representatives engage in while visiting the workplace, as well as the express language of contract provisions governing access rights.

• An employer violated a collective bargaining agreement when it denied the union president and a union official access to its plant, even though an unfair labor practice charge to NLRB had been withdrawn, where the agreement provided that "the Union shall have access to the plant, when necessary, by signing into the visitor log" (*FMS Corp.*, 129 LA 1514).

• Although an employer had agreed to grant reasonable access to employees on company property during reasonable times, the employer was justified in directing union organizers to leave the property because the union did not request access prior to showing up, an arbitrator ruled. For security reasons, the employer had a legitimate interest in knowing who would be coming onto its property and when, the arbitrator pointed out (*Alden North Shore and Alden Naperville*, 120 LA 1469).

• An agreement that required union representatives to make arrangements with an employer before entering the plant to "discuss matters of contract administration" did not allow solicitation of membership by a nonemployee union representative while visiting the plant, an arbitrator held (*Montgomery Ward & Co.*, 85 LA 913).

• Although a collective bargaining agreement stated that union agents would have access to an employer's plant during working hours to take up complaints and determine whether the contract was being complied with, an arbitrator upheld the employer's decision to bar one particular union representative from its property. The union representative had visited the company president in his office to discuss an alleged contract violation and, during a heated argument, had twisted the president's arm, poked him in the chest, and then invited him outside to settle the matter. The employer was justified in refusing to allow the representative back into the plant based on his conduct, the arbitrator held (*Glendale Mfg. Co.*, 32 LA 223).

• Another arbitrator decided that it was appropriate to suspend the visitation rights of a union business agent after his "unseemly" conduct during grievance meetings, which included loud outbursts, swearing, and threats (*Associated Hospitals of San Francisco*, 67 LA 323).

• However, where an employer repeatedly refused to give a union representative access to a plant to investigate violations of a union security clause and even had the union representative arrested for trespassing, an arbitrator ruled that the employer interfered with the union's contractual right to visit the premises. The arbitrator held the employer responsible for creating a confrontational situation where the circumstances called for "a spirit of cooperation and consideration" (*Piper's Restaurant*, 86 LA 809).

• When a college denied a candidate for union office the opportunity to meet union members before school started, it violated a contract clause that provided access for union officials as long as they did not interfere with the operation of classes, programs, and facilities, an arbitrator held. In reaching her decision, the arbitrator noted that the candidate was standing in the main corridor, the area was not congested, and the candidate was not impeding classes, traffic, or the school's sign-in process (*Bd. of Trustees of Community College Dist. No. 508*, 117 LA 1339).

• An arbitrator ruled that the adoption of a city's proposal that no union business could occur "in or on City property" would amount to discrimination against the union. He held that such a proposal would impose an undue hardship on the union in representing its membership and conducting its meetings (*City of Sallisaw, Okla.*, 111 LA 657).

• An employer committed a contract violation when it unilaterally imposed a requirement that union representatives give one-week written notice before visiting work areas, an arbitrator found. The contract allowed access to union representatives as long as their visits did not disrupt work activities. Although the contract also required permission for such visits, it did not state that the employer had to receive written notice or be alerted to union visits a certain amount of time in advance, the arbitrator pointed out (*State of New Hampshire*, 108 LA 209).

● An arbitrator ruled that an employer improperly denied a union's request for use of a former conference room for an after-hours meeting of a union's executive board. The denial, originally based on security and later on the ground that employer facilities could be used only by employees belonging to the bargaining unit, was improper, the arbitrator said. The bargaining agreement provided that the employer grant meeting space to whatever subdivision of "the union" requests it "where feasible," regardless of whether the individuals are employees, the arbitrator noted. The refusal was improper because the employer could have provided space without undue cost or inconvenience, the arbitrator said (*State of Ohio Dept. of Health, Northeast Dist.*, 97 LA 310).

E. Union Buttons and Insignia

Arbitrators tend to agree that employees have a right to wear union buttons and insignia unless the items interfere with production, discipline, or safety; are political in nature or otherwise inappropriate; cause customer dissatisfaction; or have adverse effects on patient care.

● An arbitrator held that teachers should have been permitted to wear buttons saying "Students Our Special Interest—CTA/NEA" despite the contention that the text was political and violated the collective bargaining agreement's prohibition on using the teachers' position to influence students. The arbitrator found that the message on the buttons was geared toward organizing and did not disrupt educational activities (*South Bay Union School District*, 121 LA 1812).

● An arbitrator found that an employer violated a clause in a collective bargaining agreement prohibiting discrimination against union members when it ordered employees to remove from their helmets and other equipment a union sticker stating "No one fired on my shift today!" on the grounds that it mocked the similar-sounding company safety slogan: "No one hurt on my shift today!" The arbitrator said that there was no "special circumstance" of ensuring safety that would justify such an order; the target of the union's protest was not the employer's efforts to improve safety, but rather the perceived notion that the employer attributed most accidents to employees instead of dangerous conditions; and the credible alternative reading that the union merely wanted to capitalize on the employer's catchy slogan and advance its view that less emphasis on discipline was the way to improve workplace safety (*U.S. Steel Corp.*, 121 LA 1255).

● An arbitrator held that a hospital committed a contract violation when it ordered an employee to remove a union-sponsored button that said "When Will The Shift End?" The arbitrator said that even though the employee had customer contact, the message probably would not be misread as profanity, the text was not inherently threatening, and the button itself was not unusually large or noticeable (*University of Iowa Hospitals and Clinics*, 112 LA 360).

● On the other hand, an employer had the right to prohibit phone center service representatives from wearing buttons with the inscription "Fight for My Union? Damn Right I Would" during working hours in the public area of a store, an arbitrator decided. Even though the collective bargaining agreement contained a provision barring the employer from discriminating against employees due to membership or lawful union activities, the arbitrator said the button was not banned for these reasons. Rather, the button was inappropriate because of the image the employer sought to convey to the public, the provocative nature of the message, and the manner of its presentation, the arbitrator reasoned (*Southern Bell Tel. & Tel. Co.*, 78 LA 812).

Part 13

Strikes and Lockouts

I. No-Strike Provisions

OVERVIEW

No-strike provisions are commonly included in collective bargaining agreements. In most cases, labor and management agree to surrender their respective rights to initiate strikes and lockouts at the same time that they pledge to resolve their disputes through contractual grievance and arbitration procedures.

Although no-strike provisions vary in their wording, they typically proscribe a range of conduct, such as walkouts, stay-ins, slowdowns, sympathy strikes, group absences, and orchestrated work disruptions. In general, violations of no-strike clauses occur whenever employees engage in concerted activities that interfere with production.

Even in the absence of concerted activity, employees can be found in violation of no-strike clauses. For instance, if employees decide individually to join in picketing by workers outside their own bargaining unit, they can be disciplined for participating in a sympathy strike.

No-strike pledges are not binding in all situations, however. For example, employees have a legitimate basis for leaving work or refusing to perform assigned duties when faced with hazards that pose an imminent danger to safety or health. In addition, some contracts authorize employees to avoid actions that might undermine other union members, such as handling struck work or crossing valid picket lines.

This chapter discusses the decisions arbitrators have rendered with regard to no-strike provisions, but it does not include a close examination of the penalties meted out for engaging in improper strikes. That subject is covered in a separate chapter, titled "Strike Penalties."

_____ **SUMMARY OF CASES** _____

A. Work Refusals and Disruptions

When employers and unions turn to arbitrators to decide whether no-strike provisions have been violated, the cases usually involve ambiguous actions, such as informal employee gatherings in reaction to perceived contract violations. However, arbitrators generally find that disruptions caused by refusals to work constitute violations of no-strike provisions, especially where the issues giving rise to the disruptions can be addressed through normal grievance procedures.

● An arbitration board threw out one union's argument that a stoppage has to be for an indefinite period of time to be a strike. The board reasoned that a union meeting during working hours was a strike just as certainly as the employer would have been conducting a lockout if it stopped production to hold a directors' meeting (*Atlantic Foundry Co.*, 8 LA 807).

● Another arbitrator declared that a planned mass departure from the workplace that disrupted an employer's production schedule was a work stoppage and violated a contract's no-strike clause (*Nathan Mfg. Co.*, 7 LA 3).

● A longshore union violated a no-strike agreement by withholding work in the midst of a dispute over the unlashing of cargo containers, an arbitrator ruled. The removal of the lashings was generally performed by lashing gangs supplied by the union, but in some cases the lashings were being removed by the crews of the vessels carrying the containers before they came into port. When that happened, the union refused to supply longshore workers to perform other services. Stressing the fact that disputes were supposed to be resolved through grievance and arbitration procedures rather than work stoppages, the arbitrator said the union was not justified in withholding other services because of the unlashing dispute (*Stevens Shipping & Terminal Co.*, 86 LA 373; see also 99 LA 297).

● Employees were engaged in an unlawful work stoppage when, after meeting with their supervisor about an incentive dispute, they refused to go back to work

until they concluded a half-hour session with their grievance chairman, an arbitrator ruled. The supervisor, as well as higher management officials who later came into the meeting, made it clear to the employees that they were to return to work, the arbitrator noted. Group pressure of this type to resolve grievances was completely unsanctioned by the contract, the arbitrator emphasized, concluding that the agreement provided an orderly method for settling such disputes (*Kaiser Steel Corp.*, 51 LA 1041; see also 6 LA 85).

● Despite the fact that an employer shut down a plant, an arbitrator decided that the responsibility for the incident rested with employees. The employees had conducted a stay-in, the arbitrator said, and the employer only shut down the plant after it had unsuccessfully tried to stop the action through the use of plant guards and local policemen. Noting that the employees had been apprised by both the union and the employer that the stay-in violated the contract, the arbitrator said the employer was justified in terminating them (*Chrysler Corp.*, 63 LA 677).

● Another arbitrator held an employer responsible for problems that arose when it reorganized its crane operators without notice. The operators previously had their own department from which they were assigned daily to the cranes in various other departments, but management decided to place them permanently with the other departments. When the change was made, the operators arrived to find their time cards were replaced by cards telling them to go to other locations to punch in. This caused considerable confusion, and the operators were about an hour late in starting work. Rejecting the employer's contention that the delay constituted a strike in violation of the contract, the arbitrator held that management itself caused the delay by its failure to tell the employees beforehand about their transfer (*Ford Motor Co.*, 10 LA 148).

1. Slowdowns

Rather than withholding their services completely, employees sometimes disrupt production by deliberately slowing the pace of their work. According to one arbitrator, even a pause at work that interferes with employees' duty to do their jobs can violate a no-strike clause (*Restaurant-Hotel Employers' Council of Southern California*, 24 LA 429; see also 55 LA 372, 50 LA 1157, 48 LA 1224, 41 LA 1253).

However, arbitrators do not find violations of no-strike provisions every time employees slow their rate of production. One arbitrator explained that the term slowdown, in its normal usage, implies a dispute in which employees intend to get some advantage from their action. In the case at hand, several work crews produced less than they previously had, but because there was no labor dispute, the arbitrator decided that they had not engaged in a slowdown in violation of the contract. The employees still performed at a rate that was considered satisfactory for other workers, the arbitrator noted, adding that the only fair way to judge effort and production was by the job, not by the individual (*Kelly-Springfield Tire Co.*, 42 LA 1162; see also 49 LA 1236).

B. Simultaneous Absences

Absences are sometimes orchestrated by groups of employees to express their dissatisfaction over workplace issues or to pressure employers. Unless unions can show that simultaneous absences are a coincidence and that each absent employee's excuse is legitimate, arbitrators generally consider such actions to be in violation of no-strike provisions.

● Shortly after a union meeting, a group of 20 employees in two departments failed to return to work. The employees phoned their employer individually to report that they were sick. The employer charged that the mass absences were a strike in violation of the contract, and an arbitrator agreed. Although testimony was presented to show that several of the employees actually were ill, the excuses of most were not backed up by evidence. It was this lack of proof that led the arbitrator to conclude that the mass absence was more than a coincidence and constituted a strike (*American Cyanamid Co.*, 15 LA 563; see also 54 LA 569).

● An employer's drivers who called in sick on a Saturday when they were scheduled to work overtime violated a no-strike provision, an arbitrator ruled. According to the arbitrator, the employer had established, albeit based on circumstantial evidence, that the employees' action most likely was concerted and prompted by the fact that nonunion drivers from another company facility also were working that day. Furthermore, the arbitrator noted that the employees presented no evidence to establish that they actually were sick (*Plainville Concrete Services Inc.*, 104 LA 811).

● On the other hand, an arbitrator found that employees were not engaged in an unauthorized strike when they went home because an employer representative had not unlocked the plant gate until one-half hour after the start of their shift. Despite the fact that six co-workers were responsible for preventing the gate from being unlocked on time, the arbitrator concluded that the employees would have reported to work if they had been able to enter the plant (*ACF Industries Inc.*, 87 LA 424).

● A school board did not have the right to add one day to the school schedule to make up for a day it closed the school because one-half of the workforce called in sick, an arbitrator decided. The school waited for six weeks to take action with regard to the incident, and had imposed the make-up day as a condition of contract ratification. Finding that the purpose of the additional workday was to discipline employees for the alleged one-day work stoppage, the arbitrator ruled that the attempt was untimely and, therefore, not based on just cause. While conceding that management might view the decision as rewarding illegally striking employees, the arbitrator said it was too late to determine whether there was a concerted and unlawful work stoppage because the employer did not see fit to discipline culpable employees in a timely fashion (*White Cloud Public Schools*, 72 LA 179).

C. Sympathy Strikes

Sympathy strikes are commonly listed among the activities prohibited under no-strike clauses. Unlike no-strike violations that require concerted activity by employees, bans on sympathy strikes can be violated when employees take individual action.

Refusals to cross picket lines are often equated with sympathy strikes. Unless contract provisions permit employees to honor valid picket lines established by other workers, arbitrators are likely to hold that employees violate no-strike clauses through the observance of picket lines just as if they had taken part in some other form of sympathy strike.

● An arbitrator interpreted language in a collective bargaining agreement that stated that all employees "shall man their jobs, regardless of actions which may be taken or exist by others not a party to this Agreement" as prohibiting a sympathy strike. Recognizing or refusing to cross picket lines established by other employees is "the textbook version" of a sympathy strike, the arbitrator said (*National Maintenance Corp.*, 107 LA 601).

● An electrical union violated a contract provision barring sanction of "any" strike, an arbitrator ruled, when the union's president addressed a letter to a clerical union that was picketing the employer to say the electrical union members would "support" a strike by the clerical union. During the course of the picketing, the electrical employees left with their tools and only returned to work after the strike ended. Refusing to accept the argument that the unified action of some 30 to 40 employees was based on their individual judgments, the arbitrator ruled that they acted in concert in violation of their contract's broad no-strike clause (*American Totalisator Co. Inc.*, 74 LA 377).

● A carpenters' union violated a no-strike pledge when its members refused to cross a picket line set up by another union, notwithstanding the contention that the personal convictions of individual union members prompted independent decisions to refuse to work, an arbitrator decided. Pointing out that the union admitted to doing nothing to convince its members that they should abide by the no-strike clause, the arbitrator emphasized that the union was responsible for the employees' action because it did not make a good-faith effort to get members to honor their contract. Ab-

sent a provision permitting employees to refuse to cross a picket line, the no-strike clause was binding on the employees, the arbitrator concluded (*National Homes Mfg. Co.*, 72 LA 1127; see also 75 LA 36, 68 LA 401, 54 LA 140).

● A local union's chief steward was properly terminated after she called in sick and joined a picket line at another one of her employer's facilities, an arbitrator ruled. The collective bargaining agreement at the location where the employee worked prohibited strikes and picketing, and it also required union representatives to refrain from encouraging or participating in such activities. The employee's violation of the contract by participating in a sympathy strike, coupled with her dishonesty and improper use of sick leave, justified the employer's decision to fire her, the arbitrator found (*Merck-Medco Rx Services of Texas LLC*, 110 LA 782).

● An employer properly fired a cashier who was observed briefly joining a group of security guards who were picketing the employer, an arbitrator held. The guards had abandoned their jobs and set up their picket line near the employer's main entrance. The employee joined the picketers on her day off—intermingling with them, hugging them, and holding one of their signs—but left about 10 minutes later when she was told she was being observed by management. In support of its decision to fire the employee, the employer cited one contract provision that prohibited both individual and concerted activities, including picketing, that interfered with its business, as well as a provision that said employees would be subject to immediate discharge for encouraging an unauthorized work stoppage. Agreeing with the employer that termination was warranted, the arbitrator found that the employee openly provided aid and comfort to the guards and "made a conscious decision to stand arm-in-arm with friends as a picket" (*Racing Corp. of West Virginia*, 119 LA 808).

● In another case, union members could not invoke their contractual right to observe another union's valid picket line where that union had not achieved majority status nor filed a petition with the National

Labor Relations Board to represent the employer's workers, an arbitrator found. There was no legitimate picket line to be honored, the arbitrator said, because the picketed employer was not a "direct employer" with which the union had a "bona fide" labor dispute "over wages, hours, or working conditions" (*Victory Marine & Alaska Cargo Transport*, 102 LA 421).

• Similarly, an arbitrator held that a contractual right to refuse to cross a union-authorized picket line did not apply to a situation where an employer allowed a nonunion contractor to use the bargaining unit's equipment. Eighteen employees had walked off the job over the incident, and the arbitrator upheld the discipline imposed on them by the employer. Rather than observing a picket line, the employees were protesting the equipment assignments and the loss of overtime work, which were contractual disputes that should have been resolved under the contract's grievance and arbitration procedures, the arbitrator determined (*Central Stone Co.*, 98 LA 41).

• *By contrast*, an arbitrator held that a no-strike clause that stated that a union and its members would not "authorize, instigate, aid, condone, or engage in work stoppages, slowdowns, refusals to work, or strikes" did not apply to sympathy strikes. The employer had twice failed to negotiate an express prohibition against sympathy strikes while negotiating agreements with other unions that specifically banned such an activity, the arbitrator observed (*GTE North Inc.*, 94 LA 1033).

• Even though a collective bargaining agreement had a no-strike clause, members of one union were entitled to honor the picket line of another union that had a contract with the same employer, according to an arbitrator. In this case, clerical employees of a waterfront terminal employer had gone on strike, and longshore workers refused to cross their picket line. The arbitrator ruled that the longshore workers had not violated their contract, which contained no promise to pass through another union's picket line. In view of a union's basic teaching that it cannot be used to break the strike of another union, the arbitrator added, the employer should have expected the longshore workers to observe the clerical union's picket line, which was a legitimate one that grew out of a typical labor dispute and could be observed by employees belonging to another union or another unit of the same union (*Waterfront Employers' Association of the Pacific Coast*, 8 LA 273).

• When unions representing employees of a general contractor and a mechanical contractor at a construction site honored another union's picket line directed at an electrical contractor on the same project, they did not commit no-strike violations, an arbitrator decided. The arbitrator said clauses in the other unions' contracts, which permitted employees to honor picket lines, applied to the situation at hand even though the picketing had been restricted to a separate gate of the electrical contractor. Finding that the striking union's picketing was protected primary activity, the arbitrator said the employees of the general contractor and mechanical contractor were entitled to honor such activity (*Associated General Contractors of Minnesota*, 63 LA 32).

1. Potential for Injury

Arbitrators have ruled that employees are justified in their refusals to cross a picket line where doing so would put them at risk of injury or violence.

• One arbitrator held that longshore workers properly stopped unloading barley from a vessel after a picket line was established to protest the importation of food that allegedly was priced too low. In deciding whether the workers faced a threat to their safety by crossing the picket line, the arbitrator interviewed a leader of the picketing group, who was unable to provide any assurance that the picketers would allow the workers to pass without violence or a threat of violence. Considering the "extreme emotions" involved in the situation, the arbitrator determined that the longshore workers would have faced an immediate hazard to their health and safety by crossing the picket lines (*Pacific Maritime Association*, 86 LA 1248).

• Another arbitrator decided that a utility company improperly invoked a no-strike provision to suspend linemen who refused to cross a construction-site picket line. The arbitrator ruled that the linemen did not engage in a concerted work stoppage but individually decided that carrying out their assignment would be too dangerous. The linemen's refusal to work was based on reasonable safety considerations related to the dangerous nature of the assignment and labor unrest associated with the picket line, which gave rise to reliable warnings that there would be trouble at the construction site (*West Penn Power Co.*, 89 LA 1227).

D. Dangerous Working Conditions

The courts have made it clear that employees are justified in refusing to work under "abnormally" dangerous conditions. Accordingly, arbitrators hold that work stoppages or walkouts under such conditions do not constitute violations of contractual no-strike provisions. In many cases, however, arbitrators find that employees do not face enough of a threat to safety or health to warrant work stoppages.

● An employer was not justified in discharging employees who walked off their jobs following management's failure to install fire extinguishers as ordered by an inspector from the Occupational Safety and Health Administration, an arbitrator decided. As a general rule, no employee is required to render services in a place that may be a hazard to his health and safety, the arbitrator emphasized, concluding that conditions existing at the plant were such that the health and safety of the employees were in jeopardy (*RI-JA Machining Co. Inc.*, 66 LA 474).

● An employer improperly suspended employees under a no-strike clause after they left an office building in the wake of a partial ceiling collapse, an arbitrator held. Although the undamaged areas remained available for use, building inspectors refused to guarantee the safety of the site and had been overheard threatening to shut the building down. Given the circumstances, the employees were justifiably concerned for their health and safety and acted reasonably in leaving the building, the arbitrator found. In rejecting the employer's contention that the employees had violated

the no-strike clause, the arbitrator emphasized that they had not engaged in concerted activity aimed at producing a change in the terms or conditions of employment. Noting that the employees had filed leave forms for the period in question, the arbitrator ordered the employer to grant them paid administrative leave and rescind their suspensions (*Pennsylvania Dept. of Public Welfare*, 86 LA 1032).

● Another arbitrator overturned the discharges of a handful of employees who left early on a hot summer day, finding that their individual departures could not be construed as an illegal strike because they were not engaged in concerted activity. Adding, however, that the employees did not experience health problems because of the heat, the arbitrator said they could not escape discipline simply because they were faced with uncomfortable conditions. In the absence of legitimate health or safety hazards, the employees' proper course of action would have been to file a grievance or request permission to leave, the arbitrator declared. Finding that the employees lacked proper authorization or a legitimate reason for stopping work, the arbitrator held that they deserved two-week disciplinary layoffs for leaving work without permission (*Phelps Dodge Aluminum Products Corp.*, 52 LA 375; see also 52 LA 259, 44 LA 847).

● Where it was found that employees had refused to work until management agreed never to operate under alleged dangerous conditions in the future, one arbitrator held that they were clearly engaging in an illegitimate strike. This was more than just a mere refusal to incur an undue health hazard, the arbitrator pointed out (*Ford Motor Co.*, 6 LA 799).

● A nurse's aide who cited safety concerns in refusing to perform routine duties at a nursing home was in violation of a no-strike clause, an arbitrator found. One night when the nursing home was short staffed by one aide, the employee and two other aides who were on duty decided they would only deal with emergencies, such as responding to bed alarms and patient call lights, until a fourth person could be called in. All three were discharged for violating a contract clause that prohibited strikes, slowdowns, and other work refusals. The employer later reinstated the two other aides, but it refused to give the employee another chance because she had led the improper action.

According to the arbitrator, the aides would not have been exposed to personal danger in doing their normal work. On the contrary, they actually put nursing home residents at risk by refusing to make rounds and perform routine duties, the arbitrator said. Finding, however, that the actual architect of the incident was a union staffer who had been contacted by the employee on the night in question, the arbitrator decided that discharge was excessive and ordered reinstatement without back pay (*Rittman Nursing and Rehabilitation Center*, 113 LA 284; see also 93 LA 203).

● A barge repair company properly discharged a shop steward for violating a contractual no-strike clause after he and several co-workers claimed they would not do their jobs because safety documents were not posted, an arbitrator held. For years, the employer had made the documents available in a central location instead of posting them on the vessels themselves. Citing this and other evidence, the arbitrator concluded that there were no imminent dangers that would justify a work stoppage. The steward could have filed a grievance if he were truly concerned about the postings, but instead he chose to withhold his services and encourage others to do the same, the arbitrator noted. All of the steward's activities on the day in question indicated an intent to obstruct normal operations "rather than an attempt to respond to any imminent safety concerns or potential danger to employees," the arbitrator said (*National Maintenance and Repair Inc.*, 101 LA 1115; see also 86 LA 451).

● Employees who did not report for work because their employer would not provide a nurse in the first aid room in its main building were not entitled to be paid for the time they missed, an arbitrator ruled, explaining that the employees' action violated a no-strike clause in their contract.

Although the employees were allowed to refuse work assignments on the ground that working conditions were unsafe, the arbitrator concluded that the absence of a nurse on duty did not constitute such a condition (*Quaker Oats Co.*, 69 LA 727).

E. Handling Struck Work

In the interest of preserving labor solidarity, some collective bargaining agreements contain "hot-goods" clauses that permit employees to refuse to handle work going to or coming from facilities where other workers are engaged in legitimate strikes. If contracts do not include such clauses, however, arbitrators generally agree that employees cannot refuse to handle struck work.

● Communications employees at a cable company refused to forward messages through a struck employer during a period when an emergency condition made it impossible to transmit the messages over their own company's facilities. They were suspended for refusing to handle the so-called "hot traffic."

An arbitrator held that neither the contract nor past practice gave employees the right to refuse to handle the messages bound for a struck employer. He noted that the work in question was not ordinary because it resulted from a cable break at the company. Allowing employees to refuse to handle the work would amount to adding something to the contract that was not put there by the parties, according to the arbitrator. Adding that the union should have followed the contractual grievance procedure rather than taking matters into its own hands, the arbitrator upheld the suspensions (*Commercial Pacific Cable Co.*, 11 LA 219).

● In a case where a strike against one employer caused a customer to shift work to a secondary employer, an arbitrator found a no-strike violation when an international union threatened to pull the union label on the work that was to be performed by the secondary employer. The international union improperly determined that the work was "struck work" under the contract, the arbitrator said, adding that the dispute should have been submitted to arbitration. The arbitrator apportioned almost all of the liability to the international union because the local union was the agent of the international union with respect to the union label and the use of the label was indispensable to the secondary employer's uninterrupted production (*Sterling Regal Inc.*, 69 LA 513)

II. Strike Penalties [LA CDI 118.6603; 118.666]

OVERVIEW

Employers typically discipline employees for participating in illegal work stoppages, such as wildcat strikes, or engaging in job actions that violate contractual no-strike clauses. The penalties meted out by employers can range from pay deductions for lost work time to termination of employment.

Shop stewards and other union leaders tend to face more severe penalties than rank-and-file workers, especially if they are responsible for instigating prohibited job actions. Arbitrators generally agree that union leaders have a greater degree of responsibility than fellow bargaining unit members. This is particularly true where collective bargaining agreements impose an affirmative duty on union leaders to prevent prohibited job actions or get employees back to work if they engage in unsanctioned work stoppages.

In deciding on appropriate strike penalties, arbitrators sometimes go so far as assessing damages against unions. Before arbitrators approve such penalties, however, they may require proof that unions actually endorsed the work stoppages rather than simply failing to avert employees' independent job actions. Also, if the prohibited activities occur in reaction to contract violations by employers, arbitrators are not likely to hold unions solely responsible for the resulting business losses and related costs.

[For discussions of arbitration rulings on other issues that arise in connection with strikes, see Part 2, XXI. Strike-Related Activities and A. No-Strike Provisions in this chapter]

SUMMARY OF CASES

A. Penalties Against Union Officials

Union leaders are supposed to set good examples for the rank and file to follow. Adhering to this view, arbitrators frequently uphold the penalties that employers impose on shop stewards and other union officials who instigate work stoppages or fail to fulfill contractual pledges requiring them to prevent fellow employees from engaging in prohibited strikes, slowdowns, or similar activities (101 LA 1115, 69 LA 459, 69 LA 93).

● The acting president of a local union was justly fired after he told a co-worker to refuse to perform a driving job, an arbitrator ruled. The driving job had become vacant, and another employee had successfully bid on the position. When the company failed to move the successful bidder into the position, he complained to the acting union president. The acting president then told other workers that they should stop filling in on the job, which presumably would prompt the company to place the successful bidder in the position.

After one co-worker agreed to perform the driving job two days in a row, he was told by the acting president that he could face union charges and lose his union card if he did not refuse the assignment. In firing the acting president, the company argued that his actions violated a no-strike clause, which barred slowdowns and other uses of economic force to resolve employment disputes. The arbitrator agreed, finding that the acting president's attempt at preventing the co-worker from performing the driving job was exactly the type of economic force that the contract prohibited. Even though his goal of helping the successful bidder was totally unselfish, the proper mechanism for resolving the dispute was the grievance process, the arbitrator said (*Linderme Tube Co.*, 116 LA 837).

● An employer properly discharged a chief steward for his involvement in protesting the discharge of another employee, an arbitrator ruled. The arbitrator said the steward's contention that he was just acting as a translator for Asian-born employees was not sufficient to overcome a con-

tract provision that said stewards were not authorized to take any action "interfering with the Company's business, but rather shall have the affirmative duty to attempt to stop such action . . . by all reasonable means available" (*Weber Aircraft Inc.*, 114 LA 765).

Arbitrators also sustained discharges where:

● a union steward violated a work rule and a settlement agreement by leading a work stoppage over an assignment that was allegedly contrary to past practice (*San Francisco Newspaper Agency*, 87 LA 537);

● a union steward violated a no-strike clause by attempting to impede the work of probationary employees (*Vernitron Piezoelectric Div.*, 84 LA 1315);

● a union president failed to take affirmative action to prevent a wildcat strike and to put an end to it as soon as it occurred (*Ford Motor Co.*, 41 LA 609);

● a shop steward did not make a convincing effort either to prevent a walkout or to secure a return to work after it occurred (*Gold Bond Stamp Co. of Georgia*, 49 LA 27);

● union committeemen—who probably were the instigators of a walkout—were derelict in their duty as union officers to try to get employees back to work (*Bell Bakeries*, 43 LA 608); and

● union officers failed to discharge their responsibility with regard to unauthorized work stoppages, but rather displayed a passive attitude that allowed them to be swept along in a job action by rank-and-file employees (*Drake Mfg. Co.*, 41 LA 732).

1. Discipline Other Than Discharge

Employers do not always resort to termination when union leaders incite, participate in, or fail to oppose improper strikes. The following are examples of cases in which arbitrators have upheld lesser disciplinary actions against union leaders.

● An arbitrator ruled that an employer properly imposed three-month suspensions on a union president and recording secretary who recommended through their actions that unit employees not show up for scheduled inventory overtime that they previously had volunteered to perform, notwithstanding the two officers' contention that they "never told anyone to not work" (*Zellerbach Paper Co.*, 73 LA 1140).

• An arbitrator upheld a two-week suspension as a penalty for a union official who deliberately shut off the main line that provided gas to welders. The arbitrator did not accept the employee's excuse that he did not think his action would cause "that big of a slowdown" (*CMI Load King Division*, 94 LA 87).

• Under a collective bargaining agreement with a no-strike provision, an arbitrator held that an employer properly imposed a three-day suspension on a union president who told his supervisor that he was "slowing down" in response to an earlier incident. The arbitrator emphasized that statements and conduct by a union president are more serious than statements and conduct by rank-and-file employees (*General Shale Corp.*, 80 LA 375).

• Disciplinary suspensions were in order for shop committeemen who took part in a slowdown, thus giving it their silent, if not active, approval, an arbitrator ruled. He agreed with the employer that although the committeemen did not initiate the slowdown, the fact that they did not try to stop it was a violation of obligations imposed on them under a contractual no-strike clause. Noting that the employer was unable to identify the leaders of the job action, the arbitrator reasoned that the next best approach was to make an example of those who had shirked their responsibility to lead (*Philco Corp.*, 38 LA 889).

2. Discipline Overturned or Reduced

When arbitrators refuse to uphold the discipline imposed on union leaders for their roles in improper strikes and prohibited job actions, they often do so for one or more of the following reasons:

• there were mitigating factors, such as a long work record and no prior disciplinary problems;

• employers failed to show that union officials were more to blame for the incidents than other employees;

• union officials encouraged improper activities, but no work stoppages actually took place; or

• despite unsuccessfully trying to prevent work stoppages, union officials fulfilled their obligations by urging fellow employees to stay on the job or return to work.

The following cases are instances in which arbitrators have set aside or reduced disciplinary actions that employers have taken against union leaders.

• An arbitrator decided that an employer did not have just cause to discharge a shop steward for his alleged role in a work stoppage. The arbitrator based his decision on the fact that the work interruption only lasted 10 minutes, there was no harm to the company's machinery or equipment, the purpose of the stoppage was to make the company aware of perceived mistreatment by lower-level supervisors, employees returned to work immediately when requested, the steward fully cooperated in getting the employees to return to work, and the evidence against the steward was hearsay evidence of two other employees who had a motive for trying to shift the blame for the action (*Boge North America*, 116 LA 197).

• A one-week suspension was too severe in the case of a union steward who told a co-worker to relax his production rate for his assembly job, an arbitrator ruled. There was no evidence that the employer suffered a loss of production, the arbitrator noted. Because the steward's action merely constituted an "attempt" to bring about a slowdown, he technically did not violate the contractual prohibition against strikes, slowdowns, or work stoppages, the arbitrator found (*Gehl Co.*, 73 LA 158).

• In a similar case, an arbitrator reduced the punishment imposed on a steward who urged a work slowdown in violation of a collective bargaining agreement because there was no evidence that a slowdown actually occurred (*KHD Deutz of America*, 88 LA 1230).

• Although a union steward did not fulfill his contractual obligation to deter other employees from taking part in a sickout, discharge was too severe because he was not the instigator of the incident, an arbitrator ruled. Noting that the steward told fellow employees to make their own decisions in the matter, the arbitrator concluded that the steward's inaction indirectly aided the work stoppage. Nevertheless, the arbitrator reduced his termination to a 10-month unpaid suspension while upholding the discharge of the employee who coordinated and led the sick-out (*Lockheed Martin Missiles & Space*, 108 LA 482).

● Participation by a union official in a wildcat strike was sufficient for a one-year probation but not termination, an arbitrator held, given that the union official later tried to halt the work stoppage and his employer failed to prove that he promoted the strike (*Empire-Reeves Steel Division, Cyclops Corp.*, 45 LA 560).

● An arbitrator set aside a 60-day suspension placed on a union president who failed to get workers back on the job within five minutes of a work action. The arbitrator said it was not clear whether the union president caused the wildcat strike or was simply caught up in it (*Weatherhead Co.*, 43 LA 442).

● An employer was not justified in discharging a member of a union shop committee for telling employees to slow down production, an arbitrator decided, notwithstanding the employer's contention that the employee violated a contractual provision barring the union from causing or sanctioning work stoppages, strikes, or slowdowns. Emphasizing that the employer failed to apply progressive discipline, the arbitrator concluded that the employee was not adequately warned that his conduct could result in termination (*Stevens Air Systems Inc.*, 64 LA 425).

● Another arbitrator set aside a steward's suspension because it was based on uncorroborated statements that the steward had encouraged an employee to slow down her production rate and had threatened reprisals if she failed to do so. According to the arbitrator, the evidence of misconduct was insufficient to overcome the greater latitude accorded stewards in performing the duties of their office (*Associated Wholesale Grocers Inc.*, 89 LA 227).

B. Penalties Against Employees

When rank-and-file workers participate in or incite unlawful strikes or other pro-

hibited job actions, they can face the same disciplinary penalties as union leaders. In addition, the outcome of arbitration cases involving rank-and-file employees often hinges on many of the same factors that arbitrators apply in deciding whether or not to uphold the discipline imposed on union leaders.

● An arbitrator ruled that a stevedoring company had just cause to discharge three longshoremen and a union steward for violating a no-strike clause of a collective bargaining agreement, when they refused to load a truck, and the union steward declined to direct them to cease the work stoppage per a provision in the agreement requiring that the steward "immediately instruct" employees to cease such an interruption. The arbitrator rejected the union's claim that a safety exception to the "obey now-grieve later" rule was triggered when the driver—who did not have the credential required by federal law for unescorted access to ports—drove up to the gate and then switched with the driver who had the required credential. No evidence of an abnormal safety hazard was presented and nothing in federal law providing for access to secure areas of maritime facilities prohibited the drivers from switching trucks outside the main gate of the port (*Federal Marine Terminals Inc.*, 130 LA 671).

● One arbitrator upheld the discipline imposed on employees following a slowdown even though they were down the line from the bottleneck and did not have primary responsibility for the drop in production. The arbitrator said if such employees do not call management's attention to the fact that they are not getting as much material to process, they must be regarded as "silent partners" in the slowdown, and they should be regarded as being just as much at fault as those who take the initiative in restricting production (*John Deere Harvester Works of Deere & Co.*, 27 LA 744).

● A hospital was justified in discharging three employees for participating in a sick-out that violated a no-strike clause, an arbitrator ruled. All three had refused to accept lesser penalties as part of a settlement agreement, contending that they had valid excuses for their absences. One employee, who had worked a long shift on the first day of the sick-out, claimed that her absence the next day was justified because she had swollen feet and was exhausted. The second employee claimed he was prevented from working because of a poison ivy flare-up. The third employee said his absence on the first day of the sick-out was necessary because he had to watch one of his two children, and his absence on the second day was necessary because his wife, who normally stayed at home with both kids, had a runny nose and a cough.

The arbitrator found the testimony of the three employees unconvincing for various reasons, including the fact that none of them contacted the hospital at the time of their absences to explain why they were away from work. The hospital, meanwhile, met its burden of showing that the three employees participated in the sick-out, the arbitrator said. With regard to the severity of the penalty, the arbitrator noted that the contract said employees could be fired if they violated the no-strike clause. The arbitrator also observed that termination was appropriate considering the seriousness of the employees' infraction in a hospital setting (*Washington Hospital Center*, 112 LA 495).

● Another arbitrator ruled that an employer was justified in discharging three employees, where they violated the "spirit" of a collective bargaining agreement prohibiting work stoppages by "contributing to the drumbeat" of a possible walkout by other workers (*ATC/Vancom of Las Vegas*, 119 LA 836).

● *By contrast*, an arbitrator decided that discharge was too severe for a bus driver who tried to persuade other drivers to stop work over a paycheck dispute. The arbitrator said that although the employee's actions violated the collective bargaining agreement's language, a lesser penalty was called for, since there was no interruption of bus service, and the entire incident took place over a 10 minute to 20 minute period (*Laidlaw Transit Inc.*, 117 LA 727).

● Even though an arbitrator was convinced that an employee had deliberately engaged in a slowdown, he changed the penalty meted out from discharge to a four-week layoff because of the employee's long history of satisfactory performance (*Reed Roller Bit Co.*, 29 LA 604).

● In cutting a two-week suspension in half for an employee who unsuccessfully urged a production slowdown, an arbitrator noted that the employee had a nine-year history of no disciplinary problems (*Premier Industries Inc.*, 81 LA 183).

● An arbitrator decided that discharge was too severe a penalty for a group of employees who had collectively decided not to increase their output when production standards were raised as a result of job changes. The arbitrator reduced their penalty to a month's layoff in view of their long seniority and the fact that they did not actually decrease their output (*Armour & Co.*, 8 LA 1).

● An arbitrator decided that a two-week suspension was too severe for some employees accused of inciting a wildcat strike. The strike could have occurred even without the employees' actions, the arbitrator said, noting that their co-workers probably did not need much encouragement to engage in the strike (*International Minerals & Chemical Corp.*, 28 LA 121).

● An employer could not deprive employees of their accumulated seniority because they missed a deadline for ending a wildcat strike, an arbitrator ruled. Although the employer informed all 2,500 strikers that they would be terminated if they failed to return by a certain deadline, it later decided it would also take the stragglers back but treat them as new employees. The contract said nothing about loss of seniority as a disciplinary measure, the arbitrator noted, and such a penalty was inappropriate because seniority acts as a vested right and affects the relative standing of all employees. Adding that the loss of seniority would lead to continuing dissension between the stragglers and those employees who stayed on the job or returned by the deadline, the arbitrator ordered the gradual reinstatement of the strikers in order of their seniority (*Lone Star Steel Co.*, 30 LA 519; see also 63 LA 736).

1. Selective Discipline

When considering the reasonableness of discipline imposed on employees for their roles in unlawful strikes or other prohibited job actions, arbitrators do not insist on equal treatment for everyone involved. Employers can vary employees' penalties based on their degree of participation, provided the distinctions are not arbitrary or capricious (97 LA 297, 90 LA 24, 89 LA 1296).

● An employer met its contractual obligation to impose "reasonable discipline" when it issued suspensions of between seven and 30 days to 17 employees of 138 who participated in an unauthorized strike, an arbitrator ruled. In this case, the employer classified employees according to its judgment of each employee's involvement and provided differential discipline based on that judgment. Rather than being unfair, capricious, or discriminatory, the employer made a rational decision based on its observance of employees who were active during the strike, the arbitrator found. The fact that the employer was not able to identify each employee involved in the strike did not prevent it from taking reasonable action toward those it was able positively to identify, the arbitrator declared (Super Valu Stores Inc., 86 LA 622).

● An employer had just cause to fire an employee whom it determined had participated in a wildcat strike to a greater degree than other workers, an arbitrator decided, rejecting the union's contention that the employer needed to establish the employee's participation by a preponderance of credible evidence. The employer did not have to prove that the employee participated to a greater degree than other strikers before it could impose discipline, the arbitrator said, explaining that the employer only needed to establish that it acted fairly and in good faith (Price Bros. Co., 74 LA 748).

● An arbitrator upheld the discharge of a number of employees for participating in a strike that violated a no-strike clause, given evidence that the strikers rejected pleadings of union and company officials to cease and desist the job action. However, the arbitrator reduced the discharge penalty to a disciplinary suspension for an employee who appeared at the plant on two separate days during the strike to get an explanation of a restraining order he had received in the mail, as well as for another employee who attempted to prevent the strike and who worked the first five days of the strike but missed the last three days because of threats against him and his wife (Grumman Flexible, 72 LA 326).

● An employer was justified in giving warning letters to 20 employees who affirmatively agreed to participate in an illegal work stoppage, an arbitrator said. However, the arbitrator reduced the penalty to an oral warning for another 32 employees who participated only passively. The more severe penalty for the workers given a written warning was justified because of their past disciplinary history, the arbitrator reasoned (Public Utility Dist. No. 1 of Clark County, 103 LA 1066).

● Another arbitrator set aside suspensions imposed on five employees accused of being the first to walk out of the plant during a wildcat strike because their identification was based on a supervisor's observing them from a window about 50 yards from the gate where the employees exited (W.S. Hodge Foundry Inc., 55 LA 548).

2. Pay Dispute

Disputes in the wake of strikes, slowdowns, and other job actions sometimes focus on pay issues. For example, employees might claim that they are entitled to be paid because they were prevented from working through no fault of their own, while employers might argue that they have a right to impose pay deductions that correspond with the drop in output caused by employees' actions.

● One arbitrator concluded that pay deductions were warranted in the case of an employer that docked the pay of every employee who participated in a work stoppage. The arbitrator rejected the union's contention that only those actually responsible for the stoppage should have had pay deductions. While acknowledging that it would not be fair to penalize innocent employees if they were forced to stop working because of others' activities, the arbitrator said that in this case, there was work that could have been done, so "it is quite manifest that each employee who stopped did so upon his own responsibility and should suffer any resultant consequences of such action" (*Fruehauf Trailer Co.*, 1 LA 155).

● Another arbitrator decided that when incentive employees engaged in a slowdown, they could be denied pay guarantees under an incentive plan and be paid only for actual output (*American Steel & Wire Co.*, 6 LA 392).

● In a similar case with the opposite outcome, an arbitrator said that cutting pay below guaranteed levels was a contract violation and therefore an improper penalty for a slowdown (*Jacobs Mfg. Co.*, 29 LA 512).

● An arbitrator held that an employer could not refuse payment to certain employees following a strike. The employer had broadcast a message by radio that it would be operating. Some employees showed up for work but were later told to go home, while other employees had been told by supervisors not to report for work. Both groups were entitled to be paid, the arbitrator held, because their lost time was primarily attributable to the employer's instructions, not the halt in production caused by the strike (*U.S. Steel Corp.*, 45 LA 509).

C. Amnesty Pledges

In the interest of getting operations back to normal, employers sometimes make offers of amnesty to employees who have taken part in improper strike activities. The following examples illustrate arbitration rulings that involve offers of amnesty to striking employees.

● Despite promising amnesty if employees would end a wildcat strike and get back to work "without further delay," an employer properly gave one-day suspensions to those employees who did not return to work until an hour later, an arbitrator ruled. The arbitrator said that the pledge was not a continuing offer to be accepted whenever the employees felt like returning (*Bethlehem Steel Corp.*, 47 LA 524).

● Although an employer's amnesty offer following a wildcat strike barred discipline for "passive nonviolent participation," it did not bar the discharge of two employees who tried to promote a secondary boycott, an arbitrator decided. According to the arbitrator, the evidence established

that they were guilty of concerted misconduct above and beyond actions protected by the amnesty agreement (*Falls Stamping & Welding Co.*, 48 LA 107).

● While finding that a steward had to be included in an employer's blanket offer of reinstatement following an unlawful strike, an arbitrator held that the denial of back pay was an appropriate penalty for the steward's role as the instigator of the strike (*Strombeck Manufacturing Co.*, 45 LA 47).

● An arbitrator concluded that a municipal employer violated a post-strike amnesty provision when it issued a written reprimand to a steward for allegedly failing to take the most direct route to his building-inspector field assignments and for failing to maximize inspection time. The arbitrator found that in this case, the discipline imposed was part of a pattern of retaliation against the steward for his outspokenness and union advocacy, and particularly for his actions during the recent strike (*County of Sonoma*, 96 LA 713).

D. Damage Award Penalties

Arbitrators have assessed damages against unions for their roles in improper strikes, even where collective bargaining agreements did not expressly grant the authority to do so.

● Despite a contract's silence on the issue of damage awards, one arbitrator declared that arbitral authority in the dispute resolution process inherently involves the fashioning of remedies to compensate for the violation of contractual rights. Accordingly, the arbitrator awarded a vessel owner and the contractor it engaged to perform stevedoring services damages that they sustained when longshore workers engaged in an improper work stoppage. The workers violated clear contractual language requiring them to continue to work pending the adjustment of any dispute that arose with regard to contract interpretation, the arbitrator held. Finding that the work stoppage was sanctioned, if not encouraged, by the union, the arbitrator ordered the reimbursement of the vessel owner and contractor for all of the additional expenses they incurred as a result of the work stoppage (*Farrell Lines Inc. and Maher Terminals Inc.*, 86 LA 36; see also 51 LA 500, 33 LA 574).

● A union that represented mechanics and drivers under separate agreements was liable to an employer for damages when the mechanics honored picket lines set up by the drivers after their contract expired, an arbitrator ruled. Citing a contractual no-strike clause and a provision obligating the union to see that its members obeyed all reasonable rules, the arbitrator determined that the union was required to take all reasonable steps to end strikes, but in this case the union failed to direct the mechanics to ignore the drivers' picket lines and return to work (*Westinghouse Transport Leasing Corp.*, 69 LA 1210; see also 66 LA 388, 66 LA 82).

● An employer was entitled to damages after a union steward encouraged a work stoppage in violation of a no-strike clause, an arbitrator ruled, since the steward was acting within the scope of his authority and the union was responsible for his actions as its agent. The arbitrator added that the employer was entitled to attorneys' fees in connection with the work stoppage, including the costs of legal services performed in obtaining a court order to compel arbitration over the matter (*Rust Engineering Co.*, 77 LA 488).

● In a separate case, an arbitrator awarded damages consisting of payment for required overtime and attorneys' fees after a union did not make efforts to get employees back to work when they walked off their jobs in violation of a no-strike clause. The arbitrator explained that timely completion of the project was of the essence, and requiring overtime to make up for lost work hours was reasonable. The claim for attorneys' fees also was reasonable, the arbitrator found, to cover the employer's costs for legal work involved in conducting a preliminary investigation and obtaining a court order to end the walkout (*Rust Engineering Co.*, 75 LA 189).

● As a remedy for a strike against a construction employer on a highway project, an arbitrator allowed damages including labor costs, rental value of its own equipment, rental value of rented equipment, and the prorated costs of traffic protection (*Foster Grading Co.*, 52 LA 197).

1. Partial or No Damages

Arbitrators commonly reject requests to hold unions responsible for losses incurred as a result of improper strikes. In cases where arbitrators award partial or no damages, they often do so because unions have not sanctioned employees' work stoppages or because employers, through contract violations or similar actions, have caused or contributed to the unrest that prompted the stoppages.

● In one case, an arbitrator found that employees instigated a work stoppage on their own, and their union never encouraged or endorsed the job action. In concluding that the union was not liable for damages, the arbitrator also noted that the union's initial response to the work stoppage was to tell employees to "work now and grieve later," and it immediately sought sufficient labor when confronted by the employer. The company official on the site failed to warn the employees or union representatives that it considered the refusal to accept work to be an illegal work stoppage, the arbitrator added, and the lack of similar incidents in the past made it difficult for the union to anticipate the employees' action (*Cooper/T. Smith Stevedoring Co.*, 99 LA 297).

● An arbitrator refused to assess damages against a union in connection with a work stoppage protesting an employer's subcontracting agreement with a nonunion company. The arbitrator pointed out that the employer had improperly entered into the subcontracting agreement without notifying the union and had failed to organize a pre-job conference as called for in the collective bargaining agreement (*Shook Inc.*, 91 LA 620).

● Citing an employer's shared responsibility for the underlying dispute that culminated in a shutdown, an arbitrator refused to award full compensatory damages based on a union's no-strike violation. In this case, the arbitrator allowed out-of-pocket expenses and lost profit on a specific transaction that the employer was unable to complete due to the violation, and a reasonable portion of overhead expenses and general loss of profits arising from the shutdown. The arbitrator refused, however, to allow recovery of attorneys' fees sustained in an effort to get an injunction to end the strike (*Mercer, Fraser Co.*, 54 LA 1125; see also 53 LA 869, 53 LA 542).

• In another case, an arbitrator determined that no damages were necessary because a union's improper handbilling and picketing actions, though irritating, were de minimis (*Lucky Stores Inc.*, 100 LA 262).

Part 14

Union Security

I. Union Security [LA CDI 8.01, 8.25]

OVERVIEW

Union security clauses in labor contracts can impose varying requirements with regard to union membership, dues or fee payments, and the
use of union hiring halls.

Some clauses make union membership or financial obligations compulsory for covered workers (to the extent such requirements are permitted
under state and federal law). Under union-shop and agency-shop agreements, for example, workers must become members as a condition of continued employment or make payments to the union in lieu of regular membership. When introducing union-shop agreements, employers and unions
sometimes limit membership requirements to new hires, thereby allowing
existing workers who are not members to continue their nonunion status.

Among other types of union security arrangements, maintenance-of-
membership provisions are relatively common. In general, these provisions require employees who are union members on the effective date of
a collective bargaining agreement to remain members for the duration of
the agreement. A related feature contained in many contracts is a clause
that only allows workers to discontinue their union membership if they follow specified resignation procedures during particular windows of time.

Collective bargaining agreements also can call for the use of union hiring halls. Some arrangements require employers to obtain employees
exclusively through union hiring halls, such as for intermittent work in
the construction industry. Nonexclusive arrangements allow employers to
consider candidates from other sources along with referrals from union
hiring halls.

This chapter examines various types of disputes that arise in connection with union security agreements. Some cases deal with basic ques-

tions, such as what constitutes union membership or who is covered by the agreements. For the most part, however, disputes in this area focus on the enforcement of membership and financial obligations, which can include demands on employers to discharge delinquent employees or make up for missing payments that unions are entitled to receive.

SUMMARY OF CASES

A. Membership and Employment Status

Where labor contracts include maintenance-of-membership agreements or other union security provisions, determining what constitutes union membership can become an issue. In one of the earliest labor arbitration cases, decided during World War II, an arbitrator held that all of the following conditions had to be met in order for employees to be considered union members:

• The employees must have signed an official application card showing their intention to join the union and their desire to have the union act as their representative for collective bargaining.

• The employees must have paid their first month's union dues.

• The union must have issued employees with an official receipt for the first month's dues payment.

• The union must have furnished employees with an official membership card showing that they have been accepted for membership (*Bendix Aviation Corp., Pacific Division*, 15 LRRM 2650).

Job classifications and employment status also can play a key role in deciding whether union security provisions apply to particular workers. For example, the promotion of rank-and-file workers to supervisory positions usually means they are no longer covered as bargaining unit members.

• A union did not have the right to seek the termination of a promoted employee because of his failure to pay union dues during the 60-day probationary period that applied to his new supervisory position, an arbitrator held, even though the employee continued to accumulate seniority and could decide to return to the bargaining unit. The arbitrator said that because the supervisor was not a member of the unit during the 60-day period, he had no responsibility to

remain a union member in good standing as a condition of his employment (*Electric Energy Inc.*, 92 LA 351).

• An arbitrator ruled that a radio announcer who hosted a Saturday two-hour program was an employee required to pay union dues because he was not a supervisor, he did not take to the airwaves only in emergency conditions, his program was not a fund-raising event or a mobile unit remote broadcast, he did not perform on an irregular basis, and his work was not trivial, incidental, or de minimus (*WMHT Educational Telecommunications Inc. (WMHT/WMHQ)*, 108 LA 108).

• An employer did not violate a collective bargaining agreement when it failed to apply union membership requirements to licensed vocational nurses, an arbitrator ruled, despite the union's claim that LVNs were included in the list of classifications for which the union was the exclusive bargaining representative. The arbitrator pointed out that the recognition section of the collective bargaining agreement explicitly excluded supervisors, and, under the National Labor Relations Act, LVNs working as charge nurses were considered supervisors (*Hacienda Health Care Inc.*, 101 LA 550).

• An arbitrator agreed with an employer that it was reasonable to have a unit employee (who happened to be the plant manager's son) function as a supervisory "working foreman" in light of the relatively small size of the shop involved and the lack of sufficient supervisory work available to occupy all of the employee's time, as long as he maintained his union membership. Rather than allowing only bargaining unit members to engage in unit tasks, the contract required such work to be performed by union members, the arbitrator pointed out. The arbitrator also noted that no unit employees suffered any loss of work as a result of the employee's part-time performance, and the union had not been denied any financial support it previously enjoyed (*Modesto Milling*, 78 LA 249).

● Under a contract that recognized a union as the exclusive bargaining representative of full-time employees and that permitted part-time employees to be used to augment regular staff on an on-call basis, an arbitrator decided that the union was not entitled to require a part-time employee, who was performing fill-in duties, to pay union dues and fees. The arbitrator found that the part-time employee was not subject to the terms and conditions of the contract, particularly the contract's agency-shop provisions, because he was not included in the bargaining unit (*Saginaw County Juvenile Home*, 67 LA 446).

1. Defining New Hires

Under modified union-shop agreements, which require new hires to become union members but exempt existing employees from membership requirements if they were not members at the time the agreement went into effect, disputes sometimes arise over who should be treated as a new hire. When employees transfer into the bargaining unit, for example, some arbitrators have ruled that they must be treated as new hires and required to join the union (35 LA 274, 19 LA 85, 18 LA 664).

● One arbitrator held that an employee was not required to join a union on her return to the bargaining unit from a supervisory position, because she could not be considered a "new hire" under the parties' modified union-shop agreement. The employee had been with the employer for nearly 28 years and had not been a union member before she was transferred to the salaried supervisory job, the arbitrator pointed out (*Lord Mfg. Co.*, 55 LA 1005).

● In another case, a union had a master agreement with an automobile manufacturer requiring new employees to join the union within 30 days of the date they were hired. When an entire unit was brought under the master agreement several months later, the union claimed that all of the employees in the unit had to join. An arbitrator disagreed, however, finding that the effective date of the agreement for purposes of the new unit was the date the unit came under the agreement. Consequently, the arbitrator decided that the requirement to join the union did not apply to employees who were nonmembers when the agreement took effect for the new unit (*Chrysler Corp.*, 21 LA 45).

B. Failure to Join or Pay Unions

Unions commonly call for the discharge of employees who fail to become members, maintain membership, or make dues or fee payments as required under union security clauses. In cases where employers are guilty of failing to enforce union membership and payment requirements, arbitrators sometimes hold that they are responsible for making up the missed payments.

If employees are not union members and pay agency fees in lieu of regular dues, they can object to the use of their payments for nonrepresentational activities—that is, activities not related to collective bargaining, contract administration, or grievance adjustment—in accordance with the U.S. Supreme Court's ruling in *Communications Workers of America v. Beck* (487 U.S. 735, 128 LRRM 2729 (1988)).

● An employer improperly allowed a temporary employee to continue working after 30 days without joining the union, according to an arbitrator. The arbitrator pointed out that the collective bargaining agreement provided that after 30 days, temporary employees became part of the bargaining unit and had to join the union. When the temporary employee refused to do so, the arbitrator said the employer was obligated to terminate her or transfer her to a nonunion workplace (*Mikocem LLC*, 121 LA 1377).

● An arbitrator ruled that the discharge of an employee for failure to pay delinquent union dues was with just cause, despite the employee's claim that he did not receive a copy of the union's letter to the employer requesting that he be discharged because he had moved and failed to notify the union of his address. The arbitrator pointed out that the employee's excuses did not address his failure to pay dues for several months before the grace period began or after he received the union's notice that he would be subject to discharge if he did not become current in his dues by the end of the grace period. The arbitrator also noted that the employee had himself set in motion the forces that caused his termination by choosing to revoke his authorization for dues deduction (*American Airlines Inc.*, 120 LA 1625).

● An employer violated an agency-shop provision of a collective bargaining agreement when it failed to discharge an employee who refused to pay monthly service fees to the union, an arbitrator held. The employer argued that the union's claim was defective because it had not mentioned that a fee reduction was available if the employee elected the status of an objecting nonunion fee payer, but the arbitrator rejected that argument. The union had given the employee specific information on who to contact if he had questions, and the employer could easily have secured the information about the reduction in fees if it had wanted to include such information in a letter to the employee, the arbitrator observed (*Dyncorp Wallops Flight Facility*, 101 LA 1033).

● An employer was liable to a union for the amount of unpaid union dues or agency fees that accrued from the date it violated a union security clause by refusing to discharge employees who failed to make such payments, according to an arbitrator, since the union's loss of these amounts was the direct result of the violation. The arbitrator modified the award to exclude initiation fees, however, finding that they should remain the responsibility of individual employees (*Great Western Carpet Cushion Co. Inc.*, 95 LA 1175).

● After failing to enforce a contract provision that required employees to become union members as a condition of employment, an employer had to pay as damages to the incumbent union an amount equal to the aggregate regular dues that would have been collected from one particular employee for a period beginning 30 days after the date of hire and extending to the date the employee left the bargaining unit. In explaining his decision to impose liability on the employer, the arbitrator said he

lacked the authority to require retroactive dues payments from a nonunion employee (*Servco Automatic Machine Products Co. Inc.*, 100 LA 882).

● An employer was obligated to terminate some employees after the union notified it that the employees, who were expelled from the union for nonpayment of dues, had not tendered the required dues, an arbitrator ruled. Pointing out that the demand that the employees be discharged for not paying dues was in full compliance with applicable labor laws, the arbitrator concluded that the union was not treating the employees arbitrarily or unfairly by requiring them to pay an initiation fee in order to be reinstated (*Times Journal Publishing Co.*, 72 LA 971).

● *By contrast*, another arbitrator denied a union's request to discharge five employees who failed to pay dues, initiation fees, or agency fees. The arbitrator pointed out that the union did not properly notify the employees of their right to be nonmembers, did not provide a statement of the precise amount and months for which dues were owed and the method used to calculate the amounts, and improperly attempted to assess agency fee payments that exceeded monthly dues payments (*UNDS*, 112 LA 14).

● An employee who signed an application form to become a union member at the request of a friend and in the belief that its only purpose was to get the union certified was improperly discharged for failing to pay union dues, an arbitrator ruled. Finding that the employee demanded that his application card be returned to him and that he did not intend to belong to the union in advance of the effective date of the contract, the arbitrator concluded that the employee was induced to sign the card under mistake of fact (*Rexnord Inc.*, 77 LA 1166).

● Where a collective bargaining agreement expressly exempted an employer from any liability resulting from its violations of the contract's union-security clause, an arbitrator held the employer was not required to compensate a union for lost dues after the employer violated the agreement by failing to discharge employees who did not pay their union dues (*Yukon Manufacturing Inc.*, 105 LA 339).

C. Resignations and Escape Periods

Employees can resign their full union membership under certain types of union security agreements provided they follow proper procedures. Below are examples of arbitration cases dealing with membership resignations and escape periods.

● Where a union's constitution provided for a 10-day period for resignations, an arbitrator ruled that employees who had not resigned within this period were still members and thus subject to the maintenance-of-membership clause of a collective bargaining agreement (*Bridgeport Rolling Mills Co.*, 18 LA 233).

● A municipal employer committed a contract violation when it stopped deducting dues from three employees who submitted their resignations a year after the contract had expired, an arbitrator ruled. According to the arbitrator, the agreement remained in effect while it was being renegotiated; furthermore, the employer was obligated to comply with the provision stating that dues deductions could only be revoked during a 15-day window prior to the expiration date (*City of Effingham, Ill.*, 108 LA 1131).

● Under a contract with a maintenance-of-membership provision, an employee who resigned his membership after the union called a strike during a breakdown in negotiations for a new contract was not exempt from renewing his union membership following the execution of the new labor agreement, an arbitrator ruled. The arbitrator cited the parties' agreement to adopt language similar to that of a past labor contract as indicative of their intent not to interrupt the union security provision (*Hershey Foods Corp.*, 59 LA 453).

● In the absence of a specific reference to an escape period under a new contract, an arbitrator said previous contract language on union resignations was considered to be carried forward by the terms of a renewal agreement. The agreement provided that all the provisions of the old contract should be carried forward in the new contract except those specifically modified by the renewal agreement (*Fulton Sylphon Co.*, 7 LA 286).

● Where a union's constitution and by-laws did not mention the right of members to resign, but the collective bargaining agreement contained a maintenance-of-membership clause containing an escape period and allowing employees to withdraw from union membership "if they so desire," an arbitrator ruled that withdrawal from the union was presumed to be a reserved right of members. The agreement the union made with the employer came first, the arbitrator said, regardless of the union's constitution (*Shell Oil Co.*, 14 LA 143).

● An arbitrator stated that a union could waive the delinquency of its members when no third-party interests were affected. It is proper, the arbitrator said, for a union to continue to carry members even if they are in arrears in their dues because of illness or financial difficulties, if the members do not object. If treating delinquent employees as members in good standing meant depriving them of their right to withdraw from the union, however, then they would not have to be discharged for failing to maintain their membership, the arbitrator said (*Monsanto Chemical Co.*, 12 LA 1175).

1. Premature Resignation Letters

Employees who submit their letters of resignation from union membership prior to the escape period nevertheless may be held to have effectively resigned, particularly where the letters were sent close to the escape period.

● Under a contract providing that an employee could withdraw from a union during the seven days prior to April 1 of each year, an arbitrator decided that an employee gave timely notice of resignation from the union where he spoke to union officials about resigning and handed a letter to the payroll department requesting his withdrawal from the union as of April. Notwithstanding the union's contention that the letter was untimely because it carried a date that was before the beginning of the escape period, the arbitrator concluded that the crucial date in the letter was the effective date of the withdrawal (*Continental Oil Co.*, 61 LA 610).

• Under a maintenance-of-membership agreement that provided a 15-day escape period beginning after Nov. 6, an arbitrator ruled that letters of resignation submitted by 19 employees in the period of Oct. 17 through Nov. 5 were, nonetheless, effective. In this case, the union waited until Nov. 22 before it informed the employees that their attempted resignations were not effective, saying the 15-day escape period ran from Nov. 7 through Nov. 22. The arbitrator noted that the employees obviously intended their resignations to become effective on the first possible date. He added that the union was guilty of bad faith in waiting until the last day of the escape period to inform the employees that their resignation letters were invalid (*Carson Mfg. Co. Inc.*, 52 LA 1057).

2. Verbal Resignations

Disagreements sometimes arise as to whether resignations must be in writing or whether verbal resignations are acceptable.

• After examining a union's constitution and by-laws, an arbitrator ruled that an employee was within his rights when, during a 15-day escape period, he verbally informed the chief union steward of his desire to resign from the union. The arbitrator said it was clear that the steward was a designated contact person between the union and its members. Therefore, the employee had a right to tender his resignation to the steward. The arbitrator further found that neither the constitution and by-laws nor custom and usage in the union required that a resignation be submitted in writing (*Onsrud Machine Works Inc.*, 9 LA 375).

• Another arbitrator held that "proof of knowledge held by responsible union officers, no matter how received, that a member wishes to drop out of the union" determines whether or not the employee has resigned. The arbitrator also held that the union's efforts to get the employee to sign a union membership card upon his re-hire as a new employee constituted further proof of the employee's claim that he had resigned from the union when he left the employer (*Chicago Metal Mfg. Co.*, 9 LA 429).

D. Circumvention of Union Security

In some cases, unions claim that actions taken by employers circumvent or directly violate union security agreements by taking away bargaining unit work.

• Under a contract with a union-shop agreement, an arbitrator found that an employer improperly used temporary workers to perform bargaining unit work. Citing an unprecedented rise in spending on temporary services, the arbitrator held that the employer's actions had the effect of denying full-time work and overtime opportunities to the bargaining unit. "An employer may not, by its own actions, cause understaffing or undermanning and then use that as the excuse or explanation for resorting to temporary or casual employees," the arbitrator said. While stating that it was beyond his authority to order the employer to desist altogether from the use of temporary employees, the arbitrator decided that it was appropriate to order the employer not to use temporary workers in any week that a unit employee was on layoff status or that the number of unit members fell below a certain level (*Friedland Industries Inc.*, 94 LA 816).

• A terrazzo constructor did not violate a multi-employer collective bargaining agreement when it did not hire a foreman and one tile layer or terrazzo worker from the union, an arbitrator ruled, where the agreement stated that the foreman is "excepted" from hiring requirements "where more than one Tile Layer or Terrazzo Worker is employed on the job," and only one worker was on the job (*Rosa Mosaic Tile Co.*, 126 LA 1707).

• An arbitrator ruled that a truck driver was entitled to return to work for a company—which had violated an addendum to a collective bargaining agreement by refusing to rehire him after he was removed as a union official—only whenever it needed more than one driver, because his union membership had been suspended, and other provisions of the agreement required the company to have a steward who was a union member whenever it employed at least one driver (*Jack Gibson Construction Co.*, 125 LA 1019).

• An employer was not justified in reclassifying a secretary who was the only remaining member of a bargaining unit as a production assistant, another arbitrator ruled, because the new position was outside the bargaining unit, had a lower salary, and the job duties remained the same. According to the arbitrator, taking away the employee's union representation violated the collective bargaining agreement's recognition and union security articles (*Washington Teachers Union Local 6*, 108 LA 821).

• On the other hand, an arbitrator ruled that an employer did not violate a union security provision when it subcontracted janitorial work. The arbitrator based his decision on a contract clause that said one of the considerations for granting union security was that it would lead to higher levels of efficiency and productivity. The arbitrator said that transferring janitorial work, which was marginal to the primary work of the bargaining unit, had to be viewed as permitting a "higher level of efficiency" and, therefore, in the mutual interest of the employer and the union (*Olin Corp.*, 109 LA 919).

E. Hiring Hall Arrangements

Union hiring halls can refer workers to employers on an exclusive or nonexclusive basis. Under exclusive hiring hall arrangements, employers are obligated to seek workers solely from the union, whereas nonexclusive arrangements allow employers to consider candidates from other sources as well. If employers decide not to accept union-referred workers because they are incompetent or unsatisfactory, arbitrators are likely to uphold their decisions.

• An arbitrator ruled that a subcontractor violated a project labor agreement when it failed to limit the use of its core work force on a project to five employees on a one-to-one basis with employees hired through a union hiring hall with all subsequent hiring through the union. However, damages were limited to the last full month of the subcontractor's work on the project, because the union failed to assert the hiring violations for nine months after the subcontractor began operations, and the subcontractor complied with other agreement requirements (*Spectrum Glass and Aluminum Inc.*, 127 LA 139.

• An employer committed a contract violation when it hired nonunion cement masons for an emergency job rather than going through a union hiring hall, an arbitrator ruled. Because the work had to be done the next day for safety reasons, the employer could not satisfy the hiring hall's requirement of providing 48-hour advance notice. Instead of immediately hiring nonunion workers, however, the employer should have first consulted with the union and only hired nonunion workers if it did not agree to waive the 48-hour notice provision and guarantee labor the next day, the arbitrator said (*Levernier Construction Inc.*, 113 LA 152; see also 99 LA 689, 74 LA 633).

• An arbitrator ruled that an employer improperly used nonunion employees for work instead of union members from a hiring hall. He said that even though some of the employer's competitors used nonunion workers, the parties' collective bargaining agreement and past practice carried considerably more weight than "industry practice" (*Expo Group*, 109 LA 503).

• An employer that hired union-referred employees did not have just cause to refuse the referral of a particular employee, according to an arbitrator, even though the collective bargaining agreement had a provision allowing the employer to reject any applicant, as long as it gave a written explanation of why it was doing so. The arbitrator said that giving the employer the unrestricted right to refuse referrals would allow it to "circumvent the pecking order" for referrals and would render the seniority-like structure for referrals "superfluous." As the basis for his decision, the arbitrator cited "the well-accepted arbitration principle that labor agreements must be construed as a whole so as not to render specific provisions of the agreement inoperative" (*Hubbell-Tyner Inc.*, 115 LA 114).

• An employer was not justified in rejecting inexperienced mushroom pickers referred to it by a union, an arbitrator ruled. The arbitrator said that the job description for "general labor," which includes "picking . . . and other related unskilled jobs," when read together with the collective bargaining agreement's hiring-hall provision and the employer's past practice of hiring inexperienced mushroom pickers, did not allow the employer to reject inexperienced pickers (*West Foods Inc.*, 76 LA 916).

● Under a collective bargaining agreement that allowed an employer to reject unsatisfactory applicants, an arbitrator ruled that the employer was justified in rejecting a hiring hall referral who left several questions on a job application unanswered, did not provide adequate references, and was described as a "troublemaker" and not being a "team player" by a subordinate (*Kodiak Electric Assn. Inc.*, 107 LA 1119).

● A contract provision requiring union referrals to receive "due consideration" was not violated when a newspaper rejected the union's referral for a pressman position due to reservations about the applicant's job knowledge. Instead, the newspaper hired a candidate who had directly applied to the newspaper for the position. The arbitrator explained that once the employer gave "due consideration" to the union's referral, it had met its contractual obligation and had the right to reject the union's referral for "any reason which is not in and of itself illegal" (*Cleveland Plain Dealer*, 101 LA 393).

● Under a hiring hall agreement that gave an employer the right to reject any referred employee "within its sole discretion," the employer properly dismissed two union referrals after they had been on the job one week, an arbitrator ruled. He said use of the term "reject" applied not only to the employer's right to reject a person sent from the hiring hall, but also to subsequent actions once the person was put to work. According to the arbitrator, the individuals in question were casual employees on probation, not full-time, regular employees entitled to all contractual benefits and protections (*New Orleans Public Facility Management Inc.*, 93 LA 681).

Part 15

Dues Checkoff

I. Dues Checkoff [100.020303 (public employees); 9.01 et. seq.]

OVERVIEW

Many collective bargaining agreements contain dues checkoff provisions to facilitate employees' payment of union dues and fees. Checkoff arrangements take effect for individual employees only after they give their written authorization. Their employers then become responsible for making deductions from their paychecks and forwarding the money to unions.

In addition to providing for the payment of regular union dues, checkoff arrangements can authorize employers to take deductions for other payments, such as initiation fees and special levies, as long as the authorization forms reference such payments. Although the duration of authorizations is limited to one year, checkoff provisions commonly call for automatic renewal if employees do not follow specified revocation procedures.

Disputes in connection with dues checkoff arrangements usually focus on whether appropriate amounts are being requested by unions and deducted by employers and on whether checkoff authorizations remain enforceable in certain situations, such as after employees resign from the union or leave the bargaining unit. In resolving such disputes, arbitrators routinely begin by reviewing the applicable contract language, but their decisions tend to be driven by the unique facts and circumstances of each individual case.

SUMMARY OF CASES

A. Employers' Checkoff Obligations

Although employers are responsible for giving force to dues checkoff arrangements by deducting money from employees' wages and remitting to unions the withheld funds, they sometimes disagree with the validity of unions' dues and fee assessments, claim that dues checkoff does not apply under certain circumstances, or simply make mistakes in the amounts they deduct. When such situations arise, arbitrators often are called upon to determine if employers are meeting their dues checkoff obligations and decide what, if any, corrective measures need to be taken.

• One arbitrator imposed payment responsibility on a nursing home after it allegedly failed to deduct and remit to a union correct dues and fee amounts for a period of 15 months. A checkoff agreement between the parties obligated the employer to make deductions from each employee who had voluntarily executed a signed authorization. Rather than waiting for back payments to be deducted from employees' wages, the arbitrator held, the employer should bear the financial burden of making up any amounts that were owed. High turnover rates in the nursing home industry would mean that many of the affected employees had left their jobs, the arbitrator explained, and for those who remained with the employer, it would be too severe to take 15 months worth of dues out of their paychecks all at once.

To determine the exact amounts the employer would have to pay, the arbitrator instructed the union to give the employer statements showing details of the alleged underpayments. The arbitrator said the employer could challenge the statements by showing that particular workers were not employed in the bargaining unit at the time, had not provided checkoff authorizations, or were overcharged as a result of incorrect dues calculations. The arbitrator reserved the authority to resolve any payment discrepancies that the parties could not work out by themselves (*St. Elizabeth Health Center*, 118 LA 37).

● Another arbitrator ruled that an employer violated a collective bargaining agreement when it failed to timely remit checked-off union dues and ordered the employer to make the payments, plus interest, from the date on which they were due (*Dewitt Mailing Services Inc.*, 92 LA 238).

● After an employer discovered that it had withheld too little money from employees' paychecks under a checkoff arrangement, it could not impose deductions in excess of regular dues amounts to recoup what it had agreed to pay the union, an arbitrator held. Finding that the employer had committed a contract violation by deducting additional amounts to cover the arrearage, the arbitrator ordered the employer to reimburse affected employees for any amounts withheld in excess of authorized weekly deductions (*Air Force Logistics Command*, 90 LA 481).

● An employer committed a contract violation when it decided that an orientation program fee, which the union charged new members but then refunded once they attended the orientation session, did not constitute a proper fee that could qualify for checkoff deductions, an arbitrator held. The employer contended that the amount was not an initiation fee, but rather a penalty for employees who did not attend union meetings. In deciding that the employer was obligated to deduct and remit the fee to the union, the arbitrator cited a provision of the collective bargaining agreement that said "dues and fees are to be deducted in such sums as may be established from time to time by said Local Union, and any other fees authorized by the Local Union or the International Union" (*Cosentino Price Chopper*, 98 LA 819).

● Another arbitrator rejected an employer's claim that it was not required to deduct agency fees from employees' paychecks until it had the opportunity to verify that the union was not overcharging nonmembers. The arbitrator said any challenges to the agency fee amounts charged by the union were to be asserted by the nonunion employees rather than by the employer's "own initiative" (*Lutheran Senior City Inc.*, 91 LA 1308).

● An arbitrator ruled that an employer was not justified in refusing to include a levy in the amounts deducted from employees' paychecks. While dues hikes were subject to a vote by the union membership, assessments could be levied by the local executive board without a vote. According to the arbitrator, the additional money from the levy was to be used to carry on the regular business of the local, whose treasury had been depleted by a number of strikes, and the levy was not imposed for any set length of time. Adding that the employer had not objected in the past when the union had put similar, but smaller, increases into effect, the arbitrator concluded that the employer was obligated to accept the levy in the present situation (*Bates Mfg. Co.*, 24 LA 643; see also 41 LA 65).

● An employer improperly refused to deduct two hours' pay that a union had certified as monthly dues and fair share assessments for bargaining unit members, an arbitrator decided, because the union's discretion to decide the amount of dues and assessments affecting each employee in the "same form, manner, and degree" satisfied the contract's uniformity requirement (*Rock County*, 64 LA 887).

● An arbitrator found nothing in a collective bargaining agreement to prevent a union from imposing a fivefold increase in its initiation fee, notwithstanding an employer's objection that the fee was "unreasonable and excessive" and might hinder its recruiting efforts. The arbitrator noted that neither the collective bargaining agreement nor the checkoff form said what the fee should be. Adding that the employer had no voice in setting the amount of the fee, the arbitrator concluded that the union was under no obligation to change it (*Engineering & Research Corp.*, 23 LA 410).

1. Employer Actions Upheld

Following are examples of checkoff enforcement cases in which arbitrators have ruled in favor of employers.

● An arbitrator held that an employer was not financially responsible to a union for failing to withhold dues from some workers where the failure was inadvertent, there was no concrete basis to conclude that the employer simply did not want to withhold the dues, the computers used by the employer and union had trouble communicating, and there were problems with the nature of the workers' employment status (*Bruno's Supermarkets Inc.*, 116 LA 1618).

● An arbitrator ruled that an employer was justified in refusing to calculate and deduct dues for employees using a union's percentile formula because the collective bargaining agreement required the employer to deduct an amount "designated" by the union. The arbitrator concluded that this meant that the union should give the employer the "number" that it should deduct. The arbitrator said the employer's decision was based on "rational economic grounds" since the employer contracted out the payroll function, which had the effect of reducing its costs (*Aladdin Temp-Rite LLC*, 112 LA 1105).

● An employer properly refused to honor a dues-deduction authorization for an employee who was hired as a temporary substitute for another employee who was out on medical leave, according to an arbitrator. Although the part-time employee worked for a total of one year, the arbitrator said she never met the contractual permanent-employee qualification of nine months of continuous full-time employment (*City of Saginaw*, 88 LA 901; see also 82 LA 976).

● An employer did not violate a collective bargaining agreement when it refused to honor a union dues increase that was actually an assessment to support the union's strike-benefit fund, according to an arbitrator. Despite the union's claim that the employer had acquiesced in requests for other temporary levies, the arbitrator said the employer could refuse to be a "collection agent for a particular charitable undertaking" by adding the increase to union dues that were normally checked off (*International Paper Co.*, 92 LA 760).

● An arbitrator ruled that an employer had the right to discontinue the checkoff of union dues after its collective bargaining agreement with the union had expired. The arbitrator explained that checkoff authorizations by their terms did not survive the agreement's expiration. Although the agreement stated that "authorization and assignment shall continue in full force for yearly periods and beyond the irrevocable period set forth," the arbitrator said this language did not mean that checkoff authorization would remain effective for one year beyond the expiration date of the contract unless revoked; rather, it meant that authorization lasted for one year beyond its anniversary date or until the contract terminated, "whichever date occurs the sooner" (*Texas Gas Transmission Co. Corp.*, 78 LA 1027).

B. Dues Checkoff Revocations

Employees can revoke their dues authorizations during designated "escape" periods, provided they comply with specified revocation procedures. In some cases, arbitrators hold that employers are obligated to continue deducting union dues from employees' wages if they have not properly revoked their dues checkoff authorizations.

• An employer was required to deduct union dues from the wages of an employee who gave notice to the employer that he was withdrawing from union membership, an arbitrator decided, where the checkoff agreement was renewed automatically, unless "specific" notice of revocation was communicated. According to the arbitrator, the employee's communication to both the employer and the union was to the effect that he was withdrawing his union membership, not that he was revoking his dues authorization.

Distinguishing withdrawal of membership from revocation of authorization, the arbitrator pointed out that an employee could for personal or other reasons wish to terminate his union membership but still wish to contribute to the cost of contract administration and thereby be able to claim assistance from the union in the event of difficulties with the employer. Consequently, it did not follow that withdrawal from the union necessarily implied an intent to stop paying dues, the arbitrator added. Emphasizing that revocation of the authorization required a notice sufficient to apprise the parties unequivocally of that purpose, the arbitrator concluded that at best the employee's notice indicated that he may have, or probably intended, to cancel his dues checkoff (*Asarco Inc.*, 71 LA 730; see also 72 LA 937, 71 LA 228, 70 LA 58, 41 LA 1073, 36 LA 933).

• An employer could not discontinue its deduction of union dues from the wages of employees who sought to break their ties with a union after the expiration of a collective bargaining agreement, an arbitrator ruled. The employer contended that the employees were free to resign from the union because the contract and its maintenance-of-membership clause were not in effect at the time, and it argued that the employees' dues checkoff authorizations were no longer effective after their resignations. Finding that the employees had not acted in a timely fashion, the arbitrator said their authorizations had to be revoked during escape periods that coincided with their anniversary dates. Even assuming that the employees had effectively resigned from the union, the arbitrator added, resigning was not the same as revoking their dues check-

off authorizations, which remained in effect despite the agreement's hiatus (*Washington Post Co.*, 66 LA 553; see also 90 LA 946, 88 LA 497, 66 LA 875, 55 LA 770).

• An arbitrator ruled that an employer violated the recognition clause of a collective bargaining agreement when it unilaterally ceased deducting union dues from the paychecks of eight employees who had sent the employer written notice that they resigned their union membership, which the employer interpreted as lawful revocation of its authority to deduct the employees' dues. The arbitrator held that the relevant contract provisions did not extend to circumstances where the employer unilaterally changes working conditions without advance notice to the union (*City of Kent*, 103 LA 1049).

• On the other hand, an employer properly refused to remit union dues for a part-time, nonsupervisory research attorney in a legal service plan's regional office who had revoked her dues checkoff authorization when she learned that she was not considered a member of the bargaining unit, according to an arbitrator. The arbitrator based his decision on the fact that the regional office the employee worked in was not among the offices listed in the collective bargaining agreement; the omission of layoff rights for nonsupervisory attorneys indicated a clear intention not to include them in the bargaining unit; research attorneys performed different duties than staff attorneys in the bargaining unit; and the employee's inclusion in the bargaining unit probably would have compromised her independent judgment, since she received special and confidential assignments related to staff attorneys' malpractice and ethical practices (*UAW of America Legal Services Plan*, 88 LA 1236).

C. Departure From Bargaining Unit

When employees leave the bargaining unit, do their dues checkoff authorizations remain in effect unless they are revoked? Disputes over this issue sometimes arise after employees receive promotions or experience breaks in service.

• In one case, an arbitrator ruled that an employee's discharge ended his checkoff authorization, even though the contract did not specifically cover the matter. Any other conclusion, the arbitrator commented, would lead to the "preposterous" result of having a checkoff authorization hanging in a state of suspended animation for a period of several years if a discharged employee did not think to revoke it (*Link-Belt Co.*, 16 LA 242).

• Similarly, an arbitrator held that an employer properly refused to honor an old dues checkoff authorization that had been signed by two employees before they were fired and subsequently re-employed (*Samsonite Corp.*, 53 LA 1125).

• An employer was not required to resume the deduction of union dues when two employees returned to the bargaining unit from supervisory positions, an arbitrator ruled, despite the union's contention that the supervisors had not revoked their dues checkoff authorizations. Finding that the supervisors ceased being "employees" within the meaning of the contract upon their promotions, the arbitrator concluded that they had returned to the unit as new employees who might or might not elect to execute new dues deduction authorization forms (*Armstrong Cork Co.*, 65 LA 907).

• By contrast, an arbitrator held that an employer was obligated to deduct dues in the case of employees who signed checkoff authorizations, left their employer, and then returned, even though they did not sign new authorizations on their return. The arbitrator noted that the labor agreement covering the employees provided that dues checkoff authorizations were irrevocable for one year from the date they were signed and were transferable from workplace to workplace provided that employees continued to be represented by the same local union (*Pilgrim's Pride Corp.*, 110 LA 764).

• Another arbitrator held that five promoted employees had to keep paying union dues until they either completed one year of work outside the bargaining unit or revoked their checkoff authorizations. In this case, the collective bargaining agreement stated that the continued payment of dues allowed employees to continue accruing seniority during the first year after they left the bar-

gaining unit. Notwithstanding the employer's contention that the newly promoted supervisors were no longer members of the union and had the option of paying dues or forfeiting their accumulated seniority, the arbitrator concluded that the obligation to pay dues was mandatory in light of the supervisors' existing and valid dues checkoff authorizations (*Minnesota Mining & Mfg. Co.*, 62 LA 1013).

• An employer that erroneously collected union dues from an employee after he was promoted to a supervisory position and remitted the sum to the union was not justified in later withholding an equal amount of money from the payment owed to the union, an arbitrator held, calling the union the "sole and rightful owner" of the money (*Ogden Air Logistics Center*, 75 LA 936).

D. Effect of Decertification

Arbitrators have ruled that after unions have been decertified, employers are no longer obligated to abide by dues checkoff arrangements.

• An arbitrator disagreed with a union's claim that decertification cancelled only those contract provisions concerning recognition and representation, while the rest of the contract remained in effect until the normal expiration date. The arbitrator pointed out that the contract was a bilateral agreement, and when the union no longer was able to comply with its contractual obligations as the employees' representative, the employer no longer was bound by the contract (*Ferris Sales & Service Inc.*, 36 LA 848).

• A similar decision was reached by another arbitrator when a union that lost a decertification election claimed that the voiding of a union security agreement did not affect a separate dues checkoff provision. The arbitrator based his decision on contract law and said that the commitment to pay dues was made in the light of an assumed right of the union to compel membership. Because that assumption turned out to be erroneous, the checkoff authorizations became voidable at the option of the employees (*North Hills Electronics Inc.*, 46 LA 789).

• On the other hand, an arbitrator ruled that an employer violated a collective bargaining agreement when it failed to deduct union dues and fees after a union lost a decertification election but before a state agricultural labor relations board certified the election results. The arbitrator said that even though the decertification, if upheld, would be effective as of the election date, the agreement was still in effect during the interim, both by its terms and under state law. Furthermore, no employees had filed a written notice withdrawing their dues checkoff authorizations, the arbitrator noted (*Silva Harvesting Inc.*, 88 LA 413).

Part 16

Wages and Hours

I. Work Hours & Schedules [LA CDI 100.47 (public employees); 115. 25 et seq.]

OVERVIEW

The establishment and modification of work hours and schedules are generally regarded as inherent management rights. Arbitrators tend to give employers a free hand in this area unless their authority over the scheduling of work is restricted by contractual language.

Some collective bargaining agreements expressly state that scheduling is an exclusive function of management, or they specify that references to "normal" hours do not create any workweek guarantees. However, other labor agreements set parameters for work hours, fix particular shifts, or otherwise limit employers' flexibility with regard to scheduling.

In addition to addressing basic issues surrounding the scheduling of work, this chapter examines arbitration rulings on a number of related subjects, including the following:

- notification of schedule changes;
- flexible scheduling or "flextime" arrangements;
- requirements for using time clocks;
- meal periods and breaks;
- holiday schedule changes; and
- schedule accommodations.

SUMMARY OF CASES

A. Authority Over Scheduling

Most arbitrators regard the scheduling of work as a customary function of management that can only be limited by express

contract language. In some cases, hours-of-work clauses or similar provisions restrict employers' flexibility in setting new or different schedules. However, even where collective bargaining agreements define a "normal" schedule or "regular" workweek, arbitrators often allow employers to make adjustments, especially if the changes are supported by legitimate business reasons, such as the need to reduce costs or improve operational efficiency (88 LA 129, 85 LA 18, 80 LA 472, 73 LA 621).

• An arbitrator upheld a home health care services company's right to schedule, in advance, employees for nights on-call, overflow times, and alternate times for more than three shifts in a month, where the bargaining agreement stated that an "employee cannot be mandated for more than 3 shifts/month over their regularly scheduled hours." The language was a union proposal, the union had twice failed in bargaining to expressly limit all rotational work, the union failed to explain to management the intent of its proposal, the union's chief spokesperson did not testify, and the employer believed that the "mandate" applied for shifts scheduled after the regular rotational schedule was completed and when subsequent illnesses or other absences created vacancies that volunteers could not fill (*Spectrum Health*, 128 LA 1385).

• An arbitrator ruled that airline schedules did not have to be designed to keep cabin crew and flight deck crew co-pairings under the terms of the collective bargaining agreement that allowed an airline to reschedule and reassign employees to "otherwise maintain schedule integrity." The word "otherwise" suggested a set of circumstances similar to previous more specific examples in the contract, which did not relate to the employees' schedules, but to the aircraft and passenger schedules (*Piedmont Airlines Inc.*, 127 LA 1795).

• One arbitrator upheld an employer's institution of a new shift in response to competition, citing the presence of bona fide business reasons and the absence of contractual restrictions on scheduling. "The weight of arbitral authority is that the institution, or modification of existing shifts, absent a specific contractual prohibition against it, is an appropriate exercise of managerial judgment," the arbitrator declared (*Baltimore News American*, 68 LA 1054).

• Even though a collective bargaining agreement said the "normal workweek" would be 40 hours, an arbitrator upheld an employer's reduction in the workweek to 30 hours. Use of the term "normal" in describing the workweek did not preclude a reduction in scheduled hours, according to the arbitrator, who found that significant budgetary shortfalls experienced by the employer constituted legitimate business considerations justifying the change (*City of Coquille*, 119 LA 762; see also 119 LA 513, 117 LA 446, 115 LA 1010).

• Another arbitrator upheld an employer's implementation of a schedule change that reduced overtime and no longer assured some employees of having two consecutive days off. Neither the parties' collective bargaining agreement nor the fact that employees had received consecutive days off in the past required the employer to continue such a schedule, the arbitrator found. In support of his decision, the arbitrator cited a number of earlier arbitration cases affirming that employers retain the authority to set schedules and minimize overtime unless these management prerogatives have been relinquished (*Georgia-Pacific Corp.*, 77 LA 1156; see also 77 LA 23).

• An employer had a right to schedule part-time employees for work during a newly established night shift when an abnormal situation prevented necessary work from getting completed during the day, an arbitrator ruled. The union claimed that the employer should have addressed the situation through the assignment of overtime to full-time employees, but the arbitrator said he could find no "limitation upon the Company's right to establish new, different, or additional shifts from time to time as its requirements dictate." Under the parties' collective bargaining agreement, the employer was permitted to use part-time employees on any shift to address an abnormal workload as long as they did not displace regular employees from their regularly assigned jobs, the arbitrator observed (*Associated Wholesale Grocers Inc.*, 73 LA 781).

• An employer did not commit a contract violation by implementing a new schedule of three 12-hour days Friday to Sunday and reducing the normal workweek of press department employees to a four-day schedule running Monday to Thursday, an arbitrator ruled. The employer made the changes to avoid overlapping work schedules on Friday and to reduce overtime. The arbitrator determined that the changes were permissible because the contract granted the employer the right to reduce or change schedules and did not guarantee employees' hours (*Goodman Co.*, 122 LA 543).

• An employer did not violate its labor contract or past practice by making Saturday a part of the basic workweek, an arbitrator ruled. For many years, Saturday had been treated as a regular day off, and employees had received premium pay if they worked on Saturday. Despite the duration of this practice, the arbitrator said there was no "meeting of the minds" that would make it binding, and the contract specifically reserved to management the right to direct operations and the right to schedule work. He also noted that other contract provisions said Saturday and Sunday work could be scheduled as part of the basic workweek, and overtime premiums were required for the sixth and seventh days of work, not "for Saturday or Sunday work as such" (*North Baking Co.*, 116 LA 1788; see also 73 LA 418).

• An arbitrator ruled that a utility company did not violate a collective bargaining contract when it rescheduled repair crew employees to do transmission repair work on one Saturday and did not pay them overtime. The repair work was "necessary" as it had to be completed before the start of the summer loading period, which would have been followed shortly by hurricane season, and the labor contract required overtime pay only when unnecessary work was scheduled (*Georgia Power Co.*, 128 LA 729).

• Despite contract provisions mentioning a six-day, 44-hour workweek and continuation of current employment conditions, an arbitrator upheld an employer's elimination of Saturday work schedules. The workweek clause was intended merely to set forth hours of work for purposes of computing overtime, the arbitrator found, and was not intended as a guarantee requiring the employer to schedule 44 hours of work. There had been no negotiations

of a workweek guarantee, and if there had been any such intention, it should have been stated explicitly in the contract, the arbitrator said (*Consumers Service Co.*, 29 LA 447; see also 116 LA 1633, 97 LA 39, 95 LA 482, 91 LA 1121, 83 LA 314, 10 LA 312).

• *By contrast*, an arbitrator found that an employer could not implement a reduction in hours where a contract included an explicit workweek guarantee. The employer had instituted a reduced schedule of 32 hours per week during a period when there was a significant decrease in the level of operations, but the arbitrator found that the contract provided for layoffs under such circumstances and did not allow the employer to circumvent the guarantee of a 40-hour week (*United States Steel Corp.*, 118 LA 445; see also 111 LA 902, 105 LA 347, 89 LA 1313).

• Despite the lack of a workweek guarantee, an employer that cut employees' hours to 35 per week was in violation of a collective bargaining agreement that defined the normal workweek as 40 hours, an arbitrator ruled. A relatively brief reduction in hours would have been acceptable, but continuing the reduced schedule for an indefinite period amounted to the establishment of a 35-hour workweek, the arbitrator held. The parties had not negotiated that schedule, and there was no evidence that the union had yielded its contractual entitlement to a normal workweek of 40 hours, the arbitrator found, ordering the employer to return to the former schedule (*Scrupples Inc.*, 111 LA 1209; see also 92 LA 430, 81 LA 1150, 81 LA 502).

• An airline violated a collective bargaining agreement when it rescheduled flight attendants to have them work longer hours and added legs on flights, instead of using reserve lineholders. The arbitrator found that the agreement required the airline to use reserves unless delays or cancellations were involved (*Piedmont Airlines*, 127 LA 1795 (Arb. 2010)).

• Another arbitrator decided that a contract's reference to a "regular workweek" consisting of five "regularly scheduled days" meant that an employer could not set a schedule with different starting times on different days. Varying employees' starting times on a day-to-day basis created an "irregular schedule," the arbitrator observed. In order to meet its contractual obligations, the employer was required to assign employees to schedules with "the same starting time each day, week after week," the arbitrator said (*Fort Dodge Laboratories Inc.*, 87 LA 1290).

• An arbitrator overturned an employer's scheduling of 12-hour shifts on weekends, rejecting the assertion that the employer could require the extended weekend hours indefinitely as long as it paid employees overtime. According to the arbitrator, the purpose of contractual language specifically designating regularly scheduled workdays and workweeks goes beyond the issue of providing a basis for determining overtime pay and really concerns giving employees a means of planning the time they are not regularly scheduled to work. As such, the arbitrator held that the employer could not establish regularly scheduled 12-hour shifts on weekends (*First Energy Generation Corp.*, 123 LA 1013).

• Under a contract that specifically addressed the number of days per week that certain employees would be scheduled, an employer could not unilaterally institute a three-day workweek, an arbitrator decided. The contract said certain routes for delivering the employer's product "may be operated on a 4- or 5- day work week at the Employer's option." The employer argued that the change to a three-day schedule was justified by economic reasons and constituted a legitimate exercise of its authority to operate its business in an efficient and profitable manner. Rejecting the employer's argument, the arbitrator said the fact that the parties had negotiated a workweek of four or five days for the routes in question meant that the employer's authority to institute a different schedule had been restricted (*H. Meyer Dairy Co. Inc.*, 108 LA 765).

• An employer violated a contract's work-hours clause when it scheduled stand-by assignments of one pool of refinery workers so that they were essentially on call for the majority of their days off, an arbitrator ruled. Citing contract language that forbade the employer from acting in an arbitrary or unreasonable manner, the arbitrator re-

marked that the change significantly disrupted the employees' personal lives and could not be condoned, especially in light of the fact that they had to be available to respond one-half hour before and into shift. Even though the likelihood of being called into work was not high, the arbitrator noted that workers could not "take the risk of being unavailable for work, because failure to report to work if called results in disciplinary action" (*ConocoPhillips Co.*, 122 LA 1784).

• An arbitrator overturned a schedule change that was supported by a sound business rationale but was nevertheless "unnecessary." According to the arbitrator, in the absence of specific language that limits employers in the exercise of management rights, they are generally held to an implied standard of good faith and reasonableness. In this case, however, the parties' collective bargaining agreement imposed a stricter standard on the employer's right to make schedule changes, requiring "a showing of necessity," the arbitrator noted. Concluding that the new schedule was motivated primarily by management preference and "was not necessitated by operational requirements," the arbitrator ordered the employer to return to the previous work schedule (*Southern Calif. Edison Co.*, 95 LA 221).

1. Implementation of Continuous Operations

Unions sometimes raise objections when employers implement continuous-operations schedules. Disputes surrounding such schedules often focus on how they affect employees' days off or their opportunities to earn extra pay in the form of weekend premiums and overtime compensation. As with other types of schedules, arbitrators tend to give employers quite a bit of leeway regarding the changes they implement to keep operations running on a continuous basis (114 LA 1793, 109 LA 673, 104 LA 1133, 100 LA 937, 90 LA 922).

• An employer was within its rights to implement staggered shifts to keep one of its lines operating 24 hours a day, seven days a week, an arbitrator ruled. The parties' contract had no provision mandating that employees be scheduled so that they had consecutive days off nor any requirement that they be paid overtime for weekend work when scheduled for no more than 40 hours per week, the arbitrator observed in upholding the new shifts (*Voss Steel Corp.*, 123 LA 1005).

• In a case where the management rights clause of a collective bargaining agreement gave an employer the right to schedule work and where 40 percent of its workforce had been on a seven-day workweek for many years, an arbitrator found that the employer could put the rest of its employees on the same schedule. Nothing in the contract obligated the employer to negotiate with the union about the matter, the arbitrator found (*Celanese Corp. of America*, 30 LA 797).

• An arbitrator approved an employer's setting up a seven-day, continuous-shift operation in spite of a contract clause that said the normal workweek would consist of five eight-hour days, Monday through Friday. Absent specific provisions to the contrary, the arbitrator held that the "normal week" clause should not be interpreted to bar continuous operations, largely because such a restriction would preclude the employer from introducing new products that might require extended operating hours (*Stanley Works*, 39 LA 374).

• Interpreting a similar contract clause, another arbitrator determined that an employer was required to maintain a fixed workweek. In this case, the arbitrator concluded that the employer could not unilaterally institute a continuous-operations schedule (*Traylor Engineering & Mfg. Div. of Fuller Co.*, 36 LA 687).

• An employer committed a contract violation when it converted its extrusion department to continuous operations and put employees on a rotating schedule of five consecutive workdays, an arbitrator ruled. The contract listed two schedules. One was a standard Monday-to-Friday workweek, and the other was a continuous-operations schedule that included rotating shifts of seven consecutive workdays. While acknowledging the employer's authority to operate its extrusion department on a continuous basis, the arbitrator pointed out that the employer had never before devi-

ated from the contractually specified schedules. Adding that the extrusion department itself had adhered to the schedule with seven consecutive workdays during a previous period when it operated on a continuous basis, the arbitrator said past practice weighed heavily in his decision to reject the new five-day schedule (*Genova Pennsylvania Inc.*, 99 LA 475).

2. Union Consent

Unless contract language dictates otherwise, arbitrators generally agree that employers can make schedule changes without union consent. In some cases, however, arbitrators find that union consultation, negotiations, or mutual agreement have to precede the implementation of any changes.

• Based on an employer's failure to meet with a union prior to switching maintenance employees from four 10-hour days to five eight-hour days, an arbitrator overturned the new schedule. In this case, the parties' collective bargaining agreement expressly obligated the employer to consult with the union before making schedule changes (*Willamette Industries Inc.*, 107 LA 897; see also 87 LA 9, 85 LA 1144).

• Under a contract providing that regular starting or quitting times could not be changed except by mutual agreement, an employer did not have the right to require employees to clock out at 3:30 p.m. instead of 3:20 p.m. Technically, the shift ended at 3:30, but the parties had agreed to the earlier quitting time, which was accomplished by having employees use their 10-minute afternoon break at the end of the day. In revising the schedule, the employer required employees to take the break at 2:00 p.m. and clock out at the end of the scheduled shift. According to the arbitrator, the key question in the case was the interpretation of the phrase "regular quitting time." Concluding that the plain meaning of the phrase was the time when production normally stopped, the arbitrator said the regular quitting time had been set at 3:20 by mutual agreement and could not be changed unilaterally by the employer (*Schnadig Corp.*, 83 LA 1194).

• An employer had to reach agreement with a union in order to switch from a schedule of Monday through Friday and alternate Saturdays to a schedule that would make Saturday a permanent workday and instead give employees every other Monday off, an arbitrator held. Although a different production schedule might have been needed for legitimate business reasons, the employer could not unilaterally implement the change, the arbitrator determined, noting that the parties' collective bargaining agreement established a regular workweek of Monday through Friday (*Seamless Rubber Co.*, 26 LA 758; see also 54 LA 588,).

● Another arbitrator ruled that an employer was precluded from unilaterally changing the schedules of maintenance crews to require more weekend work. The arbitrator found that management's inherent right to define the workweek was limited in this case by the fact that the parties' collective bargaining agreement listed work schedules with specificity, and the contract's management rights clause did not allow the employer to exercise its authority in a way that would contravene other provisions of the agreement. Absent the union's agreement to amend the existing language on work hours, the employer's changes constituted a contract violation, the arbitrator held. In addition, the employer's actions violated a "longstanding and apparently well-established practice of negotiating with the maintenance group concerning their work schedules," the arbitrator said (*Swift & Co.*, 122 LA 828).

● *By contrast*, an arbitrator held that an employer was not required to obtain approval from or negotiate with a union before making changes in its employees' regular workweek. Although the parties' labor contract stated that the employer and union "may negotiate" necessary schedules that differed from the standard Monday-to-Friday workweek, the arbitrator said the clause did not mean that the employer had to seek or receive the union's consent before changes could be made (*Menasco Mfg. Co.*, 30 LA 465).

● An employer did not violate a contract provision barring unilateral changes in current schedules when it began requiring file clerks to work weekends and holidays. The employer gave the union advance notice and agreed to negotiate over the impact of the change, but meetings with union representatives failed to produce agreement on the matter, the arbitrator noted. In upholding the weekend and holiday scheduling, the arbitrator pointed out that the employer was not obligated under the collective bargaining agreement to wait until the union agreed to the change before implementing it (*Veterans Administration Medical Center*, 72 LA 374).

● An employer did not violate its collective bargaining agreement when it unilaterally changed its employees' starting time from 7 a.m. to 9 a.m., according to an arbitrator. A previous contract required the employer to consult the union before making schedule changes. Although the union claimed that the provision in question had been accidentally excised from the contract, the arbitrator noted that for "every witness testifying that it was a mistake [to delete the provision], there is a witness testifying that it was not a mistake." Left to rely only on "the signed and sealed agreement," the arbitrator said the absence of the provision requiring union consultations made the employer's actions proper (*Burroughs Corp.*, 120 LA 1247).

B. Notification of Schedule Changes

Even where management retains the authority to set work hours and schedules, collective bargaining agreements commonly require employers to provide advance notice of changes. Arbitration cases that deal with claims of notification violations are relatively rare, but the issue of proper notice does surface from time to time.

● An employer committed a contract violation by failing to provide notice before assigning mine inspectors to a new "man-trip-to-mantrip" schedule that required them to enter the mine in the morning, stay with the miners, and emerge with the crew at the end of the shift, an arbitrator ruled. Under the contract, the employer had to apprise the union of any changes that were made in policies, practices, or working conditions. Notwithstanding the employer's contention that it had an inherent right to direct its workforce, the arbitrator concluded that the change in the schedule was not merely a matter of its directing workers, but also a matter of altering an established working condition (*Mine Health and Safety Administration*, 75 LA 369).

• An arbitrator upheld an employer's right to periodically change the starting time of the early day shift from 7:00 a.m. to 3 a.m., because nothing in the collective bargaining agreement prohibited the employer from establishing a shift start-up schedule that began at 3:00 a.m., no discussions took place in bargaining concerning prohibition of such a shift change, timely notice was provided to employees, and assignment was administered equitably (*Atlas Roofing Corp.*, 129 LA 1189).

• An employer's unilateral change to a 6 a.m. starting time was upheld by an arbitrator based solely on the fact that an employer provided advance notification of the change. The scheduled workday previously began at 7 a.m., but employees often started earlier than that and received overtime pay for the extra time. Although the employer cited business justifications in support of the earlier starting time, the arbitrator said the arguments for and against the change were irrelevant to the outcome of the dispute. The only contractual restriction on the employer's ability to implement a different schedule was that it had to make changes by written notice, according to the arbitrator, and the employer satisfied that requirement before putting the new starting time into effect (*Fedders-U.S.A.*, 92 LA 418).

• Under a contract that required an employer to notify a union of any change in shift start times, the employer had the right to forego notifying the union and require a new employee to start work no later than the normal shift time, an arbitrator decided. Because the new hire in effect was not already working a normal shift but was merely working for a period of time on his first day with the employer, the arbitrator said the contract clause on union notification did not apply (*Carnation Co.*, 73 LA 827).

• Although a mining company's notice regarding the scheduling of mandatory 10-hour shifts was unreasonable, the employer did not violate its labor contract when it

extended employees' workdays during a period when a mine's viability was in jeopardy, an arbitrator found. Acknowledging that the notice was inadequate and adding that the employer should have had substantial discussions with the union about the situation, the arbitrator nonetheless determined that the employer's requirement for 10-hour days was not a violation "in the face of a mine's closing," and denied the overall grievance (*Pinn-Oak Resources LLC*, 119 LA 349).

• A county prison did not violate its collective bargaining agreement when it rescheduled a part-time employee one day before he was supposed to work, an arbitrator determined. Under the parties' labor contract, work schedules were to be posted two weeks in advance, but the arbitrator said that the notice requirement applied only to full-time employees, who were guaranteed 40 hours of work per week. Despite the union's contention that a lack of notice is just as inconvenient for part-time workers as full-time workers, the arbitrator concluded that part-time employees were not contractually assured of any notice under the contract (*County of Clearfield*, 118 LA 398).

C. Flexible Schedules and 'Flextime'

In some workplaces, flexible scheduling or "flextime" policies enable employees to exercise a degree of personal preference in setting their hours of work. For example, some employees might choose early arrival and departure times, while others might start work as late as possible and stay later at the end of the workday. Once instituted, such schedules sometimes give rise to conflicts as employers attempt to restrict or otherwise change the hours employees work.

• In one case, an arbitrator found that an employer violated a memorandum of understanding when it unilaterally required employees to change their flextime schedules and denied them flextime options because there were not enough supervisors for "minimum supervisory coverage" throughout a work shift. Although the schedule came directly from the employer's flextime guidelines, which included statements about supervisor-employee ratios, those guidelines did not give the employer the authority to alter employees' hours whenever the specified ratios could not be met, the arbitrator decided, ordering the employer to meet with the union to determine a mutually acceptable remedy (*County of Alameda*, 86 LA 20).

● *By contrast*, another arbitrator held that an employer had the right to curtail the use of flextime. The employer had a policy of allowing employees to come to work as much as two hours early so they could then leave early for appointments or other reasons, but it decided to change this policy owing to a lack of supervision early in the morning. Noting that flextime had never been addressed in the parties' collective bargaining agreement, the arbitrator said his decision had to be based strictly on the principles applicable to past practice. Citing the fact that such practices must be acceptable to both parties, the arbitrator reasoned that once the employer no longer considered the flextime policy acceptable, the past practice ceased to exist. Thus, the employer had the right to set a new policy and establish it unilaterally, the arbitrator asserted. The employer's only obligation was to notify employees of the change, the arbitrator said, adding that even one week's notice would give employees enough time to change any plans they had made (*Franklin Electric Co. Inc.*, 108 LA 1020).

● A federal agency had the right to change flextime arrangements at a call center when phones were left without staff to answer them for an hour every afternoon, an arbitrator ruled. Employees wanted the employer to use answering machines for that hour, but the arbitrator said the agency had the right to determine how its mission would be accomplished. According to the arbitrator, decisions regarding the methods, means, and technology of performing the agency's mission were not mandatory bargaining subjects, and the employer was free to change its employees' work schedules to meet its operational needs (*National Aeronautics & Space Administration*, 87 LA 1017).

● An arbitrator upheld an employer's altering a rehabilitation counselor's flextime work schedule despite the employee's claim that the change was made to retaliate for his filing a grievance over another matter. The new schedule was prompted by the fact that the employee's perception of his job varied markedly from his supervisor's view of it. Although this revelation came to light because of the earlier grievance, the schedule change was made simply to correct communication problems between the employee and his supervisor and to make him more accessible to the supervisor, the arbitrator said, denying the grievance (*Vermont Social & Rehabilitation Services Dept.*, 91 LA 494).

● An employer was justified in assigning an employee a start time of 9:30 a.m. under a flextime policy, an arbitrator found. The employee's supervisor chose the time because the employee, unlike all the other workers in the unit, refused to agree to a consistent arrival time. The arbitrator said "it was never intended that individual employees should be able to exercise flextime selection without limit and without consideration for the general operation and mission" of the employer. Describing the employer's process of discussing and mutually agreeing on each employee's hours as "entirely reasonable," the arbitrator said the employer was neither capricious nor arbitrary in its demands but was merely exercising its rights (*U.S. Army Tank-Automotive Command*, 81 LA 719).

D. Use of Time Clocks

Because the installation of time clocks can be regarded as a change in employment conditions, arbitrators sometimes have to decide whether employers can act unilaterally in requiring employees to use time clocks or whether union negotiations must precede such a change. As indicated below, cases involving time clocks have produced mixed rulings.

● While expressing the view that the installation of time clocks was a mandatory bargaining subject, an arbitrator decided that a union's grievance over such a move was doomed where an employer had made its intentions known during contract negotiations. The change in policy was instituted shortly after the parties signed a new contract. The employer argued that even if the issue were a required subject of bargaining, the union had waived that right by failing to negotiate the point when it was brought up during contract talks. Emphasizing the union's failure to pursue the matter earlier, the arbitrator said the grievance process could not be used to stop a change that the union should have fought during bargaining (*Motor Wheel Corp.*, 26 LA 931).

• An arbitrator upheld an employer's unilateral installation of time clocks, rejecting the contention that the employer had to bargain with the union because it was making a change in working conditions. A key consideration in the case was the fact that the parties had negotiated a zipper clause in their contract that said no bargaining would occur during the term of the contract on any subject. Prior to signing off on the contract, the union had asked about the ramifications of the zipper clause and had been told that the clause would enable the employer to change working conditions without any discussions, the arbitrator noted. Adding that the employer had a past practice of making unilateral changes in working conditions, the arbitrator said the union failed to show that the employer violated the contract when it installed the time clocks without first bargaining with the union (*Entex Inc.*, 73 LA 330).

• Specific procedures for clocking in and out were within an employer's exclusive authority, an arbitrator decided. Even though manual time clocks had been used in the past, the arbitrator found nothing wrong with the employer's introduction of more advanced units. Pointing out that the installation of new equipment was not a condition of employment, the arbitrator said the union had no right to prevent employer's using the updated time clocks (*Babcock & Wilcox Co.*, 45 LA 897).

• An employer had the right to install a time clock outside a company bathroom and to require employees to punch their time cards upon entering and leaving to prevent the abuse of bathroom privileges, an arbitrator ruled. Rejecting the contention that the use of the time clock by female employees was "humiliating and undignified," the arbitrator said it was inconceivable that female employees under a female supervi-

sor would experience any embarrassment among practically all female employees by having to punch a time clock at the bathroom entrance (*Cagle's Poultry and Egg Co.*, 73 LA 34).

• Another arbitrator reached the opposite conclusion in a similar case, finding that requiring employees to keep time clock records of their bathroom visits exceeded an employer's authority to establish and enforce reasonable work rules. The employer argued that the rule was an appropriate means of solving the problem of too much lost work time because of loitering in bathrooms. Even though the rule may have helped improve productivity, the arbitrator rejected its implementation because it also resulted in a loss of dignity and embarrassment to employees. Although no one could blame the employer for wanting to curb wasteful activity by a small number of workers, other methods should have been found to reduce the incidence of loitering without imposing onerous and humiliating timekeeping procedures on all employees, the arbitrator concluded (*Schmidt Cabinet Co. Inc.*, 75 LA 397).

• An employer could not require the use of time clocks in conjunction with a voluntary flextime program that allowed employees to arrive anywhere between 7 a.m. and 9 a.m., an arbitrator held. Although the parties' collective bargaining agreement said employees could not be forced to punch time clocks, the employer argued that the use of time clocks by employees in the flextime program was done on a voluntary basis in exchange for the benefit of participating in the program. The arbitrator acknowledged that the employer would have a difficult time administering the program without requiring employees to punch in and out. Notwithstanding that fact, and in spite of the voluntary nature of the flextime program, the arbitrator relied on the explicit language of the contract in concluding that no employee could be required to punch a time clock (*State of New York, Department of Taxation and Finance*, 80 LA 180).

E. Meal Periods and Breaks

Disputes over the scheduling of meal periods and breaks usually focus on when they must be taken or how many breaks employees are entitled to receive per day. The outcome of such disputes typically depends on the facts and circumstances of each case.

• An employer had the right to stagger rest periods after it instituted continuous operations, an arbitrator ruled. Under the parties' collective bargaining agreement, times for rest periods were determined by foremen, stewards, and workers in each department, but this right, the arbitrator said, was dependent on the shifts and hours that were set by the employer. When management decided to switch to continuous operations, it necessarily followed that rest periods had to be staggered, the arbitrator reasoned (*Philco Corp.*, 40 LA 490; see also 88 LA 599, 75 LA 16, 62 LA 374).

• An arbitrator ruled an employer did not violate a collective bargaining agreement by unilaterally increasing the departmental shift from eight hours to eight and one-half hours through discontinuation of a 20-minute paid lunch break and addition of a 30-minute unpaid lunch break, even though an article in the agreement specified that the shift's regular hours were 3 p.m. to 11 p.m. The contract provision also gave the employer the right to "change permanently the regular hours of work" when the change in operation was necessary, an increase was required to meet customer demand and to improve production, and the employer on multiple occasions had informed the union of changes in regular hours of work (*Belleville Shoe Manufacturing Co.*, 126 LA 825).

• An arbitrator upheld an employer's establishing set periods and times for its employees to take their coffee breaks. Although employees had been accustomed to taking coffee breaks according to their individual preferences, the employer found that the practice was putting a crimp in production lines, which were being stopped because of the random nature of the employee's breaks. To remedy the situation, the employer made a rule limiting breaks to set periods in the morning and afternoon, prompting the union to protest that this amounted to a prohibited change in working conditions. The arbitrator denied the grievance, pointing out that the employer's action did not end the practice of allowing breaks but actually gave it official recognition and status (*Dover Corp.*, 33 LA 860; see also 74 LA 312, 39 LA 1265).

• Another arbitrator held that an employer could unilaterally reduce two 15-minute wash-up periods per day to two five-minute periods (*Ruralist Press Inc.*, 51 LA 549; see also 68 LA 94, 62 LA 179, 61 LA 891).

• Despite observing a single lunch period for production employees for 14 years, an employer had the right to schedule an additional lunch period so certain machines could be operated continuously, an arbitrator ruled. According to the arbitrator, deciding the number of lunch periods and how many employees would be scheduled for each period were "management prerogatives since they involve the methods of the employer's operations and the direction of the workforce" (*Zimmer Manufacturing Corp.*, 75 LA 16).

• A city government did not violate its collective bargaining agreement when it told firefighters that they could only take their lunch periods between 11:30 a.m. and 1 p.m., an arbitrator determined. Clear contract language gave the city managers the right to assign working hours, and lunch breaks were included in the definition of working hours, the arbitrator observed (*City of Broken Arrow*, 114 LA 881).

• *By contrast*, an employer that had established four half-hour lunch periods between 11 a.m. and 1 p.m. could not legitimately add a fifth half-hour period and require lunch breaks to begin as early as 10:45 a.m. and end as late as 1:15 p.m., an arbitrator ruled. Although contract language requiring a half-hour lunch period said nothing about when it should be taken, the arbitrator decided that the obligation to provide a lunch period implied scheduling it at a reasonable time, which by custom meant near the middle of the shift. In this case, the arbitrator held, past practice was so consistent that 11 a.m. and 1 p.m. had to be regarded as the outside limits for lunch periods (*Bakelite Co.*, 29 LA 555).

• Where a collective bargaining agreement provided for a 15-minute afternoon break after lunch, an arbitrator held that an employer improperly rescheduled the break for the last 15 minutes of the workday. Despite the fact that the agreement did not restrict the scheduling of rest periods except that the break could not be connected to lunch, the arbitrator said the term "rest period" meant a "short interruption during the work period," and a rest period at the end of the day could not be an interruption between periods of work. Thus, the employer could not push the afternoon break all the way to the end of the day, the arbitrator ruled (*Air System Components*, 104 LA 477).

● An employer that had a past practice of giving three paid coffee breaks to its transfer drivers improperly discontinued the third break following the effective date of a new collective bargaining agreement, an arbitrator ruled. Because the practice was of long standing and the parties specifically agreed during contract negotiations that the practice would continue under the new contract, the employer was not free to make changes without negotiating with the union over the issue, the arbitrator held (*Pacific Clay Products*, 62 LA 706; see also 73 LA 34, 62 LA 45, 21 LA 194).

● Similarly, an arbitrator held that an employer could not decide to allow fewer rest periods after it had given employees the same number of breaks for five years. Such a longstanding practice took on the status of an obligation binding on both parties, according to the arbitrator. Concluding that the number of rest breaks had become a working condition set by past practice, the arbitrator said it could not be changed unilaterally by the employer (*Formica Corp.*, 44 LA 467).

● An employer violated a contract provision requiring lunch periods to be arranged by mutual agreement between the parties when it compelled employees to operate their looms during scheduled lunch periods, an arbitrator decided. Notwithstanding the employer's contention that continuous operation of the looms was dictated by the need to maintain its competitive position in the marketplace, the arbitrator ruled that clear contract language had to be enforced unless modified by a subsequent

agreement (*Atlanta Wire Works Inc.*, 62 LA 945; see also 71 LA 1128).

● Under a contract that provided for a paid, 20-minute lunch period, an employer could not relieve most employees of all duties during lunch but require boiler firemen to keep an eye on the boilers while they ate, an arbitrator ruled. Because the contract did not make an exception to the lunch break for these employees, and because they did not receive any extra pay for having to work while eating lunch, the arbitrator reasoned that the employer had to schedule other employees to relieve the boiler firemen so they could receive the same type of lunch break as everyone else (*Ford Roofing Products Co.*, 5 LA 182).

F. Holiday Schedule Changes

If employers are concerned that very little work will get done on a day adjacent to a holiday, can they shut down operations even if unions object? Arbitrators commonly look for specific contract language concerning work guarantees when resolving disputes over employers' authority to make holiday schedule changes. [*See also* Part 9. Holidays.]

● An arbitrator upheld an employer's refusal to schedule work on Christmas Eve and New Year's Eve because of its concern that employees would start their holidays on the employer's time. The union demanded pay for the time lost, relying on a contract clause describing the hours of work as eight per day and 40 per week. The arbitrator pointed out that the contract itself said that the hours-of-work clause was not to be construed as a guarantee of any fixed amount of work, adding that the agreement also contained a reporting-pay clause that was inconsistent with the idea of a work guarantee. Noting that there was no showing of bad faith on the part of the employer, the arbitrator decided that the shutdown did not violate the contract (*Pittsburgh Screw & Bolt Co.*, 29 LA 615; see also 85 LA 398, 83 LA 314, 64 LA 287, 62 LA 1191, 29 LA 795).

● An arbitrator decided that an employer had the right to shut down its plant on the Monday preceding the Christmas Eve and Christmas holidays after the union rejected an offer to work the preceding Saturday at a straight-time rate. According to the arbitrator, the mere existence of a separate contract provision that stated that "five days, Monday through Friday, shall constitute a week's work" did not imply a guarantee of 40 hours as a standard workweek (*T M Fab Inc.*, 64 LA 287).

● An arbitrator determined that a grocery store had to close on Easter unless a competitor within a 10-mile radius was open for business the same day. The parties' collective bargaining agreement provided that no employee had to work on Easter unless a competitor was also open, which the arbitrator defined as a retail establishment offering a similarly extensive line of food and houseware products. If that condition were met, the arbitrator held, the employer would be allowed to schedule Easter as a workday. To staff the store in such a situation, the employer had to seek volunteers, the arbitrator said, and if too few people volunteered, the employer's scheduling of workers would have to start with the least senior employees (*Supervalu Holdings Inc.*, 116 LA 417).

G. Schedule Accommodations

Anti-discrimination laws can require employers to make adjustments in schedules as an accommodation for those employees whose religious beliefs or disabilities affect the days or times they can work. Such laws only require "reasonable" accommodations, however, which means that employers do not have to grant special arrangements that would cause undue hardship or damage their business. As illustrated by the examples below, arbitrators are unlikely to elevate the individual needs of employees above employers' business needs when disputes arise over accommodations.

● An arbitrator upheld a shipping company's offering of part-time work to a Seventh-Day Adventist who wanted to leave early every Friday. Under the employer's proposed accommodation, the employee would have given up his position as a full-time delivery driver and instead worked two shifts as a loader. Despite the fact that the part-time position was more strenuous and paid less, the arbitrator concluded that the employer's proposal seemed to be the only viable option. Granting the employee's request to leave early on Fridays would have meant significantly more work for the employer's dispatcher and much more overtime for other drivers, the arbitrator noted. In addition, because many commercial customers required package pickups at day's end, changing the employee's schedule would have forced a change in those pickup times, leading to a potential loss of business, the arbitrator said (*United Parcel Service*, 103 LA 1143; see also 77 LA 838).

● An employer did not violate its labor contract by altering past practice and refusing to excuse maintenance employees in a continuously operating plant from mandatory Sunday work for religious reasons, an arbitrator held. In the past, when such excused absences were allowed, the workers who filled in on the Sunday shifts had received their same, basic pay. Under a negotiated change in the way the plant operated, the employer would have been required to give replacement workers premium pay for Sunday work, "thus incurring an additional labor cost of 50 percent to 100 percent," the arbitrator said. This change would have seriously compromised the employer's operations and caused an undue hardship if the employer continued to excuse the employees from Sunday work, the arbitrator concluded (*The Goodyear Tire & Rubber Co.*, 107 LA 193).

● An employer did not violate the Americans with Disabilities Act when it issued a new rule requiring mandatory Saturday overtime on an as-needed basis for assemblers, an arbitrator ruled. Because the employer allowed assemblers to seek accommodation and placed those who had valid medical restrictions on light-duty work or in jobs where they could avoid Saturday overtime altogether, the arbitrator concluded that the new policy did not constitute a contract violation or conflict with the protections of the ADA (*Bobcat Co.*, 119 LA 817).

● An employer did not violate its labor contract when it refused to allow an employee to be paid while attending physical therapy during the workday, an arbitrator held. Such an accommodation of a temporary physical problem was not covered by the agreement, the arbitrator said, adding that it was unreasonable for the employee to receive his physical therapy on company time and then demand overtime hours to make up for the work he missed (*Johnstown America Corp.*, 114 LA 577).

● An arbitrator upheld an employer's discharge of a power company maintenance mechanic who refused to work on two Saturdays because of his religious beliefs. In this case, the employer had allowed the employee 75 straight Saturdays off by shift-swapping with co-workers, but on the days in question there was an emergency situation and no other workers were able to switch with him. The employee could have avoided the conflict in the first place by transferring to a job that required no Saturday work, the arbitrator observed. Under the emergency situation that existed on the two Saturdays in question, allowing the employee to miss work would have caused the employer undue hardship, according to the arbitrator, who added that the employee had other op-

tions while the employer had none (*Georgia Power Co.*, 94 LA 1303).

● Another arbitrator reached a similar conclusion in a case involving an employee who claimed that she could have avoided being discharged for excessive absenteeism if her employer had accommodated her religious beliefs. According to the arbitrator, the employee was aware of the attendance policy at the mushroom farm where she worked, as well as the direct conflict between her religious beliefs and her mandatory work schedule. Although her employer tried to accommodate her request to be excused from Saturday work, the arbitrator pointed out that the perishable nature of produce necessitated that it be harvested on schedule. The arbitrator found that excusing the employee from all Saturday work would have posed an undue hardship on the employer, and reassigning the employee to a position that did not require Saturday work would have violated the seniority rights of other employees (*Moonlight Mushrooms Inc.*, 101 LA 421).

II. Setting & Adjusting Pay [LA CDI 100.45 (public employees); 114.30; 114.61]

OVERVIEW

For union-represented workers, federal labor law defines "wages" as a mandatory subject of bargaining. As a result, details regarding overall pay structures and normal wage adjustments tend to get hashed out at the bargaining table without ever becoming the subject of grievances.

When pay-related issues go to arbitration, the disputes usually revolve around narrower concerns. This chapter focuses primarily on situations where employers have established or adjusted rates of pay in response to unusual circumstances, such as the creation of new jobs or job classifications, changes in workloads or duties, and the introduction of new equipment or technology.

Aside from disputes over standard rates of pay, arbitrators often resolve conflicts involving overtime pay, premium pay, reporting and call-in pay, and incentive pay. Those topics are discussed separately in other chapters.

SUMMARY OF CASES

A. Setting Rates of Pay

When employers create new jobs or combine existing classifications, they typically establish applicable pay rates only after conducting an evaluation of the duties and responsibilities for the affected positions. However, job evaluations cannot occur in a vacuum. In many cases, arbitrators emphasize the importance of making comparisons with other jobs or classifications when setting rates of pay.

● One arbitrator determined the job rate for a new classification in light of the employer's past practice, prevailing practice in comparable plants, and the effect on intra-plant wage relationships (*Wetter Numbering Machine Co.*, 13 LA 177).

● According to another arbitrator, the following factors should be considered in setting up the rate range for a new job: (1) nature of the duties and responsibilities of the job as compared to other jobs at the plant; (2) existing wage rate structure; and (3) existing method of in-grade rate progression (*Dumont Electric Corp.*, 13 LA 763; see also 62 LA 511, 62 LA 574).

• When two jobs are combined, an arbitrator said, the resulting position should be evaluated as though it were a completely new job, and the pay rate should be set accordingly (*Republic Steel Corp.*, 20 LA 370).

• An employer violated its collective bargaining agreement by setting too low a wage rate for a new job classification of repairmen/inspectors whose duties required greater levels of responsibility than other inspection jobs, an arbitrator held. Employees in the new classification took on duties that were previously performed by management, and they had to undergo special training and testing and acquire many hours of on-the-job experience in order to be certified for their new duties, the arbitrator observed. Finding that the employer deliberately withheld this requirement during wage rate talks in order to reduce the union's leverage in negotiating a wage schedule for the new position, the arbitrator boosted the hourly pay for the job (*Union Tank Car Co.*, 122 LA 876).

• An oil refinery established an appropriate rate of pay for operators in a newly reorganized sulfur recovery unit, an arbitrator held. Even though the pay rate for the new job category was the highest allowed under the parties' labor contract and the same as that of other operators, the union argued that because the reorganization allowed the unit to be staffed with fewer workers, the employer should have passed along its savings by boosting wages. The arbitrator, however, said the employer's savings were irrelevant and the pay rate was reasonable in light of the fact that it was "both symmetrical with the then-maximum wage levels of the collective bargaining agreement, and most important, was, and is, calibrated objectively to the particulars of the affected jobs" (*Valero Oil*, 124 LA 431).

• An employer that successfully negotiated for the consolidation of numerous job classifications did not commit a contract violation when it discontinued a special pay rate that had applied to four employees, an arbitrator held. Although the higher rate had been preserved for four years under the first contract that included the consolidated classifications, the employer told the union during the next round of contract talks that it would eliminate the special rate. The union claimed that the higher rate should have been grandfathered into the new contract, but it signed the pact without that language, the arbitrator noted. The union could not successfully argue that the agreement's silence on the matter meant the rate should continue, the arbitrator said, because the employer "was not silent" on the question and had made its intentions known through "clear verbal expressions" (*Lafarge Corp.*, 124 LA 537).

B. Impact of Job Duties on Pay

Arbitrators generally agree that adjustments to existing pay rates are in order when employees experience substantial changes in their job duties. For example, a material increase in workload or the addition of new responsibilities would normally justify a pay raise. *By contrast*, arbitrators are less likely to award wage adjustments in situations involving overlapping duties from different job classifications, particularly if the tasks in question have been shared or swapped back and forth over time (124 LA 782, 109 LA 984, 73 LA 892, 72 LA 816, 71 LA 59, 54 LA 250, 29 LA 226).

• A health care system did not violate a collective bargaining agreement by paying ultrasound technicians at one campus more than those at another campus, even though a 2004 agreement included wage parity across two campuses, where a 2006 amendment raised wages at one campus because units were required to perform new procedures (*Forum Health System*, 128 LA 1329 (Arb. 2011)).

• An employer did not commit a contract violation by refusing to pay cabinet makers at a higher rate when they performed certain tasks that carpenters also performed, an arbitrator ruled. The employer asserted that the tasks in question had been performed by both carpenters and cabinet makers for decades, and the arbitrator agreed that there was no "credible evidence whatsoever that this work has exclusively, or even primarily, been that of the carpenters" (*Brookhaven Science Associates LLC*, 122 LA 882).

• An employer was justified in denying lift truck operators the higher pay rate of lead checkers whenever they handled supply pallets and corrugated material, an arbitrator held. These overlapping duties made up a very small portion of the lead checkers' responsibilities, and the two groups had traditionally shared the tasks, the arbitrator noted. The union compared the situation to one in which pay rates were increased for a different group of drivers, but the arbitrator traced that wage adjustment to a change in duties following the implementation of a new computer system (*Graphic Packaging International Inc.*, 119 LA 946).

• *By contrast*, an employer could not require a technology staff development coordinator in a school district to take on teaching assignments without providing extra pay, an arbitrator held. The employee was subject to greater effort and stress as a result of the teaching assignments and, more importantly, was "performing work that he was not hired to do," the arbitrator noted. In light of the extra work, it was "equitable and just" that the employee receive extra compensation, the arbitrator said (*Hayward Unified School District*, 124 LA 187).

• A newspaper rack sales distributor was not entitled to the higher pay of a street sales manager when he did some of the manager's work on days the manager also worked, an arbitrator ruled, because the memorandum of agreement stated that employees were entitled to higher-classification pay when they assumed "the full range of responsibilities of the higher level. . . ." However the distributor was entitled to the higher pay on days that the manager was absent and the distributor assumed the full range of the manager's job (*Toledo Blade Co.*, 128 LA 1743).

• Chemical plant operators were entitled to a pay increase after taking on reporting, documentation, and safety duties that were previously performed by supervisors, an arbitrator ruled. Under the parties' collective bargaining agreement, any time an employee's job was "modified substantially," a new wage rate was in order. In this case, the employees' new duties required an extensive training period and significantly more responsibility, both of which met the definition of a substantial modification, the arbitrator determined (*Arizona Chemical Co.*, 107 LA 836; see also 107 LA 384, 101 LA 931).

• An employer committed a contract violation by adding a new category of functions to an existing job classification without addressing the issue of pay, an arbitrator decided. The employer, a manufacturer of spice products, had begun requiring employees who milled and blended the spices to perform testing duties in addition to their usual tasks. According to the arbitrator, the question of pay could not be ignored, because the parties' collective bargaining agreement specified that a "significant" change in job content would trigger an obligation on the part of the employer to negotiate with the union over wage changes (*Tone Brothers Inc.*, 116 LA 1678; see also 111 LA 39).

C. Equipment and Technology Changes

When employers introduce new equipment or technology, disagreements over pay rates often ensue. Factors that typically militate in favor of pay increases include new skill requirements, added responsibilities, and increased output, but arbitrators sometimes find that such factors are offset by a reduction in physical effort due to technological enhancements.

• An employer committed a contract violation by refusing to grant any pay increases to employees who had to learn new computer systems, hardware, and software, as well as the ways in which the new systems interfaced with other aspects of a department's work, an arbitrator ruled. The change in the employees' jobs was nothing if not "substantial," and for certain employees whose assignments changed most substantially, a raise was in order, the arbitrator said (*Cooper Industries Inc.*, 104 LA 383; see also 54 LA 418).

• An employer violated a collective bargaining agreement by failing to negotiate over new jobs created by the addition of a new press, an arbitrator ruled, finding the employer met with the union only twice, did not treat the union as an equal partner in negotiations, cut off talks and unilaterally decided not to pay employees a new rate. The arbitrator ordered the employer to return to negotiations and pay back pay retroactive to the date the press was installed, even though the agreement limited back pay to 60 days, because the agreement did not authorize the arbitrator to set a new rate (*Calumet Carton Co. Inc.*, 129 LA 1664).

• An employer's introduction of robots to perform painting tasks triggered an obligation to reconsider the wage rates of employees who had previously done the painting manually, an arbitrator ruled. Although the physical demands of the job decreased, the tasks, responsibilities, and knowledge required of the employees increased when they were retrained to operate the robots, the arbitrator observed. Concluding that the fundamental nature of the job had been altered, the arbitrator ordered the employer to meet with the union and negotiate a new pay rate for the affected employees (*ABB Power T&D Co.*, 116 LA 1161).

• A pay increase of $0.25 per hour, as opposed to the 3.5 percent raise demanded by a union, was appropriate for employees whose productivity rose 30 percent after their employer introduced new machinery, an arbitrator held. The essential nature of the jobs remained the same, and for every increase in skill or effort required, there were other aspects of the jobs that became easier and required less effort, the arbitrator pointed out. Consequently, it was difficult to see how much of the increased productivity could be "attributed to the machine itself and how much to the crew and how much of what is attributed to the crew should be reflected in increased compensation," the arbitrator said in rejecting the union's demand (*Menasha Corp.*, 108 LA 308; see also 104 LA 730, 11 LA 108).

• Another arbitrator determined that the work of employees on a platform welder was equivalent to what was delineated in the agreed-upon job description, as was the pay rate the workers received for their labors. Despite the union's claim that the platform welding machine being used was not the same type of device discussed during earlier talks over pay rates, the arbitrator said the differences were minimal and the work be-

ing done, as well as the skill levels required, were "essentially the same" as they had been (*G.H.N. Neon Inc.*, 111 LA 1117).

• An employer did not have to pay truck operators the higher pay rate earned by shipping clerks merely because the employer installed a computer system that enabled the truck operators to enter certain information online, an arbitrator found. Even though the change in job duties meant the employer was able to eliminate some shipping clerks' jobs, the truck operators were not entitled to the shipping clerks' higher pay because they did not perform all or even most of the functions that the clerk jobs required, the arbitrator said (*Union Camp Corp.*, 110 LA 820).

• Similarly, an arbitrator upheld an employer's refusal to grant an upward adjustment in the contractual wage rate of a salt mining company's bulk loaders after the installation of a new computer system. He determined that the changes in the employees' job duties were not "substantial" enough to warrant a wage increase (*Morton Salt*, 112 LA 110).

• An employer's introduction of a new handling system that lessened the physical effort required of certain workers to a "considerable extent" justified the lowering of a piece rate, an arbitrator determined. Under the parties' labor contract, the employer had the right to make reductions if they were supported by improvements in employees' working conditions, the arbitrator observed (*Dexter Co.*, 122 LA 705).

D. Impact of Job Moves on Pay

Arbitrators usually grant employers considerable latitude in making temporary assignments and initiating other job moves. What they look at more closely, however, is how equitably pay rates are applied in those situations. Some collective bargaining agreements specify in great detail how movements between and among job classifications are to be handled, while others provide only broad outlines for such changes, and it is in these instances that grievances usually arise. [See also Part VII. D. Transfer.]

• An employer was justified in cutting the wages of employees who were temporarily transferred to lower-grade jobs, an arbitrator determined. Although the parties' collective bargaining agreement required the employer to maintain employees' regular pay rates for 60 days during a temporary transfer to a lower-classified job for the employer's convenience, the arbitrator found that the focus of this case was different. The employees actually faced the prospect of layoffs, and although the new assignments were seen as temporary, the contract language governing temporary transfers did not apply in a layoff situation, the arbitrator concluded (*ADM Milling Co.*, 111 LA 274).

• An employer was within its rights to pay maintenance employees the lower wages of shipping employees when they worked in the shipping department on a weekend, an arbitrator decided. Despite the union's assertion that the employees were on temporary transfer and were entitled to their regular rate of pay, the arbitrator determined that none of the employees were forced to work on the weekend. Indeed, all were volunteers who signed up for the weekend duty to make extra money, and their temporary stint in the lower-level job was not for the employer's benefit, the arbitrator pointed out (*Celotex Corp.*, 112 LA 825).

• In another case, an arbitrator found that an employer did not violate its labor contract by reducing the wages of an employee who had transferred into a lower classification. Despite the fact that the employee had an oral agreement with the employer that he would keep the higher salary after the transfer, and even though this oral agreement had been honored for seven years, the arbitrator said that the contract was clear and prescriptive in stating that oral understandings had "no force and effect whatsoever." In spite of the factors favoring continuation of the higher rate, the arbitrator concluded that he was obliged to follow the contract (*Vons, A Safeway Company*, 121 LA 741).

• An electrician at a utility company was not entitled to be paid at a working foreman's rate when he was the senior employee on a three-person crew that performed routine maintenance on a trans-

former, an arbitrator found. Previously, the higher rate was mandated if an electrician directed a crew in the absence of a working foreman, but the contract language imposing that requirement had been replaced by a new provision that gave management the flexibility to deny the extra pay in situations where the work assignments were brief or less complex. Emphasizing that the union had been unsuccessful in its attempts to restore the former requirement, the arbitrator said the union could not extract through a grievance what it was unable to achieve in negotiations (*AEP-Public Service Co. of Oklahoma*, 123 LA 82; see also 122 LA 1207).

• An employer violated its labor contract when it failed to pay a higher wage rate to an employee who was temporarily assigned from her job as an office assistant to a higher-paying job of shift analyst, an arbitrator determined. Although she did not meet all requirements of the job nor perform every task involved, the arbitrator asserted that "a fairer reading of the concept of a transfer requires an assessment of whether the individual is performing a significant amount of work of the job classification whose functions he or she is asked to perform." Finding that the employee met the requirements, the arbitrator sustained the grievance but decided that given other factors, the employee was entitled to only 95 percent of the pay at the higher grade (*Wolf Creek Nuclear Operating Corp.*, 115 LA 641; see also 123 LA 1603, 115 LA 1300).

• A contractor that provided food services at a military base committed a contract violation by failing to pay cook I employees at the cook II wage rate when they served as primary cooks on days that the higher-paid employees did not work, an arbitrator ruled. According to the union, serving as a primary cook who prepared hot meals was the core responsibility of the cook II position and was outside the cook I job description, a view the arbitrator accepted. The employer's practice of paying cook I employees cook II rates when cook II employees were sick or on leave but not on their scheduled days off was "an artificial distinction" that was "not supported by the language of the contract, the bargaining history between the parties, or the preponderance of the evidence," the arbitrator said, ordering the employer to pay the employees the difference between their normal wages and the higher rates (*Chugach Support Services Inc.*, 123 LA 1806).

• An employer could not cut an employee's wages to a lower rate when assigning him a temporary out-of-classification job on a day when work was available in his regular job, an arbitrator ruled. Given that the temporary assignment was purely for the employer's benefit so that it could better use the employee's skills at a job other than his usual position, and because the particular type of transfer was not described in the parties' contract, the arbitrator concluded that the employee was to be paid at the higher rate (*AMG Industries Inc.*, 113 LA 77).

• An industrial air conditioning company violated its collective bargaining agreement when it refused to pay assemblers at a higher rate associated with the job of compressor repairers when the assemblers did repair work on compressors, an arbitrator held. Under the contract, there was no doubt that employees performing higher graded work, even on a temporary basis, had to be paid the wage rate of that task, the arbitrator said. Adding that it had been a common past practice to upgrade assemblers when they did repair work, the arbitrator ordered the employer to make the employees whole for the additional compensation they were wrongfully denied (*McQuay International*, 117 LA 453).

E. Pay Gaps or Inequities

The wage disputes that come before arbitrators sometimes revolve around claims of wage gaps or pay inequities. In such cases, the outcome tends to hinge on the contractual terms negotiated by the parties rather than subjective perceptions of fairness.

• An employer did not commit a contract violation by paying some employees, but not others, in excess of contractual wage rates, an arbitrator held. Four employees complained about not receiving as much pay as some of their fellow workers.

However, the hourly wages negotiated by the parties were specifically referred to as "minimum rates of pay," the arbitrator pointed out, and there were no contractual restrictions on higher pay rates. According to the arbitrator, the employer retained the right to exceed the minimum rates as long as differences in pay were not attributable to illegal discrimination, and there was no evidence of unlawful bias in this case (*Coffeyville Flour Mill Inc.*, 100 LA 561).

• Introduction of a new computer system and other job changes did not alter the fact that a union's only claim for a wage increase for certain workers was based on perceived inequity between the pay rate for workers in one department and that of workers who had less responsibility in other departments, an arbitrator said. While expressing sympathy for the union's position, the arbitrator concluded that the union was attempting to gain through arbitration what it "was unable to obtain in the negotiations involving the existing agreement" (*International Paper Co.*, 106 LA 645).

• An employer was justified in giving a new-hire wage increase, but not the general wage hike, to an employee who was hired approximately seven months prior to the effective date of a new contract, an arbitrator ruled. The parties had no practice of giving new employees the general increase, the arbitrator found. Although a management bargaining proposal had used the phrase "current employees" to discuss those who should get the general wage increase, that phrase was removed from the current agreement during contract negotiations, the arbitrator added (*COPAZ Packing Corp.*, 105 LA 1074).

• *By contrast*, an arbitrator found that a hotel violated its collective bargaining agreement when it did not apply an automatic tip policy of 15 percent to all of its servers and bartenders when it was first instituted. The collective bargaining agreement specified that workers in the same job classification were entitled to equal salary scales and that tips were to be regarded as wages. The new policy, however, remained in place for several months on a "trial" basis before the hotel extended its coverage to all servers and bartenders. Finding that the original implementation of the policy constituted a contract violation, the arbitrator ordered the hotel to provide back pay to those employees who had been affected "to their detriment" during the policy's initial trial period (*ITT Sheraton/Sheraton Bal Harbour Resort*, 102 LA 903).

F. Merit Increases

Merit increases are given not so much for how long employees work but for how well they execute their assigned tasks. Therefore, employees with similar lengths of service in equivalent positions can earn different rates of pay based on their capability and performance. One arbitrator noted that merit pay is just that—something awarded a person for meritorious service. It is not a right to which one is entitled by virtue of his presence on the payroll" (*Koehring Co.*, 65 LA 638; see also 21 LA 614, 21 LA 480, 14 LA 77).

If a collective bargaining agreement specifies that an employer has the right to give merit increases, or if a management rights clause grants authority over such matters, arbitrators tend to let employers give merit increases as they see fit. The only impediment in these cases is if employers grant merit increases in a way that is unfair, arbitrary, or discriminatory or if the increases are based on erroneous or insufficient data (70 LA 514, 69 LA 1239, 41 LA 314, 40 LA 143, 21 LA 614, 17 LA 568, 15 LA 180, 15 LA 4).

● An employer had the right to provide merit increases to employees who took on extra duties to help implement a new program at a mental health center, an arbitrator held. Despite the union's claim that a merit increase "is concerned with how an employee performs, not what is performed,"

and its assertion that at least some of the increases were mere favoritism, the arbitrator said the fundamental issue in the case was one of the employer's authority under the contract. The employer had to provide certain minimum wages, but the agreement did not specify what, if any, maximum salaries were required or allowed, the arbitrator said, noting that the lack of "contractual restraint" on the employer was buttressed by a strong management rights clause, rendering the union's claims moot (*CIT Mental Health Services Inc.*, 89 LA 442).

● A state did not violate a memorandum of understanding, which provided that during the term of the bargaining agreement a particular social worker classification would undergo a job evaluation study, when it refused to implement the results of the study that workers' point total merited an increase of one pay grade, where the memo was silent on the question of implementation, the parties never discussed the question and walked away with their own assumptions, and there had been no consistent practice of immediate implementation of such studies (*State of Iowa*, 127 LA 106).

● A state agency violated its collective bargaining agreement when it failed to give merit increases to employees whose annual reviews entitled them to merit pay but who were promoted at the same time as or shortly before their annual reviews, an arbitrator ruled. Under the contract's explicit language, any employee whose performance met or exceeded expectations was entitled to a merit increase, regardless of any other shifts, promotions, or changes in duties, the arbitrator determined, ordering the workers who met the relevant criteria to be given back pay with interest (*Florida Keys Aqueduct Authority*, 124 LA 211).

III. Overtime Work & Pay [LA CDI 115.501; 117.327; 118.658]

OVERVIEW

Disagreements involving overtime work often have to be resolved by arbitrators. Generally speaking, disputes over the assignment of overtime are most prevalent, while those addressing the appropriate compensation for the work are less common.

Arbitration cases that deal with the assignment of overtime can be divided into two groups according to whether employees want the extra work or are trying to avoid it. When grievances are filed over the distribution of desired overtime, they usually come from employees who claim that they have been bypassed for overtime assignments to which they were entitled. Grievances over mandatory overtime, on the other hand, typically question whether employers have the right to compel employees to work extra hours, or they challenge the discipline imposed on employees who have failed to perform the overtime they were assigned.

Where overtime compensation is concerned, the normal standard is to pay employees at one-and-a-half times their regular hourly wage or "straight-time" rate. However, various situations can occur in which the appropriate pay rate for overtime hours is unclear. For example, if collective bargaining agreements require premium pay for work performed on holidays, employees might claim that they should be paid one-and-a-half times the premium rate for overtime hours on holidays. The outcome of such cases typically hinges on whether collective bargaining agreements contain provisions on the pyramiding of pay, which are aimed at preventing different premium rates from being piled on top of each other for the same hours of work.

SUMMARY OF CASES

A. Mandatory Overtime

Many grievances question whether employers have the right to compel employees to work overtime or discipline those employees who refuse such duty. Where collective bargaining agreements do not specifically address management's overtime powers, arbitrators commonly rule that the reasonable imposition of mandatory overtime is a retained right of management or they find that this right is implied under other contract provisions, such as clauses recognizing management's authority to schedule work and direct the workforce or those describing normal hours and prescribing higher pay rates for extra hours (116 LA 246, 55 LA 31, 52 LA 493, 48 LA 1077).

● In one case, an arbitrator said if a contract specified what constituted a "normal" workday or "normal" workweek, he could infer that there would occasionally be "abnormal" workdays or workweeks. Such provisions did not preclude the imposition of mandatory overtime but instead affirmed the right to require overtime under certain circumstances, according to the arbitrator (*Jones & Laughlin Steel Corp.*, 29 LA 708).

● In a case where a contract stipulated that changes in work schedules had to be agreed to by both the employer and the union, an arbitrator found that an instance of mandatory overtime did not violate the parties' labor agreement. Because the overtime was for a limited, specific period and not an overall schedule change, the employer did not have to seek or receive the union's approval, the arbitrator said. In addition, under the contract's management rights clause, the employer had the right to schedule overtime as needed, the arbitrator found (*McConway & Torley Corp.*, 55 LA 31).

● Another arbitrator stated that the burden is not on an employer to find contractual provisions that expressly authorize it to require overtime work. Rather, the arbitrator said the burden rests with the union to point out any contractual prohibition against such mandatory assignments (*Seilon Inc.*, 51 LA 261; see also 105 LA 257).

● An employer that previously assigned overtime to its employees on a voluntary basis was justified in making assignments mandatory, an arbitrator decided, because there was nothing in the contract that specifically limited the employer's right to require overtime. Emphasizing the rights of management to run a plant, make rules, and set working hours, the arbitrator ruled that the employer's reasonable assignment of overtime did not violate the parties' labor contract (*Powermatic/Houdaille Inc.*, 63 LA 1).

● Similarly, an arbitrator upheld the imposition of mandatory overtime under a collective bargaining agreement that gave an employer sole discretion in scheduling production. Even though the employer had in the past met its production needs through voluntary overtime, that did not preclude its exercising a right specifically stated in the contract, the arbitrator concluded (*Colt Firearms*, 52 LA 493).

1. Disciplinary Actions

Employees can face various disciplinary consequences if they refuse overtime assignments or leave without permission when they are expected to keep working.

● In some cases, a refusal to work overtime can be grounds for discharge, especially if the incident is regarded as an act of insubordination (120 LA 399, 114 LA 415, 106 LA 475, 94 LA 1303, 85 LA 787).

● At the other end of the spectrum are cases in which a failure to work overtime is treated as an attendance violation (119 LA 1803, 114 LA 1647, 110 LA 880, 96 LA 855).

● Between these extremes are disciplinary actions such as warnings and suspensions. The latter can vary greatly in duration, from a few hours to several weeks (116 LA 1251, 115 LA 773, 107 LA 782, 86 LA 1137, 86 LA 832).

Although the refusal of overtime is typically regarded as misconduct, arbitrators often find reasons to overturn or reduce the discipline imposed by employers. Among the most common reasons are communication problems or insufficient notice from management about required overtime, inadequate or inequitable disciplinary procedures, and a failure to consider the legitimate excuses of employees who claim an inability to work (101 LA 694, 95 LA 449, 94 LA 647, 93 LA 707, 92 LA 483, 86 LA 378, 74 LA 1020, 74 LA 967, 46 LA 607).

• An arbitrator overturned a suspension imposed on an employee who failed to work beyond his normal 3 p.m. quitting time on a Friday because he had a bill he needed to pay. A company personnel manager incorrectly told the employee he could not be forced to work overtime, and the employee honestly believed the manager had the authority to excuse him from staying late. According to the arbitrator, the employee could not be held responsible for acting on wrong information from management regarding his obligation to work overtime (*Fieldcrest Cannon Inc.*, 99 LA 776).

• Discharge was too severe a penalty for an eight-year employee who refused an overtime assignment so he could be with his son at a football banquet, an arbitrator ruled. A week beforehand, the employee had told his supervisor he would need to leave by 4 p.m. to take his son to the banquet and he said he would use vacation time if necessary. On the day of the banquet, the employee had already gone beyond his normal 4 p.m. quitting time when his supervisor assigned him extra work. In spite of their prior discussion, the employee was warned that a refusal to comply would result in discipline. The arbitrator noted that a worker who receives an order from management normally must adhere to the "obey now, grieve later" doctrine. However, that was not a viable option in this case because completing the overtime assignment would have caused the employee and his son to miss the banquet. In light of these circumstances, as well as the employee's eight years of service and the fact that this was a first offense of insubordination, the arbitrator reduced the penalty to a disciplinary suspension (*Waste Management Inc.*, 103 LA 771).

• An employer had to excuse employees from failing to work daily overtime if substitutes were available to take their place, an arbitrator ruled. A "call board" listed volunteers for overtime, and the employer had made assurances during negotiations that the availability of a qualified volunteer would relieve employees of their obligation to work assigned overtime, the arbitrator found. Given that the employer already had a practice of making exceptions for employees who missed weekend overtime if someone from the call board took their place, the arbitrator said the same practice had to be applied to daily overtime (*Commercial Filters Division*, 91 LA 25).

• An arbitrator reduced the penalty of discharge to a one-week suspension in a case where a swing-shift employee disobeyed an order from his foreman to stay and work on the graveyard shift. Earlier that day, the employee had a disagreement with his supervisor about contractual requirements regarding overtime. The employee sought out a supervisor from the graveyard shift in an attempt to avoid working overtime, but that supervisor indicated that the decision was not his. He advised the employee to "do the right thing," which the employee took as permission to leave. According to the arbitrator, the "equivocal response" of the graveyard-shift supervisor did not countermand the foreman's order to work overtime. However, the employer "was not in a position to properly evaluate whether termination was an appropriate penalty," the arbitrator said, because management denied the employee a fair opportunity to tell his side of the story and failed to conduct an adequate investigation. In addition, the arbitrator said the employee's earlier disagreement with his foreman, along with other "unusual circumstances" surrounding the overtime assignment, left some doubt about whether the employee was entirely at fault (*Horizon Lines of Alaska LLC*, 120 LA 1805).

• Another arbitrator ordered reinstatement without back pay for an employee who failed to report for Saturday overtime, finding that the penalty of termination did not comport with the employer's stated system of progressive discipline (*Phillips 66 Co.*, 93 LA 707).

• Declaring that an employer had an obligation not to impose overtime in cases of sickness or physical inability to perform, an arbitrator overturned the termination of an employee who refused to work a double shift because she felt "unsafe." The employee had been ill and was excessively tired at the end of her regular shift. Though the principle of "work now and grieve later" normally requires compliance with management directives, employees need not comply if they have a reasonable good-faith belief that following those directives will be injurious to their own health and safety or the safety of others, the arbitrator explained. Finding that the employee refused the extra shift because her physical condition made the risks unreasonable, the arbitrator reduced the employee's termination to a five-day suspension (*Kaiser Aluminum & Chemical Corp.*, 92 LA 367).

● In a case involving inadequate notice of overtime as well as a medical excuse, an arbitrator held that an employer improperly disciplined an employee for refusing to work past the end of her regular shift. Under the parties' collective bargaining agreement, the employer was required to excuse employees from overtime assignments that were not scheduled in advance if the employees had a prior commitment and their inability to work was justified. The employer normally posted overtime notices before lunch but did not do so on the day in question, the arbitrator pointed out, and the employee had an appointment with her doctor following her scheduled shift, which was a justifiable excuse for not working overtime (*Lear Seating Corp.*, 98 LA 194).

● A three-day suspension was too severe for an employee who refused an overtime assignment because his child was ill, an arbitrator ruled. After being told he would need to stay late, the employee first said he was not well but retracted that claim when it appeared that his employer would require a fitness examination. The employee subsequently spoke with his wife and claimed he had to go home to attend to a sick child. The employer suspected that the employee made up the excuse. Based on the evidence, the arbitrator determined that the employee was not faced with an emergency or immediate reason to go home, but his child was in fact ill. Thus, the arbitrator reduced the discipline to a written warning (*Jefferson Smurfit Corp.*, 110 LA 276).

● *By contrast*, an arbitrator ruled a power company had just cause to issue a one-day suspension to a lineman for his poor overtime response rate under its policy providing for discipline of employees who fail to respond to 26 percent of overtime callouts when his work group's rate was below 40 percent, where he had a history of failing to meet the required percentage, the lineman had a 22.5% response rate for the first six months of the year while his group exceeded 40 percent, he offered no evidence of mitigating circumstances, and he was only the second employee to receive such a suspension in the past six years (*Ameren UE Corp.*, 128 LA 1787).

● An employer had just cause to suspend an employee who refused to work overtime, even though he was doing so to bring attention to the employer's alleged violation of the labor contract. The arbitrator ruled he was obligated to "obey now and grieve later," and his absentee record showed a calculated application of testing the limitation of absentee rules (*Haynes International*, 125 LA 1358).

● An arbitrator upheld an employer's discipline of an employee who told his supervisor he was tired, had worked enough overtime, and wanted to spend time with his family. The employee was the junior worker in his unit, and the parties' collective bargaining agreement granted the employer the right to assign overtime in reverse order of seniority if no one volunteered for the extra hours. Although the contract also stated that overtime could be declined for good cause, the arbitrator said the reasons given by the employee were inadequate. The outcome might have been different if the employee had claimed he was so tired that working would have posed a risk, but there was no evidence of an unusual safety or health hazard justifying the employee's overtime refusal, the arbitrator found (*Timken Latrobe Steel Co.*, 121 LA 1634).

● Under a contract that said employees "will cooperate" when asked to perform overtime work, an employer was justified in suspending two employees who missed hundreds of hours of scheduled overtime, an arbitrator ruled. The company's regular schedule included 12 hours of overtime per week, but each of the employees routinely skipped the extra hours. While acknowledging that overtime was not compulsory under the contract, the arbitrator said the employer was justified in imposing discipline on the two employees, because their repeated overtime refusals constituted a failure to cooperate, and they were the worst offenders of all the workers at the plant (*Hercules Machine Tool & Die Co.*, 108 LA 258).

● An employer had just cause to discharge an employee who willfully ignored three direct orders to stay late and complete repairs on a machine that had stopped working, an arbitrator decided. The employee had at least constructive knowledge that his refusal could lead to termination for insubordination, and a work rule against failing to cooperate with supervisors authorized discharge for a first offense, the arbitrator pointed out. The employee claimed that he could not work the overtime because he had to pick up his son from school. However, the arbitrator said the key question was whether the employee had a legitimate emergency, because "it does not follow that every familial problem justifies disobeying direct orders." Finding that the employee could have made alternative arrangements regarding his son but failed to do so, the arbitrator determined that the employee's conduct amounted to deliberate disobedience (*Southern Champion Tray Co.*, 96 LA 633).

2. Substantiation of Excuses

Various arbitrators have declared that it is reasonable for employers to require substantiation from employees if they claim an inability to work overtime. In some cases, a fraudulent excuse can carry more severe consequences than the overtime refusal itself.

● One arbitrator ruled that an employer was within its rights to demand documentation in support of an employee's claim that it was "too stressful" for him to work overtime. The employer had the authority to require overtime work, and it was reasonable to require documentation from an employee claiming that a medical

restriction prevented him from performing part of his ongoing responsibilities, the arbitrator held. It was also reasonable for the employer to insist on a second opinion from a clinical psychologist after the employee provided documentation from a general practitioner, according to the arbitrator (*Fairmont General Hospital Inc.*, 119 LA 134).

● An employee was properly discharged for fraudulently claiming that a migraine prevented him from working overtime on a Saturday, an arbitrator decided. The employee had complained to his supervisor about the scheduled overtime because he was planning to participate in a bowling tournament. On Saturday morning, the employee called in sick, but he still went bowling in the afternoon. When the employee received a written reprimand, he tried to challenge it by submitting a note on a physician's prescription form. The note was not signed, however, and an investigation revealed that the employee had not seen a doctor. The arbitrator upheld the employee's termination for falsification of records, finding that the doctor's excuse was a sham. "If he was well enough to bowl, he was well enough to work," the arbitrator said (*American Steel Foundries*, 113 LA 730).

● An overtime refusal was properly treated as a voluntary quit in a case where an employee claimed sickness, had been warned in the past about his failure to work overtime, and had failed to go to a medical examination arranged by his employer in order to substantiate a previous illness claim, an arbitrator ruled. Less than a month before the incident precipitating his termination, the employee had been reminded that, under company policy, a refusal to work mandatory overtime was a "voluntary quit," the arbitrator noted. In addition, the employee had been told that any claims of illness should be made before, not after, he was asked to work overtime (*Land-O-Sun Dairies Inc.*, 105 LA 740).

B. Distribution of Desired Overtime

On the other side of the coin from situations involving mandatory overtime are those in which employees want to work extra hours. Many collective bargaining agreements address employees' rights in this area by calling for the equalization of overtime or requiring employers to offer opportunities for extra hours to the most senior employees first. Other factors can also come into play. For example, collective bargaining agreements commonly separate employees by department, classification, or shift for overtime purposes or allow employers to take employee qualifications into account when deciding who will perform the work. The language of individual contracts can make all the difference in the outcome of arbitration cases that challenge the handling of overtime assignments.

• One collective bargaining agreement contained a clause requiring an employer to allocate overtime work according to departmental seniority unless strict adherence to the rule would substantially impair production. An arbitrator found that the employer violated the contract when it made no attempt to contact the senior employee from a particular department but instead gave an overtime job to an employee from another department who was already on hand performing other tasks on an overtime basis (*Harris Brothers Co.*, 53 LA 293; see also 95 LA 11).

• Under another labor agreement, an employer was required to offer overtime in seniority order to employees who held the same job title on all shifts after offering overtime in seniority order to employees working the same job on the same shift. According to an arbitrator, the employer had an obligation to assign available overtime to a senior employee who was readily present and accessible at work, because he had let his supervisor know that he wanted to work all available overtime. Consequently, the employer had to pay that employee for the overtime work he was denied (*Koppers Industries Inc.*, 119 LA 65; see also 117 LA 231).

• An arbitrator ruled an employer violated the bargaining contract, which provided that overtime be equally distributed if practicable, when it based its overtime callout for first responder assignments on the needs of the service determined by the employer, because it was often practicable

to equalize overtime in that situation. The arbitrator awarded the low persons on the overtime lists to be compensated in the amount that they would have received had the company followed proper overtime assignment (*Xcel Energy*, 125 LA 513).

• An employer committed a contract violation when it allowed an employee from one shift to trade overtime assignments with a co-worker from another shift, an arbitrator held. The contract and a memorandum of agreement together specified two different types of overtime—regular overtime, in which extra work was to be assigned solely to employees within a given department, and fill-in overtime, in which employees could take other assignments. Two separate overtime rosters were maintained, but when the employer allowed the workers to trade assignments, it enabled one of them to use his position on the regular overtime roster to perform work outside his shift, which constituted fill-in overtime whose volunteers had to be drawn from a separate list. Permitting the trade-off "contradicts the delicate contractual balance" the parties had carefully crafted in negotiations, the arbitrator said, ordering the employer to cease engaging in the practice (*PHB Inc.*, 123 LA 146).

• A beverage company did not violate a collective bargaining agreement stating that "[o]vertime will be offered to [e]xpress [d]rivers on a voluntary basis first" when it offered extra express runs to swingmen on straight-time before it offered overtime to regular express drivers who were scheduled to be off, an arbitrator ruled. The provision only required that overtime be offered to express drivers before non-express drivers, it did not prohibit the company from using straight-time swing drivers before it called in express drivers to work overtime, and the union failed to establish that there was a past practice of offering additional work to express drivers on overtime when swing drivers were available to do work (*Pepsi Beverage Co.*, 129 LA 1572 (Arb. 2011)).

• An arbitrator upheld an employer's right to use floaters on a hot team to rebuild damaged or flawed cabinet doors on overtime, instead of offering overtime to regular employees in the door department, because it was difficult to know when overtime work was needed, the number, varied processes, and time to rebuild doors could be anticipated, and management made a good faith judgment to call in the hot team (*Masterbrand Cabinets Inc.*, 128 LA 881).

• A contract called for overtime work to be performed by the classification of employees who normally performed that type of work. Given such a provision, an arbitrator ruled that it was a violation of the contract for overtime to be assigned to another classification of employees even though the job was to be performed in their work area and they had on occasion performed that particular task (*American Shipbuilding Co.*, 54 LA 1216; see also 74 LA 699).

• An employer violated its collective bargaining agreement when it scheduled weekend overtime work separately for each weekend day, resulting in a junior employee being offered more overtime than a senior employee who wanted to work as much overtime as possible, according to an arbitrator. Although the employer had a past practice of scheduling weekend overtime on a daily basis, the union had alerted the employer that it wanted to start strictly adhering to the letter of the agreement, which specified that senior employees should be given preference for overtime. The arbitrator held that the employer had to give the senior employee overtime pay for the eight hours of work he was improperly denied (*Welch Foods Inc.*, 122 LA 805; see also 91 LA 570).

• An employer committed a contract violation when it granted overtime work to an electrician who was the 16th worker in seniority in his department, an arbitrator found. The employee who was fifth in seniority complained about being bypassed, but the employer argued that he had no standing to grieve because the four electricians above him on the seniority list did not choose to file grievances. The arbitrator rejected that argument and ordered the employer to give the employee eight hours of overtime pay (*Celotex Corp.*, 63 LA 521).

• An arbitrator decided that a senior employee was improperly denied overtime after his employer posted a defective notice about the work. The employee worked in a different department from the one where the overtime was to be performed, but the notice did not properly indicate that workers from the employee's department could do the work. Consequently, the arbitrator determined that the employer committed a contract violation when it chose two of the employee's junior co-workers for the overtime (*Admiral Metals Servicenter*, 117 LA 231).

• An employer violated its labor contract by failing to canvass senior employees to seek volunteers for overtime work, an arbitrator held. When one overtime assignment became available, the employer followed the normal procedure of offering the work to senior employees. However, the process was not repeated when another assignment became available, and the employer argued that employees who had earlier refused overtime need not have been asked again. The arbitrator disagreed. Just because employees failed to agree to a prior overtime assignment, the employer was not justified in passing over them for a new overtime assignment, the arbitrator determined (*Grief Bros. Corp.*, 55 LA 384).

• On the other hand, an arbitrator found that an employer was justified in bypassing one employee and assigning overtime to a worker with less seniority in spite of a contract provision requiring overtime to be given to the most senior employee classified to do the work. Overtime was necessary for Labor Day, and it was scheduled late in the afternoon of the last working day before the holiday. Without attempting to contact the most senior employee, who had gone on his honeymoon and was not due back until after Labor Day, the foreman assigned the overtime to the second most senior worker. The employer emphasized the unreasonableness of trying to contact the senior employee throughout the holiday weekend, adding that it would be very difficult to get a substitute at the last minute if the senior employee were unavailable. The arbitrator agreed with the employer and held that the overtime was properly assigned to someone else (*Carey Salt Co.*, 51 LA 1170).

• Another arbitrator decided that an employer had the flexibility to assign extra hours on a rotating basis under a collective bargaining agreement that did not make seniority a governing factor with regard to overtime. Although the employer allegedly had a practice of taking seniority into consideration when making overtime assignments, the arbitrator pointed out that a general seniority clause in the contract only applied to promotions, layoffs, and recalls. In the absence of a specific contract provision on overtime work, the authority to decide how to assign such work "lies within the management rights of the employer," the arbitrator declared (*Armour Foods Inc.*, 85 LA 1013; see also 30 LA 177).

• In another case, even though a contract specified that overtime had to be distributed according to seniority, an arbitrator did not find a violation where a junior employee was given overtime work after a foreman discovered that the senior employee who might have been offered the overtime had already left the plant. The union argued that the foreman should have earlier sought out the senior employee to alert him to the possibility of overtime, but the arbitrator determined that there was no evidence of bad faith and denied the grievance (*Kellogg Co.*, 62 LA 1217; see also 77 LA 217).

1. Overtime Equalization

Some collective bargaining agreements provide for the equal sharing of overtime, with equalization typically limited to employees within the same job classification, department, or shift.

• An employer's failure to assign additional overtime to employees on one of its shifts violated a contract that called for equalization of overtime with consideration given to seniority, an arbitrator ruled. Management scheduled a specific overtime assignment for all first-shift employees and promised to even up the overtime of second-shift employees within the time period allotted for equalization. When management subsequently failed to do so, second-shift employees with greater seniority than some of the first-shift workers filed a grievance, which the arbitrator upheld. Under the contract, the arbitrator said, the employer was required to cross shift lines if necessary to equalize overtime with consideration to seniority (*Eaton, Yale & Town Inc.*, 54 LA 1121; see also 75 LA 608, 75 LA 275, 75 LA 99, 74 LA 699).

• An employer that failed to contact vacationing employees to determine their availability for scheduled overtime on the date they would have returned to work violated a contract requiring equalization of overtime, an arbitrator held. Although the employer normally offered overtime to workers who put their names on a roster, the arbitrator said overtime eligibility was based on employees' relative overtime accumulations, not on their having added their names to a sign-up sheet. In addition, the arbitrator noted that the employer had a past practice of contacting employees who were scheduled to work but were absent, and there was no reason to treat workers returning from vacation differently from workers who were away from the plant because of illness (*General Mills Chemicals Inc.*, 66 LA 1012; see also 76 LA 1159, 73 LA 1087).

• After failing to reach an employee about one overtime assignment, an employer committed a contract violation by not attempting to contact the employee when another overtime assignment became available 20 minutes later, an arbitrator ruled. Under the contract's overtime equalization requirements, the employee was first in line for overtime because he had accumulated the fewest hours. The employee did not answer the phone when the employer called him about the initial assignment. When the second overtime opportunity arose, the employer should have tried calling the employee again rather than assuming he was still unavailable, the arbitrator held, ordering the employer to pay the employee for the overtime hours he was denied (*Goodyear Aerospace Corp.*, 52 LA 1098; see also 76 LA 1159, 74 LA 110).

• Under a contract requiring double-time pay for hours worked in excess of 12 per day, an employer could not ignore its overtime equalization obligations in an effort to avoid paying three employees the higher rate, an arbitrator ruled. Once the three employees reached the 12-hour mark, the employer dismissed them. In their place, the employer used other workers who had accumulated more overtime but were not eligible for double-time pay. The arbitrator found that assigning the work to employees with more hours of overtime violated the equalization requirement, and he ordered the employer to pay the three employees double-time for the work they were denied (*Continental Can Co. Inc.*, 52 LA 118).

• An employer was required to assign overtime to employees who had worked the least amount of extra hours, even though they had become eligible for a higher pay rate because of how many consecutive days they had worked, an arbitrator decided. The employer could not avoid the equalization of overtime, as required under the parties' collective bargaining agreement, just because the employees would be eligible for double-time pay as a result of working a seventh consecutive day, the arbitrator found (*American Enka Corp.*, 52 LA 882; see also 54 LA 387).

• An employer did not violate an overtime equalization requirement by failing to give an employee any overtime work during a two-month period when other employees worked as much as 24 hours of overtime, an arbitrator decided. In the following two months, the employer did give the employee enough extra work to bring his overtime hours in line with those of other workers. The union claimed that the employee was entitled to pay for overtime he had missed during the first two months, but the arbitrator ruled that four months was a reasonable period in which to equalize overtime because the contract did not set any time limit (*North American Aviation Inc.*, 17 LA 320; see also 89 LA 781).

• A system for allocating overtime was not violated when one employee worked extra hours as acting supervisor while two other employees received no overtime, an arbitrator ruled. During a winter emergency at a power station, an employee on temporary assignment worked overtime for 10 days. Two mechanics who were not offered any overtime work during the emergency grieved, contending that the contract required equitable allocation of overtime hours. The arbitrator found that the agree-

ment between the parties did not require perfect equity with regard to overtime, but that the goal of the overtime system was to apportion overtime opportunities "as equitably as practicable" so that everyone in the bargaining unit had a fair chance to earn extra money. Furthermore, a previous grievance settlement cited by the union only prohibited foremen from working overtime as craftsmen, but not as supervisors. Concluding that the company had met that obligation, the arbitrator denied the grievance (*Virginia Electric & Power Co.*, 118 LA 402).

• Under an equalization system that allowed the accumulated overtime of employees in the same department to differ by up to 36 hours, an arbitrator held that the employee with the least number of hours would not move to the front of the line for overtime assignments unless the 36-hour gap had already been exceeded. The union complained about situations where the gap in employees' relative overtime accumulations exceeded the 36-hour limit after an overtime assignment was scheduled but before it was actually performed. However, the arbitrator decided that the 36-hour limit would only come into play if it had been exceeded before the work was scheduled. Once overtime work was properly assigned, management would not be required to change the assignment if the recipient's accumulated hours increased prior to the performance of the overtime to push that employee ahead of another worker by more than 36 hours, the arbitrator ruled (*National Lead Co.*, 53 LA 687).

2. Skills and Abilities

When employers face challenges over the selection or rejection of particular individuals for overtime assignments, they frequently defend their decisions by pointing to the skills and abilities of the employees who received the overtime or were bypassed for the work. The amount of leeway employers have in considering worker qualifications typically hinges on the applicable contract language.

• In one case, an arbitrator held that an employer committed a contract violation by failing on two separate occasions to call in a senior engineer to perform maintenance work on an overtime basis. The employee claimed that he was entitled to the work under new language in the parties' collective bargaining agreement requiring overtime assignments to be given to "the most senior qualified employee" within the department. The employer said the employee did not normally perform maintenance duties and was not the most qualified person for the work in question. However, the arbitrator determined that the new contract language required overtime to be given to the most senior employee who could do the work, not the most qualified individual (*City of Fergus Falls*, 110 LA 961).

● Under a collective bargaining agreement requiring overtime equalization, an employer's practice of assigning overtime to the workers in its maintenance department on the basis of their different proficiencies constituted a contract violation, an arbitrator held. The language of the contract did not allow the employer to choose the employee who was best at performing a given task if another maintenance worker was being shortchanged on overtime hours. According to the arbitrator, the employer could only make an exception to the rules on overtime equalization if an employee who lagged in overtime hours was totally unqualified to perform the necessary work (*National Lead Co.*, 53 LA 687).

● An employer improperly bypassed female employees for overtime work that involved lifting more than 50 pounds, an arbitrator ruled. In spite of a policy aimed at sparing female employees from heavy lifting, it was frequently necessary for women to lift more than 50 pounds during regular hours. The employer committed a contract violation in bypassing the female employees for the overtime assignment, the arbitrator said, because they had shown that they were able to do the required lifting (*Standard Brands Inc.*, 54 LA 732).

● Where a contract allowed employees to assert their seniority rights to obtain overtime work on their shift if management considered them "capable of handling the job," an arbitrator determined that an employer had to allow a senior employee to perform tasks outside his current job

classification. The employee had been promoted to leadman after holding other jobs in the same department. The employer had intended to limit overtime assignments for different tasks to employees currently holding the pertinent job classification, but a contract amendment aimed at establishing this restriction was ambiguous and thus did not preclude the senior employee from securing overtime work he was capable of performing in other classifications, the arbitrator said (*Lull Engineering Co. Inc.*, 85 LA 581).

● *By contrast*, an arbitrator upheld the selection of a junior employee for overtime work that involved the training of other workers on how to operate a crane, where the senior employee who contested the decision had not regularly worked on the crane for more than 15 years (*Inco Alloys International Inc.*, 108 LA 585).

● An employer did not commit a contract violation by refusing to give overtime assignments to two employees who were not skilled in the required tasks. The employees, who worked as inspectors for an auto parts manufacturer, objected to being passed over for overtime, but according to the employer, the overtime work required computer programming skills that the workers lacked. Although the contract required qualified employees with the least amount of overtime hours to be assigned any extra work that was available, that did not mean unqualified employees had to be given the overtime hours, the arbitrator said (*Tower Automotive Products Co. Inc.*, 116 LA 677).

● An employer did not violate the overtime equalization requirement of a collective bargaining agreement by assigning all the welding work on a special project to one employee, an arbitrator ruled. The employee was unique in possessing a special welding certificate that an outside consultant said was needed to do the project safely, the arbitrator observed. This was a matter of extreme importance, the arbitrator added, because the project had a direct impact on the safety of the public (*Miami-Dade County*, 119 LA 901).

● Safety was also a prominent consideration in a case where an arbitrator upheld an employer's decision to deny double-shift overtime to senior employees. Rejecting the argument that overtime had to be assigned on the basis of seniority alone, the arbitrator pointed out that the parties' collective bargaining agreement required employees to have the "skill ability" for the work being done. On the basis of this language, the employer had the discretion to decide that no employees were able to work double shifts, because doing so could create safety hazards, the arbitrator decided (*Beverage Concepts*, 114 LA 340; see also 118 LA 252, 94 LA 148).

3. Probationary, Temporary, or Transferred Workers

When questions surface about the overtime rights of probationary, temporary, or transferred workers, they commonly arise because regular employees are vying for the same extra hours. If the parties cannot agree about how overtime work should be distributed in such situations, arbitrators must step in and provide the answers.

● An arbitrator upheld an employer's assignment of overtime to a probationary employee when all permanent employees in the department already were working overtime. The parties' collective bargaining agreement stipulated that overtime was to be distributed equally among employees in a department, but it did not require the employer to seek out senior employees from other departments, the arbitrator noted. The contract language on overtime distribution was clear and unambiguous, the arbitrator said, adding that a probationary employee is still an "employee" under the contract (*Hess and Eisenhardt Co.*, 53 LA 95).

● An employer properly bypassed a senior maintenance worker and a welder when it assigned overtime work to a pair of probationary employees in its tool-and-die department, an arbitrator decided. All the regular employees in the tool-and-die department had declined the overtime. In addition, the maintenance worker and welder lacked the skills for the work in question, whereas the probationary employees were well qualified, the arbitrator pointed out. Although the parties' collective bargain-

ing agreement prohibited the scheduling of probationary workers for overtime "as long as there are employees in the plant with seniority who will work," the agreement made an exception for the tool-and-die classification, the arbitrator noted (*American Metals Industries Inc.*, 95 LA 1278).

● An arbitrator found that when overtime is to be shared equally throughout a department or work group, employees temporarily transferred to another area are entitled to overtime assignments scheduled in their regular group. To rule otherwise would mean that management could avoid giving overtime to particular employees merely by temporarily transferring them prior to assigning overtime, the arbitrator declared (*Armstrong Cork Co.*, 54 LA 252; see also 53 LA 616).

● Under a contract provision that made employees ineligible for overtime if they were not qualified to perform the work, an employer had the right to assign overtime to experienced temporary employees, an arbitrator ruled. The overtime involved filling a large order in the employer's warehouse, and the two office employees who filed a grievance had little or no experience with the required tasks. Concluding that the employer was not obligated to train office employees before using outside help, the arbitrator said the employer had the right to assign the overtime to the temporary employees absent a clear showing of discriminatory or arbitrary treatment of the regular office employees (*Nissan Motor Corp.*, 66 LA 1326; see also 72 LA 996).

● On the other hand, an employer improperly assigned overtime to temporary employees on its Valentine's Day candy production line, an arbitrator ruled. Despite the fact that the line was staffed entirely by seasonal, temporary employees, the arbitrator found that regular employees could not be denied the opportunity to perform the overtime work. The arbitrator's ruling was based on the fact that regular employees received preference over temporary workers for overtime assignments in the past. Also, the regular employees' coverage by the collective bargaining agreement meant that they were "entitled to first consideration for all contractual benefits," the arbitrator said (*Zachary Confections Inc.*, 77 LA 464).

C. Disputes Over Pyramiding of Pay

In addition to providing for overtime pay after a certain number of hours worked in a day or a week, collective bargaining agreements commonly call for other special pay rates, such as holiday and weekend premiums or premiums for the sixth or seventh day of work in the same week. Absent clear contractual prohibitions against the pyramiding of pay, arbitrators often find that overtime rates apply on top of these other rates.

● Under a contract that did not prohibit pyramiding of pay for overtime worked on premium-pay days, an arbitrator found that a holiday rate had to be treated as the base rate when computing overtime pay. Even though the contract already called for triple-time pay for holiday work, the arbitrator concluded that the holiday rate had to be multiplied by time and one-half when employees worked overtime on a holiday; hence, holiday overtime had to be compensated at four-and-a-half times the straight-time rate (*Fry's Food Stores*, 44 LA 431).

● Employees who worked on a Saturday holiday were entitled to triple-time pay, an arbitrator ruled. The employees were paid time-and-a-half wages for the Saturday holiday they worked, but they contended that they were also entitled to time-and-a-half wages for having worked more than 40 hours a week. The arbitrator ruled that a contract provision prohibiting pyramiding of overtime was applicable only to daily and weekly overtime work, not holiday work. In addition, a contract clause stated that employees were entitled to time-and-a-half "additional" wages for working certain holidays, which meant "additional to such other pay as would be received on the day involved," the arbitrator said (*Los Angeles Jewish Community Council*, 11 LA 869).

● Under a contract that provided double-time pay for holiday work and time-and-a-half for more than eight hours worked in a given day, an arbitrator allowed employees to collect triple-time pay for overtime hours worked on a holiday, because the contract did not expressly prohibit pyramiding of premiums (*Phelps Dodge Refining Corp.*, 9 LA 474).

● Despite having received time-and-a-half pay for hours worked on a scheduled day off, an employee was also entitled to overtime pay for the hours she worked in excess of 40 during the same week, an arbitrator ruled. The employee's situation was not covered by a contract provision that prohibited the payment of both daily and weekly overtime for the same hours, the arbitrator said, because the premium pay the employee received for her off-day work was not the same as daily overtime. Rather, it was analogous to "penalty pay" that an employee would receive for working on a Sunday or a holiday, the arbitrator reasoned (*Safeway Stores Inc.*, 45 LA 244).

● An employer committed a contract violation by refusing to pay an employee double time for working from 3 p.m. to 7 p.m. on the Memorial Day holiday after she had already put in an eight-hour shift that ended at 7 a.m. that day. Noting that the contract called for overtime on holidays to be compensated at a double-time rate, the arbitrator said it was "nonsensical" for the employer to argue that double-time pay was required only if the overtime hours immediately followed the scheduled hours an employee worked on a holiday (*City of Lansing, Michigan*, 123 LA 555).

● Another arbitrator determined that three separate rates applied in a situation where an employee worked from 3 a.m. to 3 p.m. on a Monday. Because the contract specified that the workweek began at 7 a.m. Mondays, the employee was entitled to double-time Sunday premiums for the four hours from 3 a.m. to 7 a.m. The employee's straight-time rate applied to the middle four hours from 7 a.m. to 11 a.m., while the last four hours, from 11 a.m. to 3 p.m., had to be paid at the time-and-a-half rate applicable to daily overtime. The arbitrator said the application of the Sunday premium rate and the regular overtime rate to different hours worked on the same day did not contradict the prohibition against pyramiding, because pyramiding would only occur if two different rates were piled on top of each other for the same hours of work (*King-Seeley Thermos Co.*, 61 LA 544).

● In another case, however, an employer properly paid employees at a time-and-a-half rate rather than a double-time rate for work scheduled on a contractual holiday, an arbitrator decided, notwithstanding the union's contention that the payment of the time-and-a-half rate was not in keeping with the intent of the contract. The parties' collective bargaining agreement included a no-pyramiding clause, and although the clause included an exception that required work performed on Sundays to be compensated at a double-time rate, it did not specify that the exception also applied to holiday work, the arbitrator observed (*Inland Container Corp.*, 63 LA 1294).

● An employer did not commit a contract violation by denying holiday premiums and only paying regular overtime rates to employees who worked on the eve of a holiday, an arbitrator held. Even though a side agreement provided for extra pay when employees worked on the eve of a holiday, the parties had changed the definition of holidays in their collective bargaining agreement to exclude holiday eves and include only those shifts that fell on the holidays themselves. Finding that the retention of contrary language in the side agreement was a mutual mistake, the arbitrator held that employees could no longer receive additional premiums for overtime work performed on holiday eves (*St. Louis Post-Dispatch*, 92 LA 23).

● An employer that paid premium rates for holiday work did not have to count those same hours as part of the 40-hour total that employees had to reach before becoming eligible for overtime pay, an arbitrator ruled. The employer's decision to stop counting employees' work hours on holidays when determining overtime eligibility was in keeping with a contract provision that prohibited the pyramiding of pay, the arbitrator concluded (*Graphic Packaging International Inc.*, 122 LA 675).

1. Unworked Holidays

Disagreements about employees' entitlement to overtime pay can also surface in connection with unworked holidays. For example, if employees have Monday off because of a holiday but then work Tuesday through Saturday, do the holiday hours have to be treated the same as time worked for overtime purposes? Arbitrators have ruled both ways on this question.

● One arbitrator determined that an employer had to treat a holiday as time worked for overtime purposes. When employees worked a Saturday during a week that included an unworked holiday, the employer argued that the holiday hours did not have to be counted as time worked. Rejecting the employer's argument, the arbitrator said the holiday had to be seen as time worked or employees would invariably lose the overtime premium when they worked the sixth day of a week that included a holiday (*Martin Aircraft Tool Co.*, 25 LA 181; see also 103 LA 614).

● Another arbitrator reached the opposite conclusion where a contract discussed the requirement of exceeding 40 hours of work in a week and stated that hours lost from the regular schedule would be treated as time worked for overtime purposes if they were lost at the request of management. The arbitrator decided that time off on a holiday was not time lost at the request of management. Rather, the arbitrator compared employees' time off on a holiday to an unworked Sunday, which would not be viewed as time worked for overtime purposes (*Goodyear Clearwater Mills*, 6 LA 117).

D. Defining 'Day' for Daily Overtime

Under collective bargaining agreements that require daily overtime once employees exceed a certain number of hours within a 24-hour period, the starting and ending times defining a day can play a pivotal role in determining employees' entitlement to overtime pay.

● In one case, an arbitrator determined that a temporary change in employees' schedule to a later starting and ending time did not trigger an entitlement to overtime pay when they reverted to their regular schedule. The employees normally worked from 3 p.m. to 11 p.m. Because of the altered schedule, however, the employees worked a shift on Tuesday that had overlapped into Wednesday by several hours. In spite of these morning hours, the arbitrator concluded that the employees were only entitled to straight-time pay when they returned to the 3 p.m. shift on Wednesday afternoon. The arbitrator's decision was based on the fact that the parties' collective bargaining agreement defined the workday for purposes of computing overtime as "24 consecutive hours commencing with the starting time on an employee's regularly assigned shift." Applying this definition, the arbitrator determined that the employees' workday on Wednesday did not begin until 3 p.m., and the earlier hours were part of the previous workday (*Chicago Pneumatic Tool Co.*, 42 LA 1240).

● In another case, a problem arose with the initiation of daylight saving time one weekend. The contract required overtime pay if employees worked more than eight hours in a day, which was defined as "24 hours beginning at the time an employee starts work on his regular or assigned schedule." When daylight saving time caused clocks to be moved ahead, the time change had the effect of shortening the period between the start of employees' Saturday and Sunday shifts by one hour. Consequently, after working a full day on Saturday, employees who returned on Sunday at their normal starting time were entitled to overtime pay for the first hour of their Sunday shifts, an arbitrator decided. The contract was very specific in defining a day as 24 hours long, and only 23 hours had elapsed between the start of the Saturday shifts and the start of the Sunday shifts, the arbitrator pointed out (*Neches Butane Products Co.*, 49 LA 1195).

E. Remedies for Overtime Violations

Reimbursement for lost wages is a common remedy ordered by arbitrators when employees have been improperly denied overtime work. As an alternative, "make-up overtime" is sometimes ordered. This type of remedy tends to be more problematic than a monetary remedy, however, because giving employees make-up work to correct past violations can run counter to normal overtime distribution procedures and affect the contractual rights of other workers.

● An arbitrator decided that overtime pay was preferable to make-up work in one case where an employer had improperly bypassed an employee for overtime and given the work to someone from a different classification. The arbitrator explained that to give the employee make-up overtime would have adversely affected the contractual overtime rights of the other employees in his classification (*Trane Co.*, 52 LA 1144; see also 96 LA 483).

● Another arbitrator gave an employer specific instructions on how to remedy a situation where an employee had been improperly bypassed for eight hours of overtime work. The employer could offer make-up overtime under the following conditions: it would have to be at a convenient time when the employee otherwise would not be working, and the overtime would have to be created specifically to compensate the employee and could not take away from his other overtime opportunities. However, if the employee left the company or was unable to work the make-up overtime within a reasonable period of time, the employer would have to provide eight hours of overtime pay without requiring him to work any make-up overtime (*Kimberly-Clark Corp.*, 61 LA 1094; see also 76 LA 10).

● In another case where an employer improperly bypassed an employee for an overtime assignment under a contract stipulating equal distribution of overtime, an arbitrator ordered the employer to grant make-up overtime. The contract failed to specify any remedy for improper overtime assignments, and the arbitrator determined that the remedy was appropriate because the bypass occurred within the same overtime equalization roster, and no inequities would result from make-up overtime. Furthermore, the bypass was unintentional, and the employee would suffer no loss of earnings as long as he received the make-up assignment within a reasonable period, the arbitrator reasoned (*Kaiser Aluminum & Chemical Corp.*, 54 LA 613).

● A series of grievances came before an arbitrator in which he found that certain employees had been denied their proper opportunity for overtime work. The employer's past practice had been to pay employees at straight-time rates in such instances. Finding, however, that the most important consideration was that the employees would have been paid at overtime rates had they worked the hours in question, the arbitrator ordered the employer to pay the employees overtime rates for the work they had been denied (*John Deere*, 20 LA 737).

• Another arbitrator held that the mistakes an employer made when assigning overtime, even though they were honest and understandable, were the employer's responsibility. Because of a computer error, an employee who should have been offered overtime was left off the list of workers assigned to Saturday work. The aggrieved employee had to be compensated, the arbitrator said, despite the fact that he should have been aware of the error and should have called it to management's attention before the scheduled overtime was performed (*Goodyear Aerospace Corp.*, 54 LA 579).

IV. Premium Pay [LA CDI 100.45 (public employees); 115.52]

OVERVIEW

Collective bargaining agreements commonly call for premium pay when employees work at undesirable times, such as nights and Sundays, or perform onerous duties.

This chapter examines disputes that can arise in connection with various types of premium pay, including shift differentials, environmental pay or "dirty work" premiums, and premiums for working weekends or a sixth or seventh consecutive day. Arbitration cases dealing with holiday premiums, meanwhile, are discussed in the chapter titled "Pay for Holiday Work."

SUMMARY OF CASES

A. Premiums Based on Day Worked

Unionized employers commonly agree to provide premium pay for work performed on certain days—such as Saturday, Sunday, or a sixth or seventh day in a row—but questions can arise as to whether the premiums apply to particular employees or to particular hours worked. For example, a common question is how to handle shifts that extend past midnight, with only a portion of employees' hours falling on a calendar day covered by premium pay requirements. As illustrated below, arbitrators do not consistently award employees premium pay in these types of cases, nor do they routinely find that employers are justified in denying premium pay.

- An arbitrator ruled that an employer was not required to pay employees premium overtime rate for working seven days in a single payroll week, where one of those days was a paid, unworked holiday, and the agreement required that the employee be regularly scheduled to work—and then be instructed not to work—on such a holiday for it to be considered a "day worked" for the purpose of applying the rate, and the grievants were not initially scheduled to work on the day at issue (*Bayer Crop-Science*, 127 LA 592 (2010)).

- When employees worked a shift that started Sunday afternoon and extended into Monday morning, they were entitled to premium pay for the entire shift, including the hours after midnight, an arbitrator decided. The arbitrator based his decision on contract language stating that all work beginning on a holiday would be paid at one and one-half times the regular straight-time rate for the entire shift. He concluded that "Sunday is a premium day, the same as a holiday. To pay overtime for an entire shift that starts on a holiday but not on a Sunday premium day would create an anomaly that is to be avoided in contract interpretation" (*Luce & Son Co. Inc.*, 117 LA 107).

● An employer committed a contract violation by denying premium pay for weekend work to employees who were assigned to a new three-day, 12-hour shift schedule, an arbitrator held. Employees who were assigned to other shift schedules remained eligible for premium pay, but the employer did not grant the weekend premiums to employees on the new three-day schedule. Finding that eligibility for premium pay was mandated by the contract, the arbitrator ordered the employer to drop the three-day schedule until a new plan could be negotiated with the union. In addition, he ruled that the employees had to be compensated for any premium pay they had been denied for work performed on weekends (*South Charleston Stamping and Mfg.*, 115 LA 710).

● Employees who worked on Sunday from 7 a.m. until 2:15 p.m. were entitled to eight hours of premium pay at a double-time rate, an arbitrator held. In overturning the employer's decision to limit the employees to seven hours of premium pay, the arbitrator found that the employer had a past practice of granting employees a full eight hours of pay whenever they worked more than four hours in a workday (*Construction Industry Combined Committee*, 69 LA 14; see also 86 LA 827).

● An arbitrator ruled that an employer improperly denied seventh-day, double-time pay to an employee who worked 10 days in an 11-day period. The arbitrator refused to accept the employer's position that the employee's seven consecutive days of work did not make him eligible for the double-time rate because they did not fall within the week encompassed by one time card. Citing the absence of clear contract

language defining the workweek, the arbitrator said the employer's interpretation would "harshly" deny the premium rate if employees worked seven consecutive days but did not start on the same day as the time card (*Earth Grains Division of Merico Inc.*, 98 LA 632).

● *By contrast*, an arbitrator decided that an employer was justified in refusing to pay a seventh-day premium to employees who worked for seven consecutive days, because they were not seven straight days during the established workweek that started on Sunday and ended on Saturday. The arbitrator pointed out that the parties had not modified the established workweek during bargaining, and the union knew what the policies were (*Gilroy Foods*, 115 LA 331).

● Another arbitrator ruled that the higher premiums required for Saturday and Sunday work did not apply to hours that spilled over to those days from shifts that began on the previous days. Although the applicable contract language stated that employees would receive time and one-half their regular pay rate for "all work performed on Saturday" and double-time for "all worked performed on Sunday," the arbitrator decided that the Saturday premiums only applied to shifts that began on Saturday, and the Sunday premiums only applied to shifts that began on Sunday. The arbitrator said his interpretation was supported by the parties' past practice for 10 years during the terms of four preceding collective bargaining agreements (*Vlasic Foods Inc.*, 74 LA 1214).

● Under a contract stating that "double-time shall be paid for all work performed on Sunday, excepting the shift that overlaps into Sunday," an arbitrator ruled that an employer was not obligated to pay a double-time premium to an employee who worked a new shift that started at 10 p.m. Sunday and ended at 6 a.m. on Monday (*Baltimore News American*, 68 LA 1054; see also 90 LA 663, 74 LA 1042).

● An employee was not entitled to time and one-half for work he performed on a Saturday, according to an arbitrator, because the collective bargaining agreement clearly stated that where Saturday work was part of an employee's regular five-day workweek, which in this case was Tuesday through Saturday, employees were to be paid on the basis of their regular hourly rate (*Western Tube and Conduit Corp.*, 99 LA 824).

● Where a contract required a double-time premium for all work performed on Sunday when it was the sixth or seventh day worked in the workweek, an arbitrator held that the double-time rate did not apply to work performed before the start of the workweek, which began at 7:00 a.m. Monday. Even though the workday was considered a 24-hour period extending from 7:00 a.m. to 7:00 a.m., the arbitrator said the pre-shift hours, being continuous with Monday, could not be considered an extension of Sunday. Moreover, past practice supported the employer's contention that employees performing the pre-shift work were entitled to time and one-half, rather than the double-time rate, the arbitrator concluded (*Certain-Teed Products Corp.*, 61 LA 689; see also 86 LA 992, 76 LA 1037).

● Without having accumulated at least 40 work hours in a week, drivers were not eligible for double-time premium pay when they worked more than eights hours on Sunday, an arbitrator ruled. Although the employer had previously paid the double-time rate in such situations, the parties' collective bargaining agreement mandated double time for Sunday work only if employees had already worked at least 40 hours, the arbitrator noted. In light of the contract's "clear and unambiguous" language, the arbitrator agreed with the employer's contention that past practice should not be the overriding factor in the case (*Jewel Food Stores*, 116 LA 349).

● An employer did not commit a contract violation by refusing to pay maintenance mechanics the same premiums for the seventh consecutive day of work as it paid two other classes of employees, according to an arbitrator. The practice remained consistent through the years, even after a provision specifying that Saturday and Sunday premiums did not apply to the mechanics had been inadvertently deleted from the parties' collective bargaining agreement. The arbitrator pointed out

that if the parties had intended to make the mechanics eligible for the premiums along with the other employees, they could have changed the agreement's provisions to specifically include the mechanics (*Quebecor World Printing Inc.*, 115 LA 865).

1. *Effect of Time Not Worked*

Employers often take the position that employees have to work a full schedule in order to qualify for seventh-day premiums and the like, but arbitrators do not always agree that time not worked due to holidays or other reasons should cost employees their eligibility for premium pay (68 LA 1006, 60 LA 387, 60 LA 187, 58 LA 685, 53 LA 855).

● In one case, an arbitrator ruled that an employer was justified in not paying employees a seventh-day premium for weeks in which one of the days was a holiday or some other day for which the employees received pay but did not work. The arbitrator pointed out that in the most recent bargaining, the parties had added a contract provision specifying that employees must actually work seven days within a week to be eligible for the seventh-day premium. The fact that the parties "substantively" changed a 30-year-old provision calling for premium pay for the seventh consecutive day to one that "clearly and literally" set forth that employees must actually work seven consecutive days in order to receive premium pay tipped the "evidentiary scales" in favor of the employer's position, the arbitrator said (*Spartan Stores Inc.*, 105 LA 549).

● After an employee received paid leave for four days of jury duty, he was not entitled to time and one-half for a Saturday shift he voluntarily worked, an arbitrator held. The collective bargaining agreement stated that employees who did not work their normal 40 hours would receive only straight-time pay for Saturday work, the arbitrator noted. He also pointed out that although the agreement specifically stated that holidays, sickness, and bereavement leave were to be considered as working time for purposes of overtime, no mention was made of leave for jury duty (*Roesch Inc.*, 92 LA 101; see also 52 LA 575, 52 LA 357).

● In a case where a collective bargaining agreement required overtime pay for hours worked on the sixth day of the week, provided that employees worked all scheduled hours on the preceding five days, an arbitrator ruled that employees recalled midweek from a long-term layoff were entitled to overtime rates for work performed on Saturday. The arbitrator explained that the term "sixth day of the week" referred to Saturday as the sixth day of the normal workweek, not the sixth day on which a particular employee may have actually worked. He said that the employer had initiated both the original interruption of the employees' work and their return to work; thus, the employees actually worked all the hours for which they were scheduled on the preceding five days in the workweek (*Hussmann Corp.*, 93 LA 675).

● An arbitrator decided that an employee's absence from his regular shift due to a snowstorm counted as time worked under an "act of God" provision and entitled him to premium pay for Saturday work. Even though 70 percent of the workforce reported to work on the day in question, the arbitrator pointed out that the employer had excused workers' storm-related absences, and the employee reasonably concluded that the snowstorm made it unsafe for him to attempt to drive to work (*Xerxes Corp.*, 89 LA 913).

2. Pyramiding of Premiums

Certain days or hours that employees work have the potential to be covered by more than one type of premium pay. For example, if employees work on a Sunday that is also a holiday, they might claim that they are entitled to Sunday premiums and holiday premiums in combination with each other.

To address such situations, some collective bargaining agreements expressly prohibit the pyramiding of premiums or establish a maximum multiplier, such as two times the regular hourly wage. Nevertheless, arbitrators are sometimes asked to make determinations regarding applicable pay rates, particularly where premium pay and overtime requirements become intertwined (99 LA 1122, 91 LA 1043, 87 LA 130).

● Where Friday was the sixth day of the workweek and employees had already received premium pay for Sunday, an employer was justified in paying employees at the straight-time rate for their Friday hours, an arbitrator ruled. Reasoning that premium pay was the equivalent of overtime pay, the arbitrator said the employees were not entitled to payment at the overtime rate for Friday after receiving premium pay for Sunday, even though they had put in 40 hours during the first five days of their Sunday-to-Friday schedule. Paying employees at the higher rate for both days would amount to pyramiding of overtime, which was prohibited by the contract, the arbitrator found. He added that his ruling was consistent with the generally accepted concept that a six-day workweek includes one overtime day (*Utah International Inc.*, 75 LA 212; see also 102 LA 83, 94 LA 271, 94 LA 52, 92 LA 23, 90 LA 225).

● *By contrast*, another arbitrator found that an employer was required to pay an employee premium rates for two separate days, despite a contractual prohibition against pyramiding. In this case, the employee was scheduled to work Monday, take Tuesday and Wednesday off, and work Thursday through Sunday. When he was also called in on Wednesday, he received time and one-half for that day, but the employer refused to pay him time and one-half for Sunday as the sixth day worked in the week. Rejecting the employer's argument that such a payment would be pyramiding, the arbitrator pointed out that there were two different days involved, and these were not, therefore, "the same overtime hours." The contract clause on pyramiding did not preclude hours counted under one provision from also being counted under any other provision. Rather, he said, the clause was intended to prevent paying a double premium in such situations as an employee working the sixth day in the workweek, that same day also happening to be his first scheduled day off (*Dow Chemical Co. Packaging Division*, 49 LA 480).

● Under a contract that did not prohibit pyramiding, an arbitrator awarded triple pay to employees at a county landfill for holiday work. One provision of the contract called for employees to receive eight hours of straight-time pay on designated holidays, and a separate provision called for employees to receive double-time pay if they worked on a holiday. The arbitrator determined that the provisions had to be read as cumulative in the absence of specific language forbidding such an interpretation; thus, employees were entitled to the straight-time pay regardless of whether or not they worked, plus the double-time rate for all hours they put in on designated holidays (*Mason County*, 97 LA 45).

B. Premiums Based on Shift Worked

Many employers pay a higher rate, such as a shift premium or shift differential, to employees who work evenings or nights. The applicable pay rates are usually spelled out in collective bargaining agreements, and employees assigned to the particular shifts are automatically compensated at the higher rates (107 LA 985, 98 LA 312, 95 LA 479, 89 LA 581, 83 LA 17, 81 LA 1118, 81 LA 903, 77 LA 1220).

• An arbitrator required a hospital to pay premium rates to orderlies who previously worked from 6:30 a.m. to 3 p.m. but had their schedules changed to include a shift that ran from 7:30 p.m. to 4 a.m. on certain workdays. The arbitrator decided that the employees were entitled to contractual premium pay for the split shift because the employees were now required to work portions of two shifts (*Miami Inspiration Hospital Inc.*, 68 LA 898).

• Under a collective bargaining agreement that provided a shift differential for night work, an arbitrator ruled that an employer violated the agreement by denying the shift differential to janitors who worked on the night shift. Although janitors had not received the differential prior to the current agreement and the subject was not mentioned during negotiations, the arbitrator explained that the contract language neglected to specifically exclude janitors from receiving the premium (*Journal-Tribune Publishing Co. of Sioux City, Iowa*, 51 LA 606).

• On the other hand, an arbitrator ruled that night-shift premiums did not apply to watchmen, even though the contract did not specifically exclude them. In this instance, the arbitrator based his decision on a past practice of several years of not paying such employees the premium (*John Lucas & Co.*, 19 LA 344).

• In another case, an arbitrator decided that an employer was not required to pay shift premiums to cleaning staff for night work because they had not received such pay in the six years that they had been covered by the contract. This past practice overrode the fact that the contract made no exceptions to the payment of premium pay for those hours, according to the arbitrator (*Morgan Engineering Co.*, 33 LA 46).

• A newspaper did not violate a collective bargaining agreement or a memorandum of understanding concerning part-time mailroom workers when it refused to pay them a night differential, according to an arbitrator. The arbitrator based his decision on a number of factors, including the following: neither document specifically addressed the matter; the union had not objected to an employer proposal to deny part-time mailroom workers the night differential when the employer first put forth the proposal; and two subsequent contract negotiations, as well as past practice, were consistent with the understanding that night differentials would not apply (*Bakersfield Californian*, 97 LA 447).

• When an employer unilaterally changed the hours of an evening shift, which had been compensated with a shift differential and which previously ran from 3 p.m. to 11 p.m., to a new schedule of 11 a.m. to 7 p.m., an arbitrator disagreed with the union's contention that employees were entitled to the shift differential for the hours of 3 p.m. to 7 p.m. The arbitrator pointed out that the shift differential was only applicable to the eight-hour evening shift and not to a few hours worked during that time span (*Diamond Shamrock Corp.*, 55 LA 827).

• In the case of an employee who worked regularly from 12:30 p.m. to 9 p.m., with a half-hour for lunch between 4:30 p.m. and 5 p.m., and where the regular second-shift hours began at 4:30 p.m., an arbitrator concluded the employee worked exactly half his hours on the day shift and half his hours on the next shift. The arbitrator pointed out that because the lunch period could not be counted as hours worked, the employee could not show that a majority of his work time was spent on the second shift and denied his claim for the second-shift premium (*Canfield Oil Co.*, 7 LA 322).

1. Calculating Overtime Pay

When calculating the overtime pay rates for employees who receive shift premiums, employers generally are required to base their calculations on the sum of the regular rate and the shift premium. When employees who normally work a day shift are occasionally assigned overtime that extends into a premium-pay shift, however, arbitrators typically rule that such employees are not entitled to have the shift differential included in their overtime pay.

● An arbitrator ruled that an employer was in error when it contended that an employee who worked on a late shift was entitled only to one-and-one-half times the day rate, instead of one-and-one-half times the sum of the day rate and the night-shift premium. The arbitrator pointed out that the differential for late-shift work had become an integral part of the employee's wage. Therefore, he said, compensation for the employee's overtime hours had to be paid at the rate of one and one-half times his full hourly wage, including the shift premium (*Public Service Electric & Gas Co.*, 2 LA 2).

● On the other hand, day-shift employees were not entitled to premium pay for the overtime they worked on a shift with a shift-differential bonus unless they worked that entire shift, an arbitrator decided. The arbitrator based his decision on the fact that the provision giving the shift differential to all employees "working the shift" was ambiguous, both parties admitted that past practice on the issue had been "all over the board" for several years, for the past year, the employer had limited premium pay to employees who worked the entire bonus shift, and such a limitation constituted a good-faith attempt to bring logic, consistency, and the "rule of reason" to an ambiguous phrase (*Brown-Forman Beverage Co.*, 103 LA 292; see also 73 LA 677).

● Employees on the first shift were not entitled to a shift differential for the hour they worked after the shift's normal quitting time, according to an arbitrator. He said that the shift differential was intended only as additional compensation for second-shift employees who had to give up their "socializing time." Occasional overtime work performed by the first shift did not alter their status as first-shift employees, and the contract specified that the second shift, not the first, was to receive the differential, the arbitrator concluded (*Ideal Corrugated Box Co.*, 46 LA 129).

● An arbitrator ruled that an employer properly paid employees who worked overtime on their day off on the basis of the shift differential applicable to the shift actually worked rather than on the basis of the shift to which they were regularly assigned. In this case, employees who regularly worked a premium-pay shift were called in on their day off to work the day shift, and the employer did not include their usual shift differential when computing the overtime pay for the day shift worked. The arbitrator upheld this procedure because the practice had been in effect for several years, and the union had never challenged it before (*Bonanza Air Lines Inc.*, 44 LA 698).

2. Shift Premiums for Unworked Hours

Arbitrators have ruled both ways over the issue of whether premium pay is required for hours that are paid but not worked.

● An arbitrator held that night-shift employees were not entitled to a night-shift differential for paid but unworked hours, such as holidays, vacations, and sick leave, where the past practice under the collective bargaining agreement had been to pay the night-shift differential only for hours actually worked. Despite the fact that the union had pointed out that similar language in another collective bargaining agreement with a different party had been interpreted to require the shift differential for all paid hours, the arbitrator concluded that it was insufficient to override an interpretation that the parties in this case had followed without complaint for many years. He said that the matter was best addressed in the next negotiating session rather than as a grievance (*Beitzell & Co.*, 74 LA 884).

• *By contrast*, another arbitrator ruled that second-shift and third-shift employees were entitled to their normal shift differentials when they were paid for vacations and holidays, because a contract provision stated that pay would be computed at the employee's regular straight-time hourly rates and be based on their regularly scheduled hours. The arbitrator said that "regular straight-time hourly rate" in the collective bargaining agreement meant the rate of pay employees got for their regular work, and the rate of pay that shift employees regularly got was the day rate, plus the differential (*Carbon County, Pa.*, 73 LA 1305).

C. Premiums Based on Type of Work

Some collective bargaining agreements require environmental pay or dirty work premiums when employees perform work under hazardous, onerous, or severe conditions. Disputes in this area often focus on whether particular job duties qualify for the added compensation or whether employees should be paid their regular wage rates.

• An arbitrator ruled that an employer violated a collective bargaining agreement in denying premium pay to employees for filming a university commencement, even though the premium rate did not apply to events filmed "for any non-profit purpose," because the commencement amounted to a "theatrical or musical production" subject to the rate, it was the parties' intent to have the determining factor be the purpose of filming, and the commencement footage was intended for reproduction and resale (*SMG*, 127 LA 443).

• An arbitrator ruled that painters were entitled to premium pay for cleaning and painting aircraft hangers, which involved extremely large building tops, high off the ground and laced with a maze of obstacles, and which were unusually hot from nearby heaters and bright from overhead lights. The arbitrator disagreed with the employer's contention that the working conditions were not excessively onerous; he concluded that the preponderance of evidence established that the job was per-

formed under "the worst conditions within recent memory . . . upon a platform which was unsteady, unsure and unstable, and that the requisite elements of both 'high pay' and 'dirty pay' were present" (*Marine Corps Air Station*, 82 LA 563).

• An employer violated a collective bargaining agreement when it implemented a rule limiting premium pay to the "actual time worked" while dressed out in full anti-radioactive contamination clothing, according to an arbitrator. The arbitrator said it did not seem "reasonable" for the employer to "effectively ignore contract language relating to premium pay areas, and equally important, to depart from a long tradition of consultation" with appropriate safety experts in developing appropriate criteria for premium pay (*Pan Am World Services Inc.*, 91 LA 859).

• On the other hand, an arbitrator ruled that metalsmiths were not entitled to environmental pay for being subjected to a considerable amount of dust, noise, and heat while working in a metal shop. Although the collective bargaining agreement provided for extra compensation for employees who were subject to "unusually severe" hazards, physical hardships, and working conditions, the arbitrator said that the conditions under which the employees worked were common to any metalworking operation and were within the employees' job descriptions (*Naval Air Rework Facility*, 73 LA 201).

• Similarly, an employer was justified in denying premium pay to workers for the cleanup of ballast tanks on a ship that had been damaged at sea or for work on a pipe system in the fuel bunker of another ship, according to an arbitrator. The arbitrator pointed out that the collective bargaining agreement was intended to embody all significant types of tasks that might warrant dirty work pay, but none of the disputed work assignments were mentioned in that listing (*Newport News Shipbuilding and Dry Dock Co.*, 77 LA 943).

1. Pay for "Extra" Responsibilities

Employees sometimes claim that they deserve additional pay based on extra work or special responsibilities they have taken on, but arbitrators frequently reject such claims.

● An employer was justified in denying bilingual premium pay to a firefighter, an arbitrator decided. The firefighter had met the requirements for such pay with regard to his demonstrated language proficiency, but he had not obtained a recommendation from the personnel director to receive the premium pay, as required under a memorandum of understanding, the arbitrator noted (*Ventura County Fire Protection District*, 79 LA 1055).

● Another arbitrator ruled that an employer properly refused to pay an employee at the assistant-foreman rate for the time the employee spent in training co-workers in the operation of a particular piece of equipment. The arbitrator pointed out that the training task was not mentioned in either the employee's or assistant foreman's job description; any past practice was contravened when the employer rescinded a previous memo permitting assistant-foreman pay for training duties, and training of co-workers had been an inherent part of employees' jobs for years. The arbitrator added that "the simple fact of training does not an Assistant Foreman make. To hold otherwise could lead to the strange result whereby many or even most members of a department, if they are engaged in even marginal training, qualify as Assistant Foreman" (*Dayton Rogers Co.*, 91 LA 1249).

● Labor relations consultants who worked for a teachers' union were improperly required to service more than the 1,500 members called for in the collective bargaining agreement, according to an arbitrator. The arbitrator decided that the consultants were entitled to premium pay for their excess workload. In the absence of any evidence that the union employing the consultants acted willfully or created other overages, the arbitrator reduced the requested premium from three times to 1.5 times the percentage of the overage based on 1,500 members (*Ohio Education Association*, 102 LA 1147).

2. *Teachers and School Employees*

● A school district should have paid teachers to serve as presenters at training day, even though there was a 20-year practice of non-payment for presenting during normal school hours, where the clear language of the agreement was that "Any teacher who serves . . . as a presenter for a workshop shall be compensated at the rate of $60 per hour. . ." an arbitrator ruled. However, the school district did not violate the collective bargaining agreement when it did not pay extra compensation to teachers who presented at a workshop for attending the "voluntary" preparation meeting, because the agreement only provided for compensation for those who presented at meetings, not for those who attended meetings about presenting (*North Shore School District*, 130 LA 144).

● An arbitrator ruled that a school bus driver should have been paid at the higher rate of "truck driver," even though there was no job description listed for that job in the collective bargaining agreement— where the agreement included a pay rate for that job—and the school board designed the truck driving job for the employee and assigned him to do that work. The absence of a job description in the agreement cannot undermine the driver's claim, the arbitrator said, and ruled the grievant was entitled to proper wages from six days before he filed the grievance until the truck driving position ended, where he could have filed timely grievance within six days of when he did (*Broward County School Board*, 128 LA 1729).

● Teaching assistants should have been paid at .5 rather than .33 the full-time equivalency rate for their work on a summer school course, an arbitrator ruled, where it was the first time the course was taught on a team basis, the professors in charge of the course were not on campus for most of the time, there was an academic integrity issue that the assistants dealt with, there were no clear written instructions on how to teach the course, and no one doubted the assistants' claimed hours (*University of Illinois*, 127 LA 263).

● *By contrast*, an arbitrator ruled that a college did not violate a collective bargaining agreement that required it to raise the salary of "any current employee whose salary would be less than the newly negotiated starting salaries" to that given new hires who had special circumstances of prior service or unique specialization, when it did not raise all faculty to the level of new hires who were brought in at a higher rate, because the agreement referred to employees similarly situated with respect either to prior experience or unique circumstances (*Community College of Beaver County*, 129 LA 1255).

• An arbitrator ruled a school district did not violate a collective bargaining agreement when it assigned a custodian to work at a football stadium, even though the utility worker job description covered stadium work and the district failed to pay the custodian at the utility worker wage rate. The arbitrator determined that the job descriptions were not part of the bargaining agreement, the union could identify no portion of the agreement that limited management's discretion as to the assignment of work, and the union presented no evidence on the pay issue (*Springfield City School District Board of Education*, 129 LA 377).

• An arbtitrator ruled that a school district did not violate a collective bar-gaining agreement that provided extra compensation for teachers who worked lunch/recess duty, when it did not provide that extra compensation for teachers who worked an activity period that occurred before or after the lunch period. Even though the district justified the distinction in pay because some of the students chose to engage in non-instructed pursuits like playing games during the activity period, many of the activities were instructional and the class sizes were generally between 20 and 30 students (*Shaler Area School District*, 128 LA 310).

• An arbitrator ruled that a high school did not violate a collective bargaining agreement when it did not adjust a teacher's pay in a master level salary schedule after he had taken additional undergraduate level courses, where the agreement—in referring to "[s]alary adjustments for advanced training"—based master level salary increases on additional credits both relating to the purpose for which the master's degree has been recognized and at a level above that of undergraduate (*Flat Rock Community Schools*, 127 LA 951).

V. Reporting & Call-In Pay [LA CDI 100.48 (public employees); 114.71]

OVERVIEW

Many collective bargaining agreements provide for reporting pay and call-in pay to address situations where employers make last-minute changes that deviate from established work schedules. Generally speaking, provisions on reporting pay mandate a minimum amount of compensation if employees show up for work but are sent home before putting in all or any of their scheduled hours. Call-in provisions, meanwhile, typically guarantee payment for a minimum number of hours if employees are asked to come to work at an unscheduled time.

Disputes over reporting pay outnumber disputes over call-in pay, as employers frequently claim that they should not be held responsible for paying employees when work becomes unavailable or operations must be halted because of circumstances beyond their control. Even if employers cannot prevent such situations, however, arbitrators expect them to give as much notice as practicable in an effort to spare employees the inconvenience of making an unnecessary trip to work.

Employers are less likely to argue that they have good cause to deny employees call-in pay. One question arbitrators sometimes have to decide is whether employees should receive call-in pay or normal overtime rates for work performed at unscheduled times. Disputes also tend to arise if employees request call-in pay when they have not done any actual work.

SUMMARY OF CASES

A. Reporting Pay and Its Exceptions

In resolving disputes over reporting pay, arbitrators must decide how much compensation, if any, employees should receive in situations where scheduled work has been cancelled. Many of these cases revolve around contractual exceptions that excuse employers from providing reporting pay if work becomes unavailable through no fault of management. Common exceptions include acts of God, power outages, equipment breakdowns, and unsafe conditions that are beyond employers' control.

• An employer was not obligated to give call-in pay to an employee who went to work, despite his contention that the employer should have talked to him personally to tell him that the shift was cancelled, an arbitrator ruled, where a manager telephoned him 13 hours before the shift and left a voice mail message. In this age of voice mail, it was not reasonable to imply a requirement that the employer speak with the employee personally, the arbitrator said (*Neenah Paper Inc.*, 129 LA 637).

• An employer did not have to provide reporting pay after an oil tank ran dry one weekend and employees refused to remain at work on Monday because they were concerned about inadequate heat, an arbitrator held. Management believed there would be enough oil to last until Monday, but a temperature drop caused the oil to run out earlier than anticipated. The company president told the employees that an oil shipment was on its way and they should either get to work or exit the premises. All the employees went home, and the employer did not pay them for that day. The arbitrator awarded the employees payment for time spent in the plant but refused to award them four hours of reporting pay because of mitigating factors in the employer's favor (*Dietz Machine Works Inc.*, 52 LA 1023).

• Employees who were required to take a random drug test after their shift ended were not entitled to four hours of reporting pay, an arbitrator ruled. Had the employees been ordered to report for a work-related appointment at a time that was "outside their standard daily work schedule," they might have been entitled to reporting pay, the arbitrator explained. In this instance, however, they were already at work and did not report to the workplace solely to submit to the test. Only when a work-related appointment is "the sole and exclusive reason" employees are required to come to or return to a facility would the provision on reporting pay be triggered, the arbitrator determined (*Sandia National Laboratories*, 123 LA 779).

• An employer that switched to a compressed workweek of four 10-hour days was not required to pay employees for a full shift when they were sent home early because of unexpected events, an arbitrator ruled. Before the implementation of the compressed workweek, employees normally worked five eight-hour days and were entitled to reporting pay of four hours if they were sent home for reasons within the control of the employer. While acknowledging that the parties' collective bargaining agreement mentioned a 10-hour guarantee under the new schedule, the arbitrator rejected the union's assertion that employees were entitled to a full 10 hours of pay when they were sent home early. Rather, he determined that the clause on reporting pay applied to such situations, requiring a minimum of four hours' pay if employees were sent home for reasons within management's control and excusing the employer from providing reporting pay if employees were sent home early through no fault of management (*Mike Sells' Potato Chip Co.*, 123 LA 1317).

• In another case, an arbitrator determined that an employer had to pay its employees for a full eight-hour shift even though they only worked seven hours before daylight savings time started and they were sent home. Although the employer claimed it was not obligated to pay for the unworked hour because the start of daylight saving time was beyond its control, the arbitrator upheld the union's position, saying the employer could have scheduled the employees for eight hours, even though it would have created confusion at the start of the next shift (*Magma Copper Co.*, 51 LA 9).

1. Power and Equipment Failures

Not all power and equipment failures are equal in the eyes of arbitrators, who must determine if such problems were truly beyond employers' control or could have been anticipated in order to avoid a last-minute cancellation of scheduled work.

• An employer was not in control of or responsible for a power failure that shut down its plant, an arbitrator determined. In a situation that could not have been anticipated, damage to the power grid precluded the employer's opening its plant for business and exempted it from having to provide four hours of reporting pay to employees, the arbitrator ruled (*E.W. Bliss Co.*, 55 LA 522).

• An arbitrator found that reporting pay was not required in a case where the local utility company had come to make repairs at an employer's plant and had assured management that power would be restored in time for the next shift. Having received these assurances, the employer was caught off guard when one of the main power lines melted down and the determination was made that power would not be restored to most of the plant for some time. According to the arbitrator, the confluence of unfortunate circumstances was beyond the employer's control and it was freed from the responsibility of having to provide reporting pay (*TRANSFAB Inc.*, 114 LA 844; see also 113 LA 823, 110 LA 794).

• A power failure in an employer's main electric feeder line qualified as an event beyond management's control that excused the employer from providing four hours of reporting pay, an arbitrator ruled. The union contended that because the burnout that precipitated the power failure took place inside the plant, its occurrence was management's responsibility and therefore was within its control. The arbitrator accepted the argument that the main feeder line was management's responsibility, but because the power failure could not have been anticipated, it was beyond the employer's control (*Erie Artisan Corp.*, 51 LA 850).

• By *contrast*, another arbitrator required an employer to provide report-ing pay to employees for work time they lost during an electrical outage. Despite contract language stating that such pay was not required when a shutdown was prompted by causes beyond the employer's reasonable control or if employees received two hours' notice, the arbitrator found that the outage was not entirely outside normal expectations. Noting that the employer had chosen an electricity service plan that resulted in relatively predictable power interruptions, the arbitrator decided that the affected employees were entitled to four hours of reporting pay (*Industrial Alloys Inc.*, 116 LA 1226).

• Another arbitrator found that an employer was obligated to provide reporting pay when production was halted by a power outage. Employees had worked for two hours before the power went out and they were sent home. The employer asserted that they were only entitled to be paid for actual time worked because the power outage was beyond its control. According to the arbitrator, the employer's obligation to provide the minimum four hours of reporting pay was triggered when they reported to work, not when the power outage occurred, and it had to pay the employees for the full four hours (*AKRO Corp.*, 102 LA 191).

• An employer was not justified in denying reporting pay when a boiler leak caused a plant shutdown, an arbitrator ruled. Although the agreement specified that the employer did not have to provide reporting pay if a lack of work was prompted by a major power interruption or equipment breakdown beyond its control, the arbitrator noted that the leak occurred following the boiler's being turned off and repaired, and such leaks were common in these situations. Although the leak itself was beyond the employer's control, the arbitrator said the employer should have foreseen the possibility of a breakdown following maintenance and made every effort to discover it in time to warn employees not to report to work (*Rubatex Corp.*, 52 LA 1270; see also 74 LA 513, 54 LA 1218).

• A collapsed flue, which prompted a plant shutdown, did not qualify as an event beyond management's control that would excuse an employer from providing reporting pay, an arbitrator held. There had been no flue inspection for three years, and the union argued that a proper inspection might have prevented the collapse. Siding with the union, the arbitrator determined that the situation was in fact within the employer's control and awarded the employees reporting pay (*Bunker Hill Co.*, 51 LA 873).

2. Severe Weather Conditions

Some arbitrators take the view that employers must be free to determine if severe weather conditions make work dangerous or impossible. Other arbitrators look to the facts and circumstances of each particular situation to decide if an episode of inclement weather constitutes a valid emergency that gives employers the right to shut down operations and refuse to pay employees who report for work.

• Employees were not entitled to reporting pay when their employer closed its plant because of freezing rain and icy roads, an arbitrator ruled. Such conditions fall under the category of acts of God, exempting the employer from providing reporting pay, the arbitrator found. The fact that the employees drove on the icy roads without difficulty on their way to the plant and had not seen any accidents was not relevant, according to the arbitrator (*Bangor Products Corp.*, 63 LA 213; see also 74 LA 191, 73 LA 962, 72 LA 845, 71 LA 1015, 71 LA 716).

• On the other hand, an arbitrator found that an employer was responsible for providing reporting pay to employees who showed up for work during a snowstorm after the employer decided to close down production because it suspected there would be substantial absenteeism. The arbitrator determined that the employer was not forced to close down but did so in anticipation of the effect of widespread absenteeism on production. That decision to stop operations was entirely within management's control and not an act of God, the arbitrator held, ordering the employer to provide reporting pay to the employees who showed up for work (*Westinghouse Electric Corp.*, 51 LA 298; see also 73 LA 627, 55 LA 685).

• An arbitrator ruled that a situation in which a heavy equipment operator who volunteered for snow/ice detail outside of his regular shift but was sent home after four and one-half hours with five hours of overtime pay was covered by a contract provision stating that an employee who "reports for work as scheduled, in inclement weather" may elect to work a full day provided productive work is available. The city he worked for violated the contract provision when it sent the employee home after a new forecast moved back the expected arrival of the storm, denying him opportunity to have the city consider the availability of productive work such as mixing material used to salt the streets (*City of Memphis*, 128 LA 1669).

3. Safety Issues

Arbitrators are usually inclined to excuse employers from providing reporting pay if they unexpectedly shut down their operations because of safety concerns. In such cases, arbitrators tend to focus on how real the dangers are and how quickly and fully employers alert their workers.

• An employer did not violate its labor contract when it denied reporting pay to employees whose evening shift was cancelled because of civil disturbances in the area, an arbitrator ruled. The agreement guaranteed employees four hours of pay unless they were denied work for reasons beyond the employer's control. When the employer had to shut down operations because of a curfew imposed by the governor, some employees arrived for work despite the employer's radio announcements about the situation. Because the curfew constituted a classic illustration of circumstances beyond management's control, the arbitrator said no minimum payments were required (*Koppers Co. Inc.*, 54 LA 408).

• In another case, an arbitrator upheld an employer's denial of pay to employees who reported for their 3 p.m. shift despite a citywide curfew starting at that hour. The employees were sent home as soon as they arrived, but they later claimed they were owed four hours of pay under a contract clause requiring reporting pay if employees were sent home for lack of work. The arbitrator interpreted "lack of work" to mean a lack of the need for the employer's product, which would require adjusting the work schedule to cut production. Because no such situation existed, the arbitrator rejected the employees' claim (*Lockheed-Georgia*, 51 LA 720).

• An arbitrator found that an employer was not obligated to provide reporting pay to employees who were sent home after several workers suddenly fell ill and the state health department advised closing the plant. When the employer shut down operations, it paid employees for the two hours worked. The arbitrator denied a grievance for four hours of reporting pay, explaining that the employer had made every effort to locate and control the source of the problem. The situation was obviously beyond the employer's control, and it was therefore not liable for reporting pay, the arbitrator concluded (*Lasko Metal Products Inc.*, 51 LA 1119).

• Denial of reporting pay met with an arbitrator's approval in a situation where an employer gave employees the option of remaining on the job after it received a bomb threat. Because similar threats on previous occasions had turned out to be hoaxes, the employer considered it likely that the latest threat was also a hoax. The employer told employees they could go home and be paid only for the time they actually spent on the premises or they could stay and work the entire shift. The union later claimed that workers were entitled to reporting pay because there was no explosion and hence no reason to send anyone home. The arbitrator denied the grievance, pointing out that if an actual explosion would exempt the employer from providing reporting pay, the same should hold true for the mere threat of an explosion. To rule otherwise, the arbitrator said, would mean that "any mischief maker could drive the corporation out of business with threats of one sort and another" (*General Cable Corp.*, 54 LA 696; see also 73 LA 1252, 62 LA 463).

• In another case, an arbitrator determined that an employer was obligated to give reporting pay to employees for wages lost during two separate bomb scares. The contract provided specific causes for lack of work where the employer was not required to provide reporting pay—"labor disputes, riots, fire, flood, tornado, lightning, power

failure, or act of God." Because the provisions were detailed and specific and given that the underlying reason in this case was not included in the list, the arbitrator found that the employer was not exempt from the contract's reporting pay requirements (*Miller Printing Machinery Co.*, 64 LA 141; see also 73 LA 280, 72 LA 1232, 69 LA 511).

• In a case involving an alarm designed to detect unsafe levels of carbon monoxide, an arbitrator decided that an employer was required to pay employees for lost work time. Employees left the area when the alarm sounded, but 20 minutes later the employer announced that the alarm had been precipitated by a malfunction and instructed employees to return to work. Seventeen refused, believing conditions were genuinely unsafe, but they asked for other work for the remaining hour of their shift. The employer refused the request, saying it could not find substitute work on such short notice. The employees later demanded the pay they had been denied for that last hour based on contract provisions stating that employees who report for their normal shift because they have not been notified to stay home are entitled to eight hours of work. The employees were justified in refusing to return to work, the arbitrator said, noting that the contract did not limit the employer's liability and ordering the employer to pay each of the 17 workers for the lost hour (*Miller Printing Machinery Co.*, 54 LA 69).

4. Disciplinary Action

Arbitrators often rule that employees are not entitled to reporting pay if they are sent home early for disciplinary reasons or suspended but report for work anyway.

• An employer was justified in refusing to provide reporting pay to two employees who were sent home a little more than an hour after their shifts started because they had threatened a supervisor, an arbitrator held. Although the parties' collective bargaining agreement contained a clause requiring reporting pay when employees were sent home early, the arbitrator said the two employees should not be rewarded for creating the problem that precipitated their "difficult" situation. The contract was not particularly clear on the issue, but the arbitrator concluded that it was not the intention of the parties in negotiating the agreement to protect or reward employees in such situations (*Unarco Industries Inc.*, 55 LA 421).

• Reporting pay was not required for an employee with a poor attendance record who was suspended following an unexcused absence, an arbitrator ruled. The employee failed to come to work one day and did not call in. When he reported to work the next day, his foreman asked him why he had been absent but did not believe his claim of having been ill. The foreman immediately sent the employee home and suspended him for three days. The arbitrator rejected the employee's assertion that he was owed four hours of pay for reporting to work before he was suspended (*Barber-Greene Co.*, 53 LA 1244).

• *By contrast*, an arbitrator found that employees were entitled to reporting pay after their employer refused to allow them to work because they had balked at complying with a modified attendance rule. The revised rule required absent employees to notify the employer at least a half-hour before the start of their shift or within two hours after the shift started if an emergency prompted the absence. Although the arbitrator found that the employer had administered the modified rule in a fair manner, he concluded that the employer had failed to give the union an opportunity to negotiate on the subject, which was enough of a reason to obligate the employer to provide reporting pay (*National Can Corp.*, 63 LA 766).

B. Notification Requirements

When arbitrators resolve disputes over reporting pay, they sometimes focus less on events prompting the cancellation of scheduled work than they do on the adequacy of employers' efforts to notify employees that they should not report to work (67 LA 1029, 67 LA 792).

• An arbitrator found that an employer made sufficient effort to notify employees that its second shift was cancelled when riots broke out throughout the city where

its plant was located. The employer issued radio announcements to warn employees that the second shift was cancelled and sent home those workers who had not heard the notice. Although the contract said employees who were sent home for lack of work were entitled to a minimum of four hours' pay unless they were notified the night before not to show up, the arbitrator found that reporting pay was not required because the employer's attempts to notify the affected employees were reasonable under the extreme circumstances, and there was no "lack of work." The arbitrator also declared that no employer should face any deterrents when confronted with a decision whether to shut down operations for the safety of its employees (*Electronic Communications Inc.*, 51 LA 692).

• A cattle slaughterhouse was justified in refusing to provide reporting pay to employees after it notified local news outlets by 11 p.m. that the following morning's shift was cancelled because of a power failure caused by severe weather conditions, an arbitrator determined. In addition to finding that the outage was beyond the employer's control, the arbitrator noted that it was the employer's habit to notify workers via local radio and television stations, which it had done in this instance (*Excel Corp.*, 120 LA 186).

• In a different case, an arbitrator awarded employees reporting pay despite their employer's efforts to alert them that its plant had closed because of a severe snowstorm. Notice of the closing was broadcast on four major radio stations, but 112 employees did not hear the announcements and were sent home after they reported for work as scheduled. Noting that the contract called for at least four hours of pay for employees who reported for their regular shift absent instructions to the contrary, the arbitrator awarded the employees reporting pay because despite the employer's efforts to notify all employees, a significant number of workers never received the instructions to stay home (*Niagara Machine & Tool Works*, 55 LA 396).

• Another arbitrator concluded that reporting pay was required in a case where employees were not given any advance notice that their employer would close its plant. The plant could have operated in spite of a heavy snowfall, according to the arbitrator, who pointed out that there were already four or five employees at work when the employer decided to close and a good percentage of the regular workforce lived within a mile of the facility (*Hamilton Press Inc.*, 65 LA 274; see also 71 LA 1106, 71 LA 551, 70 LA 150).

• An arbitrator ordered an employer to pay its night-shift employees four hours of reporting pay for showing up at the start of the day on which they were scheduled to be laid off. The employer argued that reporting pay was not required because the employees were not actually scheduled to work, but the arbitrator disagreed. Observing that the employees had reported on a normal workday, the facility was operating, work was available, and the employer had not provided adequate layoff notices, the arbitrator decided that the employer had met none of the conditions that would have exempted it from providing reporting pay (*Fritz Co. Inc.*, 101 LA 507).

• Similarly, an employer was required to give reporting pay to employees who were laid off without being informed of the layoff before the end of their previous shift, an arbitrator ruled. Although the employer claimed that ongoing financial concerns constituted "extenuating circumstances" that exempted it from contractual requirements to make such payments, the arbitrator said all layoffs relate to a lack of business, and to treat financial concerns as a defense would effectively "void all payments where a layoff is involved" (*International Playing Card and Label Co.*, 116 LA 717).

C. Call-In Pay

Provisions on call-in pay are usually triggered when employees are asked to work at unscheduled times because of unanticipated needs or emergencies. Such provisions typically guarantee payment for a minimum number of hours to compensate employees for being called in—or in some cases "called out"—to work during their off hours.

• An employer did not violate its labor contract when it refused to pay an employee who was contacted at home but rejected

an opportunity to work, an arbitrator determined. Under the parties' collective bargaining agreement, if a worker was called in to work but the assignment either was withdrawn or took less than two hours to complete, the employee was entitled to two hours' pay. Because the employee refused the assignment, the arbitrator determined that he was not entitled to call-in pay. To qualify for such pay, "employees must be given actual work to be performed," the arbitrator said (*Southwest Gas Corp.*, 119 LA 1284).

• An employer did not violate its labor contract when it paid overtime rather than call-out pay to employees who were notified on their preceding shift to report early the next day for a mandatory informational meeting before working their regular shift, where the employees were not called during unscheduled time away from work, they suffered no inconvenience as a result of the slightly earlier start time, and the employer was specifically authorized to determine starting times (*W.R. Grace & Co.*, 125 LA 1772).

• An employer did not have to provide call-in pay to employees who had been asked to work on a weekend but were sent home because of a power outage, an arbitrator found. The employees had been told that they would be needed on a Saturday, a not uncommon occurrence even though they normally worked a Monday-to-Friday schedule. After they showed up and were sent home because of the power failure, the employees claimed that they were entitled to compensation under a contract provision guaranteeing a minimum of four hours of work or four hours of pay if they were called in at some time other than their regular shift. However, the arbitrator said that because there was an established practice of extended workweeks, the employer's request to have the employees come in on the Saturday in question did not trigger an entitlement to call-in pay (*General Dynamics Corp.*, 54 LA 405; see also 84 LA 675).

• An employer violated its labor contract and contravened past practice when it refused to pay an employee four hours of call-in pay after he was called back to work for an extra shift, an arbitrator ruled. For more than 20 years, the employer had provided a minimum of four hours' call-in pay in these situations even if employees worked for a shorter period of time. In ordering the employer to pay the employee for the full four hours, the arbitrator commented that expecting an employee "to give up his free time, drive to the plant, get dressed, report to the site, clean up, and return home for an assignment that may only pay one-half hour is ludicrous" (*Consolidation Coal Co.*, 105 LA 1110; see also 103 LA 1025).

• An employee was entitled to call-in pay at a double-time rate when his employer asked him to work on a Sunday, an arbitrator held. Even though the employee was contacted about the Sunday shift on the previous day, he was scheduled to have both Saturday and Sunday off, and the contract only allowed the employer to avoid paying the call-in premium if it notified employees of newly added hours prior to the end of their last regularly scheduled shift, the arbitrator observed (*Basic Vegetable Products Inc.*, 90 LA 666).

• A natural gas company committed a contract violation by refusing to provide call-out pay to an off-duty employee who handled a problem for the employer from his home, an arbitrator ruled. The employee spent nearly three-fourths of an hour making telephone calls concerning an "emergency line locate" for a construction project. According to the arbitrator, the provision on call-out pay was designed to compensate workers for interruptions of their leisure time, and that leisure was disturbed when the employee was called on to perform work for the employer from his home, just as it would have been if he were required to make a trip to the construction site (*Columbia Gas Transmission Corp.*, 120 LA 649).

1. Overtime Versus Call–in Pay

A question that sometimes arises in connection with call-in pay is whether employers can simply compensate employees at regular overtime rates when they are asked to work unscheduled hours. Disputes of this type most commonly arise when employees work additional hours either just before or

just after shifts that have been scheduled in advance.

• Employees who were called in two hours before their normal starting time and then worked their normal shift were entitled to overtime but not call-in pay, an arbitrator ruled. Although the employees were called in before they were scheduled, the arbitrator distinguished between overtime hours and call-in hours. Overtime is time worked in a continuous stream with the regular work schedule—even if it precedes rather than follows that shift, according to the arbitrator. Call-in pay is designed to compensate employees for making a special trip to work, so employees would have to be released to leave the workplace immediately after completing an assignment to qualify for call-in pay, the arbitrator reasoned (*Owens-Illinois Inc.*, 55 LA 1121; see also 73 LA 478, 69 LA 908).

• *By contrast*, an arbitrator decided that an employee was entitled to four hours of pay for performing 30 minutes of work after the end of a holiday shift. The employee came to work on the holiday to fix a conveyor belt. He made the necessary repairs, informed his foreman that the work was completed, then clocked out. Shortly thereafter, the foreman received a call about a different problem and caught the employee as he was about to leave. The employee worked another 30 minutes to fix the new problem, for which the employer paid him 30 minutes of overtime. According to the arbitrator, however, the situation qualified as a "call-out" under the parties' collective bargaining agreement, and he awarded the employee four hours of pay for the additional work he performed (*Morton Thiokol Inc.*, 85 LA 500).

• Although an employee was entitled to four hours of call-in pay when he worked an extra hour and 30 minutes, he was not entitled to be paid for the entire four hours at a double-time rate, an arbitrator decided. The contract in this case mandated a minimum of four hours' pay for call-in situations and double-time rates for any hours worked beyond 12 in a day. When the employee was asked to work the extra time after already putting in 12 hours, he was paid double-time for the hour and 30 minutes he actually worked, but the remainder of the four-hour call-in guarantee was paid at a time-and-a-half rate. The arbitrator upheld the payment of the lower rate, finding that the extra two and one-half hours of call-in pay did not count as time worked and thus did not qualify for the double-time premium (*General Portland Cement Co.*, 53 LA 653).

2. Nonwork Activities

In some cases, arbitrators have to decide if call-in pay must be provided to employees who participate in disciplinary investigations or other activities that do not involve the actual performance of work.

• An employer was obligated to provide call-in pay to employees for the time that they were required to spend at a disciplinary investigation during their off-duty hours, an arbitrator ruled. Although the employer contended that the phrase "called back to work" applied only to situations where employees were brought back to perform production activities, that was not explicitly stated in the contract, the arbitrator noted. If there was an exception to the call-in provision for disciplinary meetings, it should have been stated in the labor agreement, the arbitrator said (*Mobil Oil Corp.*, 76 LA 3).

• An employer was required to provide call-in pay to a police officer who reported for treatment of a duty-related injury when he was not scheduled to work, an arbitrator ruled. The employee needed medical attention for a knee injury that he suffered while on duty, and a doctor ordered him to obtain physical therapy. Although it was customary to receive such treatment during regular working hours, the employee worked nights and was unable to schedule two therapy sessions while on duty. The employer argued that call-in pay was not required for the employee's therapy sessions. However, the arbitrator found that the employer expected police officers to follow their doctors' orders, which meant that the employee was obligated to obtain the therapy as instructed. Adding that the employer had a practice of counting time spent receiving medical treatment for duty-related injuries as work time, the arbitrator concluded that the employee was entitled to call-in pay for the sessions he could not schedule during his shifts (*City of Lansing, Mich.*, 83 LA 491).

VI. Incentive Pay [LA CDI 114.391]

OVERVIEW

Rather than defining the compensation of union-represented workers strictly in terms of fixed wage rates, some collective bargaining agreements establish incentive pay systems that allow employees to earn varying amounts in proportion to what they produce.

Incentive pay is usually associated with work that is repetitive, easily measured, and performed by employees at their own pace. Typically, incentive pay systems guarantee a base rate of pay and provide employees with additional earnings once their output exceeds a certain threshold. Under piecework plans, for example, employees receive a set amount per unit of output. Other incentive systems use percentages, with additional pay available to employees whose performance exceeds a 100 percent baseline. Regardless of how incentives are calculated, the end result is that higher levels of production translate into higher earnings.

Contract provisions usually impose limits on employers' ability to revise the standards governing incentive pay. When disputes arise over changes made by employers, arbitrators often hold that workers should be able to maintain the same level of earnings they had prior to the introduction of new standards (67 LA 184, 26 LA 812, 17 LA 472). Alternatively, arbitrators sometimes focus on maintaining the ratio of earnings to the effort expended, reasoning that workers should not reap undeserved benefits if employers implement operational or technological improvements that boost production without requiring any increase in effort (37 LA 669, 28 LA 129, 22 LA 450, 10 LA 20).

Aside from disputes over the establishment or revision of incentive standards and rates, other issues that arbitrators address in this area include the following:

- whether incentive rates should apply during downtime or when incentive work is not the only type of work performed by employees;
- whether employers can deny incentive pay under certain circumstances; and
- whether employees should be subject to discipline or discharge if they falsify production reports or otherwise manipulate incentive pay systems.

SUMMARY OF CASES

A. Establishing or Revising Incentive Standards and Rates

Arbitrators frequently acknowledge employers' authority to set appropriate standards and rates under incentive systems, not only for the calculation of how much pay employees can earn, but also for the speed of their work and the output levels they are expected to achieve. In general, arbitrators are more likely to uphold standards and rates put in place by employers—whether new or revised—when they are supported by time studies or other analyses and do not cause employees to suffer a loss in their earnings potential.

- One arbitrator rejected a union's claims that the incentive standards an employer established for a new box-making machine were unreasonable and inequitable. The arbitrator pointed out that the industrial engineer who developed the standards had studied and timed many other machines used in the plant over a period of more than eight years. The engineer used the same methods and procedures in developing the standards for the new machine, and he also contacted consultants and other companies that had experience with similar machines, the arbitrator observed (*Lawrence Paper Co.*, 107 LA 730).

- An arbitrator upheld a tire manufacturer's method of calculating group incentives, which based employees' pay rates on the number of tires shipped out and the overall hours that the group members needed to complete the work. The employees had complained about the employer's control over staffing levels, arguing that an overstaffed group could not keep hours low enough to maximize incentive rates. However, the arbitrator accepted the employer's explanation that the key to higher earnings under the incentive system was for employees to work better as a group. The employer's system did not restrict the group's earnings opportunity or its ability to perform at levels above 100 percent, the arbitrator found, adding that the required staffing levels could be expected to approach ideal levels as employees learned to work together in order to process more tires in fewer hours (*Pirelli Tire Corp.*, 112 LA 757).

- An employer's standard for the number of vehicle parts a crew was expected to produce per hour under a newly established incentive rate was appropriate, an arbitrator ruled. The parties' collective bargaining agreement called for the establishment of rates that would allow an average employee, working at normal incentive speed, to earn 30 percent over the guaranteed day rate for the job. The employer conducted preliminary time studies when production of the part in question began and, after various changes in how the work was performed, conducted another time study some three weeks later and set a permanent standard of 217 pieces per hour. Although the union claimed that a lower number was called for, the arbitrator found no apparent substantive errors in the time study conducted by the employer and accepted 217 pieces per hour as the appropriate standard to be used in the calculation of incentive rates for workers producing the new part (*Checker Motors Corp.*, 108 LA 1107).

- Another arbitrator held that a piece rate set by an employer after a new machine went into operation was unreasonably high, but he also rejected a union-proposed rate, finding that it was too low. Instead, after considering all the elements, including work duties performed, operating conditions, increased machine speed, and other changes, the arbitrator concluded that a number somewhere in the middle of the two was the "more realistic approach" (*Permold Corp.*, 101 LA 390).

• An employer committed a contract violation by adopting an old incentive pay rate when its press operators began working on new parts, an arbitrator ruled. The employer argued that the incentive rate was appropriate because it had been applied previously when the employees worked on the same kind of parts. However, the arbitrator said, the employer was required to treat the parts as a new product when they were reintroduced into the production process. Under the requirements of the contract, the arbitrator found, the work involved in producing the parts had to be subjected to a reasonable trial period to determine if any equipment or product changes affected the process, and the parties then had to negotiate an acceptable incentive rate, which in this case was a piecework price per 100 units of output (*Harris-Thomas Drop Forge Co.*, 110 LA 604).

1. Changing Standards or Rates

Revisions to incentive pay systems can usually be justified on the basis of substantial changes affecting how the work is performed. For example, arbitrators frequently allow employers to reduce incentive pay rates or increase production standards where the introduction of new or improved machinery or technology results in increased output without requiring an increase in effort (63 LA 384, 11 LA 432, 3 LA 677).

• In a case involving a piecework plan, one arbitrator declared that "a piece rate, once established, should not be changed unless the relevant conditions of work are subsequently changed or unless an error or oversight was made on establishing the original rate." Employees are entitled to prompt notification of a change in their pay rate, the arbitrator added, and should be informed of the results of time studies and employer allowances for factors such as fatigue and personal needs. "The essen-

tial standard should be that the employees affected should have free access to the relevant information so that any injustices in the final result may be corrected through the regular grievance procedure," the arbitrator declared (*International Harvester Co.*, 1 LA 512).

• An employer did not violate a collective bargaining agreement when, upon discovering that it had "miscalculated" earnings protection adjustment for five grievants by using a higher "special assignments" hourly rate they had received under the predecessor company rather than the rate of their regular incumbent jobs at the time the employer took over the plant and eliminated special assignments, it began calculating the adjustment based on the base hourly rate of the grievants' incumbent jobs plus the average incentive paid to employees in their respective areas, where the collective bargaining agreement provides that the adjustment must be calculated on the basis of the employee's hourly vacation rate at a time a new employer took over the plant, which was based upon the base rate of pay plus incentive earnings (*U.S. Steel Corp.*, 126 LA 993).

• An employer's revision of an incentive rate for technicians in a foundry did not violate a collective bargaining agreement that permitted adjustments to be made in conjunction with "sufficient" job changes, an arbitrator ruled. The union contended that changes in production methods and equipment that occurred around the time of the rate adjustment were not substantial enough to trigger a pay revision. However, the arbitrator found that the employer had restructured its manufacturing process over a period of more than two years, and it was this overall restructuring rather than the latest incremental changes that generated the conditions warranting a revision of the incentive system (*Mueller Co.*, 120 LA 1253).

• Where increases in production were owing to machinery and engineering changes rather than increased employee effort, an employer could adjust incentive rates without violating a contractual ban on revisions that would lessen the earnings potential of employees, an arbitrator determined.

He noted that the stated aim of the incentive agreement was to give employees more money for extra effort above normal. If the rates had remained the same, the arbitrator reasoned, earnings would have gone up in direct ratio to the increased productivity, even without any extra effort from the employees (*Libbey-Owens-Ford Glass Fibres Co.*, 31 LA 662; see also 65 LA 643).

• An arbitrator ruled that an employer did not violate a contract when it revised the production standards under an incentive system to allow less time for the work performed on a cutting machine. An upgrading of the machine to provide automatic feed without excessive jam-ups justified a review of the operation, and the change in the standard was commensurate with the degree of change in the job content, the arbitrator found (*Armstrong Tire Co.*, 95 LA 1050).

• An employer's discretion to make necessary incentive plan changes also gave it the authority to discontinue incentives for a group of employees, an arbitrator found. The employer's action followed mechanical improvements and procedural changes that substantially altered the duties of the affected employees. Pointing out that the parties' collective bargaining agreement allowed incentive plan changes following modifications in equipment, processes, or job duties, the arbitrator said the employer not only had the authority to revise incentive rates in response to changed conditions, it also had the discretion to decide that an existing incentive rate should no longer apply. In such a situation, the employer was not obligated to institute new incentives, the arbitrator found. Instead, the employer could decide that the affected employees should be paid a straight hourly wage, the arbitrator said, upholding the employees' removal from the incentive plan (*Timken Co.*, 85 LA 377; see also 79 LA 73).

• The accumulation of various job changes over more than a decade, coupled with the introduction of a new machine, justified an employer's reduction of a piece rate, an arbitrator held. The employer did not reevaluate the rate until after it introduced the new machine, but it then made

time studies that proved the work could be performed more quickly than in the past. According to the arbitrator, the employer's delay in making the studies did not preclude the rate reduction. Absent a contractual provision requiring rate adjustments in response to every minor job change, there was nothing to prevent the employer from taking years of changes into consideration once the introduction of the new machine prompted it to examine the job, the arbitrator said (*Dexter Co.*, 122 LA 705).

• A 13-month delay in establishing a new rate for a job after changes were made was allowed by another arbitrator, who found that this period of time was necessary to allow a complete restudy of the operation (*Mosaic Tile Co.*, 16 LA 922).

• *By contrast*, an arbitrator determined that an employer improperly reduced a piece rate after it had been in effect for more than two years. The parties' collective bargaining agreement prohibited changes in piece rates after they had been "definitely established," the arbitrator noted. Although the employer was entitled to a reasonable amount of time within which to discover and correct errors, two years was far more than a reasonable time limit for changing the rate, the arbitrator declared (*International Harvester Co.*, 14 LA 1010; see also 34 LA 497).

• An arbitrator ruled that an employer improperly discontinued incentive pay for some employees who were not production workers but who had been receiving incentive pay for feeding materials directly to production workers. The employer had decided to deny incentive pay to the workers on the basis of a ruling in an earlier case in which certain nonproduction workers had been removed from the incentive plan. The arbitrator pointed out that the situation in the current case differed from the earlier case in several respects: there was a substantial past practice of coverage of the disputed employees in the current case; one employee in the current case was not removed from the plan despite the fact that she did not engage in direct hand-to-hand feeding; and after the issuance of the prior award, the employer had engaged in horse trading with respect to which employees were to be included or excluded, which was an indication that the matter was one for negotiation (*Chris-Craft Industries*, 45 LA 955).

B. Accounting for Downtime and Nonproduction Tasks

Disputes concerning incentive pay frequently focus on how to treat periods when production is interrupted or employees are prevented from performing their normal incentive work. Even where employers and unions have agreed to build in allowances for machinery breakdowns, materials shortages, delays, or downtime, controversies can arise over the pay employees should receive in some circumstances.

● Employees' absences on a level three snow emergency were properly used to deny employees perfect attendance bonuses, an arbitrator ruled, because the bonus program enumerated which excused absences were not to be counted against the employee and did not include inclement weather excused absences (*H. J. Heinz Co.*, 125 LA 1738).

● However, an arbitrator ruled that an employer violated a collective bargaining contract when it denied bonus awards under a variable pay plan to strikers whose last day of work for the year was in September, where the employer had introduced the company-wide plan in bargaining and said that employees were eligible unless "they are terminated " (*PPG Industries Inc.*, 123 LA 1755).

● In one instance where incentive employees were held up for an hour and a half because their supervisor had not gotten certain equipment ready for them to use, an arbitrator ruled that they were entitled to straight-time pay for the downtime. He agreed with the union that such long periods of lost time that were the fault of management were not the kind of delays allowed for in the incentive rates (*Bethlehem Steel Co.*, 29 LA 360).

● An employer could not cease paying incentive rates for machine operators' downtime, an arbitrator ruled. The operators received an incentive rate that was 20 percent above the base rate whenever they performed their production work within specified time limits, and the same incentive rate had traditionally been applied when they performed nonproduction work during periods of downtime. The employer claimed that its obligation to pay the 120 percent incentive rate for downtime had ended when a new collective bargaining agreement took effect. However, the employer never informed the union of its intention to change the downtime compensation, and this prevented the matter from being consciously explored during contract negotiations, the arbitrator found. Without an agreement to reduce downtime compensation, the provision from the previous contract carried over to the successor contract, the arbitrator concluded (*ILPEA Industries Inc.*, 118 LA 705).

● In a ruling on the equities of a downtime situation, an arbitrator agreed with a union that incentive employees should be paid average hourly earnings rather than base rates during periods when machinery broke down (*Pantasote Co.*, 3 LA 545).

● Another arbitrator ruled the other way in interpreting a contract that stated that waiting time caused by machine breakdowns would be paid at the "regular earning rate." The arbitrator said that the employer need pay only on the basis of the hourly rate and not on the basis of average earnings (*Kensington Steel Co.*, 13 LA 391).

● An arbitrator rejected a union's claim that incentive employees deserved standard hourly rates for a delay that began in the preceding shift and continued into theirs. The union argued that the incentive plan was not in effect until a crew actually started work. But the arbitrator disagreed, saying that in the absence of contract language to the contrary, an incentive plan with built-in delay allowances must be considered as covering all delays regardless of when they start (*Kaiser Steel Corp.*, 31 LA 447).

● Under a collective bargaining agreement calling for payment of a specified hourly rate when a shortage of materials "substantially" reduced the output of employees, an arbitrator found that the hourly rate did not automatically kick in whenever a materials shortage caused employees' production to drop below the point in the incentive range that was on a level with the hourly rate. Instead, the arbitrator ruled that the hourly rate should only kick in if a materials shortage caused a drop in production that would push employees' pay below the base rate (*Maytag Co.*, 20 LA 43).

1. Disputes Over Assigned Work

Some cases center around the tasks employees are assigned and whether they can refuse work that might have a negative effect on their incentive earnings.

● After installing new equipment and changing work processes for employees covered by a piecework plan, an employer was justified in adding nonproduction duties that had traditionally been performed by workers who did not receive incentive pay, an arbitrator ruled. The employer had transitioned from manual to mechanized processes for some employees who performed casting work. Unlike their co-workers who continued to perform the work manually, the employees using the new machinery were given some cleaning and carrying chores. The arbitrator concluded that the employer acted fairly and reasonably in assigning the employees the new duties. The added tasks were less significant than those eliminated as a result of the new machinery, the arbitrator found, and contractual provisions governing incentive pay gave the employer the authority to alter work content in response to changes in equipment, processes, or other factors (*Household Manufacturing*, 80 LA 1111).

● A machine operator who worked on an incentive basis and whose machine broke down was entitled to refuse assigned work on a new machine that had the potential of diluting his earnings, an arbitrator ruled. The contract provided that the employer could offer employees alternative assignments if they reported for work and their regular work was not available, but employees could refuse such assignments and be paid only for elapsed time registered on their time cards. Rejecting the employer's contention that the employee only had the

right to refuse work at the start of his shift, the arbitrator concluded that there was no doubt as to the meaning of the contract giving the employee the right to refuse assigned work (*Mueller Co.*, 76 LA 965).

C. Determining Appropriate Rates for Mixed Work and Overtime

When employees fill in as utility workers on incentive operations in addition to their regular jobs at hourly rates, the question arises whether they should be paid their hourly rates or the incentive rates for their work.

● An arbitrator ruled that employees in a "hybrid classification" who did piecework in addition to their hourly-paid work had to be paid at least the rate of their hourly scale. He noted that under the collective bargaining agreement, regular pieceworkers customarily were paid at a straight hourly rate or at their piece rate, whichever was greater. In the absence of contract provisions covering hourly employees assigned to piecework, the arbitrator reasoned, casual pieceworkers should receive the same treatment (*John Deere Waterloo Tractor Works*, 21 LA 449).

● An arbitrator decided that electricians who were not on an incentive wage rate, but who were assigned to work with electricians who were on incentive, were not entitled to incentive pay in the absence of a past practice by which employees who were not on incentive pay were paid such a rate when working with incentive employees. Despite the union's request for the arbitrator to study "very carefully" various provisions of the parties' collective bargaining agreement, the arbitrator concluded that there was nothing in the agreement that supported the union's position (*Jessop Steel Co.*, 76 LA 641).

1. Overtime Work

Questions about appropriate pay rates also can arise when incentive employees perform overtime work.

● Under a collective bargaining agreement providing for incentive pay for production work in excess of scheduled quotas, an arbitrator held that a production employee who worked two hours of overtime daily performing maintenance work not normally required of production employees was not entitled to receive incentive pay for those overtime hours, because incentive bonuses were historically limited to the hours actually spent in production (*Brighton Electric Steel Casting*, 47 LA 518).

• Another arbitrator found that an employer committed a contract violation when it stopped including incentive hours in its calculations of overtime pay. Employees were awarded incentives in the form of added hours rather than higher rates of pay. For example, an employee could earn two incentive hours during an eight-hour shift and receive credit for 10 hours of work, with eight hours paid at straight-time rates, plus two hours paid at overtime rates. Before the employer ended this longstanding past practice, members of management met with four union officials, who agreed that incentive hours should be paid at straight-time rates and overtime rates should only apply to actual hours worked. However, the union representatives at that meeting did not include the entire shop committee, and the change was never submitted to the membership for their approval. Noting that proposals concerning wages had always been brought back to the full membership for their ratification in the past, the arbitrator said the employer had not obtained a binding agreement from the union regarding the change, and thus it had to continue the practice of paying overtime rates on incentive hours (*Kohler Co.*, 122 LA 1221).

D. Denying Incentive Pay Based on Deficiencies or Defects

Arbitrators have ruled both ways on the issue of whether incentive pay should be denied in situations involving performance deficiencies, quality defects, or the reworking of spoiled work.

• A paper company improperly withdrew an incentive bonus from employees after finding that they had left rolls of paper on the ground where they were subsequently damaged by water, instead of properly storing them on boards, an arbitrator ruled. The employer was not authorized by the collective bargaining agreement, rules and regulations, or past practice to withhold incentive bonuses for such conduct but instead was confined to normal disciplinary procedures, the arbitrator said (*Lawrence Paper Co.*, 96 LA 297).

• An employer improperly counted parts that were rejected by a customer against employees' incentive pay, according to an arbitrator. The arbitrator based his decision on the fact that the customer had designed the part incorrectly, the parts were actually manufactured by a subcontractor, and the only work the employees were responsible for was painting and shipping the parts, which they had done correctly (*Cedar Metalworks Corp.*, 115 LA 749).

• An employer could not cite Department of Transportation regulations as a basis for denying incentive pay to its drivers when their average speeds reached 50 miles per hour or more, exceeding a limit established by the employer, an arbitrator ruled. The eligibility for incentive pay was contingent on drivers committing "no serious DOT violations," but the parties had not discussed the meaning of that phrase and there was no meeting of the minds on its interpretation, the arbitrator found. Moreover, DOT regulations did not officially weigh violations as either "serious" or "minor," the arbitrator noted in overturning the denial of incentive pay based on high driving speeds (*Sherwin-Williams Co.*, 92 LA 464).

• On the other hand, an arbitrator held that an employer properly denied incentive pay to a department's employees where the quality of their product runs was unacceptable and ultimately cost the employer money. The arbitrator found that the employer was not liable under the parties' collective bargaining agreement to pay an incentive rate to employees when their work performance was substandard, even if no disciplinary action was necessary (*Lawrence Paper Co.*, 100 LA 384).

• Another arbitrator ruled that an employer was justified in paying workers a day wage, instead of an incentive rate, when reworking spoiled work, despite the union's claim of past practice, which was based on a single instance occurring three or four years previously. The arbitrator decided that the "past practice" cited by the union did not appear to have been clearly enough "enunciated" nor sufficiently "readily ascertainable" as a practice accepted by both parties to qualify as a binding past practice (*True Temper Corp.*, 80 LA 229; see also 83 LA 361).

1. Group Situations

Where employees working under a group incentive system must stop their regular production work to redo parts spoiled by one or two crew members, arbitrators must decide how the remainder of the crew is to be compensated.

● One arbitrator ruled that an employer was justified in apportioning among all employees in its production line the cost of reprocessing the work damaged by two employees. Although the union protested that penalizing all the employees for the mistakes of two was unjust, the arbitrator held that the earnings deduction was not really a penalty, but the result of an accurate count of acceptable products. Had the employees at fault been made to correct the error, he pointed out, they would have earned less than base wages, which would have been a contract violation. Furthermore, the arbitrator said, the assembly line would have been stopped and the other employees paid only base wages. He said that by continuing to operate, the line made up the reprocessing cost and still earned incentive pay (*Westclox*, 34 LA 777).

● Another arbitrator reached a different conclusion, ruling that the rest of a crew should not be penalized for work spoiled by one or two members of the group. The employees responsible for the spoiled work should be paid their hourly rate, the arbitrator said, but the others should get average earnings for the time they waited while the parts were being reworked (*International Harvester Co.*, 23 LA 184).

E. Disciplining Incentive Employees

Arbitrators commonly uphold the termination of incentive employees who falsify production records with the deliberate intent of deceiving their employers. In some cases, however, arbitrators find that employees' conduct does not warrant such severe consequences and they overturn discharge or reduce the penalties imposed by employers.

● An employee was properly terminated for the intentional falsification of records after reporting a grossly inflated level of production one day, an arbitrator ruled. The employee claimed that she had simply made a mistake, but the arbitrator found that termination was justified whether or not the employee's explanation for her incorrect production report was true. The employer did not have to tolerate such a flagrant miscount of the parts the employee had completed in light of the fact that she had worked under an incentive system for six years and could be expected to know she would be held to strict standards in recording her production, the arbitrator explained (*Madison Furniture Industries*, 88 LA 804).

● An employer had just cause to discharge four sheet metal workers who reported abnormally high output on the last day before a holiday shutdown, an arbitrator found. After they were questioned about their output, the four incentive workers admitted that they had built up a bank of completed work over the preceding weeks. The arbitrator upheld discharge, concluding that the employees entered into a concerted plan to overstate their production for the shift in question (*Dresser Industries, Inc.*, 75 LA 45).

● Another arbitrator found that the penalty of discharge was too severe for an incentive employee who understated his output on a labor reporting ticket. The employer had revised the standard for how many parts the employee was expected to work on per hour, and he reported the reduced output because he was angry and felt he was being cheated. The employer had a right to expect the accurate completion of official company documents, the arbitrator said. The employee's infraction was serious, the arbitrator added, pointing out that he could have sought redress through normal grievance procedures. In reducing the penalty to a suspension, however, the arbitrator noted that the employee did not try to cover up what he had done, he was completely honest when confronted by the employer about his actions, and his misconduct was not motivated by a desire for personal monetary gain (*Thomas Industries Inc.*, 83 LA 418).

• An employee who deliberately slowed the output of his crew after its size was reduced from four workers to three should have been disciplined rather than permanently reassigned to a position that did not offer incentive pay, an arbitrator ruled. The employee complained to his employer that there was too much work for three people to handle. According to the arbitrator, the crew reduction was appropriate in light of the fact that the employer had purchased new equipment and instituted different operating methods. Nevertheless, disqualifying the employee from his incentive position, which in turn reduced his earnings, was unduly harsh, the arbitrator held. He said the employee's deliberate failure to produce in accordance with his ability should have been viewed as misconduct warranting discipline in the form of a suspension (*Checker Motors Corp.*, 95 LA 435).

• An employee who filled out his production record to reflect completion of a specified period of incentive work, even though part of the time was spent training new employees, was improperly discharged for dishonesty, an arbitrator ruled. Emphasizing that the employer's system for recording and distinguishing between "incentive" and "training" was confusing, the arbitrator concluded that the employer charged the employee with committing a crime but failed to prove the worker's guilt beyond a reasonable doubt (*H. R. Terryberry Co.*, 65 LA 1091).

Related Arbitration Titles from Bloomberg BNA

The Common Law of the Workplace

Discipline and Discharge in Arbitration

Elkouri and Elkouri: How Arbitration Works

Fairweather's Practice and Procedure in Labor Arbitration

Grievance Guide

How ADR Works

How to Prepare and Present a Labor Arbitration Case

Just Cause: The Seven Tests

Labor Agreement in Negotiation and Arbitration

Labor Arbitration: Cases and Materials for Advocates

Labor Arbitration: A Practical Guide for Advocates

Labor Arbitrator Development: A Handbook

National Academy of Arbitrators (NAA) Proceedings

For details on these and other related titles, please visit our Web site at *bna.com/ bnabooks* or call *1-800-960-1220* to request a catalog. All Bloomberg BNA books are available on a 30-day free-examination basis.